Tony Wheeler

Tony was born in England but grew up in Pakistan, the Bahamas and the USA. He returned to England to do a degree in engineering at Warwick University, worked as an automotive design engineer, returned to university to complete an MBA in London, then dropped out on the Asian overland trail with his wife Maureen. Eventually settling down in Australia, they've been travelling, writing and publishing guidebooks ever since, having set up Lonely Planet Publications in the mid-1970s. Travel for the Wheelers is considerably enlivened by their daughter Tashi and their son Kieran.

Nancy Keller

Born and raised in northern California, Nancy earned BA degrees in history and social science, working along the way in a variety of occupations. After graduating she moved to the redwood forest and developed a serious love affair with the alternative press, doing every aspect of newspaper work from editorial and reporting to delivering the papers. She returned to university to earn a master's degree in journalism, finally graduating in 1986 after many breaks for extended stays on the west coast of Mexico. Since then she's been travelling and writing in Mexico, Central America, Europe, Israel, Egypt, various tropical South Pacific islands and New Zealand.

She is also the author or co-author of various other Lonely Planet books including *Central America on a shoestring* and the *Mexico* and *Rarotonga & the Cook Islands* tsks.

Jeff Williams

Jeff is a Kiwi, from Greymouth on New Zealand's wild West Coast. He lives in Melbourne, when not travelling, and tries to keep abreast of his toddler, Callum's, enthusiasm and exploration.

When not working for Lonely Planet he amuses himself mountaineering, skiing and birdwatching on whichever continent will have him.

From Nancy

First, greatest thanks to my co-author, Jeff Williams, to our editor Sally Steward, and to artist and mapmaker Jane Hart. All of these people have been magnificent to work with.

For their help while researching this edition of the book, thanks to the staffs of the many visitor information centres and DOC offices I visited, who were knowledgeable, friendly and patient. These local agencies, found in just about every city and town, are a tremendous resource for travellers.

Thanks also to the proprietors of the numerous hostels, backpackers, etc, who shared their hospitality, their warmth and knowledge, and provided some of the best information and travelling tips about their areas. Special thanks to Gordon Burrow of the YHA.

Special thanks for extra helpfulness in one way or another to Sharron Beh of the Auckland Visitor Centre, Diana Parr of the national DOC office, Miles Davidson of the NZ Ski Council, Dave Morgan of the NZ Mountain Safety Council, and Continental Airlines.

Thanks also to the people who took me to try all kinds of activities – daredevil and otherwise – so I could write about them – tandem skydiving, canoeing down the Whanganui River, hurtling down mountains on bicycles, white water rafting, abseiling and rafting through caves, and many others.

Warm regards also to the various people I house-sat for on this trip and wrote parts of this book on their kitchen tables while, for a welcome change, they were able to travel and I was able to stay in one spot for a while.

Deepest appreciation to my friend Mrs Tek van Asch of Takapuna, Auckland, who welcomed me into New Zealand the last time I came to write this book and who did it again this time, who was most supportive in every way. Thanks Tek. Thanks also to her husband Roland, and lovely daughters Helen and Marie.

Special thanks also to the folks at Waitomo, who once again helped to make my stay there one of the most enjoyable, interesting and memorable experiences of my stay in New Zealand.

Thanks to 'Rat' and Mark in Auckland.

From Jeff

There are so many people to thank for making my research trip to New Zealand so worthwhile.

In the South Island, my brother Mark was a great companion for the north of the South Island (as was his friend Julie); Athol & Gill Forrest (and Rachel & Glenn) who share their home away from home in Christchurch (now Auckland); Linda & Winston Monk in Greymouth for unfailing hospitality; and Alison and Callum at home.

Thanks also to Dawn Muir of the New Zealand Tourist Board; Gordon Burrow and Alan Gilbert of the YHA; Anton Wilke of Canterbury Tourism; Prue Norling of Mt Cook Airlines for plenty of travel information (and Ian Hunter of the same office for unravelling the bus enigma); Dave Hawkey and Sarah Talbot of the International Antarctic Centre; Sue McInnes of the Kaikoura Information Centre; Dennis & Rick Baumann of Dolphin Mary Charters (Dolphin Encounter), Kaikoura for the experience of a lifetime with 450 playful Dusky dolphins; Miriama Watson of Whale Watch, Kaikoura; the irrepressible Mary Anne Webber of the Marlborough District Council; Bruce Maunsell in Picton; Peter Pannell in Havelock; Paddy Giloolly in Collingwood; the staff of the Last Resort, Karamea; Henry van Asch of AJ Hackett (and Warren at the Kawarau Bridge); Judith Whittaker of the Queenstown Promotion Board; Neil Ross of Dart River Jetboat Safari; Helen Paterson of Fiordland Travel; Robyn Clarke, Visitor Information Centre, Queenstown; Anne Pullar of the Wanaka Promotion Association; the 'go-for-it attitude' of white water sledger Thierry Huet; Jill Cameron and Dorothy Piper of Tourism Dunedin; Brian, Lesley & Dave of Elm Lodge, Dunedin; the staff of Surf Rafting Dunedin Ltd for the yellow-eyed penguins; Trish Blackstock and the black stilts of Twizel; Jackie Hunter, of the Waitaki District Council, perhaps the best organised Promotions Officer I have met; Robyn Waghorn of the Methven Information Centre; Fergus and Mary Sutherland of Catlins Wildlife Trackers for unfolding the intricate mysteries of this beautiful place; Lesley Gray of Stewart Island Promotions; and the Wizard for a chuckle.

In the North Island there were also many willing helpers. Andy & Renee Wurm, Titirangi; Cheryl Lee, Whangarei Information Centre; Bill and Linley Shatwell of Arcadia Lodge in Russell; Martin at the Mousetrap in Paihia; Peter and Kerry Kitchen of Main

Street Backpackers in Kaitaia; the staff of Sand Safaris; Lyn Downey, Information Far North, Kaitaia; the greenies at the Green House, Dargaville; Roger Mulvay, Matakohe Kauri Museum; Julie Thompson, Tauranga/Mt Maunganui Information Centre; Tony Kirby, Sunshine Coast Promotions, Whakatane; Tim de Jong of East-Capers & Dreamers, Opotiki; Aly Hing and Sandra Ham of the Napier Information Centre; the staff of the Opotiki, Gisborne, Hastings and Te Urewera National Park information centres; Mark from Grand Rapids, a great thespian and travelling companion; Geoff from the Sunkist Lodge, Thames; Barbara Wilkinson of the Thames Information Centre; and the informative crew of the Coromandel & Hauraki Plains Promotion Council in Ngatea.

This Book

This book has had a varied history. Tony Wheeler did the first edition back in 1977 and the next two were updated by New Zealander Simon Hayman. The fourth edition was updated by Australian Mary Covernton, Tony Wheeler updated the fifth edition with Robin Tinker who wrote the tramping section. The sixth edition was updated by Nancy Keller, who updated this edition together with Jeff Williams.

Thanks to the many travellers who took the time to write, giving us their opinions and comments. We've taken all suggestions on board and tried to accommodate as many as possible. A list of all your names is included on pages 769 to 770.

From the Publisher

This edition was edited by Sally Steward and Jane Hart was responsible for design, illustrations and maps, with additional maps from Chris Klep, Maliza Kruh, Margaret Jung and Michelle Stamp. Margaret Jung was responsible for the cover design. Thanks for proofing assistance from Rob Flynn and Vyvyan Cayley, and thanks to Chris Lee-Ack for assisting with the colour map.

Warning & Request

Things change – prices go up, schedules change, good places go bad and bad places go bankrupt – nothing stays the same. So if you find things better or worse, recently opened or long since closed, please write and tell us and help make the next edition better.

Your letters will be used to help update future editions and, where possible, important changes will also be included in a Stop Press section in reprints.

We greatly appreciate all information that is sent to us by travellers. Back at Lonely Planet we employ a hard-working readers' letters team to sort through the many letters we receive. The best ones will be rewarded with a free copy of the next edition or another Lonely Planet guide if you prefer. We give away lots of books, but, unfortunately, not every letter/postcard receives one.

Contents

Map Legend

BOUNDARIES

— · — · — · —	.... International Boundary
— · · — · · —	.... Internal Boundary
++++++++++++	.... National Park or Reserve
– – – – – – –	.... The Equator
....	.... The Tropics

SYMBOLS

◉	NATIONAL	.... National Capital
●	PROVINCIAL	.... Provincial or State Capital
●	Major	.... Major Town
●	Minor	.... Minor Town
■		.... Places to Stay
▼		.... Places to Eat
✉		.... Post Office
✈		.... Airport
i		.... Tourist Information
⊖		.... Bus Station or Terminal
66		.... Highway Route Number
⦂ † ⊞ ♁		...... Mosque, Church, Cathedral
∴		.... Temple or Ruin
✚		.... Hospital
☀		.... Lookout
🛆		.... Lighthouse
⚑		.... Camping Area
⊤		.... Picnic Area
⌂		.... Hut or Chalet
▲		.... Mountain or Hill
⌒		.... Cave
⊢●━┤		.... Railway Station
═		.... Road Bridge
⊢┿━┤		.... Railway Bridge
⇒ ⇐		.... Road Tunnel
⤗ ⤙		.... Railway Tunnel
〰		.... Escarpment or Cliff
⌣		.... Pass

ROUTES

———————	.... Major Road or Highway
– – – – – – –	.... Unsealed Major Road
———————	.... Sealed Road
– – – – – – –	..... Unsealed Road or Track
═══════	.... City Street
++++++++++	.... Railway
●━◉━●	.... Subway
– – – – – – –	.... Walking Track
– – – – – – –	.... Ferry Route
+++++++++	.... Cable Car or Chair Lift

HYDROGRAPHIC FEATURES

	.... River or Creek
	.... Intermittent Stream
	.... Lake, Intermittent Lake
	.... Coast Line
	.... Spring
	.... Waterfall
	.... Swamp
	.... Salt Lake or Reef
	.... Glacier

OTHER FEATURES

	Park, Garden or National Park
	.... Built Up Area
	... Market or Pedestrian Mall
	.... Plaza or Town Square
	.... Cemetery

Note: not all symbols displayed above appear in this book

Introduction

Fresh air, magnificent scenery and outdoor activities are the feature attractions of New Zealand. It's not a big country but for sheer variety it's hard to beat. As soon as you reach New Zealand, you quickly see that its reputation for being 'clean and green' is well deserved. Visitors who come expecting a pristine, green, well-organised little country are not disappointed.

New Zealand is like a microcosm of all the world's attractions. Here you can tramp on the sides of active volcanoes, or in remote, rugged patches of virgin rainforest, through thermal areas of geysers and boiling mud, or kauri forests with some of the largest and oldest trees on earth. You can swim with dolphins, watch whales, see glaciers descending into rainforests, fish for trout in cold, pristine streams and see fur seals and penguins swimming around the boat as you cruise on remote fiords. If you're adventurous you can go white water rafting, cave rafting, rock and mountain climbing, tandem skydiving, skiing down long glaciers, and much more. And of course there's bungy jumping! Plus there are many chances to experience the fascinating Maori culture and the warmth of New Zealand's friendly people.

There are cities too, with some fascinating museums and a cultural life that's a lot more interesting than it was even just a few years ago. All the major cities have a great nightlife with live theatre, dancing and arty café scenes. Arts & crafts are popular and all the major cities have fine galleries.

Getting around is a breeze as there's lots of public transport and hitchhiking is reason-

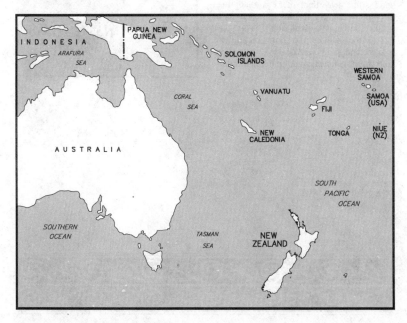

ably easy; cycling through the country is another popular way to travel. Finding accommodation is also easy and generally won't empty your wallet too quickly, although it's an idea to book ahead if you decide to go there in the high season. The food is fresh and there's plenty of it, and even the wine is excellent.

Travellers do have one consistent complaint about New Zealand, though. That is, that in their travel plans they haven't allowed themselves enough time in the country. Look at the map of the world and it doesn't appear as a big country. However, once you arrive in New Zealand, it soon becomes apparent how much there is to see and do.

If time is no object, we'd recommend allowing at least six weeks for a visit to New Zealand. Of course you can still enjoy the country if you have less time; if time is short, you might pick just a few places or activities that especially captivate your interest and focus your trip around those. On the other hand some travellers make a mad dash through the country, rushing from activity to activity, and have a great time.

This book will help to show you all there is to see and do in New Zealand, and to plan your travels. Have a great time. It's a beautiful country.

Organisation of this Book

The following map shows how we have divided the country:

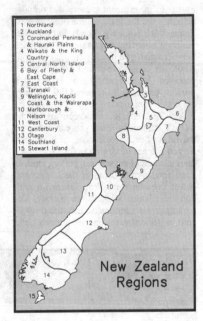

1 Northland
2 Auckland
3 Coromandel Peninsula & Hauraki Plains
4 Waikato & the King Country
5 Central North Island
6 Bay of Plenty & East Cape
7 East Coast
8 Taranaki
9 Wellington, Kapiti Coast & the Wairarapa
10 Marlborough & Nelson
11 West Coast
12 Canterbury
13 Otago
14 Southland
15 Stewart Island

New Zealand Regions

Facts about the Country

HISTORY

New Zealand's history has two distinct phases – the pre-European phase and the more recent history since the arrival of Europeans.

Pre-European History

The original inhabitants of New Zealand were known until fairly recently as Morioris, or moa hunters. Recent evidence indicates that Polynesians arrived in New Zealand in a series of migrations and that the people known as Moriories were in fact an early wave of these Polynesians and not a separate race from the Maoris, who came later. Estimates are that these first Polynesians arrived in New Zealand at least 1000 years ago.

It was these early settlers who hunted the huge flightless bird, the moa, both for food and its feathers until it became extinct. Today, the name Moriori refers to the original settlers of the Chatham Islands, who migrated there from New Zealand. Though it is popularly believed that the Moriori became extinct when the last full-blooded Moriori (Tommy Solomon) died in 1933, respected historian Michael King asserts that there are in fact a number of Moriori still living in New Zealand, though they do not advertise the fact.

Before the arrival of Europeans, the Maoris did not have writing. Instead, as in many parts of the world, their history was preserved in intricate and very specific chants and songs. A priestly class, the to-hungas, was charged with keeping the history, genealogy, stories and spiritual matters of the tribe, like living libraries. There is a rich mythology, easily as complex as anything the ancient Greeks and Romans ever came up with, which includes a panoply of gods and explanations for all kinds of natural phenomena including the creation of the earth and sky, and the creation of New Zealand.

Although the Maoris had this rich mythol-ogy, they also kept quite accurate history, though not always in the precisely dated and geographically specific ways that modern historians would do. Nevertheless there seems to be much factual truth in their account of how New Zealand was discovered by Kupe around 950 AD and how it came to be populated by Polynesians.

Kupe, a particularly brilliant Polynesian navigator, is said to have set sail from Hawai-ki, the Polynesian homeland, in the 10th century for the 'great southern land, uninhabited and covered with mists'. Despite the similar names, Hawaiki is not Hawaii; experts believe it is more likely to have been an island in the Marquesas, possibly Raiatea, in what is now French Polynesia, though no one now knows for sure exactly where Hawaiki was. (Interestingly, Hawaiki is the 'ancestral homeland' for many and various Polynesian peoples, the land they came from before they got to wherever they currently live.) The similar spelling and pronunciation of Hawaii and Hawaiki, however, suggests that another party of emigrants from Hawaiki settled in Hawaii, naming it after their home island.

Kupe is believed to have arrived in New Zealand around 950 AD. It is said that when Kupe sighted New Zealand, a huge land mass relative to most Polynesian islands, it had a white cloud stretching as far as the eye could see. Kupe named the land Aotearoa – Land of the Long White Cloud – and Aotearoa is still the Maori name for New Zealand. Kupe stayed at least several months making explorations of the coast, in some places (such as the Whanganui River in the North Island) also exploring some distance inland. He then returned to Hawaiki and told about the land he had discovered.

Centuries later, around 1350 AD, when things weren't going so well in Hawaiki – overpopulation, shortage of food and all those other familiar problems – the decision was made to follow Kupe's navigational instructions and head south. According to legends, 10 great canoes sailed to New Zealand around 1350 AD, stopping at Rarotonga along the way and setting sail from there for Aotearoa; some historians believe the Great Migration may have occurred even earlier. The names of the canoes are all remembered, and their landing points, crews and histories are also recalled. They were very large canoes, lashed together to form double-hulled vessels. The people who came on them carried with them their domestic animals (dogs and rats) and various agricultural plants including taro, yam and kumara, or sweet potato (which originated in South America – how the early Polynesians had the South American kumara is a fact historians still cannot account for). Today, every Maori still can trace their lineage back to one or another of the canoes of the Great Migration.

When the Great Migration arrived, the country was not entirely devoid of human beings; there were small groups of moa hunters, who must have arrived in earlier, smaller migrations. But the new immigrants from the great fleet soon established themselves in their adopted home, displacing or assimilating with the previous residents.

Maori culture developed without interference from other cultures for hundreds of years, with each canoe group establishing itself in its own territory. Being warriors, however, they engaged in numerous tribal battles over territory and for other reasons, with the losers often becoming slaves or food. Eating an enemy was a way not only to deliver the ultimate insult but also to take on the enemy's life force, *mana* or power.

Though remaining a Stone Age culture – it would have been difficult to get beyond that stage in New Zealand, since there are few metals apart from gold! – the Maoris evolved a culture sustained by agriculture and hunting. They had a complex social structure with tribes, sub-tribes and clans,

Maori Legend – The Creation of the Earth & Sky

In the beginning there was nothingness. Before there was light, there was only darkness.

Rangi nui, the Sky, dwelt with Papa tu a nuku, the Earth, lying over her. The two were united, and bore many children. Papa's nakedness was covered with many things begotten from her union with Rangi - land, trees, animals of the sea, and many other created things, so that she would not be naked. But all lived in utter darkness.

The principal children of Rangi (Sky-Father) and Papa (Earth-Mother) were six. They were Tawhiri matea, God of winds and storms; Tangaroa, God of the sea and of all things living in it; Tane mahuta, God of the forest and of all things that live in the forest; Haumia tiketike, God of wild plants that give food for humankind, including the fern root, berries and many others; Rongo ma Tane, God of cultivated food, including the kumara and all other plants cultivated for food by humankind; and Tu matauenga, the God of war.

After eons and eons of living in darkness, because their parents were joined together and no light had ever yet come between them, the children of Rangi and Papa could take it no longer - they wanted light. They debated what should they do. Eventually they decided that the thing to do was to separate their parents, so that light could enter the world.

They each tried, and failed, to separate Rangi and Papa. Finally it was Tane mahuta's turn to try, and he pushed and strained, his shoulders to the ground and his feet to the sky, and finally succeeded in forcing his parents apart. Light flooded into the world. Thus Tane mahuta became father of the day.

The two parents were grief-stricken at having been separated. They have been separated ever since, but their love for one another has never faded. In the beginning, Rangi shed so many tears that much of the land that had been revealed to light became covered by sea. Finally some of their children turned Papa over onto her stomach, so that Rangi and Papa would not always be looking at one another and grieving. Rangi still cries for his wife, but not as much as before when there was danger that all the land would be drowned because of his tears; his tears now are the drops of dew that form every night on Papa's back. The mists that form in the mornings in the valleys, and rise towards the heavens, are Papa's sighs of longing for her husband. ■

Maori Legend – the Creation of New Zealand

A long time after the creation of the world - after Tane mahuta had created a woman out of red earth, breathed life into her nostrils, mated with her and had a daughter, who also became his wife and bore him other daughters, and after many many other things had happened - one day the demigod Maui, who lived in Hawaiki, went out fishing with his brothers.

They went further and further out to sea. When they were very far out, Maui took out his magic fishhook - the jaw of his sorcerer grandmother - tied it to a strong rope, and dropped it over the side of the canoe. Soon he caught an immense fish, and struggling mightily, pulled it up.

This fish became the North Island of New Zealand, called by the ancient Maori 'Te ika a Maui' (the fish of Maui) or sometimes 'Te ikaroa a Maui' (the big fish of Maui). The Mahia Peninsula, on the east coast of the North Island, on the north end of Hawke's Bay, was known as 'Te matau a Maui' (the fishhook of Maui), since it was the hook with which he caught the giant fish.

The South Island was known as 'Te waka a Maui' (the canoe of Maui) - it was the canoe he was sitting in when he caught the fish. Kaikoura Peninsula, on the north-east coast of the South Island, was the seat where he sat. Another name for the South Island was 'Te wai Pounamu' (the water greenstone), since much greenstone (jade, or pounamu) was found in the rivers there.

Stewart Island, south of the South Island, was known as 'Te punga a Maui' (the anchor of Maui). It was the anchor that held the canoe as Maui fished up the giant fish. ■

and a stratified society which included a royal class, a priestly class and a class of experts in various fields, all the way down to a slave class. Genealogy *(Whakapapa)* was extremely important, since it told who was who in the tribe. Land was held communally and, as in other parts of Polynesia, each tribe and sub-tribe had a *marae*, a place of high spiritual significance where the mana and the tribe's ancestral spirits resided. On the marae elaborate meeting houses were constructed, with symbolic features including powerful wooden carvings of the ancestors, as well as woven flax wall panels and symbolic paintings.

The higher classes were decorated with intricate tattooing – the women with *moko* on the chin only, the very high-ranking men not only over the entire face but over other parts of the body as well.

They made clothing from the fur of dogs, flax, feathers and other materials; warm fur cloaks decorated with feathers can still be seen in some NZ museums. They also made greenstone (jade) ornaments and war clubs, and beautifully carved war canoes, as well as a variety of household items. Often they lived in *pa* or fortified villages. Expeditions were mounted to the South Island to find jade, but otherwise most of the tribes stayed in the much warmer North Island.

European Exploration

In 1642 Dutch explorer Abel van Tasman, who had just sailed around Australia from Batavia (modern-day Jakarta, Indonesia), sailed up the west coast of New Zealand but didn't stay long after his only attempt at landing resulted in several of his crew being killed and eaten. His visit, however, meant that the Europeans now knew of Aotearoa's existence and in those days of colonialism it also meant that they would eventually want it. Another result of his visit was a new name – he christened the land New Zealand, naming it after the Netherlands' province of Zeeland. He also left legacies in the names of Tasmania and of the Tasman Sea, the body of water between New Zealand and Australia.

The Dutch, after this first uncomfortable look, were none too keen on the place and it was left alone until British navigator and explorer Captain James Cook sailed around New Zealand in the *Endeavour* in 1769.

Since Tasman had only sailed up the west coast, there had been speculation that this could be the west coast of a large southern continent that was believed to exist. In the logical European cosmology, it was thought there must be a balance to everything and that a large southern continent must exist to offset the large land masses in the northern hemisphere. Cook sailed right around the coast of New Zealand, mapping as he went, and many places in New Zealand still bear the names that he gave them as he passed by and literally 'put them on the map'. Cook made a number of friendly contacts with the Maoris, discovered that his Tahitian interpreter could communicate with them and was impressed with their bravery and spirit, and with the potential of this lightly populated land. Having concluded his sail around the coasts of both the North and South Islands and determined that this was not the large southern continent, he claimed the entire land for the British crown and then took off for Australia. In 1777 when he published the account of his voyage, Europe learned about the idyllic land to the south.

Another European, the French explorer Jules Sébastien César Dumont d'Urville, was sailing around New Zealand at the same time as Cook but the two never did bump into one another. They came very close – even passing on one occasion in a very thick fog, neither ever seeing the other or suspecting the other was there.

When the British started their antipodean colonising they opted for the larger and even more lightly populated Australia. New Zealand's first European settlers were temporary ones – sealers (who soon reduced the seal population to next to nothing) and then whalers (who did the same with the whales). They introduced diseases and prostitution, created such a demand for preserved heads that Maori chiefs started chopping off their slaves' heads to order (previously they'd only preserved the heads of warriors who had died in battle) and worst of all they brought in European firearms. When they exchanged greenstone *meres* (war clubs) for muskets, the Maoris soon embarked on wholesale slaughter of one another. Equally or even more devastating, as in other parts of the world where indigenous people were decimated by European diseases to which they had no resistance, were the severe epidemics of diseases such as smallpox, measles, mumps, influenza, syphilis and gonorrhea experienced by the Maoris. By

1830 the Maori population was falling dramatically.

European Settlement

In 1814 the arrival of Samuel Marsden, the first missionary, brought Christianity to New Zealand and he was soon followed by other Anglican, Wesleyan Methodist and Roman Catholic missionaries. The Bible was translated into Maori, and for the first time the Maori language was written down. By the middle of the 19th century warfare had been much reduced, cannibalism fairly well stamped out and the raging impact of European diseases were also curbed. But the Maori people now found themselves spiritually assaulted and much of their tradition and culture were irrevo-cably altered. Despite the missionary influence their numbers continued to decline.

During the early 19th century European settlers were increasingly arriving in New Zealand, some on settlement campaigns organised from Britain. Unlike Australia, which was originally a British convict colony, New Zealand was typically settled by lower middle class and upper working class British – not those who were so rich they wanted to stay where they were, but those rich enough to be able to afford the passage out. Many were escaping Britain's Industrial Revolution in a sort of early 'back to the land' movement. Of course there were plenty of challenges in settling a new land, and although the land they settled on was 'purchased' by the New Zealand Association, relations with the Maoris did not always go smoothly, especially as the Maori and Pakeha (European) concepts of land ownership were quite different.

The new settlers began to demand British protection from the Maoris and from other less savoury settlers. The British were not too keen on further colonising – what with burn-ing their fingers in America, fighting in Canada, and generally stretching out their involvement in other places, not to mention having Australia to worry about. But the threat of a French colonising effort stirred them to dispatch James Busby to be the

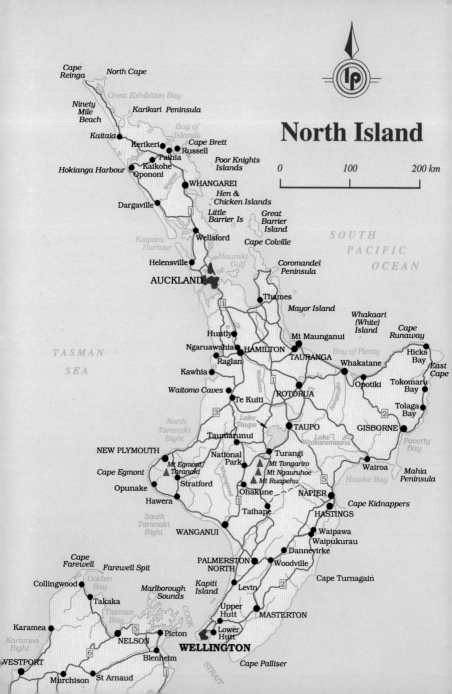

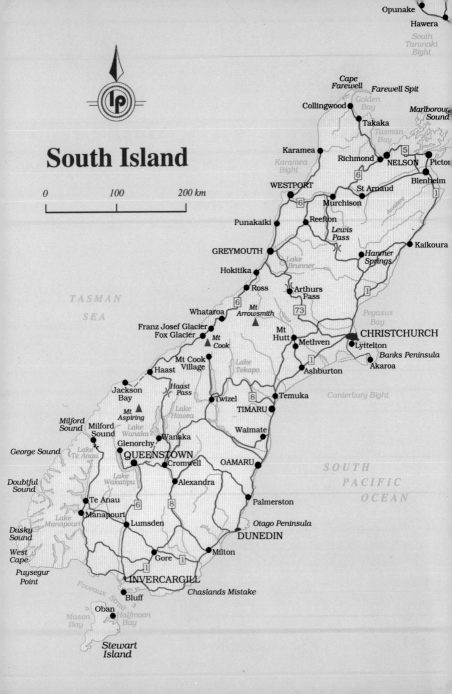

South Island

0   100   200 km

Opunake
Hawera
South
Taranaki
Bight

Cape
Farewell
Farewell Spit
Golden
Bay
Marlborough
Sound
Collingwood
Takaka
Tasman
Bay
Karamea
Richmond
NELSON
Picton
Karamea
Bight
St Arnaud
Blenheim
WESTPORT
Murchison
Punakaiki
Reefton
Lewis
Pass
Kaikoura
GREYMOUTH
Lake
Brunner
Hanmer
Springs
Hokitika
Ross
Arthurs
Pass
TASMAN
SEA
Whataroa
Mt
Arrowsmith
Pegasus
Bay
Franz Josef Glacier
Fox Glacier
Mt
Cook
Mt
Hutt
Methven
CHRISTCHURCH
Lyttelton
Banks Peninsula
Mt Cook
Village
Lake
Tekapo
Ashburton
Akaroa
Haast
Jackson
Bay
Haast
Pass
Twizel
Temuka
Canterbury Bight
Mt
Aspiring
Lake
Hawea
TIMARU
Milford
Sound
Milford
Sound
Lake
Wanaka
Wanaka
Waimate
George Sound
Glenorchy
QUEENSTOWN
Cromwell
OAMARU
SOUTH
Doubtful
Sound
Lake
Te Anau
Alexandra
PACIFIC
Lake
Wakatipu
OCEAN
Te Anau
Palmerston
Dusky
Sound
Manapouri
Lake
Manapouri
Lumsden
Otago Peninsula
West
Cape
DUNEDIN
Puysegur
Point
Gore
Milton
Foveaux Strait
INVERCARGILL
Chaslands Mistake
Bluff
Mason
Bay
Oban
Halfmoon
Bay
Stewart
Island

British Resident in 1833. The fact that this was a very low-key effort is illustrated by poor Busby even having to pay his own fare from Australia and, once he'd set up shop in Kororareka (now called Russell) in Northland, his efforts to protect the settlers and keep law and order were made somewhat difficult by his having no forces, no arms and no authority. He was soon dubbed 'the man of war without guns'.

The Treaty of Waitangi

In 1840 the British sent Captain William Hobson to replace Busby. Hobson was instructed to persuade the Maori chiefs to relinquish their sovereignty to the British crown. In part this decision was made because it was clear that there was going to be increasing emigration from Britain to New Zealand; there was an obvious need for a policy on how the Maoris and Pakehas were to relate to one another, especially regarding land deals, or chaos and war would soon be the result. A treaty was drawn up to specify the positions, the rights and duties, and a mutually agreed-upon method of land sales between the two sides.

The proposal was drawn up within a few days of Hobson's arrival in New Zealand and on 5 February over 400 Maoris gathered in front of Busby's residence at Waitangi in the Bay of Islands to hear the treaty read. The Maori chiefs had some objections, the treaty was amended, and they withdrew across the river to debate the issue throughout the night. The following day, 6 February 1840, with a truly British display of pomp and circumstance, the treaty was signed by Hobson and 45 Maori chiefs, mostly from the Bay of Islands region. Over the next seven months the treaty was carried throughout New Zealand by missionaries and officials, eventually being signed by over 500 Maori chiefs. Busby's house is now known as the Treaty House and the anniversary of 6 February 1840 is considered the birthday of modern New Zealand.

Though the treaty was short and seemed to be simple, it was a controversial document then and it has continued to be controversial

ever since. Many books have been written about all the various shades of meaning, interpretations and debates surrounding the treaty, so we won't try to go into it all here. Basically the treaty said that the chiefs ceded the sovereignty over their land to the Queen of England, in exchange for the Queen's protection in the unqualified exercise of their chieftainship over their lands, their people, their villages and all their possessions. The treaty granted to Maori people all the same rights, privileges and duties of citizenship as enjoyed by the citizens of England. The treaty also established a policy for land sales, stipulating that the Maoris were guaranteed the full, exclusive and undisturbed possession of all their lands, estates, forests, fisheries, etc for as long as they wanted, but that if and when they wanted to sell land, the Queen's agent had the exclusive right to buy it, at a price mutually agreed upon by both parties. The Queen's agent would then sell the land to the settlers in an orderly and fair fashion.

The treaty seemed to promise benefits for both sides in that it would regulate settlement and land sales, protecting the interests and rights of all concerned. Nevertheless controversy arose not only in the interpretation of the treaty – debate has raged for years as to whether the Maoris and the Pakehas, with their two different cultures and world views, had the same understanding in signing the treaty, especially since the English and Maori translations can be viewed as having some significant differences – but also in the ways in which the treaty was handled in subsequent years. When settlers arrived and needed land and the Maoris didn't want to sell, conflict inevitably resulted. The admirable idea that the government should act as a go-between in all Maori-Pakeha deals to ensure fairness on both sides fell apart when the government was too tightfisted to pay the price.

The first visible revolt came when Hone Heke, the first chief to sign the Treaty of Waitangi, chopped down the flagpole at Kororareka, upon which flew the British flag. Despite new poles and more and more guards Hone Heke or his followers managed to chop the pole down four times, and on the last occasion it was covered with iron to foil further attempts. After his final destruction of the pole in 1845, he burnt down the town of Koro-rareka for good measure. In the skirmishes that followed, the British governor put a £100 reward on Hone Heke's head, to which he brilliantly responded by offering a matching £100 for the governor's head.

This was only one in a long series of skirmishes, battles, conflicts, disputes and arguments between the Maoris and Pakehas. The original benign intent of the Treaty of Waitangi began to ebb under the pressure of ever-increasing numbers of European settlers. The Maoris in various places became increasingly alarmed at the effect the European settlers were having on the land and on their own society. The Pakehas, in turn, particularly after the administration of New Zealand passed to a settler government under the Constitution Act of 1852, increasingly disregarded the principles of fairness outlined in the treaty. Pressures between the Maoris and Pakehas finally escalated into full-fledged wars fought in many parts of the country between 1860 and 1865, wars known collectively as the Maori Wars.

In the Waikato region south of Auckland, a number of tribal chiefs united to elect a Maori King in 1859. Although the King represented only these tribes, not all the Maori people in New Zealand, the Maori kingship was accorded great respect and it was not until the 20th century, with permission of the Maori King, that Pakehas were able to settle in the Waikato/King Country region.

Although the Maoris were brilliant warriors, eventually they were worn down by sheer weight of numbers and equipment. Following the Maori Wars, with the Maori people beaten down and not able to do much about it, the Pakeha government confiscated much Maori land. The Treaty of Waitangi, which had given the Europeans the right to settle in New Zealand and had been supposed to guarantee fairness on all sides, especially as regards the acquisition of land, was completely disregarded; in 1877 Chief Justice Prendergast ruled that the treaty was 'a simple nullity'. The confiscation of Maori lands engendered extreme bitterness, not only because it completely disregarded the Treaty of Waitangi, but also because it was handled extremely unfairly. The government confiscated the best lands, leaving the worst to the Maoris, regardless of the actions of the various Maori tribes in the wars – so some of the more hostile tribes kept their lands, while some of the most benign lost their lands, simply because the government had the power to seize them.

In 1840 the capital of New Zealand was moved south to Auckland. In 1865 it was moved south again, this time to Wellington, where it has remained ever since.

Late 19th Century

The Maori Wars were the last time there was widespread and full-scale conflict within the country. Things calmed down, European settlement and influence grew, and New Zealand became an efficient agricultural country. Sheep farming, that backbone of modern New Zealand, took hold as refrigerated ships made it possible to sell NZ meat in Europe. New Zealand became what has been called 'an efficient offshore farm' in relation to England, exporting agricultural products, especially mutton, wool, sheepskins and dairy products, and importing manufactured goods. Still, remote as it was, New Zealand had to take care of its own needs to a large extent and became known as a rugged, independent little country.

Towards the end of the 19th century New Zealand went through a phase of sweeping social change that took it to the forefront of the world. Women were given the vote in 1893, 25 years before Britain or the USA, and more like 75 years ahead of Switzerland. An eminent leader at this time was Richard John 'King Dick' Seddon who, together with the Liberal Party, was responsible for many of the reforms. The range of far-sighted social reforms and pioneering legislation included old-age pensions, minimum wage structures, the establishment of arbitration courts and the introduction of child health services. The latter included the foundation in 1907 of the Plunket Society, an organisation of nurses who care for expectant mothers and young babies.

Meanwhile the Maori people floundered. New Zealand grew through immigration (a very selective immigration), but by 1900 the Maori population had dropped to an estimated 42,000 and was falling very fast. The Maoris were given the vote in 1867, but the continuing struggle to hold on to their culture and their ancestral lands sapped their spirit and energy for some time.

Early 20th Century

New Zealand had become a self-governing British colony in 1856, and a dominion in 1907. By the 1920s it controlled most of its own affairs, but it took until 1947 before it became a fully independent country.

Meanwhile New Zealand fought for the British in the Anglo-Boer war of 1899 to 1902, in WW I and WW II. The Kiwi soldiers earned great reputations for skill and bravery, and they also suffered heavy losses of life. NZ troops assisted in the European and Middle East arenas of WW II, but after 1941 when war was declared in the Pacific and New Zealand was directly threatened, a division was also established in the south-west Pacific.

During the Korean War (1950 to 1953), when New Zealand sent troops as part of a Commonwealth brigade, Australia, New Zealand and the USA signed the ANZUS defence pact. The aim of the pact was to provide mutual aid in the event of any attack. With the conceived threat of communism, New Zealand also joined the anti-communist SEATO (the South-East Asia Treaty Organisation).

New Zealand had become a member in the the South Pacific Commission in 1947, a group responsible for promoting research in the South Pacific. During the '60s and '70s an increased amount of NZ aid was directed to the Pacific countries and in 1971 New Zealand joined the South Pacific Forum, designed for Pacific governments to discuss common problems.

Late 20th Century

New Zealand's economy prospered after WW II but along with much of the rest of the world, it took a nose-dive in the '70s and '80s. The closure of much of its traditional European market for agricultural products, combined with the oil crisis price hikes of many of its mineral and manufactured imports, did not help the country's economic situation at all. Unlike Australia, New Zealand had little mineral wealth to supplement its agricultural efficiency. The inefficiencies of small-scale manufacturing that afflicted Australia were simply magnified by the even tinier population of New Zealand. Unemployment began to be an increasing problem.

Meanwhile, in the latter part of the 20th century, things finally began to turn around for the Maoris, largely due to various Maori leaders who kept pressing for justice and who would obviously never give up until their cause had been heard. In 1975, for the first time in a century, the Treaty of Waitangi which in 1877 had been ruled 'a simple nullity' was reconsidered; and the Parliament passed the Treaty of Waitangi Act, establishing a Waitangi Tribunal to investigate Maori claims against the British Crown, dating from 1975. In 1985 the act was then amended to order the Tribunal to examine claims dating all the way back to the original signing of the Treaty of Waitangi in 1840. Financial reparations were made to a number of Maori tribes whose lands were found to have been unjustly confiscated, allowing them to buy land, invest in education and do other things for the uplifting of their people. Today the Maori population is increasing faster than the Pakeha and they number 9.6% of the population of New Zealand, or around 330,000 people.

New Zealanders are proud of their record of racial harmony, despite the difficulties; there has never been any racial segregation and inter-marriage is common. In *Return to Paradise* James Michener tells of the outraged local reaction when WW II GIs stationed in New Zealand tried to treat the Maoris like American Blacks. In recent years there has been a growing interest in *Maoritanga* (Maori culture) and Maori language, literature, arts and culture are experiencing a flourishing renaissance.

Internationally, New Zealand has become one of the most interesting and important countries in the South Pacific region. It has taken a strong stand on nuclear issues, refusing entry to nuclear-equipped US warships and condemning French nuclear testing in the Pacific. Although this brave policy has caused more than a few problems for the Kiwis, they have continued to stick by it.

New Zealand's anti-nuclear stance put a sour note on its relations with the USA. Although it remains one of NZ's principal trading partners, the USA decided to suspend its obligations to New Zealand within the ANZUS defence pact after New Zealand established a policy of not allowing nuclear vessels to use its harbours. Since the USA has a policy to 'neither confirm nor deny' the presence of nuclear arms on any of its military ships, it found itself unable to use New Zealand ports without spilling the beans, and so was unwilling to continue a full defensive relation with New Zealand.

New Zealand also became a leader in the Pacific in its opposition to nuclear testing by the French at Moruroa Atoll in French Polynesia. The testing has caused radiation effects in Polynesians in the region around the test site, and radiation poisoning of fish that has even wider effects throughout the Pacific since fish can migrate some distances, but apparently none of this was of any concern to the French government. In 1985 the French sent several government-sponsored terrorist agents to New Zealand, to bomb and sink the Greenpeace ship *Rainbow Warrior* as it sat in Auckland Harbour, preparing to lead a flotilla to French Polynesia to protest against French nuclear testing. A Greenpeace photographer, Fernando Pereira, was killed in the bombing, making the action not only destruction of the ship but also murder. Two French agents were caught, tried, found guilty and sentenced to 10-year terms, but they did not end up serving out their entire terms; both were repatriated, by France, with honours, well before their time was finished. French nuclear testing at Moruroa was suspended at the time of writing, although there were proposals in France of recommencing.

In 1983 Australia and New Zealand signed a Closer Economic Relations Trade Agreement, permitting free and unrestricted trade between the two countries. As it became increasingly aware of itself as a Pacific nation rather than an 'efficient offshore farm' for the UK, New Zealand's trade with the UK declined in proportion to its increased trade with Australia, the USA, Japan and a few other South-East Asian countries. In 1987 the NZ government embarked on a plan of privatisation, selling formerly government-operated enterprises into the private sector and diminishing the welfare state.

Increasing pressures on the economy, and different ideas by different political parties as to what should be done about it, caused havoc in the government in the late 1980s. Prime Minister David Lange, who had faced increasing opposition from within his own Labour Party as a result of various economic policies, shocked the nation by resigning the prime ministership in August 1989. He was replaced by his nominee, Minister of Justice Geoffrey Palmer, but Palmer lasted only 13 months before being replaced by Michael Moore, a former Minister of Foreign Affairs. Moore was prime minister for only two months, until the general election of October 1990 when the overwhelming victory by the

National Party put Jim Bolger, leader of the National Party, in as prime minister. The economy seemed to fare even worse under the National Party, however, until in 1993 it seemed to be looking up a bit.

After the 6 November elections, when no decisive result was achieved and the whole NZ political system was left hanging in limbo, the economy responded accordingly, with the dollar sliding on world markets.

GEOGRAPHY

New Zealand stretches 1600 km from north to south and consists of two large islands and a number of smaller islands scattered around the two main ones, plus a few far-flung islands hundreds of km away: New Zealand's territorial jurisdiction extends to the islands of Chatham, Kermadec, Tokelau, Auckland, Antipodes, Snares, Solander and Bounty (most of them uninhabited) and to the Ross Dependency in Antarctica.

The North Island (115,000 sq km) and the South Island (151,000 sq km) are the two major land masses. Stewart Island, with an area of 1700 sq km, lies directly south of the South Island. The country is 10,400 km south-west of the USA, 1700 km south of Fiji and 2250 km east of Australia, its nearest large neighbour. Its western coastline faces the Tasman Sea, the part of the Pacific Ocean which separates New Zealand and Australia.

With a total land mass of 268,000 sq km, altogether New Zealand's land area is greater than that of the UK (244,800 sq km), smaller than that of Japan (377,800 sq km), and just a little smaller than that of Colorado in the USA (270,000 sq km). With only 3,435,000 people, and almost 70% of those living in the five major cities, that leaves a lot of wide open spaces. The coastline, with many bays, harbours and fiords, is very long relative to the land mass of the country.

Both the North Island and South Island have some high mountains, formed by two distinct geological processes, both associated with the westward movement of the Pacific tectonic plate.

When one tectonic plate slides underneath another one, it forms what's called a subduc-

tion zone. Geologists say that the North Island of New Zealand is on the southern reaches of the subduction zone where the oceanic Pacific plate is sliding underneath the continental plate, resulting in volcanic activity which has created a number of large volcanoes and thermal areas, and some equally impressive volcanic depressions.

A rough 'line' of volcanoes, some which are still active, extends from the steaming Whakaari (White) Island in the Bay of Plenty, south past Mt Putauaki (Edgecumbe) and the highly active thermal areas in and around Rotorua and Lake Taupo. New Zealand's largest lake, Lake Taupo was formed by a gigantic volcanic explosion in 186 AD, and still has thermal areas bubbling away nearby. South of Lake Taupo are the North Island's spectacularly large volcanoes Tongariro, Ruapehu, Ngauruhoe and the smaller Pihanga. Continuing south-west there's the lone volcanic cone of Mt Egmont/ Taranaki. They say that Port Nicholson, the bay where Wellington is, is another place formed by a giant volcanic crater, now filled by the sea. Other parts of the North Island also have evidence of volcanic activity; in Auckland, for example, there are over 50 volcanic cones, including most of its famous 'hills' (One Tree Hill, Mt Eden, etc) that rise up from the flatlands.

The North Island has some ranges of hills and mountains produced by folding and up-lift, notably the Tararua and Ruahine ranges in the southern part of the North Island. In general, though, most of the high places of the North Island were formed by volcanic activity. In the centre there's a high plateau.

In the South Island the geological process is different. Here the two tectonic plates are smashing into each other, resulting in a process called 'crustal shortening'. This has caused the Southern Alps to rise as a spine extending along virtually the entire length of the South Island. Thrust faulting, folding, and vertical slips all combine to create a rapid uplift of the Southern Alps – as much as 10 mm per year – and though the Southern Alps receive a lot of rainfall and hence a lot of erosion, their rapid rate of uplift is enough to keep pace and they are continuing to rise. Most of the east side of the South Island is a large plain known as the Canterbury Plains. Banks Peninsula, on the east coast, was formed by volcanic activity and joined to the mainland by alluvial deposits washed down from the Southern Alps.

Another notable feature of New Zealand's geography is the country's great number of rivers. There's a lot of rainfall in New Zealand (see the Climate section, Facts for the Visitor chapter) and all that rain has to go somewhere. The Waikato River in the North Island is New Zealand's longest river, measuring in at 425 km. Also in the North Island, the Whanganui River is the country's longest navigable river, which has made it an important waterway from historic times down to the present. New Zealand also has a number of beautiful lakes; Lake Taupo is the largest and Lakes Waikaremoana and Wanaka are two of the most beautiful.

FLORA & FAUNA
As is the case for most Pacific islands, New Zealand's native flora & fauna are, for the most part, not found anywhere else in the world. And, like other Pacific islands, New Zealand's native ecosystem has been dramatically affected and changed by plants and animals brought by settlers, mostly in the last 200 years. Wild pigs, goats, possums, wallabies, rabbits, foxes, dogs, cats and deer have all made their mark on the native wildlife, and blackberries, gorse, broom and the usual crop of agricultural weeds have infested huge areas of land.

Much of New Zealand's unique flora & fauna has survived, but today over 150 native plants – 10% of the total number of native species – and many native birds are threatened with extinction.

Flora
In the 1800s when the first European settlers arrived, about 70% of New Zealand was covered in native forest. Much of it was soon cleared, in some places as part of a profitable timber industry (as in the large kauri forests), in other places to make way for farming, and

in some places for both reasons. Just as the attitude towards whaling has shifted dramatically in recent years from the way it was a century ago, it's interesting to see the shift in attitude towards native forests: whereas today much of the native forest is cherished and protected in national and forest parks, the early European settlers regarded the 'clearing of the land' as a sort of mission – the first step towards 'civilising' it. Clearing was done with little regard for the consequences, and in some places serious soil erosion was a result.

Despite there not being as much native forest around as there was before the European settlers arrived, New Zealand still has some magnificent areas of native forest and bush. About 10% to 15% of the total land area of the country, or around six million hectares, is native flora, much of it in protected national parks and reserves.

The variety of vegetation types in New Zealand is enormous. Heading south from the giant kauri forests of Northland there are the luxuriant lowland kohekohe forests of the Bay of Plenty; the rainforests dominated by rimu, various beeches, tawa, matai and rata, and a great variety of tree ferns; the podocarp and hardwood forests of the lower parts of the North Island with its kahikatea, tawa, rimu, rata, and kohekohe; the summer-flowering alpine and subalpine herbfields; and the windswept scrub of the smaller islands.

In the South Island the vegetation changes dramatically as you climb into the mountains. The lowland supplejacks give way to rimu, miro, and then tree ferns at about 800 metres. Above 1000 metres the totara, wineberry, fuschias, rata and kaikomako are gradually left behind, to be replaced by subalpine scrub. At about 1200 metres the scrub gives way to the tussock grasses and alpine herbfields, and at the extreme heights only some hardy lichens hang on to the rock, ice and snow-bound peaks.

One of the more noticeable plants is the pohutukawa, known as the New Zealand Christmas tree, which explodes with brilliant red flowers around December, peppering the

The Giant Kauri

The kauri, known to science as *Agathis australis*, is the king of the North Island forests. Found only in New Zealand and in north-eastern Australia, mature kauris – sometimes as old as 1500 years – can reach a height of 36 metres with a diameter of over three metres for the first 30 metres, making them amongst the largest trees in terms of wood volume in the world. The kauri is a conifer, and thus related to the common pine trees in other parts of the world, but it has unusual long, broad and thick leaves, sometimes tinged red.

Before European settlement the kauri dominated three million hectares of forests from North Cape to Waikato. It wasn't long, though, before the Pakehas realised the value of the kauri wood, and the wholesale destruction of the great kauri forests began. Today, not much more than 10,000 hectares of mature kauri forests remain, mostly reserved in the Waipoua Forest on the west side of the Northland, although another 20,000 hectares of young kauri forest is being carefully nurtured.

The early settlers also found that the white to reddish-brown gum of the kauri could be used to make a high-quality varnish, and a huge 'gum-digging' industry arose. Trees were scarred with long V-shape grooves that oozed huge amounts of gum, and fossilised gum was also dug up from around the old stumps of burned or felled kauris – hence the name 'gum-digging'.

The first gum was exported to Sydney in 1815, and by 1895 it had become New Zealand's chief export, earning more revenue than gold. The kauri gum varnish industry collapsed in 1925 when synthetic varnishes became widely available, although gum-digging continued on a small scale into the 1960s, when gum was worth about $400 per ton.

Of course, the Maoris knew all about kauri gum long before the Pakehas discovered it. They chewed it, tattooed with it, and even made torches with it. ■

forests with colour. Another Kiwi favourite is the yellow-flowered kowhai.

Like the Australian species, most of the 72 NZ orchids are not large or brilliantly coloured; one exception is the beautiful *Earina autumnalis*, which produces heavily perfumed cream flowers at Easter.

The cabbage tree, found throughout the plains and foothills, doesn't provide cabbages, nor is it a tree; but its swordlike leaves did supply the Maoris with medicines, rope and thatching. It is common throughout the country on the plains and foothills.

The northern rata is a tall tree that begins life high in another tree, sending down aerial roots that join horizontally and gradually enclose the host in a hollow trunk. It's found throughout the North Island and along the north-western coast of the South Island. The kahikatea, or white pine, dominates the lowland forests all over New Zealand from North Cape to Bluff, often having massive buttress roots to support a 60-metre-high trunk.

New Zealand's best known palm is probably the nikau. While it is mainly a North Island species, it also occurs as far south as Greymouth, on the west coast of the South Island.

New Zealand has hundreds of species of ferns, including several species of tree ferns. Probably the best known tree fern is the silver fern, so named because of the silver colour on the underside of its fronds; just as the kiwi is the national bird, the silver fern is the national plant (yes, it's the plant that the All Blacks wear over their hearts on their rugby jerseys!).

Two plants to be wary of are the tutu and the ongaonga, or tree nettle, both tall shrubs or small trees. Every part of the tutu is poisonous, but particularly the black berries that hang invitingly in loose clusters. Unless you are a foremost expert on edible native plants, leave them all alone. The leaves of the ongaonga are covered in brittle stinging spines. If you brush against them they'll break off and stick to your skin, releasing a poison that makes you groggy and uncoordinated for several days. It's also extremely painful and can be fatal.

The matagouri, or wild Irishman, is a thorny bush of the South Island lowlands. Its incredibly hard thorns were used by the

Maoris for tattooing in pre-European times when bones were in short supply.

Another plant that was important to the Maoris in pre-European times was harakeke or flax, which they used to make rope, baskets, mats, fishing nets and clothing; the traditional Maori 'skirts' are still made of flax today. The British were so impressed with its usefulness that a huge export industry was born in the early 1800s, continuing strongly until its collapse during the depression of the 1930s. The last flax mill was closed at Foxton in 1937.

Many New Zealanders love their native forests with a passion and have an equally passionate aversion to forests of introduced species. Nonetheless various introduced species have been planted in large tracts for the timber industry. The most obvious imports are the massive plantations of radiata (or Monterey) pine and Douglas (or Oregon) fir, which supply the economically important sawn timber and paper industry. There are also a couple of beautiful stands of California redwood trees.

The Maori language has bestowed marvellous names on some of the native plants of New Zealand, names that are almost unpronounceable to Europeans – tawhairauriki, kowhai ngutukaka, whauwhaupaku, mingimingi, hangehange, kumarahou, and pua o te reinga, to name a handful. Some of the English names are nearly as colourful, and it's interesting to speculate about their derivations – gum digger's soap, wild Irishman, seven-finger, bog pine, flower of Hades and Dieffenbach's Spaniard.

Fauna

With animal life so common in New Zealand (the four-legged, off-white, woolly variety that is), it's curious to discover that there are virtually no native mammals. The first Maori settlers brought some rats and the now extinct Maori dog with them but the only indigenous mammals were bats. So you can imagine how surprised they were, the Maoris *and* the bats, when the Europeans turned up with sheep, cows, pigs and everything else

old MacDonald's farm could offer. Today the countryside supports several species of deer, rabbits, possums, goats and wild pigs – all deliberately introduced and many of which have multiplied to such an extent in the wild that they have now become harmful to the environment. Of course, there are also sheep. In fact, there are so many sheep that after lambing time the sheep population can reach 100 million, 30 sheep for every man, woman and child.

If New Zealand had few animals it had plenty of birds, which thrived with no predatory animals around. Some birds did not survive so well after predatory species were introduced; some became extinct and seven species of native birds are now on the list of endangered species. The worst affected were the flightless birds like the kakapo and takahe, which were easy prey for the introduced competitors and predators.

Other species have been affected by modern human activities. The rare brown teal's natural environment is wetlands which unfortunately have been affected by continued drainage and reclamation of swamps, and the modification of rivers for irrigation and hydroelectricity.

Common birds found all over the country include the morepork (mopoke), a small spotted owl whose call you will often hear at night; the tui, a large black bird with a white crop under its throat and a pure call; and the little fantail, which will often flit around nearby as you're tramping through bush. This habit has given the fantail the reputation of being very 'friendly' – it may be sociable, too, but it really flies along beside you to snatch up insects that fly out of the bush when you pass by.

In the high country of the South Island there's the raucous kea. Keas have a reputation for killing sheep, which makes them unpopular with farmers, but they may be just as unpopular with you as they like to hang around humans, tipping over rubbish bins, and sliding noisily down roofs at night.

Yet the mountains would be far poorer if the birds were not there to greet you with their strident call 'kee-aa' when you tramp or

climb up into their domain. Keep a close eye on your gear when they're around since they have incredibly strong beaks and will have a peck at anything, including pulling eyelets out of boots and ripping sleeping bags and tents.

Another amusing bird is the duck-like weka which hangs around campsites and rushes over to steal things when you turn your back. The weka will purloin anything it can carry in its bill – particularly if it's a shiny object – so don't leave rings and watches lying around.

Of course there are plenty of birds around the coasts, too, with seagulls, albatross, and a number of species of penguin, including the yellow-eyed penguin which is the rarest of all penguins.

The NZ bird you *won't* see is the famous moa, a sort of oversized ostrich. Originally there were numerous types and sizes, but the largest of them – the huge giant moas – were as high as four metres. They had been well and truly extinct for a few centuries by the time the Europeans turned up, but you can see moa skeletons and reconstructions in many NZ museums.

Surprisingly not extinct is the tuatara, the sole survivor of a group of ancient reptiles somewhat akin to the dinosaurs. Sometimes mistakenly referred to as a lizard, it is now found only on a few offshore islands and is absolutely protected.

New Zealand has no snakes and only one spider that is dangerous to humans, the rare katipo which is a close relative of the North American black widow and the Australian redback.

New Zealand is renowned as an angler's paradise, largely due to the introduction of rainbow and brown trout, perch, carp, Atlantic salmon and quinnat salmon to its rivers and estuaries. Native fish include the tenacious kahawai and the moki, hapuku, John Dory, gurnard and tarakihi.

Sitting at a major confluence of warm and cold ocean currents, New Zealand's offshore waters have a great variety of both tropical and cold-water species of fish. The tuna, marlin, snapper, trevally, kahawai and large sharks are tropical species; the hake and the blue and red cod are cold-water species. Some species, which can live in both warm and cold waters, are found all around NZ's coasts; they include bass, grouper and tarakihi. With thousands of km of coastline and a lot of tidal mudflats, flounder and sole are also common in coastal waters, as are crayfish (lobster).

New Zealand's unique positioning also gives it a number of areas attractive to marine mammals. In particular, the waters just offshore from Kaikoura, on the north-east coast of the South Island, have a combination of the warm and cold currents and a continental shelf that all results in abundant nutrients being swept up from the sea floor, attracting fish, squid and a number of marine mammals including dolphins, whales and seals. Kaikoura is the place on earth where the giant sperm whale is most easily seen, while dolphins of various species can be seen frolicking in all NZ's waters. Whaling was an important industry in New Zealand in the late 1800s and up until around the 1920s; today the whales, dolphins and other marine mammals attract nature-lovers from around the world.

If you hear something croaking during the night in New Zealand, you can be sure it's not one of the three species of Kiwi frogs – they lack a vocal sac, so can only produce a high-pitched squeak. They're also remarkable in not having a free-swimming tadpole stage, instead undergoing metamorphosis in a capsule. One frog is restricted to the high parts of the Coromandel Peninsula, and another to the summit of Stephens Island and remnant rainforest around Marlborough Sound.

NEW ZEALAND BIRDS

Kiwi *(Apteryx...)*

There are three species of kiwis in New Zealand - the brown kiwi *(Apteryx australis...)*, little spotted kiwi *(A. owenii)* and great spotted kiwi *(A. haastii)*.

The best known of New Zealand's birds, the kiwi has become the symbol of New Zealand. It's a small, tubby, flightless bird and, because it's nocturnal, is not easy to observe. Kiwis may have no wings, feathers that are more like hair than real feathers, short sight and a sleepy nature, but the All Blacks have nothing on them when it comes to strength of leg! The kiwi has one thing in common with Australia's equally 'cute' national symbol, the koala – a shocking temper, which is usually manifested in giving whatever or whoever it is upset with a thumping big kick. Despite the fact that night-time is when they are most active, they are still fairly lazy, sleeping for as many as 20 hours a day. The rest of the time they spend poking around for worms which they sniff out with the nostrils on the end of their long bill.

The female is larger than the male and much fiercer. She lays an egg weighing up to half a kg, huge in relation to her size (about 20% of her body weight), but having performed that mighty feat leaves the male to hatch it while she guards the burrow. When kiwi junior hatches out it looks just like a mini version of its parents, not like a chick at all, and associates only with dad, completely ignoring mother kiwi.

Although the kiwi is not endangered it is suffering from pig-hunters' dogs, the destruction of native bush, and the use of opossum traps.

Kea

Takahe

Kea *(Nestor notabilis)*

The kea is a large parrot decked out in unparrot-like drab green except for bright red underwings, that inhabits South Island high country forests and mountainous areas. They're amusing, fearless, cheeky and inquisitive birds. There are plenty of opportunities to observe them at the Fox and Franz Josef glaciers. At the car park at the terminal of the Fox Glacier they hang around waiting for tourist handouts. Signs warn you of their destructive tendencies. They make concerted assaults on campervan roof hatches as soon as the passengers have wandered off, or they ride nonchalantly on the spinning roof ventilators on tourist buses.

Tui *(Prosthemadera novaeseelandiae)*

The tui is a forest bird found throughout New Zealand. It is conspicuous by its white throat feathers. It has an extremely large repertoire of sounds and can mimic many other bird calls. You can easily see them around much of the country, including Auckland, Pelorus Sound, and Ulva Island and Oban on Stewart Island.

Takahe *(Notornis mantelli)*

This is one of the birds that disappeared and then was found again in the Murchison Mountains of Fiordland in 1948. Its habitat is tussock and small patches of beech forest. Its population is estimated to be about 160 (1991) and some of these are in captivity, especially at Te Anau Wildlife Park, Mt Bruce National Wildlife Centre and on Maud Island in the Marlborough Sounds. It is a flightless bird which feeds on tussock shoots, alpine grasses and fern roots.

Bellbird *(Anthornis melanura –* (Maori: Makomako)
This bird is common in both native and exotic forests and is easily identified by its beautiful bell-like call. It is found in all areas of New Zealand with the exception of Northland. The green of the male bird is particularly noticeable and both sexes have curved honeyeater bills and short tail feathers.

Morepork *(Ninox novaeseelandiae –* Maori: Ruru)
This bird is found throughout New Zealand with the exception of the east of the South Island. It is the only endemic owl and differs from the introduced little owl in that it has a rounded head and larger tail.

Yellow-eyed Penguin *(Megadyptes antipodes –* Maori: Hoiho)
The hoiho is the world's rarest species of penguin, its numbers having diminished because of the loss of its coastal habitat. It can still be seen along the south-east coast of the South Island (see Oamaru, Otago Peninsula and Catlins Coast). The streaked yellow head and yellow eye are its most conspicuous characteristics.

Yellow-eyed Penguin

Blue Penguin *(Eudyptula minor –* Maori: Korora)
The korora is common in coastal waters from the top of the North Island to Stewart Island. It is the smallest species of penguin and can often be seen coming ashore at night. Its upper parts are blue, underparts white and bill black. It is known as the fairy penguin in Australia.

Fiordland Crested Penguin *(Eudyptes pachyrhynchus –* Maori: Pokotiwha)
The pokotiwha lives around the south-west coasts of the South Island and around Stewart Island. It is very timid and is identifiable by its yellow crest, which is different from the markings of the hoiho. You are most likely to see them when you're travelling in the area of Milford Sound.

Kaka *(Nestor meridionalis...)*
There are two distinct species of kaka. The North Island *(N. meridionalis septentrionalis)* inhabits lowland forest in the North Island and forested offshore islands. The South Island *(N. meridionalis meridionalis)* inhabits forest in Nelson, the West Coast, Fiordland and Stewart Island. The South Island kaka is slightly larger and has a whitish crown (grey perhaps); both birds are generally bronze in colour with crimson tones on the underparts.

Morepork

Royal Albatross *(Diomedea epomorphora –*
Maori: Toroa)
These birds range throughout the world and breed on a number of the island groups to the south and east of New Zealand. There is one mainland breeding colony, at Taiaroa Head on the Otago Peninsula. They breed from October to September. There is nothing quite like seeing these enormous birds in flight, especially as they swoop past at eye level. On land they are lumbering creatures. In winter you may see a wandering albatross *(Diomedea exulans)* in New Zealand mainland waters.

Yellowhead *(Mohoua acrocephala –*
Maori: Mohua)
The mohua is fairly hard to find and if observed in a forest it is unmistakeable because of its bright yellow head. That is if you are in the ancient forests of Arthurs Pass National Park, Fiordland or the Catlins Forest (all in the South Island). If you see a similar bird in open grassland it is most likely that it is the introduced yellowhammer. The mohua is about the size of a house sparrow.

Whitehead *(Mohoua albicilla –*
Maori: Popokatea)
The whitehead inhabits forest and scrubland in the North Island only. Like the yellowhead, the most conspicuous feature is the single colour of the head. It doesn't occur north of Te Aroha except for populations on Tiritiri Island and Little Barrier.

Royal Albatross

Australasian Gannet *(Sula bassana –*
Maori: Takapu)
The takapu is becoming increasingly common around New Zealand waters and there are three mainland breeding colonies (Farewell Spit in the South Island, Muriwai and Cape Kidnappers in the North Island). The juveniles migrate to Australia and return in four years to breed. These birds dive from great heights, with wings folded back, to catch fish. Their yellow head against a white body is their most obvious feature. On land they are ungainly but in the air they are poetry in motion.

Gannet

Kakapo *(Strigops habroptilus)*
This species is severely endangered and the remaining populations are on the predator-free Little Barrier and Codfish islands. It is the largest parrot in the world, is nocturnal and flightless. There are probably only 50 or so birds left. You will only observe this bird with the assistance of the Department of Conservation.

North Island Kokako *(Callaeas cinerea wilsoni)*
The depletion of habitat and the introduction of predators have severely endangered the populations of this weak flier. It is a member of the wattle-bird family and is distinguished by its blue wattle (the skin hanging from its throat). It would most likely be observed in unmodified lowland forest of the Central North Island, Taranaki, Northland and the Coromandel. The South Island kokako, orange-wattled, is probably confined to one tiny population on Stewart Island – it may be extinct. ∎

National Parks

New Zealand has many parks: 12 national, 20 forest, three maritime and two marine, plus numerous other types of parks and reserves and two World Heritage Areas. For information including a map of locations, see the Outdoor Activities chapter.

GOVERNMENT

The government of New Zealand has been modelled on the British parliamentary system, elections being based on universal adult suffrage. The minimum voting age is 18 and candidates are elected by secret ballot. The maximum period between elections is three years, but the interval can be shorter for various reasons, such as when the government of the day needs to seek the confidence of the people on a topic of particular national importance. Voting is not compulsory, although on average more than 80% of those eligible to vote do so.

The difference between the UK's Westminster system and the NZ model is that New Zealand has abolished the upper house and currently governs solely through the lower house. Known as the House of Representatives, it has 99 member's seats, four of which were traditionally set aside for Maori representation – the Maoris were admitted to parliament in 1867 – but this is expected to change with the restructuring of the political system. The House of Representatives functions primarily to legislate and review the actions of the government in power. No tax can be imposed, nor any money spent until the house has authorised such action.

Like the UK, New Zealand is a constitutional monarchy. The traditional head of state, the reigning British King or Queen, is represented by a resident governor-general, who is appointed for a five-year term. An independent judiciary makes up another tier of government.

The government runs on a party system. The party that wins a majority of seats in an election automatically becomes the government and its leader, the prime minister. The two main parties are the National (conservative) and Labour parties.

The two-party system has traditionally made it difficult for other parties to gain much power. Nevertheless, in 1992, a new political alignment arose with a number of minor parties including the Greens, New Labour, Democrats (descended from the former Social Credit Party), Mana Motuhake and a new party, the Liberals (formed by two dissenting former National Party MPs) all joining to form a new coalition party called the Alliance. Election results in November 1993 were so close that the National Party was only voted in by a majority of one seat, ahead of the Labour Party and the smaller Alliance and NZ First parties.

After a 1992 referendum to assess the public's ideas on a number of electoral reforms, including proportional representation, new laws were submitted to a vote in the November 1993 elections. New Zealanders voted overwhelmingly for proportional representation, thus breaking down the two-party political system. The traditional four seats set aside for Maori representation will be abolished and it's likely that after the next elections a tiered system of various parties will be represented in parliament.

ECONOMY

New Zealand is a modern country which enjoys a standard of living equivalent to that of other 'developed' countries.

New Zealand's economy has suffered various slumps in recent years, and unemployment is around 11%. Nevertheless, in 1993 the economy was showing signs of recovery, with more money starting to circulate, and people seemed to be feeling a cautious optimism.

The New Zealand economy has been undergoing a radical restructuring in various ways, moving from a 'welfare state' type of government-involved economy towards a private open-market economy. The government, which went through a period of economic crisis in the past decade or so, has been pulling back and selling off many formerly government-run enterprises into private hands, including NZ Rail in 1993.

The government is also pulling back in its role of administering a 'welfare state', which is raising cries from many quarters. Controversial actions include increasing privatisation of the health system, necessitating people to spend money for health care and to buy personal health insurance, unnessary just a few years ago. Other health benefits such as automatic free accident health care and compensation, disability and unemployment payments, etc have also been reduced and/or made more difficult to get. People who once received welfare ('the dole'), for example, are now starting to be required to work in work programmes in order to receive it.

Tourism, service industries, manufacturing, small-scale industry and agriculture are all highly important in the NZ economy. In a recent count the sector of trade, restaurants and hotels accounted for the largest proportion of the gross domestic product (GDP), followed by the sector of financing, insurance, real estate and business services, followed by manufacturing, then agriculture, transport and storage, and then by food, beverages and tobacco, and a host of other smaller sectors.

With all the sheep, cattle and farms you see around New Zealand it's not surprising to find that agriculture is an important part of the economy. In strictly dollar amounts it accounts for only about 10% of the entire GDP and employs about the same percentage of the total workforce, but 53% of all land in the country is devoted to pastureland, and agricultural products such as sheep, cattle, fish and forestry products are NZ's chief exports. Farming is a scientific proposition in New Zealand, with research constantly carried out and the most modern scientific farming methods used.

In case you wanted to know, New Zealand is reckoned to have around 60 million sheep and 8 million cattle. Figures vary a lot, though, depending on what time of year you're counting – at lambing time the sheep population can rise over 100 million!

New Zealand's principal trading partners are Australia, Japan, the USA, Asia and the UK. Principal exports are meat (with beef and veal bringing in slightly more revenue than lamb and mutton), dairy products (milk, cream, yoghurt, butter and cheese), forest products (primarily coniferous sawed logs, timber and wood pulp from non-native trees planted for the timber industry), fruits and vegetables (especially kiwi fruit, apples and pears), wool and fish (including crustaceans and molluscs), in that order. Main imports are machinery and mechanical appliances, electrical machinery and equipment, and a variety of manufactured goods. Exports are higher than imports.

POPULATION & PEOPLE

The 1991 census showed New Zealand to have a population of around 3,435,000. Ethnically, 78.8% are New Zealand Pakeha, 9.6% are New Zealand Maori, 3.9% are Pacific Island Polynesian, 1.1% are Chinese, 0.8% are Indian and 5% are 'Other'. Comparing these statistics with those of five years before, a few patterns are evident. Europeans are the only group declining, percentage-wise, while Maoris, Polynesians, Chinese, Indian and 'Other' peoples are on the rise. Overall the population was up about 3.7% over five years before, when it was recorded at 3,307,000.

Many of the islands of the Pacific are currently experiencing a rapid population shift from remote and undeveloped islands to the 'big city' and Auckland is very much the big city of the South Pacific, with the greatest concentration of Polynesians on earth. It sometimes causes a great deal of argument, discussion and tension and much of it is not between the recent Pacific immigrants and the Pakeha population but between the islanders and the Maoris, or among the various island groups themselves. Asians are also becoming an important element in New Zealand immigration.

Recently, New Zealand established a 'points system' of immigration as an incentive to attract skilled people and especially finance to the country. Having large amounts of money to invest in the New Zealand economy wins you quite a few points! It is open to all nationalities and many Asians with money to invest are immigrating to New Zealand under this points system.

If Pacific and Asian immigration were to continue unchecked and the Maori population also continued to grow faster than the population of European descent, the Pakehas would eventually find themselves in the minority. Over the last 15 years or so the economic situation led to a mass exodus to Australia and further afield. In some years there was an actual population decline but recently the emigratory flow has started to slow.

With only about 12.6 people per sq km, New Zealand is lightly populated by many countries' standards (compare it to 366 per sq km in the Netherlands, 327 per sq km in Japan, 234.5 per sq km in the UK, or 26.8 per sq km in the USA) but it is much more densely populated than Australia with its stretches of empty country and 2.2 persons per sq km. The South Island once had a greater population than the North Island but now the South Island is the place to go for elbow room – the entire population of the South Island is barely more than that of Auckland. The capital is Wellington but Auckland is the largest city. The five largest cities – the only ones in the country with populations over 100,000 – are:

City	Population
Auckland	896,000
Wellington	328,300
Christchurch	308,200
Hamilton	125,000
Dunedin	114,500

Altogether the population of the 15 largest 'urban areas' comes to 68.4% of NZ's population – Auckland alone has 26% of the entire population – and if you add the 7.5% in the 15 'secondary urban areas' you have altogether accounted for 76% of the country's population. That leaves just 24% spread out around the rest of the country – that is, a lot of wide open spaces!

EDUCATION

New Zealanders place a high value on education, and virtually the entire population is literate. By law, education is mandatory and free for all children between the ages of six and 15; in fact most children enter school by the age of five, and many also have attended preschools before that, all subsidised by the state. Correspondence school is available for children who live in remote places.

New Zealand has seven universities, a number of teachers' colleges and polytechnics and one agricultural college.

A new and growing facet of education in New Zealand is that it is gaining a reputation, especially in Asian countries, as a good place to learn English. There are over 25 language schools throughout New Zealand (most of them in Auckland) and student visas are available which permit foreign students to study in New Zealand for up to four years.

ARTS

New Zealand has a multi-faceted arts scene, with both Maoris and Pakehas engaged in all kinds of traditional and modern arts.

Maori

Maori arts are dramatic in many ways, and they include various arts that people of European backgrounds might not be familiar with.

Traditionally the Maori people did not keep history using the written word; their history was kept in long, very specific and stylised songs and chants. As in many parts of the world where oral history has been practised, oratory, song and chant developed to a magnificent art in Maori culture. The many rituals associated with Maori protocol are also quite stylised – if you ever visit a marae and are greeted with the traditional *haka* (war chant) and *wero* (challenge), you will appreciate how artistic they are. The Maori arts of song and dance include some special features such as the *poi* dance and action songs. Martial arts, using a variety of traditional weapons and movements, are highly stylised and developed.

Other Maori arts include crafts such as

wood carving, bone carving and jade carving, basketry and weaving, including a distinctive form of wall panelling known as *tukutuku* which can be seen on marae and in Maori churches. Wood carvings, tukutuku wall panels and distinctive styles of painting (especially on the rafters and ceilings) can be seen in most Maori meeting houses. These traditional Maori arts are not used only on the marae, though – wood carving, bone carving, painting, basketry and various other arts are being used in both traditional and new ways, creating some vibrant art.

Drama & Dance

New Zealanders are engaged in all the traditional European-based art forms. There's a lively literary scene (see the Books & Maps section in the Facts for the Visitor chapter), there are poetry readings, many dance styles and live theatre. Wellington is particularly known for its theatre scene, with traditional as well as improvisational and avant-garde live theatre companies. Other major centres – Auckland, Christchurch and Dunedin – also have active theatre and dance scenes. Even smaller towns often actively support a community theatre group.

Music

As with theatre, so with music – the major centres have the liveliest music scenes but even smaller towns can have some interesting music on offer. Ruatoria, on the East Cape of the North Island, is not exactly New York City but it is the home town of Herbs, a popular and internationally known Maori reggae band.

There's plenty of opportunity for going out in the evening and hearing live music in the larger centres, with a choice of everything from a symphony concert, the ballet, or a rock, jazz or blues band, or even Irish music. Irish music – both the acoustic ballad minstrel variety and the rousing Irish dance band style – is very popular in New Zealand. In the larger centres you can hear Irish music any night of the week and Irish-style pubs are becoming very popular.

Rock New Zealand rock music doesn't begin and end in Dunedin, though over the last 10 years you could be forgiven for thinking so – it's true that in terms of innovative and alternative music, Dunedin is New Zealand's music capital. (See the Dunedin section in the Otago chapter for more details.)

In the '70s and '80s, Split Enz was New Zealand's best known and successful band. Originally a very unusual and eccentric group, their style became more main-stream in the '80s. Ridiculously enough, their completely apolitical song *Six Months in a Leaky Boat* was banned in England during the Falklands war of 1982.

Like many other New Zealand bands who achieved success, Split Enz based themselves in Australia and found themselves referred to as 'a great Australian band'. After the break-up of the band in the mid-'80s, band member Neil Finn formed another successful 'Australian' band, Crowded House. (At least Crowded House *did* possess some Australian members.)

Bands from New Zealand have long been renowned not only for their 'alternative' feel but also for imaginative (sometimes surreal) names. Examples (all of which are or were quite good bands) include Sneaky Feelings, Straitjacket Fits, Look Blue Go Purple and the Jean-Paul Sartre Experience (who have recently modified their name to the JPS Experience). Possibly the prize example, however, are an outfit called The Great Unwashed, who later renamed themselves The Clean – signifying a major change in musical direction, perhaps?

Art

The larger centres have a variety of museums and art galleries where the latest art can be seen, and even smaller towns often have a gallery which may combine both arts & crafts. You can find all the arts represented including painting, sculpture, ceramics and pottery, and a wide variety of handicrafts.

Although there are distinct 'Maori arts' and 'Pakeha arts', in fact there is rarely a division in who practises which arts. There are Pakeha people who enjoy carving in bone and painting in traditionally Maori styles; Maori songs, poi dances, and a little bit of Maori language are taught in schools and all New Zealand children, regardless of background, learn them. Likewise, there are many Maori people who excel in the traditionally Pakeha arts – there are Maoris in theatre, music and many other Western art forms. Dame Kiri Te Kanawa, a Maori, is one of the world's best known operatic divas, and there are many other examples.

New Zealand literature, especially, is an arena in which the Maoris are making a strong mark – though the written word was not traditionally a part of Maori culture, NZ is experiencing a movement of dynamic Maori writing in fiction, non-fiction, poetry and every other written form.

CULTURE

Culture in New Zealand has two major sides to it – the Pakeha (principally in the British colonial tradition) and the Maori. In general, the Pakeha culture predominates. Nevertheless, living side by side with it is the Maori culture, which has both traditional and modern aspects.

In fact, there is a variety of smaller culture groups living beside each other in one way or another in New Zealand. In the far north there are the descendants of the Yugoslavian Dalmatian gum-diggers, who get together and have dances in their traditional Dalmatian dress; in the far south there are the Scottish games and marching bagpipe bands that have come down from the Scottish immigrants in that region. Polynesians have brought their cultures with them – in Auckland you can go to a Samoan rugby match on Saturday afternoon, go out dancing the *tamure* at a Cook Islands nightclub on Saturday night, and go to a Tongan church with the service held in Tongan language on Sunday – then go home and watch the All Blacks on TV opening a rugby match with the traditional Maori haka. The Indians and

Chinese are New Zealand's other two major immigrant groups; in between going to your Samoan rugby match and Cook Islands dance you might stop off at a Chinese or Indian restaurant!

The intercultural aspects of New Zealand are quite regional and even local in nature. One small town on the Kapiti Coast, Otaki, has nine marae, a Maori university and a famous Maori church; Rotorua and the East Cape, also in the North Island, are well-known for their Maori culture; many other places in the North Island are, too – but then there are some regions of New Zealand, such as in the far south of the South Island, where few Maori people live and any Maori influence there would scarcely be noticed at all.

Although in many ways the various cultures live side by side without touching a great deal, there are still many points of contact. Between the two cultures, it is the Maoris who have had to make most of the adjustment to the dominant Pakeha culture – speaking English, going to school, joining the workforce, etc. Often the Maori people, collectively and as individuals, are very bicultural, living in the Pakeha way in many respects but having a separate Maori cultural life at the same time. It wouldn't be uncommon, for example, for a Maori to work all week in an office, speaking English, and then spend the weekend on a marae, speaking Maori and participating in rituals that have been passed down through many generations.

Many Pakehas have a certain awareness of Maori culture, and the awareness is gradually increasing. Most New Zealanders of every background can sing at least a few Maori songs, especially the most loved *Pokarekare ana*. Many Pakehas have visited a marae. 'Kia ora' has become the national greeting for many New Zealanders, Maori and non-Maori alike. The resurgence of interest in Maoritanga – Maori culture – with its revival of Maori culture, Maori language and Maori pride, is gradually being noticed in subtle ways throughout NZ.

Of course we don't have space here to completely describe even the two major cultures, but we'll try to point out a few of the more noticeable elements of each culture.

Pakeha

New Zealand Pakeha culture is descended from its historical roots (not so long ago) of pioneering, principally British upper-working class/lower middle-class stock, with the odd assortment of Dutch, Scottish, Dalmatian and other Europeans thrown in. A high value is placed on things like hard work, resourcefulness, honesty, fairness, independence, ruggedness and so on – all the things a rugged pioneering middle-class English culture would be expected to value.

In addition, New Zealanders are known for being a sports-loving and outdoors-loving people. Not only do they passionately love their national rugby team, the All Blacks, it isn't unusual for every member of the family to be on a sports team – the father and sons might be on rugby teams, the mother might play tennis and the daughters be on netball teams, for example – and the whole family might take off together for tramping, sailing, cycling, camping, swimming at the beach or whatever. The stereotypical 'national character' includes friendliness, helpfulness – and they drink a lot of tea and beer!

Of course anything we say will be stereotypical and won't represent everyone in New Zealand. There are probably hundreds of people who prefer indoor pursuits, would rather read poetry than hear about rugby, and would rather drink wine than tea or beer.

Maori

Probably the main feature of Maori culture today is its biculturalism – the way that Maori people, while adapting to Pakeha culture, also manage to maintain their own culture at the same time.

Maori culture is complex and no brief description here can do it justice. We'd recommend that you visit a marae if you get the chance – you will learn more about Maori culture in a few hours there than we can

explain here. There are some excellent books about many aspects of Maori culture, with guides about visiting marae, biography, autobiography, literature, ethnographical and anthropological studies, and Maori writers expounding on issues of the times all widely available. For details, see the Books section in the Facts for the Visitor chapter.

One of the most distinctive aspects of Maori culture is that it is tribal. Genealogy, *(whakapapa)* determines everyone's place in the tribe and so genealogy and family ties are critically important. The marae is the focus of Maori culture, the place where the tribe gathers. The rightful home of every member of the tribe, it is their place to stand and most fully be themselves. It is here that their ancestors are as present as the current generations, and where each Maori person fits in to the generations that have come before and those that will come after. His or her own marae is where every Maori person has the right to be heard. Increasingly, marae are also involved with education, with passing on traditional arts and knowledge.

This, too, is generalisation. Many Maori people live in close association with their marae, but then there are also many who do not, especially those who, for one reason or another, have gone to live in an area far from their marae. Some Maori people speak fluent Maori, others don't speak it at all, others are studying and trying to learn it. Some Maori people have deep connections with their family and their tribe, others don't. Some practise traditional Maori arts, others don't. There's no generalisation that can be made about a culture that will describe everyone in it, especially in a modern multi-cultural society where possibilities are so varied.

RELIGION

The most common religion in New Zealand is Christianity. The 'big three' denominations are Anglican (Church of England) with 24.7% of the population, Presbyterian with 18.3% and Roman Catholic with 15.5%. Many other denominations also have followings, with Methodists, Baptists, Mormons,

Marae Etiquette

Visitors to New Zealand have several opportunities open to them to witness fascinating aspects of Maori culture. Perhaps the best place to gain some understanding of Maoritanga is by visiting a marae. The marae is the open area in front of the *whare hui* (meeting house), but the term is often loosely used to describe the buildings as well. Either way it is a place which is sacred to the Maoris and to be treated with great respect.

Some of the many attributes of and values held on the marae include:

- That it is a place to stand *(Turangawaewae)*
- That it is a place of kinship *(Whanau-ngatanga)*, friendship *(Manaakitanga)*, love *(Aroha)*, spirituality *(Wairua)* and the life force *(Mauri)*
- Respect for elders *(Whakarongo kii nga kaumatua)*
- That it is a place where life and death merge, where the living *(te hunga ora)* give great honour to the dead *(te hunga mate)*
- The preservation and use of the Maori language *(Maori reo)*

A welcoming ritual *(Te Powhiri Ki Te Manuhiri)* is followed every time visitors *(manuhiri)* come onto the marae. They bring with them the memories of their dead. The hosts *(tangata whenua)* pay their respects to the deceased of the manuhiri, likewise the manuhiri to the tangata whenua. The ceremony removes the tapu and permits the manuhiri and tangata whenua to interact. The practice varies from marae to marae. Note that shoes must be removed before entering a whare hui.

Te Powhiri Ki Te Manuhiri may proceed as follows: A welcoming call *(karanga)* by women of the tangata whenua to the manuhiri. It could also include a ceremonial challenge *(taki* or wero).The manuhiri reply to the karanga and proceed on to the marae. They pay respect and sit where indicated, generally to the left of the whare hui (sides are as if facing outwards from the whare hui).

Welcoming speeches *(mihi)* are given by the tangata whenua from the threshold *(Taumata Tapu)* in front of the meeting house. Each speech is generally supported by a song *(waiata)*, generally led by the women. When the mihi is finished the manuhiri reply. The tapu is deemed to have been lifted from the manuhiri when the replies are finished. The manuhiri then greet the tangata whenua with handshakes and the pressing of noses *(hongi)*. In some places the hongi is a single press, in others it is press, release, press.

Before the manuhiri leave the marae they make farewell speeches *(poroporoaki)* which take the form of thanks and prayer.

The important thing to remember, as a visitor, is that once invited you are extremely welcome on the marae, as a cornerstone of Maori culture is hospitality. Once protocol has been satisfied you have become part of an extended family and the concern of the tangata whenua is you – the manuhiri. They want to see you fed and looked after, almost spoiled, because you are a guest. Such hospitality is fantastic and lucky visitors to New Zealand are increasingly being given the opportunity to enjoy it. When the roles are reversed and you are the tangata whenua, remember that the care of *your* guests becomes your No 1 concern. ■

Brethren, Jehovah's Witnesses, Pentecostals, Assemblies of God and Seventh Day Adventists all well represented, along with various other faiths including Hindus, Jews, Muslims and Baha'is. The Ratana and Ringatu faiths, also with significant followings, are Maori adaptations of Christianity.

There is also a significant number of people – 16.7% – who have no religion.

LANGUAGE

New Zealand has two official languages: English and Maori. English is the language that you usually hear spoken. The Maori language, long on the decline, is now making a comeback. You can use English to speak to anyone in New Zealand, as Maori people speak English. There are some occasions, though, when knowing a little Maori would be very useful, such as if you visit a marae, where often only Maori is spoken. It's also useful to know since many places in New Zealand have Maori names.

Kiwi English

As everywhere in the world where English is spoken, in New Zealand it is spoken in a unique way. The elision of vowels is the most distinctive feature of the Kiwi pronunciation of English. The NZ treatment of 'fish & chips', for example, is an endless source of delight for Australians when pronounced 'fush & chups'. In the North Island sentences often have 'eh!' attached to the end. In the far south a rolled 'r' is practised widely, a holdover from that region's Scottish heritage – it's especially noticeable in the Southland. There are some words in common usage which are peculiar to, or typical of, Kiwi English:

afghan – a popular home-made chocolate biscuit

All Black – a revered member of the national rugby team. The name comes from 'All Backs', which they were called by the press on an early All Black visit to England

baa – the most common greeting bleated by around 60 million Kiwis

bach – holiday home, usually a wooden cottage (pronounced 'batch')

Beehive – Parliament House in Wellington, so called because of its distinctive shape

box of birds – expression, usually a reply to 'How are you', meaning 'on top of the world'

choice – fantastic, great

ciggies – cigarettes

crib – Southland bach

cuzzies – cousins, relatives in general

dairy – a small corner store which sells just about everything, especially milk, bread, the newspaper and ice cream; a convenience store. Cows are not milked here!

DOC – Department of Conservation

coolie bin – cooler, esky – large insulated box for keeping beer, etc cold

freezing works – slaughterhouse

Godzone – New Zealand (God's own)

good as – short for 'good as gold'

good as gold – very good

greenstone – jade; pounamu

handle – a beer glass with a handle

hard case – an unusual or strong character

hokey pokey – neither mischief nor magic but a delicious variety of ice cream

hooray – a rather 'bush' way of saying goodbye

huntaway – loud-barking sheepherding dog, usually a sturdy black-and-brown hound

Instant Kiwi – state-run lottery; a chance to become an instant millionaire

Is it what! – strong affirmation or agreement; Yes isn't it!

jandals – elsewhere in the world they may be referred to as sandals, flip flops or thongs; usually rubber footwear

judder bars – bumps in the road to make you drive slowly; speed bumps

kiwi – a flightless brown bird with a long beak; it is the national symbol and the name by which New Zealanders often refer to themselves; also an adjective to mean anything of or relating to NZ. Also a member of the national Rugby League team.

kiwi fruit – once called Chinese gooseberries; a small, succulent fruit with fuzzy brown skin and juicy green flesh

lounge bar – more up-market and polite bar than a public bar; called a 'ladies' bar' in some countries

metal road or metalled road – gravel or gravelled road

motor camp – New Zealand caters well for its travelling population with a network of well-equipped camps. These have tent sites, caravan and campervan sites, on-site caravans, cabins and tourist flats

Nifty-fifty – 50cc motorcycle

Pakeha – a fair-skinned person of European ancestry

Plunket – the Plunket Society is an organisation established to promote the health of babies. There are Plunket rooms (baby clinics), Plunket nurses (baby nurses), etc.

pushchair – baby stroller

Rheiny – affectionate term for Rheineck beer

scrap – a fight, not uncommon at the pub

section – a small block of land

Steinie – affectionate term for Steinlager beer

tarseal – the bitumen surface of a road

varsity – university or uni

wopwops – in the wopwops is out in the middle of nowhere; remote

A *Personal Kiwi-Yankee Dictionary* by Louis S Leland, Jr (John McIndoe, Dunedin, 2nd edition 1990, paperback) is a fine and often hilarious book of translations and explanations of quirks between the Kiwi and Yankee ways of speaking English. Yanks will love it.

Maori

The Maoris have a vividly chronicled history, recorded in songs and chants which dramatically recall the Great Migration and other important events. It was the early missionaries who first recorded the language in a written form. They did this using only 15 letters of the English alphabet, with all syllables ending in a vowel.

The language is related to other Polynesian languages (including Hawaiian, Tahitian and Cook Islands Maori) and has some similarity to dialects found in Indonesia. It's a fluid, poetic language and surprisingly easy to pronounce if you just remember to say it phonetically and split each word (some can be amazingly long) into separate syllables.

Although the Maori language was never dead – it has always been used in Maori ceremonial events, for example – in recent years there has been a revival of interest in the language, an important part of the renaissance of *Maoritanga* (Maori culture). Many Maori people who had heard the language on maraes all their lives but had not spoken it in day-to-day living, are now studying Maori and speaking it with fluency. In many places, Maori people have got together to provide instruction in Maori language and culture for young children, so that they will grow up speaking Maori in addition to English, and be familiar with Maori tradition. It is a matter of some pride to have fluency in the language and on some marae only Maori is allowed to be spoken, to encourage everyone to speak it and to emphasise the distinct Maori character of the marae.

Pronunciation The consonants in Maori – h, k, m, n, p, r, t and w – are pronounced the same as in English. A couple of combinations, however, are pronounced in a special way. 'Ng', pronounced as in the English suffix '-ing' (singing, running, etc), can be used at the beginning of words as well as at the end; it's easy to practise this sound, just say the '-ing' over and over, isolate the 'ng' part of it, and then practise using it to begin a word rather than end one.

The 'wh' also has a unique pronunciation in Maori, generally being pronounced like a soft English 'f'. This pronunciation is used in many place names in New Zealand, especially in the North Island, where there are

place names such as Whangarei, Whangaroa and Whakapapa (all pronounced as if they began with a soft 'f'). There is some regional variation, however; in the region around the Whanganui River, for example, the 'wh' is pronounced the same as in English (as in when, why, etc) – so the Whanganui River, in the local Maori dialect, is pronounced with the English 'wh' sound rather than the English 'f' sound.

The main thing an English speaker needs to learn when learning to speak Maori is the correct pronunciation of the vowels. We can only approximate the sounds here; to really get it right, you will have to hear someone pronounce it correctly, so take what is written here only as a rough guideline.

Each vowel has both a long and a short sound. The approximate sounds are:

ā	as in 'large' (long a)
a	as in 'but' (short a)
ē	a sort of combination sound, between 'get' and 'bait' (long e)
e	as in 'get' (short e)
ī	as in 'weed' (long i)
i	as in 'it' (short i)
ō	as in 'pork' (long o)
o	a shorter sound than o
ū	as in 'moon' (long u)
u	as in 'foot' (short u)

The diphthongs are pronounced approximately like this:

ae & ai	as in 'sky'
ao & au	as in 'how'
ea	as in 'lair'
ei	as in 'bay'
eo	eh-oh
eu	eh-oo
ia	as in 'beer'
ie	as the 'ye' in 'yet'
io	as in 'ye old'
iu	as in 'cue'
oa	as in 'roar'
oe	as in 'towing'
oi	as in 'toy'
ou	as in 'sow'
ua	as in 'fewer'

Each syllable ends in a vowel and there is never more than one vowel in a syllable. There are no silent letters.

You can find a number of Maori phrasebooks, grammar books and Maori-English dictionaries if you want to study the language. Learning just a few basic greetings is an excellent thing to do, especially if you will be going onto a marae, where you will be greeted in Maori.

The *Collins Maori Phrase Book* by Patricia Tauroa (William Collins Publishers, Auckland, 1990, paperback) is an excellent book for starting to speak the language, with sections on ordinary conversation and also on how the language is used in the context of the culture, ie on a marae. *Say It In Maori* compiled by Alan Armstrong (Viking Sevenseas Ltd, Paraparaumu, 1968, paperback) is a smaller pocket-size book.

Small English-Maori dictionaries include the *English-Maori Maori-English Dictionary* by Bruce Biggs (Auckland, University Press, Auckland, 1990, paperback) and the *Revised Dictionary of Modern Maori* by PM Ryan (Heinemann Education, Auckland, 1989, paperback).

The *Dictionary of the Maori Language* by HW Williams (GP Publications, Wellington, 7th edition, 1991, paperback) is a large volume which translates only from Maori to English; it's the standard classic dictionary used by serious students of the language. The *Complete English-Maori Dictionary* by Bruce Biggs (Auckland University Press, Auckland, 1981, reprinted 1992, paperback), on the other hand, translates only from English to Maori.

Meanwhile, here are a few words you will probably run into:

atua – spirit or gods
haka – war dance
hakari – feast
hangi – oven made by digging a hole and steaming food in baskets over embers in the hole; a feast of traditional Maori foods
heitiki – carved, stylised human figure worn around the neck, usually shortened to 'tiki'
hoa – friend
hui – gather; meeting

iwi – people, tribe
kai – food, any word with kai in it will have some food connection
ka pai – good, excellent
karakia – prayer
koe – you (singular)
kaumatua – elders
koutou – you (plural)
kumara – sweet potatoes, a Maori staple food
mana – psychic power or influence
manuhiri – visitor; guest
Maoritanga – Maori culture
mere – flat, greenstone war club
moko – facial tattoo
ngati – people, tribe
o – of
pa – fortified village, usually on a hilltop
Pakeha – a fair-skinned person of European ancestry
tane – man
tangata – human beings
tangata whenua – people of the land; the local people
taniwha – fear-inspiring water spirit
tapu – holy; sacred; taboo; forbidden
te – the
tiki – an amulet or figurine, often a carved representation of an ancestor
tohunga – priest, wizard or general expert
wai – water, place names with 'wai' in them will often be on a river
whakapapa – genealogy
whare – house
whare runanga – meeting house
whare whakairo – carved house

Greetings & Small Talk

Haere mai! – Welcome!
Haere ra. – Goodbye, farewell. (from the person staying to the one going)
E noho ra. – Goodbye, farewell. (from the person going to the person staying)
Kia ora. – Hello, good luck, good health.
Tena koe. – Hello. (to one person)
Tena korua. – Hello. (to two people)
Tena koutou. – Hello. (to three or more people)
Kei te pehea koe? – How are you? (to one person)
Kei te pehea korua? – How are you? (to two people)
Kei te pehea koutou? – How are you? (to three or more people)
Kei te pai. – Very well, thank you; that is satisfactory, OK.
Ka pai. – Thank you.

Place Names

Many place names have a clear Maori influence. Maori words you may come across incorporated in New Zealand's place names include:

anatoki – axe or adze in a cave; cave or valley in the shape of an axe
awa – river or valley
ika – fish
iti – small
kahurangi – treasured possession, special greenstone
kai – food
kainga – village
kare – rippling
kotinga – cutting or massacre
koura – crayfish
manga – branch, stream or tributary
mangarakau – plenty of sticks, a great many trees
manu – bird
maunga – mountain
moana – sea or lake
moko – tattoo
motu – island
nui – big
o – of
one – beach, sand or mud
onekaka – red-hot or burning sand
pa – fortified village
papa – flat, broad slab
parapara – the soft mud used for dyeing flax
patarua – killed by the thousands, site of early tribal massacres
pohatu – stone
puke – hill
rangi – sky, heavens
rangiheata – absence of clouds; a range seen in the early morning
repo – swamp
roa – long
roto – lake
rua – hole, two
takaka – killing stick for parrot, or bracken
tane – man

tapu – sacred or forbidden
tata – close to, dash against, twin islands
te – the
totaranui – place of big totara trees
uruwhenua – enchanted objects
wahine – woman
waka – canoe
wai – water
waikaremumu – bubbling waters
waingaro – lost, waters that disappear in certain seasons
wainui – big bay or many rivers, the ocean
wero – challenge
whanau – extended family
whanga – bay or inlet
whare – house
whenua – land or country

Try a few – Whanga-roa is 'long bay', Roto-rua is 'two lakes', Roto-roa is 'long lake', Wai-kare-iti is 'little rippling water'. All those names with 'wai' in them – Waitomo, Waitara, Waioru, Wairoa, Waitoa, Waihi, and so on – all have something to do with water.

However, a little knowledge can be a dangerous thing, and words don't always mean the sum of their components. If you're interested, *A Dictionary of Maori Place Names* by AW Reed (Reed, Auckland, 2nd edition 1982, reprinted 1992, paperback) is an excellent reference for understanding Maori placenames all over New Zealand, and it's small enough to be no trouble to carry around.

Facts for the Visitor

VISAS & EMBASSIES

Everyone needs a passport to enter New Zealand. If you enter on an Australian or New Zealand passport, or any other passport containing an Australian or New Zealand residence visa, your passport must be valid on arrival. All other passports must be valid for at least three months beyond the time you intend to stay in New Zealand, or one month beyond the intended stay if the issuing government has an embassy or consulate in New Zealand that is able to issue and renew passports.

Australian citizens or holders of current Australian resident return visas do not need a visa or permit to enter New Zealand, and they can stay in New Zealand as long as they like. There is no need for Australians to have a work permit should they wish to work in New Zealand.

Citizens of the UK and other British passport holders who have evidence of the right to live permanently in the UK do not need a visa, and upon arrival in New Zealand they are issued with a permit to stay in the country for up to six months.

Citizens of the following countries do not need a visa, and upon arrival in New Zealand they are issued with a permit good for a three months' stay:

Austria, Belgium, Brunei, Canada, Denmark, Finland, France, Germany, Greece, Iceland, Indonesia, Ireland, Italy, Japan, Kiribati, South Korea, Liechtenstein, Luxembourg, Malaysia, Malta, Monaco, Nauru, the Netherlands, Norway, Portugal, Singapore, Spain, Sweden, Switzerland, Thailand, Tuvalu, USA

Citizens of all other countries require a visa to enter New Zealand, available from any NZ embassy or consular agency in the world. Visas are normally valid for a three months' stay.

To qualify for a visitor's permit on arrival, or to qualify for a visa if you need one, you must be able to show:

1. Your passport, valid for three months beyond the time of your intended stay in New Zealand.
2. Evidence of sufficient funds to support yourself in New Zealand for the time of your intended stay, without working. This is calculated to be NZ$1000 per month (NZ$400 per month if your accommodation has been prepaid) and can be in the form of cash, travellers' cheques, bank drafts or the following credit cards: American Express, Bankcard, Diners Club, MasterCard or Visa.
3. Onward tickets to a country to which you can show you have right of entry, with firm bookings if travelling on special rate air fares.

Although every visitor to New Zealand is not asked to produce all these documents, you must have them. If you don't, you may be held up at NZ customs and not allowed to enter the country, or you may not be allowed to board the plane in the first place. If you do not have sufficient funds, you can still come if you have a friend or relative in New Zealand who is willing to sponsor you, that is, who will guarantee your accommodation and maintenance.

As with almost anywhere in the world entry requirements are likely to change, so always check the situation shortly before you depart. There's nothing worse than arriving at the airport for your flight and being turned back because you don't have a visa, when you thought you didn't need one!

If you know in advance that you will want to stay longer than the permitted time, or if you intend to work or study in New Zealand, you must obtain a visa, work permit or student permit before coming to New Zealand, even if you are from a country that otherwise would not require a visa.

It is illegal for you to work in New Zealand on a visitor's permit. You can apply for a work permit either before or after you arrive, but you will be granted permission to work only if there are no suitable New Zealand job seekers who could do the job you have been offered, and you will only be able to work for the remaining time you are entitled to stay as a visitor.

You can study for up to three months on a visitor's permit, provided it is one single course of not more than three months' duration. If you want to study longer, you will need to obtain a student permit.

If you decide you want to stay longer in New Zealand, you can apply for an extension of your visitor's permit. All visitors are allowed to stay for up to nine months, provided they apply for further permits and meet normal visitor requirements. 'Genuine tourists' and a few other categories of people can be granted stays of up to 12 months.

You can apply for a work permit, a student permit or an extension of your visitor's permit at any office of the New Zealand Immigration Service. They have offices in Auckland, Manukau, Hamilton, Palmerston North, Wellington, Christchurch and Dunedin. Requirements for an extension are the same as those for your initial visa or visitors' permit.

Be careful not to overstay your time. Extensions are easy to get, provided you meet the requirements. If you overstay your permit, however, you are subject to removal from the country.

New Zealand Embassies & Consulates

New Zealand embassies and consulates in other countries include:

Australia
    High Commission, Commonwealth Ave, Canberra, ACT 2600 (☎ (6) 270 4211; fax 273 3194)
    Consulate-General, Watkins Place Building, 288 Edward St, (GPO Box 62), Brisbane, QLD 4001 (☎ (7) 221 9933; fax 229 7495)
    Consulate-General, 60 Albert Rd, South Melbourne (PO Box 7275, Melbourne, VIC 3004) (☎ (3) 696 0399; fax 696 0391)
    Consulate-General, 16th Floor, State Bank Centre, 52 Martin Place (GPO Box 365), Sydney, NSW 2001 (☎ (2) 233 8388; fax 231 6369)
    Consulate-General, Level 13, 83 Mount St (GPO Box 1166), North Sydney, NSW 2059 (☎ (2) 959 3011; fax 959 5116)
Canada
    High Commission, Suite 801, Metropolitan House, 99 Bank St, Ottawa, Ont K1P 6G3 (☎ (613) 238 5991; fax 238 5707)
    Consulate-General, Suite 1200-888 Dunsmuir St (PO Box 10071, Pacific Centre), Vancouver, BC

V6C 3K4 (☎ (604) 684 7388/2117; fax 684 7333)
France
    Embassy, 7 ter, rue Leonard de Vinci, 75116, Paris (☎ (1) 4500 24 11; fax 4501 26 39)
Germany
    Embassy, Bundeskanzlerplatz 2-10, 5300 Bonn 1 (☎ (228) 22 80 70; fax 22 16 87)
    New Zealand Consulate-General, Heimhuderstr 56, 2000 Hamburg 13 (☎ (40) 442 55510/20; fax 442 55549)
Ireland
    Consulate-General, 46 Upper Mount St, Dublin 2 (☎ (01) 762 464; fax 762 489)
Italy
    Embassy, Via Zara 28, Rome 00198 (☎ (6) 440 2928/30; fax 440 2984)
Japan
    Embassy, 20-4-Kamiyama-cho, Shibuya-ku, Tokyo 150 (☎ (3) 3467 2271/75; fax 3467 6843)
    Embassy Annex, Toho Twin Tower Building, 2nd Floor, 1-5-2 Yurakucho, Chiyoda-ku, Tokyo 100 (☎ (3) 3508 9981; fax 3501 2326)
    (NZ also has consulates in Fukuoka, Hokkaido, Nagoya, Osaka and Sendai)
Netherlands
    Embassy, Mauritskade 25, 2514 HD The Hague (☎ (70) 346 93 24; fax 363 29 83)
Switzerland
    Consulate-General, 28A Chemin du Petit-Saconnex, CH-1209 Geneva (PO Box 334, CH-1211, Geneva 19) (☎ (22) 734 95 30; fax 734 30 62)
UK
    High Commission, New Zealand House, The Haymarket, London SW1Y 4TQ (☎ (71) 973 0366/63; fax 973 0370)
USA
    Embassy, 37 Observatory Circle NW, Washington, DC (☎ (202) 328 4848; fax 667 5227)
    Consulate-General, Suite 1530, Tishman Building, 15th Floor, 10960 Wilshire Blvd, Los Angeles, CA 90024 (☎ (310) 477 8241; fax 473 5621)
    Consulate, 1674 South Parkway East, Memphis, TN 38106 (☎ (901) 575 7928; fax 575 8498)
    Consulate, 6810 51st Ave NE, Seattle, WA 98115 (☎ (206) 525 9881; fax 543 0801)

Foreign Embassies & Consulates in NZ

Foreign embassies in New Zealand are in Wellington, the capital city; see the Wellington section for details. A number of countries also have consulates in Auckland and Christchurch; see the Auckland and Christchurch sections for details on these.

DOCUMENTS

No special documents other than your passport are required in New Zealand. Since no vaccinations are required to enter New Zealand, an international health certificate is not necessary.

If you are from a country whose driver's licence is not recognised in New Zealand, you will need an International Driving Permit if you want to drive. It must be issued by your home country. See the Getting Around chapter for details.

If you'll be travelling by bus or airplane in New Zealand, get an International Youth Hostel card (called a YHA card in New Zealand) or a VIP Backpackers Card. They'll give you up to a 50% discount on domestic air travel and a 30% discount on major bus lines, plus dozens of other discounts. An ISIC card (International Student Identity Card) will also entitle you to certain discounts.

CUSTOMS

Customs allowances are 200 cigarettes (or 50 cigars or 250 grammes of tobacco), 4.5 litres of wine or beer and one 1125 ml (40 oz) bottle of spirits or liqueur. As in most places the customs people are very fussy about drugs. Like Australia they are also fussy about animal products and the threat of animal disease, which is not surprising when they've got 60 million sheep at risk.

MONEY

The currencies of Australia, the UK, USA, Canada, Germany and Japan are all easily changed in New Zealand. Westpac banks, found throughout the country, will exchange these and about 30 other currencies.

American Express, Visa, MasterCard and Thomas Cook travellers' cheques are all widely recognised. Visa, MasterCard, Australian Bankcard, American Express and Diners Club credit cards are the most widely recognised. Banks will give cash advances on Visa and MasterCard, but for American Express card transactions you must go to an American Express office. American Express has offices or representatives in Auckland, Wellington, Christchurch, Queenstown, Dunedin, Nelson, Whangarei, Lower Hutt, Rotorua, Hamilton and Pukekohe.

As in most countries, if you need to have money sent to you it's probably easiest to do it by telegraphic transfer, bank to bank.

If you're intending a long stay it may be worth opening a bank account. Westpac and the Bank of New Zealand (BNZ) are probably the two banks with the most branches throughout the country, easy to get to on your travels, and you can request a card for the 24-hour teller machines giving you access to your money anytime. The ASB issues a cash card for teller machines on the spot, which is useful, and you can even choose your own pin number.

PostBank, which was once a part of the post office but is now independent, is another bank with many branches but their services are a bit more limited.

Unless otherwise noted all prices quoted in this book are in NZ dollars.

Currency

New Zealand's currency is dollars and cents. There are five, 10, 20, 50 and 100 dollar notes and five, 10, 20 and 50 cent, $1 and $2 coins. Yes their coins will fit Australian parking meters and pay phones!

You can bring in as much of any currency as you like and unused foreign currency or travellers' cheques which you brought in with you may be exported without limitations. Unused NZ currency can be changed to foreign currency before you leave the country.

Exchange Rates

A$1	=	NZ$1.21
C$1	=	NZ$1.36
DM1	=	NZ$1.05
S$1	=	NZ$1.19
UK£1	=	NZ$2.65
US$1	=	NZ$1.78
¥100	=	NZ$1.74

Banks are open from 9.30 am to 4 pm Monday to Friday. Exchange rates may vary a few cents from bank to bank; you'll get a slightly better rate for travellers' cheques than for cash. At most banks there's no service charge for changing travellers' cheques, only a five cent stamp fee per cheque.

Costs
It is possible to travel quite economically in New Zealand, or there's plenty of opportunity to spend up. If you stay in hostels, the cost will usually be around $12 to $16 per person, per night. In motor camps, costs are about $20 to $25 for one or two people in simple cabins, about half that for camping. Basic DOC campsites are even cheaper, ranging on average from $2 to $6 per person. Guesthouses, farmstays, homestays and B&Bs typically charge around $50 or $60 a night for two, but it *can* be that much per person. Cheaper hotels are about $35/50 for singles/doubles, while motels are usually around $60 to $70 for two.

Hostels, motor camps and motels all have kitchens for guests' use, so staying in these gives you the option of doing your own cooking. Eating out can cost anywhere from around $5 for a simple takeaway meal to around $50 or $60 for two for dinner at most medium-priced restaurants.

The average long-distance (three to five-hour) bus ride might cost around $30, or half that with a YHA or VIP card. If you have a few people together, hiring a car or buying one on the buy-back system may be just as economical as taking the bus. Hitchhiking and cycling are also popular ways to get around and they don't cost a thing.

Of course one of the main reasons people come to New Zealand is to participate in the host of activities the country is known for. Some cost nothing – tramping, swimming, bird-watching or whatever. There are so many enjoyable activities that do cost something, however, that activities can end up being a major part of the travel budget.

Tipping
Tipping is not a widespread or traditional custom in New Zealand, and many Kiwis still regard it as a rather odd foreign custom

that they can't quite see the need for. Nevertheless, it is sometimes done, principally in the major centres where there's been more foreign influence. The only time you would give someone a tip is in a restaurant (not in a simple cafe) and even then, only if you feel you have received exceptional service. The tip would be about 5% of the bill.

Consumer Taxes
GST (Goods & Services Tax) adds 12½% to the price of just about everything in New Zealand. Most prices are quoted inclusive of GST but when you're paying for something beware of any small print an-nouncing that the price is GST exclusive; you'll be hit for the extra 12½% on top of the stated cost.

CLIMATE & WHEN TO GO
Lying between 34°S and 47°S, New Zealand lies squarely in the 'roaring forties' latitude, meaning it has a prevailing and rather continual wind blowing over it from west to east all year round, ranging from a gentle breeze pleasantly stirring and freshening the air, to occasional raging gales in winter.

This breeze is relatively warm and moisture-laden coming across the Tasman Sea. When it hits New Zealand's mountains the wind is swept upwards, cools, and drops its moisture, resulting in a much rainier climate on the west side of those high points than on the east side. When the wind comes up from the south, it's coming from Antarctica and is icy and cold; a southerly wind always means cold weather.

The North Island and the South Island, because of their different geological features, have two distinct patterns of rainfall. In the South Island, the Southern Alps, which make a north-to-south spine along most of the island, act as a barrier for the moisture-laden winds coming west across the Tasman Sea, creating a wet climate on the west side of the mountains and a dry climate on the east side: the annual rainfall is over 7500 mm per year on the west side but it's only about 330 mm a year on the east side, even though it's not so far away.

The South Island's geography also creates

a wind pattern in which the prevailing wind, swept upwards, cooled and losing its moisture in the form of rain or snow, blows eastwards down onto the Canterbury Plains as a dry wind, gathering heat and speed as it blows downhill and across the Canterbury Plains towards the Pacific coast. In summer this wind can be very hot, dry and fierce. Called a katabatic or foehn wind, it is similar to other famous winds in the world including the chinook wind formed by the Canadian and American Rockies. In the Grey River valley on the South Island's west coast there's another kind of downhill wind, locally called 'The Barber'.

In the North Island, the west sides of the high volcanoes get a lot more rain than the east sides, though since there is not such a complete barrier as the Alps, the rain shadow effect is not so pronounced. Rainfall is more evenly distributed over the North Island, averaging around 1300 mm per year. In the North Island there's some rainfall throughout the year – typically there are rainy days alternating with fine days, all year round – and it's enough to keep the landscape always green.

The temperature is a few degrees cooler in the South Island than the North Island, and of course it's cooler in winter (June, July and

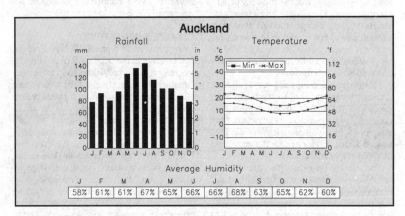

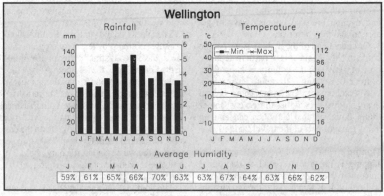

August) than in summer (December, January and February). There are several regional variations – it's quite warm and pleasant up in the Northland at any time of year, where it's almost always a few degrees warmer than the rest of the country. Higher altitudes are always considerably cooler, and it's usually windy in Wellington, which catches the winds whistling through the Cook Strait in a sort of wind tunnel from the Tasman Sea to the Pacific Ocean.

Snow is mostly seen in the mountains, though there can be snowfalls even at sea level in the South Island, particularly in the extreme south. Some of the plains and higher plateaus also receive snow in winter, notably the Canterbury Plains in the South Island and the high plateau around the Tongariro National Park in the North Island, especially on the 'desert' (east) side. Snow is seldom seen near sea level on the west coasts, and not at all in the far north.

One of the most important things travellers need to know about the New Zealand climate is that it's a maritime climate, as opposed to the continental climate typical of larger land masses. This means the weather can frequently change with amazing rapidity. We've alluded to this at many places throughout this book – it affects you in many

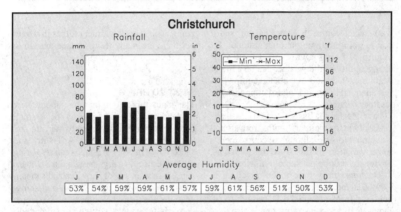

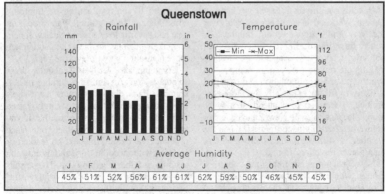

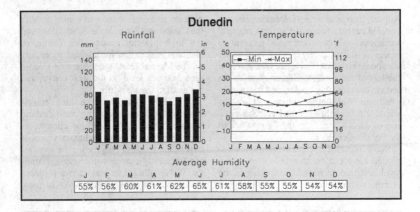

Dunedin

Rainfall · Temperature

Average Humidity

J	F	M	A	M	J	J	A	S	O	N	D
55%	56%	60%	61%	62%	65%	61%	58%	55%	55%	54%	54%

ways when you're in New Zealand, and if you're going tramping at high altitudes, for example, being aware of the extreme changeability of the weather can be a life or death matter. So it is essential to equip yourself adequately for all kinds of unpredictable weather changes.

New Zealand's busiest tourist season is generally in the warmer months from around November to April, though of course there's some variation in this – ski resort towns, obviously, will be packed out in winter.

The most busy time to be travelling in New Zealand is during the summer school holidays from around 20 December to 30 January. To a lesser extent there's also a lot of travelling going on at Easter weekend, at Labour Weekend in late October, and over the May and August school holidays. If you're travelling during the summer school holidays, when New Zealanders as well as visitors are out on the road, remember that every type of accommodation and transport is likely to fill up, especially the more economical places, so plan ahead. It may be more pleasant to visit New Zealand either before or after this hectic period, when the weather is still warm and there aren't as many other travellers around.

New Zealand is not like some countries, though, where the weather is so miserable at some times of year that there's no point in

going. You'll need warmer clothes in winter but there are many things to see and do in New Zealand all year round.

WHAT TO BRING
The main thing to remember about New Zealand is that while it may be a small compact country it has widely varying and very changeable weather. A T-shirt and shorts day at the Bay of Islands can also bring snow and sleet to a high pass in the Southern Alps. In fact, on any of New Zealand's mountains you can often meet T-shirt-and-snow-gear weather on the same day. So come prepared for widely varying climatic conditions and if you're planning on tramping come prepared for anything! Waterproof rain gear and a warm down sleeping bag will help to make your stay in New Zealand much more pleasant at any time of the year.

Come prepared for New Zealand's 'dress standards' too. An amazing number of restaurants, bars, clubs and pubs have signs proclaiming their equally amazingly varied dress rules. It sometimes seems that if you combined all the rules together (one place proclaims no denim, the next no leather, or no shirts without collars, no sandals, no gang insignia, etc) the only thing you'd be permitted to wear would be your birthday suit! Seriously though, men should bring a tie if they're planning on eating in upmarket restaurants.

Otherwise there are no great preparations to be made. New Zealand is a modern, well-organised country and you should be able to find most visitor's requirements, from film to pharmaceuticals.

TOURIST OFFICES
Local Tourist Offices

There are local tourist information centres in nearly every city or town – almost any town big enough to have a pub and a corner shop seems to have a tourist information centre. They are united by VIN, the Visitor Information Network, which strives to ensure that each of its members provides top quality information and service.

The centres have abundant information on local activities and attractions, they give out free brochures and maps, and many will even make bookings for accommodation, activities and transport. They are an excellent resource for travellers everywhere in New Zealand; make use of them.

Overseas Reps

The New Zealand Tourism Board (NZTB) has its main office in Wellington and representatives in various countries around the world. Its purpose is to promote tourism in New Zealand; you can contact them for information about travelling in New Zealand and they will send you some brochures about the country. NZTB offices include:

NZTB Head Office
  PO Box 95, Wellington, New Zealand (☎ (04) 472 8860; fax 478 1736)
Australia
  Ground Floor, 288 Edward St (GPO Box 2634), Brisbane Qld 4001 (☎ (7) 221 3176; fax 221 3178)
  Level 19, Como Office Tower, 644 Chapel St, South Yarra, Melbourne VIC 3141 (☎ (3) 823 6283; fax 823 6276)
  Downtown Duty Free House, 1st Floor, 84 Pitt St, Sydney NSW 2000 (GPO Box 614) NSW, 2001 (☎ (2) 221 7333; fax 235 0737)

Canada
  Suite 1200-888 Dunsmuir St, Vancouver BC, V6C 3K4 (☎ (604) 684 2117, ☎ freephone 1 800 888 5494; fax 684 1265)
Germany
  Friedrichstrasse 10-12, D-6000 Frankfurt/Main 1, Germany (☎ (69) 971 2110; fax 9712 1113)
Japan
  Meiji Seimei Sakaisuji Honmachi Building, 2nd Floor, 1-7-15 Minami Honmachi, Chuo Ku, Osaka-shi 541 (☎ (6) 268 8335; fax 268 8412)
  New Zealand Embassy Annex, Toho Twin Tower Building, 2nd Floor, 1-5-2 Yurakucho, Chiyoda-Ku, Tokyo 100 (☎ (3) 3508 9981; fax 3501 2326)
UK
  New Zealand House, Haymarket, SW1Y 4TQ London (☎ (071) 973 0363; fax 839 8929)
USA
  1111 North Dearborn St, Suite 2705, Chicago, IL 60610 (☎ (312) 440 1345)
  1825 North Lincoln Plaza, Suite 603, Chicago, IL 60614 (☎ (312) 587 1190; fax 587 1192)
  501 Santa Monica Blvd, No 300, Santa Monica, CA 90401 (☎ (310) 395 7480, ☎ freephone 1 800 388 5494; fax 395 5453)
  Office of the Trade Development Board, Suite 1206, 432 Park Ave South, New York, NY 10016 (☎ (212) 447 0550; fax 447 0558)

USEFUL ORGANISATIONS

A number of organisations provide useful services for travellers in New Zealand, especially the visitor information centres, the Department of Conservation (DOC) and the Automobile Association (AA). Most useful of all is the network of visitor information centres throughout the country. DOC also operates information and visitor centres in cities, towns and parks throughout New Zealand; these are great for maps and information about outdoor areas and outdoor activities, especially tramping.

The AA is a useful organisation to join if you are doing any driving; its benefits and services are described in the Car & Motorbike section of the Getting Around chapter. Like the visitor information centres and DOC offices, AA offices or agents are found in most cities and towns throughout New Zealand. In this book we've listed visitor information centres, DOC and AA offices wherever they exist. Among the three, you can find out almost anything you could want to know about New Zealand.

If you're a student of any age, or if you're under 26, the STA (Student Travel Agencies) is a good travel resource. They offer discounted airfares, sell International Student Identity (ISIC) Cards and provide other services for both international and domestic travel. STA has offices in Auckland, Hamilton, Palmerston North, Wellington, Christchurch and Dunedin.

BUSINESS HOURS
Office hours are generally Monday to Friday from 9 am to 5 pm. Most government offices are open Monday to Friday from around 8 am to 4 or 4.30 pm. Shops are usually open Monday to Friday from 9 am to 5 pm plus Saturday mornings, with 'late-night shopping' to 8 or 9 pm one night of the week, usually Thursday or Friday. Many small convenience stores (called 'dairies' in NZ) stay open much longer hours and some of the larger supermarkets now also stay open seven days a week.

HOLIDAYS
People from the northern hemisphere never seem to become completely familiar with upside-down seasons. To them Christmas simply doesn't fall in the middle of summer and how is it possible to have mid-winter cold in August? But it's worth remembering, since Christmas is in the middle of summer and the school holidays, which means lots of New Zealanders are on holiday, which in turn means crowds and higher prices. If you want to avoid the school-age hordes, they're out of captivity from mid-December until the end of January (the same time as Australian school kids) and then for a couple of weeks in May and again in August.

Public holidays include:

January
    New Year's Day and the next day (1st & 2nd)
February
    Waitangi Day or New Zealand Day (6th)
March
    Good Friday/Easter Monday (March or April)
April
    Anzac Day (25th)

June
    Queen's Birthday (1st Monday)
October
    Labour Day (4th Monday)
December
    Christmas Day and Boxing Day (25th & 26th)

CULTURAL EVENTS
A number of cultural events and festivals are held annually around New Zealand. Some of the more noteworthy ones include:

January
    Annual Yachting Regatta – Auckland
    Summer City Programme – Wellington, beginning of January to end of February – two months of festivals and entertainment around the city
February
    Marlborough Food & Wine Festival – Blenheim, 2nd weekend in February
    International Festival of the Arts – Wellington; an entire month of national and international culture (even-numbered years only)
    Art Deco weekend (third weekend) – Napier; dinners, balls, fancy dress and Deco tours
March
    Fiesta Week (mid-March) – Auckland; great fun with some terrific fireworks and the 'Round the Bays' run
    Golden Shears Sheep Shearing Contest – Masterton; a major event in this sheepish country!
    International Billfish Tournament – Bay of Islands
    Ngaruawahia Regatta for Maori Canoes – Hamilton
April
    Highland Games – Hastings
May
    National Woodcrafts Festival – Christchurch
June
    New Zealand Agricultural Field Days – a major agricultural show at Mystery Creek, Hamilton
September
    New Zealand Listener Women's Book Festival – week-long festival of women's books, with events throughout the country
November
    Canterbury Show Week – Christchurch
    International Trout Fishing Contest – Rotorua

Each province also has its own anniversary day holiday. Local holidays include:

Wellington	22 January
Auckland	29 January
Northland	29 January

Top Left: Mt Aspiring, Otago (JL)
Top Right: Sandfly Point, Milford Track, Southland (HL)
Bottom Left: Waitomo Caves, The King Country (AB)
Bottom Right: Relaxing, Tutoko Valley, Southland (JW)

Top: Milford Track, Southland (HL)
Bottom: Lighthouse, Castle Point, The Wairarapa (HL)

Nelson	1 February
Otago	23 March
Southland	23 March
Taranaki	31 March
Hawke's Bay	1 November
Marlborough	1 November
Westland	1 December
Canterbury	16 December

When these local holidays fall between Friday and Sunday, they are usually observed on the following Monday; if they fall between Tuesday and Thursday, they are held on the preceding Monday.

There are many smaller annual events held all over New Zealand; each little town seems to have its annual fair, often involving simple sports like racing horses on the beach, wheelbarrow and sugar bag races, woodchopping and sheep-shearing contests.

POST

Post offices are open from 9 am to 5 pm on weekdays. You can have mail addressed to you care of 'Poste Restante, CPO' in whichever town you require. CPO stands for Chief Post Office. Mail is usually held for 30 days.

For mail within New Zealand there are two options in how to send it. Regular postage stamps cost 40 cents; delivery time is two days between major centres, a bit longer for rural areas. Or there's Fast Post, promising next-day delivery between major centres (Auckland, Wellington, Christchurch), two-day delivery for rural areas. Fast Post stamps cost 80 cents.

For international mail, use Fast Post; just affix a Fast Post sticker or use a Fast Post envelope. The cost and approximate delivery times for international letters include:

Australia	$1	3 to 6 days
Pacific Islands	$1	3 to 8 days
UK & Europe	$1.80	6 to 12 days
USA & Canada	$1.50	4 to 10 days
Mexico & Latin America	$1.80	6 to 12 days
East Asia (China, Japan, Malaysia, Indonesia, etc)	$1.50	4 to 10 days
West Asia, India & Africa	$1.80	6 to 12 days

It costs $1 to send postcards anywhere in the world; remember to affix a Fast Post sticker.

TELECOMMUNICATIONS
Telephones

Most pay phones in New Zealand have now been converted to the card-operated type. The few coin phones still remaining are usually in the more remote areas.

The card phones accept $5, $10, $20 or $50 cards, which you can buy from any shop displaying the lime-green 'phone cards available here' sign. Phone cards are sold at many places including visitor information centres, news agencies, tobacconists, petrol stations and at many dairies, hostels and larger hotels.

To use the card phones, simply insert your card and follow the instructions on the telephone. The meter automatically deducts the cost of your call from your card, and tells you how much value your card has left when you finish the call. Phone cards are quite a collectors' item in New Zealand, so don't throw your old card away; it won't be hard to find someone who wants it.

As well as making normal local calls, you can use phone cards for making long distance calls from pay phones, including international calls. Because you can dial direct, you do not have to pay for an operator to connect you.

If you intend travelling in more remote areas, take plenty of 20 cent coins to use, as only the old-fashioned coin-operated phones may be available. You usually put your money in, dial the number, and press button A when it is answered. If there's no answer, press button B and your money will be returned.

An option for long-distance telephone calls is the call-back service. Dial 013 before you make the call and an operator will ring you back immediately after you hang up to tell you how much it cost. This service costs an extra $2.80 on top of the price for the call, but it means that many hostels, hotels and so on will allow you to place long-distance calls from their telephones, if you pay on the spot. Of course you can always just find out the rate, time yourself and pay them anyway, but many businesses will prefer you use the call-back service to be sure of the cost.

To reach the local and national operator dial 010, for directory assistance anywhere in New Zealand it's 018.

For emergencies in the major centres dial 111 and say whether you want police, ambulance or fire brigade. Emergency calls are not charged.

STD Codes

City codes, called area codes in many countries, are called STD codes in New Zealand. The entire South Island and Stewart Island are on the (03) STD code. The North Island has various regional STD codes: (09) in Auckland and the Northland, (07) in the Coromandel Peninsula, Bay of Plenty and central North Island, (06) in the East Coast, lower-central North Island and Taranaki regions, and (04) in and around Wellington. Note that you need to use the STD code even within a region if the place you're calling is a fair distance from where you are.

STD codes for every city and town are listed in the introductory pages of the telephone directory.

In this book, we have not listed the STD code for each telephone number. Unless indicated otherwise, the code for every telephone number in each chapter is given in the Information section at the beginning of the chapter. For the South Island, just remember to dial 03 for all numbers if you're not in the South Island, and if you're already there, dial the 03 code if you are calling long-distance within the island or to Stewart Island.

International Telephone Calls

Charges and instructions for direct dialling of international calls are listed in the introductory pages of telephone directories. Direct dialling is easy and can be done from private or card phones; simply dial '00' to get out of the country, then the country code, area code and number. The country code for New Zealand is 64. Country codes for some of the more frequently dialled countries include:

Australia	61
Canada	1
Germany	49
Japan	81
UK	44
USA	1

There is both a regular rate and an economy rate for telephoning to many countries; to other countries there is only one fixed rate, regardless of when you phone. Where there is an economy rate, it varies from country to country; for example, the economy hours to phone to Australia are from 11 pm to 8 am Sunday to Friday and all day Saturday; to the UK it's the same except it begins at midnight rather than 11 pm; to Germany or Japan it's every day from midnight to 8 am; to the USA and Canada it's from 10 pm to 8 am Monday to Saturday and all day Sunday. The telephone directory lists prices and economy hours for every country. Prices are charged by the minute.

A few sample prices include:

Country	Regular rate/min	Economy rate/min
Australia	$1.58	$0.99
Canada	$2.85	$1.98
Germany	$3.00	$1.98
Japan	$3.00	$1.98
UK	$2.85	$1.98
USA	$2.85	$1.98

You can make a price-required call to any another country by dialling 0160 rather than 00 to begin the call; the charge for this service is 34 cents.

For the international operator dial 0170; international directory information is 0172.

Country Direct Many countries have Country Direct services, enabling you to phone directly to the operator in that country, bypassing the operator in New Zealand. There are various times when using this service can be very convenient, such as when you want to charge a call to your telephone number in your home country. It's also often just a lot easier to communicate with the operator in your home country. Details, including the Country Direct numbers for all the various countries that have the service, can be found in the introductory pages of the telephone directory or by asking the New Zealand international operator.

If you're ringing *to* New Zealand using New Zealand's Country Direct service, you can charge the call to your New Zealand Telecom card if you have one, or to a variety of internationally recognised credit cards (MasterCard, Visa, Diner's Club and American Express) – even if the credit card comes from a country other than New Zealand.

Fax

Fax machines have become very common in New Zealand; many hotels, motels and even hostels now have fax machines. Most centres of any size have some kind of business offering fax services. Typically the charge to send a fax is about $5 plus the telephone toll charges. Receiving a fax costs around $1 per page.

TIME

Being close to the international date line, New Zealand is one of the first places in the world to start a new day. New Zealand is 12 hours ahead of GMT (Greenwich Mean Time) and UTC (Universal Time Coordinated) and two hours ahead of Australian Eastern Standard Time.

In summer New Zealand observes Daylight Saving Time, an advance of one hour, which comes into effect on the last Sunday in October and lasts to the first Sunday of the following March. Of course some other countries also have Daylight Saving Time so it's not always the same, but usually the time differences are:

When it is:	It is:
Noon in NZ	midnight in London
	8 pm in New York
	8 pm in Toronto
	5 pm in San Francisco
	10 am in Sydney
	9 am in Tokyo
	8 am in Hong Kong
	8 am in Singapore

ELECTRICITY

Electricity is 240 volts AC, 50 cycle, as in Europe and Australia, and Australian-type three-prong plugs are used.

LAUNDRY

You won't see many laundromats in New Zealand, but virtually every accommodation place provides a coin-operated washing machine and dryer where you can clean your clothes for about $2.

WEIGHTS & MEASURES

New Zealand uses the metric system for all weights, measures, distances, etc. Until 1967 it was on the British Imperial system, however, and although in ordinary day-to-day usage the metric measures are used (kilometres of distance, kilograms of fruit and vegetables, etc) you will still encounter vestiges of the old system. Measures of land are still often expressed in acres rather than hectares, if you go skydiving they'll take you up to 9000 feet rather than 3000 metres, and if you ask someone how much they weigh you might get the answer in kilos, pounds, or stone (a stone is 14 pounds).

BOOKS & MAPS
History

A History of New Zealand by Keith Sinclair (Penguin, Auckland, 1991, paperback) is a readable and entertaining general history of New Zealand, from the Maori account of the creation of the earth up to the present. *The People and the Land – Te Tangata me Te Whenua: An Illustrated History of New Zealand 1820-1920* by Judith Binney, Judith Bassett & Erik Olssen (Bridget Williams Books, Wellington, 1990, paperback) is another good history of New Zealand, with plenty of interesting illustrations.

The award-winning *Two Worlds: First Meetings between Maori and Europeans 1642-1772* by Anne Salmond (Penguin, Auckland, 1991, paperback) is an account of the first points of contact between the Maori and the European explorers, a fascinating book of two-sided anthropological history telling the story as it was experienced by both sides.

Maori: A Photographic and Social History by Michael King (Reed, Auckland, 1983, paperback) is a comprehensive illustrated history of the Maori people.

The Old-Time Maori by Makereti (New Women's Press, Auckland, 1986, paperback) is an important historical document. First published in London in 1938, the book was the first ethnographic account of the Maori people ever written by a Maori scholar. It's fascinating reading.

One of the continuously most controversial elements of New Zealand history is the Treaty of Waitangi. Many books have been written about the treaty and the debates surrounding it. One of the best is *The Treaty of Waitangi* by Claudia Orange (Bridget Williams Books, Wellington, 1987, paperback). The same author has written several other books about the treaty, including *An Illustrated History of the Treaty of Waitangi* (Allen & Unwin, Wellington, 1990, paperback).

Another significant moment in New Zealand history, noted around the world, was when Greenpeace's ship *Rainbow Warrior* was sunk by the French government in Auckland Harbour in 1985. Several books have been written about the incident; *Making Waves: The Greenpeace New Zealand Story* by Michael Szabo (Reed, Auckland, 1991, paperback) tells the story of this and other Greenpeace activities in New Zealand and the Pacific, with lots of colour illustrations.

Historical Biography Some of the most fascinating history has been told in the form of biography. *The Dictionary of New Zealand Biography* (Allen & Unwin, Wellington, Department of Internal Affairs, hardback) is a multi-volume collection of hundreds of short New Zealand biographies. Volume One, published in 1990 with over 600 biographies from the years 1769 to 1869, and Volume Two, published in 1993 with biographies from the years 1870 to 1900, are already out and a third volume is said to be on the way.

A People's History: Illustrated Biographies from The Dictionary of New Zealand Biography, Volume One, 1769-1869 selected by WH Oliver (Bridget Williams Books, Wellington, 1992, paperback) contains over 100 selected biographies of early New Zealanders, illustrated with historic photos.

Of course there are many biographies written about historical NZ figures. Three about Maori elders are particularly interesting. *Eruera: The Teachings of a Maori Elder* by Eruera Stirling as told to Anne Salmond (Oxford University Press, Auckland, 1980, paperback) won the Wattie Book of the Year Award, one of NZ's highest awards. *Te Puea* by Michael King (Sceptre, Auckland, 1977, paperback) tells the story of Te Puea Herangi, one of the most influential women in modern Maori history. *Whina*, also by Michael King (Penguin, Auckland, 1983, paperback), tells the story of Whina Cooper, another very important Maori figure, who organised her first public protest at age 18 and welcomed an international audience to the XIV Commonwealth Games in Auckland in 1990 at the age of 95.

NZ Women's Biography

The Book of New Zealand Women – Ko Kui Ma Te Kaupapa edited by Charlotte Macdonald, Merimeri Penfold & Bridget Williams (Bridget Williams Books, Wellington, 1991, paperback) is a large anthology of over 300 biographical essays of New Zealand women, a great resource.

Maori Culture

In recent years New Zealand has experienced a renaissance of interest in Maori culture, and many excellent books have been written about various aspects of it. Language books are mentioned in the Language section of the Facts about the Country chapter.

Some useful and insightful books have been written about the customs, protocol and meanings of things on the marae; it would be particularly useful to read one or more of these if you are going to visit a marae.

Te Marae: A Guide to Customs & Protocol by Hiwi & Pat Tauroa (Reed, Auckland,

1986, paperback) is a useful little 'how-to' book for non-Maoris who may be visiting a marae for the first time. It gives a background and understanding of customs and procedures on the marae, and good, readable advice about how one is to behave.

Hui: A Study of Maori Ceremonial Gatherings by Anne Salmond (Heinemann Reed, Auckland, 1976, reprinted 1990, paperback) is an excellent, more scholarly book about Maori gatherings on the marae. It's not written from a 'how-to' perspective, but as an insight into Maori culture.

Te Ao Hurihuri: Aspects of Maoritanga edited by Michael King (Reed, Auckland, 1992, paperback) is a collection of writings on many aspects of Maori culture, written by a number of respected Maori authors.

Tikanga Whakaaro: Key Concepts in Maori Culture by Cleve Barlow (Oxford University Press, Auckland, 1991, paperback) is a bilingual book in English and Maori, in which the author tells about Maori culture by taking 70 terms central to Maori culture and explaining their significance.

Maori Customs and Crafts compiled by Alan Armstrong (Viking Sevenseas Ltd, Paraparaumu, 1973, paperback) is only a small book in the Pocket Guide series but it tells a little bit about many different Maori customs and crafts, with illustrations.

Literature

New Zealand has an active literary scene, with a number of modern authors and a few old classics. Probably the most internationally known New Zealand writer is still Katherine Mansfield (1888-1923), who was born and raised in New Zealand and later moved to England, where she spent most of her short adult life and did most of her writing. Mansfield's short stories can be found in many volumes, including *The Stories of Katherine Mansfield: Definitive Edition* edited by Antony Alpers (Oxford University Press, Auckland, 1984, paperback).

Frank Sargeson (1903-82) is another classic New Zealand author. Within the country he is probably as well-known as Mansfield,

especially for his three-volume autobiography, his novels and many short stories, but since he lived all his life in New Zealand, his work did not become as widely known internationally.

The *Oxford Book of New Zealand Short Stories* edited by Vincent O'Sullivan (Oxford University Press, Auckland, 1992, paperback) is a good collection of New Zealand short stories, as is *Some Other Country: New Zealand's Best Short Stories* chosen by Marion McLeod & Bill Manhire (Bridget Williams Books, Wellington, 1992, paperback). For a wide collection of fiction by New Zealand women, try *In Deadly Earnest* collected by Trudie McNaughton (Century Hutchinson, Auckland, 1989, paperback).

For students of NZ literature there's the *Oxford History of New Zealand Literature in English* edited by Terry Sturm (Oxford University Press, Auckland, 1991, paperback), or the *Penguin History of New Zealand Literature* by Patrick Evans (Penguin, Auckland, 1990, paperback).

Maurice Shadbolt is the author of several fine historical novels about New Zealand – so far he's published nine novels, four collections of short stories and several nonfiction books. His best-known novel is probably *The Season of the Jew* (1987), which won the Wattie Book of the Year Award in 1987 and was chosen by the New York Times as one of the best books of that year.

Janet Frame is another popular novelist, poet and short story writer. Her three-volume autobiography was made famous by the film *An Angel at my Table* by acclaimed local director, Jane Campion. *Janet Frame: An Autobiography* (Random Century, Auckland, 1989, paperback) is a fascinating insight to her life, and her many works are widely available. Shonagh Koea is another popular author; her better-known works include *The Woman Who Never Went Home* (1987), *The Grandiflora Tree* (1989), *Staying Home and Being Rotten* (1992) and *Fifteen Rubies by Candlelight* (1993).

Other favourite New Zealand authors include Maurice Gee, whose novel *Going West* won the New Zealand Wattie Book

Award in 1993; Stevan Eldred-Gregg, Fiona Kidman, Robyn Hyde and Dame Ngaio Marsh.

Poetry Poet James K Baxter, who died in 1972, is possibly the best known NZ poet. Other include RAK Mason, Allen Curnow, Denis Glover, Hone Tuwhare and the animated Sam Hunt. *Contemporary New Zealand Poetry Nga Kupu Titohu o Aotearoa* edited by Miriama Evans, Harvey McQueen & Ian Wedde (Penguin, Auckland, 1989, paperback) is an excellent collection of NZ poetry, both in English and Maori.

Contemporary Maori & Pacific Literature
Te Ao Marama – Contemporary Maori Writing edited by Witi Ihimaera (Reed, Auckland, paperback) is a series of which two books have been published so far. *Volume One: Te Whakahuatanga o te Ao – Reflections of Reality* (1992) is an anthology of written and oral Maori literature; *Volume Two: He Whakaatanga o te Ao – The Reality* (1993) examines the crucial issues affecting Maori people as seen by several prominent Maori authors.

Witi Ihimaera, editor of the series, is a prolific Maori author of novels and short stories. Some of his better known novels include *The Matriarch* (1986), *Tangi* (1974) and *Pounamu, Pounamu* (1973).

Keri Hulme, author of *The Bone People* (Pan Books, London, 1983, paperback), is one of New Zealand's favourite modern authors; she received international acclaim when *The Bone People* won the British Booker McConnell Prize for fiction in 1985. She has published several other novels and books of poetry.

Alan Duff is a controversial author who writes about Maori people in modern New Zealand society. He has written two novels and one non-fiction book, all of which have generated heated debate. His first novel, *Once Were Warriors* (Tandem, Auckland, 1990, paperback) has been made into a film; his second is *One Night Out Stealing* (Tandem, Auckland, 1991, paperback). In 1993 his non-fiction *Maori: The Crisis and the Challenge* (Harper Collins, Auckland, 1993, paperback) sparked a rage of controversy.

Other significant Maori authors include novelists Apirana Taylor and Patricia Grace, and poet Hone Tuwhare.

With Auckland being the home of the largest concentrated population of Pacific islanders on earth, New Zealand also has some important Pacific Island authors. Albert Wendt, a Samoan author who is a professor of English at the University of Auckland, is one of the finest. His novels include *Leaves of the Banyan Tree* (1979), *Pouliuli* (1980), *Sons for the Return Home* (1987), *Ola* (1991) and *Black Rainbow* (1992); he has also published two poetry books and two collections of short stories.

The Shark that Ate the Sun: Ko e Ma go ne Kai e La by Niuean author John Puhiatau Pule (Penguin, Auckland, 1992, paperback) is another excellent book by a Pacific author, writing about the Pacific islanders' experience in New Zealand.

Maori Myths, Legends & Stories
A number of good books have been written about the rich legends, myths and stories of the Maori people, from the creation myth forward. An excellent one is the illustrated *Maori Myths and Tribal Legends* retold by Antony Alpers (Longman Paul, Auckland, 1964, reprinted 1992, paperback). Another smaller volume is the illustrated *Maori Myth and Legend* by AW Reed (Reed, Auckland, 1988, paperback).

Traditional Maori Stories introduced and translated by Margaret Orbell (Reed, Auckland, 1992, paperback is a fine book of Maori stories told side by side in English and Maori.

Modern Autobiography
Check out *The Life and Times of a Good Keen Man* by Barry Crump (Barry Crump Associates, PO Box 137, Opotiki, 1992, hardback). One of New Zealand's favourite characters, Barry Crump is a writer and rugged adventurer. He is the author of many popular books including *A Good Keen Man* (1960), *Hang On A Minute Mate* (1961) and

a long list of books after that, which still sell even after all these years. He is the quintessential Kiwi bushman, a living legend and a wonderful writer. (Thanks for writing your books, mate!)

Being Pakeha by Michael King (Hodder and Stoughton, Auckland, 1985, paperback) is the autobiography of one of New Zealand's foremost Maori historians, who is a Pakeha. It's an interesting position to be in and an interesting book.

Mihi Edwards is a contemporary Maori elder who writes very readable books telling the story of her life – a lot about how some of the current generation of Maori elders were raised, how they were punished if they spoke their language in school, and many other things about what it has been like to grow up Maori in Pakeha culture. The two autobiographical books published so far include *Mihipeka: Early Years* (Penguin, Auckland, 1990, paperback) and *Mihipeka: Time of Turmoil* (Penguin, Auckland, 1992, paperback).

Photography

There are innumerable coffee-table books of photographs of New Zealand. You'll find at least a dozen in almost any large bookstore in New Zealand, with titles like *New Zealand – the Glorious Islands, New Zealand – A Special Place, Beautiful New Zealand* and so on. Two of New Zealand's best photographers, Craig Potton and Robin Morrison, have published a number of books.

Art & Architecture

There are plenty of high quality art books on NZ's well-known artists. Many books have also been written about Maori arts & crafts. A truly magnificent one is *Taonga Maori: A Spiritual Journey Expressed through Maori Art* by the Australian Museum (Australian Museum, 6-8 College St, Sydney, NSW 2000; 1989, paperback). It's an impressive book with colour photographs and insightful text about some of the best Maori art in existence.

Architecture is not what people usually think of when thinking about New Zealand,

but the book *The New Zealand House* by Michael Fowler (partner in a Wellington architectural firm) & Robert van de Voort (photographer) (Lansdowne Press, Auckland, 1988, hardback) is a fascinating presentation of an amazing variety of NZ home architecture, with a wealth of colour photos of everything from grand Victorian palaces to home-made rolling caravan inventions.

Chatham Islands

Moriori: A People Rediscovered by Michael King (Viking, Auckland, 1989, hardback) tells about the Moriori people of the Chatham Islands and reveals that the truth about this people is very different from the common notions about them. The same author also wrote *A Land Apart: The Chatham Islands of New Zealand* by Michael King (text) and Robin Morrison (photographs) (Random Century, Auckland, 1990, hardback), a good book of photographs, history and stories of these remote islands.

Travel Guides

Innumerable specialised travel guides have been written about all kinds of things you can do in New Zealand. There are books about tramping, skiing, cycling, scuba diving, surfing, fishing, bird watching and many more. They're mentioned in the Outdoor Activities chapter in the appropriate sections.

The *Mobil New Zealand Travel Guides* by Diana & Jeremy Pope (Reed, Auckland, 1991, paperback) are excellent resources for historical background about hundreds of places you can visit if you're travelling around New Zealand. There's one book about the *North Island* and another about the *South Island*, both worth carrying if you like to know history, background and interesting stories about the places you visit.

The *Insight Guide – New Zealand* (Apa Productions, Hong Kong, 1992, paperback), with plenty of colour illustrations, is another guide for background about the country.

Cartoons

No overview of New Zealand publishing could be complete without mention of New Zealand's favourite comic strip, *Footrot Flats* by Murray Ball. Many books have been published of the adventures of the focal character, Dog, a mongrel black-and-white sheep dog, and his master Wal, the farmer. It's a delightful look into rural New Zealand farming life as told from the sheep dog's point of view; try to have a look at one of these books sometime while you're in New Zealand.

Bookshops

Whitcoull's and London Bookshops are two large bookshop chains with a wide selection of books, including sections specialising in New Zealand books; many of the Whitcoull's bookshops are especially good. Both have branches throughout New Zealand. Bennett's Government Bookshops, with branches in Auckland, Manukau, Hamilton, Palmerston North, Wellington, Christchurch and Dunedin are also excellent bookshops with a wide variety of books and maps about New Zealand.

Maps

Many excellent maps are widely available in New Zealand; you can easily find everything from street maps and road atlases to detailed topographical maps.

If you're a member of the Automobile Association (AA) you can go into any AA office, present your card, and get all the maps you want for free. The AA city, town, regional and highway maps are some of the best available. They also publish road atlases and large maps of the North and South Islands, which anyone can buy, member or not. The Shell road atlas, Wises maps and road atlases, and the Minimap series are also excellent; they are available at AA offices, Bennett's Government Bookshops, map shops and some other bookshops.

DOSLI (the Department of Land and Survey Information) publishes several series of excellent maps of all kinds – street, country and holiday maps, maps of national parks and forest parks, detailed topographical maps for trampers, and more. Their maps are available at DOSLI offices, at Bennett's Government Bookshops, at map shops and some other shops. Many DOC offices carry the DOSLI topographical and national park maps.

MEDIA

Newspapers & Magazines

There is no national paper although the *New Zealand Herald* (Auckland), the *Dominion* (Wellington) and the *Press* (Christchurch) all have wide circulations. Backing up the city newspapers are numerous local dailies, some OK, some not. The closest to a national weekly news magazine is the *Listener*, an excellent publication which provides a weekly TV & radio guide, plus in-depth articles on the arts, social issues and politics. The international publications *Time* and *Newsweek* are available almost anywhere.

Radio, TV & Film

There are two national noncommercial radio stations and many regional or local commercial stations, broadcasting on the AM and FM bands.

There are three TV stations (Channels One, Two & Three) plus Sky, a satellite station with three separate sections: a 24-hour CNN news section, a 24-hour sports section and a movie section.

Although New Zealand's film industry is small, it has recently produced a number of highly acclaimed films. *The Piano*, directed by Jane Campion, was a winner at the 1993 Cannes Film Festival. Seven feature films were released in 1992, including *The End of the Golden Weather* directed by Ian Mune, a tender film about early adolescence. *The Quiet Earth, Utu, Mr Wrong, Smash Palace* and *Vigil* have also won high acclaim. Yet other notable films include *The Navigator, Ngati, The Grasscutter, Starlight Hotel, Bad Taste, Goodbye Pork Pie* and *The Flying Fox and the Freedom Tree*. Even the beloved NZ cartoon character, 'Dog', has a film out – *Footrot Flats – The Dog's Tale*. Most video shops in New Zealand have at least some selection of NZ films.

HEALTH

There are no vaccination requirements to enter New Zealand. New Zealand is largely a clean, healthy, disease-free country. Medical attention is of high quality and reasonably priced but you should have medical insurance.

Travel health depends on your pre-departure preparations, your day-to-day health care while travelling and how you handle any medical problem or emergency that does develop.

Travel Health Guides

There are a number of books on travel health. *Travellers' Health* by Dr Richard Dawood (Oxford University Press, 1986, paperback) is comprehensive, easy to read, authoritative and highly recommended, although it's rather large to lug around. *Travel with Children* by Maureen Wheeler (Lonely Planet Publications, 1990, paperback) includes basic advice on travel health for younger children.

Pre-Departure Preparations

Health Insurance A travel insurance policy to cover theft, loss and medical problems is a wise idea. There are a wide variety of policies and your travel agent will have recommendations. The international student travel policies handled by STA or other student travel organisations are usually good value. Some policies offer lower and higher medical expenses options but the higher one is chiefly for countries like the USA which have extremely high medical costs. Check the small print:

1. Some policies specifically exclude 'dangerous activities' which can include scuba diving, motorcycling, even tramping. If such activities are on your agenda you don't want that sort of policy.
2. You may prefer a policy which pays doctors or hospitals direct rather than you having to pay on the spot and claim later. If you have to claim later make sure you keep all documentation. Some policies ask you to call back (reverse charges) to a centre in your

home country where an immediate assessment of your problem is made.
3. Check if the policy covers ambulances or an emergency flight home. If you have to stretch out you will need two seats and somebody has to pay for them!

Medical Kit A small, straightforward medical kit is a wise thing to carry. A possible kit list includes:

1. Aspirin or Panadol – for pain or fever.
2. Antihistamine (such as Benadryl) – useful as a decongestant for colds, allergies, to ease the itch from insect bites or stings or to help prevent motion sickness.
3. Antibiotics – useful if you're travelling well off the beaten track, but they must be prescribed and you should carry the prescription with you.
4. Kaolin preparation (Pepto-Bismol), Imodium or Lomotil – for stomach upsets.
5. Rehydration mixture – for treatment of severe diarrhoea, this is particularly important if travelling with children.
6. Antiseptic, mercurochrome and antibiotic powder or similar 'dry' spray – for cuts and grazes.
7. Calamine lotion, antihistamine or anti-itch cream – to ease irritation from bites or stings.
8. Bandages and Band-aids – for minor injuries.
9. Scissors, tweezers and a thermometer (note that mercury thermometers are prohibited by airlines).
10. Insect repellent, sunscreen, suntan lotion, chap stick.
11. Water purification tablets or other water purification system, if you'll be camping in the bush.

Health Preparations Make sure you're healthy before you start travelling. If you are embarking on a long trip make sure your teeth are OK.

If you wear glasses take a spare pair and your prescription. Losing your glasses can be a real problem, although in New Zealand you can get new spectacles made up quickly, cheaply and competently.

If you require a particular medication take an adequate supply, as it may not be available locally. Take the prescription, with the generic rather than the brand name (which may not be locally available), as it will make getting replacements easier. It's a wise idea to have the prescription with you to show you legally use the medication – it's surprising how often over-the-counter drugs from one country are illegal without a prescription or even banned in another.

Immunisations You don't need any vaccinations to visit New Zealand. It's always a good idea to keep your tetanus immunisation up to date no matter where you are – boosters are necessary every 10 years and protection is highly recommended – but even this is not strictly required.

Basic Rules
Care in what you eat and drink is the most important health rule; stomach upsets are the most likely travel health problem but the majority of these upsets will be relatively minor.

Water Tap water is clean, delicious and fine to drink in New Zealand. Water in lakes, rivers and streams will look clean and it could be OK, but since the parasite *Giardia protozoa* has been found in many New Zealand lakes, rivers and streams, water from these sources should be purified before drinking.

Water Purification The simplest way of purifying water is to boil it thoroughly, that is, for more than three minutes. Filtering is acceptable *only* if you use *Giardia* rated filters, available from some outdoor equipment retailers.

If you cannot boil water it should be treated chemically. Iodine is very effective in purifying water and is available in tablet form (such as Potable Aqua), but follow the directions carefully and remember that too much iodine can be harmful. Before buying, check the manufacturer's specifications on the packet to ensure that the tablets will kill the *Giardia* parasite.

If you can't find tablets, tincture of iodine (2%) or iodine crystals can be used. Two drops of tincture of iodine per litre or quart of clear water is the recommended dosage; the treated water should be left to stand for 30 minutes before drinking. Iodine crystals can also be used to purify water but this is a more complicated process, as you have to

first prepare a saturated iodine solution. Iodine loses its effectiveness if exposed to air or damp so keep it in a tightly sealed container. Flavoured powder will disguise the taste of treated water and is a good idea if you are travelling with children.

Nutrition If your food is poor, if you're travelling hard and fast and therefore missing meals, or if you simply lose your appetite, you can soon start to lose weight and place your health at risk.

Make sure your diet is well balanced. Meat (lamb, beef, pork and poultry) is plentiful in New Zealand; eggs, tofu, beans, lentils and nuts are also good ways to get protein. Fresh fruits and vegetables are a good source of vitamins. Also eat plenty of grains and bread. If your diet isn't well balanced or if your food intake is insufficient, it's a good idea to take vitamin and iron pills.

Everyday Health A normal body temperature is 98.6°F or 37°C; more than 2°C higher is a 'high' fever. A normal adult pulse rate is 60 to 80 per minute (children 80 to 100, babies 100 to 140). You should know how to take a temperature and a pulse rate. As a general rule the pulse increases about 20 beats per minute for each °C rise in fever.

Respiration (breathing) rate is also an indicator of illness. Count the number of breaths per minute: between 12 and 20 is normal for adults and older children (up to 30 for younger children, 40 for babies). People with a high fever or serious respiratory illness (like pneumonia) breathe more quickly than normal. More than 40 shallow breaths a minute usually means pneumonia.

Many health problems can be avoided by taking care of yourself. Wash your hands frequently – it's quite easy to contaminate your own food. Avoid climatic extremes: keep out of the sun when it's hot, dress warmly when it's cold. Avoid potential diseases by dressing sensibly. You can avoid insect bites by covering bare skin when insects are around, by screening windows or beds or by using insect repellents. Seek local advice: if you're told the water is unsafe due to currents, riptides or for any other reason, don't go in. In situations where there is no information, discretion is the better part of valour.

Climatic & Geographical Considerations
Sunburn On the beach, in the snow or at high altitudes you can get sunburnt surprisingly quickly, even through cloud. The sun is particularly dangerous here in New Zealand, where the ozone layer is said to be considerably thinner than in other parts of the world. Use a sunscreen and take extra care to cover areas which don't normally see sun – eg your feet. A hat provides added protection, and you can also use zinc cream or some other barrier cream for your nose, lips and ears. Calamine lotion is good for mild sunburn.

Cold Too much cold can be dangerous, particularly if it leads to hypothermia. Hypothermia is a real and present danger in New Zealand, due to the country's extremely changeable weather. A certain number of visitors die from hypothermia every year in New Zealand, mostly because they have gone out walking without adequate preparation, not realising that the weather can change abruptly and within the space of a few minutes a bright, warm day can change to freezing winds, rain and hail. You should always be prepared for cold, wet or windy conditions even if you're just out walking or hitching, and it's especially important if you're tramping out in the bush, away from civilisation.

Hypothermia occurs when the body loses heat faster than it can produce it and the core temperature of the body falls. It is surprisingly easy to progress from very cold to dangerously cold due to a combination of wind, wet clothing, fatigue and hunger, even if the air temperature is above freezing. It is best to dress in layers; silk, wool and some of the new artificial fibres are all good insulating materials. A hat is important, as a lot of heat is lost through the head. A strong, waterproof outer layer is essential, since keeping dry is vital. Carry basic supplies, including food containing simple sugars to generate heat quickly, and lots of fluid to drink.

Symptoms of hypothermia are exhaustion, numb skin (particularly fingers and toes), shivering, slurred speech, irrational or violent behaviour, lethargy, stumbling, dizzy spells, muscle cramps and violent bursts of energy. Irrationality may take the form of sufferers claiming they are warm and trying to take off their clothes.

To treat hypothermia, first get the patient out of the wind and/or rain, remove their clothing if it's wet and replace it with dry, warm clothing. Give them hot liquids – not alcohol – and some high-kilojoule, easily digestible food. This should be enough for the early stages of hypothermia, but if it has gone further it may be necessary to place the victim in a warm sleeping bag and get in with them. Do not rub the patient, don't place them near a fire or remove their wet clothes in the wind. If possible, place a sufferer in a warm (not hot) bath.

Motion Sickness Eating lightly before and during a trip will reduce the chances of motion sickness. If you are prone to motion sickness try to find a place that minimises disturbance – near the wing on aircraft, close to midships on boats, near the centre on buses. Fresh air and looking at the horizon or off into the distance usually helps; stale air, cigarette smoke and reading makes it worse. Commercial anti-motion sickness preparations, which can cause drowsiness, have to be taken before the trip commences; when you're feeling sick it's too late. Dramamine, sold over the counter at chemists, is the usual preferred medication. Ginger is a natural preventative and is available in capsule form.

Diseases of Insanitation
Diarrhoea A change of water, food or climate can all cause the runs; diarrhoea caused by contaminated food or water is more serious. Despite all your precautions you may still have a bout of mild travellers' diarrhoea but a few rushed toilet trips with no

other symptoms is not indicative of a serious problem. Moderate diarrhoea, involving half-a-dozen loose movements in a day, is more of a nuisance. Dehydration is the main danger with any diarrhoea, particularly for children, so fluid replenishment is the number one treatment. Weak black tea with a little sugar, soda water, or soft drinks allowed to go flat and diluted 50% with water are all good. With severe diarrhoea a rehydrating solution is necessary to replace salts and minerals. You should stick to a bland diet as you recover.

Lomotil or Imodium can be used to bring relief from the symptoms, although they do not actually cure the problem. Only use these drugs if absolutely necessary – eg, if you *must* travel. For children Imodium is preferable, but do not use these drugs if the patient has a high fever or is severely dehydrated.

Antibiotics (prescription only) can be very useful in treating severe diarrhoea especially if it is accompanied by nausea, vomiting, stomach cramps or mild fever. Three days of treatment should be sufficient and an improvement should occur within 24 hours.

Giardia This intestinal parasite is present in contaminated water; it's been found in many rivers, lakes and streams in New Zealand, so it's important to know about it if you will be out in the bush. It can be spread by any mammals such as possums, rats, mice or humans. Though drinking contaminated water is the most common way to catch *giardia*, it can also occur as a result of poor personal hygiene or unhygienic food handling.

The symptoms are stomach cramps, nausea, a bloated stomach, watery, foul-smelling diarrhoea and frequent gas. *Giardia* can appear several weeks after you have been exposed to the parasite. The symptoms may disappear for a few days and then return; this can go on for several weeks. As long as you are carrying the parasite, you risk spreading it to the environment and to other people.

Metronidazole known as Flagyl is the recommended drug, but it should only be taken under medical supervision. The treatment is simple and quick acting. If you will be out in the bush you might want to carry some Flagyl in your first aid kit. Note that antibiotics are of no use. If you suspect that you have *giardia*, see a doctor as soon as practical.

Viral Gastroenteritis This is caused not by bacteria but, as the name suggests, by a virus. It is characterised by stomach cramps, diarrhoea, and sometimes by vomiting and/or a slight fever. All you can do is rest and drink lots of fluids.

Diseases Spread by People & Animals

Tetanus This potentially fatal disease is found around the world; it's not any particular problem in New Zealand but it's still a good idea to keep your tetanus booster up to date. Tetanus is difficult to treat but is preventable with immunisation. Tetanus occurs when a wound becomes infected by a germ which lives in the faeces of animals or people, so clean all cuts, punctures or animal bites. Tetanus is known as lockjaw, and the first symptom may be discomfort in swallowing, or stiffening of the jaw and neck; this is followed by painful convulsions of the jaw and whole body.

Amoebic meningitis This very serious disease can be a danger if you bathe in natural hot thermal pools. Fortunately, it's no danger at all if you know how to protect yourself from it.

The amoeba that causes the disease can enter your body through the orifices of your head, usually the nose but occasionally the ears as well. Once it gets inside the nose it bores through the tissues and lodges in the brain. It's very easy not to catch the disease – just keep your head out of the water!

Symptoms of amoebic meningitis may have a slow onset – it could be several days or even several weeks later that the first symptoms are noticed. Symptoms may be similar to the flu at first, later progressing to severe headaches, stiffness of the neck, hypersensitivity to light, and then even coma. It can be treated with intravenous anti-amoebic drugs.

Sexually Transmitted Diseases Sexual contact with an infected partner spreads these diseases. While abstinence is the only 100% preventative, using condoms is also effective. Gonorrhoea and syphilis are the most common of these diseases; sores, blisters or rashes around the genitals, discharges or pain when urinating are common symptoms. Symptoms may be less marked or not observed at all in women. Syphilis symptoms eventually disappear completely but the disease continues and can cause severe problems in later years. The treatment of gonorrhoea and syphilis is by antibiotics.

There are numerous other sexually transmitted diseases, for most of which effective treatment is available. However, there is no cure for herpes and there is also currently no cure for AIDS, which is present in New Zealand as in most other parts of the world.

AIDS can be spread through contact with the body fluids of another person, primarily blood and semen, and can be spread through infected blood transfusions as well as by sexual contact. It can also be spread by dirty needles – vaccinations, acupuncture and tattooing can potentially be as dangerous as intravenous drug use if the equipment is not clean.

Toxic Shellfish It doesn't happen often but it has been known to occur: certain algae or other substances in sea water can cause shellfish that are normally safe to eat to become dangerous. In early 1993 this happened in the Marlborough Sounds and several people became violently ill – one or two died, and a pregnant woman lost her baby – before it was realised what was going on. Ask local advice before you eat any type of shellfish.

Cuts, Bites & Stings
Cuts & Scratches Skin punctures can easily become infected while travelling and may be difficult to heal. Treat any cut with an antiseptic solution and mercurochrome. Where possible avoid bandages and Band-aids,

which can keep wounds wet; if you have to keep a bandage on during the day to protect the wound from dirt, take it off at night while you sleep to let it get air.

Coral cuts are notoriously slow to heal, as the coral injects a weak venom into the wound. Avoid coral cuts by wearing shoes when walking on reefs, and clean any cut thoroughly.

Bee & Wasp Stings Wasps are a problem in some places in New Zealand. They are attracted to food, especially at picnic sites; late summer is the worst time of year for them. There are especially many wasps in beech forests.

Bee and wasp stings are usually painful rather than dangerous. Calamine lotion will give relief; ammonia is also an effective remedy. Ice packs or antihistamine cream will reduce the pain and swelling. If you are allergic to bee or wasp stings, carry your medication with you.

Mosquitoes & Sandflies Mosquitoes appear after dusk. They are not a big problem in some parts of the country but in certain places – notably the west coast of the South Island, and especially in summer – they can come in clouds. Avoid bites by covering bare skin and using an insect repellent. Insect screens on windows and mosquito nets on beds offer protection, as does burning a mosquito coil or spraying with a pyrethrum-based insect spray. Mosquitoes may be attracted by perfume, aftershave or certain colours. They can bite you right through thin fabrics, or on any small part of your skin not covered by repellent.

Another New Zealand insect that can drive you wild is the sandfly, a tiny black creature that is found in inland areas as well as around the coasts, where it lives in bushes, trees or grasses. Sandfly bites can be even more irritating than mosquito bites; since the insects live on the ground, sandfly bites are mainly on the feet and ankles. Wearing shoes, thick socks and plenty of insect repellent is not only advisable but practically a necessity where sandflies are present.

The most effective insect repellent is called DEET (N,N-Diethylmetatoluamide); it is an ingredient in many commercially available insect repellents. Look for a repellent with at least a 28% concentration of DEET. DEET breaks down plastic, rubber, contact lenses and synthetic fabrics, though, so be careful what you touch after using it. It poses no danger to natural fibre fabrics.

New Zealand's Department of Conservation (DOC) gave us a few other recommendations for keeping away the sandflies and mosquitoes. They say that eating plenty of vitamin B1 is an effective deterrent to sandflies, and we've heard the same thing about mosquitoes too. Externally, they recommend making up a half-and-half mixture of Dettol (the bathroom cleaner) and baby oil, and wiping it over your skin where sandflies may bite.

Other good insect repellents include Off! and Repel, which comes in a stick or a spray and will not eat through plastic the way DEET-containing repellents do.

Spiders Many types of spiders live in New Zealand but by far the most famous is the only poisonous one, the retiring little katipo spider, *Latrodectus katipo*. It has a poisonous bite that can be fatal, but though mention of its name strikes fear into the hearts of brave souls, in fact only a few deaths have ever been recorded and most of those were a long time ago. Nowadays anti-venom is available from most hospitals, and it's effective even if administered as long as three days after the bite has occurred.

The katipo is found in coastal areas in all of New Zealand except for the far south. It lives in areas just back from the high tide zone, weaving a small, dense web in driftwood, grasses or any other suitable place close to the ground. The katipo is not aggressive; it's a shy animal which only bites if disturbed.

Only the mature female spider is dangerous; she is identified by a shiny black body, about six mm long, with a bright red patch on the rear of the abdomen. The harmless mature male is identified by the presence of white markings on both sides, in addition to the red patch; the white markings are also present on the immature spiders of both sexes.

Jellyfish Local advice is the best way of avoiding contact with these sea creatures with their stinging tentacles. Stings from most jellyfish are quite painful. The most effective folk remedy for jellyfish stings, used all over the world, is to apply fresh urine to the stings as soon as possible. This is also useful if you touch stinging coral. Ammonia is also effective. Dousing in vinegar will de-activate any stingers which have not 'fired'. Calamine lotion, antihistamines and analgesics may reduce the reaction and relieve the pain.

Women's Health
Gynaecological Problems Poor diet, lowered resistance due to the use of antibiotics and even contraceptive pills can lead to vaginal infections when travelling. Keeping the genital area clean, and wearing skirts or loose-fitting trousers and cotton underwear will help to prevent infections.

Yeast infections, characterised by a rash, itch and a thick white discharge, can be treated with a vinegar or lemon-juice douche or by putting a few teaspoons of plain (not flavoured!) yoghurt into the vagina. (The bacteria that cause the fermentation of yoghurt eat yeast; it's a very effective remedy but only if used in the early stages of infection; if you let it get too severe then the yoghurt doesn't seem to help much.) Nystatin suppositories are the usual medical prescription. Trichomonas is a more serious infection; symptoms are a discharge and a burning sensation when urinating. Male sexual partners must also be treated, and if a vinegar-water douche is not effective medical attention should be sought. Flagyl is the prescribed drug.

Pregnancy Most miscarriages occur during the first three months of pregnancy, so this is the most risky time to travel. The last three months should also be spent within reasonable distance of good medical care, as quite serious problems can develop at this time. Pregnant women should avoid all unnecessary medication. Additional care should be taken to prevent illness and particular attention should be paid to diet and nutrition.

WOMEN TRAVELLERS

New Zealand is quite an easy country for women travellers, with few hassles. Women should, however, exercise the same degree of caution as they would in most other countries. We recommend that you hitchhike in company, and observe all the normal commonsense habits of safety, like not walking through isolated urban areas alone in the middle of the night, and so on.

DANGERS & ANNOYANCES

With high unemployment and an economy that has seen better days, theft is a rising problem in New Zealand. Theft from cars is a particular problem. In doing the previous edition of this book back in 1990 we drove around New Zealand for months with most of our belongings in the car and never had a problem. This time, one of our first experiences back in the country was having things stolen out of our car at night, when an apparently experienced thief went through all the cars parked in the private parking lot of a hostel, getting cameras, jackets, car radios and anything else that looked good. The policeman who came to take the report told us all that if you leave valuables in your car nowadays in New Zealand, you should expect that they will be stolen. Violent crime is not as common.

The biggest dangers in New Zealand, though, may come not from your fellow humans but from nature. Remember to take all the recommended precautions when tramping, especially in the mountains; see the Tramping section in the Outdoor Activities chapter for advice on tramping safety, and follow the advice! See the Health section for advice on health dangers.

Sharks

Sharks exist in NZ waters but they are well fed by the abundance of marine life and rarely pose a threat to humans. However attacks do occasionally occur. Take notice of any local warnings if you are planning on swimming, surfing or diving. Should you come face to face with a shark when diving, the best thing to do is move casually and quietly away. Don't panic, as they are attracted by things that thrash around in the water. Avoid swimming in places that would be obvious attractions to them as predators, such as areas where young seals or penguins are learning to swim. They are also attracted to blood, so don't swim where fish are being killed or cleaned in the sea.

FILM & PHOTOGRAPHY

Photographic supplies, equipment and maintenance are all readily available in New Zealand. You can probably find any kind of camera or equipment you're looking for, but it may cost more here than elsewhere.

Fuji and Kodak are the most popular films, with Agfa also available. Typical costs for Fuji film are around $7/9 for a roll of 24/36 colour prints, $12/18 for a roll of 24/36 colour slides (transparencies). Agfa film is available at similar prices; Kodak film may cost about $1 more.

The processing cost is around $17/20 for a roll of 24/36 colour prints, $10/15 for a roll of 24/36 colour slides. Prices can vary quite a bit from shop to shop, so if you'll be buying much film or getting much processed it might pay to shop around. One-hour photo developing shops are found all over New Zealand, but they only do prints; slide processing takes considerably longer, usually about a week.

The only notable peculiarities of taking photos in New Zealand might be if you're taking photos in the bush. Native bush in New Zealand is quite dense, and it may be darker than you think, photographically speaking. If you'll be doing much tramping in heavy bush and want to record your journey, carry a couple of rolls of 400 ASA film.

As everywhere, early morning or late

afternoon light makes for some of the most interesting shots.

LANGUAGE SCHOOLS

People from around the world, especially Asia and the Pacific countries, come to New Zealand to study English. Some of the attractions are that the country is a native English-speaking country with a high standard of education that is accredited throughout the world and it's a country which is uncrowded, clean, green and friendly. Typically each language school arranges for its students to live in homes with New Zealand families, so that English is used outside as well as inside the classroom. They also arrange a variety of extracurricular evening and weekend activities for their students.

Auckland has the highest concentration of language schools, and there are a few in other parts of the country as well. The Auckland Visitor Information Centre keeps a complete, up-to-date list.

WORK

New Zealand has a high unemployment rate, so it's fussy about foreigners coming in and taking jobs that its own citizens need. An ordinary visitor's permit or visa does not give you the right to work in New Zealand; if you work without a work permit, you are breaking the law. You can apply for a work permit before arriving in New Zealand or within the country at any office of the New Zealand Immigration Service; see the Visas & Embassies section at the beginning of this chapter for more about work permits.

One type of work that foreign visitors are often able to get in New Zealand is fruit picking. Apples, kiwi fruit and other types of fruit and vegetables need to be picked in summer and early fall, and often there are not enough New Zealanders available to make up the picking crews. Picking season is from around January to April so that's when the most work is available, though there may be some agricultural work to be done all year round. Picking is hard work and the pay is by the amount picked. If you're slow you won't make much money; speedy pickers do well.

HIGHLIGHTS

There are so many superb physical features in New Zealand that you find yourself taking the beauty of the country for granted after a while. With hundreds of km of rugged coastline and sandy beaches, lush native forest, rugged mountains and volcanoes, abundant wildlife and many other beautiful natural features, New Zealand has 'highlights' practically everywhere you turn. But if we had to pick some 'not to be missed sights or things to do in New Zealand' here's what they'd be, from north to south:

- Northland. In particular the magnificent Waipoua Kauri Forest on the west side, home of some spectacular giant 1500-year-old kauri trees; isolated beaches; the Bay of Islands on the east side; and the trip to Cape Reinga on the top.
- Visit a museum, for an insight into New Zealand culture, both Maori and Pakeha. The museums at Auckland, Wellington, Christchurch, Hamilton and Wanganui are amongst the best, but there are also interesting museums in some smaller, out-of-the-way places such as the Otamatea Kauri & Pioneer Museum at Matakohe and the Wagener Museum at Houhora, both in the Northland. Fascinating whether you're interested in present history, pioneering times or prehistory.
- Waitomo Caves, south of Hamilton. The Waitomo area is riddled with limestone caves with stalactites and stalagmites; the Waitomo Cave has the added attraction of a magnificent glow-worm grotto. Waitomo also offers amazing and unusual activities including cave rafting, abseiling 100 metres down into the Lost World cave, a variety of other caving and abseiling expeditions, horse trekking and more.
- Rotorua, central North Island. This is one of New Zealand's most interesting areas. Go there for the thermal activity (boiling mud pools, hissing geysers and eerie volcanic landscapes) and the Maori culture (don't miss the night-time Maori concerts or a *hangi*).
- Tongariro National Park, central North Island. A World Heritage Area, this park has some of the best mountain/volcano scenery in the country, excellent tramping tracks, and skiing in winter.
- Kaikoura, east coast of the South Island. Whale watching trips and swimming with dolphins have made this place famous, and there are many other activities.

- Fox and Franz Josef Glaciers, west coast of the South Island. Nowhere else do glaciers come so close to sea level so close to the equator. Steep mountains and heavy rainfall are the scientific answer but sitting in sub-tropical rainforest, looking at so much ice, drives the easy answers out of your head. To experience their full majesty, get above them in a plane or helicopter or walk on them.
- Mt Cook, west coast of the South Island. The highest mountain in New Zealand has fantastic scenery, good tramping and skiing, and the Tasman Glacier.
- Queenstown, South Island. The adrenaline capital of New Zealand. This is a resort town which offers a host of activities in a fantastic setting.
- Fiordland, south-west coast of the South Island. Similar to the fiords of Norway. Milford Sound is one of the most spectacular, with towering Mitre Peak. You won't forget the dolphins frolicking in the boat's bow wave and the absolute silence of night in this unique wilderness.
- The Catlins, south coast of the South Island. This place is a living museum, with an amazing array of flora & fauna including species not found elsewhere, tracts of rainforest, waterfalls and magnificent kelp-strewn ancient beaches. A must!
- Stay on a farm. Farm life, especially sheep farming, is what rural New Zealand is all about.
- Activities. How can we choose a highlight here? New Zealand has some of the finest tramping in the world. It also has great skiing. Plus literally dozens of activities ranging from boat trips and visits to sheep stations to shooting rapids upstream in jet-boats or downstream in inflatables, white water sledging/rafting/boogey boarding, tandem skydiving, rap jumping, mountain biking, excellent tramping, bungy jumping from two high bridges, and skiing in winter. Is tandem skydiving more thrilling than white water sledging? If you go swimming with hundreds of dolphins, will you ever forget it as long as you live? A visit to a marae may be the thing you'll treasure as your warmest memory.

ACCOMMODATION

New Zealand has a wide range of accommodation and places to stay but to all of it there is one catch: the Kiwis are great travellers. Even Australians fall behind the New Zealanders when it comes to hitting the road – a greater proportion of New Zealanders have passports than in any other country and when they are not jaunting around overseas they'll be jaunting around at home. So during the holiday season you may well find a long queue at popular places. This applies particularly to any cheap accommodation in major holiday areas. The answer is to book ahead if you are going to be arriving in tricky places on popular occasions.

Accommodation has been bracketed into several categories. First of all there are the camping grounds – motor camps and Department of Conservation (DOC) campsites. Then there are the hostels – the YHAs, YWCAs and YMCAs, and the private, independent hostels, usually called 'backpackers'. Then there are the guesthouses or B&Bs, hotels and motels. Another option is accommodation on farms or in private homes, known as 'farmstays' and 'homestays' in NZ parlance. There is considerable overlap between these various groups.

Information

To find your way around New Zealand's motor camps, hotels, motels and so on, pick up a copy of the *Accommodation Guides* published by the Automobile Association (AA). There's one for the North Island and another for the South Island. Both are revised every year and are available from any AA office. They're not a complete listing but most places are included. Copies are available free to members of the AA or to overseas visitors who belong to an automobile association enjoying reciprocal rights with the AA. Otherwise you can purchase them for a small fee.

Jason's accommodation directories are similar commercially produced guides, but they don't have as many listings as the AA books because it costs the hotel, camping ground, motel or whatever a lot of money to get into *Jason's*.

Other publications are useful for the latest rundown on hostels, Department of Conservation (DOC) campsites, and B&Bs; see them in those sections.

Camping & Cabins

If you like to camp, New Zealand is a great place for it. For the tent camper the Kiwi campsites are some of the best in the world

– which doesn't mean caravanners aren't catered for as well. Most camping grounds have facilities for tent campers, caravans and campervans, plus cabins of varying degrees of luxury and often on-site caravans.

If you are driving, cycling, hitchhiking or hiking around with a tent and sleeping bag everything will be fine – there are plenty of camping grounds and motor camps, particularly in touristy places, and they are very well equipped. Most of them have kitchens and dining areas where the cooker, hot plates, kettles and toasters are provided; you supply your own pots and pans, utensils, plates, etc. They're great places to meet people – you talk with other people while you're fixing your food, you carry on when you share a table to eat it. There are also laundry facilities and often TV rooms too. Though it's best to bring your own sleeping bag, many places will hire you linen if you're staying in cabins and haven't brought your own.

How the sites are charged varies. There may be a site charge and then an additional cost per person. Sometimes it's just a straight site charge. But most of the time it's a per person charge and that's typically around $7 to $9 per adult, half price for children. Most sites charge a dollar or two more per person if you want a powered site for a caravan or campervan as opposed to a tent site without power.

At most sites the kitchen and showers are free but you do get a few sites where there are coin-in-the-slot operated hot plates and hot showers. At most sites laundry facilities are coin operated.

New Zealand has several federations of camping grounds. Top 10 Holiday Parks is an association of the cream of the crop of the country's camping grounds, motor camps and holiday parks. Another fine federation of NZ camping grounds is the Kiwi Camps of New Zealand. There's also the Camp & Cabin Association of NZ Inc. All have brochures listing details about their members, available at member camping grounds and at visitor information centres.

If you intend to camp round New Zealand but have no camping gear you can buy it in New Zealand. Good, high quality tents and sleeping bags are available, but the prices are also high. If you're coming from North America or Australia you can get better prices in those places. Auckland, Wellington and Christchurch all have good second-hand camping and sports shops; many of the army and navy surplus shops around New Zealand also have inexpensive and/or second-hand gear.

Remember it gets cool in New Zealand in the winter, so camping becomes a lot less practical then, especially in the south. If you're well enough equipped it's not quite so bad in the north, although New Zealand's weather is very changeable.

DOC Camping Grounds The Department of Conservation (DOC) operates over 120 camping grounds all around New Zealand. There are DOC campsites in reserves and in national parks, maritime parks, forest parks and farm parks.

DOC camping grounds are of three types. Serviced camping grounds have flush toilets, hot showers, tap water, kitchen and laundry areas, outdoor lighting, picnic tables, rubbish collection, and usually have powered as well as non-powered sites. They may also have BBQ and fireplace facilities, a shop or a campervan waste disposal point. Fees are around $6 to $9 per adult, per night.

Standard campsites are more basic, with minimal facilities including cold running water, toilets, fireplaces and not much else – but they also have minimal charges, around $2 to $6 per adult.

Children aged five to 16 are charged half price at both types of sites; it's free for children under the age of five.

The third type of camping area, informal camping areas, are free. They have limited facilities, usually just a cold water tap and places to pitch tents. Sometimes the access to these types of sites is a bit more difficult – you may have to walk in, rather than drive in – but they are worth the walk if you're geared for camping.

DOC publishes a useful brochure, *Conservation Campsites*, with details on all the

DOC camping grounds throughout New Zealand. You can pick it up at any DOC office, or write for it to the Department of Conservation, PO Box 10420, Wellington.

You can check with local DOC offices for details on facilities, what you need to take with you and whether you should book in advance. Bookings can be made for all serviced camping grounds; contact the DOC office nearest the camping ground. Standard camping grounds and informal camping areas operate on a first come, first served basis, and fees are paid by a self-registration system. Since all fees are used for the maintenance of the camping grounds, and are kept as low as possible, it's important to pay them (usually into an 'honesty box') even when there's no warden present.

Back Country Huts DOC also operates numerous back country huts, most of which can only be reached on foot. See the Tramping section in the Outdoor Activities chapter for information on huts.

Cabins & Tourist Flats Many camping grounds and motor camps have cabins. Standard cabins are simply free-standing rooms with bare mattresses where you have to provide your own sleeping gear (a sleeping bag is fine) and towels, unlike a motel where all that sort of stuff is provided. Cabins can be very cheap, often around $20 or $25 for two which can make them even cheaper than hostels. They generally charge per two adults, plus so much for each additional person, but some charge per cabin and some per person. Usually you can hire sheets and blankets if you come unequipped.

Moving up from this basic standard, there is a variety of standards and prices of cabins. Often the cabins become 'tourist flats' and are equipped closer to motel standard with kitchens and/or bathrooms. You will still have to do the clean up yourself and bring your own bedding, towels and so on, although at many camps now even the bedding is included. On-site caravans (trailer homes in US parlance) are another campsite possibility. Many camping grounds also have regular motel rooms or an associated motel complex and hostel-style bunkrooms.

Hostels
Hostels offer cheap accommodation in locations all over New Zealand. At a hostel you basically rent a bed, usually for around $12 to $16 a night. Some hostels have male and female bunkrooms for 10 or more people. Others have smaller bunkrooms or 'share rooms' with three or four beds, or they may even have double or single rooms. Double and twin rooms have become more common at hostels as they are often requested by travellers, and now most hostels have at least a few double rooms available. All hostels have a fully equipped communal kitchen, a dining area, a lounge area and a laundry room.

It's a good idea to travel with your own sleeping bag if you'll be staying in hostels. The independent backpackers' prices usually assume that you have your own bedding; if you need to hire it, you'll pay a few dollars more. YHA hostels provide bedding for free, you just have to ask for it.

YHA Hostels The YHA in New Zealand produces a free annual *YHA Accommodation Guide* with details on all their hostels throughout New Zealand. You may be able to get a copy from your national YHA or you can request one from the YHA National Office, PO Box 436, Christchurch, New Zealand (☎ (03) 379 9970; fax 365 4476). It's also available at all YHA hostels and YHA travel centres throughout New Zealand.

The YHA hostels are only open to members. You can either join the YHA in your home country (don't forget to bring your membership card) or in New Zealand at any YHA hostel. There's a joining fee of $10 and annual membership is $24 for senior members (age 18 and over). Junior memberships, for ages 15 to 17, are $12 per year with no joining fee; cards are issued for free to those under the age of 15. Membership in the New Zealand YHA also allows you to use YHA hostels anywhere else in the world. Your membership also entitles you to a host

Hostelling in New Zealand
To an even greater extent than Australia the New Zealand hostel scene has gone through a real revolution in the past few years, and it continues even as we write. It's a combination of strong growth, more liberal attitudes and a new commercial approach.

Hostels have always been popular in New Zealand – after all it's a good country for backpackers. But the recent growth in demand has been phenomenal as there are now a lot more travellers. So many more, in fact, that hostels were getting booked out far in advance, which, of course, created the need for more hostels. With the YHA hostels and the private backpackers there are now hundreds of hostels all over New Zealand, in cities, towns, villages and even in rural areas. There were over twice as many hostels in New Zealand when we researched this edition of the book as there had been when we researched the previous edition. You may find there are many more again by the time you arrive.

The second factor affecting the hostel scene has been a dramatic change in the general attitude towards hostelling. The old, strict segregation by gender, lights out early, stay away all day policies are memories of a bygone era. In part it's been because people staying at the hostels demanded a more easy going approach, but also because younger-minded people have been running the hostels. The old hostel 'wardens' have even metamorphosed into 'managers'!

Finally all of these factors – growth in demand, growth in the number of hostels and therefore the competition for customers, and the need for more liberal attitudes – have come together in a new, more commercial, approach. Getting people to stay in hostels has become a commercial decision just like other businesses. If hostel A is better equipped, cheaper or a more pleasant place than hostel B then people will stay in A rather than in B. And running a hostel, many people have suddenly realised, is just as good a way of making a living as running a motel. What's the difference between a motel room for $48 with two people in it and a bunkroom for four at $12 each? Well with the bunkroom you don't have to provide a TV, telephone or attached bathroom, or launder bedding for starters!

So today hostels have become very attractive places to stay. If you're a couple you can usually get a room to yourself. You can arrive rather late at night if you've booked a room in advance. You won't be locked out if you get back from the pub late at night (but be quiet!) and you won't be pushed out the door because 'the hostel is closed from 10 am to 4 pm'.

Apart from being a highly economical form of accommodation, particularly if you're travelling solo, hostels are also a great place for meeting people and making friends. They're also wonderful information sources – almost every hostel has a notice board smothered in notes, advice and warning and the hostel managers are also often great sources of local information. Hostels also often negotiate special discounts and deals for their hostellers with local businesses and tour operators. ∎

of discounts in New Zealand, including significant discounts on travel (30% off on bus travel, 50% off on most domestic flights).

If you don't want to buy a whole year's membership, you can still stay at YHA hostels. They offer International Guest Cards and Kiwi Starter Cards for $4 per night; you pay $4 for each night you stay in a hostel and if you reach six nights, that's $24 and your card then becomes a full membership card. There are also a number of Associate YHA Hostels – these are privately owned premises which are approved by the YHA as suitable for members' use. You don't need a membership card to stay at an Associate YHA Hostel.

Particularly during school holidays and at popular hostels it is a wise idea to book ahead. You can do this either directly with the hostel in question, through the New Zealand YHA offices, or one hostel can book ahead for you at another hostel. Reservations must be paid in advance; if you're at one hostel and want to make a booking for the next one, you pay on the spot and are given a voucher, which you present upon arrival at the next hostel. If you have a credit card (Visa, MasterCard or Bankcard) you can reserve directly by phone or fax, giving details of your card. It is also possible to book from one country to another, so you can book at YHA hostels in New Zealand before you arrive in the country and also make bookings in NZ for hostels in the next countries you'll be visiting. The accommodation guide has full details on what to do.

Backpackers The numerous 'backpackers' (private or independent hostels) have basically the same facilities and prices as YHA hostels – fully equipped communal kitchens, common areas, laundry facilities and so on. Most backpackers charge extra if you need to hire bedding, so it's best to travel with your own sleeping bag.

A couple of handy brochures are useful for the latest listings of the many backpackers, which are springing up all around the country with amazing rapidity. The *New Zealand Budget Backpackers Accommodation* pamphlet, commonly known as the 'Blue Brochure', is an excellent publication, with details and prices on many backpackers throughout New Zealand. The Blue Brochure is published by Budget Backpackers Hostels NZ Ltd, led by the operators of Rainbow Lodge at Taupo in the North Island and Foley Towers at Christchurch in the South Island. It's available at scores of hostels, backpackers and information

centres around New Zealand, or you can request one from Rainbow Lodge, 99 Titiraupenga St, Taupo (☎ (07) 378 5754; fax 377 1568).

Another popular guide is the *VIP Backpackers Accommodation Guide*. Published by Backpackers Resorts of New Zealand Ltd, its 1993 booklet listed 66 hostels and backpackers from Kerikeri in the north to Invercargill in the south. All the hostels and backpackers listed here are members of the VIP network; possession of a VIP Card gives you $1 off at every hostel, plus a host of other discounts (similar to those offered on a YHA card). The VIP accommodation guide is available at VIP hostels and backpackers and at information centres around New Zealand, or you can request one from Backpackers Resorts of New Zealand Ltd, Box 991, Taupo (☎ (07) 377 1157).

Yet another brochure listing NZ hostels and backpackers is the *Backpackers Guide to New Zealand* published by ATA (c/o Post Office, Kaikoura). Unlike the other two, who list the hostels that pay to advertise in them, this one endeavours to list *all* the backpackers in NZ, with mention of them all but descriptions of its advertisers.

Youth Hostels Get A New Name

Over the next few years, youth hostels around the world will be getting a new name. The International Youth Hostel Federation (IYHF), of which the Youth Hostels Association of New Zealand (YHA-NZ) is a member, has changed its name to Hostelling International. The old familiar logo used around the world as a symbol for youth hostels – the triangle with a little house and a cockily leaning tree, has even been changed – now the tree is standing straight up.

The reason for the name change is that the term 'youth hostel' gives the impression that the hostels are only for young people, whereas in fact people of all ages are welcome. Originally, youth hostels were established in Europe as a refuge and shelter for travelling young people, but nowadays people of all ages use the hostels – in fact many older people find them excellent for budget travel.

The name change will be gradually phased in over the next few years. Meanwhile, hostels that have always been called 'youth hostels' in New Zealand are now called 'YHA hostels'. ∎

HOSTELLING
INTERNATIONAL

YMCA & YWCA Hostels There are YMCA and YWCA hostels in several larger towns which offer straightforward, no frills accommodation and are generally reasonably priced. A few are single-sex only but most take both men and women. Although the emphasis is on long-term accommodation – providing a place to stay for young people coming to study or work in the 'big city' – they are increasingly also setting aside beds for travellers.

Accommodation in these hostels is often in single or twin rooms. They have one extra plus point – they are often less crowded during the holiday seasons, when their students and long-term residents go home or go off on holiday, so their rooms tend to have space available right when every other type of accommodation is likely to fill up.

Guesthouses & B&Bs

There's a wide variation in types and standards in this category. Some guesthouses are spartan, cheap, ultra-basic accommodation, in some cases defined as 'private' (unlicensed) hotels. Others are comfortable, relaxed but low-key places, patronised by people who don't enjoy the impersonal atmosphere of many motels. Others are very fancy indeed. Many are quite posh places that specialise in fancy breakfasts. Some try to give their guests a feeling for life with a New Zealand family. Because they tend to get lumped into this one category, the 'B&B' places at the top of the heap try hard to dissociate themselves from the rock bottom guesthouses at the other end of the strata.

B&B accommodation in private homes has recently become a fashionable concept in the USA and there are now many New Zealanders offering family-run enterprises of that type. Get a copy of *The New Zealand Bed & Breakfast Book* by J & J Thomas (Moonshine Press, Wellington, paperback) with details on dozens of B&B places all over the country. This is an excellent annual book, available from most bookstores and visitor information centres.

Another development in this type of travel is that there are now many agencies specialising in booking accommodation in private homes and farms throughout the country. Many of these are B&B arrangements. The NZTB has a list of reputable agencies; check also with local visitor information centres.

Although breakfast is definitely on the agenda at the real B&B places it may or may not feature at other places in this category. Where it does it's likely to be a pretty substantial meal – fruit, eggs, bacon, toast, tea and coffee are all likely to make an appearance. Many guesthouses pride themselves on the size, quality and 'traditional value' of their breakfasts. If you like to start the day heartily it's worth considering this when comparing prices.

Guesthouses can be particularly good value if you're travelling on your own. Most hotels and motels are priced on a 'per room' basis whereas guesthouses usually charge 'per person'. Typically B&Bs cost around $30 to $50 per person. Except at the most expensive B&B guesthouses, rooms generally do not have attached bathrooms.

There's also the DB&B (dinner, bed & breakfast) plan which is popular with skiers, for example, who like to wake up, have a good breakfast, go out skiing and come back to a hot meal. Many B&Bs offer the evening meal for an extra charge. A few B&Bs offer a kitchen where guests can do their own cooking, but most do not.

There are several cooperatively produced lists of B&B accommodation – usually available from guesthouses which appear on the list, and from visitor information centres.

Hotels

As in Australia a hotel has to be licensed to serve alcohol. So at one end of the scale the hotel category can include traditional older-style hotels where the emphasis is mainly on the bar and the rooms are pretty much a sideline. At the other end it includes all the brand new five-star hotels in the big cities, hotels which are pretty much like their relations elsewhere in the world in facilities and in their high prices. In between, many places that are essentially motels can call themselves hotels because they have a bar and liquor licence. At the cheapest old-style hotels, singles might cost as low as $20 while at the most luxurious new establishments a room could cost $200 or more.

Some of the older hotels now also have 'backpackers rooms'. They are usually about the same as the regular hotel rooms except they don't have the frills – no TV, radio or what have you – and the customers provide their own towel and bedding (usually a sleeping bag). The cost is usually about half the normal hotel rate.

If you like staying in economical older hotels, a free *Pub Beds* brochure will give you a good discount when you present it at participating hotels. It's published by Pub Beds, PO Box 32-332, Auckland 9, New Zealand (☎ (09) 445 4400; fax 445 8407) and is available at many hotels and information centres around New Zealand.

Motels

Motels are pretty much like motels anywhere else in the world although NZ motels are notably well equipped. They always have tea and coffee-making equipment and supplies; usually there's a fridge and very often there's a toaster and electric frying pan if you just feel like whipping up some scrambled eggs. Even a real kitchen is not at all unusual, complete with utensils, plates and cutlery. Although long-life milk for your coffee or tea is starting to take over, at many traditional motels you'll still find a small carton of fresh milk by your door every morning.

Sometimes there's a distinction drawn between 'serviced motels' and 'motel flats'. Essentially the difference is that a motel flat has more equipment and less service. You don't get people rushing around pulling the sheets straight every time you turn round – which is just fine with me and probably with you too. A motel room typically costs around $55 to $70. Sometimes you can find them cheaper, and there are many more luxurious new motels where $70 to $100 is the usual range. There's usually only a small difference in price, if any, between a single or double motel room.

Farmstays (Farm Holidays)

New Zealand has been called the world's most efficient farm so a visit to a farm is an interesting way of getting to grips with the real New Zealand. Farmstays are a very popular activity as many farms take guests who can 'have a go' at all the typical farm activities and be treated as one of the household into the bargain. If you want to know more about it contact the NZTB or the visitor information centres. There are all sorts of farms you can choose from – dairy, sheep, high country, cattle or mixed farming farms. If you're staying in the homestead typical daily costs are in the $60 to $120 range including meals, but there are also many on a B&B only arrangement where costs may be more like $35 to $50 per day, with an extra $10 to $15 if you want dinner. Some farms have separate cottages where you fix your own food and have to supply your own bedding; these ones may charge by the week. Rates can get as cheap as $10 per night in basic sheep shearers' cottages, for example. You'll probably find that the cheapest farm holidays have to be booked when you're actually in New Zealand; only the more expensive places go looking for customers abroad.

WWOOF A very economical way to stay on a farm and actually do some work there is to join Willing Workers on Organic Farms (WWOOF), based in Palmerston North in the North Island. Membership in WWOOF provides you with a list of over 300 organic farms throughout the country where, in exchange for your 'conscientious work', the farm owner will provide food, accommodation and some hands-on experience in organic farming. Once you've made a decision about which farm you'd like to visit you have to contact the farm owner or manager directly by telephone or letter. They emphasise that you cannot simply turn up at a farm without warning.

To join WWOOF and receive the booklet, write to Janet & Andrew Strange, WWOOF, PO Box 10-037, Palmerston North, New Zealand, or telephone (06) 355 3555, for full details. The cost is $15 if you join in New Zealand. If you join from overseas, the cost is A$10 for Australia, US$10 for the USA, C$10 for Canada, £5 for the UK, DM15 for Germany, or Y1100 for Japan.

Homestays

In addition to farms there are also numerous possibilities for staying in private homes throughout New Zealand, whether in urban or rural areas. Most are B&B arrangements – see the Guesthouses & B&Bs section for additional details. Several of the agencies which handle farmstays are combination 'farm and homestay' services. Visitor information centres throughout New Zealand, especially in the smaller towns, keep lists of farmstays and homestays in their areas.

Possibilities for farmstays and homestays in New Zealand are extensive. In this book we have not even tried to list each individual farmstay and homestay; there are simply too many. Your best bet if you're interested in farmstays and homestays is to get hold of a copy of the *Bed & Breakfast Book* mentioned earlier, make contact with one of the umbrella organisations specialising in farmstays and homestays, or ask at the visitor information centre for each area.

Home Exchange

If you want to spend some time in one area, an option is a holiday home exchange. It works the same way as in other parts of the world: you pay a fee to a matching agency, they facilitiate connections between potential home-swappers, and once the connection is made, there are no more accommodation costs – it's an even swap, home for home. Home rentals can often also be arranged.

There are a couple of agencies in New Zealand that handle home exchange, and each does it a little differently. The Worldwide Home Exchange Club is a worldwide organisation with a representative in New Zealand. They offer home swapping, home rentals and 'hospitality exchange' arrangements, where you visit someone's home as their guest and they then visit yours at another time. When you sign up, you receive a booklet with listings of members' homes all around the world; it's then up to the members to make contact. Write for information and a membership blank to Worldwide Home Exchange Club, CPO Box 4433, Auckland 1, New Zealand (☎ (09) 630-8732).

The Home Swap Holiday Club is a similar organisation but it is more of a national New Zealand club. Nevertheless they say they may be able to arrange something for overseas visitors too, with direct holiday home rentals perhaps being more likely than a home swap. Contact them at Home Swap Holiday Club, PO Box 2056, Raumati Beach, Paraparaumu, New Zealand (☎ & fax (04) 298-8130).

FOOD

If you're expecting any sort of gastronomic surprises in New Zealand you may be in for a bit of a disappointment. Nowhere does New Zealand's solid English ancestry show through clearer than on the dining table. New Zealand as a whole has not had the wide variety of immigrants that has given Australians and North Americans a healthy liking for 'spicy tucker'. But if straightforward solid, honest fare like steak & chips, fish & chips, roast lamb and the like fit the bill then you won't be unhappy.

Having said that let me immediately add that the situation is quite different in the major cities, where you can find everything from Italian to Middle Eastern to Indian to Vietnamese to Mexican food. The choice of restaurants is a lot more cosmopolitan than it was even just a few years ago. Curiously, despite the proliferation of international restaurants in the larger cities, there is nothing to be seen from the Pacific Islands, the source of New Zealand's largest number of immigrants. In the hinterlands, Chinese restaurants still predominate over any other sort of overseas cuisine.

There's not much of a NZ national cuisine – no moa & chips or Auckland fried kiwi. They're big meat eaters though and a NZ steak is every bit as good as an Aussie one. Lamb, of course, is top quality and available everywhere. New Zealand is also renowned

Kiwi Fruit

New Zealand's most famous fruit, the kiwi fruit, is also known as the Chinese gooseberry. The fruit is fuzzy, brown, and about the size of a small lemon. The skin peels off to reveal its unique green flesh, high in vitamins and fibre. The name kiwi fruit was dreamed up in the 1950s.

Imported from the Yangtze Valley in China, the first kiwi fruit climbers were grown as ornamental garden vines and it was only around 50 years ago that the first attempts were made to grow them commercially. The industry grew very slowly at first; only in the last couple of decades has it finally assumed the economic importance it enjoys today. New Zealand now produces about two-thirds of all the kiwi fruit grown in the world. ∎

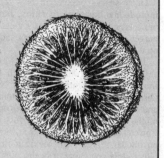

for its dairy products and the milk, cheese and ice cream are excellent.

With all that coastline it's not surprising that seafood is pretty popular. There are some fine local varieties of oyster and the now rare and expensive toheroa or slightly less pricey tuatua. In some places, such as 90 Mile Beach in the North Island, and in the right season, a few minutes of digging in the sand at the beach can yield bucketfuls of shellfish, including tuatuas; pipis and periwinkles are other favourites.

The green-lipped mussels, available all over New Zealand, are easily the best in the world and though they're exported abroad they cost a fortune if you get them in other countries – compare $5 for *eight dozen* fresh ones in New Zealand (admittedly an excellent deal) to around $15 for a dozen in Australia. Likewise Bluff oysters are hard to beat – oyster fans shouldn't leave New Zealand without tasting them. Scallops are also good eating but ask local advice before you eat them; in 1993 there was a ban on them for several months, which was later lifted. Crayfish (lobster) is a speciality in some areas. Saltwater fish favourites include hoki, hapuka, groper, snapper, and kingfish.

New Zealand also has good fresh water fish, with incredibly large rainbow and brown trout. The areas around lakes Taupo and Rotorua in the North Island are particularly famous for giant-sized trout, but in fact they are found in many places in the country.

You can't buy these trout in the shops but there are many opportunities to catch one yourself. There are a number of guidebooks about fishing in New Zealand; see the Outdoor Activities chapter.

Eels, plentiful in New Zealand's rivers and creeks, are another local delicacy, especially smoked eels. Actually smoked eels and smoked fish are both quite popular.

Fast Food & Takeaways

Starting from the bottom there are plenty of fast food joints, along with those symbols of American culinary imperialism: McDonald's, Pizza Hut and Kentucky Fried Chicken.

Of course there is fish & chips. Unlike in Australia where frying up good English fish & chips seems to be an Italian or Greek occupation, in New Zealand it's very often a Chinese one. (To the Americans in the crowd, note that 'chips' in New Zealand are the same thing as 'French fries' in the USA.)

New Zealanders are just about as tied to the meat pie as Australians but they probably do make a better job of them. To any Americans or Poms out there, the meat pie has as great a cultural significance to Australians as the hot dog does to a Noo Yorker – and is as frequently reviled for not being what it once was or currently should be.

If you want to eat fast food and takeaways Kiwi style, fish & chips and hot meat pies are about as traditionally Kiwi as you can get. Try kumara chips sometime, for a variation.

Other snacks popular in New Zealand include nachos, potato skins, battered mussels and hamburgers like the great 'Kiwi burger' with a fried egg, beetroot and salad on it.

Tastebuds Mexican Cantina, found in several places around the North Island including Whangarei, Rotorua, Napier, Gisborne, New Plymouth, Palmerston North and Wellington with more branches opening all the time, is a great local fast food chain. You can get a good meal of a taco, burrito or enchilada, served with Mexican rice and either chile con carne or beans, plus a few crispy chips and whatever 'hotness' of sauce you like, all served on a paper plate for under $6 – such a deal.

Cafes & Tearooms

New Zealand's traditional cafes or coffee shops, called tearooms, are nothing to get very excited over. They're usually open on weekdays from around 9 am to 5 pm and perhaps on Saturday morning, serving fare such as tea, scones and white bread sandwiches. Devonshire teas, which include a pot of tea, one or two scones, jam and whipped cream, are served at morning and afternoon tea time (around 10 am and 3 or 4 pm).

In the larger cities, though, an entirely different cafe scene has sprung up in just the past few years. You can now go into many cafes in the larger cities and order espresso (or cappuccino, cafe latte, etc), croissants, sinfully rich desserts, and focaccia bakes – Italian focaccia bread covered with a variety of ingredients and then baked (try the cheese and pesto one at Zoe's Cafe in Wellington). Some cafes, like the traditional tearooms, stay open only on weekdays until around 5 pm, but each city has some that are popular late-night hangouts where you can sit and drink espresso, have a dessert, listen to music and generally hang out and be cool.

Pub Food

If you move into the pubs you'll probably find some of the best value for money. Counter meals (pie & chips, stews, etc) have more or less died out, though some bars still sell pies from a pie warmer. A lot of pubs now have bistro meals – simple but good food like schnitzel, steak, fish or the like with chips (French fries) and a good fresh salad or coleslaw. Average main courses range from $8 to $12 and they are usually excellent value. Cobb & Co restaurants are a chain offering pub-style food in locations all over New Zealand. They're safe, sound and consistent and also open commendably generous hours, usually from 7 am to 10 pm seven days a week.

Restaurants

Up another jump and into the restaurants. Here there's the BYO-Licensed Restaurant split. BYOs (bring-your-own, or BYOG, bring-your-own-grog) mean that you can bring your own bottle of wine or whatever along with you and the food prices are generally a notch lower than in licensed restaurants. Check before you arrive if it is BYO or not. If you like reading about restaurants before you try them Michael Guy's *Eating Out* is an interesting guide to restaurants all over New Zealand.

Vegetarian New Zealand has a number of great vegetarian restaurants, principally in the big cities. Auckland has several cheap and excellent vegetarian restaurants including Gopals (run by the Hare Krishnas) and the Simple Cottage. In Christchurch the Mainstreet Cafe is more expensive but the food, especially the desserts, is superb.

Self-Catering

Buying your own food to cook yourself is generally far cheaper than eating out, of course, and with all camping grounds and hostels and most motels having cooking facilities it's a relatively easy alternative.

New Zealand has several large supermarket chains – Pak 'N Save, New World and Woolworth's for example – that have excellent prices and they're usually open seven days a week, with at least one or two 'late night' shopping nights when they're open until around 8 pm. The large supermarkets are not found only in large cities; sometimes there are unusually large supermarkets in a town that wouldn't seem to warrant it, like the huge Pak 'N Save supermarkets in Kaitaia and Thames, as they serve a large rural community.

When the supermarkets are shut, the good old corner dairy is the place to go. A dairy is a small shop found on many street corners throughout New Zealand, which sells milk, food, the local newspaper, chocolate, sweets – in fact a bit of everything, but mostly food lines. They're open longer hours than other shops and are far more widespread, but their selection is usually not as good as a larger shop, and their prices tend to be higher.

DRINKS
Beer & Pubs
New Zealanders are great drinkers, and both the beer and the pubs are pretty good. Almost all the beer is now brewed by only two companies. Steinlager, the various types of DB (Bitter, Export, etc) and Lion Red are probably the most popular beers. Down in the deep south you'll see some different labels like Speights, Southland Bitter and Bavarian. Bavarian used to be brewed by a private company, as was much of New Zealand's beer, before it was taken over by one of the two giants. Many a true Bavarian drinker will tell you it's not the same as in the good old days. Monteith's, from the South Island's wild west coast, is as dark as the bitumenous coal dug by the miners who drink it.

There are a smattering of small boutique breweries where the beer is made and consumed on the premises. Check out the Shakespeare Tavern & Brewery in Auckland or the popular Loaded Hog in Christchurch, Timaru and Wellington; the Loaded Hog makes four different types of grog and boasts that all are guaranteed 100% hangover-free! The Shakespeare Brewery makes six different varieties and if you manage to drink all of them in one evening you get a certificate of achievement. Probably the best of the boutique beers are from Marlborough and Nelson – Pink Elephant and Mac's. 'Dark' drinkers will appreciate the Black Mac.

Cans aren't very popular and most beer is sold in bottles anyway as they're refundable and cheaper than cans. In a pub the cheapest beer is on tap. You can ask for a 'seven', which was originally seven fluid ounces but is now a 200 ml glass, the nearest metric equivalent (it's still called a 'seven' though – old ways die hard!); a 'handle' which is a half litre or litre mug with a handle; or a jug, which is just that.

Drinks at public bars are the cheapest, while lounge or other bars tend to mark their drinks up more, but prices vary widely.

In public bars you can pretty much wear anything, but lounge bars have a lot of 'neat dress required' signs around. You sometimes get the feeling they are determined that New Zealand should be the last home of the necktie. The bars with entertainment are normally lounge bars, which can sometimes make things a bit awkward for the traveller with jeans, sandals and T-shirt.

A New Zealand invention is the Trust-operated pub which started in Invercargill.

Blarney Stone Meets Kiwiland
Irish-style pubs have become all the rage in New Zealand nowadays, not only in the large cities but in many smaller towns as well. Typically they are relaxed, low-key places to enjoy a brew, conversation and a good inexpensive meal. Most feature Irish music at least once or twice a week, but there's live music every night in many places, with acoustic Irish folk music, rousing Irish dance bands or both. Often they import their beers and ales, with kegs imported straight from England and Ireland on tap.

Naturally St Patrick's Day (17 March) is the occasion of the year in these places and there may be several days of partying leading up to the big event.

One place in Auckland, the Civic Tavern, has gone all-out and boasts an Irish pub, an English pub and a Scottish pub all under one roof! ■

For some time that stout town was 'dry' and when the prohibition was repealed they decided that pubs should be publicly owned and the profits go to the community. It worked so well that many other pubs around the country are also Trust operated.

Wines & Wineries

New Zealand also has a thriving wine-producing industry and many wineries have established international reputations, particularly for their whites. Air New Zealand has been a consistent winner of awards for the best wines served by an airline.

A few notable wine-producing areas are Henderson near Auckland, Waiheke Island just off Auckland, Martinborough in the Wairarapa region, Hawke's Bay, and Blenheim in the north part of the South Island. Winery visits and tours are popular in all these places and of course there's free wine tasting. As New Zealand wine continues to achieve a higher reputation new wineries in these and other regions will probably continue to open.

An unusual New Zealand speciality is kiwi fruit wine. There are lots of different varieties – still and bubbly, sweet and dry – and even a liqueur. You may not like it, but New Zealand's the best place to try it. It's also an interesting way to while away a few hours – taking a look at a kiwi fruit winery and having a free tasting in pleasant surroundings. The Purangi Winery near Whitianga on the Coromandel Peninsula, with an organic orchard and a variety of fruit wines and liqueurs including kiwi fruit, feijoa, passion fruit and others, is one of the most enjoyable and unique.

ENTERTAINMENT

As in many countries, there's plenty of nightlife in the major cities but not much in the small towns, where everything seems to shut with a bang after dark except the pub and the Chinese takeaway, and even they might be closed by around 9 or 10 pm. In the cities there's plenty of entertainment, with cinemas, theatre, discos, live music venues, late-night cafes and plenty more.

In spectator sports, rugby is practically a national mania, with cricket in a distant second place. It seems little boys in New Zealand learn to play rugby about as soon as they can walk, and continue to play it as late in life as they can manage. As you travel round New Zealand you'll see matches being played everywhere you go by teams of all ages. In rugby season when they're not out playing rugby, they're inside watching it on television. The All Blacks, New Zealand's national rugby team, are the national heroes.

Rugby League, a variant of rugby, is also very popular; the national team is called the Kiwis.

THINGS TO BUY

You don't go to New Zealand intending to come back with a backpack full of souvenirs – a photograph of some flawless moment may be your best reminder – but there are some things worth checking out.

Woollen Goods

You can buy beautiful woollen gear in New Zealand, of course, particularly jumpers (sweaters) made from hand-spun, hand-dyed wool. Hand-knit jumpers are something of an art form in New Zealand and although they're not cheap – they sell in tourist shops for around $200 to $300 – they are of the highest quality and great if you can afford them. Other knitted goods include hats, gloves, scarves, mufflers and so on.

Woollen Swann-Dri jackets, shirts and pullovers are so practical and warm that they're just about the New Zealand national garment in the countryside, especially if you happen to be a farmer. Most common are the red-and-black or blue-and-black plaid ones, though they do also come in a few solid colours. You can buy Swann-Dris (affectionately known as 'Swannies') in certain shops and again, though they're not cheap – a good pullover could cost you around $200 – they're top quality and if you buy one it will probably keep you from ever getting cold for at least the next decade or so.

Sheepskins

Sheepskins are also popular buys – the ones

Rugby

No book about New Zealand would be complete without mention of the national obsession – Rugby Union football. Try to escape the euphoria when the national team, the All Blacks, steamroller their international opponents into the mud of Eden Park – impossible. Look at the fear on the faces of the opposition as the All Blacks perform the fearsome haka at the start of a match and for which they have become famous.

According to tradition rugby had its beginnings in 1823 when William Webb Ellis picked up the ball during a game of soccer at Rugby School in England. The illegality of this move led to the popularity of such handling of the ball and the game was born. In 1846 the rules of rugby were published at the school. The Rugby Union was formed in 1871. Rugby was carried to the far outposts of the British Empire by British citizens travelling and living abroad.

The NZ Football Union was founded in 1892 and the country became a stronghold of the game. Interprovincial championship began in 1902 with play for the Ranfurly Shield which was donated by the then governor general, The Earl of Ranfurly. New Zealand first played in Great Britain in 1888-89 and 1905-06.

The highest level of competition for rugby is now the World Cup and, before that, countries established their supremacy after a number of test matches against each other. Test-match rugby is still intensely exciting. The World Cup was inaugurated in 1987 and hosted jointly by Australia and New Zealand – New Zealand emerged as the first world champions. It was a rather aloof team that went on to the UK in 1991 to defend it, and horror of horror, it was won by the Wallabies, the Australian team. It stuck in the craw of every observer in NZ to call them world champions.

Politics has entered the sport on a number of occasions and the apartheid debate was perhaps the most vehement example. A series tour to South Africa was postponed in 1967 because the NZ team included Maoris. A team with Maori players did tour in 1970. In 1973 the South Africans were prevented from touring but they did get to tour in 1981. Since then the Springboks have emerged from the sporting wilderness – they toured Australia in 1993 and, at the time of writing, a series against the All Blacks was planned.

The game is played on a quadrangular-shaped field. The maximum distance between the goal lines is 100 metres, the field is 69 metres wide, goalposts are 5.6 metres apart with the cross bar three metres above the ground. The object is to get the ball across the opponents' goal line and ground it (a try worth four points), or kick it over the goal posts (a conversion worth two points, a penalty worth three or a drop goal from the field worth three).

The oval ball is leather and weighs 440 gms. It is kicked off from the centre and then, by a combination of maul, ruck and scrum, is taken by one team. Without getting offside and without passing forward they attempt to get the ball to the opponents' line. Play stops only for a lineout, when the ball has gone out and is thrown back in to a line of players; a scrum when opposing forwards pack down against each other; a penalty or conversion; or for a respite to remove an injured player. Get the full bottle from someone in the pub.

There are 15 players in each side – eight forwards and seven backs. The backs include a fullback, left wing, right wing, outside centre, inside centre, fly half and scrum half. They usually have slender builds and can move quickly with the ball. Looking at a number of forward packs you could be forgiven for thinking that brawn was a prerequisite. There are two burly props, a hooker to rake the ball in the scrum, two second rowers or locks, two flankers (or breakaways) and the last man down (No 8). The last three are referred to as loose forwards.

There are approximately 11,000 clubs in NZ. The All Blacks, over the years have included many great players such as the famous lock forward Colin 'Pine Tree' Meads – 55 caps (representing New Zealand) and 133 appearances between 1957 and 1971; Brian Williams, the great winger; Don Clarke, fullback extraordinaire; Grant F Fox, fly half and still playing; Ian Kirkpatrick, a scintillating loose forward; and the great Waka Nathan. Eden Park in Auckland is the Mecca of the game, it can hold a crowd 57,000 and has been used since 1921.

Seven-a-side competition is now popular with the advent of the Hong Kong sevens tournament. The All Blacks do fairly well in this fast-running game but a strong force has been the Fijian team. The modern All Blacks are very much a melting pot of Pakehas, Maoris and Polynesians. If you're interested and there at the right time, make sure you see a game at Eden Park – tickets are available at the park itself and it's best to buy them well in advance of the game (weeks before, for the popular games).

Rugby League, with 13 instead of 15 players and slightly different rules, is also popular but not as revered as rugby. ■

sold in the top tourist shops are beautiful and pure white, with long, thick, straight combed wool. Numerous other things are made of sheepskin, including toasty warm slippers.

Greenstone (Pounamu)

Jade, called greenstone or pounamu in New Zealand, is made into ornaments, brooches, earrings, cuff links and tikis. The latter are tiny, stylised Maori figures, usually depicted with their tongue stuck out in a warlike challenge, worn on a thong or chain around the neck. They've got great *mana* or power, but they also serve as fertility symbols so beware!

Bone Carvings

Maori bone carvings are another fine Maori art form which is undergoing something of a renaissance in New Zealand. Of course the Maori artisans have always made bone carvings, but nowadays it seems you see amazingly beautiful bone carvings a lot more often. Tikis can be carved of bone as well as greenstone, though the greenstone ones are more common, and there are some very interesting human and animal figures that are carved of bone. Fishhooks, carved in a variety of traditional Maori styles, are also commonly carved of bone; a certain type of fishhook represents the legend of how New Zealand was fished up from the sea by Maui. Dolphins, sea birds and other figures are also carved of bone. Bone figures are often worn on a thong or a chain around the neck.

Paua (Abalone)

Abalone shell, called paua in New Zealand, is another substance from which beautiful carvings and jewellery are made. It's illegal to take unadulterated paua shells out of New Zealand, but you can buy pendants, earrings and many other things made of paua and take them with you with no problems. You'll probably see whole shells used as ashtrays in places where paua is plentiful, but you can't take one of those out of the country.

Wood Carvings

Another distinctive Maori art form, Maori wood carvings are worth checking out, particularly in Rotorua. In a number of places, carvers are producing tremendous forms such as leaping dolphins, in addition to the sometimes highly intricate traditional Maori carvings.

Other Arts & Crafts

New Zealanders have a reputation as great do-it-yourselfers and there are a lot of excellent shops selling art & crafts where you'll find everything from hand-painted scarves to ceramics to home-made jams and preserves, in addition to all the handicrafts previously mentioned. The quality of the pottery and weaving is particularly fine: they make good presents to take back home and don't take up much room in your pack. Nelson, in particular, is noted for its excellent pottery. The quality of the local clay has attracted many potters there.

Fashion

City Kiwis have an independent flair when it comes to fashion, and consequently there are some great little clothes shops around. In Auckland, check out Ponsonby Rd, the markets and in the centre around High and O'Connell Sts. For unique women's fashion, try boutiques Zambesi, in Vulcan Lane, and Streetlife, in High St. Both have made a name for themselves locally and overseas for their original designs.

The more mainstream quality designers congregate around the central city and Parnell districts in Auckland. Thornton Hall is a successful women's label you'll find in all the major cities.

Outdoor clothing has also become very competitive and the durable yet stylish Canterbury sports clothing label is known internationally.

Other

If you're planning a camping trip around New Zealand you can buy top quality sleeping bags, tents, clothes and other bush gear. You get what you pay for and if you don't mind paying the price you can get some of the world's best quality. The large cities have second-hand sports shops were you can sometimes pick up some good bargains.

You can find beautiful postcards everywhere you go in New Zealand and a postcard collection would make a great keepsake of the country. Books of New Zealand photography, in hardback or paperback, are sold in bookshops around New Zealand; the Whitcoull's chain has a large selection but you can find them in most bookshops. Or how about a book of *Footrot Flats* cartoons?

Of course there are also plenty of silly souvenirs. How about a little tin can that goes 'baaaa' like a sheep when you turn it over? Or a miniature sheep? Then there are the snow-domes with a flock of sheep trapped in a perpetual snow shower. And how about everything you can think of, from T-shirts to key rings, emblazoned with little cartoon kiwi birds?

Outdoor Activities

New Zealand is a haven for visitors who seek to combine adventure with the wide, open spaces.

The land, air and water are not sacrosanct, and New Zealanders and their visitors move over or through these media in just about every way imaginable. They jet-boat, white water sledge, raft, boogey board, canoe, kayak, surf, surf raft, scuba dive and ski through the water; bungy jump, parapente, skydive, abseil, fly, helicopter and barrel roll through the air; and tramp, mountain-bike, ski, horse-ride, rock climb and ice climb across and up terra firma. Not forgetting, beneath the surface – caving, cave rafting, *tomo* exploring and hydrosliding are all actively pursued.

To give you an indication of the lengths Kiwis will go to experience something different, read *Classic New Zealand Adventures* by Jonathan Kennett, Johnny Mulheron, Greg Carlyon & Malcolm O'Neill (GP Publications, Wellington, 1992, paperback). It contains every adventure from a sedate paddle down a river to wharf jumping on a bicycle, pillocking across mud flats on a rubbish tin lid, and bridge swinging on a climbing rope. Still bored? Then try a jump in the nude from the top of Maruia Falls!

The *New Zealand Adventure Annual & Directory* by John Woods (First Light Media, PO Box 31, Gisborne, 1993, paperback) is another good resource coming out annually with articles, colour photos and listings of all kinds of adventure and activity operators around New Zealand.

Tramping

Tramping, or bushwalking as it is often called, is the best way of coming to grips with New Zealand's natural beauty. It gives the traveller the greater satisfaction of being a participant rather than just a spectator.

The country has thousands of km of tracks, many well marked, some only a line on the maps. One thing that makes tramping especially attractive are the hundreds of huts available, enabling trampers to avoid the weight of tents and cooking gear. Many tracks are graded; some are easily covered by those with only moderate fitness and little or no experience, while others are more rewarding for experienced, fit walkers. Many travellers, once having tried a track, then gear the rest of their trip in New Zealand to travelling from one track to another, with side trips to see other sights. This section should open your eyes to the possibilities of tramping, but before attempting any track consult the appropriate authority for the latest information.

Information

There are literally hundreds of tracks to be enjoyed all over New Zealand. Visitors tend to want to do the 'famous' ones – the Milford, Routeburn, Abel Tasman, etc – and some of these tend to get so crowded with trampers that everyone gets annoyed, while meanwhile an equally beautiful track may exist just a few km away and nobody goes on it. Most of the time it's because they haven't heard about it.

In this chapter we give details on New Zealand's 'Great Walks', while throughout the book you'll find information on many other good walking areas and specific tracks. The Great Walks are the most famous tramping tracks in the country and they became famous because of their beauty. Their beauty does indeed make them worth going on but if you go on these tracks, please don't do so and then be upset that they are crowded – especially the Abel Tasman Coastal Track, the most popular track in New Zealand. Of *course* these tracks are sometimes crowded, especially at the height of summer – people from all over the world have come to tramp on them.

The 'most walked' tracks in New Zealand are the Abel Tasman Coastal Track, which 20,000 people walked in 1990/91; the Milford Track with 10,000; the Routeburn Track 8360; the Kepler Track 6700; the Lake Waikaremoana Track 6500; and the Tongariro Crossing 5000.

If you like tramping but want to avoid the crowds, it's worth asking at DOC offices and park headquarters for details on lesser-known tracks – they will be happy to help you plan some enjoyable walks. There are DOC offices in every city and in dozens of towns, and they all give free information about tramping in their areas. Every national park, forest park and maritime park has its own DOC headquarters and they all have information on a number of long and short walks. There are also council parks, farm parks, regional parks and more, all of which have walking possibilities.

Tracks, Huts & Wardens

The following notes on tracks, huts and wardens apply only to the popular 'tourist' tracks. If you venture off these onto any other tracks, things will be quite different. For example it may take you an hour to cover one km, huts may be eight hours or so apart, there won't be any wardens and you will have to be much better prepared. Keep these factors in mind:

• When walking allow about four km per hour on easy ground.

• Huts are usually placed three to four hours apart.

• Huts usually cater for 24, and beds are thick foam mattresses on bunks.

• Huts on the more popular tracks usually have wood stoves with gas burners.

• There is a two-night limit on huts, if they are full.

Camping on tracks is allowed on all except the Milford Track. On Great Walks tracks, where the huts can fill up, camping areas are provided beside all the huts for overflow. On the Milford Track numbers are regulated so the huts don't get overloaded.

The NZ Environmental Care Code gives guidelines for camping (get this from any

DOC office). Always leave firewood in huts for the next group, in case they arrive in heavy rain or the dark.

In the last decade or so, there has been an amazing improvement in the conditions of tracks and huts. Tracks are administered by conservation officers and wardens; the former are permanent staff, well trained and very knowledgeable. The wardens are temporary; usually employed for the summer season to keep an eye on and maintain the huts, provide track information and first aid, collect hut fees and generally be helpful to trampers.

Wardens in the national parks collect hut fees when they're on duty, from November to April. Whether a warden is present or not, it's important that you always pay your hut fees, as all huts require maintenance and this is how it is paid for. Most DOC offices in the regional centres near the start of tracks sell back country hut tickets. Check with wardens or DOC staff in the regional offices for weather forecasts and information about the track.

Getting into and out of tracks can be a real problem. Having a vehicle only simplifies the problem of getting in. Having two vehicles allows the positioning of one at each end of the track. If you have no vehicle then you have to take public transport or hitch in, and if the track starts or ends at the end of a dead-end road, hitching will be difficult. Fortunately, with the far greater number of trampers now walking New Zealand's tracks there is also more transport available.

Leave excess luggage behind or send it on to a point near the end of the track. Camping grounds and other accommodation places will often hold luggage for free. Bus companies will carry excess luggage at a very reasonable price and will hold it in their offices until it is picked up.

Surprisingly, most people on the tracks are from outside New Zealand. It's common to have a ratio of only one in 10 Kiwis in a hut, although on the Milford Track, of course, it can reach 50-50. Kiwis do tramp, but they tend to avoid the more popular tracks, seeking the really wild and untouched regions. To some New Zealanders tramping is still considered to be blazing trails through deep snow over 4000-metre-passes, sleeping out in the open during blizzards, then fording rivers neck deep, ducking to avoid the blocks of ice, all done in shorts and T-shirt.

Once on the track be careful. In good weather most of the tracks are safer than walking around town but what really makes them dangerous is New Zealand's contrary weather. A glorious walk in perfect conditions can suddenly become a fight for survival in a blizzard. An easy two-hour walk to the next hut can turn into a grim struggle against wind, wet and cold over a washed-out track and swollen rivers. Hopefully this won't happen but such unexpected and abrupt changes are common, so be prepared and be careful. Weather forecasts should be watched but taken with a grain of salt. New Zealand's prevailing weather comes from the south-west, an area which has no inhabited land and very little sea or air traffic, making accurate reporting difficult. In Fiordland it is considered that the forecast weather hits the area a day before it is forecast.

The most crowded season for tracks is during the summer school holidays – from one to two weeks before Christmas to the end of January. The couple of weeks before school breaks up in December can also be bad as many school groups are on the trails. December-January on the main trails is a good period to avoid. The best weather is from January to March, though most tracks can be walked enjoyably anytime from about November to April. June and July are considered the middle of winter and not the time to be out on the tracks. Some are closed in winter because of avalanche dangers. It's best to time your walks so that the most southerly are done in the middle of summer.

For an enjoyable tramp the primary consideration is your feet and shoulders. Make sure your footwear is adequate and that your pack is not too heavy. Having adequate, waterproof rain gear is also important, especially on the West Coast of the South Island, where you can get drenched to the skin in

minutes if your rain gear is not up to the challenge.

Above all else, *toitu te whenua* – leave the earth undisturbed.

Back Country Huts

The DOC has a network of back country huts in the national, maritime and forest parks. Hut fees range from $4 to a maximum of $20 per night for adults, paid with tickets purchased in advance at any DOC office or park visitors' centre. The tickets cost $4 each (you can buy them in booklets) and are valid for 15 months. Children under 11 years of age can use all huts free of charge. Children 11 years and older are charged half price and use a special 'youth ticket'.

Huts are classed into four categories and, depending on the category, a night's accommodation may require one or two tickets, except on Great Walks where Great Walks passes are required. On arrival at a hut, you simply date the tickets and deposit them in the box provided. Hut accommodation is on a first come, first served basis.

The best, Category One, huts have cookers and fuel, bunks or sleeping platforms with mattresses, toilet and washing facilities, and a water supply. They may also have lighting, heating, radio communications, drying facilities, and a hut warden on duty. Category One huts are found on the Great Walks, where Great Walks passes are required (see the following section). The cost

in Great Walks huts ranges from $6 to $20 per night (youths half price).

Category Two huts have bunks or sleeping platforms with mattresses, toilet and washing facilities, and a water supply. They may also include cooking and heating facilities, but you may have to provide your own cooker and fuel. The cost is $8 (two tickets) per night.

Category Three huts are more basic, with bunks or sleeping platforms (but no mattresses), toilet and water supply only. You provide your own cooker and fuel. These huts are $4 (one ticket) per night.

There is no fee for Category Four facilities, which are usually just simple shelters for getting out of the rain – no bunks or other amenities.

Camping is permitted outside the huts (but not the ones on the Milford track); the cost is $6.

If you plan to do much tramping, consider getting an Annual Hut Pass. The pass allows you to stay overnight at all Category Two and Three huts on a first come, first served basis, and to camp outside all Category One huts where this is allowed. The cost is $58 (children $29) and the pass is valid for one year from the date of purchase. It does not apply to the Great Walks.

A list of all huts and their categories is available at any DOC office. The Milford Track operates on a system all its own.

Great Walks

Several of New Zealand's most famous tracks have been designated 'Great Walks'. They are:

1. Lake Waikaremoana, Te Urewera National Park (North Island)
2. Tongariro Northern Circuit, Tongariro National Park (North Island)
3. Abel Tasman Coastal Track, Abel Tasman National Park (South Island)
4. Heaphy Track, North-West Nelson Forest Park (South Island)
5. Routeburn Track, Mt Aspiring and Fiordland National Parks (South Island)
6. Milford Track, Fiordland National Park (South Island)
7. Kepler Track, Fiordland National Park (South Island)
8. Rakiura Track (Stewart Island)

The canoe trip down the Whanganui River in Whanganui National Park in the North Island is obviously not a walk – they call it the Whanganui Journey – but it, too, is part of the Great Walks system.

Ordinary back country hut tickets and Annual Hut Passes are not valid on the Great Walks; all Great Walks require a special Great Walks Pass for that particular walk.

These are sold at local DOC offices, national park offices and other places in the vicinity of each walk; the local DOC office can advise you of all the places selling the passes.

The passes cost different amounts for different walks, but they are not expensive. They allow you either to use the huts or to camp in the designated campsites, whichever you prefer. Bring camping gear, since at peak times (summer, Easter weekend, etc) the huts can fill up.

On some tracks – the Tongariro Northern Circuit and the Whanganui Journey, for example – Great Walks passes are necessary only at certain times of year, when the tracks are busiest. During the times of year when Great Walks passes are not required on these tracks, ordinary back country hut tickets and Annual Hut Passes are accepted.

DOC Campsites
In addition to the back country huts, DOC also maintains over 100 campsites; see Accommodation in the Facts for the Visitor chapter.

Track Classification
Tracks are classified according to their difficulty and many other features – how they are marked, degree of steepness, etc. The track classification system is relatively new but you will often hear the various classifications used. They are:

1. Path. Easy and well-formed; allow for wheelchair access or to 'shoe' standard. Suitable for people of all ages and fitness levels.
2. Walking Track. Easy and well-formed; constructed to 'shoe' standard. Suitable for people of most ages and fitness levels.
3. Tramping Track. Requires skill and experience. Constructed to 'boot' standard. Suitable for people of average physical fitness.
4. Route. Requires a high degree of skill, experience and route-finding ability. Suitable for well-equipped trampers.

New Zealand Walkways
The New Zealand Walkways Commission, appointed in 1976, was set up to establish a system of NZ Walkways that would eventu-

ally link throughout the entire country. The plan of linking them all together has been abandoned, but there are still some fine walkways, especially close to urban areas where they provide good recreation for families. They are now administered by DOC.

Books
The national parks produce very good books with detailed information on the parks' flora & fauna, geology and history. DOC has leaflets available on thousands of walking tracks throughout the country, and the local DOC office is usually the best source of information on specific tracks.

Tramping in New Zealand, by Jim Du-Fresne, is another Lonely Planet guide. It has descriptions of many walks, of various lengths and degrees of difficulty, in all parts of the country.

There are plenty of other books about tramping in New Zealand. *New Zealand's Top Ten Tracks* by Mark Pickering (Heinemann Reed, Auckland, 1990, paperback) contains many of the obvious ones (Milford, Routeburn, etc). *101 Great Tramps* by Mark Pickering & Rodney Smith (Reed, Auckland, 1991, paperback) has 101 suggestions for two-day to six-day tramps around the country.

Tramping in North Island Forest Parks by Euan & Jennie Nicol (Reed, Auckland, 1991, paperback) and *Tramping in South Island Forest Parks* by Joanna Wright (Reed, Auckland, 1990, paperback) are good for shorter walking and tramping possibilities, with suggestions for everything from half-hour walks to tramps taking several days.

The Forest and Bird Book of Nature Walks by David Collingwood & EV Sale, revised by Joanna Wright (Reed, Auckland, 1992, paperback) has good suggestions for short walks, half an hour to several hours in length.

BP (Penguin) publishes a series of pocket-size paperback guides to several of NZ's most popular walking tracks. There's also a series of *Shell Guides* on the more popular tracks.

Moir's Trampers' Guide to the Southern Lakes & Fiordland by the New Zealand

Alpine Club is the definitive work on tracks in the south of the South Island. It comes in two volumes: *Northern Section: Lake Wakatipu to the Ohau Watershed* (1984) and *Southern Section: Hollyford Valley South* (1986, both in paperback).

Maps

The DOSLI (Department of Survey & Lands Information) topographical maps are the best, though stationery shops tend to have a very poor selection of them. DOSLI has map sales offices in the North Island in Auckland, Hamilton, Gisborne, Napier, Rotorua, New Plymouth, Palmerston North, Wellington and Whangarei; and in the South Island in Blenheim, Christchurch, Dunedin, Hokitika, Invercargill, Nelson and Timaru. The DOC often has a selection of DOSLI maps for sale on the tracks in its immediate area.

DOSLI has various series of maps for specific uses. 'Parkmaps' are produced for national, state and forest parks, and there are 'Trackmaps' for some of the more popular walking tracks. There are also 'Holidaymaker' maps, 'Touringmaps', 'Terrainmaps' and 'Streetfinder' maps and larger 'Aotearoa' and 'Pacific' maps covering all of New Zealand and many Pacific islands. The most detailed are the 'Topomaps' series of topographical maps. They have the best details, but the problem is you may need two or three maps to cover one track. All the maps cost $11 each.

Conservation Volunteer Programme

DOC has a programme in which you can volunteer to participate in all kinds of conservation projects. Work might include things like counting certain species of birds, guarding and protecting nesting areas at certain times of year, track and/or hut maintenance or any number of other activities. You don't get paid but you do get a chance to go to some wild out-of-the-way places and get hands-on experience in conservation. You can volunteer for any length of time.

Each DOC regional conservancy office administers the volunteer programme for its entire region. North Island conservancy regional offices are in Whangarei, Auckland, Hamilton, Rotorua, Gisborne, Napier, Turangi, Wanganui and Wellington. In the South Island they're in Nelson, Christchurch, Hokitika, Dunedin and Invercargill.

Track Safety

It's *very important* that you learn and follow some basic rules of safety if you'll be out tramping in New Zealand. Thousands of Kiwis and overseas visitors tramp in New Zealand every year without incident, but every year a few more die in the mountains – mostly completely unnecessarily, in ways that wouldn't have happened if they'd been properly informed and observant of simple safety rules.

The main thing to be aware of when tramping in New Zealand is the extremely changeable climate. New Zealand has a maritime climate, not a continental climate – which means that if you come from any of the large land masses (Australia, North America, Europe or wherever) the climate holds surprises that you won't be expecting.

Always remember that the weather can change extremely quickly. Heavy rain, snow and high winds can hit mountain areas *even in summer*, and it can happen in a matter of minutes, even on a warm sunny day. Always be mentally and physically prepared for all kinds of weather. Take along warm enough clothes, waterproof rain gear (raincoat and overtrousers) and a waterproof pack liner. If you should find your clothing and footwear are not adequate for the conditions, it's best to turn back.

Hypothermia is the main health hazard for tramping in New Zealand. Be aware of what causes it so you can avoid it, and know what to do about it if it does occur. (Hypothermia is covered in the Health section of this book; see the Facts for the Visitor chapter.)

Getting lost is another very real danger, so stick to the tracks. It is another quirk of New Zealand that getting lost in the bush is more of a danger here than in many other places. The native bush is very dense. People have become hopelessly lost even when having

'Help us warn them – DOC's plea'

Tongariro DOC staff are urging local accommodation and transport operators to frequently warn their overseas customers about the dangers of the Tongariro Mountains. This follows last week's tragedy where a young tourist froze to death on Tongariro.

On Friday 22 May the body of a young Turkish-German tourist was recovered from the slopes of Mt Tongariro by the Ruapehu Alpine Rescue Organisation working with the NZ Rail rescue helicopter.

Conservation Officer Ian Goodison of Whakapapa said:

'This person had been attempting to walk the Tongariro Crossing, a very popular summer day walk with both Kiwis and overseas visitors. He attempted the crossing by himself, during high winds with rain and snow falling, after ignoring sound advice from people experienced in local conditions. He was clad only in jeans, light upper clothing, nylon parka and sandshoes, and carried a very heavy pack containing all his travelling possessions. He appears to have been overwhelmed by the cold and subsequently died from hypothermia.

Outdoor Safety

'Visitors to Tongariro National Park are strongly advised that from May to November the walks in the mountains are in winter alpine conditions and appropriate precautions must be taken. People using the Tongariro Crossing and similar routes must not travel alone, and must be adequately dressed and equipped for alpine conditions. Mountaineering equipment such as ice axes and crampons are essential. Often it is essential to carry avalanche transceivers, shovels and probes as well.

'Even during the summer months, warm and waterproof clothing must be carried. We see many visitors who are inadequately dressed walking around in the mountains in sand-shoes and light clothing. Several months ago on Tongariro a guided party came across a lone tramper nearly dead from hypothermia. They saved his life. The whole incident would never have happened if the tourist concerned had been adequately clothed and in the company of others.

'I would like to ask operators of accommodation facilities and transport services who have frequent contact with overseas visitors to impress upon their guests that there are life-threatening risks involved in wandering around in mountains and bush alone and inadequately equipped. NZ is developing an image as a destination offering unique outdoor adventure. Many visitors have an agenda of outdoor experiences to achieve during their NZ trip, often in the form of personal challenges and exciting outdoor activities. It is often difficult to convince them that a particular action may be foolhardy and dangerous. However, I'm sure that a lonely death is not on anyone's agenda, and I hope that these unfortunate incidents will provide a clear example of what not to do in the outdoors.

'All visitors should contact a Park Visitor Centre of Information Centre before their trip for up-to-date information about weather and mountain conditions.'

Published by the Ruapehu Bulletin, Ohakune
27 May 1992
(reprinted here with permission)

(Note: This article is about Tongariro but it could just as easily have been written about any mountain region in New Zealand.) ■

set off to do something as simple as a 15-minute walk, and only been found many days later or even not at all. It sounds so strange it's almost comical, but if you spend any length of time in New Zealand and keep up with the news you'll start to notice that people go missing in the bush quite fre-

quently – and it's not always overseas visitors, either, it's often experienced trampers who know the areas they're tramping in.

Always make sure someone responsible knows where you're going, what route you intend to take, when you expect to come out, and that they must notify the police if you don't come out. Then don't forget to let them know when you've come out safely!

Fill out an intentions and/or help form at the DOC office, national park headquarters, visitors centre or whatever at the start of the trip, and write in the logbooks of huts along the way, giving the names of the members of your party and details about when you were there and where you are going when you leave. Do this even if you don't stay in the huts – it will make it far easier to find you if you should go missing.

Other safety rules include:

1. Choose a track that suits your level of fitness and experience.
2. Find out what to expect on the track. Always seek local advice about current track and weather conditions from the proper authority – the local DOC office, national park headquarters, etc – before you set out.
3. Go with at least one other person, and stay on the track.
4. Be sure to purify river or lake water before drinking it.
5. Take along a first aid kit and everything else you're supposed to – water purifier, warm clothes, etc.
6. If you meet heavy rain, and rivers in your path have risen, stay where you are until the rivers go down, retrace your tracks, or take another route. Don't ever cross a flooding river unless you are absolutely certain you can get across safely.

The NZ Mountain Safety Council has published a number of pamphlets with good information for tramping, with titles like *Bushcraft, Mountaincraft, Outdoor First Aid, Hypothermia, Survival*, etc. They are widely available at information centres, hostels, etc. DOC also has excellent safety advice and it's worth talking to them about it.

Going with tramping clubs can be a great way to tramp in New Zealand, as you'll be with like-minded people who know about the bush. Federated Mountain Clubs (PO Box 1604, Wellington) has information on local clubs all around NZ.

Department of Conservation (DOC) – Te Papa Atawhai
DOC looks after parks, tracks, walkways,

Sun Orchid

huts and general tramping facilities. It also administers hundreds of scenic, historic, scientific and nature reserves, and wildlife refuges and sanctuaries. They also have responsibility for the Subantarctic Islands and the two World Heritage areas – Tongariro National Park and Te Wahipounamu (South-west New Zealand, which incorporates Fiordland, Mt Aspiring, Mt Cook and Westland national parks).

The local DOC office is usually the best place for information on nature and outdoor attractions in any area. They produce excellent pamphlets on almost any natural attraction. In some places the visitor information centres also have the same sort of information and a collection of DOC pamphlets.

National Parks
New Zealand has many parks: 12 national, 20 forest, three maritime and two marine, plus a few other types of parks and reserves. There also two places that have been designated World Heritage Areas: Tongariro National Park in the North Island and Te Wahipouna-mu in the South Island, which incorporates four of the South Island's national parks: Westland, Fiordland, Mt Cook and Mt Aspiring.

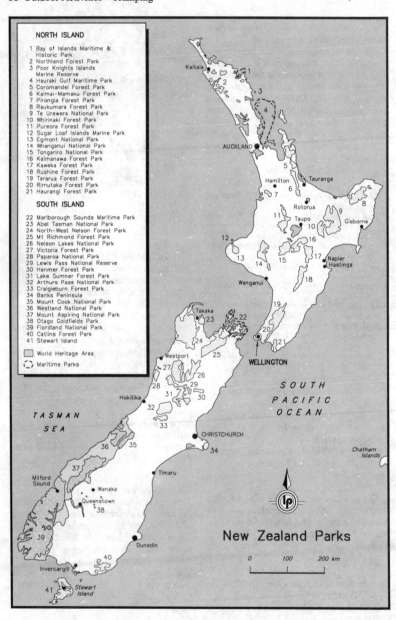

NORTH ISLAND

1 Bay of Islands Maritime &
  Historic Park
2 Northland Forest Park
3 Poor Knights Islands
  Marine Reserve
4 Hauraki Gulf Maritime Park
5 Coromandel Forest Park
6 Kaimai-Mamaku Forest Park
7 Pirongia Forest Park
8 Raukumara Forest Park
9 Te Urewera National Park
10 Whirinaki Forest Park
11 Pureora Forest Park
12 Sugar Loaf Islands Marine Park
13 Egmont National Park
14 Whanganui National Park
15 Tongariro National Park
16 Kaimanawa Forest Park
17 Kaweka Forest Park
18 Ruahine Forest Park
19 Tararua Forest Park
20 Rimutaka Forest Park
21 Haurangi Forest Park

SOUTH ISLAND

22 Marlborough Sounds Maritime Park
23 Abel Tasman National Park
24 North-West Nelson Forest Park
25 Mt Richmond Forest Park
26 Nelson Lakes National Park
27 Victoria Forest Park
28 Paparoa National Park
29 Lewis Pass National Reserve
30 Hanmer Forest Park
31 Lake Sumner Forest Park
32 Arthurs Pass National Park
33 Craigieburn Forest Park
34 Banks Peninsula
35 Mount Cook National Park
36 Westland National Park
37 Mount Aspiring National Park
38 Otago Goldfields Park
39 Fiordland National Park
40 Catlins Forest Park
41 Stewart Island

World Heritage Area
Maritime Parks

New Zealand Parks

0   100   200 km

Information DOC information centres for the various national parks and maritime parks are found at:

Abel Tasman National Park – Totaranui, Nelson, Motueka, Takaka
Arthurs Pass National Park – Arthurs Pass village
Bay of Islands Maritime & Historic Park – Russell
Egmont National Park – Dawson Falls and North Egmont on Mt Egmont/Taranaki
Fiordland National Park – Te Anau
Hauraki Gulf Maritime Park – Auckland
Marlborough Sounds Maritime Park – Blenheim
Mt Aspiring National Park – Wanaka
Mt Cook National Park – near the Hermitage Hotel
Nelson Lakes National Park – St Arnaud
Otago Goldfields Park – Dunedin
Paparoa National Park – Punakaiki
Stewart Island National Park – Oban
Te Urewera National Park – Lake Waikaremoana
Tongariro National Park – Whakapapa on Mt Ruapehu
Westland National Park – Franz Josef and Fox Glaciers
Whanganui National Park – Pipiriki

In addition to the national parks there are forest areas covering 11,850 sq km. Information is available at local DOC offices. The excellent pamphlet *Exploring New Zealand's Parks* outlines the national, maritime and forest parks.

What to Take
Equipment This list is for someone who will be sticking to the main tracks, staying in huts and tramping during the summer months. It is inadequate for snow country or winter.

Boots – light to medium are recommended. The boots should be broken in or you'll get painful blisters. Cover your heels with moleskin before you start if you think there is any chance of blisters. Feet are the greatest source of discomfort on a track and therefore should have the greatest care.
Alternative footwear – thongs (jandals)/sandals, running/ tennis shoes for strolling around the huts and if the boots become just too painful to wear.
Socks – three heavy polypropylene or woollen pairs; two to be worn at once to reduce the chance of blisters. Frequent changes of socks during the day also reduces the chance of blisters but isn't too practical.
Shorts, light shirt – for everyday wear, swimsuits for the immodest

Woollen sweater/jersey, woollen trousers – essential in case of cold weather. Some of the modern synthetics, such as polypropylene and polar fleece, are just as good as wool.
Waterproof raincoat and overtrousers. A combination of wet and cold can be fatal.
Knife, fork & spoon, cup, plate, soup bowl. (You can cut this back to knife, spoon and bowl – a bowl is multipurpose: you can eat or drink out of it, and mix things in it.)
Pot/billy (one) – 1½ to two litres capacity is sufficient
Pans (two) – 15 cm across and five cm deep is plenty. The pot and pans are adequate for two to three-course meals for two people. Preferably the pots should fit into each other and be made of aluminium for lightness.
Camping stove – Take one along, even if you'll be staying in huts. Many huts don't have cookers.
Matches/lighter – for cooking and lighting candles. Matches are a bit of a bind as it is difficult to keep them dry.
Candle – half to one candle per day, depending on how many are sharing the hut. Some huts have lanterns supplied.
Torch (flashlight) – for nocturnal toilet visits and late arrival at the hut
Toilet paper, Band-aids, insect repellent (insect repellent advice is in the Health section, Facts for the Visitor chapter).

New Zealand's Environmental Care Code

1. Protect plants and animals. Treat New Zealand's forests and birds with care and respect. They are unique and often rare.

2. Remove rubbish. Litter is unattractive, harmful to wildlife and can increase vermin and disease. Plan your visits to reduce rubbish, and carry out what you carry in.

3. Bury toilet waste. In areas without toilet facilities, bury your toilet waste in a shallow hole well away from waterways, tracks, campsites and huts.

4. Keep streams and lakes clean. When cleaning and washing, take the water and wash well away from the water source. Because soaps and detergents are harmful to water life, drain used water into the soil to allow it to be filtered. If you suspect the water may be contaminated, either boil it for at least three minutes, or filter it, or chemically treat it.

5. Take care with fires. Portable fuel stoves are less harmful to the environment and are more efficient than fires. If you do use a fire, keep it small, use only dead wood and make sure it is out by dousing it with water and checking the ashes before leaving.

6. Camp carefully. When camping, *leave no trace of your visit.*

7. Keep to the track. By keeping to the track, where one exists, you lessen the chance of damaging fragile plants.

8. Consider others. People visit the back country and rural areas for many reasons. Be considerate of other visitors who also have a right to enjoy the natural environment.

9. Respect our cultural heritage. Many places in New Zealand have a spiritual and historical significance. Treat these places with consideration and respect.

10. Enjoy your visit. Enjoy your outdoor experience. Take a last look before leaving an area; will the next visitor know that you have been there?

Protect the environment for your own sake, for the sake of those who come after you, and for the environment itself.
Toitu te whenua – Leave the land undisturbed.

Small first-aid kit – nothing fancy
Small towel – should dry quickly
Sleeping bag – warm down or Hollofill, light to medium weight, including a light stuff bag for rapid and easy packing
Pack of cards – brush up on Crib, 500 and Euchre
Pen/pencil and paper
Pot scrubber and tea towel – washing up is usually done in cold water making pot cleaning difficult
Map and compass
Water purifier (see Health Section)
Sun protectors – hat, cream, glasses
Useful books – for birdwatching, plant identification, etc
Camera, binoculars

Food It should be nourishing, tasty and lightweight:

Breakfast – the most important meal of the day:
   Muesli/porridge (quick cooking) – good with sultanas (raisins)
   Bacon & eggs – bacon in vacuum pack will last days
   Bread, butter/margarine, Vegemite or Marmite/ honey
   Tea/coffee, sugar, instant milk
Lunch – it's normally eaten between huts and therefore should not require too much preparation
   Bread/crackers, butter/margarine. (There are

some nice wholemeal crackers available, but 'Cabin Bread' is larger and stronger and so will stand up to being crammed in a pack better.)
Cheese – tasty, not bland

Dinner – must be hot and substantial
Instant soups – help to whet the biggest appetites
Fresh meat – good for the first two days
Dehydrated meals – Alliance is excellent, Vesta is OK
Dehydrated vegetables, instant mashed potatoes – check the preparation time; 20 minutes is the limit
Rice – goes with everything
Dessert – easy to cook, instant such as tapioca, custard or Instant Puddings

Snacks – important source of energy while tramping
Chocolate – 100 grams per person per day
Raisins, sultanas, dried fruit
Scroggin – combination of all the above; make it yourself
Glucose – in the form of barley sugar, glucose tablets or powder from chemists; it gives almost instant energy
Biscuits – great before bed with tea. Get a recipe for 'Tararuas', an indestructible, calorie-packed life saver
Cordial concentrate – powder; a great thirst quencher, adds flavour to purified water
Instant noodles

As all rubbish should be carried out, ensure that everything is in suitable containers. Extra lightweight metal and plastic containers are available from supermarkets and some chemists. Don't take glass bottles – transfer the ingredients, such as coffee or Vegemite, into light containers.

This list of equipment is by no means complete for a long trek, but it should get you through the first tramp without suffering from withdrawal symptoms. For a three-day tramp, one loaf of bread, 200 to 300 grams of butter/margarine and 200 grams of instant dried milk are sufficient amounts to take for one person. Since so many dishes require milk it is important not to underestimate your requirements.

Everything should be kept in plastic bags, preferably two, to protect them from the elements. Clothes must be kept dry under all circumstances. Plastic pack liners, 'survival bags', made by the NZ Mountain Safety Council, are sold in outdoors shops for about $4 and they are an excellent investment.

Made of thick plastic that will not tear, a survival bag is large enough that you can climb into it for survival if need be, or you could split it and make a shelter. If you can't find one, you could use large green plastic rubbish bags. Put the whole schemozzle into a lightweight, waterproof backpack. The total weight should not exceed 14 kg for a three-day tramp.

MILFORD TRACK
(Four days)

'The finest walk in the world' is a special track, unique in New Zealand. It is the country's best known track and one which most Kiwis dream of doing, even if it's the *only* track they ever walk. Many overseas visitors also make a special effort to do the track, sometimes planning years in advance, though sadly they often leave New Zealand without realising that many other great tracks exist.

For some walkers who have done other tracks, Milford generates a lot of bitterness because of the way it is run. It is interesting that a lot of trampers doing the Routeburn, only a few km away, move on to other tracks and refuse to do the Milford because they feel they will be ripped off. This is partly because of the enforced regulation of numbers at Milford.

However, the benefits of regulating the numbers of walkers on this, the best known track in New Zealand, outweigh the inconvenience it may cause to some individuals. Firstly, keeping the number of people going through to a reasonable level and making sure everyone is accommodated in the huts (ie no camping) means that the environment is far better protected. Secondly, whilst it means a bit more challenge in scheduling yourself to go on it, you are guaranteed that the track won't be overcrowded. Furthermore, as it is necessary to enter and leave the track by boat, tight control is essential to handle the large numbers. The high fees at Milford are required to maintain the track in pristine condition despite the crowds.

The highlights of Milford are the beautiful

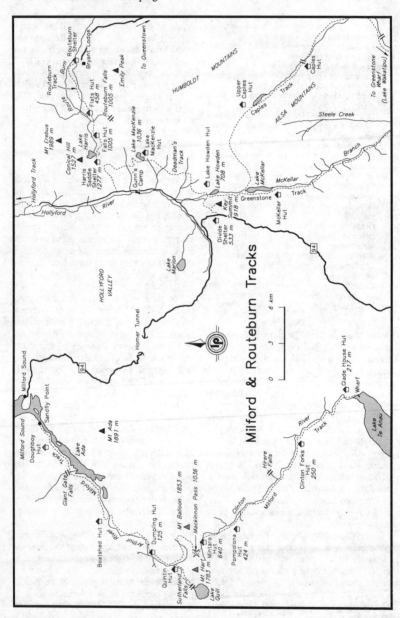

Milford & Routeburn Tracks

views from the Mackinnon Pass, the 630-metre Sutherland Falls, the rainforest, and the crystal clear streams, swarming with clever, fat trout and eels.

The track is open from early November to early April, although heavy rain can close it sooner. As a party of trampers usually leaves every day during the season, it's only possible to stay extra nights in huts if the following party does not fill the hut.

Milford is synonymous with rain: 5½ metres of it a year is only average. However, the number of rainy days is not exceptionally high, so when it does rain in this country of granite the effect is an experience not to be missed. Water cascades *everywhere* and small streams become raging torrents within minutes. A few years ago large sections of the track were washed away, as were several bridges which only hours previously had been standing several metres above the surface. The level of Lake Te Anau rose half a metre in less than eight hours. Imagine the state of any hapless trampers making their way to the next hut – and remember your raincoat! You should also pack your belongings in an extra plastic bag and send any excess luggage to Milford or leave it in Te Anau.

Costs

For independent walkers the cost of doing the walk is made up of a $70 permit fee (no concession for children), which covers three nights in the huts, plus the costs for the launch from the end of the track to Milford Sound ($19, children $11.50), the bus to Te Anau Downs ($10, children $5), the boat from there to the track ($37, children $10), and the bus back to Te Anau ($33, children $20). All this, including the permit fee, will probably come to around $170 per person (children $120). If you stay at the hostel in Milford add another $16 per night – plus food, of course, particularly at Milford.

In addition to independent trampers, organised parties are taken through by guides and they stay at a different chain of huts. These huts are usually an hour before the 'freedom walkers' huts so there is little mingling of the two. The guided walk – five days and four nights (three in huts on the track and one in Milford) – costs around $1355, somewhat less for children 10 to 15 years old (around $845). Children under 10 are not accepted.

Track Information

You can walk the track as an independent 'freedom walker' or as part of a guided tour. The track can only be done in one direction, from Lake Te Anau to Milford, and you need a permit from the Track Walking Office of the national park headquarters in Te Anau. This allows you to enter the track on a particular day and no other. As bookings can be heavy it pays to book as far ahead as possible – even several months or a year in advance is not a bad idea, especially for December and January.

Independent bookings are made through the DOC office in Te Anau (☎ 249 8514; fax 249 8515). Milford Track Guided Walk (☎ (0800) 659 255 or 249 7411) take bookings for the former option.

Walking the Track

The track follows the fairly flat Clinton River valley up to the Mintaro Hut, passing through rainforest. From Mintaro it passes over the Mackinnon Pass, down to the Quintin Hut and through the rainforest in the Arthur River valley to Milford Sound. You can leave your pack at the Quintin Hut while you make the return walk to Sutherland Falls. If the pass appears clear on arrival at Mintaro Hut make the effort to climb it, after a hot drink, as it may not be clear the next day. The view from Mackinnon Pass is the exceptional feature of the track.

Walking Times

Estimated walking times are as follows:

Boat landing at Glade House to Clinton Forks Hut	two hours
Clinton Forks to Mintaro Hut	4½ hour

Mintaro to Dumpling Hut	six hours
Side trip to Sutherland Falls	1½ hours return
Dumpling to Sandfly Point	5½ hours

Guided walkers stop at their own huts – Glade House, Pompolona and Quintin. They actually have a longer walk than independent walkers on the last day (from Quintin out to Sandfly Point).

Getting There & Away

Te Anau End InterCity has a bus from Te Anau to Te Anau Downs, to connect with the Fiordland Travel boat to Glade House at the head of Lake Te Anau, where the Milford Track begins. Other, smaller operators offer the boat trip cheaper. See the Te Anau section in the Southland chapter for details on getting to the track. There is a route, very difficult to follow and only for those with considerable experience, over the Dore Pass east of Glade House, cutting out the first boat trip.

Milford End The ferry to Milford departs from Sandfly Point at the end of the track at 2 pm. Buses from Milford take about 2½ hours to Te Anau, with a stop at The Divide, and there are connections from Te Anau to Queenstown. Hitching out is possible but requires patience. Or you can fly out from Milford to either Te Anau or Queenstown.

ROUTEBURN TRACK

(Three to four days)

The great variety of country and scenery makes the Routeburn Track one of the best rainforest/subalpine tracks in the country. Unfortunately, it has become the surrogate for those that miss out on the Milford and is thus extremely crowded in the busy season.

Up at the northern end of Lake Wakatipu, Glenorchy is a convenient base, with excellent facilities, to do the Routeburn, Rees-Dart or Greenstone-Caples tramps. The store at Glenorchy has a reasonable selection of tramping supplies – freeze-dried food, basic trampers' stodge, grains, cereals, dried fruit, a selection of fresh vegetables and fruit, eggs, frozen foods and gear like candles, pots, pans and toiletries, as well as ice cream, milk shakes and pies. There's also a pub, a good wholefood cafe, a ranger station, and a post office – there's no bank so take enough cash with you.

Track Information

There are guided four-day walks on the Routeburn which include transport between Queenstown and Routeburn Valley and between The Divide and Queenstown, accommodation, meals and guiding. See Queenstown in the Otago chapter for details on tours and DOC offices.

Walking the Track

The track can be started from either end. Many people travelling from the Queenstown end attempt to reach The Divide in time to catch the bus to Milford, connecting with the launch trip across Milford Sound. The highlight of the track is the view from Harris Saddle, or more especially from the top of nearby Conical Hill. You can see the waves breaking on the West Coast beach at Martins Bay. It is recommended that you stay an extra night at the Falls Hut, if the saddle is clouded over, in the hope of better weather the next day. The view is almost as good is the view from Key Summit, which offers a panorama not only of the Hollyford Valley but also of the Eglinton and Greenstone River valleys.

Trampers starting from Queenstown can return by the easy, flat Greenstone track (two days or one very long day) to Elfin Bay on Lake Wakatipu and then walk up the road 10 km to the bus at Kinloch (the same service that you use for the Routeburn), or charter a jet-boat back to Queenstown.

Walking Times

Estimated walking times are as follows:

Bryant Lodge/Routeburn Shelter to Flats Hut	2½ hours
Flats to Falls Hut	one hour
Falls to Harris Saddle	1½ hours

Harris Saddle to Lake Mackenzie Hut	3½ hours
Lake Mackenzie to Lake Howden Hut	three hours
Lake Howden to The Divide	one hour

Getting There & Away

Queenstown End It's possible, but difficult, to hitchhike. The Backpacker Express up to the start of the walk is probably the most popular way of getting to the trailhead. See Tramping Transport in the Queenstown section in the Otago chapter for details.

The Glenorchy Holiday Park offers special packages from Queenstown which include transport to Glenorchy, overnight accommodation and then transport to the trailhead in the morning; for more information see Glenorchy & the Rees-Dart in the Otago chapter. You can also organise to be collected from the trailheads if you do the walks in the opposite direction. The cost of transport to or from the trailheads may seem expensive but it's good value considering the state of the roads.

The Divide/Te Anau End It's possible to hitchhike from Te Anau (you have to leave in the morning) or Milford (leave early morning or mid-afternoon). Hitchhiking out is much easier, early morning to Milford, mid-afternoon to Te Anau; the object is to connect with people driving up to Milford from Te Anau for the day. There is trampers' transport between The Divide, Te Anau and Milford during the summer, with bus frequency scheduled according to the demand – inquire at the visitor centre. There are also InterCity, Mt Cook Landline and Fiordland Travel buses from Te Anau via The Divide to Milford and back every day. Check the latest schedule details so you know what time to expect the bus.

ROUTEBURN-GREENSTONE & CAPLES

An option on the Routeburn trek is to combine it with the Caples or Greenstone tracks and make a round trip. Access at the Caples and Greenstone end is at Greenstone Wharf. There is now a road from Kinloch to Greenstone Wharf which is OK, though fairly rough in spots as there are some fords to cross. The Caples and Greenstone tracks together form a loop track.

Walking the Track

Most huts have four bunks with gas stoves at higher altitudes, wood stoves elsewhere. Those at lakes Howden and Mackenzie are almost luxurious, with flush toilets, running water and even gas cookers. Huts on the Routeburn, Caples and Greenstone tracks cost $14 per night. There are some newer huts on the Caples-Greenstone route: the McKellar Hut at the southern end of Lake McKellar and the Upper Caples Hut, upriver from Kay Creek and not far down river from Fraser Creek, both of which can accommodate 20 people. The latter is particularly well designed and has a good wood stove with coal provided. At either end of the Routeburn Track, The Divide and Routeburn shelters are only day-use shelters, with no bunks or fireplaces. The Harris Saddle shelter is similar, for emergency use only.

The Routeburn Track is closed by snow in the winter and is extremely popular in January. A stretch of the track between Harris Saddle and Lake Mackenzie is very exposed and dangerous in bad weather. This section has even been closed by snow in the middle of summer, so check with the warden if the weather looks dicey.

Walking Times

Estimated walking times are as follows:

Greenstone Wharf to Caples Hut	three hours
Caples Hut to Upper Caples Hut	2½ hours
Upper Caples Hut to McKellar Saddle	3½ hours
McKellar Saddle to Lake Howden Huts	three hours

The McKellar Saddle to Lake Howden Hut walk will lead you on to the Routeburn as mentioned earlier. Other options from McKellar Saddle include turning off for The Divide before reaching Lake Howden Hut, or turning into the Greenstone Track.

GREENSTONE TRACK

This track is often used as a means of returning to Queenstown from the Routeburn, or as a loop with the Caples Track.

Track Information

Guided walks along the Greenstone Track are available – see Queenstown in the Otago chapter.

Walking the Track

It is a 13½-hour walk down the broad easy Greenstone Valley to Lake Wakatipu from Lake Howden. You can meet Lake Wakatipu at either Greenstone Wharf (where the Caples Track also begins) or at Elfin Bay. From Elfin Bay you can charter a jet-boat to Queenstown, and from Greenstone Wharf there are minibuses (Backpacker Express) to and from Glenorchy. There are several huts along the track but only a shelter at Elfin Bay. There are several tracks in the adjacent more attractive Caples Valley.

Walking Times

Estimated walking times are as follows:

Greenstone Wharf to Slip Flat bivouac	three hours
Slip Flat to Mid Greenstone Hut	3½ hours
Mid Greenstone to McKellar Hut	five hours
McKellar Hut to Howden Lake Hut	two hours

Coming from the Caples side, it's three hours from McKellar Saddle to the McKellar Hut.

KEPLER TRACK

(Four days)

This track was cut in 1986 and 1987 to give access to the Kepler Mountains at the southern end of Lake Te Anau. Like any Fiordland track the walk depends on the weather; when it's wet, it's very, very wet.

The track is top quality, well graded and gravelled, and the three large huts are well equipped, with heating and gas stoves. Hut fees are $14 per night (children $6) and hut wardens are on hand from early November to late April. Camping is permitted at Dock Bay and Brod Bay on Lake Te Anau and at Shallow Bay on Lake Manapouri.

The alpine sections of the track may be closed in winter due weather conditions; these sections also require a good level of fitness. Other sections are much easier. The first leg from the control gates to Brod Bay makes an excellent easy day trip.

Walking the Track

The walk can be done over four days and features a variety of vegetation and terrain including lakeside and riverside sections (good trout fishing!), then climbing up out of the beech forest to the treeline, where there are panoramic views. The alpine stretch between Iris Burn Hut and Mt Luxmore Hut goes along a high ridge line, well above the bush with fantastic views when it's clear. Other sections cross U-shaped glacier-carved valleys. It's recommended that the track be done in the Mt Luxmore-Iris Burn-Moturau direction.

Walking Times

Estimated walking times are as follows:

Park Visitor Centre (Te Anau) to control gates	45 minutes
Control gates to Brod Bay	1½ hours
Brod Bay to Mt Luxmore Hut	3½ to 4½ hours
Mt Luxmore to Iris Burn Hut	five to six hours
Iris Burn waterfall track	20 minutes one way
Iris Burn to Moturau Hut	five to six hours
Moturau to Rainbow Reach	1½ hours
Rainbow Reach to control gates	2½ to 3½ hours

Getting There & Away

The track is a loop, starting and finishing from the flood control gates at the southern end of the lake, within walking distance of Te Anau. Another possible starting/finishing point is about 10 km down the road towards Manapouri at the Rainbow Reach Swingbridge. See Te Anau in the Southland chapter for details of local transport services.

HOLLYFORD-MARTINS BAY-PYKE TRACK

This is a well-known track along the broad

Top Left: Seal, Moeraki, Canterbury (HL)
Top Right: Dolphin (DB)
Bottom Left: Kiwi (NZTP)
Bottom Right: Tuatara (NZTP)

Top: Hangi, Te Kaha, Coromandel Peninsula (HL)
Bottom: Te Mata o Hoturoa war canoe, Whanganui Regional Museum, Wanganui (NK)

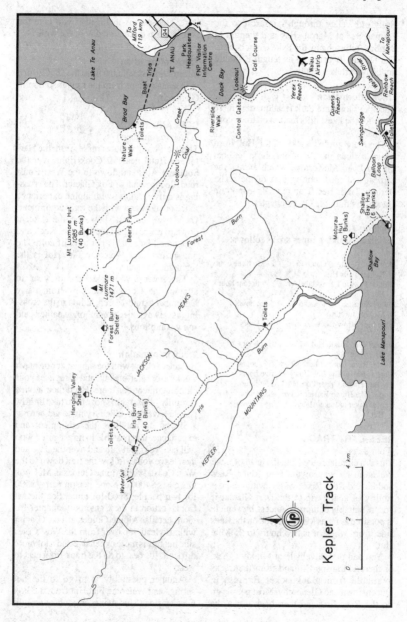

Kepler Track

Hollyford Valley through rainforest to the Tasman Sea at Martins Bay and then on to Big Bay, returning by the Pyke River back to The Divide. Because of its length it should not be undertaken lightly.

Track Information
Check at Fiordland Park Headquarters in Te Anau for the latest information on track conditions.

There are guided walks on the Hollyford which include the flight out and a jet-boat trip on Lake McKerrow, which avoids the hardest and most boring part of the walk, Demon Trail. See Tramping Transport in Queenstown, in the Otago chapter.

Walking Times
Estimated walking times are as follows:

Hollyford (Gunn's) Camp to Hidden Falls Hut	2½ to three hours
Hidden Falls to Lake Alabaster Hut	3½ to four hours
Lake Alabaster Hut to Lake McKerrow Hut	three hours
Lake McKerrow Hut to Demon Trail Hut	1½ hours
Demon Trail Hut to Hokuri River Hut	five hours
Hokuri River Hut to Martins Bay	five hours
Martins Bay to Big Bay Hut	five hours
Big Bay Hut to Upper Pike Hut	four hours
Upper Pike Hut to Barrier River	six hours
Barrier River to Lake Alabaster Hut	seven hours

REES-DART TRACK
(Four days)
This is a circular route from the head of Lake Wakatipu by way of the Dart River, Rees Saddle and Rees River valley, with the possibility of a side trip to the Dart Glacier if you're suitably equipped. Access by vehicle is possible as far as Muddy Creek on the Rees side, from where it is two hours to 25 Mile Hut.

You can park a vehicle at Muddy Creek, or there is transport to and from the tracks available from Backpacker Express in Queenstown and Glenorchy. Most people go up the Rees first and then back down the

Dart. Transport is included if you take the Fun Yak trip on the last day of the walk.

Track Information
Information is available from the DOC office in Queenstown or from the ranger station in Glenorchy.

COPLAND TRACK
(Three to four days)
This well-known route crosses from the Hermitage Hotel near Mt Cook right over the Southern Alps and down to the West Coast road, 26 km south of Fox Glacier. The crossing is only for those with alpine experience in ice or snow and with the right equipment. Once over the pass, however, the descent down to the road past the Douglas Rock and Welcome Flat Huts is not too difficult. The hot springs near Welcome Flat Hut is the highlight for many.

The most favourable time of year to attempt the Copland track is from early December to mid-March, although the crossing is always dependent on weather and snow conditions.

Track Information
Be sure to check with the ranger station at Mt Cook before starting out, and to register your climbing intentions there. Heed their advice carefully – this track is not one to take lightly, people have been killed trying to get across!

If you do not have the equipment and experience, it is possible to hire a guide who will take your party up and over the pass and then leave you to follow the trail down to the West Coast. From Alpine Guides in Mt Cook this costs $400 for a one-person party, $500 for two people, $600 for three. See the Mt Cook section in the Canterbury chapter for more details. Alpine Guides at Fox Glacier will also lead you over from the West Coast side but this is more expensive and a lot more difficult. It's best to do the track from east to west.

Another possibility is to go to the hot springs and Welcome Flat Hut from the Fox Glacier side. This makes a good overnight trip and it's an easy walk up the valley from the West Coast road.

Walking Times

Estimated walking times are as follows:

Hermitage to the Hooker Hut	half a day
Pass to Douglas Rock Hut	full day (10 hours)
Douglas Rock Hut to Welcome Flat Hut	2½ hours
Welcome Flat Hut to West Coast road	5½ hours

ABEL TASMAN NATIONAL PARK COASTAL TRACK

(Three to four days)

This track is one of the most beautiful in the country, passing through pleasant bush overlooking beaches of golden sand lapped by bright blue water. The numerous bays, small and large, make it like a travel brochure come to life.

Once little known outside the immediate area, this track has now been 'discovered' and in summer hundreds of backpackers may be on the track at any one time – far more than can be accommodated in the huts, so bringing a tent is a good idea. At other times of the year it's not so crowded.

Huts have bunks for a minimum of 16 and are equipped with wood stoves.

Track Information

The track operates on a 'Great Walks Pass' system – the cost is $6 per night on the track (children $3) whether you stay in the huts or camp. You can obtain the pass in Nelson from the DOC, in Motueka from the DOC or the Visitor Information Centre, and in Takaka at a number of places including the DOC, the Visitor Information Centre, the bus depots, the Shady Rest Hostel and the Pohara Beach Camp. All these DOC offices are sources of track information, and there's also a National Park Visitors Centre at Totaranui, open seasonally from late November to February.

Walking the Track

Several sections of the main track are tidal, with long deviations during high tides, particularly at Awaroa. As the tidal stretches are all just on the northern side of huts, it is important to do the track in a southerly direction if the low tides are in the afternoons, and from south to north if they are in the mornings. Check the newspaper, subtracting 20 minutes from the Nelson tidal times. Tide tables and advice are available at the DOC office in Motueka.

If you have the time, take additional food so that you can stay longer should you have the inclination. Bays around all the huts are beautiful but the sandflies are a problem, except at the tiny, picturesque beach of Te Puketea near the Anchorage Hut. There are some Maori rock carvings on the coast track between the Bark Bay and Awaroa Huts. They're in a cave at the extreme northern end of Onetahuti Beach, just north of the Tonga Quarry. You have to ford a small stream to reach the two caves and the spiral, abstract carvings are in the left cave, not the one half filled with water.

Kaiteriteri and Totaranui have large camping grounds; there is a smaller one at Pohara Beach, 10 km east of Takaka on the road to Totaranui. Excess luggage can be sent very cheaply by the Golden Bay Connection bus between Nelson, Motueka and Takaka. There are four-day guided walks on the track for around $525 (children $465). Or you could do the track by sea kayak. Again, see the Abel Tasman National Park in the Marlborough & Nelson chapter.

Walking Times

Estimated walking times are as follows, south to north:

Marahau to Anchorage Hut or Torrent Bay Hut	three to four hours
Torrent Bay to Bark Bay Hut	three hours
Bark Bay to Awaroa Hut	three hours
Awaroa to Totaranui	1½ hours

Getting There & Away

A variety of transport services provide access to the track and it's now easy to get in and out from Nelson, Motueka and Takaka.

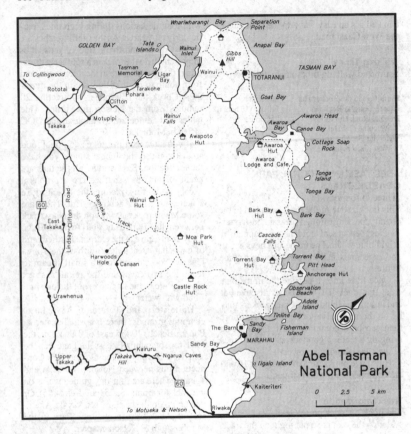

See the Abel Tasman National Park section in the Marlborough & Nelson chapter. One method of getting to the start of the track is by boat from Nelson, which eliminates the need to go by bus as you are dropped at the start of the track. Hitching is difficult going to or from either end of the track. There's a telephone at the Marahau parking area to phone for a taxi if you miss the scheduled bus. There is a great cafe at the Marahau end with all sorts of delicious goodies waiting for hungry trampers. Accommodation is at The Barn (see Abel Tasman National Park in the Marlborough & Nelson chapter).

HEAPHY TRACK
(Four to six days)

The Heaphy is one of the best known tracks in New Zealand. The track doesn't have the spectacular scenery of the Routeburn, but it still has its own beauty. Some people find it a disappointment if done immediately after the nearby Abel Tasman National Park coastal track.

The track lies almost entirely within the North-west Nelson Forest Park. Highlights include the view from the summit of Mt Perry (two-hour walk, return, from Perry Saddle Hut) and the coast, especially around the Heaphy Hut. It's worth spending a day or two resting at the Heaphy Hut, something which is appreciated by those travelling south from Collingwood. It is possible to cross the Heaphy River at its mouth at low tide, but with caution, scramble through a hole in the cliffs and come out to a wrecked Japanese squid boat.

Alternatively, take the very badly marked track (check with the DOC) over the hill to the coast, then walk south along the beach. Almost an hour up the coast is a seal colony.

It is possible to return to the Nelson/Golden Bay region by the more scenic, if harder, Wangapeka Track (about five days) starting just south of Karamea. The track now has km markers along its length; the zero marker is at the start of the track at the Kohaihai River near Karamea and the total length is 76 km.

Track Information

Send excess luggage by White Star bus between Westport and Nelson, Motueka or Takaka.

More detailed information and maps are available from the DOC offices at Nelson, Motueka, Takaka and Karamea.

Walking the Track

Huts are geared to handle 16 people. They all have gas stoves, except Heaphy and Gouland Downs which have wood stoves, and hut fees are $8 a night (children $4). Most people travel west from Collingwood to Karamea. From Brown Hut the track passes through beech forest to Perry Saddle (but don't take the shortcut going uphill, unless you are fit). The country then opens up to the swampy Gouland Downs, then closes in with sparse bush all the way to Mackay. The bush becomes more dense towards the Heaphy Hut with the beautiful nikau palm growing at lower levels.

The final section is along the coast through heavy bush and partly along the beach. Unfortunately, the sandflies are unbearable along this, the most beautiful part of the track. The climate here is surprisingly mild but do not swim in the sea as the under-

Heaphy Track

tows and currents are vicious. The lagoon at Heaphy Hut is good for swimming though, and fishing is possible in the Heaphy River.

Km Markers Brown 76, Perry Saddle Hut 61, Gouland Downs 49, Blue Duck Shelter turn-off 47, Mackay 36.5, Lewis 24, Heaphy 17, Kohaihai River 0.

Walking Times

Estimated walking times are as follows:

Brown Hut to Perry Saddle Hut	five hours
Perry Saddle to Gouland Downs Hut	two hours

Gouland Downs to Saxon Hut	1½ hours
Saxon to Mackay Hut	three hours
Mackay to Lewis Hut	three to four hours
Lewis to Heaphy Hut	two to three hours
Heaphy to Kohaihai River (track start)	five hours

Getting There & Away

Collingwood End Hitchhiking in either direction is very difficult. There's a bus service from Nelson to Collingwood with stops at Motueka and Takaka. From Collingwood you can charter the minibus to take you to the trailhead. See the Collingwood section in the Marlborough & Nelson chapter for details. There's a phone at the trailhead so you can call for the bus. There's also an airstrip nearby and it's possible to fly back from there to Karamea.

Karamea End Hitching is very difficult. You can take a taxi between Karamea and the start of the track – it can be called from the end of the track. A bus is also available (from The Last Resort) and it's possible to charter a plane back to the Collingwood end of the track. There is a bus service to Westport from Karamea; see the Westport section for details. There is a rather primitive camping ground at the Karamea end of the track and Karamea has the very popular Last Resort hostel during the busy season.

WANGAPEKA TRACK

Although not as well known as the Heaphy Track in the same park, it is a more enjoyable walk. The track starts some 25 km south of Karamea on the West Coast and runs 56 km east to the Rolling River. It takes about five days and there is a good chain of Huts ($4 to $8 per night, children $2 to $4) along the track.

Getting There & Away

Access is the same as for Heaphy Track.

STEWART ISLAND TRACKS

The northern portion of the island has a circular track (North West Circuit Tracks) but it is long, some 10 to 12 days. However, the section from Oban to Christmas Village Bay contains some very attractive, sheltered bays and bush, ideal for relaxing. The drawback is having to return along the same track.

Huts on Stewart Island walks range from the small six-bed Long Harry Hut to the relatively new and well-located Port William Hut with 24 bunks. The Port William Hut is frequently used by school parties who are expected to take tents and use them if others require the bunks. Huts cost $6 per night and have wood stoves.

Track Information

The DOC office in Oban sells three pamphlets: *Rakiura Track*, *North West Circuit Tracks*, and *Halfmoon Bay Walks*.

Walking the Tracks

From Christmas Village Bay Hut it's a 3½-hour climb to the summit of Mt Anglem (980 metres) and an outstanding view of part of the South Island and most of Stewart Island. An excursion can be made to Yankee River (four hours one way) but the track is very boggy. An old boiler at Maori Bay is a reminder of the timber milling days.

Due west of Oban is the attractive and wild Masons Bay with its extensive sand dunes. The walk between Oban and Freshwater Hut is not particularly pleasant though and tends to be boggy. It's possible to hire a small boat to North Arm Hut, cutting out the first day. From Freshwater to Masons Bay you're walking on a tractor track, firmer under foot, but it may be under water.

The Rakiura Track, between Port William Hut and North Arm, makes an interesting three-day circular tramp near Oban. Huts at Port William and North Arm have space for 30 trampers, and access to the track costs $6 per night. This is one of the Great Walks for which you require a pass.

Walking Times

Estimated walking times to Freshwater Hut and Masons Bay are as follows:

Oban to North Arm Hut	five hours
North Arm to Freshwater Hut	five to six hours

Freshwater River to Big Sandhill Hut (Masons Bay)	three to four hours

Estimated walking times for the Rakiura Track are as follows. Note that mud can lengthen these times.

Ferry terminal (Oban) to Port William Hut	four hours
Port William to North Arm Hut	six hours
North Arm Hut to Ferry terminal (Oban)	five hours

Getting There & Away

See the Stewart Island section for details. There are no roads on the island outside the immediate vicinity of Oban.

TONGARIRO NORTHERN CIRCUIT

(Three to four days)

The Tongariro National Park in the central North Island has a long, circular Round-the-Mountains Track embracing Mt Ruapehu, Mt Ngauruhoe and Mt Tongariro, requiring about five to six days to complete.

A shorter three to four-day track around the northern circuit of the park is a Great Walk. Along this route there are several possibilities for shorter walks taking from a few hours to overnight, including the famous Tongariro Crossing (read on).

Highlights of the Northern Circuit include tramping through several volcanic craters including the South Crater, Central Crater and Red Crater; brilliantly colourful volcanic lakes including the Emerald Lakes, Blue Lake and the Upper and Lower Tama Lakes; the steaming Ketetahi Hot Springs and the cold Soda Springs and Ohinepango Springs; various other volcanic formations including cones, lava flows and glacial valleys; and spectacular views extending right over Lake Taupo and as far as Mt Taranaki on a fine day.

Side trips include return walks to the summits of Mt Ngauruhoe and Mt Tongariro, to the Historic Waihohonu Hut and to Ohinepango Springs.

Track Information

Track information is available from all the Tongariro National Park visitor centres: the Whakapapa Visitor Centre (☎ (07) 892 3729) in Whakapapa Village, the Ohakune Ranger Station (☎ (06) 385 8578) in Ohakune and the Tongariro/Taupo Conservancy (☎ (07) 386 8607) in Turangi.

Check with one of these information centres for current track and weather conditions before setting out. Camping is $6.

Walking the Track

The track is served by four huts: the Mangatepopo, Ketetahi, Oturere and Waihohonu Huts. The Old Waihohonu Hut, built in 1901, has been replaced by a modern hut but the original, once a stage coach stopover, is preserved as a historic place. There are no huts in Whakapapa Village but there is a holiday park with camping and cabins, plus more expensive accommodation. Camping is permitted beside all the huts.

During the full summer season, that is from late October to 31 May, a Great Walks pass is required and must be bought in advance, whether you stay in the huts or camp beside them; the cost is $12 per night in huts or $6 for camping (children half price). Ordinary back country hut tickets and annual passes cannot be used during these months. The Tongariro National Park Visitor Centres sell Great Walks passes or can advise you of a number of other places in the area where you can purchase them.

The rest of the year, from 1 June to late October, ordinary back country hut passes or annual passes may be used; the cost is $8 per night (two tickets) for huts, $4 (one ticket) for camping. However, this track is quite different in winter, when it is covered in snow and becomes a challenging alpine trek.

Track Safety

Check with one of the DOC offices for current track and weather conditions before you set out. The weather on the mountains is extremely changeable – warm brilliant sunshine, snow, hail, wind, etc can all alternate within a few minutes of one another, at any time of year. It's a lot colder and windier on the mountains than you might expect from looking at them from down below. There's

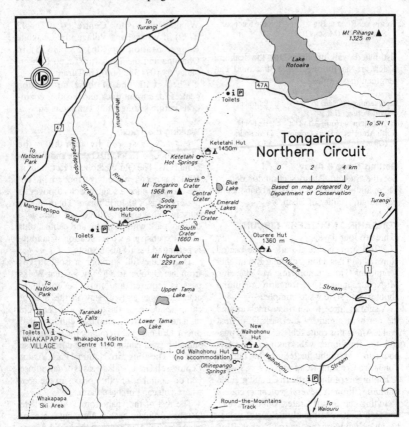

Tongariro
Northern Circuit

0   2   4 km

Based on map prepared by
Department of Conservation

no use doing the walk in rain or in clouds; in cloudy weather, visibility can be as low as a few metres around you and you can't see a thing – not even the next pole marking the track ahead of you, much less the sights.

Most difficulties on the mountains are caused by failure to bring adequate gear for the weather; check the What to Take list earlier in this chapter for what you should have in the mountains. You should boil or treat all your drinking water, even at huts, due to the presence of giardia and other parasites.

A lot of accidents occur on this track when people misjudge loose rocks – watch your step! – or, oddly enough, when people go sliding down the volcanic slopes, whether scoria or covered with snow, without checking what they'll be sliding onto or thinking how they will stop, resulting in smashing onto rocks below or falling through holes in the snow during springtime. Sounds silly, but they say that's what most of the accidents result from here. So watch out!

When climbing on Mt Ngauruhoe, watch out for the loose scoria. If people are coming up when you descend, be very careful not to dislodge rocks onto them. One little piece of scoria dislodged can collect material until it becomes a huge slide further down. Keep control as you descend – the scoria can rip you to shreds.

Around the Ketetahi Hot Springs, be careful of unstable ground caused by the thermal activity there.

In winter, ice axes, crampons, snow gaiters and snow goggles are essential, and avalanche gear including an avalanche transceiver, avalanche probe and snow shovel are advisable – plus the alpine or mountaineering experience and knowledge of how to use all these things. Unless you have alpine mountaineering experience, it's best to come with a guide in winter. Plateau Outdoor Adventure Guides (☎ & fax (07) 892 2740) make winter mountaineering and ski touring trips on the mountains.

Walking Times

Whakapapa Village to Mangatepopo Hut	two to three hours
Mangatepopo Hut to Emerald Lakes	three to four hours
Emerald Lakes to Ketetahi Hut & Hot Springs	two to three hours
Emerald Lakes to Oturere Hut	one to two hours
Oturere Hut to Waihohonu Hut	two to three hours
Waihohonu Hut to Whakapapa Village	five to six hours

Side trips from the main track include:

Mt Ngauruhoe Summit (from the Mangatepopo Saddle)	two hours return
Mt Tongariro Summit (from Red Crater)	two hours return
Historic Waihohonu Hut (from the new Waihohonu Hut)	30 mins return
Ohinepango Springs (from the new Waihohonu Hut)	one hour return

Getting There & Away

There are several points of access to this circular track. You can get onto it from Whakapapa Village; from the end of Mangatepopo Road coming into the park from SH 47; from the end of Ketetahi Rd coming in from SH 47A; or from a car park on SH 1 (the Desert Rd). Beware of leaving valuables in a parked car at any of these access points, especially at Ketetahi and Mangatepopo, as car breakins have been reported. If you have a vehicle, it may be preferable to leave it at one of the nearby towns such as National Park or Turangi from where you can take public transport to begin the track.

Various operators provide transport to Whakapapa Village and the Mangatepopo and Ketetahi Road ends; see the Tongariro National Park section in the Central North Island chapter for details.

TONGARIRO CROSSING
(Eight to 10 hours)
Often called 'the finest one-day walk in New Zealand', the Tongariro Crossing covers many of the most spectacular features of the Tongariro Northern Circuit, including the South Crater, Red Crater, Central Crater and North Crater; the Emerald Lakes and Blue Lake; the Ketetahi Hot Springs and the cold Soda Springs; and the glacial Mangatepopo Valley. On a clear day the views are magnificent.

The track passes through a variety of vegetation zones ranging from alpine scrub and tussock, to places where there is no vegetation at all on the higher altitudes, down into lush podocarp forest as you descend from Ketetahi Springs to the end of the track.

There are a couple of steep spots on the track that are a bit of a rugged climb, and a few places where you must watch your footing on loose volcanic scoria, but most of the track is not terribly difficult. It's a long, exhausting day's walk though – you'll feel you have accomplished something after you've done it.

Worthwhile side trips from the main track include ascents to the summits of Mt Ngauruhoe and Mt Tongariro. Mt Ngauruhoe can be ascended most easily from the Mangatepopo Saddle, reached near the beginning of the track after the first steep climb. The summit of Mt Tongariro is reached by a poled route taking off from Red Crater.

Ketetahi Track
If you don't want to do the entire Tongariro Crossing or if the weather is not suitable for it, the Ketetahi Hot Springs and Ketetahi Hut

can be reached by a shorter route, beginning at the Ketetahi car park at the end of the Ketetahi Road. It's about a 2½ to three hours' uphill climb to reach the hot springs from the car park, the first hour walking through lush forest and the second hour through alpine tussock; you can see the springs steaming away on the hillside above you. Going back down takes a couple of hours.

Track Information & Safety
See the Tongariro Northern Circuit track for details.

Walking the Track
The track can be done in one day. It's a long day's journey, though, and you might want to break it up. Near the start of the track is the Mangatepopo Hut; or there's the Ketetahi Hut near the Ketetahi Hot Springs, a couple of hours before the end of the track. To stay at or camp beside either hut, you must have a Great Walks pass, purchased in advance, from the end of October until 31 May; the rest of the year, back country hut tickets and annual passes are accepted.

The Ketetahi Hut, beside the steaming Ketetahi Hot Springs, is the most popular hut in the park. It has bunks to sleep 24 people, but it regularly has 50 to 60 people trying to stay there on Saturday nights and at the busiest times of year (summer and school holidays). Bunks are claimed on a first come, first served basis, so you have the best chance of getting a bunk if you arrive early. It's obviously not a bad idea to bring camping gear with you, just in case. Campers can use all the hut facilities except for the bunks, which can put a bit of a crowd on the kitchen at busy times.

Walking Times
Estimated walking times are as follows:

Mangatepopo Road end to Mangatepopo Hut	30 minutes
Mangatepopo Hut to Mangatepopo Saddle	1½ hours
(Side trip) Mangatepopo Saddle to summit of Mt Ngauruhoe	two hours return
(Side trip) Red Crater to Mt Tongariro Summit	two hours return
Mangatepopo Saddle to Emerald Lakes	1½ to two hours
Emerald Lakes to Ketetahi Hut	two to three hours
Ketetahi Hut to Ketetahi Hot Springs	15 minutes
Ketetahi Hot Springs to Ketetahi Rd end	two hours

Getting There & Away
The track begins at the Mangatepopo Road end and finishes at the Ketetahi Road end. Since it's a one-way track, it's most convenient to take public transport, which will drop you at one end of the track and pick you up at the other end. See the Tongariro National Park section in the Central North Island chapter for details on transport in and out.

Theft from parked vehicles has become a problem at both ends of the track. If you do park a vehicle here, don't leave any valuables in it.

WAIKAREMOANA: LAKE CIRCUIT
(Lake Track, three to four days)
A very attractive walk through beech forest with vast panoramas and beautiful views of the lake. The track is entirely within Te Urewera National Park, which many travellers rate as one of the most attractive parks in New Zealand.

Track Information
There is a motor camp with cabins at Waikaremoana; inquire at the visitor information centre about other campsites. To stay in the huts on the track you need to purchase a pass from the visitor information centre before undertaking the walk. This is $6 per night for adults and $3 for children as the walk is now one of the Great Walks.

Walking the Track
The track can be done from either end. Starting from Onepoto all the climbing is done in the first few hours.

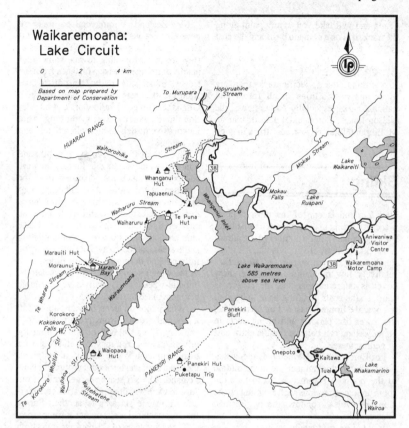

Walking Times

Estimated walking times are as follows:

Onepoto to Panekiri Hut	five hours
Panekiri to Waiopaoa Hut	four hours
Waiopaoa to Marauiti Hut	4½ hours
Marauiti to Te Puna Hut	2¾ hours
Te Puna to Whanganui Hut	two hours
Whanganui to Hopuruahine Stream Landing	two hours

Getting There & Away

There is an InterCity bus between Wairoa and Rotorua on Monday, Wednesday and Friday; it will stop at either end of the track for you. The Waikaremoana Shuttle service (☎ (06) 837 3855) operates from Tuai, stopping at Twin Lakes store, Onepoto, the motor camp, visitor information centre, Mokau landing, and Hopuruahine camp and bridge – twice daily except Wednesday and Thursday; on Thursday it is in the morning only as it does a return run to Wairoa. The cost is Tuai to Wairoa $10, Wairoa to Hopuruahine Bridge $20; Tuai to the bridge $10 and Tuai to the visitor information centre $9. During the summer months, a launch ferry service operates from the Waikaremoana Motor

Camp and will take you to any point along the track. It is on a demand basis and the cost is $15.

OTHER TRACKS

In addition to these specific tracks there are numerous possibilities in all forest and national parks, especially Arthurs Pass, the Nelson Lakes, Coromandel and, of course, Mt Egmont/Taranaki – an easy track in good weather.

Skiing

New Zealand is one of the most popular places for skiing in the southern hemisphere. For Australians it has a number of big attractions, not the least of which is that it's more reliable and cheaper than in Oz. Australia's relatively low mountains mean the snow cover is unpredictable and the season is short, so the costs of skiing have to be high to cover the limited season. For Australians, the lower lift, parking and hiring costs in New Zealand can balance out the extra cost of getting there.

For Europeans and Americans the attraction is skiing 'down under', ie in the middle of the northern summer – not to mention some unique attractions such as skiing on the slopes of a volcano or down the long Tasman Glacier runs.

In addition to downhill skiing, there are ample opportunities for Nordic, telemark and cross-country skiing, ski touring, and snowboarding. One ski area, the Waiorau Nordic Ski Area in the Pisa Range near Wanaka, specialises in Nordic skiing, but many downhill ski areas have areas with cross-country possibilities.

Heli-skiing is another attraction of New Zealand skiing. New Zealand seems to have more helicopters than it knows what to do with and in winter many are used to lift skiers up to the top of long, isolated stretches of virgin snow, or even to the tops of glaciers. The cost of these flights is surprisingly reasonable.

New Zealand's commercial ski areas are generally not very well endowed with on-field chalets, lodges or hotels. The places to stay are in surrounding towns, sometimes nearby and sometimes at a distance from the slopes. Either way, daily transport to and from the ski areas can be easily arranged. Often there's a good variety of accommodation in the nearby towns, ranging from inexpensive hostels to high-class hotels and ski lodges.

Club ski areas are open to the public and you are welcome to ski there; they are cheaper and much less crowded than the commercial ski areas. And although non-members pay a slightly higher non-members' rate, they can still work out to be cheaper than the commercial areas. These club areas usually do have accommodation at the areas, subject to availability; it may be fully booked during the busiest times, such as the winter school holidays or weekends, but mid-week you'll usually have no trouble getting a place to stay.

At the major ski areas, lifts cost about $40 a day and group lessons are around $25 a half-day, $35 a full day, or $50 an hour for private lessons. You may as well bring your own equipment if you have it, although all the usual stuff can be bought or hired in New Zealand. The ski season is generally from June to October, although it varies considerably from one ski area to another. Snow-making machines assist nature at some areas.

There are plenty of ski-package tours both from Australia and within New Zealand. Information centres in New Zealand, and the NZTB internationally, have brochures on the various ski areas and packages available, and can make bookings.

The *Skier's Atlas of New Zealand and Australia* by Sasha St Clair (1992, paperback, WSH Publishing, 1 Mulbury Lane, Wanaka, (☎ & fax (03) 443 8279) is an excellent reference book, filled with information on all the commercial and club ski areas in both New Zealand and Australia, with colour illustrations of the ski areas and ski runs, and information on heli-skiing, glacier skiing and so on.

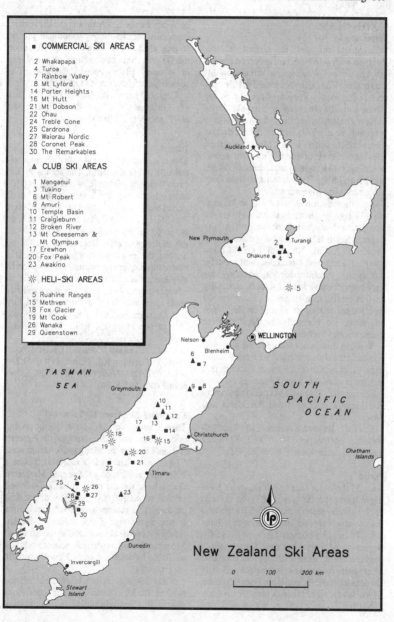

■ COMMERCIAL SKI AREAS

2 Whakapapa
4 Turoa
7 Rainbow Valley
8 Mt Lyford
14 Porter Heights
16 Mt Hutt
21 Mt Dobson
22 Ohau
24 Treble Cone
25 Cardrona
27 Waiorau Nordic
28 Coronet Peak
30 The Remarkables

▲ CLUB SKI AREAS

1 Manganui
3 Tukino
6 Mt Robert
9 Amuri
10 Temple Basin
11 Craigieburn
12 Broken River
13 Mt Cheeseman &
    Mt Olympus
17 Erewhon
20 Fox Peak
23 Awakino

☼ HELI-SKI AREAS

5 Ruahine Ranges
15 Methven
18 Fox Glacier
19 Mt Cook
26 Wanaka
29 Queenstown

Auckland

New Plymouth

Turangi

Ohakune

TASMAN SEA

Nelson

Blenheim

Greymouth

SOUTH PACIFIC OCEAN

Christchurch

Chatham Islands

Timaru

Dunedin

Invercargill

Stewart Island

WELLINGTON

New Zealand Ski Areas

0   100   200 km

NORTH ISLAND
Whakapapa

Whakapapa ski area, the largest in New Zealand with a 161-hectare groomed area, is six km above Whakapapa Village on Mt Ruapehu in Tongariro National Park. It's the end of the road – known as the Top of the Bruce – and has the most popular ski slopes in New Zealand, including a downhill course dropping nearly 800 metres over four km. There are chairlifts, T-bars, platters and rope lifts, and plenty of possibilities for snowboarding, cross-country and telemark skiing, and paragliding. The normal season is from 1 June to mid-November.

Accommodation is available at Whakapapa Village within the national park (see the Tongariro National Park section in the Central North Island chapter), or in nearby towns including National Park (12 km away), Turangi and Ohakune (each about 50 km away). Accommodation bookings are very heavy during the ski season, especially on weekends, so plan ahead. There are ski club lodges at Iwikau Village on the slopes but these are generally available only to members and friends.

You can drive yourself up to the slopes or you can take a shuttle minibus from Whakapapa Village, National Park or Turangi; taxi service is available from Ohakune.

During the ski season ski package tours to Whakapapa operate from Auckland and Wellington.

Contact: Ruapehu Alpine Lifts Ltd, Private Bag, Mt Ruapehu (☎ (07) 892 3738; fax 892 3732, snowphone (0900) 99 333).

Turoa

Around the other side of Mt Ruapehu from the Whakapapa ski area, the Turoa ski area on the south-western side of Mt Ruapehu is the country's second largest ski area. Chairlifts, T-bars and platters take you up to the beginning of a four-km run. There's also a beginner's lift, snowboarding and telemark. There is no road toll or parking fee and daily ski area transport is available from Ohakune, 17 km away, where there's plenty of accommodation – once again, accommodation

bookings can be heavy during the ski season, especially for the more economical places, so plan ahead. There are three cafeterias on the ski area. Skis can be hired on the slopes or at many places around Ohakune. The season lasts from June to late October.

Contact: Turoa Ski Resort Ltd, PO Box 46, Ohakune (☎ (06) 385 8456; fax 385 8992, snowphone (0900) 99 444).

Tukino

This is a club-operated ski area, on the eastern side of Mt Ruapehu. The area is 28 km from Waiouru, 50 km from Turangi, and it's quite remote – you have to traverse 14 km of gravel road once you leave the sealed Desert Rd (SH 1), and you need a 4WD vehicle to get in (or make a prior arrangement to use the club transport). Because access is so limited, the area is uncrowded, however it is most suitable for the beginner or intermediate skier, since there are only a couple of advanced runs. Accommodation is available at ski clubs here. It has a short season, 1 July to 1 October, because it is on the opposite side of the mountain from the prevailing winds.

Contact: Tukino Mountain Clubs Association, 11 Grendon Rd, Titirangi (☎ (04) 234 6961, (07) 854 9769, (09) 424 0609, snowphone (06) 585 6294).

Manganui Ski Area, Mt Taranaki

There's more volcano-slope skiing on the eastern slopes of Mt Taranaki in the Egmont National Park at the Manganui club ski area, 17 km from Stratford. You get to it after a 20-minute walk along the scenic Manganui Gorge from the car park. It has a T-bar and several rope lifts, and there is a day-visitor canteen. The season here is from mid-June to mid-September. There is limited accommodation on the ski area and at the Stratford Mountain House, with more accommodation available in Stratford or in New Plymouth, 60 km away.

Early summer skiing is possible off the summit of Mt Taranaki; when conditions permit, it is an invigorating two-hour climb to the crater but an exhilarating 1300-metre descent back to the area.

Contact: Stratford Mountain Club, c/o 32 Mountain Rd, RD2 Stratford (☎ (06) 765 7658).

SOUTH ISLAND
Coronet Peak

New Zealand's southernmost slopes, near Queenstown, are rated the best in New Zealand and are comparable to any in the world. There's even talk of running a future winter Olympics here. The season, mid-June to October, is reliable because of a multi-million dollar snow-making system. Access to the ski area is from Queenstown, 18 km away, and there's a shuttle bus service in the ski season. You can hitch if you leave early in the morning and depart before 4 pm to come down again. The well-heeled often catch a helicopter.

Chairlifts, T-bars and beginners' lifts take you up the slopes. The treeless slopes and good snow provide excellent skiing – the chairlifts run to altitudes of 1585 and 1620 metres. On selected evenings there is night skiing.

The ski area is operated by the Mt Cook Group and they have a licensed restaurant, overnight ski storage, a ski repair shop and ski lessons. The lift tickets are also valid at The Remarkables. For accommodation see the Queenstown section in the Otago chapter; there are active après-ski possibilities.

Contact: Mt Cook Group, PO Box 359, Queenstown (☎ (03) 442 7653/7870; fax 442 7674, snowphone (0900) 39 700, snow report (0900) 39 600).

The Remarkables

Like Coronet Peak, the Remarkables ski area is near Queenstown (23 km away), with shuttle buses running from Queenstown during the season (late June to late October). It, too, has beginner, intermediate and advanced level runs, with chairlifts and beginners' lifts. Passes for Coronet Peak and the Remarkables, including weekend and multi-day passes, can be used interchangeably at either ski area.

Both Coronet Peak and The Remarkables have designated ski school areas, with group, private, and children's lessons. The Remarkables also offers a Nordic ski school, telemark and cross-country lessons. Snowboard equipment and instruction are also available.

Contact: Mt Cook Group Ltd, PO Box 359, Queenstown (☎ (03) 442 7653/7520; fax 442 7674, snowphone (0900) 39 700, snow report (0900) 39 600).

Treble Cone

The season at Treble Cone, 29 km from Wanaka in the Southern Lake District, is from mid-June to mid-October. Reliability has been improved with the extension of snow-making to the top of the Deliverance chair. The highest of the areas in the Southern Lake area, Treble Cone is spectacularly situated overlooking Lake Wanaka. It has a chairlift, two T-bars and three beginners' lifts, and a natural half-pipe for snowboarding. Accommodation is available in Wanaka and shuttle buses run from there or from Queenstown, 1½ hours away (see also Parapenting/Paragliding in this chapter).

Contact: Treble Cone Ski Area, PO Box 206, Wanaka (☎ (03) 443 7443; fax 443 8401, snowphone (0900) 39 000).

Cardrona

Cardrona is 33 km from Wanaka and is open from mid-June to mid-October. It's a relatively new ski area with three chairlifts and a couple of beginners' lifts. It has numerous runs to choose from over variable terrain suitable for beginning, intermediate and advanced level skiers. Buses run from Wanaka during the ski season, or from Queenstown, about 1½ hours away. There is a licensed cafeteria in the main facilities complex.

Cardrona has acquired a reputation for its services offered to disabled skiers. The ski area is close to the Waiorau Nordic Area.

Contact: Cardrona Ski Resort, PO Box 117, Wanaka (☎ (03) 443 7411, 443 7341; fax 443 8818, snowphone (0900) 39 000).

Waiorau Nordic Area

New Zealand's only commercial Nordic ski area is 26 km from Wanaka, on the Pisa Range high above Lake Wanaka. There are 25 km of groomed trails and thousands of hectares of open rolling country for the ski tourer. Huts with facilities are dotted along the top of the Pisa Range. So whichever Nordic or cross-country discipline you are into – skating, day or overnight touring, telemarking, cross-country downhill – it is catered for here. The season is from late June to late September.

Alpine Recreation Canterbury (☎ (03) 680-6736; fax 680-6765) operates guided ski tours in the Lake Tekapo high country and Mt Cook National Park.

Contact: Waiorau Nordic Ski Area, Private Bag, Wanaka (☎ (03) 443 7542; fax 443 7541, snowphone 443 7544).

Awakino

This is a club ski area on Mt St Mary in the Waitaki, about 12 km from Kurow, 45 km from Oamaru and 66 km from Omarama. Awakino is known to get the odd powder blast during southerly storms but essentially it is for intermediate skiers. The season is from July to October. Although it has just two rope lifts, most of the runs are for intermediate and advanced skiers. There is also good cross-country skiing nearby. There's accommodation 500 metres below the main rope lift or at Kurow or Omarama. Access to the area is by 4WD.

Contact: Waitaki Ski Club, PO Box 191, Oamaru (☎ (03) 436 0771).

South Canterbury Region

There are three ski areas in South Canterbury – Ohau, Mt Dobson and Fox Peak. The Mt Dobson and Fox Peak ski areas are between Fairlie and Tekapo, on the main Christchurch to Mt Cook road. Both towns are good bases for skiing in this region.

Ohau, a commercial ski area 45 km from Twizel and the most distant from Christchurch, has the longest T-bar in the southern hemisphere. It is situated on Mt Sutton and has a large percentage of intermediate and advanced runs, plus excellent terrain for snowboarding, telemark, and cross-country skiing to Lake Dumb Bell. Accommodation is available at the Lake Ohau Lodge, 15 minutes from the slopes, or in Twizel, 50 minutes away. Ski season is from July to October.

Contact: Ohau Ski Area Ltd, PO Box 51, Twizel (☎ & fax (03) 438 9885).

Mt Dobson, a commercial ski area 26 km from Fairlie and 47 km from Lake Tekapo, has New Zealand's largest learners' area, with possibilities also for intermediate and advanced skiers, in a three-km wide basin. From the summit of Mt Dobson, on a clear day you can see Mt Cook, the Pacific Ocean and the Southern Alps. Accommodation is in Fairlie and Lake Tekapo. The season is from late June to mid-October.

Contact: Mt Dobson Ski Area Ltd, Alloway Rd, Fairlie (☎ & fax (03) 685 8039, snowphone (0900) 39888).

The **Fox Peak** club ski area, 23 km from Fairlie in the Two Thumb Range, has five rope lifts. Skid Row, the learners' lift, is free. There is good ski touring from the summit of Fox Peak and paragliding is also popular here. There's accommodation at the ski area at Fox Lodge, or in Fairlie, 40 minutes away. The season is from early July to late September.

Contact: Fox Peak Ski Club, PO Box 368, Timaru (☎ (03) 688 0703, snowphone 685 8539).

Mt Hutt

Mt Hutt is one of the highest ski areas in the southern hemisphere and is rated as one of the best in New Zealand. It's 104 km west of Christchurch and you can get there by bus from Christchurch or from local accommodation centres Methven and Ashburton.

Mt Hutt has beginner, intermediate and advanced level slopes, with a quad and a triple chairlift, three T-bars, various other lifts, and heli-skiing from the car park to slopes further afield. Instruction is offered at all levels, and there's also racing and racing instruction.

The ski season here is very long, usually

from early May to mid-October, and is made reliable by extensive snow-making facilities. There's a variety of accommodation in Methven, 24 km away, or you can stay at Ashburton, 34 km from Methven on the main Christchurch to Dunedin road.

Contact: Mt Hutt Ski & Alpine Tourist Co, PO Box 14, Methven (☎ (03) 302 8811, 308 5074; fax 302 8697, snowphone 302 8605).

Erewhon

The Erewhon club ski area must be one of the best gems in New Zealand. It is based on Mt Potts, above the headwaters of the Rangitata River, and is about 75 km from Methven. It has four rope lifts and one learners' lift. Accommodation and meals are available from a lodge at Mt Potts, eight km from the ski area. It has a good mix of beginning, intermediate and advanced slopes, with snowboarding and telemark also popular. Transport by 4WD is essential, and can be arranged through the club. The season is from early July to October.

Contact: Erewhon Ski Club, 45 Matilda St, Timaru (☎ (03) 684 7032, snowphone 303 9736 on holidays & weekends).

Mt Olympus

Hard to find, but worth the search, is Mt Olympus, 66 km from Methven and 12 km from Lake Ida. This club area has four lifts which lead to a number of intermediate and advanced runs. It is on the south side of the Craigieburn Range, and the southerly aspect means that there is often good powder. Snowboarding is accepted, there are good telemark areas and cross-country trails to other areas. Accommodation is available on the area and in a lower lodge, or there's accommodation in Methven. 4WD is advised from the bottom hut. The season is from early July to October.

Contact: Wind Whistle Winter Sports Club, PO Box 25055, Christchurch (☎ (05) 166 6838, snowphone (03) 366 5865).

Porter Heights

The closest commercial ski area to Christchurch, Porter Heights is 35 km from the nearest town, Springfield, and about 90 km from Christchurch on the Arthurs Pass road. The 720-metre 'Big Mama' run is the longest and steepest run in New Zealand. There are three T-bars, one platter lift and a learners' lift. There's a half-pipe for snowboarders, plus good telemark areas, and ski touring out along the ridge. The season runs from mid-June to mid-October. Accommodation is available on the area or in neighbouring Springfield. The Snowman Shuttle & Tours (☎ (03) 364 8887) provides economical transport to and from the ski area.

Contact: Porter Heights Skifield, PO Box 536, Christchurch (☎ (03) 379 7484, (05) 163 7731; fax (03) 366 6061, snowphone (03) 366 5865).

Arthurs Pass & Craigieburn Regions

There are five ski areas in the Arthurs Pass and Craigieburn regions.

Temple Basin, the most distant from Christchurch, is a club area just four km from the Arthurs Pass township. It is a 45-minute walk uphill from the car park to the lift area where there are three rope lifts. From the summit of Mt Temple, on a clear day, you can see all the way from the Tasman Sea to the Pacific Ocean. At night there's flood-lit night skiing. Accommodation is available at two lodges on the area, or in Arthurs Pass. The season is from early July to October.

Contact: Temple Basin Ski Club, PO Box 1228, Christchurch (☎ (03) 332 1725; fax 337 2110, snowphone 366 5865).

The **Craigieburn Valley** ski area, centred on Hamilton Peak, is 40 km from Arthurs Pass, 48 km from Springfield and 110 km from Christchurch. It is one of New Zealand's most challenging club areas, with mostly intermediate and advanced runs. It is a pleasant 10-minute walk through beech forest from the car park to the ski area. The season is from early July to mid-October.

Contact: Craigieburn Valley Ski Club, PO Box 2152, Christchurch (☎ & fax (03) 318 8711, snowphone 328 7555).

It is possible to ski from Craigieburn Valley to the **Broken River** club ski area, 50 minutes away, where the ski passes are interchangeable; it will take twice that time to ski back, so plan accordingly. Otherwise access to Broken River is unsealed for the last six km, after which it's a 15-minute walk to the lodges and a further 10-minute walk to the ski area. Accommodation is available in three lodges, or you can stay in Springfield, 40 minutes away; it's 1½ hours to Christchurch. The season is from late June to late October.

Contact: Broken River Ski Club, PO Box 2718, Christchurch (☎ (05) 168 8713, snowphone (03) 366 5865).

Another good club area in the Craigieburn Range is **Mt Cheeseman**, 30 km from Springfield and 112 km from Christchurch. The ski area, based on Mt Cockayne, has a T-bar and a poma serving the wide, sheltered basin. Accommodation is available at two lodges at the area, or in Springfield. The season is from early July to late September.

Contact: Mt Cheeseman Ski Club, PO Box 22-178, Christchurch (☎ & fax (03) 379 5315, (☎ (05) 168 8794, snowphone (03) 366 5865).

The fifth ski area is **Mt Olympus**, mentioned earlier.

Hanmer Springs Region

There are three ski areas near Hanmer Springs.

Amuri, a club area based on Mt St Patricks, is 27 km from Hanmer Springs and has a poma and a rope lift, leading to runs suiting all types of skiers. There's accommodation at the area, or you can stay in Hanmer Springs, 45 minutes away. The season is from early July to mid-September.

Contact: Amuri Ski Area, PO Box 129, Hanmer Springs (☎ & fax (03) 315 7125, snowphone 315 7401).

New Zealand's newest commercial ski area is **Mt Lyford**, 75 km from Hanmer Springs, 37 km from Waiau, and 3.5 km from Mt Lyford Village, where accommodation is available. It has skiing at all levels, basin and off piste telemark, 15 km of groomed trails for cross-country skiing, and a natural half-pipe for snowboarding. Mt Lyford has been built in conjunction with a wilderness retreat

where there is ice skating, fishing, golf and hot pools. It is open from early June to mid-October. The **Mt Terako** ski area is being developed nearby and has separate access to Mt Lyford.

Contact: Mt Lyford Ski Area, Private Bag, Waiau, North Canterbury (☎ (03) 343 0248, fax 343 0784, mobile (025) 315 6178, ☎ & fax (03) 315 6178, snowphone (025) 330 999).

Nelson Region

In the north, near St Arnaud in Nelson Lakes National Park, there are two ski areas.

The **Rainbow Valley** commercial ski area is just outside the park. There is a double chair and a T-bar which lift skiers to the top of a spacious bowl, a learners' lift, and it's good for cross-country skiing. Accommodation is available in St Arnaud, 56 km away, or in Nelson or Blenheim, each 1½ hours away. The season is from mid-June to mid-October.

Contact: Rainbow Valley Ski Area, Private Bag, St Arnaud (☎ & fax (03) 521 1861, snowphone (0900) 39 555).

Mt Robert, a club area inside the park, 15 km from St Arnaud, has two lodges right at the ski area, but it's a 1½-hour walk from the car park, seven km from St Arnaud, to reach it. On weekends a helicopter lift is available from the car park. This area is known for its powder and there are many cross-country opportunities for the suitably equipped. The season is from mid-June to late October.

Contact: Nelson Ski Club Inc, PO Box 344, Nelson (snowphone (03) 548 8336).

HELI-SKIING

If you want to try heli-skiing New Zealand is a great place for it. Harris Mountains Heli-Skiing, based in Wanaka and Queenstown, has been suggested by many to be the pick of the bunch. It operates from July to October over a wide area with over 100 peaks and 200 runs to choose from in The Remarkables, the Harris Mountains, the Buchanans Range, and The Branches, plus the Tyndall Glacier.

In Wanaka, they can be contacted through the Wanaka Travel Centre, 99 Ardmore St, PO Box 177, Wanaka (☎ (03) 443 7930/7277, fax 443 8876). In Queenstown contact them through the Queenstown Information Centre on the corner of Shotover and Camp Streets (☎ (03) 442 6722).

Other heli-skiing companies in the South Island include:

Southern Lakes Heliski, based in Queenstown (☎ (03) 442 6222; fax 442 7867)

Heli-Guides New Zealand, based in Queenstown (☎ & fax (03) 442 8151, ☎ 442 3208)

Alpine Guides Westland, based in Fox Glacier (☎ (03) 751 0825)

Alpine Guides Mt Cook, based in Mt Cook Village (☎ (03) 435 1834; fax 435 1898)

Methven Heliskiing/Alpine Guides, based in Methven (☎ (03) 302 8108)

Mt Hutt Helicopter, based in Methven (☎ (03) 302 8401; fax 302 8102)

In the North Island, Snowrange Heliskiing does guided heli-ski trips to the Ruahine Ranges, south-east of Mt Ruapehu, operating from July to October. They are based in Taihape (☎ (06) 328 2869; fax 388 1011).

GLACIER SKIING

Although it is not strictly necessary to fly up to the **Tasman Glacier** (people have been known to walk!) this is really a ski resort for the jetsetter only – skiing down from the upper reaches of the Tasman Glacier usually requires a flight up from Mt Cook airfield in a ski-plane. You need to be a fairly competent skier as well as a rich one to savour this unique skiing experience. The lower reaches of the glacier are almost dead flat and are usually covered in surface moraine so you must either walk out – or fly once again. In exceptional circumstances the run down the glacier can be 20 km in length, although it's usually less than 10 km. Still quite an experience.

Count on around $495 for a flight up, the guide fee, two runs down the glacier and the flight back. You must have a guide with you – contact Alpine Guides Mt Cook, based at Mt Cook Village (☎ (03) 435 1834; fax 435 1898). The season is from mid-July to late October.

Other glaciers that can be skied on Mt Cook include the **Murchison Glacier** and **Mannering Glacier**.

On the other side of the divide, the Fox Glacier Wilderness Skiing – Alpine Guides Westland (☎ (03) 751 0825) operate in Westland National Park, in the **Fox Glacier** and **Franz Glacier** névés. The season is from August to December.

Other Activities

MOUNTAINEERING

New Zealand has a rich history of mountaineering, as it is an ideal training ground for greater adventures overseas. The Southern Alps offer a great number of challenging climbs, and are studded with a number of impressive peaks.

It is not a pursuit for the uninitiated as it is highly challenging, very physical and contains a number of dangers – fickle weather with storms, winds and extreme cold; avalanches; rotten, loose rock and the ever-present danger of rockfall; the possibility of falling; and equipment failure, all factors that can lead to accidents.

Don't be put off, though, as proper instruction and training will allow you to enjoy the mountains, aware of their pitfalls, and enable you to make commonsense decisions which enhance your safety and thus appreciation of the mountain environment. A list of recommended companies which give instruction in mountaineering is included at the end of this section.

The Mt Cook region has always been the focus of climbing activity in New Zealand, and the history of NZ climbing is inextricably linked to it. On 2 March 1882, William Spotswood Green and two Swiss alpinists, after a 62-hour epic, failed to reach the summit. Three local climbers, Tom Fyfe, George Graham and Jack Clarke, spurred into action by the news that two well-known European alpinists, Edward Fitzgerald and Matthias Zurbriggen, were coming to attempt Cook, set off to climb it before the visitors. On Christmas day 1884 they ascended the

Hooker Glacier and north ridge, a brilliant climb in those days, and stood on the summit of Aoraki (Mt Cook).

In 1913, Freda du Faur, an Australian, was the first woman to reach the summit. In 1948, Edmund Hillary's party climbed the south ridge. Hillary went on to become, with Tenzing Norgay, the first to the summit of Mt Everest in the Himalaya. Since then most of the daunting face routes have been climbed. An extremely lucky Geoff Wayatt climbed the east face the day before a recent huge landslide (see Mt Cook in the Canterbury chapter). The Mt Cook region has many great peaks – Sefton, the beguiling Tasman, Silberhorn, Elie de Beaumont, Malte Brun, Aiguilles Rouges, Nazomi, La Perouse, Hicks, De la Beche, Douglas and the Minarets. Many of the peaks can be ascended from Westland National Park, and there is a system of climbers' huts on both sides of the divide.

Mt Cook is only one of a number of outstanding climbing areas. The others extend along the spine of the South Island from Tapuaenuku (in the Kaikouras) and the Nelson Lakes peaks, in the north, to the rugged mountains of Fiordland.

Arthurs Pass is an outstanding climbing area. There are a number of challenging routes on Mt Rolleston and 'away from it all' climbs on Mts Carrington and Murchison. To the south lie the remote Arrowsmiths, with true wilderness climbing possibilities.

Beyond the Cook region is Mt Aspiring National Park, centred on 'the Matterhorn of the South' Mt Aspiring, and the Volta, Therma and Bonar ice fields which cling to its sides. This is the second centre of mountaineering in New Zealand, and there are possibilities for all levels of climbs on Aspiring, Rob Roy, Avalanche, Liverpool, Barff, and peaks around the Olivine Ice Plateau. To the south, in the Forbes Mountains is Mt Earnslaw, flanked by the Rees and Dart rivers.

Fiordland is not without its impressive peaks. The mightiest of these is Tutoko, the centrepiece of the Darrans Range, just to the north of Milford Sound. There are some

walks in this area but, generally, if you wish to explore the Darrans you are forced to climb up sheer granite walls. This is the remotest and most daunting region of New Zealand, and the domain of the skilled, confident mountaineer.

For those seeking to learn the necessary skills, here's a list of climbing schools:

Mt Cook & Westland National Parks
Alpine Guides Mt Cook (☎ (03) 435 1834; fax 435 1898), PO Box 20, Mt Cook Village (mountaineering courses and Copland Pass)

Alpine Guides (Westland) (☎ (03) 751 0825; fax 751 0857), PO Box 38, Main Rd, Fox Glacier (ski mountaineering, mountaineering and Copland Pass)

Alpine Recreation Canterbury (☎ (03) 680 6736; fax 680 6765), PO Box 75, Lake Tekapo (ski touring, high altitude pass crossing – Ball Pass, mountaineering courses)

Southern Alps Guiding (☎ (03) 435 1890), PO Box 32, Mt Cook (private guiding)

Mt Aspiring National Park
Aspiring Guides (☎ (03) 443 7930; fax 443 8876) (heli-skiing, mountaineering courses, guiding)

Mountain Recreation (☎ & fax (03) 443 7330), PO Box 204, Wanaka (also guiding for Cascade Saddle crossing – Matukituki to the Rees-Dart, mountaineering courses, high altitude walks in upper Matukituki)

Mountain Works (☎ & fax (03) 442 7329), PO Box 647, Queenstown (for Mt Earnslaw and Copland Pass)

ROCK CLIMBING
This sport has increased in popularity in New Zealand. No longer is it just considered practice for mountaineering, it is now an activity in its own right. There are a number of companies set up to take beginners out for their first climbs, with all attention being paid to safety.

In the North Island, popular climbing areas include the Mt Eden Quarry in the heart of Auckland, and Whanganui Bay and Motuoapa in the vicinity of Lake Taupo. About 10 km south of Te Awamutu, the Wharepapa Rock Climbing Field with 42 rock climbs ranging from beginners' level to advanced, attracts rock climbers wanting to practise their skills.

The South Island has a great number of areas. Above Christchurch, in the Port Hills, there are a number of climbs, and 100 km away on the road to Arthurs Pass is Castle Hill and a number of great friction climbs. For the more adventurous there are the long, extreme routes of the Darrans, a range blessed with New Zealand's best rock.

RAP JUMPING

This is a variation on abseiling or rapelling. Instead of the traditional face to the wall, feet first approach of descent, you go almost head first, face out. The Bay of Islands, Wanaka and Queenstown (again!) are good places to experience rap jumping and there are operators there willing to teach you to come to grips with gravity.

CAVING

There are plenty of caving opportunities in New Zealand, as this is also a popular activity amongst local outdoor enthusiasts. Auckland, Westport and, of course, Waitomo are all areas where you'll find both active local clubs and organised tours.

MOUNTAIN-BIKING & CYCLE TOURING

This mode of transport has taken off with phenomenal fury. Mountain bikes are seen everywhere, used either for recreation or as a form of daily transport.

New Zealand, with its great scenery as well as off-road possibilities, is great biking country. Many choose mountain bikes or touring cycles as the preferred mode of transport around New Zealand – the bike allows them to get off the beaten track, or to amble along at a leisurely pace.

Most towns have mountain bikes for hire – a good way to see the towns and their attractions as well as to take off into the countryside. Bikes can be hired by the hour, day, week or month; you can hire the bike alone, or hire a bike with a bike/bus option, or even go on an organised bicycle tour. The various options are discussed under Cycling in the Getting Around chapter.

If you'll be cycling through New Zealand, get a copy of *Cycle Touring in New Zealand* – *including both North & South Islands* by Bruce Ringer (Hodder & Stoughton, Auckland, 1989, paperback). With maps and suggestions for long-distance cycle tours as well as short side trips, it tells you all you need to know about cycling through New Zealand, including where the steep hills are! *Classic New Zealand Mountain Bike Rides* by Paul Kennett, Patrick Morgan & Jonathan Kennett (GP Publications, Petone, 1991, paperback) is another good cycling book, suggesting a wide variety of short and long rides all over New Zealand.

For downhill fans, various companies will take you up to the top of mountains, hills and volcanoes (Mt Ruapehu, Otago Peninsula, Remarkables) so that you can hurtle down without the usual grunt of getting uphill beforehand.

Many routes which were traditionally walked are now being biked. One thing to remember, though, is *never* to bicycle on walking tracks in national parks. Bicycles quickly damage the tracks, which are expensive and a lot of work to maintain. DOC, therefore, who puts in and maintains the tracks, will charge you a huge fine if you're seen bicycling on a track. They take this very seriously and *will* fine you if you're caught. Cycling on roads in national parks is OK.

HORSE-RIDING

There are numerous places where you can see the countryside by horse in New Zealand, on anything from half-hour rides to 12-day treks. In the South Island, all-day adventure rides on horseback are a great way to see the surrounding country in Kaikoura, around Mt Cook, Queenstown and Dunedin. There are many treks offered in Westland, from all-day rides at Punakaiki, and excursions up to 12 days long at the Waitaha Valley, Ross.

At Franz Josef Glacier you can take a 2½-hour tour through rainforest. In Otago, near Wanaka, the more adventurous shouldn't miss out on an overnight wilderness pack trip, or a mountain and river trek.

In the North Island, Taupo has options for wilderness horse-trekking and for rides in the hills overlooking the thermal regions.

The Coromandel Peninsula and Waitomo are also good places for horse-trekking.

There are many more options available, so check the index for individual mentions in this book, and ask at the local information centres for lists of operators.

BIRDWATCHING

New Zealand is a birdwatcher's paradise in many ways. In such a small area there are many unique endemic species, a number of interesting residents and wave upon wave of visitors. It is as famous for extinct and point-of-extinction species as it is for existing species.

The extinct species can't be 'watched' but a tour through museums, into caves where their bones are found and into former habitats is fascinating. These were the islands of the giant four-metre-tall moa and the Haast's eagle which was large enough to have preyed upon it; the remarkable huia with its vastly different male and female beaks; and the beautiful Auckland Island merganser. The number of species on the point of extinction and the frenzied efforts to rebuild their populations is also a captivating story. Included are the takahe (believed extinct until found in the remote Murchison Mountains in Fiordland), New Zealand bushwren, Chatham Islands black robin, black stilt, kakapo, blue-wattled kokako and the New Zealand dotterel. (See the Canterbury chapter for more information on the black stilt and Stewart, Chatham & Outer Islands chapter for the black robin.)

Any visiting birdwatcher will not be disappointed by the more accessible species. The kiwi is probably the most sought after species to observe and you are guaranteed to see the Stewart Island sub-species at all times of the year.

Other birds sought after are the Southern royal albatross (found in a mainland colony on the Otago Peninsula), the white heron or kotuku (found near Okarito in Westland), the cheeky kea which ranges throughout the Southern Alps, the yellowhead or mohua seen in the remote Catlins, Fiordland crested penguin, yellow-eyed penguin (seen in colonies along the south-eastern coast of the South Island), Australasian gannet (at Farewell Spit, Muriwai and Cape Kidnappers), wrybill, oystercatcher, and in the forests the kereru or New Zealand pigeon, rifleman, tui, kaka and the saddleback.

There is no shortage of places to see birds. Some of the best are Ulva Island (near Stewart Island); the Catlins Forest Park and south-east coast; Fiordland and the forests of Westland; Otago Peninsula; Cape Farewell; the Marlborough Sounds; Te Urewera National Park; the Firth of Thames (Miranda Naturalist's Trust); Opoutere and the Coromandel; and the forests and coasts of Northland. There are a number of islands established as wildlife refuges where threatened birds are being protected: you will need special permission to visit these.

There are a number of field guides for birdwatching in New Zealand. Jeff, an avid birder, reckons the two that a real twitcher should carry around are *A Field Guide to New Zealand Birds* by Geoff Moon (Reed, Auckland, 1992, hardback) and *Birds of New Zealand: Locality Guide* by Stuart Chambers (Arun Books, Hamilton, 1989, paperback). Both have excellent colour photos of the birds in their natural environments and lots of good information about them; the *Locality Guide* also gives valuable practical information on how and where to find each species anywhere in New Zealand.

See the Flora & Fauna section in our Facts about the Country chapter for descriptions of various birds.

MAZES

For some reason, Kiwis are mad on mazes, and there are some spectacular ones built as tourist attractions around the country. When they tired of ordinary mazes they made three-dimensional ones, most of which are incredibly convoluted – the original three-dimensional maze, at Wanaka in the South Island, can take hours to work through. There's even a waterslide maze at the Olympic swimming pool in Dunedin.

The Fairbank Maze, opposite the airport at Rotorua, is the largest hedge maze in New

Zealand, with a 1.6 km pathway. Te Ngae Park, three km beyond the Rotorua airport, is a three-dimensional, 1.7 km wooden maze similar to the one at Wanaka.

There are usually other facilities that make them great fun for families. Recently New Zealand has even started to export its mazes – a maze craze has developed in Japan where Kiwi consultants advise on the designs.

Water Activities

JET-BOATING
New Zealand is the home of the amazing jet-boats, invented by CWF Hamilton in 1957. An inboard engine sucks water into a tube in the bottom of the boat, and an impeller driven by the engine blows it out a nozzle at the stern in a high-speed stream. The boat is steered simply by directing the jet stream.

The boats are ideal for use in shallow water and white water because there are no propellers to damage, there is better clearance under the boat, and the jet can be reversed instantly for quick braking. The instant response of the jet enables the boats to execute 360° spins almost within the length of the boat. All that adds up to some hair-raising rides on NZ rivers.

The Shotover and Kawarau rivers near Queenstown in the South Island are popular jet-boating rivers, with the Dart River less travelled but also good. In the North Island, the Whanganui, Manganui-a-te-Ao, Motu and Rangitaiki Rivers are popular for jet-boating; the Huka Jet, operating near Taupo, is also popular.

Just about every riverside and lakeside town throughout New Zealand has a jet-boat company that runs trips, sometimes in combination with other adventure activities such as bungy jumping, flightseeing and rafting.

RAFTING
There are almost as many white water rafting possibilities as there are rivers in New Zealand. And there is no shortage of compa-

nies willing to take you on a heart-pounding, drenching, exhilarating and spine-tingling ride down some of the wildest and most magnificent rivers in the world. The Shotover and Kawarau rivers in the South Island, popular for jet-boating, are also popular for white water rafting, as is the less accessible Landsborough River (often reached by helicopter or light plane). Canterbury has the Rangitata River, considered one of the island's best, and with two companies operating on it.

The north of the South Island has great rafting possibilities, such as the Buller, Karamea and Gowan rivers. Details about all the companies offering trips can be found in the respective sections. The West Coast has the Hokitika and Waiho rivers, plus plenty of other exciting rafting possibilities.

In the North Island there are plenty of rivers, like the Rangitaiki, Wairoa, Motu, Tongariro, Rangitikei and Ngaruroro, that are just as good. There is also the Kaituna Cascades near Rororua, with a seven-metre waterfall, the Okere Falls, as its highlight. This is perhaps NZ's bumpiest raft ride, with 15 drops in 40 minutes, a fact which necessitates the allocation of two guides to each boat instead of the usual one. The drop over the six-metre Tawhai Falls in Tongariro National Park is another dramatic drop.

The rivers are graded from one to six, with six meaning 'unraftable'. The grading of the Shotover canyon varies from three to five plus depending on the time of year, the Kawarau River is rated four, and the Wairoa River is graded three to five. On the rougher stretches there's usually a minimum age limit of 12 or 13 years. The rafting companies supply wet suits and life jackets.

Rafting trips take anything from one hour to three days and cost between about $75 and $130 per person per day, depending on whether or not helicopter access is involved. Spring and summer are the most popular rafting times.

CANOEING & KAYAKING
An open two-person canoe, called simply a canoe or sometimes an Indian canoe in other

parts of the world, is called a 'Canadian canoe' in New Zealand. A kayak, a smaller, narrower one-person craft which is covered except for a hole for the paddler to sit in, is often called a 'kayak' in New Zealand but it can also be called a 'canoe'. It's a good idea to specify whether you mean a 'Canadian canoe' or a 'kayak' when talking about river trips in this country.

Many companies offer canoeing and kayaking trips on the same rivers where rafting is popular. You can go for a few hours of quiet paddling or white water excitement in hired canoes or kayaks without a guide, or take longer solo or guided camping trips with fishing and other activities thrown in.

Canoeing is especially popular on the Whanganui River in the North Island, where you can hire a canoe for days at a time; there are many other possibilities. Canoeing is also popular on lakes, notably Lake Taupo, and on lakes not far from Christchurch.

Kayaking is a very popular sport. Commercial trips (for those without their own equipment) are offered on a number of rivers and lakes in the North and South Island. One of the best is with Down to Earth Adventures on the Matukituki and Makarora rivers near Wanaka.

Sea Kayaking

Sea kayaking is relatively new in New Zealand but those who have tried it rave about it. Popular sea kayaking areas are the Bay of Islands (with trips departing from Paihia) and Coromandel in the North Island, and in the South Island the Marlborough Sounds and along the coast of the Abel Tasman National Park, where sea kayaking has become a viable alternative to walking on the Abel Tasman Coastal Track (see those sections for further details).

Fiordland has become a popular destination for those wishing to hone their sea kayaking skills. There are tour operators in Te Anau and Manapouri who can arrange trips in the lakes and fiords.

RIVER SLEDGING

This is a relatively new sport in 'find the new quick buzz' New Zealand. Discard the raft, kayak, canoe, lilo or inflated inner tube if you think they lack manoeuvrability. Instead, grasp a responsive polystyrene sled or a modified boogey board, flippers, wet suit and helmet, a positive attitude, and go for it.

In the North Island, the Rangitaiki River near Rotorua seems to be the river to hurl yourself down, with the aptly named Jeff's Joy being the pick of nine or so rapids on the most popular stretch. In the South Island, the Kawarau near Queenstown is both boogey boarded and sledged. The Chinese Dogleg, not far from the bungy bridge, provides all the fun (see the Wanaka and Queenstown sections for more information about the lunatic antics of Serious Fun and Frogz have More Fun). Don't continue downriver from the Dogleg. Pull out as a big surprise awaits around the corner – this can be safely observed from the Cromwell-Queenstown road!

CAVE RAFTING

Yet another variation on the rafting theme is not true rafting at all, but it is very unusual and exciting. It's known as 'Black-Water Rafting' at Waitomo in the North Island, and as 'Underworld Rafting' at Westport or 'Taniwha Adventure Caving' at Greymouth in the South Island.

It involves donning a wet suit, a lighted hard hat and a black inner tube and floating on underground rivers through some spectacular caves. An added attraction is seeing glow-worms, those fascinating insects, glowing away like a Milky Way of stars in the bowels of the earth.

SCUBA DIVING

Scuba diving also has its devotees. The Bay of Islands Maritime & Historic Park and the Hauraki Gulf Maritime Park in the North Island, and the Marlborough Sounds Maritime Park in the South Island, are obvious attractions but there are many more diving possibilities around both islands. Even Invercargill, with its notoriously cold water, has a club!

New Zealand has two marine parks, which

are protected marinelife reserves – interesting for diving. The Poor Knights Islands Marine Reserve is around the Poor Knights Islands off the coast near Whangarei, north of Auckland. This reserve is reputed to have the best diving in New Zealand, and French naturalist Jacques Cousteau rates it one of the 'top 10' diving spots in the world. The Sugar Loaf Islands Marine Park, another interesting reserve, is off Back Beach in New Plymouth, not far from the city centre.

Fiordland in the South Island is a surprisingly interesting place for diving. The diving here is most unusual because the extremely heavy rainfall leaves an actual layer of freshwater, often peaty brown, over the saltwater. You descend through this murky and cold freshwater into amazingly clear and warmer saltwater. The freshwater cuts out light which discourages the growth of seaweed and this provides ideal conditions for the growth of black coral, which can be found much closer to the surface than is common elsewhere in the world. Leave it there, though. It's 100% protected in New Zealand.

Fiordland also has plenty of crayfish (lobster) and amazing pods of dolphins who display great interest in the relatively rare appearance of scuba divers. It also has areas of protected black coral, *Antipathes fiordensis*, white when alive but black when dead; snake stars which symbiotically live on the coral; and brachiopods, true living fossils.

Coastal Fishes of New Zealand: A Diver's Identification Guide by Malcolm Francis (Heinemann Reed, Auckland, 1988, paperback) is a field guide to all the fishes a diver in New Zealand is likely to encounter, with colour photos of the fishes in their natural environment.

SURFING

With its thousands of km of coastline, New Zealand has excellent surfing possibilities. Swells come in from every angle and while any specific beach will have better surfing at some times of the year than at others, there's good surfing to be found *somewhere* in New Zealand at any time of the year.

A few spots recommended by surfies are:

North Island
Auckland area (within two hours drive of the city)
    West coast: Piha, Raglan, Muriwai
    East coast: Whangamata, Matakana Island
Gisborne
    City beaches, Mahia Peninsula
Taranaki
    Stent Rd, Puniho Rd, Greenmeadows Point

South Island
Dunedin
    Sandfly Bay, Long Point, Lobsters near Akatore River
Kaikoura
    Meatworks, Mangawhau Point, Mangamanu Reef
Westport
    Westport beaches, Tauranga Bay

According to the surfing grapevine, Auckland is the best surfing area in the North Island, and Dunedin the best in the South Island, especially in summer and autumn, but there are hundreds of possibilities. There are guidebooks on surfing in New Zealand. Look for *The New Zealand Surfing Guide* by Mike Bhana (Heinemann Reed, Auckland, 1988, paperback) with details about surfing at beaches all around New Zealand including what times of year to surf where, where to find right-hand and left-hand breaks, tidal advice and more.

FISHING

New Zealand is renowned as one of the great sport-fishing countries of the world, thanks largely to the introduction of exotic rainbow trout, brown trout, quinnat salmon, Atlantic salmon, perch, char and a few other fish. The lakes and rivers of central North Island are famous for trout fishing, especially Lake Taupo and the rivers that feed it. The rivers and lakes of the South Island are also good for trout, notably the Mataura River in Southland.

The rivers of Otago and Southland, in southern South Island, have some of the best salmon fishing in the world.

Saltwater fishing is also a big attraction for Kiwi anglers, especially in the warmer waters around the North Island where surfcasting or fishing from boats can produce big

catches of grey mullet, trevally, mao mao, porae, John Dory, gurnard, flounder, mackerel, hapuku, tarakihi, moki and kahawai. The Ninety Mile Beach and the beaches of the Hauraki Gulf are good for surfcasting.

The colder waters of the South Island, especially around Marlborough Sounds, are good for snapper, hake, trumpeter, butterfish, ling, barracouta and blue cod. The Kaikoura peninsula is great for surfcasting.

It is not easy to hire fishing gear in New Zealand, so bring your own if you can. Rods and tackle may have to be treated by NZ quarantine officials, especially if they are made with natural materials such as cane or feathers.

If you want to fish on inland waters you will need a fishing permit. They are available for particular regions and are available for a day, a week, a month or a season. If you plan to do a lot of fishing in different areas, you can get a special tourist licence that is valid throughout most of New Zealand for one month. Special tourist fishing licences are available only at Tourism Rotorua; see the Rotorua section for details. Local visitor information centres and DOC offices can give you more information about fishing licences and regulations.

Many books have been written about fishing in New Zealand. John Kent has written both the *North Island Trout Fishing Guide* (Heinemann Reed, Auckland, 1988, paperback) and the *South Island Trout Fishing Guide* (Hienemann Reed, Auckland, 1990, paperback). Tony Orman, a renowned NZ fisherman and author, has written *21 Great New Zealand Trout Waters* (David Bateman, Auckland, 1993, paperback) as well as *Fishing the Wild Places of New Zealand* (Bush Press, Auckland, 1991, hardback) telling not only how to catch fish but also relating some of the author's adventures fishing in many of New Zealand's wilderness areas. For surfcasting, check out *Surfcasting: A New Zealand Guide* by Gil Henderson (David Bateman, Auckland, 1991, paperback).

MARINE-MAMMAL WATCHING

Kaikoura, on the north-eastern coast of the South Island, is the centre of marine-mammal watching in New Zealand. One company operates daily whale-watching tours, two offer swimming with dolphins, and another two seal swimming.

The main attraction is the sperm whale, which is the largest toothed whale on earth, but there's also a lot of other beautiful wildlife to be seen on the tours: Hector's dolphin (the smallest and rarest of all dolphins), the dusky dolphin (found only in the southern hemisphere, often in huge groups), the NZ fur seal, the orca or killer whale (the largest of all dolphins), common dolphin, pilot whale, blue penguin, the royal albatross, mollymawk and many other sea birds.

Nature being what it is, there's no guarantee of seeing any specific animal on any one tour, but it's fairly certain that something of interest will be out there any time you go. In general, the sperm whales are most likely to be seen from October to August, and orcas from December to March. Most of the other animals are seen all year round.

There is also swimming with dolphins in the North Island at Whakatane, Paihia and Whitianga; in the North Island it's mainly interaction with bottlenose dolphins.

Whales & Dolphins of New Zealand & Australia: An Identification Guide by Alan N Baker (Victoria University Press, Wellington, 1990, paperback) is a guide for identifying the species, with details on dorsal fins and so on, but it's sort of a ghoulish book since all the photos of animals show only dead ones!

MAMMALS SEEN IN NEW ZEALAND WATERS

Perhaps one of the greatest delights of a trip to New Zealand, especially the South Island, is a chance to observe the wealth of mammalia seen in New Zealand waters. There are 76 species of whales and dolphins on this globe and New Zealand, as small as it is, is blessed by the fact that 35 of these species have been observed in its waters. Kaikoura is particularly blessed as nearly half of that number of whales and dolphins, our cousins, have been seen in waters off its shores.

Of the 66 species of toothed whales and dolphins, the largest and the smallest are seen in New Zealand waters – the sperm whale and the Hector's dolphin. Then there are the baleen whales, seals and sea lions.

No longer does the blood of these species stain our waters as an indication of short-term reward. The whales, dolphins, seals and sea lions attract not the bludgeon and harpoon but the entranced eyes of observers from all round the world. The tourist dollars pouring into Kaikoura are worth many times those made by the slaughter of marine mammals for their oils and skins.

Not often seen, but occasionally observed in waters off Auckland Island in New Zealand's Subantarctic dependencies, is the spectacled porpoise *(Australophocaena dioptrica)).*

MYSTICETI – BALEEN WHALES

Humpback Whale *(Megaptera novaengliae)*

Sadly, sightings of humpbacks are rare. There is a group which migrates from Tonga to Antarctic waters via the coast of New Zealand. Once there were an estimated 100,000 in the world's oceans, now the number is believed to be about 2000. These whales sieve their food through baleen (fine whalebones), hence their classification. The males are a little smaller than the females who usually reach 16 metres in length and about 50 tonnes in weight. Humpbacks have unique tail fluke patterns, flippers (about a third of their body length) and throat grooves.

These whales are also known for their songs, sung during courtship by the male to woo females. The song is the same, with just small changes, or signatures, from whale to whale.

Migratory groups are seen in the Kaikoura area in June and July.

Humpback Whale

ODONTOCETI – TOOTHED WHALES & DOLPHINS

Orca *('Killer Whale' – Orcinus orca)*

The orca are the largest of the dolphins and among the largest predators on earth, feeding on other dolphins and whales, as well as seals, sea birds, penguins and sharks. They grow up to 9.5 metres in length (females seven metres) and 8000 kg in weight (females 4000 kg).

They are distinguished by their huge dorsal fins, often reaching nearly two metres in length. The New Zealand pods (groups) have not been extensively studied. Both sexes have up to 12 pairs of teeth in each jaw. The orca vocalises both for socialising and as a means of keeping contact when foraging for food. There is no record of an unprovoked attack by an orca, as powerful as it is, upon humans.

Long-Finned Pilot Whale *(Globicephala melas)*

Of the two species of pilot whale, the long and short-finned, it is the long-finned which is seen the most in New Zealand waters. This is the species which has become notorious for large-scale 'beachings'. Long-finned pilot whales grow to over six metres in length (females up to 5.5 metres) and 3000 kg (females 2500 kg). The bulk of their diet is squid, plentiful along the coast of New Zealand.

Dusky Dolphin *(Lagenorhynchus obscurus)*

Dusky dolphins can reach lengths of over two metres, but they usually average 1.6 to 1.8 metres. What they lack in size they make up for in spirit. These are the most playful and those which 'dolphin swimming' participants are likely to encounter. While in the water, you will probably see them executing leaps such as head-first re-entry leaps, noisy leaps and somersaults, especially the head over tail.

They feed on small schooling fish, and often round up hundreds of fish in a tight ball, from which the pod takes turns at feeding. They congregate near the shore from late October to May; the pods then break up as winter comes on and the dolphins move offshore.

Dusky Dolphin

Hector's Dolphin *(Cephalorhynchus hectori)*

Named after zoologist Sir James Hector, these dolphins are confined to New Zealand waters. They have a rather dumpy shape, a distinctive rounded fin and reach a length of only 1.4 metres. Like the dusky they feed on small schooling fish, but they stay relatively close to shore all year round. Even though they are the world's rarest dolphin there is a good chance that you will see them when travelling in the South Island. Kaikoura, Banks Peninsula and Porpoise Bay (Southland) are all good locations.

Some years back Greenpeace reported that around Banks Peninsula 230 Hector's, about 30% of the population of the area, had been killed in gill nets over a four-year period. Fortunately, DOC has since declared Banks Peninsula a marine mammal sanctuary, with restrictions being placed on netting. What about the rest of New Zealand, or is it goodbye to the Hector's for the sake of a bag of fish?

Sperm Whale *(Physeter macrocephalus)*

This is the largest of the toothed whales, the male often reaches up to 20 metres in length; the female is much smaller with a maximum length of 12 metres. This is the whale that 'watchers' come to Kaikoura to see – or at least see 10% of the whale, as this is all that is seen from the boats until the whale dives and then exposes its tail flukes. Males weigh from 35-50 tonnes and females just over 20 tonnes, and both live up to 70 years. They dive for long periods, usually around 45 minutes.

They are hard to locate in the open ocean and the only real giveaway is the blow from their spout or their sonar clicks, detected with hydrophones. Because they require a huge feeding area for each individual they are normally seen singly. The visitors to the Kaikoura area are identified by the markings on their tail flukes. These whales have a single blowhole, offset on the left side of their head.

Bottlenose Dolphin *(Tursiops truncatus)*
This is the 'Flipper' dolphin and it is one of the larger species, often reaching four metres, although those seen in New Zealand waters are about 3.5 metres. They are very gregarious but occasionally they go 'solo', like Maui, the bottlenose dolphin that you are likely to see at Kaikoura.

It is the bottlenose that is most recorded in history, probably because of its commensal fishing activities with humans. They are also know to cooperatively feed among themselves, after encircling a shoal of fish.

Common Dolphin *(Delphinus delhis)*
These are the most widespread of dolphins, occurring throughout the world. They grow up to 2.5 metres, although are likely to average just over two metres. They dive to nearly 300 metres and can stay underwater for five or so minutes. Near Kaikoura, they are often seen alongside pods of duskys, but are considered more an offshore (pelagic) species. Common dolphins are recognisable by the golden coloration on their sides. Again, squid is a favoured food and its abundance off NZ's coastlines probably accounts for the presence of this species – they are opportunistic feeders.

Southern Right Whale Dolphin *(Lissodelphis peronii)*
Like their whale cousins, these dolphins do not have a dorsal fin. More common in subantarctic waters, they are only occasionally seen in waters off the main islands of New Zealand. They are thought to reach lengths of three metres and are very fast swimmers, travelling through the water in a series of bounces.

SEALS
New Zealand Fur Seal *(Arctocephalus forsteri)*
This is the seal most commonly seen in New Zealand waters. Mature male seals (bulls) are about two metres in length, and females (cows) are about 1.6 metres; average weight is about 140 kg. Once slaughtered in their thousands for their dense, luxuriant two-layered skins, fur seals are now thriving as a protected species. More often than not you see them basking on rocks, and they will probably enter the safety of the water if you get too close. Fur seals look much different from sea lions in that they have a broader bear-shaped head, prominent ears and larger front flippers. The pups are born in the summer months.

You can swim with them in a number of locations, especially near Kaikoura. They are a popular distraction for sea kayakers in the Abel Tasman National Park, and you are bound to see them in Milford Sound if you take one of the boat trips.

New Zealand Fur Seal

Elephant Seal *(Mirounga leonina)*
This seal, with its distinctive trunk-like nose is not commonly seen in New Zealand waters. There is one small breeding colony at the Nuggets, Southland, in the fauna-rich Catlins (see the Catlins in the Southland chapter). It is found in its thousands on New Zealand's Subantarctic islands.

SEA LIONS
Hooker's Sea Lion *(Neophoca hookeri)*
The Hooker's sea lions are visitors to the South Island, and the place you are most likely to see them is on beaches in the Catlins (see the Catlins in the Southland chapter). They are much larger than the New Zealand fur seal. ∎

Aerial Activities

BUNGY JUMPING

Bungy jumping was made famous by Kiwi A J Hackett's bungy dive from the Eiffel Tower in 1986. He teamed up with New Zealand's champion speed skier, Henry van Asch, and looked for a way to make commercial jumping safe. Hackett and van Asch now operate bungy jumping companies in New Zealand, Australia and France, and they are continually on the lookout for spectacular eyries for clients to leap off. The company alone has sent many thousands of people hurtling earthward from bridges over the Shotover and Kawarau rivers near Queenstown, in Normandy, France, and even from a tower in Cairns, Australia, with nothing between them and kingdom come but a gigantic rubber bungy cord tied to their ankles.

The jump begins when you crawl into the preparation area, get your ankles strapped up with a towel for padding, and have adjustments made to the cord depending on your weight. You then hobble out to the edge of the jumping platform, stand looking out over thin air, and get ready to jump. The crew shout out 'five, four, three, two, ONE!' and you dive off and are flying. Likely as not you will dunk head first into the river below before soaring upwards again on the bungy. The daring choose the 'escalator' and step off to watch the bridge above disappear rapidly, before the cord turns them 180° and they hurtle back up towards the bridge, upside down.

After bobbing up and down like a human yo-yo, you finally settle down, grab the pole held up to you by the crew down below, and are pulled into a rubber raft. There you're unstrapped and towed back to dry land. No doubt about it, it's a daredevil sport, and the adrenaline rush can last for days. But it's all very well organised, with every possible precaution and attention to safety. In fact, Hackett's rightly boast that their jump is fully approved to the NZ Safety Standards.

The historic Kawarau Suspension Bridge, near Queenstown, attracts the most jumpers; it's 43 metres above the Kawarau River. A more spectacular dive spot is Skippers Canyon Bridge, 71 metres above a narrow gorge on the Shotover River, also near Queenstown (see Queenstown in the Otago chapter).

You'll pay upwards of $89 for a bungy jump, which includes a bungy T-shirt that can only be obtained by actually doing the jump. It's even more expensive at the Shotover bridge, but there the price includes transport to the rather remote jump site ($145). You can also arrange for still photos or a video of your jump, to impress the folks back home.

Jumping is also done in the North Island at Taupo, where there's a bungy platform jutting out from a cliff 45 metres above the Waikato River, and from a 43-metre bridge (the same height as the Kawarau Bridge) over the Rangitikei River near Mangaweka (see Mangaweka in the Central North Island chapter). You can bungy off the Waiau River Bridge near Hanmer Springs, and off the Nagumo Bridge, 44 metres over the spectacular Deep Gorge, a 25-minute drive east of Masterton. In late 1993 the Manga-weka people were creating an even higher, 75-metre, 'Mega-bungy' jump at Mokai. It will be the highest jump in the country.

There's also a bungy jump site at Freeman's Bay in Auckland, where people jump from a crane. It's a chance to see or experience bungy jumping but if you'll be going to some of the other places, the higher jumps over wild river gorges are a lot more spectacular.

PARAPENTING/PARAGLIDING

This is perhaps the easiest way for humans to fly, without the problems faced by Icarus. After half a day of instruction you should be able to do limited solo flights. Before you know it you could be doing flights from 300 metres.

The best place to learn the skills necessary to operate your parapente/paraglider is Wanaka. Initial instruction is conducted at

Mt Iron, just outside the town and the long jumps are from the road up to Treble Cone ski field (often up to six minutes air time). Communication between instructor and student is via a radio in your helmet.

A half day at Mt Iron costs about $70, and a full day which includes Treble Cone is about $140. If you want a taste of flying without instruction consider taking a tandem flight from Treble Cone. Contact Air Action (☎ 443 9193); Richard, the senior instructor, is one of New Zealand's most experienced pilots and his knowledge instils confidence (see Wanaka and Queenstown in the Otago chapter).

AERIAL SIGHTSEEING

Planes and helicopters abound in all parts of New Zealand, and there are plenty of pilots willing to take you for sightseeing trips (called flightseeing by the locals).

The incredible contrast in scenery and the spectacular mountain ranges make New Zealand one of the best places for aerial sightseeing. Some of the best trips are around the Bay of Islands, the Bay of Plenty, Tongariro National Park and Mt Taranaki in the North Island, and Mt Cook and the West Coast glaciers and fiords in the South Island. You can even arrange to be flown up to the top of the glacial ski fields, from where you have a clear run all the way down to the bottom.

If you get down to the south-western coast of the South Island, try to fit in a flight up the fiords; the scenery is sensational and you can often combine the flight with a trip on the water to see other places of interest.

Most aerial sightseeing companies operate from the local aerodrome. Ask at the local tourist office for information; in some places you can just turn up at the aerodrome during daylight hours and arrange a trip on the spot. We have included details of flight operators in the relevant sections in this book.

SKYDIVING

A lot of the aerial sightseeing companies also operate skydiving courses and trips. Many visitors are taking the 'ultimate' jump in tandem with a fully qualified instructor. It is not cheap, usually around $175, but the thrill is worth every dollar.

You can go tandem skydiving in the North Island at Taupo, Rotorua, at Parakai near Auckland, at Paraparaumu near Wellington and at Hastings near Napier. In the South Island there's tandem skydiving at Nelson, Christchurch and Queenstown. It's a popular activity in all these places and since it's a fairly new activity in New Zealand, probably it will start being done at even more places.

An extra bonus is that by going up to skydiving height you also get in some great aerial sightseeing, so if you're only going to do it once, you might want to pick the place you would most like to see from a bird's eye view.

Getting There & Away

ARRIVING IN NEW ZEALAND

See the Visas section in the Facts for the Visitor chapter for information on what you will need when you arrive in New Zealand.

TRAVEL INSURANCE

However you're travelling, it's worth taking out travel insurance. Work out what you need. You may not want to insure that grotty old army surplus backpack – but everyone should be covered for the worst possible case: an accident, for example, that will require hospital treatment and a flight home. It's a good idea to make a copy of your policy, in case the original is lost. If you are planning to travel for a long time, the insurance may seem very expensive – but if you can't afford it, you certainly won't be able to afford to deal with a medical emergency overseas.

AIR

The overwhelming majority of visitors to New Zealand arrive by air. There are three airports that handle international flights – Auckland, Wellington and Christchurch. Most international flights go through Auckland; certainly if you're flying from the USA or Canada you're going to arrive in Auckland. Wellington airport has limited runway capacity and international flights are all to and from Australia. Flights to and from Christchurch are also mainly with Australia although there are some connections to other countries.

There are some special ticket types and definitions which may be of interest to visitors to New Zealand:

Circle Pacific Tickets

Circle Pacific tickets use a combination of airlines to circle the Pacific, combining Australia, New Zealand, North America and Asia. You can start and finish the circle at any point; the circle goes from the US west coast via various islands in the Pacific to New Zealand, on to Australia, to Asia and back to the west coast. Typically the fare for a Circle Pacific ticket is around A$2500 to A$3000, or US$2000 to US$2500.

Circle Pacific tickets usually have some sort of advance purchase requirement and there will probably be restrictions on changing your route once you've bought the ticket. Typically, you're allowed four stopovers but additional stopovers can be included at extra cost. You will have to complete the circuit within a certain period of time, usually six months, though one-year tickets are also available.

Air New Zealand has an excellent 'Coral Route' departing from Los Angeles which doesn't include Asia but does include New Zealand, Australia and many small Pacific islands. See the Coral Route section under to/from the USA.

Round the World Tickets

Round the World (RTW) tickets have become very popular in the last few years and they can be useful to visit New Zealand in combination with other destinations. Airline RTW tickets are often real bargains, and can work out no more expensive or even cheaper than an ordinary return ticket. They work particularly well from Europe – having come halfway round the world to New Zealand in one direction you might just as well continue the same direction! Prices start at about UK£850, A$1800 or US$1300.

As with Circle Pacific tickets you can join the loop at various places around the world. You can use a RTW ticket to make stops in Asia, Australia, New Zealand, the USA and Europe.

The official airline RTW tickets are often put together by a combination of two airlines, and permit you to fly anywhere you want on their route systems so long as you do not backtrack. Other restrictions are that

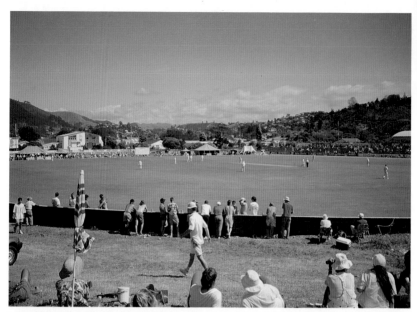

Top: Australia vs New Zealand One-Day International, Nelson (JW)
Bottom: Sports Day, wood-chopping, Waitomo (NK)

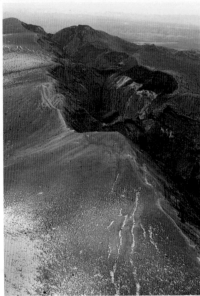

Top: The Bath-House (Museum of Art & History), Rotorua (TW)
Bottom Left: Mt Tarawera, Rotorua (TW)
Bottom Right: Hell's Gate, Rotorua (CH)

you (usually) must book the first sector in advance and cancellation penalties then apply. There may be restrictions on how many stops you are permitted and usually the tickets are valid for 90 days up to a year. An alternative type of RTW ticket is one put together by a travel agent using a combination of discounted tickets.

To/From Australia

The number of air routes between Australia and New Zealand has proliferated in the last few years. The NZ cities with flights to or from Australia are Auckland, Christchurch and Wellington. Australian cities with flights to or from New Zealand are Adelaide, Brisbane, Cairns, Canberra, Coolangatta (Gold Coast), Hobart, Melbourne, Perth and Sydney.

Some examples of regular one-way/return economy fares are A$520/650 from Sydney, A$600/720 from Melbourne, flying into Auckland; flying into Christchurch or Wellington can cost anywhere from around A$50 to A$150 more. In the high season, such as over the December-January summer school holidays, the fares are about A$200 higher. Fares from Brisbane or Hobart are similar, from Adelaide costs slightly more.

It's much cheaper to take an Advance Purchase Excursion (Apex) fare which can get you to New Zealand and back for little more than a regular one-way fare. With these fares you must book and pay for your ticket at least seven days prior to departure and once the tickets are issued cancellation charges apply should you wish to change your reservation or if you fail to fly. Insurance is available to protect against the advance purchase cancellation fees. With an Apex fare the minimum stay in New Zealand is six days (two days if one is a Saturday), the maximum can vary from around one to three months.

The fare depends on the day you fly out as well as where you fly to and from. The year is divided up into peak, shoulder and off-peak times, which can vary with the airline. Typical off-season low-cost fares from a travel agent specialising in discount tickets – about the cheapest fares you'll find, in other words – would cost around A$350/400

one-way/return from Sydney to Auckland, A$400/570 from Sydney to Christchurch or Wellington. From Melbourne the equivalent fares would be A$365/430 to Auckland, A$465/550 to Christchurch or Wellington. Fares in the high season will cost more, so it pays to plan your flight dates carefully. If you visit New Zealand in the summer, leaving just a day earlier in December or later in January could save you about A$150.

If you're travelling from Australia to the US west coast via New Zealand, the high season is different – there may be many high, shoulder and low-season times marked throughout the year, depending on the airline – but generally the high season is during the US summer (June, July and August). Low season fares can be around A$1000/1900 one-way/return, high season fares can be more like A$2200 return, but special excursion fares and other specials are almost always on offer too, which can bring the price as low as about A$800/1500 for one-way/return from Sydney, Brisbane or Melbourne.

RTW fares departing from Australia, which can include a stopover in New Zealand, vary with the season. The northern hemisphere summer (June, July and August) is usually the high season for RTW fares; they cost around A$2000 to A$2300 in high season but the price can be a few hundred dollars less in the off-season. Depending on where you want to go, how many stops, time of year, etc you could probably pay anywhere from around A$1800 to A$3000.

In Australia, STA and Flight Centres are major dealers in cheap airfares. They have branches in all the major cities. Otherwise, check the travel agents' ads in the Yellow Pages and ring around.

To/From the USA

Most flights between the USA and New Zealand are to/from the USA's west coast. Most go through Los Angeles but some also arrive and depart from San Francisco. If you're coming from some other part of the USA, your travel agent can arrange a discounted 'add-on' fare to get you to the city of departure.

Several excursion (round-trip) fares are available with various airlines. The lower priced ones will have more restrictions and advance purchase requirements, and have a shorter term of validity; a one-year ticket will cost more than a ticket good for only a month or two. Cheaper regular excursion fares cost about US$1170 in the low season, US$1470 in the high season. The more expensive excursion fares are around US$1500 and US$1800. The same excursion fares continuing to Australia after New Zealand cost US$100 more. Cheaper 'short life' fares are frequently offered, for only limited periods.

You can do better than these straightforward fares with travel agents. The easiest way to get a cheap airfare from the USA is through a travel agency selling discounted fares; these fares can be around US$750 return from Los Angeles or around US$1050 return from New York.

The Sunday travel sections of papers like the *New York Times*, the *Chicago Tribune*, the *Los Angeles Times* or the *San Francisco Examiner* always have plenty of ads for cheap airline tickets and there are often good deals on flights across the Pacific, especially in the west coast papers. Even if you don't live in these areas, you can have the tickets sent to you by mail.

Two of the most reputable discount travel agencies in the USA are STA and CIEE/Council Travel Services. Both of these are international travel agencies with a number of offices throughout the USA and in other countries. Both started out as student travel agencies. While they both still specialise in student travel, honouring and selling the International Student Identity Card (ISIC), they also offer discount tickets to non-students of all ages. You can contact their national head offices to ask about prices, find an office near you, purchase tickets by mail or buy an ISIC card.

STA Travel
    5900 Wilshire Blvd, Suite 2110, Los Angeles, CA 90036 (☎ (213) 937 1150; fax 937 2739). Telephone sales: (800) 777 0112, (212) 986 9643)

CIEE/Council Travel Services
    205 East 42nd St, New York, NY 10017 (☎ (212) 661 1414; fax 972 3231)

STA has offices in Los Angeles, San Francisco, Berkeley, Philadelphia, New York, Boston and Cambridge. Council Travel has offices in all these cities and in 20 others around the country. Both agencies have good fares on offer.

The magazine *Travel Unlimited* (PO Box 1058, Allston, MA 02134) publishes details of the cheapest air fares and courier possibilities for destinations all over the world, departing from the USA.

If you want to visit other Pacific destinations on your way to or from New Zealand, compare carefully the stopover possibilities offered by each airline. Air New Zealand flights offer an excellent variety of stopover options on their Coral Route. Other airlines fly to New Zealand for the same price, or sometimes cheaper, but with more limited stopover options.

The Coral Route Air New Zealand operates a special 'Coral Route' through the Pacific, departing from Los Angeles, which has some excellent stopover options. Their basic return (round-trip) LA-Auckland-LA flight is US$798 if you fly direct with no stopovers. On the Coral Route, you pay US$898 LA-Auckland-LA with one stopover, and you can add on additional stopovers for US$100 each.

Stopover possibilities include Honolulu, Tahiti, Rarotonga, Western Samoa, Tonga and Fiji and you can ask for as many or as few as you like, with a few restrictions in how you can organise your routing (there's no direct flight between Honolulu and Tahiti, for example). They also have arrangements with other airlines whereby they can add the Solomon Islands, Vanuatu and New Caledonia as further stopover options. Check with Air New Zealand for details on these, as these fares are outside their basic Coral Route fare structure.

On any of their USA-New Zealand flights, whether it's a direct flight or one with stopovers, you can pay an extra US$100 to add Australia on as another stopover option. There's no limitation how long you can stay at any stopover point, as long as you finish your entire trip in one year.

To/From Canada

In Canada, the student and discount travel agent is Travel CUTS, which has about 35 offices around Canada. Once again, you don't have to be a student to use their services. Their primary offices in the west and east will give you the address of their office nearest you:

Travel CUTS
　602 West Hastings, No 501, Vancouver, BC V6B 1P2 (☎ (604) 681 9136; fax 683 3567)
　187 College St, Toronto, Ontario M5T 1P7 (☎ (416) 979 2406; fax 979 8167)

The *Vancouver Sun* and the *Toronto Globe & Mail* carry travel agents' ads. The magazine *Great Expectations* (PO Box 8000-411, Abbotsford BC V2S 6H1) is useful.

Most flights coming from Canada will have at least one stopover on the way to New Zealand. See the USA section; much of the same advice applies, especially as regards stopover options. There are many stopover possibilities, so investigate the options.

To/From the UK

London-Auckland return tickets can be found in London bucket shops for around UK£950. Some stopovers are permitted on this sort of ticket. Depending on which airline you come with, you may fly across Asia or across the USA. If you're coming across Asia you can often make stopovers in places like India, Bangkok, Singapore and Australia; coming across in the other direction, stopover possibilities include places like New York, Los Angeles, Honolulu or a variety of Pacific islands. Stopover options will vary depending on which airlines you fly with; investigate the options.

Since New Zealand is about as far from Europe as you can get, it's not that much more to fly right on round the world rather

than backtracking. The regular airline RTW tickets that go through the South Pacific generally cost around UK£1930 but agents can organise an RTW route from around UK£850 to UK£1130.

There has always been cut-throat competition between London's many 'bucket shops', and London is an important European centre for cheap fares. There are plenty of bucket shops in London and although there are always some untrustworthy operators most of them are fine. Look in the listings magazines *Time Out* and *City Limits* plus the Sunday papers and *Exchange & Mart* for ads. Also look out for the free magazines widely available in London – start by looking outside the main railway stations. The Globetrotters Club (BCM Roving, London WC1N 3XX) publishes a newsletter called *Globe* which covers obscure destinations, and they can help in finding travelling companions.

Two good, reliable low-fare specialists are Trailfinders in west London, which produces a lavishly illustrated brochure including air fare details, and STA with a number of branches in London and around the UK. Look for them at:

Trailfinders
　46 Earls Court Rd, London W8 (☎ (071) 938 3366)
STA
　74 Old Brompton Rd, London SW7 (☎ (071) 581 4132; fax 581 3351)
　117 Euston Rd, London NW1 (☎ (071) 465 0484; fax 388 0944)

Most British travel agents are registered with the ABTA (Association of British Travel Agents). If you have paid for your flight to an ABTA-registered agent who then goes out of business, ABTA will guarantee a refund or an alternative. Unregistered bucket shops are riskier but also sometimes cheaper.

To/From Europe

Frankfurt is the major arrival and departure point for flights to New Zealand, with connections to other European centres.

There are many bucket shops where you

can buy discounted air tickets in mainland Europe. In addition to the bucket shops, STA and Council Travel, the international student and discount travel agencies also have a number of offices in various European countries. Any of their offices can give you the details on which office might be nearest you. Their offices include:

STA
> c/o Srid Reisen, Berger Strasse 118, 6000 Frankfurt 1, Germany (☎ (69) 43 01 91; fax 43 98 58)
> c/o SSR Reisen, Leon Hardstrasse 10, 8001 Zurich, Switzerland (☎ (1) 242 3000)
> c/o Voyages Decouvertes, 21 Rue Cambon, 75001 Paris, France (☎ (1) 42 96 16 80; fax 42 61 00 01)

Council Travel
> 18 Graf Adolf St, 4000 Dusseldorf 1, Germany (☎ (211) 32 90 88; fax 32 04 75)
> 31 Rue St Augustin, 75002 Paris, France (☎ (1) 42 66 20 87), tel & fax 44 95 95 75)

To/From Asia

There are far more flights to New Zealand from Asia than there were only a few years ago. There are direct flights to Auckland from Tokyo, Nagoya, Taipei, Hong Kong, Singapore and Denpasar/Bali, and connecting flights from Sapporo, Fukuoka, Seoul, Bangkok, Kuala Lumpur and other places. Most of the connecting flights have stopovers in Australia. There are also a few direct flights to/from Christchurch including flights to/from Tokyo and Singapore.

From Tokyo, Apex return fares vary from around 196,000 yen to 276,000 yen depending on the season. From Kuala Lumpur, Malaysia, you can get return fares for around M$2925 and Malaysia is a popular place for fare discounting. From Singapore return fares start from around S$2625. Hong Kong is another popular fare discounting centre and discounted return tickets to New Zealand cost around HK$10,200 in the high season, HK$8400 in the low season.

Ticket discounting is widespread in Asia, particularly in Hong Kong, Singapore and Bangkok; Hong Kong is probably the discount air ticket capital of the region. There are a lot of fly-by-nights in the Asian ticketing scene so a little care is required. STA,

which is reliable, has branches in Hong Kong, Tokyo, Singapore, Kuala Lumpur and Bangkok.

You can pick up some interesting tickets in Asia to include Australia and New Zealand on the way across the Pacific. See Circle Pacific Tickets.

SEA

Cruise ships apart, there are no longer any regular passenger ship services to New Zealand and these days arriving on some romantic tramp steamer (something you can still do in various Pacific Island nations) is pretty much a thing of the past. Ditto for the idea of working your passage.

Even working your way across the Pacific as crew on a yacht is much more difficult to arrange now than it used to be. There are many yachts sailing around the Pacific but nowadays they're usually only willing to take on experienced yachties as crew.

To try your luck finding a yacht, you have to go to the appropriate port at the appropriate time. There are lots of favourite islands, ports and harbours where you're likely to find yachts, such as Sydney and Cairns in Australia; Bali in Indonesia; various ports in Fiji or Tahiti; Hawaii, San Diego or San Francisco in the USA. In New Zealand, popular yachting harbours include the Bay of Islands and Whangarei (both in the Northland), Auckland and Wellington.

Yachts tend to move around the Pacific with the calendar – they sail with the prevailing winds, they stay out of the typhoon areas when it's cyclone season so there are certain times when you're more likely to find yachts. From Fiji, October to November is a peak departure season as cyclones are on their way. March-April is the main departure season for yachts heading to Australia. Be prepared for rough seas and storms crossing the Tasman Sea.

TOURS

Tours to New Zealand can be arranged from outside the country. Contact the NZTB, which handles international promotion of tourism for New Zealand; their addresses around the world are listed in the Facts for the Visitor chapter.

LEAVING NEW ZEALAND

As in Australia, STA and Flight Centres International are popular travel agents specialising in discount fares. Flight Centres have some of the cheapest fares, and they have branches throughout New Zealand. STA has offices in Auckland, Hamilton (Waikato University), Palmerston North, Wellington, Christchurch and Dunedin. Their head office in Auckland (see the Auckland section) can give you details on all of them.

Here are some sample one-way/return discount fares offered from Auckland, quoted in NZ dollars:

Auckland to:	High Season	Low Season
Frankfurt	$1265/2345	$1040/1995
New York	$1220/2320	$1220/2200
Los Angeles	$939/1738	$939/1599
San Francisco	$939/1738	$939/1599
Vancouver	$1030/1830	$1030/1690
Honolulu	$985/1265	$985/898
Fiji	$734/720	$734/605
Singapore	$760/950	$760/950
Bangkok	$869/1085	$869/1085
Hong Kong	$1040/1285	$987-1185
Tokyo	$985/1375	$887/1265
Sydney	$423/520	$423/445

Melbourne	$515/750	$515/650
Brisbane	$510/750	$510/620
Cairns	$678/1015	$678/920

There's a $20 departure tax at the airport.

WARNING

This chapter is particularly vulnerable to change – prices for international travel are volatile, routes are introduced and cancelled, schedules change, rules are amended, special deals come and go, borders open and close. Airlines and governments seem to take a perverse pleasure in making price structures and regulations as complicated as possible and you should check directly with the airline or travel agent to make sure you understand how a fare (and ticket you may buy) works.

In addition, the travel industry is highly competitive and there are many lurks and perks. The upshot of this is that you should get opinions, quotes and advice from as many airlines and travel agents as possible before you part with your hard-earned cash. The details given in this chapter should be regarded only as pointers and cannot be any substitute for your own careful, up-to-date research.

Getting Around

AIR

Although New Zealand is a compact country and ground transport is generally quite good there are still places where flying can make a lot of sense, particularly if you've already done the same journey by land. Travel by land and sea between the North and South Islands can take a couple of days altogether. By air the same trip could be done in an hour or two and actually cost less. There are also great views to be enjoyed, particularly if your flight takes you over the mountains or volcanoes. Another time flying makes a lot of sense is when you have limited time to spend in the country. A variety of discounts can make flying in New Zealand quite economical.

New Zealand has two major domestic airlines: Air New Zealand and Ansett New Zealand. Several smaller airlines – Mt Cook Airline, Eagle Air and Air Nelson – are partly owned by Air New Zealand and have been grouped together as 'Air New Zealand Link' to complement the regular Air New Zealand services. With a host of connecting flights, the Air New Zealand National & Link network covers the country quite completely. Ansett's coverage is more limited but they, too, have many useful flights.

Discounts

Air New Zealand has regular listed economy fares, but it also has discounts which make it virtually unnecessary to ever have to pay the full fare.

If you purchase your tickets before you arrive in New Zealand you can save 12½% off the full fare, as the government's 12½% GST tax is usually charged when you buy the tickets in New Zealand.

On the other hand, the various discount fares available can save you even more than that, some being up to 50% off the regular fare, while some fares, such as the Air New Zealand Visit New Zealand fare, are GST exempt for visitors. These all have certain requirements, which are spelled out in the airlines' timetables. Conditions for equivalent fares are the same on both airlines, and it's best to book as far in advance as possible.

Both Air New Zealand and Ansett New Zealand offer very good deals if you have an International Student Identity Card (ISIC), a Youth Hostel (YHA) card or a VIP Backpackers card, giving you a 50% discount on standby flights. There's usually no problem getting a seat, except at the busiest times such as school holidays, Monday morning commuter flights and the like. It could be worth getting one of these cards just to save on airfares if you'll be doing much flying.

Airpasses

There are airpasses available based on a coupon system and available for all major flight destinations in New Zealand. The tickets are in the form of 'flight sector coupons'. Each flight uses up between one and four coupons, depending on how many sectors there are to the flight, ie how many stops it makes. So, if you were to take a direct flight from Rotorua to Christchurch, for example, it would cost you one coupon, but if you took a flight that transfers through Wellington, it would cost you two coupons. The passes can be open dated and even once you've set your dates, they can be changed again at little or no extra charge.

Ansett's routes are much more limited than Air New Zealand's, but you can change your itinerary anytime upon payment of a $25 surcharge. With Air New Zealand your route can be changed without penalty prior to starting the travel, but once you have taken your first flight, you cannot change your routing. Full refunds will be given prior to use of the coupons, but there is no refund after you've taken your first flight.

Air NZ Explore New Zealand Airpass – can only be bought outside NZ; minimum three coupons, maximum eight

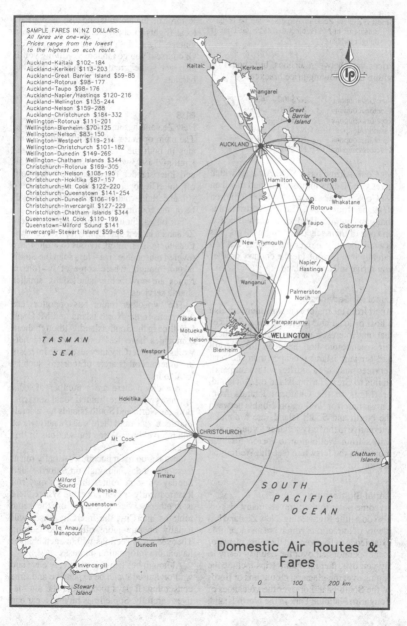

SAMPLE FARES IN NZ DOLLARS:
All fares are one-way.
Prices range from the lowest
to the highest on each route.

Auckland-Kaitaia $102-184
Auckland-Kerikeri $113-203
Auckland-Great Barrier Island $59-85
Auckland-Rotorua $98-177
Auckland-Taupo $98-176
Auckland-Napier/Hastings $120-216
Auckland-Wellington $135-244
Auckland-Nelson $159-288
Auckland-Christchurch $184-332
Wellington-Rotorua $111-201
Wellington-Blenheim $70-125
Wellington-Nelson $83-150
Wellington-Westport $119-214
Wellington-Christchurch $101-182
Wellington-Dunedin $149-269
Wellington-Chatham Islands $344
Christchurch-Rotorua $169-305
Christchurch-Nelson $108-195
Christchurch-Hokitika $87-157
Christchurch-Mt Cook $122-220
Christchurch-Queenstown $141-254
Christchurch-Dunedin $106-191
Christchurch-Invercargill $127-229
Christchurch-Chatham Islands $344
Queenstown-Mt Cook $110-199
Queenstown-Milford Sound $141
Invercargill-Stewart Island $59-68

TASMAN SEA

SOUTH PACIFIC OCEAN

Domestic Air Routes & Fares

0   100   200 km

Ansett NZ New Zealand Airpass – can be bought outside or in NZ (subject to 12½% GST tax if bought in NZ)

Prices vary between airlines, but should be within the following price brackets:

3 sectors/coupons	NZ$400 – 435
4 sectors/coupons	NZ$520 – 580
5 sectors/coupons	NZ$630 – 725
6 sectors/coupons	NZ$730 – 840
7 sectors/coupons	NZ$820 – 980
8 sectors/coupons	NZ$900 – 1120

Mt Cook Airline has a Kiwi Air Pass which gives you 30 days almost unlimited travel on Mt Cook Airline services for $999 (children $749, age four to 14). The only restriction is that you can only fly once in each direction on each of their scheduled flights. This pass is available only to overseas visitors, but you can buy it either outside the country or after you arrive in New Zealand.

Local Air Services

Apart from the major operators there are also a host of local and feeder airlines. Services that may interest travellers include Southern Air's economic hop between Invercargill and Stewart Island (cheaper than the boat services and a favourite with trampers), flights to Great Barrier Island off Auckland, or flights to the Chatham Islands from Christchurch or Wellington. Flights between the North and South Islands are a popular alternative to the ferry services – you can hop across from Wellington to Picton for little more than the ferry fare (see the Wellington section for details).

Aerial Sightseeing

At some point in their travels many visitors also do a little flightseeing. New Zealand has plenty of attractions which are an incredible experience to fly over and there are plenty of local operators all over the country ready to fly you over them. Popular trips include the flights over the glaciers, mountains or fiords of the South Island or over the volcanoes of Tongariro National Park in the North Island.

Rotorua on the North Island also has various local flights to enjoy including flights in a vintage Tiger Moth biplane and aerobatics. Of course if you go tandem skydiving you'll also get some great flightseeing into the bargain.

BUS

New Zealand has an extensive bus network. The main operator is InterCity, which operates in both the North and South Islands. Until mid-1993 when the New Zealand Rail and Interislander ferry services were sold off, InterCity operated all three systems; it's still uncertain what the effects of the sale will be on the country's transport network.

For buses, though, InterCity is still New Zealand's largest operator. With a few exceptions there is an InterCity bus to almost any town of reasonable size – less so in the South Island, though, where some of its former routes are now being handled by smaller shuttle services.

The two other major bus operators are Newmans in the North Island and Mt Cook Landline in the South Island. Although these companies have less extensive route networks than InterCity they also have interests in numerous other areas of tourism, such as local tours.

In addition there are a number of local operators with more limited local services. Both the North and South Islands have small shuttle services and there's also a network of 'alternative' buses – see the sections in this chapter.

Services on main bus routes usually run at least once a day, although on Saturday and Sunday on some routes the buses may run less frequently or even not at all. Where there is another service operating on the same route as InterCity, the InterCity buses will usually operate more often. The Getting There & Away sections within each chapter have more information on buses.

Although bus travel is relatively easy and well organised it can be expensive and time consuming. It pays to consider the alternatives carefully. Sometimes buying a car can

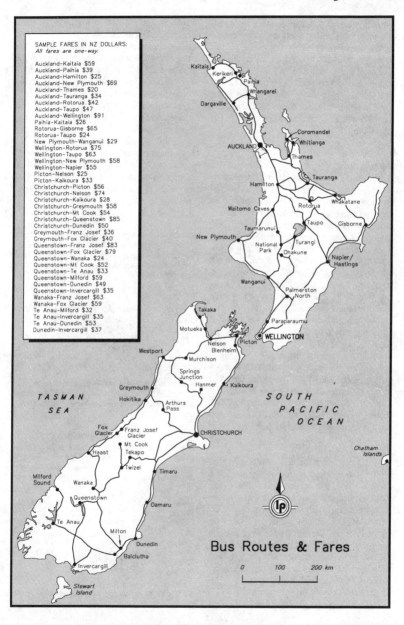

SAMPLE FARES IN NZ DOLLARS:
All fares are one-way.

Auckland-Kaitaia $59
Auckland-Paihia $39
Auckland-Hamilton $25
Auckland-New Plymouth $69
Auckland-Thames $20
Auckland-Tauranga $34
Auckland-Rotorua $42
Auckland-Taupo $47
Auckland-Wellington $91
Paihia-Kaitaia $26
Rotorua-Gisborne $65
Rotorua-Taupo $24
New Plymouth-Wanganui $29
Wellington-Rotorua $75
Wellington-Taupo $63
Wellington-New Plymouth $58
Wellington-Napier $55
Picton-Nelson $25
Picton-Kaikoura $33
Christchurch-Picton $56
Christchurch-Nelson $74
Christchurch-Kaikoura $28
Christchurch-Greymouth $58
Christchurch-Mt Cook $54
Christchurch-Queenstown $85
Christchurch-Dunedin $50
Greymouth-Franz Josef $36
Greymouth-Fox Glacier $40
Queenstown-Franz Josef $83
Queenstown-Fox Glacier $79
Queenstown-Wanaka $24
Queenstown-Mt Cook $52
Queenstown-Te Anau $33
Queenstown-Milford $59
Queenstown-Dunedin $49
Queenstown-Invercargill $35
Wanaka-Franz Josef $63
Wanaka-Fox Glacier $59
Te Anau-Milford $32
Te Anau-Invercargill $35
Te Anau-Dunedin $53
Dunedin-Invercargill $37

Bus Routes & Fares

0   100   200 km

actually work out cheaper than travelling by bus (see the Driving section). Slowness of travel seems particularly prevalent on the once-a-day InterCity services where the bus also operates as a means of local communication, picking up and dropping off mail at every little town along the way. Frequent stops at small cafes for cups of tea also slow things down, so it can take a long time to get anywhere.

Discounts

Although fares do vary from company to company they are generally fairly close and seem to play leapfrog with one another. The fares on the Bus Routes & Fares chart are indicative of the normal, standard fares. Due to competition, however, all the major bus lines offer a variety of discounts. If you are travelling by bus in New Zealand, knowing which discounts are being offered by which companies can cut your travel costs by as much as 50%. All the bus companies have free timetable booklets detailing all their discounts, where they travel and when, and it pays to get hold of these booklets and study them. You'll never have to pay full fare if you know how to get the discounts.

Most of the following discounts apply only to trips that would otherwise cost $20 or more. Group discounts are also available. InterCity 'Saver 30', Newmans and Mt Cook 'Budget Fares' offer a 30% discount; you must book ahead (the earlier the better) to get a spot, and buy your ticket at least one full day before you travel.

Other discounts include a 30% reduction on the standard fare for anyone with a YHA card, a VIP Backpackers card, a New Zealand Budget Backpackers Pass or an Independent Travellers Discount card. Discounts of 30% are also given for those over 60 years of age, for the blind or disabled, and for going and returning by the same route all on the same day. Students with a student identity card (the ISIC card is fine) receive a 20% discount, and holders of a YHA Travelcard receive a whopping 50% discount.

Travelpasses

The major bus lines also offer a variety of discount travelpasses. The passes allow for extra days in between bus trips; for example, you have 14 days in which to use the eight day InterCity Travelpass, rather than having to travel every day for eight days.

As with any unlimited travelpass of this type you have to do lots of travelling to make it pay off – they're best for people who want to see a lot within a short time. If you feel a Travelpass is what you'll need, be prepared to do a lot of pre-planning to work out an itinerary you can stick to. Also it's often necessary to book ahead on the buses to be sure of a seat.

InterCity New Zealand Travelpass – unlimited travel on any InterCity bus or train and (at the time of writing) on the Interislander ferry between the North and South Islands. Children under five travel free; those between five and 15 pay 67% of the adult fare. Costs are:

Days of Travel	InterCity NZ Travelpass	Complete in:
8 days	$396	14 days
15 days	$492	22 days
22 days	$644	31 days

Newmans Stopover Pass – $99; 14 days travel in all parts of the North Island except the Northland region; you can travel only in one direction, ie no backtracking

Newmans Flexi Pass – One Island Pass for either the North or South Island, or a Two Island Pass good for both islands; valid for three months; travel can be at any time within the three-month period. The cost is:

Days of Travel	One Island Pass	Two Island Pass
7 days	$329	$364
10 days	$380	$420
15 days	$450	$495
20 days	$540	$580
25 days	$650	$675
30 days	$720	$750

Mt Cook's Kiwi Coach Pass – covers both islands and includes a one-way air flight between Wellington and either Nelson or Blenheim; buy overseas or in NZ; children half price. The cost is:

Days of Travel	Kiwi Coach Pass	Complete in:
7 days	$398	11 days
10 days	$477	16 days
15 days	$553	23 days
25 days	$692	35 days
33 days	$735	45 days

Northliner Express – several discount passes for the Northland; valid 14 days from date of purchase; unlimited travel on various routes. Costs are Bay of Islands pass $49; Northland pass $79; Loop pass $69.

Shuttle Buses

There are a number of small shuttle bus companies offering useful services throughout the country. Typically they are smaller, cheaper and friendlier than the regular large buses. Some of them are designed especially with foreign travellers and/or backpackers in mind, and have lots of little 'extras' that make them especially attractive. Some shuttles operate useful routes especially for trampers, others are simply useful, operating on routes that the large bus companies do not serve.

Following are a few examples. In the North Island there are also shuttles around the East Cape, around Coromandel Peninsula, and up in Northland. In the South Island there are shuttles between Christchurch and Akaroa, and between Westport and Karamea.

North Island

Kiwi Safaris – 'Mud & Worm Loop' circle trip Auckland, Waitomo, Rotorua, Te Aroha & Thames (or reverse – it makes the loop in both directions); great entertainment on board; free pick-up & drop-off

Alpine Scenic Tours – between Turangi & National Park with stops at various spots in the Tongariro National Park that are especially useful for trampers, with extension services up to Taupo & Rotorua

C Tours – shuttle from New Plymouth to Rotorua, with a one-hour stop at Waitomo; gets you there faster than if you took the major bus lines

South Island

Kiwi Backpacker Track Special – from Queenstown to the Routeburn Track & Milford Sound

Skyline Connections' Abel Tasman Bus Services – Abel Tasman Track

Nelson Lakes Transport – between Nelson & St Arnaud for the Nelson Lakes National Park

Leisuretime Activities – between Tekapo & Mt Cook via Twizel & Glentanner

Coast to Coast Shuttle & Alpine Coach & Courier – both cross the South Island between Christchurch & Greymouth

New Zealand Shuttles – from Picton down the east coast as far as Oamaru

Skyline Connections – between Picton & Motueka (via Nelson) along the scenic Queen Charlotte Drive

'Alternative' Buses

In addition to the regular bus services and the shuttle buses, there are yet more buses in New Zealand, which for want of a better term we call 'alternative' buses. Several such bus companies operate tours lasting for several days in various parts of the country. In some places, notably the west coast of the South Island, these can be the best way of seeing the area if you don't have your own wheels, as hitchhiking is difficult and the more conventional bus services simply whiz past many of the most attractive spots.

On all these trips, the buses are comfortably fitted out, the atmosphere is casual and there are plenty of stops to see the sights along the way, plus stops for walks, picnics, boat cruises, recreational activities and so on. Usually all you need to bring is a sleeping bag, plus the usual travelling gear such as good walking shoes, warm clothes and rain gear, and your own food. Accommodation costs are extra; low-cost overnight accommodation is pre-booked, usually at hostels (the cost is about $10 to $13 a night), with an option to camp if you have your own tent ($7 or $8 a night). The exception is the Flying Kiwi bus, a 'rolling travellers home' which comes equipped with bunks and tents, included in the price.

Except for the Southern Explorer, which operates only in summer from October to May, all the buses operate all year round, with more frequent departures in summer.

Often they have negotiated special deals so you can get discounts on activities, accommodation, etc as you travel with them.

All the buses have pamphlets detailing their itineraries, departure times, and costs. Contact numbers are listed here for direct bookings. Many can also be booked through hostels and visitor information centres. All require advance booking, and usually a deposit. Be sure you understand the refund policy when you make your booking, in case you decide to cancel later on.

Kiwi Experience – Nth & Sth Islands; 15 routes; minumum of two to 18 days to complete one route, depending on the route; tickets valid for three to six months, so you can complete your travel any time within that period. For reservations: Auckland, 36 Customs St East, (PO Box 1553, ☎ (09) 366 1665); Wellington (☎ (04) 385 2153); Christchurch (☎ (03) 311 0550); and in Sydney, Australia, (☎ (02) 368 1282).

Magic Bus – Nth & Sth Islands, affiliated with InterCity buses. Bookings: at any hostel, or by telephoning Auckland (☎ (09) 358 5600); Taupo (☎ (07) 378 9032); Wellington (☎ (04) 387 2018); Picton (☎ (03) 573 6855); Nelson (☎ (03) 548 3290); Queenstown (☎ (03) 442 8178); Christchurch (☎ (03) 377 0951), Dunedin (☎ (03) 477 9238).

North Cape Green Beetle – Nth Island; departs from Auckland for the Northland region. Contact them in Auckland at the Outdoor Adventure Co (☎ (09) 358 5868); in Wellington at the Port Nicholson YHA Hostel (☎ (04) 801 7280); or in Queenstown at Backpacker Specialists (☎ (03) 442 8178).

Awesome Tours – Nth Island, affiliated with Kiwi Experience; Northland; tour lasts three days but passes are good for three months. Bookings: (☎ (03) 366 1665).

West Coast Express – Sth Island; six days Nelson to Queenstown via the West Coast route; cost $99; you can depart from either end of the line. For bookings in Nelson contact the Nelson YHA Hostel (☎ (03) 548 8817), or Tasman Towers (☎ (03) 548 7950); in Queenstown contact the Queenstown YHA Hostel (☎ (03) 442 8413) or Backpacking Specialist (☎ (03) 442 8178); or you can book at any of the hostels in Wanaka or in Auckland at the Outdoor Adventure Co (☎ (09) 358 5868).

Southern Explorer – Sth Island; four-day trip from Queenstown to Dunedin via Te Anau, Milford Sound, the 'southern scenic route' to Invercargill, through the Catlins and on to Dunedin; cost $110;

for $130 you can continue on from Dunedin to Queenstown or Te Anau. One-day sections available for individual day prices ($18 to $36). Bookings can be made in Queenstown at the Backpacking Specialists (☎ (03) 442 8178) or in Te Anau at the Te Anau Motor Park (☎ (03) 249 7820).

Flying Kiwi – the 'rolling travellers home'; includes bunks, tents, hot shower and kitchen, enabling the bus to camp out in some idyllic remote places and still keep everybody comfortable. They carry mountain bikes, a seven-metre Canadian canoe, a windsurfer, fishing gear and more. Sth Island trips include: 14-day Southern Exposure winter trip for $680; 17-day South Island summer trip for $890; and 24-day Grand Traverse trip for $1150. In the Nth Island they operate an eight-day Northern Wanderer trip; a four-day Northern Express trip, and a Northern Loop trip combining both. They also do various combinations of the Nth Island and Sth Island trips. Contact them at 2 Canterbury St, Picton (☎ & fax (03) 573 8126).

TRAIN

The InterCity bus company, which for years operated the network of InterCity buses, New Zealand Rail trains and the Interislander ferry service between the North and South Islands, sold the train and ferry network to an American company just as we were about to go to press. In late 1993 it wasn't clear how this would affect transport in New Zealand. The facts presented here were accurate before and shortly after the sale – our best advice would be to read what's here, take it as a general guide and pick up a copy of the New Zealand Rail timetable at your earliest convenience. It lists routes, times, fares etc and will contain current information.

There are just a few main train routes: Auckland to Rotorua, Auckland to Tauranga, Auckland to Wellington, Wellington to Napier, Picton to Christchurch, Christchurch to Greymouth, and Christchurch to Invercargill. See the relevant city sections for details. On a map you might notice quite a number of other branch railways, but these no longer have passenger trains.

The elimination of many of the smaller halts has made train travel a reasonably speedy method of getting from place to

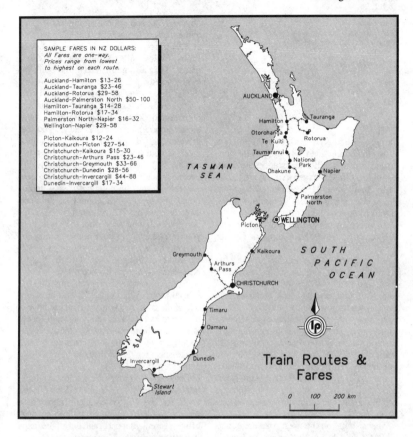

SAMPLE FARES IN NZ DOLLARS:
*All Fares are one-way.
Prices range from lowest
to highest on each route.*

Auckland-Hamilton $13-26
Auckland-Tauranga $23-46
Auckland-Rotorua $29-58
Auckland-Palmerston North $50-100
Hamilton-Tauranga $14-28
Hamilton-Rotorua $17-34
Palmerston North-Napier $16-32
Wellington-Napier $29-58

Picton-Kaikoura $12-24
Christchurch-Picton $27-54
Christchurch-Kaikoura $15-30
Christchurch-Arthurs Pass $23-46
Christchurch-Greymouth $33-66
Christchurch-Dunedin $28-56
Christchurch-Invercargill $44-88
Dunedin-Invercargill $17-34

Train Routes & Fares

0   100   200 km

place, and the trains are modern and comfortable. Trains in New Zealand have only one class. Fares are often cheaper than bus fares on the same routes. NZ Rail publishes a handy timetable booklet with current details on routes and fares. Since the major bus companies do the same, it's easy to compare routes, fares and convenience of departure times.

NZ Rail operates a nationwide Central Reservations Centre (☎ freephone (0800) 802 802; fax (04) 498 3721) open every day from 7 am to 9 pm. Reservations can also be made at any NZ Rail or accredited travel agent, and since it's a freephone number, many hostels and information centres will also make reservations for you.

Discounts

Like the major bus services, the rail services also offer a variety of discounts. A limited number of discounted seats are set aside on each train.

Advance booking is required for all these fares and the sooner you make your reservation, the better your chances are of getting the cheapest seats.

Super Saver Fare	50%
YHA Travelcard holders	50%
Blind or disabled travellers	50%
Saver Fare	30%
YHA card holders	30%
People over 60	30%
One-day excursion trips	30%
Economy Fare	20%
Students	20%

CAR

Driving around New Zealand is no problem – the roads are good and very well signposted, traffic is light and distances are short. Petrol (gasoline) is expensive – at around $1 a litre, that's about US$2.30 for a US gallon. Prices vary slightly from station to station, city to countryside, but only by a few cents; the average costs per litre might be around 93c for unleaded, 97c for super or 53c for diesel.

Kiwis drive on the left, as in the UK, Australia, Japan and most of South-East Asia, and there's a 'give way to the right' rule. This is interpreted in a rather strange fashion when you want to turn left and an oncoming vehicle is turning right into the same street. Since the oncoming vehicle is then on your right you have to give way to them. Ask a New Zealander to explain it to you before setting off! Some visitors have commented that New Zealand driving is terrible but probably most people find the driving in other countries terrible in one way or another.

Speed limits on the open road are generally 100 kph, in built-up areas the limit is usually 50 kph although in some places you may see a sign announcing LSZ. This stands for Limited Speed Zone and it means that although the speed limit in that zone is normally 100 kph, the speed limit is 50 kph when conditions are unsafe due to bad weather, limited visibility, pedestrians or cyclists or animals on the road, excessive traffic, or poor road conditions.

If you'll be driving in New Zealand, pick up a copy of *The Road Code* (Wellington: GP Publications, 1992, paperback). It will tell you all you need to know and though it costs around $15 it's well worth the investment –

obviously a good understanding of the rules of the road could save your life. It's available at AA offices, Bennett's Government Bookshops, Whitcoull's Bookshops and other places. They also publish a similar book for motorcyclists.

The drivers licences of Australia, USA, Canada, UK, Germany, the Netherlands, Switzerland, South Africa, Namibia and Fiji are all honoured in New Zealand; you can drive in NZ for up to one year with any of these. If your licence comes from any other country you'll need an International Driving Permit in addition to your regular licence. Get this in your home country, as International Driving Permits cannot be obtained directly from the NZ Automobile Association (AA). If you need one, they will help you to send away to your home country for one and have it mailed to you, or they will tell you everything you must do to obtain a New Zealand drivers licence.

To drive a motorcycle you must have a special motorcycle licence. If you are from one of the countries whose drivers licence is honoured by New Zealand, your motorcycle licence will be honoured too, otherwise you must have an International Driving Permit which specifies that it licences you to drive a motorcycle.

Excellent road maps are readily available in New Zealand; see Books & Maps in the Facts for the Visitor chapter. If you're a member of the AA you can go into any AA office, present your card, and get all the maps you want for free. There are a number of other useful benefits of AA membership including emergency breakdown services, free technical advice about your car, free legal assistance if you should get a traffic ticket, help in understanding the NZ driving rules, and so on.

Membership in the AA costs $66 per year plus a joining fee of $20, but if you can show you're a foreigner they have a special overseas visitors' rate of six months' membership for $50. The AA has reciprocal rights with the automobile associations of many countries, so if you are a member of an equivalent organisation overseas, you probably qualify for free reciprocal benefits from the AA in New Zealand. Remember to bring your card!

The AA also operates a mobile car inspection service, a very useful service if you're buying a used car. Details are given in the Buying a Car section.

Car Rental

The major operators – Avis, Budget, Hertz – have extensive fleets of cars in New Zealand with offices in almost every town. Typical costs for unlimited distance rental of a small car (Toyota Corolla, Mitsubishi Mirage) are around $125 to $150 per day, with a minimum rental of three days.

Medium-sized cars (Toyota Corona, Ford Telstar) are typically around $150 to $190 per day with unlimited km. In addition there's a daily insurance charge of around $20 a day.

Apart from the three major international operators there are also a number of others. Their rates often undercut the major operators but there may be more restrictions on use, and one-way rentals may not always be possible. All sorts of special deals are available. Sometimes you may find special one-way rental deals available when a company ends up with too many cars banked up at one place and too few at another. Operators often want cars to be shifted from Wellington to Auckland and from Christchurch to Picton – most renters travel in the opposite directions. Usually you must be at least 21 years old to rent a car in New Zealand and sometimes there will be an insurance excess if you're under 25.

Campervan Rental

Renting a campervan (also known as mobile homes, motor homes or, in US parlance, RVs) is an enormously popular way of getting around New Zealand. In some popular but out-of-the-way areas of the South Island almost every other vehicle seems to be a campervan.

With a campervan you have your transport and accommodation all in one neat package. At night you just find a campsite, connect up to the campsite power system, put a bucket

under the drain from the sink and you're at home. Of course you don't even have to find a campsite, you can simply find a quiet place off the road in many areas. Apart from transport and accommodation, you've also got your own kitchen on wheels.

There are numerous companies renting campervans and their costs vary with the type of vehicle and the time of year. For a basic van, suitable for two people, the cost could be around $100 per day during the low season (usually from 1 October to 30 April), $160 per day in the high season (usually from 1 May to 30 September). Some operators break the year into three seasons – low (1 May to 15 October), high (20 December to 31 March) and shoulder (the rest of the year). Shoulder season prices will fall somewhere between the high and low season rates. The costs in the high season can be as much as two or three times the low season rates.

For details on companies renting campervans in Auckland, see that chapter in the Getting There & Away section.

Although they're good fun and a pleasant way of seeing New Zealand, measured strictly on a cost basis they're not the cheapest way of getting around with a rental vehicle. You could rent a car and spend the night in camping ground cabins – even in motels at the high season when campervans are expensive – at comparable or lower costs.

Whether you rent a campervan or not, watch out for the colourful and exotic housetrucks you occasionally see around New Zealand. These individually built constructions often look like a collision between an elderly truck and a timber cottage, sometimes complete with shingle roof and bay windows! Many of these uniquely Kiwi contraptions look far too fragile for road use but they seem to travel all over the country.

Motorcycle Rental

It's also possible to hire a motorcycle for touring in New Zealand. Most of the motorcycle hire shops are in Auckland, and Christchurch has a few too; see those sections for details. You can hire anything from a little 50cc moped or 'Nifty-fifty', for zipping around town, to a big 750cc touring motorcycle.

As with cars, you can find motorcycles to buy on the buy-back system. Remember you will need a motorcycle licence; a car licence might get you by if you want to do something like toodle around on a moped, but if you want to drive a regular motorcycle (rental bikes are usually from 250cc to 750cc in size) then you'll have to have a motorcycle licence. See this Driving section for a list of which countries' drivers licences are honoured in New Zealand.

Buying a Car

If you're planning a longer stay and/or if there is a group of you, buying a car and then selling it again at the end of your travels can be one of the cheapest ways of seeing New Zealand. You're not tied to the bus schedules, nor do you find yourself waiting by the roadside with your thumb out looking for a ride.

Since most travellers arrive in New Zealand at Auckland, that's where most look to buy a car. Fortunately this is easy to do; it seems the city is inundated with cars for sale.

There are many ways to buy cars in Auckland. One of the most convenient for travellers is the 'buy-back system', where you buy a car from a dealer who guarantees to buy the car back from you at the end of your travels. The amount they offer to buy the car back from you depends on how long you've had the car and how far you've driven it. They may give you considerably less than you paid for it – maybe about 50% if you've had the car for a long time and taken it all around the country – but it still may come out cheaper than hiring a car or even taking the bus. Some dealers give you the right to sell the car to anyone else you like – a very convenient option since it means you can try to sell the car elsewhere and get the best price you can, but if you can't sell it or it seems to be taking a while, you know you can always take it back where you got it. Even if you are not obligated to sell the car back to them, they are obligated to buy it back from you if

you want to sell it back to them – that's the agreement.

The dealers who sell cars on the buy-back system are listed in the Auckland section. There is at least one similar dealer operating in Christchurch – Wheels (☎ (03) 366 4855) at 20 Manchester St. The Christchurch tourist information centre or the hostels there can probably tell you if there are others.

There are also many other ways of buying and selling cars in Auckland. You can find cars in the newspaper small ads just like anywhere else in the world. The *New Zealand Herald* carries such ads every day but they have an entire special car section on Wednesday. Other useful Auckland publications with car ads include the *Trade & Exchange*, coming out on Thursday, and the *Auto Trader*.

There are a number of car fairs in Auckland, where private individuals bring their cars to sell. It might be good to ring ahead to be sure the one you choose is still operating before you go out there, or the Auckland Visitor Information Centre should have current information. Come early, between 8 and 9.30 am, for the best choice of cars. Alternatively, you could try the car auctions.

Newmarket car park car fair; Broadway Ave near the corner of Khyber Pass Rd (☎ (09) 524 9183): Saturday mornings

Oriental Market carpark car fair; Britomart St at Customs St East (☎ (09) 524 9183): Saturday

North Shore car fair; at the car park on Wairau Rd in Takapuna (☎ (09) 480 5612): Saturday

Manukau car fair; South Auckland, in the parking lot of the giant shopping mall near the Manukau motorway offramp (☎ (09) 358 5000): Sunday

Ellerslie Racecourse car fair; near the Greenlane roundabout (☎ (09) 810 9212): Sunday

Turner's Car Auction (☎ (09) 525 1920), McNab St in Penrose; several times a week, with a special day set aside for budget vehicles

Hanmer Auctions (☎ (09) 579 2344), 830 Great South Rd, Penrose; also holds auctions several times weekly

The car fairs and auctions have lots of cars available from around $1000 to $4500. These are the real cheapies; a good, late-model used car from a dealer could cost around $8500 (with warranty).

In general, the cheapest prices are found at the auctions, where car after car is whizzed past a group of bidders, bids are taken, and the car is sold to the highest bidder – all within about 30 seconds. Next cheapest prices will be found at car fairs, where you have more time to browse around. You might try buying at an auction, and selling at a fair, to get the best overall deal. If you do buy at an auction, come early to inspect the vehicles before the hectic bidding starts.

Another way to find cheap cars for sale is to look on the notice boards of hostels, where you'll often see ads from other travellers keen to sell their cars and move on. Though less so than Auckland, Christchurch is another popular arrival and departure point, it has lots of cars, and the dry climate keeps them fairly rust free.

Make sure any car you buy has a WOF (Warrant of Fitness) and that the registration lasts for a reasonable period. You have to have the WOF certificate proving that the car is roadworthy in order to register it, and the WOF must be current (not more than 28 days old). To register a car, both you and the seller fill out a form which is filed at any post office. Registration can be purchased for either six months or a year.

Auckland has a very useful mobile inspection service, Car Inspection Services Ltd (☎ (09) 309 8084), who come to wherever you are and perform a thorough inspection on any car you are considering buying. The cost is $69 but it's worth it. The AA also does car inspections; the cost is the same for their mobile inspection service, or about $10 cheaper if you bring the car to an AA-approved mechanic. Since AA is a nationwide organisation, AA inspections are available all over New Zealand. The car fairs and auctions have inspection services standing by to provide on-the-spot inspections and since they're right there, they charge a reduced rate. It's a good idea to fork over the cost to get a car inspected if you're thinking of buying it; the money you spend doing that could save you buying a car that could drain

you of hundreds of dollars in repair bills later on. Another wise precaution before you buy a car is to ring the freephone Credit Check telephone number (☎ (0800) 658 934). With the licence plate and chassis numbers, they can confirm the ownership of the car and tell you if any outstanding debts are owed on it.

Car prices in New Zealand, which a few years ago were amazingly expensive due to high duties, have come down remarkably due to large numbers of used cars from Japan having been shipped to New Zealand. Although a few years ago when this started (around 1990) people shied away from the Japanese imports because of uncertainty about the availability of spare parts and other things the cars might need, by now there are so many Japanese imports in the country that you should have no problem finding anything you need for them.

Carshares
Travelpool (☎ (09) 307 0001), is a company based in Auckland which organises carshares countrywide. Drivers looking for riders to share expenses ring Travelpool with details of where they'll be going and when; travellers looking for a ride also ring the service to see if anyone is going their way. If a match is made, the traveller pays a commission for the service, the driver and traveller are put in contact, and they work out an arrangement for sharing costs for the trip. Even with the commission fee, sharing no more than the cost of petrol for the journey can still work out a lot cheaper than the bus, especially if there are a few people sharing the cost.

BOAT
Inter-Island Ferries
The Interislander ferry service, operating between Wellington in the North Island and Picton in the South Island, is covered in detail in the Wellington section.

Other regularly scheduled inter-island ferry services in New Zealand include those to the various islands off Auckland; see the Islands off Auckland section in the Auckland chapter.

Ferries also connect Stewart Island with the mainland at Bluff, near Invercargill; see the Stewart Island section for details.

Other Water Transport
There are various places where transport is more convenient by water than by land, especially in the Marlborough Sounds area where a number of places to stay can only be reached by water. Regular launch and water taxi services operate along the coast of the Abel Tasman National Park, departing from Nelson.

Other convenient ferry services include the ferries to Russell on the east side of the Northland, including the passenger ferry from Paihia and the car ferry crossing over from Opua. On the west side of the Northland is the convenient car ferry from Rawene to Kohukohu.

In other places transport over lakes is a significant way to get around and see things, such as at Queenstown, Taupo and Lake Waikaremoana. Sometimes the most interesting things to see are reached by water rather than by land; cruises on Milford and Doubtful Sounds in Fiordland National Park in the South Island, and on the Bay of Islands in the Northland are especially popular.

Sea kayaking has become increasingly popular in New Zealand in the last few years and now there are sea kayaking operators in many places. Sea kayaking is covered in the Outdoor Activities chapter and in all the relevant places throughout this book.

BICYCLE
In recent years there has been a marked increase in the number of cyclists touring New Zealand. You seem to see touring bicycles almost everywhere, especially in summer. There are lots of hills, so it's hard going at times, but it's a compact country and there's always plenty of variety. Many cyclists call New Zealand a cyclists' paradise – it's clean, green, uncrowded, unspoiled, friendly, there are plenty of places where you can camp out or get cheap accommodation in hostels, plenty of fresh water, the climate

is not too hot or too cold, the roads are good, bikes (whether to rent or buy) and cycling gear are readily available, as are bicycle repair services – you get the idea. Pick up a copy of *Cycle Touring in New Zealand* by Bruce Ringer (Auckland: Hodder & Stoughton, 1989, paperback) – it's full of useful information for cyclists, like where the steep hills are!

Apart from giving you independence from public transport or hitching, cycling also gives you the ideal means of getting around once you get to your destination. If you do get fed up with cycling you can always take it along on public transport for a while, or ship it ahead to a destination up the road and catch up with it when you get there.

The best way to carry a bike on public transport is often on one of the shuttle buses or 'alternative' buses; you can bus it on the major bus lines or on the train, but they'll only take it on a 'space available' basis (meaning it may not get on) and you'll have to pay extra for it (around $10). Many of the shuttle or 'alternative' buses, on the other hand, make sure they always have enough storage space to accommodate bikes and they usually will take them along as baggage for free. Kiwi Experience has a bus-bike plan in which you can bike or bus as much as you like (read on).

Many international airlines will carry your bicycle at no additional cost as 'sporting equipment'. Remember to bring your helmet, as NZ regulations require that you wear one.

Many bicycle rental operators in New Zealand offer daily and weekly bicycle hire, with negotiable monthly rates. Bicycle rental is listed in the Getting Around sections of cities and towns throughout this book. Costs vary widely – daily rates can be anywhere from around $10 to $25, weekly rates anywhere from around $50 to $125, and monthly rates anywhere from around $120 to $360; it all depends what kind of bike you get and where you get it from. A bit of time spent comparing prices will probably be time well spent. Practically all rental companies also have bicycle touring gear available –

panniers, tool kits, tents and, of course helmets, which are compulsory.

The Kiwi Experience bus people offer a bus-bike combination called Wild Cycles. When you hire a mountain bike from them, it also entitles you to send your luggage on ahead of you on their bus services at no extra cost. You also have the option of buying bus vouchers ($110 for five vouchers, $210 for 10 vouchers) which are each good for one day's travel on Kiwi Experience buses, giving you the option of taking the bus whenever you want – such as in bad weather, or over particularly long or difficult cycling stretches, or if you simply get tired of pedalling for a while and want a rest. You can start and end your tour at Auckland, Wellington, Queenstown or Christchurch, meaning you don't have to backtrack with the bike. Their bikes are good quality, fully-equipped, mountain bikes and their cost is about at the top of the bike-hire rate heap in the country: the cost is $25 a day, $125 a week, $240 for two weeks and $360 for three to five weeks, which isn't such a good deal for three weeks but at five weeks for the price of three it suddenly looks a lot better. They will make suggestions on cycling routes geared to your interests, cycling ability and fitness. For further details contact Wild Cycles (☎ (09) 366 1665, freephone (0800) 656 548).

Bicycle Tours of New Zealand (☎ & fax (09) 276 5218, mobile ☎ 026 354 6134) at 22 Walmsley Rd, Otahuhu, opposite the train station (PO Box 11-296, Auckland 1131) has much cheaper prices: the cost by the day/week/month is $15/50/120 for a women's bike; $15/60/150 for a men's bike; $20/70/180 for a mountain bike; plus they hire other types of bikes including racing bikes and tandems. Panniers, tents etc are available for hire and they also offer a number of free services including luggage storage, mail processing, message recording, maps, and route suggestions.

Pedaltours (☎ (09) 302 0968; fax 302 0967) at PO Box 37-575 Parnell, Auckland, offers a variety of guided cycle tours but they're not cheap – the cost is from $1595 for an eight-day tour around various areas in the North Island up to $4495 for a 19-day Grand Tour of the South Island. A vehicle goes along with the bikes to carry luggage and give you a rest from cycling if you like.

Of course you can also buy bicycles in New Zealand but prices are high for new bikes. If you want to 'own your own' you're better off bringing one in, or buying a used one. Hostel notice boards frequently have signs offering mountain bikes for sale, or check the newspaper small ads. You'll probably find the most bikes available are in Auckland and Christchurch.

HITCHING

Overall, New Zealand is a great place for hitching and, although almost anybody who does a fair amount of hitching will get stuck somewhere uncomfortable for an uncomfortably long period of time, most travellers rate it highly. It's pretty safe, the roads are not crowded but there are just enough cars to make things fairly easy, and the locals are well disposed towards hitchhikers.

The usual hitching rules apply. If you're standing in one spot, pick your location so drivers can see you easily and stop safely. Some hitchhikers report they have better luck hitching while walking alongside the road than when standing planted in one spot. You may find you have better luck getting picked up if you stand in a 50 kph speed zone rather than a 100 kph zone, as it's easier for the cars to stop. Often you'll have better luck the earlier it is in the day.

In larger towns it usually pays to get out

of town before starting to hitch, either by local bus or walking. You may pick up a lift on the way out, but don't count on it, it's much harder to get a ride in town with a pack. On the other hand on the open road, it's a lot easier to get a lift if you're wearing a pack. Learn which rides not to take – not just crazy drivers but also rides that leave you at inconvenient locations; wait for the right one.

Dress for the occasion – not in your fancy clothes ('they can afford to take the bus') or too shabbily ('don't want them in my car'). If someone else is already hitching on the same stretch of road remember to walk ahead of them so they get the first ride, or leave the road until they get a ride. Most importantly, be cautious and careful – there are some unpleasant people on the road in New Zealand just as there are anywhere else in the world. During our last visit two Swedish hitchhikers tossed their backpacks in the back of a car which stopped for them, and the car immediately drove off leaving them standing by the roadside, totally ripped off.

Generally hitching on the main routes in the North Island is good. In the South Island hitching down the east coast from Picton through Christchurch to Invercargill is mostly good. Elsewhere in the South Island there are hundreds of km of main roads with very little traffic. Expect long waits – even days – in some places. It's a good idea to have the InterCity, Newmans and Mt Cook timetables with you so you can flag a bus down if you're tired of hitching. Make sure you show the driver the colour of your money. Quite a few drivers have been stopped by hitchhikers who have then decided they can't afford the fare, so some bus drivers are wary about stopping unless they know you're prepared to pay.

It's easier hitching alone if you are male. Unfortunately, even though New Zealand is basically a safe country for women, a woman on her own may experience some tricky – if not dangerous – situations. Better to travel with someone else if possible. Many hostels have local hints for hitching (such as what bus to get out of town, where to hitch from) on their notice boards.

Please note that hitching is not always a safe way of getting around. Just because we explain how it works doesn't mean we recommend it.

LOCAL TRANSPORT
To/From the Airport
In all the large cities and even many smaller ones, shuttle services operate to and from the airports. Shuttle services are good value, costing less than taxis when there are one or two people going to the airport, though if you have a group of around four people together to split the cost a taxi can work out about the same.

Bus
There are bus services in most larger cities but with a few honourable exceptions they are mainly daytime, weekday operations. On weekends and particularly on Sunday buses can be very difficult to find.

Train
The only city with a good suburban train service is Wellington, with regular trains up the main corridors to the north. It's the only electrified railway in New Zealand.

Taxi
Although there are plenty of taxis in the major towns they rarely 'cruise'. If you want a taxi you usually either have to phone for one or go to a taxi rank.

Bicycle
Bicycles can be rented by the hour, day or week in most major cities and in many smaller locales. Rentals by the week for longer trips are becoming more common. See the Bicycle section earlier in this chapter.

TOURS
Tours can sometimes be a useful way of getting around, especially if you're travelling in an area that is otherwise hard to reach, or when you have limited time, or when you want the benefit of commentary. Backpacker types often use the 'alternative' buses as a

sort of informal tour; see these in the Bus section.

Otherwise there are a variety of more conventional tours. Thrifty Tours, operated by InterCity, are indeed thrifty, using a combination of tour buses and public transport to create a variety of short and long tours all over New Zealand. Mt Cook Line, operators of the Mt Cook Landline bus network and Mt Cook Airline, also offers a variety of tours around New Zealand. Gray Line is another major tour operator, offering a variety of one-day tours in various cities and towns, plus inter-city tours. All of these are major companies which can be contacted through virtually any travel agent or visitor information centre in New Zealand, or through travel agents or the NZTB before you arrive in New Zealand.

NORTH ISLAND

Auckland

On the shores of Waitemata and Manukau harbours, Auckland is almost surrounded by water and covered in volcanic hills. It is the main entry point for visitors to New Zealand, with people arriving from all over the world. It has many things to see, lots of accommodation and restaurants, and some good places for night-time entertainment.

Auckland is also the biggest city in New Zealand (population 896,000) and in recent years has become the 'big city' for the Polynesian islands of the South Pacific. So many islanders from New Zealand's Pacific neighbours have moved to Auckland that it now has the largest concentration of Polynesians in the world, and more recently it has been attracting immigrants from Asia as well. All the foreign influences help to give Auckland a much more cosmopolitan atmosphere than other cities in New Zealand.

Sprawling between the two large harbours Auckland, like Sydney, has a lot of enthusiastic yachties who sail back, forth and around on weekends and make it look very picturesque – the city is nicknamed 'the City of Sails'.

Also like Sydney it has a harbour bridge, which was opened in 1959 with due pomp and ceremony and four traffic lanes. Probably to no one's surprise it was discovered that the reason not many people lived on the North Shore was because there hadn't been a bridge, and as soon as there was one, so many people moved there to live that the bridge wasn't big enough. Fortunately, the Japanese came to the rescue and 'clipped' two more lanes on each side (known locally as the 'Nippon Clippons') to convert it to eight streams of cars.

History

Maoris settled in the Auckland area as early as 1350 AD. Other Maori peoples desired the fertile land in succeeding years, and eventually the volcanic cones around the area were topped by pas (fortified Maori settlements).

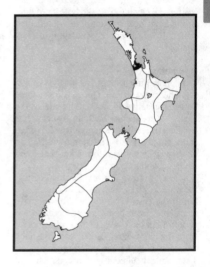

However, tribal wars and epidemics ravaged the settlements and by 1840, when Europeans came to settle here, the area was almost deserted.

From early colonial times the colonial administrative centre of New Zealand had been in the Northland at Russell, but after the signing of the Treaty of Waitangi in 1840, Captain William Hobson, New Zealand's first governor, decided to move the capital south to a more central position. The site of Auckland was chosen principally for its fine harbour and good soil and in September 1840 officials came down from Russell to formally proclaim Auckland as capital of New Zealand. Governor Hobson named the new settlement after his former commander, Lord Auckland, who was at that time the Viceroy of India and a British hero. The new settlement did not get off to as prosperous a start as was hoped, however, and 25 years later, in 1865, the capital was moved once again, this time south to Wellington.

Later in the century, a gold rush in the Thames goldfields and a great increase in the area's agricultural production did much to revive Auckland. Since the turn of the century the city has been the fastest growing city in New Zealand, and it now holds just over 25% of the entire population of New Zealand.

Orientation

The commercial heart of Auckland is Queen St, which runs from Queen Elizabeth II Square – usually called 'QE II Square' by the locals – near the Ferry Building by the waterfront, up (literally) to Karangahape Rd (often called simply 'K Rd'), passing Aotea Square on the way, with the information centre and the large Aotea Centre.

The Downtown Airline Terminal is near the waterfront; the railway station is about a km to the east. Long-distance buses arrive and depart from both places; the airport is about 21 km south-west of the centre. Not far from the city centre, Parnell and Ponsonby are popular restaurant and shopping areas. There's plenty of good accommodation right in the city centre, in Parnell nearby, and in other nearby districts.

To the east of Queen St is Albert Park, a popular lunch-time haven for city workers and students and the venue for free rock concerts on Sunday afternoons in summer. Beyond the park is Auckland University, the largest in New Zealand, where visitors are welcome to most activities.

Quay St runs along the waterfront, and Customs St is parallel, one block inland; it's called Customs St East on one side of Queen St, Customs St West on the other.

Information

All telephone numbers in Auckland have an 09 prefix if you are calling them from a long distance (even within the region).

Tourist Information The Auckland Visitor Centre (☎ 366 6888; fax 366 6893) is at 299 Queen St on Aotea Square. The centre has all sorts of information about Auckland, the surrounding area, and all of New Zealand, and

can supply the answers to most visitors' questions. The friendly and helpful staff also make bookings for every form of transport, tours, activities, accommodation and about anything else you can think of in New Zealand, and they keep an up-to-date list of all kinds of activities. The office is open every day from 9 am to 5 pm.

Another branch of the same office (☎ 366 0691) is in a kiosk on Queen Elizabeth II Square at the foot of Queen St. It, too, is open every day from 9 am to 5 pm.

Other visitor information centres in the Auckland area include the Manukau Tourist Information Centre (☎ 275 5321; fax 275 5578) located on George Bolt Memorial Drive, between the city and the airport; centres at the airport in both the Domestic (☎ 275 0789) and International (☎ 275 6467) Terminals; and the Takapuna Visitor Information Centre (☎ 486 8670) on Hurstmere Rd in Takapuna, on the North Shore.

The Department of Conservation (DOC) information centre (☎ 307 1465; fax 377 2919) in the Sheraton complex on the corner of Karangahape Rd and Liverpool St has a wealth of information and maps on all of New Zealand's national parks, forest parks, walkways and tracks, nature reserves, etc. If you are interested in doing some walks or experiencing some of NZ's amazing natural areas, drop in here when you arrive in the country and they'll help you to plan an itinerary to suit your interests, guiding you to areas off the beaten track as well as providing information on the more popular places. From October to Easter the office is open Monday to Friday from 8.30 am to 5.30 pm, with additional Saturday hours of 10 am to 1 pm from December to February. From Easter to October it's open Monday to Friday, 9 am to 4.30 pm.

The Automobile Association (AA) office (☎ 377 4660; fax 309 4563) is at 99 Albert St, on the corner of Albert and Victoria Sts. If you're a member of an equivalent overseas auto club you can use its services; it has free accommodation and campsite directories for both islands, and excellent maps. It's open Monday to Friday from 8.30 am to 5 pm. In the same building, the Department of Land and Survey Information (DOSLI) (☎ 377 1899; fax 307 1025) sells a complete selection of DOSLI maps including topographical maps, national park maps, street maps, road atlases and so on. It's open Monday to Friday from 8 am to 4.30 pm.

Also check out the annual *Auckland A to Z Visitors Guide* booklet, the monthly *Auckland Great Time Guide* booklet, and the weekly *Auckland Tourist Times* newspaper. All are free at the Visitor Centre and all contain useful information for visitors.

Money The Bank of New Zealand branch at the airport is open for all international arrivals and departures.

In the centre, the Downtown Airline Terminal on Quay St has an automatic 24-hour change machine – stick in notes of Australia, Canada, Japan, UK, USA, Japan, Germany, France, Italy, Switzerland and a few other countries and it will pop you out the equivalent amount in New Zealand money.

Nearby at the Ferry Building on Quay St, Interforex changes money every day from 8 am to 8 pm. Thomas Cook has Bureaux de Change on the corner of Queen and Customs Sts, at 96 Queen St, and at 107 Queen St. Travelex changes money in the Ansett Travel Shop at 75 Queen St, as does the Westpac Bank at 79 Queen St. The Regency Duty Free Shop in the Finance Plaza on the corner of Queen and Victoria Sts also changes money. Otherwise you can change money at any bank Monday to Friday from 9 am to 4.30 pm.

The American Express Travel Services Office (☎ 379 8243; fax 303 4046) is at 101 Queen St, while the American Express Card Division (☎ 367 4567; fax 367 4558) is at 67-69 Symonds St.

Post A number of post offices are scattered around the city centre. Poste Restante is held at the CPO in the Bledisloe Building in Wellesley St West, near the corner of Queen St. Post offices are open Monday to Friday from 9 am to 5 pm.

Consulates Although Auckland is the largest city in New Zealand it is not the capital, that honour goes to Wellington. Most diplomatic offices are in the capital but there are a number of consulates in Auckland. These are some of them, but there are more; the Auckland Visitor Centre keeps a complete list. They include:

Australia
> Union House, 32-38 Quay St, City (☎ 303 2429)

Canada
> 9th Floor, Jetset Centre, 48 Emily Place, City (☎ 309 3690)

Cook Islands
> 330 Parnell Rd, Parnell (☎ 309 1875)

Denmark
> 273 Bleakhouse Rd, Howick (☎ 537 3099)

Finland
> 10 Heather St, Parnell (☎ 309 2969)

Germany
> 5th Floor, 52 Symonds St, City (☎ 377 3460)

Ireland
> Dingwall Building, 87 Queen St, City (☎ 302 2867)

Japan
> 6th Floor, National Mutual Building, 37-45 Shortland St, City (☎ 303 4106)

Netherlands
> 7th Floor, 90 Symonds St, City (☎ 379 5399)

Sweden
> Targetti House, 60 Parnell Rd, Parnell (☎ 373 5332)

UK
> Fay Richwhite Building, 151 Queen St, corner Queen & Wyndham Sts, City (☎ 303 2973)

USA
> General Building, corner Shortland & O'Connell Sts, City (☎ 303 2724)

Travel Agencies Naturally Auckland is full of travel agencies; there are probably hundreds. Several of them specialise in domestic travel within New Zealand, including adventure travel, young peoples' and backpackers travel, making bookings for all activities, tours, transport, accommodation, etc within New Zealand. They will take the time to go over your plans with you, see what your interests are and how much time you have, and help you to set up a plan. Sometimes you can get discounts if you book through them. Several have offices at the larger hostels.

The Auckland Central Backpackers

Travel Centre (☎ 358 4874; fax 358 4871) is downstairs at the Auckland Central Backpackers at 9 Fort St, just off Queen St. They're open every day from 8 am to 8 pm and they welcome travellers to use it as a resource centre as well as a travel agency – you're welcome to come and ask anything you want to know about travel in New Zealand, even if you're not buying anything. Independent Travel Services (☎ 303 3442; fax 303 3443) on the ground floor of the Central City Backpackers (CCB) at 26 Lorne St offers similar services and it's open every day from 8 am to 7 pm.

The YHA Travel Centre (☎ 379 4224; fax 366 6275) at 36 Customs St East, on the corner of Gore St, provides the same services, with discounts for YHA members. It's open Monday to Friday from 9 am to 5 pm. Another YHA Travel Centre is in the lobby of the Auckland City YHA Hostel (☎ 309 2802; fax 373 5083) on the corner of City Rd and Liverpool St. In addition to domestic travel, the YHA Travel Centre also handles international air tickets, with good prices for students and young people.

The Outdoor Adventure Co (☎ 358 5868; fax 358 5878) in the Ferry Building on Quay St also specialises in NZ travel. They're open Monday to Friday from 9 am to 5.30 pm, weekends from 9.30 am to 4 pm, with longer hours in summer.

The Student Travel Agency (STA) International Travellers Centre (☎ 309 9995; fax 309 9829) is at 10 High St. It has free information and makes bookings for international travel only. It's open from 9 am to 5 pm Monday to Friday. Other good places to check for cheap international airfares are Flight Centres (☎ 358 0074, 377 4655) with several offices around Auckland, and Skytrain (☎ 309 6896, 302 2014; fax 302 2015) at 37 High St.

Airlines Auckland is the main arrival and departure point for international airlines although there are also flights through Wellington and Christchurch, principally from Australia. International and domestic airlines serving Auckland include:

Aerolineas Argentinas
1 Queen St (☎ 379 3675)
Air New Zealand
Queen Elizabeth II Square, Quay St; 139 Queen St; 264 Karangahape Rd; Airport Domestic Terminal (☎ 357 3000)
Air Pacific
404 Queen St (☎ 379 2404)
Ansett New Zealand
75 Queen St (☎ 302 2146)
British Airways
corner Queen & Customs Sts (☎ 367 7500)
Canadian Airlines International
44-48 Emily Place (☎ 309 0735)
Cathay Pacific
191 Queen St (☎ 379 0861)
Continental Airlines
99 Albert St (☎ 379 5680)
Delta Airlines
87 Queen St (☎ 379 3370)
Garuda Indonesia
120 Albert St (☎ 366 1855)
Japan Airlines
120 Albert St (☎ 379 9906)
Mt Cook Airline
75 Queen St (☎ 309 5395)
Polynesian Airlines
283 Karangahape Rd (☎ 309 5396)
Qantas
154 Queen St (☎ 379 0306, freephone (0800) 808 767)
Singapore Airlines
West Plaza Building, corner Albert & Fanshawe Sts (☎ 379 3209)
Thai Airways International
22 Fanshawe St (☎ 377 3886)
TWA
69 Beach Rd (☎ 373 4826)
United Airlines
7 City Rd (☎ 379 3800).

Local airlines operating from Auckland include:

Great Barrier Airlines
Auckland Domestic Terminal (☎ 275 9120)
Gulf Island Air
Waiheke Island (☎ & fax 372 7428)

Bookshops Whitcoull's at 186 Queen St is a huge bookshop with good sections on New Zealand books, travel books, fiction and anything else you can think of. The Faraway Places bookshop in Exchange Lane, 95 Queen St opposite Fort St, specialises in travel guides to New Zealand, the Pacific and the world, and has plenty of maps; they also carry foreign language books (new, used and trade-ins) and Lonely Planet books in several languages. Bennett's Government Bookshop at 25 Rutland St, opposite the library, has a good selection of books about New Zealand, Maori subjects, travel guides and maps. Among these three, you can probably find any book you can think of about New Zealand.

For second-hand books, try Bloomsbury Books upstairs at 10 O'Connell St off Shortland St, David Thomas' Bookshop at 2 Lorne St near the corner of Victoria St, Jason Secondhand Books at 50 High St beside the Simple Cottage vegetarian restaurant, or the Anah Dunsheath Bookshop on High St near Vulcan Lane. Other second-hand book dealers include the Old Book Cellar at 13 Commerce St, the David Young Bookshop at 82 Victoria St West, the Rare Book Shop at 6 High St, St Kevins Arcade at 183 Karangahape Rd and Stratford Books in the QE II Square.

Downstairs in the cellar of the Old Customs House, corner of Customs St West and Lower Albert Rd, the Pathfinder Bookshop has a large collection of New Age books, as does Goodey's New Age Bookshop, at 20 Chancery St half a block off High St. The Polynesian Bookshop at 283 Karangahape Rd has an excellent selection of books on the islands of the South Pacific.

Newspapers The *Auckland Tourist Times* is a useful free weekly newspaper of visitor information, events and activities in the city. The *New Zealand Herald* is the Auckland morning daily.

Maps The mini-map series is very handy for finding your way around Auckland – small enough for a pocket, yet detailed enough to show everything. You can get good maps of Auckland and other places in New Zealand from the Auckland Visitor Centre, the AA, DOSLI (see Tourist Information), Bennett's Government Bookshop and the Faraway Places bookshop. The free tourist information booklets *Auckland A to Z Visitors Guide*

and the *Auckland Good Time Guide* contain good maps of the city centre.

Sports Shops Auckland has a good variety of sports shops where you can buy camping and sports equipment. Second-hand sports shops include the Sports Bazaar on the corner of Karangahape and Gundry Rds and the 2nd Hand Sports Shop at 14 Upper Queen St.

The Auckland Domain

Covering about 80 hectares, the Auckland Domain, near the centre of the city, is a lovely public park that's worth wandering through to take a look at the Winter Gardens and the Auckland Museum. It's a pleasant walk down through the Domain and back through the university grounds and Albert Park to Queen St.

Auckland Museum

If you're only going to see one thing in Auckland, see one of Auckland's magnificent museums. The Auckland Museum in the Domain has a tremendous display of Maori artefacts and culture: pride of place goes to a magnificent 25-metre-long war canoe, but there are many other examples of the Maoris' arts and lifestyle. The museum also houses a fine display of South Pacific items and NZ wildlife, including a giant moa model, and displays thousands of other interesting objects from around the world.

An excellent one-hour guided tour of the Maori exhibits, followed by a half-hour performance of traditional Maori music and dance, costs $6.50 (children $1.50, students & seniors $5.50, family $13). The tours begin at 10.30 am and 12.45 pm daily. These are a good introduction to Maori culture, and apart from Rotorua this is about the only chance you'll get to see Maori culture so well represented on a regular basis.

The museum is open from 10 am to 5 pm daily; admission is free. It's about a 25-minute walk from Queen St up through the Domain, or you can catch bus Nos 63, 64 or 65 from the Downtown Bus Terminal, or the Bus-A-Bout or United Airlines Explorer bus.

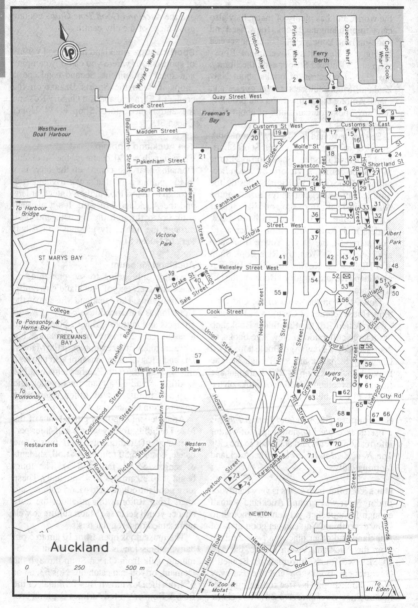

Westhaven
Boat Harbour

Wynyard Wharf

Hobson Wharf

Princes Wharf

Ferry
Berth

Queens Wharf

Captain
Cook
Wharf

Jellicoe Street

Freeman's
Bay

Quay Street West

Beaumont Street

Madden Street

Pakenham Street

Gaunt Street

Halsey Street

Customs St West

Customs St East

Fort

Shortland St

Albert
Park

Fanshawe Street

Victoria
Park

Victoria Street

To Harbour
Bridge

ST MARYS BAY

Street West

Wellesley Street West

Drake St

Sale Street

Cook Street

College Hill

To Ponsonby &
Herne Bay

FREEMANS
BAY

Franklin Road

To Ponsonby

Union Street

Nelson Street

Hobson Street

Vincent Street

Greys Avenue

Mayoral
Drive

Myers
Park

Queen Street

City Rd

Restaurants

Collingwood Street

Anglesea Street

Ponsonby Road

Picton Street

Hepburn Street

Howe Street

Wellington Street

Western
Park

Day St

Pitt Street

Road

Karangahape

Hopetoun Street

NEWTON

Newton

Upper Queen Street

Symonds Street

Great North Road

To Zoo &
Motat

Road

To
Mt Eden

Auckland

0   250   500 m

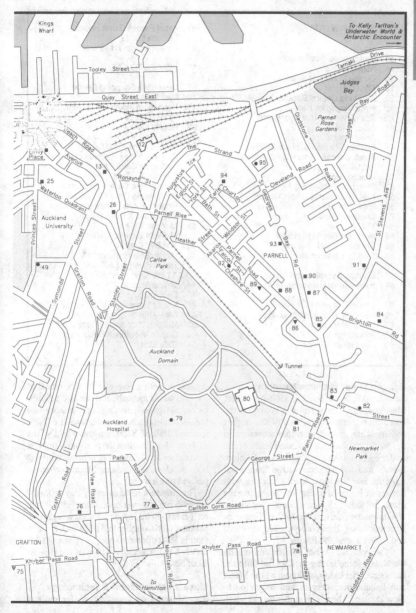

■ PLACES TO STAY

4	Travelodge
13	Harbourview Station Hotel
14	Aspen Lodge
16	Queen St Backpackers
18	Regent Hotel
23	Auckland Central Backpackers (ACB)
25	Hyatt Kingsgate Hotel
26	Downtown Backpackers Hostel
41	Albion Hotel
42	Abby's Hotel
47	Central City Backpackers (CCB)
53	Aotea Central Square Backpackers Hostel
55	Imperial Hotel
57	Freeman's Travellers' Hotel
58	Kiwi Hilton Backpackers Hostel
62	Park Towers Hotel
63	Chateau Maples
64	YMCA
65	Auckland City YHA Hostel
66	Sheraton Hotel
68	Railton Travel Hotel
76	YWCA
77	Georgia Backpackers Hostel
81	International Backpackers-Alan's Place
84	Chalet Chevron
85	Parnell's Village Motor Lodge
87	Leadbetter Lodge
88	Parnell Inn
90	City Garden Lodge
91	Ascot Parnell Guest House
93	Lantana Lodge
94	Parnell Lodge YHA Hostel

▼ PLACES TO EAT

7	Downtown Shopping Centre
10	Kiwi Tavern
15	Poppadom Indian Restaurant
27	Hotel De Brett
28	Rupina Cafe
29	Kerouac
30	BNZ Tower & Food Court
32	Simple Cottage Restaurant, La Cucina Cafe, Paneton & Periwinkles Cafe
33	Hard to Find Cafe & Badgers
34	Boulangerie Croix du Sud & 61High St
35	Finance Plaza (Tapas Bar, Margarita's & Food Court)
36	Mexican Cafe & Midnight Express Cafe
38	The Bird Cage
42	Middle East Restaurant & Tony's Steak & Seafood
43	A Little Italy
44	Strand Arcade
45	Civic Tavern
46	Krautz Expresso Bar & Ferlinghetti's
47	Cafe Aroma, Tony's Restaurant
53	Mekong Vietnamese Restaurant & Gopals Vegetarian Restaurant
54	Cafe Efes

Hobson Wharf Maritime Museum

New in August 1993, the Hobson Wharf Maritime Museum at Hobson Wharf on the downtown waterfront is one of the largest and most interesting maritime museums in the world, exploring a thousand years of the seafaring history of this Pacific island nation. It's an unusual and innovative 'hands-on' museum and maritime learning centre with dozens of impressive displays including the giant 76-foot (25-metre) outrigger canoe *Taratai* that modern navigator Jim Siers constructed using thousand-year-old methods and sailed across the Pacific.

Other vessels are both inside and out on the water, some taking visitors out onto the harbour. Other exhibits illuminate the Maori and Pakeha discovery of and migration to New Zealand; there's an authentic old whaling station with a 26-metre lifesize mural of a sperm whale and calf, and hands-on exhibits on navigation, fishing, oral history and NZ genealogy. Also here are the New Zealand Hall of Yachting, the world's first jet-boat (the *Hamilton Jet)* invented in New Zealand in 1957, a sailing school, working boat builders, sail makers, Maori craftspeople and much more.

The museum is open every day from 10 am to 5 pm, staying open later, until 9 pm, on Friday, Saturday and Sunday nights in summer (1 November to 31 March). Admission is $9 (children to age 17 & seniors $4, family $18). You can get here on the Bus-A-Bout bus.

Museum of Transport & Technology

The Museum of Transport & Technology

58	Caravanserai Tea House & Merchant Mezze Bar	19	Tepid Baths ('The Teps')
59	Mosquito Cafe	20	Turners & Growers Building & Watershed Theatre
60	Baan Thai Restaurant	21	Bungy Jumping Site
61	Espresso Temple & Cafe Hasan Baba	22	Shakespeare Tavern & Brewery
69	Verona Cafe	24	Rugby Pub Tavern
70	McDonald's	31	STA
72	El Inca	35	Finance Plaza (Tapas Bar, Margarita's & Food Court)
73	Restaurant 360°		
74	Urbi et Orbi Cafe	37	Automobile Association (AA) & DOSLI
75	Maharajah Indian Restaurant		
86	Kebab Kid	38	The Bird Cage
89	Parnell Village	39	Victoria Park Market
		40	Kitty O'Brien's Irish Pub
		45	Civic Tavern
	OTHER	48	Auckland City Art Gallery
		49	Maidment Theatre
1	Hobson Wharf Maritime Museum	50	Bennett's Government Bookshop
2	Dockside Markets	51	Public Library
3	Ferry Building	52	CPO
5	Downtown Airline Terminal & The Rock Garden	56	Aotea Square, Auckland Visitors Information Centre & Town Hall
6	Queen Elizabeth II ('QE II') Square & Information Kiosk	67	Department of Conservation (DOC)
		71	Mercury Playhouse Theatre
7	Downtown Shopping Centre	72	El Inca
8	Downtown Bus Terminal	78	Carlton Club Tavern
9	YHA Travel Centre & Blarney Stone Irish Pub	79	Wintergardens
		80	Auckland Museum
10	Kiwi Tavern	82	Ewelme Cottage
11	China Oriental Market	83	Kinder House
12	Railway Station	92	Rick's Blue Falcon
17	Old Customs House	95	Nags Head Tavern

(MOTAT) is out at Western Springs, on the Great North Rd. It has many interesting exhibits including one about pioneer aviator Richard Pearce. It's quite possible that this eccentric South Island farmer actually flew before the Wright brothers, but to Pearce a mere hop off the ground wasn't flying and he made no personal claims. During his life he produced a steady stream of inventions and devices, though not surprisingly he was a lousy farmer!

Another section of Motat, the Sir Keith Park Memorial Airfield features displays of rare and historic aircraft. Admission to Motat includes admission to the airfield, and the museum runs electric trams regularly to the site, one km away. Trams also operate every 10 minutes between Motat and the zoo, costing $1 return.

Motat is open from 9 am to 5 pm weekdays and 10 am to 5 pm on weekends and holidays; admission is $8.50 (children $4.50, seniors $6.50, family $17). Get there on a Pt Chevalier bus No 045 from the city, departing from Customs St West, or on the Bus-A-Bout.

Auckland Zoo

The Auckland Zoo is on Motions Rd off Great North Rd in the same area as Motat and is connected to it by a regular tram service. It has a nocturnal house (day is night) where you can see kiwis foraging for worms. Kiwis are not in fact rare, it's just that they are rarely seen in their natural setting because of their nocturnal habits. There's also a large walk-through aviary where you can observe native birds. Amongst the real rarities in the zoo are the tuataras, the prehistoric NZ reptiles. The usual lions, hippos, rhinos, etc can also be seen.

The zoo is open every day from 9.30 am to 5.30 pm (last admission 4.15 pm); entry is $9 (children $4.50, seniors $5, family $24). The Pt Chevalier bus No 045 from Customs St West will get you to both Motat and the zoo, as will the Bus-A-Bout.

Kelly Tarlton's Underwater World & Antarctic Encounter

New York may have mythical crocodiles in its sewers but Auckland certainly does have sharks in its stormwater tanks. At Orakei Wharf on Tamaki Drive, Kelly Tarlton's is a unique aquarium housed in old stormwater holding tanks. An acrylic tunnel runs through the aquarium and you travel through on a moving footpath, with the fish swimming all around you. You can step off at any time to take a better look and the whole place is designed to recreate the experience of scuba diving around the coast of New Zealand. The aquarium is divided into two sections, a reef fish area and a sharks and stingrays area. Kelly Tarlton's was devised and developed by NZ diver Kelly Tarlton who unfortunately died in 1985, only seven weeks after his aquarium opened.

Opened in December 1993, the Antarctic Encounter is a new part of Kelly Tarlton's and it's the only place of its kind in the world. It's not a display but rather a complete Antarctic environment. Going through a replica of Scott's 1911 Antarctic hut, you then climb aboard a heated Snow Cat, the type of vehicle used in Antarctica, and enter an environment where a penguin colony lives at -7°C, then go through an attack by an Orca killer whale and on to a very cold below-the-ice aquarium full of life that exists below the Antarctic ice cap. Finally there's a visit to an Antarctic scientific base of the future, and exhibits on the history of Antarctica.

One ticket admits you to all parts of Underwater World; the cost is $15 (children $7.50). It's open every day from 9 am to 9 pm. You can get there on bus No 72, 73, 74 or 75 from the Downtown Terminal, or on the United Airlines Explorer bus or the Bus-A-Bout.

Auckland City Art Gallery

The Auckland City Art Gallery is two blocks off Queen St, on the corner of Wellesley St East and Kitchener St, beside Albert Park. The gallery has an extensive collection of NZ art including many works by Colin McCahon and Frances Hodgkins, along with international works and occasional special exhibits. It's open every day from 10 am to 4.30 pm; admission is free.

Historic Buildings

There are a number of restored and preserved colonial-era historic buildings around the city. The oldest building in the city is **Acacia Cottage** in Cornwall Park at the foot of One Tree Hill. Built in 1841 by Sir John Logan Campbell and his partner William Brown, the cottage originally stood near where Shortland St is today.

Highwic, at 40 Gillies Ave, Epsom, and **Alberton**, at 1 Kerr-Taylor Ave, Mt Albert, on the corner of Kerr-Taylor Ave and Mt Albert Rd, are both large houses of wealthy mid-Victorian New Zealanders, originally built in the 1860s, added on to with time, and ultimately bequeathed to the Historic Places Trust. **Ewelme Cottage**, at 14 Ayr St, Parnell, off Parnell Rd, was built by a clergyman in the 1860s, of fine native kauri wood. All are open daily from 10.30 am to noon and from 1 to 4.30 pm. A combined ticket to visit all three historic places is $7 (children $2). Otherwise it costs $2.50 (children 50c) to visit Ewelme Cottage, $3.50 (children $1) to visit each of the others.

Just five doors from Ewelme Cottage, **Kinder House** at 2 Ayr St on the corner of Parnell Rd is a fine example of early (1857) architecture and contains two galleries of artwork and memorabilia of the Rev Dr John Kinder. His original watercolours are found in the Auckland City Art Gallery, and his original photos are in the Auckland Museum, with photographic reproductions here. The restored home is open Monday to Friday from noon to 3 pm, depending on the availability of staff; admission is $1 (children 50c).

Renall St, coming off Ponsonby Rd, has been declared a conservation area by the Auckland city council, and is a registered place of historic interest for its 19th century atmosphere. The houses along this block are still used as private homes and are not open to the public, but you can stroll along and see the 20 or so early artisans' houses and the larger Foresters' Hall at No 5.

Mt Wellington Stone Cottage is at the Shopping Centre in Panmure. To get there take Bus Nos 51 and 52, from the Downtown Bus Terminal. There are several of the early **'Fencible Cottages'**, including one from the 1840s, at Jellicoe Park, Quadrant Rd, Onehunga. It's open from 1.30 to 4.30 pm on weekends. To get there, take Bus Nos 301 and 302 from Victoria St East.

In south-east Auckland, **Howick Colonial Village** in Lloyd Elsmore Park, Bells Rd, Pakuranga is a restored village of the 1840 to 1880 period, on the old military settlement of Howick. It has over 20 restored colonial buildings including a thatched sod cottage, forge, schoolhouse, village store, church and settlers' houses. It's open from 10 am to 4 pm daily; entry is $6 (children $3, seniors $5, family $18). Take the Howick bus from the Downtown Bus Terminal, phone 534 5059 for details.

Parnell

Parnell is an old inner suburb, only a km or two from the centre, where there was a concerted effort to stave off the office developers and restore the old houses and shops, many of them with a decidedly eccentric touch. Parnell now has one of the most appealing streets in New Zealand with lots of arts & crafts shops, good (and expensive) restaurants, galleries and trendy Kiwis. It's a great place to have a snack in one of the open-air cafes and people-watch. Everything here is open seven days a week. You can walk to Parnell from Queen St in about 20 minutes (it's a pleasant walk through the Domain) or take bus No 63, 64 or 65 from the Downtown Bus Terminal. The United Airlines Explorer bus and the Bus-A-Bout make regular stops at Parnell Village.

The Parnell Rose Gardens on Gladstone Rd, Parnell, has harbour views and is in bloom from November to March. The United Airlines Explorer bus or the Bus-A-Bout bus will drop you there.

Swimming & Thermal Pools

There are swimming pools in the city and various swimming centres outside. The Tepid Baths, locally known as 'the Teps', is in the heart of the city on the corner of Customs St West and Hobson St, two blocks from Queen St. It has a large indoor swimming pool, a spa pool, saunas and steam room. Admission to all of these is $5.50 (children $3.50, seniors $4), or $3.50 (children $1.50) for the swimming pool only. Also here is a health and fitness centre where you can work out for $10 a day or $55 a month. The Teps is open from 6 am to 10 pm weekdays, from 8 am to 7 pm on weekends and holidays.

Other pools in the city include the Olympic Pool in Newmarket, the Parnell Baths on Judges Bay Rd in Parnell with a saltwater pool right on the waterfront (closed in winter), the heated Point Erin pool on Shelly Beach Rd in Herne Bay, and the Takapuna Pools on Killarney St in Takapuna on the North Shore.

The Aquatic Park at Parakai, 45 km northwest of Auckland (bus No 069 from the Downtown Bus Terminal), has indoor and outdoor hot mineral pools and various waterslides. The centre is open from 10 am to 10 pm daily; admission is $8 (children $4) and a day pass on the waterslide is an extra $5. You can stay there at the Aquatic Park Holiday Camp (☎ 420 8884, ☎ & fax 420 8998); the cost of $8.50 per person in tent sites or caravan sites includes free admission to the pools. There are also three motels nearby.

The Waiwera Thermal Pools, another big complex of hot pools with waterslides and several sizes and temperatures of pools, are at Waiwera, 48 km north of Auckland (bus No 895 from the Downtown Bus Terminal).

It's open daily from 9 am to 10 pm, Friday and Saturday until 11 pm; admission is $9 (children $5). One of the most popular attractions of the pools is that every night they show a movie on the big screen – just like in the cinema except here you watch it from the hot pool! The film is included in th $9 admission price. There's accommodation at Waiwera – see the Northland chapter for details. Within walking distance of Waiwera is the Wenderholm Regional Park with a good beach, estuary, lawns, trees and bushwalks.

The Miranda Hot Springs on the Miranda coast road, off the Thames/Pokeno Rd, is about an hour's drive from Auckland. It has open and covered hot pools, private spas, children's play areas, and campsites with power. It's open from 10 am to 9 pm daily; admission is $5 (children $2.50, seniors $3.50, private spas $3 extra).

Beaches

Auckland is known for its fine and varied beaches dotted all around the harbours and up and down both coasts. You can run around them with 80,000 fit New Zealanders in the 'Round the Bays' run which is held in March every year – one of the largest fun runs in the world.

East coast beaches include Judges Bay, Kohimarama, Mission Bay, Okahu Bay and St Heliers Bay, all accessible from Tamaki Drive. Mission Bay is the most popular in summer, with a park area, sidewalk cafes and a good ice-cream shop. With most east coast and harbour beaches, swimming is better at high tide. Buses along Tamaki Drive leave from the Downtown Bus Terminal: Nos 71, 76 and 770.

Popular north shore beaches include Takapuna and Milford. To get to them, take Bus Nos 83 or 85, departing from Victoria St West.

There's good surf on west coast beaches within an hour's drive from the city. Try Bethells where the water is often very rough, Karekare, Muriwai, and Whatipu, with good day walks in the area. These beaches are all less than 50 km from the city centre, and most have surf clubs near the shore. Serious surfers in the Auckland area recommend Piha and Raglan on the west coast and Tawharanui, east of Warkworth, on the east coast. See the Around Auckland section for more on Piha and Whatipu, and the Around Hamilton section for more on Raglan.

Auckland Observatory

The Auckland Observatory, in the One Tree Hill Domain, off Manukau Rd, is open to the public from 7.30 to 10 pm every Tuesday and Thursday evening with an illustrated talk on some aspect of astronomy and, on clear nights, viewing by telescope and help in finding the southern hemisphere constellations. Admission is $6 (children $3, family $15). To get there, take bus Nos 302, 304, 305 or 312 from Victoria St East.

One Tree Hill & Mt Eden

One Tree Hill is a small (183 metres) extinct volcano cone which, like the other extinct volcano cones in the Auckland area, was used by the Maoris as a fortified pa. This was the largest and most populous of the Maori pa settlements, and you can still see the terracing and dugout storage pits they made, and look down into the crater. One Tree Hill was named for a sacred totara tree which stood on the hilltop until 1876, now replaced by a huge pine tree. Get there on bus Nos 302, 304, 305 or 312 from Victoria St East.

You get a good view of the city from One Tree Hill but the view from Mt Eden, the highest volcanic cone in the area at 196 metres, is the best in Auckland. From Mt Eden you can see the entire Auckland area, all the bays, both sides of the isthmus, and scope out the coast-to-coast walkway. You can also see the old Maori pa terracing and storage pits and look 50 metres down into the volcano's crater. It's worth the trouble to get up there. You can drive to the top or take bus No 274 or 275 from Customs St East.

Markets & Flea Markets

Victoria Park Market on Victoria St West opposite Victoria Park is a big outdoor market, open every day from 9 am to 7 pm.

There's a lively atmosphere, with outdoor cafes and entertainment on weekends. It's about a 20-minute walk from the centre, heading west on Victoria St from Queen St, or you can take Bus No 005 from Customs St West (this bus does not run on weekends), the United Airlines Explorer bus or the Bus-A-Bout.

The China Oriental Market on Quay St, a few blocks east of the centre, is another interesting market, housed in a huge brightly coloured warehouse with lots of imported goods shops, international food concessions, unusual merchandise and some good deals. It's open every day from 10 am to 6 pm, and on Sunday there's a flea market from 10 am to 3 pm.

Dockside Markets at Princes Wharf on the downtown waterfront is a similar place with arts & crafts, ethnic food stalls and street entertainment, plus fresh fish, fruit and vegetables. It's open on Friday, Saturday and Sunday from 9.30 am to 6 pm. Take the Bus-A-Bout and get off at the Maritime Museum.

On Sunday from around 7 am to 2 pm a couple of other markets are held: the Ponsonby Market in the Upper Queen St Council Car Park, and the Total Concept Market in the Britomart Car Park upstairs on the 2nd floor above the bus terminal.

There are also a number of weekend flea markets in the city and surrounding suburbs. Sunday mornings are the most popular time, with markets held from around 7 am to noon at the Avondale Racecourse in Avondale, the Mt Wellington Flea Market in the Big Fresh car park on the corner of Mt Wellington Highway and Penrose Rd, the Panmure Flea Market at the Panmure Community Hall on Pilkington Rd in Panmure, and the Takapuna Flea Market in the Central car park in Anzac St, Takapuna, opposite the Police Station. The Otara Flea Market, one of the largest flea markets in New Zealand, is held every Saturday from around 6 am to noon in the car park between the Manukau Polytec and the Otara Town Centre on Newbury St in Otara.

Many other local and theme markets specialising in arts & crafts, antiques, clothing, home produce or what-have-you, are held monthly; the Auckland Visitor Centre keeps an up-to-date list.

Parks & Walks

Pick up a copy of the ARA pamphlet guide to the Auckland Regional Parks from the Auckland Visitor Centre, the DOC information centre or from the Regional Parks Central Office on the ground floor of the Regional House on the corner of Pitt and Hopetoun Sts in the centre (π 366 2166). The colour pamphlet contains photos, details of facilities and activities, and maps for over 20 parks in the Auckland area. Some allow camping, others are interesting day parks.

The Auckland Visitor Centre also has information on the many central city parks and on good walks around the city and the surrounding areas. There are walks along the city waterfront, coastal walks, country and bush walks, and walks in the Waitakere Ranges west of Auckland.

There's a Coast to Coast Walkway marked out between the Waitemata Harbour on the east coast and the Manukau Harbour on the west. The walkway encompasses Albert Park, Auckland University, the Auckland Domain, Mt Eden, One Tree Hill and other points of interest, keeping as much as possible to reserves rather than city streets. Total walking time is four hours at an easy pace; the route intersects or comes near to city bus routes at many points along the way so there's plenty of opportunity to make it a shorter walk. Pick up a Coast to Coast Walkway pamphlet from the Auckland Visitor Centre or DOC information centre before you start out; it points out many details of historical interest along the way.

Amusement Parks

Rainbow's End Adventure Park on the Great South Rd (corner of Wiri Station Rd) at Manukau is a large amusement park with lots of rides and entertainment, open every day from 10 am to 5 pm. Super passes for $24 (children $19) are good for unlimited rides, all day long; otherwise, a $10 admission includes two rides and extra rides are $4 each. Take bus Nos 447, 457, 467, 487 or 497 from the Downtown Bus Terminal or take the Manukau exit off the Southern Motorway and drive 400 metres to the park.

Expo Pavilion

At the Expo Pavilion of New Zealand you can see the New Zealand exhibits from the 1988 World Expo in Brisbane, Australia. It contains a variety of entertainment including four audiovisual theatres, horse riding, fishing and mini-golf, an animal farm and live entertainment on weekends. Tours are conducted hourly on the hour from 10 am to 4 pm; the cost is $8 (children $4). The Expo Pavilion is on Montgomerie Rd off George Bolt Memorial Drive, the route from the city to the airport. Get there on the Airporter bus, which leaves from the Downtown Airline Terminal.

Bungy Jumping

World Bungee, the crew who did the bungy jump at the opening ceremony of the 1990 Commonwealth Games, does bungy jumping from a crane over Freemans Bay, near the downtown waterfront. They go every day in summer, with more limited hours in winter. The cost is $62 to jump; you may want to ring (☎ 303 0030) to schedule a jump to avoid having to wait in a queue. The jumps from bridges over river gorges, are more spectacular than this jump off a crane, and if you'll be travelling around New Zealand you should probably do one of those, but if this is your only chance then you might as well do it here – or at least have a look. Both the United Airlines Explorer bus and the Bus-A-Bout stop at the bungy site.

Other Things to Do

Auckland has no shortage of outdoor activities to enjoy. Kayak hire, sea kayaking and white water kayaking trips and classes can be organised by Ray Button Adventures (☎ 419 0796). Sailboards, mountain bikes and camping gear can be hired from Windsurf Kiwi (☎ & fax 629 0952). Diving trips are organised by the Dive Centre (☎ 444 7698) in Takapuna, the Diving Network (☎ 367 5006) in Howick and other operators.

Marco Polo Tours (☎ 426 8455) based at Orewa, north of Auckland, does snorkelling trips to Goat Island.

The Auckland Climbing School (ACS) Adventures (☎ 837 3620) conduct six-hour courses in rock climbing, abseiling, kayaking, caving, mountaincraft and more. 4 Track Adventures (☎ 480 3233) do four-wheel motorbike safaris in the Woodhill Forest on Auckland's west coast. There are also many possibilities for horse-riding, tennis, golf and other sports in and near Auckland. The Auckland Visitor Centre and the various agencies specialising in NZ adventures can tell you about these and many other activities, and they will make bookings.

Scenic Flights

There are scenic flights over Auckland and the islands of the Hauraki Gulf. Auckland Scenic Air Safaris (☎ 298 5210) does 50-minute scenic flights over Auckland for $75 per person, a one-hour flight to the west coast for $85 per person, or a 1¼ hour flight over the Firth of Thames and the Coromandel Peninsula to the eastern side of the peninsula for $115 per person; they will also make flights further afield. Christian Aviation (☎ 298 9846) based at Ardmore Airfield does scenic and charter flights.

Or you can go flightseeing by helicopter. The Helicopter Line (☎ 377 4406), Auckland Helicopters (☎ 256 0648) and North Shore Helicopters (☎ 426 8287) all do flightseeing trips over the city for $72 per person, and trips further afield. There are plenty of other flightseeing operators; the Auckland Visitor Centre has all the details and can make bookings.

Tandem Skydiving & Other Airborne Activities

The Parakai Parachute Centre (☎ 838 6963) at Parakai, about 30 km north-west of Auckland near Helensville, does tandem skydiving every day, weather permitting. The cost is $175; for an extra $10 they'll provide return transport to/from Auckland. Parakai Aerial Adventures, at the same telephone and

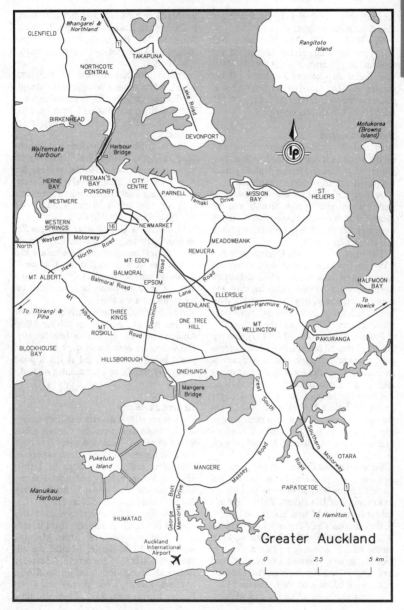

Greater Auckland

0   2.5   5 km

location, does aerobatics. Flight training is also done at the airfield.

Sky Bird (☎ 529 2230, after hours 528 7594) provides hang gliding instruction and tandem hang gliding. Sky Cat (☎ 528 7594) does flights on – believe it or not – a flying catamaran! They say it's the only flying catamaran in the world. Balloon Safaris (☎ 415 8289) does hot-air balloon trips.

Harbour Cruises

Auckland offers almost as many things to do on the water as it does on land, with a great variety of cruises and ferries departing from the piers on the downtown waterfront.

A ferry across the harbour to Devonport makes an interesting trip. There's also the *Kestrel* jazz ferry on Friday and Saturday evenings. See the Devonport section later in this chapter for details.

The Pride of Auckland Company (☎ 373 4557) has five large sailing yachts (you can't miss them on the water with their distinctive blue-and-white-striped sails) making 1½ hour 'experience sailing' cruises ($30), two-hour luncheon cruises ($46) and three-hour dinner cruises ($75) around the harbour.

Fullers Cruises (☎ 377 1771), having absorbed several other harbour boat companies, now has the largest selection of cruises available. They do inner harbour cruises including a 2½ hour coffee cruise ($18), a 1½ hour luncheon cruise ($38), and longer cruises to various Hauraki Gulf islands. On the outer island cruises you can make it a day trip or get off on the island and return whenever you want. Children go for half price on all Fullers cruises.

Fullers Harbour Explorer cruise gives you an all-day boat pass for $17 and you can get on and off the boat as often as you like; it makes stops at Devonport, Kelly Tarlton's Underwater World and Rangitoto Island. Fullers also does half-day or full-day trips to Waiheke Island for $20 with optional tours on the island, including an Eagle Explorer tour for $9 or a vineyard tour for $15, and day trips to Great Barrier Island for $50 with an optional bus tour on the island for $17.

Fullers also does a Sunday and Wednes-

day Mail Run trip which goes from Auckland to Devonport, Rakino, Motutapu, Motuihe, Islington Bay, Rangitoto, Devonport and back to Auckland; the cost is $16 and the trip takes all day.

Fullers also has services to Rangitoto Island, while another company, the Rangitoto Express (☎ 372 6892) operates ferries to both Rangitoto and Rakino Island – see the Rangitoto section later in this chapter for details.

Ferries go between Auckland and Birkenhead during the morning and afternoon rush hours, making a stop at Northcote along the way. They leave from opposite the Downtown Airline Terminal and take 15 minutes each way; the fare is $6 return, $3.50 one way (half price for children).

In summer, a host of other boats ply the harbour (they don't call this the City of Sails for nothing!) and you can even take a trip around the harbour on the tug *William C Daldy* on summer Sundays. The Auckland Visitor Centre has plenty of information on the various cruises available.

Auckland makes particularly good use of its fine harbour on the annual Auckland Anniversary Day Regatta in late January. The waters are dotted with more boats than you'd believe possible and if it's a good windy day, there'll be a fair number of dunkings!

Te Aroha Cruises

The historic (1909) wooden auxiliary schooner *Te Aroha* sails from the Captain Cook Wharf in central Auckland every few days from November to April on a variety of interesting cruises. Day trips to Tiritiri Matangi, Waiheke, Browns Island, Rakino, Motutapu and Ponui Islands depart every day in January and cost $25 to $35.

Other trips last for several days and visit a number of islands. A three-day Bird Islands of the Gulf tour lands on Tiritiri Matangi, Kawau and Little Barrier Islands; the all-inclusive cost is $375 per person. A four-day Botanical Special tour landing on Tiritiri Matangi, Kawau, Little Barrier and Great Barrier Islands costs $495. They also do a three-day Backpackers Special Inner Gulf Cruise for $245 with stops at Waiheke, Tiritiri Matangi and Kawau Islands, passing close to a number of other islands along the way. Plus there are other cruises further afield to the Bay of Plenty ($495), the Coromandel ($235) and a four-day annual pilgrimage to Totara North in the Northland, the place of the schooner's 1909 launching ($450).

You can sleep in two-person cabins or on the deck under the stars. There's plenty of time to explore on the various islands, lots of good food and drink, diving, snorkelling and fishing and if you like you can even help out on deck with the sails. All in all these people do great trips. Check with the NZ Adventure Centre (☎ 309 9192; fax 309 9824) in the Downtown Shopping Centre in QE II Square for bookings and schedules.

Organised Tours

You can do your own tour of several major attractions around Auckland by getting a Bus-A-Bout All Day Bus Pass for $10 (children $5). It departs from the Downtown Airline Terminal on Quay St hourly on the half hour from 9.30 am to 3.30 pm, making a circular route with stops at Kelly Tarlton's Underwater World, the Parnell Rose Gardens, Parnell Village, Auckland Museum, Auckland Zoo, Motat, Victoria Park Market, the Bungy Jumping site, Hobson Wharf Maritime Museum, and back to the Downtown Airline Terminal. You can get off wherever you wish and get on the bus when it comes around the next hour. You can join the tour at any point along the way, getting your ticket from the bus driver.

The United Airlines Explorer bus costs the same and does basically the same thing; it goes to all the same places as the Bus-A-Bout, with the exception of Motat and the zoo. The double-decker bus departs from the Ferry Building hourly on the hour from 10 am to 4 pm every day.

The Gray Line (☎ 377 0904) three-hour morning or afternoon Auckland Highlights tour costs $37, an Auckland Panorama tour costs the same, and there's another afternoon tour covering different attractions for $32. A lunch-time harbour cruise costs $20. You can combine all three and 'do' all of Auckland in a day for $83, or combine any two (children half price). Offering similar tours for the same prices is Great Sights South Pacific (☎ 377 0904).

Various other operators also have bus tours of the city and further afield. Scenic Tours (☎ 634 0189) offers a three-hour City Highlights tour twice daily for $32, plus various tours combining this with cruises on the harbour. Gray Line, Great Sights and Scenic Tours all offer a number of additional tours further afield, including tours to Waitomo, Rotorua and the Bay of Islands.

Super Shuttle Tours (☎ 307 5210) offer half-day sightseeing tours of Auckland for $22, and a Sunday tour for $48 (children half price). ABC Tours (☎ 302 1100) offer half-day ($30) and full-day ($60) tours of the city sights; the full-day tour includes a cruise across the harbour to Devonport. Kiwiland Explorer (☎ 307 6828) does two-hour tours for $25.

World of Nature (☎ 846 4986) does a variety of half-day Auckland Wildlife Tours and Auckland Garden Tours for $45. Bush & Beach Nature Tours (☎ 478 2882) offer full-day, small-group nature tours for $79. The Antipodean Explorer (☎ 302 2400, mobile (025) 926 896) offers small-group full-day tours to west Auckland for $55. The Antipodean Explorer and Bush & Beach both visit a gannet colony at Muriwai and go through the native bush of the Waitakere Ranges; both tours have an excellent reputation.

There are many other specialised tours around Auckland including golf and fishing tours. In winter there are ski tours to the North Island ski areas, principally Whakapapa. The Auckland Visitor Centre can tell you about various specialised tours.

The Old Devonport Ferry & Coach tour (☎ 373 3776, ext 878) makes an enjoyable way to visit Devonport, just across the harbour. You ferry to Devonport and when you get there, a van is waiting to take you around Devonport's many sights, including the summits of North Head and Mt Victoria, two volcanic cones with excellent views which are quite a climb otherwise. The van tour takes about an hour, and if you jump right back on the next ferry to Auckland the total time is about 1¾ hours, but you're welcome to stay in Devonport as long as you like before catching the ferry back to Auckland. The tour departs from the Auckland Ferry Building hourly on the hour from 10 am to 3 pm; the cost is $20 (children $10, family $50).

If you're already in Devonport, you can take the van tour only – just show up at the wharf about 25 minutes past the hour, from 10.25 am to 3.25 pm; the cost is $15 (children $6).

Many other tours depart from Auckland to places all over New Zealand; the Auckland Visitor Centre should have details on all of them. One of the more economical is Thrifty Tours (☎ 478 3550 or any InterCity office or travel agent), offering a wide range of tours incorporating travel on public transport with accommodation and guided tours at several stopoff points.

Backpackers tours departing from Auckland include the North Cape Green Beetle (☎ 358 5868) and Awesome Adventures (☎ 366 1665), both offering tours of Northland; Kiwi Experience (☎ 366 1665); and Kiwi Safaris (☎ freephone (0800) 800 616). See the Getting Around chapter for details on these and others.

Annual Events

A number of annual events are held in Auckland. Some of the more important ones are mentioned here but there are plenty of others; the Auckland Visitor Centre keeps a complete list of annual and current events, and can supply exact dates. Annual events include:

January
    Benson & Hedges Open Tennis Tournament; Amway Classic Tennis Tournament; Opera in the Park; Auckland Anniversary Day Regatta
February
    Ports of Auckland Festival; Devonport Food & Wine Festival; New Zealand Golf Open

March
    Around the Bays Fun Run; New Zealand Ironman Competition; Royal Easter Show
June
    New Zealand Boat Show; 'Local Flavours' Arts Festival; Stitches & Crafts Festival; Rothmans International Car Rally
July
    Great New Zealand Crafts Show
September
    New Zealand Home Show
November
    Great New Zealand Crafts Show
December
    Nissan Mobil 500 Series

Places to Stay

Camping & Cabins There are camping grounds and motor parks both north and south of the city centre, many very convenient to the centre.

North of the city, the four-star *Auckland North Shore Caravan Park, Cabins & Motel* (☎ 419 1320, 418 2578; fax 480 0435) is at 52 Northcote Rd in Takapuna, four km north of the Harbour Bridge; take the Northcote Rd exit and it's 700 metres west of the motorway, beside Pizza Hut. Accommodation includes tent and caravan sites at $16/22 for one/two people, cabins ranging from $27/37 to $45/55, tourist flats and leisure lodges at $60/66, and motel units at $66/80 for one/two people.

Also in Takapuna, the *Takapuna Beach Motor Camp* (☎ 489 7909) is at 22 The Promenade, Takapuna, eight km from the CPO and right on the beach on the north shore, with a view of Rangitoto Island. It's an easy walk to the shops and centre of Takapuna, and a 10-minute drive or bus ride into Auckland centre. Tent sites are $11/17 for one/two people, powered sites are $27 for two on the waterfront, $22.50 for two in other sites, and they also have cabins at $31.50 for two and on-site caravans at $40 for two. It's the usual story – supply your own bedding, cutlery, etc.

Further north of Auckland, the *Tui Glen Camping Park* (☎ 838 8978; fax 837 3080) is beside the swimming pool complex at Henderson, in the wine country 13 km northwest of Auckland. Sites are $6 per person, $9 with power. Cabins are $35 for two, and they also have tourist flats at $48.

South of the city centre, the closest camping to the city is the fine *Remuera Motor Lodge* (☎ 524 5126; fax 524 5639) at 16 Minto Rd, off Remuera Rd. It's eight km from the CPO, a six-minute drive, or 20-minute bus ride from the centre on the yellow bus route, Nos 64 and 65, departing every 20 minutes from the Downtown Bus Terminal. It's a quiet, secure camp with plenty of trees and a rural feel, at the end of the street so there's no traffic passing by, and in addition to the usual comforts it also has a large swimming pool, a wood-burning BBQ, and it's just 100 metres from shopping and the bus stop. Tent and powered sitess are $11 per person with discounts available, there's a self-contained bunkroom with beds at $20 per person, or tourist flats at $60 for two.

The *Avondale Motor Park* (☎ 828 7228) at 46 Bollard Ave, off New North Rd, is nine km from the CPO but fairly close to Motat and the zoo. Sites are $8 per person, $9 with power, and they also have on-site caravans at $25/33 for one/two people, cabins at $30/42 and tourist flats at $40/52.

The *Manukau Central Caravan Park* (☎ & fax 266 8016) at 902 Great South Rd, Manukau, is a quiet place, away from the motorway. Tent sites are $8 per person, powered sites $15/18 for one/two people, powered en-suite sites are $19/22, and they also have cabins at $20/28, on-site caravans at $30/36, and tourist flats at $45 or $50.

The *Meadow Court Motor Camp* (☎ 278 5612) is also in Manukau at 630 Great South Rd, two minutes from the Manukau city centre and not far from the airport; it's handy to Rainbow's End amusement park. Sites here cost $7 per person, $8 with power.

New Zealand Holiday Parks (☎ 298 0599/0499; fax 537 0782) at 4 Cunningham Place off the Great South Rd in Takanini, is about 18 km south of Auckland. Campsites are $8 per person, $10 with power, on-site caravans are $20 for one or two people and cabins are $35.50 for one or two.

The *South Auckland Caravan & Camping Park* (☎ 294 8903; fax 294 8122) is on Ara-

rimu Rd, 200 metres off the Great South Rd at Ramarama, 35 km south of Auckland city centre. It's a large park on a 48-hectare dairy farm 500 metres from the Ramarama motorway offramp. You can walk around on the farm, see the dairy operations, enjoy the private lake, and it also has a colour TV room, fish & chips, shops and a laundry. Tent sites are $8/14 for one/two people, powered sitess are $12/16, and cabins and on-site caravans are $20/25.

The Auckland Regional Council operates about a dozen camping grounds in the regional parks around Auckland. Some are accessible by vehicle, others are reached by tramping; many are in coastal areas. Information about these camping grounds is available in the *Camping in the Great Auckland Outdoors* and the *Auckland Regional Parks* pamphlets published by the Auckland Regional Council, available from the Auckland Visitor Centre or directly from the Auckland Regional Council (☎ 366 2166) on the ground floor of the Regional House on the corner of Pitt and Hopetoun Sts.

Hostels Auckland has been experiencing a boom in the hostel scene in the past few years. If you don't like the first hostel you land at, by all means shop around – there are plenty of good ones to choose from and the standards of most of them are pretty high. The international YHA has two hostels in Auckland – one in the city centre, another in Parnell – and the rest are independent hostels, known here as 'backpackers'.

The prices given here are summer prices. Even though there are so many hostels to choose from, they may still all be full in summer. In winter there are fewer travellers, it's not so hectic, and most hostels give about a 25% discount off their normal prices. Sometimes the hostels have touts and vans waiting at the airport to meet incoming flights; they'll give you a free ride into town and they may offer cheaper prices to people from straight off the plane as an inducement to come to their hostel.

Some of the hostels, notably the Auckland City YHA, the Auckland Central Backpackers and the Central City Backpackers (CCB) have travel agency services downstairs in the lobby. They specialise in travel within New Zealand, with an emphasis on travel options and activities of interest to hostellers and backpackers. All the hostels have kitchens where you can do your own cooking; a few have bistros as well.

Hostels – City Centre Just off Queen St and right behind the Sheraton Hotel, the *Auckland City YHA Hostel* (☎ 309 2802; fax 373 5083) on the corner of City Rd and Liverpool St has 75 rooms with 140 beds. Many of the rooms – mostly twin, double and family rooms – have great views of the city and harbour. The nightly cost is $19 in double and twin rooms ($16 in winter), $25 in single rooms. The cafe on the ground floor serves economical meals and snacks, and there's a YHA travel agency in the lobby. The hostel is open 24 hours. You can book in advance from YHAs overseas, and from here you can book ahead to YHAs in other countries.

Opposite one another near Fort St on the corner of Queen St, situated right in the city centre at the bottom of Queen St, are two large hostels. The *Queen St Backpackers* (☎ 373 3471; fax 358 2412) at 4 Fort St sleeps 90 people; opposite this at 9 Fort St, the *Auckland Central Backpackers* (☎ 358 4877; fax 358 4872) has room for 300 hostellers. It has many amenities including made-up beds, a cafe and bar, a video theatre, upstairs outdoor decks, a bicycle workshop where you can use tools and get help with fixing your bike, and a popular backpackers travel agency downstairs. The cost is the same at both hostels: $16 per person in four-bed dorms, $18.50 in double or twin rooms and $22 in single rooms.

Another good, large hostel is the *Central City Backpackers (CCB)* (☎ 358 5685; fax 358 4716) at 26 Lorne St. It sleeps 120 and has all the usual amenities including a backpackers' travel agency downstairs. The cost per person is $12 to $16 in dorm rooms, $18 in double or twin rooms and $25 in single rooms, with discounts for weekly stays.

On the 2nd floor, 295 Queen St, just a couple of doors down the hill from Aotea Square, the *Aotea Central Square Backpackers Hostel* (☎ 303 3350) is another very centrally situated hostel, sleeping 50 or 60 hostellers in rooms that are basic but OK, the kitchen and lounge areas can get crowded, but the same could be said about many other big city hostels. The cost of $13/17.50 per person in double/dorm rooms includes a continental breakfast.

When our researcher visited the *Kiwi Hilton* (☎ & fax 358 3999) at 430 Queen St, they found it basic, despite its good location on Queen St. It sleeps 70 and it can certainly get crowded, particularly in the kitchen area. Nevertheless it's a place to stay right in the centre of Auckland and lots of people must like it just fine as at times they are so packed in that it's popularly rumoured people have even been seen sleeping on the billiard table. The cost of $13 in dorm rooms, $15 in twin rooms and $17.50 in double rooms includes a continental breakfast.

Getting off Queen St, a much smaller hostel, the *Downtown Backpackers Hostel* (☎ 366 1444) is conveniently situated at 6 Constitution Hill, near Auckland University. It sleeps 18 people with three double rooms, one twin and two dorms; the cost per person is $13/15 in dorm/double rooms; $25 single for a double room to yourself. Parking is available and there are fruit trees and a BBQ, in a parklike setting.

The *Georgia Backpackers Hostel* (☎ 309 9560) located at 189 Park Rd on the corner of Carlton Gore Rd, Grafton, is opposite the Auckland Domain, about a five-minute walk to the Olympic Swimming Pool and a 10-minute walk to upper Queen St or the supermarket. It sleeps about 45 hostellers in a converted older house; the cost is $10 or $13 in a nine-bed dorm room, $15 in double rooms.

Nearby, the *YWCA* (☎ 379 4912; fax 358 1628) at 10 Carlton Gore Rd, Grafton, is mostly long-term accommodation for young women but it also has a few rooms for travellers. Inside the house (females only) it's $17 per person in single or twin rooms, linen included. Out the back there's a small cottage which takes men and women travellers, the cost is $10 with your own sleeping bag or $15 with linen included. The office is open Monday to Friday from 8 am to 6.30 pm, weekends and holidays from 8 to 10 am and 4.30 to 6.30 pm. Take a Hospital bus No 283 from the city terminal, or bus No 274 or 275 from Customs St.

The *YMCA* (☎ 303 2068; fax 377 6770) is in a tall, modern building on the corner of Pitt St and Grays Ave. It has space for 130 men and women, all in single and twin rooms; the cost of $20 per night, linen included, remains the same all year round. Economical meals are served in the cafeteria, and you can use the health and fitness centre for a small fee.

Hostels – Parnell There are also some good hostels in Parnell, one of Auckland's more stylish districts. From the city centre, you can walk there (a 20-minute walk) or take bus No 635, 645 or 655.

The *Parnell Lodge YHA Hostel* (☎ 379 0258/3731; fax 358 4143) is at 2 Churton St on the corner of Earle St, three short blocks east of Parnell Rd. It sleeps 81; the cost is $16 in dorm rooms ($13 in winter), $18 per person in doubles and twins.

Three backpackers hostels are found on St Georges Bay Rd, which branches off from Parnell Rd at the top of the hill by the library. The first one you come to as you head down the hill is the *Leadbetter Lodge* (☎ 358 0665) at 17 St Georges Bay Rd. It's a homely, quiet hostel sleeping 28; the cost is $13 in dorm and family rooms, $15 and $17.50 per person in double and twin rooms.

Next along, the *City Garden Lodge* (☎ 302 0880) at 25 St George's Bay Rd is a fine hostel in a large, elegant old home originally built for the Queen of Tonga. The cost is $14 in dorm rooms, $12.50 or $17.50 per person in double rooms.

Further down the hill at 60 St George's Bay Rd, *Lantana Lodge* (☎ 373 4546) is a small hostel sleeping 20; the cost is $13 in dorm rooms, $15 per person in doubles and twins.

When we visited, the cleanest backpackers we found in Parnell was the *International Backpackers – Alan's Place* (☎ & fax 358 4584) at 8 Maunsell Rd, in a quiet residential location beside the Auckland Domain, near the Auckland Museum. In the past the large brick building provided student housing for the Blind Foundation; it feels a bit institutional but it's very clean, well-kept and there's plenty of space for everyone, with a lounge, TV room, large kitchen and dining area, and a reading room, with central heating and plenty of off-street parking. It sleeps 70 people in 35 rooms; the cost is $12 in dorm rooms, $14 per person in doubles and twins, and $18 in single rooms, with discounts if you stay or month.

Hostels – Mt Eden The Mt Eden district, about a 20-minute walk or five-minute bus ride from the city centre, has two good hostels. You can take bus Nos 274 and 275 from the downtown bus terminal or bus Nos 255 to 258, 265 or 267 from the St James Theatre on Queen St.

The *Eden Lodge Tourist Hostel* (☎ 630 0174) at 22 View Rd, Mt Eden is a very 'up-market' hostel. Billed as a 'jetsetters 5-star hostel' it's in a huge colonial-era home, surrounded by gardens and filled with antique furnishings, original art, and many large pleasant spaces. It sleeps only 20, so there's plenty of space for everyone. The cost is $14 in four-bed dorms, $16 per person in double rooms and $20 in single rooms, or $12 in a bunkroom out behind the house. Buses stop on the corner of Mt Eden Rd and View Rd.

Further up the hill, *Berlin Lodge* (☎ 638 6545) is at 5A Oaklands Rd, Mt Eden, just off Mt Eden Rd, in a quiet tree-lined residential street at the foot of Mt Eden; the bus stops at the Mt Eden shops on the corner, 100 metres away. German, French and English are spoken here. The cost is $10 and $12 in dorm rooms, $14 in share rooms (up to four beds), $15 per person in twin and double rooms, and $20 or $25 in single rooms. Ring for free pick-up.

Hostels – Other Areas A couple of other hostels are situated in suburban areas a bit farther from the city centre. *Plumley House Backpackers* (☎ 520 4044) at 515 Remuera Rd on the corner of Ladies Mile is a large hostel in a former colonial mansion. Rates per person are $13 in dorm rooms, $16 in double rooms or $18 in single rooms, with a 10% discount for weekly stays. Bus Nos 635, 643, 644, 645, 653 or 655 all come from the city centre and they also provide free pick-up from the city centre.

The *Ivanhoe Lodge* (☎ 846 2800; fax 846 7288) is at 14 Shirley Rd in Western Springs, near Motat and the zoo. It's a large 80-bed hostel with a bar, pool table, games room and sauna. The cost of $10 to $14 in dorms, $17 in double or $20 in single rooms includes breakfast, and if you stay for a week you get one day free. To get there, take bus No 045 to Grey Lynn shops, then walk down Turangi Rd to No 42C, following the signs. They make a courtesy trip into town each morning, returning in the afternoon.

Hostels – Near the Airport Near the airport are a couple of places with backpackers rooms as well as motel units. The *Airport Skylodge International* (☎ 275 1005; fax 275 1003) at 144 McKenzie Rd, Mangere has hostel facilities at $20 per person. They offer a free shuttle service to/from the airport, eight minutes away.

The *Skyway Lodge* (☎ 275 4443; fax 275 5012) at 30 Kirkbride Rd, Mangere, five minutes from the airport, has bunkroom accommodation at $15 per person, and they, too, offer courtesy airport transport.

Guesthouses Guesthouses/bed & breakfasts (B&Bs) are popular in Auckland and there are quite a few of them, some in and near the city centre, some in quiet residential areas a short distance away. All the ones mentioned here are attractive, clean, comfortable and friendly, with a 'home away from home' feeling, and the room rate includes a substantial breakfast. Most have off-street parking and a 'no smoking in the

house' policy, with smoking areas provided outside. Unless mentioned otherwise, the rooms usually have shared bathroom facilities. The ones in residential areas are all near convenient bus routes into the city.

In the city centre, *Chateau Maples* (☎ & fax 358 2737) at 100 Greys Ave is only about 300 metres from Queen St, but since it's set in a park, it's still quiet and private. The cost is $50/75 for singles/doubles.

Also in the city centre, the *Aspen Lodge* (☎ 379 6698; fax 377 7625), looking out on a delightful little park at 62 Emily Place, is about a five-minute walk from Queen St; singles/doubles here are $45/65.

Still quite central, about a 10-minute walk from Queen St, the *Freeman's Travellers' Hotel* (☎ 376 5046; fax 376 4052) at 65 Wellington St, Freeman's Bay, has a private garden area behind the house and 12 rooms at $38/60 for singles/doubles, plus two serviced two-bedroom apartments at $68/74.

The attractive and a bit posh Parnell district is about a 20-minute walk from Queen St, an attractive walk through the Auckland Domain, and there are also frequent buses (Nos 635, 645 or 655 from the Downtown Terminal).

Parnell has two good guesthouses, both with private bath in every guest room. The *Ascot Parnell* (☎ 309 9012; fax 309 3729) at 36 St Stephens Ave, off Parnell Rd, is a long-running favourite in Auckland, with 11 guest rooms in a restored historic home. The cost is $75/103 for singles/doubles. Nearby, *Chalet Chevron* (☎ 309 0291) at 14 Brighton Rd has beautiful views over the harbour; the cost is $45 or $56 in single rooms, $90 in double rooms, with one smaller double at $72.

The *Heathmaur Lodge* (☎ 376 3527) at 75 Argyle St, Herne Bay, is in a large old three-storey mansion, a two-minute walk to a sandy beach, an easy walk to restaurants and a 10-minute ride to the city centre. With the water nearby, an open view, quiet neighbourhood, spacious accommodation and homely atmosphere, it seems far removed from the big city even though it's so close. Basic room rates are $35/50 for share-facility rooms, add $10 for private bathrooms, with lower weekly rates. The price includes breakfast and if you like you can pay $10 extra and have dinner with the family.

Mt Eden is another residential district with two attractive guesthouses. The *Bavaria B&B Hotel* (☎ 638 9641; fax 638 9665) at 83 Valley Rd is a lovely place with a private sun deck and garden; both English and German are spoken. Its 11 rooms, all with private bath, include some larger rooms. High-season prices are $49 to $59 for singles, $79 to $89 for doubles, but substantial discounts are offered for longer or repeat stays, off-season stays, and so on. Also in Mt Eden, the *Pentlands Tourist Hotel* (☎ 638 7031) at 22 Pentland Ave, off Valley Rd, has a large outdoor grounds with a tennis court, a BBQ area and picnic tables, and a large lounge area with a pool table and open fire; the cost is $39/59 for singles/doubles.

To get to Mt Eden, take bus Nos 274 and 275 from the downtown bus terminal or bus Nos 255 to 258, 265 or 267 from the St James Theatre on Queen St.

Aachen House (☎ 520 2329; fax 524 2898) at 39 Market Rd, Remuera, about four km from the centre, is a bit further out but it's worth the trip. A fine old Victorian home with just seven guest rooms and a lot of style, it's set in half an acre of private garden at the foot of Mt Hobson. Inside it has spacious rooms and many fine touches, including original NZ art works. Singles/doubles are $54/72.

Also in Remuera is the Remuera House (☎ 524 7794) at 500 Remuera Rd, an attractive English-style guesthouse with B&B at $39/58 for singles/doubles.

Hotels Several hotels are conveniently situated in the heart of the city. The *Albion Hotel* (☎ 379 4900; fax 379 4901), on the corner of Wellesley St West and Hobson Sts, has 20 rooms in a restored older building done up with a bit of style. Single/double rooms, all with private bath and many other amenities, are $70/75.

In the same price range, *Abby's Hotel*

(☎ 303 4799; fax 302 1451) on the corner of Wellesley St West and Albert St has rooms with private bath at $79. There's a good selection of bars and restaurants here and the only real drawback is that the rooms are extremely compact, postage-stamp size.

More expensive, but an excellent place to stay, the *Imperial Hotel* (☎ 357 6770; fax 357 6793) at 131-139 Hobson St has 58 rooms, all with private bath and other amenities, priced at $135.

The *Park Towers Hotel* (☎ 309 2800; fax 302 1964) at 3 Scotia Place, just off Queen St, has a simple, student-like decor. Rooms with private bath are $130.

Nearby, the *Railton Travel Hotel* (☎ 379 6487; fax 379 6496) located at 411 Queen St is cheaper but the rooms are quite basic. There are three categories of rooms here: economy rooms with shared facilities cost $48/65 for singles/doubles, rooms with private facilities are $66/86, and business rooms with more amenities are $75/90 for singles/doubles; all prices include a cooked breakfast. There's a smorgasbord dinner every night for $18.

Opposite the railway station, the *Harbourview Station Hotel* (☎ 303 2463; fax 358 2489) at 131 Beach Rd looks like an older place from the outside but on the inside it's all been freshly renovated, the rooms are looking good and each has its private bath. The cost is $50/70 for singles/doubles.

If you want Auckland's best you can move right up into the *Hyatt* (☎ 366 1234; fax 303 2932) on the corner of Princes St and Waterloo Quadrant, the *Centra* (☎ 302 1111; fax 302 3111) at 10-20 Gladstone Rd, Parnell, the *Travelodge* (☎ 377 0349; fax 307 8159) at 96-100 Quay St, or the *Parkroyal* (☎ 377 8920; fax 307 3739) in Customs St East, all with rooms at about $200 a night; to the *Sheraton* (☎ 379 5132; fax 377 9367) at 83 Symonds St with rooms at $300 a night, to the *Pan Pacific* (☎ 366 3000; fax 366 0121) in Mayoral Drive where rooms are $360, or the top of the heap, the *Regent* (☎ 309 8888; fax 379 6445) on the corner of Albert and Swanson Sts, where double rooms are $400 a night – much more for a suite, of course!

Motels Auckland has over 100 motels, so it's hard to make any particular recommendations. Generally costs start from around $55 for singles, $65 for doubles or twins. Some of the camping grounds have tourist flats or motel units (see Camping & Cabins).

Several areas reasonably close to the city have a good selection of motels. *Parnell's Village Motor Lodge* (☎ 377 1463; fax 373 4192) at 2 St Stephens Ave, on the corner of St Stephens Ave and Parnell Rd, has 17 units in an older building and a newer extension, with studio units at $67, larger studios at $85, or one-bedroom units at $95. Some of them are quite spacious – sizes range from single to a big family unit sleeping nine – and all are self-contained and very well-equipped.

Going down Parnell Rd towards the city the *Parnell Inn* (☎ & fax 358 0642) at 320 Parnell Rd is another reasonably priced motel with 16 rooms at $55/68 for singles/doubles, with a 20% discount for stays of a week or more. You can bargain for a discount here.

Another alternative is Jervois Rd in Herne Bay, taking off from the junction with Ponsonby Rd. There are a number of places along here or off Jervois Rd along Shelly Beach Rd. This is close to the southern end of the Harbour Bridge. At 6 Tweed St, which in turn is off Shelly Beach Rd, the *Harbour Bridge Motel* (☎ 376 3489; fax 378 6592) has singles/doubles at $55/68, with larger family units available. It's an older (1886) building full of character and style with a newer extension. There's an outdoor BBQ, an attractive garden, and it's a convenient location. You can bargain for a rate here and probably get it.

Also in Herne Bay, the *Sea Breeze Motel* (☎ 376 2139; fax 376 3177) at 213 Jervois Rd is near beaches, fishing and tennis courts, restaurants and shops, and a bus stops outside the door. They have studio units for $73 and one-bedroom units for $81. The *Abaco Spa Motel* (☎ 376 0119; fax 378 7937) at 59 Jervois Rd has units from $85 to $99.

Continue north across the Harbour Bridge and there are more motels in Takapuna or Birkenhead. The *Mon Desir Motel* (☎ 489 5139; fax 489 8809) at 144 Hurstmere Rd, Takapuna, is right on the beachfront, with a beautiful view of Rangitoto Island; amenities include an outdoor pool, sauna, four bars and a restaurant. Single/double rooms are $100/115 and they also have suites. Also in Takapuna, the *Takapuna Beach Motel* (☎ 489 7126; fax 489 8563) on The Promenade, half a block from Takapuna Beach, has units at $105.

If you have an early flight to catch and want to stay out near the airport there are lots of motels in Mangere, particularly along Kirkbride Rd and McKenzie Rd. Almost every one of them manages to get the words 'airport' or 'sky' into their names and most of them are from around $70 a night. The *Skyway Lodge* (☎ 275 4443; fax 275 5012) at 30 Kirkbride Rd has a share-facility lodge with single/double rooms at $35/45, a bunkroom with beds at $15 per person, and two-bedroom family units starting at $64 a double. There's a swimming pool, sauna and TV lounge, and courtesy transport to/from the airport, five minutes away.

Also near the airport, the *Airport Skylodge International* (☎ 275 1005; fax 275 1003) at 144 McKenzie Rd has standard units at $64, family units at $101 and hostel facilities at $20 per person. They, too, offer courtesy airport transport.

Places to Eat

Once the home of overwhelming blandness, Auckland has undergone a culinary revolution in the last decade or so. There are now all sorts of dining possibilities. Unlike some cities, there are no distinct ethnic areas – you can find almost anything almost anywhere.

In the city centre, a number of good cafes and good but inexpensive restaurants are scattered along High St/Lorne St, running parallel to Queen St, one block over. Of course there are plenty of places to eat on Queen St, too; some characterful little places are on Queen St up the hill a bit, towards Karangahape Rd ('K Rd'). Other districts in the city with good cafes and restaurants include K Rd, Ponsonby and Parnell.

Fast Food Food courts are popular for quick eating in Auckland. At the foot of Queen St, the Downtown Shopping Centre on QE II Square, on the corner of Queen St and Customs St West, has the *Upstairs Downtown Food Court*. The lower ground floor of the *BNZ Tower* on the corner of Queen St and Shortland St/Swanson St also has a good food court. The *Finance Plaza* on the corner of Queen St and Durham St has a food court up on the 4th floor, by the *Tapas Bar* which is also great for economical meals. In Queen St down from Wellesley St, the *Countrywide Bank Centre* also has a food court.

In case you were wondering, yes, Auckland has *McDonald's*, quite a number of them in fact. You'll find one in the QE II Square Upstairs Downtown Food Court, another up on the 4th floor of the Finance Plaza on Queen St, another about halfway up Queen St between Victoria and Wellesley Sts, and yet another just around the corner on Karangahape Rd. The one on K Rd is open every day from 7 am until midnight.

There's a *Wendy's* upstairs in Queen St, just down from Wellesley St. In the same block but a bit further down the hill, opposite McDonald's, there's a *Pizza Hut* downstairs in the Strand Arcade.

Cafes & Cheap Eats There are numerous places in the city where you can dine inexpensively. Along High St/Lorne St, the little *Cafe Aroma* at 18 Lorne St has good food at good prices; on weekdays it's open from 7 am for breakfast, closing around 5 pm (7.30 pm on Friday). Down the road, the *Krautz Expresso Bar* at 2 Lorne St is also popular, with tables inside and in a pleasant little courtyard out the back.

In the next block, on the corner of High St and Victoria St East, *Boulangerie Croix du Sud* is a French bakery with a good selection of croissants, breads, baguette sandwiches and lunch-time snacks. Next door, *61 High St* at yes, 61 High St, is good for sandwiches at lunch time, as is the *Periwinkles Cafe* opposite.

Also here near the High St/Victoria St East

corner, next door to one another, *Paneton* at 60 High St and *La Cucina* at 58 High St are popular sidewalk cafes with espresso, sandwiches, focaccia bakes and so on. Paneton is also a bakery, with wholemeal baked goods. Further down High St, *Rakino's* upstairs on the 1st floor at No 35 is another cafe.

Still on High St/Lorne St, the *Simple Cottage* vegetarian restaurant (see Vegetarian) is good, as is *Ferlinghetti's*.

Vulcan Lane is a picturesque little alleyway running between High St and Queen St. Two sidewalk cafes, *Kerouac* and the *Rupina Cafe*, are opposite one another in Vulcan Lane. *Kerouac* is open from 7 am to 5 pm weekdays (later on Friday), 9 am to 4 pm on weekends, and they pride themselves on their breakfasts. The *Rupina Cafe* is open from 9 am to 9 pm weekdays, 24 hours on weekends. Both places are great for atmosphere and they're likely to be playing some fine jazz music when you show up.

Several other good places are up the hill on Queen St, between Aotea Square and K Rd. The *Caravanserai Tea House* at 430 Queen St is a casual, relaxing Middle Eastern caravanserai or way-station for relaxation and revitalisation of weary travellers where you can get a good lunch for $5, a *meze* combination platter for $10, or just hang out over coffee. Next door, the *Merchant Mezze Bar* is a similar place with good atmosphere, good music and good food. They serve light meals and snacks, mostly based on Middle Eastern and North African ideas, plus wines, beers and coffees.

In the same block, the *Mosquito Cafe* at 436 Queen St is another atmospheric little restaurant/cafe, specialising in Fijian and African food at good prices.

Keep on going up Queen St and you reach some more good cafes and restaurants. The *Baan Thai* restaurant on the corner of Queen St and Turner St is open for dinner every night, with plenty of vegetarian and meat selections. A little further up the hill, the *Cafe Hasan Baba* has Turkish food and a beautiful full-wall mural of the Blue Mosque in Istanbul. Up the block a bit more, the *Espresso Temple* at 486 Queen St is a hip little cafe featuring 'cool coffee, kai and music'. Live music is featured on a regular basis.

In Karangahape Rd, the *Verona Cafe* at 169 K Rd and *Urbi et Orbi* at 361 K Rd are two popular cafes, both open long hours.

Also don't forget the *University Cafeteria*, on the university campus, as another city cheap eats possibility.

The cheap eats and late nights quandary can be solved by *The White Lady* mobile hamburger stand on Shortland St off Queen St. It's open 6 pm to 3 am Monday to Wednesday, until 3.30 am on Thursday, and 24 hours on weekends and holidays. A variety of burgers start at $4, there are plenty of toasted sandwiches, or you can splurge all the way up to $10 for a big steak.

Cafe Forte on the corner of Fort and Commerce Sts, one block off Queen St, is open 24 hours; it's a very simple place to get breakfast or basic meals and snacks any time of the day or night.

Markets The large markets have plenty of possibilities for interesting and inexpensive eating. The *Victoria Park Market* has several eating places including *Rick's Café Américain*, which is open all day from 7.30 am and has live music, mostly jazz, in the evening. The *China Oriental Market* on Quay St and the *Dockside Market* on Princes Wharf also have good, cheap eats.

Opposite the Victoria Park Market, the *Bird Cage* on the corner of Victoria St West and Franklin Rd is most known for its jazz but it's also a restaurant, priding itself on its good-value $5 cooked breakfasts. It's open weekdays from 7.30 am until late, weekends from 9.30 am until late.

Pub Food The various city pubs are another economical eating possibility, particularly at lunch time. The three pleasant pubs at the *Shakespeare Brewery*, on the corner of Albert and Wyndham Sts, all serve food, as does the bistro of the *London Bar* up on the 1st floor at Wellesley St West near the corner of Queen St. The *Blarney Stone Irish Pub* at 50-52 Customs St East has good lunch and dinner menus, with special low-cost back-

packers meals. The English-style *Nags Head Tavern* on St Georges Bay Rd near The Strand, at the bottom of the hill in Parnell, serves lunch, dinner and snacks in its restaurant section, and is especially popular at lunch time. Upstairs in the Downtown Airline Terminal on Quay St by the waterfront the *Rock Garden* serves lunch and dinner both inside and out on the patio, catching the breeze off the sea.

Backpackers Meals Lots of international backpackers and budget travellers visit New Zealand, and most of them arrive and depart from Auckland. This means that there are almost always lots of international backpackers around Auckland, whether they're just arriving in the country, or about to leave, or just sticking around the city for a while. A couple of places have been set up just to serve them, providing inexpensive meals and an atmosphere that backpackers would like.

The two backpackers bars, *Tapas Bar* and the *Kiwi Tavern* (see Entertainment), both serve good inexpensive meals. They both have a menu of $5 meals, plus specials throughout the week (pizza night on Tuesday or whatever).

Some of the larger downtown hostels have cafes. The *Cafe at the World's End* is in the Auckland Central Backpackers at 9 Fort St, near the lower end of Queen St, and there's also a cafe downstairs at the Queen St Backpackers across the street. Or there's the *Simply Delicious Cafe* in the Auckland City YHA Hostel, on the corner of City Rd and Liverpool St further up the hill just off Queen St; it's open only for breakfast and dinner in winter, for lunch too in summer.

Restaurants There are many good restaurants around the centre, and they don't have to be expensive.

Tony's at 27 Wellesley St West must be doing something right because they've been carrying on unchanged while plenty of other places have come and gone. They have a basic steakhouse menu which also features NZ lamb dishes and pastas. A good steak dinner, with starter and dessert, may cost around $30, or about $12 for lunch. There's another *Tony's* at 32 Lorne St and the very similar *Lord Nelson Steak House* at 39 Victoria St West.

The *Mekong* up on the 4th floor at 295 Queen St has been consistently voted the 'best ethnic restaurant in Auckland' by all and sundry. It's got a varied collection of Vietnamese specialities with main courses around $15 and smaller portions at $8.50; it's open every day from 4 pm onward.

A number of places in the city provide Italian food, including *A Little Italy* at 43 Victoria St West where you can get good pizzas or pasta.

For Mexican food, the *Mexican Cafe* upstairs at 67 Victoria St West has a fun, casual atmosphere; its bar and its restaurant sections are equally popular, it's not too expensive and there are plenty of vegetarian and meat dishes to choose from. Another fine Mexican restaurant, the tiny *Hard to Find Cafe* at 47 High St has a bright Mexican decor and healthy food. It is indeed hard to find, tucked away back from the street in an arcade. Main courses are around $15 at either place; both are open for dinner every night, for lunch Monday to Friday.

You can go Chinese at anything from cheap takeaways to flashy restaurants. The *New Orient Chinese Restaurant* in the Strand Arcade on Queen St has a buffet lunch from noon to 2.30 pm Monday to Friday for $14; dinner nightly with dancing every night except Sunday, when there's a $19 buffet dinner.

There are several fine Indian restaurants around town; the *Poppadom* and the *Maharajah* have both won awards for the 'best Indian restaurant in Auckland'. The *Poppadom* downstairs at 55 Customs St East near Queen St has à la carte selections or an ample combination banquet for $14 at lunch time, $24 at dinner. The *Maharajah* at 19 Khyber Pass Rd is also very popular. Both are open every night for dinner and in the daytime for lunch on weekdays.

The *Middle East* at 23A Wellesley St West is a tiny place and usually pretty crowded.

Deservedly so since the food is excellent and economical – the usual Lebanese specialities (schwarma, kebabs, felafel) at around $4 to $7 for snacks or $14 to $16 as full meals with salad and pita bread. Check out their great collection of camel art. Also on Wellesley St West, *Cafe Efes* at No 58 has Mediterranean food – Turkish, Greek, Lebanese, etc – and belly dancing on Friday, Saturday and Sunday nights. It has excellent prices, with a $6 lunch special, vegetarian main courses for about $8.50 to $13, meat main courses for about $10. Both places are open for dinner every night, for lunch on weekdays only.

For authentic Turkish food, try the similarly priced *Midnight Express Cafe* at 59 Victoria St West, near the Mexican Cafe. It has great food and great atmosphere, with a beautiful mural of sunset in Istanbul, good music, regular tables in front and low tables with cushions in the rear. It's open from 11 am to 11 pm on weekdays, weekends from 5 to 11 pm.

Several glossy places provide drinks and meals with a stylish air. Try the Wine Bar in the *Hotel De Brett* on the corner of High and Shortland Sts or *Cheers Cafe & Bar* at 12 Wyndham St, just off Queen St, open every day of the year from 11 am to 1 am. The *Cin Cin Brasserie & Bar* in the Auckland Ferry Building at 99 Quay St has a fine view of the ferries and harbour; it's open from 10 am to around 3 am.

If you want to splurge on a meal in a unique setting with a magnificent view over the city, try the revolving *Restaurant 360°* on the top floor of the Telecom Building in Hereford St, off Karangahape Rd. The restaurant takes one hour to make a complete 360° revolution, giving you a view of the entire city as you go round. The food is a lavish all-you-can-eat buffet which costs $18 at lunch time, $25 to $28 at dinner, $20 at Sunday brunch, or $12 for late supper on Friday and Saturday nights from 10 pm until late. Children are charged $1 for each year of their age, up to 12 years.

Surprisingly, despite the big Polynesian population there's no Polynesian restaurant as yet.

Vegetarian On Queen St just a couple of doors down the hill from Aotea Square, *Gopals* upstairs on the 1st floor at 291 Queen St is run by the Hare Krishnas. At this relaxed, comfortable place Indian vegetarian food is served and you can get snacks, à la carte meals, a student brunch for $4, lunch for $5 or an all-you-can-eat buffet for $7.95. It's open for dinner from 5 to 8.30 pm every night, for lunch from noon to 2.30 pm on weekdays.

The *Simple Cottage* at 50 High St is another popular vegetarian place with good, economical vegetarian food and some fine desserts. It's open long hours, from 9 am to 9 pm Monday to Saturday, 3 to 9 pm Sunday. Across the road and down a bit is *Badgers* at 47 High St, a tiny place with a good variety of wholesome vegetarian food to take away or eat there. Hot lunches are about $3 to $5.50, salads an extra $4. It's open Monday to Thursday from 10 am to 8 pm, Friday until 9 pm.

Across Victoria St, *Ferlinghetti's* at 12-14 Lorne St is a small cafe with organic vegetarian and vegan food.

Restaurants – Parnell There are all sorts of restaurants along Parnell Rd in Parnell. They range from pizzerias to pub food specialists to Chinese takeaways to espresso coffee shops and a number of Italian restaurants.

Starting at the top of the hill and working our way down, the *Kebab Kid* opposite the library near the top of the hill at 363 Parnell Rd is small and nothing much to look at, but it's been voted one of the top spots of its kind in Auckland, with tasty Middle Eastern food to take away or eat there and prices lower than most places in town, even though it's in fancy Parnell. You can get a *meze* selection of five salads for two people for $13 or a simple salad, felafel or meat-filled pita for around $6. The Kebab Kid is open every day from noon until around 10 or 11 pm.

The Parnell Village conglomeration of shops has some good medium-priced restaurants hidden away, several with tables in open courtyards so you can enjoy the fresh air. There's *Papagayo* for Mexican, Filipino and Spanish food, *Valerio's* for Italian food, *Thai Friends* for Thai food and *New-Ko-A* for Japanese and Korean food. The bright and pleasant *Konditorei Boss* German pastry shop/cafe is highly enjoyable for European pastries, espresso concoctions and light meals. Tucked away in the rear of Parnell Village, is the arty little *Boardwalk* vegetarian cafe.

Hidden behind some other shops but also worth looking for is the *Elephant House Crafts Centre and Vegetarian Cafe*, down the hill a bit at 237 Parnell Rd, with a greenhouse-like cafe area loaded with plants. The *Parnell Coffee House* on the corner of Parnell Rd and Gibraltar Crescent is another pleasant place for a coffee.

The *Oak and Whale* at No 269 was once a straightforward pub but has now been upgraded to a large, popular restaurant with an interesting menu, a wine list, and occasional live music. Next door, *La Trattoria Cafe* at 259 Parnell Rd is a fancy Italian/continental restaurant with dining inside or out on a torch-lit patio. Less expensive Italian places along Parnell Rd include the *Italian Cafe & Bar* at No 207, *Portofino* at No 158, *Portobello* at No 131, *Chianti* at No 115 and the *Milano* at No 111. Several of these places are combination Italian restaurants/pizzerias where you can take the food away or dine there.

Ajo at 161 Parnell Rd and *Cafe Birak* nearby are two trendy new places with eclectic menus. The large *Maruhachi Restaurant* on the corner of Parnell Rd and Akaroa St is a Japanese restaurant with a sushi bar, tempura and teppanyaki.

Restaurants – Ponsonby Ponsonby is one of Auckland's most popular restaurant districts, with numerous restaurants and cafes offering all sorts of cuisines strung out over many blocks along Ponsonby Rd, interspersed with many other kinds of businesses. You can walk along here in the daytime or evening and see what captures your fancy.

Beginning on the corner of Ponsonby Rd and Jervois Rd, *The Gluepot* has reasonable pub food and snacks. Around the corner and one block down on Jervois Rd are three good places. The *Shahi Cafe* at 26 Jervois Rd is a good, inexpensive Indian restaurant and takeaway, with seating upstairs in the restaurant and a takeaway counter downstairs by the door. Nearby is the *Cheminée Cafe* at No 32, and a little further along at No 42 Jervois Rd is the famous *Death By Chocolate*, featuring expensive but fantastic chocolate desserts.

Heading down Ponsonby Rd from the Ponsonby Rd/Jervois Rd corner, one block down is Pompallier Terrace with a couple of fine places to eat, both near the corner of Ponsonby Rd. *Freiya's* is probably one of Auckland's most interesting restaurants, serving Parsee food – it's one of only two Parsee restaurants in the southern hemisphere. They explain that over 1000 years ago, a small group of Zoroastrians who became known as Parsees migrated from the province of Pars in ancient Persia and landed on the shores of western India, eventually developing a unique cuisine blending Caspian and Indian influences. The restaurant is small and has a fine atmosphere, with good music playing and wonderful aromas in the air; it's very popular so you may want to reserve a table (☎ 376 3738). Main courses are around $15 and they also do takeaways. It's open for dinner Tuesday to Sunday from 6 pm.

Opposite Freiya's, *Java Jive* has a reasonably priced menu with a selection of meat and vegetarian dishes, plus strong coffees and good desserts. Live music starts every night around 9.30 or 10.30 pm (see Entertainment); the restaurant/cafe opens every night at 6 pm. They have a great collection of jazz and blues music, a good jazz/blues mural and other jazzy art.

Cafe Cezanne at 296 Ponsonby Rd is a small, casual place with a great atmosphere and good food at good prices. Breakfasts, light meals, gourmet burgers and unusual pies are served all day, all at around $7, and there's a good dinner menu, late night desserts and espresso. Someone will come around to your table and serve you bottomless cups of coffee. The cafe is open from 8

am to midnight every day, closing later (around 1.30 am) on weekends. Next door the *Cafe Mediterranean*, open every day from around noon until 1 am, has Middle Eastern takeaways from about $5 to $7 but it's lots more expensive if you sit down to eat in the restaurant. The *Expresso Love* coffeehouse and the Turkish *Cafe Hasan Baba* are across the road.

The *Musical Knives* at 272 Ponsonby Rd is a good vegetarian cafe and restaurant with an innovative menu that changes every fortnight; it's open every day from 10 am to 3 pm, and from 6 to 10.30 pm, except Sunday nights. *Fed Up* at No 244, open for dinner every night and for brunch on weekends, is kind of shabbily kitsch but there's real art on the walls and real food at reasonable prices as well. The dishes are imaginative, well-prepared and great value. Next door, the *Bake Haus* has wonderful baked goods of every description.

The *Star Horse* at 185 Ponsonby Rd near the corner of Franklin Rd offers a Chinese all-you-can-eat buffet for only $8.90 from 5.30 to 10 pm every evening and, naturally, it's always busy. Another place where you can get cheap Chinese food is the *East Ocean Chinese Takeaway* at No 268. In the fast food and takeaways category, also along here is a *Kentucky Fried Chicken*, a number of pizzerias and Italian restaurants.

Two of the trendiest spots in Auckland on our most recent visit, both sort of a mixture of bar-cafe-restaurant, were the *Tuatara* at 198 Ponsonby Rd and *SPQR* at 150 Ponsonby Rd. We could barely squeeze through the door of the *Tuatara* on a Thursday night; it's open every day from 11 am (10 am on weekends) until around midnight or 1 am. The smaller *SPQR* is open every day from 8 am to 2 am. Opposite SPQR, the *Atomic Cafe* is open from 7.30 am during the week, a bit later on weekends; next door is the *Ponsonby Natural Foods* grocery store.

The *Open Late Cafe* at 134A Ponsonby Rd on the corner of Picton St is a popular cafe in the evening, with meals, good desserts and coffee, and it is indeed open late – until 3 am on weeknights, 4 am on weekends.

Entertainment

Auckland has a good variety of places to go after the sun sets. The Auckland Visitor Centre in Aotea Square keeps a complete up-to-date list of all the city's activities and events including music, concerts, theatre, opera, dance, sports and anything else you can think of. The entertainment section in the Saturday *Herald* also gives a good run-down on events for the week.

Whatever you're doing late at night in Auckland, keep your eye on the time if you're dependent on public transport – the buses finish at about 10.30 pm, Sunday at 7 pm.

English, Irish & Scottish-Style Pubs The
Civic Tavern at 1 Wellesley St West near the corner of Queen St is 'Auckland's British Pub' with three bars on three floors, each specialising in a different part of the UK. Upstairs is the *London Bar*, an English-style pub with a live jazz band Tuesday to Saturday nights, a bistro open for lunch and dinner every day except Sunday, and a selection of 140 beers from around the world, including English ale on tap. *Murphy's Irish Bar* on the ground floor has an Irish band Thursday to Saturday nights and on Sunday afternoons. Downstairs, *Younger's Tartan Bar* is a Scottish-style bar with a Celtic band Thursday to Saturday nights and a selection of 120 to 140 different Scotch whiskies and 70 malts.

The *Shakespeare Tavern & Brewery* on the corner of Wyndham and Albert Sts brews six different brews on the premises, including three ales, one stout, one lager and one ginger beer. If you can drink all six in one night you get a certificate of achievement! Here too there are three different bars on three floors. It's a popular spot, featuring live music on weekends and poetry readings on Monday nights.

Kitty O'Brien's Irish Pub at 2 Drake St, Freemans Bay, is on the corner of Drake and Wellesley Sts near the Victoria Park Market. Live music, usually Irish, is featured every night except Monday. The *Blarney Stone Irish Pub* at 50-52 Customs St East in the centre features live music, usually Irish and rock, on Thursday to Saturday nights and on Sunday afternoons.

In Parnell the *Nags Head Tavern* at the bottom of St George's Bay Rd near The Strand is a popular English-style pub where it's a challenge to squeeze through the door on Friday nights. It has live music on Wednesday and Friday nights and on Sunday afternoons, with lots of acoustic and Irish music. Meals are served in a restaurant section off to one side.

The *Albion Hotel* on the corner of Wellesley St West and Hobson St has live Irish folk music on Tuesday nights, another band on Friday nights.

Jazz & Blues *Java Jive* at 12 Pompallier
Terrace, just off Ponsonby Rd in Ponsonby, has live music every night, mostly jazz and blues. Sunday is country music night, Monday is blues jam night, and there's always good music playing. Around the corner, *The Gluepot* on the corner of Ponsonby Rd and Jervois Rd has live music every night, with jazz and blues once in a while.

The *Bird Cage* on the corner of Victoria St West and Franklin Rd, opposite the Victoria Park Market, features live jazz and blues on Thursday and Friday nights and on Sunday afternoons in the conservatory. Half a block away, on Victoria St West on one side of the Victoria Park Market, *Rick's Café Américain* has live music, mostly jazz, every night except Friday and Saturday. In Parnell another Rick's, *Rick's Blue Falcon* at 27 Falcon St one block off Parnell Rd has live jazz or blues every night, with a jazz jam on Tuesday.

The *London Bar* in the Civic Tavern at 1 Wellesley St West near the corner of Queen St has a jazz combo Tuesday to Saturday nights. The *Shortland Bar* downstairs at the Hotel De Brett on the corner of Shortland and High Sts has live jazz on Friday and Saturday nights.

The *Kestrel* 'jazz ferry' runs back and forth between Auckland and Devonport from 7 pm until midnight on Friday and Saturday evenings, with a jazz band on board, dining and a dance floor. See the Devonport section for details.

Latino & Salsa *El Inca* at 373 Karangahape Rd is a lively place with salsa music for dancing from Thursday to Sunday nights, with no cover charge. A restaurant area is in the rear.

Backpackers Bars/Cafes Auckland has some popular backpackers hangouts with good cheap food, casual friendly atmosphere, and entertainment.

The *Tapas Bar* up on the 4th floor of the Finance Plaza on the corner of Queen St and Durham St has disco music and dancing every night and it's an enormously popular spot with backpackers, with a good $5 lunch and dinner menu, and various weekly specials including $5 all-you-can-eat buffet nights. It's open every day from 11 am until 3 am Sunday to Wednesday, until 6 am Thursday to Saturday nights. Also up here on the 4th floor are *Margarita's* with live music on weekends, and the *Club Plaza Disco*.

The *Kiwi Tavern*, in Britomart Place, just off Customs St West opposite the China Oriental Market, has three separate floors with the Moa Bar on the ground floor, the Haka Bar on the 1st floor with occasional live music and the Loft Bar upstairs where you can hang out, relax, play pool or darts, have a coffee or beer, read international newspapers, hire bicycles, leave off your luggage, check out the travellers' notice board and generally take it easy. The Kiwi Tavern is open every day from 8 am to 3 am, later in summer.

Right downtown on Fort St just off Queen St, *Park in the Bar* downstairs at the Queen St Backpackers and the *Bar at the World's End* in the Auckland Central Backpackers are other popular backpackers hangouts. The Bar at the World's End has an outdoor 7th-floor rooftop deck with tables and BBQs all year round, plus an indoor restaurant and a bar with weekly pool competitions. It's a bar especially for backpackers and all are welcome, guests and non-guests alike.

Rock, Disco & Other Rock venues tend to come and go but one of the most popular has long been *The Gluepot* on the corner of Ponsonby Rd and Jervois Rd in Ponsonby. They have live music of one kind or another every night – rock, jazz, blues or whatever – with three separate venues that may all have something going on at once. Larger rock concerts are held at *The Power Station* at 33 Mt Eden Rd in Mt Eden.

Next door, the *Rugby Pub Tavern* at 51 Fort St is a rugby hangout, with rugby on big screen TV. The *Carlton Club* on the corner of Broadway and Khyber Pass in Newmarket is a popular rugby and sports bar; the *Rock Garden* (read on) is also into sports.

The *Hotel de Brett* on the corner of Shortland and High Sts in the city has six pubs and bars, including the *de Brett Wine Bar* that's a popular meeting place with good food, the upstairs *House Bar* set up like an original 1930s cocktail bar, the downstairs *Shortland Bar* with jazz music on weekends, and various bars with pool tables and so on. The *DOS Bar* ('Department of Sound') upstairs in the Hotel de Brett has a DJ disco on Friday and Saturday nights.

Galatos is a nightclub in the Old Customs House building on the corner of Customs St West and Albert St. *Abby's Hotel* on the corner of Wellesley St East and Albert St has several bars featuring live entertainment. The *Shakespeare Brewery* also has music.

The *Sugar Reef* in the Civic Theatre on Queen St is a rock/disco venue with a trendy mid-20s crowd, as is *Steelz* nightclub, with disco on weekends, at 184 Victoria St West. *Le Bom* at 51 Nelson St and *The Venue* also have rock. The more upmarket *Rock Garden* upstairs in the Downtown Airline Terminal on Quay St has light rock and jazz music on weekends (nothing too heavy here), and it's also into sports, sponsoring various teams. Up on Karangahape Rd, try the *TNT* nightclub.

Auckland's two leading gay bars are in the large, glossy building on the corner of Albert and Wolfe Sts, opposite the Regent Hotel. *The Staircase* is a popular nightclub, disco and bar, while *The Bar* is a more low-key bar and gathering place. Both are up on the 1st floor; the entrance to The Staircase is a doorway on Albert St, while the entrance to The Bar is a doorway around the corner on Wolfe St. The *Midnight Club* at 37 Albert St is another popular gay bar. *Alfie's* in the Century Arcade on High St, formerly Auckland's most popular gay bar and disco, is still there but it's been a bit eclipsed by the other places.

In the 'other' category is the *Espresso Temple* at 486 Queen St, a hip little cafe with eclectic live music several nights a week and a weekly lunch-time pianist.

Poetry The *Shakespeare Tavern Brewery* on the corner of Albert and Wyndham Sts has poetry readings every Monday night. Over in Devonport, the *Masonic Tavern* on the corner of Church St and the waterfront parade has poetry readings on the first Wednesday of each month.

Theatre There are various live theatre venues around the city centre. They include the *Mercury Playhouse* (☎ 303 0693) in France St, Newton, off Karangahape Rd, the *Galaxy Theatre* (☎ 302 0095) in the Old Customs House on the corner of Customs St West and Albert St, and the *Maidment Theatre* (☎ 379 3685) on the corner of Princes and Alfred Sts. The *Watershed Theatre* (☎ 357 0888) in the Turners & Growers Building on the corner of Customs St West and Market Place specialises in alternative theatre.

Other Entertainment The Aotea Centre in Aotea Square on Queen St is a venue for all kinds of performances and concerts; stop by or phone for their current schedule (☎ 309 2678). Also check out the Auckland Philharmonia Orchestra (☎ 638 7073), the New Zealand Symphony Orchestra (☎ 358 0952) and the New Zealand Ballet Co (☎ 358 3580).

Auckland University has a restaurant, pub, live music, plays, film series, lectures, and more. Art films can be seen at the University or at the *Vogue, Academy, Capitol* or *Bridgeway* theatres, the last being in Northcote.

Many good cinemas around the city show first-run films; check the newspaper for listings.

Several of the harbour boats offer evening entertainment, with dinner and dancing cruises.

Getting There & Away

Air Auckland is the major arrival and departure point for international flights to/from New Zealand. See the Information section for airline office locations, and the Getting There & Away chapter for information on international flights.

Air New Zealand, Ansett New Zealand and Mt Cook Airline connect Auckland with the other major centres in New Zealand. See the introductory Getting Around chapter for fare details. A number of local operators also have flights in and out of Auckland.

The Auckland airport is 21 km south-west of the centre. It has two terminals – an International Terminal and a Domestic Terminal. A free shuttle service operates between the two, and there's also a signposted footpath.

Each terminal has a tourist information centre (International Terminal ☎ 275 7467, Domestic Terminal ☎ 275 0789, ext 8943). At the International Terminal there's a free telephone for making accommodation bookings, and a bank open to change money for all arriving and departing flights. Both terminals have left luggage facilities and there are also a few rent-a-car desks, though you'll get much better rates from rent-a-car companies in town.

Bus InterCity buses have services from Auckland to just about everywhere in New Zealand. See the relevant sections for details. InterCity buses operate from the Auckland InterCity Travel Centre (☎ 358 4085) beside the railway station. The office is open Monday to Thursday from 7.45 am to 5.30 pm, Friday 7.45 am to 6 pm, and weekends from 8 am to 2.30 pm.

Newmans buses (☎ 309 9738) operate from the Downtown Airline Terminal, Quay St and their buses go just about everywhere in the North Island. Northliner Express buses

(☎ 307 5873) also operate from the Downtown Airline Terminal, with services heading north from Auckland to Whangarei, the Bay of Islands and Kaitaia.

A number of backpackers buses operate in and from Auckland; all offer door-to-door service, picking you up and letting you off at any hostel in Auckland, and they can be cheaper, friendlier and more fun than the commercial bus companies. They include:

Kiwi Experience (☎ 366 1665)
  Goes to many places all over New Zealand
Green Beetle (☎ 358 5868)
  Goes to Northland
Awesome Adventures (☎ 366 1665)
  Tour of Northland
Kiwi Safaris (☎ freephone (0800) 800 616)
  Does a 'Mud & Worm Loop' circle from Auckland to Thames, Te Aroha, Rotorua, Waitomo and back to Auckland (or vice versa) .
Sunkist Lodge Bus Services (☎ (07) 868 8808)
  Operating from the Sunkist Lodge hostel in Thames, it offers service from Auckland to Thames and on to Whitianga
C Tours (☎ (06) 758 1777, freephone (0508) 224 422)
  Based in New Plymouth, does daily runs between Auckland and New Plymouth, stopping at Hamilton and Waitomo on the way

Train Trains arrive and depart from the railway station (☎ freephone (0800) 802 802) on Beach Rd. You can phone for reservations and information every day from 7 am to 9 pm.

Two trains operate between Auckland and Wellington, about a 10-hour trip. The Overlander train runs every day, departing both ends in the morning and arriving around dinnertime. The Northerner is an overnight train operating every night except Saturday, departing each end in the evening and arriving early in the morning.

The Geyserland train operates twice daily between Auckland and Rotorua, a four-hour trip. The Kaimai Express train operates daily between Auckland and Tauranga, a 3½ hour trip with a stop in Hamilton on the way.

Hitching As usual, it's easier hitching if you get out of town before starting to hitch, but if you want to hitchhike from town use the Beaumont St motorway ramp near Victoria Park to go north, the Grafton Bridge ramp behind the hospital to go south.

Otherwise, to get out of the urban sprawl and start hitching northwards take a bus from the Downtown Bus Terminal to Waiwera (bus No 895), Hatfields Beach (bus No 894), Orewa (bus No 893) or Silverdale (bus No 899). All leave about six times a day and cost about $5. Alternatively, you can take an hourly bus to Albany for about $3 and start hitching from there.

To get a good early start hitching north, you can bus to Orewa, stay overnight there (the Marco Polo hostel is very convenient) and be on the highway first thing in the morning.

Going south, take any southbound long-distance bus and get off at the Bombay Hills crossroads. Buses leave many times daily; the cost is around $10.

Getting Around
Airport Transport The Auckland Airport is 21 km south-west of the centre. Door-to-door airport shuttle servicse include Super Shuttle (☎ 307 0500), Johnston's Shuttle Express (☎ 256 0333) and Airport Shuttle (☎ 576 8904). The cost between the airport and the city centre is around $15 for one person, $20 for two, $25 for three. Super Shuttle offers a backpackers rate of $9 one-way ($14 return) if you're going to or from a hostel.

A shuttle bus runs every half hour between the airport and the Downtown Airline Terminal (☎ 275 9396, 275 7685), starting at 6.30 am and finishing at 8.45 pm, with scheduled stops along the way. The cost is $9 one-way, $14 return, and the trip takes about 40 minutes.

Bus Local bus routes operate every day from around 6.30 am to 10.30 pm, finishing earlier (around 7 pm) on Sunday.

The Downtown Bus Terminal is on Commerce St, between Quay St and Customs St East, but not all buses leave from here. Local bus route timetables are available from the bus terminal, from newsagents, from the

Auckland Visitor Centre, or you can phone Buz-a-Bus (☎ 366 6400) for information and schedules. It operates from 7 am to 7 pm weekdays, until 9 pm on Friday, from 8 am to 7 pm on Saturday and 8 am to 6 pm on Sunday, although on weekends you may have trouble getting an answer as there aren't enough people to answer the phone. There's a bus information kiosk at the Downtown Bus Terminal open 7 am to 6.45 pm Monday to Friday, 8.30 am to 5 pm on weekends. The Bus Place at 93 Victoria St on the corner of Hobson St is another source of information, open from 8.15 am to 4.30 pm Monday to Friday. The *Auckland Busabout Guide* gives bus routes and departure points to the city's major attractions.

Inner city fares cost 40 cents, further distances cost $1, then $2 and so on. Busabout passes are available for unlimited daily bus use from 9 am onwards (anytime on weekends) for $8 (children $4). The passes can be bought on board the bus. Weekly passes are also available or there are family passes for $12.

Taxi There are plenty of taxis in Auckland but, as elsewhere in New Zealand, they rarely cruise. You usually have to phone for them or find them on taxi ranks.

Ferry For harbour ferry information phone 373 3776 for the Devonport ferry, 828 9003 for the Birkenhead ferry, and Fullers at 377 1771 or 373 3776 for information on ferries to Waiheke, Rangitoto, Great Barrier and other islands. See also the Harbour Cruises section.

Car & Campervan Rental The major rental operators plus a host of smaller ones have offices in Auckland, many of them at Mangere, near the airport. They include:

*Abcam	☎ 378 6391
Ace	☎ 378 8002
Action	☎ 267 5881
*Adventure	☎ 275 8994
Affordable	☎ 630 1567
Airport	☎ 446 0610
Alternative	☎ 373 3822

Avis	☎ 379 2650
*Avon	☎ 275 0194
Backpackers	☎ 358 0188
Bays Rentals	☎ 308 9004
Big Save	☎ 303 3928
*Blue Sky Motorhomes	☎ 827 6399
*Budget	☎ 379 6768
Care	☎ 303 0100
*Cheapa	☎ 827 4577
Clifton	☎ 489 6939
Dizzy Duck	☎ 377 8088
Dollarsave	☎ 480 9881
Economy	☎ 275 3777
*Gypsy Hire	☎ 480 5098
Henderson	☎ 838 8089
Hertz	☎ 303 4924
*Horizon	☎ 307 8226
Ideal	☎ 262 0464
*Leisureport	☎ 275 3013
Letz	☎ 275 6890
*Matthew	☎ 256 0555
*Maui	☎ 275 3013
McDonalds	☎ 276 8574
Metropolitan	☎ 630 2030
*Mt Cook	☎ 377 8389
Nationwide	☎ (0800) 803 003
National	☎ 275 0066
*Newmans	☎ 303 1149
North Harbour	☎ 486 0972
*Pegasus	☎ 358 5757
Percy	☎ 303 1122
*Realistic	☎ 302 2985
Rent-a-Dent	☎ 524 8891
Rent-a-Wreck	☎ 357 0019
*Rock Bottom	☎ 622 1592
Route 66	☎ 480 9881
Russells	☎ 836 3309
*Scotties	☎ 630 2625
Southern Cross	☎ 275 3099
*Suntrek	☎ 520 1404
Takapuna	☎ 486 5555
*Take It Easy	☎ 817 4387
Thrifty	☎ 358 4488
Ultra	☎ 275 3580
*Value	☎ 360 0099
*Wenderkreisen	☎ 810 9582

*All the ones with an asterisk have campervans as well as rental cars.

Car Buy-Backs If you're planning to tour the country for a while, it may work out cheaper to buy a car on the buy-back system – you buy the car from a dealer who guarantees to buy it back from you when you're ready to sell. You can get cars on this system in any price range, from old clunkers to top-line cars. (See the Getting Around chapter for more details about car buy-backs, fairs, auctions and ads.) Places in Auckland that sell cars on the buy-back system include:

Budget Car Sales
    12 Mt Eden Rd, City (☎ 379 4120)
Chris Stephen Motors
    155 Wairau Rd, Takapuna (☎ 443 0112)
Clarkes
    251 Great South Rd, Greenlane (☎ 520 2003)
Downtown Rentals
    2 Lower Hobson St, City (☎ 303 1847)
Geraghty McGregor Motors
    335 New North Rd (☎ 307 6700)
Rex Swinburne Motors
    825 Dominion Rd, Mt Roskill (☎ 620 6587)
Rock Bottom Rentals
    49 Nielson St, Onehunga (☎ 622 1592)

Motorcycle Rental If it's just a small scooter you're looking for, the Mobil Service Station (☎ 358 5757) at 48 Customs St East will hire you a scooter for $25 for 24 hours. Only a car drivers' licence is needed.

For larger motorcycles there are plenty of options. As with bicycles, some will hire you the motorcycle, others will sell it to you on a buy-back system, guaranteeing to buy it back from you for a fixed rate depending on how long you're keeping it. They usually hire anything from around a 250cc to a 750cc size.

Bill Russell Motorcycles (☎ 377 8739) at 24 Mt Eden Rd, Mt Eden sells 250cc to 750cc motorcycles on the buy-back system; occasionally they also have scooters. When they buy it back from you they deduct about $600 for one month, $800 for two months or $1000 for three months. Insurance is not included in this rate, but they will help you arrange insurance when you buy the bike, and they can also advise you about getting a motorcycle drivers' licence.

Mike Vinsen Suzuki (☎ 378 4095) at 300 Great North Rd, Grey Lynn hires motorcycles and sometimes mopeds and scooters. They also sell motorcycles and cars on the buy-back system.

Other places that hire motorcycles include Colemans Suzuki (☎ 303 1786) at 538 Ka-

rangahape Rd, Graeme Crosby (☎ 376 3320) at 299 Great North Rd, and Clifton Rentals (☎ 489 6939) in Shakespeare Rd, Milford.

Bicycle Rental Several companies around Auckland hire bicycles, usually mountain bikes, by the day, week, month or longer. They also hire all the gear you need for longer journeys – helmets, panniers, tents and so on. Most will help you work out a cycle touring route.

Some operate on a buy-back system. This can work out to be cheaper than hiring, if you're planning to tour around the country for a while.

The Penny Farthing Cycle Shop (☎ 379 2524, 379 2002; fax 309 1559) on the corner of Symonds St and Khyber Pass Rd hires mountain and hybrid bikes. The Mountain Bike Hire Co (☎ 358 4885) hires 21-speed mountain bikes in five sizes and they offer free delivery to wherever you're staying.

Bicycle Tour Services (☎ & fax 276 5218, mobile (026) 354 6134) at 22 Walmsley Rd, Otahuhu, opposite the railway station, hires mountain bikes, racing bikes, tandems and others by the day, week or month, and they'll help you make a touring itinerary for no extra charge. The Mobil Service Station (☎ 358 5757) at 48 Customs St East hires mountain bikes by the day, week or month and their prices are very competitive.

Cycle Xpress (☎ 379 0779) at 11 Beach Rd hires and sells new and used bikes and offers to buy them back on the buy-back system. Pack 'n Pedal at 16 Anzac St, Takapuna (☎ 489 6907) and at 436 Broadway in Newmarket (☎ 522 2161) hires and sells bikes on the buy-back system and also sells cycling gear and camping equipment.

Pedaltours (☎ 302 0968; fax 302 0967) at 28 Birdwood Crescent, Parnell offers guided group cycling tours of both the North and South Islands, and you can hire a bike from them even if you don't join one of their tours.

Another option for bicycle hire is the Kiwi Experience (☎ 366 1665), who hire out mountain bikes in connection with their bus services. Vouchers are available which will allow you to take their buses when you want (like over the hilliest parts or in bad weather) and they offer free delivery of your luggage ahead of you, meaning you don't have to carry it all on the bike. You can hire the bike and drop it off at various points around the country including Auckland, Wellington, Queenstown and Christchurch.

Around Auckland

REGIONAL PARKS

The Auckland Regional Council administers 21 regional parks around the Auckland region, all within 15 to 90 km of the city (20 minutes' to 1½ hours' driving time). There are several coastal and beach parks with swimming and surfing beaches, plus bush parks, a kauri park, the Waitakere Ranges west of Auckland, and a gannet colony at Muriwai on the coast north-west of the city. All the parks have good walks and tramping tracks, ranging from 20 minutes to several hours in length; several allow camping.

An Auckland Regional Parks pamphlet with photos, descriptions and a list of facilities available in each regional park is available from the Auckland Visitor Centre, the DOC information centre, or directly from the Regional Parks Central Office (☎ 366 2166) on the ground floor of the Regional House on the corner of Pitt and Hopetoun Sts.

VINEYARDS

New Zealand's wines have earned themselves an excellent worldwide reputation and there are numerous vineyards in the Auckland area. A leaflet available from the Auckland Visitor Centre details the vineyards, their addresses, opening hours and shows their locations on a map. A number are within walking distance of Henderson, which you can reach by public transport. Other fine vineyards are found on Waiheke Island, half an hour's boat ride from Auckland.

DEVONPORT

Devonport is an attractive suburb on the tip of Auckland's North Shore peninsula. It was one of the earliest areas of European settlement and with its many well-preserved Victorian buildings it retains a 19th-century atmosphere. Nowadays it also has a tourist atmosphere – it's the most popular excursion from Auckland centre, only 15 minutes away on the hourly ferry – and has lots of small shops, arts & crafts galleries, cafes and takeaways in the area surrounding the ferry dock.

Devonport also has several points of interest. Two volcanic cones, **Mt Victoria** and **North Head**, were once Maori pa settlements – you can see the terracing they made on the sides of the cones. Mt Victoria is the higher of the two, with a great 360° view and a map at the top pointing out all the landmarks and giving the names of the many islands you can see. You can walk or drive to the summit of Mt Victoria; the road is open all the time except from 6 pm to 7 am Thursday, Friday and Saturday.

North Head, on the other cone, is a historic reserve riddled with old tunnels built at the end of the last century due to fears of a Russian invasion. The fortifications were extended and enlarged during WW I and WW II but dismantled after WW II. Some of the old guns are still up here and a ranger is on hand with historical info. The reserve is open to vehicles every day from 6 am to 6 pm, to pedestrians until 10 pm.

The **waterfront promenade** of Devonport, with a view back towards the city, makes a good stroll. Near the ferry wharf is a childrens' playground and a large lawn area where families picnic on sunny days.

Walk west from the wharf along the promenade (left as you come out the doors of the wharf building) for about five blocks until you reach the navy base, then turn right into Spring St, and about a block away at the end of the street you'll come to the small **Naval Museum**, open from 10 am to 4.30 pm daily; admission is free but donations are appreciated.

On the other hand, if you turn right as you

exit the wharf building, walk along the waterfront promenade until you reach the foot of North Head, turn left into Cheltenham St and walk another five short blocks, you'll come to **Cheltenham Beach**, a lovely little beach with a superb view of Rangitoto Island.

Places to Stay

Devonport is an enjoyable place to stay, outside the city but within easy reach of it, and it has several good, small B&B guesthouses to choose from.

Pride of place goes to the *Peace & Plenty Inn* (☎ 445 2925; fax 302 0389) at 6 Flagstaff Terrace, very centrally situated just a one-minute walk from the ferry wharf – it's just one door off from Victoria Rd, facing the little triangular grassy park. In a restored historic New Zealand kauri house built around 1890, it's one of the most artistically and unusually decorated places we've seen, and they make good breakfasts too. The cost for B&B is $65 to $85 single, $95 to $125 double, in four attractive guest rooms, three with open fireplaces, all with shared or private bath.

Near the attractive Cheltenham Beach, *Devonport Villa* (☎ 445 2529; fax 486 8505) at 21 Cheltenham Rd is in an Edwardian villa with a swimming pool and four guest rooms priced from $60 to $75 for singles, $85 to $100 for doubles.

Down the other end of Cheltenham Beach, *Cheltenham by the Sea* (☎ 445 9437) at 2 Grove Rd just off Wairoa Rd, is a homely guesthouse in a family home; the cost is $45/65 for singles/doubles in three guest rooms, each with private entrance but all sharing the bath facilities. Around the corner, the *Trout & Kiwi* (☎ 445 1025; fax 445 4080) at 28 Ascot Ave on the corner of Wairoa Rd has just two guest rooms, each with its own private bath, at $60/80 for singles/doubles.

You'll see the *Esplanade Hotel* (☎ 455 1291; fax 445 1999) as soon as you get off the ferry – it's directly opposite the dock, on the corner of Victoria Rd and Queen's Parade. It's the only hotel in Devonport but it has definitely seen better days; the cost of $30/40 in single/twin rooms, $65 in the double suite, seems quite high considering the building's tired feeling.

Places to Eat

Devonport has a number of good restaurants and cafes to choose from, especially on Victoria St, the street heading inland when you come from the ferry wharf. The wharf building itself has a small food court with fast food counters, plus an upstairs restaurant, an ice cream counter and a sweets shop.

Heading up Victoria St from the wharf are several good restaurants and cafes. The first one you come to, the *Devonport Bar & Brasserie* at 5-7 Victoria Rd lets you know right on the door that 'a good standard of dress and behaviour is required' – so if you want to act crazy, don't come here! Further along Victoria St at No 55 are *Death by Chocolate, Delissimo Pizza* and the *Shamiana* Indian restaurant. Opposite at No 14, the *Left Bank* restaurant, cafe and bar in a converted old bank building has a pleasant courtyard out the back, meat dishes and a vegetarian dish changing daily. Next door is the *Devonport Delicatessen* and beside it the *Devonport Cafe*.

Opposite these, *Something Fishy* at No 71 is an expensive but good seafood restaurant. Also in Devonport's 'expensive but good' category are the *Low Flying Duck* at 99 Victoria St, winner of a recent 'best restaurant in Auckland' award, and the *Porterhouse Blue* restaurant at 58 Calliope Rd. Good, inexpensive food is served at *Garcia's Authentic Mexican Restaurant* at 161 Victoria Rd, open for dinner every night except Sunday.

For pub food, the *Masonic Tavern*, on the corner of Church St and the waterfront parade, a few blocks east of the docks, serves with lunch from noon to 2.30 pm, dinner from 5 pm Monday to Saturday. It has a relaxed local atmosphere and good views of the harbour.

Over on Cheltenham Beach, *McHugh's of Cheltenham* restaurant right on the beach at the end of Cheltenham Rd is an attractive licensed restaurant with a fine view of the beach and of Rangitoto Island offshore. It's open every day from noon to 2 pm for a buffet lunch which costs $18 on weekdays, $20 on weekends, and there's also a Sunday dinner buffet from 6 pm on for $25. Reservations are a good idea here (☎ 445 0305).

Entertainment

The *Masonic Tavern* has live bands on Friday night, and poetry readings on the first Wednesday of every month. The *Esplanade Hotel* has live music on Friday and Saturday nights.

The *Kestrel* 'jazz ferry' is also a good time. See the following section for more information.

Getting There & Away

Boat The Devonport ferry departs from the Auckland Ferry Building hourly, on the hour, from 6.15 am to 11 pm (midnight on Saturday, 10 pm on Sunday), leaving the Devonport dock to go back to Auckland hourly on the half hour, with more frequent sailings during commuter hours (6.15 to 9.15 am and 3 to 6.30 pm on weekdays). The return fare is $6 (children $3, family $14.50).

On Friday and Saturday evenings the *Kestrel*, a historic (1905) ferry sometimes affectionately called the 'jazz ferry', goes back and forth across the harbour from Auckland to Devonport, departing hourly from each side (Auckland on the hour, Devonport on the half-hour) from 7 pm to midnight. An open ticket for $6 (children $3) entitles you to go back and forth as many times as you like, or you can stay on the ferry all evening – there's a jazz band for dancing, a restaurant for dining, and all in all it's a very pleasant evening. Reservations are recommended for dining on the ferry (☎ 377 1771), but are not needed otherwise.

The Fullers Harbour Explorer stops at Devonport, Kelly Tarlton's Underwater World and Rangitoto Island; an all-day pass entitles you to jump on and off the boat wherever you like. Fullers (☎ 377 1771) has information on all the Devonport ferries.

You can also visit Devonport on an Old Devonport Ferry & Coach Tour from Auckland; see Auckland, Organised Tours.

Bus Buses to Devonport run regularly from the Downtown Bus Terminal in Auckland, but the ferry crossing is quicker – it's 10 or 15 minutes on the ferry, about 25 minutes by bus.

PIHA & WHATIPU

Piha, about 40 km west of Auckland, is a seaside village of maybe 500 to 1000 souls (many artists, craftspeople and alternative types), that comes alive in summer with hundreds of beachgoers, holidaymakers and surfers. In summer, in addition to the beach life, there's tennis, lawn bowling, live bands playing on weekends at the surf club, and lots of partying going on. Surfing competitions are held in Piha, and there are many good bushwalks through the surrounding Waitakere Ranges and along the rocky coastline. All in all it's a very enjoyable, picturesque spot, a refreshing change from Auckland.

A bus connects Piha with Auckland, but not very frequently – it runs on Friday all year round, leaving Auckland at 8.25am and 6.30 pm, and returning to the city at 9.40 am and 8 pm. There's also a bus on Sunday in summer between Labour Weekend (late October) and Easter, heading out to the beach at 10 am and returning at 3.30 pm. The trip takes about an hour and departs from the Downtown Bus Terminal in Auckland.

The *Piha Domain Campground* (☎ 812 8815) right on the beach is open all year round and has tent sites at $12.50 for two, powered sites at $15 for two, and on-site caravans at $30 for two. This is the only official accommodation in Piha, but several Piha residents have a caravan or two renting for about $10 to $12 per person a night; it's a good way to meet the locals as well as to enjoy Piha.

Another attractive spot is Whatipu, on the northern side of Manukau Harbour at Manukau Heads, 40 km from Auckland via Titirangi and Huia, about a 50-minute drive from the city. The *Whatipu Lodge* (☎ & fax 811 8860), in a quiet and isolated area good for tramping and fishing, has basic non-powered campsites at $8 per vehicle (up to four people), plus hostel-style accommodation with single, twin and double rooms at $18 per person. Take the bus to Huia and they'll come to pick you up.

Islands off Auckland

The Hauraki Gulf off Auckland is dotted with islands. Some are within minutes of the city and are popular for day trips. Waiheke Island in particular is a favourite weekend escape and has become almost a dormitory suburb of the city. Waiheke also has some fine beaches and hostels so it's a popular backpackers destination. Great Barrier Island, once a remote and not much visited island, is also becoming a popular destination. The islands are generally accessible by ferry services or light aircraft. There are a couple of 'getting there is half the fun' possibilities, like the elderly wooden auxiliary schooner *Te Aroha*.

Forty-seven islands are included in the Hauraki Gulf Maritime Park, administered by DOC. Some are good sized islands, others are simply rocks jutting out of the sea. The islands in the park are roughly classified into two categories: recreation islands and conservation islands. The recreation islands can be visited, transport is available to them, and their harbours are dotted with yachts in summer. The conservation islands, on the other hand, have severely restricted access. Special permits are required to visit some of them, and others cannot be visited at all, since these islands are refuges for the preservation of plant and animal life, especially birds, that are sometimes extremely rare or even endangered species.

Information
The Hauraki Gulf Islands are administered by DOC, so the DOC information centre in Auckland is the best place for information. It produces leaflets on several of the islands and can tell you about natural features, walk-

ways, camping and so on. The Auckland Visitor Centre is the place to go for information on the more commercial aspects of the islands – hotels, ferry services, etc. If you're planning to spend some time exploring, look for the DOSLI maps on Waiheke Island and Great Barrier Island.

RANGITOTO & MOTUTAPU ISLANDS
These two islands, joined by a causeway, are part of the Hauraki Gulf Maritime Park. Rangitoto is just 10 km from the city. The youngest of the 50 or so volcanic cones in the Auckland region, Rangitoto rose from the sea only about 600 years ago, in a series of volcanic explosions. The last eruption was 250 years ago. Rangitoto is the short version of Nga Rangi-itotongia-a-Tama-te-kapua, a name meaning 'the days of Tama-te-kapua's bleeding', as the chief of the *Arawa* canoe was wounded here.

Rangitoto is a good place for a picnic. It has lots of pleasant walks, a saltwater swimming pool, barbecues near the wharf and a great view from the summit of the 260 metre cone. Lava caves are another attraction. There's an information board with maps of the various island walks and a shop which is open while cruise ships are at the island.

The hike from the wharf to the summit takes about an hour and is worth it for the fine view. Up at the top, a loop walk goes around the crater's rim. The walk to the lava caves branches off the summit walk and takes 15 minutes one way. There are plenty of other long and short walks on the island, with several short and easy enough for children. Be sure to bring water if you're planning to do much tramping – on a sunny day the black lava gets pretty hot. You need good footwear as the whole island consists of lava with trees growing through it – no soil has developed as yet.

Motutapu, in contrast, is mainly covered in grassland, grazed by sheep and cattle. The island was bought from the Maoris in 1842 for 10 empty casks, four double-barrelled shotguns, 50 blankets, five hats, five pieces of gown material, five shawls and five pairs of black trousers. There's an interesting

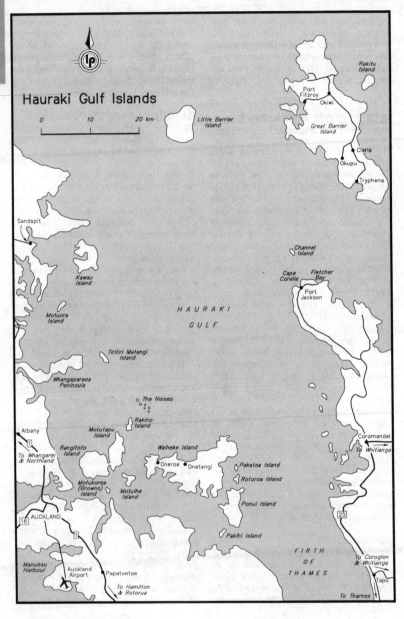

Hauraki Gulf Islands

0   10   20 km

Rakitu Island

Port Fitzroy
Okiwi

Great Barrier Island

Claris

Okupu

Tryphena

Little Barrier Island

Sandspit

Channel Island

Cape Colville
Fletcher Bay

Port Jackson

Kawau Island

Motuora Island

HAURAKI GULF

Tiritiri Matangi Island

Whangaparaoa Peninsula

The Noises

Rakino Island

Albany

Motutapu Island

Coromandel

To Whitianga

To Whangarei & Northland

Rangitoto Island

Waiheke Island

Oneroa   Onetangi

Pakatoa Island

Rotoroa Island

Motukorea (Browns) Island

Motuihe Island

16

AUCKLAND

Ponui Island

1

25

Pakihi Island

Manukau Harbour

Auckland Airport

Papatoetoe

FIRTH OF THAMES

To Hamilton & Rotorua

To Coroglen & Whitianga

Tapu

To Thames

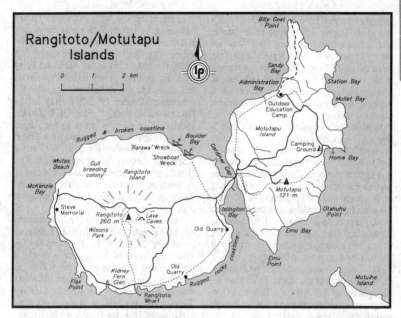

three-hour round trip walk between the wharf at Islington Bay and the wharf at Home Bay. Islington Bay, the inlet between the two islands, was once known as 'Drunken Bay' as sailing ships would stop here to sober their crews who had over-indulged in the bars of Auckland.

Places to Stay

There's a DOC campsite at Home Bay on Motutapu Island. Facilities are basic, with only a water tap and toilet provided at this fairly rudimentary campsite. Bring your own cooking equipment as open fires are not permitted. Camping fees are $3 per night. For more information contact the island's Senior Ranger (☎ 372 7348) or the DOC in Auckland.

Getting There & Away

The ferry trip to Rangitoto from the Ferry Building in Auckland takes about an hour. Fullers (☎ 377 1771) has ferries departing

every day at 9.30 am, midday and 2.30 pm. They depart from Rangitoto for the return trip at 10.30 am, 1 pm and 3.30 pm, with an extra departure leaving the island at 5 pm on Sunday. The return fare is $16 (children $8).

Fullers' Harbour Explorer ferry stops at Rangitoto Island and other places; see the Auckland Harbour Cruises section.

The Rangitoto Express, operated by Sinclairs Ferry Division (☎ 372 6892, 473 6977), is another service to Rangitoto and it, too, departs from the Auckland Ferry Building. It operates only on Friday, Saturday and Sunday, but in winter it may be going on Sunday only. The cost is $12 return (children $5). Reservations are required on this ferry. Some of the Rangitoto Express ferries continue from Rangitoto to Rakino Island, another hour further on.

WAIHEKE ISLAND

Half an hour's ferry ride from Auckland, Waiheke (population 6000) is the most visited of the gulf islands and at 93 sq km it's one of the largest. It's reputed to be sunnier and warmer than Auckland and there are plenty of beaches, so it's a popular day trip from the city. There's also plenty of accommodation should you want to stay longer. The atmosphere on Waiheke is very relaxed, the beaches are great, and it's an excellent place for taking it easy.

Waiheke has for many years been attracting all kinds of artistic and 'alternative lifestyle' folk – there are more artists per sq km here than you'll find almost anywhere else in New Zealand. Their work can be seen around the island in a number of galleries, craft shops and other places. In addition there's a lot more cultural life here than you would expect on an island with such a small population. The island also has a fair number of farmers, retirees and people who commute the half-hour to work in the city.

The island's main settlement is Oneroa, at the western end of the island. From there it's fairly built up through Palm Beach to Onetangi in the middle. Beyond this the eastern end of the island is lightly inhabited. The island is very hilly so riding around on a bicycle can be hard work. The coastline is an interesting mixture of coves, inlets and private little beaches.

Waiheke was originally discovered and settled by the Maoris. Legends relate that one of the pioneering canoes came to the island, and traces of an old fortified pa can still be seen on the headland overlooking Putiki Bay. The Europeans arrived with missionary Samuel Marsden in the early 1800s and the island was soon stripped of its kauri forests. It's still good for bushwalking, however.

Information

The Waiheke Island Visitor Board Information Centre (☎ 372 9999) is in the Pendragon Mall, a newish pink shopping centre right on the main road in Oneroa. It has maps and information about the island, and makes bookings for tours and accommodation. It also keeps a large binder full of contact information and examples of the artwork of many of Waiheke's artists and craftspeople.

In Auckland, the Auckland Visitor Centre has plenty of information about the island, and they can book any activity or accommodation. The Outdoor Adventure Co (☎ 358 5868; fax 358 5878) in the Auckland Ferry Building also has plenty of information on the island and can make bookings. The NZ Adventure Centre (☎ 309 9192) in the Downtown Shopping Centre, QE II Square, specialises in package tours to the island. The Auckland Central Backpackers Travel Centre (☎^358 4874; fax 358 4871) at the Auckland Central Backpackers Hostel, 9 Fort St, just off Queen St, also has plenty of information about the island and can make bookings for all activities and accommodation.

The *Gulf News* is a weekly newsmagazine of island events. *Waiheke Island – A Tour*, an interesting little booklet produced by the Waiheke Historical Society, is available at the Waiheke information centre and at the museum. You can use it to make your own tour or just to learn about the island. *Island Time – a visitor's guide to Waiheke*, available at the bookshop in the Pendragon Mall opposite the information centre, is another useful source of information about the island. Several Waiheke residents have written about the island and you may find some of their works in this bookshop.

There's also a Waiheke radio station, the community-owned and operated 93.8 Gulf FM.

In Oneroa there's a post office, banks and a 24-hour automatic teller machine. Basic post office services – postage stamps and letterboxes – are also available at the general stores at Palm Beach, Ostend, Onetangi and Rocky Bay. Waiheke is a local telephone call from Auckland.

Artworks Living Art Centre

The Artworks Living Art Centre (☎ 372 6900) has a variety of hands-on galleries where you can make pottery, arts & crafts. The work of some of the island's artists is displayed in the upstairs art and crafts galleries, and concerts and performances are held in the theatre. Artworks is on Ocean View Rd

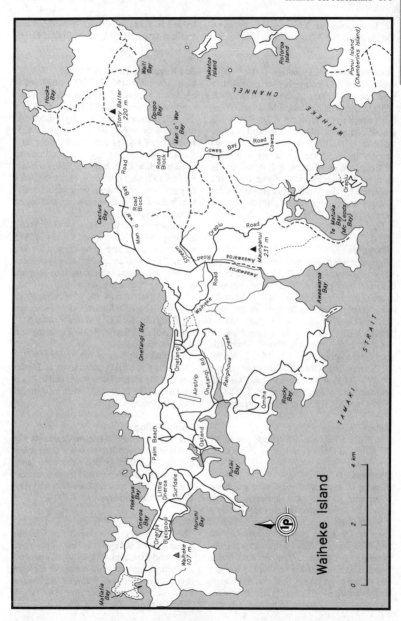

Waiheke Island

on the corner of Kororoa Rd, between Oneroa and the Matiatia Wharf; it's open every day from 10 am to 5 pm.

Historic Village & Museum
On the road to Onetangi, between the airstrip and the golf club, is the small Historic Village and Waiheke Island Museum. There isn't much to the Historic Village – it's just an old cottage, an old woolshed and a couple of baches – but the little museum is interesting enough, with historic photos and relics of the old days on the island. Admission is free, with donations gratefully accepted. It's operated by the Waiheke Island Historical Society and is open from 11 am to 2 pm on weekends most of the year, every day during school holidays.

Vineyards
Vineyards are fairly new on Waiheke, but already some of their wines have won international recognition. Three fine wineries were operating on our last visit to Waiheke, with more scheduled to open in the near future. All offer tours and tastings are by appointment; you can come on your own or on a vineyard tour (see Tours). Vineyards include the Peninsula Estate (☎ 372 7866) at 52 Korora Rd, Oneroa; Goldwater Estate (☎ 372 7493) at 18 Causeway Rd, Ostend; and the Stonyridge Vineyard (☎ 372 8822) at 80 Onetangi Rd, right beside the airstrip.

Marae
The Piritahi Marae in Blackpool, just down the hill from Oneroa, welcomes visitors.

Beaches
Popular beaches with good sand and good swimming include Oneroa Beach and the adjacent Little Oneroa Beach, Palm Beach in a lovely little cove, and the long stretch of sand at Onetangi Bay. A number of the beaches have shady pohutukawa trees growing in the sand. You can find nudist beaches at Palm Beach and on the western end of Onetangi Beach. Surf skis and boogie boards are hired on Onetangi Beach from the Onetangi Store, and a fellow who comes around in a van in summer hires these and surfboards too. There's snorkelling at Hekerua Bay and Enclosure.

Sea Kayaking, Boats & Sailing
Gulf Adventures (☎ 372 7262 or 627 9666) operate a variety of popular sea kayaking services including surf kayak hire for $25 a day, sea kayak hire for $35 a day, guided one to three-hour beginners' kayak trips for $25, Eskimo roll classes for $25 per hour, and guided full-day sea kayak expeditions to Pakatoa Island on Sunday for $60. Free taxi service to/from your accommodation, plus free taxi service between your accommodation and the ferry when you arrive and depart from the island, are included.

Wilderness Expeditions (☎ 372 9020, bookings 377 1771) hire sea kayaks for $35 a day, tents and camping equipment for $10 a day. They also do guided sea kayak tours for $65 per person (minimum four people), and fishing boat charters.

Ross Adventures (☎ 357 0550, after hours 410 4743), based at Matiatia, do half-day sea kayaking trips for $25, full-day trips for $55, lunch included. They also do kayak trips on Great Barrier Island.

Hauraki Gulf Sailing Adventures (☎ 372 7320) do day sailing adventures to Hooks Bay (for the Stony Batter walk) and to Pakatoa Island. The cost is $35, with an optional lunch on Pakatoa.

Horse-Riding
The Shepherd's Point Riding Centre (☎ 372 8104) at 6 Ostend Rd, between Ostend and the airstrip, offers guided rides over farmland, bush and beaches, and lessons are also available. They also do farmstays and residential riding holidays.

Walks
There are plenty of good walks on Waiheke – a system of walkways is being developed all around the island. Pick up a walks pamphlet from the information centre, or look for the mimeographed *Waiheke Walkways*, available at several places around the island.

In Onetangi there's a forest and bird

reserve with several good walks, one of them a walk up to three large kauri trees. For coastal walks, there's a good, well-marked track right around the coast from Oneroa Bay to Palm Beach. It's about a two to 2½ hour walk; at the Palm Beach end you can jump on a bus to come back to town. Another good coastal walk begins at the Matiatia ferry landing; take off to the left (north) from the landing and you can walk around this section of the coast and be back at the landing in about an hour.

Probably the favourite walk on the island is the Stony Batter walk. At the eastern end of the island, the farmland derives its name from the boulder-strewn fields. There's an interesting walk leading to the old WW II gun emplacements with their connecting underground tunnels and sweeping views. (As fortune would have it, these guns never fired a shot during the war.) The site is reached along the private road to the Man 'o War Station, but vehicles are not permitted to go beyond a certain point. From the gun emplacements you can continue walking north to Hooks Bay or south to Opopo Bay. From the entrances the walk over a private road to the site takes 1½ hours each way (about 20 minutes by bicycle). From the site it's an additional 1½ hours return to either of the bays. Cactus Bay is a fine little beach near the northern road end.

Other Things to Do

Waiheke has clubs for a variety of sports and activities – croquet (☎ 372 7637), badminton (☎ 372 8208), bridge (☎ 372 8740), Hatha yoga (☎ 372 7138), aerobics (☎ 372 6192) and many others. *Island Time – a visitor's guide to Waiheke* has listings for all these and many other activities on the island. Visitors are usually welcome to join in.

The Waiheke Golf Club (☎ 372 8886) is on the road between Ostend and Onetangi, just past the Historical Village & Museum. Visitors are welcome; there's a $10 green fee and clubs are available for hire.

The Film Society (☎ 372 8275, 372 5321) brings an interesting variety of films to the

island – international films, art films and what have you.

There's a weekly market at Ostend Hall on the main road in Ostend from 7 am to noon on Saturday mornings. It has a produce market (fresh fruits and vegetables), flea market, baked goods, and miscellaneous stuff; it's best to get there early.

Scenic Flights

Scenic flights are operated by Gulf Island Air (☎ & fax 372 7428). The costs are $30 per person for a Waiheke scenic flight, $50 per person for a gulf scenic flight.

Tours

Fullers Island Explorer bus is popular for day trips to Waiheke. It meets you at the ferry and takes you on a one-hour tour of the island, after which you can either return to the ferry and go back to Auckland, spend time on the island anywhere you choose and return to the ferry with the bus later on in the day, or hang onto your ticket and jump on and off the bus as many times as you like, all day long. The ticket costs $9 (children $5) and can be purchased together with your ferry ticket.

Several small local operators offer minibus tours of the island. The Waiheke Island Shuttle Express (☎ 372 7756) offers Waiheke Lifestyle Tours for $10 per person, Island Vineyard Tours also for $10, or a combination of both tours for $16.

Gulf Adventures (☎ 372 7262, 627 9666), who also operate the Dial-a-Cab taxi service, offer Waiheke tours starting at $5 per person if you have a minimum of four people wanting to go – showing you as much as possible for the fare price. They, too, offer special interest tours of the island – vineyard tours, bush & beach tours, or whatever. They also do farm visit tours, including a farm BBQ lunch, for $25 per person.

Tour Waiheke (☎ 372 7151) and Gulf Adventures both do tours to Stony Batter, taking you on a trip around the island, dropping you off at the entrance to the Stony Batter walk, and arranging to pick you up

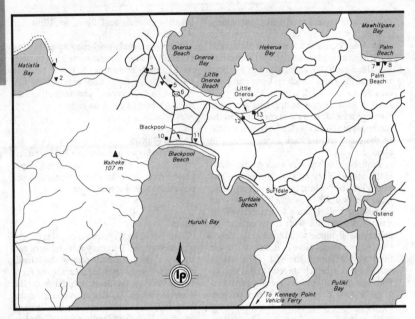

PLACES TO STAY

7   Palm Beach Backpackers &
    Palm Beach Lodge
9   Waiheke Island Resort & Conference
    Centre
12 Punga Lodge
13 Waiheke Island Backpackers -
    Hekerua House
14 McGinty's Lodge
15 Waiheke Island YHA Hostel
16 Roanna-Maree Motel &
    Strand Cafe & Onetangi Store
17 Onetangi Hotel
19 Midway Motel & Cabins

PLACES TO EAT

2   Harbour Master's Bar & Grill
8   Pacific Cafe & Palm Beach Store
11 Fig Tree Cafe

OTHER

1   Matiatia Ferry Wharf
3   Artworks Living Art Centre
4   Pendragon Mall, Visitor Information
    Centre, Earthsea Cafe, Aoreno's
    Pizza & Bookshop
5   Oceanview Mall, Vino-Vino Bar &
    Cafe, Poppy's Ice Cream Cafe &
    Pickle Palace Deli
6   Post Office
10 Piritahi Marae
18 Ostend Hall, RSA
20 Waiheke Forest & Bird Reserve
21 Kauri Grove
22 Shepherd's Point Riding Centre
23 Stonyridge Vineyard & Croquet Club
24 Waiheke Island Museum &
    Historic Village
25 Waiheke Golf Club

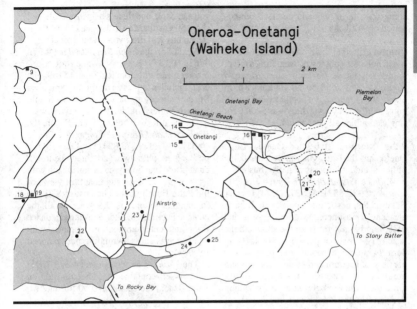

Oneroa-Onetangi
(Waiheke Island)

0   1   2 km

Piemelon Bay

Onetangi Bay

Onetangi Beach

14
Onetangi
15

16
17

20
21

18 19

Airstrip

23

22

24 25

To Stony Batter

To Rocky Bay

later. The cost is \$15 or \$20 (children half price).

The mailman, Peter Ward (☎ 372 7802) takes up to three people out with him on the Monday to Friday mail run. It's an excellent tour – he stops at many scenic spots to give you a look, stops to chat with the locals, and tells stories about the island as you go around it. The trip takes from about 8.30 am to noon and costs \$10. Arrange in advance for him to pick you up.

You can do your own self-guided tour by hiring a bike, scooter, motorcycle or car from down by the ferry wharf; pick up a copy of the booklet *Waiheke Island – A Tour* from the visitor information centre, and off you go.

Annual Events

Summer events include the Waiheke Jazz Festival held just after Christmas each year, and the Onetangi Beach Races in February with horse racing on Onetangi Beach. The Waiheke Arts & Crafts Fair is held on Labour Weekend in late October.

Places to Stay

Waiheke has three good hostels, two of them with camping, plus a couple of motels, a lodge and two posh resorts. The hostels are in Little Oneroa, Palm Beach and Onetangi. The motels are found in Palm Beach and Ostend. Palm Beach also has the two more upmarket resorts.

Many of the island residents offer home-stays, farmstays, B&B arrangements, or private self-contained houses, baches or flats. There's a lot of variety and the cost is anywhere from \$10 to \$200 a night. Over 40 such places have joined to form the Waiheke Island Homestay Association; contact the association through the Waiheke Information Centre (☎ 372 9999) in Oneroa and someone will help to match you with the type of place you are looking for. The Auckland Visitor Centre also keeps a current list of homestays, farmstays and other accommodation on Waiheke.

Oneroa Principal town of Waiheke, Oneroa is still not a very big town. Straddling a ridge, it has sea views on both sides. *Hauraki House* (☎ 372 7598) at 50 Hauraki Rd, in Sandy Bay, Oneroa, is a popular B&B guesthouse with good views; the cost is $40/60 for singles/doubles all year round.

Little Oneroa Just beyond Oneroa, Little Oneroa has the Little Oneroa Beach and one of the island's few areas of native bush.

Waiheke Island Backpackers – Hekerua House (☎ 372 8371; fax 372 7174) is at 11 Hekerua Rd, nestled in native bush. It has a pleasant atmosphere, swimming pool and deck, and it's not far from the shop and the beach. The cost per person is $14/15/16 in dorm/twin/double rooms, camping is $10 per person. In summer they do barbecues and meals on weekends and occasionally throughout the week. From the ferry landing you can take the Palm Beach bus and get off at Hekerua Rd, just up the hill from Oneroa ($2), or the shuttle bus will bring you to the door ($3). Phone ahead from Auckland to make sure there's room, as this is a popular place. Substantial discounts are offered if you book through the downtown hostels or the Outdoor Adventure Co at the Auckland Ferry Building.

Also in Little Oneroa, *Punga Lodge* (☎ 372 6675) at 223 Ocean View Rd has three double rooms and two twin rooms in a tranquil bush setting. The summer rate from December to Easter is $55/70 single/double for B&B, with discounts the rest of the year.

Palm Beach Palm Beach is in a beautiful little cove. Right on the beach, the *Palm Beach Backpackers* (☎ 372 8862; fax 379 2084) at 54 Palm Rd is associated with the posh Palm Beach Lodge and you can hire all its 'extras' like windsurfers, kayaks, mountain bikes and so on. The cost is $16 per person in four-bed share rooms, $20 in double rooms, or there's camping at $15 per site. It has a small cafe plus a kitchen where

you can cook, and there's a licensed cafe and shop 50 metres down the road. The Palm Beach bus will drop you on the corner.

Next door, the *Palm Beach Lodge* (☎ 372 7763; fax 379 2084) is a much more up-market place with double rooms at $160. The cost includes an assortment of activities. Special discount packages are available through Fullers, the ferry company.

On the hill overlooking Palm Beach, the *Waiheke Island Resort & Conference Centre* (☎ 372 7897; fax 372 8241) at 4 Bay Rd is a posh resort with two and three- bedroom chalets and one honeymoon suite, each with its own private deck and beautiful views of the Palm Beach cove. The cost of $80/100 for singles/doubles is the same in all the chalets. Facilities include a restaurant, dance floor and entertainment in summer, with tennis courts and a swimming pool planned for 1994.

The *Waiheke Beach Lodge* (☎ 372 7695) has two self-contained townhouses right on Palm Beach; the cost is $40/60 for one/two people.

Ostend Ostend village has shops, a couple of places to eat and the Saturday morning market. In the centre of the village, the *Midway Motel & Cabins* (☎ & fax 372 8023) at 1 Whakarite Rd, has cabins with shared kitchen and bath facilities at $15 per person, plus $5 extra the first night if you need to hire linen, and self-contained motel units at $45/55 for singles/doubles.

Onetangi Onetangi has a long sandy beach, popular in summer for swimming, surfing, windsurfing and other activities; surf skis, surfboards and boogie boards are available for hire.

The *Waiheke Island YHA Hostel* (☎ 372 8971) on Seaview Rd in Onetangi is up on the hill overlooking the bay; it's a bit of a hike to the shop so take your food with you when you go. The cost is $14 a night and all the rooms are twin rooms. The YHA offers two and three-night discount packages including the return ferry fare and the return bus fare on the island. The last stop on the

Onetangi bus route is at the bottom of the hill, or you can take the shuttle from the ferry to the door.

Right on the beach, the *Roanna-Maree Motel* (☎ & fax 372 7051) has a swimming pool, spa pool and 18 well-equipped double and family units priced at $80 in high season, with discounts the rest of the year. It is conveniently situated beside the Onetangi Store and the Strand Cafe; the Onetangi bus stops at the door.

Places to Eat
Oneroa There are plenty of places to eat at Oneroa, including a string of snack bars and takeaways. The *Earthsea Cafe* in the Pendragon Mall in the centre of town has healthy, natural foods at inexpensive prices; they make tasty nachos, serve fresh seafood, and there's a wide selection of breakfasts, teas, soya and dairy smoothies, and espresso coffees. Also in the mall, *Aoreno's Pizza* is good for pizza.

Across the street in the Oceanview Mall, the *Vino-Vino Bar & Cafe* is a popular bar and gathering place and it also serves good food, with an outdoor deck with a beautiful view over Oneroa Bay. It's open from 11 am to 10 pm, every day in summer, Wednesday to Sunday in winter. There are plenty of other places to eat in Oneroa, including *Poppy's Ice Cream Cafe*, the *Pickle Palace Deli* and *Schooner's*, but the *Earthsea, Aoreno's* and *Vino-Vino* are the ones that people rave about.

Down the hill from the centre of Oneroa, the *Fig Tree Cafe* is near the waterfront on the corner of the Esplanade and Moa Ave in Blackpool, between Surfdale and Oneroa. It has good food – with steak and other meats, seafood and vegetarian dishes. Dinner main courses are around $20. Inside there's an attractive decor, candlelight in the evening, and outside there's a pleasant dining courtyard. It's open for lunch and dinner every day from December to February, with more limited hours in winter. Although it's small, it's one of the island's favourite restaurants, so reservations are recommended (☎ 372 6363).

Matiatia At Matiatia not far from the ferry wharf, the large *Harbour Master's Bar & Grill* has several dining areas including a restaurant, bar meals, and an outdoor garden and swimming pool area under shady trees with a view of the bay, beautiful in summer. Winner of the NZ Lamb Cuisine award, the restaurant is open for lunch and dinner every day in summer, Wednesday to Sunday in winter, with entertainment on weekend nights – live bands, disco, a dance floor, and a karaoke.

Palm Beach The *Pacific Cafe* at 39 Palm Rd, right by the beach at Palm Beach, has a cafe menu with a salad bar, outdoor barbecues in summer, mulled wine in winter, and everything in the house is priced under $10. There's live music on Sunday afternoons, backgammon nights, and an outdoor dining area. Next door, the general store offers takeaways and groceries.

Ostend In the centre of Ostend village, the *RSA* serves good, cheap pub food, with steak & chips for $7 and a pitcher of beer for $1.50. Opposite this is a *Chinese takeaway*.

Onetangi At the Onetangi Store right by the beach, the *Strand Cafe* does takeaways and sit-down meals, with seating inside or outside, opposite the beach. It's open all day every day, all year round. The Onetangi Store also hires wave skis and boogie boards, videos and video players, and sells postage stamps and groceries.

Rocky Bay The tiny *Top Nosh Cafe* at the Rocky Bay Store has just a few tables but they make good hamburgers, desserts and takeaways. It's open every day from 9 am to 6 pm.

Entertainment
The *Harbour Master's Bar & Grill* in Matiatia has dancing and live bands on weekend nights, plus a karaoke. The *Pacific Cafe* in Palm Beach has live music on Sunday afternoons.

Music concerts, dances, plays and other

events are staged from time to time at the Artworks Living Art Centre in Oneroa.

Getting There & Away
Air Gulf Island Air (☎ & fax 372 7428) offers flights to/from Waiheke. One-way/return cost is $35/59 to Ardmore Aerodrome in Papakura, $50/89 to Auckland Airport, $35/65 to Coromandel and $43/75 to either Thames or the North Shore. They also do charter flights and scenic flights. The airstrip is between Ostend and Onetangi.

Boat The *Quickcat* is a modern, high-speed 500-seat catamaran ferry service out to the island. It zips you out in about half an hour at a return cost of $20 (children $10). On the island, buses connect with all arriving and departing ferries; a combination ferry/bus return ticket costs $21 if you take the bus to Oneroa, $23 if you bus to anywhere else on the island's bus routes, or $29 for the Fullers Explorer plus tour plus return ferry. Children go for half price on all Fullers services, or there's a special return family rate of $48. You can take your bicycle along on the ferry for an extra $4 return. There are six sailing times every day; phone Fullers (☎ 377 1771, 373 3776) for schedule information. From Auckland the ferry departs from the Auckland Ferry Building; on Waiheke the ferries arrive and depart from Matiatia Bay at the western end of the island.

If you've got your own car the Subritzsky Shipping Company (☎ 534 5663) operates a vehicle ferry between Waiheke and the mainland. It departs from Half Moon Bay on the Auckland side two or three times every day, landing and departing from Kennedy Point on the island; it also has services between Half Moon Bay and Matiatia, or between Wynyard Wharf and Matiatia. The voyage takes about 1½ hours. The cost is $55 each way ($110 return) for a car and driver, plus $10 for each additional passenger; motorcycles cost $30 each way ($60 return). Bookings must be made in advance.

The Waiheke Island Backpackers – Hekerua House (see Places to Stay, Little Oneroa) has a package sailing trip which includes the ferry from Auckland to Waiheke, bus to the hostel, one night's accommodation, and then an all-day sail from Little Oneroa Bay to Coromandel, making a stop at either Stony Batter or Pakatoa Island on the way. The cost is $89 including one night's accommodation (of course you can stay additional nights if you like) and you can do it from either direction, starting from Auckland or Coromandel.

Getting Around
Bus Two bus routes operate on the island, both connecting with the arriving and departing ferries. The Onetangi bus goes from the Matiatia wharf, though Oneroa, Surfdale and Ostend, ending at Onetangi. The Palm Beach bus goes from Matiatia through Oneroa, Blackpool, Little Oneroa, Palm Beach and Ostend, ending at Rocky Bay. The fare on either bus is $1 from the ferry to Oneroa, $3 right to the end of the line. You can buy bus tickets from Fullers when you buy your ferry ticket.

Shuttle Two companies operate door-to-ferry, ferry-to-door shuttle bus services: Waiheke Island Shuttle Express (☎ 372 7756) and Tour Waiheke Shuttle (☎ 372 7151). Both charge about the same prices – $3 to Little Oneroa, $5 to Palm Beach or Onetangi – with discounts when there's more than one person going. Both companies also do island tours.

Taxi Two taxi services operate on Waiheke: Waiheke Taxis (☎ 372 8038) and Dial-a-Cab (☎ 627 9666). If you have a group of four together, taking a taxi may cost about the same as the bus.

Rental Vehicles Waiheke Rental Cars (☎ 372 8635) has an office by the ferry wharf at Matiatia Bay. They hire cars, Jeeps and utes (pickup trucks) for $40 per day plus 35c/km, or $12 per hour plus 35c/km. Minibuses cost $60 per day plus 40c/km, or $15 per hour plus 40c/km. Motorcycles are $45 for 24 hours or $35 for half a day; 50cc scooters are $15 for two hours, $20 for four hours or $25 for all day. They also hire mountain bikes at $10 for four hours or $15 per day. A full tank of petrol is included with all vehicle hire.

Bring your driver's licence if you want to hire a motor vehicle. Foreign licences are OK but they can't hire you a vehicle if you have no licence at all.

Hitching Hitching around the island is very easy, many people find it the best way to get around.

PAKATOA ISLAND
Pakatoa Island is a small tourist resort 36 km out from Auckland and just off the east coast of Waiheke. The resort has a restaurant, bar, coffee shop, swimming pool and various sporting facilities. There are great views of the gulf and across to the Coromandel Peninsula from the island's high point.

Places to Stay
The *Pakatoa Island Resort Hotel* (☎ 372 9002; fax 372 9006) is the only place to stay on the island. The cost is $108 per apartment for one or two people; children stay free and seniors receive a 15% discount. Meals are available at $15 for breakfast, $25 for dinner, and each of the 62 apartments also has its own kitchenette so you can do your own cooking if you like.

Getting There & Away
Boat If you'll be staying at the resort, they'll send a boat to pick you up from downtown Auckland; the cost is $45 per person return. Otherwise you can make day trips to Pakatoa on sailing cruises or by sea kayak from Waiheke.

KAWAU ISLAND
Kawau is near the coast, well to the north of the islands off Auckland. It's reached by turning off SH 1 at Warkworth and travelling a few km east to Sandspit, 45 km from Auckland, from where the ferry departs.

On Kawau Sir George Grey's historic home, Mansion House, was used as a hotel for many years. It has now been restored to its original state and is open to the public as a museum. Sir George, an early governor of New Zealand, built Mansion House in 1846. There are many beautiful walks on Kawau, starting from Mansion House and leading to beaches, an old copper mine, and a lookout. You'll see numerous wallabies around here – they're not native to New Zealand so they're an unusual sight in this part of the world.

Places to Stay
There is no accommodation at Mansion House but there are several places to stay at Vivian Bay, on the north side of the island, and a couple of others on Bon Accord Harbour.

The least expensive accommodation on the island, suitable for backpackers, is the *Katy Clark Homestay* (☎ 422 8835), with two simple and self-contained cabins, each sleeping four, on the water in Harris Bay, Bon Accord Harbour. It's right over the water – the tide laps up under the floor – and the cabins have electricity, showers and kitchen; bring your own sleeping bag and food. The cost is $20 for two people, $40 for four, with discounts for longer stays.

The *Cedar Lodge* (☎ 422 8700) on the waterfront at Smelting Cove, Bon Accord Harbour, has two self-contained suites, each sleeping four; the cost is $60 for one or two people if you do your own cooking, $78 per person with all meals included.

Vivian Bay is the only sandy bay with accommodation on the island; attractions include a white sandy beach, swimming, fishing, snorkelling and bush walks. On Vivian Bay, *Kawau Island Cottages for Couples* (☎ 422 8835) has three chalets on the beach; the cost is $160 a double, with all meals included. Also right on the beach at Vivian Bay, *St Clair Lodge* (☎ 422 8850) has space for about 14 people in twin and double rooms; the cost is $85 per person, including all meals.

Getting There & Away
Boat The Kawau Island Mansion House Ferryboat Company (☎ 425 8006; fax 425 7650) operates ferries to Kawau from

Sandspit, a few km from Warkworth, which is about an hour's drive north of Auckland on SH 1. The ferries take about 45 minutes to reach the island and the fare is $20 return (children $10). Departures are several times daily.

They also operate a daily mail run cruise, departing from Sandspit at 10.30 am; it delivers the mail and freight to up to 63 wharfs and pontoons along the west side of the island, stopping at the Mansion House and at many coves, bays and inlets. A full commentary on the island is given as you go. The cost is $29 (children $10).

The same company also operates other cruises from Sandspit, including champagne luncheon cruises and dinner cruises, both costing $39 (children $19).

Another company, Kawau Provedores (☎ 425 6169, mobile (025) 960 910) also operates ferries from Sandspit to Kawau; the journey takes somewhat longer (1½ hours) and costs $15 return (children $8). It departs every day at 10 am, with an additional sailing at 2 pm in summer. They also offer a combined three-hour lunch and Mansion House cruise; the cost is $32.

Check your connections when getting to Sandspit from Auckland if you're using public transport, as it is not always easy. Buses heading north on SH 1 stop at Warkworth, but then you still have to get to Sandspit.

Gubbs Motors (☎ 425 8337) has buses to Sandspit. Their buses to Warkworth depart from the Auckland Downtown Bus Terminal a couple of times every day, continuing from Warkworth to Sandspit; the cost is $15 from Auckland to Warkworth, $5 from Warkworth to Sandspit. They also offer service on request just between Warkworth and Sandspit. Otherwise the ferry company may be able to help you with transport from Warkworth if you let them know in advance that you'll need it.

The schooner Te Aroha stops at Kawau on some of its cruises.

GREAT BARRIER ISLAND

Great Barrier Island (population 1100), 88 km from the mainland, is the largest island in Hauraki Gulf. Tramping, cycling, swimming, fishing, scuba diving, boating, sea kayaking and just relaxing are the popular activities on the island. With a small population living on the 110-sq-km island, there's plenty of open space. Great Barrier has hot springs, historic kauri dams, a Forest Sanctuary, and a network of tramping tracks. The west coast has safe sandy beaches; the east coast beaches are good for surfing. Because there are no possums on the island to eat it, the native bush is lush, green and thick.

The island was named by Captain Cook. Later it became a whaling centre, a number of ships were built there and the island has also been the site for some spectacular shipwrecks including the SS Wairarapa in 1894 and the Wiltshire in 1922. There's a cemetery at Katherine Bay where many of the victims of the Wairarapa wreck were buried.

Great Barrier Island is decidedly isolated, there are periodic complaints in the Auckland papers about how lousy the roads are and how the government on the mainland forgets about the islanders' existence. The island doesn't even have a pub. Tryphena is the main town, and arrival and departure port. Whangaparapara is an old timber town and the site of the island's whaling activities of last century. The Great Barrier Forest between Whangaparapara and Port Fitzroy has been developed for tramping and there has been much reforestation on the island. There are hot springs off the Claris-Whangaparapara road.

In summer from around mid-November to Easter the island is a very busy holiday destination, especially from 20 December to the end of January, over Easter, and at Labour Weekend at the end of October. It is very crowded with visitors at these times and if you must come then, make sure you have your transport, accommodation and activities booked in advance.

Information

The Outdoor Adventure Company (☎ 358 5868; fax 358 5878) in the Ferry Building on Quay St in Auckland has plenty of informa-

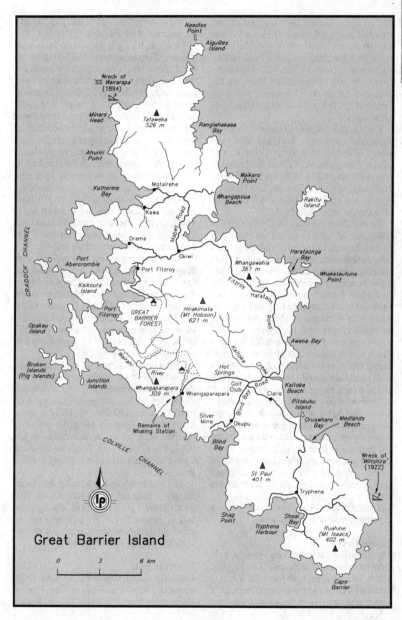

Great Barrier Island

0   3   6 km

tion on Great Barrier Island, especially on activities you can do there. They can tell you just about anything you'd want to know about the island, and can make bookings for all island activities. The NZ Adventure Centre (☎ 309 9192; fax 309 9824) on the ground floor of the Downtown Shopping Centre in QE II Square offers package tours to the island.

The Auckland Visitor Centre and the DOC information centre in Auckland also have plenty of information about Great Barrier Island. The Auckland Central Backpackers Travel Centre (☎ 358 4874; fax 358 4871) at the Auckland Central Backpackers Hostel, 9 Fort St, just off Queen St, also has plenty of information about the island.

On the island, the main DOC office (☎ 429 0044; fax 429 0071) is in Port Fitzroy, a 15-minute walk from the ferry landing. It has information and maps on the island, collects camping fees and sells hut tickets, and it has a good camping ground. It's open Monday to Friday from 8 am to 4.30 pm, with weekend hours during the height of summer. Another DOC ranger is in Whangaparapara; the office is open irregular hours.

In Tryphena, Safari Tours & Travel operates a Great Barrier Island Information & Travel Office at the Stonewall Store (☎ 429 0448) and they also do bus tours, transport, and hire cars, mountain bikes and kayaks.

There's no power on the island, so bring a torch (flashlight) with you when you go. Most people on the island generate their own power by using solar, wind or diesel energy, but there are no street lights anywhere. Automatic telephone service has just come to the island within the past few years; although card phones are present, phone cards are not always available so you might want to bring one with you too. Food is available but more expensive than on the mainland.

Things to Do

The island is great for walking; you can walk from the west coast to the east coast in a day. There are amazing canyons, lush virgin forest with kauri and pohutukawa trees, great views, and remains of the kauri dams from

the old logging days. At Whangaparapara are the remains of an old whaling station.

Mountain biking is popular on the island. There is diverse scenery, and biking is not too difficult here, even though the roads are unsealed. Here is one popular ride: you can cycle from Tryphena to Medlands Beach in about an hour, stop for a swim, then cycle another hour to the hot springs; from there it's another half-hour to accommodation in Whangaparapara. You could catch the ferry out from Whangaparapara, or continue another day cycling through the forest up to Port Fitzroy, stopping on the way for a hike up to the kauri dams on a good, well-marked 4WD track. It's about a three to 3½ hour ride, not counting stops, but allow all day if you're going to the kauri dams. You can send your luggage ahead of you on the bus if you don't want to lug it around on the bike.

Port Fitzroy is good for sea kayaking, with deep clear water and lush forest. Two-day sea kayaking trips around Port Fitzroy and four-day trips taking in the surrounding coastline are organised by Outdoor Adventures in the Auckland Ferry Building, with overnight stays in cabins. Ross Adventures (☎ 357 0550, after hours 410 4743) conduct two to seven-day sea kayaking trips.

Scuba diving is good on the island, with some of the most varied diving in New Zealand. There's pinnacle diving, shipwreck diving, lots of fish, and great visibility, with over 33-metre (100-foot) visibility at some times of year; February to April is probably the best time of all. Aquaventure (☎ 429 0033; fax 429 0077) in Tryphena conducts diving trips and also offers diving instruction.

The best beach on the island is Medlands Beach; Whangapoua and Kaitoke are also good. There's good surfing at Whangapoua and at Awana Bay – Whangapoua has an excellent right-hand break, while Awana has both left and right-hand breaks.

Places to Stay

DOC Camping Grounds & Huts DOC operates camping grounds at Port Fitzroy, Harataonga Bay, Medlands Beach, Awana

Beach and Whangaparapara, all with basic facilities including water and pit toilets. Fires are permitted on the island only in the designated fire places in the camping grounds, and even then, only if DOC has provided the firewood – you're not allowed to chop or gather wood to make fires. It's a good idea to bring your own cooker. Camping is not allowed outside the designated camping grounds without a permit from DOC. Camping costs are $3 per adult, or $2 if you bring your own cooker.

Port Fitzroy and Whangaparapara have basic huts in bush settings, each an hour's walk from the nearest wharf. Each hut sleeps up to 24 people in two bunkrooms; facilities include cold water, pit toilets and a kitchen with a wood stove but no pots and pans. Bring your own sleeping bag and cooking equipment. The cost is $8 (two tickets); hut tickets are available on the island but not all the time, so it's probably best to obtain your hut tickets or annual hut pass before you go to the island. From November to January the huts are very busy; accommodation is first come, first served, so the early birds get the bunks!

Hostels Three places at Tryphena offer hostel-style accommodation. *Pohutukawa Lodge* (☎ 429 0211) on the Tryphena beachfront is an associate YHA hostel, meaning you can stay with or without a YHA card. Bunks are $13 per night ($15 for non-YHA members), you can fix your own food and there's a shop at the lodge, plus restaurants nearby. Fishing and diving trips are arranged from the hostel.

Out on Cape Barrier Rd, the *Shoal Bay Holiday Park* (☎ 429 0485) has beds for $16 (see Cabins & Baches). The *Sunset Beach Motels* (☎ 429 0568) – the only motel listed for the island – has hostel accommodation for $15 per person. If you wish to splurge, their motel rooms are $85 a double.

The *Fitzroy Hostel* (☎ 429 0055) at Fitzroy, has beds for $12 per person, and they'll let you use their dinghies.

On Mason's Rd at Medlands Beach, the *Rangimarie Farmlet* (☎ 429 0320), with

organically grown fruit and vegetables, is in a rural setting about five minutes from the beach. The cost is $20 per person.

Lodges In addition to the hostel, the *Pohutukawa Lodge* (see Hostels) also has a separate lodge with three self-contained double/twin rooms; the cost for B&B is $55/85 for one/two people in summer, $45/55 in winter.

Pigeons Lodge (☎ 429 0437) at Shoal Bay on the beachfront is in a bush setting, five minutes' walk to the beach; the cost is $80 for two. Very central, *Tipi & Bob's Holiday Lodge* (☎ & fax 429 0550) has motel-type accommodation 50 metres from the sea, with a garden bar, restaurant and takeaways. Units cost $77 per night most of the year, rising to $99 on summer weekends. Their dinghy is available for free to guests.

At Whangaparapara Harbour, the *Great Barrier Lodge* (☎ 429 0351) at the water's edge has nine double, twin and family rooms; the cost is $39 per person. Two self-contained cabins cost $69 and $79 for two. It's a good base for a tramping holiday and you can relax in the restaurant or bar after a day's walk.

At Kaianara Bay, Port Fitzroy, the *Jetty Tourist Lodge* (☎ 429 0050) near the water has double and twin rooms at $99. All the units are self-contained and there's a restaurant in case you don't want to cook. On the other hand you may want to cook up the day's catch taken in sheltered Fitzroy Harbour.

The *Paradise Park Lodge* (☎ 429 0352) at Medlands, has self-contained units set in 10 acres of park-like grounds; the cost is $90 for two. You can cook your own meals or dine in the restaurant (see Hostels for details on cheaper accommodation at Medlands).

Cabins & Baches Out at Shoal Bay on Cape Barrier Rd is the *Shoal Bay Holiday Park* (☎ 429 0485), with cabins sleeping four; the cost of $16 per person includes linen and blankets. The two self-contained chalets cost $65 for two.

Often holiday baches and caravans, all privately owned and maintained, are available to visitors. Some are listed below but this list is by no means all that is available. Safari Tours & Travel (☎ 429 0448) keep a comprehensive list so check with them; they will also provide transport. Most of these places are in Tryphena.

Jenny Frost's (☎ 429 0445); $80 double
Crosswinds Homestead (☎ 429 0557); $49 per person
Kowhai Cottage (☎ 429 0473); $80 double
Lovell's Holiday Bach (☎ 429 0468); $60 2 or 4
Macadamia Heights (☎ 429 0497); chalet $99
Nancy's Nest (☎ 429 0433); $80 double
Pa Beach Chalets (☎ 429 0483); $99 double
Shalom (☎ 429 0556); chalet $99
Tom & Rose Bone (☎ 429 0479); $60 double
Bubbles Wheeler's (☎ 429 0530); $80 double
Whale Cottage (☎ 429 0211); $80 for four
The Granny Flat (☎ 429 0451); $65 double
Sherwood Orchids (☎ 429 0445); $80 double B&B

Places to Eat
There aren't many restaurants on the island, so all the places to stay make provisions for their guests to eat, one way or another, providing meals, or a place for their guests to cook, or both. *Tipi & Bob's* in Tryphena have a garden bar, restaurant and takeaways. Social clubs in Tryphena and Claris are places you can go for a meal; they serve meals on weekends all year round, on weekdays too in summer.

Food is of course available in grocery stores but it's more expensive than on the mainland, so you may want to bring food with you.

Getting There & Away
Air Great Barrier Airlines (☎ 275 9120) fly twice daily from the Air New Zealand Domestic Terminal at Auckland Airport to Claris, and in summer to Okiwi as well. The flight from Auckland takes half an hour and costs $89 one-way, $170 return on weekdays, $119 return on weekends, or there's a fly-boat combination whereby you fly one way and go by boat the other way for $119 any day. The airline operates a free transfer bus from Claris to Tryphena and from Okiwi to Port Fitzroy.

Boat Fullers Cruises (☎ 377 1771) operate ferries between Auckland and Great Barrier Island several times weekly, stopping first at Tryphena and then at Port Fitzroy. The voyage takes two hours and costs $99 (children $49). Fullers also make a day trip cruise to the island, departing from the Auckland Ferry Building at 9 am and returning by 6 pm; the cost is $50 (children $25) with an optional $17 bus tour.

Most of the Fullers ferries depart from Auckland in the morning, but the Friday night ferry departs in the evening. This one does not always continue to Port Fitzroy, so if you're trying to go there, make sure you check in advance.

A 22-foot (7.3 metre) open rigid-hulled inflatable boat (the same kind of boat as is used for whale watching) operates between Fletcher Bay on the Coromandel Peninsula and Tryphena. You must book ahead for this service, as it goes on demand rather than on schedule (weather permitting). The crossing takes about 30 minutes (15 minutes in fine weather) and costs $35. Phone the Sunkist Lodge in Thames (☎ (07) 868 8808) to book a trip. The same people have also worked out a discounted route going on their boat from Fletcher Bay to Tryphena, from there joining the Fullers cruise to Auckland, all for $70, a $20 discount from normal prices.

You can take a car to the island on the Gulf Trans car ferry (☎ 373 4036). One-way trips take about six hours and cost $470 for a car and driver, $40 for each extra adult and $25 for each extra child. The ferry departs from Wynyard Wharf in Auckland every Tuesday at 7 am, returning from Fitzroy every Wednesday at 9 am.

The 1909 schooner *Te Aroha* also comes to Great Barrier Island; see *Te Aroha* Cruises in the Auckland section.

Getting Around
Roads on the island are rough and ready. From Tryphena in the south to Port Fitzroy in the north is about 47 km by gravel road, or 40 km via Whangaparapara using the walking tracks. The roads are so bad that you may decide walking is a good idea!

A bus operates from Tryphena through

Claris and Okiwi to Port Fitzroy and back once a day, its departures scheduled to co-incide with the arrivals and departures of the ferry. You can arrange to send your luggage on ahead on this bus if you like, a convenient service for trampers and cyclists. If the place where you're staying knows you're coming and they're not on a bus route, they will come to pick you up.

Safari Tours (☎ 429 0448) hire cars, mountain bikes and kayaks. They are based at the Great Barrier Island Information and Travel Office at the Stonewall Store in Tryphena. There are a handful of taxis on the island but they aren't cheap.

OTHER ISLANDS

Dotted around Rangitoto-Motutapu and Waiheke or further north are many smaller islands. They include:

Motukorea Island

South of Rangitoto, the small island of Motukorea, or 'Island of the Oystercatcher', is also known as Browns Island. It was settled by Polynesians by about 1300 AD, who had developed three fortified pa settle-ments on the volcanic cones by 1820. It was purchased from the Maoris by John Logan Campbell and William Brown in 1839, before the founding of Auckland, and used as a pig farm. It's now part of the Hauraki Gulf Maritime Park. The old wharf collapsed long ago and along the west coast lie the rotting wrecks of five old ferries that were run aground and abandoned.

Motuihe Island

Halfway between Auckland and Waiheke, this small two-sq-km island with its fine beaches is a popular day trip from the city. At one time the island was used as a quaran-tine station and the cemetery at the north-western tip has graves of victims of the 1918 influenza epidemic. In WW I it was used as a prisoner-of-war camp and it was from here that the German captain Count Felix von Luckner made a daring but ultimately unsuc-cessful escape.

The peninsula pointing out north-west has

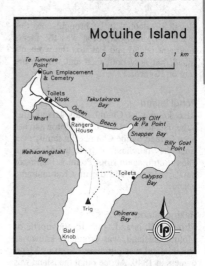

fine sandy beaches on both sides so one side is always sheltered from the wind. On a sunny weekend there may be over 500 boats anchored in the bay! There are several walking tracks on the island; it takes about three hours to walk all the way around.

Places to Stay If you want to stay overnight on the island, ask DOC about their basic camping ground and farmhouse. You can reach them at the kiosk on the island (☎ 534 8095), or check with the Auckland DOC office.

Getting There & Away Fullers (☎ 377 1771) stops at Motuihe on its Sunday and Wednesday mail run (see Auckland Harbour Cruises). In summer they may go more often; check with them for the current schedule.

Rotoroa Island

Another small island, just off the east coast of Waiheke Island between Pakatoa and Ponui Islands, Rotoroa is a private island which has belonged to the Salvation Army since 1907. The Salvation Army uses the island for a residential treatment programme for recovering alcoholics, and it is officially illegal for alcohol to be brought onto this island. Originally Rotoroa was the men's treatment island and Pakatoa the women's island, but now both men and women are here on Rotoroa.

Ponui Island

Also known as Chamberlins Island, this larger island is just south of Rotoroa and has been farmed by the Chamberlin family ever since they purchased it from the Maoris in 1854. South again from Ponui is Pakihi, or Sandspit Island, and the tiny Karamuramu Island.

Rakino Island

This small island, just to the north of Motutapu Island, was originally known as Hurakia and was purchased from its Maori owners in 1840. At one point the island was used for prisoners taken in the Maori Wars. The island has sandy beaches, rugged coast-

lines and deep-water coves. Beyond Rakino there is a cluster of tiny islands collectively known as The Noises.

Getting There & Away The Rangitoto Express ferry (☎ 372 6892) comes to Rakino after stopping at Rangitoto Island, but not on all of its sailings – it stops at Rakino only once on Friday, once on Saturday, and twice on Sunday, so if you want to make it a day trip, Sunday is your day. After stopping at Rangitoto it takes about another hour to reach Rakino; the return fare from Auckland is \$22 (children \$10). Reservations are required.

Fullers (☎ 377 1771) stops at Rakino on its Wednesday and Sunday mail run (see Auckland Harbour Cruises).

Tiritiri Matangi

Part of the Hauraki Gulf Maritime Park, this island, about four km off the coast of the

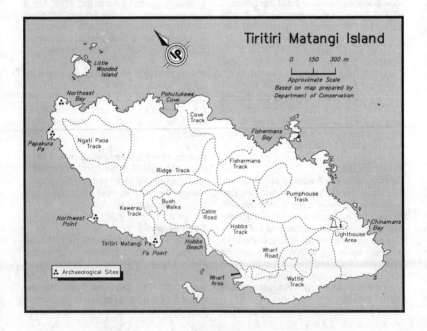

Tiritiri Matangi Island

Whangaparaoa Peninsula, is further north, about halfway between the islands close to Auckland and Kawau Island.

The 220-hectare island is an 'open sanctuary' where native wildlife is protected but visitors are permitted. The island has some original coastal broadleaf forest with large pohutukawa trees and also some re-vegetated forest. Native birds, including many rare species, thrive on the island and are practically tame, since there is nothing to threaten them. They include takahes, black robins, bellbirds, brown teal ducks, parakeets (kakarikis), whiteheads, saddlebacks, tuis, wood pigeons, little spotted kiwis and many other species. Ornithologists from all over the world come to the island to birdwatch.

There are a number of good walks on the island. Starting from the wharf there are one, two and three-hour walks, and in a day you could explore most of the coastal and ridge walks.

Places to Stay Camping is absolutely prohibited on the island, in the interest of protecting the wildlife, but visitors are welcome to stay overnight in the lighthouse keeper's house. The cost is $15 per person and the house has a kitchen and everything you need. Bring all your own food, though, as there is no shop on the island. Phone ahead for reservations (☎ 479 4490).

Getting There & Away Day trips to the island are made most Sunday, with departures from Auckland or from Gulf Harbour near Orewa; the island's DOC officer (☎ 479 4490) will have details. The *Te Aroha* schooner also comes here (see Auckland – *Te Aroha* Cruises).

Little Barrier Island

Little Barrier Island, 25 km from Kawau Island, is one of New Zealand's prime nature reserves, being the last area of NZ rainforest that remains unaffected by humans, deer or possums. Several rare species of birds, reptiles and plants, live in the varied habitats on the volcanic island. Access to the island is strictly restricted and a DOC permit, very difficult to obtain, is required before any landing is made on this closely guarded sanctuary.

The easiest (and perhaps even the only) way to gain access to this island is to come on a *Te Aroha* cruise, where the DOC permit is already arranged (see Auckland – *Te Aroha* Cruises).

Motuora Island

Motuora Island is halfway from Tiritiri Matangi to Kawau. There is a wharf and a camping ground on the west coast of the island but there is no regular ferry service to Motuora. A camping permit can be obtained from the ranger on Kawau Island (☎ 422 8882), or you can just show up and get your permit from the caretaker there. The camping cost is $3 per person.

Mokohinau Islands

These are the most remote islands of the Hauraki Gulf Maritime Park, 23 km northwest of Great Barrier Island. They are small, low-lying islands receiving little rain. They are all protected nature reserves, requiring a permit for landing.

Northland

Northland is a special part of New Zealand. This place is a cradle of both Maori and Pakeha culture; and here legend intertwines with reality. In the far north is the tail of the fish (the North Island) which Maui brought up from the sea. A journey to the end of the road brings you to the junction of two worlds – this world where all is transitory and the spirit world where all endures.

Geographically, the region is shaped like a finger pointing north from Auckland. Often referred to as the 'winterless north', its climate tends to be mild compared to the rest of New Zealand. It's a popular holiday resort area with beaches and water sport activities, and close enough to the big city for weekend trips. As emphasised before, Northland is also modern New Zealand's cradle – it was here that Europeans first made permanent contact with the Maoris, here the first squalid sealers' and whalers' settlements were formed, and here the Treaty of Waitangi was signed between the settlers and the Maoris. To this day there is a greater proportion of Maoris in the Northland population than elsewhere in New Zealand.

Many travellers to the region only visit the rather touristy Bay of Islands, which is a shame since there are so many other beautiful and interesting places around Northland.

A good way to travel around Northland is in a westerly direction. If you go west via Matakohe Kauri Museum you'll be able to learn about the big trees before you actually see them in Waipoua Kauri Forest; you reach the Hokianga, Kaitaia and Far North Maori communities on your way up, giving you the chance to learn some aspects of Maori culture before reaching the place where the spirits depart from this world – at least one marae orientation visit is a must at this stage; and you can enjoy the beautiful, though touristy, Bay of Islands as you head back south.

Information
One particularly useful pamphlet to have

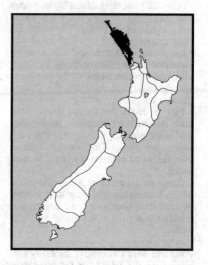

with you is the *Northland Great Time Guide*, available from most visitor information centres.

The 09 telephone prefix applies for Auckland and all points north from there. We have not included it with each telephone number here, so remember that, if you are phoning long-distance within the region, you'll need to dial 09 first.

Getting Around
In addition to the regular bus services there are other services catering specifically for the backpacking visitor.

Transit New Zealand have promised that the road through the western forests will be sealed by the end of 1994; this will make SH 12 an excellent loop through Northland, especially for tourists driving their own vehicles.

The main bus line serving Northland is Northliner Express (☎ Auckland 307 5873; Kerikeri 438 3206; Kaitaia 408 0879). This

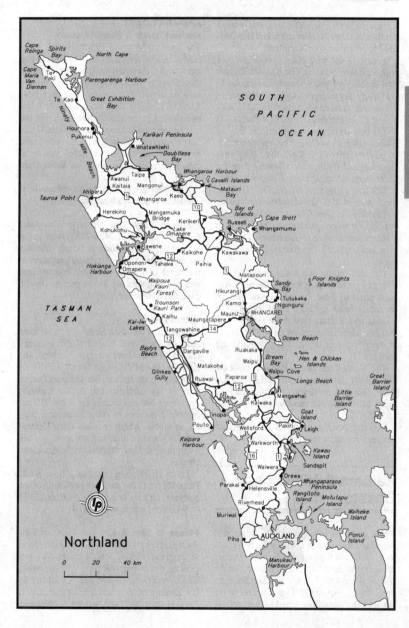

SOUTH
PACIFIC
OCEAN

Cape Reinga
Spirits Bay
North Cape
Cape Maria Van Diemen
Te Paki
Parengarenga Harbour
Te Kao
Great Exhibition Bay
Houhora
Pukenui
Ninety Mile Beach
Karikari Peninsula
Whatawhiwhi
Doubtless Bay
Awanui
Taipa
Mangonui
Whangaroa Harbour
Cavalli Islands
Kaitaia
Matauri Bay
Ahipara
Whangaroa
Kaeo
Tauroa Point
Herekino
Mangamuka Bridge
Kerikeri
10
Bay of Islands
Cape Brett
Russell
Whangamumu
Kohukohu
Lake Omapere
Rawene
Kaikohe
Kawakawa
Hokianga Harbour
Opononi
Omapere
Taheke
12
Paihia
1
Matapouri
Poor Knights Islands
Waipoua Kauri Forest
Hikurangi
Sandy Bay
Tutukaka
Ngunguru
Trounson Kauri Park
Kamo
Kai-Iwi Lakes
Kaihu
Maunu
WHANGAREI
TASMAN SEA
Tangowahine
Maungatapere
14
Ocean Beach
Baylys Beach
Dargaville
Ruakaka
Bream Bay
Hen & Chicken Islands
Matakohe
Waipu
Waipu Cove
Great Barrier Island
Glinkes Gully
Ruawai
Paparoa
12
Longs Beach
Little Barrier Island
Tinopai
Kaiwaka
Mangawhai
Pouto
Wellsford
Goat Island
Pakiri
Leigh
Kaipara Harbour
Warkworth
Kawau Island
Sandspit
16
Waiwera
1
Whangaparaoa Peninsula
Parakai
Helensville
Orewa
Rangitoto Island
Motutapu Island
Waiheke Island
Riverhead
Muriwai
Ponui Island
Piha
AUCKLAND
Manukau Harbour

Northland

0   20   40 km

service follows the east coast, but with a number of other smaller operators it is possible to reach most of Northland.

Access to the west coast is possible now with a number of buses. The Kaipara Klipper (☎ 438 6111) gets you to Dargaville from Auckland every day except Saturday (it also serves Whangarei for when you want to switch coasts).

The 15-seater West Coaster (☎ Paihia 402 7857) bus service travels from the Bay of Islands (Paihia) to Dargaville on weekdays. It passes through Kaikohe, Rawene, Opononi and the forests, allowing time for photo stops at the big trees. A one-way ticket is $32 and a day return from Dargaville to the forests is $16. On Monday, Wednesday and Friday the West Coaster also travels via Brnderwyn where passengers can transfer to a Northliner service to Auckland. This service has replaced the former Kauri Coast liner.

The one place that most travellers are trying to get to is Cape Reinga, the northernmost point of New Zealand – a number of operators head up here from the Bay of Islands and Kaitaia (see those sections for details). More information on getting to out of the way places is included in the relevant sections.

The North Cape Green Beetle Shuttle (☎ 358 5868) departing from Auckland, has three, five and six-day tours which include many of Northland's most interesting sights and activities.

See the Auckland and Getting Around chapters for more tour possibilities.

Kaipara & Hibiscus Coasts

There are two possibilities for the drive from Auckland to Wellsford, where the two roads join – you have the option of following either the Kaipara coast (SH 16) on the west or the Hibiscus coast (SH 1) on the east. Both are great drives, especially if you turn off to see some of the attractions listed in this section.

KAIPARA COAST
Muriwai Beach & Gannet Colony
The road to Muriwai Beach is well signposted at Waimauku on SH 16. Unless you are a surfer, the main attraction here will be the colony of Australasian gannets (*Sulidae sula bassana*). The colony was once confined to a nearby rock stack but now it has overflowed to the shore cliffs, even past the barriers erected to keep observers out. If you haven't seen these beautiful birds before take the opportunity to see them here – you are at close range, looking down on them from above.

The other attraction is the ice-cream shop, a must to visit in midsummer.

Place to Stay The *Muriwai Waterfront Camp* (☎ & fax 411 7426/7763) is set in the Regional Park at Muriwai Beach (about a 40-minute drive from Auckland), adjacent to the beach and an 18-hole golf course. Tent and powered sites are $8 per person, on-site caravans $10 per person.

Helensville
This town is less than an hour's drive from Auckland and well placed at the southern end of New Zealand's biggest harbour, the Kaipara. The MV *Kewpie Too* (☎ 420 8466) does trips from Helensville as far as Dargaville at the northern end of the harbour. Four-hour harbour cruises are about $10 per person; a number of other interesting trips are available. About four km from Helensville, at Parakai, there are hot springs – see Swimming & Thermal Pools in the Auckland chapter.

From Helensville you can follow South Head Rd out to the southern peninsula of the Kaipara Harbour, or continue north on SH 16 to Wellsford where you join SH 1.

Places to Stay & Eat The *Point of View Backpackers* (☎ 420 7331) is a small place; with great views, which costs $15 per person; the owner will pick up from town. The *Grand Hotel* (☎ 420 8427), Railway St, has accommodation and a restaurant. Out at Parakai there are three motels – *Hinemoa,*

Mineral Park and *Moturemu Lodge*. The *Aquatic Park Holiday Camp* (☎ 420 8884) is adjacent to the thermal complex. Here a tent site is $8.50 per person, with the added incentive of free admission to the hot pools.

HIBISCUS COAST

This beautiful coast is a favourite with local holidaymakers, especially those from Auckland. In this respect summers are really busy. At other times of the year it is a great place to be and there are many scenic walks to do. These are outlined in *Walks of the Hibiscus Coast* – three bush, two country and eight coastal walks are described; the leaflet is free from tourist offices. Remember that tidal information is most important for any of the coastal walks – inquire about tide charts at visitor information centres.

Whangaparaoa Peninsula

The first major holiday area you reach, north of Auckland when travelling up SH 1, is the Whangaparaoa Peninsula. This is a haven for lovers of water-based activities – windsurfers flock to Manly Beach, boaties leave from the Weiti River and Gulf Harbour, and swimmers find great beaches around the tip of the peninsula. Actually this peninsula area is now established as Shakespeare Regional Park. Many native bush birds and waders can be seen here and the native forests of the park contain karaka, kowhai, taraire and old puriri. A number of walking tracks traverse the park.

Orewa

In the neighbouring town of Orewa, there is a statue of Sir Edmund Hillary, one of the first two humans to stand on top of Mt Everest. To get around Orewa, Silverdale and the Whangaparaoa Peninsula, you can take the free Joybus which operates in summer months – it does a 16-km round trip taking 45 minutes and starting just outside Hillary House in Hillary Square. Wenderholm Regional Park, eight km north of Orewa, has splendid views, bushwalks, beach swimming, and picnic spots.

Places to Stay The *Marco Polo Backpackers Inn* (☎ 426 8455), is at 2a Hammond Avenue, Hatfields Beach, Orewa. It is clearly signposted from the highway – an AA sign with 'Hostel'. Take Auckland city bus Nos 894, 895 or 899 as they stop right in front. At this purpose-built hostel dorm beds are $13, and twins/doubles are $16 per person; a single costs $25. In addition to supplying lots of good advice, the owners can organise snorkelling trips to nearby Goat Island marine reserve ($25). They are also opening another hostel in early 1994: *Pillows* will also cater for backpackers and will cost $14 for a dorm bed, $17 for a twin and $25 a single; inquire at the Marco Polo.

In addition, Orewa has about 10 *motels* and three *motor camps/camping grounds*. The motels vary wildly in charges but a campsite will cost between $8 and $9 per person.

Waiwera

The Waiwera Hot Pools are in the coastal village of Waiwera, 48 km north of Auckland on SH 1. For information on the pools see Swimming & Thermal Pools in the Auckland chapter.

Places to Stay & Eat Near the hot pools are a range of accommodation choices. The town has two hotels, two motels and a caravan park. At the *Waiwera Thermal Caravan Park* (☎ 426 5270), on the beachfront, there are a number of on-site vans available at $12 per person; the pools are free to people staying here.

Moir Hill Walkway

A few km before you reach Warkworth there is a waterfall, lookout and views of the Hauraki Gulf from the Moir Hill Walkway. The track is directly off the main road so the bus services can drop you there. The return trip takes three to four hours and walking boots are only necessary in winter. Just north of the walkway is New Zealand's satellite tracking station.

Sheepworld

Four km north of Warkworth, Sheepworld is an unabashedly touristic attraction demonstrating many aspects of NZ sheep farming, including sheepdog manoeuvres, shearing, and things you can try for yourself such as carding, spinning, weaving, feeding tame sheep and lambs. There's even a video of a year in the life of a sheep, starring 'Gladys'! It's open daily from 9 am to 5 pm, with show times at 11 am, 1 and 3 pm; admission is $6 (children $4).

Places to Stay & Eat Warkworth has a hotel, a licensed tourist establishment, one lodge, five motels, and three camping grounds in the vicinity. Beef, lamb and seafood dishes are served at the *Landfall Restaurant*, Elizabeth St. The *Copper Kettle Dairy* has been recommended for its home-made cakes. On Queen St there are a number of places – *Cafe Cats* for pasta and seafood, *Geppetto's Expresso Cafe* for that long black with an extra long 'nose', and the *Kowhai Dairy* for breakfast or a salad lunch. *Grumpy's* in the Walton Park Motel, Walton Avenue, claims 'great hospitality' in spite of its name.

Dome State Forest

The Dome State Forest is 10 km north of Warkworth and 12 km south of Wellsford, on SH 1. The 401-hectare forest was logged about 90 years ago and is now protected and regenerating. There's a walking track to the Dome summit (336 metres) departing from the car park opposite Kraacks Rd on SH 1. It takes about an hour's steady walking to reach the summit, with great views of the Hauraki Gulf and beyond. Another 800 metres past the summit is the Waiwhiu Kauri Grove, a stand of 20 mature kauri trees which the loggers didn't take.

As you continue north on SH 1 you'll pass the Sunnybrook Scenic Reserve, another lovely spot.

Sandspit

East of Warkworth, a few km from the main road, is Sandspit, where a ferry service departs for Kawau Island. (See the Islands

off Auckland section in the Auckland chapter for more details.) The Sandspit turn-off also leads up to Goat Island, a scenic reserve of the Hauraki Gulf Maritime Park; inquire at the Marco Polo at Hatfields Beach about snorkelling trips to this reserve.

LEIGH TO BREAM BAY

Less frequented than the main road north is the scenic route from Warkworth out to Leigh on the east coast, and then north via Mangawhai and Waipu to Bream Bay. This route is very scenic and you can see out to the Hen & Chicken Islands. There are a number of places where you can relax, off the not-so-beaten path along this route. Additionally there are many fine walks and great birdwatching opportunities.

Pakiri Beach

The beach at Pakiri is known for its white sands. A good way to see this area of unspoilt beach and the forests behind is on horseback. About a three-minute walk from the beach is the *Pakiri Farmstay* (☎ 422 6275), on Rahuikiri Rd. There is a variety of accommodation on this farm – cabins are $67 for two; a double room in the farmstay is also $67, including meals; and a bunkroom bed is $15. Really want to get away from it all? Then rent the gypsy wagon out at the beach for $40. There are 45 horses on the farm. You can go riding for 1½ hours for $20; a day trip which includes lunch is $70. Watch out for Pupu, the magpie which thinks it owns the place.

Mangawhai Cliffs Walkway

The Mangawhai Cliffs Walkway leads from Mangawhai Heads to Bream Tail (1½ to two hours one way), giving extensive views both inland and of the Hauraki Gulf islands. The return trip can be made around the foreshore at low tide when the sea is not rough.

Brynderwyn Hills Walkway

Also in the same area is the Brynderwyn Hills Walkway (eastern section), starting from the Mangawhai-Waipu Cove road. It's an easy two-hour return climb affording panoramic views of Northland and the Hauraki

Gulf from the highest point. The road continues to Langs Beach, where it's possible to camp, before it rejoins the main highway at Waipu.

Waipu & Bream Bay

Near the mouth of the Waipu River there is an estuary which is home to many species of wader birds. If you are lucky you can see the rare New Zealand dotterel, variable oyster-catchers and fairy terns. The Ebb & Flow Backpackers (☎ 432 0217) is well situated overlooking the Waipu River estuary on Johnsons Point Rd. A bunk bed in this place costs $10, and twins and doubles are $15 per person. The Ebb & Flow has all facilities but don't expect trees – it sits on a rise overlooking the estuary where you can fish, birdwatch or snorkel until your heart is content. The view from the verandah includes the Hen & Chickens and Sail Rock, as well as Bream Head. For $35 you can do a tour of the Waipu Caves. George, your blind guide, ensures part of the tour fee goes to the Royal Guide Dog Society. At nearby Waipu Cove there is a motel and a motor camp.

At Uretiti DOC have a campsite. Book with them on (☎ 438 0299); sites cost $5 for adults and $2.50 for children. You can buy camping supplies from the Four Square store.

In Waipu town itself there is an unusual small museum. The House of Memories has displays relating to early Nova Scotian settlers of Waipu and the surrounding district. Admission is $2; children $1.

Western Route

There are two main routes from Auckland through Northland to the top of New Zealand. The simplest and fastest route is to head straight up through Whangarei on the eastern side of the peninsula, through the Bay of Islands to Kaitaia.

The west coast route is slower – the road is unsealed for a stretch – and longer, but it takes you through Dargaville, the Waipoua Kauri Forest and the remote and scenic Hokianga Harbour. To reach Northland you can go through Helensville or Warkworth to Wellsford and then on to Brynderwyn, 112 km north of Auckland, from where you choose the east or west coast route.

Matakohe

Turning off at Brynderwyn for Dargaville you pass through Matakohe, where the **Otamatea Kauri & Pioneer Museum** has a strange and wonderful collection of kauri gum in the basement. It also has lifelike displays of various aspects of the life of the kauri bushpeople and an extensive photographic collection. It's a superb museum, well worth the short detour to see it.

The museum shop has some excellent bowls and other items crafted from kauri wood. They're expensive but very well made. Look for the items made of 'swamp kauri', ancient kauris which lay in swamps for thousands of years, their gum-saturated wood still remaining in good condition. The museum is open daily from 9 am to 5 pm; admission is $5 (children $1.50).

When we visited a major new wing was being added. The main feature of the new area will be a slab of kauri which is over 22 metres long, and its stump which is four metres high. There will also be a staircase and mezzanine area which looks out on to the surrounding countryside – it is due to open at the end of June 1994.

Facing the museum is the **Matakohe Pioneer Church**, built between 1866 and 1867 of local kauri wood. When the tiny church was built it served as the interdenominational church for both Methodists and Anglicans, as well as the town hall and schoolhouse for the pioneer community. Later on a schoolhouse was built and you can see it on the far side behind the museum. The Pioneer Church was renovated in 1978 and is once again in use. The large brick Coates' Memorial Church nearby was built in 1950.

Places to Stay Near Matakohe are two backpackers. The *Old Post Office Guesthouse* (☎ 431 7453) is at Paparoa, seven km from Matakohe. It is a very pleasant hostel with all the facilities; a share room is $12 and single/twin/double rooms are all $15 per person. The pleasant outdoor roof area overlooks a sylvan valley. At Ruawai, west of Matakohe on the main road to Dargaville, is the *Ruawai Travellers Hostel* (☎ 439 2283). All beds cost $15 in this clean place which has the drawback of being on the main road. Pluses are free linen and laundry facilities.

DARGAVILLE

Dargaville (population 4900), 185 km north of Auckland, is named after its founder, Joseph McMullen Dargaville (1837-96), who was born in Ireland and came to New Zealand in the 1860s when the kauri timber trade was at its height. Seeing potential in this site at the confluence of the northern Wairoa River and Kaihu Creek, he bought 171 acres in 1872 for £1 an acre, and laid out a private town. The river town at the heart of the kauri district became an important centre for the seagoing exports of kauri timber and gum, and at one time it was the busiest port in New Zealand.

As the kauri forests were decimated, Dargaville continued its central role and today is the principal service centre of the predominantly agricultural Northern Wairoa area. It has an active Dalmatian (Yugoslav) community. As in many other parts of Northland, these people are descendants of the 19th-century immigrant gumdiggers who came from the coast of Dalmatia, in Yugoslavia.

Information

There's a handy little information centre (☎ 439 8360) on Normanby St in the town centre. It's open all year from 8.30 am to 5 pm Monday to Friday, with additional summer hours of 9 am to 3 pm on weekends (summer only) and public holidays. This office also houses the AA, making it convenient for picking up AA maps and other publications.

Northern Wairoa Museum

Dargaville's eccentric little museum is not of

■ PLACES TO STAY

1	Kauri House Lodge
2	Glendene Motel
3	Best Western Parkview Motel
4	Selwyn Park Camping Ground
5	Hobson's Choice Motel
6	Dargaville Motel
16	Northern Wairoa Hotel
18	Central Hotel
19	Green House YHA Hostel
22	Mangawhare Commercial Hotel

▼ PLACES TO EAT

7	Ocean Beach Fisheries & Takeaways
8	Lorna Doone
10	New Asian Cuisine
11	Bella Vista & Golden Lion
14	Papa's Pizza
15	Alpha Home Cookery
20	Mangawhare Fast Foods
21	River Road Dairy
23	Lighthouse Cafe

OTHER

9	Woolworths
12	Bus Station
13	Information Centre & Automobile Association (AA)
17	Public Toilets
24	Northern Wairoa Museum

the same standard as Matakohe but it's still worth visiting. Maori exhibits include a gigantic 18th-century war canoe found buried in sand dunes, the only surviving one made in pre-European times from stone tools. There are also early settlers' items, kauri gum samples and historical photographs. The highlight of the museum is the maritime section. Hundreds of ships were built and worked on in the Kaipara Harbour, which was also notorious for shipwrecks.

The museum is at the top of a small hill in Harding Park on the outskirts of town, about three km from the centre. In front of the museum are the masts from the *Rainbow Warrior*. An exhibit tells the day-by-day story of the attack on the conservation flagship and the subsequent investigation which

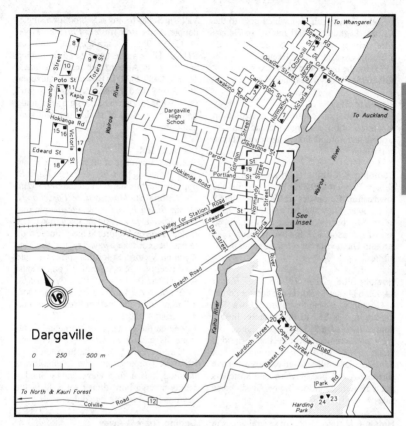

Dargaville

0   250   500 m

To North & Kauri Forest

NORTHLAND

revealed the first case of international terrorism to occur in New Zealand. The museum is open daily from 9 am to 4 pm; admission is \$2.50 (children 50 cents).

Harding Park

Harding Park is an interesting area as it is the site of an old Maori pa, Po-tu-Oterangi. Tucked into the bottom of the hill is an early European cemetery. There are great views over Dargaville and the surrounding countryside from the park, and picnic areas have been set up near the museum. The Light-

house Restaurant adjoining the museum takes maximum advantage of the view.

Cattle Sale

Every Monday from 11 am to 1 pm there's a roundup and cattle sale at the Mangawhare cattle yards. You're welcome to attend, just don't make any sudden movements!

Tours

Check with the information centre for a couple of excellent tours of the area. One tour visits the Waipoua Kauri Forest, the Trounson Kauri Park, and the Kai-Iwi Lakes;

the other is a beach tour which goes to the Kaipara Lighthouse and returns to Dargaville driving along the beach. The tour operators are Kauri Coast Excursions (☎ 439 7133) for the beach trip and Maxi's Tours (☎ 439 6695) for the forest and lakes.

Places to Stay
The information centre has a leaflet on accommodation in Dargaville and can also arrange accommodation in homes and farms in the area.

Camping & Cabins Both are available at *Selwyn Park* (☎ 439 8296), 1.5 km from the town centre. Campsites are $7 per person, $9 with power. They also have simple cabins at $8 to $14 per person and fully equipped tourist cabins at $37 for two persons. (See Around Dargaville for other camping possibilities.)

Hostels The *Green House YHA Hostel* (☎ 439 6342) at 13 Portland St on the corner of Gordon St, is near the centre of town. The nightly cost is $13 in this pleasant hostel; doubles/twins are $15 per person. One of the great pleasures for the traveller is the odd game of No 8 pool – the good news is that this place has a full-size table. They also have surfboards and free bicycles, and hostellers get a 10% discount on Baylys Beach horse rides.

Hotels & Motels There are several hotels in and near Dargaville. The *Northern Wairoa Hotel* (☎ 439 8923) on Hokianga Rd has single rooms at $27, and twin rooms at $40. At the *Mangawhare Commercial* (☎ 439 8018) on River Rd, Mangawhare, DB&B rates are $50. The *Central Hotel* (☎ 439 8034) at 18-22 Victoria St has single/double rooms at $40/70, breakfast included.

The *Kauri House Lodge* (☎ 439 8082) on Bowen Rd is a more expensive place with rooms at $80/90, each with bathroom. The rooms in this old colonial homestead are all furnished with antiques, and there's a swimming pool.

The *Dargaville Motel* (☎ 439 7734) at 217 Victoria St has rooms at $48/60 for a single/double. At the *Best Western Parkview Motel* (☎ 439 8339) at 36 Carrington St, rooms are $71/79. There's a restaurant and swimming and spa pools. Also in town are the *Glendene Motel* (☎ 439 7424) in Bowen Rd, with units at $35/49 and *Hobson's Choice Motel* (☎ 439 8551) Victoria St, with a swimming pool and a variety of studio, one and two-bedroom units.

Places to Eat
There are a number of takeaway places and cafes, including the *Chicken Inn* on Kapia St opposite the bus station, and the *Bella Vista* on Victoria St. *Mangawhare Fast Foods, Ocean Beach Fisheries & Takeaways*, and *River Road Dairy* are on the main roads. The *Golden Lion* on Victoria St has Chinese food to eat there or take away. Try also the *New Asian* on Victoria St for that spring roll and fried rice; they're open until 10 pm. Wanna some pizza? Try *Papa's Pizza* on Victoria St.

The *Northern Wairoa Hotel* has pub food, a Friday night smorgasbord and huge Sunday roasts – the latter for $12. The *Lorna Doone* on the corner of Victoria and Gladstone Sts, and the *Lighthouse* up on the hill in Harding Park beside the museum, both have good reputations. The *Lighthouse* is licensed, has a fine view, and a Sunday family smorgasbord dinner for $18; in the daytime it offers cafe fare only.

Getting There & Away
Bus The bus stop is on Kapia St. There's a bus route from Auckland via Dargaville to Paihia Monday to Friday. The two operators are the Kaipara Klipper and Mains Coachlines. There are also weekday buses to Whangarei which continue to Auckland. From Dargaville it's 3¼ hours to Auckland, four hours to Paihia, and one hour to Whangarei.

AROUND DARGAVILLE
Kaipara Lighthouse
A worthwhile trip from Dargaville, if you can find a way to get there, is the 71-km run south-east to Kaipara Lighthouse; the last 6.5

km is on foot along the foreshore. If you don't have wheels check with the information centre about tours that go there. Built in 1884, the lighthouse has been restored to its original condition.

Ocean Beach

Only 15 minutes from Dargaville is Ocean Beach, the site of many shipwrecks. It's said that the hulks of a French man o' war and an ancient Spanish or Portuguese ship can occasionally be seen. A French boat sank off Baylys Beach in 1851; you can read about it at the Dargaville museum.

Ocean Beach is over 100 km long and is the longest stretch of beach in the country that you could drive a vehicle on, although this is not the best idea for your car since the salt water is corrosive and the soft sand can trap the car in the incoming tide. But it is a very long, smooth stretch of beach. There is access at Baylys Beach (14 km west of Dargaville), Glinks Gully, Mahuta Gorge and Omamari – the main road does not touch the beach.

Horse rides on Baylys Beach are a popular activity from Dargaville. For $25 you get half a day of riding plus transport to and from Baylys Beach. You can book at the Green House Hostel – there's a 10% discount for hostellers – or phone 439 6730.

Places to Stay The *Baylys Beach Motor Camp* (☎ 439 6349) at Baylys Beach, 14 km from Dargaville, has tent sites at $8 per person and cabins at $26 to $28 for two.

DARGAVILLE TO HOKIANGA

En route to the big trees from Dargaville you can make a number of excursions. There are many walks you can undertake in Waipoua Kauri Forest as well as in the smaller reserves. Any visit to this area should be preceded by a visit to the Kauri Museum in Matakohe. An excellent set of brochures *Walks of the Kauri Coast Northland 1, 2 & 3* are available from the information centre in Dargaville. They cover more than 28 walks, including all the main walks in Waipoua Kauri Forest.

Kai-Iwi Lakes

Only 34 km north of Dargaville are three superb freshwater lakes called the Kai-Iwi Lakes (Taharoa Domain) and, although they've been developed as a resort for swimming, trout fishing and so on, the area is still relatively unspoilt. The lakes are Kai-Iwi, Taharoa and Waikere. The largest of the lakes, Taharoa, is fringed with pines and dotted with gleaming white sand beaches.

A walking track leaves from the Kai-Iwi Lakes out to the coast, then north along the beach to Maunganui Bluff where it climbs to the summit and drops down to the beach again. The track continues past the Waikara Beach campsite to the Kawerua campsite and on to Hokianga South Head near Omapere. Allow three days for this walk if you plan to do it all (it can also be done in shorter sections) and make sure you organise to cross the Waipoua and Waimamaku rivers at low tide.

You can get more information from the Dargaville information centre or the DOC visitor centre at Trounson Kauri Park or in Waipoua Kauri Forest. Activities and bylaws are outlined in a pamphlet *Taharoa Domain: Kai-Iwi Lakes* available from visitor information centres.

Places to Stay There are two rustic *camping grounds* at the Kai-Iwi Lakes, one at Pine Beach right on the main lake, and another at Promenade Point (book these at the information centre). They have toilets, cold showers, fireplaces, and no power points, and cost $5 per person.

For those wishing to stay on a farm there is the *Kaihu Farm Hostel* (☎ 439 4004), 33 km north of Dargaville on SH 12. Share, twins and doubles are all $14 in this 20-bed place. They have a small shop where you can stock up before going on one of the many bushwalks in the area. Waipoua Kauri Forest and Kai-Iwi lakes are both close by.

Trounson Kauri Park

Heading north from Dargaville you can take a route passing by the 573-hectare Trounson Kauri Park, 40 km north of Dargaville.

There's an easy half-hour walk leading from the parking and picnic area by the road, passing through beautiful forest with streams and some fine kauri stands, a couple of fallen kauri trees and the 'four sisters' – two trees each with two trunks. There's a ranger station and camping in the park.

Guided night-time nature walks are available in Trounson. Contact Vaughan Darby (☎ 439 0627). You'll see a wide variety of nightlife; including a North Island brown kiwi if you're lucky.

Places to Stay The turn-off for the Trounson Kauri Park is 32 km north of Dargaville. Just after the turn-off, the *Kauri Coast Motor Camp* (☎ 439 0621) is in a lovely riverside spot which is central to the lakes, the kauri forest, and generally everything of interest around the area. They do bushwalks, pony rides, river, lake and sea fishing. Per-person rates are $8.50 in tent or powered sites, $13 in basic cabins, or $18 in self-contained cabins.

There's also a DOC *camping ground* at the Trounson Kauri Park (☎ 439 0615). It's a beautiful place, ringed by superb kauris. Sites are $6 per person, with or without power. They have put in cabins and the cost of these is $8 per person, $4 for children or the whole place for $60 a week.

Waipoua Kauri Forest

The road north enters the Waipoua Kauri Forest 50 km out of Dargaville. The Waipoua Kauri Forest Sanctuary, proclaimed in 1952 after much public pressure and antagonism at continued milling, is the largest remnant of the once extensive kauri forests of northern New Zealand. There is no milling of mature kauri trees nowadays, except under extraordinary circumstances such as for the carving of a Maori canoe. Milling in the Puketi Forest was stopped some years back not only to protect the kauri but also because this area was the home of the rare native bird, the kokako.

The road through the forest passes by some splendid huge kauris. Turn off to the

forest lookout just after you enter the park – it was once a fire lookout and offers a spectacular view. A little further north another turn-off leads to the park Information Centre (☎ 439 0605), which in addition to plenty of information also has excellent exhibits on kauri trees, the history of the kauri in New Zealand and on native birds and wildlife. Nearby is Maxwell Cottage, a tiny hut used by the first ranger, now set up as an interesting little museum. Here you can pick up a brochure on the park which tells the full story of the trees. A fully grown kauri can reach 60

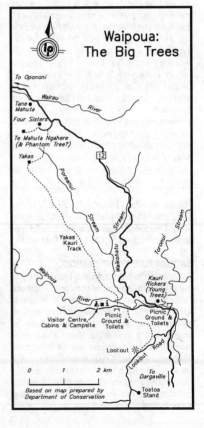

Waipoua:
The Big Trees

metres and have a trunk five metres or more in diameter. They are slow growing and some kauris are over 1500 years old.

Several huge trees are easily reached from the road. Te Matua Ngahere, the 'father of the forest', has a trunk over five metres in diameter, believed to be the widest girth of any kauri tree in New Zealand. This massive tree is a short drive then a 10-minute walk from the main road. Close by are the Four Sisters, a graceful collection of four tall trees in close proximity. Also near Te Matua Ngahere is the Phantom Tree, believed to be the second largest in the forest. It was 'lost' for a number of years but has since been rediscovered – DOC will tell us about it when new paths and walkways are constructed.

From the same access road you can follow a half-hour walking track to the Yakas Tree, the eighth largest kauri in New Zealand, and continue if you like for the whole two to three-hour trek to the park information centre.

Further up the road is Tane Mahuta, 'lord of the forest', the largest kauri tree in New Zealand, which stands close to the road and is estimated to be 1200 years old. At 52 metres, it's much higher than Te Matua Ngahere but doesn't have the same impressive bulk – although its cubic volume is said to be even greater.

On the southeastern boundary of the Waipoua Kauri forest is the 250-hectare McGregor Memorial Reserve. It contains regenerating kauri and podocarp forest and is the habitat of the kiwi and kauri snail. As manuka (tea-tree) is an ideal cover under which native trees grow it is being planted over former grassland in the reserve. To reach the reserve turn off SH 12 onto Marlborough Rd, about one km south of Katui Homestead. The entrance to the reserve is four km down Marlborough Rd.

Places to Stay There is plenty of accommodation right in the heart of the forest. Next to the Waipoua River and just past the information centre, there are *campsites* and *cabins* available. The cabins have showers as well as kitchen facilities; the cost is $12 per adult

Bellbird

and $6 per child. The campsites (with shared showers and toilets) are $6 for adults and $3 for a child. A furnished three-bedroom lodge is also available; bookings through DOC (☎ 439 0605).

Near Waimamaku, just north of the Waipoua Kauri Forest, the *Solitaire Guesthouse* (☎ 405 4891) is a B&B in a well restored old kauri house for $34/56 a single/double, or $51/90 with dinner. It's a pleasant, friendly place with plenty of good walks, horseriding and surfcasting off the beach.

Hokianga Harbour

Further north the road winds down to the Hokianga Harbour and the tiny twin townships of Omapere and Opononi. Hokianga is a popular area for city slickers wishing to escape to an alternative lifestyle, but it's still fairly unspoilt – much less commercial than the Bay of Islands – and a good place for travellers who want to take time out and drift for a while.

As you come up over the hill from the south there's a rest stop on Pakia Hill with a great view of the harbour; it's worth a stop.

Further on down the hill, two km west of

Omapere, Signal Station Rd leads out to the **Arai-Te-Uru Recreation Reserve & Lookout**, on the South Head of the Hokianga Harbour. It's about a 30-minute walk from Omapere, or if you're driving, a five-minute walk from the car park to the Signal Station Point which overlooks the harbour entrance, the massive sand dunes of the North Head, and the turbulent confluence of the harbour and the open sea. There's a swimming beach here, people fish off the rocks, and it's also the northern beginning/ending point of the Hokianga-Waipoua Coastal Track.

OMAPERE

There's a tiny museum at Omapere, on the main road through town, which also houses the Hokianga Visitors Information Centre (☎ 405 8869). Opening hours are very limited in winter, longer in summer.

Places to Stay & Eat

In town there are the *Motel Hokianga* (☎ 405 8847) and the *Omapere Tourist Hotel, Motel & Caravan Park* (☎ 405 8737). Expect to pay about $68 a double in the former and $8 each for a tent site in the latter. The prices drop down considerably in the off season (June to August) at the Motel Hokianga – you may get a unit for $170 per week.

For a dining splurge there is the fancy *Harbourmaster's Restaurant* at the Omapere Tourist Hotel & Motel, where you can eat indoors or outside, watching the boats and all the activity in the bay.

The Omapere Village Shopping Centre has takeaways, a bakery and store. About two km outside Omapere heading south the *Panorama Restaurant* has, yes, a panoramic view of the harbour, whether from inside or out on the deck. It serves light meals and takeaways plus home-baked goods and a separate dinner menu.

OPONONI

Only 3.5 km past Omapere the road passes through the tiny settlement of Opononi. The stone walls along Opononi's seafront were constructed from rock ballast used in timber ships which were sailed out from Sydney by convicts.

Back in 1955 a dolphin paid so many regular, friendly visits to the town that it became a national attraction. Opo, as the dolphin was named, played with children and learned to perform numerous tricks with beach balls. Unfortunately, Opo was killed, some say accidentally, by illegal dynamite fishers. A sculpture of Opo marks the dolphin's grave outside Opononi's pub. You can see a video of Opo at the Hokianga Visitors Information Centre & Museum in Omapere.

Cruises & Fishing

Both of the Opononi hostels have boats and they frequently take hostellers out for fishing and shellfish excursions and on trips across to the North Head sand dunes. A water taxi operated by the owner of the Taha Moana Motel (☎ 405 8824) is available for harbour cruising, water-skiing, parasailing and trips across to the dunes.

The MV *Sierra* is a 40-foot (12-metre) boat built of local Hokianga kauri wood in 1912, at the end of the logging boom. The boat plied the Hokianga Harbour for 42 years, carrying passengers and freight and, after a varied history including a sojourn in Auckland, is now once again operating in the harbour. It is licensed to carry 39 passengers and does several enjoyable cruises including the historic 'mail run', departing from Opononi and stopping at wharves in Te Karaka, Rawene, Kohukohu and Horeke. It costs about $75 to hire the whole boat to make the full return cruise, less if you just want to stop off somewhere (if the boat is near full expect to pay about $10). The boat also does twilight cruises, sandhill excursions, fishing, a tavern run (there are five on the harbour), and private charters. Phone 405 8702/8753 to check details, which vary with the seasons.

Fishing and shellfishing are excellent around the Hokianga Harbour. Fishing trips are easily arranged; even fishing off the wharf or the rocks near the harbour entrance is not bad.

Walks

Hokianga-Waipoua Coastal Track The Hokianga-Waipoua Coastal Track begins/ ends at the South Head of the Hokianga Harbour and extends southwards along the coast – it's four hours to the Waimamaku Beach exit, six hours to the Kawerua exit which also has a campsite and hut, 12 hours to the Kerr Rd exit where there's a campsite at Waikara Beach, or you could continue the entire 16 hours (allow about three days) to the Kai-Iwi Lakes. Pick up a brochure from any information centre or DOC office in Northland for details.

Other Walks In addition to the Hokianga-Waipoua Coastal Track there are several shorter local walks. Cemetery Rd is on the eastern outskirts of Opononi. From this road you can make a half-hour climb up **Mt Whiria**, one of the oldest unexcavated pa sites, with a splendid view of the harbour.

Two km east of Opononi the Waiotemarama Gorge road turns south for six km to the **Waiotemarama bush track**. This track climbs to Mt Hauturu, 680 metres high. It's a four-hour walk to the summit (eight hours return), but there's a shorter loop walk starting from the same place which takes only about two hours and passes a picturesque waterfall and kauri trees. The highest point in Northland, Te Raupua (781 metres), is nearby but there is no regular route.

Between Waima and Taheke is the **old Waoku coach road**, once the sole route to Dargaville and, because of the rainfall, only open during summer. The track at the end of the road leads to some old, handmade culverts and excellent views of the valley. It takes about three hours there and back. If you continue to follow it, it winds south to Tutamoe and then west to Wekaweka Valley. You can enter the track from Waoku Rd or from Wekaweka Rd, and it can take a full or a half-day to do the trek depending where you start and finish; there's another branch of the track that winds down through the Mataraua Forest. Get information from DOC before starting out.

Other Things to Do

There are several opportunities for horse-riding in the area – inquire at the Hokianga Visitors Information Centre .

The Heritage Restaurant & Art Gallery at the Opononi Resort Hotel – Motel has a display of artwork done by locals.

Places to Stay

Hostels The *Opononi YHA Hostel* (☎ 405 8792) is two km east of Opononi at Pakanae, it's the second driveway from the highway on Waiotemarama Gorge Rd. It's a good, rustic hostel, in the former old Pakanae schoolhouse, but a little far from the town. It costs $10 per night ($14 for nonmembers), or $25 in total if you're staying for three nights. The dorm rooms are basic but it has a large airy kitchen and a quiet location.

Te Rangimarie – The House of Harmony (☎ 405 8778) is more convenient than the YHA hostel. The cost is $12 a night in dorm or double rooms. It's up the steep driveway beside the South Hokianga War Memorial Hall in the centre of Opononi.

Hotels & Motels In central Opononi, the *Opononi Resort Hotel – Motel* (☎ 405 8858) has one-bedroom motel units for $74; with two bedrooms they're $85, less in winter. Most of the hotel rooms share facilities and cost $25/35, or $45 a double with private bath. They also have a backpackers section, where beds are just $12 a night.

Also in Opononi the *Taha Moana Motel* (☎ 405 8824) has one-bedroom units at $58 a double, two-bedroom units at $85 for two ($10 each extra adult), remaining the same all year.

Camping & Cabins The *Opononi Beach Motor Camp* (☎ 405 8791) has campsites at $8 per person, $9 with power, and a handful of on-site caravans at $12 per person. There are also a couple of chalets sleeping four at about $35 per unit. This camp is closed from May until Labour weekend (late October).

Places to Eat

On the main road in Opononi the *Blue Dol-*

phin Restaurant has burgers, sandwiches and other light meals, plus a separate dinner menu. You can eat indoors or out on the deck overlooking the harbour. The *Heritage Restaurant & Art Gallery* at the Opononi Resort Hotel – Motel has basic food at moderate prices.

Not surprisingly, most of the restaurants here specialise in seafood, and it's excellent. If you are looking for entertainment in either Omapere or Opononi then try the karaoke night at the Opononi Resort Hotel – 'great' crooned one reader. The South Hokianga RSA (☎ 405 8723) accepts nonmembers and the attraction at these places is really cheap beer and a kitbag of reminiscences.

Getting There & Away
Bus InterCity buses stop at Omapere and Opononi on their Monday-to-Friday run between Dargaville and Paihia, each about two hours distant. The bus driver heading south through the Waipoua Kauri Forest will pick you up in the morning, drop you off in the forest, and arrange to pick you up for the return trip in the afternoon.

KAIKOHE
Kaikohe is one of the central towns in Northland as it is on SH 12, close to the divergence of SH 1 and SH 10. If you are getting around on public transport, it is more than likely that you will pass through Kaikohe. The AA agent (☎ 401 1803) is at 5 Dickson St. The main thoroughfare is Broadway and the accommodation and eating places are spread along it. Included are the *Kaikohe Hotel* (☎ 401 1563) and the *Kaikohe RSA & District Services Ltd* (☎ 401 0149). The room rates are $30/40 for a single/double in the former and $45/65 for a single/double in the latter. Not far away, at 36 Raihara St, is the *Motel New Haven* (☎ 401 1859) where twins or doubles are $65 to $70.

ROUTES TO KAITAIA
From the Hokianga you can head north to Kaitaia and the Ninety Mile Beach or east to the Bay of Islands. There are two routes north to Kaitaia. The longer and busier route

goes via Kaikohe and is easier for hitchhikers. The alternative route is 70 km shorter and takes you on the Rawene-Kohukohu ferry.

The ferry departs from Rawene every hour on the half-hour between 7.30 am and 5.45 pm and goes from the Narrows on the Kohukohu side at 7.45 and 8.30 am and then every hour from 9 am to 6 pm. The starting time may be an hour later and finishing time an hour earlier in winter; the crossing takes 20 minutes. Fares are $9 for cars ($12 return), $2 for people (includes return).

Rawene
While you wait for the ferry at Rawene you can visit historic Clendon House, open from 10 am to 4 pm daily, except Thursday and Friday (from June to August it is open only on weekends). Admission is $2 (children $1). Clendon House was built by James Clendon, an early trader, who settled in the Bay of Islands in 1832. He was the first US consul in New Zealand and probably built this house after 1866 when he moved to Rawene to take up the position as Resident Magistrate of the Hokianga Harbour region.

Outside the Westpac Bank is *Te Hawera*, an old Maori dugout waka (fishing canoe), distinguishable by its lack of carved ends.

Rawene is a pleasant little settlement – you might decide to stay longer than just the wait for the ferry. Tiny though it is, Rawene is full of history. It's the third oldest European settlement in New Zealand, and in addition to Clendon House there are plenty of other historic buildings. The Wharf House, now housing a restaurant, is the oldest building in Rawene and has been a hospital, a private home, and many other things during its long lifetime. The hotel, too, is a historic place, built in the 1870s.

Places to Stay & Eat Rawene has a *motor camp* (☎ 405 7720) in Marmon St just off Manning St, with tent sites at $8 per person ($9 with power), cabins at $15 per person, and two self-contained units at $20 per person. The *Masonic Hotel* (☎ 405 7822), just a few steps up from the ferry landing, has rooms from $30/50.

You can get an excellent feed of fish & chips at the *Wharfhouse Takeaways*, near the water's edge and just off Parnell St.

Mangungu Mission
In 1828 the Wesleyan Missionary Society established a settlement at Mangungu on Hokianga Harbour. The mission house, built between 1838 and 1839, was in service until 1855. The Hokianga chiefs signed the Treaty of Waitangi in this building in 1840. In 1855 the house was dismantled and shipped to Auckland but in 1972 the Historic Places Trust had it returned to Mangungu. The mission house is now three km west of Horeke, which you can get to by turning off either SH 1 (Ohaeawai to Kaikohe) or SH 12 (Rawene to Kaikohe).

The mission house is open weekends and during the school holidays from noon to 4 pm. If you wish to learn more about the fascinating history of Hokianga obtain a copy of *Hokianga: A Visitors' Guide* (Eric Harrison, Auckland, 1992).

Kohukohu
This pleasant town is in a very quiet backwater on the north side of Hokianga Harbour. It is a good example of a completely preserved town with a number of old, historic kauri buildings. There are a number of kauri villas over 100 years old and other fine buildings including the Masonic Lodge, Anglican Church and old school.

Places to Stay & Eat Kohukohu is one of those places that allows you to get away from it all for a while. Backpackers are spoilt here. The *Kohukohu Tree House* (☎ 405 5855) is undoubtedly one of the finest backpackers retreats in the country. Constructed of wood and stained glass, it is nestled in the hills not far from the waters of Hokianga Harbour and two km from the northern ferry terminus. It is not expensive either – twins/triples are $13 per person, two private sleep-outs can be yours for $32 a double and normal doubles are $15 each person. Even the showers,

including the small 'Japanese' one, are wood-lined. The main room is like no other; and if you wish to tax the brain there are plenty of books and board games available. Bone-carving is also a popular pastime here – carve your own gifts for $30 which includes tuition and materials.

Two B&Bs in Kohukohu have been recommended: *Catherine Bawden* (☎ 405 5534) in Hawkins Rd and *Jackie Kelly* (☎ 405 5815), Rakautapu Rd.

Ngawha Springs
Near Kaikohe is Ngawha Springs which has a series of hot springs of varying temperatures at the Domain Pool – pick one to suit your mood. It's very basic but it's a great way to spend a bleak day and only about three km off the main road. Admission is $2.

Forest Scenery
To get to the Omahuta Forest, turn off just south of Mangamuka Bridge. The Mangamuka Gorge picnic area on the south side of the hill is also worth a stop as it is in a lovely forest setting next to a stream; there is good swimming nearby. The Raetea Forest recreation area on the northern side of the range is also a good spot for a rest.

The Far North

KAITAIA
Kaitaia, the second-largest commercial centre in the north, is a small, pleasant town with all visitor facilities. It has a large shopping centre, post office, banks, library, museum and information centre. It is the jumping-off point for trips up Ninety Mile Beach to Cape Reinga. Buses leave Kaitaia every morning on this trip – see the following section on Ninety Mile Beach.

Entering Kaitaia you'll see a welcome sign in three languages – Welcome, Haere Mai (Maori) and Dobro Dosli (Dalmatian) – as many Maoris and Dalmatians live in the area. Both groups are culturally active, with a Maori marae and a Yugoslav Cultural Club being the focus of activities.

Information

The Northland Information Centre (☎ 408 0879) is in Jaycee Park on South Rd. They have information on Kaitaia and the entire Far North region. They also book accommodation, tours and activities for the Far North. The office is open from 8.30 am to 5 pm on week days and 8.30 am to noon on Saturday and Sunday.

Far North Regional Museum

The Far North Regional Museum near the information centre houses an interesting collection including a giant moa skeleton, various bits and pieces from shipwrecks, and the Northwood Collection – hundreds of photographs taken around 1900 by a professional photographer. The giant 1769 de Surville anchor, one of three the explorer lost in Doubtless Bay, is one of the museum's prize pieces. On weekdays it's open from 10 am to 5 pm, 1 to 5 pm on weekends, with extended summer hours. Admission is $2 (children 50 cents).

Far North Community Centre Mural

The unusual three-dimensional mural at the Far North Community Centre is an exceptional combination of painting, sculpture, backlighting and other innovative techniques, together paying tribute to the Far North region. Three-dimensional scenes include a Maori canoe on a turbulent sea, whalers, kauri forestry, and others.

The community centre is open from about 8.30 am to 5 pm Monday to Friday, but is also open on many evenings and weekends for various functions. It's just a short walk around the corner from the visitor information office and the museum.

Sullivan's Nocturnal Park

In Fairburn, about a 20-minute drive from Kaitaia, Sullivan's Nocturnal Park (☎ 408 4100) is open every day from noon to midnight. The main attraction is a glow-worm grotto beside a waterfall; in the dark of night you're taken on a guided nature walk for a close-up view of the glow-worms in their natural habitat. There's also a nocturnal kiwi room and areas for picnics in the daytime. Entry is $6 for adults, $3 for children.

To reach the park from Kaitaia, go eight km south-east on SH 1, turn left at the Fairburn signpost and continue for another nine km. Coming from Taipa it's about a half-hour drive. It is open daily from 9.30 am until 10 pm.

Kaitaia Walkway

The Kaitaia Walkway, also known as the Kiwanis Bush Walk, makes a good day trip and has excellent views. Originally planned as a road, the track has a gentle gradient along its nine km, and you should allow five hours to walk it. To get to there head south from Kaitaia on SH 1 for three km, then turn right into Larmer Rd and follow it to the end. Her you'll find the Kiwanis Club Bush Camp Hut, where you can stay overnight if you've made prior arrangements.

The track finishes at Veza Rd, off Diggers Valley Rd, which can be an awkward place to get out of as there is no transport and it is quite a long way from the main road. There is a good short walk from the Larmer Rd end to the lookout or Kauri grove. Inquire at the local DOC office for further information.

Tours

Kaitaia is a small town but it's quite a centre for tours to surrounding areas, notably Cape Reinga and the gumfields of Ahipara. See the section on Ninety Mile Beach for information on tours to that region.

Other popular tours from Kaitaia are operated by Tall Tales Travel 'n Tours, based at both the Main Street Hostel (☎ 408 1275) and an office at 123b Commerce St (☎ 408 0870; fax 408 1100).

The trip to Te Rarawa Marae with Tall Tales is fascinating and informative. Peter, the guide, is attuned to all nuances of the interrelationship of past and present, legend and fact, marae protocol, Maori culture, etc. I would recommend such a learning experience before you venture further north to

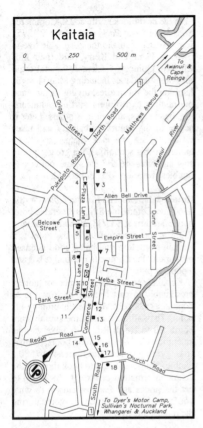

Kaitaia

0   250   500 m

To Awanui & Cape Reinga

■ PLACES TO STAY

1 Capri Motel
2 Main Street Backpackers
6 Kaitaia YHA Hostel
13 Kaitaia Hotel

▼ PLACES TO EAT

3 Sea Dragon
4 Beachcomber
7 Steve's Snapper Bar
10 Time Out Cafe
11 White Lady Pie Cart

OTHER

5 Kaitaia Travel Bureau
8 Pak 'n Save Supermarket
9 Post Office
12 Four Square Supermarket
14 Yugoslav Cultural Club
15 Far North Regional Museum
16 Northland Information Centre
17 Far North Art & Crafts Gallery
18 Far North Community Centre

NORTHLAND

Spirits Bay and Cape Reinga – the journey will have far more meaning. The interpretation of the carvings, paintings and weaving inside the whare hui (meeting house) is particularly important as it enmeshes myriad aspects of life, death and the hereafter. Of great interest are the panels depicting the Earth Mother (Papatuanuku) and Sky Father (Rangatira) and the creation of the earth and sky. The last panel is intriguing – it encourages you to look beyond. Try for yourself. The marae and culture tour costs $20 per person.

Peter's suggestions for some preparatory

reading include *Te Marae: A Guide to Customs & Protocol*, Hiwi & Pat Tauroa (Heinemann Reed (division OUP), Auckland, 1990), *Tikanga Whakaaro: Key Concepts in Maori Culture*, Cleve Barlow (OUP, Auckland, 1992), and the *Oxford Maori Picture Dictionary: He Pukapuka Kupuahua Maori*, Pita Cleave & EC Parnwell (OUP, Auckland, 1991).

The Pupuharakeke Trail, or Snail Trail, is operated by guides from the Ngati Kuri tribe and includes a fascinating one to four-day traverse of Maori land in the very Far North above Parengarenga Harbour. Highlights are views of the silica sands of Te Kokota, pupuharakeke (flax snail), the money tree and the Kurahaupo rock where one of the Great Migration canoes was tied up. The cost is $65 per day; all accommodation, meals and transport included.

Tall Tales have a number of other trips more designed to stimulate adrenaline flow than to arouse the grey matter. For $100 you can ride your own quad (four wheeler) motorbike through the gumfields and up and down the sand dunes near Ahipara; a share bike is only $75 per person. Their 4X4 Landcruiser trip, or Tu Tu (Mucking About) tour crosses the gumfields, beach and sand dunes. Time is left for sand tobogganing down 80-metre sand dunes. The cost of tu tu-ing is $45 per person.

There is another Funbus operator (Tu-Tu Seaspray Trail) (☎ 406 0838) which does a similar trip – sand tobogganing, swimming and a barbecue to finish the day; $45 for adults, $25 for children.

Other Things to Do

It's easy hitching a ride out to the beach at Ahipara, 14 km west of Kaitaia. Ahipara is the southernmost section of Ninety Mile Beach and is popular with locals and visitors. Here there's fishing, surfing, horse-riding, a motor camp and lots of picnicking and playing around on fine days.

The Aero Club (☎ 406 7320) will take you for a one-hour flight up to Cape Reinga and back, or for any other scenic or charter flight. It's quite economical if you can get a group of three together.

There's a park and children's playground on Commerce St between the museum and the visitor information centre. Further down in the park, opposite the Far North Community Centre, the Far North Arts & Crafts Gallery has many unusual items.

Every year a special marathon is conducted along the length of Ninety Mile Beach. It celebrates the legend of Te Houtaewa. This great runner ran the length of the beach from near Te Kao to Ahipara to steal kumara from the Rarawa people, returning with two full baskets after being angrily pursued.

Places to Stay

Hostels Kaitaia has two excellent hostels. The *Kaitaia YHA Hostel* (☎ 408 1840) is very central at 160 Commerce St (the main drag). It sleeps 39 and since there are plenty of twin rooms and family rooms you have a pretty good chance of getting a room to yourself. The cost is $13 a night.

In the next block north, at 235 Commerce St, is *Main Street Backpackers* (☎ 408 1275). It's privately run and the hospitable live-in owners, Peter and Kerry (and their kids Chelsea, Quincey, Ossie and Waiata) organise many activities including Maori hangis, lamb on the spit parties, diving, fishing and pig-hunting expeditions, surfing, windsurfing, bushwalks, and various others. Peter is active in the Maori community and takes visitors to see the local marae (see Tours earlier in this section). It's a great place to stay and rates are $13 for share rooms, and doubles/twins are $15 per person.

Hotels & Motels The *Kaitaia Hotel* (☎ 408 0360) on Commerce St is a venerable hotel with 30 rooms at $33/38, all with bathroom. Right at the centre of town, the hotel is a Kaitaia institution and has a good licensed restaurant plus a house bar, a lounge bar and a popular pub.

Kaitaia has a surprising number of motels, presumably in part because the town is so popular as a Ninety Mile Beach jumping-off point. They all exist along the stretch from South Rd to North Rd. They have various amenities such as swimming pools, saunas, spas, gyms, etc, and rates from $40 to $80 a double. Your best bet is to book through the visitor information centre (☎ 408 0879) to get the prices and features closest to what you're looking for. Otherwise you can ring the motels directly:

Best Western Wayfarer Motel	☎ 408 2600
Kaitaia Motor Lodge	☎ 408 1910
Kauri Lodge Motel	☎ 408 1190
Loredo Motel	☎ 408 3200
Motel Capri	☎ 408 0224
Northerner Motor Inn	☎ 408 2800
Orana Motor Inn	☎ 408 1510
Sierra Court Motor Lodge	☎ 408 1461

There are a few B&B inns around the Far North region, and these, too, can be booked through the visitor information centre.

Camping & Cabins *Dyer's Motor Camp* (☎ 408 0333) at 67 South Rd on the southern end of town, and the basic *Pine Tree Lodge*

Motor Camp (☎ 409 4864), 18 km west on the coast at Ahipara, each have tent and powered sites at $8.50 per person.

The *Park Ninety Mile Beach* (☎ 406 7298) is 18 km north on the Cape Reinga road at Waipapakauri Ramp and has tent and powered sites at $9 per person, basic cabins at $28 for two and fully equipped tourist cabins at $40 for two. There's a licensed restaurant on the premises; lamb on the spit is the speciality.

Places to Eat

The *Steve's Snapper Bar* at 123 Commerce St is good and economical, with a big serving of fish & chips for just $3. It's across the road and a little down from the YHA and although it's essentially a takeaway place you can eat your 'takeaways' there. They also do fried chicken and pizzas and they sell fresh fish. Further up the main road, towards SH 1 the *Sea Dragon* has Chinese takeaways. There is another *Sea Dragon*, this time a restaurant, further down Commerce St – locals report that the cooks aren't too heavy handed on the MSG. *VIP Takeaways* is another good spot for fish & chips and there are several other takeaways around town.

There are also a few good cafes, including the *Time Out Cafe* right in the centre of town with an excellent selection of inexpensive food and a comfortable atmosphere. The *Kauri Arms Tavern*, the *Collard's Tavern* and the *Kaitaia Hotel Pub* all serve pub food. For a late-night bite the *White Lady Pie Cart*, just off Commerce St, is open some nights until 3 am and also serves nonalcoholic drinks.

For a fancier meal try the award-winning, licensed and BYO *Beachcomber* on Commerce St.

Pak 'N Save is a gigantic supermarket on the main drag. Prices are lower here than anywhere else and it attracts customers from far and wide. There are two Four Square stores – Shaw's in the main street, and another by the Plaza. Also look for the large *bakery* on Commerce St; it has a good selection of baked goodies. It's open from about 6 am.

Entertainment

For years Kaitaia had only one bar and pub, at the *Kaitaia Hotel*, but the town now has three pubs including the *Kauri Arms Tavern* on Commerce St and the *Collard's Tavern* on the northern side of town. With the competition they all have to try harder and now they all bring in live bands on the weekends. The bar at Collard's has a huge screen which draws in the rugby devotees in winter.

Getting There & Away

Air Eagle Air (☎ 407 7411) has one daily flight between Kaitaia and Auckland, with connections to other centres, and weekday flights to Whangarei.

Bus InterCity (☎ 408 0540) leaves from the Kaitaia Travel Bureau on Blencowe St. Northliner also leaves from the same place. Several daily buses go between Kaitaia and Auckland via Doubtless Bay, the Bay of Islands and Whangarei. Travel time is 30 minutes to Doubtless Bay, 2½ hours to Paihia, 3½ hours to Whangarei or seven hours all the way to Auckland. The Cape Reinga tours leave from the visitor information centre, or they'll pick you up from your accommodation.

Getting Around

The major rental car companies have agents in Kaitaia: Budget is at Star Garage (☎ 408 2510), Avis is at the Kaitaia Travel Bureau and Hertz is at Kaitaia Toyota (☎ 408 0440). Haines Haulage (☎ 408 0116) provides airport transport for $5 per person.

NINETY MILE BEACH

The west coast tip of Northland – ending in Cape Reinga – is known as Ninety Mile Beach. When they metricate it to Ninety Kilometre Beach the name will be a lot more accurate as it's a good bit short of 90 miles! Private vehicles are prohibited on the beach so the trip can only be made by bus, and these trips are very popular. The buses travel up the beach and down the road, or vice versa, depending on the tides.

The bus trips start from Kaitaia, Doubtless Bay and the Bay of Islands. It's preferable to start from Kaitaia or Doubtless Bay since they're that much closer to Cape Reinga – two of the small, local operators start out from both places, one from Kaitaia only. Going from the Bay of Islands you have a couple of hours extra travel at each end of the day to contend with, and you're limited to going with a larger, more commercial tour company.

If you're staying a while in the Cape Reinga-Ninety Mile Beach area, a network of tracks has been opened up connecting the various beaches, and there are a couple of campsites with road access. You can walk down the Ninety Mile Beach but you'll need to be well prepared as there are no huts, and although it may not be as long as 90 miles it certainly seems like it to walk! The main attraction of the Far North is the coastline, which is scattered with beautiful beaches – far too many to mention here.

The Aupouri Forest, about 75 km long and five km wide, covers two-thirds of the western side of the peninsula. It's an exotic forest, mostly pine, planted for timber. Kauri forest used to cover the area, in fact traces have been found of three separate growths of kauri which were buried and then grew up again. This was a fruitful area for gumdiggers, as was most of the northern region. On the northern edge of the Aupouri Forest a volcanic rock formation called The Bluff is part of a 36-hectare private reserve used for fishing by the Maori tribe living in nearby Te Kao. A colony of white-fronted terns can be seen just past the Bluff on a prominent sandspit.

North of The Bluff, the Te Paki Reserves are public land and you can go where you wish there, just leave the gates as you found them and don't disturb the animals. There are about seven sq km of giant sand dunes on either side of where the Te Paki stream meets the sea; a stop to take flying leaps off the dunes is one of the highlights of the locally operated tours.

For details of walking tracks in the area inquire at the DOC shop and information centre at Cape Reinga or at DOC Whangarei.

Wagener Museum & Subritzky Homestead

The Wagener Museum at Houhora is an astonishing place, with over 50,000 items on display, spanning almost nine centuries. Worldwide nature exhibits include a five cm mouse deer and 30 cm insects; an 1878 Symphonion is among a collection of antique gramophones, player pianos and other musical instruments that the guide will play for you. Other operational antiques include various inventive washing machines, telephones, clocks and carriages. Top quality Maori carvings are found both inside and outside, and the prehistory and old photographs section is equally interesting. A number of the interesting prehistoric items were excavated from the Mt Camel pa site. The kauri gum exhibit includes some intriguing knick knacks fashioned for local shows.

It's open daily from 8 am to 5.30 pm (with reduced hours in winter); admission is $5 if you are with a tour, $6 if you are not (children $2.50).

The Subritzky homestead was built between 1860 and 1862. It is interesting as an example of pioneering ingenuity. It was constructed of local kauri and the different widths of timber, just as cut from the log, can be seen in the flooring. Note also the worn door thresholds, the huge doorlocks and equally large keys, and the carefully grooved edges of the ceiling boards.

Tours

Several small, locally owned tour operators run from Kaitaia and Doubtless Bay up to Cape Reinga (☎ 408 1778), 27 South Rd, Kaitaia, have small buses which carry between 12 and 19 people. In a day trip they leave from Kaitaia and take in the Aupouri Forest, the beach, Te Paki Stream, sandhills, Cape Reinga, Tapotupotu Bay, Rarawa Beach and Houhora Heads (the Wagener Museum and Subritzky Homestead). The cost is $45 for adults and $22 for children (discounts for backpackers should be $40 or $37 without lunch).

Nor-East Coachlines (☎ 406 0244) is

another good local company, operating from Mangonui. Nor-East goes to the same places as Sand Safaris for about the same price.

Other small-group local tours to the Cape Reinga area include Tall Tales Travels 'N Tours, based at Kaitaia's Main Street Hostel (see the Tours section for Kaitaia). Cuzzy Leisure Tours (☎ 408 1853), 169 Commerce St, Kaitaia, are another small, friendly outfit.

Fullers and King's tours come from the Bay of Islands only. In addition to being a bit more costly these tours are also more formal, done in big buses with a time schedule to adhere to.

Of course you could go up to Cape Reinga on your own, there's no bus but there are rental car companies in Kaitaia if you didn't bring your own, and even hitching is not too difficult. The main advantage with a tour is that you'll see the best parts of the region, learn something about it, and especially in the 4WD vehicles you can go to places you'd never reach by car. Driving on the beach is something you wouldn't want to inflict on your own car (it causes rust) and car rental companies strictly disapprove: in a car you have to stick to the roads. Motorcycling on the beach would be OK but if you try this take it slow and be extra careful, a few bikers have been killed when they suddenly rode into washouts or soft sand. If you want to spend more time than the one-day tour allows, you can make arrangements with one of the smaller tour operators for you to get off the tour and be picked up on another day.

Places to Stay

If you do plan to stay on the cape there are several DOC campsites in the Cape Reinga area. There's a site at *Spirits Bay*, with cold water and limited toilet facilities, and another at *Tapotupotu Bay*, with toilets and showers; neither has electricity and you should bring a cooker with you as fires are not allowed. Both bays are infested with mosquitoes and biting sandflies, so come prepared with coils and insect repellent.

Spirits Bay is a sacred area to the Maoris – in Maori folklore, the spirits departing from the dead come here and leap off the

cliffs into the sea, leaving New Zealand to return to the legendary homeland Hawaiki.

There's another DOC campsite at *Rarawa Beach*, three km north of Ngataki, with water and toilet facilities only. No prior bookings can be made and no open fires are permitted. Cooking is confined to gas cookers only because of the high fire risk.

The *Pukenui Lodge Motel & Backpackers Hostel* (☎ 409 8837), is the northernmost accommodation in New Zealand, in a lovely setting overlooking Pukenui Harbour. The motel has singles, twins or doubles for $60; $12 for each extra person. The hostel is in a separate house behind the motel. It's pleasant, comfortable and homely, with dorm rooms at $12.50 and twins/doubles at $15 per person. Cape tours pick up from here.

Follow Lamb Rd west about 500 metres and there's the *Pukenui Motor Camp* (☎ 409 8803) with tent and powered sites at $7.50 per person, on-site caravans at $12 to $17.50 per person and a tourist flat at $40 for two. *Northwind Backpackers* (☎ 409 8515) of Henderson Bay will pick you up from Pukenui and take you to the east side of the peninsula; accommodation is $12.50 per person.

The *Houhora Camping Ground* (☎ 409 8564) is opposite the Wagener Museum. It's an attractive location but with minimal facilities – no power and cold showers only. Nonetheless rates are low and if you happen to be towing a boat there's a boat ramp here. At the turn-off to the museum from the highway the *Houhora Chalets Motel* (☎ 409 8860) has six A-frame units for $45/60 for singles/twins or doubles. This and other local motels can be booked through the visitor information centre in Kaitaia (☎ 408 0879).

Places to Eat

Opposite the Pukenui Lodge, on the corner of Lamb Rd and the main highway, is *Fork of the North's* restaurant, tearoom, takeaway and shop.

KARIKARI PENINSULA

Remote Karikari Peninsula, sandwiched between the Aupouri Peninsula and Doubtless Bay, has a number of great beaches and secluded bays, including Rangiputa and Matai Bay. Matai Bay is especially lovely, with its tiny 'twin coves'.

A range of accommodation types is found on the peninsula. There is a DOC campground at *Matai Bay* (☎ 402 2100). During the Christmas holidays it is very popular, but usually not full at other times of the year. There is a good walking track from the end of the beach which takes you up onto the southern peninsula. The cost at this place is $6 for adults and $3 for children.

The *Karikari Motor Camp* (☎ 408 7051) is off Matai Bay Rd at Karikari Bay. A campsite is $9.50 per day for two adults and three children, and cabins and caravans are $26. There are two lodges at Rangiputa as well as one motor inn on the peninsula.

DOUBTLESS BAY

From Kaitaia it's about 40 km to Doubtless Bay, heading north a few km to Awanui and then turning east on SH 10. The bay gets its unusual name from an entry in Captain Cook's logbook, where he wrote down that the body of water was 'doubtless a bay'. The area is much less touristed than the Bay of Islands, it has plenty of unspoiled scenic beauty and a few good activities and places to stay. Tours to Cape Reinga depart from here (Nor-East) and take only about half an hour longer in travel time than if you go from Kaitaia.

The area is full of tiny picturesque bays and coves. On the northern and western sides the bay is bounded by the Karikari Peninsula. Other beaches circle the bay and include the popular beach resorts of Taipa, Cable Bay and Cooper's Beach. Mangonui, the principal town, is a charming historic village. The whole area is great for fishing and shellfishing, boating, swimming and all other watersports.

Taipa

According to Maori legend, Taipa is the place where Kupe, the original Polynesian discoverer of New Zealand, first set foot on the new land in about 900 AD. Today it has a fine beach, a harbour where the Taipa River meets the sea, and several motels and motor camps. You can get a good view overlooking Taipa by turning off the main road onto Bush Point Rd.

East of Taipa is Cable Bay, once the home of the longest cable in the world: from 1902 to 1912 a cable stretched 3500 nautical miles from here to Queensland, Australia. The cable station was closed down in 1912 when another cable was laid between Sydney and Auckland. Today Cable Bay and Cooper's Beach are popular beach resorts, especially during the summer.

It's about a 30-minute drive from Taipa to Sullivan's Nocturnal Park in Fairburn (see Kaitaia), turning from SH 10 onto Peria Rd and continuing for about 24 km.

Rangikapiti Pa

Between Cooper's Bay and Mangonui is the Rangikapiti Pa Historic Reserve, with ancient Maori terracing and a spectacular sweeping view of Doubtless Bay. There is a walkway from Mill Bay, just west of Mangonui, to the top of the pa.

Mangonui

Mangonui, the principal town of Doubtless Bay, is a tiny, picturesque historic village. It has all the basic services and a few interesting spots to visit. The Mangonui wharf has a small saltwater aquarium and there's good fishing off the wharf. The name Mangonui means 'Big Shark' – this may mean we're not the only ones who know about the abundance of fish here!

The Mangonui Courthouse is a historic reserve and the nearby Wharf Store has a variety of arts & crafts. Dances are held on Saturday nights at the Mangonui War Memorial Hall, beginning at 8 pm.

Also at Mangonui is the attractive little Mill Bay, dotted with tiny boats; you can take Silver Egg Rd out to the Mill Bay's Mangonui Cruising Club and an assortment of historical markers. This was the spot where Mangonui's first European settler made his base, and the whaling boats replenished their water from this stream.

You can drive the backroads in between Taipa and Mangonui in search of art & crafts. Included in this 50-km drive, which is outlined in the pamphlet *Craft Trail Inland: Taipa to Mangonui*, is the Kohumaru Cooperative, where there is a picnic area and farm animals.

Places to Stay

Hostels The *Old Oak Inn* (☎ 406 0665), 19 Beach Rd, in Mangonui is an 1861 kauri house with hostel accommodation from $13.50 in dorms, $16 per person in twins/doubles and $20 for a single. It's a pleasant small lodge with a seafood restaurant and an arts & crafts shop. Many inexpensive activities are organised from the hostel including canoe and kayak trips around the inner harbour and mangrove swamps, fishing trips, and excursions to Sullivan's Nocturnal Park in nearby Fairburn. They hire mountain bikes and kayaks for $5 a day. It takes just a couple of hours to bike to the Karikari Peninsula and the area has many other good spots to visit. It has received several readers' recommendations.

Just behind Cafe Nina is the recently renovated *Mangonui Waterfront Backpackers* (☎ 406 0347). Share rooms are $12.50 per bed, doubles $15 and twins $13.50 per person.

Hotels & Motels In Mangonui the historic *Mangonui Hotel* (☎ 406 0003) is comfortable and refurbished, with regular rooms at $35 for a single and $37 per person for a double or twin (breakfast included).

There are many motels in the area including the Mangonui Motel (☎ 406 0346) in Mangonui, the *Blue Pacific Motel* (☎ 406 0010) and the *Taipa Sands Motel* (☎ 406 0446) in Taipa and the *Driftwood Lodge* (☎ 406 0418) in Cable Bay. The *Cooper's Beach Motel* (☎ 406 0271) is popular and has typical rates at about $55 a double.

Bookings for all accommodation in the area can be made through the visitor information centre (☎ 408 0879) in Kaitaia.

Camping & Cabins As mentioned earlier there's a DOC campsite at Matai Bay on the Karikari Peninsula. Across the peninsula the *Karikari Bay Motor Camp* has on-site caravans, cabins, tent and boat hire, and there's also the *Tokerau Beach Motor Camp* (☎ 408 7510).

At Cooper's Beach, the *Cooper's Beach Motor Camp* (☎ 406 0597) is one of the largest camping spots in the area, with one km of private beach. Campsites are $9 per person, $10 with power; on-site caravans are $28 for two people, and two bedroom self-contained units sleeping four are $32. Two travellers we met described this place as the most unfriendly they had ever been in – you may have better luck.

Similar holiday camping grounds are dotted around the bay. In Taipa are the *Blue Pacific Caravan Park* (☎ 402 7394) and the *De Surville Holiday Park* (☎ 406 0656). On Hihi Beach, 11.5 km from Mangonui, is the *Hihi Motor Camp* (☎ 406 0307).

Places to Eat

In Mangonui the *Cafe Nina* is a cosy little cafe with good food at reasonable prices, the kind of place you can sit around and listen to good music, drink cappuccino and have a game of chess or backgammon. Unfortunately, the pizzas here are pricey as a small is $12.50, a medium $19 and a large $33 – makes you wonder how a bit of dough and a scattering of cheese, seafood perhaps and vegetables can cost so much.

Similar in style is the *Purple Parrot* in the Old Post Office. Nachos with the works are $7.50 and the ubiquitous 'death by chocolate' $5; all breakfasts are $6.50.

Also in Mangonui, *Harbour View Takeaways* has tables indoors or out on the deck overlooking the harbour. The *Mangonui Fish Shop* hangs out over the water near the wharf and in addition to fresh shellfish and smoked fish it serves award-winning fish & chips and seafood salads.

For a step up the *Mangonui Hotel* has a restaurant with an outdoor BBQ area to one side, and the *Old Oak Inn* has an à la carte seafood restaurant. At Cooper's Beach the

Cooper's Beach Motel has the *Pamir Restaurant* with steak and seafood.

Entertainment
This is not exactly Auckland for entertainment but there is a pub at the *Mangonui Hotel* and a Saturday night dance at the *Mangonui War Memorial Hall*.

Getting There & Away
Bus InterCity buses pass through Mangonui twice a day on the Bay of Islands-Kaitaia route. The travel time is 30 minutes to Kaitaia, passing through Mangonui mid-afternoon; two hours to Paihia, leaving Mangonui at around 10.30 am.

WHANGAROA
The main road to the Bay of Islands passes close to Whangaroa, where in 1809 the ship *Boyd* was set alight, eventually sinking near Red Island. The area was once well known for its kauri forests. The timber was milled at Whangaroa and across the harbour at Totara North, often ending up as sailing vessels.

Whangaroa is six km off the main road and is a popular game fishing centre. The outer harbour is surrounded by high, rugged cliffs and curious hills. The domed summit of St Paul's, above the town to the south, offers fine views.

When we passed through it seemed the entire town was up for sale, with a number of key businesses changing hands.

Information
The Boyd Gallery (☎ 405 0230) is a gallery, dairy and general store which also houses the town's informal tourist information office. They make bookings for harbour cruises, fishing trips and other activities and can also book accommodation around Whangaroa. It's open every day, from 8 am to 5 pm in winter, from 7.30 am to 7 pm in summer.

Cruises & Fishing
Sea Fever Cruises operate two-hour cruises on the harbour; the cost is $25 for adults and $12.50 for children. Several other boats are available for line and deep sea fishing, water-skiing and diving. Diving expeditions to the sunken *Rainbow Warrior* at the Cavalli Islands just off the coast are especially popular – Diving Network Matauri Bay (☎ 367 5066) has been recommended. You can book boats through the Marlin Hotel or the Boyd Gallery. Much of the harbour is completely unspoilt since there is no road access to it.

In the holiday season a lunch cruise goes out to the famous Kingfish Lodge, a licensed fishing lodge accessible only by boat, with a lovely private beach, a seafood restaurant and a two-hour walking track to Tauranga Bay (four hours return). You can also go there on the MV *Friendship*, taking the morning harbour cruise out and being picked up again on the return of the afternoon harbour cruise.

The *Snow Cloud*
A lot of travellers have raved about trips aboard the yacht *Snow Cloud* which operates out of Whangaroa Harbour. Its owners are enthusiastic sailors and offer trips out to the Cavalli Islands where there are excellent beaches, diving spots, snorkelling and walks. Four Seasons Yacht Charters (☎ 405 0523) charge a mere $40 for a full-day trip which includes lunch, and morning and afternoon teas. More often than not, in summer you'll get back late and they will help cook fish (which you caught) for dinner.

Sea Kayaking
The area around Whangaroa Harbour is ideal for exploration by sea kayak. *Coastal-Combers* (☎ 405 0381) are located out on the coast, about 20 minutes from Whangaroa and an hour north of Paihia; they offer a free pick-up service from Kaeo if you stop a minimum of two nights. This coast is magical, with bays, beaches, sea caves, tunnels and islands to explore. The kayak tours 'comb' the coast, visiting different areas each day for a reasonable $50 per day. If you are lucky you may even have the opportunity of paddling in the expanse of beautiful Whangaroa Harbour.

Walks

The St Paul's Walk begins from Whangaroa Harbour and takes about half an hour, climbing to the St Paul's Scenic Reserve for a splendid view of the bay.

On the northern side of the harbour the Wairakau track goes from Totara North to Pekapeka Bay (1½-hour walk). The track leads to DOC's Lane Cove Cottage; book this through DOC Kerikeri (☎ 407 8474). The marked track begins from the signpost near the church hall on Campbell Rd in Totara North and passes through farmland, hills, flats, shoreline, the Wairakau Stream, and Bride's Veil Falls before arriving at Lane Cottage, built in 1922.

There's a day walk on Mahinepua Bay, heading out onto Hororoa Point. From the Kingfish Lodge a two-hour track comes out at Tauranga Bay. There are also many enjoyable walks in the Puketi and Omahuta Kauri forests, about 20 km south-west of Whangaroa.

Other Things to Do

For a scenic drive passing by many of the area's most beautiful spots, depart from Whangaroa, stopping first at Tauranga Bay, then Mahinepua Bay, Te Ngahere, and perhaps a short detour to Matauri Bay, emerging on SH 10 just south of Kaeo. All these bays have fine beaches (see Matauri Bay & the *Rainbow Warrior*) later in this chapter.

Guided horse-trekking expeditions go through native and pine forest and up to scenic lookout points.

Lane's Mill at Totara North is an old mill which is open in the summer to show visitors how the mill used to work.

Places to Stay

Camping & Cabins The *Whangaroa Motor Camp* (☎ 405 0306) costs $7.50 per person for tent sites, $9 for caravan sites; there are a number of cabins. The camp is about 2.5 km before the wharf.

Other nearby motor camps are at Matauri Bay, Taupo Bay and Tauranga Bay. The *Tauranga Bay Holiday Park* (☎ 405 0436),

at Tauranga Bay Beach, 17 km from Kaeo has sites for $8 ($8.50 with power) and cabins for $28.50 for two people ($8.50 each extra adult). Like a lot of places it applies minimum unit rates in summer.

Hostels The *Sunseeker Lodge* (☎ 405 0496), is up on a hill about 500 metres beyond the wharf, with a great view of the harbour, and an outdoor BBQ and lawn area to enjoy it from. The cost is $13 in dorms, and doubles and twins are $17 per person. They provide a free pick up and drop off from Kaeo, and can provide information on tours, etc.

At Totara North the *Historic Gumstore Hostel* (☎ 405 1703) dates from 1890 and has hostel accommodation from $9, with dorms and two private rooms; doubles/twins are $12.50 to $15 per person. You can rent dinghies here and they also do fishing trips. You don't have to go far either as the mangrove-fringed creek is right beside (almost underneath) the old store.

About 24 km south of Mangonui on SH 10 there is the *Kahoe Farm Hostel* (☎ 405 1804). Although the setting of the farm is nothing special there is plenty to do in close proximity. The Lane Cove walk is not far away, Mt Patukohatu (329 metres) is just behind the farm and sacred Tara Tara rock can be seen from here. They organise horse treks, sailing (on the *Snow Cloud*) and kayaking. A bed in a share room is $13 and doubles/twins are $15 per person. Camping, perhaps in a spot of your choosing closer to the bush, is $7.50 per person. Meals of the day, such as excellent pizzas, are between $6 and $12.

The *Lane Cove Cottage* on the western arm of the harbour is operated by DOC. The cost is $8 a night and it can only be reached by the two-hour Wairakau Track from Totara North, or by boat. There are showers and flush toilets, but you have to bring your own cooker. Make arrangements first at the DOC office in Kerikeri.

Hotels & Motels Right by the wharf the *Marlin Hotel* (☎ 405 0347) has share-facility rooms at $30/40 for singles/doubles, one twin room with private facilities at $45 and a one-room self-contained flat for $50. The hotel has one of the town's two restaurants and the pub, and it also has diesel for boats, petrol for cars, and dive tank filling. The *Motel Whangaroa* (☎ 405 0022) and the *Truant Lodge Motel* (☎ 405 0133) have motel rooms at about $56 and $73 respectively. At the *Kingfish Lodge* (☎ 405 0164), reached by boat, double rooms are $75, with lower off-season rates.

Places to Eat

The *Marlin Hotel* has dinner main courses costing about $14, and it serves breakfast and lunch too. The Truant Lodge Motel also has a *restaurant* but ring ahead to see when it is open. Catch the water taxi to the *Kingfish Lodge* where you can dine in the waterside bistro – this place is not only meritorious for its setting but also for its food as it has received two Taste NZ awards.

AROUND WHANGAROA
Puketi & Omahuta Kauri Forests

The Puketi Forest and the Omahuta Forest comprise one large forest area about 20 km south-west of Whangaroa, with kauri sanctuaries and other native trees, camping and picnic areas, streams and pools, and viewpoints.

The two forests are reached by several entrances and contain a network of walking tracks varying in length from 10 minutes to two days. A pamphlet detailing the tracks and features of the forests is available from any DOC office. Camping is permitted in Puketi Forest and there is a trampers' hut. Costs in the hut are $5 per adult ($2 per child). Book at the DOC office in Kaikohe (☎ 401 0109).

Matauri Bay & the *Rainbow Warrior*

The trip out to Matauri Bay is one of the surprises of Northland. The view from the ridge above the bay is superb with the beach, Cavalli Islands and headland way down below. The Cavalli Islands are the last resting place of the Greenpeace flagship *Rainbow Warrior* and there is a monument to that vessel at the top of the headland.

To get to Matauri Bay either take the coastal route east of Whangaroa or turn off

---

The *Rainbow Warrior* Trail

New Zealand is seldom mentioned on the world stage. With a population of three million and relative isolation it remains, in many eyes, a small, almost inconsequential Pacific nation. In 1985 an explosion in Auckland Harbour changed that status for a month or so. French saboteurs, with the sanction of their government, attached explosives to the side of the Greenpeace flagship *Rainbow Warrior* and effectively sank her. In the explosions one green campaigner, Fernando Pereira, was killed. The two saboteurs were captured, tried and found guilty. In a farcical turn of events they were imprisoned on a French Pacific island as if they had just won a trip to Club Med. Within two years and well before the end of their sentence, they returned to France to receive a hero's welcome.

The whole event was planned through the French government and their secret service and organised by several agents, none of whom, apart from the two saboteurs, have been brought to justice.

Northland was the stage for all this. It is believed that explosives for the sabotage were delivered by yacht (which had picked them up from a submarine) from Parengarenga Harbour in the Far North. They were driven to Auckland in a Kombi van of which just about everyone in the north knew the existence, but not the purpose of. Bang, an innocent man dead, and international outrage – Auckland Harbour is in the news.

The skeletal remains of the *Rainbow Warrior* were taken to the waters of the beautiful Cavalli Islands, where treasures should be buried. The masts of this oceanic crusader were sent to the Northern Wairoa Museum in Dargaville. The memory of the photographer who died, Fernando Pereira, endures in a peaceful bird sanctuary in Thames. The haunting memorial to the once-proud boat sits in peace atop a Maori pa site at Matauri Bay. ■

south of Kaeo towards Otoroa – it is hard to get lost. You won't regret the drive along the coast as there are many fine bays including Piapia, Wainui and Mahinepua. Take a detour to Tauranga Bay – it's well worth it.

There are a couple of accommodation options in Matauri Bay. The *Matauri Bay Holiday Park* (☎ 405 0525) has sites for $8.50 ($11 with power), and on-site caravans for $20/30 to $40 for one/two persons. The *Oceans Beachfront Hoilday Village* (☎ 405 0417) has four comfortable units and a lodge which sleeps 14. They also have a licensed *restaurant*. To get there turn left at the headland (with the monument) and go as far as the end of the road.

Bay of Islands

The Bay of Islands was the site of New Zealand's first permanent European settlement and today it has become one of the country's major tourist attractions.

DOC have produced an excellent booklet *The Story of the Bay of Islands Maritime and Historic Park*. If you are exploring in depth as you travel then buy a copy. Its frontispiece is haunting: 'Whatungarongaro te tangata toitu te whenua' (People are perishable but the land endures).

Orientation
The townships around the Bay of Islands are all on the mainland, there are no island resorts. To the north is Kerikeri – 'so nice they named it twice', claim the tourist brochures. Paihia, the main centre on the bay, is virtually continuous with Waitangi. A little south of Paihia is Opua from where a car ferry shuttles across the Waikare Inlet to take you to Russell. You can also reach Russell from Paihia by road but it's a long and roundabout route.

Information
There are visitor information centres at Paihia, Russell and Kerikeri, and DOC

offices at Russell and Kerikeri – see those sections for details.

Cruises
The Bay of Islands is a very popular holiday area, so there's quite a bit to see and do. Nearly 150 islands dot the waters of the bay – it's aptly named.

The best way to introduce yourself to the area is to spend the money and take a cruise. Fullers (☎ 402 7421) and Kings Tours and Cruises (☎ 402 8288) operate very popular regular cruises and they're supplemented by a host of other cruises from smaller operators.

Best known of the cruises is Fullers 'cream trip' which has had quite a history. Back in 1920 Captain Lane started a boat service around the bay, picking up dairy products from the many farms. As more roads were built and the small dairy farms closed, the cruise became less and less of a working trip and more of a tourist one. The trip takes about five hours and passes a number of historical sites including Captain Cook's landing spot of 1789 and Otehei Bay where westerns' writer Zane Grey went big game fishing. Other cruises follow a roughly similar pattern.

Weather permitting, the cruises may go through the Hole in the Rock off Cape Brett and stop at a deserted island bay for lunch. If you're not planning to bring your own lunch make sure you order it in advance. The cruises go past Te Hue where the French navigator Marion du Fresne was killed by Maoris in 1769.

Fullers operate the 'cream trip' daily, and it lasts from 10 am to 3.30 pm (between October and May) for $49 per person (children $25). In the off-season the trip goes four times a week – Monday, Wednesday, Thursday and Saturday.

At the same price Fullers also have a Cape Brett trip from 9 am to 1 pm and again from 1.30 to 5.30 pm; this timing allows for an hour stopover at Otehei Bay on Urupukapuka Island. A 'subsea adventure' in a tourist submarine can be combined with the other cruises for $10 (children $5).

NORTHLAND

NORTHLAND

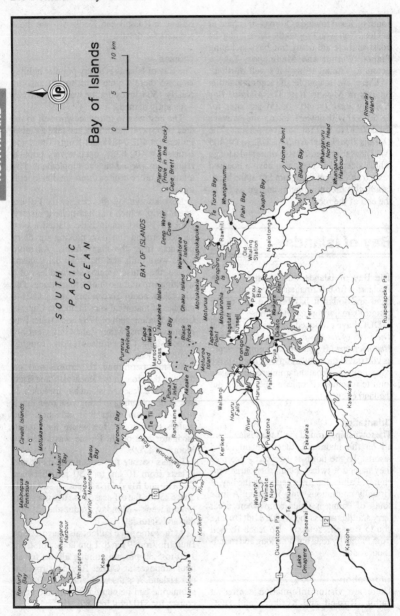

Bay of Islands

Kings have a similar schedule and one of the attractions of their cruise is a remotely operated underwater video camera, 'The Rover', which allows you to view below the water without leaving your seat.

If you're staying at a hostel book through them and you'll get a discount (about 15%). All the Fullers cruises depart first from Paihia and then from Russell about 15 minutes later, so you can start off from either side, and if you like you can get off on the opposite side from where you began. Kings depart from Waitangi, then Paihia followed by Russell.

There are all sorts of smaller cruises, line and big game fishing trips, sailboat charter operators and so on in the Bay of Islands. The hostels here generally fix up cheaper trips.

R Tucker Thompson

This tall sailing ship sails between November and April from Russell. It is run by Fullers (☎ 402 7421, 403 7866) and costs $65 (children $35), with morning tea and lunch included. You can help set the sails or take the helm and enjoy the sailing of a bygone age. The return ferry ticket from Paihia to Russell is included in the price.

Sailing

There is plenty of opportunity to go sailing in the Bay of Islands. Fullers *R Tucker Thompson* has been mentioned, but there are many other operators:

Carino & Carino New Zealand: a 40-foot (12-metre) keel yacht and 42-foot catamaran operating out of Russell (full day $48 and meal $10; ☎ 403 7230)

Great Escape Charters: bareboat yacht charters, 16-foot (five-metre) two berth and 20-foot (six-metre) three berth yachts operating out of Kerikeri (two berth $70 and three berth $90 per 24 hours; ☎ 407 8920)

Place in the Sun: operates out of Russell and occasionally detours to Fiji (cruises from $30 for a half day, $150 for 24 hours; ☎ 403 7008)

Rainbow Yacht Charters: bareboat, instructional trips and skippered yachts operating out of Paihia (price on application; ☎ 402 7821)

Straycat Day Sails: a day trip in a catamaran departing from Russell, Kerikeri and Paihia ($60 includes lunch; ☎ 407 7342)

Vigilant: this is a luxury cruise during which you can help sail a beautiful yacht – operating from Russell (price on application; ☎ 403 7596)

Sea Kayaking Trips

Sea kayaking trips in the bay have become very popular, with a number of operators offering trips that are highly recommended by travellers. Coastal Kayakers (☎ 402 8105 or 403 7957 after hours) does a trip around the mangrove forests up to Haruru Falls, passing right underneath the falls, and out to Motumaire Island all in one day. The cost of $60 for the full-day trips may be less if you book through a hostel.

Bay of Islands Sea Kayakers (☎ 402 8105) organise extended kayaking/camping trips around the islands, with overnight stops on Urupukapuka Island; a three-day trip costs

The Hole in the Rock

about $170 and their short trip to Haruru Falls costs $30.

They also have independent rentals – a double kayak or Canadian is $45 for a half day and $80 for a full day.

Over in Russell there are more operators. Kaptain Kayak (☎ 403 7584), near the corner of Matauwhi Rd and Florence Ave, hire out kayaks and canoes in addition to mountain bikes and windsurfers. Ring them for details of extended guided tours. The Bay of Islands Kayak Co (☎ 403 7672) is run by the very friendly hosts at the Lanes Rd Farm (see Places to Stay in Russell). Their guided sea kayak trips are from $55 per day and they also arrange independent rentals. If you want to sea kayak as well as snorkel, sunbathe, swim, walk and skinny dip (optional) then try The Outer Edge Adventure Company (☎ 402 8147); phone them for further details.

Cape Reinga Trips & Other Tours

It's easier to make trips up 90 Mile Beach and to Cape Reinga from Kaitaia or Doubtless Bay than from the Bay of Islands. However, if you do go from the Bay of Islands, King's Tours & Cruises (☎ 402 8288) has trips departing from Paihia and Kerikeri daily at 7.30 am, returning at 8.30 pm, and stopping at about 15 different locations including the Puketi Kauri Forest. The cost is $52 (children $26) but if you have taken their Cape Brett tour you can get a twin tour package for $80 (children $40). Fullers (☎ 402 7421) charges $75 (children $42) for a similar trip with lunch thrown in. Their deluxe version at $85 includes entry to the Wagener Museum, and Sullivan's Glow Worm Grotto & Kiwi House.

Fullers have a shorter trip which includes Kerikeri and the Puketi Forest. It's about four hours in duration and costs $35 (children $17). Kings have concocted an interesting half-day tour which includes less-visited attractions – the Opua-Kawakawa Vintage railway, the Kawiti Glow Worm Caves and the Ruapekapeka Pa site. This trip costs $37 for adults and $20 for children.

Flying over the Bay of Islands is magnificent and surprisingly inexpensive: you can take a short aerial tour (about 15 minutes) for $29; if you take the 30-minute Cape Brett option it is $56. Book flights through the hostels, the visitor information centre, Fullers or phone 402 8170.

Getting There & Away

Air Mt Cook Airline (☎ 402 7421) has daily flights to Kerikeri from Auckland and Rotorua, but the closest that Air New Zealand can get you is Whangarei. Great Barrier Airlines (☎ 275 9120) costs less than Mt Cook and it comes up from Auckland to Paihia daily during the summer, by charter only the rest of the year.

The Holiday Shoppe in the Maritime Building, Paihia, does all air and bus bookings.

Bus All the buses serving Paihia arrive and depart from the Maritime Building by the wharf, and all bookings and tickets can be arranged from the visitor information centre there.

InterCity has buses several times daily from Auckland to the Bay of Islands, via Whangarei and Opua. The trip takes about four hours to Paihia (5½ hours on the slower bus with more stops) and about 30 minutes later it stops in Kerikeri before continuing north to Kaitaia, two hours further on.

Another route is a four-hour trip going from Paihia to Dargaville via the Waipoua Kauri Forest – it is called the West Coaster (see the introductory Getting Around section for Northland).

Northliner has an Auckland-Whangarei-Bay of Islands video bus service. It departs from the Downtown Airline Terminal in Auckland and stops at the Paihia Maritime Building, Haruru Falls, Puketone Junction and Kerikeri. There's a connecting service to Russell and also a direct Whangarei-Russell service. Northliner's service is more direct than InterCity (not so many stops) but it goes only once a day, except for Saturday when it doesn't go at all.

Getting Around

A passenger ferry connects Paihia with

Russell. It departs from Paihia from 7.20 am to 6.45 pm (to 10 pm in summer); from Russell from 7 am to 6.10 pm. The fare is $5 return ($6 with Fuller's) or $3 one way.

Three ferries (*Waimarie*, *Bay Belle* and the *Blue Ferry*) operate on average every 20 minutes from Russell to Paihia in summer. A crossing is made on the half hour in winter by two of them. Be careful that you don't have to wait as the Fullers ticket is not interchangeable – perhaps singles in either direction is the best option if time is paramount.

To get to Russell with your car you cross from Opua to Okiato Point using the car ferry (see Getting There & Away for Russell for more details).

There's also a water taxi (☎ 403 7123, 403 7378) for getting around the bay.

BAY OF ISLANDS MARITIME & HISTORIC PARK

The Bay of Islands Maritime & Historic Park is comprised of about 40 different sites extending all the way from Mimiwhangata Bay in the south to Whangaroa Harbour in the north. Marked walks of varying levels of difficulty (many very easy) take anywhere from 10 minutes to 10 hours and include tramps around islands, Maori pas and other historical sites, scenic, historic and recreational reserves and the Mimiwhangata Marine Park.

The Bay of Islands Maritime & Historic Park visitor information centre is at Russell (☎ 403 7685). DOC Kerikeri (☎ 407 8474) can also supply you with information. If you're coming directly up from Auckland you might check with the DOC office there, on Karangahape Rd. There are a number of good books which will guide you in the right direction. *The Story of the Bay of Islands Maritime & Historic Park*, produced by DOC, is indispensable. You can also get the two useful pamphlets *Huts & Camping* and *Walking* from the DOC visitor information centre.

Places to Stay

The DOC office in Russell has details of accommodation in the park. Get a copy of *Huts & Camping: Bay of Islands Maritime & Historic Park*. The *Cape Brett Hut* is a very popular destination. You can arrange to walk there and stay in the hut by ringing 403 7923; the cost per night is $4 for adults and $1.50 for children. A 'koha' or donation should be made to the Maori landowners. Find out about this when you inquire about hut bookings.

Camping is permitted at most of the bays on *Urupukapuka Island* but you must make your own transport arrangements and be completely self-sufficient. You need food, stove and fuel and a shovel for digging a toilet.

Also popular are the *Mimiwhangata Cottage & Lodge* in the coastal Mimiwhangata park. This park is about equidistant from Russell or Whangarei on the east coast. Both the cottage and the lodge can accommodate eight persons easily and bookings are made in seven day blocks; understandably both are very popular. From June to October the cottage is $250 per week and the lodge is $450; at other times the cottage is $350 and the lodge $550. Linen is provided in the lodge. Both places can be booked in Russell (☎ 403 7685).

PAIHIA & WAITANGI

The main town in the area, Paihia, was settled by Europeans as a mission station in 1823 when the first raupo (bullrush) hut was built for the Reverend Henry Williams. Paihia still has a pretty setting but the missionary zeal has been replaced with an equally fervent tourist industry. Nevertheless it's basically an accommodation, eating and tours centre and a good starting point to see the rest of the Bay of Islands.

Adjoining Paihia to the north is Waitangi, the site of the historic signing of the 6 February 1840 treaty between the Maoris and the representatives of Queen Victoria's government. Since this is such an important part of NZ history, Waitangi is a particularly interesting place to be on New Zealand Day, 6 February.

Information

Most of the information places are conveniently grouped together in the Maritime Building right by the wharf in Paihia. Here you'll find the Bay of Islands Visitor Information Centre (☎ 402 7426), Marsden Rd, which can give information, advice, and make bookings for everything in the region. Also in the Maritime Building are the Fullers and King's offices for cruises and tours, a fishing centre for fishing boat bookings, the bus station, and the terminal for the ferry to Russell. The offices are open every day from 8 am to 5 pm.

Waitangi National Reserve

The Treaty House in Waitangi has special significance as the starting point for the European history of New Zealand. Built in 1832 as the home of British Resident James Busby, eight years later it was the setting for the signing of the historic Treaty of Waitangi. The house, with its beautiful sweep of lawn running down to the bay, is preserved as a memorial and museum.

A few metres across the lawn, the magnificently detailed Maori Whare Runanga (Meeting House) was completed in 1940 to mark the centenary of the treaty. The carvings represent the major Maori tribes.

Down by the cove is the largest war canoe in the world, the Maori war canoe *Ngatokimatawhaorua*, named after the canoe in which the Maori ancestor Kupe discovered New Zealand. It too was built for the centenary, and a photographic exhibit details how the canoe was made from two gigantic kauri trees. The canoe is launched every year on 6 February (New Zealand Day) for the annual treaty-signing commemoration ceremonies.

Beyond the Treaty House a road climbs Mt Bledisloe, from where there are commanding views of the area. Beginning from the visitors' centre, a walking track takes off through the reserve, passing through the mangrove forest around Hutia Creek and on to Haruru Falls. The walkway has a boardwalk among the mangroves so you can explore them without getting your feet wet.

The walk to the falls takes about 1½ hours one way.

Admission to Waitangi Reserve is $5 (children free) and it's open from 9 am to 5 pm daily. At the visitors' centre where you enter the reserve an audiovisual presentation relating the story of the developments surrounding the signing of the treaty begins every half-hour.

Dolphin Swimming

This is a popular and fast growing activity in a country blessed with many types of marine mammals (see Kaikoura in the South Island). To be feasible such an activity must have a contact success rate – in the Bay of Islands it was said to be 93% for trips in '92 to '93. The dolphins most often observed are the commons and the bottlenose, although it is likely that you will see other marine mammals.

Dolphin Discoveries (☎ 403 7350) got this activity underway in this region in 1991 and now conduct up to three trips daily in the spotting season (October to February); all equipment is provided.

Fullers run Dolphin Adventures. The cost for these three-hour trips is $65 for adults and $35 for children.

Kelly Tarlton's Shipwreck Museum

Beached beside the bridge over the Waitangi River is the barque *Tui*, an old sailing ship, imaginatively fitted out as a museum of shipwrecks. It's open from 9 am to 5.30 pm daily (the cafe hours are 10 am to 10 pm), with extended hours during holiday periods; admission is $5 (children $2.50). Recorded sea chants, creaking timbers and swaying lights add to the eerie mood as you look at the collection of over 1000 bits and pieces diver Kelly Tarlton dragged up from wrecks around the coast.

Haruru Falls

A few km upstream from the *Tui* are the very attractive Haruru Falls, also accessible via the walkway through the Waitangi National Reserve. At the foot of the falls there's good swimming, several motor camps, a licensed

NORTHLAND

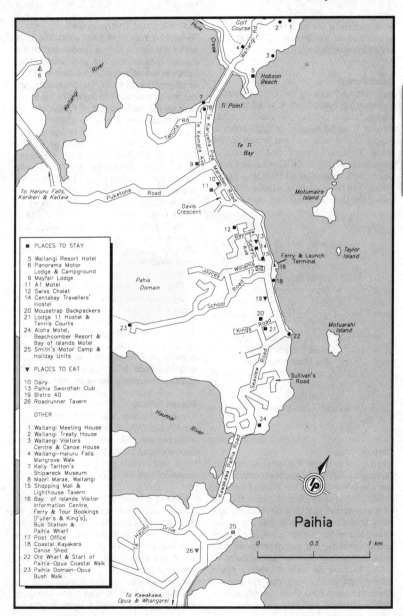

PLACES TO STAY

5 Waitangi Resort Hotel
6 Panorama Motor
   Lodge & Campground
9 Mayfair Lodge
11 A1 Motel
12 Swiss Chalet
14 Centabay Travellers'
   Hostel
20 Mousetrap Backpackers
21 Lodge 11 Hostel &
   Tennis Courts
24 Aloha Motel,
   Beachcomber Resort &
   Bay of Islands Motel
25 Smith's Motor Camp &
   Holiday Units

PLACES TO EAT

10 Dairy
13 Paihia Swordfish Club
19 Bistro 40
26 Roadrunner Tavern

OTHER

1 Waitangi Meeting House
2 Waitangi Treaty House
3 Waitangi Visitors
   Centre & Canoe House
4 Waitangi-Haruru Falls
   Mangrove Walk
7 Kelly Tarlton's
   Shipwreck Museum
8 Maori Marae, Waitangi
15 Shopping Mall &
   Lighthouse Tavern
16 Bay of Islands Visitor
   Information Centre,
   Ferry & Tour Bookings
   (Fuller's & King's),
   Bus Station &
   Paihia Wharf
17 Post Office
18 Coastal Kayakers
   Canoe Shed
22 Old Wharf & Start of
   Paihia-Opua Coastal Walk
23 Paihia Domain-Opua
   Bush Walk

Paihia

restaurant and a tavern. If you wish to kayak to the base of the falls see Sea Kayaking earlier in this chapter.

Opua Forest

Just behind Paihia is the Opua Forest, a regenerating forest with a small stand of kauris, and a number of walking tracks ranging from 10 minutes to three hours in length. If you walk up from School Rd for about 20 minutes, you'll find a couple of good lookout points. DOC publishes pamphlets with details on all the Opua Forest walks. You can also drive into the forest by taking the Oromahoe Rd west from Opua.

Boats

There are small boats for hire at both ends of the Paihia beach. You can hire powerboats for $30 an hour or $100 for four hours – plus fuel. Contact Charter Pier (☎ 402 7127). All these prices will vary tremendously with the seasons – summer is definitely the high season around here for both attractions and prices.

At the more ecologically appropriate end of the boating scale there are a number of sailboat and yacht charter operators on the bay (see Sailing earlier in this Bay of Islands section), while Smith's Camp have small dinghies for hire. At the Waitangi end of the beach three-metre catamarans cost $50 for a half day.

Diving

Moving from above the water to under it, there is a handful of companies available to get you below the surface. Paihia Dive Hire (☎ 402 7551) on Williams Rd hires full sets of scuba gear to qualified divers. They also offer scuba and snorkelling courses, tank filling and scuba gear servicing, a dive shop, and diving trips, including expeditions to the sunken *Rainbow Warrior*. Bay Guides (☎ 402 7906), in addition to abseiling and hiking trips, guide diving trips. All levels of divers are catered for. Their trips depart from Paihia wharf daily all year round.

Walks & Other Things to Do

There is a variety of good short and long walks around the Bay of Islands and on the islands themselves. The park information centre in Russell and DOC Kerikeri have lots of information on walks. You could start with the two-minute stroll to the top of the headland on the southern end of Paihia, or take the mangrove walk near the *Tui* barque, or the coastal walk from Paihia to Opua.

For a walk with a difference go to Bay Guides (☎ 402 7906) – you can combine the walks with abseiling from various cliffs. The cliffs range in height from 10 metres to the spectacular 30-metre Rainbow Falls; you get wet on the last abseil but no previous experience is necessary.

The Cape Reinga Camping & Tramping Company (☎ 402 7426) will guide you further afield. An overnight trip to the Cape Reinga area costs $99, all meals and accommodation included.

There are various possibilities for horse-riding in the area; hostels or the information centre can fix you up. Lane's Rd Farm Horse Treks (☎ 403 7672) have a couple of great treks near Russell. In addition to diving equipment, you can rent fishing tackle and bicycles from Paihia Dive Hire. The hostels and Mountain Bike Adventures (☎ 402 6777) also hire bicycles or arrange trips.

Places to Stay

The Bay of Islands Visitor Information Centre (Paihia Wharf) will tell you what is available and make bookings. They're particularly good for B&B bookings which can be a worthwhile deal in Paihia, where accommodation is often quite expensive.

Camping & Cabins There are many camp-sites around Paihia and Waitangi, most of them a few km back from the coast near the Haruru Falls. The *Panorama Motor Lodge & Caravan Park* (☎ 402 7525), beside the river and facing the falls, has tent and powered sites at $9 per person in peak summer season, and motel units at $89 at peak season but $50 at other times. The camp is well equipped with a large swimming pool, bar and restaurant, and their own charter boat which does full-day cruises.

The *Twin Pines Tourist Park* (☎ 402 7322) on Puketona Rd at the falls has tent and powered sites at $8.50 per person, cabins and on-site caravans at $17.50 per person, and more expensive tourist flats. Next door the *Falls Caravan Park* (☎ 402 7816) has tent and powered sites at about the same rates. At Puketona Junction there's another camping ground, *Puketona Park*.

The *Bay of Islands Holiday Park* (☎ 402 7646) is three km from the falls, 6.5 km from Paihia on Puketona Rd, and has tent and powered sites at $8.50 per person, cabins at $30 for two persons.

The *Smiths Holiday Camp* (☎ 402 7678) is at a lovely spot right on the waterside, 2.5 km south of Paihia towards Opua. Tent and powered sites are $9 per person, cabins are $36 for two, motel units are $68 a double and there are also tourist cabins and tourist flats. It has its own beach, dinghies for hire, a camp store and a courtesy car.

Hostels There is no YHA hostel in Paihia (it's out at Kerikeri) but there are three good private hostels. All of them make bookings for local activities at significantly discounted prices, and they all have bicycles for hire.

The most unusual of the hostels is *The Mousetrap* (☎ 402 8182), at 11 Kings Rd. It is run by one of the characters of backpackers accommodation in New Zealand. Martin is Bavarian and, until some unfeeling council officials deemed otherwise, was accompanied by a pet pig wherever he went. The building is also unusual – it was built by a sea captain who designed it to look like a ship. It has small galley kitchens, a verandah shaped like a bridge, a lookout on the roof and a crow's nest BBQ area. The ship is not spartan – it has all the facilities including two living areas, one with TV and the other without, and there is a Cardphone downstairs for ship-to-shore communication. The costs are $13 for a dorm bed; doubles and twins $15 per person.

The *Lodge Eleven* (☎ 402 7487) on the corner of Kings and MacMurray Rds is a comfortable, clean place, charging $13 a night in dorm rooms or $16 per person in share, twin and doubles. Each room has its own toilet and shower and there are communal kitchen, BBQ and lounge facilities. They have their own boat for fishing and sightseeing trips (share petrol, $45 for four people), a courtesy car and a friendly atmosphere. The staff speak several languages. It is next to the tennis courts and you can hire gear and play a game for $5.

The *Centabay Travellers' Hostel* (☎ 402 7466) at 27 Selwyn Rd, just behind the shops and a short stroll from the Maritime Centre is a spacious hostel with a large recreation area. It has undergone extensive renovations recently. The nightly cost is $13 in bunkrooms, and $16 per person in double and twin rooms.

Down at the Waitangi end of Paihia the *Mayfair Lodge* (☎ 402 7471) at 7 Puketona Rd has bunkroom beds for $12, twins/doubles for $13/14 per person (rates increase in summer). It's well equipped with the usual kitchen and lounge facilities, billiards and table tennis, BBQ and even a spa pool.

Guesthouses Several B&B guesthouses are found around Paihia and the Bay of Islands; the information centre makes referrals and bookings. *Abba Villa* (☎ 402 8066) at 21 School Rd is one of the Paihia B&B places; rates are $42/68 for singles/doubles. *The Cedar Suite* (☎ 402 8516), 5 Sullivans Rd, is a slice of luxury at $74 for your own fully self-contained studio apartment.

Hotels If you really want to spend, there's plenty of opportunity. The *Waitangi Resort Hotel* (☎ 402 7411) is in a fine setting, north across the bridge with an excellent restaurant, bar, heated pool and room prices for around $118 to $130. Suites are much more.

Motels With about 40 motels to choose from you'd think the competition would keep prices down but they're as expensive as anywhere. Motels stand shoulder to shoulder along the waterfront and minimum double rates are around $75 to $95 during the peak summer season, dropping to $50 or $65 during the off season. Rates tend to vary with the room, the season, current demand and probably a few other secret factors as well.

With so many to choose from, the best advice is probably to ask the visitor information centre, cruise the motel strip looking for a vacancy sign or simply take pot luck. On the plus side most of the Paihia motels offer pretty good standards and most have good kitchen facilities. A few likely places to try, listed with their high season rates (winter rates will be lower) are:

A1 Motel (or Aywon) (☎ 402 7684), Davis Crescent; $70 for doubles

Ala-Moana Motel (☎ 402 7745), Marsden Rd on the waterfront; $65 to 110 for doubles or twins

Aloha Motel (☎ 402 7540), Seaview Rd; swimming pool, spa, games room and video, $56 singles, $79 to $124 doubles, with units up to three bedrooms and sleeping up to nine people for $124 to $247

Ash Grove Motel (☎ 402 7934), Blackbridge Rd, Haruru Falls; swimming pool, spa pool and three hectares of land, $87 doubles

Blue Pacific Motel (☎ 402 7394), corner of Marsden and Puketona Rds; a double at peak times is $94

Dolphin Motel (☎ 402 8170), 69 Williams Rd; singles/twins are $66/77

Swiss Chalet Lodge Motel (☎ 402 7615), 3 Bayview Rd; $105 to $195 in peak season

Places to Eat

Takeaways & Cheap Eats There are a number of takeaway places scattered around, particularly in the shopping centre opposite the Maritime Centre and the post office.

The *Cafe Over the Bay,* upstairs diagonally across from the Maritime Building, has a good view of the bay and good food too, with lots of European dishes (mostly French and Italian). Lunches are about $6 to $10, dinners $17, or just have a pastry and cappuccino. Does Italian pavlova tempt you? Also upstairs here is the *Lighthouse Tavern Bars & Restaurant,* including *Alby's Bistro.*

At 41 Williams Rd, *Esmae's* is open for dinner and tends to be more expensive; mains are about $16 to $22 and entrees half that range.

Restaurants There are quite a number of restaurants where the prices are somewhat higher, with main courses averaging around the $20 mark. *Tides*, on Williams Rd, is one of the better places and has an early-bird $27 three-course special if the order is placed before 7 pm.

Bistro 40 on Marsden Rd has an attractive decor, it's in a converted old home with areas indoors and out on the brick patio overlooking the sea. One of our readers from Oklahoma described the food as superb and, after sampling the mussels, I would reiterate this comment. Unfortunately, it is one of those stingy places that charges $3.50 extra for the salad or vegetables and, get this, $1.50 for a bread roll!

The *La Scala* licensed restaurant on Selwyn Ave is about the priciest place in town, with a mixed seafood platter for two at about $75.

There are two fancy restaurants out at the Waitangi Resort Hotel. Both *The Waitangi Restaurant* and the *Rangatira Room,* are expensive (main courses around $16 to $30) but actually not so much more than some of the places in town. There is a cheaper bistro for the impecunious.

Entertainment

The *Lighthouse Tavern* upstairs on Marsden Rd has various sections including a restaurant, bars and a pub, and it features live bands. At Haruru Falls the *Twin Pines* has a tavern and entertainment on weekends. They brew their own Putt's No 1 lager and No 1 ale. The *Roadrunner* is a pub about a five-minute drive south of Paihia en route to Opua.

The *Waitangi Resort Hotel* has a couple of public bars in a separate building, and the expensive Wharetapere piano bar in the hotel itself. Fullers has evening cruises with entertainment and dancing on the *Tiger Lily III* from December to March.

Getting There & Away

For information on travel to/from Paihia, see the Getting There & Away entry under the Bay of Islands heading.

RUSSELL

A short ferry ride across the bay is Russell, originally a fortified Maori settlement which spread over the entire valley, then known as Kororareka.

Russell's early European history was turbulent. In 1830 it was the scene of the 'war of the girls', which occurred when two Maori girls from different tribes each thought they were the favourite of a whaling captain. This resulted in conflict between the tribes, which the Maori leader, Titore, who was recognised as the chief of chiefs in the area, attempted to resolve by separating the two tribes and making the border at the base of the Tapeka Peninsula. A European settlement quickly sprang up in place of the abandoned Maori village.

In 1845 the government sent in soldiers and marines to garrison the town when the Maori leader, Hone Heke, threatened to chop down the flagstaff – symbol of Pakeha authority – for the fourth time. On 11 March 1845 the Maoris staged a diversionary siege on Russell. It was a great tactical success, with Chief Kawiti attacking from the south and another Maori war party attacking from Long Beach. While the troops rushed off to protect the township, Hone Heke felled the hated symbol of European authority on Maiki Hill for the final time. The Pakehas were forced to evacuate to ships lying at anchor off the settlement. The captain of HMS *Hazard* was wounded severely in the battle and the first lieutenant ordered the ships' cannons to be fired on the town, during the course of which most of the buildings were razed.

Russell today is a relaxed, peaceful and pretty little place. It's a marked contrast to the neon hustle of Paihia across the bay.

Information

The Tourist Information Office (☎ 403 7596), run by Bradley's, is out at the end of the pier. There's a Fullers office (☎ 403 7866) at the land end of the pier.

The excellent Bay of Islands Maritime Park visitor information centre (☎ 403 7685) is next to the Captain Cook Memorial

Museum and has displays about the area and lots of information on nature, camping, walks, snorkelling, diving and many other activities throughout the 40 or so separate far-flung regions of the park. The centre is open every day from 9 am to 5 pm (May to August until 4.30 pm) and has an audiovisual show beginning every half-hour.

Get a copy of the excellent pamphlet *Russell Heritage Trails* which outlines one walking tour of town and three driving tours on the peninsula.

Captain Cook Memorial Museum

The Captain Cook Memorial Museum was built for the bicentenary of his Bay of Islands visit in 1769. It's small but it houses maritime exhibits, exhibits relating to Cook and his voyages, and a fine 1:5 scale model of his barque *Endeavour* – a real working model – in addition to a collection of early settlers' relics. The museum is open from 10 am to 4 pm every day; admission is $2.50 (children 50c).

Pompallier House

Close by and on a lovely waterfront site, is Pompallier House, built to house the printing works for the Roman Catholic mission founded by the French missionary Bishop Pompallier in 1841. It also served as a tannery and only in the 1870s was converted to a private home. It is one of the oldest houses in New Zealand and has a small museum. It's currently undergoing restoration and is due to reopen in 1994; check at the information office. You can look at this place from the gate at the right-hand end.

Flagstaff Hill

Overlooking Russell is Maiki (Flagstaff) Hill, where Hone Heke made his attacks – this, the fifth flagpole, has stood for a lot longer than the first four. The view is well worth the trouble to get up there, and there are several routes to the top. If you're walking, you can take the track west from the boat ramp along the beach at low tide, or up Wellington St at high tide. The track passes through the Kororareka Point Scenic Re-

NORTHLAND

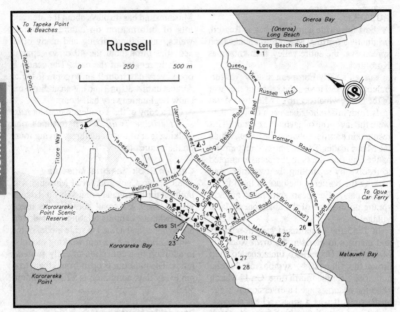

Other Things to See & Do

Christ Church in Robertson Rd, Russell is the oldest church in New Zealand. Built in 1835, it is suitably scarred with musket and cannon ball holes, and it has an interesting graveyard. Note the many tapestry pew cushions which depict familiar bay scenes.

Clendon Cottage was built by James Clendon, US Consul, 1839, who later moved to Rawere (see Clendon House) as Resident Magistrate.

Out at Lanes Rd Farm (☎ 403 7673) you can go horse-riding through a particularly beautiful part of the peninsula – the treks pass through bush, mangroves and along beaches. Often they swim the horses, depending on the tide. The cost is $25 for a two-hour trek ($20 for guests staying at the farm).

Tours & Cruises

Russell Mini Tours (☎ 403 7866) depart from Fuller's, fronting the pier, several times

serve. Alternatively you can simply walk to the end of Wellington St and take the short track up the hill from there, about a 30-minute climb. If you want to drive up to the summit, drive up Tapeka Rd.

Oneroa Bay

About one km behind Russell to the east is Oneroa Bay, with a beautiful beach known variously as Oneroa Bay Beach, Donkey Beach or Long Beach. It's about a 15-minute walk from the Russell wharf, heading over the hill on Long Beach Rd. When you reach the summit of the hill, at the intersection with Queen's View Rd, there's a tiny old graveyard with benches and a good view of Oneroa Bay. Take a turn here and go about a block up Queen's View Rd to where it meets Oneroa Rd and the view is even better – a sweeping vista of both sides of the peninsula. There's an unofficial nudist beach past the rocky outcrops on the northern end of the main beach.

■ PLACES TO STAY

3   Russell Holiday Park
4   Mako Motels
5   Russell Lodge
8   Duke of Marlborough Hotel
11 Duke's Lodge
21 Hananui Lodge
25 Motel Russell (Best Western)
26 Arcadia Lodge

▼ PLACES TO EAT

9   Duke of Marlborough Tavern & Bistro
10 RSA
12 Quarterdeck Restaurant
14 Verandah Cafe
16 Trader's Cafe
18 The Restaurant, Swordfish Club &
    Strand Cafe
19 The Gables

    OTHER

1   Adobe Cottage
2   Maiki (Flagstaff) Hill & Lookout
6   Boat Ramp
7   Police Station
13 Fuller's & Russell Mini Tours
15 Four Square Store
17 Christ Church
20 Public Toilets
22 Museum
23 Tourist Information Office &
    Ferry Terminal
24 Maritime Park Visitor Information
    Centre & Captain Cook Museum
27 Pompallier House
28 Clendon Cottage

each day and cost $8 (children $4) for a one-hour tour of the town and Long Beach. All the Fullers cruises out of Paihia pick up passengers at Russell about 15 minutes after their Paihia departure. You can charter yachts out of Russell, just as from Paihia.

Places to Stay

Camping & Cabins The *Russell Holiday Park* (☎ 403 7826), on Long Beach Rd, is centrally located, with tent and powered sites at $9 per person, cabins with kitchen and sleeping four to six people at $34 to $36 for

two ($10 each extra adult), and tourist flats at $49 for two. The *Orongo Bay Holiday Park* (see Hostels) also has campsites.

Hostels Four places around Russell offer hostel-style accommodation. *Orongo Bay Holiday Park* (☎ 403 7704) is three km south of Russell on the road to the Opua car ferry – it's an easy hitch if you don't have a car but they also provide a free pick-up service if you arrive in Russell by ferry. Orongo Bay is an Associate YHA Hostel, the nightly cost is $12 in one to four-bed rooms whether you're a YHA member or not. They also have camping in tent sites at $6 per person, powered sites $7. There's a swimming pool, a TV/games room, and good bikes for hire at $10 per day.

The *Arcadia Lodge* (☎ 403 7756) is on Florance Ave, about a 10-minute walk from the wharf. It's a splendid place up on a hill, with a magnificent view over Matauwhi Bay and several decks to enjoy it from. Each unit has its own kitchen; toilets and showers are shared. A bed in a share room is $14, and singles/doubles/twins are all $18 per person; The price usually drops in the off season. Bill and Linley go out of their way to make sure this 1890s Tudor-style house is a 'home away from home'.

Two blocks behind the wharf on the corner of Beresford and Chapel Sts, *Russell Lodge* (☎ 403 7640; fax 403 7641) has budget units, each with four bunks and private toilet, at $12.50 per person most of the year, $15 during the summer rush, or you can get the whole unit for $35. They have a large fully equipped kitchen area with a pool table in the middle of it. The motel units, sleeping four to six people, start from $60. There's an extensive outdoors recreation area with a swimming pool. They have a small shop where you can buy packaged backpackers supplies.

Just 10 minutes from Russell is the *Lanes Rd Farm* (☎ 403 7672) which occupies 40 hectares of historic farmland. They will pick up from Opua by boat or Russell by vehicle. Backpackers can stay here for $15 and twin/double rooms are $20 per person. The attraction of this place is its location and the wealth of adventure activities that spring from that. They also run the Bay of Islands Sea Kayaking Co (see Sea Kayaking earlier in this Bay of Islands section) and a horse trekking business. In addition they have a free dinghy and they organise barbecues on their boat, the *Opua Duck*. They are fitting out a van so they can travel further afield with their visitors.

Hotels & Motels The fine old *Duke of Marlborough Hotel* (☎ 403 7829), right on the waterfront, would certainly be the place to stay if money was no object. This is a place with some real old-fashioned charm. They have 'budget' rooms from $68 and better single/double rooms for $90 to $130. All rooms have private facilities, tea/coffee and a colour TV.

The *Duke's Lodge* (☎ 403 7899) beside the hotel was once part of the hotel but now it's under separate management and is more of a straightforward motel, with a swimming pool in the central courtyard and rates of $95 to $120 in summer (these are reduced considerably in the off season).

Motels in Russell generally cost from around $60 a night, particularly during the summer season when minimum rates often apply. There are about ten motels and the same general advice applies as for the Paihia motels. You can book through the Bay of Islands Visitor Information Centre in Paihia.

Places to Eat
There are several cafes and takeaways in Russell, including the waterfront *Strand* with sandwiches, snacks, a courtyard at the back and a verandah in front. They serve great lunches and a good-value soup of the day. Beside the Strand is a *health food shop* with a selection of pitta sandwiches including felafel. Back a block are the pleasant *Verandah Cafe* and the *Traders Cafe* with indoor and patio sections.

The *Duke of Marlborough Tavern* has typical pub food in its family pub section, with main dishes around $10. There's more 'refined' dining in *Somerset's Restaurant* at the Duke of Marlborough Hotel on the waterfront. The Duke has now opened a cheaper family dining area with a bar. Also on the waterfront are the *Quarter Deck Restaurant* with main courses from $16 to $25 and the expensive and licensed *Gables*, with main courses up around $19 to $23. Both of these places are well recommended and have friendly hosts.

Entertainment
The 'new' *Duke of Marlborough Tavern* was the first pub in New Zealand to get a licence, back on 14 July 1840. Its three predecessors all burnt down. The tavern, in the block behind the hotel, has both a family pub and a more serious, perhaps 'rougher', bar. If you want cheaper beer then get one of the RSA members to sign you in to their very friendly club.

Getting There & Away
Basically your choices are to come on the ferry from Paihia (see that section for details), to drive or hitch in via the Opua car ferry, or take the Northliner bus.

Fullers run a continuous shuttle service during the day from Opua to Okiato Point, still some distance from Russell. This ferry operates from 6.30 am to 8.50 pm (9.50 pm on Friday). The one-way fare is $6 for a car and driver, $9 for a campervan and driver, $3 for a motorcycle and rider, plus $1 for each additional adult passenger. InterCity go to Paihia, from where you catch the ferry. There's a much longer dirt road which avoids the Opua ferry, but it's a long haul to Russell via this route.

OPUA
As well as being the car ferry terminus, Opua is a busy deep sea port from which primary produce (meat, wool and butter) is exported. The town was established as a coaling port in the 1870s when the railway line was constructed. Before the wharf was built, after WW I, the coal was transported out to ships on lighters (flat-bottomed barges). Today, the occasional cruise ship may be seen alongside the wharf, as well as many local and

overseas yachts during the summer. If you're trying to hitch a ride to faraway places this could be a good spot to look. Yachties are sometimes willing to take more crew.

The Opua Forest, for the most part a re-generating forest, is open to the public. There are lookouts up graded tracks from the access roads and a few large trees have escaped axe and fire, including some fairly big kauris. You can enter the forest by walking in from Paihia on School Rd (see Paihia), driving in from Opua on the Oromahoe Rd, or a couple of other access roads. Get a leaflet from the visitor information centres in Paihia, Russell or Kerikeri.

Vintage Railway

There's a historic steam train service which operates from Opua to Kawakawa which runs everyday except Friday in summer, and Saturday to Tuesday in winter. The trip takes 45 minutes each way and a single/return costs $8/15 (children $5/8).

Places to Eat

At Opua there's the *Ferryman's Restaurant & Bistro* by the car ferry dock. The restaurant section is expensive but the bistro is a great place to sit out by the waterside and enjoy a light meal, sandwich or burger.

KERIKERI

Nestled into the northern end of the bay, Kerikeri is an attractive town with a sleepy, laid-back atmosphere. The word *kerikeri* means 'to dig' and it was right here, in 1820, that the first agricultural plough was intro-duced to New Zealand, and here that the Maoris grew large crops of kumaras (sweet potatoes) before the Pakehas arrived.

Today it is still primarily an agricultural region, with kiwi fruit, citrus and other orchards. Large numbers of itinerant farm-workers congregate in Kerikeri for the six-week kiwi fruit harvest beginning the first week in May, but orchard work of one kind or another is usually available all year round except perhaps during February. It is also a centre for a wide variety of arts & crafts.

Kerikeri is significant in NZ history. It became the site of the country's second mission station when the Reverend Samuel Marsden chose the site at the head of the Kerikeri inlet under the protection of the Maori chief, Hongi Hika. In November 1819 the Reverend John Butler arrived at the site and set up the mission headquarters. New Zealand's oldest wooden building, Kemp House, and its oldest stone building, the Stone Store, were part of the mission station and are still in superb condition.

Kerikeri is occasionally subject to flood-ing and in March 1981 it was inundated when the river burst its banks.

Information

There is a visitors centre near the Stone Store – across the bridge at Rewa's Maori Village. Information on walking tracks and huts is available from DOC Kerikeri (☎ 407 8474).

Stone Store

The Stone Store is the oldest stone building in New Zealand; construction began in 1833 and was completed in 1836. It is currently undergoing restoration and will be com-pleted early 1994. It is still open to the public and there is a small interpretative display there; entry is free during restoration.

Kemp House

Near the Stone Store is Kemp House – New Zealand's oldest surviving building, a remarkable fact given that it is constructed of wood. It was erected in 1821 by John Butler, who was the first head of the Church Missionary Society's new station. It is still complete with original fittings and chattels. It's open daily from 10 am to 12.30 pm and 1.30 to 4.30 pm; admission is $3.50 (students and children $1). Get a copy of the informa-tive pamphlet *Kemp House*.

Rewa's Maori Village & Visitors' Centre

Just across the river from the Stone Store, Rewa's Maori Village is built on a site thought to have been occupied at one time by Chief Rewa. The various buildings are an authentic reproduction of a *kainga*, a pre-

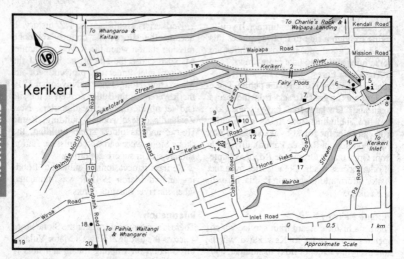

European unfortified Maori village, with various habitations, kitchen buildings, storerooms and so on, and exhibits of the many plants the Maoris used. It's open every day, admission is $2 (children 50c) and there are fine views across the inlet.

Waimate Mission House

This is New Zealand's second oldest surviving house. Built of kauri between 1831 and 1832, it was the Anglican Waimate Mission from 1832 to 1841 and the home of New Zealand's first Anglican bishop, Bishop Selwyn, from 1842 to 1844. It can be reached from SH 1 between Ohaeawai and Okaihau by turning off at Te Ahuahu. It can also be reached from SH 10 by turning off at Puketona. It is open daily, except Thursday and Friday, from 10 am to 12.30 pm and 1.30 to 4.30 pm. Adjacent to the building are the Church of St John the Baptist (1871) and a Sunday school building of the 1880s. An admission fee is charged.

Not far from the mission is *The Old Store*, on Te Ahuahu Rd, which is open for lunch, and morning and afternoon teas. Try the kumara and celery soup followed by blueberry and apple pie.

Walks

Just up the hill behind the Kerikeri Stone Store Tearooms is a marked Historical Walk which takes about 10 minutes and leads to Kororipo Pa, the fortress of Maori chief Hongi Hika, from which huge warfaring parties of Maoris once departed on raids, terrorising most of the North Island. The walk emerges near the St James Anglican church, built in 1878.

Across the bridge from the Stone Store is a verdant scenic reserve with several marked tracks. There's a four-km Kerikeri River track leading to Rainbow Falls, passing by the Wharepoke Falls (Fairy Pools) along the way. Alternatively you can reach the Rainbow Falls from Waipapa Rd, in which case it's only a 10-minute walk to the falls. The Fairy Pools are great for swimming and picnics and can be reached from the dirt road beside the YHA Hostel if you aren't up to the hike along the river.

Arts & Crafts

The Kerikeri area is home to many artists and artisans. Several shops display their work, and in most you can see work in progress, especially pottery. On Kerikeri Rd at the

■ PLACES TO STAY

7   Kerikeri YHA Hostel
9   Homestead Lodge & Restaurant
12 Cottle Court Motel
13 Aranga Holiday Park
16 Pagoda Lodge Caravan Park
17 Hone Heke Lodge
19 Hideaway Lodge, Adventure Park
20 Puriri Park

▼ PLACES TO EAT

1   Adam & Eve's Restaurant
6   Stone Store Tearooms & Restaurant

    OTHER

2   Rainbow Falls
3   Scenic Reserve & Carpark
4   Kemp House
5   Rewa's Maori Village &
    Visitors' Centre
6   Stone Store & Museum
8   Kororipo Pa
10 Price Choppers
11 New World Supermarket
14 Post Office, Bus Station
15 Public Toilets
18 The Orange Centre

northern end of town there's Red Barn
Pottery; at the south side, also on Kerikeri Rd
is The Studio and the Kauri Workshop. North
of Kerikeri, Earthlight Pottery on Waipapa
Rd, Lilly's Pots near the junction of SH 10
and Waipapa Rd, and Northland Woodcraft
Workshop at Waipapa Landing have crafts
on display. On SH 10 there are several good
shops including the Origin Art & Craft Co-
Operative with many kinds of crafts; Blue
Gum Pottery; the Orange Centre (the Fraser
McKenzie Gallery); and the Potting Shed
with pottery and weaving.

Other Things to See & Do
At the Orange Centre (☎ 407 9397) you can
learn about citrus fruits and take a $3 tour of
the orange, kiwi fruit and other orchards in
the 'orange-mobile'. The tour also includes
a visit to the shed where fruits are graded and
sized. The Orange Centre is by the Kerikeri

crossroads on SH 10, open daily from 9 am
to 5 pm.

For children the Adventure Park on Wiroa
Rd has 2½ hectares of good old-fashioned
amusements. It's open daily from 10 am to 5
pm (summer only); admission is $3. Kids
will also like the Kerikeri Orchard Railway
on SH 10.

The Aero Club at the Kerikeri Airport, on
Wiroa Rd six km west of town, does scenic
flights and charters. Kerikeri Tours (☎ 402
8511 or 407 8606) does half-day tours of
Kerikeri. You can hire a row boat and explore
the Kerikeri Inlet in front of the Stone Store.

Places to Stay
Camping & Cabins There are several
camping grounds at Kerikeri. The *Pagoda
Lodge Caravan Park* (☎ 407 8617) is on Pa
Rd at the inlet near the Stone Store. Campsites are $8.50 per person, tourist flats $30 to
$50 for two, and they have free dinghies and
canoes that you can use to explore the inlet.

The *Aranga Holiday Park* (☎ 407 9326)
is on Kerikeri Rd in a lovely setting beside
the Puketotara River, only five minutes' walk
from town. Tent or powered sites are $7.50
per person, cabins are $28 for two people. A
tourist flat with private facilities is $47 for
two. The *Hideaway Lodge* (☎407 9773) on
Wiroa Rd has campsites (see also Hostels).

Hostels Since Kerikeri is a centre both for
tourists to the Bay of Islands and for itinerant
agricultural workers, its hostels attract both
kinds of people. If you're looking for orchard
work some of the lodges may be able to help
you find it.

The *Kerikeri YHA Hostel* (☎ 407 9391) is
on the main road (Kerikeri Rd). The nightly
cost is $13 and various trips are organised
from the hostel, including full-day Bay of
Islands sailing trips, kayaking and horse-
riding. The lounge room is spacious and
decorated with murals.

The *Hone Heke Lodge* (☎ 407 8170; guest
☎ 407 7682) is on Hone Heke Rd in a quiet
residential area about 10 minutes' walk from
the town centre. The cost per person is $11
in bunkrooms, $15 per person in twin or

double rooms; double rooms with ensuite are $20.

The *Hideaway Lodge* (☎ 407 9773) is on a 3½-hectare orchard on Wiroa Rd, west of and out beyond the SH 10 junction. It's four km from town but they offer free rides to town twice daily and they also hire bicycles ($5 per day). The per-person cost is $9 to $11 in dorm rooms, $12 to $15 in twin or double rooms, and there's a big field where campsites are $7 per person. There's a swimming pool, BBQ, games room and so on, plus sports gear and activities. This is a big place which may hold 150 people during picking season, as it's the main accommodation available for itinerant orchard workers.

The *Puriri Park* (☎ 407 9818) is a different kind of place, also in an orchard, but all on a very small scale, with a comfortable cottage behind the family home offering bunks in triple rooms at $13 per person, or $16 per person for a couple to have the room to themselves. The cottage is pleasant, with kitchen and sitting areas, and you can use the swimming pool, walk through the orchard and go on some nearby bushwalks. Puriri Park is just past the Orange Centre on SH 10 heading towards Paihia. It has been highly recommended from a number of readers.

Guesthouses The *Puriri Park* (see Hostels) also has 'homestay' rooms in the family home at about $30/42 for singles/doubles, or $42/64 with breakfast. Another option out in the country is *Puketona Lodge* (☎ 402 8152), Puketona Rd (eight km on the way to Kerikeri from Paihia). Check with the visitor information centre in Paihia for other B&B homestays in the area.

Motels Several motels are found along Kerikeri Rd. Near the youth hostel, *Kemp Lodge* (☎ 407 8295) is small, with a swimming pool and three chalets costing $60 for singles, $68 to $78 for doubles during the high season; off-season rates will be lower. Next door the *Abilene Motel* (☎ 407 9203) has a swimming pool and 10 units, two with private spa pools, at $65/72. The *Cottle Court Motel* (☎ 407 8867) has units at $66/78.

The *Central Motel* (☎ 407 8921) has 14 units with features like a waterbed suite, swimming and spa pools, colour TVs and so on. Summer rates start at $70, dropping to $65/70 in winter. There are plenty of other motels.

Places to Eat
Kerikeri has several fast food places and cafes. On the main road the *Calypso* has good fish & chips and other takeaways. Cafes include *Goodies Cafe*, with sandwiches, snacks and cakes, and *Food Affair*. *As You Like It* is an attractive, mainly vegetarian restaurant off the main road with tables indoors or out on the brick courtyard.

Across from the Stone Store the *Stone Store Tearooms & Restaurant* is open daily from 9 am to 9 pm. It's a lovely spot to eat indoors or out on the verandah overlooking the lawn and the boats moored in the inlet. They have a great selection of mains and desserts in the evening.

More expensive places include *Adam & Eve's Restaurant* (licensed) five minutes out of town on Waipapa Rd; the *Homestead Hotel* out of town on Homestead Rd; and out on SH 10 on the road to Paihia, *Taylor's Licensed Cafe & Restaurant* which has standard food of the steak, chicken and seafood variety.

Getting There & Away
Bus InterCity and Northliner buses come and go from Travel Lee's (☎ 407 8013) on Cobham Rd, just off Kerikeri Rd in the town centre, stopping at Kerikeri half an hour after Paihia. InterCity buses heading north and south stop through several times daily. Kerikeri is the northern end of the line for Northliner buses, which come once a day every day. See Getting There & Away, Bay of Islands, for more details on long-distance buses.

Both companies have buses departing from Kerikeri in the morning for the half-hour trip to Paihia, returning in the late afternoon, every day except Sunday.

Top: Cape Reinga, Northland (JW)
Middle: Mt Ruapehu, Tongariro National Park (RS)
Bottom: Wainui Inlet, Golden Bay, Marlborough (VB)

Top: Stone Store, Kerikeri, Northland (TW)
Bottom: South of Coromandel, Coromandel Peninsula (TW)

Eastern Route

This description assumes that you are heading back in the direction of Auckland from the Bay of Islands to complete the loop around Northland.

In particular, there are two very scenic drives out on the east coast. There's the back road from Russell to SH 1, and the drive out to Tutukaka from Hikurangi on SH 1 which loops around to Whangarei. Out to sea are the Poor Knights islands.

South via Whangaruru

If you head directly south from Russell there's a long stretch of dirt road before you get back on the main road, but it is quite a beautiful route. There's access to the **Ngaiotonga Scenic Reserve** which preserves a good example of the mixed forest that once predominated throughout Northland. There are two short walks, suitable for families, here. They are the 20-minute **Kauri Grove Nature Walk** and the 10-minute **Twin Bole Kauri Walk**, both providing good opportunities to see fine specimens of these majestic trees. There's a longer walk passing through the Ngaiotonga reserve before heading into the Russell Forest.

The trip north from this area to **Whangamumu Scenic Reserve** is well worth the time. The reserve is accessible by foot or sea and there is a 'back to nature' camping area at the main beach. There are over 40 prehistoric sites on the peninsula and the remains of an unusual whaling station. A net, fastened between the mainland and Net Rock, was used to ensnare or slow down whales so the harpooners could get an easy shot in. The whales taken were mainly humpbacks and in 1927 over 70 whales were trapped in this fashion.

The **Whangaruru North Head** is worth visiting for its landscape and sheltered waters. Pohutukawa, puriri and kowhai abound here and many bird species can be seen in the area; the rare convolvulus *Calystegia marginata* grows in the forest.

You can camp at Whangaruru North Head (the camp fees are $5 for an adult and $2.50 for a child).

A recent addition to the park system in this area is the **Mimiwhangata Coastal Park** near Helena Bay. You can stay in either the DOC lodge or cottage here (see Places to Stay in Bay of Islands Maritime & Historic Park). If you can, do so because this is a truly scenic part of the coastline, with coastal dunes, pohutukawa, jutting headlands and picturesque beaches. Birdwatchers will be pleased to know that there is a chance of glimpsing the rare brown teal here.

Tutukaka Coast

At Hikurangi on SH 1 you can turn off and take a very scenic route to Whangarei. It's a superb but little known way to head back. When driving from Hikurangi the first place you come to on the coast is Sandy Bay surf beach. You can turn off before the coast and head north to Whananaki, where you can go horse-trekking on a little frequented piece of the east coast. There is a succession of idyllic bays from here on – Woolley's, Whale (reached after a 10-minute walk), Matapouri, Church, Kowharewa, Pacific, Dolphin and Whangaumu (Wellingtons) bays. There is much scope for walking, boating, swimming and, perhaps most popularly, fishing in this area.

Tutukaka is the home of the Whangarei Deep Sea Anglers Club and the marina here is cluttered with all types of boats. The large town of the area is Ngunguru, a few km south of Tutukaka. Here you'll find all the facilities you need, such as food outlets, accommodation, petrol, laundromat and sports complex.

Places to Stay & Eat At Ngunguru there is *Coastal Backpackers* (☎ 434 3419), Waitoti Rd, where all accommodation is $12 per person. This is a quiet farm and I had the place all to myself for one cold evening in winter.

Up at Whananaki, at *Whananaki Trail Rides* (☎ 433 8299), you can get a bed for $10 and camping is free. The plus is that you can horse trek through some 'top' country for a reasonable price ($24 for two hours, a two-day trek is $90).

Hungry? Don't like seafood? Then head on south. If you love seafood, welcome to paradise. The places to go for a meal are the *Tutukaka Hotel*, *Snapper Rock Cafe* and the *Whangarei Deep Sea Anglers Club*. If you catch fish then Smoking Jacko Hawkins (☎ 434 3948) will smoke them for you.

WHANGAREI

Back on the main road you soon reach Whangarei (population 40,000), the major town of Northland and a haven for yachts. Boats from around the world are moored in Town Basin, an attractive area right on the edge of the town centre. The beaches at Whangarei Heads about 35 km east of town are incredibly scenic, with many tiny bays and inlets, although they are somewhat difficult to reach if you don't have your own transport. The climate and soil combine to make this city a gardener's paradise, reflected in the many parks and gardens which thrive in this city.

Whangarei is more than just Northland's largest city. If you have transport and want to stick around for a couple of days you'll find plenty to do in both the city and the surrounding area.

Information

The Whangarei Visitor Information Centre (☎ 438 1079) is at Tarewa Park, Otaika Rd, on SH 1 at the southern entrance to town. It's open every day from 8.30 am to 5 pm and the staff are very helpful and friendly, with good maps and suggestions on things to do in the area. The AA office on James St near the mall also has good maps of town and of the surrounding region. There is a cafe which overlooks a very 'kid-friendly' park.

The DOC office (☎ 438 0299) at 149-151 Bank St has information on camping, recreational activities, maps and hut tickets, as well as an environmental shop with posters, publications, T-shirts and souvenirs.

Cafler Park

Cafler Park spans a little stream in the centre of town. It has well-tended flowerbeds, a conservatory and fernery. The Margie Maddren Fernery & Snow Conservatory is New Zealand's only all-native fernery and has over 80 varieties on display. Both are open daily from 10 am to 4 pm; admission is free.

Clock Museum

If you're interested in time and timepieces don't miss one of Whangarei's claims to fame, the Clapham Clock Museum in Cafler Park. It has an awesome variety of clocks – big, small, musical, mechanical or just plain weird, all ticking away furiously. Altogether there are over 1300 timepieces, with about 900 clocks and 400 watches. The museum custodian will show you around and demonstrate various oddities. Don't worry, clepsydra, skeleton, speaker's, 'nark', chess, gravity, tower, coconut, balloon, grandfather, 400-day and hickery dickery dock are all types of clock. The museum is open from 10 am to 4 pm everyday; admission is $3.50 (children $1.20).

Northland Regional Museum

A few km west of Whangarei, on the Dargaville road, is Maunu. The main attraction here is the Northland Regional Museum, open from 10 am to 4 pm daily. The museum is set in a large park which includes the 1885 Clarke Homestead, where the attendant gives you a guided tour explaining how the homesteaders lived and settled in the area 100 years ago. The museum domain also includes a kiwi house, an old locomotive which runs through the park during the summer, an abandoned mercury mine and more. Admission is $5 and that gets you into everything.

'The Quarry'

The Northland Craft Trust, or 'The Quarry' as it is informally known, is about 500 metres west of the town centre in an old converted quarry. It's a cooperative of artists and artisans of every description, with many studios where work is in progress and a showroom where the wares are exhibited and sold. Each summer their summer school attracts both

NZ and international artists and artisans. From the town centre head west on Rust Ave, which becomes Selwyn Ave, and The Quarry is a couple of blocks further on.

It is open daily from 10 am to 4 pm, with hours extended over the summer.

Whangarei Falls

The Whangarei Falls are very photogenic, with the water cascading over the edge of an old basalt lava flow. Adjacent to the Ngunguru Rd, in the suburb of Tikipunga about five km north of the town centre, the falls may be reached by catching a Tikipunga bus and walking the last bit. There's no bus on weekends. There are three natural swimming pools in the river, and numerous picnic spots within the domain.

A H Reed Memorial Kauri Park

The A H Reed Memorial Kauri Park spans a pretty stream and has a waterfall, several easy walkways and over 50 kinds of native trees including punga, totara and a few large kauris (some up to three metres in diameter). It's about five km from the town centre, going out Whareora Rd.

Scenic Reserves & Walks

There are two scenic reserves handy to the centre of town, on the hills on either side of the valley. Coronation Scenic Reserve, on the west, has a lookout, an old pa site, Maori pits and an old gold mine, as well as lots of bush. It is accessible from Kauika Rd.

On the eastern side is the Parahaki Scenic Reserve. There is a road to the summit of Parahaki, turning off Riverside Drive (the road towards Onerahi and the airport). Three tracks lead down from the summit, two finishing at Mair Park and one at Dundas Rd.

The Onerahi Mangrove Walk in Onerahi is an easy, level walk along an old (1880) railway embankment, lasting two hours and passing through mangrove swamps and over a harbour bridge. The pathway can be entered from the end of Cockburn St on one side, or from the end of Waimahanga Rd on the other side. If you're coming from town on the bus, take the Onerahi bus and get off at Handforth St, then turn into Cockburn St off Handforth.

There's a shorter, 15-minute mangrove walk over boardwalks in the centre of town, just behind the Olympic swimming pool.

Ten minutes up from Dundas Rd are some falls, with lots of glow-worms on the cliffs nearby, making a good evening walk. As a round trip from the bottom it takes about 20 minutes to reach the falls. Information on these and other walks is available from the visitor information centre and DOC.

In particular, the visitor information centre provides a number of Community Services Department pamphlets entitled *Walks* which have maps, access information and features.

Other Things to See & Do

In addition to the Ted Eliott Memorial Pool Complex with its Olympic-size indoor and outdoor pools, saunas and spas, there are many other places where you can do any one of a number of energetic things – bowling, netball, squash, square dancing and other activities. In fact, Whangarei has the highest number of clubs per capita in New Zealand.

The Whangarei Tramping Club (☎ 436 1441) and YWCA Tramping Club (☎ 438 2926) both welcome visitors. If you prefer to take a horse try Whananaki Trail Rides (☎ 433 8299) or the Whangarei City Riding Centre (☎ 437 5710).

Scenic flights taking up to three people are about $35 to $45 per person for flights of 45 minutes to one hour; phone 436 0707 after 5 pm for details.

For the aesthete, there's an art gallery behind the library, and another at the historic Reyburn House.

Places to Stay

Camping & Cabins There are two *DOC camping grounds* near Whangarei. One is on the east coast, north of Whangarei, at Otamure Bay, Whananaki; and the other is at Uretiti on Bream Bay, just off the highway between Waipu and Whangarei.

The *Alpha Caravan Park* (☎ 438 9867) at 34 Tarewa Rd is the most centrally located

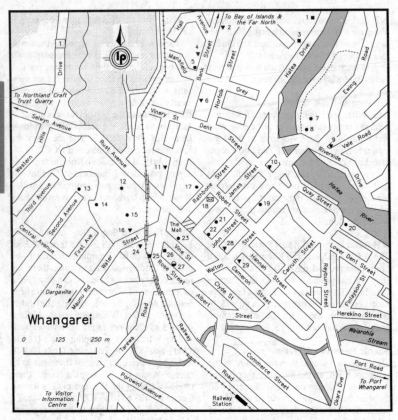

Whangarei

0   125   250 m

To Bay of Islands &
the Far North

camp, less than a km from the town centre. Camping is $7 per person, $9 with power, cabins are $35 to $38 for two, and self-contained units are $50 for two. The *William Jones Park* (☎ 437 6856) on Mair St, 2.5 km from the town centre by Mair Park, has tent or powered sites at $6.50 per person, cabins at $22 for two people ($15 each extra adult).

The *Otaika Motel Caravan Park* (☎ 438 1459) 136 Otaika Rd at the southern entrance to Whangarei, with tent and powered sites at $7.50 per person, well-equipped tourist flats at $33/40 for one/two people and motel units at $48/60.

The *Whangarei Falls Motor Camp* (☎ 437 0609) near the falls, five km from the town centre, has tent and caravan sites at $7.50 per person, a hostel-style bunkroom at $13, doubles/twins for $16 per person, and cabins at $24/32 for one/two people, most sleeping up to four and some sleeping up to six. They have swimming and spa pools, and in summer a big barbecue twice a week for just $7. Phone for free pick-up if you don't have wheels; they're a little way out of town.

The friendly owners organise diving (see Poor Knights later in this chapter), fishing trips, horse rides and visits to the Abbey

■ PLACES TO STAY

1   Hatea House Hostel
3   Settler's Motor Inn
26 The Grand Establishment Hotel
29 Settler's Hotel

▼ PLACES TO EAT

2   Kentucky Fried Chicken
4   McDonald's
6   Pizza Hut
9   Mooring's Restaurant
10 Reva's Pizza Parlour
11 Plume's Restaurant
16 Brasserie
24 Taste Spud
25 King Dragon
28 Full Circle
29 Al's Diner

OTHER

5   Department of Conservation (DOC)
7   Olympic Swimming Pool
8   Mangrove Boardwalk
12 Forum North Cultural Centre
13 Cafler Park, Fernery & Conservatory
14 Clapham Clock Museum
15 Civic Arcade
17 Taxi Rank, Public Toilets
18 Post Office
19 Pak 'N Save Supermarket
20 Reyburn House Art Gallery
21 Air New Zealand Link, Eagle Air,
    Automobile Association (AA) &
    Ansett (Roseman & Warren)
22 The Mall
23 Dolphin Bar
27 City Bus, InterCity & Northliner Bus
    Station

Caves. The cave trips are $8 per person, all equipment provided. These are undeveloped caves and in the two-hour excursion you walk through water and scramble over rocks while interesting features are pointed out to you.

Other camping and caravaning sites include *Kamo Springs Caravan Park* (☎ 435 1208) at 55 Great North Rd, Kamo; the *Blue Heron Holiday Park* (☎ 436 2293), on Tamaterau Beach; and *Tropicana Holiday Park* (☎ 436 0687) on Whangarei Heads Rd by the beach, 10 km from Whangarei.

Hostels The *Hatea House Hostel* (☎ 437 6174) at 67 Hatea Drive is a small, friendly hostel with only 13 beds (two bunkrooms, a twin and a double room) in a converted family home by the Hatea River, one km from the centre. Rates are $13 per person and they do kayaking ($15 per trip) and boating on the river and out to the sea. If you are in your own car, getting in and out of this place is difficult as it is on a blind bend on Hatea Drive.

Apart from Hatea House there is precious little hostel accommodation in central Whangarei. The nearest other places are Whangarei Falls (see Camping & Cabins) to the north and Waipu to the south (see Waipu & Bream Bay earlier in the chapter).

Hotels & Motels Whangarei has a surprisingly large number of hotels and motels. The *Grand Establishment Hotel* (☎ 438 4279) on the corner of Bank and Rose Sts was once a grand place in the old style, with high gilt carved ceilings, red plush carpet, statues and so on – Queen Elizabeth II even stayed here on her first visit to New Zealand in 1954 (see the photo in the lobby). There's a restaurant and several bars, and rooms cost $56/75 for singles/twins.

Whangarei's budget motels generally cost from around $55 to $65 for a double. The following have been recommended: *Motel 6* (☎ 438 9219), 153 Bank St; *Burgundy Rose* (☎ 437 3500), 15 Lupton Avenue; *Hibiscus Motel* (☎ 437 6312), 2 Deveron St; *Redwood Lodge Motel* (☎ 437 6861), Hatea Drive & Drummond St; *Regency* (☎ (09 438 3005), 11 Cross St; and the *Continental Motel* (☎ 437 6359), 67 Kamo Rd.

Places to Eat

Takeaways & Fast Food You can have a pleasant and economical lunch on a sunny day in Whangarei's Mall, tables and chairs provided – the *Sidewalk Cafe* is popular. *Taste Spud* on Water St has about 20 different kinds of baked potatoes, a few Mexican and

Indian snacks and a sit-down counter. *Something Else* in the Civic Arcade is another pleasant place, with healthy food (good soups, salads and cakes) to take away or eat there. Locals say *Moorings* on Riverside Drive, with a restaurant and takeaway section, has the best fish & chips in Whangarei. Some aficionados of the fish & chip may dispute that claim – *Al's Diner*, in Walton St, would be on an equal footing.

Fast-food fans can find a *McDonald's*, a *Kentucky Fried* and a *Pizza Hut*, all a km or so from the town centre on the main road heading north. New Zealand's answer to the high-profile chains, *Georgy Pie*, has made it to Whangarei.

A huge Pak 'N Save supermarket between Walton and Carruth Sts has the lowest prices in town. There is a Big Fresh on Port Rd and Woolworths on Kamo Rd.

Pub Food The *Forum Bistro* in the Forum North civic centre has typical pub meals. There's a *Cobb & Co* restaurant at the Kamo Hotel, 567 Kamo Rd, about two km north of the town centre, with the usual Cobb & Co menu.

Restaurants The *Reva's Pizza Parlour* on Dent St near the yacht basin has an art gallery, spontaneous musicianship and an international clientele of boaties, yachties and other travellers and artistic folk. *Moorings Restaurant* on Riverside Drive just across the harbour has good seafood meals. For ethnic food try the *King Dragon Chinese* in town.

For a fancy night out Whangarei has several possibilities including *Cafe Monet* at 144 Bank St and the *Classic Cafe* at 1D Grant St in the Kamo suburb on Whangarei's northern side. At 2 Bank St the *Ivory Room Restaurant* in the Grand Hotel serves breakfast, lunch and dinner daily, with a $12 Sunday night smorgasbord.

Three places in Whangarei have made it into the Taste New Zealand hall of culinary fame and fall into the expensive category. *The Full Circle*, 74 Cameron St, specialises in local produce including Bream Bay scallops and smoked hoki. The *Water Street Brasserie* has an outdoor courtyard for summertime dining; it is closed on Monday. At 63 Bank St you will find *Plumes Restaurant*. If your expense account allows it then your tastebuds will be well rewarded. Does pork fillet stuffed with feijoa, honey and pinenuts, baked and served in a sweet & sour sauce tempt you?

Entertainment

The best music places are out of town. The *Tutukaka Hotel*, north-east of town, and the *Parua Bay Hotel*, south-east at Whangarei Heads, are popular on weekends. Closer in, the *Onerahi Hotel* and the suburban *Tikipunga Tavern* on Denby Crescent have entertainment.

The Grand Hotel has a disco in Oscar's Bar and a duo singing in The Corner Bar; the Dolphin Bar is a popular nightclub and cabaret venue; and the *Forum Bar* in the Forum North Cultural Centre also has live music, all from Wednesday to Saturday nights. The *Settlers Motor Inn* and the *Kamo Hotel* also have music from time to time.

Getting There & Away

Air Eagle Air, Air New Zealand and Ansett share about six flights daily between Auckland and Whangarei, with connections to other centres. Roseman & Warren Travel (☎ 438 4939) in the James St Arcade is the agent for Eagle Air, Ansett and Air New Zealand.

Bus The InterCity bus depot (☎ 438 2659) is on Rose St. InterCity has frequent buses between Auckland and Whangarei, continuing north to the Bay of Islands, Hokianga Harbour and Kaitaia, with another route to Dargaville. From Whangarei it's three hours to Auckland, 1½ hours to Paihia, 3½ hours to Kaitaia or an hour to Dargaville.

Northliner has a daily bus service Auckland-Whangarei-Bay of Islands, with a route to Kerikeri via Paihia or directly to Russell on the Opua ferry. The bus operates from the Northliner Terminal (☎ 438 3206) in Rose St.

Hitching Being the only big town between Auckland and the Bay of Islands, and the principal town of the region, Whangarei is a very busy spot for hitchhikers going north and south.

Heading north, the best hitching spot is on SH 1 just after the Three Mile Bush Rd intersection, in the Kamo suburb about five km north of the town centre. Any Kamo bus from the town centre will drop you there. Heading south, the best hitching spot is on SH 1 opposite Tarewa Park or, second best, about 500 metres further south, by the New World supermarket.

Getting Around

Whangarei Bus Services (☎ 438 3104) operates a limited local bus service. On Saturday the problem is particularly acute and there are no buses at all on Sunday. The Onerahi bus route serves the airport on this same schedule. Rental cars are available from Avis (☎ 438 2929), Budget (☎ 438 7292) and Rent-a-Cheapie (☎ 438 7373).

AROUND WHANGAREI
Whangarei Heads

There is magnificent scenery at Whangarei Heads, though it's hard to get to without a car as there is no bus; hitching should not be too difficult, especially on weekends. On the way is the Waikaraka Scenic Reserve on Mt Tiger, with excellent views (turn-off at Parua Bay).

There are great views from the top of 419-metre Mt Manaia. The trail to the top starts from the main road beneath the mountain (but it's easy to miss), and you climb up through forest. Close to the top are cables to help you scale a steep rock. Two hours of hard work will get you to the summit where there are incredible views of the sea, the mountains, the surrounding dairyland and, just as a contrast, the oil refinery at Marsden Point. DOC advises that the track requires great care, a fair degree of agility and a reasonable head for heights. This walk, and many others, are outlined in the free DOC pamphlet *Walks in the Whangarei District*.

Marsden Point

New Zealand's oil refinery is at Marsden Point, across the harbour from Whangarei Heads. They have an information centre (☎ 432 8194) you can visit to learn about oil refining; there is a 130-sq-metre scale model of the refinery, accurate down to the last valve and pump. The centre is open from 10 am to 4 pm, daily.

New Zealand Fudge Farm

On SH 14, at Tangiteroria, between Whangarei and Dargaville, is the home of 'creamy farm-fresh fudge'. Fudgeaholics can satisfy their addiction from 9.30 am to 4.30 pm, Thursday to Sunday.

Poor Knights Islands Marine Reserve

The Poor Knights Islands Marine Reserve, 24 km off Northland's east coast, was established in 1981. The reserve is reputed to have the best scuba diving in all New Zealand and has been rated by many as one of the top diving spots in the world.

The two large islands (Tawhiti Rangi and Aorangi) were once home to members of the Ngati-wai tribe, but since a massacre in the early 1800s by a raiding party, the islands have been tapu. You are *not* allowed to land on the islands – but you can swim around them.

As the northern islands are bathed in a subtropical current, varieties of tropical and subtropical fish not seen in other coastal waters are observed by divers. The waters are clear and there are none of the problems with sediment that there are on the mainland. The underwater cliffs drop steeply, about 70 metres, to a sandy bottom, where there is a labyrinth of archways, caves and tunnels, packed with a bewildering variety of fish.

As the islands are relatively isolated from the mainland they have acted as a sanctuary for flora & fauna, the most famous example of which is the prehistoric reptile, the tuatara.

Diving trips depart from Whangarei, Tutukaka and elsewhere. The *Pacific Hideaway*, operated by the Bells, is a fully-equipped dive boat. You can book this at the Whangarei Falls Motor Camp (☎ 437 0609);

at $75 per day – two dives, a deep one and a shallow one are guaranteed for this price. A four-day course, with practical and theory lessons, is also conducted, with two days of diving included at the Poor Knights.

Aqua Action (☎ 434 3867; fax 434 3202) operate out of Tutukaka. They have a two-dive day for $75 and a three-dive day for $90

– anyone in the know realises that this is good value. They also cater for dedicated free divers, stopping at three different Poor Knights' sites for $55. Like the Bells they conduct courses leading to full accreditation.

Contact the Whangarei DOC office for more information on the islands.

Waikato & the King Country

The Waikato and the King Country regions lie south of Auckland. Heading from Auckland past the outer suburbs, within about an hour you enter the fertile plains of the Waikato, one of the world's richest dairying and agricultural regions.

The Waikato region encompasses the central and lower reaches of the Waikato River, New Zealand's longest river, which starts in the central North Island, flows out from Lake Taupo and meets the sea here on the west coast. The Waikato region includes four plains and Hamilton, New Zealand's fifth-largest city, is its major centre. Further south is a historic region known as the King Country, extending roughly from the towns of Otorohanga in the north to Taumarunui in the south, and from western Lake Taupo to the coast.

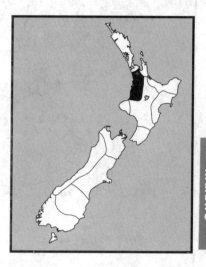

WAIKATO

HISTORY

The Waikato region was cultivated by the Maoris in pre-European times, with archaeological evidence showing that thousands of hectares were under cultivation with kumaras (sweet potatoes) and other crops.

When the Europeans settled in Auckland in 1840, relations with the local Maoris were peaceful at first; missionaries in the 1830s introduced European crops and farming methods to the Waikato region, and by the 1840s the Maoris were trading their agricultural produce with the European settlers in Auckland.

Relations between the two cultures soured during the 1850s, however, largely due to the Europeans' eyeing of the Maoris' land for settlement. By the early 1860s the Waikato Maoris had formed a 'King Movement' and united to elect a king. The movement probably stemmed both from a need for greater organisation of the Maori tribes against the Pakeha invaders and from a desire to have a Maori leader equivalent to the British Queen when dealing with the Pakehas.

The first Maori King, King Potatau Te Wherowhero, was a paramount high chief of the Waikato tribes when he was made King in 1859. He died one year later at the age of about 85 and was succeeded by his son, the second and most widely known Maori King, Matutaera Te Wherowhero, commonly known as King Tawhiao, who ruled for the next 34 years until his death in 1894.

The King Movement was a nationalistic step on the part of the Maoris, who were unwilling to sell or otherwise lose their homeland to the Europeans. The Europeans, however, were equally unwilling to take no for an answer, and in July 1863 they sent a fleet of gunboats and small craft up the Waikato River to put down what they regarded as the 'open rebellion' of the Maori King Movement. After almost a year of warfare known as the Waikato Wars, involving many historic battles, the Europeans finally won in April 1864 and the Maoris retreated south to the area now known as the King Country,

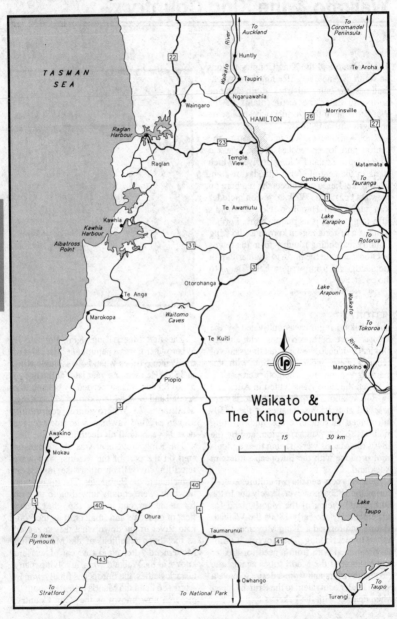

WAIKATO

Te Arikinui Dame Te Atairangikaahu

The Maori 'King Movement', in which local chief, Te Wherowhero, was elected as the first Maori king in 1859, is still very much alive among the Waikato Maori tribes. Te Arikinui Dame Te Atairangikaahu, who currently holds the title of Maori Queen, is the sixth in the line of succession.

Her father, Koroki Mahuta, was the fifth Maori King. When he died in 1966, there was widespread concern over who his successor should be, since he had no sons - but two daughters, Tura and Piki. There had been a Maori king since 1859, but never a Maori queen.

According to ancient tradition, if an *ariki* (the first-born of a noble family) had no sons, the office of chief would have been passed on to a close male relation upon the death of the chief. Therefore it was a great matter to decide - should the inherited royal office be passed on to one of Koroki Mahuta's descendents, although they were women, or should it be passed to someone else?

After much discussion and debate, the Maori chiefs and elders decided that the office should pass to Piki, Mahuta's daughter. Princess Piki became the first Maori Queen on 23 May 1966.

In 1970 Queen Elizabeth II conferred upon her the title Dame Commander of the British Empire, and her official title became Te Arikinui Dame Te Atairangikaahu.

Although many Europeans misunderstand her position, believing her to be Queen of all the New Zealand Maoris just as Queen Elizabeth II is Queen of all of the UK, in fact Te Arikinui Dame Te Atairangikaahu is Queen only of the tribes who united to form the Maori King Movement in the 1850s. She is head of the Tainui tribal confederation, which consists of four major tribes: the Waikato, Maniapoto, Hauraki and Raukawa. This is one of New Zealand's largest Maori confederations, estimated to contain around 70,000 to 75,000 people (out of the entire Maori population of around 330,000).

Te Arikinui Dame Te Atairangikaahu's marae is the magnificent Turangawaewae Marae, beside the Waikato River in Ngaruawahia. If you are travelling through Ngaruawahia on SH 1, you can see the marae as you cross the bridge over the river. The Queen has houses in various places significant to her people - for example, there is a house for the Maori Queen beside the Maketu Marae in Kawhia, where the *Tainui* canoe is buried.

Te Arikinui Dame Te Atairangikaahu is an eloquent speaker and a gracious leader who is much loved by her people. She uses her influence to try to promote equality between Maoris and Pakehas - mutual understanding and mutual respect for each culture and each people. ∎

WAIKATO

where the Europeans dared not venture for several more decades.

Information

In general, the Waikato and King Country telephone numbers have an 07 prefix if you are calling them from a long distance (even within the regions), so we haven't included the prefix with each telephone number. Where the prefix is different, it is included with the number but again, you only need to use it if you're not calling locally.

AUCKLAND TO HAMILTON

The trip to Hamilton by road from Auckland takes about 1½ hours and there are a few points of interest along the way. If you're a steam train enthusiast you can pause at the **Glenbrook Vintage Railway** (☎ (09) 236 3546), where on Sunday and public holidays from Labour Weekend in late October to Queen's Birthday in early June you can take a 12-km steam train ride. From 26 December to 4 January the line operates every day. The rides depart every half hour from 11 am to 4 pm and take 45 minutes return; the cost is $8 (children $3, family $20). To get there follow the yellow signs after leaving the Southern Motorway at Drury, 31 km south of Auckland, and head for Waiuku. There is also an **animal farm and deer park** at Glenbrook.

Te Kauwhata, 67 km south of Auckland and just off SH 1, is a good place for a bit of wine tasting. From here the road follows the Waikato River all the way to Hamilton. Along the way is **Huntly**, a coal-mining town with the large Huntly Power Station (☎ 828 9590) which can be visited by appointment – free 1½ to two-hour guided tours are offered for groups of one to 60 people. You will need to arrange it a couple of days in advance.

At the lookout on SH 1, a couple of km north of the town, there are a restaurant, a crafts shop and the **Pukeroa Native Timber Museum**, open every day from 9.30 am to 5 pm, with samples of woodturning and all kinds of New Zealand and exotic timbers. Also at Huntly is the **Huntly Mining & Cultural Museum** at 26 Harlock Place, open from 10 am to 3 pm every day except Monday.

South of Huntly the road enters Taupiri Gorge, a gap through the ranges. On your left as you emerge from the gorge is a Maori cemetery on the hillside.

Ngaruawahia, 19 km north of Hamilton on SH 1, is an important centre for the Waikato Maori people and the home of the Maori Queen, Te Arikinui Dame Te Atairangikaahu. A few hundred metres off SH 1, beside the river on River Rd, is the impressive Turangawaewae Marae.

If you're fit, there is an excellent view from Taupiri Mountain, and on the opposite side of the river there are also good views from the Hakarimata Track. The northern end leads off Parker Rd, which can be reached by crossing the river at Huntly and following the Ngaruawahia-Huntly West Rd. The southern end meets the Ngaruawahia-Waingaro Rd just out of Ngaruawahia. To walk the length of the track takes seven hours.

A shorter walk, and easier to get to if you have no transport, is a three-hour return trek from Brownlee Ave, Ngaruawahia, to Hakarimata Trig (371 metres). The top part of this is fairly steep but the view is rewarding. Tracks from each access point meet at the trig.

About 25 km west of Ngaruawahia are the popular Waingaro Hot Springs (see the Around Hamilton section).

Hamilton

New Zealand's largest inland city and fifth-largest overall, Hamilton (population 125,000) is 129 km south of Auckland. Built on the banks of the Waikato River, it is the Waikato region's major centre, and in the past few decades the city has undergone spectacular growth.

Archaeological evidence shows that the Maoris had long been settled around the Hamilton area, but when the Europeans arrived, the site was deserted. European settlement was initiated by the 4th Regiment of the Waikato Militia, who were persuaded to enlist with promises of an acre (less than half a hectare) in town and another 50 acres in the country. The advance party, led by Captain William Steele, travelled up the Waikato River on a barge drawn by a gunboat and on 24 August 1864 went ashore at the deserted Maori village of Kirikirioa. The township built on that site was named after Captain John Fane Charles Hamilton, the popular commander of HMS *Esk* who had been killed in Tauranga at the battle of Gate Pa four months earlier on 30 April.

The Waikato River was once Hamilton's only transport and communication link with other towns including Auckland, but it was superseded by the railway in 1878, and later by roads.

Orientation & Information

Running north to south a block from the Waikato River, Victoria St is the main drag of the commercial centre; you'll find most things you'll need on or near this busy thoroughfare.

The Hamilton Visitor Centre (☎ 839 3360; fax 839 0794) is in the City Council Building in Garden Place, between Victoria and Anglesea Sts right in the centre of town. It's open weekdays from 9 am to 4.30 pm, 10 am to 2 pm on Saturday, Sunday and public holidays. It has information on Hamilton, Waitomo and the Waikato region and also sells bus, train and Interislander ferry tickets, and postage stamps.

The DOC office (☎ 838 3363; fax 838 8004) on the ground floor of the BDO House at 18 London St, near the river, has maps and information on the natural attractions of the region, including the Pirongia Forest Park, the Coromandel and south to the Pureora

Forest Park. It's open Monday to Friday from 8.30 am to 4.30 pm.

The Map Shop (☎ 838 2489) in Victoria St facing Ward St, operated by DOSLI, has maps of every description on New Zealand and most other parts of the world – topographic maps, forest and national park maps, street maps, etc. It's open Monday to Friday from 9 am to 5 pm, Saturday 10 am to 12.30 pm.

The AA (☎ 839 1397) on the corner of Victoria & Bryce Sts is open weekdays from 8.30 am to 5 pm. Campus Travel (☎ 856 9588) at Waikato University on Knighton Rd is an agent for STA, the international student travel agency. The CPO is in Victoria St, opposite Garden Place.

Waikato Museum of Art & History

The Waikato Museum of Art & History is an excellent museum in an attractive, modernistic building on the corner of Victoria and Grantham Sts near the river. It has a good Maori collection, with lots of carvings and the impressively large and intricately carved *Te Winika* war canoe, dating from 1836. The canoe has had an eventful history and has now been beautifully restored, a project detailed in photos along the wall. The art collection includes interesting paintings, and the museum also sponsors numerous concerts and other events. It's open every day from 10 am to 4.30 pm; admission is $2 (children 50c, students and seniors $1, Monday free). The attractive Museum Cafe, open the same hours as the museum, is worth a visit too.

Gardens, Parks & Walks

The huge Hamilton Gardens complex contains about 100 different theme gardens – rose gardens, a riverside magnolia garden, a scented garden, cacti and succulents, vegetable and glasshouse gardens, carnivorous plants, and many more, with new ones still under construction. The complex is on Cobham Drive on the east side of the Cobham Bridge, and can be reached by walking south from the city centre along the river walkway.

The gardens are always open; admission is free.

Other relaxing spots are Hamilton Lake (Rotoroa) and the green domains along the Waikato River. Walkways pass through verdant parks and bushy areas on both sides of the river all the way from Cobham Bridge to Whitiora Bridge (both beyond the limits of our map) and there are a couple of sandy riverside beaches right in town. The area below the traffic bridge (Bridge St) is particularly attractive. Embedded in the riverbank walkway are the remains of the gunboat SS *Rangiriri*, which played a part in the Maori Wars in 1864.

The visitor centre has a free map showing the walkways around the lake, along the river and down to Hamilton Gardens. The DOC office has info on many other walks in and around Hamilton.

Hilldale Zoo Park

Hilldale Zoo Park, with 40 species of animals, is quite good, though really more fun for the kids. The zoo is eight km from the city centre – take SH 23 west towards Raglan, turn right at Newcastle Rd and then right again onto Brymer Rd. The zoo is open from 9 am to 5 pm every day; admission is $6 (children $3).

National Agricultural Heritage

The interesting National Agricultural Heritage complex incorporates the Clydesdale Agricultural Museum, the National Dairy Museum, a Heritage Village with historical buildings, and farm animals the kids can touch and feed. It's open every day from 9 am to 4.30 pm; admission is $3 (children and seniors $1.50, wagon rides $1, swimming pool 50c).

The complex is on Mystery Creek Rd at Mystery Creek, 16 km south of Hamilton and 1.5 km south-east of Hamilton airport. Transport is easy with a vehicle but it's a little difficult to get there by public transport. Buses run via the airport turn-off but that still leaves you four km away. A taxi from the airport or from town might be the best option.

WAIKATO

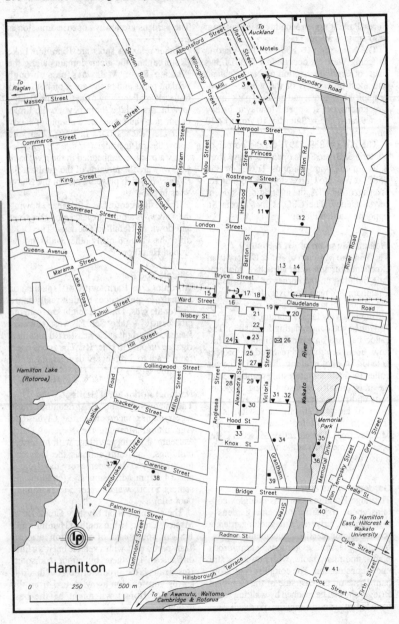

Hamilton

0   250   500 m

To Raglan
To Auckland
Motels
To Te Awamutu, Waitomo,
Cambridge & Rotorua
To Hamilton
East, Hillcrest &
Waikato
University
Hamilton Lake
(Rotoroa)
Memorial
Park

■ PLACES TO STAY

1 Hamilton YHA Hostel
27 Commercial Establishment Hotel,
   Cobb & Co & Freemans Bar
33 Grand Central Private Hotel
37 YWCA
39 Riverview Private Hotel
40 Parklands Travel Hotel/Motel

▼ PLACES TO EAT

2 Pizza Hut
4 Kentucky Fried Chicken
5 Harwood's Restaurant
6 Cask & Grill, Tosca's Restaurant &
   Royal Thai Restaurant
7 Seddon House Restaurant
9 Mandarin Restaurant
10 Totally Burgered &
   Death by Chocolate
11 Oss's Bar
13 Gino's Portofino Restaurant & AA
14 Governor's Tavern
16 Fox & Hounds, Centreplace Food
   Court & Village 5 Cinemas
17 French Bakery
19 McDonalds
20 Eldorado's, No 8 &
   Adriana's Restaurants
22 Singapore Restaurant
25 Gelato Arlecchino

27 Commercial Establishment Hotel,
   Cobb & Co & Freemans Bar
28 Tastebuds Mexican Cantina
29 Metropolis Cafe
31 Hungry Horse Restaurant &
   Exchange Tavern
32 Left Bank Cafe
41 Boonjo

OTHER

3 Pak 'n Save Supermarket
8 Founders Theatre
12 Department of Conservation (DOC)
13 AA, Gino's Portofino Restaurant
15 Hamilton Transport Centre
16 Fox & Hounds, Village 5 Cinemas &
   Centreplace Food Court
18 Centreplace Shopping Mall
19 The Map Shop & McDonald's
21 Air New Zealand & Legends Disco
23 Garden Place
24 Hamilton Visitor Centre
26 CPO, Down Under Bar
27 Commercial Establishment Hotel,
   Cobb & Co & Freemans Bar
30 Vinnie's Rock Bar, Shakes Disco
31 Hungry Horse Restaurant &
   Exchange Tavern
34 Waikato Museum of Art & History
35 SS *Rangiriri*
36 Riverboat Cruises
38 Hamilton Operatic Society

WAIKATO

Temple View

People interested in comparative religious studies might want to take a trip to Temple View, eight km south-west of Hamilton, site of the South Pacific's principal Mormon Temple and college. Only Mormons are allowed inside the temple itself but there is a Visitors' Centre, open from 9 am to 9 pm daily, with large pictures of the temple's interior, videos, tours and brochures all telling the story of this temple and of the Mormon faith. The staff is gracious and friendly. To get there, catch the Temple View bus from the Hamilton Transport Centre.

Cruises

River cruises on the Waikato River are a popular attraction. The historic paddleboat MV *Waipa Delta*, which made its first voyage on the Waikato River in March 1877, departs from Memorial Park, on the riverbank opposite the town centre. There are morning and afternoon tea cruises for $18, a luncheon cruise for $30, and a moonlight cruise for $39 ($49 on Saturday). Children aged five to 12 are half price. Reservations are recommended (☎ 854 9415, 854 9419).

Other Things to Do

The information centre can supply details on many things to do around Hamilton if you have the time, including river and lake amusements, horse-riding, ice skating, a grand-prix raceway, 10-pin bowling and more. Waterworld Te Rapa on Garnett Ave is a large complex in pleasant surroundings with several indoor and outdoor pools and waterslides. Day tours operate to the Waitomo Caves.

Events

In recent years Hamilton has been promoting itself as an events centre; if you're in New Zealand for a while you'll notice it seems there is always something or other going on in Hamilton. Check with the visitor centre for current schedules.

Among the more notable annual events are the hot-air balloon festival held in March or April; the New Zealand National Agricultural Field-days in mid-June; the Antique Fair and New Zealand Crafts Show in July; the Waikato Home & Garden Show and the Waikato A&P (Agricultural & Pastoral) Show in October; the Rose Show and Toy Fair in November; and there are plenty more.

Places to Stay

Camping & Cabins Hamilton has a couple of camping grounds on the east side of the river, two or three km from the city centre. The *Municipal Camp* (☎ 855 8255; fax 855 3865) on Ruakura Rd in Claudelands, two km east of the centre, has tent sites at $10/13.50 for one/two people, powered sites at $13/16.50, standard cabins at $17/24, family cabins at $28/34 and tourist cabins at $30/38.

The *Hamilton East Tourist Court* (☎ 856 6220) on Cameron Rd, three km east of the centre, has tent sites at $13, powered sites at $16, standard cabins at $32, tourist cabins at $39 and tourist flats at $48; all prices are for two adults. It's on the city bus route, take the University or Peachgrove Rd lines from the Hamilton Transport Centre.

The *Narrows Park Christian Camp* (☎ 843 6862) is 11 km south of Hamilton, near the Hamilton Airport and adjacent to the Narrows Golf Club. It's owned and operated by the Presbyterian Church but anyone is welcome to stay there. Tent sites are $6 per person, powered sites $8 per person, and cabins are $30 for two people.

Hostels The *Hamilton YHA Hostel* (☎ 838 0009) at 1190 Victoria St is beside the river

a few blocks north of the city centre, a pleasant 15-minute walk along the river. The cost is $14/16 per night in dorm/double rooms.

The *Silver Birches* (☎ 855 6260) at 182 Tramway Rd is a small hostel sleeping just seven to nine people in double, twin and triple rooms. It's run by a friendly European couple, with German, Swiss-German and French spoken as well as English. It's an attractive place with a beautiful garden and honey fresh from the bees; the cost is $15 per night. It's in the eastern suburbs of Hamilton, about seven km from the centre, which is a bit inconvenient but they do hire bicycles, and the local No 11 Fairfield bus route from the Hamilton Transport Centre stops half a block away, on the corner of Tramway and Marden Roads. To get there on your own, head east over the river on the Boundary Rd bridge, keep going about six km until you reach Tramway Rd, turn left and go another couple of blocks.

The *YWCA* (☎ 838 2219; fax 847 1750) on the corner of Pembroke and Clarence Sts, about one km from the city centre, takes both men and women casuals when there is room. The rates are $12.50 a night with your own sleeping bag, $20 a night with linen provided, or $76 weekly, all in single or double rooms with shared kitchenettes.

The *Parklands Travel Hotel/Motel* (see Hotels) and the *Riverview Private Hotel* (see Guesthouses) have budget backpackers rooms at $15 per person.

Hotels & Guesthouses *The Silver Birches* (see Hostels) has a couple of separate self-contained guesthouse apartments. One sleeps one or two people and costs $55; the other sleeps two or three and costs $60 to $70. Meals are not included but you can cook your own.

The old-fashioned *Grand Central Private Hotel* (☎ 838 1619) at 27 Hood St looks like it may have already seen its best days but it is indeed quite central. Its prices of $30/45 for singles/doubles include a cooked breakfast served in the dining room from 6 to 8 am. It takes permanent residents as well as casuals and the weekly rate is $95/170 for singles/doubles.

Around the corner near the Waikato Museum, the *Riverview Private Hotel* (☎ 839 3986) at 60 Victoria St is a similar place with small, simple rooms for $25 per person including breakfast, which is served at 7 am (8 am on weekends). There's also a backpackers rate of $15 per person if you supply your own linen and don't take the breakfast; there's a kitchen where you can do your own cooking. Or there's a weekly B&B rate of $95 per person.

Right in the city centre on Victoria St near the corner of Collingwood St, the *Commercial Establishment* (☎ 839 1226; fax 838 0777) has private-facility rooms at $55, shared-facility rooms at $25/35 for singles/doubles, and suites at $65. Also here are a Cobb & Co restaurant and the Freemans Bar.

The *Parklands Travel Hotel/Motel* (☎ & fax 838 2461), just across the river at 24 Bridge St, has hotel rooms at $25 per person ($35 with cooked breakfast), motel units at $40 to $55 single, $55 to $60 double, and a budget bungalow where beds are $15 a night in single, double or dorm rooms.

Motels Hamilton has plenty of motels, particularly along Ulster St, the main road into the city from the north. In fact Hamilton has one of the biggest concentrations of motels in New Zealand. The *Parklands Travel Hotel/Motel* is OK (see Hotels). Some other moderately priced places, all on or near Ulster St, include:

Abbotsford Court Motel (☎ 839 0661; fax 838 9335), 18 Abbotsford St, just off Ulster St, private spa pool, $58/69 for singles/doubles

Bavaria Motel (☎ 839 2520; fax 839 2531), 203-207 Ulster St, spa pool, $60/72 for singles/doubles with discounts for longer stays

Classic Motel (☎ 849 6588), 451 Ulster St, swimming and spa pools, $50/58

Mariner Motel (☎ 838 1769; fax 838 0374), 257 Ulster St, swimming and spa pools, $55/65

Farmstays & Homestays The visitor centre has listings for farmstays and homestays in the Waikato region.

Places to Eat

Snacks & Fast Food The modern *Centreplace* shopping centre is a good place to go for a quick and cheap meal. On the ground floor is an international food court with a variety of counters offering Italian, Lebanese, Chinese and Singaporean food, the *Fishpot Cafe*, the *Charcoal Chicken Joint*, a delicatessen and a sweets shop. Also on the ground floor, the *Whole Food Cafe* has pies, samosas and the like, to take away or eat there. On the mezzanine level is the pleasant *Chequers Coffee Lounge*. Just outside the centre at 68 Ward St there's a *French Bakery*.

Another fine place for a daytime meal is the *Museum Cafe* at the Waikato Museum of Art & History on the corner of Victoria and Grantham Sts. It has gourmet food and desserts but it's not expensive, and there's a peaceful ambience with seating indoors or on the shaded balcony overlooking the river. It's open every day from 10 am to 4.30 pm.

Tastebuds Mexican Cantina in the Farmers Building on Collingwood St on the corner of Alexandra St serves Mexican snacks like nachos, tacos, enchiladas, burritos and so on to take away or eat there. It's a casual place with a colourful decor where you can get a full meal for less than $6. It's open every day from 11 am to around 7 or 9 pm.

Nearby, the *Metropolis Cafe* at 241 Victoria St near Collingwood St is a hip cafe with lunches, dinners, snacks, rich desserts and espresso. It's open every day from 11 am until late, except that it opens on Sunday at 6 pm and closes on Monday at 6 pm.

In the Garden Place on Victoria St the *Gelato Arlecchino* has pizza, coffee and Italian gelato; there's another branch in the Centreplace international food court.

Totally Burgered at 789 Victoria St boasts 17 varieties of gourmet char-grilled burgers including a couple of chicken burgers and a tofu burger for the vegetarians in the crowd. It's a popular spot open every night from 5.30 to 9 pm and from noon to 2 pm Tuesday to Friday.

A couple of doors away, *Death by Chocolate* at 783 Victoria St serves only desserts;

WAIKATO

if you don't mind spending at least $12.50 for the cheapest dessert on the menu, or $15 for the Death by Chocolate namesake dessert, plus $2.50 for a cup of coffee to go with it, you'll probably like it.

And yes, the big three American fast food chains are all represented in Hamilton. There's a *McDonald's* right in the centre on the corner of Victoria St and Claudelands Rd, possibly the busiest street corner in Hamilton. About five blocks north, on Ulster St just where it takes off from Victoria St, there's a *Pizza Hut* and a *Kentucky Fried Chicken*.

Pub Food Moving on to pub food, there's a popular *Cobb & Co* in the Commercial Establishment on the corner of Victoria and Collingwood Sts, open from 7 am to 10 pm daily with the usual Cobb & Co menu. A block away, the *Hungry Horse* is a similar restaurant/bar serving dinner every night and lunch every day except Monday.

The friendly Olde English-style *Fox & Hounds* in Ward St does pub lunches and ploughmans' platters. Nearby, the *Governors Tavern* on Bryce St by the river has indoor areas plus a riverside garden bar, pleasant in summer; lunch and dinner are served on Thursday, Friday and Saturday. *Oss's Bar* at 711 Victoria St has a good selection of inexpensive bar meals with tasty food, huge portions and interesting dishes you don't usually see in pubs, as well as all the old favourites.

Restaurants Hamilton has plenty of good restaurants. *Eldorado's Mexican Restaurant* at 10 Alma St has great atmosphere and serves large portions of tasty Mexican and Tex-Mex food. Dinner main courses cost around $13 to $20, or you can get lunch for about $6 to $11. It's open every day from 11.30 am until around 10 or 11 pm, until 3 am on Friday and Saturday.

Next door at 8 Alma St is the *No 8 Restaurant* with innovative Italian-style cuisine at around the same prices as Eldorado's; it's open for dinner every evening except Sunday. Next door again, *Adriana's Cafe & Restaurant* at 6 Alma St is an authentic Italian BYO with a relaxed atmosphere and interesting art on the walls, open for dinner every evening but Monday; Italian is spoken.

Gino's Portofino at 8 Bryce St is a bit more expensive but it's popular with the yuppie crowd for Italian and continental cuisine, with a beautiful mural on the wall and main courses around $20, plus pizzas and vegetarian selections. It's open every day from noon to 11 pm.

The *Mandarin Restaurant* at 63 Rostrevor St just off Victoria St is a most enjoyable Chinese restaurant, with good value all-you-can-eat smorgasbord meals plus an à la carte menu. The smorgasbord dinner for $15 features over 20 dishes, the smorgasbord lunch for $10 has 12 dishes, and there's free dessert, tea and coffee. It's open for dinner every night from 5.30 pm, for lunch on weekdays only.

The *Singapore Restaurant* on Garden Place, Victoria St, is another Chinese restaurant but since the food features that spicy Malaysian flavour it's a good change from the usual Chinese dishes. Across the river, *Boonjo* at 316 Grey St has a spartan decor but a good reputation for its Malaysian food; there's a set dinner for $16 or you can order curries and other Malaysian delicacies from the à la carte menu. It's a casual BYO open for dinner every night except Sunday.

Other good restaurants include *Tosca's*, a bar & grill steak-and-seafood restaurant in the rear of the *Cask & Grill* at 931 Victoria St, and the upstairs *Royal Thai* at 937 Victoria St, with genuine Thai cuisine. Opposite this is another Thai restaurant, the *Sala Thai*.

There are plenty of places you can spend more money in Hamilton if you want to pull out your fancy clothes and go up-market. Top of the top include the *Left Bank Cafe* beside the river on Marlborough Place just off Victoria St, *Harwoods* at 24 Liverpool St and *Seddon House* at 67 Seddon Rd. Finally, don't forget the meals served on the MV *Waipa Delta* (see Cruises).

Entertainment
Pubs, Bars & Nightclubs Just as there are plenty of places to eat in Hamilton, there are

also plenty of places to go out for a good time. The *Fox & Hounds* in Ward St just off Victoria St is a popular Olde English-style pub with 27 varieties of imported beer, plus Newcastle Brown, Guinness and cider on tap, pub lunches, and live entertainment on Wednesday and Thursday nights. Nearby, the *Governors Tavern* on Bryce St, beside the river, has live bands on Wednesday and Thursday nights and on Saturday afternoons from 4 to 8 pm; the riverside garden bar is lovely in summer.

Freemans Bar in the Commercial Establishment on the corner of Victoria and Collingwood Sts has live bands for dancing on Thursday, Friday and Saturday nights, plus other entertainment on Wednesday nights. The *Exchange Tavern* at 188 Victoria St has bands for dancing on Friday and Saturday nights. The *Cask & Grill* at 931 Victoria St has live jazz and blues on Friday nights. *Oss's Bar* at 711 Victoria St is a popular sports bar with good bar meals and occasional entertainment on Tuesday, Saturday and Sunday nights.

The *Down Under Bar* downstairs in the rear of the Post Office building on Victoria St has live bands for dancing on Friday and Saturday nights, but they warn that 'a high standard of dress is required' – men must wear collars, no work boots, etc.

At the opposite end of the spectrum of fussiness about dress codes, *Vinnie's Rock Bar* at 30 Alexandra St has live rock bands Wednesday to Sunday nights from around 9.30 pm to 3.30 am; it's a popular rock venue for the early 20s age group, as is the *Shakes* disco upstairs, open Wednesday to Saturday nights until around 3 or 5 am. *Legends* upstairs over the Air New Zealand office in Ward St is another disco.

Cinema & Theatre The newish *Village 5 Cinemas* upstairs in Ward St has five movie theatres showing the latest films. Live theatre venues include the *Founders Memorial Theatre* (☎ 838 6600) in Tristram St, the *Riverlea Theatre & Arts Centre* (☎ 856 5450) in Riverlea Rd off Cambridge Rd, and

the *Hamilton Operatic Society* (☎ 839 3082, 839 0215) at 59 Clarence St.

Getting There & Away

Air The Air New Zealand office (☎ 839 9835, after hours 839 9800) at 33-35 Ward St near Victoria St is open Monday to Friday from 8.30 am to 5 pm. They have direct flights to Auckland, Christchurch, Dunedin, Kaitaia, Palmerston North, Wellington and Whangarei, with connections to several other centres. Kiwi West Aviation (☎ freephone (0800) 505 000) has Monday to Friday flights to New Plymouth.

Bus All local and long-distance buses arrive and depart from the Hamilton Transport Centre on the corner of Anglesea and Ward Sts. Newmans (☎ 838 3114) and InterCity (☎ 834 3457) have separate counters; the InterCity counter also sells train tickets and Interislander ferry tickets. It's open Monday to Friday from 8 am to 5.15 pm, Saturday 9.30 am to noon, and Sunday from 10 am to noon and from 3.45 to 5.15 pm.

Frequent buses make the connection between Hamilton and Auckland (two to 2½ hours). Buses also depart for Thames (1½ to two hours), Tauranga (two hours), Whakatane (3½ hours), Opotiki (4½ hours), Rotorua (1½ hours), Taupo (two to 2½ hours), Waitomo (1½ hours), New Plymouth (four hours) and Wellington (8½ to nine hours),

A number of local bus operators run regular services to nearby towns including Raglan, Huntly, Te Awamutu, Morrinsville, Te Aroha and Thames.

The Kiwi Safaris bus (☎ freephone (0800) 800 616) operating between Auckland, Waitomo, Rotorua, Te Aroha and Thames will pick you up or drop you off by arrangement wherever you're staying in Hamilton, a convenient service which is both cheaper and more fun than the larger bus companies if you're going to these destinations.

Train The day and evening trains between Auckland and Wellington stop at the Frankton railway station outside the city, but no tickets are sold there – for train tickets you must go to the InterCity desk of the Hamilton Transport Centre on the corner of Ward and Anglesea Sts (see Bus).

The Geyserland train running twice daily between Auckland and Rotorua, and the daily Kaimai Express train between Auckland and Tauranga stop at both the Frankton station and an underground station below the Hamilton Travel Centre. To get between the two stations you must walk (about 20 minutes) or take a taxi.

Hitching Hamilton is a bit spread out, and from the centre it's a distance to good hitching spots on the outskirts. It may be best to take a local bus to the edge of town and hitch from there.

Heading south to Waitomo or New Plymouth, catch a Glenview bus to the outskirts. For hitching to Rotorua, Taupo, Tauranga or Wellington, catch a Hillcrest bus and get off by the Hillcrest School. Hitching north to Auckland is easiest if you take a Huntly bus to the outskirts or to Huntly.

From Hamilton, SH 1 leads north to Auckland and east towards Cambridge, Tauranga, Rotorua, Taupo and Wellington. SH 3 heads south towards Te Awamutu, Otorohanga, Waitomo, the Tongariro National Park and New Plymouth. SH 26 heads north-east to Te Aroha and the Coromandel Peninsula, while SH 23 heads west to Raglan.

Getting Around
Airport Transport Hamilton Airport is 12 km south of the city. The Airport Shuttle (☎ 847 5618) offers a door-to-door service between the city and the airport for $7 per person.

Bus Hamilton has a good city bus system but it only operates on weekdays, with services from around 7 am to 5.45 pm, Friday until 8.45 pm. On weekends you'll have to walk or take a taxi. All local and long-distance buses arrive and depart from the Hamilton Transport Centre on the corner of Ward and Anglesea Sts. You can buy a four-ride pass for $3, otherwise a single ride is $1.80.

A complete timetable of local city bus routes plus local buses ranging further afield (to Raglan, Huntly, Te Aroha, Thames, etc) is available at the Hamilton Transport Centre or from the visitor centre. Both places can answer any questions you may have about buses; for bus information, ring the visitor centre (☎ 839 3360), Busline (☎ 856 4579) or Hamilton City Buses (☎ 846 1975).

Car Rental There are many car rental agencies, including Rent-a-Dent (☎ 839 1049) which is more economical than most.

Around Hamilton

WAINGARO
The Waingaro Hot Springs is a popular day trip from Hamilton, with three thermal mineral pools of varying temperatures ranging from 32°C to 42°C, private spa pools, giant waterslides, children's play areas, barbecues, animals and a deer park. The complex is open every day from 9 am to 10 pm; admission is $5 (children $2.50).

You can stay near the hot springs in the *Waingaro Hot Springs Motel & Caravan Park* (☎ & fax 825 4761). Campsites with power cost $9 per person, on-site caravans are $29/38 for one/two people and motel units are $65/70. To get there, turn west at Ngaruawahia, 19 km north of Hamilton, and go 23 km; it is clearly signposted.

RAGLAN
On the coast 48 km west of Hamilton, Raglan (population 2700) is Hamilton's closest and most popular beach. A relaxed little town on a beautiful harbour, Raglan is known for its 'alternative lifestyle' ambience. The town is a popular beach resort in summer, quieter the rest of the year.

Raglan is world famous for its surfing, attracting top surfers from around the world to Te Manu Bay and Whale Bay, especially in summer when international ProAm surfing competitions are held here, though

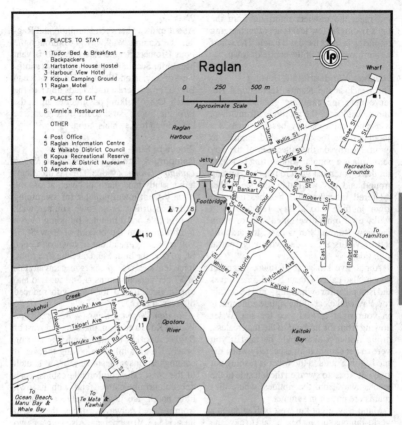

Raglan

PLACES TO STAY
1 Tudor Bed & Breakfast - Backpackers
2 Hartstone House Hostel
3 Harbour View Hotel
7 Kopua Camping Ground
11 Raglan Motel

PLACES TO EAT
6 Vinnie's Restaurant

OTHER
4 Post Office
5 Raglan Information Centre & Waikato District Council
8 Kopua Recreational Reserve
9 Raglan & District Museum
10 Aerodrome

WAIKATO

there's good surfing here all year round. The sheltered inner harbour is good for windsurfing, and there's also a variety of swimming beaches.

Information

The Raglan Information Centre (☎ 825 8129) is at 31 Bow St, right in the centre of town, on the left if you're coming from Hamilton; look for the flag saying 'Waikato District Council'. Here you can pick up free maps of the town and the region and find out everything you want to know about the area. The office is open Monday to Friday from

8.30 am to 4.30 pm, closing for an hour at lunch time from 12.30 to 1.30 pm.

Museum

The small Raglan & District Museum on Green St has exhibits on the history of the Raglan area. It's open every day during the summer school holidays, less frequently the rest of the year.

The Wharf

A pleasant and relaxing thing to do in Raglan is to walk down to the wharf around sunset and meet the trawlers returning from the day's fishing. A few locals are often hanging around to inspect the day's catch. The wharf is four blocks east of the centre of town.

Beaches, Windsurfing & Surfing

The beach at the Kopua Recreational Reserve near the camping ground, a five-minute walk over the footbridge from town, is a safe, calm estuary beach which is a popular place for children and families to swim. Nearby on the other side of the tiny peninsula is a popular windsurfing beach; to get there you must go through the camping ground and pay a $1 day use fee. Other sheltered inner-harbour beaches close to town include Cox's Bay, reached by a walkway from Government Rd or from Bayview Rd, and Puriri Park, towards the end of Wallis St, a safe swimming spot at high tide.

About five km west of town, Ngarunui Beach, also called Ocean Beach, has waves and is popular for swimming – just be certain you stay well clear of the riptide zone that is on your right as you face the sea. Water flowing from the harbour to the sea creates a strong riptide which could be fatal if you were to get caught in it, especially when the tide is going out and the water is rushing out to sea. It's best to swim on the left side of the beach, away from the riptides, where lifeguards are posted in summer.

Manu Bay, eight km west of Raglan, is a world-famous surfing beach, said to have the longest left-hand break in the world. Featured in the 1966 cult surfing film *Endless Summer*, this was the beach where a surfer caught a wave which he was still riding about 10 minutes later. The very long, uniform waves at Manu Bay are created by the angle at which the ocean swell, coming in from the Tasman Sea, meets the coastline here. Whale Bay, a couple of km further west of Manu Bay, is another excellent surfing spot.

Ruapuke Beach, a rugged stretch of coastline still further past Whale Bay, is good for surfcasting but not so good for swimming due to treacherous cross-currents; it can be reached from Ruapuke Rd.

Walking

About midway between Hamilton and Raglan, the Karamu Walkway goes through the Four Brothers Scenic Reserve. The Bryant Memorial Scenic Reserve is nine km southwest of Raglan on Whaanga Rd, past Ocean Beach. From there a track leads down to the beach. Other walking possibilities are in the Pirongia Forest Park, south of Raglan; see the Raglan to Kawhia section.

Places to Stay

Camping & Cabins The beachside *Kopua Camping Ground* (☎ 825 8283) is on a sheltered, sandy inner-harbour beach across the estuary from town, popular for swimming and windsurfing. From town you can walk to it in five or 10 minutes by going over a footbridge from the bottom of Bow St; if you're driving, head out of town on Green St, go over the bridge and take the first right. It has tent sites at $6 per person, caravan sites at $7 per person, cabins at $40 for two and tourist flats at $50 for two, with reduced off-season rates.

Raglan Wagon Cabins (☎ 825 8268) on Wainui Rd is a cheerful place six km west of Raglan, two km before Manu Bay surfing beach. Up on a hill overlooking the sea, it commands a magnificent view of this stretch of the coast. The comfortable cabins, each one colourfully painted and with its own little porch, are imaginatively constructed from restored railway carriages; the cost in these is $12.50 per person. Also here are two self-contained houses at $20 per person and plenty of tent sites at $5 per person. There's a kitchen and TV lounge and the friendly owner, who you may find working away converting more old railway carriages into cabins, has a copy of the *Endless Summer* surfing film on video.

Hostels & Guesthouses The *Tudor Bed & Breakfast-Backpackers* (☎ 825 8771) is on Wallis St facing the wharf, four blocks east of the centre of town. It's a well-equipped little place with kitchen and sitting areas, a free laundry, and just one double room, one twin room and one single room. Bed &

breakfast is $28/42 for singles/ doubles; if you bring your own sleeping bag and make your own breakfast then it's $14 per person.

The *Hartstone House* (☎ 825 8670) at 15 John St is a hostel with a bunkroom sleeping nine, and a spa pool for relaxing those tired muscles after a long day at the beach. The cost is $12 per night.

Hotels & Motels The *Harbour View Hotel* (☎ 825 8010) on Bow St in the centre of town has single/double rooms at $38/48. Across the bridge on the west side of town, the peaceful *Raglan Motel* (☎ 825 8153) at 14 Wainui Rd is right on the shore of the estuary, with singles/doubles at $50/60.

Places to Eat

Vinnie's on Green St is the favourite restaurant in town, receiving rave reviews from locals. The *Bow St Cafe* and *Seagulls* are also good, but everyone will tell you that Vinnie's is the place to go.

Entertainment

There's occasional live music the *Harbour View Hotel* on Bow St.

Getting There & Away

Local buses serving Raglan depart from the Hamilton Transport Centre.

RAGLAN TO KAWHIA

The back roads between Raglan and Kawhia, on the coast 55 km to the south, are slow and winding, but scenic and enjoyable for travelling off the beaten track. Good gravel roads, they take a while to traverse – allow at least 1½ hours' driving time between Raglan and Kawhia, not counting stops. There's not much traffic, so hitching is probably not a good idea – you need to be cycling or have a vehicle.

There are two routes between Raglan and Kawhia. From Raglan you can head west along the coast, out past Ocean Beach, Manu Bay and Whale Bay, and keep following the coast road until it turns inland and meets the interior road at Te Mata, 20 km south of Raglan. Along the way is the *Ruapuke Motor*

Camp near the beach at Ruapuke. Alternatively, from Raglan you can head towards Hamilton and take the signposted Te Mata-Kawhia turn-off.

About 12 km south-west of Raglan is **Mt Karioi**. You can make a good round-the-mountain drive, over mostly gravel roads, in a couple of hours from Raglan.

Along this route the **Te Toto Track**, starting from the Te Toto car park on Whaanga Rd (the coast road) on the western side of Mt Karioi, is strenuous but scenic, ascending steeply from the car park to a lookout point (two hours) followed by an easier stretch up to the summit of Mt Karioi (one hour). From the east side of the mountain, the **Wairake Track** is a steeper two-hour climb to the summit. You can combine the two tracks, going up one side and down the other in about four hours, but you will have to arrange transport at both ends as there is no public transport.

Mt Karioi is in one part of the Pirongia Forest Park; a larger part lies within the triangle formed by the towns of Raglan, Kawhia and Te Awamutu, with the 959-metre summit of **Mt Pirongia** clearly visible throughout the district. Tracks going through the forest park lead to the summit of Mt Pirongia – the mountain is usually climbed from Corcoran Rd on the Hamilton side. There's a hut near the summit if you want to spend the night. Maps and information about the Pirongia Forest Park are available at the DOC office in Hamilton. The township of Pirongia is 32 km south-west of Hamilton.

At Te Mata, 20 km south of Raglan, the lovely **Bridal Veil Falls** drop 55 metres over a sheer cliff into a cool pool. The route to the falls is clearly signposted in Te Mata. From the car park it's an easy 10-minute walk through native bush to the top of the falls, with a further bush walk leading down to the pool, where you could swim to cool off.

KAWHIA

The west-coast port of Kawhia (population 450), a peaceful little town on the Kawhia Harbour, is 55 km south of Raglan, 57 km west of Otorohanga and 66 km west of Te

Awamutu. The harbour is large, with many fiord-like extensions, but its entrance is narrow – the people of the *Tainui* canoe missed it on their first trip down the coast around 1350 AD, and Captain Cook also missed it when he sailed past about four centuries later in 1770, naming Albatross Point on the south side of the harbour but failing to note the harbour itself.

The main reasons people visit Kawhia are to see its historical sites, to go fishing – the town is known for its excellent fishing – and to have a relaxing time at the beach. Kawhia's main event of the year is the whale-boat rowing regatta on New Year's Day, an annual event which has been held since early this century and draws thousands of visitors.

Information
Kawhia has no information centre, but you can pick up a map, information and pamphlets about the town at the little museum beside the wharf, or at the Kawhia Motel. A public noticeboard in the centre of the tiny town has a map showing the locations of places of interest and places to stay.

Museum
The Kawhia Regional Museum Gallery is in the historic former Kawhia County Building just north of the wharf, in the centre of town. It has some interesting exhibits about the town and is a source of information, with pamphlets about Kawhia's history, its fishing and its attractions, including a map of the town. The museum is open on Saturday and Sunday most of the year – from 11 am to 4 pm from 1 November to 28 February, and from noon to 4 pm from 1 March to 31 October, opening every day from 25 December to 12 January. If you're there at another time, however, one of the people who run the museum will be happy to come down and open it for you; ring Diana & Jim (☎ 871 0714), Heather (☎ 871 0783) or Joyce (☎ 871 0703). Admission is free but donations are welcomed.

Walkway & Marae
From the museum and the wharf, a pleasant walk extends seaward along the coast, passing the historic Tangi te Korowhiti pohutukawa tree (it's unmarked) and leads to the impressive Maketu Marae. The swimming spot in front of the pohutukawa trees is popular with children. You are welcome to continue on the road, through the marae grounds, to the wooden fence behind the marae. Here, behind the fence, are the two stones, Hani and Puna, marking the burial place of the *Tainui* canoe. The marae's meeting house, Auaukiterangi, named for Hoturoa's father, is impressively carved; you must usually make arrangements a day or two in advance to visit it. Visits to this and other maraes around Kawhia can be arranged through the museum.

Forest & Beach
Behind Kawhia, the Tainui Kawhia Forest is a pine timber forest, which you can go through to reach the town's favourite open-sea beach, Ocean Beach, about three km behind the town. About two hours on each side of low tide you can find the Puia Hot Springs in the sands – just dig a hole and you have your own little natural spa. The coast is reputed to be dangerous for swimming. There's a driveable track over the dunes.

Fishing & Horse-Riding
Kawhia has great fishing of all kinds – shellfishing, surfcasting, fishing off the wharf, or fishing-boat trips. Two boats (☎ 871 0723, 871 6305) offer fishing trips inside the harbour and deep-sea fishing outside the harbour, whichever you prefer. Horse-riding can be arranged through the Beachside Store & Tearooms (☎ 871 0705) in the centre of town.

Other
There's a nine-hole golf course up on a hill above the town at the top of Pearl Ave, affording a fine view of the town and the harbour. Lawn and indoor bowling and tennis are found at the Bowling Club on the corner of Hoturoa St and Rosamund Terrace.

The *Tainui* Canoe

Though it's only a small town, Kawhia has an illustrious history. It was here that the *Tainui* canoe, one of the canoes of the Great Migration of around 1350 AD, made its final landing.

Before the *Tainui* canoe departed from the Maoris' homeland island of Hawaiki, the priests there prophesied that the departing canoe would eventually come to a favourable place where its people would make a new home, have a good life and prosper. Their prophecy went something like this:

Te Tauranga mou e Tainui	Your resting place Tainui
Ko te Taihauauru	Is the west coast
Ka whia te mataitai	(There is) an abundance of shellfish
Ka whia te ika	An abundance of fish
Ka whia te kai.	An abundance of food.

The priests told the leaders of the *Tainui* canoe what landmarks to look for, which would signify that they had arrived at the new home they were destined to find.

The *Tainui* canoe left Hawaiki, stopping at Easter Island, Raiatea (an island in French Polynesia) and Rarotonga (the principal island of the Cook Islands) as it crossed the Pacific. It landed in New Zealand at Maketu on the Bay of Plenty, accompanied by the *Arawa* canoe. The *Arawa* canoe stopped there, its people becoming the Arawa people, a large Maori tribe who still live in the Bay of Plenty and Rotorua areas today.

The leaders of the *Tainui* canoe, however – Hoturoa, the captain and Rakataura, the expert tohunga or high priest – knew that the *Tainui's* home was destined to be on the west coast. So the *Tainui* canoe took off again and persevered on. The story of how it found its final resting place is a long and heroic story. Seeking first one way and then another to get to the west coast, the Tainui people finally dragged their canoe overland at Manukau Harbour, near Auckland. Setting off south in search of the prophesied landmarks, they journeyed all the way to the South Island, still without finding their place. They turned around and came north again, still searching, and finally recognised their prophesied new home at Kawhia Harbour.

When they landed the canoe, they tied it to a pohutukawa tree on the shore, naming the tree Tangi te Korowhiti. Though the tree is not marked, it still grows with a few other pohutukawa trees on the shoreline between Kawhia town and the Maketu Marae; you can easily see it. At the end of its long voyage, the *Tainui* canoe was dragged up onto a hill and buried. After burying the canoe, Hoturoa and Rakataura placed sacred stones at either end to mark its resting place. Hani, on higher ground, is the stone marking the bow of the canoe, and Puna, the lower stone, marks the stern. These sacred stones are still there, a powerful remembrance to the Tainui people. You can walk up behind the marae and see the stones behind a wooden fence.

The prophecy that this place would be a good home for the long-journeying Tainui people did come true for them. Kawhia Harbour indeed turned out to be abundant with shellfish, fish and food. Today the Tainui tribe extends over the entire Waikato region, over the Coromandel Peninsula, north to Auckland and south to Lake Taupo and south past Mokau on the coast. Kawhia, the Maketu Marae and the burial place of the *Tainui* canoe are supremely sacred to all the Tainui people.

Another point of historical significance for Kawhia is that it was once the home of Te Rauparaha, the great Maori warrior. When pushed out of Kawhia by warring Waikato tribes in 1821, Te Rauparaha moved southwards, making his base on Kapiti Island off the west coast of the southern North Island, from there making raids all the way down to the South Island. Te Rauparaha now lies buried opposite the historic Maori church in Otaki, a town on the Kapiti Coast. See the Kapiti Coast section in the Wellington chapter for more on Te Rauparaha. ■

WAIKATO

Places to Stay

Camping & Cabins Kawhia has three camping grounds, which are practically deserted in winter but can all be full at busy periods in summer. The *Forest View Motor Camp* (☎ 871 0858) on Waiwera St is a good camping ground with tent sites, caravan sites and cabins, as is the *Beachside Motor Camp* (☎ 871 0727) on the beachfront. The *Kawhia Motor Camp* (☎ 871 0774) on Karewa St is smaller and simpler, with just tent sites and caravan sites.

Hotels & Motels The *Kawhia Hotel* (☎ 871 0700) in the centre of town is about the first thing you'll see when you enter the town. Its emphasis is more on its pub than on accommodation, but it does have a few rooms available at $25 per person. The *Kawhia Motel* (☎ 871 0865) is a friendly place in the centre of town on the corner of Jervois and Tainui Sts with units at $50/60 for singles/doubles.

Places to Eat

There's a general store and a grocery store in the centre of Kawhia where you can buy groceries; the tearoom off to one side of the Beachside Store is the only place in town you can sit down and get a hot meal, though it's only takeaway food (burgers, toasted sandwiches, hot pies, etc). A shop selling fresh fish is about a block away, near the wharf.

Getting There & Away

Bus You can take a bus between Kawhia and Te Awamutu with Kawhia Bus & Freight (☎ 871 0701, mobile (025) 966 754) every day except Sunday, when they do not operate. The bus departs from the stores in central Kawhia at 7 am for the trip to Te Awamutu. In Te Awamutu it departs from in front of the Bed-A-Buy Furniture Store on the corner of Arawata and George Sts, one block from the CPO roundabout, leaving at 10.30 am Monday to Friday, at 10 am on Saturday, for the return trip to Kawhia. The fare is $6 each way.

Road The 50-minute drive to Kawhia from Te Awamutu or Otorohanga is a scenic route offering fine views of the harbour as you approach the coast. Along the way is the Te Kauri Park Nature Reserve, with a one-hour walk from the road to a kauri grove – they say that Kawhia Harbour marks the southernmost limit that kauri trees grow naturally, though you rarely see the trees outside the Northland.

You can also reach Kawhia by the coastal back roads, either south from Raglan or north from Waitomo and Te Anga. The road to Te Anga is a good sealed road, as is the road heading inland to Te Awamutu and Otorohanga; the road heading from Kawhia north to Raglan is a good gravel road, winding and slow to traverse, but very scenic.

The circular drive from Waitomo out along the Marokopa Rd to Te Anga, north to Kawhia, inland to Otorohanga and back to Waitomo is a lovely scenic drive, as is the circle from Hamilton to Raglan, south to Kawhia passing the Bridal Veil Falls, inland to Te Awamutu and back to Hamilton. Or you can go all the way from Te Anga to Raglan on the coast, passing through Kawhia on the way. Some travellers enjoy driving or cycling down the coastal back roads all the way from Raglan in the north to Awakino and Mokau in the south, finally coming to New Plymouth (or vice versa, south to north). The road from Te Anga south to Awakino is unsealed for most of the way so it's slow going, but it's a scenic journey off the beaten track.

TE AWAMUTU

Midway between Hamilton and Otorohanga on SH 3, about 30 km from either place, Te Awamutu (population 1750) is a service town for the local dairy-farming community. Te Awamutu is noted for its rose gardens – in fact it calls itself the Rose Town of New Zealand. The **Te Awamutu Rose Garden** with over 2000 rosebushes is on SH 3, on the corner of Gorst Ave, opposite the information centre. November to April is the time to see the roses at their best; a Rose Festival is held in November each year.

There was a Maori settlement here in pre-European days, and Te Awamutu was an important site in the Waikato wars – you can still see the flat-topped hill where there was a fort. After the wars, it became a frontier town. The name Te Awamutu means 'river cut short', since the river above this point was unsuitable for canoes.

Information

The Te Awamutu Information Centre (☎ 871 3259), on the corner of Gorst Ave and SH 3, opposite the Rose Garden, is open every day from 9 am to 4.30 pm.

Museum

The Te Awamutu District Museum in the Civic Centre on Roche St houses a fine collection of Maori *taonga* (treasures), the centrepiece of which is the Uenuku:

Uenuku is one of the traditional Maori gods or spirits and it is said to manifest as a rainbow. The spirit of Uenuku is said to have been brought to New Zealand on the *Tainui* canoe. This Maori totara carving, probably the oldest in New Zealand, was made to contain this spirit. The carving was made using only stone tools.

Jennifer Evans, Te Awamutu District Museum

The museum is open Tuesday to Friday from 10 am to 4 pm; Saturday, Sunday and public holidays from 2 to 4 pm.

Other Things to See & Do

On the third Sunday of each month, from 10 am to 4 pm, the **Waikato Railway Museum** has the biggest static display of large steam locomotives in New Zealand. Railway enthusiasts can ring the information centre to inquire about the possibility of other opening times.

Every Thursday from around 10 am to 3 pm, farm animals are auctioned off at the Te Awamutu Sale, held at the sale yard on Gorst Ave, just past the information centre and the Rose Garden. It's a rural event which visitors often find fascinating.

Beginning behind the Rose Garden and opposite the sale yard, the **Pioneer Walk** goes beside the river for about 1.5 km to Memorial Park and the **Aotearoa Centre**, where there's a Maori carving and weaving institute where you can see the work in process.

The Pirongia Forest Park is 12 km west of Te Awamutu. About 10 km south is the **Wharepapa Rock Climbing Field**, with 42 rock climbs ranging from beginner's to advanced levels.

Places to Stay

The *Selwyn Park Motor Camp* (☎ 871 7478)

on Gorst Ave behind the information centre has tent sites, powered sites and cabins. *Rosetown Lodge* (☎ 871 7650) at 494 Kihikihi Rd, on SH 3 one km south of the centre of town, is a small hostel sleeping eight in a large bunkroom out behind the house. The cost is $14 per person in the bunkroom, or $7.50 per person for tent sites.

Motels in Te Awamutu include the *Rosetown Motel* (☎ 871 5779; fax 871 6800) at 844 Kihikihi Rd, the *Road Runner* (☎ 871 7420) at 141 Bond Rd and the *Park Lodge Motel* (☎ 871 5179) on the Main Ohaupo Rd.

Places to Eat

There are several places to eat in Te Awamutu, including a *Kentucky Fried Chicken*. The *Gold Star Restaurant & Takeaways* on Alexandra St, the town's main commercial street, is about 1½ blocks from the SH 3 roundabout. It's good for Chinese food, with an all-you-can-eat smorgasbord for $11 at dinnertime, or $7 to fill up just one plate. They also have regular New Zealand-style takeaways and good ice cream. It's open every day from 11.30 am until around 10 pm.

Getting There & Away

Buses and trains between Auckland and Wellington stop at Te Awamutu, as do local buses between Te Awamutu and Hamilton. See the Kawhia section for details on buses between Te Awamutu and Kawhia.

MORRINSVILLE

About 33 km north-east of Hamilton on SH 26, the road leading to Te Aroha and the Coromandel Peninsula, Morrinsville (population 5600) is a small centre for the Waikato dairying industry. In fact its tourist literature boasts that 'there are more cows within a 25 km radius of Morrinsville than in any other part of the world'! To reassure the city folks it also states, 'Our retailers are not country bumpkins'. It's a friendly town, with gardens dotted around. The **Morrinsville Museum & Pioneer Cottage** on the corner of Lorne and Anderson Sts is open on Sunday afternoons from 1.30 to 4 pm.

Ask at the Morrinsville Information Centre (☎ 889 5575) in Thames St, the main street through town, for anything you want to know about Morrinsville; it's open every day from 10 am to 4 pm.

The town's clothing, ceramics and mushroom producers offer tours on specified days of the week; tours can be arranged through the information centre. A couple of scenic reserves are nearby, or you could climb **Mt Misery** for a view over the town.

The Morrinsville Camping Ground (☎ 889 6462) in Cureton St, set in a peaceful part of the town's recreation grounds near the Olympic pool, the tennis courts and children's playgound, has tent and powered sites. Homestays and farmstays in the area, enabling visitors to experience farming and small-town life first-hand, can be arranged through the information centre or through George & Ann Tomsett (☎ 887 5873).

Buses and trains going between Hamilton and Te Aroha or Thames on the Coromandel Peninsula stop in Morrinsville.

TE AROHA
Te Aroha (population 3700), 55 km northeast of Hamilton on SH 26, is at the foot of the mountain of the same name. Te Aroha means 'love', since this is where Kahu-matamomoe sat on the summit of Mt Te Aroha and was filled with love for the land and people of Te Paeroa-o-Toi.

From the summit on a clear day you can see as far as Tongariro and Mt Egmont/Taranaki so it's well worth the climb. Te Aroha also has other good bush walks, some hot mineral and soda pools in the domain to relax in afterwards, and a couple of museums.

Orientation & Information
The clock tower at the intersection of Whitaker and Kenrick Sts marks the centre of town. From this intersection, Kenrick St is SH 26 heading south-west to Hamilton, and Whitaker St is SH 26 heading north to Paeroa and Thames. Whitaker St is the town's 'main drag', with most businesses found along it. The Domain, a large park on Whitaker St a block or two south of the clock tower, con-

tains most of the town's attractions including the Te Aroha Museum, the hot spa baths, a geyser, and walking tracks to Mt Te Aroha, a restaurant and the information centre and DOC offices.

The Te Aroha Information Centre (☎ 884 8052), on Whitaker St in the Domain, is open Monday to Friday from 10 am to 4.30 pm, Saturday and Sunday from 10 am to 3 pm. It also serves as the town's AA agent.

There's a DOC office (☎ 884 9303) in the Domain, near the spa baths. It's open Monday to Friday from 8 am to 4.30 pm, every day during school holidays, with maps and information on Mt Te Aroha and the Kaimai-Mamaku Forest Park.

Museums
The **Te Aroha Museum** in the Cadman Building in the Domain, occupying the town's original bathhouse building, has exhibits on the mining and agricultural development of the town. It's open on weekends and public holidays for most of the year, daily during the summer school holidays; opening hours are 1 to 3 pm from April to September; and 1 to 4 pm from October to March. Admission is $1 (children 50c).

Cobbers Museum at 60 Kenrick St is a private agricultural and colonial museum, which an avid collector put together at home until it got so extensive he decided to open it to the public. It's open on weekends from 10 am to 5 pm, weekdays in the evening after 5.30 pm, or by arrangement (☎ 884 8769).

History fans might also like to see New Zealand's oldest **organ**, the 1712 Renatus Harris pipe organ in St Mark's church.

Hot Pools & Geyser
The Hot Soda Water Baths in the Domain at the foot of Mt Te Aroha have two types of thermal water: hot soda water and hot mineral water. All the baths are in private hot-tub pools; the cost is $3.50 (children $2) for half an hour's soak, but only $2.80 if you show your YHA card. The baths are open every day from noon to 9 pm; it's a popular place so if you want to go on the weekend it

might be good to book yourself a spot in advance.

Behind the hot pools is the Mokena geyser, said to be the only hot soda water geyser in the world. It's quite active, going off about every half hour or so.

Walking Tracks

The walking tracks going up Mt Te Aroha start at the rear of the Domain, from behind the hot pools and geyser. It takes about an hour on a relatively easy track to ascend to the Bald Spur Lookout, also called the Whakapipi Lookout (350 metres); after that it's another two hours' steep climb to reach the summit of Mt Te Aroha (950 metres). The climb is worth it for the magnificent view.

Other tramping possibilities and things to see in the outdoors around Te Aroha include Wairongamai, five km south of town off Loop Rd, with many old relics of the gold mining era; the Killarney Lakes, three lakes 11 km south of town; and the Wairere Falls, two waterfalls, 73 and 80 metres high, which are 26 km south of Te Aroha.

Other Things to Do

There's trout fishing all year round in the Waihou River; get a fishing licence from Cockerton's Variety Store.

Places to Stay

Camping & Cabins The *Te Aroha Holiday Park* (☎ 884 9567), about two km west of Te Aroha on Stanley Rd after the racecourse, has a swimming pool, tennis courts, children's playgrounds, farm visits, car rental and more, plus they provide free pick-up from the town centre. Tent sites are $7 per person, powered sites $7.50 per person, standard cabins are $17/22.50 for one/two people, fancier cabins are $25/32, and tourist flats are $32/39.

Hostels The *Te Aroha YHA Hostel* (☎ 884 8739) on Miro St, a few blocks from the centre of town, is a pleasant small hostel (just 12 beds) and costs $10 a night. Family rooms and free bicycles are available. It has heaps of information about Te Aroha and has

organised YHA discounts to various places around town including the hot spa pools and the Blue Lady Takeaways.

Hotels & Motels The Palace Hotel (☎ 884 9995) on Whitaker St by the clock tower has rooms at $35/60 for singles/doubles. The *Te Aroha Motel* (☎ 884 9417) at 108 Whitaker St has units at $55/66.

Farmstays The information centre can provide referrals for farmstays in the area.

Places to Eat

Try the *Bank Cafe* in the historic old bank building on Whitaker St; it's a cafe in the daytime and a restaurant at night. Next door, the *Blue Lady* is basically a takeaway but it has a couple of tables so you can eat your 'takeaways' there if you like. In the Domain there's the pleasant *Domain Restaurant*.

Getting There & Away

Bus Kiwi Safaris (☎ freephone (0800) 800 616) will pick you up or drop you off at the information centre or wherever you're staying in Te Aroha, but you must book in advance. It stops at Te Aroha on its daily circle trip – Auckland, Thames, Rotorua, Waitomo, Auckland circuit (or the other way around) – making it a most convenient service if you're going to one of those destinations.

Daily InterCity buses, departing from the bus stop on Kenrick St, go to Rotorua (1½ hours), but if you want to go to Auckland on public buses you'll have to change buses at Hamilton.

If you're going to Hamilton (one hour), take the weekday local or InterCity buses departing from the bus stop on Kenrick St. InterCity buses operate weekdays between Hamilton and Thames, stopping at Morrinsville, Te Aroha and Paeroa on the way.

CAMBRIDGE

On the Waikato River 20 km south-east of Hamilton, Cambridge (population 700) is a small, peaceful town with a charming rural English atmosphere. Cricket is played on the village green in the centre of town. Cambridge is famous for the breeding and training of thoroughbred horses.

Information

The Cambridge Information Centre (☎ 827 6033; fax 827 3505) on the corner of Victoria and Queen Sts is open Monday to Friday from 8 am to 4.30 pm. They can give you lots of information on the town including free maps, information on walks, arts & crafts and antiques shops, etc.

Things to See & Do

Cambridge has a number of arts & crafts and antiques shops. Best known is the award-winning **Cambridge Country Store**, with a great variety of merchandise in an attractive building converted from the town's old Presbyterian church. You'll see it on SH 1 in the centre of town; it's open every day from 8.30 am to 5 pm. Another old church worth seeing, also on SH 1, is the 100-year-old **St Andrew's Anglican Church**, a white church with a beautiful wooden interior with fine stained-glass windows and a high steeple sheathed in copper. The outside is beautiful but it's still a surprise to see the beauty of the interior.

The **Cambridge Museum**, occupying the historic 1909 former Cambridge Courthouse building on Victoria St, is open Tuesday to Saturday from 10 am to 4 pm, Sunday and public holidays from 2 to 4 pm. **Te Koutu Lake** at the Te Koutu Park in the centre of Cambridge is a peaceful bird sanctuary.

Other attractions in Cambridge include jet-boat and drift-boat rides on the Waikato River, visits to the Cambridge dairy factory, and walking on tracks along both sides of the Waikato River and around Te Koutu Lake. The information centre has free pamphlets showing all the town's walking tracks.

There are also walks further afield. From SH 1 take the turn-off at Cambridge and in about a five-minute drive you'll reach the Maungakawa Scenic Reserve, a regenerating forest with some exotic timber species and a fairly easy short bush walk. From the eastern side of Mt Maungakawa, a track

suitable for experienced trampers ascends from Tapui Rd; it takes half a day to walk there and back. Also about a five-minute drive from town, Mt Mungatautri is another good walking spot; it takes about 1½ hours to climb to the summit.

Places to Stay

Camping & Cabins The *Cambridge Domain Motor Camp* (☎ 827 5649) in Scott St, Leamington, about 1.5 km from the centre of town, has tent sites at $6.50 per person, powered sites at $7.50 per person and cabins at $10 per person.

Hostels The *Cambridge Country Lodge* (☎ 827 8373) is a pleasant hostel in a rural setting on a two-hectare farmlet 100 metres down Peake Rd, turning off from SH 1, a km north of Cambridge. They offer courtesy transport to the Hamilton railway station, Hamilton airport and Cambridge buses; bicycles are also available to help you get around, and there are fresh eggs and vegetables from the farm. You can do your own cooking or home-prepared meals are available. The cost is $12 per person with your own sleeping bag in single, double and dorm rooms, $14/25 for singles/doubles with a made-up bed.

Hotels & Motels Hotels include the *Masonic Hotel* (☎ 827 5500) in Duke St East with single/double rooms at $30/45 and the *National Hotel* (☎ 827 6731) in Lake St with singles/doubles at $32/55.

Motels in Cambridge tend to be a bit expensive, around $55 to $65 for singles, $75 for doubles; they include the *Cambrian Lodge Motel* (☎ 827 7766, 827 6019) at 63 Hamilton Rd, the *Captains Quarters Motor Inn* (☎ & fax 827 8989) at 57A Hamilton Rd, the *Colonial Court Motel* (☎ 827 5244) at 37 Vogel St and the *Leamington Motel* (☎ 827 4057, 827 4725) at 90 Shakespeare St. Other places are more expensive.

Farmstays Ask at the information centre for referrals to farmstays in the area.

Getting There & Away

Local buses to Cambridge operate from the Hamilton Transport Centre. Long-distance buses from Hamilton to Rotorua or the Bay of Plenty stop in Cambridge.

KARAPIRO & ARAPUNI

Karapiro, furthest downstream of a chain of hydroelectric power stations and dams on the Waikato River, is 28 km south-east of Hamilton, eight km past Cambridge, just off SH 1. The road passes over the dam and the lake is popular for aquatic sports. For camping at the lake, the Karapiro Lake Domain (☎ 827 4178) beside the lake has tent sites, powered sites and bunkrooms.

Arapuni, the first government-built hydroelectric station on the river, is 66 km from Hamilton via Te Awamutu. Take SH 3 to just south of Te Awamutu, and turn left (east) at Kihikihi. It is also accessible from Karapiro or Tirau on SH 1. The dam was built across the Arapuni Gorge and is worth a look. Visitors are allowed access to most of the works.

The King Country

The King Country is the region just south of the Waikato region. It includes the Otorohanga, Waitomo and Taumarunui districts; it has no major cities, but its principal towns are Otorohanga, Te Kuiti and Taumarunui. Travelling south from Hamilton, Otorohanga is the first town you'll reach when you enter the King Country.

The King Country is named after the Maori King Movement, which developed in the Waikato in the late 1850s and early 1860s. When King Tawhiao and his people were forced to move from their Waikato land after the Waikato Wars of 1863 to 1864 against British troops, they came south to this region which was as yet unaffected by Pakeha invasion. Legend has it that King Tawhiao placed his white top hat, symbol of the kingship, on a large map of New Zealand and declared that all the land it covered

would be under his mana or authority. The area coincided roughly with the present-day districts of Otorohanga, Waitomo and Taumarunui, extending westwards to the coast and eastwards as far as Lake Taupo.

For several decades the King Country remained the stronghold of King Tawhiao and other Maori chiefs, who held out there against the Pakehas longer than the Maoris did anywhere else in New Zealand. This area was forbidden to the Pakehas by Maori law until the 1880s, and was even then not much penetrated by Pakehas until, with the consent of the Maori chiefs, the Auckland-Wellington Main Trunk Railway Line entered the region in 1891. The earliest Europeans to settle in Otorohanga were timber millers, the first of them arriving in 1890. The laying of the railway to form a continuous line from Auckland to Wellington in 1908 finally marked the end of the region's isolation, though even today a powerful Maori influence is still present.

From 1884, when Pakehas were allowed into the district, until 1955, the King Country was 'dry' (alcohol was prohibited). This condition was apparently imposed by Maori chiefs when they agreed to the Europeans building the railway through their country, opening it up even more to the outside world. Needless to say there are now numerous hotels everywhere, so you won't go thirsty.

OTOROHANGA

Otorohanga (population 2600), in the upper Waipa basin, is on SH 3, 59 km south of Hamilton and 16 km from Waitomo Caves. Principally a dairying and sheep farming community, it is the northernmost township of the King Country. Most people pass through Otorohanga on the way to the Waitomo Caves, or stay overnight in Otorohanga and use it as a base. It's a convenient base for visits to Waitomo, Kawhia and Pirongia.

The name Otorohanga means 'food for a long journey'. Legend says that a Maori chief who was on his way to Taupo passed through Otorohanga carrying little food, but that through magic incantations he was able to make the food last for the journey.

Orientation & Information

SH 3 is the main road through town; it's called Maniapoto St for the few blocks that it passes through town.

The Otorohanga Visitor Information Centre (☎ 873 8951; fax 873 8398) on the corner of Maniapoto and Tuhoro Sts is open Monday to Friday from 9 am to 5 pm, Saturday and public holidays from 10 am to 3 pm and Sunday from 11 am to 2 pm. In this small town the information centre serves a variety of functions: in addition to giving information about Otorohanga, Waitomo and places nearby, it is also the AA agent, the agent for InterCity and Newmans bus tickets, train and Interislander ferry tickets, and the InterCity, Newmans and Waitomo Shuttle bus stop.

The post office is on the corner of Maniapoto and Ballance Sts. Public toilets are opposite the railway station.

Kiwi House

The well-signposted Otorohanga Kiwi House is the town's main attraction and worth a visit. In a kiwi house night and day are reversed, so you can watch the kiwis in daytime under artificial moonlight. There are also various other native birds including some keas, which more than live up to their reputation for being inquisitive. The walk-in aviary is the largest in New Zealand. Other birds you can see include morepork owls, hawks, wekas; reptiles include tuataras.

The Kiwi House is open from 10 am to 5 pm every day, except from June to August when it closes at 4 pm. The last admission is half an hour before closing time. Admission is $6 (children $2).

Historical Society Museum

Near the Kiwi House is the Otorohanga Historical Society Museum (☎ 873 8758, 873 8462) in the Old Courthouse on Kakamutu Rd. It's open from 2 to 4 pm on Sunday, but at other times ring up and the friendly old guy who maintains it will wander over and open it up for you. Make a donation; it's a nice little local museum.

Other Things to See & Do

There is a **deer park** near the Kiwi House. It's basically a high-fenced paddock where you can look at the deer from a distance, and there's also an enclosure with peacocks and ducks. There's no entry charge but there is a donation box. Between the deer park and the Kiwi House are kiwi breeding pens and the **Rhododendron Gardens.**

Nearby there's an outdoor Olympic-size **swimming pool** open daily in summer, from around December to the end of March, and an indoor heated pool open every day from 1 May to 20 December; opening times are available on leaflets at the pool. Admission is $2 (children $1, family $5).

The **Otorohanga Sale,** the biggest in the King Country area, is held every Wednesday at the Otorohanga Sale Yards on the corner of Otewa Rd and the Old Te Kuiti Rd, on the south side of town. Sheep, cattle, pigs, farm equipment and actually just about anything goes on auction; the bidding gets in good swing by about 10 am and goes on until the sale breaks up around 2 pm or so. Visitors usually find it fascinating.

The Otorohanga County Fair is held the first weekend in February at the Island Reserve on the south side of town.

Places to Stay

Camping The *Otorohanga Kiwitown Caravan Park* (☎ 873 8214, freephone (0800) 808 279; fax 873 8214) is on Domain Rd, adjacent to the Kiwi House – you can hear the kiwis calling at night. There's a BBQ area, with free wood for BBQs; tent sites are $6.50/12 for one/two people, powered sites are $14, and on-site caravans are $26 for two people.

Hostels The *Otorohanga Associate YHA Hostel* (☎ 873 8908) is in a private home at 70 Main North Rd, about a km north of the CPO on SH 3. It sleeps eight and the cost is $12 per night. Try to arrive before 8.30 pm. Since this is an associate YHA hostel, you can stay with or without a YHA card.

Art Deco architecture, Napier, East Coast
Top photograph (TW)
Other Photographs (JW)

Top: Wellington (RS)
Bottom: Jerusalem, Whanganui River Road, Central North Island (NK)

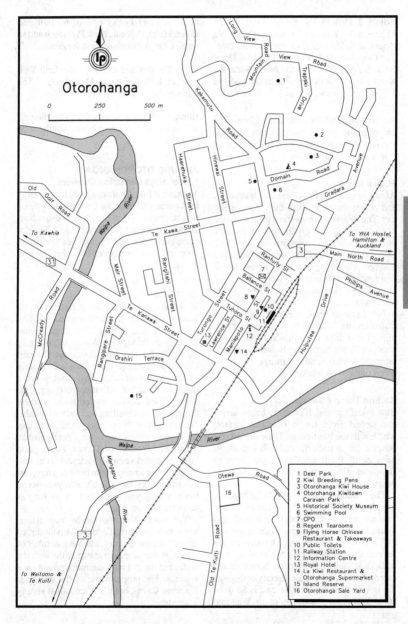

Otorohanga

0   250   500 m

To Kawhia

31

Old Golf Road

Waipa River

Kakamutu Road

Haerehuka Street

Hinewai Street

Long View Road

Mountain View Road

Trapski Drive

View Road

Gradara Avenue

Domain Road

● 1

● 2

● 3

▲ 4

● 5   ● 6

Te Kawa Street

McCready Road

Main Street

Rangitahi Street

Te Kanawa Street

Rangiare Street

Orahiri Terrace

● 15

Turongo Street

Lawrence St

Tuhoro St

Maniapoto

Ranfurly St

Ballance St

St

7 ✉

8 ▲

9

10

11

12

13 ■

▲ 14

To YHA Hostel,
Hamilton &
Auckland

3

Main North Road

Phillips Avenue

Huipurea Drive

Waipa River

Mangaorongo River

Otewa Road

Old Te Kuiti Road

16

3

To Waitomo &
Te Kuiti

1 Deer Park
2 Kiwi Breeding Pens
3 Otorohanga Kiwi House
4 Otorohanga Kiwitown
   Caravan Park
5 Historical Society Museum
6 Swimming Pool
7 CPO
8 Regent Tearooms
9 Flying Horse Chinese
   Restaurant & Takeaways
10 Public Toilets
11 Railway Station
12 Information Centre
13 Royal Hotel
14 La Kiwi Restaurant &
   Otorohanga Supermarket
15 Island Reserve
16 Otorohanga Sale Yard

Hotels & Motels The *Royal Hotel* (☎ 873 8129) on Te Kanawa St has single/double rooms at $35/50, or $65 with private bath. The *Otorohanga & Waitomo Colonial Motel* (☎ & fax 873 8289) on the Main North Rd about a km north of town has units at $63 to $73 for one person, $70 to $80 for two.

Farmstays & B&Bs A number of farms and homes in the area welcome guests for B&B and farmstay arrangements. The information centre keeps a current list.

Places to Eat

Along Maniapoto St are several takeaways and coffee shops, most of them open every day. The *Regent Tearooms* is a pleasant place open every day from 6 am to 5 pm, until 7 pm on Friday. Other tearooms include *Dot's Dairy Coffeepot* and the *Troubador Coffee Lounge*. Also along here is the *Flying Horse Chinese Restaurant & Takeaways*. The *Otorohanga Workingmens Club* also has a restaurant.

For a fancier meal, the licensed *La Kiwi* restaurant on Maniapoto St is open every night for dinner. The *Royal Hotel* on Te Kanawa St has bistro meals, a licensed restaurant, a pub, and a lounge bar with entertainment on weekends.

Getting There & Away

Bus InterCity and Newmans buses arrive and depart from the information centre, which sells the bus tickets. There are several buses a day in each direction. It's about 30 minutes to Waitomo Caves, one hour to Hamilton, 3½ hours to Auckland and three hours to New Plymouth.

The Waitomo Shuttle (☎ 873 8279/8214, freephone (0800) 808 279) is the most convenient service between Otorohanga and Waitomo, picking you up and dropping you off wherever you wish. Departures are several times daily in each direction, with additional times on request; bookings are essential and can be made directly or through the information centre. The cost is $6 to or from Waitomo. Once you're in Waitomo

there are several other options for transport to Auckland, Rotorua, New Plymouth and so on; see the Waitomo section for details.

Train The day and evening Auckland-Wellington trains stop at Otorohanga. The railway station is in the centre of town.

Hitching Hitching is easy from Otorohanga, whether you're heading north, south, or to Waitomo.

AROUND OTOROHANGA
Otorohanga Carnation Growers

Ten km out from Otorohanga on the highway to Kawhia (SH 31), the Otorohanga Carnation Growers (☎ 873 7400) have about 10,000 sq metres of glasshouses. They're open every day and visitors are welcome; they ask that you telephone before you arrive.

WAITOMO

Waitomo (population 300) is famous for its limestone caves; the whole region is riddled with caves and strange limestone formations. Tours through the Waitomo Cave (also called the Glow-worm Cave), the Ruakuri Cave and the Aranui Cave have been feature attractions for decades. In recent years a whole new batch of activities has cropped up – organised caving expeditions, rafting through caves, abseiling and various combinations of the three, plus horse trekking, white water rafting and more. There's also an excellent Museum of Caves, some good bush walks and a newish backpackers hostel. Visitors used to stop for an hour or a day, just to see the caves; now there's plenty to choose from to keep you enthralled for as long as you care to keep going.

The name Waitomo means *wai*, water; *tomo*, hole or shaft. It's aptly named: dotted throughout the countryside are a number of tomos, shafts dropping abruptly through the surface of the ground into underground cave systems. The proper name of the village is Waitomo Caves, but it's often called simply Waitomo.

Rivers going underground, great springs emerging from the ground, independent hollows and basins instead of connecting valleys, deep potholes and vast caves, isolated tower-like hills...these are some of the distinctive features of karst, the name given to the kinds of country that owe their special characteristics to the unusual degree of solubility of their component rocks in natural waters.

from *Karst* by J N Jennings, Australian National
University Press, Canberra, 1971

Information

Waitomo is eight km west of the main highway, SH 3. The information centre is at the Museum of Caves (☎ 878 7640; fax 878 6184) in the centre of the village, half a km before the Glow-worm Cave. The museum also serves as the post office and as the booking agent for most of the activities and transport around Waitomo; most transport stops outside the door. It's open every day from 8.30 am to 5.30 pm; until 5 pm in winter from Easter to the end of October; and later, until around 8 pm, in January.

Still more caving information is available at the Waitomo Caves – Tomo Group Hut (see Hostels).

Groceries are available at the general store beside the museum, but the choice is wider at nearby towns like Otorohanga or Te Kuiti. If you're planning to camp or stay at a hostel and prepare your own food it's worth bringing supplies with you.

Museum of Caves

If you want to find out more about caves, visit the excellent Waitomo Museum of Caves. You'll learn about how caves are formed, the fauna and flora that live in caves, the history of caves and cave exploration. Exhibits include a cave model, fossils of extinct birds and animals that have been discovered in caves, and a cave crawl for the adventurous. There's also a 27-minute audiovisual presentation about caving, and 10-minute videos about glow-worms and the many other natural attractions found in the Waitomo area.

The museum is open every day from 8.30 am to 5.30 pm; until 5 pm in winter from Easter to the end of October; and later, until

around 8 pm, in January. Admission is $3.50 (children free); admission is also included free with various activities, or you can get a 'museum-cave special' for $16.50 (children $8.50) if you visit the Glow-worm or Aranui caves (read on).

Between the museum and the general store there's a carved Maori canoe and some limestone formations with interesting plaques telling about karst and the area's limestone geology.

The Caves

There are three major touring caves in Waitomo – the Waitomo (Glow-worm), the Aranui, and the Ruakuri.

The Waitomo Glow-worm Cave had been known to the local Maoris for a long time, but the first European to explore it was English surveyor Fred Mace, who was shown the cave on 28 December 1887 by the Maori chief Tane Tinorau. Mace prepared an account of the expedition, a map was made and photographs given to the government, and before long Tane Tinorau was operating tours of the cave. So by now, people have been touring the cave for over a century.

The Glow-worm Cave is a big cave with the usual assortment of stalactites and stalagmites, until you board a boat and swing off onto the river. As your eyes grow accustomed to the dark you'll see a Milky Way of little lights surrounding you – these are the glow-worms. You can see them in other caves and in other places around Waitomo, and in other parts of New Zealand, but the ones in this cave are still something special to see; conditions for their growth here are just about perfect, so there is a remarkable number. The tour takes about 45 minutes.

The Aranui and Ruakuri caves are three km further up the road from the Glow-worm Cave. The Ruakuri Cave is an active cave, with large, dripping caverns where stalactites and stalagmites are still being formed, plus other interesting formations including straws, cave coral, flowstone, rimstone and columns. It also has glow-worms (not as many as in the Waitomo cave, but they're here), fossils of scallops as big as your hand,

KING COUNTRY

KING COUNTRY

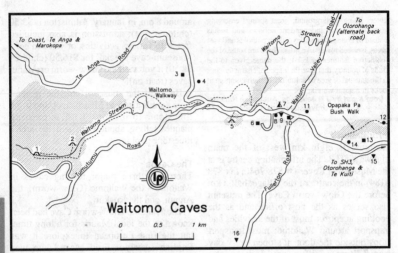

Waitomo Caves

0   0.5   1 km

1   Ruakuri Cave, Ruakuri Natural Bridge
    & Ruakuri Scenic Reserve
2   Aranui Cave
3   Waitomo Caves – Tomo Group Hut
4   Tokikarpu Marae
5   Waitomo Glow-worm Cave & Grotto
6   THC Waitomo Caves Hotel
7   Waitomo Caves Motor Camp
8   Waitomo Museum of Caves,
    Information Centre &
    Waitomo Down Under
9   Waitomo General Store & Tearooms
10 Waitomo Guest Lodging
11 Rabbit World
12 Opapaka Pa
13 Juno Hall
14 Ohaki Maori Village & Crafts Centre
15 Merrowvale Tearooms
16 Roselands Restaurant

and a river running through, where if you're lucky you may be able to stand on a bridge and see the lights of the Black Water Rafters coming through. The tour takes about an hour.

The Aranui Cave is different from the other caves; its beauty is more delicate, with thousands of tiny, hollow 'straw' stalactites hanging from the ceiling, and there's no river running through. It takes about 45 minutes to tour this cave. Transport to the Aranui Cave is not included with the tour ticket. You may be able to catch a ride with the tour guide or other visitors, but if not you'll have to hitch or walk.

All three caves have their own distinct characteristics and beauty, and all are worth seeing. A walk-through cave tour seems very tame if you've been on some of the other caving activities around Waitomo, but these are still beautiful caves to see. The Glow-worm cave is the most popular cave and its tours, with their large crowds of tourists, may seem like a bit of a tourist rush-through; it's unfortunate that this is all that many people ever see of the Waitomo area – arriving in a big tour bus around lunch time, being shuttled through the one cave and off again. If you do visit this cave, try to go on the first tour of the day – you'll get to visit some smaller caverns that the big groups later in the day can't enter for fear of depleting the oxygen supply.

The Waitomo and Aranui caves can be visited independently or you can get a combined ticket for both. Tickets are sold at the

Glow-worms

Glow-worms are the larvae of a type of gnat called a fungus gnat, which looks much like a large mosquito except without mouth parts. The larvae glow-worms have luminescent organs which produce a soft, greenish light. Living in a sort of 'hammock' hanging down from an overhang, they weave sticky threads which hang down and catch unwary insects attracted by their lights. When an insect flies towards the light, it gets stuck in the hanging threads and becomes paralysed, after which the glow-worm reels the thread up and then eats the insect.

The larval stage lasts for six to nine months, depending on how much food the glow-worm gets – the more food, the quicker it can mature. When the glow-worm has grown to about the size of a matchstick it goes into a pupa stage, much like a cocoon. The adult fungus gnat emerges about two weeks later.

The adult of the species may be caught and eaten by the larval glow-worm. Even if it avoids that fate, the adult insect does not live very long because it does not have a mouth; it emerges, mates, lays eggs and dies, all within about two or three days. The sticky eggs, laid in groups of 40 or 50, hatch in about three weeks to become larval glow-worms.

Glow-worms thrive in moist, dark caves, but they can survive anywhere if they have the requisites of moisture, an overhang to hang from, and insects to eat. Waitomo is famous for its glow-worms but you can see them in many other places around New Zealand, both in caves and outdoors. Similar glow-worms exist in south-east Australia but the New Zealand variety is a distinct species, *Arachnocampa luminosa*.

When you come upon glow-worms, don't touch their hammocks or their hanging threads, try not to make loud noises, and don't shine a light right on them. In daylight their lights fade out, and if you shine a torch right on them they will dim their lights. It takes the lights a few hours to become bright again, during which time the glow-worm will catch no food. The glow-worms that shine the brightest are the ones that are the hungriest. ∎

KING COUNTRY

Glow-worm Cave & Grotto, 500 metres past the Museum of Caves. Entry to just one cave costs $14.50 (children $7.25), the combined two-cave ticket is $22 (children $11, family $50). There's also a 'lunch-cave special' offering one cave tour and a BBQ lunch at the THC Waitomo Caves Hotel for $31 (children $16), and a 'museum-cave special' for one cave tour and a visit to the Museum of Caves for $16.50 (children $8.25).

The 45-minute tours of the Glow-worm Cave depart every day on the hour from 9 am to 4 pm, with the last tour of the day at 4.30 pm. From late October to Easter there's also a 5.30 pm tour, and there may be even more at the height of the summer season. Aranui Cave tours begin at 10 and 11 am and at 1, 2 and 3 pm, and also take about 45 minutes.

One-hour tours of the Ruakuri Cave operate on the hour from 9 am to 4 pm every day. Tickets are sold at the Museum of Caves; the cost is about $10 for a cave tour alone, or $12 for a combined museum-cave ticket.

Check out the large Tane Mahuta carving outside the Glow-worm Cave ticket office. It was commissioned in 1987 for the centennial of the first recorded exploration of the Waitomo (Glow-worm) Cave and has many interesting figures relating to the area and the caves. A pamphlet explaining the various details of the carving is available at the Glow-worm Cave ticket office and at the Museum of Caves.

Cave Activities

Black Water Rafting I & II Black Water Rafting started in Waitomo in 1987 and quickly became one of New Zealand's most popular adventures.

Black Water Rafting I is a three-hour trip down a subterranean river through the Ruakuri Cave, expertly guided and organised in groups of no more than 12 at a time. First you get into a wetsuit and caver's helmet with a light on the front, grab a black inner tube, and you're off on a trek through the cave which involves leaping over a small waterfall, floating through a long glow-worm covered passageway, and plenty of Kiwi-style joking and laughs. At the end of the journey there's a hot shower and soup to warm up your innards, but in the wetsuit you probably won't get too cold.

The $50 fee includes admission to the Museum of Caves for more education on glow-worms and caves, and altogether it's well worth the outlay. Trips leave from the museum several times daily; because it's so popular, you should book as far in advance as you can – about a week in advance on weekends and in summer, if possible – to be sure of getting a spot. Bookings are made at the Museum of Caves. This tour is raved about by just about everyone who goes on it.

More recently another trip, called Black Water Rafting II, has been added. It goes through a different part of the Ruakuri Cave and it's a lot more caving adventure – an all-day caving expedition, it includes all the features of BWR I but also involves abseiling into the caves, with abseiling instruction before you take off. The trip takes six hours; the cost is $100.

Black & White Rafting Waitomo Rafting operates 3½-hour white water rafting trips on the Grade 4 Mokau River, with morning and afternoon trips departing from the Museum of Caves. By itself it costs $50, but you can also do a Black & White Rafting combination trip, featuring both White and Black Water Rafting, for $95; altogether it's a full 7½ hour day. A visit to the Museum of Caves, where the bookings are made, is included with either one.

Waitomo Down Under Waitomo Down Under operates a variety of adventures. Their three-hour Cave Tubing trip is similar to Black Water Rafting; wearing a wetsuit and caving helmet, you go through the Te Ana Roa cave ('long cave') in inner tubes, going over *two* waterfalls (one on a slide) and getting a good close-up view of some glow-worms along the way. It, too, ends with a hot shower, hot soup and tea, and includes a visit to the local marae along with some Maori culture; the cost is $45.

Waitomo Down Under also does a 1½-hour Adventure Caving trip through a different cave which includes glow-worms and a crystalline white section known as 'The Pretties'. The entrance is a bit of a tight squeeze but it opens up after that. Or they can take you on a free-hanging 20-metre abseil down into a tomo, good for first-time abseilers – they give you all the abseiling instruction you need and it takes about an hour or two.

The cost for the Adventure Caving trip is from $25, the abseiling is from $40, but you can do all three of their activities for $100, whether on the same day or different days. They also offer horse trekking tours from $20.

The Waitomo Down Under office (☎ & fax 878 6577) is next door to the Museum of Caves. Make bookings directly with them, not at the museum. It is operated by descendants of Tane Tinorau, the Maori chief who introduced Fred Mace to the Waitomo Cave and who led tours there a century ago.

Lost World And now...to try to describe the indescribable.

This is what the first explorers had to say about it:

'... Soon we came to the first tomo many hundreds of feet deep. We cleared the growth of fern which surrounded it, and made our way down to a ledge of rock overhanging a cave. Mr Pavet was first down and his calls of delight we thought were only a hoax, but as each of us came to the brink of the chasm we fairly shouted with delight and astonishment. We had fallen upon a "wonderland". The sight that met our view was enchanting. Fairyland was before us. Away down, near what appeared to be its very depths was a large plateau of moss and ferns, but so far down that they appeared only small topped matter showing all the tints of green. As we looked we more than half expected to see the pixies come dancing out. This is no imagination. It was fairyland without fairies.'

excerpt from The King Country Chronicle, 16 December 1906.

We found it about the same when we went through.

With 100 metres (300 feet) of free-hanging abseiling to get into the Lost World cave, this is the deepest commercial abseil in

New Zealand, and quite possibly the deepest commercial abseil into a cave in the world. It won the New Zealand Tourism Award, and it's right up there as one of the most amazing things you can do in this country. And you don't need any prior abseiling or caving experience to do it – the guides are the best professionals around and they're used to dealing with first-timers.

There are two ways to visit the Lost World. The principal trip is a two-day affair, with about five hours of professional abseiling instruction on the first day and a nine-hour physical and emotional experience on the second day. This is when you abseil down into the cave, then by a combination of walking, rock climbing, spider-walking, inching along narrow rock ledges, wading and swimming through a subterranean river and assorted other caving manoeuvres, you take a three-hour journey through a magnificent 30-metre-high cave to get back out, passing thousands of glow-worms, fossilised oysters the size of dinner plates, amazing rock and cave formations with stalactites, stalagmites, flowstone and all the rest, waterfalls and more. The cost is $395, it goes twice a week and you'll never forget it.

The other option is a tandem abseil into the cave. It's the same awe-inspiring abseil, but you do without the day of instruction because you go down with a professional guide right beside you on another rope, telling you how to do it as you go. When you reach the bottom, you walk for just half an hour into the cave, passing the 'Jesus Rock' made famous in photographs, and then just before reaching the point where the underground river starts, you climb up via another amazing vertical cavern to get back to the surface. The tandem trip takes only four hours and costs $195.

The Lost World can also be visited as a 'Gruesome Twosome' combo with the Haggas Honking Hole trip; read on. Bookings for all Lost World trips are made at the Museum of Caves.

Haggas Honking Hole Yet another amazing trip presented by the Lost World people, this four-hour caving trip includes professional abseiling instruction followed by a caving trip with four abseils, rock climbing, and going along a subterranean river with waterfalls. Along the way you see glow-worms and a variety of cave formations – stalactites, stalagmites, columns, flowstone, cave coral and all the rest. It's a good experience for seeing real caving in action – you're using caving equipment and going through caverns of various sizes, squeezing through some tight spots and narrow passageways as well as traversing huge caverns.

These trips go every day. The cost is $95; or you can do a 'Gruesome Twosome' combining this with the Lost World tandem abseil for $250. Both four-hour trips, they can be done together on one day, or on different days.

Ohaki Maori Village & Crafts Centre

The Ohaki Maori Village is a replica of a pre-European Maori pa. It's also a centre for traditional Maori arts & crafts, with demonstrations and displays of Maori weaving and a shop where the arts & crafts are sold. The centre is open every day from 10 am to 4.30 pm. Admission to the Maori village is $2.50 (children $1.50), a weaving demonstration is $5 (children $1.50), or you can do both for $6 (children $2). The centre is two km from Waitomo village, on the road leading to the highway.

Also here is a one-hour return track to the Opapaka Historic Pa Site, up on a hill behind the centre; see Bush Walks.

Rabbit World

In a red barn about 400 metres before you reach Waitomo village, Rabbit World is a centre for products made with the fur of special German Angora rabbits. It's mostly a shop selling raw Angora fibre, yarn and crafts; for $3 (children 50c) you can have a short tour to see the rabbits, and if you're there at the right time (usually around 1 pm, but times vary) you can see how the rabbits are shorn. It's open every day from 9 am to 5 pm.

Horse-Trekking

Waitomo Horse-Trekking operates from the Juno Hall hostel (see Hostels), with a variety of rides and overnight treks through Waitomo wilderness areas. The cost is $20 for a one-hour ride, $30 for two hours, $50 for a half day, and $70 for a full-day ride. Waitomo Down Under also does horse treks.

Bush Walks

The Museum of Caves has free pamphlets on various walks in the area, and there are some good ones. One is a 15-minute forest walk at the Glow-worm Cave ticket office, where there's a grove of California redwood trees. Also from here, the five-km, three-hour Waitomo Walkway takes off through farmland and follows the Waitomo Stream to the Ruakuri Scenic Reserve, where a half-hour return walk passes by the river and caves and a natural limestone bridge.

This half-hour return walk in the Ruakuri Scenic Reserve can be done by itself, beginning from the Ruakuri and Aranui Caves car park; it's a beautiful bush walk by day and after dark you can see thousands of glowworms along the path. Be sure to bring a torch (flashlight) if you come at night as it's very dark in this bush.

A one-hour return walk, the Opapaka Pa Bush Walk takes off from the car park of the Otaki Maori Village & Crafts Centre, leading up to a pre-European Maori pa site on a hill. Plaques along the way describe traditional Maori medicinals found in the forest, traditional forest lore and the pa site itself.

Many other good walks are found west of Waitomo on the Marokopa Rd; see Around Waitomo for more on these.

Other Things to Do

There's golf, squash and bridge at the Waitomo Golf Course on SH 3 heading north towards Otorohanga.

Places to Stay

Camping & Cabins The *Waitomo Caves Motor Camp* (☎ 878 7639) is opposite the general store, which is where you book into the camp. Campsites cost $6 per person, or $7 with power. It also has cabins at $10 or $15 for one person and $8 or $10 per person if you're sharing.

Both the hostels will also allow you to pitch a tent.

Hostels The Waitomo Caves Associate YHA Hostel (☎ 878 8227; fax 878 8858) is at the THC Waitomo Caves Hotel right in the centre of Waitomo, in a separate building that once served as the staff housing. It sleeps 25, the cost is $15 per night, and since it's an associate YHA hostel you can stay with or without a YHA card.

Juno Hall (☎ 878 7639) is on the main road in from the highway to the caves, opposite the Merrowvale Tearooms, one km before the Museum of Caves. It sleeps 30 people and is quite popular; the cost per person is $13 in dorm rooms, $16 in twin or double rooms, or $6.50 for tent sites. They operate a courtesy van to the hitching spot at the junction of SH 3, to the caves and to the pub; they also do horse trekking, hunting and fishing trips.

Two km further on past the Glow-worm Cave, the *Waitomo Caves – Tomo Group Hut* (☎ 878 7442) has more rustic hut-style accommodation, also with room for 30 people (lots more with a squeeze). The cost is $8 per night; you can pitch a tent on the lawn for the same price. Bring your own sleeping bag. If you're walking up to the hostel from the village, buy some goods at the store or you'll have a two-km walk back from the hostel.

The hostel is also the clubroom of the Hamilton Tomo Group, the largest caving club in New Zealand. If you're lucky you may be invited on a caving trip to one of the many non-tourist caves in the area, particularly on weekends when the hostel fills up with cavers. The hut has detailed maps on many caves but it's not advisable to go off caving alone in the area. Caves can be dangerous: some have networks spanning several km and people have been lost underground. Altogether there are over 100 km of caves in the Waitomo region, many still unexplored, so there's ample field for caving adventure.

Guesthouses & Farmstays *Waitomo Guest Lodging* (☎ 878 7641) is conveniently situated just 100 metres from the Museum of Caves in the centre of the village. It's a pleasant, friendly B&B with four guest rooms, each with private bath. Bed & breakfast costs $25 or $30 per person.

Several homes and farms in the area offer lodging and B&B arrangements. Check with the Museum of Caves, where many are listed.

Hotels The *THC Waitomo Caves Hotel* (☎ 878 8227; fax 878 8858) in the centre of the village is a historic hotel built in 1908 to accommodate tourists coming to visit the caves, and extended in 1928. It has standard rooms at $90, premium rooms at $130, but also some economy rooms at $30 if you bring your own sleeping bag, $35 with linen. The economy rooms are popular so if you want one of these, be sure to book ahead. Children age 14 and under stay for free.

Motels There are a couple of motels out on SH 3 at the junction of the Waitomo turn-off, eight km from Waitomo. The *Glow Worm Motel* (☎ & fax 873 8882) on the corner of the two roads has units at $55/65 for singles/doubles. About 100 metres south on SH 3, the *Caves Motor Inn* (☎ 873 8109; fax 878 8872) has a variety of accommodation including cabins at $13 per person, lodge rooms at $20/32 for singles/doubles, standard units at $45/55 and premium units at $55/65. They also have a bar and restaurant.

Places to Eat

Snacks & Fast Food The general store beside the Museum of Caves is open every day, with a tearoom off to one side where you can get inexpensive meals to take away or eat there. *Merrowvale Tearooms*, two km from the caves out towards the main highway, has both indoor and patio seating and is open every day from 9 am to 5 pm for breakfast, lunch and Devonshire teas.

The *THC Tavern* near the Museum of Caves offers inexpensive BBQ dinners for $6 but only when the Kiwi Experience bus is in town.

Restaurants For more elegant dining the *THC Waitomo Caves Hotel* has the *Fred Mace Restaurant*, which in addition to its regular menu also has a BBQ lunch buffet for $18 and a Sunday night carvery for $20. Or you can get a 'lunch-cave special' where you get lunch and a cave tour for $31 (children $16); tickets are available at the Glowworm Cave.

Roselands Restaurant is another good place for a meal at lunch time, with an ample BBQ lunch of steak or fish, a salad buffet, dessert and coffee for $20 in an attractive setting with garden, veranda or indoor seating. To get there from Waitomo village, go 400 metres towards the highway (east), then follow the signs for three km. It's a beautiful place and a good lunch, worth the trip out there. It's open every day from 11.30 am to 2.30 pm.

Entertainment

The *THC Tavern* is a popular spot in the evening. It often has a live band on Saturday nights, and on the nights the Kiwi Experience bus is in town it puts on a good BBQ dinner. About once a month it features bar games like glow-worm plucking off the ceiling, horizontal bungy jumping, dry surfboard riding, tug-of-war, bucking bronco and other shenanigans.

Getting There & Away

Bus The Waitomo Shuttle operates between Waitomo and Otorohanga. The cost is $6 between Otorohanga and Waitomo, $4 from Waitomo to the SH 3 turn-off. It runs on a regular schedule, but will do extra trips by request. Bookings are essential and can be made through the Waitomo Museum of Caves, the Otorohanga Information Centre, or directly through Otorohanga Taxis (☎ 873 8279, 873 8214, freephone (0800) 808 279).

KING COUNTRY

They'll pick you up, and drop you off wherever you wish.

On weekdays Perry's Bus makes a round trip from the coast to Te Kuiti on the Marokopa Road – see the Marokopa Road section for information.

For transport farther afield, the Kiwi Safaris bus includes Waitomo on its 'Mud & Worm Loop' – so from Waitomo you can take it either to Rotorua or to Auckland. The cost is $17 to Rotorua or $22 to Auckland, making it about half the price of the larger buses. They'll pick you up and drop you off wherever you're staying, and they offer free bicycle transport, free drinks on board, plus books, magazines and good music – such a deal. Make bookings at the Museum of Caves or phone them directly on their freephone number (☎ (0800) 800 616).

C Tours operates a round-trip service between New Plymouth and Rotorua, stopping at Waitomo on the way for a one-hour tour of the Glow-worm Cave. It departs from New Plymouth at 7 am, arrives in Waitomo at 9.30 am, departs from Waitomo an hour later and arrives in Rotorua at 12.30 pm. It departs from Rotorua at 1.30 pm, arrives at Waitomo at 3.30 pm, departs Waitomo an hour later and arrives in New Plymouth at 6.30 pm. The cost is $23 from Waitomo to Rotorua, $45 from Waitomo to New Plymouth, or $68 between New Plymouth and Rotorua. Make bookings at the Museum of Caves or in New Plymouth (☎ (06) 751 1711). The service runs only twice weekly, on Tuesday and Friday, and offers door-to-door service to your accommodation.

InterCity has round-trip excursion bus services to the Glow-worm Cave from Auckland and Rotorua. You only get to spend an hour at the caves so it's a very rushed trip. If you are already in Otorohanga you can catch the InterCity bus to the caves as it passes through at about noon. Since the Auckland and Rotorua excursion buses arrive and depart from the caves at the same times, you could arrive on the bus from Auckland and leave an hour later on the bus to Rotorua, or vice versa. You can also take these buses just one way to or from Waitomo. Leaving

Waitomo, both buses depart from the Glow-worm Cave at 1.30 pm every day. Regular full fare is $41 to Auckland or Rotorua.

Kiwi Experience and Magic Bus also come to Waitomo.

Otherwise, frequent bus services along SH 3 will drop you at the Waitomo turn-off, eight km from Waitomo.

Hitching Hitching to Waitomo from the turn-off on SH 3 is usually pretty easy, as is hitching around Waitomo once you're out there. Hitching out towards Te Anga and Marokopa can be more difficult because there's so little traffic.

Getting Around

Bicycles Mountain bikes can be hired from the Museum of Caves. Since the region is hilly this may be only for the stout of heart and leg.

AROUND WAITOMO

There are many scenic reserves around the Waitomo area; the Waitomo Museum of Caves has plenty of printed information about them.

Marokopa Road

Heading west from Waitomo, the Marokopa Road follows a rewarding and scenic route with a couple of natural beauties worth visiting. Ask at the museum for the booklet *A Trip Through Time* by Peter Chandler, founder of Black Water Rafting, with suggestions for a four to six-hour exploration of the 53-km road from Waitomo to Kiritehere on the coast. Of course you can also visit just the major sights but it's a great little booklet if you want to do more.

On weekdays Perry's Bus makes a round trip from the coast to Te Kuiti on the Marokopa Road, passing through Waitomo at about 8.30 am on the way to Te Kuiti. It departs from the Te Kuiti railway station at 1 pm for the return trip, reaching Waitomo about half an hour later and continuing on to Taharoa on the coast. Iron sands are being mined at Taharoa but it is not really worth the trip out.

Tawarau Forest

Various walks take off from the Alpiger Hut in the Tawarau Forest, about 20 km west of Waitomo village (see Places to Stay). There's a one-hour walk from the hut to the Tawarau Falls and other longer walks.

Mangapohue Natural Bridge

The Mangapohue Natural Bridge Scenic Reserve, 26 km west of Waitomo, is a 5½-hectare reserve with a giant natural limestone bridge formation, which is a 20-minute walk from the road on a wheelchair-accessible pathway. At times you may see cavers practising their manoeuvres by dangling from the summit on ropes. You can easily walk to the summit. On the far side, big rocks full of oyster fossils jut up from the grass. At night you'll see glow-worms.

Marokopa Tunnel

Not far from the Natural Bridge, the Marokopa Tunnel is another massive limestone formation – a natural tunnel 270 metres long and 50 metres high at its highest point, going right through a limestone hill. Limestone formations, fossils and glow-worms can be seen in the tunnel.

The tunnel is on private land, but you can see it by going with Marokopa Tunnel Treks (☎ & fax 876 7865), operated by the friendly farming couple who own the land. Every day at 10.30 am they conduct guided walks through the tunnel, departing from their farmhouse near the Mangapohue Natural Bridge car park and leading on a bush walk beside the Marokopa River, then up a small tributary to the tunnel. A picnic lunch and afternoon tea are provided; plan to spend about 3½ to four hours. The cost is $18 ($10 for students aged 11 to 17, under 11 free). Torches are provided. Look for the sign at the Mangapohue Natural Bridge car park.

Piripiri Caves

About four km further west is the Piripiri Caves Scenic Reserve, where a 30-minute track leads to a large cave containing fossils of giant oysters. Bring a torch if you want to explore the cave.

Marokopa Falls

The impressive 36-metre Marokopa Falls are 32 km west of Waitomo. You can view them from the road above, or walk to the bottom on a track starting just downhill from the roadside vantage point.

Marokopa & Te Anga

To get to Marokopa village, on the coast 48 km from Waitomo, turn left (south-west) just past the tavern at Te Anga, 30 km west of Waitomo. Incidentally, the pleasant Te Anga Tavern is worth a stop if you've worked up a thirst. The whole Te Anga-Marokopa area is riddled with caves.

The bitumen road ends just out of Marokopa, but it is possible to continue, on a difficult but scenic road, 60 km further south until you meet SH 3 at Awakino.

From Te Anga you can also turn north on a different road leading to Kawhia, 53 km to the north (see the Around Hamilton section). The loop from Waitomo to Te Anga to Kawhia to Otorohanga and back to Waitomo is a favourite scenic drive. You can extend it by continuing up the scenic back road from Kawhia to Raglan, seeing the Bridal Veil Falls on the way.

Places to Stay About 20 km west of Waitomo, the Alpiger Hut is a DOC-operated hut in the Tawarau Forest; the turn-off to the hut is well-signposted at Appletree Rd. The hut is an old farmhouse, built by a Swiss farmer named Alpiger. A number of walking tracks to waterfalls and other attractions, 20 minutes to three hours in length, take off from the hut. Back-country hut tickets or an annual hut pass, available at any DOC office, are required. The DOC office in Te Kuiti has pamphlets and information on the hut and on the Tawarau Forest.

In Te Anga, the *Bike 'n Hike* (☎ 876 7362) is a small backpackers operated by an outdoorsy fellow knowledgeable about caving, geology and fossils who will take you on walks and bicycle tours to see waterfalls, fossils, limestone formations and glow-worms, plus fishing, hunting, abseiling and anything else you can think of. Mountain bikes are available for hire.

About 10 km south of Te Anga on the road to Marokopa, *Hepipi Farm* (☎ 876 7861) offers B&B at $40 per person or DB&B (dinner, bed & breakfast) at $45 per person. They also have three self-contained units at the beach in Marokopa; the cost is $35 per unit, each sleeping four or five people.

Also at the beach in Marokopa, the *Marokopa Motor Camp* (☎ 876 7546) has tent sites at $5 for two people, caravan sites at $10 for two, an on-site caravan at $25 for two and a cabin at $35 for two.

TE KUITI

Te Kuiti (population 4750) is 19 km south of Otorohanga on SH 3 and 19 km from the Waitomo caves. While Te Kuiti has little of particular attraction for visitors, it does have basic services and makes another convenient base for visiting Waitomo.

There are several versions of how the town got its name. One version is that Te Kuiti is short for Te Kuititanga, 'the narrowing in', referring not only to the narrowing of the Mangaokewa Valley here but also to the confiscation of Maori property after the Waikato wars. Another historian writes that the original name of the town was Te Kuiti O Nga Whakaaro O Te Iwi, meaning 'the narrowing down of thoughts of the people'.

Locals will proudly tell you, however, that the town is named for Te Kooti, a prominent Maori rebellion leader who came here in 1872, seeking refuge from the Pakehas, and remained for a number of years. The magnificently carved Te Tokanganui a Noho Marae, overlooking the south end of Rora St, was a gift Te Kooti left to his hosts, the Ngati Maniapoto people.

Te Kuiti got its nickname, 'The Shearing Capital of the World', because many champion sheep shearers have come from here.

Orientation

SH 3 passes right through Te Kuiti, but the commercial part of town is centred along Rora St, running parallel to SH 3 (called Carroll St as it passes through town) one

block over, on the east side of the railway tracks. The information centre, the railway station, the post office, the long-distance and local bus stops, and most restaurants, shops and other businesses are all found on or near Rora St.

Information

The Te Kuiti Information Centre (☎ 878 8077; fax 878 5280) on Rora St in the centre of town is open Monday to Friday from 8.30 am to 5 pm, Saturday 9 am to noon. In January it's also open on Sunday from 9 am to noon. The information centre has information on Waitomo and the surrounding area as well as Te Kuiti, homestays and farmstays, and it's also the AA agent for the town.

The DOC office (☎ 878 7297) at 78 Taupiri St, one block east of Rora St, is open Monday to Friday from 8 am to 4.30 pm. It has plenty of maps, brochures and information on the area's natural attractions, including short and long walking tracks, scenic reserves, and forests such as the large Pureora Forest Park. If you're in the area in summer, ask about the summer programme of nature activities.

Gardens

If you're a garden fan, ask the information centre for their King Country Gardens brochure, giving details on 20 private gardens you can visit in the region.

On the south side of Te Kuiti, The Birches (☎ 878 6314) at 9 Hardy St is a lovely one-acre garden created by Don and Marie Lewis, with dozens of varieties of fuchsias, orchids, birches (of course) and many other species of flowers and trees. The cost is $3 for a tour around the garden, or if you'd like to have lunch too it's $10, by prior arrangement. Please telephone before you arrive.

Te Kuiti Muster

On the first weekend in April (or the following weekend, if Easter falls then) the Te Kuiti Muster is a popular annual event featuring all kinds of entertainment including sheep and goat shearing championships, a country parade, arts & crafts, live music, sheep races, Maori culture groups, BBQs and hangis, a duathlon, a town-wide bargain day, a tour of the Te Tokanganui a Noho marae (circumstances permitting) and more. Some years a steam locomotive comes from Auckland for the day.

Things to See & Do

The Mangaokewa River winds through the town, with a pleasant riverside walkway good for a stroll. Beside the river, the Mangaokewa Scenic Reserve, three km south of town on SH 30, has picnic and BBQ areas, a waterhole for safe swimming, and overnight camping.

On the north-western boundary of Te Kuiti, the 52-hectare Brook Park Recreation Reserve is an attractive park with a number of walking tracks leading to the summit of the Ben Lomond hill. Besides affording a fine view, the hill is the site of the historic Matakiora Pa, constructed in the 17th century by Rora, son of Maniapoto. Camping is permitted in the park.

The Te Kuiti Lookout, on Awakino Rd

(SH 3) as it climbs out of town heading south, provides a great view over the town, especially at night with the sparkling lights stretching out below.

There's an open-air swimming pool on the corner of Hinerangi St and Alexandra St, open every day during summer from Labour Day in late October until around mid-March. Admission is $1.

The Waitomo Community Cultural & Arts Centre on the corner of King and Jennings Sts is the town hall and venue for events of all kinds.

Places to Stay

Camping & Cabins The *Domain Motor Camp* (☎ 878 6223) on the north side of town beside the Mangaokewa River, about 800 metres north of the information centre, is a peaceful camping ground with tent sites at $5.50 per person, powered sites at $6.50 per person, on-site caravans at $15/20 for one/two people, and cabins at $22 for two.

Camping is also permitted at the Brook Park Recreation Reserve on the north-western boundary of Te Kuiti, and at the Mangaokewa Scenic Reserve beside the Mangaokewa River three km south of the town on SH 30 (see Things to See & Do); both have BBQs, picnic areas and toilets, but no other facilities. Payment is by donation.

Hotels & Motels On Rora St in the centre of town, the *Te Kuiti Hotel* (☎ 878 8172) has 33 rooms, all with private facilities; the cost is $45/55 for singles/doubles.

The *Panorama Motel* (☎ 878 8051; fax 878 8872) at 59 Awakino Rd (SH 3), about 1.5 km south of town, has a filtered swimming pool and a panoramic view over the town. The cost is $59/69 for singles/doubles in motel units or serviced units.

Farmstays & B&Bs Several farms and private homes in the area welcome guests for farmstays and B&B arrangements; the information centres in Te Kuiti, Otorohanga and Waitomo all keep current lists.

KING COUNTRY

KING COUNTRY

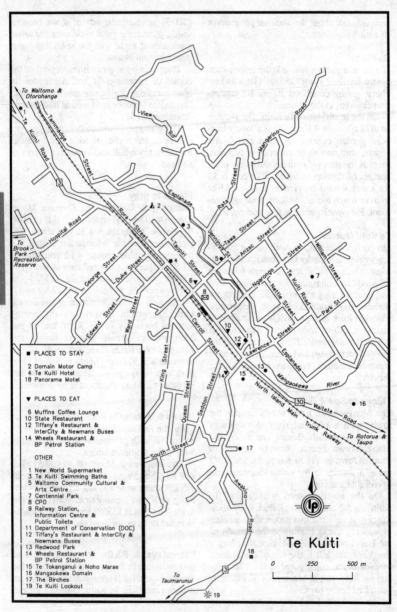

■ PLACES TO STAY

2 Domain Motor Camp
4 Te Kuiti Hotel
18 Panorama Motel

▼ PLACES TO EAT

6 Muffins Coffee Lounge
10 State Restaurant
12 Tiffany's Restaurant &
    InterCity & Newmans Buses
14 Wheels Restaurant &
    BP Petrol Station

OTHER

1 New World Supermarket
3 Te Kuiti Swimming Baths
5 Waitomo Community Cultural &
  Arts Centre
7 Centennial Park
8 CPO
9 Railway Station,
  Information Centre &
  Public Toilets
11 Department of Conservation (DOC)
12 Tiffany's Restaurant & InterCity &
   Newmans Buses
13 Redwood Park
14 Wheels Restaurant &
   BP Petrol Station
15 Te Tokanganui a Noho Marae
16 Mangaokewa Domain
17 The Birches
19 Te Kuiti Lookout

Te Kuiti

0   250   500 m

Places to Eat

The *Muffins Coffee Lounge* at 7 King St, half a block from Rora St, is a simple place with delicious food; it's open Monday to Friday from 8.30 am to 5 pm, Saturday 9.30 am to noon.

The *State Restaurant* at 199 Rora St also has good food, with a takeaways counter and a good menu with reasonable prices in the sit-down restaurant section. It's open every day from 10 am to 8 pm, until 9 pm on Friday.

Also on Rora St, *Tiffany's Restaurant* is conveniently open long hours, from 8 am to 11 pm every day; this is also the town's 'bus station', with bus tickets sold here and the long-distance buses stopping at the door.

Wheels Restaurant beside the BP Petrol Station on the south end of Carroll St is a friendly, casual restaurant popular with the locals and with travellers passing through. It has both European and Chinese food, with a restaurant and a takeaways section. It's open every day from 6 am to 9 pm, until 10 pm on Friday and Sunday nights.

The large New World Supermarket on SH 3 on the northern outskirts of town is a good place to buy groceries; many people from Waitomo come here to do their weekly shopping. Otherwise there are markets, dairies and a bakery along Rora St in the centre of town.

Getting There & Away

Bus InterCity and Newmans buses arrive and depart from Tiffany's Restaurant on the south end of Rora St; the ticket office (☎ 878 8872), which sells train and Interislander ferry tickets in addition to bus tickets, is open Monday to Friday from 8.30 am to 5 pm.

Long-distance bus services include those to New Plymouth (two hours), Taumarunui (one hour) or north to Hamilton (1½ hours) and on to Auckland (3¾ hours).

Buses also operate in the local region. A Perry's bus, operating Monday to Friday only, comes into town from the coast along the Waitomo-Marokopa Road each morning and departs from the railway station on Rora St at 1 pm for the return trip, heading all the way out to the coast at Taharoa, past the

Waitomo Caves, Te Anga and the other scenic attractions along the Waitomo-Marokopa Road.

Train The railway station is on Rora St in the centre of town, but it's not here that you buy railway tickets; they are sold at Tiffany's Restaurant (☎ 878 8872) on the south end of Rora St. The Auckland-Wellington trains stop at Te Kuiti.

Hitching Hitching is easy around Te Kuiti, and from Te Kuiti to Waitomo Caves.

AROUND TE KUITI
Pureora Forest Park

The large Pureora Forest Park, about 50 km east of Te Kuiti, has camping, lodge and hut facilities, swimming, fishing, and long and short forest treks, including tracks to the summits of Mt Pureora (1165 metres) and Mt Titiraupenga (1042 metres). Hunting is permitted in the northern section of the park, designated as a recreational hunting area, but you must obtain a permit from the park headquarters. The DOC office in Te Kuiti has pamphlets, maps and information on the park.

TAUMARUNUI

Taumarunui (population 6100) is the southernmost of the King Country's three major towns. It is a quiet but pleasant little town on SH 4, 82 km south of Te Kuiti and 43 km north of the town of National Park. Its name, meaning 'big screen', comes from an episode in the town's history when a Maori chief, Pehi Taroa, was dying and asked for a screen to shade him from the sun. They say that he died before the screen was in place, still asking for it with his final words – *taumaru nui*.

History

Situated at the confluence of the Whanganui and Ongarue Rivers, both major transport waterways, Taumarunui was already an important settlement in pre-European days. It was also significant as the historical meeting place of three important Maori tribes: the

Whanganui tribes, the Tuwharetoa and the Maniapoto.

As in the rest of the King Country, European influence in Taumarunui came late; Pakehas did not settle in the area until the 1880s and even then it remained until the early 20th century, when the Main Trunk Railway Line came south from Te Kuiti in 1903, before their settlements began to flourish. It took off rapidly, though – in the same year that the railway line reached the town, riverboat service coming from the coast at Wanganui was extended up the Whanganui River to Taumarunui.

Immediately this link, running all the way from Auckland to Wanganui, became a much travelled route, not only for commerce but also for tourism; see the Whanganui National Park section of the Central North Island chapter for more on this period in the history of the river and Taumarunui's role in it. Taumarunui became an important railway town, with timber from the area's sawmills freighted out.

Today the town still attracts travellers, not so much for the town itself as for its role as a jumping-off point to other places. Cherry Grove at the confluence of the two rivers is a popular departure point for canoe trips on the Whanganui River; see the Whanganui National Park section in Central North Island for details. The town is also the northern end of the Stratford-Taumarunui Heritage Trail.

Orientation & Information

The commercial part of town is a few blocks stretching east from the Ongarue River, between the Whanganui River and the highway, SH 4. The highway is called Hakiaha St as it passes through town; it is the town's main drag and you'll find everything you need on or near it.

The Taumarunui Information Centre (☎ 895 7494) is at the railway station on Hakiaha St in the centre of town. It's open Monday to Friday from 8 am to 5 pm, Saturday and Sunday from 10 am to 4 pm. It's also the agent for AA and for InterCity bus and train tickets. It has a good selection of maps, including a useful map of the town, and an interesting operating model of the Raurimu Spiral, 37 km to the south.

There's a DOC office (☎ 895 8201) at Cherry Grove, beside the river. The post office is on Miriama St, one block off Hakiaha St, between Manuaute and Hikaia Sts.

Walks

The information centre has suggestions for several enjoyable walks around Taumarunui. A pleasant walkway extends east along the Whanganui River from Cherry Grove to the Taumarunui Camping Ground, about three km away. Another track leads to the Rangaroa Domain with a good view over the town, its rivers and mountains; go over the railway line, up The Incline and through the native bush behind the scout den to reach it. The Te Peka Lookout across the Ongarue River on the west side of town is another good vantage point.

For even better views extending all the way to Tongariro National Park in the south, climb to the summit of the flat-topped Mt Hikurangi (770 metres) north-east of the town. The curious hill can be seen from far and wide. Before climbing, you must first ask permission from the owner, Mr Skelton (☎ 895 3031).

The Ohinetonga Scenic Reserve on the banks of the Whakapapa River, 26 km south of town at Owhango, has bush walks lasting from one to three hours.

Raurimu Spiral

Even if you're just passing through the town, stop by the information centre to see the operating model of the Raurimu Spiral, a feat of train engineering that was declared a 'wonder of the world' when it was completed early this century. While you're there, pick up a pamphlet telling the story of how the spiral with its three horseshoe curves, one complete circle and two short tunnels, allowed the sections of the Main Trunk Railway coming south from Auckland and north from Wellington to finally be joined at Horopito in 1908. At Raurimu, 37 km south of Taumarunui and six km north of National

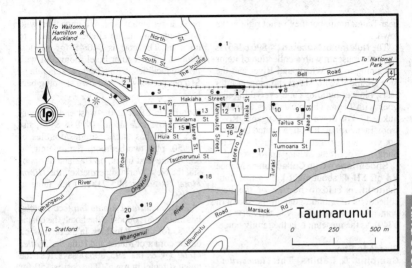

1 Rangaroa Domain
2 Kelly's Riverside Motel
3 Pioneer Jet Boat Tours
4 Te Peka Lookout
5 New World Supermarket
6 Public Toilets
7 Railway Station & Information Centre
8 Main Trunk Cafe
9 Central Park Motor Inn
10 Maata Park
11 Grand Lodge Hotel
12 Willows Restaurant
13 Taumarunui Alpine Inn &
     Pinnacles Restaurant
14 Hilton Motel
15 Tattles Motel
16 CPO
17 Taumarunui Domain
18 Rod McLiesh Reserve
19 Cherry Grove
20 Department of Conservation (DOC)

Park, there's a lookout with a view of the Raurimu Spiral.

If you're going by train along this stretch you'll go through the spiral anyway, but if you happen to be travelling by some other means, there's still an easy way you can take

the spiral if you start from Taumarunui. The trains coming from north and south arrive at National Park at the same time. Taumarunui is the next station to the north, an hour's ride from National Park, passing through the spiral. If the trains are running on time – but *only* if they are – you can take the train from Taumarunui south to National Park, change trains and come back north again, passing through the spiral twice. The cost is $10 each way. Check with the information centre, where train tickets are sold, to see if the trains are on time.

River Trips

Canoe, kayak, rafting and jet-boat trips on the Whanganui River all depart from Taumarunui. See the Whanganui National Park section for details.

Stratford-Taumarunui Heritage Trail

See the Taranaki chapter for details on this interesting route between Taumarunui and Stratford, in the Taranaki region.

Museums

There are a couple of interesting museums

near Taumarunui, but they're not right in the town.

The **Nukunuku Museum** (☎ 896 6365) is a private museum with a collection of items pertaining to the Whanganui River and the area around it, with Maori and pioneer artefacts, pioneer buildings and everything that goes with them. The museum is at Nukunuku, 17 km down the Whanganui River from Taumarunui. It's often visited by river, but you can also get to it by road – it's on Saddlers Rd, off the Whanganui River Rd.

Shoebridge's Gun Collection on Mahoe Rd off SH 4, about eight km east of Taumarunui, is said to be one of the best collections of antique guns in the southern hemisphere. Ring before you arrive (☎ 896 6749), as the museum is in the family home.

Places to Stay

Camping & Cabins The *Taumarunui Camping Ground* (☎ 895 8514) is on the banks of the Whanganui River near SH 4, three km east of town. It has tent sites at $7 per person, powered sites at $8 per person, cabins at $17/27 for one/two people, and a family unit at $45. You can get a special backpackers rate of $12 per person in the cabins if you ask. Features of the camp include kayaks and bicycles for hire, bush walks, overnight tramping and guided tours.

Backpackers The Grand Lodge Hotel and the Taumarunui Alpine Inn both have good budget backpackers rooms (singles, doubles and twins) in addition to their regular hotel rooms; see Hotels.

Hotels The *Grand Lodge Hotel* (☎ 895 7876) is right on the main drag, Hakiaha St, opposite the railway station in the centre of town. It has a kitchen where you can do your own cooking, a TV lounge and a laundry. Hotel rooms are $25/36 for singles/doubles, or there's a backpackers rate of $15 per person with your own sleeping bag.

The *Taumarunui Alpine Inn* (☎ 895 7033; fax 895 7031) on the corner of Marae and Miriama Sts, one block off the main drag, is more attractive and up-market; it has a spa

pool, a restaurant and a lounge bar with entertainment, but no kitchen for guests to cook in. The cost is $40/45 for singles/doubles in its regular hotel rooms, all with private facilities, with a backpackers rate of $16 per person with your own sleeping bag.

Motels On SH 4 at the west end of town, *Kelly's Riverside Motel* (☎ 895 8175; fax 895 9089) has studio singles/doubles at $45/50, plus two-bedroom family units at $55. In the next block, on Hakiaha St opposite the New World supermarket, the *Hilton Motel* (☎ & fax 895 7181/2) has units at $52/59.

The *Taumarunui Alpine Inn* (see Hotels) has motel units opposite the hotel; the cost is $45/55 for singles/doubles. In the next block on the corner of Marae and Huia Sts, *Tattles Motel* (☎ & fax 895 8063) says it's 'the quietest motel in town'. The cost is $50 for regular units, $60 for family units, and there's a villa for groups of six or seven.

The *Central Park Motor Inn* (☎ 895 7132; fax 895 7133) on Maata St just off Hakiaha St is the luxury spot in town, with a swimming pool, sauna, spa pool, tennis courts, a BBQ and a licensed restaurant; units range from $50 to $90.

Places to Eat

The *Main Trunk Cafe* on Hakiaha St on the east end of town is in a brightly painted, red, antique (1913) railway passenger car, now restored and converted to a cheerful cafe. It's open 24 hours every day, with menu of fish & chips, burgers, sandwiches and the like. There are also plenty of other tearooms, takeaways and cafes along Hakiaha St and down the side streets, including three Chinese restaurants.

For a fancier meal there's the licensed *Pinnacles Restaurant* at the Taumarunui Alpine Inn on the corner of Marae and Miriama Sts, with a $10 smorgasbord lunch and a $17.50 smorgasbord dinner, plus bar meals. The *Willows Restaurant* upstairs on Hakiaha St opposite the railway station is also licensed and features a chef's grill, salad and dessert bar for $20 plus an à la carte menu.

The New World Supermarket on the west end of Hakiaha St is a good spot to pick up groceries and picnic food to take by the river.

Entertainment

The lounge bar at the Taumarunui Alpine Inn has live music for dancing on Thursday, Friday and Saturday nights, karaoki on other nights.

Getting There & Away

Bus & Train Buses and trains travelling between Auckland and Wellington all stop at the railway station at Taumarunui. The station also houses the information centre, which is where you buy your tickets.

Hitching Hitching is easy heading north or south on SH 4. It is a lot more difficult to get a ride on the Stratford-Taumarunui Road, as there is so little traffic.

Taranaki

The Taranaki region juts out into the Tasman Sea on the west coast of the North Island about halfway between Auckland and Wellington. The region takes its name from the large Mt Taranaki volcano, also called Mt Egmont, whose massive cone dominates the landscape. Conditions are excellent for agriculture and dairy farming, with rich volcanic soil and a climatic pattern of abundant rainfall.

The names Taranaki and Egmont are both widely used around the region, with Taranaki being the traditional Maori name for the volcano (there are several theories as to its meaning) and Egmont being the name Captain James Cook gave it in 1770, after the Earl of Egmont who had encouraged his expedition. Today the region is called Taranaki, the cape is called Cape Egmont, and the waters on either side of the cape are called the North and South Taranaki bights. Egmont National Park remains the name of the national park, but in 1986 the New Zealand government ruled that Mt Taranaki and Mt Egmont are *both* official names for the volcano itself.

In addition to the obvious attraction of Egmont National Park – Mt Taranaki is the 'most climbed' mountain in New Zealand – the region is also popular for its world-class surfing and windsurfing beaches.

Information
See the following sections for details. Most of this region's telephone numbers have an 06 prefix if you are calling them from a long distance (even within the region).

New Plymouth

Principal centre of the Taranaki region, New Plymouth (population 48,700) is about equal distance from Auckland (373 km) and Wellington (357 km). An attractive coastal city,

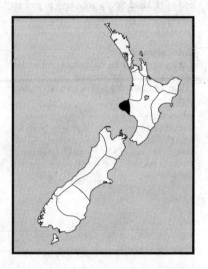

with Mt Taranaki towering behind it and surrounded by rich agricultural and dairy lands, New Plymouth makes a convenient base for visiting the Egmont National Park.

History
Archaeological evidence shows that the Taranaki region was settled by Maoris from early times. In the 1820s the Taranaki Maoris took off to the Cook Strait region in droves to avoid a threatened attack by the Waikato tribes, but it was not until 1832 that the Waikato tribes attacked and subdued the remaining Te Ati-awa tribe, except at Okoki Pa (New Plymouth) where whalers had joined in the battle. So when the first European settlers arrived in the district in 1841, the coastlands of Taranaki were almost deserted. Initially it seemed there would be no opposition to land claims, so the New Zealand Company was able to buy extensive tracts from the Te Ati-awa who had stayed.

When the other members of the Te Atiawa and other tribes returned after years of exile and slavery they objected strongly to the sale of their land. Their claims were substantially upheld when Governor Fitzroy ruled that the New Zealand Company was only allowed to retain just over 10 sq km around New Plymouth – of the 250 it had claimed. The Crown slowly acquired more land from the Maoris, but the Maoris became increasingly reluctant to sell and the European settlers increasingly greedy for the fertile land around Waitara, just north of New Plymouth.

The settlers' determination finally forced the government to abandon its policy of negotiation, and in 1860 war broke out. For 10 years the Maoris kept the military engaged in guerrilla warfare. During this time settlers had moved in on Waitara and were in control there, but the Maoris came and went as they pleased throughout the rest of the province. The Taranaki chiefs had not signed the Treaty of Waitangi and did not recognise the sovereignty of the British Queen, so they were treated as rebels. By 1870 over 500 hectares of their land had been confiscated and much of the rest acquired through extremely dubious transactions.

The Taranaki province experienced an economic boom with the discovery of natural gas and oil at Kapuni in 1959 and more recently at the Maui natural gas field off the coast of South Taranaki.

Orientation & Information

Devon St (East and West) is New Plymouth's main street; its central section is a mall.

The New Plymouth Information Centre (☎ 758 6086; fax 758 1395) on the corner of Liardet and Leach Sts is open Monday to Friday from 8.30 am to 5 pm, weekends and public holidays 10 am to 3 pm, with a computerised telephone information line operating 24 hours a day. The office staff is very helpful and they have lots of free printed information including a good city map and up-to-date details on restaurants and places to stay.

There's a DOC office (☎ 758 0433; fax 758 0430) at 220 Devon St West, open Monday to Friday from 8 am to 4.30 pm. The AA office (☎ 757 5646) is at 49-55 Powderham St. There are plenty of banks in the centre; the Devon Hotel (☎ 759 9099) at 390 Devon St East will cash travellers' cheques on the weekend.

Museums & Galleries

The **Taranaki Museum** on Ariki St between Brougham and Egmont Sts has an interesting collection of Maori artefacts, wildlife exhibits including moa and whale skeletons, and an early colonists' exhibition. The museum is open Tuesday to Friday from 10.30 am to 4.30 pm, weekends and public holidays from 1 to 5 pm; admission is free, donations welcomed.

The **Govett-Brewster Art Gallery**, on the corner of Queen and King Sts, is a renowned contemporary art gallery with a good reputation for its adventurous shows. Fans of abstract animation on film should seek out the films of Len Lye, pioneer animator of the 1930s, whose works are held here and shown from time to time. It's open Monday to Friday from 10.30 am to 5 pm, Saturday and Sunday from 1 to 5 pm; admission is free except during some special exhibitions.

Historic Places

If you like historic sites, pick up a free New Plymouth Heritage Walkway leaflet from the information centre, which outlines a self-guided tour of 30 historic sites around the city centre. Some are mentioned here but there are plenty of others.

Richmond Cottage, on Ariki St on the corner of Brougham St, was built in 1853. Unlike most early cottages, which were timber, Richmond Cottage was sturdily built of stone. From June to October it's open Friday from 2 to 4 pm, Saturday and Sunday from 1 to 4 pm. From November to May it's also open Monday and Wednesday from 2 to 4 pm. Admission is $1 (children 20c).

St Mary's Church, on Vivian St between Brougham and Robe Sts, is the oldest stone church in New Zealand, built in 1846. Its graveyard has numerous interesting grave-

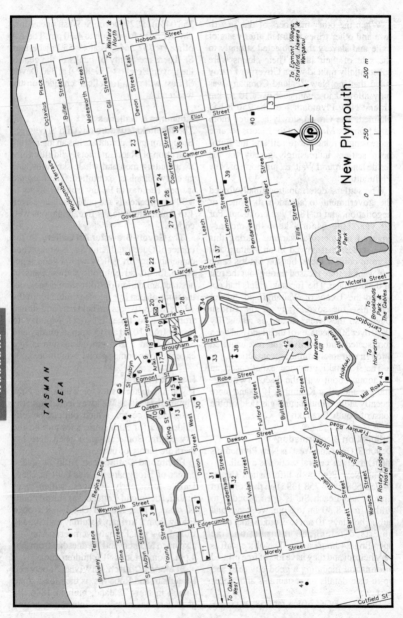

■ PLACES TO STAY

2	Mid City Motel
3	Aotea Lodge
14	White Hart Hotel
18	Royal Hotel
25	State Hotel, Cobb & Co Restaurant
31	Braemar Motor Inn
32	Balconies B&B
39	Inverness City Budget Lodge
40	Central Motel
43	Hostel 69

▼ PLACES TO EAT

11	Down to Earth
16	Black Olive Restaurant
19	Bellissimo Licensed Cafe
21	The Duke Cafe/Bar
23	Kebab Connection
24	Tastebuds Mexican Cantina & Gareth's Restaurant
25	State Hotel & Cobb & Co Restaurant
26	The Steps Restaurant
27	Kentucky Fried Chicken
29	L'Escargot Restaurant
34	The Mill Cafe/Bar
36	McDonald's

OTHER

1	Kawaroa Park & Petrocorp Aquatic Centre
4	Monument
5	InterCity Bus Station
6	The Rocks
7	City Centre Mall & Pak 'n Save Supermarket
8	Stage II Nightclub
9	Richmond Cottage
10	Newmans Bus Station
12	Department of Conservation (DOC)
13	Govett-Brewster Art Gallery
15	Opera House
17	Taranaki Museum & Public Library
20	CPO
21	The Duke Cafe/Bar
22	White Star Bus Stop & Avis Rent-A-Car
28	Air New Zealand
30	Clocktower
33	Automobile Association (AA)
34	The Mill Cafe/Bar
35	Woolworth's Supermarket
37	New Plymouth Information Centre
38	St Mary's Church
41	Churchill Heights
42	New Plymouth Observatory

TARANAKI

stones of early settlers and of soldiers who died during the Taranaki wars. Impressed by their bravery, the British also buried several of the Maori chiefs here.

Beside Brooklands Park, **The Gables** is an early hospital built in the late 1840s. In 1854 a notable Maori chief died here from wounds received in a tribal feud. The hospital consequently became tapu, which saved it during the Taranaki wars as its forbidden status prevented the Maoris from burning it down! It's now a medical museum and the home of the local arts society, with regular exhibitions. It's open Saturday to Tuesday from 1 to 5 pm, Wednesday and Friday from 10.30 am to 5 pm, and Thursday from 10.30 am to 4 pm.

On Devon St at the eastern end of town is the **Fitzroy Pole**, erected by Maoris in 1844 to mark the point beyond which Governor Fitzroy had forbidden settlers to acquire land. The carving on the bottom of the pole depicts a sorrowful Pakeha topped by a cheerfully triumphant Maori.

If you're wandering around the city, have a look at the curious transparent **clocktower** on the corner of Devon St West and Queen St. It was erected in 1985 to replace the old post office tower which was demolished 16 years earlier.

Marsland Hill & Observatory

The New Plymouth Observatory is on Marsland Hill off Robe St. Public nights are held every Tuesday, and include a planetarium programme and viewing through a six-inch refractor telescope if the weather is clear; times are from 7.30 to 9.30 pm from March to October, 8 to 10 pm during daylight saving time from November to March. The cost is $2 (children $1).

Also on Marsland Hill is a carillon, and St

Mary's Church is directly below. You'll get fine views from the hill over the central city.

Power Station

At the western end of town is the New Plymouth Power Station, designed to run on oil or gas. The original intention was to burn coal, but the discovery of natural gas in Taranaki changed this. The station is dominated by its towering 200-metre chimney. Free one-hour tours are conducted at 10 am on Wednesday and at 2 pm on Sunday.

Paritutu & Other Viewpoints

Above the power station is Paritutu, a steep hill with a magnificent view from the top. The name means 'rising precipice' and it's worth the tiring but quick scramble to the summit. Not only do you look down on the station but out over the town and the rocky Sugar Loaf Islands rising just offshore.

Yet another good viewpoint is Churchill Heights, with a trig marker on top showing directions and distances to places near and far. You can walk up from Morley St or drive up from the entrance on Cutfield St.

Arts & Crafts Centre

Just below the Paritutu car park and within easy walking distance, is the Rangimarie Arts & Crafts Centre on Centennial Drive. It features a display of traditional Maori arts & crafts and you can watch the members working on their carving, weaving and other skills. It's open from 8.30 am to 4 pm on weekdays, and by appointment on weekends.

Parks

New Plymouth is renowned for its superb parks. **Pukekura Park**, a 10-minute walk from the city centre, is worth a visit, with 49 hectares of gardens, bush walks, streams and ponds and a kiosk cafe. Display houses with orchids and other exotic plants are open every day from 10 am to noon and 1 to 4 pm. Rowboats on the lake can be hired on weekends, holidays and on summer evenings. The lights and decorations in Pukekura Park from mid-December to early February are worth

making a special trip to see, as hundreds of people stroll through the park in the evening to enjoy them.

Adjoining Pukekura is **Brooklands Park,** another lovely park, and between the two, the Bowl of Brooklands, an outdoor soundshell in a bush and lake setting. Brooklands Park was once the land around an important early settler's home; the fireplace and chimney are all that remain of the house after the Maoris burnt it down. Highlights include a 2000 year old puriri tree, a rhododendron dell with over 300 varieties of rhododendrons, The Gables historic hospital (see Historic Places) and beside it, a children's zoo open daily from 9 am to 6 pm.

On the waterfront is **Kawaroa Park**, with green areas, squash courts and the Petrocorp Aquatic Centre which has a waterslide, an outdoor swimming pool, and an indoor pool open all year. Also on the waterfront in the central city area is Pukeariki Landing, a historic area with a number of sculptures on display.

Walks

The information centre has leaflets on good walks around New Plymouth, including coastal walks and others through local reserves and parks, in addition to the Heritage Walkway already mentioned. The Te Henui walkway, extending from the coast at East End Reserve to the city's southern boundary, is one of the most interesting and varied. The Huatoki Valley walkway, following the Huatoki Stream, makes an attractive walk to the city centre if you're staying at one of the hostels (Hostel 69 or the Rotary Lodge) and there are plenty of others. Not to mention, of course, the many good walks on Mt Taranaki.

Sugar Loaf Islands Marine Park

New Plymouth has parks not only on land but also offshore. The Sugar Loaf Islands Marine Park, established in 1986, includes the rocky islets offshore from the power station, Back Beach on the west side of Paritutu, and the waters up to about a km offshore. The islands are a refuge for birds, seals and marine life; the greatest number of seals present is from August to October but some are there all year round.

Activities in the park include boating and sailing, diving, bird watching, pole fishing, surfing and beach walks. Boat trips to the islands are popular in summer. Happy Chaddy's Charters (☎ 758 0228, 751 1174) depart from Lee Breakwater hourly, 8.30 am to 5.30 pm; the cost is $15/7 per adult/child. Peak Charters (☎ 758 5921, 755 2169) also make hour-long trips to the islands for $10/5 per adult/child.

Beaches, Surfing & Windsurfing

Besides being beautiful to look at, the Taranaki coastline is a world-class surfing and windsurfing area. In the New Plymouth area, Fitzroy and East End beaches are at the eastern end of town. Fitzroy is a surfing beach and can be reached by bus from New Plymouth. There's also good surf at Back Beach, by the Paritutu Centennial Park at the western end of town, and at Oakura, 15 km west of New Plymouth. There are no buses to Oakura but hitchhiking is easy.

The Sirocco Windsurfing Shop & School, also called the Coastal Surf Shop (☎ 752 7562) on SH 45 just before Oakura, hires surfboards and sailboards and offers instruction in the same. It's also a good source of up-to-the-minute information on wind and surf conditions. If you don't get the shop you can ring John (☎ 752 7800), manager of the Wave Haven Hostel in Oakura, who is the windsurfing instructor.

Aerial Sightseeing

Several operators offer scenic flights around the area including flights over the snow-capped summit of Mt Taranaki – superb if the weather's clear. They include Kiwi West Aviation (☎ 0800-505 000), the New Plymouth Aero Club (☎ 755 0500) and the Stratford Aero Club (☎ 756 6628, 756 7771).

Organised Tours

Neuman's Sightseeing Tours (☎ 758 4622) at 78-80 Gill St – not the national Newmans bus line – offers a variety of 16 local sightseeing tours, ranging from a $30 half-day scenic city tour to a full-day tour around Mt Taranaki or down the Stratford-Taumarunui Heritage Trail for $60. Tubby's Tours (☎ 753 6306), who operate the daily shuttle service to Mt Taranaki, offer city sights tours for $25, half-day ($40) and full-day ($60) tours; C Tours (☎ 751 1711) also offer similar tours at similar prices.

Places to Stay

Camping & Cabins There are several camping grounds within easy reach of the city centre. The *Belt Rd Seaside Motor Camp* (☎ & fax 758 0228, freephone 0800-804 204) at 2 Belt Rd is on a bluff overlooking the port, 1.5 km west of the centre. The prices for one/two people are $10/14 in tent sites, $12/16 in powered sites, $15/20 in backpackers cabins, $25 in standard cabins with fridge and colour TV, $25/36 in cabins with private kitchen, or $25/34 in on-site caravans.

The *Aaron Court Caravan Park* (☎ & fax 758 8712) at 57 Junction Rd is on SH 3, three km south of the city centre. Rates for one/two people are $8/12.50 for tent sites, $15 for powered sites, $25/28 in cabins and $46 in tourist flats.

In Fitzroy, 3.5 km east of the town centre, the *Fitzroy Camp* (☎ 758 2870) is at the end of Beach St, beside a good surfing beach. It has tent sites at $11/13 for one/two people, powered sites at $13/15, cabins and on-site caravans at $25/31. Also in Fitzroy, *Princes Tourist Court* (☎ 758 2566) at 29 Princes St has tent sites at $7/14, powered sites at $10/16, cabins ranging from $24 to $29 for singles or $29 to $40 for doubles, tourist flats at $35/46, and motel units at $42/55.

Heading around the coast in the other direction, the *Oakura Beach Camp* (☎ 752 7861) is an attractive camp right on Oakura Beach, a beautiful beach for surfing and windsurfing. The turn-off to the beach is one km west of Oakura, which is 15 km west of New Plymouth. To get there, turn seaward onto Wairau Rd, then left at the beach onto Tasman Parade. The costs for one or two

TARANAKI

people are $12.50 in tent sites, $14 in powered sites or $44 in on-site caravans.

Hookner Park (☎ 753 9506, 753 9168) at 551 Carrington Rd is a quiet, peaceful camp on a commercial dairy farm 10 km south of the town centre. Campers are welcome to join in the farm life. The costs for one/two people are $8/16 in tent sites, $10/16 in powered sites, $15/25 in cabins or $25/30 in on-site caravans.

Hostels The *Rotary Lodge II* (☎ 753 5720) at 12 Clawton St is a tranquil 22-bed hostel in large park-like grounds with a stream running through. It's a fair way (1.5 km) from town, but you can make the 15-minute walk on a pleasant streamside walkway, or they will pick you up from the bus station, free of charge, when you arrive. The cost is $13/14 in dorm/double rooms, or $10 for tent sites. It's an associate YHA hostel, so you can stay with or without a YHA card. They also offer mountain bike hire.

About the same distance from the centre, *Hostel 69* (☎ 758 7153) at 69 Mill Rd is another small, pleasant hostel with convenient services including mountain bike hire, free pick-up when you arrive and free rides to good hitching spots when you leave. It's a friendly place with a large well-kept garden, and if it's not raining there's a fine view of Mt Taranaki. The cost is $13/14 in dorm/double rooms.

More central, the *Inverness City Budget Lodge* (☎ 758 0404) at 48 Lemon St is in a large, stately old home; the cost is $15 in single rooms, $13 in double or triple rooms. It was up for sale on our last visit; you might ring ahead to make sure it's still operating.

The *Wave Haven Hostel* (☎ 752 7800) is on SH 45 three km west of Oakura, a beach community 15 km west of New Plymouth, on the corner of Main South Rd and Ahu Ahu Rd. It's a friendly, relaxed and comfortable home-style place popular with surfers, windsurfers and other outdoorsy types; it's near a world-class surf break, and windsurfing instruction operates from the hostel. The cost is $13 in bunkrooms, $15 in shared or double rooms.

Guesthouses *Balconies Bed & Breakfast* (☎ 757 8866) at 161 Powderham St is a fine B&B with singles/doubles at $35/55. Also central, the *Aotea Lodge* (☎ 758 2438) on the corner of Young and Weymouth Sts has single/double rooms at $22/35 without meals or $30/50 with breakfast included; dinner is also available, or there's a weekly rate of $125.

Other B&Bs include the *Brooklands B&B* (☎ 753 2265) at 39 Plympton St near Brooklands Park off Brooklands Rd, the extension of Victoria Rd, with singles/doubles at $35/55. The *Home Stay B&B* (☎ 758 6090) at 481 Mangorei Rd, beside the Tupare Gardens on the outskirts of New Plymouth, has B&B at $30/50.

The information centre can make recommendations for other B&Bs, homestays and farmstays in the area.

Hotels There are several old-style hotels around central New Plymouth. The *White Hart Hotel* (☎ 757 5442) on the corner of Devon St West and Queen St has singles/doubles at $25/40. The *Royal Hotel* (☎ 758 0892) on the corner of Brougham and Ariki Sts has singles/doubles at $25/50. Or there's the *State Hotel* (☎ 758 5373; fax 758 5371) on the corner of Devon St East and Gover St, with singles/doubles at $38/50 and a Cobb & Co restaurant.

More modern, the *Braemar Motor Inn* (☎ 758 0859; fax 758 5251) at 157 Powderham St has hotel rooms at $44/49 and motel rooms at $70/79.

Motels New Plymouth has plenty of motels, starting from around $55/60 and up. The *Mid City Motel* (☎ & fax 758 6109) on the corner of St Aubyn and Weymouth Sts is reasonably central, with singles/doubles at $60/65. The *Central Motel* (☎ & fax 758 6444) at 86 Eliot St, a few blocks east of the centre, is small but convenient, with units at $57 for singles, $65 or $70 for doubles. The *Timandra Unity Motel* (☎ 758 6006) at 31B Timandra St off Coronation Ave, the extension of Eliot St, has singles/doubles at $53/63.

The *Aaron Court Motel* (☎ & fax 758

8712) at 57 Junction Rd is at the Aaron Court Caravan Park, on SH 3 three km south of the centre; motel units are $55/62 or there are tourist flats at $46. At Oakura, a pleasant beachside community 15 km west of New Plymouth, the *Oakura Beach Motel* (☎ 752 7680) on Wairau Rd has singles/doubles at $52/62.

Places to Eat

Snacks & Fast Food New Zealand is a small country and New Plymouth is a small city but the *McDonald's* on the corner of Leach and Eliot Sts is absolutely huge. There's an equally large *Kentucky Fried Chicken* on the corner of Courtenay and Gover Sts, and a *Pizza Hut* about three km east of the town centre on the corner of Sackville St and Clemow Rd in Fitzroy. There are plenty of Chinese takeaways around the centre, especially on Devon St.

Opposite the Kentucky Fried Chicken, the *Steps Restaurant* at 37 Gover St is a popular wholefoods restaurant with good food and a pleasant atmosphere. There are plenty of inexpensive selections on the blackboard menu and you can eat there or take away. It's open every day; weekdays it opens at 8 am, closing at 4 pm Monday to Wednesday, 7 pm on Thursday and 9 pm on Friday. Saturday and Sunday it's open from 10 am to 2 pm.

The *Tastebuds Mexican Cantina* on Devon St East near the corner of Gover St is a good, inexpensive place for Mexican-style snacks or meals. It's set up for takeaways or there's plenty of space to eat there at the brightly painted tables. It's open every day from 11 am until late, except Sunday when it opens at 4.30 pm. Nearby is *Kiwi Taco* with similar fare.

In the same block, the *Kebab Connection* at 211A Devon St East features doner kebab and other Middle Eastern takeaways, or you can use their $2 delivery service (☎ 757 8158). It's open Monday to Friday from 11.30 am to 2 pm and from 4.30 to 8.30 pm, Saturday and Sunday 11.30 am to 9.30 pm.

In the City Centre shopping mall on Gill St there's a food court with Chinese, Italian,

seafood, wholefood, sandwich and dessert counters.

Also in the City Centre shopping mall, the large Pak 'n Save supermarket is recommended by locals as one of the best places in town for grocery shopping. Another large supermarket, Woolworth's is on Leach St between Eliot and Cameron Sts, beside McDonald's. Or for wholefoods there's *Down to Earth*, a bulk wholefoods grocery on the corner of Devon St West and Morley St which also features 'healthy takeaways'.

Up in Pukekura Park, the *Park Kiosk* has good snacks in beautiful surroundings.

Pub Food *The Mill* cafe/bar on Courtenay/Powderham St on the corner of Currie St, popular for its evening entertainment, has a dining area with bar meals always available; it's open every day except Sunday, from 11 am until late.

There's a *Cobb & Co* restaurant on the corner of Devon St East and Gover St, with the usual Cobb & Co menu; it's open Monday to Friday from 7.30 am to 2.30 pm and 5 pm until late, Saturday and Sunday from 8 am until late.

Restaurants The *Black Olive Restaurant* on Egmont St near the corner of Devon St West has a curious menu, half with absolutely straightforward pub-style dishes like schnitzel, steak and ham steak, and half with Indonesian dishes. Main courses cost $14 to $20 and it's licensed or BYO.

The *Bellissimo Licensed Cafe* upstairs at 36E Currie St is another licensed or BYO restaurant, with a varied menu and local guitarists playing in the evening. You can come for snacks, meals or just coffee or a drink; it's open Wednesday to Sunday evenings from 5 pm until late.

Other quality licensed restaurants include *Gareth's* at 182 Devon St East, or the 'genuinely French' *L'Escargot* in a historic building at 37-39 Brougham St.

Entertainment

The *Brooklands Bowl* at the entrance to Brooklands Park is a large, fine outdoor theatre. All kinds of concerts are held here; the information centre will have current schedules and ticket prices. At the *Opera House* on Devon St West you can see not only operas but every other kind of performance as well.

The *Mill* cafe/bar on the corner of Courtenay/Powderham St and Currie St was the most popular place for a night out on our last visit to New Plymouth, with live music Wednesday to Saturday nights in two separate parts of the building. One section has live rock music for dancing, while the other is a popular disco, open Thursday to Saturday from around 10 pm to 4 am. Bar meals are available and it's known for having something enjoyable for all ages.

Other popular dancing spots include *The Duke* cafe/bar upstairs on Devon St East near the corner of Currie St, and the *Stage II* nightclub at 51 Gill St near Liardet St; both have rock music for dancing Thursday to Saturday nights from around 9 pm to 3 am.

The *Royal Hotel* on the corner of Brougham and Ariki Sts has music for dancing on Tuesday and Friday nights. The *White Hart Hotel* on the corner of Devon St West and Queen St has live bands in the bar on Friday nights. Or there's *The Rocks* upstairs over the Super Liquor Store on the corner of St Aubyn and Egmont Sts, a pub with bands, a dance floor, and a great view of the sea.

Getting There & Away
Air Air New Zealand (☎ 758 7674, 757 9057) at 12-14 Devon St East, has direct flights several times daily to Auckland, Nelson and Wellington, with connections to other centres. Kiwi West Aviation (☎ freephone (0800) 505 000) offers weekday flights to/from Palmerston North and Hamilton.

Bus The InterCity bus station (☎ 757 6929) is beside the waterfront on St Aubyn St, near Egmont St. The Newmans station (☎ 757 5482) is about a block away on the corner of Queen and King Sts. Both companies have several buses daily heading north to Hamil-

ton (four hours) and Auckland (5¾ hours), and south-east to Wanganui (2½ hours) and Palmerston North (five hours), from where buses proceed south to Wellington or east to Napier and Gisborne.

Don't confuse the national Newmans bus line that operates long distance services with the local Neuman's bus line that does sightseeing tours.

White Star buses (☎ 758 3338) depart from the Avis Rent-A-Car office at 25 Liardet St. They operate every day except Saturday, with two buses a day heading to Wellington via Wanganui and Palmerston North.

C Tours (☎ 751 1711) have shuttle buses twice weekly (Tuesday and Friday) heading to Waitomo, spending an hour there for a caves tour, and continuing on to Rotorua. Travel time is 2½ hours to Waitomo, 5¼ hours to Rotorua, and even counting the hour at Waitomo it still comes out to be the quickest way to travel by bus from New Plymouth to Rotorua, since you don't have to transfer at Hamilton. You can go for the whole trip or only as far as Waitomo if you want to stay there. The shuttles return to New Plymouth from Rotorua, via Waitomo, on the same day.

Hitching If you're hitching north towards Auckland, a good hitching spot is on Courtenay St about 1.5 km east of the centre; anywhere from about Hobson St eastwards is good, the further out the better. Courtenay St becomes Northgate as it heads out of town.

Hitching south towards Wanganui, a good hitching spot is on the corner of Coronation Ave and Cumberland St, about 1.5 km south of the centre; Coronation Ave is the southern extension of Eliot St.

To hitch west around the Taranaki coast towards Oakura, head west out of town on Devon St West, which becomes South Rd. Hitching is good on the corner of South Rd and Barrett Rd, four km from the centre, or anywhere along South Rd.

Getting Around
Airport Transport The New Plymouth airport is 11 km east of the centre. Withatruck

(☎ 751 1777) operates a shuttle service to and from the airport; the cost is $10.

Bus City buses operate every day except Sunday, with buses to Fitzroy, Waitara and a few other places. The information centre has local bus timetables.

Tubby's Tours (☎ 753 6306) operates a daily shuttle service from New Plymouth to Mt Taranaki; see the Mt Egmont/Taranaki section for details.

AROUND NEW PLYMOUTH

Egmont National Park, of course, is the primary attraction of the New Plymouth area, but there are several other places of interest. Those mentioned here are all within about 20 km of New Plymouth; Hurworth, the Pouakai Zoo Park and the Pukeiti Rhododendron Trust can all be reached by heading south from the centre on Carrington Rd. Other attractions, further afield, are mentioned in the Around Taranaki section later in this chapter.

Tupare

Tupare, seven km south of New Plymouth, is a fine three-storey Tudor-style house surrounded by 3.6 hectares of lush English garden. It's part of the Queen Elizabeth II National Trust; look for it at 487 Mangorei Rd on the Waiwhakaiho River. The garden is open every day from 9 am to 4 pm; admission is $5 (children free).

Hurworth

This early homestead, at 552 Carrington Rd about eight km south of New Plymouth, dates from 1856. Its pioneer builder and first occupant, Harry Atkinson, later became premier of New Zealand four times. The house was the only one at this site to survive the Taranaki wars and is today owned by the New Zealand Historic Places Trust. It's open Wednesday to Sunday from 10 am to 4 pm; admission is $2.50 (children 50c).

Pouakai Zoo Park

Further on towards Pukeiti is the Pouakai Zoo Park at 590 Carrington Rd, about 10 km

south of New Plymouth. Formerly a wildlife reserve, it became a zoo in 1987 and has won an award for its contribution to the conservation of New Zealand wildlife. It's open every day; admission is $3.50 (children 80c).

Pukeiti Rhododendron Trust

The Pukeiti Rhododendron Trust is a 400-hectare garden surrounded by native bush, renowned internationally for its large collection of species of rhododendrons and azaleas. Peak flowering of rhododendrons generally takes place in September, October and November, though it's worth going up any time of the year. Pukeiti is 20 km south of New Plymouth; to get there, just keep following Carrington Rd all the way from town. The road passes between the Pouakai and Kaitake ranges, both part of Egmont National Park, but separated by the Trust. Pukeiti is open every day from 9 am to 5 pm; admission is $6 (children free).

Lake Mangamahoe & TATATM

If you're heading out towards Stratford or North Egmont on SH 3, stop off at Lake Mangamahoe, about 9.5 km south of New Plymouth. The lake is the setting for many famous photographs of Mt Taranaki, reflected in its waters.

Opposite the lake, on the corner of SH 3 and Kent Rd, is the Taranaki Aviation, Transport and Technology Museum (TATATM), with vehicles, railway and aviation exhibits, farm equipment, household and other items. It's open Sunday and most public holidays from 10.30 am to 4.30 pm; admission is $3 (children 50c, family $7).

Waitara

Waitara is 13 km east of New Plymouth on SH 3. If you turn off SH 3 at Brixton, just before Waitara, and head seven km south, you'll reach the site of the Pukerangiora Pa. It's beautifully situated on a high cliff by the Waitara River, but historically it was a particularly bloody battle site.

Rafting and canoeing on the Waiwhakaiho and the Waitara rivers are popular local activities. For details, phone Waiawaka Rafting/ Canoeing (☎ 755 2068).

Just beyond Waitara on SH 3 heading east from New Plymouth is the Motunui Methanex Synthetic Fuels Plant (Synfuel). Opened in 1986, it was the world's first plant to convert natural gas to petrol (gasoline) and it remains the world's largest methanol production facility. Natural gas is piped here from the Maui natural gas field, 34 km offshore from Cape Egmont; the synthetic fuel produced here meets 30% of New Zealand's petrol needs. You can stop by the visitors' centre near the plant's main entrance to see exhibits on the plant; it's open every day from 8 am to 5 pm and admission is free.

Mt Egmont/Taranaki

The Taranaki region is dominated by the massive cone of 2518 metre Mt Taranaki – a dormant volcano that looks remarkably like Japan's Mt Fuji or the Philippines' Mayon. After a long-standing dispute about whether the volcano should be called Taranaki, its Maori name, or Mt Egmont, the name it was given in 1770 by Captain James Cook, the New Zealand government settled the dispute in 1986 when it ruled that both names are official.

Geologically, Mt Taranaki is the youngest of a series of three large volcanoes on one fault line, the others being Kaitake and Pouakai. Mt Taranaki last erupted 350 years ago, but it is regarded as being dormant rather than extinct. The top 1400 metres is covered in lava flows and there are a few that descend to 800 metres above sea level. An interesting feature is the small subsidiary cone on the flank of the main cone and two km south of the main crater, called Fantham's Peak (1962 metres).

There's a saying in Taranaki that if you can see the mountain it's going to rain, and if you can't see the mountain it's already raining! There is some truth in this. The mountain is one of the wettest spots in New Zealand with about 7000 mm of rain recorded annually at North Egmont (compared with 1584 mm in nearby New Plymouth), as the mountain catches the moisture-laden winds coming in from the Tasman Sea and sweeps them up to freezing heights.

Naturally it tends to be quite windy up there too. Nonetheless it doesn't rain *every* day and the volcano is truly a spectacular sight on a clear day, even if it does try to cover itself in protective cloud.

History

Mt Taranaki was supremely sacred to the Maoris, both as a burial site for chiefs and as a hideout in times of danger.

According to legend, Taranaki was once a part of the group of volcanoes at Tongariro. He was forced to leave rather hurriedly when Tongariro caught him with the beautiful Pihanga, the volcano near Lake Taupo – who was Tongariro's lover.

So angry was Tongariro at this betrayal that he blew his top (as only volcanoes can when upset) and Taranaki took off for the coast. Fleeing south in anger, pain and shame, the defeated Taranaki gouged a wide scar in the earth as he fled, meeting the sea at Wanganui and then moving still further west to his current position, where he's remained in majestic isolation ever since. Some time later, Tongariro sent a river of cool water out from his side to heal the scar in the earth that Taranaki's flight had left, and this water, the Whanganui River, still flows.

The Maoris did not settle the area between Taranaki and Pihanga very heavily, perhaps because they feared the lovers might be reunited with dire consequences. Most of the Maori settlements in this district were clustered along the coast between Mokau and Patea, concentrated particularly around Urenui and Waitara.

The Egmont National Park was created in 1900 and is the second-oldest national park in New Zealand.

Information

If you plan to tramp in Egmont National Park, get hold of local information about current track and weather conditions before

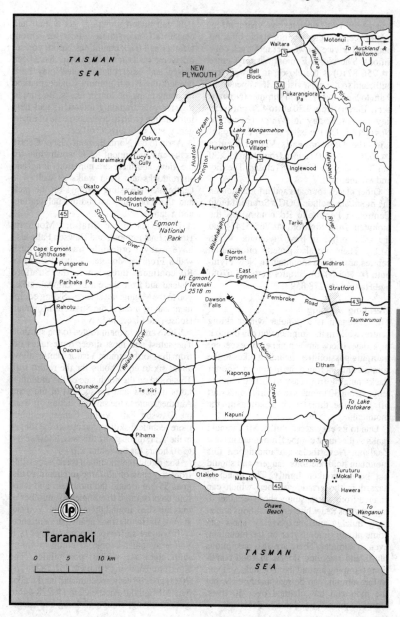

TASMAN SEA

Motonui
To Auckland & Waitomo
Waitara
3
NEW PLYMOUTH
Bell Block
3A
Pukarangiora Pa
Waitara River
Oakura
Huatoki Stream
Carrington Road
Lake Mangamahoe
Hurworth
Egmont Village
Tataraimaka
Lucy's Gully
3
Inglewood
Manganui River
Okato
Pukeiti Rhododendron Trust
Egmont National Park
Waiwhakaiho River
Tariki
45
Story River
North Egmont
Cape Egmont Lighthouse
East Egmont
Midhirst
Pungarehu
Mt Egmont/Taranaki 2518 m
Dawson Falls
Stratford
Parihaka Pa
Pembroke Road
43
To Taumarunui
Rahotu
Waiaua River
Oaonui
Kaponga
Kapuni Stream
Eltham
Opunake
Te Kiri
To Lake Rotokare
Kapuni
Pihama
3
Normanby
Turuturu Mokai Pa
Otakeho
Manaia
45
Hawera
Ohawe Beach
3
To Wanganui

Taranaki

0   5   10 km

TASMAN SEA

TARANAKI

you set off. DOC operates two visitor information centres on the mountain, offering maps and advice on weather and track conditions. The North Egmont Visitor Centre (☎ 756 8710) is the closest to New Plymouth, and so the most visited. It is open from 9 am to 5 pm every day in summer (November to Easter), from 9.30 am to 4.30 pm every day except Friday in winter (Easter to November). On the other side of the mountain, the Dawson Falls Visitor Centre (☎ (025) 430-248) is open from 9 am to 5.30 pm Thursday to Monday (closed Tuesday and Wednesday).

Other places for maps and information on the mountain include DOC's Stratford Field Centre on Pembroke Rd coming up the mountain from Stratford (☎ 765 5144) and the DOC office in New Plymouth (☎ 758 0433). There are also general information centres around the mountain in New Plymouth (☎ 758 6086), Stratford (☎ 765 6708) and Hawera (☎ 278 8599).

Tramping & Skiing

The mountain is a popular winter skiing centre, while in the summer you can climb it in a day. There are a number of excellent tramping possibilities including hikes to the summit or right round the mountain. Shorter tracks ranging from easy to difficult and in length from 30 minutes to several hours start off from the three roads heading up the mountain.

Due to its easy accessibility, Mt Taranaki ranks as the 'most climbed' mountain in New Zealand. Nevertheless, tramping on this mountain holds definite dangers and should not be undertaken lightly. The principal hazard is the erratic weather, which can change from warm, sunny shorts weather to raging gales and white-out conditions amazingly quickly and unexpectedly; snow can come at any time of year on the mountain, even in summer. There are also precipitous bluffs and steep icy slopes. In good conditions tramping around the mountain, or even to the summit, can be reasonably easy, but the mountain has claimed over 50 lives. Don't be put off, but don't be deceived.

If you intend tramping, get a map and consult a Conservation Officer for current weather and track conditions before you set off. Some tracks marked on maps have been closed and other planned ones may have opened; the North Egmont Chalet, marked on many maps, no longer exists. Be sure to register your tramping intentions and help information (who to contact in case of emergency, etc) with a DOC office.

A trip to the North Egmont Visitor Centre at the end of Egmont Rd is worthwhile for the view, and there are numerous long and short tracks and bush walks as well. The centre has interesting displays on the park and the mountain, an audiovisual feature, and a cafe.

The roads to the Stratford Mountain House, East Egmont, and Dawson Falls also have many worthwhile tracks and bush walks. From the Mountain House, Pembroke Rd continues three km to the Stratford Plateau and from there a 1.5 km walk takes you to the Maunganui ski area. Skiing equipment can be hired at the Stratford Mountain House (see Places to Stay).

There are two main routes to the summit. The safest and most direct route takes off from the North Egmont Visitor Centre; allow about six to eight hours for the return trip. This route on the north side of the mountain loses its snow and ice soonest in the year. Another route to the summit, taking off from the Dawson Falls Visitor Centre, requires more technical skill and keeps its ice longer in the year; if you go up this way, allow seven to 10 hours for the return trip.

The round-the-mountain track, accessible from the ends of all three mountain roads, goes 55 km around the mountain and takes four days or more to complete. A number of huts are sited around the mountain. You can start or finish this track at any park entrance.

If you are an inexperienced climber or if you want other people to climb or tramp with, there are various possibilities. The Stratford Tramping Club (☎ 762 7822, 764 7028) goes on easy, medium and hard walks. The Mt Egmont Alpine Club (☎ 278 4460) goes tramping, climbing, skiing and canoeing. DOC can put you in contact with other tramping clubs in the area. Mountain Guides Mt Egmont (☎ 758 8261, 762 4752) offer guided trips to the summit all year round.

Places to Stay

Most visitors stay in New Plymouth, the nearest large town to the park, from where there's a convenient daily door-to-door shuttle service to the mountain. Other options are to stay in the park itself or in other nearby towns around the mountain.

Camping, Huts & Bunkhouses There are a number of tramping huts scattered about the mountain, administered by DOC and reachable only by trails. Most cost $8 a night (two tickets, which can be purchased from any DOC office), but some cost only $4 (one ticket). You provide your own cooking, eating and sleeping gear, they provide bunks and mattresses, and no bookings are necessary, it's all on a first come, first served basis.

The Camphouse, a bunkhouse beside the North Egmont Visitor Centre (☎ 756 8710), has bunks at $8, with hotplates for cooking and hot showers; bring your own sleeping bag and kitchen utensils.

By the Dawson Falls Visitor Centre (☎ (025) 430 248), *Konini Lodge* has bunkhouse accommodation at $12 per person. Bring your own sleeping bag, food supplies and kitchen utensils.

There are motor camps at New Plymouth, Stratford, Eltham, Hawera, Opunake, Oakura and Waitara, but camping is not encouraged within the park itself – you're supposed to use the tramping huts.

Guesthouses The *Dawson Falls Tourist Lodge* (☎ & fax 765 5457) beside the Dawson Falls Visitor Centre is an attractive European alpine-style lodge with lots of carved wood and painted decorations, good views, comfortable rooms and sitting rooms and a dining room where guests dine all together. Rates are $80/100 for singles/doubles, meals extra. A courtesy car will meet public transport in Stratford.

On the eastern side of the mountain, the

Mountain House Motor Lodge (☎ & fax 765 6100) on Pembroke Rd, about 15 km up the mountain from Stratford, has standard rooms at $82, deluxe rooms at $95 and chalet cabins with kitchens at $75. They hire skis in winter for use at the nearby ski area.

Getting There & Away

There are several points of access to the park, but three roads lead almost right up to where the heavy bush ends. Closest to New Plymouth is Egmont Rd, turning off SH 3 at Egmont Village, 12 km south of New Plymouth, and heading another 16 km up the mountain to the North Egmont Visitor Centre. Pembroke Rd enters the park from the east at Stratford and ascends 18 km up to East Egmont, Stratford Mountain House, the Plateau car park and the Maunganui ski area. From the south-east, Manaia Rd leads up to Dawson Falls, 23 km from Stratford.

Public buses don't go to Egmont National Park but Tubby's Tours in New Plymouth (☎ 753 6306) operates a daily door-to-door shuttle bus from New Plymouth to the mountain. The cost is $10 one way or $15 return, whether you return on the same or a different day. Tubby's also offers guided tours of the mountain, as do the other New Plymouth tour companies.

An alternative shuttle from New Plymouth to the park is with John Morton (☎ 758 2315), who goes up early each morning and returns in the late afternoon.

AROUND TARANAKI

Mt Taranaki is the principal attraction but there are also other places of interest around the Taranaki region.

There are two principal highways around the mountain. SH 3, on the inland side of the mountain, is the most travelled route, heading south from New Plymouth for 70 km until it meets the coast again at Hawera. The coast road, SH 45, heads 105 km around the coast from New Plymouth to Hawera, where it meets up again with SH 3. A round-the-mountain trip on both highways is 175 km, although shortcuts can be taken. A Taranaki Heritage Trails booklet, available free from information centres and DOC offices, points out many places of interest.

Stratford

Stratford (population 5650), 40 km south of New Plymouth on SH 3, is named after Stratford-upon-Avon in England, Shakespeare's birthplace, and almost all its streets are named after Shakespearean characters. There is an Information Centre (☎ 765 6708) on Broadway, the main street; a DOC Field Centre (☎ 765 5144) on Pembroke Rd, heading up to Mt Taranaki, and an AA office (☎ 765 7331) at 298 Broadway North.

On SH 3 one km south of the centre, the Taranaki Pioneer Village is a four-hectare outdoor museum featuring 50 historic buildings and other items pertaining to the heritage of the Taranaki region. It's open every day from 10 am to 4 pm; admission is $5 (children $2, family $12).

At Stratford is the turn-off for Pembroke Rd, heading up the mountain for 18 km to East Egmont, the Stratford Mountain House and the Maunganui ski area. Stratford is also the south end of the Stratford-Taumarunui Heritage Trail.

Accommodation in Stratford includes hotels, motels, B&Bs and the *Stratford Holiday Park* (☎ 765 6440) in Page St beside the King Edward Park and an indoor heated swimming pool, with tent sites, powered sites, cabins, tourist flats and a bunkhouse.

Stratford-Taumarunui Heritage Trail

From Stratford, the Whangamomona-Tangarakau Gorge route (SH 43) heads off towards Taumarunui in the central North Island. The route has been designated a Heritage Trail, passing by many historic sites including the historic town of Whangamomona, Maori pa sites, small villages, waterfalls, abandoned coal mines and small museums. You can pick up a free Heritage Trails booklet from information centres or DOC offices in Stratford, Taumarunui or New Plymouth giving details of 32 places of interest along the route; keep an eye out for the blue and yellow Heritage Trail signs along the way, with explanatory plaques.

It takes a minimum of 2½ to three hours to drive the 150 km from Stratford to Taumarunui (or vice versa), as the road winds through hilly bush country and 30 km of it is unsealed. Nevertheless it's a good trip if you can put up with the road. It's best to start early in the day; allow at least five hours for the trip if you plan to make stops to see the historic sites. Fill up with petrol from the Stratford or Taumarunui ends, as petrol stations are limited once you're on the road. This is definitely a way to get right off the beaten track in New Zealand.

Eltham & The Lakes

About 10 km south of Stratford is Eltham, well known for its cheeses. Eleven km southeast down the Rawhitiroa Rd is Lake Rotokare, the largest stretch of inland water in Taranaki, where there's a 1½ to two hour walk around the lake through native bush. The artificial Lake Rotorangi, 46 km long and popular for boating and fishing, is also nearby, with cruises operating on the lake.

HOLLARD GARDENS

On Manaia Rd three km north of Kaponga, which is about 13 km west of Eltham on the road to Opunake, are the large Hollard Gardens, administered by the Queen Elizabeth II National Trust. It's most colourful from September to November when the rhododendrons are in bloom but many other plantings provide colour all year round. The vast array of rare plants make it a horticulturalist's delight, with posted half and one-hour walks through various gardens. It's open every day from 9 am until dusk; admission is $5 (children free).

Manaia Rd continues north right into the Egmont National Park, leading up to Dawson Falls.

Kapuni

About seven km south of Kaponga is Kapuni. Natural gas discovered at Kapuni was the first such find of any size in New Zealand. It is now piped to Auckland and Wellington. Oil condensate is also piped from Kapuni to New Plymouth, from where it is shipped to

New Zealand's oil refinery at Marsden Point near Whangarei, north of Auckland.

Hawera

Hawera (population 11,050) is on the coast 70 km south of New Plymouth and 90 km from Wanganui. It has an Information Centre (☎ 278 8599) at 55 High St (beside the water tower) and an AA office (☎ 278 5095) at 121-123 Princes St.

Elvis fans might be interested in visiting the Kevin Wasley Elvis Presley Memorial Room (☎ 278 7624) at 51 Argyle St, with a collection of Elvis records and souvenirs. You need to ask that you please telephone before you arrive.

Hawera also has the excellent Tawhiti Museum, a private collection of remarkable exhibits, models and dioramas covering many aspects of Taranaki heritage. The life-like human figures were cast from real people around the region; it's quite a unique museum. A bush railway operates the first Sunday of each month and every Sunday during school holidays. The museum is on Ohangai Rd near the corner of Tawhiti Rd, four km from town. It's open Friday to Monday from 10 am to 4 pm, but on Sunday only in winter (June, July and August).

Two km north of Hawera on the Turuturu Road are the remains of the pre-European Turuturu Mokai Pa. The reserve is open to the public every day. The Tawhiti Museum has a model of the pa.

Accommodation in Hawera includes hotels, motels and the *King Edward Park* camping ground (☎ 278 8544) on Waihi Rd, adjacent to the park, gardens and municipal swimming pool, with tent sites, powered sites, cabins and on-site caravans.

Oakura

If you're starting round the mountain from New Plymouth on the coast road, SH 45, the first settlement you'll come to is the small town of Oakura (population 970), 15 km west of New Plymouth, known for its beautiful beach – great for swimming, surfing and windsurfing. Oakura has a town pub with an attractive beer garden, there's a crafts shop called the Crafty Fox open every day, a surfing and windsurfing shop, and accommodation including a good hostel, motor camp and motel (see the New Plymouth section).

Lucy's Gully

Lucy's Gully, 23 km from New Plymouth on SH 45, is one of the few places where exotic trees are being maintained in a national park. A pleasant picnic area, it is also the start of a couple of tracks into the Kaitake Ranges. Further along SH 45, turn west at Pungarehu onto Cape Rd to reach the Cape Egmont Lighthouse, an interesting sight but not open to visitors.

Parihaka

Inland a km or two from Pungarehu is the Maori village of Parihaka (population 100), formerly the stronghold of the Maori prophet and chief Te Whiti and once one of the largest Maori villages in New Zealand. Te Whiti led a passive resistance campaign against the ruthless land confiscation that was taking place with the expansion of European settlement. In the last military campaign in Taranaki, Te Whiti was defeated and jailed, and in 1881 Parihaka was razed. The heavily armed troops found themselves opposed only by dancing children.

The spirit of Te Whiti still lives on, and his descendants and followers meet at Parihaka annually; it is not open to the public. Many other places in Taranaki are steeped in their Maori past.

Oaonui

Further south along the coast is Oaonui, the landfall of the gas pipeline from the Maui platform and the site of the onshore processing plant. A model room is open to visitors daily from 8.30 am to 4.30 pm.

Opunake

Opunake (population 1600) is the largest town on the the west side of the mountain. There's a fine beach in the small Opunake Bay, a peaceful place good for swimming and surfing; right on the beach, the *Opunake Beach Motor Camp Resort* (☎ 761 8235) has tent sites, powered sites, on-site caravans, and backpackers accommodation for $10 per night. In town, the *Opunake Motel and Opunake Backpackers* (☎ 761 8330) has motel units, a cottage and a large house for backpackers out the back.

Coromandel Peninsula & Hauraki Plains

South-east of Auckland lie the very flat Hauraki Plains, and the Coromandel Peninsula, a rugged, densely forested region with very little flat land, where rivers force their way through gorges and pour down steep cliffs to the sea. The Coromandel Forest Park stretches almost the entire length of the peninsula. It's an intensely scenic area, isolated and well worth going to before it becomes spoilt by tourism. There are a number of small towns scattered up and down both sides of the peninsula along the coast.

North of Coromandel township, towards the tip of the peninsula, there is a wealth of possibilities, including the rugged Moehau Range and isolated Fletcher Bay.

South of the peninsula is the pancake flat Hauraki Plains and to the west the bird-watchers' heaven, the Firth of Thames.

Information

Most of this region's telephone numbers have an 07 prefix if you are calling them from a long distance (even within the region), so we haven't included the prefix with each number. Where the prefix is different, it is included with the number.

Getting There & Away

Bus The InterCity (well, a collection of operators holding InterCity concessions) bus station (☎ 868 67251) is on Queen St at the old railway station. Buses operate between Auckland, Thames and Whitianga daily – these are run by Sunkist Bus Services (☎ 868 8808); it's a 1½-hour trip from Auckland to Thames and another 1½ hours to Whitianga, the ticket is valid for three months, and the cost is $65. The trip can include the peninsula loop (including Fletcher Bay) for an extra $20.

Once in Thames there is a good network established so you can reach the far flung parts of the peninsula. Murphy's (☎ 867

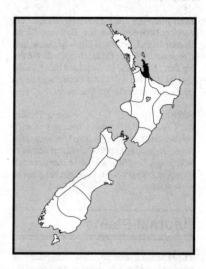

6829) travel between Thames, Coromandel, Whitianga, Tairua and back to Thames, everyday except Saturday; the loop cost is $35. If you wish to go further afield, say into the Kauaeranga Valley or to Fletcher Bay, then the Sunkist Lodge (☎ 868 8808) can arrange transport. There is daily transport to the Kauaeranga Valley at 1.30 pm daily, and trips go to Fletcher Bay daily in the peak season, or otherwise on Monday, Wednesday and Friday (May to October). As part of the Auckland loop, but not including the peninsula loop, the all-up cost for the valley and Fletcher Bay is $82.

Connections can be made to Rotorua with Kiwi Safaris Hot Mud Safaris (☎ (0800) 800 616) who do an Auckland-Thames-Te Aroha-Rotorua loop. Similarly, there is an Auckland-Thames-Tauranga loop with Bayline Coaches (☎ 578 2825). Get a copy of the *Coromandel Peninsula Bus Services* pamphlet.

COROMANDEL

To reach Cook's Beach, Hahei and Hot Water Beach you can use Bev's Lookabout Tours (☎ 866 3917), which operates out of Ferry Landing, just across from Whitianga.

Boat Plans are afoot to consolidate the boat service between Fletcher Bay and Great Barrier Island. This will allow an Auckland-Coromandel-Great Barrier loop, with the last leg from the island to Auckland being on the QuickCat. This will make a cycle tour of the peninsula particularly attractive.

Hitching Hitching is OK between Thames and Coromandel but can sometimes be difficult beyond there. Be prepared for long waits if you're heading up to Colville or across to Whitianga. Traffic is sparse on the east coast except at holiday periods, so hitching can be slow going.

Hauraki Plains

The Hauraki Plains cover the triangular area bounded by Miranda on the south-west of the Firth of Thames across to Waihi by the east coast and then down to the southern apex at Paeroa and Te Aroha, which are inland. To know more about the area, get a free copy of *Hauraki: Part of the Coromandel Experience*.

MIRANDA

Avid birdwatchers will love this area as it is one of the most accessible places to study birds. There is a vast 8500-hectare mudflat on the western side of the Firth of Thames, teeming with aquatic worms and crustacea, which attracts many thousands of Arctic nesting shore-birds over the Arctic winter.

The two main species are the bar-tailed godwit and the lesser knot, but it isn't surprising to see turnstones, curlew sandpipers, sharp-tailed sandpipers, and the odd vagrant red-necked stint and terek sandpiper.

Interestingly too, Miranda attracts internal migrants after the godwits and knots have departed. These include the South Island pied oystercatcher and the wrybill from South Island breeding grounds, and banded dotterels and pied stilts from both main islands. The wrybill, as its name suggests, is distinguishable by its blackish-brown bill which curves to the right at its tip.

For information on this avifauna extravaganza, visit the modern Miranda Naturalists' Trust Education Centre, just north of Miranda. More interesting facets of the birds characterisitics and the secrets of their migration are outlined in the pamphlet *Shore Bird Migration to and from Miranda*.

Places to Stay & Eat

The *Miranda Naturalists' Trust* have clean, modern accommodation with all facilities at their Education Centre. A bed here costs a very reasonable $12.50 for nonmembers ($7.50 for members), and the same for campers. To become a member of the trust costs $20 per year.

Not far south of the centre is the *Miranda Hot Springs Oasis* (☎ 867 3055) where a campsite is $7.50 per person, a powered site $15 for two and on-site caravans $35 for two. Entrance to the hot pools is included in the price (incidentally this is the largest hot pool in New Zealand); a joyous soak after a day out on the mudflats observing birds. Dinner that evening could be complemented with fresh cheese from *Miranda Valley Cheese*, open from 9 am to 6 pm.

Alternatively, head north to Kaiaua to sample the lemon fish, snapper and mussels at the local *fish & chip shop*. They claim to be NZ's best and at least one reader, a resident of Grand Rapids, Michigan, agrees.

Ngatea

Originally known as 'Orchard', Ngatea is the hub of the Hauraki Plains and it is 24 km north-west of Paeroa. Before the draining of the plains, access to Ngatea was by small steamer. Wilderness Gems, 13 River Road, is a haven for rockhounds. There is some accommodation and a few cafes here. The *Ngatea Hotel* (☎ 867 7189) has singles/doubles for $33/50 and the *Thames Valley Motel* (☎ 867 7189) has units for $40/60.

PAEROA

The Maori name for the Coromandel range was Te Paeroa-o-Toi or 'The Long Range of Toi' and local Maoris are believed to be descendants of the *Arawa* and *Tainui* canoes of the Great Migration fleet. In the days before the plains were drained Paeroa was a thriving port, and evidence of this can be seen in the Paeroa Historical Maritime Park. The main display here is the double paddle steamer *Kopu* which once operated between Paeroa and Auckland but there are other interesting displays for maritime lovers, including the 'cream boat' *Scotty* and the navy diving tender HMNZS *Manawanui*.

NZ's own soft drink 'Lemon & Paeroa' had its beginnings in this town but all that is left now is one discarded giant empty bottle, left here after Gulliver's travels.

The Paeroa Information Centre (☎ 862 8636) is on Belmont Rd (SH 2) and is open daily. The small museum is open Monday to Friday from 10.30 am to 3 pm and admission is $2 for adults and 50c for children.

Karangahake Gorge

The Karangahake Gorge Historic Walkway along the Ohinemuri River was commenced when the Paeroa to Waihi railway line was closed in 1979. Waikino is at the eastern end of the gorge and the only remaining building there, after floods in 1981, was the Waikino Hotel.

The visitor centre in Waikino, now the terminus of the six-km Waihi-to-Waikino vintage railway, has information on the history and walks of the area. The booklet *Karangahake Gorge Historic Walkway* by Derek Beisly, and the DOC pamphlet of the same name, outline several easy walks in the area and suggest some harder ones.

Three of the highlights of the walkway are the **Owharoa Falls** and the Talisman and Victoria **gold battery sites**. There is a small museum and craft shop in Waikino; admission is $5 for adults and $1 for children.

Places to Stay & Eat

The *Backpackers' Paradise* (☎ 862 6609) is at 3 Seymour St (behind the Caltex service station), where beds are $12 or a campsite is $6; sheets and blankets are provided free as is tea, coffee and Milo. In addition to this place there's the *Paeroa Hotel* (☎ 862 7099); and the *Casa Mexicana Motel* (☎ 862 8216); *Paeroa Motel* (☎ 862 8475); and *Racecourse Motel* (☎ 862 7145). All the motels are about $60/70 for singles/doubles.

There are several places to eat in Paeroa. On Belmont Rd are the *Tui Coffee Lounge* and the *Four Seasons Chinese Restaurant & Takeaways*. On Normanby Rd (SH 2) are the *Criterion Dairy* and the *Cosy Kitchen Tearooms*.

Talisman Tearooms & Crafts at Waikino serves light lunches and afternoon teas; it is open from 9.30 am to 5 pm daily.

WAIHI

At Waihi, once a booming gold-mining town, there's a good **museum** with superb models and displays about the local Martha Hill Mine. The Waihi Information Centre (☎ 863 6715) is on Seddon St; you can get information here about the Waihi Gold Mining Company as well as other attractions in the district. The museum is on Kenny St and is open from 10 am to 4 pm Monday to Friday and from 1.30 to 4 pm on weekends.

The large **Martha Hill mine** is now operating again after a long hiatus; there are weekday tours by prior arrangement (☎ 863 8192). If you want to learn more, read about it in the glossy *Martha Hill Mine – Waihi: Information Guide*.

Railway buffs, gathered together as the **Goldfields Steam Train Society** (☎ 863 8251), have acquired eight km of track between here and Waikino, and run trains between the two townships. To get to the train station turn off SH 2 at Wrigley St and proceed to the end.

From 10 am to 4 pm, November to April, you can visit the **Waihi Waterlily Gardens** out on Pukekauri Rd.

Places to Stay & Eat

There is plenty of accommodation available in and around Waihi, especially out at Waihi Beach which is 11 km east of the town.

COROMANDEL

Motor camps include: *Waihi Motor Camp* (☎ 863 7654), 6 Waitete Rd; *Waihi Water-lily Gardens Holiday Park* (☎ 863 8267), Puke-kauri Rd; *Athenree Motor Camp* (☎ 863 5600), Waihi Beach; *Beachaven Camp & Caravan Park* (☎ 863 5505), Leo St; *Bowen-town Motor Camp* (☎ 863 5381), Waihi Beach South; and *Waihi Beach Holiday Park* (☎ 863 5504), adjacent to Ocean Beach. Expect to pay about $7 for a campsite in town and an extra $2 if you are out at the beach; on-site caravans are generally $30 for two at all the camps.

There are also two motels and a hotel in town and another motel out at the beach.

On Haszard St is *Jacqui's Tearooms & Restaurant*, a BYO place which is open for breakfast, lunch and dinner. More famous is the quaint *Grandpa Thorn's Restaurant & Craft Shop*, 4 Waitete Rd. This log-cabin place has full à la carte menu and has won many awards. Coromandel mussels and local scallops are specialities. Local crafts are displayed and sold here.

Coromandel Peninsula

The Coromandel Peninsula comprises all the land mass and islands north of the Hauraki Plains and south of Great Barrier Island. The main towns are, in a clockwise direction following SH 25, Thames, Coromandel, Whitianga and Whangamata. You can cross the peninsula using either of three very scenic roads – the 309 Road, Tapu-Coroglen Rd or SH 25A. This chapter follows the west coast from Thames to Fletcher Bay in the north, and then the east coast from the top to Waihi – the scenic routes across the penin-sula are also described.

The Coromandel Peninsula is not the place to go if you're looking for lively enter-tainment, but if you're in the mood for lying around on beaches, fishing, lazing and walking it's superb. It is very much one of the last bastions of those seeking an alterna-tive lifestyle, away from the bustle of Auckland, a serenity only briefly punctuated by the hordes of Christmas holidaymakers.

HISTORY

Maoris have lived on the peninsula since the first settlers arrived, and the sheltered areas of the east coast supported a large popula-tion. This was one of the major moa-hunting areas of the North Island, although people also drew on the many other food sources available through fishing, sealing, bird-hunting and horticulture.

The European history of the peninsula and the plains to the south is steeped in gold-mining, logging and gum-digging. Gold was first discovered in New Zealand at Coro-mandel in 1852 by Charles Ring, but the rush was short-lived once the miners found it was not alluvial gold but gold to be wrested from the ground by pick and shovel. More gold was discovered around Thames in 1867 and over the next few years other fields were proclaimed at Coromandel, Kuaotunu and Karangahake. In 1892 the Martha mine at Waihi began production; by the time it was closed in 1952, around $60 million of gold had been taken. Interest in minerals is still strong today because the area is also rich in semi-precious gemstones like quartz, agate, amethyst, jasper, chalcedony and carnelian. In fact, if you walk along Te Mata beach you will probably stumble over some agate.

Kauri logging was a big business on the peninsula for around 100 years. Allied to the timber trade was ship building which took off after 1832 when a mill was established at Mercury Bay. By the 1880s Kauaeranga, Coroglen (Gumtown) and Tairua were the main suppliers of kauri to the Auckland mills. Things got tougher once the kauri around the coast became scarce due to indis-criminate felling, and the loggers had to penetrate deeper into the bush for the timber. The problems of getting it out became more and more difficult. Some logs were pulled out by bullock teams; others had to be hauled to rivers and floated out after dams had been built; tramways were built on the west coast; but by the 1930s the logging of kauri on the peninsula had all but finished.

COROMANDEL

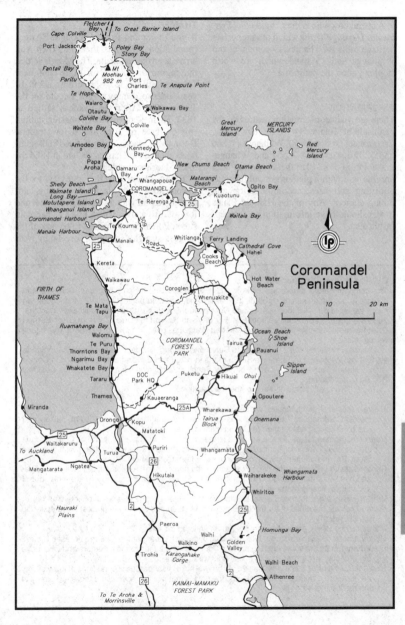

Fletcher Bay
To Great Barrier Island
Cape Colville
Port Jackson
Poley Bay
Stony Bay
Fantail Bay
Parītu
Mt Moehau 982 m
Port Charles
Te Anaputa Point
Te Hope
Waiaro
Waikawau Bay
Otautu
Colville Bay
Waitete Bay
Colville
Great Mercury Island
MERCURY ISLANDS
Amodeo Bay
Kennedy Bay
Red Mercury Island
Papa Aroha
Oamaru Bay
New Chums Beach
Otama Beach
Shelly Beach
Waimate Island
Whangapoua
Matarangi Beach
Opito Bay
Long Bay
COROMANDEL
Motutapere Island
Kuaotunu
Whanganui Island
Te Rerenga
25
Coromandel Harbour
Te Kouma
Waitaia Bay
Manaia Harbour
Manaia
Whitianga
Ferry Landing
Cathedral Cove
Hahei

Coromandel Peninsula

Kereta
Cooks Beach
0   10   20 km

Waikawau
Coroglen
Hot Water Beach

FIRTH OF THAMES
Whenuakite

Te Mata Tapu
Ruamahanga Bay
Waiomu
COROMANDEL FOREST PARK
Ocean Beach
Shoe Island
Te Puru
Tairua
Thorntons Bay
Pauanui
Ngarimu Bay
Whakatete Bay
Slipper Island
Tararu
DOC Park HQ
Puketu
Hikuai
Ohui
Thames
Kauaeranga
Opoutere
Miranda
25A
Oronga
Wharekawa
Tairua Block
Onemana
Kopu
Matatoki
Waitakaruru
25
Puriri
Whangamata
To Auckland
Turua
26
Mangatarata
Ngatea
Hikutaia
Wainarakeke
Whangamata Harbour
Hauraki Plains
2
Whiritoa
Paeroa
25
Waikino
Waihi
Homunga Bay
Tirohia
Karangahake Gorge
Golden Valley
Waihi Beach
26
2
Athenree
KAIMAI-MAMAKU FOREST PARK
To Te Aroha & Morrinsville

COROMANDEL

A useful brochure is the *Coromandel Peninsula: Heritage Trails* which outlines urban heritage trails for Thames, Coromandel and Whitianga and 15 spots which are worth stopping at on the peninsula.

INFORMATION

There are visitor information centres on the peninsula at Thames (☎ & fax 868 7284), Coromandel (☎ 866 8598), Whitianga (☎ 866 5555), Tairua (☎ 864 7055) and Whangamata (☎ 865 8340); these centres will provide you with a plethora of publications outlining activities, accommodation and dining choices. Any of the Hauraki Plains towns should have information on the peninsula also.

THAMES

If you're coming from Auckland, Thames (population 6,500) is the first town you arrive at on the peninsula. The Maoris settled the region and lived on high land near Thames until the 1820s, returning about 10 years later to occupy a new pa site on the Thames flat. After the Pakehas settled in 1833, Thames consisted of a mission station, two or three pa sites and a few traders. During the Maori Wars of the 1860s gunboats shelled the Thames pa, and in 1864 the local Maoris surrendered.

Today Thames is the gateway to the Coromandel Peninsula, a rather sleepy, laid-back little port with a small fishing fleet and lots of privately owned boats. The main street, Pollen St, is claimed to be one of the longest straight shopping streets in New

---

Cycling in the Coromandel

The compact nature of the peninsula makes it an ideal place for a cycling tour. Some people choose to get their bikes dropped off in Thames and then do a peninsula circuit. It is becoming much easier to do a full loop – Auckland-Coromandel-Great Barrier Island-Auckland – now that there are transport possibilities from Fletcher Bay and then on the QuickCat from Great Barrier. Once the mountain-bike track over the Moehau Range has been completed a full peninsula circuit will be possible.

The most preferred route is Thames to Coromandel along the coast; Coromandel to Whitianga via 309 Rd; Whitianga to Tairua via SH 25 or the ferry to Ferry Landing and then taking in Cook's Beach, Hahei, Cathedral Cove and Hot Water Beach and rejoining the road at Whenuakite. Only 309 Rd is not sealed.

The following are notes on each of the road sections:

Hauraki Plains: straight, sealed, with no steep hills
Thames to Coromandel: Thames has a busy residential area; the coast road is flat, narrow and has blind bends; last section to Coromandel is steep but sealed
North of Coromandel: to Colville the road is steep and narrow in places; north of Colville roads are unsealed and more suited to mountain bikes; there's a new mountain-bike track from Stony Bay to Fletcher Bay, which is well away from Coromandel Walkway
Coromandel to Whitianga: the two roads across the peninsula are unsealed; SH 25 is the longer and has two steep hills; 309 Rd is potholed and has corrugations but there are a number of accessible, scenic features
Whitianga to Tairua: this road is sealed and has one steep hill; the reverse direction is harder
Kopu to Hikuai: not suitable for the beginner as it is steep and slippery in places; more suited to the fit cyclist
Maratoto/The Wires: the walking tracks are off-limits to cyclists
Whangamata: there are large hills on both sides of Whangamata; in the forests around Whangamata are some great mountain bike tracks; the bush around Opoutere and Ohui have dirt and clay single-tracks with occasional water crossings
Karangahake Gorge; this road is sealed all the way but it is dangerous in conditions of low visibility as there are a number of blind bends; the plus is that it is flat, scenic and there are plenty of interesting rest stops ■

COROMANDEL

Zealand. Out on the Firth of Thames there is an excellent bird-watching hide dedicated to the *Rainbow Warrior*.

Information

The Thames Information & Public Relations Centre (☎ 868 7284) is in Porritt Park at 405 Queen St, which runs along the coast parallel to Pollen St. The people here are extremely friendly and they're a mine of information about the whole peninsula. The centre is open from 9 am to 5 pm on weekdays, and from 10 am to 3 pm on weekends.

The DOC office (☎ 868 6381) in the Kauaeranga Valley is open from 8 am to 4 pm Monday to Friday. There's an AA office at 424 Pollen St, and the CPO is on Pollen St, between Mary and Sealey Sts.

Gold-Mining Relics

You can see some of the town's gold-mining history at the beginning of Tararu Rd, at the northern end of town. The Hauraki Prospectors' Association has set up a stamper battery here and there's a gold mine close by which you can look over on request. During the summer from 10 am to 4 pm they offer two tours daily except on Sunday; the cost is $4 (children $1).

Around the end of the 1800s Thames was actually the biggest town in New Zealand, with over 100 hotels. There are still a number of fine old hotels like the Brian Boru on Pollen St; they're a solid reminder of the town's goldrush prosperity. The popular Sunkist Lodge is just one of the venerable hotel buildings.

Museums

The **Mineralogical Museum**, on the corner of Brown and Cochrane Sts, has the most comprehensive collection of NZ rocks, minerals and fossils in the country. It's open most of the year from Wednesday to Sunday, from 11 am to 4 pm (in winter it is usually Tuesday to Sunday from 11 am to 3 pm); admission is $2 (children $1). Ask someone here and they may be able to put you in touch with one of the local prospectors so you can go fossicking. Next door is the **Thames School of**

Mines which operated from 1886 to 1954. It is being restored by the Historic Places Trust.

The local **Historical Museum**, on the corner of Cochrane and Pollen Sts, is open from 1 to 4 pm everyday; admission is $2 (children 20c).

Agatha Christie Weekends

Twice a month the Brian Boru Hotel becomes the scene of a murder, and each of the 30 to 45 guests is a suspect, when the Agatha Christie weekend takes place. Guests arrive on Friday evening for dinner and spend the Saturday on guided visits around the Coromandel Peninsula. On Saturday evening they don fancy-dress costumes, and the mystery begins. Likely as not there will be a fire (with the cooperation of the local fire brigade), and with a dead body the race is on to guess 'whodunnit'. The successful sleuth wins $200. On Sunday everyone joins in a 'postmortem' over a big breakfast.

These weekends have been gaining local and international attention, winning awards for their entertainment value and attracting visitors from many countries. The price of $300 covers everything for the whole weekend, including the use of a fancy-dress costume if you don't happen to have your own. Phone the hotel (☎ 868 6523) for reservations.

Other Things to See & Do

You can walk or drive to Monument Hill – a WW I peace memorial – up Waiotahi Creek Rd from the northern intersection of Pollen St and SH 25 for a good view of Thames, the Hauraki Plains to the south and the Hauraki Gulf to the north.

Another good vantage point is Totara Pa Hill, a lookout over the Waihou Valley and the Hauraki Plains. Several Maori intertribal battles were fought in this area; if you look carefully you will see the remains of fortifications and deep trenches. Nowadays there's a cemetery on the pa site. Take Te Arapipi Rd to get there. About three km behind Thames there is a short 2½-to-three hour walk to the Rock's Goldmine; get information from the Dickson Holiday Park.

COROMANDEL

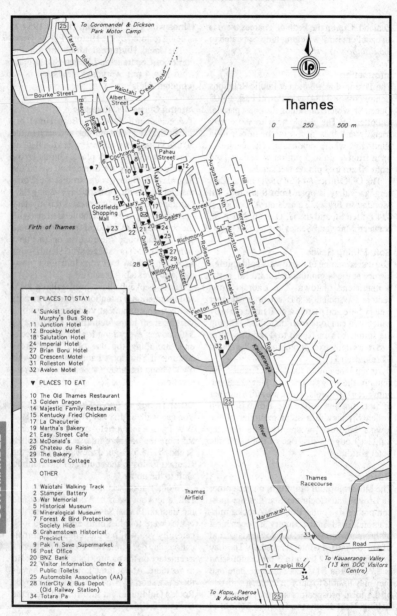

Thames

0   250   500 m

Firth of Thames

COROMANDEL

■ PLACES TO STAY

4 Sunkist Lodge &
  Murphy's Bus Stop
11 Junction Hotel
12 Brookby Motel
18 Salutation Hotel
24 Imperial Hotel
27 Brian Boru Hotel
30 Crescent Motel
31 Rolleston Motel
32 Avalon Motel

▼ PLACES TO EAT

10 The Old Thames Restaurant
13 Golden Dragon
14 Majestic Family Restaurant
15 Kentucky Fried Chicken
17 La Chacuterie
19 Martha's Bakery
21 Easy Street Cafe
23 McDonald's
26 Chateau du Raisin
29 The Bakery
33 Cotswold Cottage

OTHER

1 Waiotahi Walking Track
2 Stamper Battery
3 War Memorial
5 Historical Museum
6 Mineralogical Museum
7 Forest & Bird Protection
  Society Hide
8 Grahamstown Historical
  Precinct
9 Pak 'n Save Supermarket
16 Post Office
20 BNZ Bank
22 Visitor Information Centre &
  Public Toilets
25 Automobile Association (AA)
28 InterCity & Bus Depot
  (Old Railway Station)
34 Totara Pa

Scenic flights are offered by the Thames Air Service or you can go gliding for about $45 per half-hour. Various horse treks go up into the bush. The visitor information centre can recommend a good scenic drive around Thames, outlined on a free map. There's also a nice drive to Kauaeranga Valley through bush country.

The Thames Society of Arts & Crafts is open on weekends in winter, longer hours in summer, showing locals' work at the Old North School on Tararu Rd, north of Thames. If you like arts & crafts ask the visitor information centre for a pamphlet called the *Coromandel Craft Trail*, showing the locations of arts & crafts galleries all over the peninsula – there are many. For those who like a bargain, Pollen St has an abundance of second-hand shops and also a book exchange.

You can hire kayaks (☎ 867 7037) for $20 per day for river or coastal trips.

Places to Stay

Camping & Cabins The *Dickson Holiday Park* (☎ 868 7308) is three km north of Thames, in an attractive quiet valley beside a stream four minutes from the beach. Camping costs $7 per person, or a bit more with power. Bunkroom accommodation costs $10, cabins start from $32 a double, and a tourist flat with bathroom and colour TV costs $48 a double. It's a pleasant site with a swimming pool and free bicycles. Telephone for courtesy pick-up.

There are numerous other campsites on the coast north of Thames – see the North of Thames section.

Hostels The *Sunkist Lodge* (☎ 868 8808; fax 868 7426), 506 Brown St, is a pleasantly relaxed hostel. A dorm bed costs $13, and twins and doubles are $17 per person. The upstairs verandah is a fine place to laze on a sunny afternoon or to watch the sunset over the placid Firth of Thames; there is a pool table in the lounge downstairs. The fine old building was the Lady Bowen Hotel from 1868 to 1952 and it's reputed to have a resident ghost.

The friendly manager, Geoff, seems to know more about the Coromandel than most and has seen to it that there is a proper network of accommodation and transport for independent backpackers coming to the area. You can arrange transport into the Kauaeranga Valley and also hire mountain bikes for long or short-term explorations from this hostel. Geoff runs Fletcher Bay Hostel as well and can arrange it so that you can walk from Stony Bay to Fletchers Bay where accommodation will be available.

Hotels There are still enough hotels remaining from the goldrush days to give Thames a good representation in this category. The *Brian Boru Hotel* (☎ 868 6523), 200 Richmond St, on the corner of Pollen St, has single/double rooms for $65/88, or $97 for two with a private bathroom. In the off season you might get budget rates if you ask. The *Imperial Hotel* (☎ 868 6200), on the corner of Sealey and Pollen Sts, has single/double rooms at $33/50.

The *Junction Hotel* (☎ 868 6008) is on the corner of Pollen and Pahau Sts and, like a lot of hotels feeling the pinch, has set aside space for backpackers ($25 for a twin room) – we didn't get to see them as they were 'busy' but judging by the public bar downstairs it looks like the place is a bit rough. Another cheap hotel is the *Salutation* (☎ 868 6488), 400 Mary St, where single/ double rooms cost $20/40. Again, band noise of the 'grunge' variety may disturb your sleep here.

Motels There are plenty of motels in Thames and north along the coast towards Coromandel. None of them are bargains; count on at least $60 for a single or $70 for a double. You could try the *Brookby Motel* (☎ 868 6663) at 102 Redwood Lane or the *Crescent Motel* (☎ 868 6506) on the corner of Jellicoe Crescent and Fenton St. The *Coastal Motor Lodge* (☎ 868 6843), three km north of Thames on SH 25, is considerably more expensive at $92/105 for a single/double, but it's very attractive and pleasantly situated.

Ask at the visitor information centre for a current listing of all the motels.

Places to Eat
Snacks & Fast Food There are a number of takeaways on Pollen St and there are plenty more scattered around town. Along Pollen St you have: *The Bakery*, a bakery and coffee lounge open every day of the week where you can get baked goodies, light meals and takeaways; *La Chacuterie* prepare open sandwiches, hot continental food, soups and coffee; *Martha's Cafe* sells bread, croissants, light lunches and good espresso; *Peanutz Health Food Deli* for all your health foods and vegetarian pies; and *Rob's Burger Bar* for that post-public bar snack.

The big Pak 'N Save Supermarket on Queen St has the lowest prices in the area – a good place to stock up on provisions before tackling one of the great Coromandel tramping trips.

KFC and *McDonald's* have made it to the Coromandel; both are close to the Goldfields Mall. In the mall itself is a *Robert Harris Coffee Shop* and a number of other lunchtime outlets which sell a big range of food.

Restaurants The licensed *Old Thames Restaurant* on Pollen St has steak, seafood and various pizzas at $10 to $12 for a medium, $12 to $15 for a large. It also has Bluff oysters – not to be missed if you haven't tried them. It's open from 5 pm every day, seven days a week. *The Majestic* is a family restaurant, on Pollen St diagonally opposite the post office; hearty seafood meals are about $10 to $15 per person.

The Hotel Imperial, also on Pollen St, has the *Pan & Handle* bistro and the more expensive *Regency Room*. The restaurant at the *Brian Boru Hotel* serves a fancy three-course dinner for $30, or you can have à la carte meals. The flounder in this restaurant, which is a Thames' speciality, has been recommended. There's just one Chinese restaurant, the *Golden Dragon*.

The *Chateau du Raisin* is a wine bar where meals are served – as you would expect, they have a good selection of NZ wines.

One of our favourites is the *Easy Street Cafe*, strangely in Sealey St, which is fully licensed and open for lunch and dinner. They experiment with the menu here and offer some excellent combinations. Just out of town, on Maramarahi Rd, you'll find the fully licensed *Cotswold Cottage*. They serve a good menu which combines a number of seafoods and game caught locally.

COROMANDEL FOREST PARK
There are over 30 walks and tramps through Coromandel Forest Park, covering the area from the Maratoto Forest, near Paeroa, to Cape Colville; the most popular region is the Kauaeranga Valley which cuts into the Colville Range behind Thames. There are many old kauri dams in the valley: the Tarawaere, Waterfalls, Dancing Camp, Kauaeranga Main, Moss Creek and Waterfalls Creek dams. You are requested not to climb on them.

Information
All the walks are outlined in the excellent DOC pamphlet *Coromandel Recreation: A Forest and Coastal Experience*, free from DOC offices and visitor information centres.

Sunkist Lodge Hostel in Thames also has lots of walking information. Ask for specific information on any tracks you're planning to use, as some are in very poor condition and may be hazardous.

The DOC visitor information centre, formerly the Coromandel Forest Park headquarters (☎ 868 6381), is in the Kauaeranga Valley about 15 km from Thames. It is open on weekdays from 8 am to 4 pm, as well as on weekends in the summer.

Places to Stay
There are DOC camping grounds at various places throughout the Coromandel Forest Park. You'll find them on the west coast and northern tip of the peninsula at Fantail Bay, Port Jackson and Fletcher Bay and at Stony Bay and Waikawau Bay on the east coast. All have only a nominal fee, and you don't have to book.

Eight of the camping places are up the Kauaeranga Valley ($3 for adults and $2 for children) as are the only two DOC huts on the peninsula; the nightly cost for these is $8. Get a copy of DOC's *Camping in the Kauaeranga*.

Getting There & Away

The headquarters and main entrance to the park are reached from the southern edge of Thames along Kauaeranga Valley Rd. There are other minor access points around the peninsula; ask at the visitor information centre in Thames for details.

NORTH OF THAMES

North from Thames, SH 25 snakes along the coast for 32 km past lots of pretty little bays and beaches on one side and bush on the other. Fishing and shellfishing are excellent all the way up the coast, and the landscape turns crimson when pohutukawa trees bloom in the summer.

Along the way you pass through Whakatete, Ngarimu Bay, Te Puru, Tapu and other small settlements. The **Rapaura Watergardens**, six km inland from Tapu on the Tapu-Coroglen Rd, are open 10 am to 5 pm daily from 1 October to 30 April; admission is $5 (children $1) and there are tearooms. Also on the Tapu-Coroglen Rd is the 'square' kauri tree.

Places to Stay

There is one hostel and a number of motels and campsites along the coast between Thames and Coromandel.

Camping & Cabins The *Boomerang Motor Camp* (☎ 867 8879) in Te Puru, 11 km north of Thames, has camping facilities, cabins and on-site caravans. Another couple of km north is the *Waiomu Bay Holiday Park* (☎ 868 2777) which has camping, on-site caravans, cabins, tourist flats and motel units. Further north towards Coromandel, at Tapu, the *Tapu Motor Camp* (☎ 868 4837) has campsites, on-site caravans and cabins; the backpackers rate is $9 per person in bunkrooms or caravans.

Hostels In Tapu, 22 km north of Thames, the *Te Mata Lodge* (☎ 868 4834) has rustic hostel-style accommodation set in the bush, for $12. There are plenty of bush walks, including one to the beach, and a couple of rivers good for swimming. To get there go 1½ km north past Tapu on the coast road, turn inland immediately past the concrete bridge down Te Mata Creek Rd, and follow the road to the end. There's a sign on the gate. The very friendly proprietor takes guests on bush walks and often has school groups in.

A much smaller place is the *Tapu Tramstay* (☎ 868 4881), five minutes up the Tapu-Coroglen Rd from the Tapu Store; the charge per night is $15 for each person.

Motels Motels along the coast include *Puru Park* (☎ 868 2686) at Te Puru, 11 km north of Thames; the *La Casa Guesthouse* (☎ 868 2326), which has a Mexican restaurant and is also in Te Puru; the *Seaspray Motel* (☎ 868 2863), on the coastal road at Waiomu, 14½ km north of Thames; and the *Santa Monica Motel* (☎ 868 2429), is at Ruamahanga Bay.

COROMANDEL

When you get to Wilsons Bay the road leaves the coast and cuts through hills and valleys until you arrive at the next major town, Coromandel, 55 km north of Thames, named after HMS *Coromandel* which visited the harbour in 1820 to pick up a load of kauri spars for the navy. It was here, on Driving Creek, three km north of the township, that kauri mill owner Charles Ring discovered gold in 1852. At the height of the goldrush the town's population rose to over 10,000, but today it's a soporific little township of fewer than 1000 souls.

Information

The Coromandel Information Centre (☎ 866 8598) is in the Thames-Coromandel District Council building on Kapanga Rd. In summer it's open from 9 am to 4 pm every day except Sunday; the rest of the year it's open from 10 am to 3 pm, Monday to Friday. The centre has many useful leaflets on the surrounding

COROMANDEL

area, and makes bookings for all the accommodation in town.

In their booklet *Visiting the Town of Coromandel* there's a walking tour of the town – Historic Coromandel – which points out historic attractions, including Charles Ring's cottage.

Historic Buildings

The **Coromandel Mining Museum** on Ring's Rd is in a building erected in 1898 to house the Coromandel School of Mines. On display are exhibits pertaining to early gold-mining and the colonial era. In summer it's open daily from 10 am to noon and from 2 to 4 pm; admission is $2 (children free). In winter it opens by arrangement.

The **Coromandel Stamper Battery** (☎ 866 8765), also on Ring's Rd, demonstrates ore-crushing to extract gold and shows various amalgamation processes. In summer it should be open from 1 to 3 pm daily, and tours are offered for $3; in winter it's open by arrangement. Best to check at the visitor information centre as the hours vary.

Craft Gallery

Coromandel is a centre for potting and weaving. Go into the Coromandel Craft Gallery on Wharf Rd and, if you want to see more of any particular potter's or weaver's work, check whether you can go to their home – most of the local potters welcome visitors. Among the craft shops in the town, True Colours is a good place to see weaving in progress.

Driving Creek Railway

Driving Creek, three km north of Coromandel, is where Charles Ring discovered gold. It is now the site of various fascinating enterprises masterminded by one of Coromandel's leading artists, Barry Brickell (☎ 866 8703).

Brickell is a potter who, upon discovering excellent clay on his land, had to find a way to get it down the hill to his kiln. So he built his own railway to do it. The Driving Creek Railway runs up steep grades, across three high trestle bridges, along a spiral and a double switchback, and through two tunnels! It's a 50-minute round trip and Brickell takes visitors up to the top at 5 pm daily from Christmas to Easter, on weekends, or by arrangement during the rest of the year. The cost is $6 for adults and $3 for children. Also at Driving Creek are Brickell's pottery stall, native forest restoration project, and an environmental history museum is planned for the top of the railway.

Walks

Coromandel is in the middle of a region abounding in natural beauty, scenic reserves, and attractive bush walks. The visitor information centre has a big map on the wall showing all the scenic reserves and the two Farm Park Recreation reserves with camping (at Cape Colville and Waikawau Bay). Get a copy of the DOC *Coromandel Recreation* pamphlet and their booklet *Walking in Coromandel.*

A few of the more notable walks in the area include a three-km walk from Coromandel to Long Bay through a grove of large kauris, and a climb through Whangapoua State Forest to the 521-metre Castle Rock on 309 Rd. There are many old abandoned gold mines in the area and these, too, make for good explorations.

Places to Stay

The Information Centre can make bookings for any accommodation in Coromandel.

Camping & Cabins There are several motor camps in and around Coromandel. The *Coromandel Motel & Holiday Park* (☎ 866 8830), 400 metres from the post office, has campsites for $10 per person ($3 with power); cabins cost $25/35 for one/two people, and motel units cost $62/79. Off-season and family tariffs are available.

On the beachfront three km west of Coromandel there's camping at *Long Bay* (☎ 866 8720). Camping costs $8.50 per person; on-site caravans are camp charges plus $15. At Shelly Beach there is a *Motor Camp* (☎ 866 8988), which is five km north of Coro-

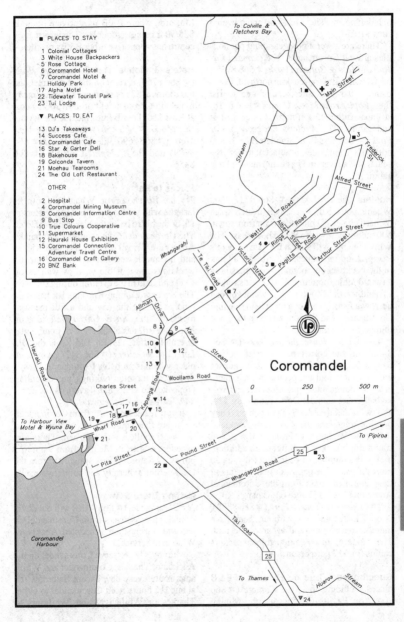

■ PLACES TO STAY

1 Colonial Cottages
3 White House Backpackers
5 Rose Cottage
6 Coromandel Hotel
7 Coromandel Motel &
   Holiday Park
17 Alpha Motel
22 Tidewater Tourist Park
23 Tui Lodge

▼ PLACES TO EAT

13 DJ's Takeaways
14 Success Cafe
15 Coromandel Cafe
16 Star & Garter Deli
18 Bakehouse
19 Golconda Tavern
21 Moehau Tearooms
24 The Old Loft Restaurant

   OTHER

2 Hospital
4 Coromandel Mining Museum
8 Coromandel Information Centre
9 Bus Stop
10 True Colours Cooperative
11 Supermarket
12 Hauraki House Exhibition
15 Coromandel Connection
   Adventure Travel Centre
16 Coromandel Craft Gallery
20 BNZ Bank

Coromandel

COROMANDEL

mandel; normal sites are $7.50 and powered sites $10.50.

There are several other camping possibilities around Coromandel. The *Oamaru Bay Tourist Flats & Caravan Park* (☎ 866 8735), on Oamaru Bay seven km north of Coromandel, has campsites, cabins and tourist flats. *Papa Aroha Motor Camp* (☎ 866 8818) at Papa Aroha, 12 km north, has campsites and cabins. The *Angler's Lodge & Motor Park* (☎ 866 8584) at Amodeo Bay, 18 km north of Coromandel, is adjacent to both the beach and a river and has campsites and one cabin.

Hostels The *Tui Lodge* (☎ 866 8237), 600 Whangapoua Rd, is a small hostel in an orchard chalet, 10 minutes' walk from town, 500 metres past where SH 25 heads east. The Whitianga bus will stop at the gate or there's free pick-up on request. It's $13 for a bunk in the backpackers room, $14 per person in a twin/double room in the chalet. It's run by a friendly retired couple from whom you can borrow a fishing rod, or a bicycle to ride into Coromandel, and find out all about the good things to do in the area.

The *White House Backpackers* (☎ 866 8468), on the corner of Frederick St and Ring's Rd, is a collection of three houses which sleep about ten people in each; there is a TV lounge and a quiet lounge, and volleyball court outside. Dorm rooms are $10, and twins and doubles $15 per person. They provide transport one way from Auckland (Monday, Wednesday, Friday only) if you stay a minimum of two nights. In addition, they sell a number of peninsula trips (as do most places on the peninsula); inquire about their Peninsula Pass from the Coromandel Adventure Travel Centre on Kapanga Rd.

The *Tidewater Tourist Park* (☎ 866 8888), is on Tiki Rd near the harbour. They have motels, tourist flats and a paraplegic unit. The modern, fully equipped backpackers cabins for $12 per person.

Guesthouses There are a number of B&B places including the *Rose Cottage* (☎ 866 7047) on Pagitts Rd opposite the Mining Museum, where B&B in a private home is $25/50 for singles/doubles. The information centre has about five other B&Bs on file.

Hotels & Motels The *Coromandel Hotel* (☎ 866 8760) is right on the main street and has rooms at $25 per person. There are many motels in Coromandel but most rooms cost at least $60. Possibilities include the *Wyuna Bay Motel* (☎ 866 8507), the *Harbour View Motel* (☎ 866 8690), the *Alpha Motel* (☎ 866 8709) and the *Colonial Cottages* (☎ 866 8856).

Places to Eat

Try the *Bakehouse* on Wharf Rd, with its lasagne with smoked snapper and oysters at $8, or the bistro bar at the *Coromandel Hotel*. The *Coromandel Cafe* near the Coromandel Adventure Travel Centre has sandwiches and hot meals and is open from 7 am on weekdays most of the year, as well as on weekends and in the evening during summer. The *Success Cafe* on Kapanga Rd has light lunches during the day and a full menu at night, and the *Star & Garter Deli*, also on Kapanga Rd, has a selection of continental fare and coffee. Out on Tiki Rd is the *Old Loft Cafe & Gallery* (☎ 866 8427), a seafood place which is probably Coromandel town's finest restaurant; bookings are essential. Opposite the Golconda Tavern is the *Moehau Tearooms & Takeaways*.

If you're heading north from Coromandel, be aware that you can't buy stores or food beyond Colville, so stock up here. There's an excellent market in Main St from 9 am to 3 pm every Saturday. Buy some fish from the local fishing fraternity and cook it yourself.

Getting There & Away

Air Coromandel (☎ 866 4016) will put down or pick up passengers from Coromandel on demand during their scheduled Auckland-Whitianga service.

Murphy's buses serve Coromandel on the Auckland, Thames, Coromandel and Whitianga route every day, except Saturday. It's about 1¼ hours from Coromandel to either Thames or Whitianga, and 3½ hours to

Auckland (see the Getting There & Away section at the end of this chapter).

Coromandel Super Tours (☎ 866 8800) operate a twice-daily scheduled service from Coromandel to Thames; the cost is $10 one way and $16 return (children $6 and $10).

BEYOND COROMANDEL

From Coromandel you can continue north to Colville and Port Jackson or take either of two routes across to Whitianga and Mercury Bay on the east coast.

The road heading north is sealed to Colville, but it's rough going beyond that and hitching north of Colville may not be so easy. The road ends at Fletcher Bay, from where it's about a 2½ to three-hour walk to Stony Bay on the east coast, where the road starts again. Sometimes, groups who have access to transport drive as far as possible and walk the rest of the way, with a driver meeting them on the other side. There is camping at Port Jackson, Fletcher Bay, Waikawau Bay and Stony Bay.

From Coromandel south-east to Whitianga there are two possible routes. SH 25 is longer (46 km, 1¼ hours) but the road is sealed and it's also the more scenic route, along the coast with exquisite beach views. The other road is Highway 309, locally known as 309 Rd.

Colville

This place, 85 km north of Thames is the 'end of the road' – the sealed road, that is. It was formerly known as Cabbage Bay, so named by Cook who insisted that his crew eat the leaves of native cabbage trees, to guard against scurvy. Now it is home to alternative-lifestylers, a small wholefood cafe and a cooperative store. The store stocks anything and is self-help – muesli, dried fruit and nuts abound.

Colville Backpackers & Farmstay (☎ 866 6820) is on a 1260-hectare farm. A bed in the backpackers cottage is $13 to $15 per person, the bush lodge is $13 per person or $50 for the whole place, the cottage with all amenities (sleeps seven) is $70 per night, and

camping is also available. Ring ahead to get directions.

Fletcher Bay

This is the true end of the road, sealed or otherwise – a real Land's End. Fletcher Bay is a magic place with deserted beaches, forest and coastal walks, sea kayaking, fishing trips, boat rides to Great Barrier, mountain biking, no end of native birds and splendid views across to Great Barrier, Little Barrier and Cuvier islands.

It is possible to do the three-hour Coromandel Walkway in a couple of ways: you can be dropped off by boat at Stony Bay and walk back to Fletcher Bay; or you can get a lift to Stony Bay and then walk around to Fletcher Bay. The walk is suggested in a south to north direction as there is regular transport out of Fletcher Bay, but not Stony Bay. A lot of people elect to walk both ways. It is an easy, pleasant walk with great coastal views and then an ambling section across open farmland. A mountain-bike track is being constructed on the flanks of Mt Moehau which will connect Stony Bay to the Fletcher Bay end of the walkway.

The Sunkist Lodge operates the *Fletcher Bay Backpackers* (☎ 866 8989), a comfortable small 16-bed place perched up on a hill overlooking the farm and beach. It has all the facilities and, judging by the visitors' book, it is very popular as people keep coming back. The cost per night is $14 and transport from Thames with Sunkist is very reasonable.

SH 25 to Whitianga

If you continue on SH 25 east of Coromandel you come to Te Rerenga, almost on the shore of Whangapoua Harbour. The road forks here; if you head north you come to the end of the road at Whangapoua and if you continue east you can visit the beachside towns of Matarangi, Kuaotunu, Otama and Opito before heading south to Whitianga. Off Opito Bay is the spectacular **Needle Rock**, so named because the hole through the rock is tapered in the shape of the eye of a needle.

From Whangapoua you can walk along

the rocky foreshore to the isolated, pristine **New Chum's Bay**. The walk takes about 30 minutes and starts by the picnic area at the end of the road.

The Woodfish Farm (☎ 866 5566/5377) is on SH 25, 19 km from Coromandel and 27 km from Whitianga. It's on a beautiful promontory jutting out into Whangapoua Harbour – the farm is surrounded by water on three sides. Guests are welcome to stay in the flat behind the farmhouse for $12 per person. You have the run of the farm, boats and fishing tackle to use, fresh vegetables, tropical fruits, milk straight from the cow and Pacific oysters in the sand just outside the flat.

309 Road

Highway 309 (locally known as 309 Rd) is shorter way to Whitianga (32 km, 45 minutes) but it's rather rough going as the road is unsealed. It's a bush road which is generally not as scenic as SH 25, unless you want to get out and do some walking. It does have some excellent spots including the **Chiltern Scenic Reserve**, **Waiau Falls**, a grove of large kauri trees, and a two-hour return walking track to the summit of **Castle Rock**.

The **kauri grove** is particularly interesting as there is a Siamese kauri, which forks just above the ground. The roots of the kauri are protected by a system of boardwalks.

The 309 Honey Cottage (☎ 866 5151) is about 12 km from Whitianga on 309 Rd. It's a lovely place, relaxing and scenic, with 40 hectares of farm and bush. The cost is $15 a night in an old kauri cottage beside a river, or you can camp for $10 a night. There are plenty of farm animals about, and there's a glass beehive where you can see bees at work (in spring). Activities include rafting, horse-riding and bushwalking. There's no bus but they will pick you up in Whitianga if you phone.

WHITIANGA

The pleasant Whitianga area of Mercury Bay has a long history, by NZ standards. The Polynesian explorer Kupe landed near here around 950 AD and the area was called Te Whitianga-a-Kupe (the Crossing Place of Kupe). Prior to that the land was abundant with moas and there is evidence that there were early moa hunters here 2000 years ago.

Mercury Bay was given its modern name by Captain Cook when he observed the transit of Mercury while anchored in the bay in November 1769.

Whitianga is the main town on Mercury Bay. The bay itself is attractive and there are seven good beaches all within easy reach of the town. Buffalo Beach, Whitianga's principal frontage onto the bay, takes its name from HMS *Buffalo*, wrecked there in 1840.

The town is a big game-fishing base for tuna, marlin, mako (blue pointer shark), thresher shark and kingfish. It is very much a tourist town, whose small population of about 2000 swells to mammoth proportions during the January holidays.

Information

There's a Whitianga Information Centre (☎ 866 5555) on the main street (66 Albert St) right in the centre of town. In summer it's open from 8 am to 5 pm every day, except Sunday when it opens from 9 am to 3 pm. Winter hours are from 9.30 am to 4.30 pm Monday to Friday and 9.30 am to 12.30 pm on Saturday; closed Sunday.

Museum

The little Mercury Bay Historic Society Museum opposite the ferry wharf has some interesting exhibits, including many historic photos of Mercury Bay and the kauri logging era. Mining, blacksmithing, the colonial era, Maori carvings, and the story of the HMS *Buffalo* and other shipwrecks are also represented. The jaws of a 1350-kg white pointer shark caught in the Hauraki Gulf in 1959 hang on the wall overlooking all.

The museum is open in summer from 10 to 3 pm daily. Winter hours are shorter: 11 am to 2 pm, three days a week. Admission is $2 (children $1).

Ferry Landing

From The Narrows on the southern side of town you can take a passenger ferry which takes five minutes to cross over to Ferry Landing, site of the original township on the southern side of Mercury Bay. A one-way crossing costs 75c (children 40c), with an extra 30c for bicycles. The ferry does not take cars, but you can drive to Ferry Landing on a circuitous route around the bay to the south, via Coroglen.

In summer the ferry runs continuously from 7.30 am to 10.30 pm. In winter the ferry runs from 7.30 am to noon and from 1 to 6.30 pm, with evening crossings by arrangement.

Bicycles can be hired from beside the store in Ferry Landing. You can walk, cycle or drive to a number of excellent spots on this side including Cook's Beach, Lonely Bay, Front Beach and Flaxmill Bay. The view from Shakespeare's Lookout, on top of the white cliffs you see when you look across the river from Whitianga, is particularly lovely, a great spot to see all of Mercury Bay with its many beaches and coves.

The stone wharf at Ferry Landing was built in 1837 by Gordon Browne, who had a trading post, warehouse and boat building business. Stone for the wharf came from Whitianga Rock, a pa site of which Captain Cook said 'the best engineers in Europe could not have chosen a better site for a small band of men to defend against a greater number'.

Purangi Winery

Purangi Winery (☎ 866 3724), six km south of Ferry Landing, is a mellow, rustic winery which makes wines (kiwi fruit, feijoa, passion fruit and apple) and liqueurs (kiwi fruit, feijoa and tamarillo) from a totally organic orchard. The organic beers (Bavarian lager and dark ale) and sparkling cider are also recommended. There's free tasting and also a good inexpensive restaurant with seating indoors or out under the vines, with lots of vegetarian dishes and summer barbecues with a big salad bar. The winery is open from 9 am to 9 pm daily. If you telephone ahead you can arrange to be picked up from the ferry at 11.30 am, 2.30 or 6.30 pm, and be returned to the ferry after your visit.

The Purangi Winery also organise a 1½-hour winery cruise on the Purangi River; the cost for backpackers is $15.

Other Things to Do

Popular trips from Whitianga include trips to Cathedral Cove and Hot Water Beach, where thermal waters are brewing just below the sand. You can go down on the beach two hours before and after low tide, dig a hole in the sand and sit in your own little natural spa pool; allow about 15 minutes to prepare your pool. The *Hahei Explorer* (☎ (025) 424 306), a rigid inflatable, operates daily scenic trips to Cathedral Cove and Hot Water Beach – landings are made whenever the sea allows.

Things to Do

Whitianga has many activities for visitors and the information centre can supply details on all of them. On the water there are scenic yacht trips, cruises, kayak trips, fishing excursions, water-skiing, sailing, jet-boating and safe swimming. In summer you can fish off the wharf. River rafting is popular on the nearby Waiwawa River.

Back on land there are horse treks, bus tours, and numerous scenic drives and walks. The Buffalo Beach Tourist Park has a hot thermal swimming pool called Champagne Springs, due to open in 1994. If you don't want to spend all your time on water or land you can take to the air for 'flightseeing' excursions.

Recently, Dolphin Quest (☎ 866 5555) commenced a 'swim with the dolphins' experience. The bottlenose dolphins were once regular visitors close inshore but now you need to go to them. Wet suits, snorkels and flippers are supplied; the cost is $75 for a three-hour trip.

Walks

Mercury Bay is rich in interesting walks. Watch your step, however, some of the mine shafts are quite deep. One of the more popular gold mines is reached by an enjoyable two-hour walk along a stream. The track starts on Waitaia Rd, about 14 km north-east of Whitianga. Many other good walks are across the river, five minutes away by ferry.

COROMANDEL

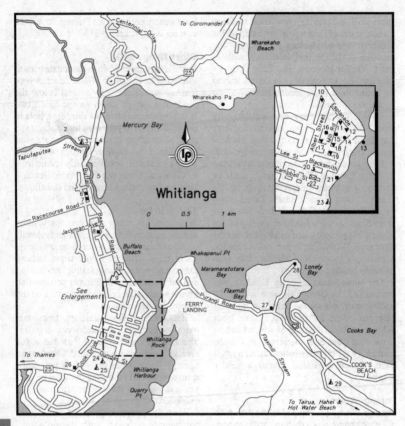

The visitor information centre has details on local walks including the Whitianga Rock Scenic & Historic Reserve. Again, obtain a copy of DOC's *Coromandel Recreation*.

Horse-Trekking

There are a number of places where you can go horse-trekking on the Coromandel's east coast. The Twin Oaks Riding Ranch (☎ 866 5388) is 10 minutes north of Whitianga on the Kuaotunu Rd; Summit Ranch (☎ 866 4418), which also has backpackers accommodation ($8); and Rangihau Ranch (☎ 866 3875) are both on the Tapu-Coroglen Rd –

costs for horse-trekking are about $20 per hour or $35 for a half day.

Places to Stay

Camping & Cabins At the *Buffalo Beach Tourist Park* (☎ 866 5854) opposite Buffalo Beach and on Eyre St, camping costs $8.50 per person ($8 in winter); it's a couple of dollars more with power. Shared accommodation costs $14 per person in bunkrooms; twin rooms are $17 per person.

Other similarly priced campsites include the *Waters Edge Lodge* (☎ 866 5760), the *Harbourside Holiday Park* (☎ 866 5746) and

■ PLACES TO STAY

1   Whitianga Holiday Park
3   Aladdin Motor Camp
6   Seabreeze Motels
7   Bailey's Motel
8   Coromandel Backpackers
9   Buffalo Beach Tourist Park
15 Seafari Motel
16 Central Park Motel
21 Whitianga Motel
23 Water's Edge Motel
24 Mercury Bay Motor Camp
25 Harbourside Motor Camp
26 Cosy Cat Guest House
29 Cook's Beach Motor Camp

▼ PLACES TO EAT

4   Back Porch Licensed Restaurant
10 Beach Cafe
11 Cook's Cove
12 Angler's Cove
17 PJ's Bistro & Bar & Chinese Takeaways
18 Snapper Jack's
19 Bay Bakery

OTHER

2   Buffalo Beach Scenic Reserve & Big Kauri Tree
5   Recreation Reserve (NZ Dotterel Nesting Site)
13 Passenger Ferry Service to Ferry Landing
14 Museum
20 Information Centre, Cardphone, Bus Stop & Public Toilets
22 Post Office
27 Shakespeare Cliff Scenic & Historic Reserve
28 Captain Cook's Memorial

the *Mercury Bay Motor Camp* (☎ 866 5579), all on Albert St; the *Whitianga Holiday Park* (☎ 866 5896) at the northern end of Buffalo Beach; and the *Aladdin Motor Camp* (☎ 866 5834) on Bongard Rd.

Hostels *Coromandel Backpackers Lodge* (☎ 907) 866 5380), 46 Buffalo Beach Rd, is a converted seaside motel. The nightly cost is $13 in a dorm room or $15/16 per person

in a double/twin room. They have free kayaks and surfboards, and you can also hire out bicycles, catamarans and a 4WD vehicle for tours of the region. The catamaran is $17 per person and there is no time limit. Just opposite this place is a bird sanctuary – nesting place of the rare New Zealand dotterel. Caspian terns and oystercatchers can be seen.

Summit Ranch (☎ 866 4418) is a horse-trekking place which also has backpackers accommodation for $8. You'll find it on the Tapu-Coroglen Rd.

Guesthouses The small and pleasant *Cosy Cat Cottage* (☎ 866 4488), 41 South Highway, is an unusual B&B guesthouse – it's absolutely loaded with cat art. There are cats on everything from the sheets to the placemats at the dinner table, and literally hundreds of cat statues. Single rooms cost $40 and double or twin rooms cost $30 per person, including a cooked breakfast. There are a number of other B&Bs; inquire at the visitor information centre.

Hotels & Motels The *Whitianga Hotel* (☎ 866 5818) on Blacksmith Lane has rooms at $30 to $45 for singles, $45 to $55 for doubles or twins; the more expensive rooms have private bathrooms.

Whitianga has about 20 motels. Most are in the $60 and upwards bracket but there are cheaper ones too; some of them reduce their rates as far as $40 in winter.

On Buffalo Beach Road there are *Baileys' Motel* (☎ 866 5500) at No 66 on the beachfront and the *Seabreeze Motel* (☎ 866 5570) at No 71. The *Seafari Motel* (☎ 866 5263) is at 7 Mill Rd, and the *Central Park Motel* (☎ 866 5471) is nearby at 6 Mill Rd. Another is the *Water's Edge Lodge* (see Camping & Cabins).

Places to Eat
There's a choice of several takeaways: pizzas at *The Bay Bakery*, good pub food at the *Whitianga Hotel*, a *Chinese takeaway* on Albert St, or fresh seafood meals and the most popular takeaway fish & chips in town

from *Snapper Jacks* seafood restaurant also on Albert St.

There are many restaurants around the harbour end of town, with seafood featuring heavily on the menu. On the Esplanade there are *Angler's Cove*, which has an adjoining ice-cream parlour; the *Harbour View Continental Cafe*; and *Cook's Cove*, which has won awards for its food. At the back end of Albert St is the *Beach Cafe*, a BYO place recommended for its pasta, and *PJ's Bistro & Bar*, 31 Albert St, lunches, bar meals from $4 and dinner. *The Back Porch Restaurant* is an à la carte licensed place attached to the Mercury Bay Beachfront Resort, on Buffalo Beach Rd; diners get great views out over the bay and mains cost from $15 to $20.

Purangi Winery, south of Ferry Landing, has excellent food and wine, great atmosphere and it's not expensive. See the Purangi Winery section for details. There are also a number of more expensive restaurants – check with the information centre.

Entertainment

PJ's Bistro & Bar, upstairs in Albert St, features the dreaded karaoke. The *Whitianga Hotel* has live music in summer, and there is good pub entertainment in the nearby town of Coroglen. When asked if there were any other choices, a resident said: 'Get real, this is Whitianga!' Looks like a seafood meal is the go then.

Getting There & Away

Murphy's buses call into Whitianga twice a day; departing at 8 am and 12.50 pm, but do check as the schedule may change. These buses connect with services to Auckland, Tauranga and Rotorua; Thames to Whitianga is $15.

Three days a week there is a service from Opoutere to Whitianga; bookings are essential and for departure times inquire at the visitor information centre.

WHITIANGA TO WAIHI

The coast is wild and there are spectacular beaches all the way from Mercury Bay to Waihi, including Hahei, Hot Water Beach where thermal waters heat the sea, Tairua, Pauanui, Opoutere, Whangamata and Orokawa.

Cook's Beach, Hahei & Hot Water Beach

This section of the coast is a popular area. Cook's Beach, as well as a number of other beaches, is accessible from the Stone Steps Wharf at Ferry Landing. Cook is believed to have careened the *Endeavour* in nearby Flaxmill (or Homestead) Bay.

The offshore islands provide protection for the beaches around Hahei. At the eastern end of the beach is a former Maori pa, which still has much evidence of the elaborate terracing used as fortifications. To the north of Hahei is Cathedral Cove, accessible only at low tide through a gigantic arched cavern which separates it from Mares Leg Cove. This headland was also the site of a Maori pa. To the south of Hahei is the Hot Water Beach.

Places to Stay Sites at the *Hot Water Beach Motor Camp & Thermal Pools* (☎ 866 3735) cost $8 per person, more with power. There's also the *Cook's Beach Motor Camp* (☎ 866 5469) and the *Hahei Holiday Tourist Park* (☎ 866 3889) which has campsites, cabins and tourist flats.

There's a variety of backpackers accommodation. The *Summer House* (☎ 866 3886), in Margaret Place ,on the corner of Pa Rd, is being upgraded so that it can accommodate more people. The cost is $8 for a campsite, or $13/15 for singles/twins. The friendly host organises wine-tasting trips at the Purangi Winery and therapeutic visits to Hot Water Beach. The *Hahei Holiday Tourist Park* (☎ 866 3889) also has backpackers accommodation at $12 per person. The *Tatahi Lodge* (☎ 866 3992), on Grange Rd, also has cheap accommodation with full facilities; the cost is $16 per person.

The luxury end of the market is looked after by the *Hay-Lyn Park Lodge* (☎ 866 3888) at Hahei Beach; they also have a coffee shop.

Tairua & Pauanui

Welcome to the playground of the rich and famous. If New Zealand's downmarket version of Australia's Gold Coast or the US's Miami Beach sounds like your scene then this split-asunder twin-town could be what you are seeking.

The highlight of Tairua is probably the climb to the top of Paku (an old pa site) and the views of the estuary, beaches, islands and Pauanui that you get from the top.

For the 'outdoor adventure of your life' according to the publicity, you could go on one of Doug Johansen's (☎ 864 8731) scenic treks and tours. This 'Kiwi Dundee' knows where the crocodiles are, as well as historic goldmines, kauri dams, aspects of the peninsula's flora & fauna, and Maori medicines and foods.

CHH Forests Limited provide free information on activities within the Tairua Forest Block, as well as printed directions for a self-guided walk to the Luck at Last mine site.

Places to Stay & Eat You have the choice of five motor camps in this area; a campsite is about $9 to $10 per person and each place usually has on-site caravans and cabins available. On SH 25 in Tairua you'll find *The Flying Dutchman* (☎ 864 8448), recognisable by the dolphins swimming on its walls. There is a balcony area leading off the recreation room (where there is a free pool table), and adequate bathroom and kitchen facilities; the cost is $15 per person in twin/double rooms.

Rooms at the *Sir George Grey Hotel* (☎ 864 8451), on Main Rd in Tairua, are $25. There are at least eight motels or lodges in Tairua and Pauanui; inquire at the visitor information centre (Pauanui Activity Booking Centre; ☎ 864 7101) in the Pauanui shopping centre about their location and current rates.

On Pauanui Boulevard near Pauanui Beach is *Keith's Licensed Restaurant*. The place serves a wide range of New Zealand foods, has a great wine selection and has won a stack of awards.

Opoutere

This is the site of one of the best situated youth hostels in New Zealand. Additionally, about a 15-minute walk from the road is the Wharekawa Wildlife Refuge, the breeding ground of the endangered New Zealand dotterel and variable oystercatcher. Keep dogs out of here and don't cross into the roped-off area during the breeding season. There are only about 1200 of this species of dotterel left in the world. There is a Monday to Friday Waihi to Opoutere Shuttle – it departs at noon.

The *Opoutere YHA Hostel* (☎ 865 9072) is a fine place to get right away from it all. It's in a country setting, almost encircled by native bush and overlooking Wharekawa Harbour. You can take one of the hostel's kayaks and paddle around, and there are plenty of bushwalks. The cost is $12 per night in dorms, $16 per person in doubles, or you can set up a tent on the expansive lawn for about $10. The management are friendly and informative.

Just down the road from the Opoutere YHA Hostel is the *Opoutere Park Beach Resort* (☎ 865 9152) with campsites at $7.50 per person.

Whangamata

This is a summertime paradise, having a four-km beach, a sheltered harbour and, for surfers, an excellent break by the bar. Otherwise, it is an unprepossessing hotch potch of single-storey buildings exuding an air of the temporary. The Whangamata PRO & Information Centre (☎ 865 8340) is on Port Rd by the wharf. They will provide information on all activities in the area and may have supplies of the excellent DOC pamphlet *Maratoto: the Wires Recreation Area* which outlines the Wires and Wentworth walking tracks.

Places to Stay & Eat The *Pinefield Holiday Park* (☎ 865 8791), Port Rd, has sites for $9, cabins and tourist flats at $38/48 for two people. Similarly, the *Whangamata Motor Camp* (☎ 865 9128), Barbara Ave, has sites for $8 each person and cabins for $33 for

COROMANDEL

two. Whangamata has a *backpackers* (☎ 865 8323) at 227 Beverly Terrace. It must be the worst signposted place in the entire backpacking universe – to get there turn off the main highway at the hostel symbol (near Mum's Corner Store) and follow the road to Ocean Rd where you turn right; turn left at the first turn, then left again into Beverly Terrace; it's the blue-and-white place. All accommodation here is $15 per person.

The *Port City Chinese Restaurant*, at 600 Port Rd, also has a takeaway section. The *Whangamata Hotel*, on the main highway three km north of town, serves bistro meals and has a family garden bar.

Getting There & Away A bus service (☎ 865 8613) operates between Whangamata and Waihi from Monday to Friday. On Monday, Wednesday and Friday there is a bus between Opoutere and Whangamata.

Bay of Plenty & East Cape

This chapter covers the East Cape and Bay of Plenty, from where it adjoins the Coromandel & Hauraki Plains near Katikati in the west, across to its eastern extremity near Opotiki.

The Bay of Plenty is split into western and eastern areas, with Tauranga-Mt Maunganui being the focal point of the west, and Whakatane-Opotiki being the centre of the east. Since most trips around the East Cape generally commence from the Bay of Plenty, the cape has also been included in this chapter, its western sweep being a continuation of the Bay of Plenty.

Information

Most of this region's telephone numbers have an 07 prefix if you are calling them from a long distance (even within the region), so we haven't included the prefix with each number. Where the prefix is different, it is included with the number.

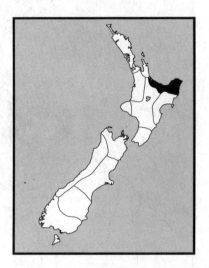

Western Bay of Plenty

The western region of the Bay of Plenty extends from Katikati and Waihi Beach to Papamoa and Te Puke on the coast, and south to the Kaimai Ranges.

Captain Cook sailed into the Bay of Plenty on the *Endeavour* in October 1769, giving it its name because of the numbers of thriving settlements of friendly Maoris he encountered (and the amount of supplies they gave him). It was a sharp contrast to the 'welcome' he received from the Maoris of Poverty Bay several weeks earlier, when lives were lost and no food was available.

The area is not as popular with tourists as the far more commercial Bay of Islands, but in summer it hums along rather nicely. It enjoys one of the highest proportions of sunny days in New Zealand, the climate is consistently mild all year round, and in summer the coastal towns and beaches are popular with Kiwi holiday-makers.

The region is rapidly becoming the horticultural centre of New Zealand, with its main exports being kiwi fruit and timber products, including logs and woodchips. There is a growing mineral water industry, with springs being 'tapped' all over the place. Naturally there are several hot mineral spas around.

TAURANGA

Tauranga (population 68,000), the principal city of the Bay of Plenty and the largest export port in New Zealand is – like the rest of the towns in the region – thriving economically.

Tauranga is a Maori name meaning the 'resting place for canoes', for this was where some of the first Maoris to arrive in New Zealand landed. Nowadays 530 cargo vessels dock here each year.

Tauranga is one of New Zealand's principal kiwi fruit and orchard regions. There's

Tuhua
(Mayor)
Island

Waihi Beach

Matakana
Island

Katikati

Tauranga
Harbour

Omokoroa

KAIMAI-
MAMAKU
FOREST
PARK

TAURANGA

McLaren
Falls

To
Matamata

29

To Hamilton

5

Ngongotaha

Mamaku

Mt
Ngongotaha
757 m

KINLEITH
FOREST

1

30

ROTORUA

Ngakuru

Lake
Ohakuri

Waikite
Valley

Waimangu

Waiotapu

Reporoa

5

To Taupo

Waikato
River

MT MAUNGANUI

Papamoa

Maketu

Te Puke

Paengaroa

Mangorewa River

Kaituna River

33

Okere
Falls

Lake
Rotorua

Hell's
Gate

Lake
Okareka

Blue
Lake

Green
Lake

Lake
Tarawera

Lake
Okataina

Tarawera
Falls

Mt Tarawera
1110 m

Lake
Rotomahana

Lake
Rerewhakaaitu

Rerewhakaaitu

38

Murupara

KAINGAROA
FOREST

Whirinaki
River

Minginui

Motiti
Island

Pukehina Beach

Pukehina

2

Otamarakau

Pikowai

Matata

ROTOEHU
FOREST

Lake
Rotoehu

Lake
Rotoma

Lake
Rotoiti

KAWERAU

TARAWERA
FOREST

MATAHINA
FOREST

Lake
Aniwhenua

Galatea

BAY
OF
PLENTY

Moutohora
(Whale) Island

Thornton

WHAKATANE

Edgecumbe

Ohope

Ohope
Beach

Te Teko

Awakeri
Hot Springs

Ohiwa
Harbour

Taneatua

Kutarere

Lake
Matahina

Waimana

Waimana
River

Whakatane
River

Rangitaiki River

UREWERA

NATIONAL
PARK

Ruatahuna

To
Lake
Waikaremoana

Tauranga
River

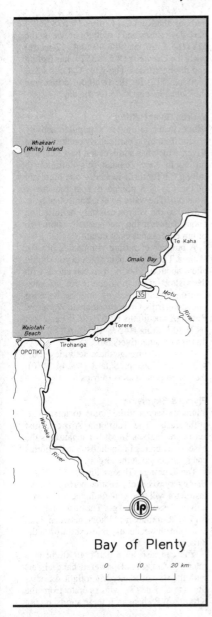

Whakaari
(White) Island

Te Kaha

Omaio Bay

35   Motu

River

Waiotahi
Beach   Torere

Tirohanga   Opape

OPOTIKI

Waioeka

River

Bay of Plenty

0   10   20 km

often work available when kiwi fruit is being picked (May and June) but you may be able to find orchard work of some kind at almost any time of the year. Check with the hostels for orchard work contacts.

Information
The Tauranga Information & Visitors Centre (☎ 578 8103) is on The Strand by Coronation Pier. It's open from 8 am to 5 pm on weekdays, 8 am to 2 pm on Saturday and Sunday; in the busy summer period, late November to the end of February, hours are extended to 7 pm. It would be worth your while obtaining a copy of their annual *Tauranga District Visitors' Guide*.

The DOC office (☎ 578 7677) on the corner of McLean and Anson Sts is open from 8 am to 4.35 pm, Monday to Friday. There's an AA office on the corner of Cameron Rd and Hamilton St.

Historic Attractions
The **Historic Village** (☎ 578 1302) on Seventeenth Ave features restored period buildings, vintage vehicles, farming equipment, an 1877 steam locomotive, an old tugboat, a Maori culture section, and relics from the gold-mining era. It's open from 9 am to 5 pm every day (until 6 pm in summer); admission is $6 (children $2; $13.50 for a family).

Te Awanui, a fine replica Maori canoe, is on display in an open-sided building at the top end of The Strand, close to the centre of town. Continue uphill beyond the canoe to **Monmouth Redoubt**, a fortified site during the Maori Wars. A little further along is **Robbins Park**, with a rose garden and hothouse.

The **Elms Mission Station House** on Mission St, was founded on the site in 1835, and the present house was completed in 1847 by a pioneer missionary. It is furnished in period style. The grounds contain gardens and several historic buildings. Tours are by prior arrangement; admission is free. The mission house is still used as a private residence but you're welcome to wander around the gardens and chapel.

BAY OF PLENTY

There's also the historic **Brain Watkins House**, built in 1887, near the corner of Elizabeth St and Cameron Rd. It's open on Sunday; a donation is requested.

Mineral Pools

There are four hot pools in the area. Fernland Spa & Swimming Pools, two km down Cambridge Rd off Waihi Rd, has public and private hot pools. In addition there are the Welcome Bay Hot Pools, Bayshore Leisure Park and Mt Maunganui Hot Salt Pools; for rates and location inquire at the visitor information centre.

Walks

There are many walking possibilities in the region. A good number of these are outlined in the free pamphlet *Walkways of Tauranga & the Western Bay of Plenty*, available from visitor information centres. Over 20 walks, in Tauranga and Mt Maunganui (including the fascinating **Waikareao estuary**) and further afield, are described. Each is accompanied by a handy map. The backdrop to the Western Bay of Plenty is the rugged 70-km long **Kaimai-Mamaku Forest Park**, with tramps for the more adventurous; DOC should be able to provide more detailed information on walks in this area. **McLaren Falls**, in the Wairoa River valley, 11 km from Tauranga just off SH 29, is worth a visit. There's good bushwalking, rock pools and, of course, the falls. It's picturesque, but not exactly awe-inspiring.

Sea Activities

Tauranga is surrounded by water, so if you like the sea you'll find plenty to do. Charter and fishing trips operate from Tauranga all year round. During the summer the place comes alive with sea activities of all kinds including jet-skiing, water-skiing, windsurfing, parasailing, diving, surfing, swimming, line fishing, deep sea fishing and harbour cruises. Ask at the visitor information centre for the latest information, and see the Around Tauranga section for details about trips to Mayor Island.

There are two recommended tours on the harbour: the Kiwi Cat Cruises (☎ 578 5381) have day cruises and a twilight cruise on the MV *The Spirit*; and the 40-foot (12-metre) yacht the *Camdella* (☎ 578 3579) has fishing and diving cruises. The Kiwi Cat costs $20 (children $12) for the two-hour cruise and the *Camdella* costs $45 for the day.

Wairoa River Rafting

White water rafting is a popular activity around Tauranga, particularly on the Wairoa River, which has some of the best falls and rafting in New Zealand. It's definitely a rafting trip for thrill-seekers – one highlight of the trip is a plunge over a four-metre waterfall! The water level is controlled from a dam, so the Wairoa can only be rafted on about 26 days in the year – usually about two or three weekends each month.

A number of rafting companies ply the Wairoa. The cost is about $60 and you should allow about 2½ hours. You can check with the visitor information centre for information on rafting operators and the dates of upcoming trips. Operators include Woodrow Rafting Expeditions (☎ 576 2628) and Wet 'N Wild Rafting (☎ 578 4093). All of them do trips on other rivers too.

If you can't arrange these activities yourself contact Shamus Safaris (☎ 544 2410); they organises all sorts of trips.

Flying & Skydiving

Tauranga seems to be home to lots of air enthusiasts. The Tauranga Airport, just across the harbour in Mt Maunganui, is the base for a number of air clubs. Scenic flights can be arranged at the airport.

The Tauranga Glider Club (☎ 576 7729) flies every weekend, weather permitting. An instructor will take you gliding and give you a flying lesson as you go. The cost is $30 for a 15 to 20-minute trip. Phone between 9 am and 5 pm on weekends, or just show up at the airport.

You can also do a half-hour flight in a microlight (a sort of powered hang-glider) with the Bay of Plenty Microlight Association (☎ 575 8877), who operate from the airport's WPS hangar. If these sports are not daredevil enough there's also skydiving (☎ 571 8633); you train in the morning and jump in the afternoon. Tandem skydiving is extremely popular in New Zealand. For information and booking ring 571 8633; the cost is $170 for this buzz of a lifetime. Parapenting is yet another way to get airborne. Parapenting Papamoa (☎ 575 8360) run courses; the first course is $100 or $180 for a couple. Soar together!

Places to Stay

Camping & Cabins The *Mayfair Caravan Park* (☎ 578 3323) is on Mayfair St, off Fifteenth Ave, beside the harbour. Tent facilities are limited. Powered sites cost $8 per person and cabins sleeping two cost $28 per night.

The *Silver Birch Motor Park & Thermal Pools* (☎ 578 4603) is at 101 Turret Rd (the extension of Fifteenth Ave) by the Hairini Bridge to Maungatapu. Sites here cost $9, cabins cost from $37 for two, and there are also tourist flats and motel flats. Campers have free use of the thermal mineral swimming pool, and there is also a boat ramp, canoes for hire, and lots of recreational facilities.

The small waterside *6th Avenue Tourist Court* (☎ 578 5709) is close to the centre on Sixth Ave. Campsites cost $16 for two and cabins cost $33 and $45 for two. You can hire bedding and cooking gear if you don't have your own.

At the *Palms Holiday Park* (☎ 578 9337), 162 Waihi Rd, about four km south of the town centre, caravan sites cost $8.50 per person and on-site caravans cost $33 for two. The *Bayshore Leisure Park* (☎ 544 0700), on SH 29, has sites for $8 per person and cabins for $28 for two. This place has its own mineral pools.

Hostels Tauranga's YHA hostel is called the *Waireinga YHA Hostel* (☎ 578 5064). At 171 Elizabeth St, it's superbly situated almost on the banks of the Waikareao Estuary, very close to the centre of Tauranga. It's a small, modern hostel with dorm, family and double rooms. The nightly cost is $14, or you can

pitch a tent on the lawn for $10. There's a BBQ, bonfire and volleyball areas, bicycle hire ($8 per day), and they organise rafting trips to the Wairoa River. If you're coming into town by bus, ask to get off at First Ave.

Unfortunately, the once excellent *Botanical Rd Backpackers* has closed. Along with the YHA, there are three choices now. The *Bell Travellers' Lodge* (☎ 578 6344) at 39 Bell St is four km from the town centre. You can phone for a free pick-up when you arrive and get free transport to the bus or hitching spot when you leave. It's a purpose-built hostel opened in early 1989, so everything is still clean and new, and it's pleasantly situated on three hectares of land. The hostel is well equipped with heating in all the rooms, a big kitchen and lounge with fireplace, colour TV, gas BBQ, and friendly hosts. Bunkroom accommodation costs $13.50 per night, a private room with bath costs $30/32 for singles/doubles, or you can pitch a tent for $7 per person. They, too, offer weekly rates for orchard workers (about $66). Their motor boat should be up and running in 1994 for waterskiing, diving and sightseeing trips.

The *Apple Tree Cottage* (☎ 576 7404), 47 Maxwell St, Pillans Point at Otumoetai, has accommodation for $15 per night which includes the great NZ breakfast; otherwise it costs $12.

Motels There are over 30 motels around Tauranga, with prices averaging around $60/70; inquire at the visitor information centre.

The old *Strand Motel* (☎ 578 5807), 27 The Strand, right up at the Robbins Park end, is rather plain and straightforward but very conveniently located. The *6th Avenue Motel* (☎ 578 5709), on the waterfront next to the Sixth Ave camping ground, has doubles for $62.

The *Bluewater Motel* (☎ 578 5420), 59 Turret Rd, has single rooms, doubles and twins. All the double rooms have a sitting room too and there's a tepid thermal swimming pool, private spa pool, children's play area, and a dinghy. A similar place is the *Savoy Motel* (☎ 578 6435), 53 Turret Rd.

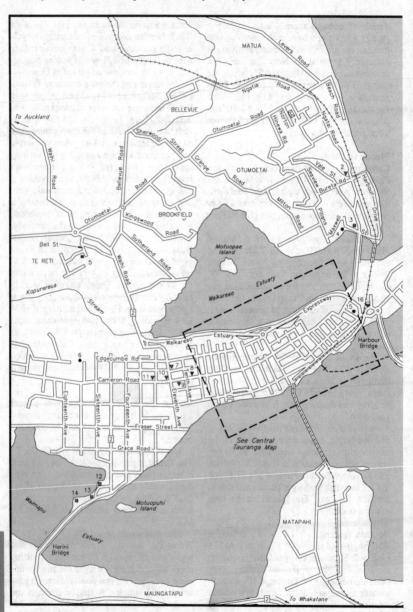

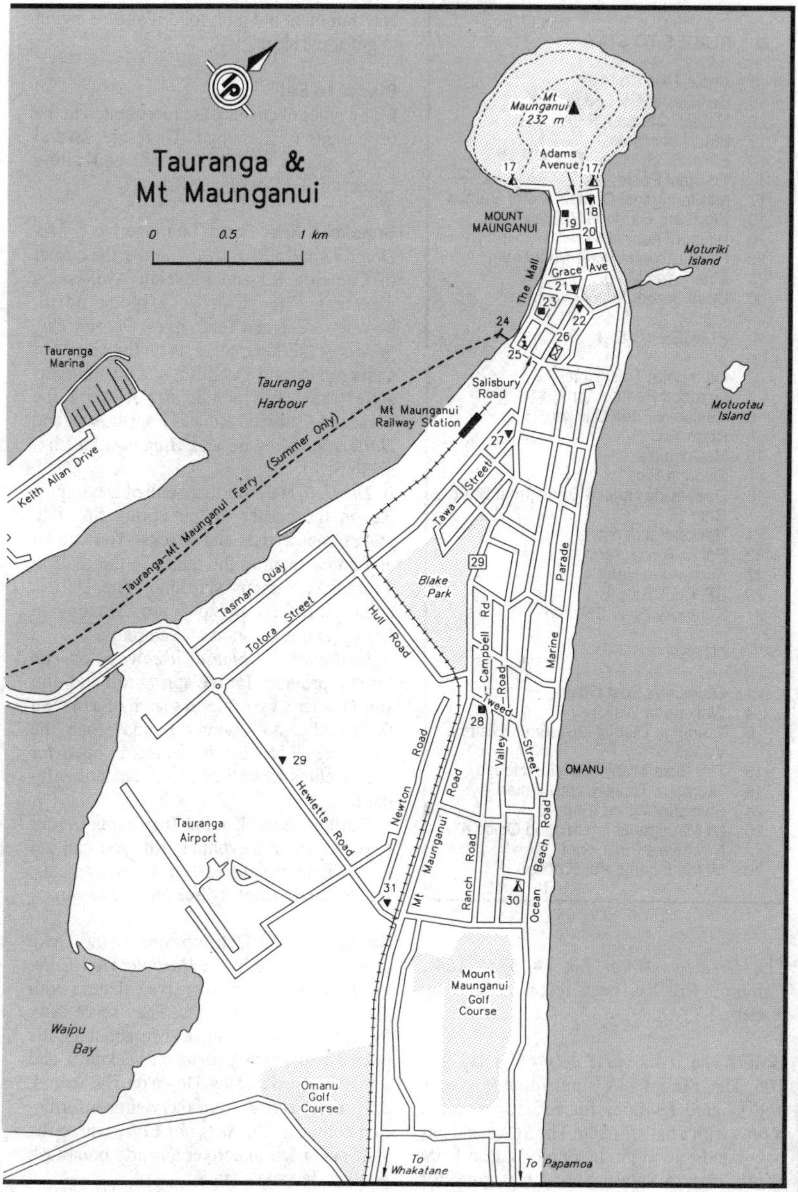

Tauranga & Mt Maunganui

0   0.5   1 km

Mt Maunganui 232 m

Adams Avenue

17   17

MOUNT MAUNGANUI

18
19   20

Grace   Ave
21
23   22
25   26
24

Moturiki Island

The Mall

Salisbury Road

Mt Maunganui Railway Station

27

Motuotau Island

Tauranga Marina

Tauranga Harbour

Tauranga–Mt Maunganui Ferry (Summer Only)

Tava Street

Keith Allan Drive

Tasman Quay

Totara Street

Hull Road

Blake Park

29

Campbell Rd

Reed

Marine Parade

28

Newton Road

Valley Road

OMANU

Hewletts Road

29

Mt Maunganui Road

Ranch Road

Ocean Beach Road

Tauranga Airport

31

30

Waipu Bay

Mount Maunganui Golf Course

Omanu Golf Course

To Whakatane   To Papamoa

■ PLACES TO STAY

3 Apple Tree Cottage
5 Bell Travellers' Lodge
12 Mayfair Caravan Park
13 Bluewater Motel
14 Silver Birch Motor Park & Thermal Pools
17 Mt Maunganui Domain Motor Camps
19 Elizabeth Gardens Holiday Park
20 Wainui Thermal Motel
23 Fawlty Towers Waterfront Motel
28 Bluehaven Motel
30 Cosy Corner Motor Camp

▼ PLACES TO EAT

2 Otumoetai Trust Hotel
7 Linardos Restaurant
8 Kentucky Fried Chicken
9 Pizza Hut
10 McDonald's
11 Georgie Pie
18 Oceanside Hotel & Beachfront Bar & Grill
21 Upstairs at Jimmy's
22 Palms Restaurant
27 Anchor Inn Hotel
29 BP Truck Stop
31 Kentucky Fried Chicken

OTHER

1 Otumoetai Post Office
4 Waikareoa Walkway
6 Tauranga District Museum & Historic Village
15 The Elms Mission Station House
16 Tauranga Travel Centre (InterCity)
24 Salisbury Wharf (Ferry)
25 Mt Maunganui Information Office & Newlove's Bus Depot
26 Mt Maunganui Post Office

The *Greerton Motor Inn* (☎ 578 8164), Cameron Rd, has been recommended by readers.

Hotels The *St Amand Hotel* (☎ 578 8127) at 105 The Strand has single/double rooms with shared facilities for $35/50 or single rooms with a bath for $30. The St Amand has live bands at night in Scotty's Bar from Wednesday to Saturday, which is great for

entertainment but a bit loud if you're trying to get some sleep.

Places to Eat

Many types of cuisines are represented in the restaurants of Tauranga. There are several eating places on The Strand, and along Cameron and Devonport Rds.

Snacks & Fast Food Tauranga has a *McDonald's* and a *Pizza Hut*, both on the corner of Cameron Rd and Eleventh Ave, and a *Kentucky Fried Chicken* a block north, between Ninth and Tenth Aves. *Georgie Pie*, the quick NZ alternative, is on the corner of Cameron Rd and Twelfth Ave. Other burger-style takeaways include *Big Al's*, on the corner of Cameron Rd and Fourth Ave, and *Hatters*, on Grey St, and *Munchies*, in Elizabeth St.

The Deli, at the northern end of Devonport Rd on the corner of the Spring St Mall, makes sandwiches and snacks. You can sit and enjoy them at the tables in the mall in Tauranga's famous sunshine. The Deli is open from 8.30 am to 5 pm, Monday to Friday, and until noon on Saturday.

Harbourside Chinese Takeaways, on The Strand, provides for the spring roll and dim sim fanatics. If you are in search of a bite on the usually slow winter Sunday then the *Captain's Table*, by the wharf, is open for fish & chips as well as other standard cafe-bar fare.

During the week at the *Trust Bank Centre Food Court*, 2 Devonport Rd, you can get seafood, international foods, roast meats, salads, sandwiches, coffee and ice cream.

Cafes Near the Deli, upstairs in the Deka department store, is the *Harbour View Cafe*, an enjoyable and inexpensive cafeteria with a sweeping harbour view. They serve tasty food at great prices; lunch costs about $5. It's open from 9 am to 3.30 pm on weekdays, and until 2 pm on Saturday. Down on The Strand, diagonally across from the visitor information centre, is the *Seafront Cafe,* where the staff never fail to deliver a hearty breakfast, good coffee and a smile.

At 82 Devonport Rd is the gourmet *Le Cafe*, a European-style cafe with attractive decor and umbrella tables on a terrace overlooking the bay. Prices are a bit higher; lunch starts at $6 for a smoked salmon and cream cheese bagel or $9 for focaccia with roast pork, blue cheese and pears. It's open from 8 am to 4.30 pm Monday to Saturday.

Upstairs at 77 Devonport Rd, *Eastcoasters* is a spacious, popular place specialising in Mexican and Tex-Mex food, light meals, burgers, and huge sandwiches, with something to please both vegetarians and meat-eaters. It's not exactly cheap but the servings are huge and it's got great atmosphere. I don't think their magic mushy burgers are similar to those in Bali. It is open from Tuesday to Sunday for dinner from 6 pm.

There is another Mexican place, *Amigo's Mexican Cantina*, down near the canoe at the end of The Strand.

Pub Food The St Amand Hotel on The Strand has standard lunch and dinner pub meals in the sidewalk *Browsing Cafe/Bar*. The *Mainbrace Restaurant & Bar* inside the hotel is a bit more fancy, with lunch and dinner pub meals every day except Sunday,

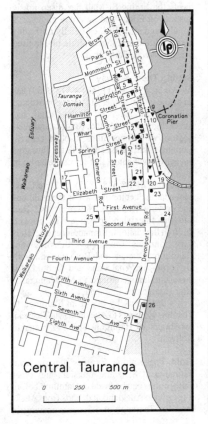

Central Tauranga

0   250   500 m

PLACES TO STAY

5   Strand Motel
11 St Amand Hotel
17 Waireinga YHA Hostel
24 Tauranga Motel
26 Harbourview Motel
27 6th Avenue Tourist Court

▼ PLACES TO EAT

6   Amigo's Mexican Cantina
7   Indigo Jones
10 Captain's Table
12 Seafront Cafe & Baywatch Brasserie
13 Harbour View Cafe
18 Le Cafe
19 Harbourside Brasserie & Bar
20 Bella Mia
21 Eastcoasters
25 Crisanta's

OTHER

1   Monmouth Redoubt
2   Botanic Gardens
3   *Te Awanui* Canoe
4   Department of Conservation (DOC)
8   Automobile Association (AA)
9   Tauranga Information & Visitors Centre
13 Deka
14 The Mall & Dolphin Bas Relief
15 Mid-City Tavern
16 Post Shop
22 Westpac Plaza
23 Air New Zealand Link

BAY OF PLENTY

when they serve a smorgasbord dinner for $18.50 from 6 to 9 pm.

There's also a *Cobb & Co* at the Greerton Motor Inn in Cameron Rd, south of the town centre. The *Otumoetai Trust Hotel*, Bureta Rd, wins the award for best value for money in Tauranga. The $2.50 salads are huge, a veritable bucket of kumara chips is $2.50, as are the open beef sandwiches – two courses for $5!

Restaurants The *Baywatch Brasserie & Bar*, on the corner of The Strand and Wharf St, was touted by a number of locals as the best place to dine. The menu is certainly innovative, combining a number of international treatments of local produce – kapiti camembert chargrilled and served with banana and tomato salad on a plum sauce, for instance. Also you can get a wide selection of good coffee types here.

For Italian food try *Linardos* licensed and BYO restaurant, on the corner of Eleventh Ave and St John St, with pastas, fettucine and spaghetti for $15; mains such as scaloppini are $19. A two-course set menu is $17.50 and a three-course is $22.50. For pizzas, as well as other pasta dishes, try *Bella Mia*, at 73A Devonport Rd.

You can get a variety of south-east and east Asian dishes (but not Chinese) at *Crisanta's*, 271 Cameron Rd.

The Garden Restaurant at the Otumoetai Trust Hotel in Bureta Rd is a bit inconvenient unless you have private transport, but it's good value. It's open every night from 5 to 9 pm.

You can dine inside or outside, overlooking the water, at the *Harbourside Brasserie & Bar* in the Old Yacht Club Building, The Strand Extension, from 11.30 am until late. A three-course meal costs from $35 to $40 here but the choice of dishes is good and combines a variety of local produce; they have a supper menu as well. More expensive than the Harbourside is *Indigo Jones* fully licensed restaurant and wine bar, at 59 The Strand. The snack meals in the wine bar are reasonably priced but nearly all the mains in

the restaurant start at about $20; a set three-course lunch is $21.

Entertainment
Several hotel bars have live entertainment nightly from Wednesday to Saturday. *Scotty's* is in the St Amand Hotel on The Strand. In Harington St there's *Harrington's Nightclub*; the *Abbey Road* has an entrance on Devonport Rd and another on The Strand Extension; and *No 19* is on Wharf St with an entrance at street level for the street-wise. At 132 Devonport Rd there is *Muzowz* downstairs and *Crossroads* upstairs.

The *Mid City Tavern* where The Strand meets the Spring St Mall has disco music upstairs on Friday and Saturday nights. It's popular and crowd-ed, especially on Friday nights, although it looks a little on the tired side nowadays. Party on dudes!

Getting There & Away
Air Air New Zealand Link (☎ 578 0083) has an office on the corner of Devonport Rd and Elizabeth St. Air New Zealand Link has direct flights to Auckland, Rotorua and Wellington, with connections to other centres. Tauranga's airport is actually not at Tauranga but at Mt Maunganui, just across the harbour.

Bus InterCity (☎ 578 2825), in Dive Crescent near the centre of town, is the main bus line serving Tauranga. Newmans, NZ Rail and the InterIslander can all be booked through the visitor information centre. Inter-City connects Tauranga with Auckland, Hamilton, Thames and Rotorua, and with Gisborne via Whakatane and Opotiki. All these bus lines continue to Mt Maunganui after stopping in Tauranga.

It's 2½ hours by bus from Tauranga to Thames, 4½ hours to Auckland (via Thames), two hours to Hamilton, and 1½ hours to Rotorua.

Train The Kaimai Express departs from Tauranga at 8.30 am; transfers and other connections can be made in Hamilton before it goes on to Auckland. It departs from Auckland for Tauranga at 5.50 pm, arriving in

Tauranga at 9 pm; there is a bar on board and snacks are served; inquire at the visitor information centre about the latest schedules.

Car The Bay of Plenty is about 200 km south-east of Auckland by the shortest route (SH 2) which takes about three hours by car. From Rotorua it's a mere 55 minutes along SH 33 and from Hamilton it's a two-hour drive down SH 1, turning onto SH 29 at Tirau.

Getting Around
To/From the Airport The Tauranga Airport Shuttle (☎ 578 6086) costs $7 per person, door to door.

Local Transport Tauranga has a local bus service which provides transport to most locations around the area, including Mt Maunganui and Papamoa. The ferry service to Mt Maunganui, discontinued when the new harbour bridge was built, now operates in summer; the cost is $5 per adult. The harbour bridge has a $1 toll in each direction for cars, but it's free for bicycles and pedestrians.

There are two taxi companies in Tauranga: Citicabs (☎ 577 0999) and Tauranga Taxis (☎ 578 6086).

Car Rental Several rental car operators have offices in Tauranga, including Budget and Avis. Probably the most economical is Rent-a-Dent. The information centre has more details.

MT MAUNGANUI
The town of Mt Maunganui stands at the foot of the 232-metre hill of the same name (also called The Mount, and the name Maunganui means 'large mountain'). It's just across the inlet from Tauranga and its fine beaches make it a popular holiday resort for Kiwis. Like Tauranga, Mt Maunganui is built on a narrow peninsula. It has been recently joined to Tauranga by a harbour bridge, making it much more accessible.

The down side of the drive to the Mount is the unsightly industrial area that they have

routed the road through, reminiscent of the factory-pocked towns of the eastern US seaboard.

Information
The Mt Maunganui Information Office (☎ 575 5099) is on Salisbury Avenue. It's open in summer from 8.30 am to 7 pm on weekdays, and from 8.30 am to 12.30 pm on Saturday. In winter it's open only from 8.30 am to 4.30 pm on weekdays; fewer hours on Saturday; and closed on Sunday. However, these times may change. The Tauranga Information Centre also has information on Mt Maunganui.

Things to See & Do
There are hot saltwater pools at the foot of The Mount, on Adams Ave – the pools are open daily from 8 am to 10 pm and admission is $2.50 for adults, $1.50 for senior citizens and children. Nearby is Moturiki Island, which is actually joined to the peninsula. Walking trails go up and around Mt Maunganui and you can climb around on the rocks on Moturiki (see *Walkways of Tauranga & the Western Bay of Plenty*, free from the visitor information centres). The beach between Moturiki and Mt Maunganui is good for surfing, bodysurfing and swimming.

The Tauranga Airport, at Mt Maunganui, is the base for a number of airborne activities – see the Tauranga section for details.

Places to Stay
Camping & Cabins Mt Maunganui is a popular summer resort so there are plenty of campsites. At the foot of The Mount, the *Mt Maunganui Domain Motor Camps* (☎ 575 4471) has waterfront sites at $16 for two people; cheaper rates apply from after Easter to late October.

At the *Cosy Corner Motor Camp* (☎ 575 5899), 40 Ocean Beach Rd, campsites cost $9 per person and on-site caravans are $34 for two. At 75 Girven Rd, the *Golden Grove Motor Park* (☎ 575 5821) has sites for $9 per person, and on-site vans and cabins at $32 for two.

BAY OF PLENTY

The *Ocean Pines Motor Camp* (☎ 575 4265) on Maranui St has campsites for $9 per person. On-site caravans cost $34.50 for two, and tourist flats cost $50 for two.

On The Mall, overlooking Pilot Bay on the Tauranga side of the peninsula, the *Elizabeth Gardens Holiday Park* (☎ 575 5787) has caravan sites for $9 per person. On-site caravans cost $38 for two and tourist flats cost $42 to $50 for two adults; they also have a backpackers bunkhouse, sleeping eight, in which a bed costs $15.

Hotels The only hotel accommodation at the moment is at the rather expensive *Hotel Mt Maunganui* (☎ 575 5089), Girven Rd, where the Monday to Friday tariff for a double room is $86; on weekends it is $10 less.

Motels There aren't as many motels in Mt Maunganui as there are in Tauranga. *Fawlty Towers Waterfront Motel* (☎ 575 5883) at 28 The Mall, facing the harbour, is expensive from Christmas to March but the rest of the year units are considerably cheaper; the peak rate is $67.50 a double.

The *Bluehaven Motel* (☎ 575 6508) at 10 Tweed St has single/double rooms for $50 to $57/60 to $69. *Wainui Thermal Motel* (☎ 575 3526) at 35 Maunganui Rd has singles/doubles for $55/68; and the *Outrigger Motel* (☎ 575 3250), 48 Marine Parade, has more expensive singles/twins or doubles at $68/78 to $85.

Places to Eat

There are many takeaways around town where you can get burgers, pizzas, Chinese and Mexican food, fish & chips and the like, particularly along Maunganui Rd.

Fast-food addicts can go to *Kentucky Fried Chicken* on the corner of Newton St and Hewletts Rd or *McDonald's* in the Bayfair Centre. A different sort of traveller, the 'truckie', heads to the *BP Truck Stop* on Hewletts Rd. The *Beachfront Bar & Grill*, next to the Oceanside Hotel on Ocean Beach Rd, is open for lunch and dinner serving safe, trusted dishes such as steak, burgers and seafood basket. The food at *Palms Restau-*

rant, on Maunganui Rd, is more imaginative and more international in taste.

Upstairs at Jimmy's, 19 Pacific Ave, is a fun dining-out place, being both a brasserie and bar with music most nights. For more late-night entertainment Frampton's 'comes alive' at the *Anchor Inn*, a popular meeting spot for locals; pub meals are also served here.

Getting There & Away

Air The Tauranga airport is actually at Mt Maunganui; see the Tauranga section for flight details and how to get To/From the Airport.

Bus Long-distance buses serving Tauranga also stop at Mt Maunganui, in front of the visitor information centre. Newlove's buses cross the harbour bridge from Tauranga.

Car You can reach Mt Maunganui across the harbour bridge from Tauranga, or from the south via Te Maunga on SH 2. If you're driving across the harbour bridge there's a $1 toll in each direction. Watch where you park your car – the parking inspectors descend like greedy locusts upon any improperly positioned vehicle.

Ferry This only operates in the summer from Salisbury Wharf, Mt Maunganui, Tauranga; the fare is $5.

AROUND TAURANGA
Katikati

In the past few years Katikati (to locals, Catty-Cat) on the Uretara River has become an open-air art gallery and many of its buildings are adorned with murals. Two good ones are Athenree Homestead and Waitekohe School c. 1914. There's an excellent small brochure 'Mural Town: Katikati' available from the Visitors' Centre (☎ 549 1658), Cherry Court – this bunch of volunteers would rate among NZ's friendliest and most helpful. Who else would hunt out a kiwi-fruit corer for a hapless American visitor?

Off SH 2 not far from Katikati, the Katikati Bird Gardens are a bird sanctuary and botanic gardens, open daily (except during July). Admission is $4.50 for adults and $1.50 for children.

Also in Katikati is the World of Horses (☎ 548 04040), open 10 am to 4 pm daily. here you can do coastal and cross-country trekking, learn-to-ride sessions and twilight rides.

Places to Stay & Eat The *Sapphire Springs Holiday Park* (☎ 549 0768) is set in 78 hectares of bush which backs on to the Kaimai Ranges. Tent sites are $8 per person, powered sites $2 extra per person, cabins $30 for two, tourist flats $50 for two, and motels $65 for two. A bunk bed in the lodge is $12.50; the springs are free to visitors but there are private spas available. About four km south of Katikati is the *Fantail Lodge* (☎ 549 1581) where B&B is over $90; the lodge has an adjoining restaurant. In town is the *Katikati Motel* (☎ 549 0385) where singles/ doubles are $59/68.

There are about 10 *homestays/farmstays* in the area; inquire at the visitor centre.

There is no shortage of good eating places in the Katikati region. On the main road through town there are a number of eateries including the *Cherry Court Coffee Lounge*, *Jacko's* and *The Roadhouse*. The *Forta Leza Restaurant* on the main road has an impressive menu, and even features West Coast whitebait (see Whitebait in the West Coast & Glaciers chapter); this place is open seven nights a week from 6 pm. Another top-notch place is *The Vineyard Restaurant* on Morton Estate – entrées are $8.50, mains $18 and desserts $8.50 – that's $35 for a three-course meal.

Attached to the World of Horses complex is the popular Irish *Trimble's Brasserie & Bar*, open noon until late, Tuesday to Sunday.

Omokoroa

This town is midway between Katikati and Tauranga, and is situated on a promontory which protrudes well into the sheltered harbour. *Plummers Point Caravan Park* (☎ 548 0669) has natural hotwater mineral pools, and sites for $8.50 per person, cabins

for $35 for two. The *Omokoroa Tourist Park* (☎ 548 0857) has sites for the same price, cabins for $30 or $32 for two, or tourist flats for $45 or $49 for two; they have three mineral pools.

On The Esplanade you can eat at *Seajay's*, open for morning and afternoon teas, light luncheons and à la carte evening meals.

Kiwi Fruit Wineries

Prestons Kiwi Fruit Winery, on Belk Rd off SH 29, is just one place where you can sample this uniquely NZ wine. They're open 10 am to 4.30 pm, Monday to Saturday. There are a number of other wineries in the district; inquire at the visitor information centre.

Tuhua (Mayor) Island

Tuhua (Mayor) Island is a dormant volcano about 40 km north of Tauranga in the Bay of Plenty. There are walking tracks through the now overgrown crater valley and an interesting walk around the island. The north-west corner is a marine reserve but specialist groups can seek permission to land there. (Permission needs to be from the Maori Trust Board – inquire at the Tauranga visitor information centre.)

Places to Stay You need a permit from the Maori Trust Board in Tauranga to land on the island or to camp there, but you can arrange this through the boat company on Coronation Pier.

The Tauranga Game Fishing Club on Coronation Pier has for some years operated the *Mayor Island Lodge*; its future is a little uncertain so inquire at the visitor information centre about the latest developments.

Getting There & Away Cruises to the island operate from Coronation Pier in Tauranga, going out via Mt Maunganui at 7 am and returning at 7 pm. The trip takes about three hours in each direction. The cost is $35 (children $25) for a day trip, or $50 (children $30) if you go out on one day and return on another. A $3 landing fee is included in the cruise costs.

The cruises operate daily between Boxing Day (26 December) and 6 February. Between Labour weekend (at the end of October) and Boxing Day they go three days a week – usually Saturday, Sunday and Wednesday. The rest of the year they may operate only sporadically or not at all, depending on weather conditions. Private boats may sometimes take passengers, and there is speculation that a sea plane service may start up. Contact the Tauranga visitor information centre for latest details.

Minden Lookout

From Minden Lookout, about 10 km from Tauranga, there's a superb view back over the Bay of Plenty. To get there, take SH 2 to Te Puna and turn off south on Minden Rd; the lookout is about four km up the road.

Papamoa

Papamoa, 13 km south of Mt Maunganui, is blessed with miles of beaches; fishing for tuatua is popular when the tide is right. There are a couple of motor camps at Papamoa, all of them along Papamoa Beach Rd. They are the *Papamoa Beach Holiday Park* (☎ 542 0816) and *Beach Grove Holiday Park* (☎ 542 1337); campsites are about $9 at each place and both have cabins as well. You can get takeaways from a number of places on Beach Rd; and the *Papamoa Family Tavern* has bistro meals.

Te Puke

Hailed as the 'Kiwi Fruit Capital of the World', Te Puke (population 7000) is not as bad as its civic plaudits have made it sound. There is much native bush nearby and the town is not far from several good beaches and exciting rivers. The Te Puke Visitor Information Centre (☎ 573 9172) is at 72 Jellicoe St and has lots of information on activities and sights in the surrounding area.

Kiwi Fruit Orchards The Bay of Plenty is kiwi fruit country and there are several places where you can learn a little more about this fruit that is so important for New Zealand's economy.

Kiwi Fruit Country (you won't miss the garish 'big kiwi fruit' sign, which looks like a green-dyed sectioned human kidney) is on SH 33, six km east of Te Puke and 36 km from Tauranga. You can visit the orchards and shop, see a video about kiwi fruit and sample some kiwi fruit or kiwi fruit wine. There's a $3 entry fee to get into the complex. If you want to take a kiwi-kart ride through the orchards and see how the fruit is grown and packed, tours operate mostly during May and June when the kiwis are in fruit, and cost $8 (children $4). Kiwi Fruit Country is open daily from 9 am to 5 pm.

Other Things to Do Longridge Park, 12 km south of Te Puke on SH 33, is a more extensive farm with tours, walks and other activities including jet-boating and white water rafting. It's designed to show the entire range of diversity of NZ farming and in addition to kiwi fruit and other orchards it has cattle, sheep, goats, and even forestry. It's open from 9 am to 5 pm; admission is $4 for adults, $2 children. The best time to see kiwi fruit picking and packing is during May and June.

Longridge Jets (☎ 533 1515) does jet-boating on the Kaituna River near Te Puke, east of Tauranga. This river is renowned as having the most exciting white water in New Zealand. The cost for a 45-minute trip is $45 for an adult and $25 for a child (minimum $90 or two adult passengers).

Places to Stay & Eat The *Te Puke Holiday Park* (☎ 573 9866) has campsites for $7.50 per person, hostel-style accommodation for $12 per person, and on-site caravans and cabins for $32 for two. At 173 Jellicoe St is the *Beacon Motel* (☎ 573 7824) which has singles/doubles for $54/68 to $74.

There are a number of takeaways and tearooms on Jellicoe St, a *restaurant* out at Kiwi Fruit Country and you can get a hearty Devonshire tea at *Windrest Cottage* at 15 Moehau St.

Maketu

There's a Maori pa site at Town Point, near

the township of Maketu, north-east of Te Puke, where you can see some ancient carvings. Maketu was the landing site of the *Arawa* canoe, more than 600 years ago, and there is a stone monument on the foreshore which commemorates this. The name Maketu comes from a place in Hawaiki. The small Maketu visitor information centre (☎ 533 2343) can't be missed, if for nothing else than the beautiful mural which decorates its front.

In Bledisloe Park, three km from Maketu, is the gun pit – still intact – from where, on 22 April 1864, Lieutenant-Colonel Thomas McDonnell and 12 Europeans fought a pitched battle against 600 Maoris. To get to Maketu from Tauranga, take SH 2 through Te Puke and turn left into Maketu Rd just past Rangiuru.

Eastern Bay of Plenty

The eastern Bay of Plenty extends from Maketu and Pukehina to Opotiki, in the far east of the bay, and takes in Whakatane and Ohope. At the southern apex of the triangle is Murupara and the Whirinaki Forest. The western flank of East Cape, traditionally included in this area, is treated separately in the East Cape section.

WHAKATANE
Whakatane (population 13,000), the principal town on the eastern side of the Bay of Plenty, is much smaller than Tauranga on the western side. It's on a natural harbour at the mouth of the Whakatane River and is the main centre of the Rangitaiki agricultural and milling district. In common with the rest of the Bay of Plenty, Whakatane has a favourable climate all year round and many visitors are attracted to the sunny beaches, especially in summer.

History
The history of Whakatane began with the landing of the *Mataatua* canoe at the mouth of the Whakatane River in about 1350 AD, during the Great Migration. A Maori settlement was established and the site remained an important Maori centre. As late as the turn of the century there were still only a few European residents. However, when the Europeans realised the richness of the land they began to settle the area and in 1914 Whakatane was formed into a town district, becoming a borough three years later.

Information
There's a small but very well-organised visitor information centre (☎ 308 6058) behind the Civic Centre on Boon St and half a block off The Strand, the town's tiny main street. The centre is open from 9 am to 5 pm on weekdays. From late October to Easter it also opens from 9 am to 2 pm on Saturday. They have printed information on just about everything – places to stay, a diner's guide, things to see & do including a four-day series of pamphlets, and tour operators to Whakaari (White) Island. The AA office is opposite the visitor information centre on Boon St and there's a DOC office (☎ 308 7213) a block away at 28 Commerce St, open from 8 am to 4.30 pm, Monday to Friday.

Whakatane Museum
The small Whakatane Museum is in Boon St beside the playground, about a block from the visitor information centre. It has photographic and artefact exhibits on early Maori and European settlers, and the natural environment, including the smoking Whakaari (White) Island volcano just offshore. It's also a centre of historical research, with an archives of historical publications. It's open from 10 am to 4 pm daily.

Pohaturoa
Just to one side of the traffic circle on the corner of The Strand and Commerce St is Pohaturoa, a large rocky area which is an important Maori sacred site. The coastline used to come right up to here and there's a

Whakatane

0   250   500 m

Approximate Scale

tunnel in the rock where baptisms and other rites were performed. Today the rock is set apart in a little park, with a plaque explaining its historical and religious significance. Also in the park are a Maori canoe, carved benches, and a monument to a chief of the Mataatua tribes.

Dolphins Down Under

Well-known dolphin expert Barbara Todd and her partner Roger Sutherland have started a dolphin-swimming operation in Whakatane. Barbara knows about as much about marine mammals as is possible, having devoted her adult life to their study. There are daily three-hour trips, October to mid-May, with Dolphins Down Under (☎ 308 4636/4635), 92 The Strand, subject to weather; the price is $70 inclusive. You will see many pelagic bird species and, if you are lucky, whales. They will pick you up in Rotorua if you come to Whakatane to do their trip and stay overnight in their backpackers accommodation, and then return you to Rotorua.

Other Things to See

The Tasman Pulp & Paper Mill (☎ 323 3999) also has free daily tours, starting at 2 pm weekdays, or times can be arranged.

The Whakatane Astronomical Observatory (☎ 312 4618) in Hurunui Ave, Hillcrest, opens to the public every Tuesday evening at about half an hour after sunset, weather permitting.

There's a botanical gardens at the river end of McGarvey Rd, beside a children's playground. Lake Sullivan, a swan lake, is on King St.

The Awakeri Hot Springs, 14.5 km from Whakatane on SH 30, the main highway to Rotorua, has a hot springs, spa pools, picnic areas and a motor camp. Also nearby are the Tarawera Falls and Mt Putauaki (Edgecumbe), a nearly perfect archetype of a volcanic cone commanding a panoramic view of the entire Bay of Plenty from the top. You need a permit to climb it; contact Tasman Forestry (☎ 323 4599). Putauaki is closed to 4WD vehicles.

PLACES TO STAY

6   Commercial Hotel Backpackers
8   Whakatane Hotel
19 Whakatane Camping Ground
25 Bay Private Hotel
26 Dolphins Down Under
    Backpackers' Hostel

PLACES TO EAT

1   The Reef Licensed Cafe
7   Buccaneer Restaurant
8   Why Not Cafe
10 Wedgewood Food Court
12 Go Global
16 Harry's Place
17 New Hong Kong Chinese Restaurant
    (Takeaways behind on Boon St)
24 Cornell's Restaurant
27 Kentucky Fried Chicken
28 McDonald's
29 Surf 'n' Turf

OTHER

2   Public Toilets
3   Muriwai Cave
4   Mataatua Park
5   Public Toilets
9   Dolphins Down Under
11 Pohaturoa Rock
13 Visitor Information Centre &
    Public Toilets
14 Department of Conservation (DOC)
15 Museum & Gallery
18 Automobile Association (AA)
20 Puketapu Lookout
21 Wairere Falls
22 Papaka Redoubt
23 InterCity Bus Depot

Walks

The information centre and DOC have lots of information on walks. An interesting 2½-hour Town Centre Walk encompasses a number of scenic and historic spots including a historical cave, a waterfall, lookout, redoubt, the Pohaturoa rock and a big game fishing facility.

Other notable walks include the 3½-hour Kohi Point Walkway, Nga Tapuwae-o-Toi (The Sacred Footsteps of Toi), through the Kohi Point Scenic Reserve, passing many attractive sites including lookouts and the Pa of Toi, reputedly the oldest pa site in New Zealand. Other walkways are the Ohope Bush Walk, the Mokorua Scenic Reserve, Latham's Track and the Matata Walking Track. The 300-metre White Pine Bush Walk, starting about 10 km from Whakatane, is suitable even for people in wheelchairs and the elderly.

Other Things to Do

Check with the visitor information centre about the wide variety of activities in and around Whakatane. Possibilities include hunting trips, horse treks and bushwalking. There are also numerous water activities including trout or sea fishing, diving and kayak trips, windsurfing and swimming. Jet-boat and white water rafting tours are made from Whakatane on the Rangitaiki, Wairoa, Motu, Whirinaki and Waimana rivers. Pohutukawa Tours (☎ 308 6495) have been recommended; they do half-day, full-day and overnight tours.

During January the Whakatane DOC offers a very cheap summer programme, visiting many of the area's most interesting sites.

Places to Stay

Camping & Cabins The *Whakatane Camping Ground & Caravan Park* (☎ 308 8694) in McGarvey Rd beside the Whakatane River has recreational facilities, a swimming pool and a spa pool. Tent or powered sites are $8 per person, on-site caravans are $25 for two, and cabins are $30 for two. The *Motor Lodge Park* (☎ 308 5189) in the south of town off Valley Rd has campsites at $10 per person.

The *Awakeri Hot Springs* (☎ 304 9117), 16 km from Whakatane on SH 30, the main highway to Rotorua, is a popular hot springs and has a motor camp. Tent and caravan sites cost $8 per adult, cabins cost $30 for two and tourist flats cost $45 for two.

Hostels The operators of Dolphins Down Under have set up, at 11 Merritt St, a small *backpackers* (☎ 308 4636) which is only a two-minute walk from the centre of town. The cost of accommodation is $13 in a dorm room or $15 per person in a twin or double room. See also Whakatane and Commercial hotels in the next section.

Hotels The old art deco *Whakatane Hotel* (☎ 308 8199) on The Strand has single/double rooms for $30/40, or $37/45 with private facilities. The *Commercial* (☎ 308 7399), on Strand East, has singles/doubles for $35/50. It is understood that both these places were tapping in to the lucrative backpackers market as from 1994; check prices at the visitor information centre. The *Bay Private Hotel* (☎ 308 6788) at 90 McAllister St has B&B for $43 or $50 per person. The more expensive rooms have private bathrooms.

Motels There are a number of motels in and around Whakatane, especially at Ohope Beach (see Ohope Beach in this section), 6.5 km to the east. Rates begin at around $60/70 for singles/doubles. The best motel prices are at the motor camps, all of which have motel units (see Camping & Cabins). The *Awakeri Hot Springs* has singles/doubles for $50/60, and the *Whakatane Motor Lodge* has units at $45. Otherwise there are no particular bargains.

Homestays & Farmstays Ring ☎ 308 7955 for listings for homestays and farmstays on farms, orchards, in town, or out at Ohope Beach. The visitor information centre has an extensive list.

Places to Eat
Most of Whakatane's eating places are in the shopping area along The Strand. You can get an adequate meal at the *Wedgewood Food Court*, *Sammies Cafe* or the *Strand Cafe*. *McDonald's* and *Kentucky Fried Chicken* are both near the intersection of Commerce St and Domain Rd. Try *Harry's Place*, in Boon St, for good old-fashioned burgers with the lot or *Dago's Famous Pizzeria* for crusty

pizza base adorned with the Super Special mix.

The *New Hong Kong Restaurant*, half a block off The Strand on Richardson St, has Chinese food, with a separate counter for takeaways straight back through the block in Boon St. You can get a hearty steak meal at the *Buccaneer Restaurant*, between the Quay and The Strand; continental food at *Go Global*, on the corner of Commerce St and Shapley Place; and vegetarian food at the popular *Why Not Cafe*, which is attached to the Whakatane Hotel. Also, *Cornell's Restaurant* in Commerce St has a well-priced, comprehensive menu.

Getting There & Away
Air Air New Zealand Link has daily flights linking Whakatane to Auckland, Wellington and Wanganui, with connections to other centres. Contact the visitor information centre or one of the travel agents on The Strand.

A Whakatane-based and owned airline, Tranz Air (☎ 308 6656), has a weekday service to Auckland with three return flights daily. The office is at the Whakatane Airport, about five km west of Whakatane on SH 2.

A taxi service (☎ 307 0388) is available to get you to and from the airport and the cost is $17; many motels/hotels have courtesy vehicles. There is no local suburban bus service.

Bus The InterCity bus depot (☎ 308 8208) is in Pyne St (Bay Coachlines). InterCity has buses connecting Whakatane with Rotorua and Gisborne, with connections to other places; all buses to Gisborne go via Opotiki. Newman's have a return service – Rotorua to Gisborne via Whakatane – book at InterCity. It's two hours to Tauranga or Rotorua, about an hour to Opotiki, and another 2½ hours from Opotiki to Gisborne via the Waioeka Gorge route (SH 2). Buses around the East Cape originate from Opotiki and Gisborne (see Getting There & Away for the East Cape).

Ohope Beach

The town of Ohope and its fine beach is seven km 'over the hill' from Whakatane. It is a pleasant area in which to spend a few days, with all types of accommodation available, and there are a number of walks in the area.

Places to Stay & Eat The *Ohope Backpackers* (☎ 312 5173), 1A West End, has bunks or double rooms for $13 per person. This place is a grand three-storey building which has beach views from the verandah; it has a lawn area in front where you can soak up some sun as you write letters or read a good book.

There are two motor camps: *Ohope Beach Holiday Park* (☎ 312 4460), Harbour Rd, has sites for $10 per person, cabins for $34 for two ($39 if they are on the beachfront) and tourist flats for $45 for two; and the *Surf 'n Sand Holiday Park* (☎ 312 5884), on the beachfront in central Ohope has sites for $9 per person, on-site caravans for $30 for two, cabins for $30 to $35 for two and tourist flats for $52 for two. There are about eight motels, most of them along West End, costing about $55/65 for singles/ doubles; and a number of homestays.

If you are after takeaways then there is the *Pink Caddyshack* on Pohutukawa Ave or *Ohiwa Oyster Farm* on Wainui Rd; a licensed *restaurant* is attached to the Ohope Beach Resort.

WHAKAARI (WHITE) ISLAND

Whakaari, or White Island, is an active volcano smoking and steaming away just 50 km off the coast from Whakatane. It's a small island of 324 hectares formed by three separate volcanic cones, all of different ages. Erosion has worn away most of the surface of the two older cones and the youngest cone, which rose up between the two older ones, now occupies most of the centre of the island. Hot water and steam continually escape from vents over most of the crater floor, and temperatures of 600°C to 800°C have been recorded. The highest point on the island is Mt Gisborne at 321 metres. Geolog-

ically, White Island is related to Whale Island and Mt Putauaki (Edgecumbe), as they all lie along the same volcanic trench.

History

Before the arrival of Europeans the Maoris caught sea birds on the island for food. In 1769 Captain Cook named it White Island because of the dense clouds of white steam hanging above it.

The first European to land on the island was a missionary, the Reverend Henry Williams, who landed in 1826. The island was acquired by Europeans in the late 1830s and changed ownership a number of times after that. Sulphur production began but was interrupted in 1885 by a minor eruption, and the following year the island was hurriedly abandoned in the wake of the Tarawera eruption. The island's sulphur industry was resumed in 1898 but only continued until 1901, when production ceased altogether.

In the 1910s further mining operations were attempted and abandoned due to mud flows and other volcanic activity, and ownership of the island continued to change. In 1953 White Island was declared a Private Scenic Reserve.

The island is still privately owned and the only way you can land on it is with helicopter or boat tours which have arranged permission. For a more detailed history of the island ask the Whakatane visitor information centre for their excellent pamphlet, *History of White Island 1769-1966*.

Getting There & Away

There are several operators taking trips to White Island including the following:

Island Princess (☎ 312 4236): a seven-hour cruise including a full meal – $60 for adults, $30 for children

White Island Volcano Adventure (☎ 307 0663): 2½-hour helicopter flight including guided tour of the island – $225 per person, minimum of four people

Kahurangi (☎ 323 7829): four-hour trip in a 20-foot (six-metre) foil cat – $66 per person, minimum of four people

Bell Air (☎ 308 6656): 45-minute scenic flights over White Island for $95 per person, minimum of two people, but with no landing

Pee Jay (☎ 312 9075): this trip in a 40-foot (12-metre) luxury sportcruiser costs $75 per person, finger food is served

All trips incur a $10 landing fee, often not included in the quoted price. This fee goes to the Presbyterian Child Relief Fund and collection is administered by the Department of Conservation. A landing by boat is definitely weather- dependent.

MOUTOHORA (WHALE) ISLAND

Moutohora (sometimes spelt Motuhora), or Whale Island, is nine km north of Whakatane and has an area of 414 hectares – somewhat larger than White Island. It was known to the Maoris as Motuhora Island and is still referred to by both the Maori and English names. Its English name comes from its shape, resembling a humpback whale. It's another volcanic island, on the same volcanic trench as White Island, and along its shore are hot springs which can reach 93°C. The summit is 350 metres high and several historic sites including an ancient pa site, an old quarry, and a camp are found around the island.

The Whakatane DOC office has a pamphlet on the interesting facets of Whale Island. A few notable events include pre-European Maori settlement, a 1769 landing by Captain Cook, and an 1829 Maori massacre of sailors from the trading vessel *Haweis* while it was anchored at Sulphur Bay. A whaling venture was started and abandoned in the 1830s. In the 1840s the island passed into European ownership and is still privately owned, although since 1965 it has been an officially protected wildlife refuge administered by DOC.

Whale Island is principally a haven for sea and shore birds, some of which are quite rare. Some of the birds use the island only for nesting at certain times of the year, while others are present all year round. Perhaps the most interesting aspect of the avifauna is the large colony of grey-faced petrels, estimated to number 10,000.

The island's protected status means landing is restricted and there are also restrictions on what you can do there – smoking is not allowed, for example, due to the destruction a fire would wreak.

Getting There & Away

The Whakatane DOC, in conjunction with the Coastguard, operates tours to the island at Christmas time. The cost is $30 and the trips last all day – these are the only trips which have permission to land on the island.

MURUPARA & WHIRINAKI

At the south of the eastern Bay of Plenty triangle is the forestry town of Murupara and the 54,000-hectare Whirinaki Forest Park. Access is off SH 38 via Te Whaiti to Minginui, the forest headquarters. Just before Minginui is the *Whirinaki Recreation Camp* (☎ 366 3601) and in Minginui is the *Ohu Forest Users' Camp*; both cost $5 per night for adults and $2.50 for children. Down by the Whirinaki River, at the Mangamate Waterfall, there is an informal camping area; a tent site is $5.

For more information about this excellent forest park get a copy of the booklet *Tramping & Walking in Whirinaki Forest Park*; it costs $1 and includes details of the excellent walk into the depths of the park via Te Hoe and Te Wairoa huts.

There are all types of accommodation in Murupara as well as four food outlets. The *restaurant* in the Murupara Hotel serves bistro meals.

OPOTIKI

Opotiki (population 5500), the easternmost town of the Bay of Plenty and centre of a prosperous horticultural, dairying and sheep farming district, is the gateway to the spectacular East Cape road and the wild, rugged forests and river valleys of the Raukumara and nearby ranges. People also come to visit the nearby beaches in summer – there are good surfing beaches at Ohiwa and Waiotahi. A road from Opotiki crosses over the

Opotiki

0   0.5   1 km

■ PLACES TO STAY

2 Opotiki Holiday Park
4 Masonic Hotel
5 Opotiki Hotel & Backpackers
11 Central Backpackers
13 Patiti Lodge
15 Magnolia Court Motel
17 Ranui Motels

▼ PLACES TO EAT

6 Opotiki Bar & Grill
12 Ocean Seafoods
14 Dannie's & Hot Bread Shop

16 Bee Bee's Diner

OTHER

1 Wharf and Boat Ramp
3 Opotiki Historical &
   Agricultural Society Museum
7 Visitor Information Centre &
   Department of Conservation (DOC)
8 East Cape Bus Depot & InterCity
9 Dreamers & East-Capers
10 Post Office & Public Toilets
18 Access to Adventure Rafting
19 Waioweka Rest Area
20 Hospital

BAY OF PLENTY

Motu Hills through beautiful bush scenery – the road is unsealed and there's not much traffic.

There are several explanations for the name Opotiki but the most likely is that it was the place of a chief named Potiki. The area was settled from at least 1150 AD, two hundred years before the Great Migration. Consequently many of the pa sites around this area have a long history.

In the mid-1800s Opotiki was the centre of Hauhauism, a Maori doctrine advocating, amongst other things, the extermination of Europeans. In 1865 the Reverend Karl Volkner was murdered in his church, St Stephen the Martyr, which culminated in the church being transformed into a fortress by government troops.

Travelling east from Opotiki there are two routes to choose from. SH 2 crosses the spectacular Waioeka Gorge. There are some fine walks of one day and longer in the Waioeka Gorge Scenic Reserve; ask at the visitor information centre or DOC for information. The gorge gets progressively steeper and narrower as you travel inland, before the route crosses typically green, rolling hills, dotted with sheep, on the descent to Gisborne.

The other route east from Opotiki is SH 35, around the East Cape, described fully in its own section.

The Opotiki Visitor Information Centre (☎ 315 8484) is on the corner of St John and Elliot Sts. DOC (☎ 315 8484) have an office in the same building. The centre does bookings for a range of activities, provides loads of free information brochures and can organise visits to a local marae.

Each year Opotiki hosts a section of the gruelling Rothman's Car Rally, and every second year has a popular Fibre & Fleece Show.

Hukutaia Domain

Just over seven km from Opotiki is the fascinating Hukutaia Domain which has one of the finest collections of native plants in New Zealand, many of the species rare and endangered. One example, a puriri tree – named

Taketakerau – is estimated to be over 2000 years old. The remains of the distinguished dead of the Upokorere sub-tribe of the Whakatohea were ritually buried beneath it. The tree is no longer tapu as the bones of the dead have been reburied elsewhere. See if you can find *Coriaria pottsiana*, named after the first chairman of the Domain, Norman Potts. For instructions of how to get to the Domain get a pamphlet from the visitor information centre.

Adventure Activities

The aptly named Dreamers and East-Capers (☎ 315 5577), opposite the visitor information centre in St John St, organise a variety of mountain-bike trips in the bush around Opotiki. Their single-track trip follows a scenic river valley and passes through patches of virgin bush – watch the slippery bridges or you will end up in the creek like I did! They have a fully escorted trip on the Old Motu coach road which takes in awesome drops, native bush and breathtaking views; the cost is between $30 and $55, depending on numbers. The six-day, five-night 'Search for the Source of the Sun' trip sees Tim and Paula fill their van up with mountain bikes, snorkelling gear, kayaks and fishing rods for your use – you stop where you like along the coastal road and do whatever takes your fancy. Discounts are given on all trips if you bring your own bike.

Places to Stay

Camping & Cabins The *Opotiki Holiday Park* (☎ 315 6050) on the corner of Grey St and Potts Ave, one block from the post office, has powered sites and tent sites for $7 per person and a bunkroom for $10 per person. For two people, cabins cost $23 and tourist flats cost $34.

There are several beachfront camping grounds near Opotiki. The *Island View Family Holiday Park* (☎ 315 7519), on Appleton Rd, four km from town, has campsites and cabins. The *Tirohanga Beach Motor Camp* (☎ 315 7942) on the East Coast Rd, six km from town, has campsites, cabins and tourist flats. Also on the East Coast Rd,

12 km from Opotiki, the *Opape Motor Camp* (☎ 907) 315 8175) has campsites and an on-site caravan.

Hostels The town has a number of backpackers places. Out at Waiotahi Beach, about five minutes west of Opotiki, is the *Opotiki Backpackers Beach House* (☎ 315 5117). It is a nice small place with adjoining kitchen and recreation room; the $12 beds are in the loft. It has a 'top' little outdoor area and will one day have a cafe overlooking the beach.

Out at the Waiotahi Estuary, and well-signposted off SH 2, is *Eastland Backpackers* (☎ 315 4870); it is a new, comfortable place which costs around $13 per night. They will pick you up from, and return you to, Opotiki for free.

In town there are two places. The *Opotiki Hotel* (☎ 315 6078) in Church St, has backpackers' beds for $10 or $15 if you require bedding. There are handbasins in all rooms but the toilets and showers are shared (see also Hotels). More of a backpackers than the hotel is *Central Backpackers* (☎ 315 5165), 30 King St. It has two very ordinary dorm rooms at the front and the kitchen and shower area seemed very small – they were working on it when we visited so hopefully the facilities will be improved. It costs $12 per night per person.

Hotels Opotiki has a couple of hotels. The *Opotiki Hotel* has backpackers accommodation. The *Masonic Hotel* (☎ 315 6115), also in Church St, has singles/doubles for $30/40. The *Patiti Lodge Travel Hotel* (☎ 315 6834) at 112 Ford St has single/double rooms for $30/45; you can order meals here for extra.

Motels The *Ranui Motels* (☎ 315 6669), at 36 Bridge St, has singles/doubles for $52/62; and at the *Magnolia Court Motel* (☎ 315 8490), on the corner of Bridge and Nelson Sts, singles/doubles are $64/72.

Places to Eat

Although not exactly gourmet capital of the Bay, Opotiki does have a small range of places to eat. *Dannie's & Hot Bread Shop*, near the corner of St John and Bridge Sts is one combination fast-food place; another is *Ocean Seafoods* on Church St for battered mussels & chips. For a hearty breakfast go to *Bee Bee's Diner* on Bridge St – they also serve full meals at other times of the day. On Looney's Rd (I'm serious), out at Waiotahe, you'll find the *Cottage Garden Cafe*, a place for afternoon and Devonshire teas. The *Opotiki Hotel* serves bistro meals as does the *Masonic*. For Kiwi fare there is the *Opotiki Bar & Grill* on Elliott St.

One day there will be a cafe at Waiotahi Beach. The project has started but isn't being pushed through at great speed. 'Cafe sin Nombre' is awaiting completion of the kitchen, arrival of a cook, permits, and so on.

Getting There & Away

The InterCity bus depot (☎ 907) 315 6146) is on Elliott St. InterCity has buses connecting Opotiki with Whakatane (one hour), Tauranga (three hours), Rotorua (three hours), and Auckland (7½ hours via Rotorua).

The Super Shuttle operates from Gisborne to Opotiki to Rotorua via the Waioeka Gorge once daily; it arrives in Opotiki about 10 am. The longer route to Gisborne (about eight hours), along the coast around the East Cape, can still be done by using a combination of local bus services (see Getting There & Away for East Cape in this chapter); it certainly should not be missed as it is one of the highlights of any visit to this region.

East Cape

The East Cape is one of the most scenic, isolated and least known regions of the North Island. The small communities scattered along the coast are predominantly Maori and the pace of life is peaceful and slow. Geographically, the area has few natural harbours and, until the road network was completed, goods had to be loaded off the beaches onto waiting barges. The interior is still wild bush, with the Raukumara Range extending down the centre of the cape. The western side of the range is divided into several state forest parks: Ruatoria, Raukumara, Urutawa, Waioeka and Mangatu.

The coast is now circled by 330 km of highway, SH 35, which took decades to build. It is an excellent road open all year round, making the coast more accessible than it ever has been. The drive is worth it if only for the magnificent views of this wild coast, dotted with picturesque little bays, inlets and coves that change aspect with the weather – on a sunny day the water is an inviting turquoise colour, at other times a layer of clouds hangs on the craggy mountains rising straight up from the beaches and everything turns a misty green. Dozens of fresh clear streams flow through wild gorges to meet the sea. During the summer the coastline turns crimson with the blooming of the pohutukawa trees lining the seashore.

It is possible to get all the way round the cape using local transport services (see Getting Around in this section).

OPOTIKI TO EAST CAPE

This trip is well described in *Opotiki & East Coast*, a comprehensive pamphlet available free from the Opotiki Visitor Information Centre. Along the first stretch of road from Opotiki there are fine views across to the steaming White Island volcano. At the Waiaua River is the right turn-off for the road to Gisborne via Toa Toa and the **Old Motu Coach road**, probably more suited for mountain bikes.

The beaches at **Torere** and **Hawai** are steeply shelved and covered with driftwood – good spots for seascape photography. About 45 km from Opotiki the road crosses the **Motu River**, famed for its jet-boating, white water rafting and kayaking possibilities.

. Some 25 km further on is **Te Kaha**, once a whaling centre but now a popular holiday spot – the small town has all the necessary facilities including a pub, store and accommodation. A succession of picturesque bays, including the beautiful Whanarua Bay, are passed before **Whangaparaoa (Cape Runaway)** is reached. You cannot miss the

Raukorore Anglican Church, nestled under Norfolk pines on a lone promontory, about 100 km north of Opotiki. Cape Runaway can only be reached on foot; seek permission before going on to private land.

Hicks Bay (once named Te Wharekahika) gets its name from a crew member of the Cook's *Endeavour*. It is a magnificent place, complemented by nearby Horseshoe Bay, remote and far away. Nearly 10 km 'round the corner' as you turn south-east is the sizeable community of **Te Araroa** where you turn off for East Cape lighthouse, the most easterly in the world. Hicks Bay Backpackers Lodge conduct trips to the lighthouse; these trips are 2¼ hours and cost $15 – you have to climb the 686 steps up to the light on your own and the best time to do it is before sunrise.

Places to Stay & Eat

There is no shortage of budget and other accommodation along the cape's western side. In addition to Tirohanga Motor Camp and its soulmate at Opape, there is *Coral's B&B* (☎ 315 8052), also in Opape. Famished? – then the fish & chips at *Torere Seafoods* are legendary. At Maraenui there is the *Oariki Homestay* (☎ 325 2678) where they make their own cheeses and wine; they have a fully equipped cottage or rooms in the house.

Te Kaha is the central point on the west side of East Cape. The *Te Kaha Holiday Park* (☎ 325 2894) has campsites, cabins and tourist flats, and the *Te Kaha* (☎ 325 2837) has budget accommodation and the usual hotel bedrooms (singles/doubles are $30/48 and budget beds are $12). At pretty Whanarua Bay there is the new *Rendezvous on the Coast Holiday Park* (☎ 325 2899) where sites were, for a short opening time in 1993, $12 for two or $4 for children; expect them to rise.

At Waihau Bay there are two accommodation places: the *Waihau Bay Holiday Park* (☎ 325 3844), Oruati Beach, with campsites, cabins and on-site caravans; and the *Waihau Bay Lodge* (☎ 325 3804) where singles/doubles are $45/65.

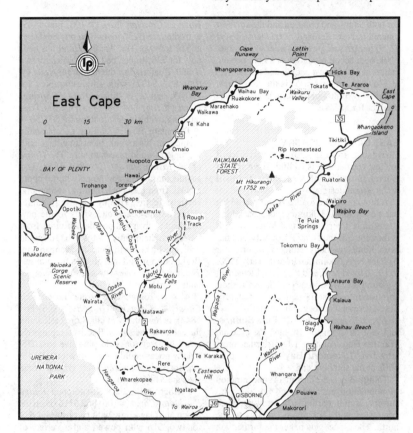

East Cape

0   15   30 km

On the northern tip of the cape are Hicks Bay and Te Araroa, both beautiful areas convenient for an overnight stopover. (Note that the prefix for telephone numbers is now 06.) At Hicks Bay there is a well-signposted private hostel, the *Hicks Bay Backpackers Lodge* (☎ (06) 864 4731), on Onepoto Beach Rd fronting the sea. It's a small, simple place with a bunkroom off to one side of the home of the exceptionally friendly hosts. The nightly cost is $13 in dorms or $15 per person in doubles. They organise trips for fishing, diving, shellfish collecting, and visits to the East Cape lighthouse and the Waiherere Falls. Boogie boards and surf skis are provided and there are also good bush walks in the vicinity.

Also at Hicks Bay, on the hill overlooking the bay, is the more expensive *Hicks Bay Motel Lodge* (☎ (06) 864 4880) with double rooms starting at $70.

Te Araroa Holiday Park (☎ (06) 864 4873), midway between Te Araroa and Hicks Bay, is another lovely spot, in a sheltered 15-hectare parklike setting with excellent surfing, swimming and fishing, bushwalking, hunting and horse-riding. The park has lots of amenities, with recreational facilities for both adults and children and the smallest cinema in New Zealand. It has tent sites at $6.50 per person, powered sites at $1 more, bunkroom accommodation at $9 per person, cabins at $30 for two people and tourist flats at $45. Also in Te Araroa is the *Kawakawa Hotel* (☎ (06) 864 4809) which has singles/doubles for $25/41.

EAST CAPE TO GISBORNE

Going south from Te Araroa the first place of interest you come to is **Tikitiki**. The Anglican Church is well worth visiting for its Maori architectural design.

A few km off the road is **Ruatoria**, which has powerful Mt Hikurangi as a backdrop. Ruatoria is a very important Maori town. It is the centre of the Ngati Porou tribe and has been home to many eminent Maoris. Sir Apirana Ngata, politician from the early 1900s to 1930, lived here, and the brave Lieutenant Ngarimu VC was born here. It had a short sojourn into Rastafarianism, which pro-duced the popular reggae band Herbs.

About 25 km south is **Te Puia Springs**, and, not far from the springs, the pleasant **Waipiro Bay**. Another 10 km further on is attractive **Tokomaru Bay** with sweeping cliffs at the southern end.

Tolaga Bay is the next main concentration of population and, although popular with surfers, is not particularly exciting when contrasted with Tokomaru or bays to the north. The aspect gets better the further you get from town towards the beach. South of Tolaga Bay is a small settlement called Whangara, the setting for Witi Ihimaera's wonderful fictional work *The Whale Rider*. This is a great little book to read for a feel of the Maori culture and mythology of the area. After passing Tatapouri and Wainui beaches you reach Gisborne (covered in the East Coast chapter).

Places to Stay

Heading south along the east coast from Te Araroa you come to the Waiapu River and the town of Tikitiki. There's the *Waiapu*

Hotel & Caravan Park (☎ (06) 864 3745) with sites at $10.50 for two, or powered sites at $12 for two. The *Waiapu Hotel* has beds only for $26; dinner, bed & breakfast for two is $90. Ruatoria has the *Manutahi Hotel* (☎ (06) 864 8437) with singles/doubles for $30/45; and at Te Puia is the *Hot Springs Hotel* (☎ (06) 864 6861), a Historic Trust building, with singles/doubles for $35/50.

Tokomaru Bay is another exceptionally scenic spot. It's a small, pleasant village with a couple of good places to stay. The *House of the Rising Sun* (☎ (06) 864 5858) is a small, comfortable and homely hostel about a block from the beach. Hiking, swimming, surfing, tennis, fishing, cycling, horse-riding on the beach and visits to the new beachside pub are all popular activities from the hostel; the nightly cost is $13. To find it, walk one block north from the Mangahauini Bridge, turn inland and go up a few houses. The hostel's the one with a wooden man out on the porch.

Also in Tokomaru Bay are the *Mayfair Cabins & Camping Ground* (☎ (06) 864 5843), behind the Mayfair Store (ask about the cabins at the store). Rooms sleeping two cost $20, larger ones sleeping five cost $35, but the prices could be less in winter. Out at Anaura Bay there is a *camping ground* where sites are $14 for two.

Further south, the well-equipped *Tolaga Bay Motor Camp* (☎ (06) 862 6716) is on the beach at Tolaga Bay, with campsites at $14 for two, $16 with power, and a variety of cabins and on-site caravans all at around $23 to $26 for two. The *Tolaga Inn* (☎ (06) 862 6856), an old historic building, has singles/doubles for $30/55.

INLAND: THE RAUKUMARA & WAIOEKA

Inland the Raukumara Range offers tramp-ing (including the highest mountain in the range, Hikurangi, at 1752 metres), hunting and white water rafting on the Waioeka and Motu rivers – contact Motu River Expedi-tions (☎ 308 7760) for more information on rafting the rivers in the region. The most popular access to this rugged, untamed region is via SH 2 (the Waioeka Gorge Rd), the 144-km road which connects Opotiki to Gisborne at the base of the East Cape triangle.

Access to Adventure (☎ 307 0743), based in Opotiki, operate rafting adventures on the Motu river. They specialise in a two-day trip from Opotiki using 4WD, raft and jet-boat. The cost is $300 per person. They also have a one-day trip on the Lower Gorge of the Motu.

There are many great walks in this region and DOC have quite a deal of information on possibilities. See their *Raukumara Forest Park* and the *Waioeka Gorge Scenic Reserve* pamphlets. The rare blue duck may be seen in the Raukumara, and Hochstetter's frog *(Leiopelma hochstetteri)*, is quite common in the park. Some parts of the region are penetrable by mountain bike, others are certainly not. Consider this region one of New Zealand's last frontiers, as wild as sections of South Westland and Fiordland – a must for those with a sense of adventure.

There are a couple of interesting accommodation possibilities along this road: the *Wairata Station Farmstays* (☎ 315 7761) is 43 km and the *Matawai Hotel* (☎ (06) 862 4874) is 76 km from Opotiki.

GETTING AROUND
Bus
The whole of SH 35 around the cape is connected by various local services; these may change, so contact the Opotiki Visitor Information Centre.

Fastways (☎ (06) 868 9421) connect Gisborne to Hicks Bay; the cost is $15. From Hicks Bay/Te Araroa there is a backpackers special (☎ 315 6350), part of a freight service offered by Eastland Backpackers; the cost is $26.

The loop is completed by the Super Shuttle which operates round Gisborne-Opotiki-Rotorua each day. This bus goes via Whakatane as well and reaches Opotiki in time to connect with the service to Hicks Bay (Rotorua to Opotiki is $37 and Rotorua to Gisborne is $32). East Coast Tours (☎ (09) 473 1721) cover the whole of the East Cape in their loop – Napier, Gisborne, Hicks Bay, Opotiki, Tauranga, Thames, Kaiaua, Auckland, Cambridge, Rotorua and Taupo.

Hitching
Hitching around the cape was once notoriously slow, with not much traffic passing by. Many locals say the hitching situation really isn't that bad. Of course there would be more traffic in summer than in winter. There are regular transport services if you get stuck.

Central North Island

The Central North Island region is famous throughout the world for its geysers, hot springs, mud pools, shimmering lakes, trout fishing, tramping and a host of other activities. The region is also of great significance to the Maori population, whose presence dates back to its discovery and exploration by Maoris in the 14th century.

It's still an active volcanic area and there have been some massive eruptions in relatively recent times. The towns of Rotorua and Taupo are the centres of a thriving tourist industry, catering for a whole range of tastes.

Information

Central North Island telephone numbers have an 07 prefix if you are calling them from a long distance (even within the regions), so we haven't included the prefix with each telephone number. The Wanganui area numbers have an 06 prefix, and this is indicated in the text.

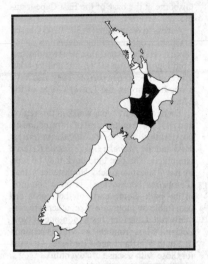

Rotorua

Rotorua (population 65,000) stands 280 metres above sea level on the shores of the lake of the same name. It's 109 km south-east of Hamilton, 368 km west of Gisborne, and 85 km north of Taupo. Rotorua is probably the most popular tourist area of the North Island, if not of New Zealand. Despite a strong smell of rotten eggs, Rotorua has a lot going for it, including:

- The most energetic thermal activity in the country – bubbling mud pools, gurgling hot springs, gushing geysers, evil smells. It's sometimes nicknamed 'Sulphur City' and some say it's sitting on a time bomb.
- A large Maori population whose cultural activities are among the most interesting to be seen in New Zealand.
- The world's best trout fishing and some interesting trout springs and wildlife parks.

Despite all these attractions and the consequent hordes of tourists it's not too much of a rip-off. In fact there are many enjoyable things you can do around Rotorua that don't cost a cent – there are magnificent walks, lakes and forests to visit, waterfalls, a fine museum, steamy areas and just spending time along the Rotorua waterfront.

New Zealand's main belt of volcanic activity stretches in a line from White Island, north of the Bay of Plenty, down to the Tongariro National Park. At one time it must have continued even further, as Mt Egmont/Taranaki is a dormant volcano and Wellington Harbour is the flooded crater of a long-extinct volcano. Rotorua is the most active area; all around the city, steam drifts up from behind bushes, out of road drains and around rocks.

History

The district of Rotorua was probably first settled during the middle of the 14th century by descendants of the navigators who arrived at Maketu in the central Bay of Plenty in the *Arawa* canoe from Hawaiki. Originally they were of the Ohomairangi tribe, but soon after they reached Maketu they changed their tribal name to Te Arawa to commemorate the vessel that brought them so far in safety. Much of the inland forest was explored by Ihenga in the late 14th century and it was he who discovered and named the lakes of Rotorua and many other geographical features of the area. The name Rotorua means 'the second lake' (*roto* means lake; *rua*, two) as it was the second lake that Ihenga discovered.

In the next few hundred years various sub-tribes spread into the area and as they grew in numbers, they split into more sub-tribes and began to fight over territory. In 1823 the Arawa lands were invaded by the Ngapuhi chief, Hongi Hika, of Northland. Although their primitive stone weapons were no match for the newly acquired muskets of the Ngapuhi, the Arawa managed to rout the Northlanders and force them to withdraw.

The first Pakeha to visit Rotorua was a Dane, Philip Tapsell, who set up a trading station at Maketu and gave the Maoris guns in exchange for flax, which he exported to Sydney where it was used to make rope. In 1831 Thomas Chapman, a missionary, visited Rotorua, returning to settle permanently in 1838, a date signifying the beginning of European occupation.

During the 1850s, wars erupted between the Arawa and the Waikato tribes. In 1867 the Waikato tribes attacked in retaliation for the part the Arawa had played in preventing the east coast reinforcements getting through for the Maori King movement. In the course of these wars the Arawa threw in their lot with the government and thus gained the backing of government troops.

With the wars virtually over in the early 1870s European settlement around Rotorua took off with a rush, particularly as the army and government personnel involved in the struggle had broadcast the scenic wonders of the place. People came to take the waters in

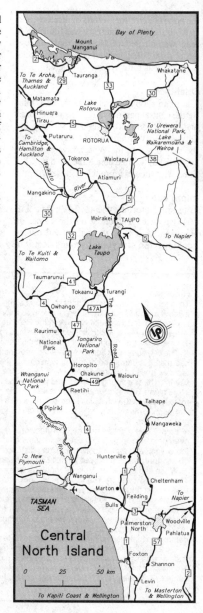

the hope of cures for all sorts of diseases, and so Rotorua's tourist industry was founded. A road was cleared in 1884 to make access easier from Auckland and in 1894 the Auckland-Rotorua railway was completed.

Orientation

The main shopping area is down Tutanekai St, the central part of which is a parking area and pedestrian mall. Fenton St starts in the Government Gardens by the lake and runs all the way down to the Whakarewarewa (just say Whaka) thermal area three km away. It's lined with motels for much of its length.

Information

Tourism Rotorua (☎ 348 5179; fax 348 6044) is at 67 Fenton St on the corner of Haupapa St. It has information and makes bookings for everything around Rotorua (tours, events, concerts and hangis, accommodation, transport, etc) and also has travel agency services for domestic and international travel. The DOC information office is also here, a comprehensive map shop, a restaurant and other services for travellers including showers, luggage storage, fishing licences, phone cards and postage stamps. It's open every day from 8 am to 5.30 pm.

The AA (☎ 348 3069) on the corner of Hinemoa and Hinemaru Sts is open Monday to Friday from 8.30 am to 5 pm. The American Express agent is Galaxy Travel (☎ 347 9444) at 411 Tutanekai St. Thomas Cook has a foreign-exchange desk in the Air New Zealand office, or there are plenty of banks that will change foreign currency. The CPO is on Hinemoa St between the Tutanekai Mall and Amohia St.

Thermalair is a useful free weekly news-

Hinemoa & Tutanekai

The story of Hinemoa and Tutanekai is one of the most well-known lovers' tales in New Zealand. It is not a legend but a true story, though you may hear variations on the story. The descendents of Hinemoa and Tutanekai still live in the Rotorua area today.

Hinemoa was a young woman of a sub-tribe that lived on the western shore of Lake Rotorua. Tutanekai was a young man of the sub-tribe that lived on Mokoia Island, in the lake.

The two sub-tribes sometimes visited one another, and that was how Hinemoa and Tutanekai had met. But though both were of high birth in their respective tribes, Tutanekai was illegitimate and so, though the family of Hinemoa thought he was a fine young man, and though they could see that the two young people loved one another, they were not in favour of them marrying.

At night, Tutanekai would play his flute on the island, and sometimes the wind would carry his melody across the water to Hinemoa. In his music she could hear his declaration of love for her. Her people, meanwhile, took to tying up the canoes at night to make sure she could not take off and go to him.

Finally one night as she heard Tutanekai's music wafting over the waters, Hinemoa was so overcome with longing that she could stand it no longer. She peeled off her clothes to get rid of the weight, and set off to swim the long distance from the shore to the island. In some versions of the story she also buoyed herself up with calabash gourds.

When she arrived on Mokoia, Hinemoa was in a quandary. She had had to shed her clothing in order to swim to the island, but now there, she could scarcely walk into the settlement naked! She sought refuge in a hot pool and tried to figure out what to do next.

Time passed and eventually a man came to fetch water from a cold spring beside the hot pool. In a deep man's voice, Hinemoa called out, 'Who is it?' The man replied that he was the slave of Tutanekai, come to fetch water. Hinemoa reached out of the darkness, seized the calabash and broke it. This happened a few more times, until finally Tutanekai himself came to the pool and demanded that the interloper identify himself. He was amazed when it turned out to be Hinemoa.

Tutanekai stole Hinemoa into his hut. In the morning, when Tutanekai was sleeping very late, a slave was sent to wake him and came back reporting that someone else was also sleeping in Tutanekai's bed! The two lovers emerged, it was discovered what Hinemoa had done in order to come to Tutanekai, and their union was celebrated. ■

paper and guide for visitors to Rotorua; you can pick up a copy at Tourism Rotorua and at other places around town. The excellent *Gateway to Geyserland* map, available for $1 at Tourism Rotorua, has a good map of the city on one side and the surrounding area on the other.

Lake Rotorua

Lake Rotorua is the largest of 12 lakes in the Rotorua district. It was formed by an eruption and subsequent subsidence of the area. There are various cruises on the lake, all departing from the Rotorua Lakefront jetty at the end of Tutanekai St. Or you can hire a speed boat or jet cat yourself.

Cruises to Mokoia Island on the *Ngaroto* launch operate every day during summer and holiday times. The boat goes hourly so you can stay on the island anywhere from one to five hours, coming back when you like. The cost is $20 for the return trip.

The *Scatcat* motorised catamaran does cruises to Mokoia Island including guided tours of the island, and two-lake cruises over Lake Rotorua, through the Ohau Channel and onto Lake Rotoiti.

The *Lakeland Queen* paddle steamer does one-hour luncheon cruises on the lake every day; the cost is $25 with lunch or $14 for the cruise only (children half price). Morning, afternoon and dinner cruises operate on demand.

The four-passenger *Hovershuttle* hovercraft does cruises along the lakefront to Sulphur Flats for $20, plus other cruises on Lake Rotorua and Lake Rotoiti.

A number of fishing boats operate from the jetty; see Fishing.

Ohinemutu

Ohinemutu is a Maori village by the lake in Rotorua. Ohinemutu means 'the place of the young woman who was killed', a name given to it by Ihenga in memory of his daughter.

The historic Maori **St Faith's Anglican Church** by the lakefront has a beautiful interior decorated with Maori carvings, woven tukutuku panels, painted scrollwork and stained-glass windows. Christ wearing a Maori cloak is etched on a window so that he appears to be walking on the waters of Lake Rotorua. Seen from this window, it's surprising how much Lake Rotorua does resemble the Sea of Galilee. The church was built between 1914 and 1918 and its history is told inside. It's open every day from 8.30 am to 5 pm.

Opposite the church is the impressive Tamatekapua meeting house, built in 1887. Named for the captain of the *Arawa* canoe, this is an important meeting house to all Arawa people. Maori concerts are held here every evening at 8 pm. Also in this complex are the Ohinemutu Craft Centre and the Te Huia Souvenir Shop.

Museums

The **Bath-House**, Rotorua's excellent art and history museum, is housed in a Tudor-style building in the Government Gardens, and yes, it was once used as a bath house, around the turn of the century. It's a dynamic museum with fascinating exhibits on the local Te Arawa Maori people, the 1886 Mt Tarawera eruption with videos about how it happened, the Pink and White Terraces, the history of this building, and changing exhibits. It's open every day from 10 am to 4.30 pm; admission is $2 (children $1, family $5).

In the gardens around the Bath-House are typical English things like croquet lawns and rose gardens – not to mention atypical steaming pools!

Te Amorangi Museum has Maori and colonial artefacts, working demonstrations of agricultural machinery, and a miniature steam railway which is operated on the second Sunday each month. The museum is in Robinsons Ave near the airport at Holdens Bay, six km from central Rotorua, and is open from 1 to 4 pm on Sunday and holidays; admission is free.

Whakarewarewa

Whakarewarewa is Rotorua's largest and best-known thermal zone and a major Maori cultural area. It's OK if you can't get your tongue around Whakarewarewa – many people call it simply 'Whaka'. On the other hand, even the name Whakarewarewa is actually short for the place's real name, Te Whakarewarewatangaoteopetauaawahiao, meaning 'the gathering together of the war forces of Wahiao'. See if you can get your tongue around that!

Whakarewarewa's most spectacular geyser is Pohutu (Maori for 'big splash' or 'explosion'), an active geyser which usually erupts at least once an hour. Pohutu spurts hot water about 20 metres in the air but sometimes shoots up over 30 metres in brief 'shots'. The average eruption lasts about five to 10 minutes, though the longest one is reputed to have lasted for 15 hours! You get an advance warning because the Prince of Wales' Feathers geyser always starts off shortly before Pohutu.

Other Whaka attractions include the Maori Arts & Crafts Institute with working craftspeople, an art gallery, a replica Maori village, kiwi house and a Maori concert held every day at 12.15 pm. There are lots of Maori concerts around Rotorua but the daily one at Whaka is rated one of the best.

Whaka is three km south of the town centre, straight down Fenton St. City buses drop you near a rear entrance, or the Sightseeing Shuttle bus will drop you at the main gate. Whaka is open daily from 8 am to 5 pm; admission is $10 (children $4, family $26). The cost to see the Maori concert is the same price, but if you want to see the reserve and the concert there's a combined ticket for $18 (children $7, family $48).

Thermal Pools

Of course you won't want to visit Rotorua without taking a dip in some thermal pools.

The Polynesian Pools, off Hinemoa St, are open daily from 9 am to 10 pm. The first building in Rotorua, a bath house, was opened at these springs in 1882 and people have been swearing to the health-giving properties of the waters ever since. There are several pools in the complex including the Priest and Radium Hot Springs adult pools ($6), a separate pool for adults and children ($7, child $2, family $15), private pools ($7, child $2, family $15 for half an hour) and a sauna ($6). Towels and swimsuits can be hired for $2 and Aix massage is available by appointment.

For ordinary swimming there's the Aquatic Centre, with a 50-metre outdoor pool, a 25-metre indoor pool, a recreational pool and various activities for children. All the water is heated to a pleasant 34°C. It's open every day from 6 am to 8.30 pm; admission is $2.50 (children $1.20, family $6). The centre is on Tarewa Rd, near Kuirau Park.

The Waikite Thermal Mineral Baths is an open-air natural mineral pool (39°C) with medicinal mineral waters, out in Waikite, a rural area. To get there, go 30 km south on SH 5 (the highway to Taupo), to a signposted turn-off which is opposite the turn-off to Waiotapu. The pool is another six km down this road. It is open every day from 10 am to 9.30 pm; admission is $4 (children $2).

Orchid Gardens

The Orchid Gardens in Hinemaru St house not only an extensive orchid hothouse blooming all year round but also a Microworld display, where you can get a microscopic view of living reptiles and insects, and a big water organ.

Performing to Schedule

How does the Lady Knox geyser manage to perform so neatly to schedule? Simple – you block it up with some rags so the pressure builds up and you shove a couple of kg of soap powder in to decrease the surface viscosity. And off it goes.

This scientific principle of the relation of soap powder to surface viscosity of geysers was discovered by some early Pakehas who thought it would be a great idea to use the hot water in the ground here to wash their clothes. ∎

Stay on the Footpaths!
Be sure that you stay on the footpaths when you walk in thermal areas around Rotorua and elsewhere in New Zealand. All thermal areas have signs advising you to do this, and there's a very good reason for it – the ground around thermal areas can look exactly like solid ground, but be hollow underneath – it can be actually only a very thin crust, over what may be boiling water or boiling mud underneath. People who didn't know this have fallen through into boiling water and boiling mud more times than we'd like to know. So stay on the footpaths! ■

Water organs are very unusual. There are only a few in the world and this is the only one in New Zealand. The sound is not actually produced by the water. The organ is really a huge fountain with over 800 jets putting on a magnificent 15-minute show of water swirling, leaping and making generally graceful, ballet-like movements up to four metres high, all choreographed to symphonic music and accompanied by a light show turning the water into changing colours.

The water organ plays every hour on the hour from 9 am to 5 pm. The complex is open from 8.30 am to 5.30 pm daily; admission is $7.50 (children $3, family $18). There's a cafe at one end of the hothouse where you can enjoy classical music along with the orchids.

Trips & Tours

There are many trips and tours in and around Rotorua, going to volcanic and thermal sites, out into the mountains and forests, up Mt Tarawera, across lakes and down rivers – tours in vans, 4WD vehicles and on bicycles – there's something for every taste. Tourism Rotorua can give you the rundown on any tours, and all tours can be booked through their office, or through the place you're staying.

Mud 'n Mountain (☎ 345 3264) does some of the most adventurous tours, visiting places way out in the bush including Mt Tarawera, forests, sink holes, a disappearing river, waterfalls and thermal areas, including a dip in some secluded hot springs. It's a fun tour with many surprises along the way and the guides have a lot of bush knowledge. A Bare Bones Budgeter tour from noon to 7 pm

costs $65, or there's the Longest Day tour from 8 am to 8 pm for $90.

Carey's Capers (☎ 347 8035) is a popular trip emphasising visits to most of Rotorua's favourite volcanic and thermal attractions, with a dip in an isolated hot water stream along the way. The cost is $40 for a half-day trip, $60 for a three-quarter day and $80 for a full-day tour.

Colin Carey, who operates Carey's Capers, has made quite a name for himself as a tour operator and now he also does a variety of other popular tours. His full-day Get Volcanic tour visits several volcanic and thermal sites in the morning, then heads up Mt Tarawera in a 4WD vehicle in the afternoon. The cost is $100 for the full day. Tarawera Gold (☎ & fax 347 1199) is another good trip, taking a guided walk through the Waimangu Valley in the morning, then boating on Lake Rotomahana and finally going up Mt Tarawera by 4WD; the cost is $130.

The World Famous Waimangu Round Trip (☎ & fax 347 1199) is called 'world famous' because that's the way this trip has been billed ever since it began in 1903. A historic trip, its emphasis is on the story of the 1886 Mt Tarawera eruption. It takes you through the Waimangu Volcanic Valley, over Lake Rotomahana past the Steaming Cliffs and the site of the Pink and White Terraces, walking across the isthmus to Lake Tarawera, a boat trip on that lake, a visit to the Buried Village, and then a ride past the Blue and Green Lakes back to Rotorua where the tour concludes with a dip in the Polynesian Pools. The cost is $90 for the full day.

Tamaki Tours (☎ & fax 349 2417; fax 346 2823) is a Maori-owned operation with morning and afternoon tours to some of the area's favourite places. The guides are friendly, knowledgeable and fun; their Maori perspective gives the tours an interesting slant. Morning tours are $60, afternoon tours $40, or you can combine the two for a full-day tour for $80. They also do an all-day Adventure Action Tour involving a 4WD trip up Mt Tarawera for $90, and a two-day Volcanic Wilderness Safari tour by 4WD, horseback and rafting, starting by going up Mt Tarawera and then through bush in remote Te Urewera National Park; the cost is $300. Their excellent Twilight Cultural Tour features a Maori hangi and concert on a marae; see Entertainment.

Other tours go up to the top of Mt Tarawera. Mt Tarawera 4WD Tours (☎ 357 4026, mobile (025) 955 634; fax 348 1226) is popular, with morning and afternoon trips; the cost is $52 (children $26, family $135). Tarawera Mountain Sightseeing Tours (☎ 348 5179) also does the trip for the same price.

4WD Bush Safaris (☎ 332 5748, mobile (025) 927 818) makes three trips a day – morning, afternoon and evening – over some very rugged tracks through native bush. The 3½ hour trips can involve wheel-spinning, mud-throwing and rut-gouging, and you can drive it yourself or they drive; the cost is $52, including refreshments at a bush cabin.

All Terrain Tours (☎ 362 8548) does mountain bike tours in the Whakarewarewa Forest Park, and longer trips through Te Urewera National Park and further afield.

There are plenty of other tours around Rotorua's more sedate attractions such as the Agrodome, thermal areas, and so on; Inter-City, Gray Line and Taylor's are three established companies and there are plenty more. Tourism Rotorua can give you all the details. Another option is to take the Sightseeing Shuttle bus and visit them on your own; see the Getting Around section.

White Water Activities

Several rafting companies make white water rafting trips on the Rangitaiki River (Grade Three to Grade Four). Half-day trips, with a barbecue afterwards, cost around $65. The trips depart from the Rangitaiki River Bridge in Murupara but if you don't have wheels they'll provide transport from Rotorua for an extra $5. Contact River Rats (☎ 347 6049), The Rafting Company (☎ 348 0233) or the White Water Excitement Co (☎ 358 5868).

Shorter and more dramatic rafting trips over the seven-metre Okere Falls, off SH 33 about 16 km north-east of Rotorua, are immensely popular. Time on the river is about 40 minutes, going over the seven-metre falls, another three-metre falls, and various rapids; the cost is $45. Kaituna Cascades (☎ 357 5032) was the first company to start making this trip, and it's still going strong; several other companies have since jumped on the bandwagon.

White Water Sledging (☎ 349 6100) operates trips on the Rangitikei, Tarawera and Kaituna Rivers; the cost is around $50 to $85 and the trips last anywhere from 30 minutes to 2½ hours.

Waka Hikoi (☎ 362 7878) operates half-day guided kayak journeys on Lake Rotoiti for $45 per person.

Fishing

And, of course, there's trout fishing. You can hire guides or go it alone, but remember you need a licence and there are various regulations about how you may catch the trout. The guided fishing trips aren't cheap (about $25 per hour per person, or $65 per hour per boat) but they all but guarantee that you'll catch a fish. Plan to spend about two or three hours. Ask at Tourism Rotorua or at the Rotorua Lakefront for fishing boat operators. Of course you can also just wander down to the lakefront and fish, as long as you have a fishing licence and you do it in the fishing season (October to June).

You can get your fishing licence directly from a fishing guide or from Tourism Rotorua. Rotorua district fishing licences cost $8 per day, $22 per week, $30 per month or $46 for the whole season. Tourism Rotorua also sells special tourist fishing licences which, for $60, allow you to fish not only in the Rotorua district but anywhere in New Zealand for a whole month.

Aerial Sightseeing

All Rotorua's attractions can be seen from the air and some, like the Tarawera volcano, are best observed from above. Flights depart either from the airport or by floatplane from the lake and are reasonably priced, from around $50.

Volcanic 'Wunderflites' (☎ 345 6079), operating from a hangar near the Rotorua Airport, are particularly popular. They will fly you up and over the awesome chasm of Mt Tarawera on a half-hour flight for $99 (children $65). For an additional fee you can land beside the volcano and wander up to look over the edge. They also have longer flights over the lakes, out to White Island, and even down to Mt Ruapehu and Mt Ngauruhoe in the Tongariro National Park.

A Rotorua flightseeing favourite is White Island Airways (☎ 345 9832) who do Tiger Moth flights over the city for $88, over Mt Tarawera for $175 or, if your stomach is strong, they'll take you up for some aerobatics for $125. You're out in the open air in a Tiger Moth but in your flight suit, leather helmet and goggles you'll feel as warm as the Red Baron. They also have a modern 10-seater de Havilland Dove; in this a Mt Tarawera trip costs $105 or you can take trips further afield, including to White Island, for $225.

Also departing from the Wunderflites hangar are Aerobatic Thrillseekers (☎ 345 6077/6079), making 15-minute aerobatic flights in a little red Pitts Special two-seater plane for $130.

The Helicopter Line (☎ 347 6086) operates from the City Helipad on Te Ngae Rd near the centre. Other helicopter flightseeing operators include Marine Helicopters (☎ 357 2512) based at the Agrodome, and Tarawera Helicopters (☎ 348 1223). Volcanic Air Safaris (☎ 348 9984/4069) do helicopter and floatplane flights departing from the Rotorua Lakefront.

Tandem Skydiving

You can go tandem skydiving from the Rotorua Airport (☎ 345 7520) for $195, or $170 if you book through a hostel. In addition to the obvious thrill of the skydiving itself, the flight includes some amazing views over all the lakes of the region, Mt Tarawera, White Island in the Bay of Plenty, east to Gisborne and south to Mt Ruapehu. It's an experience you won't soon forget.

Other Things to See

There's a Leisure World amusement park off Te Ngae Rd on the outskirts of town, with rides, a big waterslide and mini-golf. It's open every day from 10 am until 5 or 6 pm and you pay $2 to $5 per ride, or $8/10 for a half/full day on the waterslide. Nearby is a golf course with driving, rifle and pistol ranges.

Putt Putt Mini Golf on the corner of Te Ngae Rd and Marguerita St has two 18-hole miniature golf courses, bumper boats and a Grand Prix raceway.

Little Village is an 'olde worlde' village replica at 15 Tryon St, opposite the THC International Hotel.

On the outside wall of the police station opposite Tourism Rotorua is a mural depicting New Zealand's Maori and Pakeha heritage.

You can go horse-riding over farmland at The Farmhouse, 17 km north of Rotorua, off Sunnex Rd on the western side of Lake Rotorua.

The Blue Lake has lots of summertime activities including water-skiing, jet-skis, parasailing, etc. The Green Lake, though, is sacred to the Maori people and you're not allowed to go on it.

Places to Stay

With all the Rotorua region's tourist attractions, it's not surprising that it is well endowed with places to stay. Hot mineral pools are a bonus in many establishments, no matter how humble, and almost every place is thermally heated.

Camping & Cabins Rotorua has a very good selection of campsites, although some are

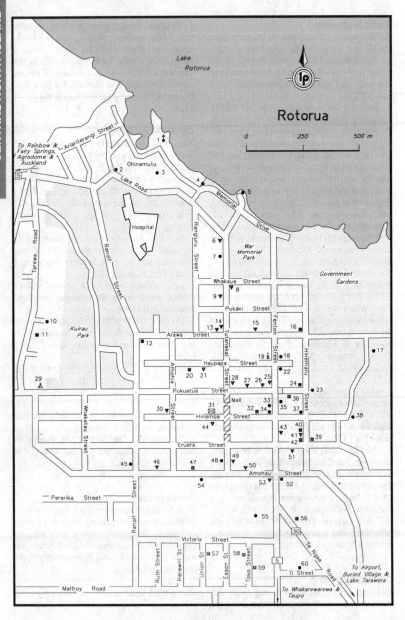

Rotorua

0   250   500 m

■ PLACES TO STAY

11	Kiwi Paka Hostel
12	Arawa Lodge Motel
16	Princes Gate Hotel
20	Ivanhoe Lodge
24	Sportsman's Hotel
29	Autohaven Camping Ground
32	Grand Establishment Hotel, Cobb & Co & Wheeler's Nightclub
36	Rotorua Central Backpackers
39	Hyatt Kingsgate Hotel
40	Eaton Hall Guest House
42	Rotorua YHA Hostel
47	Spa Backpackers Lodge
56	YWCA
57	Funky Green Voyager
58	Tresco Guest House
59	Morihana Guest House

▼ PLACES TO EAT

6	Pizza Hut
8	Lady Jane's Ice Cream Parlour
9	Lewisham's Austrian Restaurant
13	Roundabout Bar & Cafe
14	The Coffee Bean
15	Alzac Cafe
21	Floyd's Cafe
23	Orchid Gardens
25	Tastebuds Mexican Cantina
26	Pizza Forno, Country Kitchen & Cameron's Bar & Grill
27	Gazebo Restaurant
28	Lataika Lebanese Takeaway & Charcoal Chicken Joint
30	Zanelli's Restaurant
32	Grand Establishment Hotel, Cobb & Co & Wheeler's Nightclub
39	Smacker Jack's
41	Shanghai Chinese Restaurant
43	Chez Bleu
44	Smacker Jack's
46	Kentucky Fried Chicken
49	Churchill's Bar & Wimpy's
50	Taste Tease
51	Korea House Restaurant
53	McDonald's

OTHER

1	St Faith's Anglican Church
2	Lake Tavern
3	Tamatekapua Meeting House
4	Soundshell
5	Rotorua Lakefront
7	Woolworth's Supermarket
10	Aquatic Centre
17	The Bath-House Museum of Art & History
18	Civic Theatre
19	Tourism Rotorua
22	Police Station
23	Orchid Gardens
31	CPO
32	Grand Establishment Hotel, Cobb & Co & Wheeler's Nightclub
33	Ansett New Zealand
34	Air New Zealand, Mt Cook Airline & Thomas Cook
35	Link Rent-a-Car
37	Automobile Association (AA)
38	Polynesian Pools
45	3 Guys Supermarket
48	Galaxy Travel & American Express Agent
49	Churchill's Bar & Wimpy's
52	Pac 'n Save Supermarket
54	Rotorua Travel Centre & Long-distance Bus Depot
55	Supermarket
60	Ace of Clubs & Rent-a-Dent

simply 'caravan only' places. Almost all have cabins.

Closest to the centre is the *Autohaven Camping Ground* (☎ 348 1886) at 129-137 Pukuatua St, beside Kuirau Park. It has tent sites at $6.50 per person, powered sites at $8 per person, backpackers beds from $10 a night, and tourist flats at $40 for two.

Two km from the centre, Whittaker Rd off Lake Rd has two good camping grounds near Lake Rotorua. The *Cosy Cottage International Holiday Park* (☎ 348 3793; fax 347 9634) at 67 Whittaker Rd may be the only place in the world with heated tent sites – the warmth from under the ground gradually warms your tent at night. They also have a mineral pool, a heated swimming pool, canoes to loan and bicycles and fishing tackle for hire. Tent sites are $8.50 per person; powered sites $18, on-site caravans $28, tourist cabins $35, and tourist flats are $46 to $52, all these prices are for two.

The *Lakeside Thermal Holiday Park* (☎ & fax 348 1693) at 54 Whittaker Rd, beside the lake, has hot mineral pools and spas. Tent sites are $7.50 per person; powered sites $18, on-site caravans $30, cabins $35, tourist flats $45 and chalets are $49, all prices for two people.

The *Rotorua Thermal Holiday Park* (☎ 346 3140; fax 346 1324), on the southern end of the Old Taupo Rd opposite the golf course, is a large, modern camp with hot mineral pools and a heated swimming pool. Tent and caravan sites are $8.50 per person; campervan sites $10 per person; standard log cabins $18.50/30 for one/two people; facility log cabins $24/36; and tourist cabins are $25/35. They also have a hostel with beds at $12 and a lodge with B&B at $26 per person, linen included. There's a bus service which stops at the gate.

If you don't mind staying a little further out, there are many more camps and cabins in the area. The *Holdens Bay Holiday Park* (☎ & fax 345 9925) at 21 Robinson Ave is about 500 metres from Lake Rotorua, 6.5 km from central Rotorua on SH 30. It has tent and powered sites at $9 per person; standard cabins at $23; lodge cabins at $30; tourist cabins at $32, and tourist flats at $50, all prices for two people. Again there's a swimming pool, hot mineral pools, billiard table, children's playground and so on, making it a pleasant place to stay.

The *Blue Lake Holiday Park* (☎ 362 8120; fax 362 8600) is on Tarawera Rd on the shores of the Blue Lake, 10 km from the centre of Rotorua. Kayaks, Canadian canoes, fishing boats, fishing tackle and track road bicycles are all available for hire. Tent sites are $8.50 per person, powered sites $9 per person, standard cabins $26, tourist cabins $35, tourist flats $54 and motel units $70, all prices for two people.

There are a couple of places to camp at Ngongotaha, eight km from Rotorua on the western shore of Lake Rotorua, and plenty more places nearer and further from the city. All in all there's no shortage of campsites in the area, and the following is a list of some possibilities:

Redwood Holiday Park (☎ 345 9380; fax 345 4157)), three km from the Rotorua town centre at 5 Tarawera Rd, Ngapuna, at the intersection of Te Ngae Rd; camping from $10/15, also cabins, tourist flats and motel units

All Seasons Holiday Park (☎ & fax 345 6240), 7.5 km from the town centre on Lee Rd, Hannahs Bay, off SH 30, opposite the lakefront; camping from $8 per person, also tourist flats, cabins with en-suite bathrooms, and a lodge

Rainbow Resort (☎ 357 4289; fax 357 2118), eight km from the town centre at 24 Beaumonts Rd, Ngongotaha, close to the lake; camping from $8 per person, also on-site caravans, cabins and tourist flats, with free canoes and fishing rods

Waiteti Trout Stream Holiday Park (☎ 357 4749), beside Waiteti Stream at 14 Okana Crescent, Ngongotaha; camping from $8.50 per person, also on-site caravans, cabins and tourist flats

Willow Haven Holiday Park (☎ 357 4092), 31 Beaumont Rd, Ngongotaha, on the lakefront; camping from $8 per person, also self-contained chalets and tourist flats

Greengrove Holiday Park (☎ 357 4429), corner Hall & School Rd, Ngongotaha; camping from $7 per person, also cabins and tourist flats

Kiwi Ranch Holiday Camp (☎ 345 6799), Rotokawau Rd, Tikitere, opposite Hell's Gate; camping from $6.50 per person, also cabins and tourist flats

Merge Lodge (☎ 362 0880), SH 30 on the shore of Lake Rotoma; camping from $19 for two, also on-site caravans

Rotoma Holiday Park (☎ 362 0815; fax 362 7763), on Manawahe Rd, 100 metres off SH 30 on the west end of Rotoma Scenic Reserve, 36 km from Rotorua; camping from $8 per person, also on-site caravans and a cottage

Lake Rotoiti Lakeside Holiday Park (☎ & fax 362 4860), 21 km from Rotorua on Okere Rd, Okere Falls, on the shore of Lake Rotoiti, 1.5 km from Okere Falls; camping from $8.50 per person, also cabins

Ohau Channel Lodge and Tourist Cabins (☎ 362 4761), 17.5 km from Rotorua on Hamurana Rd, at the northern end of Lake Rotorua between Lake Rotorua and Lake Rotoiti; camping from $5.50 per person, also cabins and tourist flats

Fisherman's Lodge (☎ 362 8754), on old mission site at Lake Tarawera, surrounded by native bush, bush walks, peaceful and quiet, a two-minute drive or 20-minute walk from the lake; camping $7 per person, also cabins, self-contained cabins and tourist flats

Waikite Valley Thermal Pool Camp (☎ 333 1861), in Waikite Valley, 35 km south of Rotorua, six km from Waiotapu turn-off; camping from $8 per person, includes unlimited use of a hot mineral pool.

Hostels The *Rotorua YHA Hostel* (☎ 347 6810) is on the corner of Eruera and Hinemaru Sts, close to the town centre. Formerly known as the Colonial Inn, it has plenty of twin and family rooms, a thermal spa pool, and it's open all day. The nightly cost is $16 in dorm rooms, $18 in double rooms, with a special winter rate of $14.

Rotorua Central Backpackers (☎ & fax 349 3285) at 10 Pukuatua St is an upmarket hostel, with spacious rooms and a spa pool in a classic older building with plenty of character. The cost is $14 per person in dorm rooms, $16 in share rooms and $18 in doubles and twins. It's very centrally situated, yet because it's in a parking street there is little street noise.

The *Ivanhoe Lodge* (☎ 348 6985) at 54 Haupapa St is older but also central. Accommodation is in rooms or cabins; the cost is $13 per person in dorms, $14 in twin, $15 in double and $18 in single rooms. It has a video, a house bar and billiard table, a spa pool (swimming gear unnecessary) and bicycles for hire.

The *Kiwi Paka* (☎ 347 0931; fax 346 3167) is at 60 Tarewa Rd, near Kuirau Park a km or so from the town centre. Here, too, there's a thermal pool; you can hire bicycles, and the lodge has a courtesy van. The cost per person is $18 in singles, $14 in doubles or $13 in larger rooms. There's also a big lawn area where tent sites are $6 per person and campervan sites are $8 per person.

Smallest of Rotorua's hostels is the funky little *Funky Green Voyager* (☎ 346 1754) at 4 Union St. In a quiet residential neighbourhood 200 metres behind the bus station, the hostel is homely, casual and well cared-for, with just 16 beds in double and dorm rooms, a spacious back yard, hundreds of tapes and books, and plenty of information available on Rotorua and the East Cape. The cost is $14 per night.

The *YWCA* (☎ 348 5445) at 6-8 Te Ngae Rd has casual accommodation for women and men in single and double rooms for $18 per person, or in a large dorm room for $12 ($1 more if you hire linen), or $75 per week. The Y provides accommodation for students

during the school year; you can stay during that time if they have space. The summer school holiday from mid-November to mid-February is their least busy time – right when everything else is packed.

Also in transition on our last visit was the *Spa Backpackers Lodge* (☎ 348 3486; fax 346 0485) at 69 Amohau St, opposite the bus station. It was very run-down on our visit; after a long period of neglect, it had been taken over by new owners just five days before we showed up. It's a convenient location and we're wishing them the best in their efforts to get the place fixed up. There are plenty of single and double rooms; the cost is $13 in dorms, $14 in twin/doubles and $18 in single rooms.

Guesthouses There are a number of guesthouses and B&B places around Rotorua, including a couple on Toko St. Although it's reasonably central, Toko St is a quiet street and well away from the tourist hustle of central Rotorua. At 3 Toko St there's the *Tresco Guest House* (☎ & fax 348 9611), where B&B costs $45/68 for singles/doubles. There are sinks in the rooms and it's a neat, tidy and comfortable place. The same can be said for the *Morihana Guest House* (☎ 348 8511) a bit further down at 20 Toko St. Single/double rooms here cost $42/65, including breakfast. Both places have hot mineral pools.

Eaton Hall (☎ 347 0366; fax 348 6287) at 39 Hinemaru St, centrally located opposite the Hyatt Kingsgate, is a comfortable, homely guesthouse with B&B at $45/68 for singles/doubles, lower in the off-season. Book ahead in summer, as this is a popular place.

Hotels Right in the centre on the corner of Hinemoa and Fenton Sts the *Grand Establishment* (☎ 348 2089; fax 346 3219) has single/double rooms with private facilities for $45/54, plus some budget rooms at $29 for one or two people. Rooms have tea and coffee-making equipment and there's a laundry, sauna, a Cobb & Co Restaurant and the Wheeler's Nightclub.

Conveniently situated on the corner of Hinemaru and Pukuatua Sts, the *Sportsman's Hotel* (☎ 348 1550; fax 348 1688) has single/double rooms at $43/51; here there's the Dobbo's Sports Bar and a large thermal pool.

The very fancy *Princes Gate Hotel* (☎ 348 1179; fax 348 6215) at 1 Arawa St on the corner of Hinemaru St is a beautiful, luxurious grand hotel with crystal chandeliers, canopies over the beds, an elegant restaurant and bar, a health facility and much more. Single/double rooms are normally $80/100 (meals not included) but in winter when it's not too busy they offer a B&B special at $45 per person, on a twin-share basis.

Rotorua has some big hotels, to cater for those big tour groups. There's a *Quality Inn*, *Sheraton Rotorua*, *THC Rotorua*, *Geyserland Resort* and even the *Hyatt Kingsgate*. At these establishments even singles can cost $150 to $200 per night. Still, that's nothing on the wonderful but expensive *Solitaire Lodge* (☎ 362 8208; fax 346 1324) at Lake Tarawera where singles/doubles including all meals cost around $350/700 a night!

Motels There are plenty of motels in Rotorua and the competition has kept some of the prices down. Several of the campsites have motel-style rooms as well as their cabins and tourist flats. Fenton St, as it heads south from town, is a 'motel row' with dozens of motels. Just a few of the cheaper places to try in Rotorua include:

Aywon Motel (☎ 347 7659; fax 348 4066), 18 Trigg Ave; studio and one-bedroom units $66/76 for singles/doubles, spa units $82/92, two-bedrooms $103
Bel Aire Motel (☎ 348 6076), 257 Fenton St; $45/61
Colonial Motel (☎ & fax 348 4490), 22 Ranolf St; $62 single or double
Eruera Motel (☎ 348 8305), corner Eruera & Hinemaru Sts; $43/51
Forest Court Motel (☎ 346 3543), 275 Fenton St; $45/54
Havana Motor Lodge (☎ 348 8134; fax 348 8132), 12 Whakaue St; $55/68
Kiwi Lodge (☎ 349 1991; fax 349 1992), 279 Fenton St; $50/55 for one night, $45/50 for two nights or more

Lake Lodge Motel (☎ 348 5189; fax 348 5188), 16 Lake Rd; $60/65
Manhattan Motel (☎ 348 1623; fax 348 5483), 130 Hinemoa St; $65 single or double
Monterey Motel (☎ 348 1044; fax 346 2264), 50 Whakaue St; singles $45, doubles from $55
Tom's Motel (☎ 347 8062; fax 347 0078), 6 Union St; from $60 single or double
Waiteti Lakefront Motel (☎ & fax 357 2555), Arnold St, Ngongotaha, on the lakefront; $65/69

Farmstays & Homestays There are many possibilities for staying on farms or in private homes around Rotorua. Ask at the Tourism Rotorua office (see Information) a couple of days in advance; they have listings and will make bookings.

Places to Eat
Snacks & Fast Food Rotorua has plenty of snack and fast food places. One of the most popular is the *Tastebuds Mexican Cantina* at 93 Fenton St, near the corner of Pukuatua St. It's a tiny, casual and inexpensive place for Mexican food to take away or eat there; you can get a filling meal there for less than $6.

The *Lataika Lebanese Takeaway* at 284 Tutanekai St near the corner of Pukuatua St is another good place, with economical Middle Eastern vegetarian and meat selections to take away or eat there. Next door, the *Charcoal Chicken Joint* is mainly a takeaway but it has a few seats if you want to eat there; the specialties are charcoal-grilled chicken and hot carvery sandwiches.

Pizza Forno at 31 Pukuatua St makes pretty good pizzas, to eat there or take away; phone for free delivery (☎ 347 9854). Two doors away, *Country Kitchen* does good sandwiches. *The Coffee Bean* at 189 Tutanekai St near the corner of Arawa St also makes good sandwiches, and good breakfasts too; it's open from around 7 am to 3 pm, every day but Sunday.

Most of the tourist attractions have cafes but the one at the *Orchid Gardens* on Hinemaru St is especially enjoyable, and it's not expensive. It's at one end of the large indoor orchid garden; you can see the garden and listen to classical music while eating a light meal or tasty dessert. It's open every day from 8.30 am to 5.30 pm.

Taste Tease at 48 Amohau St near Fenton St is a bakery with European-style pastries, open every day from 6 am to 6 pm.

The American 'big three' are all represented in Rotorua. There's a large *McDonald's* on the corner of Fenton and Amohau Sts. *Kentucky Fried* is further west on Amohau St, and *Pizza Hut* is on Tutanekai St, up near the lake.

Chez Bleu on Fenton St near the corner of Hinemoa St doesn't look that flash but locals swear it makes the best burgers in town. It's open long hours, from 10.30 am to midnight on weekdays, until 4.30 am Thursday to Saturday nights. Another late-night fast food outlet is *Smacker Jack's* on Hinemoa St opposite the CPO, with a takeaway counter and a slightly more expensive eat-in menu. It's open from 10 am to 11 pm Monday to Wednesday, until 4.30 am Thursday to Saturday, and from 9.30 am to 9 pm on Sunday. There's a *Wimpy* as well, on Tutanekai St near Amohau St.

Pub Food Yes there's a *Cobb & Co*; it's in the Grand Establishment Hotel on Hinemoa St between Tutanekai and Fenton Sts. It has the usual Cobb & Co menu and it's open the usual Cobb & Co hours of 7.30 am to 10 pm, seven days a week.

The *Roundabout Bar & Cafe* upstairs at 83 Arawa St is a cafe, bar, resource centre and general hangout for backpackers and travellers; the operators are ex-hostel people who thought Rotorua needed a place for backpackers to hang out. It has a good menu with plenty of inexpensive meals and snacks; also here are a travellers' noticeboard, games; fax and phone services, and discounted tour tickets. It's open every day from 11.30 am until late.

Churchill's Bar at 426 Tutanekai St is another good place for a meal. A comfortable English-style bar, it serves up a lot of lunches and finger foods in big, satisfying portions; food is always available. *Cameron's Bar & Grill* upstairs on the corner of Fenton and Pukuatua Sts serves lunches and dinners.

Restaurants Naturally there are plenty of restaurants in Rotorua. The licensed *Shanghai Chinese Restaurant* at 41 Hinemaru St is good value, with inexpensive all-you-can-eat smorgasbord meals at lunch and dinnertime and plenty of vegetarian and meat selections. It's open for lunch and dinner every day (except no lunch on Sunday). Around the corner, the *Korea House Restaurant* at 16 Eruera St is a pleasant restaurant serving Korean food.

The *Alzac Cafe* at 59-61 Arawa St is a European-style cafe where you can come for a meal or just to hang out over coffee. The menu is 'California-style', emphasising fresh ingredients and eclectic international dishes.

Lewisham's Austrian Restaurant at 115 Tutanekai St specialises in traditional Austrian-Hungarian food. *Zanelli's* at 23 Amohia St is an Italian dinner house, with good Italian gelati to round out your meal. The *Gazebo Restaurant* at 45 Pukuatua St is a popular restaurant with a menu featuring French, Asian and European food. *Floyd's Cafe* at 44 Haupapa St is also good, with an eclectic menu.

Entertainment

Maori Concerts & Hangis Maori culture is a major attraction in Rotorua, and although it's decidedly commercialised it's a worthwhile investment to get out and enjoy it. There are two big activities – concerts, and hangis or feasts – and in many cases the two are combined.

A hangi is a Maori earth oven – a large pit is dug and a fire is lit to heat stones placed in the pit. Then food in baskets, covered with wet cloths, is buried with earth and steamed to perfection.

The concerts are put on by local people and they seem to get as much of a kick out of them as you will. Chances are by the time the evening is over you'll have been dragged up on stage, experienced a Maori *hongi* (nose-to-nose contact), joined hands for a group sing-in, and thought about freaking out your next-door neighbour with a haka when you get home. Hakas are war dances which are intended to demonstrate how tough you are. The high point of the haka is to stick the tongue out as far as it will go with the eyes opened wide, demonstrating derision and aggression. Other features of a Maori concert are poi dances, action songs and hand games.

Poi dances are performed by women only and consist of whirling round the poi (balls of flax fibre that are swung and twirled on lengths of string). Action songs are a recent addition to the Maori activities – story-songs illustrated by fluid hand and arm movements. There are also hand games – a reaction sharpening pastime. The best game is where the two players make rapid gestures and try to catch their opponent making the same one!

Basically your choice is whether you want to attend a concert only, or a concert and hangi combined.

For concert only, one of the best performances is presented every evening at 8 pm at the impressive Tamatekapua Meeting House in Ohinemutu, opposite St Faith's Church down by the lake. The cost is $12 (children $6) if you show up at the door or if you book directly (☎ 348 4894, after hours 348 6456), but only $7 if you buy your ticket at any hostel.

Another option for concert only is the daily concert at 12.15 pm at Whakarewarewa, which costs $10 (children $4, family $26) by itself or $18 (children $7, family $48) if you combine it with a visit to the thermal reserve (see Whakarewarewa).

For a combined concert and hangi, Tamaki Tours (☎ & fax 346 2823, 349 2417) do a magnificent Twilight Cultural Tour, picking you up at your accommodation and taking you to a marae on the shore of Lake Rotoiti for a memorable cultural experience. Along the way they explain the traditional customs involved in visiting a marae – the wero (challenge), the welcome, the protocol for speaking on the marae – and a 'chief' is chosen among the group to represent the visitors. Following the concert, everyone goes outside and watches as the food is uncovered from its underground oven and

then brought inside for a feast in the marae's dining hall. The cost is $45 and well worth it.

The Tumuni Cultural Experience (☎ & fax 347 1199, 347 8035) does a similar concert and hangi combination; the cost is $42 and includes transport.

Several of the big hotels in Rotorua also offer Maori concerts and hangis. They attract hundreds of tourists each year – even hundreds each week, during busy times. They present professional tourist performances and the traditional hangi foods, but they certainly don't dig holes out the back to cook all that food in, and so the flavour is not the same. When they're not fully booked, you can arrange to attend the performance only, skipping the hangi if you prefer. Big hotels with concerts and hangis include:

Hyatt Kingsgate, Eruera St (☎ 348 1234)
  concert $19, concert & hangi $38
Lake Plaza, Eruera St (☎ 348 1174)
  concert $17.50, concert & hangi $35
Quality Hotel, Fenton St (☎ 348 0199)
  concert $25, concert & hangi $35
Regal Geyserland Hotel, Hemo St (☎ 348 2039)
  concert $10, concert & hangi $32
Sheraton Rotorua, Fenton St (☎ 348 7139)
  concert $22, concert & hangi $39
THC International Hotel, Froude St (☎ 348 1189)
  concert $18.75, concert & hangi $37

Pubs & Nightclubs Rotorua has a selection of places for going out for a good time in the evening. *Churchill's Bar* at 426 Tutanekai St is a safe, relaxed English-style bar with over 100 bottled beers, Gisborne Cider and Irish Guinness on tap, English ale, Scottish beers Youngers and Tartan, and over 40 New Zealand wines. On Wednesday nights there's a Scottish songster; they serve good food.

Cameron's Bar & Grill upstairs on the corner of Fenton and Pukuatua Sts has game nights during the week and live bands on weekends. They, too, serve food, and boast Guinness on tap plus over 100 spirits and beers including 31 Scotches!

The *Cobb Bar* at Cobb & Co in the Grand Establishment Hotel on Hinemoa St between Tutanekai and Fenton Sts has live bands

Wednesday to Saturday nights. Also at the Grand Establishment, *Wheeler's Nightclub* is a disco popular with young people, open Wednesday to Saturday nights. The *Ace of Clubs* on Ti St, off Fenton St about 500 metres south of McDonald's, is another disco popular with young people, open Wednesday to Saturday nights until 4 am.

Dobbo's Bar at the Sportsman's Hotel on the corner of Hinemaru and Pukuatua Sts is a sports bar with live bands for dancing on Thursday, Friday and Saturday nights.

For just hanging out, don't forget the *Roundabout Bar & Cafe* upstairs at 83 Arawa St, with games and an ambience catering to travellers.

Getting There & Away

The Tourism Rotorua office (see Information) books and sells tickets for every form of transport serving Rotorua – air, bus, shuttle, train, or anything else you can think of. It's a convenient service.

Air The Air New Zealand and Mt Cook Airline office (☎ 347 9564) on the corner of Fenton and Hinemoa Sts is open Monday to Friday from 8.30 am to 5 pm; they also have a counter at the airport (☎ 345 6176) open from 6.30 am to 7 pm, seven days a week. They offer daily direct flights to Auckland, Christchurch, Mt Cook, Queenstown, Taupo and Wellington, with connections to other centres.

Ansett New Zealand (☎ 347 0596) has a city office at 113 Fenton St, open Monday to Friday from 8.30 am to 5 pm, and an airport ticket counter (☎ 345 5348) open every day. Ansett offers daily direct flights to Christchurch, Queenstown and Wellington, with connections to other centres.

Bus InterCity long-distance and tour buses arrive and depart from the Rotorua Travel Centre (☎ 349 0590) on Amohau St between Tutanekai and Amohia Sts. InterCity has daily buses to and from Auckland (four hours), Wellington (5½ hours), Taupo, Tauranga, Whakatane and Hamilton (all

1½ hours), Waitomo and Opotiki (both 2½ hours).

On the east coast routes, InterCity goes daily to Gisborne (five hours) via Opotiki and to Napier (3½ hours) via Taupo. A Monday, Wednesday, Friday service operates between Rotorua and Wairoa on the east coast, departing from Wairoa at 8 am, stopping at Lake Waikaremoana at 9.05 am and arriving in Rotorua at 12.45 pm. It departs from Rotorua for the return trip at 2.15 pm, stops at Lake Waikaremoana at 5.50 pm and arrives at Wairoa at 7 pm. (This route was not listed in the InterCity timetable, but it was operating; you might want to check to be sure it's going.)

Newmans buses arrive and depart from the Tourism Rotorua office. Newmans buses go from Rotorua to Hamilton, Auckland, Taupo, Wellington, Palmerston North (5½ hours), Tauranga, Whakatane, Gisborne and Napier (3½ hours).

Several convenient smaller buses, often cheaper and more enjoyable than the major buses, also serve Rotorua. They offer free pick-up and delivery to wherever you're staying; all you need do is book in advance.

Kiwi Safaris (☎ freephone (0800) 800 616) serves Rotorua on its 'Mud & Worm Loop', making a daily circle from Auckland to Thames, Te Aroha, Rotorua, Waitomo and back to Auckland, and vice versa. It's an excellent service, with free bicycle transport, free soft drinks, music and things to read.

Vanway Tours (☎ 346 1341) does a shuttle service from Rotorua to Waitomo and Auckland.

B&P Shuttle (☎ 348 2302, mobile (025) 971 791), affectionately known as 'the Pink Bus', operates a twice-daily shuttle service between Rotorua and Taupo. The cost is $14 to go one-way, or $14 for a return trip from Rotorua to Huka Falls and back on the same day.

C Tours (☎ New Plymouth (06) 751 1711) operates a Tuesday and Friday service from New Plymouth to Waitomo and on to Rotorua, departing from New Plymouth in the morning and returning from Rotorua by the same route in the afternoon.

Super Shuttle (☎ 349 3444) operates a daily except Saturday shuttle service between Rotorua and Gisborne, via Opotiki and Whakatane.

Train The railway station is on Dingsdale Rd off Lake Rd, about one km north-west of the centre. A shuttle service between the centre and the station serves all arriving and departing trains (see Getting Around). The station opens only when trains are departing. Buy train tickets not at the railway station, but at Tourism Rotorua (see Information) or the Rotorua Travel Centre (see Buses).

The Geyserland Express train operates twice daily between Auckland and Rotorua, stopping at Hamilton on the way. Travel time from Rotorua is two hours to Hamilton, four hours to Auckland.

Hitching Hitching to Rotorua is generally not bad except on SH 38 from Waikaremoana – once past Murupara heading out that way, count on about three cars per hour going past (that's if you're lucky!), although more people will stop than on the major roads.

The hitching problem out of Rotorua is often just the sheer number of backpackers leaving town. You may have to simply join the queue and wait.

Getting Around
To/From the Airport The airport is about 10 km out, on the eastern side of the lake. Airport Shuttle (☎ 346 2386, mobile (026) 956 810) offers a door-to-door shuttle service to/from the airport, as does Super Shuttle (☎ 349 3444). The cost is $8 for the first person, $2 for each additional passenger in the group. A taxi from the centre to the airport costs about $15.

To/From the Railway Station Rotorua's railway station used to be in town but now it has moved to the outskirts. Reesby Coachlines (☎ 347 0098) do a shuttle service for all arriving and departing trains, going between the railway station, the Tourism Rotorua office (see Information) and the Rotorua Travel Centre (see Buses).

Bus Rotorua Sightseeing Shuttle (mobile (☎ (025) 957 399) makes a constant loop every day from 8.15 am to 5.10 pm. The route begins at the Tourism Rotorua office and goes to the Whakarewarewa thermal reserve, back to Tourism Rotorua again, then on to the Orchid Gardens, the Polynesian Pools, the Bath-House museum, Rotorua Lakefront, Skyline Skyrides, Rainbow Springs, Agrodome, and back to Tourism Rotorua. Half-day passes for up to five hours cost $14, full day passes for up to nine hours are $20 (children half price), and you can jump on and off wherever you like. Ring for hotel pickup.

Reesby Coachlines (☎ 347 0098) operates several suburban bus routes Monday to Friday, with limited Saturday service. Route 3 runs to Whakarewarewa, Route 2 along the lake side to Rainbow Springs.

Car Rental Rotorua has a host of rental car companies. The competition is fierce and they all seem to offer 'specials' to try to undercut the others. Rent-a-Dent (☎ 349 1919) on Ti St is more economical than most, and in addition to cars they also have station wagons, mini buses and eight-seater 4WD vans, if you want to get a group together. Phone them for free delivery.

Link Rent-a-Car (☎ 347 8063) at 108 Fenton St is similarly priced, and you can sometimes get backpackers discounts. When available, they do a backpackers deal for relocating cars to Auckland, whereby you drive the car to Auckland for them and pay only for insurance and fuel.

Moped Rental Link Rent-a-Car (☎ 347 8063) at 108 Fenton St hires mopeds from October to April.

Bicycle Rental Rotorua is fairly spread out and public transport is not that good, so a bicycle is a nice thing to have. Lady Jane's Ice Cream Parlour (☎ 347 9340) on the corner of Tutanekai and Whakaue Sts hires mountain bikes, 10-speeds and tandems. The cost is $6/25 per hour/day for mountain bikes, $5/12 for 10-speeds, and $5 per hour for tandems. A deposit is required and some hostels get a 10% discount.

The Ivanhoe Lodge (see Hostels) hires bicycles at $12 per day. They will hire bicycles to anyone, not only their guests.

AROUND ROTORUA
Hell's Gate
Hell's Gate, 'Tikitere', another highly active thermal area, is 16 km east of Rotorua on the road to Whakatane (SH 30). The reserve covers 10 hectares, with a 2.5 km walking track to cover the various attractions including the largest hot thermal waterfall in the southern hemisphere. Guide sheets are printed in eight languages, including Australian! It's open daily from 8.30 am to 5 pm; admission is $9 (children $4).

George Bernard Shaw visited Hell's Gate in 1934. 'I wish I had never seen the place,' he said. 'It reminds me too vividly of the fate theologians have promised me.'

Waimangu Volcanic Valley
The Waimangu Volcanic Valley is another interesting thermal area. A walk through the valley, an easy downhill stroll, first passes the Waimangu Cauldron – a pale-blue lake steaming quietly at 53°C – and many other interesting thermal and volcanic features. Waimangu means 'black water', as much of the water here was a dark muddy colour. In this valley the Waimangu Geyser used to perform actively enough to be rated the 'largest geyser in the world'. Between 1900 and its extinction in 1904 it would occasionally spout jets nearly 500 metres high!

The walk continues down to Lake Rotomahana, 'warm lake', from where you can either get a lift back up to where you started or take a half-hour boat trip on Lake Rotomahana, taking you past steaming cliffs and the former site of the Pink and White Terraces.

The Waimangu Volcanic Valley is open every day from 8.30 am to 5 pm. The cost is $9 (children $4) for the valley walk only; it's $25 (children $7) for both the valley walk and boat trip. Or you can come to the valley on the Waimangu Round Trip tour (see Tours). It's an advantage to come with a guide, as there is so much interesting history here if only you have someone to point it out and tell you the stories. It's a 20-minute drive from Rotorua, going 19 km south on SH 5 (the road towards Taupo) and then five to six km from the marked turn-off.

Waiotapu
Also south of Rotorua, Waiotapu, 'sacred waters', is yet another thermal area worth visiting. It has many interesting features including the large, effervescently boiling Champagne Pool, craters and blowholes, colourful mineral terraces and other rock formations, and the Lady Knox Geyser which spouts off (with a little prompting) punctually at 10.15 each morning and gushes for about an hour. It opens daily at 8.30 am, closing in summer at 8 or 8.30 pm, in winter at 4.30 or 5 pm, depending on the weather. Admission is $7.50 (children $2.50, family $18). To get there, go 30 km south on SH 5 (the road towards Taupo), turn off at the marked turn-off and go two more km. (The turn-off for the Waikite Thermal Mineral Baths is also there; see Thermal Pools.)

Trout Springs
There are several trout springs around Rotorua – the springs run down to Lake Rotorua and the trout, lured perhaps by the free feeds waiting for them from the tourists, swim up the streams to the springs. They are not trapped there; if you watch you may see a trout leaping the little falls to return to the lake or come up to the springs. Try to latch on to a bus tour group or ask one of the people there to explain things – after about half an hour you'll be able to tell a rainbow trout from a brown trout, a male from a female, and a young one from an old one.

The Rainbow and Fairy Springs Trout Sanctuary and Wildlife Park is the best known of the trout springs. There are a number of springs (one with an underwater viewer), an aviary and a nocturnal kiwi house. The first time I was there a male kiwi was being 'introduced' to a female kiwi and getting a damn good kicking for his troubles!

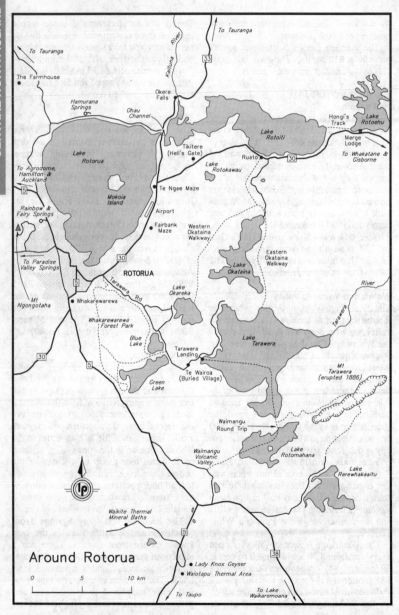

Around Rotorua

0   5   10 km

Say 'hi' to Ray Punter, the knowledgeable 'keeper of the trout'. At the springs you'll also find eels, wallabies, deer, birds, sheep, wild pigs and other native and introduced animals, now all found wild in New Zealand.

The springs are four km north of the city centre, on the west side of Lake Rotorua – take SH 5 as if you were going to Auckland or Hamilton; or catch the Sightseeing Shuttle Bus which makes a stop here. They are open from 8 am to 5 pm daily; admission is $9.70 (children $3, family $23) and also entitles you to visit Rainbow Farm across the road.

Rainbow Farm has a farm show with sheep shearing, sheep dogs and a chance to try your hand at milking a cow. There are shows three times daily and also horseback riding, 4WD farm tours and free farm walks.

Paradise Valley Springs are similar trout springs, set in an attractive six-hectare park with various animals, including a pride of lions. If you've never been in a lion's cage this is your chance – the cubs, from a few weeks to a few months old, are kept in an enclosed area and you can go in and play with them to your heart's content. The springs, 13 km from Rotorua on Paradise Valley Rd, at the foot of Mt Ngongotaha, are open daily from 9 am to 5 pm; admission is $8.50 (children $3).

Skyline Skyrides

Skyline Skyrides is on the west side of Lake Rotorua, near the Rainbow and Fairy Springs. Here you can take a gondola ride up Mt Ngongotaha for a wide view of the lake area, and once up there go flying 900 metres back down the mountain on a luge (a sort of sled without snow) or a flying fox, coming back up again on a chairlift. Also up there are a cafe and a restaurant for twilight dining. The gondola costs $8.50 (children $3, family $20) for the return trip and the luge is $3.50 for one ride, less per ride for multiple trips. It's open from 10 am daily.

Also at the top is a simulator, a contraption introduced at the Brisbane Expo in 1988 and developed from the principles of flight simulators used in training military pilots. You can sample various thrills including down-

hill skiing, car and motorcycle speedway racing, jet-boating down the Shotover River, helicopter flying over Mt Tarawera and, of course, a tear across the skies in a fighter plane. Each ride is about four minutes long and costs $6 (children $4.50). It operates daily from 9 am to 5 pm.

Also here is an 18-hole mini-golf course, a human gyroscope, a New Zealand Experience audiovisual show, an ice cream shop and a herb & crafts shop with one-hour tours of the herb gardens for $8, or three-hour hands-on craft and herb tours for $30.

Agrodome & Trainworld

If seeing the millions of sheep in the NZ countryside has stimulated your interest in these animals and their relation to New Zealand, visit Agrodome. Going to see a bunch of sheep seems a rather strange thing to do in New Zealand, but for $8.50 (children $4) you get an interesting, educational and entertaining one-hour show at 9.15 am, 11 am and 2.30 pm daily. There's sheep shearing and sheep dogs displaying their expertise; by the time you're through you may even be able to tell the difference between some of the 19 breeds of sheep on show.

Outdoors are some life-size moa replicas. You can hire horses for guided tours of the 120-hectare farm; Riverdale Farm tours are $10 or it's $16.50 for both the tour and the farm show. Agrodome is seven km north of Rotorua on SH 1, and again, the Sightseeing Shuttle bus can drop you off here.

Beside the Agrodome is Trainworld, an interesting place with one of the largest '00'-gauge model railways in the world. About 750 metres of track take 20 to 30 trains at a time whizzing around a 102-sq-metre model, which is as fascinating as the trains themselves. The whole thing is dubbed 'a journey through Britain' and the intricately detailed model portrays the towns, villages, countryside and rail centres of Britain. It's open from 9.30 am to 4.30 pm daily; admission is $7.50 (children $3, family $16).

Mazes

Near the airport are a couple of large mazes. The Fairbank Maze, opposite the airport, is the largest hedge maze in New Zealand, with a 1.6 km pathway. There's also an orchard, gardens, ponds, picnic areas, birds and animals. The maze is open from 9 am to 5 pm daily; admission is $3 (children $1.50).

Te Ngae Park, three km beyond the airport, is a three-dimensional, 1.7-km wooden maze similar to the original Wanaka maze in the South Island. It's open every day from 9 am to 5 pm; admission is $4 (kids $2).

Buried Village

The Buried Village is reached by a 15-km scenic drive along Tarawera Rd, passing the Blue and Green Lakes. On display are many artefacts unearthed from the village, displays on the Mt Tarawera eruption which buried the village in ash, and excavated buildings – you may see excavations still in progress. Of particular interest is the story of the tohunga, Tuhoto Ariki, who foretold the destruction of the village; his house has been excavated and is here on display.

Many other interesting things are on view at the Buried Village and there's also a good bush walk through the valley to Te Wairoa Falls, dropping about 80 metres over a series of falls. The village is open from 8.30 am to 5.30 pm daily (9 am to 4.30 pm, June to August); admission is $7 (children $2, family $16).

Lake Tarawera

About two km further on past the Buried Village is Tarawera Landing on the shore of

---

The Eruption of Mt Tarawera

In the 19th century, Lake Tarawera near Rotorua was a major tourist attraction. It attracted visitors from around the world to see the Pink and White Terraces, regarded as one of the seven wonders of the world - impressively large and beautiful terraces of multi-levelled pools, formed by silica deposits from thermal waters which had trickled over them for centuries. The Maori village of Te Wairoa, on the shores of the lake, was New Zealand's principal tourist resort, being the base from where Sophia, a Maori guide, took visitors on boat trips over the lake to view the terraces. Mt Tarawera towered over the lake and, although the Maoris believed that a powerful fire spirit lived inside the mountain, the mountain loomed silently there, just as it does today.

One day in June 1886, Sophia took a party out on the lake as usual, to go to see the terraces. As they were on the lake, suddenly they saw a phantom Maori war canoe gliding across the water. The Maori boatmen paddling the phantom canoe were paddling very fast. It was an ancient kind of war canoe - but this kind of war canoe had never existed on this lake. It was seen by all the people in the tourist boat - both Maori and Pakeha.

To Maori people, the appearance of a phantom Maori war canoe is an omen of impending disaster. Back at Te Wairoa, an old tohunga, Tuhoto Ariki, said the sighting of the canoe foretold disaster. He predicted that the village would be 'overwhelmed'.

Four days later, on 10 June 1886, in the middle of the night, there were earthquakes and loud sounds and the eruption of Mt Tarawera suddenly lit up the sky, with fire exploding from many places along the top of the mountain. By the time it was finished, six hours later, over 8000 sq km had been buried in ash, lava and mud, the Maori village of Te Wairoa was obliterated, the Pink and White Terraces were destroyed, 153 people were killed, Mt Tarawera was sliced and opened along its length as if with a huge cleaver, and Lake Rotomahana was formed.

Excavations were carried out at Te Wairoa to save the survivors. The guide Sophia became a heroine because she saved many people's lives, giving them shelter in her house.

The old tohunga, however, was not so fortunate. His house was buried in volcanic ash, with him trapped inside. The Maori people working to rescue the survivors refused to dig him out. They feared he had used his magic powers to cause the eruption - he had been saying for some time that the new orientation of the villagers towards tourists and a money economy were not traditional, and that neglect of the old traditions would anger the fire spirit inside the mountain. Finally, after four days had passed, he was dug out by Europeans, who took him to be cared for in Rotorua. He died a week later, at the age of around 104. ■

Lake Tarawera. Tarawera means 'burnt spear', named by a visiting hunter who left his birdspears in a hut and, on returning the following season, found both the spears and the hut had been burnt.

At 11 am daily a launch leaves from here and crosses over Lake Tarawera towards Lake Rotomahana. It stays on the other side for about 45 minutes, long enough for people to walk across to Lake Rotomahana, then returns to Tarawera Landing. Altogether the trip takes 2½ hours; the cost is $15 (children $7.50, family $35). A shorter 45-minute cruise on Lake Tarawera departs at 1.30, 2.30, 3.30 and 4.30 pm; the cost is the same as for the 2½-hour trip.

Boats departing from Tarawera Landing also provide transport to Mt Tarawera and to Hot Water Beach on Te Rata Bay, a beach on Lake Tarawera with hot thermal waters and a basic DOC campsite.

Parks & Walks

Whakarewarewa Forest Park, on the southeast edge of town, is a forest of trees planted earlier this century as an experiment to find the most suitable species to replace New Zealand's rapidly dwindling and slow-growing native trees.

The Forestry Corporation Visitor Information Centre (☎ 346 2082) in the park has a woodcraft shop, displays and an audiovisual on the history and development of the forest. Check in here if you want to go walking – there are many walks ranging from half an hour to four hours in length, including some great routes to the Blue and Green Lakes. Several walks start at the Visitor Centre, including a half-hour Redwood Forest Walk through a grove of large California redwood trees. The Visitor Centre is open Monday to Friday from 8 am to 5 pm, weekends and holidays from 10 am to 4 pm.

About 50 km east of Rotorua, signposted off the main road, is the Whirinaki Forest Park, a native podocarp (conifer) forest with walking tracks, scenic drives, camping and huts, lookouts, waterfalls, the Whirinaki River, and some special areas including the Oriuwaka Ecological Reserve and the Arahaki Lagoon. The Whirinaki Field Centre (☎ 366 3601) is adjacent to Minginui Village. Ask about the fine Whirinaki-Te Hoe Loop Walk, a four-day loop walk with seven huts that starts in some of New Zealand's finest podocarp forest and proceeds over mountains and through a series of river valleys.

DOC operates a volunteer programme in the Whirinaki Forest Park in which you do basic work on tracks, hut cleaning, weed control, etc. Volunteer assignments are for about a week, with extensions possible; you pay DOC $25 and supply your own food and sleeping bag and DOC provides you with transport out to the bush and accommodation for the week. It's about an hour's drive from Rotorua. Contact the Whirinaki Field Centre or the DOC office in Rotorua about two weeks in advance of when you'd like to go. It's not 'all work and no play'; you do get time off to relax and it's a chance to get way out in the bush and to learn about conservation in New Zealand.

Other walks in the Rotorua area include the 22.5 km Western Okataina Walkway from Lake Okareka to Ruato, through native bush. There's public transport past the Ruato end only; the whole walk takes about six hours, and you need good boots or stout shoes.

There is also an Eastern Okataina Walkway, going along the eastern shoreline of Lake Okataina to Lake Tarawera – about a 2½-hour, eight-km walk. At one time you had to walk out the same way you walked in but now a connecting track has been added, making it possible to do a two-day walk from either Lake Okataina or Ruato to Lake Tarawera and camp overnight at a DOC campsite ($5 per site), from where you can walk another hour to the Tarawera Falls. The next day you could hike up Mt Tarawera, with a choice of three exit points, but you must obtain permission to hike on Mt Tarawera (DOC can tell you how).

If you do go tramping on Mt Tarawera, take some water as it's a scarce resource up there. Watch what streams you drink from anywhere in the area; being a thermal area much of the water isn't pure. Good tramping shoes are essential – it's easy to slip on the volcanic scoria. As with other mountains in New Zealand, the weather on Mt Tarawera can be very changeable, so bring warm and waterproof clothing to protect you against wind and rain. It's not a hard walk (about 2½ to three hours each way) and no technical expertise is required.

There is no public transport, and the Eastern Okataina Walkway isn't a loop walk, so you must arrange transport at both ends, or meet the Tarawera Launch at the Tarawera outlet for transport back to the Tarawera Landing. The same launch can take you to various good places around Lake Tarawera including Hot Water Beach, with hot water in the lake and a DOC Campsite ($5 per site). Get a map from Tourism Rotorua before starting out.

You can go out to the Okere Falls, about 16 km north-east of Rotorua, on SH 33 – the turn-off is well signposted, just past the Okere Falls Store, and it's about a 30-minute walk through native podocarp forest to reach the falls. This is the seven-metre falls that the rafting companies are taking people over, so you may see a raft going over the falls. Several other walks are also here, including walks up the Kaituna River to Hinemoa's Steps and some caves.

Other short walks can be made around Lake Okataina, Mt Ngongotaha (just north of Rotorua), and Lake Rotorua. The DOC office at Tourism Rotorua has information on these and other walks, and excellent maps. Ask DOC about their special activities programmes for visitors.

Orakei Korako

Orakei Korako is one of New Zealand's finest and most active thermal areas. It is about a 45-minute drive south of Rotorua, heading towards Taupo. Orakei Korako is about a 25-minute drive north of Taupo; see the 'Around Taupo' section later in this chapter.

Taupo

Taupo (population 18,500), 85 km south of Rotorua, is claimed to be the world's trout fishing capital. If you thought those trout in the Rotorua springs looked large and tasty, they're nothing compared to the monsters here. All New Zealand's rainbow trout are descended from one batch of eggs brought from California's Russian River nearly a century ago. The lakes here are everything a trout could dream of, and so some trout grow to a prodigious size. International trout-fishing tournaments are held in Lake Taupo each year on Anzac weekend, on or around 25 April.

Lake Taupo is in the geographical centre of the North Island. The largest lake in New Zealand, it is 606 sq km in area and 357 metres above sea level. The depression Lake Taupo occupies is thought to have been formed by a gigantic volcanic explosion and subsequent subsidence. Pumice from this explosion is found as far away as Napier and Gisborne and forms a layer – in some places just one cm thick, in others metres – over a vast area of the central North Island. Historical chronicles of darkened skies in the daytime and blood-red sunsets were recorded in around 186 AD in as faraway places as China and Rome, and are believed to refer to the effects of the Taupo explosion in the atmosphere.

Taupo is built on the north-east corner of Lake Taupo, where the Waikato River, the lake's only outlet, flows out of the lake. At 425 km, the longest river in New Zealand, the Waikato leaves the lake at the township, flows through the Huka Falls and the Aratiatia Rapids, and on through the heart of the northern North Island before finally reaching the west coast at Waikato Heads just south of Auckland.

Taupo has many attractions for visitors, with things to see and do in town, out on the lake, up in the air, and in Wairakei Park, stretching north along the Waikato River. It's a relaxed town and a good base for the area.

History

Back in the mists of time a Maori chief named Tamatea-arikinui visited the area and, noticing that the ground felt hollow and that his footsteps seemed to reverberate, called the place Tapuaeharuru – 'resounding footsteps'. Another source of the name comes from the story that Tia, who discovered the lake, slept by it draped in his cloak, and it became known as Taupo-nui-a-Tia, 'the great cloak of Tia'. Taupo, as it became known, was first occupied by Europeans as a military outpost during the Maori Wars. Colonel J M Roberts built a redoubt in 1869 and a garrison of mounted police remained there until the defeat of the rebel warrior Te Kooti, in October of that year.

In the 1870s the government bought the land from the Maoris, who asked that it be named Bowen in honour of Governor Sir G F Bowen who visited the lake in 1872. While this was agreed to, it was never carried out. Taupo has grown slowly and sedately from a lakeside village of about 750 in 1945, to a resort town with a permanent population of 18,500 which swells to over 45,000 at peak holiday times. The town is on the lakefront where SH 1, the main road from the north, first meets the lake.

Information

The Taupo Information Centre (☎ 378 9000; fax 378 9003) is on Tongariro St near the corner of Heu Heu St, in a section of the Great Lake Centre. It's a useful place which does bookings for all accommodation, activities and attractions in the area, for all buses, trains and the Interislander ferry, provides general information and sometimes sells events tickets. It also offers useful services such as currency exchange on the weekends, and sells fishing licences, back country hut passes, postage stamps, phone cards and souvenirs. You can pick up a good free city map and it also has DOC maps and DOC information. The centre is open every day from 8.30 am to 5 pm.

Nearby, the AA Travel Centre (☎ 378 6000) at 93 Tongariro St has an AA travel agency and all other AA services. It's open Monday to Friday from 8.30 am to 5 pm, Saturday 9 am to 1 pm. The CPO is on the corner of Horomatangi and Ruapehu Sts.

If you're interested in knowing more about Taupo's history, look for the book *The Remotest Interior – A History of Taupo* by Barbara Cooper (Moana Press, Tauranga & Wellington, 1989, paperback). It's a fascinating book telling the history of the area all the way from the violent volcanic formation of the lake and volcanoes, to the time when Taupo was considered 'the remotest interior' of the North Island, up to modern times.

Taupo Regional Museum & Art Gallery

Behind the information centre in Tongariro St, the Taupo Regional Museum & Art Gallery has many historical photos and mementos of the 'old days' around Lake Taupo; exhibits also include Maori carvings, moa bones, the biggest stuffed trout you ever saw, and an excellent 3D model of the entire Lake Taupo and Tongariro National Park region. The museum is open Monday to Saturday from 10.30 am to 4.30 pm; admission is free.

Cherry Island

In the middle of the Waikato River not far from the centre of town, the Cherry Island Tourist Park is a small, low-key trout and wildlife park alright for families with small children but not so thrilling for adults – the 'wildlife' consists of a couple of goats, pigs, etc, and peacocks, pheasants, pigeons and ducks. The island is reached by a footbridge and is open daily from 9 am to 5 pm; admission is steep at $7.50 (children $3.50, family $22). To get there, head out on Spa Rd about one km from the centre, turn left into Motutahae St then right into Waikato St.

Taupo Bungy

The Taupo Bungy site is on Spa Rd, opposite Cherry Island about a km from the centre. Jumpers leap off a platform jutting 20 metres out over a cliff and hurtle down towards the Waikato River, 45 metres below. There are plenty of vantage points for a good view of the jumpers. The cost for a jump is $85 but there are a bewildering array of discounts; if you're staying at a hostel in town, if you are in a group of three or more, if you came to town on certain buses, or whatever, you'll pay less. The office (☎ 377 1135; fax 377 1136) is open every day from 9 am to 5 pm.

Other Things to See in Town

Taupo Mini-Golf is on the lakefront on the corner of Lake Terrace and Titiraupenga St. The 18-hole mini-golf course is open every day from 9 am until late; the cost is $5.50 (children $3, family $15). Trainsville, upstairs at 35A Heu Heu St, is a model railway exhibition in a shop for model trains and airplanes; the cost is $2.50 (children $1) to see the model railway.

Under the SH 1 bridge over the Waikato River in Taupo are control gates regulating the level of Lake Taupo and the amount of flow down the Waikato River through its string of hydroelectric power stations. Just up the hill from here is the turn-off to Acacia Bay, a pleasant peaceful beach a little over five km west of Taupo. There's a short walk from here to Little Acacia Bay.

Thermal Pools

The A C Thermal Baths (☎ 378 7321) are at the top of Spa Rd, about two km east of the town centre. There's a big swimming pool heated to 35°C with a 'Roaster Coaster' waterslide, private mineral pools and a sauna. It's open from 8 am to 9 pm every day and until 10 pm over the Christmas holidays. Admission is $4 (children and pensioners $2, family $10), saunas are $4, and for an extra $3 you can use the waterslide all day long.

The De Brett Thermal Pools (☎ 378 8559) are on the Taupo-Napier Highway (SH 5), one km from the lake. The large outdoor pool is divided into two sections, one side at 36°C and the other at 40°C, with a big hot waterslide. There are a number of private pools with different temperatures; the ones on the end are quite hot. The pools are open from 8 am to 9.30 pm daily and admission is $4 (children $2); it's 50c more to use the private

pools for as long as you want. The De Brett Family Leisure Park motor camp and the De Brett Thermal Hotel are nearby.

Lake Cruises

Three boats specialise in cruises on the lake: the *Barbary*, the *Spirit of Musick* and the *Ernest Kemp*. The *Barbary*, built in 1926, is a 50-foot (15-metre) ocean-going racing yacht once owned by Errol Flynn. 'Barbary Bill', the skipper, is much loved by tourists and locals alike and his trip is probably the most popular. The *Spirit of Musick* is an elegant 44-foot (13-metre) ketch. The *Ernest Kemp* is a different kind of boat, a replica 1920s steam ferry.

All three boats offer similar cruises, visiting a modern Maori rock carving beside the lake. The carving is on private land so it cannot be reached by foot; the only way to see it is by boat. In summer all three boats offer morning, afternoon and evening cruises; they sail in winter too but usually only once or twice a day. The cruises last about 2½ to three hours; the cost is $20 (children $10) on all the boats and they all leave from the wharfs at the Taupo Boat Harbour, off Redoubt Rd. Bookings for all the cruises can be made at the Taupo Information·Centre or at the launch office by the wharfs (☎ 378 3444). You may receive a discount if you book through a hostel.

Fishing

There are a number of fishing guides and charter boat operators in Taupo; check with the information centre. A trip will probably cost about $60 per person. If you're staying at one of the hostels you can book fishing boat trips through them. They usually have the best prices around – around $60 an hour for the whole boat, which can hold up to six people sharing the cost. Count on a fishing trip lasting around two or three hours. If you go on a boat trip they'll supply all the gear, and you can get your fishing licence through them.

Taupo is world-famous for its trout fly fishing. Fly fishing is the only kind you can do on all rivers flowing into the lake, and in a 300-metre radius of the river mouths. Spin fishing is allowed on the Waikato River (flowing *out* of the lake) and on the Tokaanu tail race, flowing into the lake from the Tokaanu Power Station. On the lake, both spin fishing and fly fishing are allowed. Several fly fishing guides operate around Taupo, some of them very good, but the price is not cheap – around $200 a day, everything included.

If you're going it on your own, you can hire fishing tackle at Bob Sullivan's Taupo Sports Depot (☎ 378 5337, after hours 378 5550) on Tongariro St, by the waterfront. The cost is $10 per day for spinning gear or $30 per day for fly gear. It's open from 8.30 am to 5.30 pm Monday to Thursday, 8.30 am to 7 pm on Friday, 8.30 am to 12.30 pm on Saturday and from 10 am to noon on Sunday.

You can get your fishing licence there or from any other sports shop, from the information centre, or from the launch office at the harbour. Fishing licences for fishing on Lake Taupo and the nearby rivers cost $8 per day, $22 per week, $30 per month or $46 for the entire year (1 July to 30 June). There's also a special tourist fishing licence, valid for one month anywhere in New Zealand, available for $60, but you can only get it from the Tourism Rotorua office in Rotorua.

Anytime you go fishing, be certain you have your fishing licence and that you obey all the rules. Fishing is taken very seriously around these parts, and there are fines of thousands of dollars for violation of fishing regulations. All the rules you need to know are written on your fishing licence.

Water Activities

Southern Lights Expeditions (☎ 377 0297) operates kayak tours on Lake Taupo in summer. The cost is $55 for a 3½ to four hour trip to the Maori rock carvings, starting from the boat ramp at Acacia Bay. The tour includes a guide, a gourmet picnic lunch, and plenty of time for fishing, swimming and a leisurely paddling pace. They also do a 1½ to two hour evening paddle at sunset for $25, and a two-day Western Bay Explorer trip to

Lake Taupo's western bays for $205. Bookings can be made directly, through the information centre, or through the hostels.

The Acacia Bay Lodge (☎ 378 6830) at 868 Acacia Bay Rd in Acacia Bay hires motorboats at $24 per hour, rowboats at $12 per hour, Canadian canoes at $12 per hour, and kayaks at $10 per hour. It takes about one hour to go from there to the Maori rock carvings in a motorboat.

The Two Mile Bay Catamaran & Keeler Centre (☎ 378 3299, mobile (025) 967 350) at Two Mile Bay, south of Taupo, hires Canadian canoes, windsurfers, catamarans and sailboats.

During the summer there are lots of activities on Lake Taupo including swimming, water skiing, windsurfing, paragliding and sailing. The information centre has details on all of them.

Several white water rafting companies operate from Taupo with one-day trips on the Tongariro and Rangitaiki rivers, longer trips on other rivers. Book these trips through the hostels or the information centre.

Aerial Sightseeing & Gliding

You can go for a scenic flight on the float-plane from the lakefront, next to Taupo Boat Harbour (☎ 378 7500/9441), with Taupo Air Services (☎ 378 5325) from Taupo Aerodrome, or with Darren's Wonderflights operated by De Brett Aviation (☎ 378 8559, mobile (025) 966 172) based at the De Brett Thermal Pools and Motor Camp on SH 5, the Taupo-Napier Rd. They all offer similar flights for similar prices, ranging upwards from about $20 (children $10) for a short flight around the Taupo area to about $96 (children $48) for flights across Lake Taupo over Tongariro National Park, or north to Rotorua.

Helistar Helicopters (☎ 374 8405, after hours 377 1280), with an office and helipad on the Huka Falls Rd north of town, offers a variety of scenic helicopter flights including an eight to 10-minute flight over Taupo and the many sights of Wairakei Park for $55 per person. Ask them about their special 'Wild

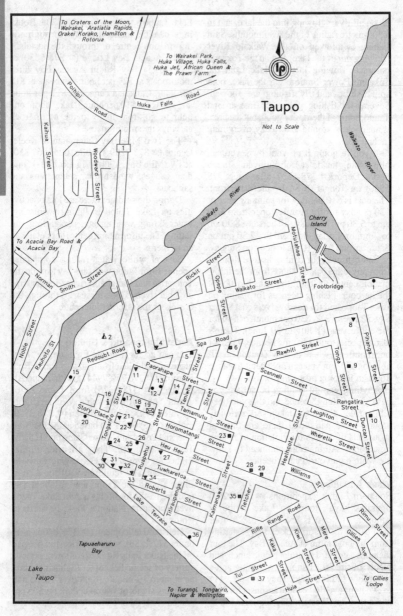

To Craters of the Moon,
Wairakei, Aratiatia Rapids,
Orakei Korako, Hamilton &
Rotorua

To Wairakei Park,
Huka Village, Huka Falls,
Huka Jet, African Queen &
The Prawn Farm

Taupo

Not to Scale

Huka Falls Road

Waikato River

Pohipi Road

Kaihua Street

Woodward Street

To Acacia Bay Road &
Acacia Bay

Cherry
Island

Footbridge

Norman Smith Street

Noble Street

Rajholo St

Redoubt Road

Rickit Street

Oepe Street

Waikato Street

Motuhahe Street

Pihanga Street

2

3

4

Spa Road

5

6

Rawhiti Street

Tonga Street

8

9

15

Paorahape Street

11

13

12

14

Tamihana Street

7

Scannell Street

Rangatira Street

16

17

18

19

Tamamutu Street

Laughton Street

10

Story Place

20

Tongariro Street

21

22

Horomatangi Street

23

Duncan Street

Wheretia Street

Heathcote Street

24

25

26

Ruapehu Street

Heu Heu Street

27

28

29

Williams St

30

31

32

34

Tuwharetoa Street

Kaimanawa Street

35

Fletcher

Rimu Street

33

Roberts Street

Titiraupenga Street

36

Lake Terrace

Rifle Range Road

Kewa Street

Kiwi Street

Mere Street

Gillies Ave

Gillies

Tapuaeharuru
Bay

Lake
Taupo

Tui Street

37

Huia Street

To Gillies
Lodge

To Turangi, Tongariro,
Napier & Wellington

1

■ PLACES TO STAY

2 Taupo Motor Camp
5 Burke's Backpackers
6 Rainbow Lodge
7 Continental Motel
9 Taupo Cabins
10 Berkenhoff Lodge
23 Taupo Associate YHA Hostel
24 Lake Hotel, Cobb & Co & Freeman's
   Bar
28 Bradshaw's Bed & Breakfast
29 Dunrovin Motel
35 Mountain View Motel
37 Courtney Motel

▼ PLACES TO EAT

3 Woolworth's Supermarket
4 Cafe Delight
8 Gee Dub's Cafe & Spa Bakery
11 Pizza Man
14 Pak 'n Save Supermarket
18 D21 Deli & Lunch Bar
21 Olive Branch Delicatessen &
   Shawarma Bar
22 Happy Heart Wholefood Cafe
24 Lake Hotel, Cobb & Co &
   Freeman's Bar

25 Hudder's Licensed Cafe
27 Margarita's Mexican Restaurant
30 Nonni's Cafe & Restaurant, Echo Cliff
   Licensed Restaurant, JD's
   Takeaways, Safari Joe's Bar & Grill,
   Red Barrel & Blacksmith's Arms
31 Kentucky Fried Chicken
32 Pizza Hut
33 Maxi's
34 McDonald's

   OTHER

1 Taupo Bungy
12 Taupo Travel Centre
13 Cycle World
15 Launch Office & Harbour
16 Taupo Information Centre &
   Great Lake Centre
17 Automobile Association (AA)
   Travel Centre
19 CPO
20 Taupo Regional Museum & Art Gallery
26 Trainsville
30 Bob Sullivan's Taupo Sports Depot
36 Taupo Mini-Golf

Ride' for backpackers, covering the same area for the same price but flown quite differently – bring along your airsickness pills for this one! German, French, Dutch and Spanish are spoken.

The Taupo Gliding Club (☎ 378 5627) goes gliding every Sunday (when the weather is suitable) at Centennial Park on Centennial Drive, about five km up Spa Rd from the centre, out past the AC Baths. They're out there from around 10 am until dark and they'll take you gliding for about $40 for a 20-minute ride.

Tandem Skydiving
Taupo Tandems (mobile (☎ (025) 428 688) does tandem skydiving trips for $170. In addition to the skydiving itself, you get a brilliant view over Lake Taupo and the entire region.

Horse-Trekking
Taupo Horse Treks (☎ 378 0356, 374 8403, after hours 377 0296) based on Karapiti Rd (the road leading to Craters of the Moon) is good for horse-trekking, with healthy, shiny, well-cared-for horses. Most popular is their two-hour horse trek, going through some fine forest and providing good views over the Craters of the Moon area. The cost is $20 per hour, but there's a special price of $33 for two hours if you ask for the backpackers special. The cost includes return transport from town.

Escape to the Wilderness (☎ 378 9276) does two-day horse treks in the Kaimanawa Ranges, going from Lochinvar Station to Wilderness Lodge for an overnight stay. The cost of $150 includes return transport from Taupo, bunkhouse accommodation, meals, guide, the horse and all gear.

Honey Hive New Zealand and the Huka

CENTRAL NORTH ISLAND

Village Riding Centre at Huka Village also do horse-riding, but their rides are just walks along the road.

Walks

You can walk all the way from Taupo to Aratiatia. From the centre of town head up Spa Rd by Woolworth's, passing by the Taupo Bungy site. Turn left at County Ave and continue through Spa Thermal Park at the end of the street, past the skateboard bowl and over the hill, following the rough roadway to the left until you hit the track.

The track follows the river to Huka Falls crossing a hot stream and riverside marshes en route. It's about a one to 1½-hour walk from the centre of Taupo to Huka Falls, depending on your walking speed. From Huka Falls you can cross the footbridge along the seven-km Taupo Walkway to Aratiatia (another two to 2½ hours). There are good views of the river, Huka Falls, and the power station across the river. It's easy walking.

If you're going to Craters of the Moon as well you can make it a round trip, using the walkway in one direction between Taupo and Aratiatia, and the road in the other direction. You would need all day, and should time it so you're at Aratiatia at 2.30 pm when the control gates are open, and at Wairakei when the Geothermal Visitors Centre is open.

Another walk worth mentioning is Mt Tauhara, with magnificent views from the top. Take the Taupo-Napier Highway (SH 5) turn-off, two km south of the Taupo town centre. About six km along SH 5, turn left into Mountain Rd. The start of the track is signposted on the right-hand side. It will take about two hours to get to the top, walking slowly.

A pleasant walkway goes along the lakefront to the south of town all the way from the Taupo lakefront to Four Mile Bay. It's a flat, easy walk and it's public access beach all along here. Heading south from Taupo, there's a hot water beach on the way to Two Mile Bay. At Two Mile Bay the walkway connects with the Lions Walk, going from Two Mile Bay (3.2 km south of Taupo) to

Four Mile Bay (6.4 km). Anywhere along here you can easily get back to SH 1, the lakeside road.

There are plenty of other good walks and tramps in the area, including river, lake, forest and mountain walks. Pick up a copy of the *Walking Trails* booklet from the Taupo Information Centre.

Tours

Walter's Backpackers Tours are run by a delightful, spry old fellow who is also Taupo's radio weatherman and foremost cyclist. He does three-hour tours of the local sights (Huka Falls, Aratiatia, Craters of the Moon, Mt Tauhara and so on) for $15, plus full-day trips further afield to Tongariro National Park for $35. Book directly with him (☎ 378 5924), through the hostels, or through the information centre.

Paradise Tours (☎ 378 9955) does 2½ hour tours of the Taupo sights for $24 (children $10), plus half-day tours to Orakei Korako and other tours. Central Plateau Tours (☎ (025) 949 113, after hours 377 0774) does morning and afternoon tours to Orakei Korako, the Aratiatia Rapids and other places; the cost is $45. Rapid Sensations (☎ 378 7902, or (025) 928 366) does guided mountain-bike tours through Wairakei Park.

Places to Stay

Camping & Cabins Camping is free beside the river about 1.5 km south of the Huka Falls towards Taupo. There are also lots of motor camps in and around Taupo, and around the shores of the lake. Several are on the lakeside to the south of Taupo, heading towards Turangi; these are mentioned in the Turangi section.

The *Taupo Motor Camp* (☎ & fax 377 3080) is on Redoubt St by the river, conveniently near the centre of town. It has tent and powered sites at $8 per person, cabins at $13.50/26 for one/two people, four-berth cabins at $38 for four, and on-site caravans at $35 for two.

Taupo Cabins (☎ 378 4346) at 50 Tonga St doesn't have camping but it has a variety of cabins. The cheapest and most basic ones are $8.50 per person, with your own sleeping bag. Or there are tourist cabins at $35 and tourist flats at $45. TVs, bedding and towels can be hired. It's about 1.5 km from the CPO.

The *Taupo All Seasons Holiday Park* (☎ 378 4272) is at 16 Rangatira St, on the corner of Matipo St. It, too, is about 1.5 km from the centre. It has a hot thermal pool and a variety of accommodation including tent and powered sites at $8 per person, standard cabins at $10 per person, tourist cabins at $30 for two, tourist flats at $40 for two, and a 40-bed lodge.

The *De Brett Family Leisure Park* (☎ & fax 378 8559) is beside the De Brett Thermal Pools, one km from the lake on SH 5, the Taupo-Napier Rd. Campsites are $8.50 per person, 50c more with power, some cabins are $15 per person, others are $45 for two, leisure lodges are $50 for two, and motel units are $58 to $68 for two.

The *Hilltop Motor Caravan Park* (☎ 378 5247) at 39 Puriri St, off Taharepa Rd, has hot mineral spas and a cold swimming pool. Tent sites are $7 to $8 per person, caravan sites $8 to $9 per person, and cabins and on-site caravans are $25 to $35 for two.

The *Lake Taupo Holiday Park* (☎ 378 6860; fax 378 2377) is on Centennial Drive off Spa Rd, opposite the AC Thermal Baths and the Taupo Golf Club, about two km from the CPO. It's a seven-hectare park with tent and caravan sites at $8 per person, family cabins at $35 for two and tourist flats at $45 for two.

Acacia Holiday Park (☎ 378 5159) on Acacia Bay Rd, three km west of the town centre, has tent and powered sites at $8.25 per person, cabins at $25.50 for two, on-site caravans at $33 for two and tourist flats at $45 for two.

The *Wairakei Thermal Valley Motor Camp* (☎ 374 8004) is a small, peaceful camp in the Wairakei Thermal Valley north of Taupo. It has tent and powered sites at $6 per person, plus a couple of on-site caravans.

The *Windsor Fishing Lodge & Caravan Park* (☎ 378 6271) at Waitahanui, 12 km south of Taupo on SH 1, has tent sites at $8 per person, powered sites at $15 for two, cabins at $20/25 for one/two people, and two-bedroom motel units at $55 for two.

Hostels Several of Taupo's hostels, particularly the Rainbow and Sunset Lodges, arrange a host of activities at significantly discounted prices. Be sure to ask about this when you check in; there are lots of possibilities!

The *Taupo Associate YHA Hostel* (☎ 378 3311) on the corner of Kaimanawa and Tamamutu Sts is handy both to the town and the lakefront. It also has the best view of any hostel in Taupo, with second-floor decks looking out over the lake and south to the volcanoes of Tongariro National Park. There are plenty of decks and spaces for hanging out and meeting other travellers. The cost is $14 in all rooms, with two or three people per room.

Rainbow Lodge (☎ 378 5754; fax 377 1568) at 99 Titiraupenga St is a busy and popular hostel with an excellent reputation among travellers – so much so that it's often full in summer and it's a very good idea to book ahead at that time. There's a large communal area, a sauna and a games area; mountain bikes, fishing tackle and camping gear are available for hire, and they offer free luggage storage. The cost per night is $10 in large bunkrooms, $13 in smaller bunkrooms, $15 in twin and double rooms.

Nearby, *Burke's Backpackers* (☎ & fax 378 9292) at 69 Spa Rd has a hot spa pool, mountain bike hire, colour TV/video, and beer and wine available. The cost is $10 to $13.50 per person in dorm rooms, $15 in doubles and twins.

Berkenhoff Lodge (☎ 378 4909; fax 377 2365) on the corner of Duncan and Scannell Sts is a bit of a distance from the centre but they offer free pick-up when you arrive and free bicycles once you're there. It was formerly a private hotel, so the rooms all come with private bath; there's also a bar and games room, and plenty of off-street parking. The cost is $10 in bunkrooms, $13.50 in twins and doubles.

The *Sunset Lodge* (☎ 378 5962) at 5

Tremaine Ave, about two km south of the town centre along the lakeside road, is the smallest hostel in Taupo with 23 beds, and also the closest to the lake, 100 metres away. It has a comfortable atmosphere and friendly owners who offer lots of free services including free pick-up, shuttles to Craters of the Moon and the De Brett Thermal Pools, free bicycles, fishing tackle and an inflatable boat, a dinghy and a windsurfer you can take out on the lake. The nightly cost is $10 to $13 per person in bunkrooms, $14 to $15 in double or twin rooms.

Howard's Wairakei Lodge (☎ & fax 374 8265, mobile (025) 992 046) is at 10 Maire St in Wairakei Village, about six km north of Taupo near the junction of SH 5 to Rotorua and SH 1 to Hamilton. It's a large 120-bed hostel on 1.5 hectares of trees and lawn, originally built as a hostel for workers on the geothermal power plant. The cost is $12 per person in four-person bunkrooms, $15 per person in twin rooms and $20 in single rooms. Tent and caravan sites, all without power, are $8 per person. There's a takeaways restaurant on the premises; bicycles and 50cc scooters are available for hire.

Guesthouses Taupo has two pleasant, comfortable guest houses to choose from. *Bradshaw's Bed & Breakfast* (☎ 378 8288) at 130 Heu Heu St has a tearoom where all meals are available. B&B is $30 to $35 per single and $50 to $55 for twins or doubles; half the rooms have private facilities.

Gillies Lodge (☎ & fax 377 2377) at 77 Gillies Ave has panoramic views over the town and lake. Amenities include a bar and a spa pool, and evening meals are available. The cost is $45/63 for singles/doubles, including continental breakfast.

Hotels In the centre of town, the *Lake Hotel* (☎ 378 6165; fax 377 0150) on the corner of Tongariro and Tuwharetoa Sts has rooms at $15 per person with shared facilities and TV lounge, $30/45 for singles/doubles with private bath. The hotel has a Cobb & Co restaurant and the popular Freeman's Bar.

The *De Brett Thermal Hotel* (☎ 378 7080;

fax 378 4174) is three km from the town centre on SH 5, the Taupo-Napier Rd, one km from the lake and just a few metres from the De Brett Thermal Baths. It's a grand old hotel built in 1889, with a variety of accommodation including budget rooms at $18/30 for singles/doubles with shared bathroom, $25/35 with private bathroom, and regular rooms with private bath, TV, etc at $40/55. They also have four-person bunkrooms at $12.50 per person if you bring your own sleeping bag. There's a restaurant, and entertainment in the lounge bar (see Entertainment). A courtesy van is available for pick-up when you arrive.

The *Spa Hotel* (☎ 378 4120), two km from the CPO on Spa Rd, is opposite the AC Baths and it has its own heated outdoor and thermal indoor pools. The hotel is built on a historic site – this was the site of the Armed Constabulary during the Maori Wars in the 1860s – and there's an early 19th century Maori meeting house on the premises. Budget 'constabulary rooms' are $35/45 for singles/doubles; there are also chalets at $50/70. Before you decide that the Spa Hotel is your kind of place, see the description under Entertainment.

If money is no object and you're looking for the height of understated luxury, one of New Zealand's most expensive hotels is just outside Taupo. The *Huka Lodge* (☎ 378 5791; fax 378 0427) at Huka Falls has singles for $675 and doubles for $1000 a night!

Motels Taupo is packed with motels and as in Rotorua, the competition tends to keep prices down, although many of them have minimum rates during holiday periods. Economical, good-value motels include the *Dunrovin Motel* (☎ 378 7384) at 140 Heu Heu St, the *Continental Motel* (☎ 378 5836) at 9 Scannell St on the corner of Motutaiko St, and the *Golf Course Motel* (☎ 378 9415) at 123 Tauhara Rd, all similarly priced, with singles/doubles for around $50/60.

The *Courtney Motel* (☎ 378 8398; fax 378 9789) at 15 Tui St has a variety of units including studio units at $56/65 for singles/doubles, and one, two and three-bedroom units at $70 for two, $11 each extra person. The *Mountain View Motel* (☎ 378 9366; fax 377 3076) at 12-14 Fletcher St has singles at $45, doubles from $65 to $75.

Places to Eat

Snacks & Fast Food Taupo has the usual collection of sandwich places and takeaway bars. Down by the lakefront are a *Pizza Hut* and a *Kentucky Fried Chicken* side by side, and a *McDonald's* on the corner of Ruapehu St. Also along here is *Maxi's*, a 24-hour dairy/cafe with takeaways and inexpensive sit-down meals. On Tongariro St near the lakefront, *JD's Takeaways* does good fish & chips.

The *Happy Heart Wholefood Cafe* has delicious, inexpensive food with both vegetarian and meat selections. It's in the Marama walking arcade between Heu Heu and Horomatangi Sts, in the block between Tongariro and Ruapehu Sts. In the same block of Horomatangi St, the *Olive Branch Delicatessen* at No 19 has tasty food to take away or eat there, with some interesting selections like spicy Mexican stuffed potatoes and rich pastries. Nearby, the *Shawarma Bar* at 3 Horomatangi St has a selection of inexpensive middle eastern food, with vegetarian and meat selections, primarily to take away – it has just two stools if you want to eat there. Also in this same block of Horomatangi St, the *D21 Deli & Lunch Bar* has a wide selection of sandwiches and snacks to eat there or take away.

Over on Spa Rd, *Cafe Delight* behind Woolworth's is good for breakfast and lunch – they'll cook you up whatever you want if they have the ingredients for it. It's open Monday to Friday from 6.30 am to 3.30 pm. Opposite this, on Spa Rd near the Tongariro St roundabout, the *Pizza Man* is popular for pizzas and they also have a selection of $5 meals (lasagne, ravioli, nachos, chili con carne, curry, etc) to take away or eat there – you can phone for free delivery (☎ 378 3400) on orders of $15 or more.

Further up Spa Rd, *Gee Dub's Cafe* on the corner of Spa Rd and Pihanga St is good for

burgers, fish & chips and toasted sandwiches. The *Spa Bakery* in the same small shopping centre has good sandwiches and baked goods.

A large *Pak 'n Save* supermarket covering practically an entire block is on Paorahape St between Ruapehu and Taniwha Sts. The large *Woolworth's* supermarket is on the corner of Tongariro St and Spa Rd. Both are open seven days a week.

Pub Food There's a *Cobb & Co* in the Lake Hotel on the corner of Tongariro and Tuwharetoa Sts, open from 7.30 am to 10 pm daily with the usual Cobb & Co menu (steaks, salad bar, etc).

The *Red Barrel*, the popular restaurant/pub on the lakefront, serves bar meals. Nearby on the lake end of Tongariro St, *Safari Joe's Bar & Grill* has a menu featuring five kinds of steak, plus other foods. The *Spa Hotel* has a bar menu in the evening with dishes like fish & chips, pie and chips, sausage and chips or steak and chips.

Restaurants *Margarita's* at 63 Heu Heu St is a popular restaurant/bar with good Mexican food and great atmosphere, with music and a colourful Mexican decor featuring bright Aztec-style artwork. Regular dinner main courses are $12 to $19 but you can order from the special $5 backpackers menu. There are a few not-so-Mexican selections on the menu too. Margarita's is open every day from 4 pm to 2 am, with happy hours from 5 to 7 and 9 to 10 pm every night.

Hudder's Licensed Cafe at 22 Tuwharetoa St is a small licensed and BYO restaurant featuring an eclectic menu, giant portions, and various specials including 'two meals for the price of one' on Rocky's Ribs on Tuesday nights, free Steinlager with every steak on Wednesday nights, and free dessert with every main meal ordered between 4 and 6 pm, every day.

On the lakeside corner of Lake Terrace and Tongariro St, *Nonni's* is open every day as a cafe during the daytime, starting from 7 am, and an Italian dinner house in the evening. Just around the corner on the

Tongariro St side, the *Echo Cliff Licensed Restaurant* is a more up-market restaurant upstairs with a good view over the lake; count on spending around $25 for a three-course meal.

If you're going up-market, the *Edgewater Restaurant* at Manuel's Resort Hotel on the lakefront is an elegant and expensive but top-notch award-winning restaurant specialising in New Zealand food. Also here at Manuel's, *Pepper's Brasserie* is a more reasonably priced family restaurant (dinner mains around $20, pastas $15), and the same award-winning chef cooks for both. Both restaurants have a fine view of the lake, especially beautiful around sunset.

Entertainment

The *Great Lake Centre* (☎ 377 1200) on Tongariro St has a 350-seat theatre and a 500-seat hall for performances, exhibitions, conventions and events of all kinds. The information centre will have the current schedule.

The *Red Barrel* on the lakefront near Tongariro St is a lively pub, good for socialising, dancing and meeting the locals. It has live bands for dancing on Wednesday, Friday and Saturday nights. Nearby, the upstairs *Blacksmith's Arms* restaurant/bar has live entertainment and dancing on Thursday, Friday and Saturday nights. Both places are open every day from noon until 2 am.

Around the corner on the lake end of Tongariro St, *Safari Joe's Bar & Grill* is another pleasant hangout; you might catch Howard Morrison's backup band playing here on Friday nights. Further along on Tongariro St on the corner of Tuwharetoa St, *Freeman's Bar* has live bands for dancing on Thursday, Friday and Saturday nights.

De Brett's Thermal Hotel, three km from the centre and one km back from the lake on SH 5, the Taupo-Napier Rd, has a home-style country &western band in the lounge bar on Thursday nights; the atmosphere is casual and friendly and anyone can come and sit in for a song. On Friday, Saturday and Sunday nights they have other live music.

There are live bands every Friday and Saturday night at the *Spa Hotel*, two km east of the town centre along Spa Rd, opposite the AC Baths. Actually the Spa Hotel is entertainment all by itself. The cavernous public bar is definitely a fishin', huntin' and shootin' hangout. There are trophy heads mounted around the wall and the toilets are labelled 'stags' and 'hinds'. Nobody seems to buy beer in less than a litre jug at a time but you feel unsteady on your feet even without any beer on board since the carpet seems to be underlaid with about five cm of foam rubber. Must make for softer landings when you fall over.

Getting There & Away

Air Air New Zealand and Mt Cook Airline (☎ freephone (0800) 800 737) have direct flights to Auckland, Kaitaia, Rotorua and Wellington, with connections to other centres. Taupo Air Services (☎ 378 5325) has a Monday, Wednesday and Friday flight to Auckland.

None of these airlines has an office in town; their offices are at the airport. In town, their ticketing is handled through travel agencies, including the AA Travel Centre (see Information), Budget Travel (☎ 378 9799) at 37 Horomatangi St, and the James Holiday Shoppe (☎ 378 7065) in the same block of Horomatangi St.

Bus Taupo is about halfway between Auckland and Wellington. Being at the geographical centre of the island, it's a hub for bus transport.

Long-distance buses including InterCity, Newmans, Magic Bus and Alpine Scenic Tours arrive and depart from the Taupo Travel Centre (☎ 378 9032) at 17 Gascoigne St. The travel centre also sells tickets for trains and the Interislander ferry, and they will make bookings for accommodation and sightseeing.

InterCity and Newmans have several daily buses to Turangi (45 minutes), Auckland (five hours), Hamilton (two to three hours), Rotorua (one to 1½ hours), Tauranga (2½ hours), Napier (two hours), Wanganui (five hours), Palmerston North (three to 4½ hours, depending which bus) and Wellington (6½ hours).

Alpine Scenic Tours (☎ 378 6305) operates a daily shuttle service between Taupo and Turangi, connecting with their other shuttle service going from Turangi to National Park. This includes several stops in the Tongariro National Park, including the walking tracks. They also operate a Monday to Friday shuttle service between Turangi and Rotorua, stopping in Taupo on the way.

B&P Shuttle (☎ 348 2302, mobile (025) 971 791), affectionately known as 'the Pink Bus', operates a twice-daily door-to-door shuttle service between Taupo and Rotorua. Bookings can be made at the information centre on Tongariro St.

In winter, ski shuttle services operate between Taupo and the Whakapapa Ski Area, a 1¼ hour trip. They go every day and may include package deals for transport and ski hire. Bookings can be made from the information centre or from the hostels.

Getting Around
To/From the Airport The airport is six km south of Taupo. Taupo Taxis (☎ 378 5100) operates a door-to-door airport shuttle service; the cost is $6. A taxi trip costs about $15.

Bus Central Plateau Tours (24 hours (☎ 377 0774, mobile (025) 949 113) operates a door-to-door shuttle bus to the African Queen, Huka Jet-Boats and the Prawn Farm; the cost is $4 per person one way, $8 return, and bookings are essential.

The same company also operates a daily shuttle service to Orakei Korako; the cost is $7.50 one-way, $15 return.

Bicycle Mountain bikes can be hired from Cycle World (☎ 378 6117, after hours 378 0429) at 126 Ruapehu St, opposite the large Pak 'n Save supermarket. The cost is $15 for half a day, $25 for a full day.

Rapid Sensations (☎ 378 7902, mobile (025) 928 366) does guided mountain bike tours through Wairakei Park, or they'll also

hire you a mountain bike and let you do your own explorations.

AROUND TAUPO
Wairakei Park
Crossing the river at Tongariro St and heading north from town on SH 1, there are a number of interesting places to visit. Take the first right turn after you cross the river and you'll be on Huka Falls Rd, which passes along the river. At the end, turn left, back onto the highway, and you'll pass other interesting spots on your way back to town. We'll describe the attractions here in the order you'll reach them following this route. You could also do the loop in the other direction, going up the highway first and back down Huka Falls Rd. The whole area is called Wairakei Park, or the Huka Falls Tourist Loop.

There's no public transport serving this route, though this is an obvious need. A shuttle bus goes to the Prawn Farm and Huka Jet/African Queen dock (see Getting Around) and a couple of tours will take you to a few places along here. Otherwise you can walk (see Walks), hitch or hire a bicycle to come out for the day. Several of the hostels have bicycles, and guided bicycle tours are also available.

Huka Village
About 2.5 km from the centre of town, the first attraction you come to after turning onto Huka Falls Rd is Huka Village, a replica of an early New Zealand pioneer village. A number of historic buildings were restored and moved to the site and it functions as a working craft village with a farrier, blacksmith, potters and other craftspeople. There's also an aviary, a deer park and honey centre. Activities include horse-riding, river rafting, farmstays, hunting, fishing and launch cruises. The village is open in summer from 9 am to 5 pm daily and in winter from 9 am to 4 pm; admission is $4.50 (children free).

Huka Falls
A little further along Huka Falls Rd are the

CENTRAL NORTH ISLAND

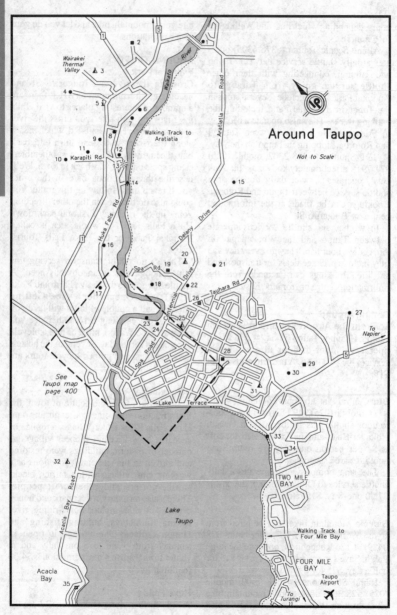

Around Taupo

Not to Scale

■ PLACES TO STAY

2 Howard's Wairakei Lodge
3 Wairakei Thermal Valley Motor Camp
19 Spa Hotel
20 Lake Taupo Holiday Park
25 Taupo All Seasons Holiday Park
26 Golf Course Motel
28 Gillies Lodge
29 De Brett Thermal Hotel
31 Hilltop Motor Caravan Park
32 Acacia Holiday Park
33 Manuel's Resort Hotel, Edgewater
    Restaurant & Pepper's Brasserie
34 Sunset Lodge
35 Acacia Bay Lodge

▼ PLACES TO EAT

33 Manuel's Resort Hotel, Edgewater
    Restaurant & Pepper's Brasserie

OTHER

1 Aratiatia
4 Wairakei Geothermal Power Project
5 Wairakei Geothermal Visitor Centre
6 Wairakei Prawn Farm
7 African Queen & *Huka Jet*
8 Honey Hive New Zealand
9 Wairakei International Golf Course
10 Craters of the Moon
11 Taupo Horse Treks
12 Helistar Helicopters & Cafe
13 Huka Falls Lookout
14 Huka Falls
15 Taupo Gliding Club, Racecourse &
    Motor Racing
16 New Zealand Woodcraft
17 Huka Village
18 Spa Thermal Park
21 Taupo Golf Club
22 A C Thermal Baths
23 Cherry Island
24 Taupo Bungy
27 Mt Tauhara Walk
30 De Brett Thermal Pools &
    De Brett Family Leisure Park

spectacular Huka Falls, *hukanui* in Maori meaning 'great body of spray'. A footbridge crosses the Waikato River above the falls, which plunge through a narrow cleft in the rock, dropping about 24 metres in all. The water here is incredibly clear and turquoise on a sunny day and it's worth making the trip to see.

Honey Hive New Zealand
Passing by the office and helipad of Helistar Helicopters (see them under Scenic Flights) you come to Honey Hive New Zealand, five km north of Taupo. It has three viewing hives (a glass hive, a commercial hive and a bush hive) set up for viewing, plus educational videos about bees and a number of honeys for tasting. It's open from 9 am to 5 pm every day; admission is free.

New Zealand Woodcraft
Further along you come to New Zealand Woodcraft, a showroom and workshop where you can see woodturning in action,

talk to the woodturner, choose your own piece of wood and watch it be woodturned, or if you know how to do it you can try the lathe yourself; they also offer woodturning instruction. They use all native New Zealand timbers and they say this place has the largest collection of native New Zealand woodturnings in the southern hemisphere. You can buy woodturned items here, and woodturning blanks of native New Zealand timbers to take home. It's open every day from 8 am to 5 pm; admission is free.

African Queen & Huka Jet
Next along, nine km north of Taupo, Huka Jet and the African Queen share a dock on the river. Together they make a bit of a strange pair, exemplifying 'the old and the new' of New Zealand river boating.

The African Queen (☎ 374 8338) is actually the historic MV *Waireka*, a 62-foot (18.6-metre), 46-passenger riverboat built by Yarrow & Co in England in 1908. It was once part of the A Hatrick & Co riverboat fleet operating on the Whanganui River (see the Whanganui National Park section for more on the history of this riverboat fleet). After over 85 years of continuous service, the boat is still operating. It makes cruises daily at 10 am and 2 pm, and in the evening by floodlight, with times varying according to the season; the cruises all cost the same at $18 (children $8).

Partly inspired by the engineering of riverboats like the *Waireka*, which has a draught of only 12 inches (30.5 cm) laden, New Zealander CWF Hamilton was inspired to invent the jet-boat in 1958. The *Huka Jet* (☎ 374 8572) departs from the same dock for a 30-minute ride down to the Aratiatia Dam and up to the Huka Falls. Trips go half-hourly all day long; the cost is $39.50 (children $20).

Wairakei Prawn Farm

Almost next door to the Huka Jet and the African Queen, the Wairakei Prawn Farm (☎ 374 8474) is the world's only geothermally heated freshwater prawn farm. Interesting guided tours of the prawn farm show you where and how the prawns are grown, and tell you about their life cycle. The tours last 20 to 25 minutes and depart every hour on the hour from 11 am to 4 pm; the cost is $3.

If all the talk about prawns makes you start thinking about lunch, rest assured – prawns are always available here for eating, though they don't give out free samples. There's a prawn BBQ daily from noon to 3 pm (the cost is $20), and a prawn dinner is served every evening (bookings essential). Or you can do a combination 'Huka Prawns Cruise' combining the African Queen cruise with the BBQ lunch; the cost is $38 (children $15). Or you can have a snack of prawns for about $9. The Prawn Farm is open every day from 9 am to 9 pm.

North of the Prawn Farm, Huka Falls Rd comes out onto the highway, SH 1, near the junction where SH 1 veers off towards Hamilton and SH 5 heads north to Rotorua. Either way will get you to a turn-off for Orakei Korako (see the Around Taupo section),

since Orakei Korako lies between the two highways, but the highway to Hamilton is the shorter one to take for Orakei Korako.

Head north a few km on SH 5, the route towards Rotorua, and you'll come to the turn-off for Aratiatia.

Aratiatia

Two km off SH 5 are the Aratiatia Rapids, a spectacular part of the Waikato River until the government, in its wisdom, plonked a power house and dam down here, shutting off the water to the rapids. To keep the tourists happy they open the control gates at 10 am and 2.30 pm daily. That's the time to be there to see the water flow through, and there are three good lookout points to see it from. It's all open land, with no admission charge.

From Aratiatia, if you're doing the loop, head back down the highway, SH 1, towards Taupo and you'll pass some amazing thermal areas. If you're coming into Taupo from Rotorua or Hamilton, you will pass all these places as you approach Taupo.

Wairakei Thermal Valley

If you are not too distracted by all the steam from the Geothermal Power Project, you'll see a 1.5-km road on your right leading to the Wairakei Thermal Valley. Wairakei, like Orakei Korako, gets its name from being the place where the waters were used as mirrors. This is the remains of what was once known as Geyser Valley. Before the geothermal power project started in 1959 this was one of the most active thermal areas in the world, with 22 geysers and 240 mud pools and springs. Now the neighbouring geothermal power project has sucked off the steam, and only eight or nine mud pools remain active. There's a bush walk to the Huiata pools but they're only active after a heavy rain. Entry is $5 (children $1) and it's open from 9 am to 5 pm every day, later in summer. Also here is the Barn Tearooms and a pleasant motor camp.

Wairakei Geothermal Power Project

New Zealand was the second country in the world to produce power from natural steam.

If you dive into all that steam you will find yourself at the Wairakei Geothermal Power Project which generates about 150,000 kW, providing about 5% of New Zealand's total electrical power.

The Wairakei Geothermal Visitor Centre is close to the road, where you can make an educational stop between 9 am and 4.30 pm daily. Information on the bore field and power house is available and an audiovisual is shown up until half an hour before closing time. You can drive up the road through the project and from a lookout see the long stretches of pipe, wreathed in steam.

Just south of here is the Wairakei International Golf Course.

Craters of the Moon

Craters of the Moon is an interesting and unexploited thermal area where admission is free. The area is well fenced for safety purposes, but not overdone as commercially exploited thermal areas can be. It's run by the DOC and is open from dawn to dusk. Be careful when you leave your car as things have been stolen from cars here.

Craters of the Moon is signposted on SH 1 about five km north of Taupo. It's the last sight you'll come to if you've done the loop in the way we did – or the first, if you're going in the other direction.

Orakei Korako

Between Taupo and Rotorua is one of the finest thermal areas of New Zealand – Orakei Korako. Its remoteness is what stops people going there, but it's worth the trip if you can make it. It's 23 km off the Rotorua-Taupo highway and 14 km off the Hamilton-Taupo highway or 37 km from Taupo itself – that is, about a 25-minute drive north from Taupo or a 45-minute drive south from Rotorua.

After the destruction of the Pink and White Terraces by the Tarawera eruption, Orakei Korako was possibly the best thermal area left in New Zealand and one of the finest in the world. Although three-quarters of it now lies beneath the waters of artificial Lake Ohakuri, which was formed by a hydroelec-

tric dam, the quarter that remains is the best part, and still very much worth seeing.

A well laid out walking track takes you around the large, colourful silica terraces for which Orakei Korako is famous, as well as geysers and Aladdin's Cave – a magnificent natural cave with a pool of jade-green water. The pool is said to have been used by Maoris as a mirror during hairdressing ceremonies; the name Orakei Korako means 'the place of adorning'.

You can get to Orakei Korako by shuttle bus from Taupo (see Taupo's 'Getting Around' section), otherwise you can go on a tour, or you could probably manage to hitch there. The admission charge of $10 (children $4, family $25) includes entry to the valley, the cave, and a boat ride across Lake Ohakuri. Canoes and dinghies are available for hire, and there are jet-boat rides, and two hot tubs. It's open from 8.30 am to 4.30 pm (4 pm in winter) every day.

There is accommodation at Orakei Korako if you want to spend the night (☎ 378 3131; fax 378 0371). An 18-room lodge, with two to six beds per room, has shared kitchen and bath facilities; all the kitchen equipment is there, you just have to bring your own food and bedding. The cost is $16 per person. There are also tourist flats sleeping six people at $40 for two. If you have a tent or caravan you can stay overnight for free.

Turangi

On the south shore of Lake Taupo, on the northern end of the Tongariro National Park, Turangi (population 3850) is a new town, developed for the construction of the hydroelectric power station, built here in 1973. It's a good access point for the tracks at the northern end of the park. It also has some of the most famous trout fishing in the world (the Tongariro River is world renowned), a trout hatchery where you can learn about trout, a power station offering free tours, and some thermal hot pools at nearby Tokaanu with a small thermal area alongside that's free to walk through, and plenty of other good walks.

Turangi is the name of the town (named after a Maori chief); Turangi/Tongariro is the name of the local area, which includes Turangi, Tokaanu and the lakeside villages heading up around the east side of Lake Taupo towards Taupo. You'll see both names used around the area.

Information

The excellent Turangi Information Centre (☎ 386 8999; fax 386 0074) is opposite the Turangi Shopping Mall, just off SH 1. It has a detailed model of the Tongariro National Park and lots of information on the area's many activities. The office also makes bookings for activities, accommodation and transport bookings. It has many useful maps of the region including one showing all the trout pools on the Tongariro River, maps of the Tongariro National Park and Kaimanawa

---

Trout

The Department of Conservation (DOC) operates three trout hatcheries in New Zealand – one in Wanaka in the South Island, one near Rotorua and the one in Turangi. The Wanaka hatchery is more for salmon than trout, while the two North Island hatcheries are almost exclusively for rainbow trout. There are other private hatcheries, some of which obtain their eggs from the DOC operations.

The first brown trout eggs arrived in New Zealand from Tasmania in 1867. They had originally come to Australia from England. Rainbow trout eggs first arrived from California in 1883. Hatcheries were established at that time to rear the first young fish, and although many fish are hatched naturally nowadays, there is still a need for artificial hatcheries. This is because New Zealand's lakes and rivers may be ideal for trout but some of them have insufficient good spawning grounds. Plus there's a lot of fishing going on (although there are tight limitations on the number of fish that can be caught).

In the wild, fully grown trout migrate each winter to suitable spawning beds. This usually means gravel beds in the upper reaches of rivers and streams. Here a female fish makes a shallow depression and deposits eggs which are quickly fertilised by an attendant male fish. The female fish then sweeps gravel over the eggs. Over two or three days this process is repeated to create a redd with several pockets of eggs. All through this process the fish do not feed and a female fish may lose one-third of her body weight by the time she returns to the lake. Male fish are in even worse shape because they arrive at the spawning grounds before the females and leave afterwards.

Less than 1% of the eggs survive to become mature fish. The eggs may be damaged or destroyed by movement of the gravel and even when hatched they may be eaten by other fish, birds or rats. Even other trout will happily make a meal of them.

Because there were only a few shipments of eggs originally, from which all today's trout are descended, New Zealand's rainbow trout are considered to be a very pure strain. The hatchery eggs are collected by capturing fish during their spawning run. Eggs are gently squeezed from a female fish and milt from males added and stirred together in a container. Incubator trays containing about 10,000 eggs are placed in racks and washed over by a continuous flow of water.

After 15 days the embryo fish eyes start to appear and by the 18th day the embryos, previously very sensitive and frail, have become quite hardy. They'd better be because on that day the eggs are poured from a metre height into a wire basket. Any weak eggs are killed off by this rough treatment, ensuring that only healthy fish are hatched out. The survivors are now placed 5000 to a basket and about 10 days later the fish hatch out, wriggle through the mesh and drop to the bottom of the trough. They stay there for about 20 days, living off the yolk sac.

When they have totally absorbed their yolk sac they are known as fry and although they can be released at this stage they are normally kept until they are 10 to 15 cm long. At this time they are nine to 12 months old and are known as fingerlings. They are moved outside when they are about four cm long and reared in ponds. Fingerlings are transported to the place where they will be released in what looks rather like a small petrol tanker, and simply pumped out the back down a large diameter pipe! ■

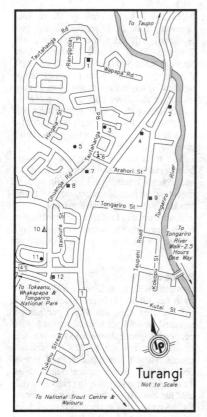

Turangi
Not to Scale

To National Trout Centre & Waiouru

1   Bellbird Lodge
2   Sportsmans Lodge
3   Avis Rent-A-Car &
    Alpine Scenic Tours
4   Tongariro River Motel
5   Turangi Shopping Mall & CPO
6   Turangi Information Centre &
    Automobile Association (AA)
7   Aurora Lodge
8   River Rats Lodge
9   Creel Lodge
10 Turangi Holiday Park
11 Department of Conservation (DOC)
12 Anglers Paradise Motel

Forest Park, and a DOC leaflet showing walks in and around the Turangi and Tongariro regions. The centre is open every day from 9 am to 5 pm.

During the ski season, the information centre has weather, road conditions and ski reports, and they always have fishing reports.

The DOC Tongariro/Taupo Conservancy office (☎ 386 8607; fax 386 7086) near the junction of SH 1 and Ohuanga Rd is open the usual DOC hours of 8 am to 4.30 pm, Monday to Friday. It offers a good summer activities programme from 26 December to mid-January.

The information centre is the AA agent for the town. The post office and several banks are in the Turangi Shopping Mall, opposite the information centre.

Remember, if you'll be doing any fishing, you must obtain a licence. Licences are available at the information centre, at the 24-hour petrol station, at Sporting Life and Griegs Sports in the Turangi Shopping Mall, and at many other places around the area.

Tongariro National Trout Centre
Four km south of Turangi on SH 1 is the Tongariro National Trout Centre, an important trout hatchery. It's open every day from 9 am to 4 pm and entry is free. There's an underwater viewing area, keeping ponds, a pleasant picnic area and then you could try your hand on the real grown-up thing in the Tongariro River which runs close by.

Tokaanu
About five km out of Turangi on the road round the western side of Lake Taupo towards Taumarunui is this pleasant little pioneer settlement (population 200) with an interesting thermal area. There's a posted walk around the bubbling mud pools and beside this, the Tokaanu Thermal Pools with hot pools and a sauna. The walk is free, the public pool costs $2.50 (children $1), private pools are $3.50, and it's $6 for the sauna (children $2.50). The pools are open every day from 10 am to 9 pm, the private pools until 9.30 pm. Take a look at the interesting

exhibits about the history of this thermal area.

The Tokaanu Visitor Centre at the Tokaanu Power Station off SH 47 is an interesting place to visit if you like this sort of thing. It has exhibits and a 17-minute documentary about the power station and the Tongariro Power Scheme, followed by a free 15-minute tour through the power station. Hydroelectric power is very important to New Zealand – 80% of the country's power is hydroelectrically generated. This power station was built in 1973 and 10% of the North Island's power is produced here. The Visitor Centre is open Monday to Saturday from 10 am to 4 pm.

There's not much else to see in Tokaanu but if you want to stay over, there are various accommodation possibilities including a motor camp, a lodge and a motel.

There's easy lake access here in Tokaanu – the road is opposite the Tokaanu Hotel – with much bird life on the shore.

Walks

Turangi is handy to walks in the Tongariro National Park, and there are a number of other good walks closer in. Pick up the DOC *Turangi Walks* leaflet from the DOC office or the information centre. Notable walks include a Tongariro River Walkway (three hours return), a Tongariro River Loop Track (one hour), Hinemihi's Track near the top of Te Ponanga Saddle (15 minutes return), a walk on Mt Maunganamu (40 minutes return) and a walk around Lake Rotopounamu, which abounds in bird life (20 minutes to the lake, then 1½ hours around the lake). Off SH 47 there's a walk to see the Te Porere Redoubt, a historic site (30 minutes return; for more information, see Walks, Tongariro National Park in this chapter). Closer in, there's the thermal walk beside the Tokaanu Thermal Pools (20 minute loop track, wheelchair accessible). There are plenty of other walks too, especially in the Kaimanawa Forest Park.

Other Things to Do

Turangi is a popular base for lake and river fishing, walking and rafting. River Rats, operating from the River Rats Lodge (see Hostels), will take you rafting on the Tongariro River, as will Tongariro River Rafting (☎ 386 6409, mobile (025) 428 198). All rafting trips and other activities can be booked through the information centre. Guests at the River Rats Lodge receive a guests' discount on their rafting trips and many other activities. Check with them for the activities they do – it's not just a rafting company anymore.

The information centre also arranges horse treks, hunting and fishing trips, cruises and charter boats, scenic minibus tours, mountain biking, kayaking, scenic flights and anything else you can think of.

Aluminum dinghies with outboard motors can be hired from Braxmere Lodge in Waihi Village, three km south-west of Tokaanu off SH 41.

Places to Stay

Camping & Cabins *Turangi Holiday Park* (☎ & fax 386 8754) is on Ohuanga Rd, off SH 41. Tent sites are $7.50 per person, powered sites $8 per person, cabins $14.50 per person, other cabins are $34 for two, and on-site caravans are $32/38 for one/two people. There's also a backpackers rate of $6/12.50 per person in tent sites/cabins. Towels, bedding and sleeping bags are available for hire. At one time this was quarters for the power station construction workers, which accounts for the large number of cabins.

At Tokaanu the *Oasis Motel & Caravan Park* (☎ 386 8569; fax 386 0694) on SH 41 has campsites at $6.50 per person, $8 with power, cabins at $15 per person, studio units at $45/50 for one/two people, and family units at $55/63. They also have hot pools and spa pools.

There are several other campsites out of Turangi on the lakeside road to Taupo. The *Motuoapa Domain Camp* (☎ 386 7162), eight km out at Motuoapa, has campsites at $7.50 per person. The *Tauranga-Taupo Lodge & Caravan Park* (☎ 386 8385; fax 386 8386), 11 km north of Turangi at

Tauranga-Taupo, offers campsites, cabins, tourist flats, family units and bedroom units. Or there's the *Motutere Bay Caravan Park* (☎ 386 8963), 17 km north at Motutere Bay, with tent/caravan sites at $6/7.50 per person and tourist flats at $40 for two. It has some campsites right on the lake edge, others across the road with a bit of a view; the lake edge sites cost $1 more. Fishing tackle and licences are available.

Hostels Right in the centre is the *River Rats Lodge* (☎ 386 7492; fax 386 0106) on Ohuanga Rd, a large place with 3.8 hectares of grounds and 196 beds in a number of separate accommodation blocks. Facilities include sauna, spa, a licensed restaurant, bar, BBQ, guests' kitchen, a TV room and more. A wide variety of activities can be arranged at a discount, including white water rafting trips. The costs are $14 per person in shared rooms with your own sleeping bag, $20 with linen provided, and they also have tourist cabins at $45 for two and en-suite motel units at $65 for two. Tent sites are $7 per person, powered sites $18 for two. A daily all-you-can-eat continental breakfast is $5.

In contrast, the *Bellbird Lodge* (☎ 386 8281, mobile (025) 996 494) at 3 Rangipoia Place is a small, homely hostel with just 12 beds and a spacious lounge area and kitchen. The cost is $15 per person in twin, double and dorm rooms. They do fishing trips on the lake for $15 per person/per hour.

Hotels, Motels & Lodges There are plenty of motels and fishing lodges in Turangi. This is a very popular area for trout fishing and, like the campsites, some of them are round the lakeshore towards Taupo. The Turangi Information Centre does bookings for all the area's accommodation.

The *Sportsmans Lodge* (☎ 386 8150) at 15 Taupehi Rd has rooms sharing a communal kitchen and TV lounge at $35/45 for singles/doubles, with a $5 discount if you stay for two nights or more. The *Aurora Lodge* (☎ 386 0115; fax 386 0815) on the corner of SH 1 and Pihanga Rd has studio units at $55/60 for singles/doubles; there's a

spa pool, house bar and licensed restaurant. The *Creel Lodge* (☎ & fax 386 8081) at 165 Taupehi Rd has bedroom and family units at around $55/70 for singles/doubles. The *Tongariro River Motel* (☎ 386 8555; fax 386 0146) on the corner of SH 1 and Taupehi Rd has studio units at $55/67.50, bedroom units at $67.50 and family units at $75 for two.

There's some interesting accommodation in nearby Tokaanu including the *Tokaanu Lodge* (☎ 386 8572; fax 386 8592) with three private mineral pools, a covered outdoor pool, a fish cleaning area and a fish freezer/smoker. The cost is $72 for one-bedroom units, $105 for two-bedroom family units. Also at Tokaanu is the *Oasis Motel* (see Camping & Cabins).

Places to Eat
The Turangi Shopping Mall has two large supermarkets, both open seven days a week, and a variety of places to eat. *Vaughan's Takeout* is a good takeaway. *L Jay's Cafe*, opposite the information centre, is also good. Simple cafes include *Coffee Time*, the *Mountains Cafe* and the *Hong Kong Chinese Takeaways*. *Valentino's* and *El Burcio* are good Italian restaurants, solid reminders of the many Italian construction workers here at the time the power station was built.

Entertainment
The hotel taverns in Turangi and Tokaanu sometimes have live bands; check with the information centre.

Getting There & Away
Bus InterCity and Newmans buses stop at the Avis Rent-A-Car office (☎ 386 8918) on the corner of Ohuanga Rd and Ngawaka Place. Tickets for buses, trains and the Inter-islander ferry are sold at this office, and at the information centre. The Avis office is open Monday to Friday from 8 am to 5 pm.

Auckland-Wellington and Rotorua-Wellington buses running along the eastern side of the lake to/from Taupo, 45 minutes to the north, all stop at Turangi.

Getting Around

Also operating from the Avis Rent-A-Car office, Alpine Scenic Tours (☎ 386 8918, after hours 386 8459/8055, Taupo 378 6305) runs a shuttle service several times daily between Turangi and National Park, stopping along the way in the Tongariro National Park – at the Ketetahi trail head, the Mangatepopo trail head, Whakapapa Village (the Chateau), and in winter the Whakapapa Ski Area (Top of the Bruce). It's an excellent service for skiers and trampers. They also operate services to/from Taupo and a Monday to Friday service to/from Rotorua.

Tongariro National Park

Tongariro, established in 1887, was New Zealand's first national park. It was given to the country in September 1887 by Horonuku Te Heuheu Tukino, a far-sighted paramount chief of the Ngati Tuwharetoa people who realised that this was the only way to preserve an area of such spiritual significance in its entirety. The name Tongariro originally covered the three mountains of the park (Tongariro, Ngauruhoe and Ruapehu) and means *tonga*, south wind; *riro*, carried away. The story goes that Ngatoro-i-rangi was stuck on the summit and almost perishing from the cold. He called to his sisters in Hawaiki for fire and his words were carried to them on the south wind.

With its collection of mighty (and still active) volcanoes, Tongariro is one of the most interesting and spectacular parks in New Zealand. In the summer it's got excellent walks and tramps and in the winter it's an important ski area.

There are two main ski areas – the Whakapapa Ski Area up above Whakapapa Village on the north side of the park and the Turoa Ski Area on the south side of the park near Ohakune. The Tukino Ski Area on the east side of Mt Ruapehu is a private club ski area and much less popular, requiring a 4WD vehicle to get to it and having only three rope tows once you're there. See the Skiing section in the Outdoor Activities chapter for more details on skiing in the park.

Mt Ruapehu is the highest of the volcanoes at 2797 metres and is still active – it's also the site for all the ski runs. The upper slopes were showered with hot mud and water in the volcanic activity of 1969 and 1975, and in December 1988 the volcano threw out some very hot rocks. The long, multi-peaked summit of Ruapehu shelters Crater Lake, which you can climb up to if you're well prepared.

Between 1945 and 1947 the level of Crater Lake rose dramatically when eruptions blocked the overflow. On Christmas Eve 1953 the overflow burst and the flood that resulted led to one of New Zealand's worst disasters. The torrent swept away a railway bridge moments before a crowded express train arrived and in the resulting crash 153 people lost their lives.

Mt Tongariro, at 1968 metres, is another old volcano but it is still considered active – it last erupted in 1926. It has a number of coloured lakes dotting its uneven summit as well as hot springs gushing out of its side at Ketetahi. The Tongariro Crossing, a magnificent walk, passes beside the lakes, right through several craters, on to the hot springs, and down the other side through lush native forest; details on this famous walk are given in the Tramping section of the Outdoor Activities chapter.

Mt Ngauruhoe is much younger than the other volcanoes in the park – it's estimated to have formed in the last 2500 years and the slopes to the 2291 metre summit are still perfectly symmetrical. In contrast to Ruapehu and Tongariro which have multiple vents, Mt Ngauruhoe is a conical, single-vent volcano. It can be climbed in summer, but in winter and under snow conditions it is definitely suitable only for experienced mountaineers. It's a very steep but rewarding climb. Between Ngauruhoe and Ruapehu are the Tama Lakes, explosion craters which have filled with water.

Information

In Whakapapa Village, on the north side of

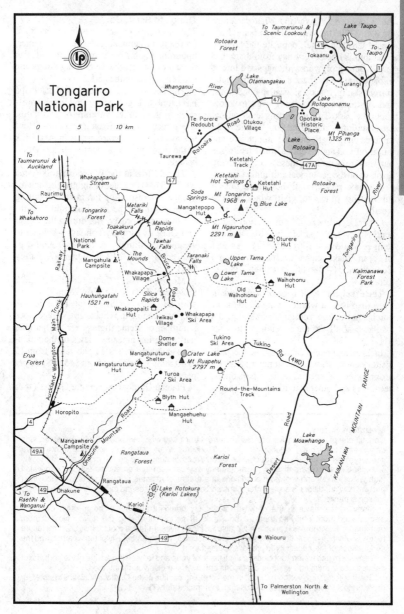

Tongariro
National Park

0   5   10 km

To Taumarunui &
Scenic Lookout

Lake Taupo

Rotoaira
Forest

Whanganui   River

Lake
Otamangakau

To
Taumarunui &
Auckland

Whakapapanui
Stream

Raurimu

To
Whakahoro

Tongariro
Forest

Matariki
Falls

Toakakura
Falls

National
Park

Mahuia
Rapids

Tawhai
Falls

Mangahuia
Campsite

The
Mounds

Hauhungatahi
1521 m

Whakapapa
Village

Silica
Rapids

Whakapapaiti
Hut

Iwikau
Village

Erua
Forest

Dome
Shelter

Mangaturuturu
Shelter

Mangaturuturu
Hut

Horopito

Turoa
Ski Area

Blyth Hut

Mangaehuehu
Hut

Mangawhero
Campsite

Rangataua
Forest

Rangataua

Ohakune

To
Raetihi &
Wanganui

Karioi

Lake Rotokura
(Karioi Lakes)

Karioi
Forest

To Palmerston North &
Wellington

Te Porere
Redoubt

Otukou
Village

Rotoaira

Taurewa

Lake
Rotoaira

Opotaka
Historic
Place

Mt Pihanga
1325 m

Ketetahi
Track

Ketetahi
Hot Springs

Ketetahi
Hut

Rotoaira
Forest

Soda
Springs

Mt Tongariro
1968 m

Blue Lake

Mangatepopo
Hut

Mt Ngauruhoe
2291 m

Oturere
Hut

Taranaki
Falls

Upper Tama
Lake

Lower Tama
Lake

New
Waihohonu
Hut

Old
Waihohonu
Hut

Whakapapa
Ski Area

Tukino
Ski Area

Tukino Rd (4WD)

Crater Lake

Mt Ruapehu
2797 m

Round-the-Mountains
Track

Lake
Moawhango

Kaimanawa
Forest
Park

KAIMANAWA   MOUNTAIN   RANGE

Tokaanu

Turangi

Lake
Rotopounamu

To
Taupo

Waiouru

Main Trunk Railway

Auckland–Wellington

Ohakune   Mountain   Road

Desert   Road

Bruce   Road

Rotoaira   Road

Tongariro   River

the park, the Whakapapa Visitor Centre (☎ 892 3729; fax 892 3814) is behind the Grand Chateau Hotel, opposite the holiday park, and is open every day from 8 am to 5 pm. It can supply you with maps and lots of information on the park and its walks, huts, current skiing, track and weather conditions, and anything else you may want to know about the park. Two interesting audio-visual presentations, including an excellent 27 minutes on the park and a 15-minute presentation on volcanoes, cost a small fee to see but they're worth it; these and the many displays on the geological and human history of the park, plus a small shop, make this an interesting place to visit whatever the weather.

Other Department of Conservation visitor centres serving the park include the Ohakune Ranger Station (☎ (06) 385 8578; fax 385 8128) in Ohakune and the Tongariro/Taupo Conservancy (☎ 386 8607; fax 386 7086) in Turangi.

The excellent DOSLI *Tongariro National Park* map is well worth having a look at or purchasing before you go off trekking. It's available at all the park visitor centres for $11.

In December and January, ask the park visitor centres about their summer activities programme of special walks, heli-bikes, heli-hikes and other activities.

Things to See & Do

The most popular activities in the park are tramping in summer and skiing in winter; opportunities for both are magnificent. But there are several other interesting things you can see and do in the park.

The Grand Chateau Hotel in Whakapapa has a nine-hole golf course and tennis courts open to the public, with hire of golf clubs, tennis racquets, etc. Even if you can't afford to stay at the hotel, you can stop in for a drink in the lobby just to savour the elegant atmosphere.

The ski lifts at the Whakapapa Ski Area (☎ 892 3738) operate for sightseeing and for trampers' transport up the mountain during the peak summer periods from mid-December to early February, and during the Easter and Queen's Birthday holidays – subject to weather conditions. A return (round-trip) ride costs about $12 (children $7, family $31).

Mountain Air (☎ 892 2812, (06) 522 9734, mobile ☎ (025) 976 978 or 976 979), with an office on SH 47 near the SH 48 turn-off heading to Whakapapa Village, does a number of scenic flights over the national park, offering amazing views of the volcanoes and their craters. Flights range from 15 to 40 minutes and cost from $45 to $100 per person.

Plateau Outdoor Adventure Guides (☎ &

Mountain Safety

Consult one of the park visitor centres for current track and weather conditions before embarking on any track in the park, especially the high-altitude tracks, and make sure someone knows where you're going and when you expect to be back. Weather conditions on the mountains are highly changeable; a pleasant hike on a warm sunny day can turn to a gruesome fight for survival in high winds, snow and white-out conditions in a matter of minutes *at any time of year*. In winter and in snow conditions ice axes, crampons and alpine mountaineering experience are necessary for some tracks.

Many of the walks in the park are stunningly beautiful and not to be missed. Don't be discouraged from enjoying them – thousands of people (including us) have enjoyed them immensely. Nevertheless, people have also lost their lives on these mountains, often by failure to follow obvious precautions. It's easy to underestimate the changeability of the weather, and the seriousness of the necessity to prepare yourself for it.

Take warm and waterproof clothing at all times of year, and to heed the advice of the park visitor centres about track and weather conditions and anything else you might need.

See the Tongariro Northern Circuit in the Tramping section of the Outdoor Activities chapter for more on this track, the Tongariro Crossing, and track safety. ∎

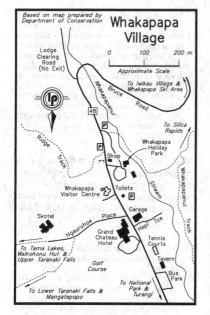

Based on map prepared by Department of Conservation

Whakapapa Village

fax 892 2740), based at Raurimu six km north of National Park township, offers a wide variety of activities around Tongariro National Park, Whanganui National Park and the surrounding region. Some of their specialties include canoeing, white water rafting and tandem rafting on the Tongariro, Whakapapanui, Upper Rangitikei, Ngaururoro, Whanganui and Manganui-A-Te-Ao Rivers; waterfall kayaking over the six-metre Tawhai Falls; winter and summer mountaineering, tramping and ski touring expeditions; rock climbing, abseiling and caving in the Okupata cave system; horse trekking; and if you can think of any other outdoor adventures they'll do those too.

To the east of Mt Ruapehu is an area known as the Rangipo Desert. It's not a desert in the true sense of the word, but was so named because of its desert-like appearance caused by its cold, exposed, windswept situation. SH 1, going down the east side of the national park, is called the Desert Rd.

Walks

The park visitor centres at Whakapapa, Ohakune and Turangi have maps, brochures and current information on a number of interesting short and long walks in the park. Be sure to ask them about current track and weather conditions before you set off.

The Tongariro Crossing, known as 'the finest one-day walk in New Zealand', is described in the Tramping section of the Outdoor Activities chapter. Along with the Tongariro Northern Circuit track of which it is a part, it has been designated one of New Zealand's 'Great Walks'.

If you're a keen tramper you can do the entire Round-the-Mountains Track, circling around both Mt Ruapehu and Mt Ngauruhoe; this track has eight huts, it can be accessed at various points around the national park and it requires about five to six days to complete. Consult with one of the park visitor centres about current track and weather conditions and for a map before embarking on this track.

A number of fine walks begin at or near the Whakapapa Visitor Centre and from the road leading up to it; these are covered here. Several other good walks take off from the Ohakune Mountain Rd, leading from Ohakune up to the Turoa Ski Area; they are covered in the Ohakune section.

Walks from Whakapapa Village include:

Whakapapa Nature Walk – A 15-minute round-trip track suitable for wheelchairs, beginning about 200 metres above the Whakapapa Vistor Centre. The track passes through beech forest and a number of gardens demonstrating the various vegetation zones of the park.

Mounds Walk – A 20-minute return walk, beginning four km below the Whakapapa Visitor Centre on SH 48. An interpretive track passing beside volcanic mounds deposited thousands of years ago, offering explanations and good views.

Tawhai Falls – A 20-minute return walk, beginning 3.5 km below the Whakapapa Visitor Centre on SH 48, leads to this six-metre waterfall.

Ridge Track – A 30-minute return walk, beginning 100 metres above the Whakapapa Visitor Centre, climbs through beech forest to alpine shrublands for panoramic views of Mt Ruapehu, Mt Ngauruhoe and the surrounding area.

Silica Rapids – A 2½ hour, eight km loop track beginning 200 metres above the Whakapapa Visitor Centre, this track goes to the Silica Rapids, named for the silica mineral deposits formed here by the rapids on the Waikare Stream. A waterfall and other interesting alpine features are passed along the way; the final two km is back down the Bruce Rd above Whakapapa Village.

Whakapapanui Track – Starting from the same point as the Silica Rapids track, this two-hour, six-km return track follows the Whakapapanui Stream beside the road; one hour is walked along the stream, the other along the road.

Whakapapanui Gorge – Not on a formed track, this is a full-day trip, for which you'll need boots. Follow the road above the Chateau up to the footbridge across the Whakapapanui Stream. Don't cross the bridge, but go to your left and follow the stream, rock-hopping up until you eventually enter the gorge itself with a sheer precipice at its head.

Taranaki Falls – A two-hour, six-km loop track, beginning at Ngauruhoe Place, 100 metres below the Whakapapa Visitor Centre, goes to the 20-metre Taranaki Falls on the Wairere Stream.

Tama Lakes – Beginning at the same place as the Taranaki Falls track, this 16-km track to the Tama Lakes takes about five to six hours return. On the Tama Saddle between Mt Ruapehu and Mt Ngauruhoe, the Tama Lakes are great for a refreshing swim in summer. The upper lake affords fine views of Mt Ngauruhoe and Mt Tongariro. Beware of windy conditions on this walk, as the Tama Saddle acts as a wind funnel for the prevailing westerly winds.

Whakapapaiti Valley – This five-hour, 10-km walk begins at Scoria Flat, five km above Whakapapa Village on Bruce Rd, and ends at Whakapapa Village. It follows the Round-the-Mountains Track for a short distance, then descends to the Whakapapaiti Hut and on down the valley, crossing the Whakapapaiti Stream, finally descending through beech forest back to Whakapapa Village. A bridge in one spot has been washed out, so you may have to wade across the stream after heavy rain.

Crater Lake – The walk to Crater Lake in the crater of Mt Ruapehu begins at Iwikau Village, at the top of Mt Bruce Rd above Whakapapa village, and takes about seven hours return (about four hours up, three hours down). It's definitely not an easy stroll; the track is not marked so you must be especially wary of white-outs and of your route when coming back down. Even in summer, there may be ice and snow to get through; check with the Whakapapa Visitor Centre for current weather conditions before you set off. Boots, sunglasses and windproof clothing are always essential; ice axes and crampons may be needed.

If the chair lift at Whakapapa Ski Area is operating, you can use it to help you get up the mountain; in that case, the walk to the crater takes only about three hours (two hours up, one hour down). It is also possible to reach Crater Lake starting from the Ohakune side, but from this side the track is steeper and ice axes and crampons are necessary all year round since you must climb up a steep glacier. If you do start from the Ohakune side, allow at least five hours up and three hours to get back down. Most people find it much better to start from the Whakapapa side.

Other good walks start from the car park at the end of the six-km Mangatepopo access road, which enters the park from SH 47. The Mangatepopo Hut, not far from the car park, makes a convenient place to stay. Walks beginning here include:

Soda Springs – This one-hour, four-km track goes to Soda Springs, a cold spring making a small waterfall.

Mangatepopo Saddle – Continuing on past Soda Springs, another half-hour's steep climb brings you to the Mangatepopo Saddle, between Mt Tongariro and Mt Ngauruhoe, with fine views.

Mt Ngauruhoe – Summit From the Mangatepopo saddle, it's about another 1½-hour climb on loose scoria to the 2287-metre summit of conical Mt Ngauruhoe. It takes only about half an hour to descend back down the mountain; altogether it's about a six to seven-hour return walk from the Mangatepopo car park to the summit.

Tongariro Crossing – If you continue from the Mangatepopo Saddle, you can do the Tongariro Crossing; see the Tramping section of the Outdoor Activities chapter. The crossing takes you over Mt Tongariro to the Ketetahi Hot Springs, but you can also reach the springs from the Ketetahi access road coming from SH 47A:

Ketetahi Hot Springs – From the car park at the end of the Ketetahi access road it's about a 2½ to three-hour uphill climb to the Ketetahi Hot Springs, which you can see steaming on the side of Mt Tongariro; it takes a couple of hours to get back down. The route passes through lush podocarp forest and alpine scrub and tussock.
There's a hut near the hot springs where you can spend the night if you like, or camp out beside the hut; for most of the year (late October to 31 May) you must purchase a Great Walks pass in advance if you want to spend the night. See the Ketetahi Track & Tongariro Crossing in the Tramping section of the Outdoor Activities chapter for more details.

Still more tracks take off from SH 47, on the north side of the park:

Mahuia Rapids – About two km north of the SH 48 turn-off leading to Whakapapa Village, SH 47 crosses the Whakapapanui Stream just below these rapids, which can be seen from the car park on the south side of the road.

Matariki Falls – A 20-minute return track through private farmland to see the Matariki Falls takes off from SH 47 about 200 metres from the Mahuia Rapids car park.

Te Porere Redoubt – The Te Porere Redoubt Historical Reserve near the junction of SH 47 and SH 47A preserves the redoubts built by Te Kooti's forces at the end of the Maori land wars; this was the site of the last pitched battle of the wars in 1869. Very different from the ancient Maori pa, Te Porere was typical of the fortification that followed the introduction of firearms. The earthworks have been restored.

If you're looking for more information about the battle, with maps, try to get hold of *War in the Tussock* by Ormond Wilson (Govt Printer, Wellington, 1961, paperback).

Lake Rotoaira – On the shores of Lake Rotoaira, on the north side of the park, are some interesting excavations of a pre-European Maori village site.

Lake Rotopounamu – A beautiful, secluded lake set in podocarp forest on the saddle between Lake Rotoaira and Lake Taupo, Lake Rotopounamu can be reached by a 20-minute walk from SH 47. The lake is on the west side of Mt Pihanga – see the Taranaki chapter for the legend about Tongariro, Taranaki and Pihanga. You can walk around the lake in 1½ hours – no camping though.

Places to Stay
The choice at Tongariro is whether you want to stay actually in the national park or outside the park in one of the nearby small towns. Within the park itself, Whakapapa Village has an expensive hotel, a motel and a motor camp. Also in the park are two Department of Conservation campsites, one near National Park and one near Ohakune, and nine huts which are accessible only by walking tracks. Small towns near the park include National Park, Ohakune and Turangi; see the separate sections on each of these towns for accommodation possibilities there.

Camping, Cabins & Huts The popular

Whakapapa Holiday Park (☎ & fax 892 3897) is up the road from the Grand Chateau Hotel, opposite the Whakapapa Visitor Centre. Tent and powered sites cost $9 per person, cabins are $33 for two and tourist flats are $50 for two, with prices the same all year round. From December to June there's also a special backpackers share rate of $12.50 per person in cabins.

Scattered around the park's tramping tracks are nine huts, with access by foot only. The cost is $8 (two tickets) in huts, $4 for camping beside the huts, with back country hut tickets and annual hut passes both acceptable. However, in the summer season from the end of October to the end of May a Great Walks or campsite pass is required for the four Tongariro Northern Circuit huts, which include the Ketetahi, Mangatepopo, Waihohonu and Oturere huts; the cost is $12 per night in huts, $6 per night for camping. Back country hut tickets and annual hut passes are not valid in these huts during this period. The rest of the year, these huts are on the same system as all the other huts in the park.

All the park visitor centres have information on huts and can sell hut tickets or Great Walks passes, or provide information on several other places in the area where Great Walks passes can be bought.

Also in the park are two basic DOC campsites with cold water and pit toilets; the cost is low and you place your money (about $2) into an honesty box. The Mangahuia Campsite is on SH 47, between National Park and the SH 48 turn-off heading to Whakapapa. The Mangawhero Campsite is near Ohakune, on the Ohakune Mountain Rd heading up to Mt Ruapehu.

Hotels & Motels At Whakapapa Village the *Grand Chateau Hotel* (☎ 892 3809, freephone (088) 733 944; fax (0800) 733 955) is indeed a grand hotel; apart from the Hermitage at Mt Cook it is the best known hotel in New Zealand. Built in 1929 in an opulent style, it has been well preserved and is priced accordingly. For most of the year, standard rooms are $107, premium rooms are $158;

from mid-July to the end of September 'economy' rooms are $113/158 for singles/doubles, premium rooms are $169 during the week and $248 on Friday or Saturday nights. There are also more expensive suites and villas. Discount packages are sometimes available.

Behind the Chateau is the *Skotel* (☎ 892 3719; fax 892 3777) with both deluxe and budget accommodation. From the end of October to early July, hostel-style twin rooms are $20/36 for singles/doubles, standard rooms are $65 and deluxe rooms are $90. In winter, from early July to the end of October, hostel-style twin rooms are $74, standard rooms are $120 and deluxe rooms are $160. They also have self-contained chalets sleeping six people; these cost $90 in summer, $220 in winter. There's a communal kitchen for the regular rooms (you provide crockery and cutlery, they provide pots and pans), as well as a sauna, spa pool, gym, games room, restaurant and house bar.

Places to Eat

There's a reasonable selection of food in the Whakapapa Store if you're preparing your own – as usual it's more expensive than down the road. It's 16 km down the road to National Park, the nearest crossroads town. The store also has takeaways.

The *Skotel* has a licensed family restaurant and house bar, serving all meals. The restaurant at the *Whakapapa Tavern*, opposite the Chateau, may be open only in winter.

Of course the fancy place to eat is at the *Grand Chateau Hotel*. Its *Ruapehu Room* is an elegant restaurant serving all meals, including a Saturday night buffet for $28 and a Sunday lunch buffet for $24 (children half price) – an excellent chance to fill yourself up on all kinds of exotic and tasty foods that you usually can't afford. Also at the Chateau, the *Carvery* is a less expensive family restaurant, open seasonally.

During the ski season there is a takeaway food van at Whakapapa Village, and if you're skiing there is food available at the Top of the Bruce where the lifts and tows start.

Getting There & Away

Bus Alpine Scenic Tours (☎ 386 8918, 378 6305) operates an inexpensive shuttle bus with several daily round trips between Turangi and National Park, stopping at Whakapapa Village, the Mangatepopo car park (for the start of the Tongararo Crossing track) and Ketetahi car park (for the Ketetahi Hot Springs track or the end of the Tongariro Crossing) along the way. They will go up to the ski area at the Top of the Bruce above Whakapapa by request; their services also continue north from Turangi to Taupo and Rotorua. Since seats are limited, book in advance to guarantee yourself a spot.

From National Park township there are a few other options in getting to the park, at the same places (Whakapapa, Mangatepopo and Ketetahi); see the National Park section for details. Transport is also available from Ohakune; see the Ohakune section for details.

Car The park is encircled by roads. SH 1 (at this point it's called the Desert Rd) passes down the eastern side of the park. SH 4 passes down the western side. SH 47 crosses the northern side and SH 49 the southern side. The main road up into the park is SH 48 which leads to Whakapapa Village, continuing further up the mountain as Bruce Rd to the Top of the Bruce and the Whakapapa Ski Area. The Ohakune Mountain Rd leads up to the Turoa Ski Area from Ohakune in the south-west.

Hitching From whichever direction you come, hitching to Whakapapa is never that easy because traffic is usually so light. If you're coming south from Turangi use the shorter saddle road, SH 47A – the locals no longer use the SH 1 to SH 47 route.

Getting Around

In winter there's a shuttle service from Whakapapa up to the ski runs at the Top of the Bruce. It will pick you up anywhere around Whakapapa, which in this small village mainly means from the Chateau and the Skotel or the holiday park.

AROUND TONGARIRO NATIONAL PARK
National Park

The small settlement of National Park (population 200) is at the junction of SH 4 and SH 47, 43 km south of Taumarunui, 35 km north of Ohakune and 15 km from Whakapapa Village. It's not of any great interest in itself but it makes a convenient base for visits to the north end of Tongariro National Park. Several daily shuttle buses from here serve both ends of the Tongariro Crossing walking track, Whakapapa Village and the Whakapapa Ski Area in winter. This being the closest town to the popular Whakapapa Ski Area, it tends to fill up during ski season, but it's very quiet the rest of the year.

National Park also makes a convenient base for a variety of other outdoor activities including canoe trips on the Whanganui River; see the Whanganui National Park section for details on river trips. Or you can hire bicycles, go on off-road motorbike excursions, horse-trekking, kayaking over a six-metre waterfall or a number of other activities.

Orientation National Park township is only a few square blocks hugging the west side of SH 4, at the junction of SH 47 which leads to Whakapapa Village, Turangi and Taupo. From SH 4, turn into the town on Carroll St, about three blocks north of the BP petrol station; most of the places to stay are on this street, which runs just four blocks from the highway on one end of the town to the railway tracks at the other end. The National Park Store is on Carroll St opposite the Ski Haus hostel; the post office and tearooms are there at the store, and InterCity buses arrive and depart from the bus stop outside. The railway station is about three blocks back from the highway. Ski hire is available at several shops in the township.

Activities You can make a good four to five-hour return walk from National Park township to the 50-metre Tupapakurua Falls, going on a good trail through heavy bush; follow Fisher Rd out of town.

Chalet on the Rocks (see Places to Stay)

organises a variety of guided mountain bike tours which you can do either with your bike or theirs. Half-day tours are $25 with your bike, $45 with theirs; full-day tours are $35 with your bike or $70 with theirs. Howard's Lodge hires bicycles to its guests for $20 per day. Both Howard's Lodge and the Ski Haus also hire tramping boots and other gear for going on the Tongariro Crossing or other treks.

Go For It Tours (☎ 892 2705) at the Petticoat Junction building, which is also the railway station, does guided off-road trail bike motorcycle tours. The cost is $45 for a 1½ to two-hour tour, $80 for half a day or $125 for an all-day tour.

Plateau Outdoor Adventure Guides (☎ & fax 892 2740), based six km north of National Park at Raurimu, offers a wide variety of outdoor adventure trips in the area; see the Tongariro National Park section.

Waterfalls Wonderland (☎ 895 4894) operates a 4WD back country tour pointing out many interesting features of the area including the Tupapakurua Falls and other waterfalls, fossils, native flora, fauna and more. Weather permitting, the tour departs from the National Park Store on Carroll St at 10 am on weekends, and will go on weekdays too by request. The cost is $45 per person.

You can use the spa pool at the Ski Haus whether you're a guest there or not. The cost is $2 per half hour; it's very popular so book ahead to be sure of getting a space.

Places to Stay Accommodation here gets very full during the ski season, so book ahead.

Camping & Cabins The *Ski Haus* has tent sites at $7 per person, or powered sites at $7 per person plus $5 per site. *Howard's Lodge* has tent sites at $8 per person. See them under Hostels. *Fletcher's Ski Lodge & Motel* also has tent sites.

The *Discovery Caravan Park* (☎ 892 2744; fax 892 2603) is beside the Discovery Lodge on SH 47, 6.5 km from National Park township and 6.5 km from Whakapapa

CENTRAL NORTH ISLAND

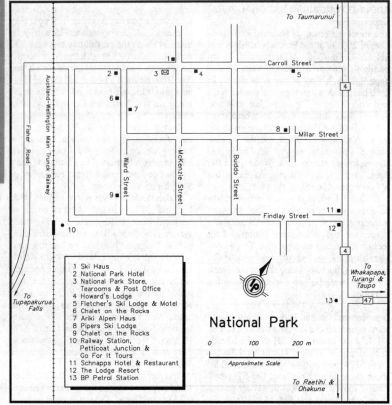

1 Ski Haus
2 National Park Hotel
3 National Park Store,
   Tearooms & Post Office
4 Howard's Lodge
5 Fletcher's Ski Lodge & Motel
6 Chalet on the Rocks
7 Ariki Alpen Haus
8 Pipers Ski Lodge
9 Chalet on the Rocks
10 Railway Station,
    Petticoat Junction &
    Go For It Tours
11 Schnapps Hotel & Restaurant
12 The Lodge Resort
13 BP Petrol Station

National Park

0   100   200 m

Approximate Scale

To Taumarunui
Carroll Street
4
Millar Street
Findlay Street
4
To Whakapapa, Turangi & Taupo
47
To Raetihi & Ohakune
To Tupapakurua Falls

Village. Tent or powered sites cost $8 per person. Cabins sleep two people; the cost is $12.50 per person.

Hostels The *Ski Haus* (☎ & fax 892 2854) is on Carroll St opposite the National Park Store, about three blocks west of the highway. Its many amenities make it a popular spot; there's a spa pool, a billiards table, a sunken fireplace area in the attractive lounge and a house bar. There's a kitchen where you can do your own cooking plus a restaurant with good food at reasonable prices. A variety of activities can be organ-

ised from the hostel including horse treks, canoeing and river rafting, trail bike trips and more. They also provide a convenient daily transport service to Whakapapa Village ($4 each way), the Whakapapa Ski Area ($12 return), and the Ketetahi and Mangatepopo road ends for trampers on the Tongariro Crossing ($15 return).

From November to June rates at the Ski Haus are $12/15 per person in dorm/double rooms; in winter it's $15/20 per person. In the ski season they also offer B&B at $35/40 per person, which is available every day and compulsory on weekends. In winter the Ski

Haus is very popular with skiers, especially on weekends, so if you want to avoid the crowds, come during the week.

Also on Carroll St, just a block from the highway, *Howard's Lodge* (☎ & fax 892 2827) is another good hostel with similar amenities including a spa pool, BBQ, ski hire, bicycle hire and comfortable lounge and kitchen areas. You can do your own cooking all year round, and inexpensive meals are also available. They provide the same transport for the same prices as the Ski Haus, plus free transport coming from Taupo each Monday. In summer from December to May, the cost is $12/15 per person in dorm/double rooms; in winter from June to November it's $15/25.

Similar prices are also available at several other places in town; read on.

Hotels, Chalets & Motels The *National Park Hotel* (☎ 892 2805; fax 892 2746) on Carroll St near the railway tracks has bunkroom accommodation at $10 per person if you bring your own sleeping bag, $15 per person with linen included. Regular hotel rooms are $20/30 for singles/doubles. Prices remain the same all year round. There's a kitchen where guests can cook, plus a pub.

Near the hotel, on Ward St, *Chalet on the Rocks* (☎ 892 2938, mobile (025) 446 025) has two self-contained three-bedroom houses with single and double rooms, and everything you need. Meals are available on request and they also organise bicycle tours. The cost is $10 per person in summer, $20 in winter.

Also on Ward St, the *Ariki Alpen Haus* (☎ & fax 892 2801) is open only in ski season. It sleeps 14 to 19 people and offers accommodation in the European tradition, similar to a homestay, with beds from $25 per person. Meals are also available, with B&B at $45 per person midweek, $55 on weekends, or dinner, bed & breakfast at $65 midweek, $80 on weekends. They have a sauna, spa pool and ski hire shop where guests receive discounts on ski hire.

Fletchers Ski Lodge & Motel (☎ & fax 892 2846, bookings in Auckland (09) 479 2987)

on Carroll St near the highway offers motel and lodge accommodation, plus spa pools, billiards, volleyball, BBQ, fireplace lounge, etc. In summer, lodge rooms are $12 per person, motel units are $50 or $60. In winter the prices rise to $20 per person in the lodge, $80 for studio units, $100 in motel units. They also offer a variety of convenient discount plans including weekend and midweek packages if you stay for two or five nights, and dinner, bed & breakfast plans. In summer, guests can cook in the kitchen; in winter, it's a restaurant.

The *Mountain Heights Lodge* (☎ 892 2833) on SH 4, two km south of National Park township, has motel units at $50 in summer, $110 in winter from November to mid-June. They also have lodge accommodation open only during ski season, with a variety of twin rooms and bunkrooms; the cost is $40 per person for dinner, bed & breakfast.

Discovery Lodge (☎ 892 2744; fax 892 2603) on SH 47, 6.5 km from National Park township and 6.5 km from Whakapapa Village, has chalets and motel units in addition to the camping and cabins also on the premises. In summer, motel units are $50 to $66 and chalets are $66. In winter, motel units are $82 to $123, chalets are $112 to $123; all prices are for the first two people. It has a covered swimming pool (heated in winter), two spa pools, a licensed restaurant, bar, and a weights room. A kitchen is available to guests but you must bring all your own kitchen gear.

Six km south of National Park on SH 4, the *Erua Ski Lodge* (☎ 892 2894, bookings New Plymouth (06) 758 7144) is open only during the height of the ski season, from around mid-July to the end of October. Accommodation includes self-catering lodge beds at $16.50 per night with your own sleeping bag, dinner, bed & breakfast plans at $39 per person, and studio tourist flats with kitchen at $95 for the unit. There's a minimum stay of two nights; they provide ski hire, ski instructors and ski area transport.

At Raurimu, six km north of National Park on SH 4, the *Slalom Ski Lodge* (☎ 892 2855, bookings at Auckland (09) 379 8886) has accommodation in summer at $11 per person with your own sleeping bag, $15 with linen provided. During the ski season B&B is $30 per person, linen included; if it's not too busy you can also get bed only for around $22 per person. There's a sauna, ski hire, and transport to the ski area can be arranged. They also offer weekend all-inclusive ski packages coming from Auckland, with transport included.

Places to Eat All the accommodation places in National Park make provisions for their guests' meals, with meals provided, kitchens where you can do your own cooking, or both.

The bar and restaurant at the *Ski Haus* are open to guests and non-guests alike. Its restaurant is open all year round; several other places to stay have restaurants open only in winter. *Schnapps* on the highway wasn't open on our last visit but it, too, provides meals and refreshments, plus hotel accommodation.

Getting There & Away National Park is midway on the daily Auckland-Wellington bus and train routes from either city.

Bus Daily InterCity buses arrive and depart from the National Park Store on Carroll St. Tickets are sold at the Ski Haus, opposite the store. The trip either north to Auckland or south to Wellington takes about five hours.

Alpine Scenic Tours (☎ 386 8918/6305) operates several daily shuttle buses making a round trip between Turangi and National Park, with stops at Whakapapa Village, the Whakapapa Ski Area by request, the Mangatepopo and Ketetahi car parks for transport to the Tongariro Crossing track, and on from Turangi to Taupo and Rotorua. Since seating space is limited, book in advance to assure yourself a spot.

Tongariro Track Transport (☎ 892 2610) operates a daily shuttle bus from behind the National Park BP petrol station on the highway to either end of the Tongariro Crossing track, stopping at Whakapapa Village on the way. The Ski Haus and

Howard's Lodge provide similar services; see them under Hostels.

During ski season most of the accommodation places make some provision for transport to the Whakapapa Ski Area.

Train Trains running north and south between Auckland and Wellington stop at National Park once in the middle of the day and once in the middle of the night, heading in both directions. Train tickets and Interislander ferry tickets are sold not from the railway station, but from the Ski Haus on Carroll St, about three blocks from the station.

Around National Park

Horopito A few km south of National Park on SH 4 is a monument to the Last Spike – the spike that marked the completion of the Main Trunk Railway Line connection between Auckland and Wellington in November 1908, a most significant event which opened up transport to, communication with, and settlement of the central North Island. A plaque at the monument relates how they had struggled to complete the line ever since the 1860s.

Raurimu Spiral The Raurimu Spiral, six km north of National Park on SH 4, is an amazing feat of railway engineering. There's a lookout near the highway. You can see an operating model of the spiral at the Taumarunui Information Centre; see the Taumarunui section for more about the spiral.

Ohakune

Ohakune (population 1300) is the closest town to the Turoa Ski Area on the south side of Mt Ruapehu. It's a pleasant little town with lots of motels and even more restaurants. It's very much a skiing town – a lot of effort goes into catering for those snow-season big-spenders. Most of the businesses in town rely on the few months of ski season, from mid-June to late October, and in fact many don't even bother opening up outside this season.

Recently, though, there's been a push to

try to attract tourists year-round, and there are many outdoor activities that can be enjoyed anytime.

While you're in town check out the Big Carrot on SH 49, paying homage to the town's primary agricultural product. The Weather Stone on Thames St is another oddity of the town. Kids will like the old tank in the children's play park on Clyde St.

Orientation & Information Ohakune has two separate business districts. One is on the north end of town by the railway station; this end is lively during ski season but many of the businesses there are closed the rest of the year. The commercial district in the south end of town is the part that functions all year round; here you'll find the information centre, the post office, banks, the supermarket, the chemist and other shops and services. Both ends have restaurants and places to stay. Ohakune Mountain Rd leads up the mountain to the Turoa Ski Area; several good walking tracks are marked along the way.

The information centre, called the Ruapehu Visitor Centre (☎ (06) 385 8427; fax 385 8527) is at 54 Clyde St on the south end of town. It has lots of brochures and an excellent three-dimensional model of the Tongariro National Park – great for tracing where you're going to walk. They also do bookings for all the area's activities and accommodation, for InterCity buses and for the train. In winter from June to October it's open Monday to Friday from 8 am to 5.30 pm, Saturday 9 am to 4 pm and Sunday from 9 am to 2 pm. The rest of the year it's open weekdays from 9 am to 4.30 pm, Saturday 9 am to noon and Sunday from 9 to 11 am.

The AA office (☎ 385 8151) is opposite, at 51 Clyde St on the corner of Goldfinch St; it's open Monday to Friday from 9 am to 5 pm. The post office is on Clyde St in the next block, on the corner of Rata St.

The Ohakune Ranger Station (☎ (06) 385 8578; fax 385 8128) is on Ohakune Mountain Rd on the north side of town, across the railway tracks. It's open Monday to Friday from 8 am to 4.30 pm and offers maps,

current weather reports and other advice about this side of the Tongariro National Park. Stop in here before doing any tramping.

The Turoa Ski Area operates an information line (☎ (06) 385 8456) with up-to-the-minute information on ski and road conditions.

Walks The Ohakune Mountain Rd goes 17 km from the north end of Ohakune to the Turoa Ski Area on Mt Ruapehu. Several walking tracks take off from this road, going to various points in the Tongariro National Park. Stop by the Ohakune Ranger Station at the bottom of this road for maps and information about the tracks before you set off. Remember that weather on the mountains is highly changeable, so come prepared for all weather, and let someone know where you're going and when you'll be back.

Two of the most delightful walks are the short 15-minute Rimu Track and the longer 1½-hour Mangawhero Forest Walk, both departing from opposite the Ohakune Ranger Station. They both pass through a lovely section of native forest; the Rimu Track is marked with plaques pointing out various features of the forest.

Other popular tracks leading from Ohakune Mountain Rd include a 1¼-hour return walk to the Waitonga Falls, beginning 11 km past the Ranger Station, and the five-hour return walk to Lake Surprise, beginning 15 km past the Ranger Station. If you continue past the falls on the Waitonga Falls track, you'll be on the Round-the-Mountains Track (see the Tongariro National Park section). Other tracks taking off from the Mountain Rd include a 10-minute return walk to the Mangawhero Falls and a four to five-hour walk on the Old Blyth Track.

There's no regularly scheduled transport up the mountain to these tracks, and hitching is chancey because there's not much traffic. The Snowliner Shuttle (see Getting Around) operates transport to the tracks. Or you could go to the top with a bicycle (see Cycling) and do some tramping on your way back down.

CENTRAL NORTH ISLAND

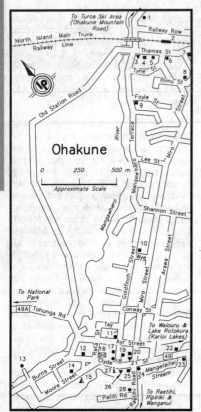

Ohakune

0   250   500 m

Approximate Scale

■   PLACES TO STAY

4   Turoa Ski Lodge, La Pizzeria,
     Coyote Bar & Grill, Steak & Salad
8   Rimu Park Lodge
9   Sunbeam Lodge
10 Hobbit Motel Lodge
12 Ohakune YHA Hostel
14 Mountain View Motel &
     Acacia Lodge Motel
15 Ohakune Motor Camp
20 Alpine Motel & Sassi's Bistro
22 High Country Cabins
25 Ohakune Hotel & Cleches Cafe & Bar

▼   PLACES TO EAT

2   Railway Station & Cafe Loco
3   The Powder Keg & Powderhorn Ski
     Shop
4   Turoa Ski Lodge, La Pizzeria,
     Coyote Bar & Grill, Steak & Salad
20 Alpine Motel & Sassi's Bistro
21 Alpine Wine Bar & Restaurant
25 Ohakune Hotel & Cleches Cafe & Bar
26 Stutz Cafe

     OTHER

1   Ohakune Ranger Station
2   Railway Station & Cafe Loco
3   The Powder Keg & Powderhorn Ski
     Shop
5   Weather Rock
6   Hot Lava Nightclub
7   Ohakune Action Park
11 The Ski Shed
13 Maungarongo Pa
16 Post Office
17 Cinema
18 Automobile Association (AA)
19 New World Supermarket
23 The Big Carrot
24 BP Petrol Station & Dairy
27 Ruapehu Visitor Centre
28 Swimming Pool

There's also a little bush walk in the small park on Clyde St, on the south end of town.

Cycling The Powderhorn Ski Shop (☎ 385 8888) hires mountain bikes at $10 per hour, $25 for half a day or $35 per day. A cheaper and highly enjoyable way to do some cycling in Ohakune is to go with Ride the Mountain (☎ (06) 385 8257), who for $15 will take you in a van to the Turoa Ski Area at the top of the Ohakune Mountain Rd and set you loose with a bicycle, helmet and all the other gear you need. It takes half an hour to get up there and all the time you want to get back down;

they're pretty easy-going and usually don't mind if you go for a tramp or a little extra bike riding, as long as you check with them in advance.

Be sure not to take a bicycle on any of the trails in the national park; it's a heavy fine if you're caught!

Ohakune Action Park The Ohakune Action Park at the eastern end of Thames St is operated by the Rimu Park Lodge (see Hostels). Activities include a 'high wire flyer' – a flying fox with a bicycle on top of the wire – grass skiing, an indoor shooting gallery, and the Ultimate Game played with teams and dye-pellet guns.

Scenic Flights Aerial sightseeing trips over the Tongariro and Whanganui National Parks are available; ask about them at the Ski Shed on the corner of Goldfinch and Ayr Sts (☎ 385 9173). Charter flights and flying instruction are also offered.

Lake Rotokura (Karioi Lakes) Lake Rotokura is about 11 km south of Ohakune on SH 49, at Karioi in the Karioi Forest, about a km from the Karioi turn-off. It's called Lake Rotokura on the map and the sign but it's actually two lakes not one, and the locals call them the Karioi Lakes. Karioi means 'places to linger', and they couldn't be more aptly named. They are two little jewels, one above the other, great for picnicking, fishing and relaxing.

Other Things to Do Ask at the information centre about activities around Ohakune, there are many and they can give you the run-down on who is doing what. There's horse-trekking, white water rafting, fishing, canoe, kayak and jet-boat trips on the nearby Whanganui River, golf and more. Or you could go for a hot swim at the Powder Keg restaurant/bar.

The Powderhorn Ski Shop (☎ 385 8888) on the corner of Thames St and Mangawhero Terrace hires mountain bikes, roller blades, ice axes and crampons in addition to ski gear. They also have a try-out programme for ski gear in which you can hire it first and if you buy it, the rental cost goes towards the price. YHA members receive a 20% discount on ski gear hire at the Ski Shed on the corner of Goldfinch and Ayr Sts.

Places to Stay Finding a place to stay is no problem in summer, but during the ski

season you should definitely book ahead, especially for any economical accommodation, for which there is much demand. On weekends and over the school holidays you probably won't find a spare bed unless it's quite expensive, but even during the middle of the week it's still a good idea to book. The places mentioned here are suggestions, but there are also more places both in Ohakune and in Raetihi, 11 km west. The information centre has information and can make bookings for all of them.

Camping & Cabins The *Ohakune Motor Camp* (☎ (06) 385 8561) at 5 Moore St near the centre is a pleasant camp beside a gurgling stream, with plenty of trees and green areas and a comfortable TV lounge-dining room. Tent sites are $6.50 per person, powered sites $16 for two, and cabins or on-site caravans are $15 per person. They offer caravan and vehicle storage for $10 a week while you're off trekking or doing other activities.

The *Raetihi Motor Camp* (☎ (06) 385 4176; fax 385 4059) in Raetihi, 11 km west of Ohakune, is a friendly camping ground with tent sites at $7 for one or two people, powered sites at $15 for two and cabins or on-site caravans at $10 to $12.50 per person. They offer free glow-worm tours and feeding of wild possums in the evening, and there are squash and tennis courts, swimming pools, a roller skating rink and a children's playground nearby. This is also a popular and inexpensive place to hire canoes or kayaks for trips on the Whanganui River. Caravan storage is available for $5 per week.

The *Mangawhero Campsite* is a simple DOC camping ground on Ohakune Mountain Rd. Facilities include cold water and pit toilets; the cost is $2 per night.

They don't have camping but the *High Country Cabins* (☎ (06) 385 8608; fax 385 8550) on Clyde St near the Big Carrot has plenty of cabins. The cost is $10 per person in summer, $20 in winter, but only $15 if there's a group of three or more. Bookings are essential in ski season.

Some other places also have cabins; see the following sections.

Hostels The *Ohakune YHA Hostel* (☎ (06) 385 8724) is on Clyde St, near the CPO and information centre. It's a good hostel with twin, triple and bunkrooms; you have your own room key so you can come and go as you wish. During ski season it is very heavily booked so at that time you should book ahead. The nightly cost is $14.

Nearby, the *Alpine Motel* (see Motels) has a separate backpackers in the rear, where rates are $15 per person (except in the ski season).

At the north end of town, the *Rimu Park Lodge* (☎ & fax (06) 385 9023) at 27 Rimu St is in a comfortable restored 1914 villa in a secluded spot just a two-minute walk from the railway station, restaurants and nightlife. It's restful in summer, popular with skiers in winter, but it still has that peaceful atmosphere even in winter when the town is buzzing. The cost is $14/16 per person in share/double rooms during summer. In the ski season it's a B&B, known for its excellent hearty breakfasts changing daily; the cost then is $28/32 per person in share/double rooms.

A number of cabins, motels and lodges in town offer backpackers accommodation; see them in the other sections.

Hotels, Motels & Lodges In the south end of town, the *Ohakune Hotel* (☎ & fax (06) 385 8268) on the corner of Clyde St and Raetihi Rd has single rooms at $30, doubles at $40 or $50, with prices remaining the same all year.

Nearby, the *Alpine Motel* (☎ & fax (06) 385 8758) at 7 Miro St is a popular place, with studio units, family units, chalets and a separate backpackers in the rear, plus a spa pool and a popular restaurant/bar. The cost for one or two people is $55 in summer, $75 to $95 in winter; out in the backpackers there's a rate of $14 except in the ski season.

Also in the south end of town, the *Mountain View Motel* (☎ & fax (06) 385 8675) at 2 Moore St opposite the motor camp has

motel units at $45 in summer, $70 in the ski season for one or two people. They also have more economical cabins with summer/winter rates at $15/17 per person, and a bunkhouse with summer/winter rates at $12/15 per person; bring your own sleeping bag and kitchen utensils.

Next door, the *Acacia Lodge Motel* (☎ (06) 385 8729; fax 385 8347) at 4 Moore St has kitchen units at $65/95 in summer/winter; serviced units at $55/85 in summer/winter; with a $10 mid-week discount in winter.

Between the south and north ends of town, the *Hobbit Motel Lodge* (☎ (06) 385 8248; fax 385 8515) on the corner of Goldfinch and Wye Sts has motel units at $65/75 for singles/doubles in summer, $95 during the ski season. They also have bunkrooms at $17 in summer with your own sleeping bag, $20 with linen provided; in the ski season they're from $25 with linen provided.

The *Sunbeam Lodge* (☎ (06) 385 8470; fax 385 8662) at 178 Mangawhero Terrace is another place with a variety of accommodation. In summer, they have backpackers accommodation at $10 per person, lodge rooms at $30 and $40 for one or two people, $50 with private facilities, studio units at $55 and motel units at $65. In winter, the lodge rooms are $61, $85 with private facilities, studio units are $99 and motel units are $141.

The *Turoa Ski Lodge* (☎ (06) 385 8274) at 10 Thames St is on the north end of town, right in the thick of the winter restaurant and nightlife scene, with a popular licensed restaurant of its own. It's open only during the ski season; the cost is $43.50/87 for singles/doubles, or there's a bunkroom at $18 per person.

Four km east of town on SH 49, the *Mt Ruapehu Homestead* (☎ & fax (06) 385 8799) is another place with a variety of accommodation and a licensed restaurant; they also organise plenty of activities through their Ruapehu Outback Adventures. They have lodge rooms at $30/42 per person in summer/winter, motel units at $40/60 per person in summer/winter, and a bunkroom with accommodation from $20 per person all year round. You can phone for free pick-up from town when you arrive.

Places to Eat There are two distinct restaurant sections in Ohakune. The one on the north side is active during the winter with the après ski crowd, but in summer there's just about nothing open. The places on the south side of town are open all year round. Many of the motels also have restaurants.

On the south side, the pleasant *Stutz Cafe* on Clyde St is open every day from breakfast until dinner, with European food, Chinese food, pizza and a takeaways section. Nearby, *Cleches Cafe & Bar* at the Ohakune Hotel on the corner of Clyde St and Raetihi Rd is also open long hours, from 7 am to 9 pm every day except Sunday, when it opens at 4 pm. On the opposite corner, the *Alpine Wine Bar & Restaurant* is open for wining and dining every evening. Half a block away, *Sassi's Bistro* at the Alpine Motel on Miro St is also open for dinner every evening, all year round; it's a pleasant little place with a varied, changing blackboard menu with something to suit all budgets.

On the north end of town there are many popular restaurants along Thames St including *La Pizzeria* which does pretty good pizzas; next door, the *Coyote Bar & Grill* is also good. Or there's the licensed restaurant at the *Turoa Ski Lodge*, and the nearby *Steak & Salad*. *Cafe Loco* in the railway station is Ohakune's 'alternative' restaurant, featuring wholefoods and an interesting menu with both vegetarian and meat dishes.

The most popular place on Thames St on our last visit was *The Powder Keg* on the corner of Thames St and Mangawhero Terrace. Especially popular for its bar, the yuppie après-ski hangout, it's also popular for its restaurant with good food and for its indoor heated swimming pool. It's hard to squeeze in the door here at times.

Entertainment Ohakune is known for being a good-fun place in the nightlife department during the ski season; the rest of the year it's pretty quiet. The *Hot Lava* nightclub on Thames St is a popular spot, open every night

during the ski season with live music on weekends and disco music on other nights; in the summer it opens as a disco on weekends only. Other places with live music in the ski season include the *Powder Keg, Turoa Ski Lodge* and *Coyote Bar & Grill*, all on Thames St, and the *Ohakune Hotel* on Clyde St in the south part of town. Also in the south part of town, the cinema on Goldfinch St is open all year round.

Getting There & Away There are several ways to get to and from Ohakune.

Bus InterCity buses serve Ohakune every day except Saturday, arriving and departing from the Ruapehu Visitor Centre, which sells the tickets. The Kiwi Experience bus also comes here.

Train The Auckland-Wellington trains stop at Ohakune. Buy tickets at the Ruapehu Visitor Centre, not at the railway station. The railway station is at the north end of town.

Getting Around There's plenty of transport available between Ohakune and the Turoa Ski Area during the winter, with several companies all charging $14 for round-trip door-to-door transport from wherever you're staying; the place you stay will arrange transport for you. It's also easy to hitchhike up to the ski area in winter, even with your skis.

Operated by Turoa Taxis, the Snowliner Shuttle (☎ (06) 385 8573, mobile (025) 435 550) offers a variety of transport around the area. In winter, the one-way/return cost is $8/14 to the Turoa Ski Area, $10/20 to Raetihi, $12/24 to Karioi and $15/25 to the Whakapapa Ski Area. In summer they offer a drop-off and pick-up service from Ohakune to all the trail heads in the Tongariro National Park, and to various spots serving the Whanganui National Park including Taumarunui and Pipiriki. For one to three passengers the cost is $18 to the Blyth Track, $24 to the Lake Surprise Track. YHA members receive a discount.

Waiouru

At the junction of SH 1 and SH 49, on the Desert Rd 27 km east of Ohakune, Waiouru (population 3300) is primarily an army base. In a large grey concrete building with tanks out front, the Queen Elizabeth II Army Memorial Museum tells the history of the New Zealand Army in times of war and peace, with an extensive collection of artefacts from early colonial times to the present and a 23-minute audiovisual presentation. It's open every day from 9 am to 4.30 pm; admission is $7 (children $3, family $15).

Mangaweka

A tiny town located on SH 1, 52 km south of Waiouru, Mangaweka's most noticeable attraction is the Aeroplane Cafe, a cafe in an old DC-3 plane right beside the highway, open every day.

Beside the plane, Rangitikei River Adventures (☎ & fax (06) 382 5747, after hours 522 8362) offers various activities including a 43-metre bungy jump over the Rangitikei River. This is the same height as the famous Kawerau Bridge jump at Queenstown, and they have plans in the works for a 75-metre jump at Mokai which will be the highest jump in New Zealand – four metres higher than the jump at Queenstown's Skippers Canyon. The cost is $70 for the Rangitikei River jump, about $130 for the Mokai jump.

They also do a number of river trips on the Rangitikei River including jet-boat trips and rafting trips ranging from Grade Two Plus to Grade Five. Booking is essential for all their activities.

Places to Stay Rangitikei River Adventures can arrange accommodation starting from $10 per night. Or there's the *Puha Palace* (☎ (06) 382 5818), a comfortable hostel occupying a historic 1895 wooden house that was once the home of New Zealand poet Sam Hunt. It's on a corner of Kawakawa St one block off the highway, opposite the post office, the DOC office, an antiques shop and a pub; a cafe is in the next block. The cost of $15 with your own sleeping bag, $20 with linen provided, is the same in double or dorm

rooms and includes breakfast. The people at the hostel and also the DOC across the street can tell you about various other activities around Mangaweka. The DOC office also has referrals for farmstays and country cottages around the area.

Whanganui National Park

Whanganui National Park, established in December 1986, is New Zealand's second youngest national park. Its main attraction is the Whanganui River, which winds its way 329 km from its source on the flanks of Mt Tongariro in the central North Island to the Tasman Sea at the city of Wanganui. The river is not the longest in the country – that honour goes to the Waikato River to the north – but the fact that it is the longest *navigable* river in the country has been shaping the destiny of the river for centuries. Historically a major route for travel between the sea and the interior of the North Island, first by the Maori and then by the Pakeha, the route was eventually superseded by rail and road. In recent years, however, recreational canoe, kayak and jet-boat enthusiasts have once again made the river a popular thoroughfare.

In 1993 the stretch of the river from Taumarunui south to Pipiriki, including an 87-km section of river between Whakahoro and Pipiriki that runs through an area that's untouched by roads, was added to the New Zealand Great Walks system and called the 'Whanganui Journey'. A Grade Two river, the Whanganui is easy enough to be enjoyed by people of any age, with or without previous canoeing experience, yet there is enough movement and small-size rapids to keep it interesting. A canoe trip down the river is a great way to relax in one of New Zealand's last great wilderness areas.

Other attractions of the park include two very good walking tracks, the Matemateaonga Walkway and the Mangapurua Track.

Fishing and hunting are also popular sports in the park.

History

In Maori legend, the Whanganui River was formed when Mt Taranaki, after his fight with Mt Tongariro over the lovely Mt Pihanga, fled the central North Island and headed for the sea, leaving a long gouge in the earth in his wake. When he reached the sea he turned westwards, finally coming to rest in the place where he stands today. Mt Tongariro sent forth cool water from his side, to flow down and heal the wound in the earth – and so the Whanganui River was born.

The river was settled from very early in New Zealand's history. The great Polynesian explorer Kupe explored some distance upriver from the river's mouth in around 900 AD. Maori genealogy traces a group of people living on the river from about 1100 AD.

Major Maori settlement began along the river in around 1350 AD, and flourished along the river in pre-European days. There were three separate tribes, each on a different section of the river, but collectively they were called Te Atihau Nui A Papa Rangi. Even back then, the river was a major route from the sea to the interior.

The first European to travel the river was Andrew Powers in 1831, but he didn't do it of his own free will – he was brought up the river as a captive by some Maori of the Ngati Tuwharetoa tribe, taking him from the coast to their home at the south end of Lake Taupo via the Whanganui and Manganui-O-Te-Ao Rivers.

European influence did not begin on the river until missionaries arrived in the 1840s. Notable missionary figures included the Anglican Rev Richard Taylor who came to the river in 1843 and explored it extensively; at the Maoris' request he bestowed new names on many of their settlements. Hiruharama (Jerusalem), Ranana (London), Koriniti (Corinth) and Atene (Athens) still survive today, though the population along the river has dwindled from its former numbers; the populations of Peterehema (Bethlehem), Hiona (Mt Zion), Raorikia (Laodicia), Karatia (Galatea) and Ramahiku (Damascus) have drifted away.

Another notable missionary on the river was the French Catholic missionary Suzanne Aubert, called Mother Aubert or, fondly, Mother Mary or Mother Mary Joseph, who established the Daughters of Our Lady of Compassion in Hiruharama (Jerusalem) in 1892. St Joseph's, the Catholic church built in 1892, is still the most prominent feature of the town and the large, white wooden convent still stands in a beautiful garden beside it.

Transport on the river had always been by canoe, until a couple of isolated voyages were made up the river by steamer in the mid-1860s during the Hauhau war. This was a war when, encouraged by some Maoris who had come from the Taranaki region, some of the river tribes joined in the Hauhau Rebellion – a Maori movement seeking to oust Europeans from New Zealand.

In 1886 the first commercial steamer transport service was established by a Wanganui company, but its vessel the *Tuhua* was wrecked beside Moutere Island a few years later in 1890. The following year, Alexander Hatrick, an Australian entrepreneur in Wanganui, began operating the 100-foot (33-metre), 250-passenger *Wairere* on the river.

This was the first of what later grew to a fleet of 12 A Hatrick & Co vessels operating along connecting parts of the river all the way from Wanganui to Taumarunui. The riverboats served a number of needs: in addition to moving passengers, cargo and farm produce in and out for the river communities, they also provided transport from the sea to the interior of the country, especially after 1903 when the Main Trunk Railway reached Taumarunui from the north.

Tourism was another major development on the river. Internationally advertised, tourist trips on the river became so popular that by 1905, 12,000 tourists a year were making the trip upriver from Wanganui or downriver from Taumarunui to Pipiriki House, a magnificent 65-room hotel in

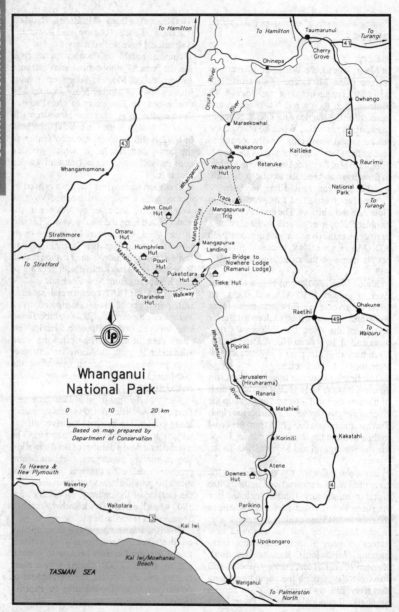

Whanganui
National Park

0   10   20 km

Based on map prepared by
Department of Conservation

Pipiriki. Many tourists also stayed at the Houseboat *Makere*, a double-decker, 92-foot (30.5-metre) floating hotel anchored at Maraekowhai at the confluence of the Whanganui and Ohura Rivers from 1904 to 1927. The Whanganui River came to be known as 'the Rhine of New Zealand' or, as New Zealand was also called in those days, 'the Rhine of Maoriland'.

The engineering feats and skippering ability required to operate the steamboats and paddle steamers on the river became legendary, spawning something like the lore that Mark Twain made famous on the Mississippi River. Modern-day canoeists often wonder at how they were able to get the steamers up the river at all; it required some imaginative engineering feats in some places, such as cables and man-made channelling of the river's currents.

Around 1918, land along the river above Pipiriki was given as grants to returning WW I soldiers. It was a rugged, difficult area to settle, a major challenge to clear, and eventually the combined factors of isolation, economic difficulty (especially in the 1930s Depression), declining soil fertility and continual physical hardships such as floods, road washouts, erosion, etc became too much for the settlers. Some families struggled for as long as 30 years to make a go of their farms, but by the early 1940s, only a few farms remained.

One of the most famous features of the river, the Bridge to Nowhere, was built in 1936 as part of a road from Raetihi to the river. It stands as mute testimony to the efforts to settle the region which finally proved too much. The track from the river's Mangapurua Landing to the bridge takes about 40 minutes to walk (1½ hours return), and though it is only a walking track now, it follows what used to be a 4½-metre-wide roadway leading down to the riverboat landing. The Matemateaonga Walkway and the Mangapurua Track, which continues another 19 hours from the Bridge to Nowhere to Whakahoro, also follow former roads, now being reclaimed by the forest.

By 1959, when the Pipiriki Hotel burned

to the ground, roads and the Auckland-Wellington Main Trunk railway line had made the interior of the North Island more easily accessible. Many of the riverboats had gone out of service and the last of them made its final voyage in 1959.

Today only one vessel of the old fleet still operates on the river: the *Otunui* makes trips every day on the lower reaches of the river, departing from a dock below the City Bridge in Wanganui. Another of the old fleet, the MV *Ongarue*, has been restored and is on display at Pipiriki, where you can walk through and read about the history of the boat and the A Hatrick & Co riverboat fleet. More recently, the *Waimarie*, which had sunk at its mooring in Wanganui in 1952, has been raised, and a restoration project is underway to get the old vessel running again on the river (see Wanganui). The MV *Waireka*, another of the old Hatrick fleet, has been moved from the Whanganui River and now operates tourist cruises at Huka Falls near Taupo.

Information
Maps, brochures and information about the park are available at the DOC offices in Wanganui (☎ (06) 345 2402; fax 345 8712), Pipiriki (☎ (06) 385 4631) and Taumarunui (☎ 895 8201). Tourist Information Centres in the area – at Wanganui, Raetihi, Ohakune and Taumarunui – also have some information on the park.

Good books about the river, available locally, include the *Guide to the Whanganui River* by the New Zealand Canoeing Association, PO Box 284, Wellington (6th edition, 1992, paperback) and *The Wanganui River – a scenic, historic and wilderness experience* published by the Department of Lands and Survey (DOSLI), PO Box 5014, Wellington (2nd edition, 1982, paperback). The Canoeing Association's *Guide* is an excellent companion to take along on canoe trips. *Walks In and Around Whanganui National Park*, a small paperback booklet published by the Department of Conservation, is good if you want to do some walking or tramping.

Canoe & Kayak Trips

The most popular part of the river for canoeing and kayaking is the section from Taumarunui to Pipiriki. Entry to the river is made from the boat ramps at Taumarunui (Cherry Grove), Ohinepa and Whakahoro. You can make a one or two-day trip on the river by entering at Taumarunui or Ohinepa and coming out at Ohinepa or Whakahoro. Once you head downstream from Whakahoro, however, you're committed to being on the river for a few days because there's no more road access to the river until you reach Pipiriki, 87 km further downstream.

The minimum time to allow is about one day from Taumarunui to Ohinepa, one day from Ohinepa to Whakahoro, and then about three days from Whakahoro to Pipiriki. The entire stretch from Taumarunui to Pipiriki takes about five days and this is quite popular. Of course if you have the time, taking a bit longer – five days from Whakahoro to Pipiriki, for example – can make it a more relaxing trip and allow you more time for interesting explorations of tributaries, caves and other features along the river, or just for relaxing and enjoying the scenery.

Below Pipiriki the river widens out, the current is more sluggish and when you are about 30 km from the sea it begins to get tidal. We didn't try it but they say that paddling a canoe in the tidal zone can be difficult, especially when you have to paddle against a strong incoming tide in order to get downstream!

The season for canoe trips is usually from around September to Easter, with the most crowded time being during the December-January school holidays. It is possible to go in the off-season – you'd have a good chance of travelling down the river and never seeing another soul, though of course the weather would be colder, the days shorter, and the winter currents more swift. If you do go during cold weather you should probably wear a wetsuit in case of capsizing – cold, wet clothes in cold weather in this wilderness could be not only highly unpleasant but hazardous to your health.

Canoe and kayak operators will provide you with everything you need for the journey, including life jackets and waterproof drums for your clothing and food – if you should capsize in rapids, you'll be very glad you had them. Most operators also have tents, sleeping bags and other camping gear for hire at very reasonable rates.

Prices range from about $15 to $30 per day for single-person kayaks, $30 to $35 per day for two-person Canadian canoes, when transport is not included in the price. However, you must of course get yourself, your gear and the canoe to and from the starting and finishing points of your trip. Transport in and out can be just as costly as the canoes themselves; the cost may be around $25 to $40 per person, depending where you're starting out from. One operator in Wanganui was charging $100. Some operators include the transport cost into the bargain when they hire the canoes. If you're comparing prices among different companies, ask about transport in and out and figure this amount into the overall cost of the trip.

Another option is a guided canoe or kayak trip. On these, there are one or more guides and everything is provided for you – usually all you have to bring is your own clothes, and a sleeping bag if you have one. They do the cooking, setting up and taking down of tents, etc. Transport, food and all other expenses are included in the trip cost. Typical prices are around $180 to $220 per person for a two-day guided trip, $270 per person for a three or four-day trip, and $475 to $550 per person for a five-day guided trip,

Some operators seem to give better deals than others, however some may give better equipment. Canoe and kayak operators that offer both independent hiring and guided trips include:

Plateau Outdoor Adventure Guides, PO Box 29, National Park (☎ & fax 892 2740)
Yeti Tours, PO Box 140, Ohakune (☎ (06) 385 8197; fax 385 8492)
Paterson's Canoe Hire, RD 3, Wanganui (☎ (06) 343 7195)
Rivercity Tours, PO Box 4224, Wanganui (☎ (06) 344 2554; fax 347 7888)

Whanganui River Experiences, PO Box 377, Wanganui (☎ freephone (0800) 808 686, after hours (06) 345 7933)

Water Based Recreation, 6 Spur Grove, Titahi Bay, Wellington (☎ & fax (04) 236 8687)

Operators offering only independent canoe and kayak hiring include:

Pioneer Jet-Boat Tours, PO Box 399, Taumarunui (☎ 895 8074)

Wades Landing Outdoors, RD 2, Owhango (☎ 894 5995)

Raetihi Motor Camp, SH 4, Raetihi (☎ (06) 385 4176; fax 385 4059)

Te Awa Kaitangata, 10 Rawhiti Place, Wanganui (☎ (06) 345 2824, 342 5509)

Operators offering only guided trips include:

Canoe Safaris, PO Box 180, Ohakune (☎ (06) 385 8758, mobile phone (025) 431 215)

Hikoi Tours, PO Box 24, Wanganui (☎ (06) 345 0945; fax 345 8727)

Camp 'n Canoe, RD 29, Kaponga, Taranaki (☎ (06) 764 6738)

Jet-Boat Trips

Jet-boats are another alternative for getting around on the river. Quite different from canoe trips, jet-boat trips are loud and fast – and they give you a chance to see parts of the river in just a few hours that would take you days to cover in a canoe or kayak. Jet-boat trips depart from Pipiriki, Taumarunui and Whakahoro. All the jet-boat operators will provide transport to the river ends of the Matemateaonga Walkway and the Mangapurua Track.

From Pipiriki Departing from Pipiriki, you can take a 20-minute return trip to the Drop Scene for $25 per person, a 40-minute return trip to the Manganui-A-Te-Ao tributary for $30 per person, or a four-hour return trip to the Bridge to Nowhere for $60 per person (children half price).

Jet-boat operators in Pipiriki include:

Bridge to Nowhere Jet-Boat Tours, PO Box 192, Raetihi (☎ & fax (06) 385 4128)

Pipiriki Tours, PO Box 4182, Pipiriki (☎ & fax (06) 385 4733)

From Taumarunui From Taumarunui you can do anything from a short 20-minute jet-boat tour for $16 per person to a two-day trip to Wanganui. Jet-boat operators in Taumarunui include:

Pioneer Jet-Boat Tours, PO Box 399, Taumarunui (☎ 895 8074)

From Whakahoro Whakahoro is a bit off the beaten track – it's a long drive down an unsealed road to get there, whichever way you come – but once you're there, you'll find a couple of jet-boat operators, including:

Ivan Rusling, Whakahoro; mailing address RD 2, Owhango (☎ 896 6233)

Jet Way Safaris, Oio Rd, Whakahoro; mailing address RD 2, Owhango (☎ 895 5076, ☎ & fax 896 6260); also offers hunting safaris and accommodation

From Wanganui From Wanganui you can do a combined land and jet-boat tour, going up the Whanganui River Rd from Wanganui to Pipiriki and then on a jet-boat trip from there. Operators offering these and other jet-boat tours from Wanganui include:

Rivercity Tours, PO Box 4224, Wanganui (☎ (06) 344 2554; fax 347 7888)

Road & River Tours, PO Box 4182, Mid-Avenue, Wanganui (☎ Wanganui (06) 344 2554; fax 347 7888, Pipiriki ☎ & fax 385 4733)

Te Awa Kaitangata Jet-Boat Tours, 10 Rawhiti Place, Wanganui (☎ (06) 345 2824, 342 5509)

Hikoi Tours, PO Box 24, Wanganui (☎ (06) 345 0945; fax (06) 345 8727).

Other River Trips

In addition to the *Otunui* which makes daily trips from Wanganui, a couple of other larger vessels also make occasional trips on the river.

In the summer you can have a five-day trip on the MV *Wakapai*, which holds 15 people, for about $520 (children $320), everything included. Phone Mr Winston Oliver (☎ (06) 385 4443) for schedule and bookings.

The *Adventurer*, a 30-foot (nine-metre) motorised vessel holding 10 people, plies the river between Whakahoro and Wanganui, making two-day trips for $300 per person and four-day trips for $500 per person, everything included. Contact Colin (☎ (06) 345 7933 or freephone (0800) 808 686).

Boating on the River

You will see much bird life on the river during the daytime, and probably hear morepork owls and kiwis calling at night. You may possibly see a small bat or two flitting around at dusk. Once abundant with fish, there are fewer living in the river now, but there are some trout, and freshwater crayfish. The river has abundant eels, especially at certain times of the year when they migrate to the sea – though the eels live in fresh water for most of their lives, they migrate downriver to spawn in the sea, the young later hatching and swimming upriver to live in fresh water.

Wild goats are a common sight along the river; an introduced species, they are considered a threat to the forest because they are so efficient at stripping and killing the native vegetation. Fallow deer and wild pigs are also present in the bush. Hunting for goats, fallow deer and wild pigs in the park is permitted and even encouraged; you just need a permit from the Department of Conservation. Hunting is prohibited near the river from 1 October to 30 April, the main season for canoeists.

Another animal you'll see at night is the possum. As in many other parts of New Zealand, the introduced possum has become so abundant here that it has become a serious pest.

The native bush is thick podocarp-broadleaf forest, with many types of trees and ferns including New Zealand's national symbol, the silver fern. Much of the land was cleared in the settlement efforts earlier this century, but the bush is now reclaiming the land that people once struggled so hard to clear. Occasionally you will see poplar and other introduced trees along the river, evidence of where people planted them in settlements that have long since vanished.

There are also traces of former Maori settlement along the river in various places, with pa sites, old kainga (village) sites, and the unusual Hauhau niu poles of war and peace at Maraekowhai, at the confluence of the Whanganui and Ohura rivers, where the *Makere* Houseboat was moored for many years. The Ratakura, Reinga Kokiri and Te Rerehapa Falls, all near Maraekowhai on the Ohura River, were popular places for Maori to come to catch small 'tuna riki' eels. Several of the landings marked along the Whanganui River's banks were once riverboat landings. The small but fascinating Nukunuku Museum beside the river at Nukunuku, just downriver from Ohinepa, is a popular feature of river trips beginning at Ohinepa or Taumarunui.

River Safety & Etiquette As river trips become more popular, it is essential that everyone using the river have patience and a congenial attitude towards other river users. Although the river flows through a wilderness area, that doesn't necessarily mean you won't see anyone. At the height of summer, you may see plenty of people plying the river in canoes, kayaks and jet-boats. Keep a good attitude, and remember that this river has been a major route for human travel in one way or another for centuries.

Also remember that motorised and non-motorised craft are equally entitled to use the river. Whichever type of craft you're in, treat people in the other type with consideration and goodwill.

A few simple 'rules of the road' on the river make travel safer and more pleasant for everyone. When an oncoming craft is approaching, keep to the right, unless you are already so far to the left that you'd have to cross in the path of the oncoming craft. In that case, just move far enough over to the left to allow room for the oncoming craft to pass by. If someone has to give way to allow the other to pass, the craft heading downriver towards the sea has the right-of-way.

If you're in a canoe or kayak and a jet-boat is approaching from either direction, you should move to the true right of the river – 'true right' is the side of the river which would be on your right if you were facing downstream – and allow the jet-boat to travel on the true left. Unless, of course, you are already so far to the true left side of the river that you would have to paddle into the path of the oncoming jet-boat to get to the true right side!

Jet-boats are supposed to slow down when they pass canoeists, but in some cases they may not be able to do so. If you're in a canoe or kayak and a jet-boat passes by, you can minimise the effect of the wake by turning at right angles to it. If the jet-boat does slow down for you, remember that it has little control once it's come off its hydroplane. Let it overtake you as soon as possible.

When beaching a canoe or kayak, especially at the end of the day, pull it well clear of the water and secure it tightly. Water levels on the river are extremely changeable and can rise quickly, especially when it's raining – and even if the weather is clear where you are, you don't know if it could be raining further upstream.

Don't drink the river water unless you boil it. Clean drinking water is available at huts and at the posted campsites, where rain water is collected in tanks. Water from the tributary streams may be safe to drink, but use your own judgement.

Tramping

There are various tramping possibilities in the park. Probably the most famous and most travelled is the 40-minute bush walk from the river's Mangapurua Landing to the Bridge to Nowhere, 30 km upstream from Pipiriki.

The Matemateaonga Walkway and the Mangapurua Track are excellent for longer tramps. Both are one-way tracks beginning (or ending) at remote spots on the river, so you must arrange for jet-boat transport to or from these ends of the tracks. Any jet-boat operator on the river will do this.

Several good walks are found along the section of river between Pipiriki and Wanganui; see the Whanganui River Rd in the Around Wanganui section for details on these. The DOC offices in Wanganui, Pipiriki and Taumarunui have information, maps and brochures on all the walking tracks in the area.

Matemateaonga Walkway Taking four days to complete, the 42-km Matemateaonga Walkway has been described as one of New Zealand's best walks. Nevertheless it is not widely known and does not attract the crowds that can form on some of New Zealand's more famous tracks, probably due to its remoteness.

Penetrating deep into bush, wilderness and hill country, the track follows an old Maori track and a disused settlers' dray road between the Whanganui and Taranaki regions. It traverses the Matemateaonga Range along the route of the Whakaihuwaka Rd, started in 1911 to create a more direct link from Stratford to Raetihi and the Main Trunk Railway. The track was cut and was to be widened to a road, but the outbreak of WW I interrupted the plans and the road was never completed.

The track passes through thick bush and regenerating bush. Much of it follows the crest of the Matemateaonga Range. On a clear day, a 1½-hour side trip to the summit of Mt Humphries affords a panoramic view of the Whanganui region all the way to Mt Taranaki and the volcanoes of Tongariro National Park. There's a steep section between the Whanganui River (75 metres above sea level) and the Puketotara Hut (427 metres), but much of the track is easy walking. There are five huts along the way.

Mangapurua Track The Mangapurua Track is a 40-km track between Whakahoro and the Mangapurua Landing, both on the Whanganui River. The track runs along the Mangapurua and Kaiwhakauka Streams, both tributaries of the Whanganui River, passing through the valleys of the same names. Between these valleys a side track leads to the Mangapurua Trig, at 663 metres the highest point in the area, from where you can see all the way to the volcanoes of the Tongariro and Egmont national parks on a clear day. The route passes through land that was cleared for farming by settlers earlier this century, and later abandoned. The famous Bridge to Nowhere is 40 minutes from the Mangapurua Landing end of the track.

The track takes 20 hours and is usually walked in three to four days. Apart from the Whakahoro Hut at the Whakahoro end of the track there are no huts, but there are many fine places for camping. Water is available from numerous small streams. There is road access to the track at the Whakahoro end, and from a side track leading to the end of the Ruatiti Valley-Ohura Rd coming from Raetihi.

Places to Stay

Within the park there are campsites, back country huts and a lodge. Along the stretch of river south of Pipiriki, there are several other accommodation possibilities; see Whanganui River Rd in the Around Wanganui section for details on these.

Camping & Huts The park has nine huts and numerous campsites. Along the upper section of the river between Whakahoro and Pipiriki are three Category Two huts: the Whakahoro Hut at Whakahoro, the John Coull Hut and the Tieke Hut. Along the Matemateaonga Walkway are five huts, but only three of them – the Puketotara, Pouri and Omaru Huts – are good Category Two huts. The other two, Humphries Hut and Otaraheke Hut, are simpler huts, with only two bunks. On the lower part of the river, Downes Hut is on the west bank, opposite Atene.

During the summer season from 1 October to 30 April, a Great Walks hut and campsite pass is required for boat trips on the river involving overnight stays in the park between Taumarunui and Pipiriki; the rule applies only to this stretch of the river. The pass is valid for six nights and seven days and allows you to stay overnight in the huts, in campsites beside the huts or in other posted campsites along the river. Camping alongside the river in the park is only permitted at these designated campsites, in order to prevent environmental damage.

The Great Walks passes cost $25 if purchased in advance, $35 if purchased on the spot (children aged 11 and up half price, under 11 free). They are available at all DOC offices and information centres in the region.

Note that back country hut tickets and annual hut passes are not acceptable during the months that Great Walk passes are required. Also note that during this time, there will be hut wardens on duty and river patrols by Conservation Officers – so you'd better have your pass!

Great Walk passes are not required in the off-season from 1 May to 30 September. During this time, the cost is $8 (two tickets) in huts, $4 (one ticket) for camping beside the huts, and free for camping along the river at the designated campsites. Annual hut passes are also acceptable at this time.

For huts and camping in other parts of the park, back country hut tickets and annual hut passes are acceptable all year round.

Revenue from the sale of tickets and passes goes toward the maintenance of huts and campsites in the park.

Lodge The *Bridge to Nowhere Lodge*, also called the *Ramanui Lodge* (☎ & fax (06) 385 4128) has lodge accommodation at $52 per person, meals included. It's quite remote, 21 km upriver from Pipiriki, near the Matemateaonga Walkway; the only way to get there is by river or by tramping. They will arrange for you to come in from Pipiriki by jet-boat. A variety of activities is offered including canoeing, jet-boat trips, guided wilderness treks and hunting trips.

Getting There & Away

If you're going on a canoe or kayak trip, the canoe company will make some arrangement for transport to get you and the canoe to and from the river.

Camp 'n Canoe (☎ (06) 764 6738) RD 29, Kaponga, Taranaki, offers transport in and out to both ends of the Matemateaonga Walkway for $128 per person. You can check with the DOC and information centres at Stratford in Taranaki, as well as the usual ones for the park, to see if anyone else is also offering this service.

There's road access to the river at Taumarunui, Ohinepa and Whakahoro. Whakahoro is a long drive in through a remote area, along a road that is unsealed for much of its distance; roads leading to Whakahoro take off from Owhango or Raurimu, both on SH 4. There isn't any further road access to the river until you reach Pipiriki, 87 km downstream from Whakahoro. From Pipiriki, the Whanganui River Rd heads south 79 km to Wanganui and east 28 km to Raetihi.

The only way to reach any part of the river by public transport is at Taumarunui, served by buses and trains, and at Pipiriki, where the mail-run bus makes a round trip coming up from Wanganui on weekdays. See the Taumarunui and Wanganui sections for details on these.

Wanganui

Midway between Wellington and New Plymouth, Wanganui (population 41,500) is an attractive coastal city on the banks of the Whanganui River. Its tourist brochure proclaims it as 'The Friendly City' and the people really do seem very friendly and helpful.

The Whanganui River, which enters the sea at Wanganui, is the longest navigable and the second-longest river in New Zealand. It starts off on Mt Tongariro and travels 329 km, passing through the Whanganui National Park named for the river, to its mouth in the Whanganui basin. The estuary, over 30 km long, is the area known to the early Maoris as Whanganui, meaning 'great estuary' or 'great wait'.

History

Kupe, the great Polynesian explorer and navigator, is believed to have travelled up the Whanganui River for about 20 km around 900 AD. There were Maoris living in the area around 1100 AD, and they fully established themselves in the area soon after the great Polynesian migration from Hawaiki around 1350 AD. By the time the first European settlers came to the coast around the late 1830s there were numerous Maori settlements scattered up and down the river.

European settlement at Wanganui was hastened along when the New Zealand Company was unable to keep up with the supply and demand for land around Wellington. In 1840 many Wellington settlers moved to Wanganui and founded a permanent settlement there, the signing of the deed being conducted on the site now known as Moutoa Gardens.

The settlement was initially called Petre

Whanganui or Wanganui?

In recent years there's been a movement to change the spelling of 'Wanganui' to 'Whanganui'. Supposedly the name should have been spelled with the 'h' all along, but it somehow got left out when the name of the Petre settlement was changed to Wanganui, the historical Maori name of the river.

In most usages of the name the 'h' has now been officially restored, including the Whanganui River, the Whanganui River Rd, the Whanganui National Park and the Whanganui Regional Museum. Only the city itself, Wanganui, still clings to the old spelling.

An interesting note is that, unlike in most of the rest of New Zealand, the Maori tribes in the river area pronounce the 'wh' sound the same as in English – as in 'when', 'why', etc – rather than as an 'f'. Therefore, the correct pronunciation of the Whanganui River is 'WHANGA-nui', not 'WANGA-nui' or 'FANGA-nui'.

The word Whanganui means 'great wait'. The name of the Whanganui River, then, is sometimes translated to mean 'the river of great waiting'. Since 'whanga' can also mean 'estuary', the name may also refer to the river's large tidal zone, extending over 30 km upstream from the river's mouth. ■

CENTRAL NORTH ISLAND

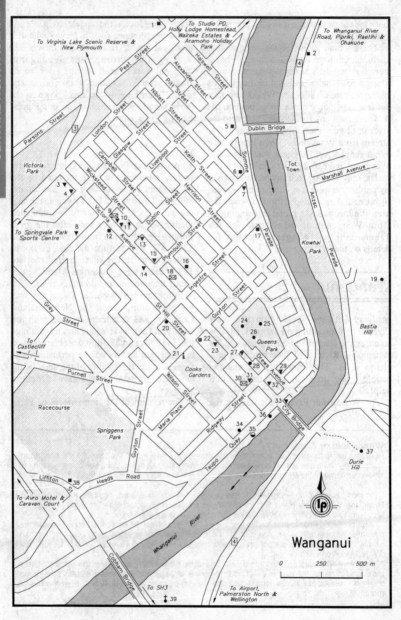

To Virginia Lake Scenic Reserve &
New Plymouth

To Studio PD,
Holy Lodge Homestead,
Waireka Estates &
Aramoho Holiday
Park

To Whanganui River
Road, Pipriki, Raetihi &
Ohakune

Dublin Bridge

Somme

Tot
Town

Marshall Avenue

Kowhai
Park

Anzac

Parade

Victoria
Park

To Springvale Park
Sports Centre

Parsons

Street

Peat

Street

London

Street

Glasgow

Street

Campbell

Street

Wicksteed

Street

Victoria

Avenue

Niblett

Street

Pitt

Street

Alexander

Street

Hadwell

Street

Liverpool

Street

Keith

Street

Harrison

Street

Dublin

Street

Plymouth

Street

Ingestre

Street

Guyton

Street

St Hill

Street

Grey

Street

To
Castlecliff

Purnell

Street

Racecourse

Spriggens
Park

Maria Place

Wilson

Street

Guyton

Street

Ridgway

Quay

Cooks
Gardens

Queens
Park

Drews

Avenue

Bastia
Hill

City Bridge

Durie
Hill

Liffiton

St

To Avro Motel &
Caravan Court

Heads

Road

Taupo

Cobham Bridge

To SH3

To Airport,
Palmerston North &
Wellington

Whanganui

River

Wanganui

0   250   500 m

■ PLACES TO STAY

1 River City Motel
2 Acacia Park Motel
5 Astral Motel
6 Riverside Inn & YHA Hostel
12 Midtown Motor Inn
16 YWCA Hostel
17 Riverside Motel
22 Grand Hotel & Cobb & Co Restaurant
38 Coachman's Lodge

▼ PLACES TO EAT

3 Greenhouse Restaurant
7 Riverside Restaurant & Bistro
8 Collegiate Motor Inn &
   Golden Oaks Restaurant
10 Wing-Wah Chinese Restaurant
11 McDonald's
13 Cameron House Restaurant
14 Kentucky Fried Chicken
15 Pizza Hut
22 Grand Hotel & Cobb & Co Restaurant
23 Dr Johnson's Coffee House & Air
   New Zealand
27 Oriental Chinese Restaurant & Taxi-
   bus stop
29 Moose McGillicuddy's

31 Chamomile Cafe &
   Cables Restaurant & Bar
32 George's Fish & Chips
33 Quay Cafe & Bar

OTHER

4 Woolworth's Supermarket
9 Small Post Office
18 Mid-Avenue Post Office
19 Water Tower
20 Department of Conservation (DOC)
21 Information Centre
23 Air New Zealand &
   Dr Johnson's Coffee House
24 Whanganui Regional Museum
25 Sarjeant Gallery
26 War Memorial Hall
27 Taxi-bus stop &
   Oriental Chinese Restaurant
28 Automobile Association (AA)
29 Moose McGillicuddy's
30 CPO Post Office
33 Quay Cafe & Bar
34 Foodtown Supermarket & K-Mart
35 InterCity & Newmans Bus Station
36 Otunui Paddle Wheeler Dock
37 Durie Hill Elevator
39 Pukiti Maori Church (St Paul's)

after one of the directors of the New Zealand Company, but his name wasn't destined to last on the maps for long. In 1844 it was changed to Wanganui, the name Kupe had given the river.

When the Maoris understood that the gifts the Pakehas had presented them were in exchange for the permanent acquisition of their land, seven years of bitter opposition followed. The Pakehas brought in thousands of troops to occupy Queen's Park, and the Rutland Stockade dominated the hill. Ultimately, the struggle was settled by arbitration and when the Maori Wars were waged with the Taranaki tribes, the Wanganui Maoris actively assisted the Pakehas.

Orientation & Information
Victoria Ave is the main shopping street; most points of interest are along or close to this busy avenue.

The Information Centre (☎ (06) 345 3286) is on Guyton St between St Hill and Wilson Sts, 1½ blocks from Victoria Ave. It's open Monday to Friday from 8.30 am to 5 pm, Saturday and Sunday from 10 am to 2 pm, with extended hours during the summer. The people there are very helpful and there's a great model of the country from Wanganui right up to the Tongariro National Park.

The DOC office (☎ 345 2402; fax 345 8712) on the corner of Ingestre and St Hill Sts, open Monday to Friday from 8 am to 5 pm, is a good resource for maps, pamphlets and information on the Whanganui National Park, Whanganui River Rd, and natural attractions around Wanganui.

The CPO is on Ridgway St, half a block off Victoria Ave. The Mid-Avenue post office is four blocks away on Victoria Ave between Plymouth and Ingestre Sts, and there's another small post office on the corner of Victoria and Liverpool Sts. The AA office (☎ 345 4578) is at 78 Victoria Ave.

Whanganui Regional Museum

The Whanganui Regional Museum, opposite the War Memorial Hall on Wicksteed St near Maria Place, is one of the largest and best regional museums in New Zealand; if you've not had the chance to study Maori culture elsewhere, stop here. Apart from the Maori collection, which includes a large magnificently carved war canoe, other fine carvings and some nasty-looking meres – those elegant but lethal greenstone clubs – the museum also has good colonial and wildlife collections, particularly the selection of moa skeletons. The museum is open Monday to Friday from 10 am to 4 pm, weekends and holidays 1 to 4 pm; admission is $2 (children 60c, family $5).

Sarjeant Gallery

On the hill beside the museum is Wanganui's equally good art gallery, with an extensive permanent exhibition, as well as frequent special exhibits. It's open Monday to Friday from 10.30 am to 4.30 pm, weekends and public holidays 1 to 4.30 pm; admission is free, donations gratefully accepted.

War Memorial Hall

Opposite the Museum is the War Memorial Hall, with a concert chamber, convention hall and pioneer room. The public library is up behind the gallery.

The *Waimarie*

On the riverbank beside Taupo Quay is the old *Waimarie* side-paddle steamer, currently being restored.

The 102-foot (34-metre), 260-passenger vessel has had a long history on the Whanganui River. In 1900, the Upriver Settlers Company ordered the vessel from Yarrow & Co Ship Builders of London. It was sent to New Zealand in pieces and assembled on the riverbank at Wanganui, where it was launched the same year. Originally named the *Aotea*, when the vessel was bought two years later by A Hatrick & Co and added to the Hatrick fleet of riverboats it was re-christened the *Waimarie*, meaning lucky.

The *Waimarie* plied the river for over 50 years until 1952, when it sank at its original berth, remaining submerged for another 40 years until January '93 when it was raised for restoration. The restoration programme is expected to take three to five years, with the goal of getting the *Waimarie* functioning again on the river. You can stop by and see how the progress is getting on.

The *Otunui*

Another of the old Hatrick Whanganui riverboat fleet, the 55-foot (16-metre), *Otunui* paddle wheeler also has a long history on the river, beginning in 1907 when it was shipped in pieces from England, reassembled at Hatrick's Foundry in Wanganui and commissioned on 2 February 1908. After plying the Whanganui River for 40 years, the vessel had a varied history which included being sunken for 20 years, relocated to other parts of the North Island around Taupo and Rotorua, and finally returned to Wanganui in 1984, where it was restored and is once again in service and capable of carrying 85 passengers.

You can take a three-hour river cruise on the *Otunui* any day of the week. Departing from the City Marina beneath the City Bridge, the *Otonui* sails twice a day, at 10 am and 2 pm, during summer (1 December to Easter), and once a day, at 1 pm, the rest of the year. The boat is owned and operated by Jack Dodd, affectionately known as 'Captain Jack'; you can ring him (☎ 345 0344) for current prices or to schedule additional trips.

Other River Trips

A variety of other river trips are possible – by canoe, kayak, jet-boat or motorised vessel, starting further up the river in the Whanganui National Park. See the Whanganui National Park section for details.

Parks

Wanganui has several parks right in the city centre including the pleasant park in which the museum, gallery and war memorial hall are situated. The complex is on a small hill right beside the town centre.

If you cross the City Bridge at the end of Victoria Ave and turn left, there's a pleasant riverside park, Kowhai Park, extending all the way up to and beyond the Dublin Bridge, with an arboretum, plantings of exotic trees, a rose garden and a children's section with a Tot Town Railway, bumper boats, mini-golf and an imaginative playground. The Glenlogie Rose Gardens are on the corner of Anzac Parade and Marshall Ave, opposite Kowhai Park.

The Virginia Lake Scenic Reserve (Roto-kawau), about one km from the top end of Victoria Ave on SH 3 heading towards New Plymouth, is a beautiful reserve of 18½ hectares with a lake, various theme gardens, a walk-in aviary, numerous statues, and the Higginbottom Fountain, colourfully lit up at night. The winter gardens and aviary are open from 10 am to 4 pm daily, and the rest of the reserve is always open.

Durie Hill & Bastia Hill
Take Victoria Ave across the river from the town centre and immediately to the left you'll see the carved gateway to the Durie Hill elevator. You can follow a tunnel into the hillside and then, for $1, ride up through the hill to the summit 65 metres above.

There are two viewpoints at the top: a lower one on the top of the lift machinery room, and a higher 31-metre watchtower built from fossilised shellrock. This higher one, the War Memorial Tower, is visible from anywhere in town; it closes at 6 pm, but you can go up the other one anytime. From here there's a fine view over the town and all the way to Mt Taranaki, Mt Ruapehu or the South Island if the weather is clear.

In summer the elevator operates Monday to Friday from 7.30 am to 7 pm, Saturday 9 am to 8 pm and Sunday from 1 to 6 pm. In winter it closes a bit earlier, at 6.30 pm, on weekdays and Saturday.

Bastia Hill, with a large water tower, is another good viewpoint. You can climb up the water tower on a spiral staircase, but only

to the first couple of levels; after that a steel gate keeps you from reaching the top.

Putiki Church
If you turn right after the Victoria Ave bridge and continue for a km or so you come to Putiki Church, also called St Paul's Memorial Church. It's a plain little place from the outside but the interior is magnificent, completely covered in Maori carvings and tukutuku wall panels. The church is usually open during the day but if it's locked you can ask for the key at the caretaker's house on the corner of Anaua St and SH 3, a couple of doors away.

Holly Lodge Estate
Six km upstream from the Dublin St Bridge, the Holly Lodge Homestead is a historic old homestead by the river. The homestead is open every day from 8 am to 8 pm; you can reach it by road, or come on the *Otunui* paddle wheeler. Out on the grounds are a swimming pool and a playground for the kids. Admission is free.

Waireka Estate
About two km further along the river, that is, eight km upstream from the Dublin St Bridge, the Waireka Estate is a 19th century homestead with a fascinating private museum collection. The original settler was George Sinclair Robertson, of a Scottish family who settled here in 1876; the present house, built in 1912 to replace the first one, has been kept in the family and is being restored by John and Margaret-Anne Barnett, she being a great-granddaughter in the family.

A visit to the estate begins with a tea at which John, very amiable and knowledgeable, relates history and stories of the homestead. He then takes you on an interesting tour of the museum collection, with items from New Zealand and around the world, topping it off by firing a cannon out on the lawn. It's an enjoyable time and well worth the $3 (children $1) admission.

The *Otonui* paddle steamer comes to Waireka Estate, and this is the best way to visit; otherwise, phone the estate (☎ 342 5729) and schedule a visit, probably to coincide with the *Otonui*'s arrival.

Other Things to See

The information centre has maps outlining a Golden Arrow Scenic Drive (you can't miss the golden arrows as you explore around town) and several scenic or historic walks in and near Wanganui.

If you prefer sightseeing from the air, the Wanganui Aero Club (☎ 345 0914) offers a variety of flights including a 20-minute tour over Wanganui for $20 per seat, a 50-minute trip up the Whanganui River to the Bridge to Nowhere for $70 per seat, and trips further afield to Tongariro National Park and Lake Taupo. Wanganui Aero Work (☎ 345 3994) offers Tiger Moth flights at $70 for a 15-minute flight.

The Splash Centre in the Springvale Park Sports Centre off London St is a large indoor heated swimming pool open Monday to Friday from 6 am to 8 pm, Saturday and Sunday 9 am to 6 pm, all year round. Admission is $3 (children & seniors $1.50, family $8).

Studio PD (☎ 343-9479), beside the river at 348 Somme Parade on the corner of Cedar Drive, shows the art of Peter Donne who has won many honours for his creations. These include bone carvings, paintings, and several other art forms including jewellery and T-shirt art. The studio is open Sunday from 2 to 5 pm, and whenever the sign says 'open', and at other times by request.

Tours

A very interesting trip up the Whanganui River Rd can be made with the weekday mail run, going up the river from Wanganui to Pipiriki Monday to Friday. The mailman, Don Adams, will pick you up at around 7.30 am and take you on an all-day trip up the river, stopping at many interesting and historic sites along the way including the Kawana Flour Mill, the Jerusalem church, the Koriniti Marae and other places, telling you along the way about the past and present of the river area. Coffee and tea is provided,

but bring your own lunch – you'll get back to town around 3 or 4 pm. The cost is $20 per person, with an optional half-hour jet-boat trip from Pipiriki to Drop Scene for another $30. Contact Don (☎ (06) 344 2554; fax 347 7888) to make a booking for the journey; it's a very popular trip so it never hurts to book as far in advance as you can.

Don Adams' family also operates Rivercity Tours (same ☎ & fax) which offers additional tours up the Whanganui River Rd and on to the Drop Scene or the Bridge to Nowhere by jet-boat, returning to Wanganui via SH 4. Lunch is included; the cost is $75 per person if you go to the Drop Scene, $110 per person if you go all the way to the Bridge to Nowhere.

Other tours are operated by Ash's Transport (☎ & fax 343 8319, mobile phone (025) 958 693). Their 1½-hour City Tour departs at 1.30 pm Monday to Thursday, other days by arrangement; the cost is $10 (children $5, family $25). At the same prices they also operate a morning tour to the Holly Lodge and Waireka Estates. Or there's a 'Higginbottom Fountain By Night' tour for $3 (children $2, family $8) and other inexpensive tours further afield to Bushy Park, Ashley Park and the Bason Botanical Reserve (see Around Wanganui). Pickup is available on all their tours. Ash's Transport also operates the airport and bus station shuttles and they proudly state that they'll strive to take you anywhere you want to go.

Places to Stay

Camping & Cabins Closest in is the *Avro Motel & Caravan Court* (☎ (06) 345 5279; fax 345 2104) at 36 Alma Rd, 1.5 km from the city centre. It has 10 powered sites at $12/18 for one/two people plus motel units at $60/70; there's an indoor spa pool, filtered swimming pool and children's playground, but unlike most motor camps it has no kitchen facilities.

The *Aramoho Holiday Park* (☎ (06) 343 8402) at 460 Somme Parade, six km north of the Dublin St Bridge, is a peaceful, parklike camp on the town-side bank of the Whanganui River. It has tent sites at $8/14 for one/two people, powered sites at $9/15, cabins from $15/23 to $18/31, tourist flats at $46 and chalets at $49. Canoes are available for hire. Local Aramoho buses run there every day except Sunday.

Other camps and cabins are at Castlecliff, a seaside suburb eight km from the centre. The local Castlecliff bus runs there every day except Sunday. The *Castlecliff Camp* (☎ (06) 344 2227) by the beach on the corner of Karaka and Rangiora Sts has tent sites at $7 per person, powered sites at $15 for two, backpackers cabins at $14/24 for one/two people, larger cabins at $28 for two and on-site caravans at $14/28.

Also in Castlecliff, the *Alwyn Motel & Cabins* (☎ (06) 344 4500) opposite the beach at 65 Karaka St doesn't have camping but it does have cabins at $16 per person, tourist flats at $45 and motel units at $58. All the cabins have private kitchens, and there's a swimming pool. If you don't have your own bedding you can hire it there and they also offer free pick-up from Wanganui when you arrive.

The *Mowhanau Camping Ground* (☎ (06) 342 9658) at Kai-Iwi (Mowhanau) Beach is a simple beachside camp with tent sites at $5.50/11 for one/two people, powered sites at $13. The turn-off for the beach is 5.5 km north-west of Wanganui on SH3, the road to New Plymouth, then another nine km out to the beach; this is one of Wanganui's most attractive beaches.

Hostels The *Riverside Inn* (☎ (06) 347 2529) at 2 Plymouth St opposite the river is a friendly hostel with a pleasant courtyard, off-street parking and accommodation in dorm rooms or cabins. The cost is $13 for YHA members, $14 for non-members; since it's an associate YHA hostel, you can stay with or without a YHA card. Don't confuse it with the Riverside Motel nearby on Somme Parade.

The *YWCA Hostel* (☎ (06) 345 7480) at 232 Wicksteed St is in a stately old homestead right in the centre of town. The cost is $12 per night with your own sleeping bag, $14 with linen provided, and they accept both women and men.

Guesthouses The *Riverside Inn* (☎ (06) 347 2529) at 2 Plymouth St opposite the river is a B&B inn in a restored Victorian home; the cost is $38/50 for singles/doubles including a continental breakfast. There's a hostel in the rear part of the building. Don't confuse it with the *Riverside Motel* nearby on Somme Parade.

Hotels The *Grand Hotel* (☎ (06) 345 0955; fax 345 0953) at 99 Guyton St on the corner of St Hill St is about the only hotel of the old school still surviving in Wanganui. Singles/doubles are $50/60; all rooms have private facilities and there's a Cobb & Co restaurant downstairs.

Motels There are plenty of motels in Wanganui; the information centre can supply details on all of them, and may even be able to get you a special deal.

The *River City Motel* (☎ & fax (06) 343 9107) at 59 Halswell St is attractively situated on a quiet tree-lined street at the foot of St John's Hill; the cost is $55 for one or two people. The *Mid Town Motor Inn* (☎ 345 8408; fax 345 8406) at 321 Victoria Ave has units at $55. *Coachman's Lodge* (☎ (06) 345 2227) at 30 Liffiton St beside the racecourse has singles/doubles at $45/55.

The *Astral Motel* (☎ (06) 347 9063; fax 347 8653) at 45 Somme Parade on the corner of Dublin St, by the Dublin St Bridge, has units at $55 and $60. Across the river, the *Acacia Park Motel* (☎ (06) 343 9093) at 140 Anzac Parade has studio units at $50/55, $60 with kitchen. The *Alwyn Motel & Cabins* and the *Avro Caravan Court* also have motel units (see Camping & Cabins).

Places to Eat

Snacks & Fast Food The *Chamomile Cafe* on the corner of Victoria Ave and Ridgway St is a pleasant cafe with a good selection of light meals and snacks. *Dr Johnson's Coffee House* in the Tudor Court on Victoria Ave between Guyton St and Maria Place is a courtyard cafe.

George's Fish & Chips on Victoria Ave between Ridgway St and Taupo Quay is said by locals to have the best fish & chips in town; it has both restaurant and takeaway sections. It's open from 8 am to 7 pm every day except Friday, when it's open until 9 pm.

The big three American fast food chains are all represented in Wanganui, within a couple of blocks on Victoria Ave. *Pizza Hut* is on the corner of Victoria Ave and Plymouth St, *Kentucky Fried Chicken* is almost opposite, and *McDonald's* is in the next block, between Dublin and Liverpool Sts.

Pub Food There's a *Cobb & Co* tucked away in the recesses of the Grand Hotel on the corner of Guyton St and St Hill St, a block from Victoria Ave, with the usual Cobb & Co menu and hours.

The *Riverside Restaurant & Bistro* on the corner of Plymouth St and Somme Parade has a bistro and beer garden with a blackboard menu; lunch and dinner are served every day.

Moose McGillicuddy's and the *Quay Cafe & Bar* also are popular places for meals; see Entertainment.

Restaurants Wanganui has several good restaurants if you're willing to pay the price. *Cables* on the corner of Victoria Ave and Ridgway St has plenty of atmosphere. So does the *Riverside Restaurant* on the corner of Somme Parade and Plymouth St by the river; it offers smorgasbord lunches every day except Saturday, and there's also a bistro and beer garden section. The *Greenhouse Restaurant* on the corner of Victoria Ave and London St is good for steak dinners.

The *Golden Oaks Restaurant* at the Collegiate Motor Inn at 122 Liverpool St is a bit on the expensive side but it has ample smorgasbord dinners on Friday, Saturday and Sunday nights, and buffet lunches on Friday and Sunday.

For Chinese food try *Wing-Wah* on Victoria Ave between Dublin and Liverpool Sts; or there's the *Oriental Chinese Restaurant &*

Takeaways at 5 Maria Place, near the museum. At either place you can get Chinese food to eat there or take away.

If you want to pull out all the stops and splurge, head for *Cameron House* at 281 Wicksteed St on the corner of Dublin St. It's a consistently award-winning restaurant with an elegant atmosphere in a classic converted home, open for lunch Tuesday to Friday and for dinner Tuesday to Saturday.

Entertainment

The *Quay Cafe & Bar* on the corner of Victoria Ave and Taupo Quay is a popular place with a variety of entertainment including live music on weekend nights, live classical music nights, jazz jam nights, chess and backgammon nights, a soap box night, guest chefs once a month, and so on. It's open Monday to Saturday from 11 am to 3 am, Sunday from 11 am to midnight.

Moose McGillicuddy's on the corner of Rutland St and Drews Ave is a traditional Irish-style bar & grill with good food and live dance music on Friday and Saturday nights. It's open Monday to Saturday from 11.30 am to 3 am, Sunday from 2 pm to 3 am.

Getting There & Away

Air Air New Zealand (☎ 345 5518/5593) at 133 Victoria Ave has daily direct flights to Auckland, Paraparaumu and Wellington, with connections to other centres.

Bus InterCity and Newmans buses operate from the Wanganui Travel Centre (☎ 345 4433) on Taupo Quay between St Hill and Wilson Sts, beside the river. Both companies operate buses to Auckland (eight hours) via New Plymouth (2½ hours) and Hamilton (four hours), to Palmerston North (1½ hours) and on to Wellington (four hours) or Napier (4½ hours). They also have services north to Tongariro, Taupo and Rotorua, but you have to transfer at Bulls, on the way to Palmerston North.

White Star buses (☎ 345 7612) operate from a bus stop in front of the Avis Rent-A-Car office at 161 Ingestre St, with buses to

New Plymouth, Palmerston North and Wellington.

The mail-run bus (☎ 344 2554) heads up the Whanganui River Rd to Pipiriki and back on weekdays; see Tours.

Car Between Wanganui and the centre of the North Island the highway (SH 4) passes through the Paraparas, an area of interesting papa hills with some beautiful views, and also passes close by the impressive Raukawa Falls and along the Mangawhero River Gorge.

Alternatively you can take the Whanganui River Rd – see the Around Wanganui section. This is a popular scenic drive, with points of interest marked along the way.

Getting Around

To/From the Airport The Wanganui Airport is about four km from the town centre, across the river and out towards the sea. Ash's Transport Services (☎ 343 8319, mobile (025) 958 693) operates a shuttle service to the airport, the bus station and other points around town. They also operate a shuttle service to the airport at Palmerston North.

Bus Wanganui Taxi-Buses (☎ 345 4441) operates several local bus routes including routes to Castlecliff, to Aramoho and others, all departing from the taxi-bus stop on Maria Place near Victoria Ave. They operate Monday to Friday from 7 am to 6 pm, with more limited service on Saturday and no service at all on Sunday. There's a flat fare of $2 to go anywhere in town, with discounts for children, students and seniors. You can pick up a schedule at the information centre.

AROUND WANGANUI
Whanganui River Road & Pipiriki

The Whanganui River Road, running along the Whanganui River most of the way from Wanganui to Pipiriki, is a scenic and historic area worth making the detour to see. The Department of Conservation has dubbed it 'The River Road Scenic and Historic Drive', with plaques along the river pointing out sites of scenic and historic interest. The River

Rd meets SH 4, the highway from Wanganui to the centre of the North Island, 14 km north of Wanganui and again at Raetihi, 91 km north of Wanganui.

It takes about 1½ to two hours to drive the 79 km between Wanganui and Pipiriki – that's not counting stops. If you come on the mail-run bus from Wanganui to Pipiriki the trip will take most of the day, but you'll have the benefit of lots of social and historical commentary. The full circle from Wanganui to Pipiriki to Raetihi and back down SH 4 through the scenic Paraparas and the Mangawhero River Gorge to Wanganui takes about four hours. The River Rd is also becoming increasingly popular with cyclists as an alternative route to SH 4.

See the Whanganui National Park section for more about the history of the river.

Information Pick up a copy of the DOC pamphlet *The River Road Scenic and Historic Drive*, available at the DOC offices and information centres in Wanganui and Pipiriki. It gives a map and commentary about various interesting spots along the road.

A Motorist's Guide to the Wanganui River Road by Judith Crawley (Whanganui historical Society, Wanganui, 3rd edition, 1987, paperback), a 40-page booklet available for $4.95 at the same places is even better, with much more detail.

Things to See The introduction to Judith Crawley's booklet says 'a story could be told at every bend as the river winds its way to the sea', and it seems to be true. Black posts topped in red along the roadway let you know that a plaque is coming up, telling about interesting historic and other sites along the river.

Space prevents us from telling everything here, but if you pick up Crawley's booklet or go on the mail-run bus from Wanganui you'll learn a lot. A few notable sights include the Maori villages of Atene (Athens), Koriniti (Corinth), Ranana (London) and Hiruharama (Jerusalem) where you can visit the historic Catholic church; the historic flour mill at Ranana; the Operiki Pa and other pa sites; the Aramoana hill from where there's a panoramic view; and Pipiriki.

Pipiriki Pipiriki is beside the river at the north end of the River Rd, 79 km from Wanganui and 28 km from Raetihi. This is the ending point for canoe trips coming down the Whanganui River; see the Whanganui National Park section for information on canoe and kayak trips, and jet-boat rides departing from Pipiriki.

The Pipiriki DOC office (☎ (06) 385 4631) is open Monday to Friday from 8 am to 5 pm with maps and information on the river and the Whanganui National Park, though it's not guaranteed someone will always be there during these hours.

The Colonial House in Pipiriki is a historic house now converted to a museum with many interesting exhibits on the history of Pipiriki and the river. If it's locked, ask at the DOC office and they'll be happy to open it for you.

Beside the Colonial House, some old steps and foundations are all that remain to mark the site of the old Pipiriki House hotel, a glamourous 65-room wooden hotel popular with tourists around the turn of the century. Pipiriki was a bustling place served by several river steamers and paddleboats back then, with 12,000 tourists a year recorded in 1905. A local Maori group was constructing a smaller hotel on the site on our last visit. Opposite the Colonial House is a public shelter.

Another interesting historic relic at Pipiriki is the MV *Ongarue*, a 60-foot (20-metre), 65-passenger riverboat that was once one of the A Hatrick & Co riverboat fleet. Built by Yarrow & Co in London in 1903 and shipped in sections to Wanganui where it was assembled, the riverboat plied the river from 1903 to 1959, when the Pipiriki House burned down and the Hatrick riverboat fleet ceased operating. The vessel was restored in 1983 and is now on display on land, about 50 metres from the turn-off to the DOC office.

Walks The Wanganui Information Centre and DOC have brochures on a couple of good walks starting from the Whanganui River Rd. Or ask them for the DOC booklet *Walks In and Around Whanganui National Park*, with details on these and other walks along the river.

The Aramoana Walkway begins across the road a few metres south of the Aramoana Lookout, near the southern end of the Whanganui River Rd three km north of its junction with SH 4. A seven-km, 2½-hour loop track, the walkway passes through farmland and forest to higher ground from where there's a panoramic view of the river area and all the way to Mt Ruapehu to the north, Mt Taranaki to the west and Kapiti Island to the south. Other features include fossilised cockle shell beds, evidence that this land now 160 metres high was once at the bottom of the sea. Take drinking water, warm clothing and be prepared for mud after wet weather.

The Atene Skyline Track begins at Atene (Athens), on the River Rd about 22 km north of the SH 4-River Rd junction. The 18-km track takes six to eight hours and features native forest, sandstone bluffs, and the 523-metre Taumata Trig, commanding broad views. The track ends back on the River Rd, two km downstream from where it began.

Places to Stay There are various places to stay along the River Rd. The nuns at the Catholic church in Hiruharama (Jerusalem) take in travellers. Accommodation is in a large room with curtains you can pull around your area for privacy; the cost is around $10 a night.

Beside the river at Ranana, the *Kauika Campsite* (☎ (06) 342 8133/8762) has hot water showers, kitchen and laundry facilities. Tent sites are $6 for two people, powered sites $10 for two.

The Ahu Ahu Ohu (☎ (06) 345 5711) PO Box 4239, Wanganui, is a remote farming community four km up the Ahu Ahu Stream from where it meets the Whanganui River at the Te Tuhi Landing, between Atene and Koriniti. In case you haven't heard of it before, Maori-English dictionaries say an ohu is a 'band of people; working party; working bee'. This small community, established in 1976, is working 30 hectares of a 250-hectare parcel, with agriculture and farm animals. They welcome visitors – WWOOFers, backpackers, campers and farmstays. Be sure to contact them before you arrive; they'll meet you at the Te Tuhi Landing.

At Pipiriki there's a DOC campsite with toilets and cold water; not far away there's a basic shelter but it's not designed as accommodation – basically just a place to get out of the rain. Another basic DOC campsite is the Otumaire Camping Site between Atene and Koriniti. DOC also operates the Downes Hut near Atene but it's across the river, so you need a boat to reach it.

Getting There & Away

Tours There are various ways of getting up and down the Whanganui River Rd. One of the most convenient and congenial is with the mail-run bus, which goes from Wanganui to Pipiriki on weekdays and takes passengers along with the mail for an interesting tour. See this and a couple of other tour possibilities under Tours in the Wanganui section.

Car There's petrol available at Raetihi on the north end of the journey and at Upokongaro and Wanganui on the south end, but nowhere in between. So make sure you have enough petrol in your tank before you start out!

Cycling This route is becoming a favourite of cyclists. SH 4 is also fine, but the River Rd has less traffic and is generally considered more interesting.

Hitching Since there's not much traffic on the River Rd, hitching along here is a dubious proposition.

Other Parks & Reserves

Heading north-west from Wanganui on SH 3 as if you were going to New Plymouth, after about 5.5 km you reach Rapanui Rd.

Turn towards the sea on this road and you come to some pleasant spots.

First is the **Westmere Reserve & Wildlife Refuge**, where there's lots of birdlife and a 40-minute lakeside walk around Lake Westmere.

Next along, **Bason Botanical Reserve** is a 25-hectare botanical reserve with a lake, conservatory, gardens of many kinds, a deer park, a lookout tower and an old homestead. The reserve is open every day from 9.30 am until dusk; the conservatory is open from 10 am to 4 pm on weekdays and from 2 to 4 pm on weekends and public holidays.

At the end of Rapanui Rd, nine km from the SH 3 turn-off, **Mowhanau Beach**, also called **Kai Iwi Beach**, is a beautiful beach. The Mowhanau Creek meets the sea here and provides a safe place for children to swim, and there's also a motor camp and scenic papa cliffs.

Bushy Park Bushy Park is 24 km north-west of Wanganui. Following the signs as if you were going to New Plymouth, take SH 3 to Kai Iwi, turn off where you see the signs and go eight km further on a sealed side road. Operated by the Royal Forest & Bird Protection Society, the park is a 96-hectare scenic reserve with spacious grounds, picnic and BBQ areas, bush walks and a historic 1906 homestead. It's open for day use every day from 10 am to 5 pm; admission is $3 (children $1, family $7).

If you want to stay the night there's a variety of accommodation available (☎ (06) 342 9879). The homestead is an interesting place to stay since it's like staying in a well-preserved museum. Single/double rooms are $35/40 most of the week, $5 extra on Friday and Saturday nights. They also have an 11-bed bunkroom at $10 per person, and caravan and tent sites at $10 per site.

Ashley Park Ashley Park (☎ (06) 346 5917), 34 km north-west of Wanganui on SH 3, is another attractive park, with gardens and trees surrounding a picturesque lake. Activities include fishing, eeling, birdwatching, and kayaking on the lake. There's also an antiques & crafts shop and Devonshire teas. The park is open for day use every day from 9 am to 5 pm; admission is free.

Here, too, there's a variety of accommodation if you want to stay over; you're welcome to join in the farm activities with the sheep, cattle, deer and other animals, and you can also go boating on the lake, hunting or hire a three-wheeler. Two motel units in a peaceful setting above the lake are $65 for two people; B&B in the house is $30 per person, with dinner by arrangement. Farmstays are $30 for two. They also have basic cabins at $11 per person and for camping there are powered sites at $10/14.50 for one/two people and unlimited tent sites at $6 per person.

Lake Wiritoa About 12.5 km south-east of the city, off SH3, Lake Wiritoa is popular for swimming and water skiing. To get there, turn left at Kaitoke Lake and keep going past it to Lake Wiritoa.

Palmerston North

On the banks of the Manawatu River, Palmerston North (population 73,000) is the principal centre of the Manawatu region and a major crossroads of the southern North Island. With Massey University, the second-largest university in New Zealand, and several other colleges also based here, Palmerston North has the pleasant, relaxed feel of a rural university town.

Orientation & Information
The wide open expanse of The Square, with seven hectares of gardens and fountains, is very much the centre of Palmerston North. Most things of interest in the town are on or within a few blocks of The Square. You can get your bearings from a lookout on top of the Civic Centre building in The Square, open 10 am to 3 pm on weekdays.

The Information Centre (☎ (06) 358 5003) in the Civic Centre building on The Square has plenty of information on the area, and free city and country maps. It's open Monday to Friday from 8.30 am to 5 pm, Saturday and Sunday 10 am to 2 pm.

The DOC office (☎ 358 9004; fax 358 9002) is at 717 Tremaine Ave, on the north side of town. It's open Monday to Friday from 8 am to 4.35 pm. There's an AA office (☎ 357 7039) at 185 Broadway on the corner of Amesbury St, two blocks from The Square.

The CPO is in Princess St between Main St and Broadway Ave, one block off The Square. Bennett's Government Bookshop at 38-42 Broadway near the Downtown Arcade is one of the better bookshop chains in New Zealand.

STA (☎ 359 2512), the student and youth travel agency, has an office at 8 Fitzherbert Ave just off The Square.

Palmerston North is the home base of WWOOF (Willing Workers on Organic Farms, PO Box 10-037, ☎ (06) 355 3555). See the Facts for the Visitor chapter for information on WWOOF.

Museums & Galleries
The **Science Centre & Manawatu Museum** share a large building on the corner of Church and Pitt Sts, one long block from The Square. Admission is $6 (children, students and pensioners $4, pre-schoolers $2, family $15). The museum specialises in the history of the Manawatu region, including its Maori history, culture and art. It's open every day from 10 am to 5 pm. Admission is free to the museum.

Around the corner is the modern and spacious **Manawatu Art Gallery** at 398 Main St West. It's open Tuesday to Friday from 10 am to 4.30 pm, weekends and public holidays 1 to 5 pm; admission is free, donations welcome.

On the south-western corner of The Square, the **Square Edge Community Arts Centre** contains many small shops featuring a variety of arts & crafts, a women's bookshop, a good bulk wholefoods grocery store, and the pleasant wholefoods Sage Cafe. The centre is open Monday to Thursday from 10 am to 5 pm, Friday 10 am to 8 pm and Saturday 10 am to 2 pm.

Rugby fans will like the **New Zealand Rugby Museum** at 87 Cuba St, a few blocks from The Square. This interesting museum contains exhibits and memorabilia relating to the history of rugby in New Zealand from the first game played in the country, in Nelson in 1870, up to the present. It also has mementos from every country where rugby is played, and videos of the most famous international games. The museum is open Monday to Saturday from 10 am to noon and 1.30 to 4 pm, Sunday 1.30 to 4 pm; admission is $2 (children 50c).

Park & Walkway

The Esplanade Park is a beautiful park stretching along the shores of the Manawatu River, a few blocks south of The Square. At the park are gardens, bush walks, a nature trail, an aviary, a conservatory and lathe house, rose gardens, a playground, a miniature railway and a miniature golf course.

The Manawatu Riverside Walkway & Bridle Track, extending 10 km along the Manawatu River, passes through the park.

Lido Swimming Complex

Adjacent to Esplanade Park, the large Lido Swimming and Recreation Centre on Park Rd has indoor and outdoor pools, sauna and spa. It's open weekdays from 6 am to 7 pm, weekends and public holidays 8 am to 7 pm; admission is $2.30 for swimming (children & seniors $1.20, family $5.80), or $4.60 for using the spa and sauna, with swimming included.

Palmerston North Showgrounds

About six blocks west of The Square, on Waldegrave & Cuba Sts, the Palmerston North Showgrounds complex contains over 20 venues ranging over 17½ hectares of grounds. It includes the Manawatu Sports Stadium and other stadiums, rugby and other sports fields, a speedway stockcar track, concert halls and more. Check with the Showgrounds (☎ 356 1505) or the information centre for the current schedule.

Other sports venues include the Awapuni Racecourse for thoroughbred horse racing, and the Manawatu Raceway on Pioneer Highway for trotting and greyhound racing.

Places to Stay

Camping & Cabins The *Palmerston North Holiday Park* (☎ (06) 358 0349; fax 358 2372) at 133 Dittmer Drive, off Ruha Place and Park Rd, is pleasantly situated beside the Lido Swimming Centre and Esplanade Park, about two km from The Square. It has tent sites at $7.50 per person, powered sites at $17 for two, cabins at $23 to $39 for two and tourist flats at $52 for two.

Hostels The *Peppertree Hostel* (☎ (06) 355 4054) at 121 Grey St, at the junction with Princess St, is a pleasant hostel with a well-appointed kitchen, off-street parking and a homely atmosphere. The cost is $14 per night, or $7 for tent sites; they offer free pick-up from anywhere in town and since it's an associate YHA hostel, you can stay with or without a YHA card.

King St Backpackers (☎ (06) 358 9595) at 95 King St is a larger hostel upstairs in a converted former hotel, 1½ blocks from The Square. The cost is $12/15/20 per person in dorm/double/single rooms, with reduced weekly rates.

Five blocks west of The Square, *Manawatu Backpackers* (☎ (06) 355 2130) at 267 Main St West on the corner of Domain St is another upstairs hostel in a converted former hotel. It's all been refurbished and the effect is quite cheerful. The cost is $15 per person with your own sleeping bag, $20/40 for singles/doubles with linen, or $35 per room with linen and private bath. Downstairs there's an Irish bar with live music on Friday and Saturday nights.

Guesthouses The *Chaytor House* (☎ (06) 358 6878) at 18 Chaytor St is in a pleasant tree-lined street a couple of blocks south of The Square; B&B is $35/55 for singles/doubles. *Grey's Inn* (☎ (06) 358 6928; fax 355 0291) at 123 Grey St, at the junction with Princess St, is an attractive, homely guest

To Railway Station,
DOC Office &
Wanganui

To Napier

To Wellington
via Foxton

To Massey University &
Wellington via Levin

Palmerston
North

0   250   500 m

Approximate Scale

Manawatu   River

The Esplanade

Manawaroa
Park

Ongley
Park

Fitzherbert
Park

Featherston Street

Bourke Street

Campbell Street

Lombard Street

Taonui Street

Walding Street

Rangitikei Street

Waldegrave Street

Cuba Street

George St

Coleman Pl

King Street

Broadway Avenue

Queen Street

Grey Street

Amesbury St

Main Street

Victoria Avenue

Church Street

Dahlia Street

Princess Street

The Square

Pitt Street

Linton Street

Chaytor St

Fitzherbert Avenue

Ferguson Street

South Street

Hereford Street

Worcester Street

Cook Street

Church Street

Main Street West

College Street

Savage Crescent

Ruha Place

Park Road

Huia Street

Te Awe Awe Street

Ada Street

Oxford Street

Morris Street

College Street

Milverton Avenue

Colombo Street

Ranfurly Street

Batt Street

CENTRAL NORTH ISLAND

■ PLACES TO STAY

2   Peppertree Hostel & Grey's Inn
3   Broadway Motel
5   King St Backpackers
7   Consolidated Mid City Motel
21 Empire Hotel &
    Cobb & Co Restaurant
24 City Court Motel
35 Manawatu Backpackers &
    Cafe de Paris
36 Masonic Hotel & Cheers Nightclub
40 Chaytor House
41 Emma's Place
43 Palmerston North Holiday Park

▼ PLACES TO EAT

6   Regent Arcade, Celtic Inn & Sun Sing
    Chinese Restaurant
10 Downtown Arcade & Food Court &
    Downtown Cinema 6
16 Deano's Bar & Grill
17 Costa's Restaurant (upstairs)
18 Pizza Piazza
21 Empire Hotel & Cobb & Co Restaurant
23 McDonald's
25 Kentucky Fried Chicken
29 Square Edge Community Arts Centre
    & Sage Cafe
30 Fat Ladies Arms
31 Puddleducks, Old Istanbul, Truelife
    Bakery & Takeaways
35 Manawatu Backpackers &
    Cafe de Paris

OTHER

1   Chantelle's Nightclub
4   Automobile Association (AA)
6   Regent Arcade, Celtic Inn & Sun Sing
    Chinese Restaurant
8   CPO
9   Air New Zealand &
    Ansett New Zealand
10 Downtown Arcade & Food Court &
    Downtown Cinema 6
11 Palmerston North Travel Centre &
    Bus Depot
12 Level One Nightclub
13 Palmerston North Showgrounds
14 New Zealand Rugby Museum
15 Three Guys Supermarket
19 Information Centre & Civic Centre
20 White Star & local bus stop
22 Abbey Theatre
26 Municipal Opera House
27 Plaza Shopping Centre
28 STA
29 Square Edge Community Arts Centre
    & Sage Cafe
30 Fat Ladies Arms
32 Manawatu Art Gallery
33 Globe Theatre
34 Manawatu Museum & The Science
    Centre
36 Masonic Hotel, Cheers Nightclub
37 Centrepoint Theatre
38 Foodtown Supermarket & K-Mart
39 Pak 'n Save Supermarket
42 Lido Swimming & Recreation Centre

house with B&B at $45/67. Or there's *Emma's Place* (☎ (06) 357 5143) at 250 Fitzherbert Ave with B&B at $30/40.

Hotels The *Empire Hotel* (☎ (06) 357 8002; fax 357 7157) on the corner of Princess and Main Sts has nine rooms with private bath, off-street parking and a Cobb & Co restaurant downstairs; singles/doubles are $58/65. The *Masonic Hotel* (☎ (06) 358 3480) at 249 Main St West near the corner of Domain St has single/double rooms at $40/50. Opposite this, the *Manawatu Backpackers* (see Hostels) is a pleasant converted hotel.

Motels Palmerston North has a wide selec-

tion of motels. The *Consolidated Mid City Motel* (☎ (06) 357 2184; fax 359 0777) at 129 Broadway Ave is conveniently situated just one long block from The Square; singles/doubles are $57/62. Further along at 258 Broadway Ave, the *Broadway Motel* (☎ (06) 358 5051/2) has rooms at $59 for one or two people.

There's a 'motel row' on Fitzherbert Ave, south of The Square; motels along here are a bit more expensive. They include the *Quality Inn* (☎ (06) 356 8059) at No 110, the *Hibiscus Motel* (☎ (06) 356 1411) at No 248, the *Avenue Motel* (☎ (06) 356 3330) at No 116, the *Rose City Motel* (☎ (06) 356 5388) at No 120, the *Coachman Motel* (☎ (06) 357 3059) at No 134 and the *Tokyo Motel* (☎ (06) 356 7074) at No 167.

Places to Eat

Palmerston North has a great number of good, inexpensive places to eat. Right on The Square and within about a block of it are many enjoyable places worth trying.

Snacks & Fast Food The *Sage Cafe* in the Square Edge Arts Centre at the south-western corner of The Square is a pleasant wholefoods cafe, open Monday to Thursday from 8 am to 4 pm, Friday 8 am to 8 pm and Saturday from 8 am to 2 pm. Also in the Square Edge Arts Centre, *Calico Pie* is a bulk wholefoods market. Nearby at 49 The Square, the tiny *Truelife Bakery & Takeaways* also specialises in wholefoods.

Also along the south-west side of The Square, *Puddleducks* at 42 The Square is a popular cafe for lunches and teas. Beside it, *Old Istanbul* is a kebab house for takeaways or to eat there.

Pizza Piazza at 16-17 The Square makes pretty good pizzas; it's open every day from 11 am and special features include a $5 lunch-time special and free delivery (☎ 358 7424).

On Broadway Ave half a block from The Square, the *Downtown Arcade* has a food court with a central dining area surrounded by takeaway counters including Italian, Chinese, fish & chips, delicatessen, coffee and ice cream counters. Opposite this at 69 Broadway, *Sun Sing* is a popular Chinese buffet restaurant open every day from 9 am to 9 pm.

There's a *McDonald's* on the south-east corner of The Square and a *Kentucky Fried Chicken* a few blocks away on Princess St.

Pak 'N Save and *Foodtown* are two huge supermarkets on Ferguson St. You can walk through to them from the Plaza Shopping Centre entrance on Church St near The Square.

Pub Food & Restaurants *Deano's Bar & Grill* on the corner of Coleman Place and George St, just a short block off The Square,

is a popular bar & grill with enjoyable atmosphere; specialties are its steak dinners and economical lunches. It's open every day from 11 am to 3 am.

The *Celtic Inn* in the Regent Arcade between Broadway and King Sts is a small Irish-style pub serving lunches and dinners plus a variety of snacks. The *Fat Ladies Arms* on Linton St on the corner of Church St is a bar & grill with meals and snacks, plus live music in the Yeeehaaa Bar (see Entertainment).

A bit classier atmosphere for an evening out is *Costa's* upstairs at 282 Cuba St, open every evening from 6 to 10 pm.

There's a *Cobb & Co* in the Empire Hotel on the corner of Princess and Main Sts, open from 7.30 am to 10 pm every day with the usual Cobb & Co menu.

Entertainment

The *Fat Ladies Arms* on Linton St on the corner of Church St, half a block from The Square, is a good-fun pub with live dance music in the Yeeehaaa Bar & Grill section; there's a quieter wine bar in another section and an area for dining. It's open every day except Monday, from 4 pm until late.

The *Celtic Inn* in the Regent Arcade between Broadway and King Sts is a small, pleasant, low-key Irish-style pub with live music on Friday and Saturday nights. The larger *Cafe de Paris* beneath the Manawatu Backpackers at 267 Main St West on the corner of Domain St is another Irish-style pub with live dance music on Friday and Saturday nights.

Apart from pubs, Palmerston North also has several nightclubs including *Cheers* in the Masonic Hotel on Main St West, *Madison's* upstairs on The Square near McDonald's, *Chantelle's* on the corner of Rangitikei and Featherston Sts, and *Level One* upstairs over the Bacchus Restaurant on Cuba St.

Palmerston North has three live theatres including *Centrepoint Theatre* (☎ 358 6983) on the corner of Pitt and Church Sts, the *Globe Theatre* (☎ 358 8699) on the corner of Pitt and Main Sts, and the *Abbey Theatre* (☎ 357 7977) in a converted abbey on

Church St near the corner of Ashley St, a block from The Square. The *Municipal Opera House* (☎ 358 1186) is opposite, on the corner of Church and Ashley Sts.

The *Downtown Cinema 6* upstairs in the Downtown Arcade on Broadway Ave, half a block from The Square, has six movie theatres showing the latest films.

Getting There & Away

Air Milson Airport on the northern outskirts of town is a new, modern airport bigger than you'd expect from the size of the town; planes often get diverted here when the weather at Wellington Airport is bad. A \$3 departure tax for all flights is charged to raise funds for the airport's construction.

Air New Zealand (☎ 356 4737, 351 8800) on the corner of Princess and Main Sts has daily direct flights to Auckland, Christchurch, Hamilton, Kaitaia, Nelson, Queenstown and Wellington, with connections to other centres.

Ansett New Zealand (☎ 355 2146) is at 50-52 Princess St, near the Air New Zealand office. It has daily direct flights to Auckland, Christchurch, Queenstown and Wellington, with connections to other centres.

Kiwi West Aviation (☎ freephone (0800) 505 000) operates Monday to Friday only, with two flights a day to New Plymouth and on to Hamilton.

Bus InterCity, Newmans and Tranzit Coachlines buses operate from the Palmerston North Travel Centre (☎ 351 6831, 357 7079) at 279 Cuba St, 1½ blocks from The Square. InterCity and Newmans buses go from Palmerston North to most places in the North Island; Tranzit Coachlines operates one route only, from Palmerston North through Masterton to Wellington.

White Star buses (☎ 358 8777) operate from a bus stop in front of the Courthouse, on Main St near The Square, with buses to Wellington, Wanganui and New Plymouth.

Many direct Auckland-Wellington services bypass Palmerston North, stopping instead at nearby Bulls. The Wellington-Napier buses do stop at Palmerston North.

Travel times from Palmerston North are 1½ hours to Wellington or Wanganui, 3½ hours to New Plymouth, three hours to Napier, and eight hours to Auckland via Taupo and Hamilton.

Train The railway station is off Tremaine Ave, about a dozen blocks north of The Square. Train tickets are sold not at the railway station, but at the Palmerston North Travel Centre on Cuba St (see Buses).

Trains between Auckland and Wellington stop at Palmerston North, as do trains between Wellington and Napier. The Auckland-Wellington trains run twice daily in each direction (morning and evening); from Palmerston North it's about two hours to Wellington and 8½ hours to Auckland. The Wellington-Napier train runs once daily in each direction, taking two hours to Wellington and three hours to Napier.

Getting Around

Bus Local mini-buses operate from a bus stop in the middle of Main St, on the east side of The Square. They operate Monday to Friday from 7 am to 6 pm, Saturday at 10 am and 1 pm, and not at all on Sunday. All rides cost \$1; there are buses out to Massey University but none to the airport. A taxi to the airport costs about \$7.

AROUND PALMERSTON NORTH
Tokomaru Steam Engine Museum

The Tokomaru Steam Engine Museum, in Tokomaru on SH 57 about 20 km south of Palmerston North, exhibits a large collection of working steam engines and locomotives. It's open every day from 9 am to noon and from 1 to 3 pm; admission is \$5 (children \$2).

Gardens

The Cross Hills Gardens, with one of New Zealand's largest and most varied collections of rhododendrons and azaleas, is five km north of Kimbolton, on SH 54 about a 45-minute drive north of Palmerston North. It's open from 10.30 am to 5 pm every day during the blooming season from September to April.

There are also a number of other gardens in the area; ask the information centre for their Garden Tour pamphlet.

Walks

The information centre and DOC office in Palmerston North have leaflets detailing a number of scenic and nature reserves, walkways, lakes and so forth in the area, many with camping and huts.

Jet-Boating

North of Palmerston North, SH 2 heading to Napier runs through the spectacular Manawatu Gorge. Manawatu Jet Tours (☎ (06) 326 8190, 358 4188) operate jet-boat

trips on the river, and will arrange transport for small groups from Palmerston North for no extra cost.

Horse-Trekking

There are various riding possibilities around Palmerston North. Timeless Horse Treks (☎ (06) 506 6157) operates from their stables 500 metres from the Ballance Bridge, on the Woodville side of the Manawatu Gorge. The information centre has details on other stables in the area.

Beaches

Himatangi Beach (29 km west of town) and Foxton Beach (40 km) are popular beaches near Palmerston North.

East Coast

This chapter includes three of the major cities of the North Island and their adjoining bays – Gisborne and Poverty Bay, and Napier and Hastings and Hawke Bay. In the latter case the actual bay is known as Hawke Bay and the area, Hawkes Bay. Like the East Cape, it is an area full of interest, with the sea on one side and towering forested hills in the hinterland. It is also a place of contrasts, from the Art Deco and Spanish Mission-style architecture of bustling Hastings and Napier to the serene, primeval forests that girt Lake Waikaremoana in Te Urewera National Park.

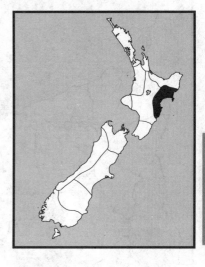

Information
Telephone numbers in this region have an 06 prefix if you are calling them from a long distance (even within the region).

GISBORNE
Gisborne (population 30,000) is New Zealand's most easterly city and one of the closest to the International Date Line. Therefore, dawn in Gisborne marks the new day for most of the world. It is 368 km east of Rotorua and 220 km north of Napier. It was here that Captain Cook made his first landfall in New Zealand on 9 October 1769. He named it 'Poverty Bay' and the spot was declared a national historic reserve in 1990. One of the panels records: 'Close to this place, Maori and Pakeha began to learn about each other, exchanged gifts and mourned the deaths which had occurred'.

Around Gisborne there are fertile alluvial plains which support intensive farming of subtropical fruits, maize and market-garden produce and vineyards. Recently, kiwi fruit and avocados have been important crops. The city itself is right on the coast at the confluence of three rivers, the Turanganui, Waimata and Taruheru. Often described as the city of bridges, it is also noted for its fine parks and recreational facilities.

History
European settlement of the region was very slow; Pakehas left much of the country unexplored until late in the 19th century. A man of considerable drive, John Williams Harris, was first to purchase a small area on the west bank of the Turanganui River. He later erected the first European-style house and store, before setting up the region's first whaling venture. In 1839 he began pastoral farming up the Waipaoa River near Matunuke which, today, is probably the oldest continued farming operation in New Zealand.

As whaling became increasingly popular the missionaries began to move into the area. Two of them, Father Baty and Reverend William Colenso, were the first Europeans to tramp into the heart of Te Urewera and see Lake Waikaremoana. Another, the Reverend William Williams, established the first mission station at Matunuke, south of the Waipaoa, in 1840.

459

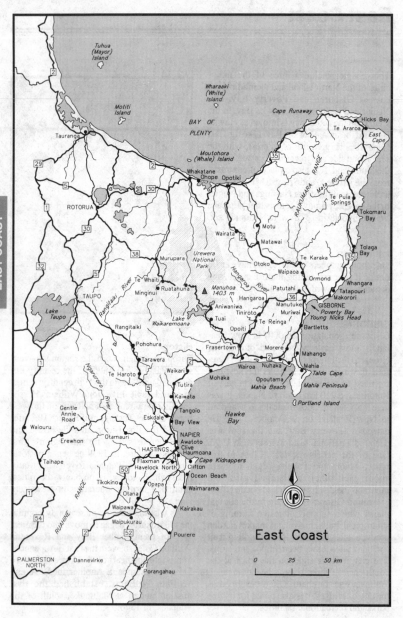

East Coast

0   25   50 km

Gradually more Pakehas arrived but there was no organised settlement. Several factors mitigated against it, the main one being that the Maoris were opposed to the idea. When the Treaty of Waitangi was signed in 1840 many chiefs from the east coast did not acknowledge the treaty, let alone sign it. Another factor was that the first governor of New Zealand to visit the region, Gore Browne, was not given much of a welcome, and so he warned against unauthorised European settlement in the region. More importantly, during the 1860s, there were numerous battles with the Maoris which further curbed European settlement.

The Hauhau insurrection that began in the Bay of Plenty reached its height at the battle of Waerenga-a-hika in November 1865. By the following year the government had crushed opposition and transported a number of the survivors, including the charismatic Maori leader Te Kooti, to the remote Chatham Islands. This paved the way for an influx of Europeans who brought with them their flocks of sheep.

Even today, however, much of the pasture land is leased from the Maoris and a large part of it is under their direct control. Unfortunately, the pioneer farmers were so anxious to profit from the land they ripped out far too much forest cover, with disastrous results. Massive erosion occurred as the steeply sloping land was unable to hold the soil after heavy rains.

To fully appreciate Gisborne's integral part in the history of New Zealand, get a copy of the booklet *Gisborne Historic Trail* from the visitor information centre for $2 then follow the guided walk in it. It covers aspects of Maori culture, Cook's arrival, European settlement, the growth of the port, city buildings of the Victorian and Edwardian eras and the establishment of industry in the area.

Information

The Eastland and Gisborne District Visitor Information Centre (☎ 868 6139) is at 209 Grey St. Look for the fine Canadian totem pole beside it. In winter (from Easter to late October) it's open from 9 am to 5 pm on weekdays, 10 am to 4 pm on weekends. The rest of the year it's open from 9 am to 6 pm daily; except for the December-January school holidays when it's open from 9 am to 9 pm daily. The office has useful brochures, good city maps and, importantly, information on clubs and organisations in the district. Children (and a fair number of adults) love the mini-golf course behind the centre.

The DOC office (☎ 867 8531) at 63 Carnarvon St is open from 8 am to 4.30 pm on weekdays; they request that you first seek information on parks and walks from the visitor information centre which stocks all the pamphlets. The AA is near the corner of Disraeli St and Palmerston Rd. There's a laundromat on the corner of Gladstone Rd and Carnarvon St.

Museum & Arts Centre

That Gisborne and the surrounding district are strongly influenced by Maori culture is clearly exhibited at the small Gisborne Museum & Arts Centre at 18 Stout St. The gallery has changing exhibitions of local, national and international art, and the museum has numerous displays relating to the east coast Maori and colonial history, as well as geology and natural history exhibits. Outside there are more exhibits – a sled house, stable, Wyllie Cottage (first house on the site, 1870), and Lysnar House with working artists' studios. This house, built in the 1890s, is not open to the public.

The museum is open from 10 am to 4 pm Monday to Friday, 2 to 4.30 pm on weekends and public holidays; admission is $3.50 (children $1.50). The Star of Canada Maritime Museum (read on) is behind this one, the same ticket admits you to both museums.

Maritime Museum

One wild night in 1912 the 12,000-ton ship *Star of Canada*, out of Belfast, Northern Ireland, was blown ashore on the reef at Gisborne, quite close to where Captain Cook made his landing. Although the ship was only three years old, all attempts to refloat it failed and eventually whatever equipment could be salvaged was removed, including

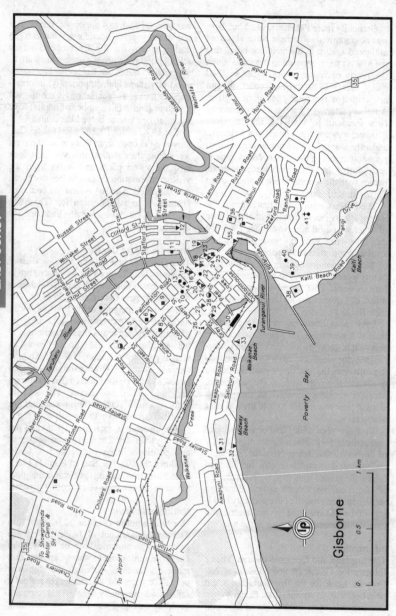

Gisborne

■ PLACES TO STAY

1   Gisborne Backpackers'
2   Sandown Park Motor Inn
6   Record Reign Hotel
8   Aloha Travel Lodge
9   Royal Hotel
25 Albion Hotel & Downtown Backpack
33 Waikanae Beach Holiday Park
36 Green Gables Travel Hotel
37 Gisborne YHA Hostel
43 Gisborne Hotel

▼ PLACES TO EAT

7   Snackisfaction
12 Pinehurst Manor Restaurant
15 McDonald's
16 Robert Harris Coffee Shop
17 Odeon Coffee Lounge
18 Mega Bite
19 The Marina Restaurant
20 Lyric Cafe
21 China Palace
23 Tastebuds Mexican Cantina
24 Scotty's Bar & Brasserie
27 Kentucky Fried Chicken

29 Pizza Hut
32 Pete's on the Beach
35 Wharf Cafe

OTHER

3   Botanic Gardens
4   Dominion Roadliners Bus Station
5   Automobile Association (AA)
10 Clock Tower
11 Museum, Art Gallery & *Star of Canada*
13 Post Office & Balcony Bar
14 Air New Zealand Link
22 Public Toilets
26 Visitor Information Centre & Public
    Toilets
28 InterCity Bus Depot
30 Railway Station
31 Olympic Pool
34 Young Nick's Statue
38 Cook National Historic Reserve
39 Waikahua Cottage Site
40 Kaiti Hill Lookout
41 Toko Toru Tapu Maori Church
42 Te Poho-o-Rawiri Marae & Meeting
    House

EAST COAST

the ship's bridge and captain's cabin, which the salvager brought ashore to win a bet that it couldn't be done.

At the waterside he sold the 26-ton bridge for £104 and it was eventually installed on the corner of Childers Rd and Cobden St. It sat there for 15 years until in 1927 the second owner's daughter got married and needed a home. Additional rooms were added and the *Star of Canada* became the best known home in Gisborne.

When the owner died in 1983 she left her unique home to the city and it was moved to its present site, restored and made into a museum. There are displays on Maori canoes, early whaling and shipping and Captain Cook's Gisborne visit but the most interesting items relate, of course, to the *Star of Canada*.

The Star of Canada Maritime Museum is directly behind the Museum & Arts Centre. They're open the same hours, and one ticket admits you to both museums. It costs $2.50 for adults, $1 for children.

Statues & Views
There's a statue of 'Young Nick' (Nicholas Young), Cook's cabin boy, in a little park on the northern side of the rivermouth, just off Waikanae Beach. He was the first member of Cook's crew to sight New Zealand. Across the bay are the white cliffs which Cook named 'Young Nick's Head'.

Across the river on the foreshore at the foot of Kaiti Hill is a monument to Captain Cook, near the spot where he first set foot on New Zealand on 8 October 1769 (9 October in 'ship time' in Cook's journal, but actually it was the 8th). Not far across the road from the monument is the site of Waikahua Cottage, which once served as a refuge during the Hauhau unrest.

From the top of Titirangi (Kaiti Hill) there's a fine wide-angle view of the area. There's a walking track up from the Captain Cook monument which starts near Waikahua Cottage. If you're driving up, turn onto Queen's Drive from Ranfurly Rd. Near the top is another monument to Captain Cook, this one with a fine statue of the captain. Down on Kaiti Beach, low tide attracts a wealth of birdlife including stilts, oyster-catchers and pelagic visitors.

At the 135-metre summit is the James Cook Observatory, with a sign proclaiming it the 'World's Easternmost Observatory'. The Gisborne Astronomical Society (☎ 868 8653) meets here at 7.30 pm on the last Wednesday of the month; all are welcome.

Another good view of Gisborne is from Gaddum's Hill. To get there head out to the suburb of Kaiti on Wainui Rd (SH 35 heading to East Cape), turn inland onto De Lautour Rd and follow it up the hill. It's a short walk from here to the trig station, a nine-km return trip from Gisborne.

Poho-o-Rawiri

Also at the foot of Titirangi is the Poho-o-Rawiri Maori meeting house, one of the largest meeting houses in New Zealand. It has a richly decorated interior and its stage is framed by carved *maihi* (ornamental carved gable boards) – it is, in essence, a meeting house within a meeting house. The human figure kneeling on the right knee with right hand held upwards is the *tekoteko* (carved figure) representing the ancestor who challenges those who enter the marae. It is open daily at any time except when a function is in progress; seek permission from the Ngati Porou urban marae to enter this shared place (inquire at the visitor information centre). A little Maori church, Toko Toru Tapu, stands on the side of Titirangi, not far from the meeting house.

The leaflet *Tairawhiti – Heritage Trails: Gisborne District* contains a wealth of information on historic sites in this ancestral land of the Maori. It covers from the tip of East Cape to the south of Poverty Bay and lists 31 places of interest.

Gardens

In the Gisborne region there are a number of attractive gardens. The **Eastwoodhill Arboretum** (☎ 863 9800), 35 km from town, is open to the public year round from 10 am to 4 pm. It contains the largest collection of northern hemisphere temperate trees, shrubs and climbers in New Zealand. To get there follow the Ngatapa-Rere road; there is a 45-minute marked track through the trees. The **Hackfalls Arboretum** (☎ 863 7091) is 61 km from Gisborne near the Kaikore and Karangata lakes – turn off Ruakaka Rd onto Berry Rd. It has a large collection of oaks, poplars and maples, including an outstanding collection of Mexican oaks; there is an admission charge.

The **Whangara Country Gardens** comprise three different gardens in Panikau, Hikatu and Wensleydale, all off SH 35 via Panikau or Waimoko Rds. Visits are by appointment only and a $3 entrance fee is charged to adults for upkeep of the gardens. Contact Panikau (☎ 862 2683), Wensleydale (☎ 862 2697), and Hikatu (☎ 862 2850).

The **Coastal Home Gardens** at Bremdale (☎ 837 8729), Mangarara (☎ 837 8738) and Ohopo (☎ 837 8848) are more for the lovers of flowering plants. They are all accessible off SH 2 on the way to Napier from Gisborne; the entrance fee for each is $3.

Other Things to See & Do

You can swim right in the city at Waikanae Beach – in fact there's good swimming, fishing and surfing all along the coast. On Midway Beach there's an Olympic swimming complex with a big waterslide and children's playground. The Botanic Gardens are beside the river off Aberdeen Rd.

If you happen to be in Gisborne around the peak of the summer holidays, check out the DOC's programme of walks and talks. Transport to walks is by private car but sharing is encouraged so you should be able to get a ride without any trouble. The Gisborne Canoe & Tramping Club (☎ 868 4741) also makes outings.

The Motu and Waioeka rivers are both in the Gisborne district; ask at the visitor information centre about white-water rafting trips. The centre also has information on walks, horse-trekking, fishing and hunting, or more genteel pursuits such as visiting the many wineries and coastal home gardens (see Gardens earlier) around Gisborne.

The wineries include Matawhero Wines, Riverpoint Rd; The Millton Vineyard, Papatu Rd; Landfall, SH 2; Parker Methode Champenoise, Banks St; and Harvest Wines, Bell Rd. There is also a brewer of natural beers, the Sunshine Brewing Company, in Disraeli St.

Near the A&P Showgrounds in Makaraka there's the East Coast Museum of Transport & Technology (ECMOT). In summer it's open from 1 to 4.30 pm on Saturday and from 10 am to 4.30 pm on Sunday.

At Matawhero, a few km south along SH 2, there is a historic Presbyterian Church. It was built from 1865 to 1866, originally as a school-room, but has also been a church, meeting place and hospital. It was the only building in the immediate vicinity to survive the conflicts of 1868, and is one of a handful still standing from this period.

Tours

A number of operators conduct tours around the Gisborne area. Nomad Off-Road Tours (☎ 862 3857) take you to the Tarndale Slip, Mangatu Forest and a working farm. Eastland Outback Tours (☎ 867 7001) tailor-make tours to suit your interests – wineries, historic places and areas of unspoilt bush. Cosmac Tours (☎ 868 4139) concentrate on the Gisborne area, and Sandown Safaris (☎ 867 9299) organise trips for guests of the Sandown Park Motor Inn.

Places to Stay

Camping & Cabins The *Waikanae Beach Municipal Camp* (☎ 867 5634) is on Grey St at Waikanae Beach, very near the centre. Sites cost $14 a night for two people, cabins range upwards from $20 for two, and tourist flats are $46 to $48.

The *Showgrounds Park Motor Camp* (☎ 867 4101), at Makaraka near the showgrounds, is cheaper for camping – only $10.50 for two; $12.50 with power – but it's not so conveniently central. The cabins here are also cheap at $15 to $20 for two people but they're pretty spartan. This camp is closed for four days in October, at showtime.

Going south, there is no more of this type of accommodation until Morere.

Hostels The *Gisborne YHA Hostel* (☎ 867 3269) is at 32 Harris St, 1.5 km from the town centre across the river, in a big rambling old home with spacious grounds. The nightly cost is $13/15 for a single/double and you can hire a bicycle to get around. Advance bookings are essential from Christmas to the end of January.

There are two other backpackers places. *Gisborne Backpackers* (☎ 867 7141) is at 690 Gladstone Rd, about two km from the town centre. A dorm bed is $13, as are doubles and twins per person; camping on the lawn is $8 per person. It is a large place with a big games room, and full laundry and kitchen facilities. If you ring you can get picked up from the bus depot; most of the buses stop outside.

The *Downtown Backpack* (☎ 867 9997) is part of the Albion Club Hotel at 13 Gladstone Rd. It costs $10 per person but the noisy bar below the rooms could be a bit of a problem.

Guesthouses There are a number of B&Bs and guesthouses in and around Gisborne; inquire at the visitor information centre. Guesthouses include the *Green Gables Travel Hotel* (☎ 867 9872) at 31 Rawiri St, Kaiti, across the river from the city centre, with singles/doubles at $35/58, including breakfast.

Repongaere (☎ 862 7717), near Patutahi, is a different, more upmarket B&B. If you are looking for a retreat where three excellent meals are served daily then this could be the place; the cost is $200 a double.

Hotels Gisborne once had several fine old hotels. Most of them have now closed down, but two of the oldest, both in Gladstone Rd, are still here. The *Royal* (☎ 868 9184) has single/double rooms at $29/43. The *Record Reign* (☎ 867 3701), at No 355, has similar accommodation. The two top hotels are the *Gisborne Hotel* (☎ 868 4109), in barbed-wired Kaiti, and the *Sandown Park Motor Inn*, Childers Rd – both cost $85 for a single or double although they have cheaper weekend or off-season rates.

Motels Most Gisborne motels start from around $60 for singles and $70 for doubles – they are fairly inflexible with these rates as demand for this type of accommodation is high. Marginally cheaper ones include the *Coastlands Motel* (☎ 868 6464) at 114 Main Rd, the *Endeavour Lodge* (☎ 868 6075) at 525 Gladstone Rd, and the *Highway Motel* (☎ 868 4059) at 60 Main Rd.

Places to Eat
Snacks & Fast Food There's the usual selection of sandwich places, particularly along Gladstone Rd, or try Peel St, up towards McDonald's, where there are two excellent upmarket sandwich places. *Mega Bite* has good hot lunches (quiche, samosas and the like), sandwiches, rolls, and drinks, and it's a relaxed and pleasant place to eat them. A larger meal, coffee included, is about $12.

Opposite this, in the centre leading to McDonald's, is the *Robert Harris Coffee Shop* with an equally good selection of sandwiches. Here you can eat inside or out in the open air mall.

Snackisfaction in Gladstone Rd is a breakfast and lunch place open from 6.30 am weekdays (closed weekends) with good food at low prices. It has one picnic table if you want to eat there, otherwise it's takeaway.

Apart from the *McDonald's*, with its main entrance on Bright St, there are also *Pizza Hut* and *Kentucky Fried Chicken* on Grey St near the visitor information centre. A *Georgie Pie* will open soon.

As usual there are a number of Chinese takeaways. The most popular is *China Palace* in Peel St, where you can choose any three items for $5.50, any five items for $8.50, and eat there or take it away for the same price. It's open from 9.30 am to 11 pm Monday to Saturday, 4.30 to 11 pm on Sunday, and has a more expensive licensed restaurant upstairs.

Light Meals & Pub Food At 124 Gladstone Rd the *Lyric Cafe* is a fine, old-fashioned seafood restaurant with a variety of meals at around $12. They have a separate takeaways counter. A block up from the Lyric, and across the road the *Odeon Coffee Lounge* offers similar fare at much the same prices. The *Cook's Galley Restaurant* in the Royal Hotel in Gladstone Rd between Cobden and Derby Sts has the usual pub food menu, as does the *Record Reign Hotel* in the next block. Down at the Gisborne wharf the *Wharf Cafe* serves meals, decadent desserts, coffee and local wine by the glass.

Restaurants The *China Palace* in Peel St is one of Gisborne's most popular restaurants. The upstairs licensed section is open nightly from 6 pm with main courses at around $14, or there's a Sunday smorgasbord for $19 (children half price). If you eat downstairs it costs much less. In Derby St there is another Chinese place *Meng Yee's Gourmet*.

Tastebuds Mexican Cantina on the corner of Lowe St and Reads Quay is part of a chain of popular Tex-Mex places, serving nachos, burritos, tacos and enchiladas. *The Marina*, wonderfully situated beside the river is expensive in the evening, but the à la carte lunches are a reasonable $12.50.

Pete's on the Beach, on Midway Beach, is a seafood and steak restaurant, open for lunch and dinner; *The Grapevine* (you must have heard about it somewhere?), 96 Derby St, has Italian and Mediterranean cuisine; and the *Incognito Brasserie* (hard to find?), 90 Peel St, has a range of continental dishes at about $20 for a main course. The top of the town's dining pile is the *Pinehurst Manor*, at 4 Clifford St, which is a winner of several Taste NZ and lamb cuisine awards and justifiably so. About five km out of town, on Bell Rd, Matawhero, is the *Harvest Cider Barn*. It is open mainly for lunch but on Thursday you can partake of the $14.50 all-you-can-eat spit roast; cold beer and cider are available.

Entertainment
Longjohn's in the Sandown Park Motor Inn

on Childers Rd, the *Albion Club*, Gladstone Rd, and the *Gisborne Hotel* on Huxley Rd have live music most weekends. The *Tatapouri Hotel* on the main road in Tatapouri, about 12 km north of Gisborne, is one of the region's most popular and enjoyable nightspots, right on the beach with both indoor and outdoor bars.

You find the dinkum band followers at *Brix* in Derby St, and the young trendy set at *Club 2000*, part of the Incognito complex on Peel St. During the summer holidays local bands, musicians and poets perform in the parks.

Getting There & Away
Air The Air New Zealand Link office (☎ 867 9490) is at 37 Bright St. They have daily direct flights to Wellington and Napier, with connections to other centres.

Bus The InterCity depot (☎ 868 6196) is on the corner of Bright St and Childers Rd.

You can approach Gisborne from four directions. From Napier in the south it's a pleasant 216-km, three-hour trip on a road which runs close to, but rarely right on, the coast. InterCity has buses along this route, originating in Gisborne and continuing south past Napier to Palmerston North and Wellington. Dominion Roadliners (☎ 868 9083), with a terminal at 411 Gladstone Rd, also has buses to Napier. Both lines stop at Wairoa.

Coming from Rotorua, Auckland and other points north, the most direct route is via Opotiki along the Waioeka Gorge. From Gisborne by this route it's 2½ hours to Opotiki, five hours to Rotorua, 10 hours all the way to Auckland. InterCity has one bus route between Gisborne and Auckland via Opotiki.

An alternative but much longer route runs from Opotiki around the coast of East Cape. See the Bay of Plenty & East Cape chapter for details on East Cape buses. The East Cape route, although longer, is one of the most scenic routes of the North Island.

The third route from Rotorua to Gisborne runs through the Te Urewera National Park, passing by Lake Waikaremoana and joining the Napier route at Wairoa, 97 km south of Gisborne. It's about 3½ hours by car between Gisborne and Waikaremoana but there is no direct bus. To travel this way by public transport involves connecting from the Napier-Wairoa-Gisborne InterCity or Dominion Roadliners bus to the Monday-Wednesday-Friday InterCity bus between Rotorua and Wairoa. Check the schedules carefully to make the connection in Wairoa. Between Wairoa and Murupara there is about 120 km of unsealed road. On Thursday there is a Tuai-Wairoa shuttle (see Te Urewera National Park in this chapter).

Hitching Hitching is OK from the south, and not too bad through Waioeka Gorge to Opotiki – it's still best to leave early. To hitch a ride out head along Gladstone Rd to Makaraka, a few km south, where you turn left for Wairoa and Napier, or right for Opotiki and Rotorua. Hopefully you may get a ride before you walk as far as Makaraka but most of Gladstone Rd is a built-up area.

Hitching from Wairoa to Waikaremoana is hard going. Gisborne is actually just off SH 36 around East Cape, so if you're hitching around East Cape head out along the Wainui road.

Getting Around
There's a city bus service, Gisborne Taxi Buses (☎ 867 2222). The buses run only on weekdays, and only until about 6 pm (some routes until about 8 pm on Friday). There is a shuttle bus (☎ 867 4765) to Gisborne airport. There are various rental car companies including Budget, Avis and Hertz. Check out Rent-a-Wreck (☎ 867 7947) for the lowest prices, with special one-way rates to Auckland.

GISBORNE TO WAIROA
Heading south towards Napier you have two choices. The bus follows the SH 2 coastal route, passing close to the Wharerata Forest Reserve, Morere Hot Springs and the Mahia Peninsula before meeting SH 36 in Wairoa. SH 36 is the inland route and is equally scenic (see Inland Route in this section).

Wharerata Walkway

The walkway is located within the Wharerata State Forest, near SH 2 and 45 km south of Gisborne. The track is 10.3 km long, about six hours return, is well marked and follows the Waiau River for much of its length. At the southern end of the track is a monument to 22 people killed in the Kopuawhara flash flood disaster of February 1938, during construction of the East Coast Main Trunk line.

Morere Hot Springs

The Morere Hot Springs, with various pools and bush walks, are 56 km south of Gisborne on SH 2, a popular day trip from Gisborne. There are three good walking tracks nearby – the 20-minute Nikau loop track, the two-hour Ridge track and the 2½-hour Mangakawa track. In summer (November to April) the springs are open from 10 am to 9 pm and in winter the hours are the same except it closes an hour earlier. The cost is $3 (children $1.50) in the public pool, $4 (children $2) in private pools.

Places to Stay & Eat The *Morere Camping Grounds & Tearooms* (☎ 837 8792) has campsites at $10 for two, $14 with power; on-site vans at $10 per person and a cabin at $20 for two. For backpackers, there is the *Peacock Lodge* (☎ 837 8824), about two minutes' walk from SH 2, in Morere. It sleeps twelve, in twins and doubles (no dorm beds) and is close to the pools, pub and walks. This old colonial farmhouse has a spacious lounge, fully equipped kitchen and a large, wide verandah – it costs $13 per person. Beside the hot springs the *Morere Springs Tavern* has a small restaurant.

Mahia Peninsula

At the northern end of the sweep of Hawke Bay is the superb, windswept and wild Mahia Peninsula – *mahia* translates as 'indistinct sounds', although the peninsula is said to be named after a place in Tahiti. There are long, curving beaches popular with surfers, clear water for diving and fishing, bird-watching at Mangawhio Lagoon and walks to a number of reserves. The isthmus was once an island, but sand accumulation has formed New Zealand's largest tombolo landform (where a sand or shingle bar ties an island to another island or the mainland). The Mahia is a magical, atmospheric place, majestic in either sun or storm.

Places to Stay The *Mahia Beach Camp* (☎ 837 5830) at Mahia has camping at $8 per person, cabins at $35 for two and motel-style units for $65 a double. On the shores of Opoutama Beach is the *Blue Bay Motor Camp* (☎ 837 5867) which has sites for $8 per person and a cottage for $13.50 per person (sleeps six, minimum charge $35). Some six km from Opoutama is the *Tunanui Farmstay* (☎ 837 5790) which has a fully self-contained cottage sleeping six – there is a lot to do in the area and the view out over the Mahia Peninsula is stupendous.

Inland Route (SH 36)

Along SH 36, the inland route to Wairoa and Napier, there are also several things to see and do. You can climb up **Gentle Annie Hill** for a good view over the Poverty Bay area. **Doneraille Park** (53 km from Gisborne), a native bush reserve, is a popular picnic spot with good swimming when the water is clear. There's fine trout fishing at **Tiniroto Lakes**, 61 km from Gisborne, and about 10 km further on, the **Te Reinga Falls** are worth the few hundred metres detour off the main road.

Wairoa

The two highways, SH 2 and SH 36, merge in Wairoa. Wairoa (population: 5200) is 98 km south of Gisborne and 118 km north of Napier and is the southern gateway to Te Urewera National Park. The reconstructed lighthouse by the river used to shine from Portland Island at the tip of the Mahia Peninsula. It was built in 1877 of solid kauri and its lens was provided by a French firm. Not far east of Wairoa is the Whakaki Lagoon, an important wetlands area renowned for its bird populations.

Get a copy of the free pamphlet *Wairoa Heritage Trails* which outlines a number of places of interest in the Wairoa, Nuhaka, Mahia and Morere areas.

Places to Stay If you have to wait in Wairoa to get a bus up to Te Urewera the *Riverside Motor Camp* (☎ 838 6301) is a pleasant place on the banks of the Wairoa River with campsites for $8 and cabins for $15 per person. The *Clyde Hotel* (☎ 838 7139), Marine Parade, has singles/doubles for $25/50; and the *Ferry Hotel Motel* (☎ 838 8229), Carroll St, has singles/doubles for $40/50. There are two other *motels* in town.

Getting There & Away There is a daily InterCity service between Gisborne and Napier which passes through Wairoa. The bus departs for Napier at 11 am and for Gisborne at 3.45 pm; the agent is W&W Buses (☎ 838 6049). There are two services into Lake Waikaremoana (see Getting There & Away for Te Urewera National Park in this chapter).

WAIROA TO NAPIER
Scenically this is a good road but in actuality it is so badly looked after by the responsible authorities that it is hard to look out of the car window at anything other than the white line. There are, however, some great reserves along this stretch of road to relax frayed drivers' nerves.

The five reserves and walkways mentioned in DOC's *Napier-Tutira Highway: Hawkes Bay Reserves and Walkways* are all accessible from SH 2. **Lake Tutira** is a bird sanctuary and two good walks lead from it – the Waikopiro Circular track and the Tutira Walkway. The **Hawkes Bay Coastal Walkway** is 12 km from SH 2, down Waikari Rd. The walkway is 16 km, goes from the Waikari River to the Aropaoanui River, and involves equal portions of boulder hopping, track walking and beach walking.

Off Waipati Rd and 34 km from Napier is the **Waipatiki Scenic Reserve**; the **White Pine Bush Scenic Reserve**, 29 km from Napier, is notable for the dominant kahikatea (white pine); and the **Tangoio Falls Scenic Reserve**, two km south of White Pine has

the Te Ana Falls, stands of ponga and wheki-ponga and podocarps. The White Pine and Tangoio Falls reserves are linked by the Tangoio Walkway, which follows Kareaara Stream.

TE UREWERA NATIONAL PARK
The Lake Waikaremoana and Te Urewera National Park turn-off (SH 38) is 97 km south of Gisborne at Wairoa, on the road towards Napier. This is a marvellous area of bush, lakes and rivers, with lots of tramps ranging from half an hour to several days, and plenty of birds, trout, deer and other wildlife. See the Outdoor Activities chapter for details on the Waikaremoana Lake Circuit.

An alternative and excellent walk is the Waipai-Ruapani circuit walk. It is a six to seven-hour, 17-km round trip which passes through beautiful mixed beech and podocarp forest, swampy basins and by lakes Ruapani and Waikareiti (obtain the track notes from the visitor information centre). There are at least twenty other walks along the park's 600 km of tracks.

Information
The Te Urewera National Park has two ranger stations. There's one in Murupara (☎ (07) 366 5641), and one within the park itself at Waikaremoana (☎ 837 3803). This latter is the park's visitor information centre and has interesting displays. They have information on the many walking tracks, campsites and huts around the park, and during the summer they offer an excellent, inexpensive programme of guided walks and talks. The visitor information centre in Gisborne also has information on the park.

Bay Kayaks (☎ 837 3737) operate tours on the lake. Their daily guided tour costs $70 (minimum of four) and traverses the northern part of the lake to Mokau Inlet; an adventure weekend is $190; three to four-day guided tours cost from $250 to $320; and there is a tramp-paddle option allowing you to, say, walk three sections of the track and kayak one for variety.

Places to Stay

There are various camps and cabins spaced along SH 38, including a camp, cabins and motel 67 km inland from the Wairoa turn-off. There are several huts along the walking tracks, costing $6 per night ($3 for children). DOC also maintains a number of minimal facility campsites around Lake Waikaremoana, where it costs only $2 to camp. All the ranger stations have information on camping.

On the shore of Lake Waikaremoana the *Waikaremoana Motor Camp* (☎ 837 3826) has campsites at $6.50 per person, $7.50 with power, plus 12 cabins at $27 for two, 10 chalets at $45 for two, two motel units at $53 for two, and a family unit sleeping up to seven people at $75 for four adults.

At Tuai, just outside the southern entrance to the park there is a *motor camp* and the *Tuai Lodge*.

On the northern edge of the park there is a range of accommodation. There are *motels* at Ruatahuna, Taneatua and Murupara and a *hotel* at Murupara. For details of the accommodation available in the Whirinaki Forest see Murupara & Whirinaki in the Bay of Plenty & East Cape chapter. At Galatea, on the Whakatane-Murupara road, the *Urewera Lodge* (☎ (07) 366 4556) has a three-bedroom cottage with two to four bunks in each room. The cost is $22 per person, a bit less in the off-season from June to August, with discounts for weekly stays.

Getting There & Away

InterCity buses run the five-hour trip between Rotorua and Wairoa on Monday, Wednesday and Friday. They depart from the Waikaremoana Camp store for Rotorua at 9.05 am, and for Wairoa at 5.30 pm. The Waikaremoana Shuttle service does a return trip, Tuai to Wairoa, on Thursday; on all other days, except Wednesday it does a shuttle through the park (see the Outdoor Activities chapter).

Most of the way between the Onuka Rd (past Frasertown) and the town of Murupara through the park, about 120 km, is unsealed, winding, extremely scenic and beautiful and, therefore, very time consuming. There is

very little traffic on this road, making it a slow go for hitching.

NAPIER

Napier (population 51,500) is a fascinating place, architecturally rich, blessed with a Mediterranean-type climate, beautiful beaches and attractive Marine Parade, good restaurants and a friendly, content population. It is a great city to visit but try to avoid domestic holidays when it becomes crowded and accommodation is expensive.

History

Long before Captain Cook sighted the area in October 1769, the Maoris found a plentiful source of food in the bay and the hinterland. The Otatara Pa, with its barricades now rebuilt, is one of the pre-European sites of habitation. The French explorer Jules d'Urville, using Cook's charts, sailed the *Astrolabe* into the bay in 1827. After whalers started using the safe Ahuriri anchorage in the 1830s, a trading base was established by one Captain Barney Rhodes in 1839. The town was planned in 1854, named after the British general and colonial administrator, Sir Charles Napier, and soon flourished as a commercial centre for the region.

In 1931 Napier was dramatically changed when a disastrous earthquake, measuring 7.9 on the Richter scale, virtually destroyed the city. In Napier and nearby Hastings over 250 people died, but in partial compensation the waterlocked city suddenly found itself 40 sq km larger. The quake heaved that amount of water-covered land above sea level! In places the land level rose by over two metres. The Napier airport is built on that previously submerged area. The rebuilding programme that followed has left us with one of the best examples of a planned Art Deco city in the world. In 1968 the city's boundaries were extended to include Taradale and reclamation of the harbour is still occurring, some 60 years after the quake.

Orientation

It used to be hard to find your way around Napier because of a lack of street name signs but this has been rectified. If you can't see the name on a sign look down at the sidewalk corner – they have resumed this method of street naming in the centre of town. At the northern end of town Bluff Hill looms, acting as a natural boundary between the centre and the Ahuriri and port areas; Marine Parade with its many attractions is the eastern boundary and the main part of town is tucked up in this north-east corner.

The prime commercial streets are Hastings and Emerson Sts; Emerson St has been developed into a pedestrian thoroughfare with clever paving and street furniture to complement its many remaining Art Deco features.

Information

Napier's helpful and well-informed visitor information centre (☎ 835 7182), at 100 Marine Parade, is close to the town centre. It's open from 8.30 am to 5 pm on weekdays, 9 am to 5 pm on weekends and public holidays (extended to 8.30 pm in the Christmas Holidays). The AA office is a couple of blocks away on Dickens St.

The DOC office (☎ 835 0415) is also on Marine Parade, in the Old Courthouse beside the museum. It's open from 9 am to 4.15 pm Monday to Friday, and has plenty of information on walkways around Napier, the Cape Kidnappers' gannet colony, and the Kaweka and Ruahine forest parks, both about 50 km west of Napier and both with walking tracks and huts. If you're here in January ask about their summer outdoor activities programme.

DOC is also a focal point for a wide range of outdoor activity organisations including tramping, canoeing, white water rafting, diving and angling clubs, any of which you're welcome to attend.

There is a very informative Environment Centre at Clive Square West. Open from 10 am to 4 pm weekdays and 10 am to noon on Saturday, it offers a free use reference library.

Art Deco

The earthquake and fire of 1931 had a very interesting side effect. Most of the older brick buildings collapsed, while survivors were mainly new buildings of reinforced concrete. Two frantic years of reconstruction saw Napier rebuilt in the years from 1931 to 1933. The result is that much of the city architecture of Napier dates from the narrow period of the late 1920s through to the early 1930s – the peak years for Art Deco. In fact Dr Neil Cossons, past president of the British Museums Association, has stated:

Napier represents the most complete and significant group of Art Deco buildings in the world, and is comparable with Bath as an example of a planned townscape in a cohesive style. Napier is without doubt unique.

The Napier Art Deco Trust which promotes and protects the city's unique architectural heritage. You can take a guided 'Art Deco walk' starting from the Desco Centre (☎ 835 0022), 163 Tennyson St. The Art Deco Trust tours start at 2 pm and take two hours – including a half-hour introduction, one-hour walk and a half-hour video and cup of tea/coffee to conclude. The cost is $5 for adults, while children, probably not that interested in architecture unless they are budding Frank Lloyd Wrights, can follow their parents round for free.

If your Napier visit doesn't coincide with the guided walks you can guide yourself with a walk leaflet available from the visitor information centre, Desco Centre or the museum. There's also a $2.50 Scenic Drive map to guide you on a drive around many examples of Art Deco and Spanish Mission-style architecture around Napier and Hastings.

The Desco Centre has a book on Napier's Art Deco architecture and some excellent postcards and posters. Many of the finest buildings are very well preserved and looked after.

As you walk around town, look for Art Deco motifs on the buildings, such as zig-zags, lightning flashes, geometric shapes and rising suns. The soft pastel colours are another Art Deco giveaway, and it has only been recently that the restorers have started

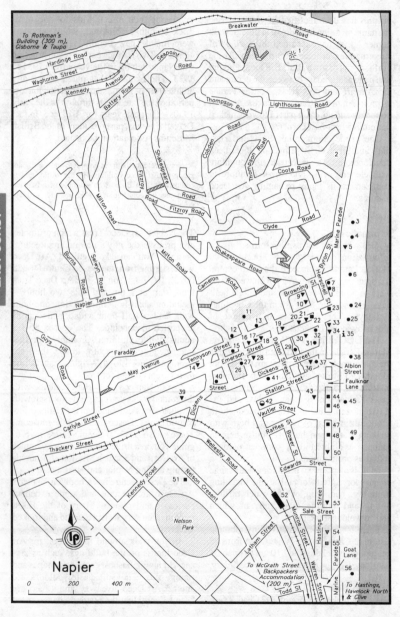

Napier

0   200   400 m

To Rothman's
Building (300 m),
Gisborne & Taupo

Breakwater Road

Hardinge Road

Waghorne Street

Kennedy Avenue

Seapoint Road

Battery Road

Shakespeare Road

Fitzroy Road

Milton Road

Burns Road

Selwyn Road

Napier Terrace

Guys Hill Road

Faraday Street

May Avenue

Tennyson Street

Emerson Street

Dickens Street

Carlyle Street

Thackery Street

Wellesley Road

Kennedy Road

Nelson Crescent

Nelson Park

Thompson Road

Lighthouse Road

Cobden Road

Thompson Road

Coote Road

Fitzroy Road

Clyde Road

Shakespeare Road

Cameron Road

Browning St

Hastings St

Byron St

Marine Parade

Station Street

Vautier Street

Raffles St

Bower St

Edwards Street

Latham Street

Munroe Street

Sale Street

Hastings Street

Goat Lane

Warren Street

Marine Parade

Albion Street

Faulknor Lane

Dalton Street

To McGrath Street
Backpackers
Accommodation
(200 m)

Todd St

To Hastings,
Havelock North
& Clive

EAST COAST

■ PLACES TO STAY

22	Criterion Backpackers' Inn
23	Masonic Hotel
44	Waterfront Lodge
46	Pinehaven Private Hotel
47	Napier YHA Hostel
48	Sea Breeze B&B
51	Gardener Court
55	Mon Logis

▼ PLACES TO EAT

5	Beaches Restaurant
9	Zeffirelli's Ristorante Italia
10	Black Market Cafe
14	Kentucky Fried Chicken
16	Deco's Bar & Grill &
	Gumnuts Restaurant
17	Antonio's Pizza Parlour
18	Food for Thought
19	National Cafe
20	Ju Ju's
21	Talking Dogs Pizza
23	Masonic Hotel Cobb & Co
28	Juices & Ices
30	Alfresco's
33	Bucks Great Wall Restaurant
34	Marnies Seafood Bar & Grill
36	Golden Crown Restaurant
39	McDonald's
43	Jenny's Cuisine
50	Stables Cafe
53	Pizza Hut
54	Restaurant Indonesia

OTHER

1	Bluff Hill Lookout
2	Centennial Gardens
3	Kiwi House
4	Swimming Pools
6	Pania of the Reef Statue
7	Department of Conservation (DOC)
8	Hawkes Bay Museum
11	Tiffen Park
12	Desco Centre & Art Deco Tours
13	Municipal Theatre
15	Napier Environment Centre
24	*Veronica* Bell
25	Sound Shell & Colonnade
26	Clive Square & Carillion
27	Taxi Stand
29	Ocean Boulevard Mall
31	Post Office
32	Telephones
35	Napier Visitor Information Centre
37	Air New Zealand Link
38	Sunken Gardens
40	Public Car Parking
41	Automobile Association (AA)
42	Newmans & Dominion Roadliners
	Bus Depot
45	Public Car Parking
49	Marineland of New Zealand
50	Stables Waxworks
52	Railway Station &
	InterCity Bus Station
56	Hawkes Bay Aquarium

EAST COAST

using them for Napier's buildings – originally they were a monochrome plaster. There are some excellent Art Deco buildings along Emerson St, including the **Provincial Hotel**, **Ju Ju's Cafe** (formerly the Ziggurat), the **Kidsons & Hursts buildings**, the **Criterion Hotel** and the **ASB Bank** (formerly T&G Insurance). On Dalton St the **Hotel Central** (now the Countrywide Bank) is a superb example of the style both externally and inside the foyer and stairs. Round the corner on Dickens St look for the extravagant Moorish and Spanish Mission-style building which used to be the **Gaiety de Luxe Cinema**. On the corner of Dickens and Dalton Sts is the State Cinema – take in a Bogart movie.

At 163 Tennyson St the **Desco Centre** faces Clive Square. It used to be the Napier Fire Station and the doors are now in. At the intersection of Tennyson and Hastings Sts are more fine buildings, particularly the block of **Hastings St** from Tennyson St to Browning St. Look at Alsops storefront in particular, the window exhibit is terrific. On Marine Parade the **Soundshell** is Art Deco as is the paving of the plaza which used to be a skating rink. From here you can admire the Art Deco clocktower (neon lit at night) of the ASB building and also the **Masonic Hotel**.

In the third week of February, Napier holds an Art Deco weekend where there are dinners, balls and much fancy dress.

Marine Parade

Rubble from the destroyed buildings was used to form a new Marine Parade that runs along the seashore. Many of Napier's attractions are found along here and there are also parks, sunken and scented gardens, amusements including a waxworks, mini-golf, swimming pools and skating rink. The statue of Pania of the Reef, a sort of Maori equivalent of Copenhagen's Little Mermaid and a symbol of the town, is found at the parade's northern end. The stony beach along Marine Parade has big waves but a strong riptide makes it unsafe for swimming.

Recently a new complex, The Stables, was opened by pop star Shakin' Stevens at 321 Marine Parade. Attractions include Earthquake '31, a simulation of the quake; historic movie and video footage before and after the quake; a Waxworks and a coffee lounge. The complex is open from 9 am to 5 pm daily, and the cafe has a barbecue on from 5 to 8 pm, Friday to Sunday.

Marineland & Aquarium

On Marine Parade, Marineland of New Zealand has a collection of performing seals and dolphins. It is open daily from 10 am to 4.30 pm, with shows at 10.30 am and 2 pm (additional shows in summer). Admission is $7.50 (children $3.75, family $19) and includes entry to the Lilliput animated village.

Not far away on the parade, the Hawkes Bay Aquarium is claimed to be the largest in Australasia. It has a wide variety of fish, sharks, turtles and other animals including New Zealand's unique tuataras. It's open daily from 9 am to 5 pm, with extended hours in summer. Feeding time is 3.15 pm, admission is $6.50 (children $3.25, family $17).

Hawkes Bay Museum & Cultural Trust

Also on Marine Parade is the excellent art gallery and museum. The museum has displays of Maori artefacts, European antiques, Art Deco items and they show a 20-minute audiovisual of the 1931 earthquake and a 20-minute video on the reconstruction after the quake. The exhibition is entitled 'The Newest City on the Globe'.

The museum's small exhibit of Maori art is one of the best in New Zealand, consisting entirely of the art of the east coast's Ngati Kahungunu tribe, one of New Zealand's largest tribes, and designed by a Ngati Kahungunu artist. Another 20-minute audiovisual shows the art and culture of this important tribe – the exhibition is entitled Nga Tukemata, 'The Awakening'. The museum is open from 10 am to 4.30 pm on weekdays and from 1 to 5 pm on weekends; admission is $2 (children free). You can buy good quality souvenirs in the museum's shop.

Kiwi House

There are kiwis at nocturnal centres all over New Zealand but the Kiwi House in Napier is the only place in the world where you can actually touch a kiwi. Every day at 1 pm there's a half-hour show with an educational talk on kiwis and afterwards everyone gathers around to touch the unusual bird, which doesn't feel at all as you'd expect. After that, at 2 pm, it's feeding time and sometimes the children can come in to feed the birds.

The centre has other animals and birds as well, including moreporks, barn owls, sugar gliders, night herons, bush geckoes and whistling frogs. It's open daily from 11 am to 3 pm; admission is $3 (children $1.50).

Bluff Hill Lookout

There's an excellent view over all of Hawkes Bay from Bluff Hill, 102 metres above the Port of Napier. It's a sheer cliff-face down to the port, however, and rather a circuitous route to the top. Coming from Marine Parade, turn inland onto Coote Rd, take the third right onto Thompson Rd, turn right onto Lighthouse Rd and follow it around until you reach the Bluff Hill Domain and Lookout. It's open every day from 7 am until one hour after sunset.

Otatara Pa

This is the largest and perhaps most impressive of the pre-European Maori pa sites in the region. It is a terraced pa on a site selected for its defensive qualities, as it is on high ground overlooking the Tutaekuri River. The surrounding area was rich in shellfish and fish, and kumara was cultivated on nearby hillsides. There is a one-hour walking track through the area. The site is administered by DOC and the local people of the Waiohiki Marae. To get there follow Springfield Rd through Taradale.

Water Sports & Other Activities

Fishing trips and pleasure cruises from Napier are popular and there are night cruises when there's sufficient demand. There are also numerous other water activities including windsurfing, kayaking, canoeing, parasailing, jet-boating, jet-skiing, knee-boarding, water-skiing and so on – ask at the visitor information centre to find the current operators. Many of them operate from near the harbour. Although the beach along Marine Parade is not good for swimming, there's great swimming and surfing on the beach up past the port.

The swimming pool on Marine Parade costs just $1. The Onekawa Pool Complex is larger and fancier, with waterslides and other attractions. Entry is $1 to the Olympic outdoor pool (open in summer only) or $1.70 (children $1) to the indoor pool, open all year.

More activities can be found at Riverland (☎ 834 9756), where there's horse-trekking and white-water rafting. They have backpackers accommodation at $10 a night (camping $7 a night) if you want to stay overnight or longer. Hawkes Bay Jet Tours (☎ 879 7032) does trips on the scenic Ngaruroro River which range from 35 minutes to one day (including an overnight stay option).

Tours

Bay Tours (☎ 843 6953) does 4½ hour Hawkes Bay tours including a scenic tour and a wine tour, each costing $34; they have a shorter tour which costs $25. The Hawkes Bay Highlights tour costs $34 and includes Hastings, Havelock North and Te Mata peak. Eastland Tours (☎ 844 8806) has Vince's Vineyard tour for $20 and the Wine & Deco Tour for $18.

The visitor information centre has a leaflet with a map of wineries in the Napier and Hastings area if you want to do a winery tour on your own.

Places to Stay

Camping & Cabins Napier has a number of campsites but none of them conveniently located if you don't have transport. Closest to the centre is *Kennedy Park* (☎ 843 9126) off Kennedy Rd at Marewa, 2.5 km from the central post office. Sites cost $8 per person with power. There are also some basic huts at $25 for two, cabins at $36 for two, and tourist flats at $55 for two.

The *Westshore Holiday Camp* (☎ 835 9456) is on Main Rd near Westshore Beach, four km north of town. Campsites here are $7 per person, $8 with power, cabins are $23 to $28 for two and there are also tourist flats.

At Taradale, 6.5 km out, *Taradale Holiday Park* (☎ 844 2732) at 470 Gloucester St has sites at $7.50 per person, $8 with power, plus on-site caravans at $37 for two and a variety of cabins at $39 to $48 for two. Near Clive there's the *Clive Motor Camp* (☎ 870 0609) which has sites for $5.50 per person; powered sites are $1 more.

Hostels The *Napier YHA Hostel* (☎ 835 7039), 277 Marine Parade, costs $14 a night. Close to the beach and opposite Marineland, it's more luxurious than most hostels because it is a converted guesthouse. Most of the 45 beds are in twin rooms and the kitchen, dining room and recreation area are all separate, making it more spacious. All rooms have their own keys, 24-hour access, and they also have bicycles for hire.

Right in the centre the *Criterion Backpackers Inn* (☎ 835 2059), at 48 Emerson St, is upstairs in what was formerly the Criterion Hotel, an Art Deco building (restored in 1991 after a fire in November 1990). It has the usual kitchen and dining facilities plus a large recreation area, and downstairs are a bistro and bar, The Cri. The nightly cost is

EAST COAST

$13 in the dormitory, $14 in twin rooms and $15 in double rooms.

The *Glenview Farm Hostel* (☎ 836 6232) is a peaceful and pleasant farm hostel on a 722-hectare hill-country sheep and cattle station, where horse-riding and walking are popular activities. You can join in the farm activities, and go hunting for geese or eels. The cost is $11 a night. The hostel is 31 km north of Napier off SH 2. A yellow AA sign at the junction of Arapaoanui Rd says 'farm hostel'; go two km towards the sea on this road and you're there. The owner provides free pick-up from this junction if you phone ahead.

At 19 McGrath St, there is *Backpackers' Accommodation* (☎ 835 3901) where bunk beds are $10 per night; the room has a separate laundry and kitchen. The *Waterfront Lodge* (☎ 835 2732) – see Guesthouses – has some budget beds for $15.

Guesthouses Since it is a summer resort of the old-fashioned school, Napier has some good old guesthouses, particularly along Marine Parade beside the beach. However, as this is a large and busy thoroughfare, it can be quite noisy. The *Pinehaven Private Hotel* (☎ 835 5575), 259 Marine Parade, has single/twin or double rooms at $38/60; it's strictly a non-smoking place. The front rooms have fine views of the seafront. There's the cheaper *Waterfront Lodge* (☎ 835 3429) at 217 Marine Parade with single/twin or double rooms at $30/45 including breakfast (see also Hostels in this sectiion).

Also on Marine Parade, at No 415, is the charming French-style *Mon Logis* (☎ 835 2125), built in 1915 as a private hotel; save it for that special occasion as singles/twins or doubles are $110/140.

Opposite Marineland, also well sited on the parade, is the *Sea Breeze B&B* (☎ 835 8067). It has a laundry, kitchen and a lounge room with a great view; singles/doubles are $30/50.

Hotels Cheaper hotels include the *Taradale Hotel* (☎ 844 2338), in Gloucester St, Taradale, which has single/double rooms at $38/42. At the *Victoria Hotel* (☎ 835 3149) on Marine Parade, singles are $40 to $55, doubles $65.

The fine old *Masonic Establishment* (☎ 835 8689) on the corner of Marine Parade and Tennyson St is very central. The rooms with bathroom are $77/94 for singles/doubles but there are budget rooms with ensuite at $51/54. Freeman's Bar is underneath so the rooms can be noisy.

Motels There are over 25 motels in and around Napier, particularly around Westshore, and most charge around $70 or more for a double. The *City Close Motel* (☎ 835 3568) at 16-18 Munroe St is conveniently located and has single/double rooms at $56/68. The *Snowgoose Lodge Motel* (☎ 843 6083), at 376 Kennedy Rd, has single/double rooms at $63/74. Also on Kennedy Rd, at No 335, is the *Tropicana Motel* (☎ 843 9153) with singles/doubles at $56/63. The *Links Motel* (☎ 835 3174), Te Awa Ave, three km south of Napier, is a good budget option with singles/doubles for $52/62. The *Gardener Court Motel* (☎ 835 5913) is a little closer to town at 16 Nelson Crescent; singles/doubles are $60/70. Inquire at the visitor information centre for more details of the many other motels and find out about off-season rates.

Places to Eat
Fast Food & Takeaways There are plenty of sandwich places along Emerson St and the sandwiches here are often pretty good. Places to try include *Food for Thought* at 204 Emerson St for healthy sandwiches and snacks. Other possibilities in Emerson St include the *National Cafe* for fish & chips and other snacks.

Back on Emerson St, opposite the Cri on Market St is *Talking Dogs Pizzeria* with small/medium/large pizzas from $7/13.50/19 – they encourage you to create your own from their list of ingredients. *Antonio's Pizzas* is further down Emerson St near Clive Square. Right on the corner of Clive Square *Juices & Ices* has sandwiches and salads, plus sweet and savoury crepes and desserts including home-made ice cream, milkshakes and fruit smoothies.

Of course there are plenty of Chinese restaurants and takeaways in Napier. Try the *Golden Crown* on Dickens St which does both. There is also a takeaways attached to *Buck's Great Wall Restaurant*, on the corner of Emerson St and Marine Parade.

And yes, there is a *McDonald's* in Napier, it's on Thackeray St down past Clive Square, and nearby a *Kentucky Fried Chicken* on Carlyle St. There's also a *Pizza Hut* on Marine Parade.

Pub Food There's a *Cobb & Co* in the fine old Masonic Establishment looking out onto Marine Parade. It's open the usual seven days a week, 7.30 am to 10 pm, and is good value. The *Victoria Hotel* at 76 Marine Parade also has a restaurant with the pub food regulars. *Deco's Bar & Grill*, in the Provincial Hotel, is licensed and has a standard, reasonably priced dinner menu.

Cafes There is a fine line between what is a cafe and what is a restaurant in this town. Some of the places which could be construed to be cafes are included here. *Brodskie's*, 136 Emerson St, does breakfasts, lunches and evening snacks. You can relax over a game of chess or backgammon while you sip cappuccino. Also on Emerson St, at No 242, is *Cafe Bizarro* with arty surroundings and a great salad bar. *Alfresco's*, upstairs at 65 Emerson St, has a good range of food and great liqueur coffees. The *Black Market Cafe*, 53 Hastings St, can deliver contraband food items at all times of the week. On Tuesday evening they have a theme night and the menu could feature Cajun, Mexican or Italian fare.

The brunch at *Jenny's Cuisine*, Hastings St, is phenomenal. Only once in my life has a cafe served a breakfast too large for me to devour – it included a veritable cornucopia of local fruit, slathers of bacon, eggs and toast. They also do great desserts in the evening.

Restaurants Further out at 409 Marine Parade the *Restaurant Indonesia* is a small BYO with attractive decor and interesting food. Their rijstaffels, that Dutch-Indonesiansmorgasbord blend, are $20 for 13 dishes, $30 for 19 dishes and $23.50 for 12 totally vegetarian selections. It's open from 6 pm, Monday to Saturday.

You can get more vegetarian food from *Gumnuts* in the Art Deco Provincial Hotel – this is the only exclusively vegetarian and seafood place in town and it is open Thursday to Saturday from 6 to 10 pm.

On Emerson St the 1st-floor *Ju Ju's* is a truly international licensed restaurant serving Italian, French, Chinese and Thai food. Not only is the food stylish, so is the Art Deco building itself and the internal fittings to go with it. The *Harston's Cafe* at 17 Hastings St has a pleasant atmosphere and serves large portions of basic Tex-Mex food for about $12. The *Tastebuds Mexican Cantina*, at 80 Dalton St near the State Cinema, offers the usual Mexican dishes. *Zeffirelli's Ristorante Italia*, 23 Hastings St, is a BYO place that is popular with the locals.

For more traditional fare try *Marnie's Seafood Bar & Grill*, in Hastings St next to the ASB; it specialises in seafood for lunch and dinner. Three of the upmarket places are the *Bayswater on the Beach*, Hardinge Rd; and *Pierre sur le Quai*, 63 West Quay; and *East Pier*, also on Hardinge Rd.

Entertainment

Popular rock pubs include the *Shakespeare Hotel* on Shakespeare Rd and the *Onekawa* in, you guessed it, Onekawa. The *Criterion Hotel* in Emerson St has bands in the Sportsman's Bar Wednesday to Saturday, the *Masonic* has jazz or guitars Thursday to Saturday, and out by the port the *Iron Pot Cafe* is also popular for jazz, blues and rock which plays from 7 pm to 1 am Wednesday and Thursday, and until 3 am Friday and Saturday nights.

Freeman's in the Masonic and *The Cri* have replaced the discos of the 1980s as the nocturnal set's venues. *The Wine Bar*, 88 Dickens St, is a more restrained place with

Art Deco decor; light snacks are available and there is music nightly.

Getting There & Away
Air Air New Zealand (☎ 835 3288) is on the corner of Hastings and Station Sts. They have direct flights to Auckland and Wellington several times daily, with connections to other centres. Air New Zealand Link connect with New Plymouth, Auckland and Wellington. There are daily services to Gisborne with Cookson Air (☎ 835 6692).

Bus InterCity buses (☎ 835 3199) operate from the railway station in Munro St. They have services to Auckland (seven hours), Hamilton (4¾ hours), Rotorua (3¼ hours), and Tauranga (five hours) via Taupo (two hours). There's also a north-south route to Gisborne (3¾ hours), Palmerston North (3½ hours) and Wellington (six hours).

Newman's (☎ 835 2009) are in Station St. Routes head north to Taupo, Hamilton and Auckland; to Rotorua via Taupo; through Palmerston North and Wanganui to New Plymouth; and to Wellington via Palmerston North.

Dominion Roadliners (☎ 878 3231) have regular buses between Gisborne, Wairoa and Napier with services on to Wellington. From Wairoa, you can catch an InterCity bus to Rotorua via Waikaremoana on Monday, Wednesday and Friday. The Dominion Roadliners operate from the Newman's depot in Napier.

All the long-distance buses coming to Napier continue for the extra half-hour ride to Hastings.

Train The railway station (☎ 834 2720) is in Monroe St. The Bay Express train operates daily between Napier and Wellington, with several stops including Hastings and Palmerston North on the 5½ hour run.

Hitching Hitching is OK around here. If you're heading north catch a long distance bus and get off at Westshore, or try thumbing closer in. If you're heading south stick to SH 2. The alternative inland route, SH 36, is much harder going with very little traffic.

Getting Around
To/From the Airport There's an airport shuttle bus (☎ 870 0700) which costs $8 (children $4). A taxi to the airport costs about $12. The Napier Taxi Service (☎ 835 7777) goes to and from the airport and operates local tours.

Bus Nimbus (☎ 877 8133) operates the suburban bus services on weekdays, with regular buses between Napier and Hastings via Taradale, plus other local services. There's no service at all on weekends. All the local buses depart from the State Theatre on Dickens St, between Dalton and Munroe Sts.

Bicycle Rental Napier Cycle World (☎ 835 9528) at 104 Carlyle St hires 10-speeds and tandems at $10 for a half-day and $14 a day. There are a number of other bicycle places as the terrain around here suits this mode of transport; inquire at the visitor information centre.

AROUND NAPIER
Gannets & Cape Kidnappers
From October until late April one of Hawkes Bay's most dramatic sights is at the Cape Kidnappers' gannet sanctuary. These large birds usually make their nests on remote and inaccessible islands but here they nest on the mainland and are curiously unworried by human spectators (see also Muriwai in the Auckland chapter and Cape Farewell in the Marlborough & Nelson chapter).

The gannets (takapu) usually turn up in late July after the last heavy storm of the month. Supposedly, the storm casts driftwood and other handy nest-building material high up the beach so very little effort has to be expended collecting it! In October and November eggs are laid, which take about six weeks to hatch. By March the gannets start to migrate and by April only the odd straggler will be left.

You don't need a permit to visit the gannet

sanctuary and the best time to see them is between early November and late February. You can get to Cape Kidnappers (so named because Maoris tried to kidnap a Tahitian servant boy from Cook's expedition here) by several methods.

From Sullivan's Motor Camp out at Te Awanga, 21 km from Napier, you can ride on a tractor-pulled trailer along the beach for $14 (children $11) with Gannet Beach Adventures (☎ 875 0898). The guided return trip takes about four hours altogether and departs about two hours before low tide at the cape.

Alternatively you can walk along the beach from Clifton, just along from Te Awanga. The eight-km walk takes 1½ to two hours and you must leave no earlier than three hours after high tide and start back no later than 1½ hours after low tide. It's another eight km back and there are no refreshment stops so go prepared!

You can also get to Cape Kidnappers with Gannet Safaris (☎ 875 0511) from Summerlee Station beyond Te Awanga. The tour travels 18 km over farmland in a 4WD coach, departing daily at 1.30 pm and taking about an hour each way, with an hour at the sanctuary. A minimum of six people is required for the trip, and the cost is $35 (children $17.50). This trip operates only from October to April.

You can find out the tide schedule for Cape Kidnappers in Napier from the visitor information centre or DOC, or ask at Clifton. There is a rest hut, with refreshments, at the colony. This is also a place to see (or, even better, to avoid) New Zealand's only poisonous spider, the katipo. The natural habitat of this spider is in the driftwood above the high tide mark, so leave it alone!

DOC, which administers the reserve, has a handy leaflet on the gannet colony and how to get to it. They also have booklets titled *The Cape Kidnapper Gannet Reserve* and *The Geology & Fossils of the Cape Kidnappers Area*. Whichever route you take to the gannets there is no public transport to Te Awanga or Clifton from Napier, but you should be able to hitch.

Places to Stay There are a couple of places to stay in the area. At Te Awanga, there is *Sullivan's Motor Camp* (☎ 875 0334); sites are $12/13 for two without/with power, and cabins are $24 to $30 for two. At Clifton, is the *Clifton No 2 Reserve* – sites are $12.50 for two, bunk beds $7 per person and cabins $24 for two.

Arts, Crafts & Antiques

Many craftspeople reside in the Hawkes Bay region. A number open their studios to the public. They range from Wairoa in the north to Waimarama and Waipukurau in the south. Get a copy of the informative *Hawkes Bay Arts & Crafts Guide* from the visitor information centres. There are also a number of antique dealers, offering 'earthquake specials', and these are listed in the *Napier Antique Trail* leaflet.

Wineries

The Hawkes Bay area is one of New Zealand's premier wine-producing regions and there are a number of vineyards you can visit and taste the wines. They include Brookfields Vineyards at Meeanee, Mission Vineyards at Taradale (the oldest vineyard in the country), Esk Valley Estate Winery, Vidal's of Hawkes Bay and Ngatarawa Wines in Hastings, Te Mata Estate Winery and Lombardi Wines in Havelock North and McDonalds Wines in Taradale.

The Napier and Hastings visitor information centres have the *Guide to Hawkes Bay Wineries*, which details opening hours. The Hawkes Bay Vintners produce a leaflet *Taste our Tradition* and a handy eight-page *Guide to the Wineries of Hawkes Bay*. The Hawkes Bay Charity Wine weekend is held at the end of October.

A number of the wineries are open for lunch – the Mission is open year round; Brookfields daily in December and January and Friday, Saturday and Sunday for the rest of the year; and the Esk Valley in January and December.

A fine way of visiting the wineries is on a bicycle, since most of them are within easy cycling distance and it's all flat land. Bicycles can be hired in Napier (see Getting Around) and there are a couple of tour operators (see Tours for Napier).

Te Mata Peak

Te Mata Peak is about 31 km south of Napier, 11 km from Hastings. It rises up in some dramatically sheer cliffs to the Te Mata trig, 399 metres above sea level, commanding a spectacular view over the Heretaunga Plains to Hawkes Bay. On a clear day you can see all of Hawkes Bay up to the Mahia Peninsula, and to Mt Ruapehu in the Tongariro National Park. You can also see oyster shells in the rocks at your feet!

Te Mata Peak is part of the 98-hectare Te Mata Park, with several walkways. You can drive right up to the trig at the summit.

If you're lucky you may see some highly skilled hang-gliders in action at Te Mata – the peak is a favourite spot for hang-gliding. In addition to the thrill of leaping straight out over a vertical cliff with nothing but fresh air under them for 399 metres or so, gliders get remarkable possibilities from the updraughts breezing in from the Pacific Ocean, just a few hundred metres away. A local reported that on one occasion a Te Mata Peak glider got stuck in an updraught for over three hours!

Peak Paragliding (☎ (025) 441 572) offer tandem paraglider flights along the spectacular cliffs of Te Mata peak; if the flight lasts less than 15 minutes you get it for free. If you are airborne for more than 15 minutes it will cost $90; there are also 10-km cross country flights for $150.

HASTINGS

Hastings (population: 40,000), 20 km south of Napier, is the growth centre of the Heretaunga Plains. It has many interesting examples of Art Deco and Spanish Mission-style architecture – it shared the same fate as Napier in the 1931 earthquake, the whole town was practically reduced to rubble and a similar rebuilding programme ensued. The central Civic Square is particularly attractive, with the Art Deco clocktower as its centrepiece; across the road there is an array of fine Spanish Mission-style buildings.

Hastings is a flat country town but it does have a number of attractions worthy of mention, including several wineries and the NZ Breweries Hawkes Bay Brewery. Hastings is a centre for agriculture, particularly orchards, with numerous roadside stands on the outskirts selling fresh produce. At harvest season there's lots of agricultural work to be found.

Orientation & Information

The Hastings Visitor Information Centre (☎ 876 0205) in Russell St is open from 8.30 am to 5 pm on weekdays, and from 10 am until 3 pm on Saturday and Sunday. They have a good city map outlining a scenic drive around Hastings, Havelock North and Flaxmere with many examples of Art Deco and Spanish Mission-style architecture and other points of interest, including Te Mata Peak. Garden lovers should obtain the free pamphlet *Hastings: Parks and Amenities*. Walking around Hastings is easy, but there is a one-way street loop which can confuse visiting motorists. The AA office is at 124 Market St North.

Historic Buildings

The legacy of the 1931 earthquake is an impressive collection of Art Deco and Spanish Mission-style buildings in and around Hastings. Features to look for in the Westend buildings are the Villa d'Este, the doorway of Kiwi Cycles, the chimney on Duckworth's building, Gloucester House and the two magnificent skylights in the Telecom Centre. In the Eastend collection there is the interior of Holden's Building, the Carlsson Flats, the Art Deco lines of Stitches and the post office (on the corner of Russell and Queen Sts).

In the south of the town seek out John Hill Ltd, the house in Pepper St, and Tong & Peryers. There is a particularly fine collection of Spanish Mission-style places along Russell St, from Eastbourne to Heretaunga Sts, including the magnificent bronze shop-front of the DIC Building (formerly Wester-man's).

At 1.30 pm on the second Sunday of each month a guided walk starts from the Hawkes Bay Exhibition Centre (next to the public library); the cost is $4.

Fantasyland
Travelling with children? In the 27-hectare Windsor Park, two km from the town centre on Grove Rd, Fantasyland is a leisure park. It has a miniature of the Disneyland castle, a Mother Hubbard's shoe, merry-go-round, pirate ship, Noddy Town, go carts, bumper boats, other boats you can take out on the swan lake fronting the castle, a flying fox, narrow gauge train rides, and much more. It's open every day and admission is $2.50 (children free). Also in Windsor Park is a swimming pool, skating rink, motor camp and more.

Exhibition Centre
The Hawkes Bay Exhibition Centre in the Civic Square, Eastbourne St, is associated with the Hawkes Bay Museum in Napier. The Exhibition Centre hosts a wide variety of changing exhibitions and the admission fee depends on what's showing at the time. It's open from 10 am to 4.30 pm on weekdays and from noon to 4.30 pm on weekends and holidays.

Havelock North
This town is only a few km east of Hastings but is worth a visit for its gardens, wineries and, if you have children, the Keirunga Park Railway. Here you get the chance to take your kids for a ride on nearly a km of track on miniature trains. The *Havelock Village Restaurant*, 5 Napier Rd, is open for lunch and dinner and serves a range of Pacific rim and continental dishes.

Places to Stay
Camping & Cabins In Windsor Park, adjacent to Fantasyland, the swimming pool and other attractions, *Hastings Holiday Park* (☎ 878 6692) has campsites at $15/16 for

two without/with power. Cabins are $25 for two, and tourist flats are $31 to $45. The camp is in Windsor Ave, 2.5 km from the post office.

The *Raceview Holiday Park Motel* (☎ 878 8837) at 307 Gascoigne St, adjacent to the racecourse, has camping at $13, on-site caravans at $25, and tourist flats at $47 – again all prices are for two people.

Hostels Hastings has two backpackers places. The *Hastings Backpackers Hostel* (☎ 876 5888), 505 Lyndon Rd East, has dorm beds for $12. It is in a suburban area, not far from the city centre. *AJ's Lodge* (☎ 878 2302), a spacious Edwardian house, is on the western side of the city, at 405 Southland Rd. They have 'affordable backpackers rates' – probably $12 to $13 for a dorm bed

Hotels & Motels There are several hotels and motels, plus many home and farmstays available around Hastings. The *Pacific Hotel* (☎ 878 3129), corner of Heretaunga and Market Sts, has beds for $15 per person. At 114 Heretaunga St, the *New Grand Travel Hotel* (☎ 878 4363) has backpackers beds at $10 to $15, and singles/twins for $30/44.

There are more than a dozen motels. A couple with reasonable tariffs are: *Aladdin Lodge Motel* (☎ 876 6736), 120 Maddison Ave, has singles/doubles for $46/66; the *Hastings Motel* (☎ 878 6243), 1108 Karamu Rd, costs $55/65; and *Motel Mecca* (☎ 878 3192), 806 Heretaunga St East, is $58/68.

Places to Eat
Hastings has the usual assortment of take-aways, cafes, etc, but the ice cream at *Rush Munro's Ice Cream Garden*, Heretaunga St West, is a real treat – home-made, loaded with fresh fruit, and very rich. People come from great distances for this ice cream, which you can only get at the garden itself, a local institution since WW II.

St Vineés Wine Bar & Cafe, 108 Market St South, provides both burger-type snacks and more substantial meals; it is open Monday to Saturday for lunch and Tuesday to Saturday

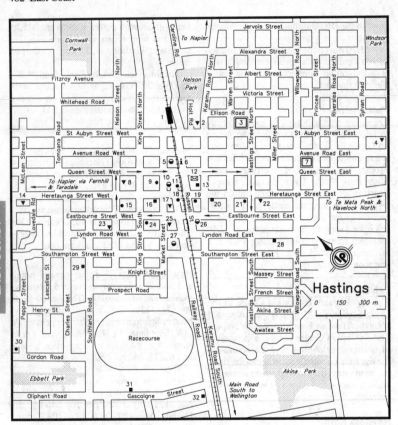

for dinner. For good old NZ fare go to *Toady's Licensed Cafe*, 103N Nelson St, for fillet of fish, schnitzel and a variety of steak dishes. Not for herbivores! Hawkes Bay's Pub of the Year in 1992 was the *Cat & Fiddle Ale House*, 502N Karamu Rd – good pub food but be careful that the dish doesn't run away with the spoon.

The *Old Flame Restaurant*, on the corner of Lyndon Rd and Nelson St, offers smorgasbords with the dangerous 'all-you-can-eat' option. Lunch, served Wednesday to Friday and Sunday, is $15; and dinner, seven nights a week, is $25 (children are charged $1 for each year of their age up to 12). At 913 Aubyn St is Vidal's Winery and attached to this is the *Barrel Room Restaurant*, open for lunch Monday to Friday and for dinner, Monday to Saturday. You can order wines at your table at cellar door prices.

Getting There & Away

It's easy to get to Hastings by bus from Napier, a half-hour away. Nimbus (☎ 877 8133) operates a frequent local bus service from Napier but only on weekdays. All the long-distance buses going to Napier continue to Hastings.

■ PLACES TO STAY

13	New Grand Hotel
16	Pacific Hotel
20	Albert Hotel
28	Hastings Backpackers' Hostel
29	AJ's Lodge
31	Raceview Holiday Park Motel
32	Clansman Motel

▼ PLACES TO EAT

2	Cat & Fiddle Alehouse
4	Vidal's Winery & Restaurant
8	Toady's Licensed Cafe
14	Rush Munro's Ice Cream Garden
17	St Vineés Wine Bar & Cafe
22	Lilac Continental Home Cookery
23	The Old Flame Restaurant
25	Spur's Licensed Restaurant

OTHER

1	Railway Station
3	NZ Breweries Hawkes Bay Brewery
5	Dominion Roadliners
6	Hastings Visitor Information Centre
7	Queen's Square
9	Automobile Association (AA)
10	Air New Zealand Link
11	Public Toilets
12	Post Office
15	Art Deco Building (Tong & Peryer's)
18	Hastings Clocktower (c 1930s)
19	Spanish Mission-style Buildings
21	Spanish Mission-style Buildings
24	John Hill Ltd
26	Nimbus Buses
27	Newman's Coachlines & Tours
30	Art Deco House

EAST COAST

REGIONAL HAWKES BAY

The main populated area of Hawkes Bay is concentrated around the Napier-Hastings conurbation. Regional Hawkes Bay does extend much further, however, both south and inland. In fact, the inland region provides some of the best tramping in the North Island in the remote, untamed Kaweka and Ruahine ranges. The main towns of this area are Waimarama on the beach and Waipawa and Waipukurau, south on SH 2.

Walks & Drives

DOC have produced an excellent series of pamphlets on the ranges. See *North-east Kaweka, Makahu Saddle, Southern Kaweka, South-east Ruahine, Mid-east Ruahine* and *Western Ruahine*.

Two excellent beach walks are outlined in the *Hastings Heritage Trails: Waimarama* – they are the walk from Waimarama south to the geologically interesting Karamea (Red Island), and the walk from Ocean Beach to Rangiika, passing the White Cliff (be careful with the tides and seek local advice).

The leaflet *Hastings District Heritage Trails: Inland Patea* describes the old Maori track from the bay into Inland Patea, a vast region which stretches from Ruapehu to Taihape and across to the gorges of the Wanganui River. The route is now a road which heads from Fernhill near Hastings via Omahu, Okawa, Otamauri, Blowhard Bush and the Gentle Annie towards Taihape. It is a three-hour return car journey to the top of the Kawekas.

Wellington, the Kapiti Coast & the Wairarapa

Wellington, the capital city of New Zealand, is situated on a beautiful harbour at the southern tip of the North Island. Approaching it from the north you will pass through one of two regions – the Kapiti Coast on the west side or the Wairarapa on the east side. Both areas have some interesting places to visit.

Information

Telephone numbers in this region have an 04 prefix if you are calling them from a long distance (even within the region).

Wellington

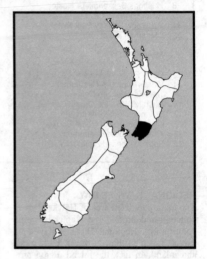

Wellington (population 328,300) takes part in friendly rivalry with larger Auckland. The town is hemmed in by its magnificent harbour, with buildings marching picturesquely up the steep hills. It's a lively city with plenty to see and do; a centre for culture and the arts, restaurants and cafes, nightlife, activities of many kinds, and home to the country's government and national treasures. Many travellers pass through Wellington as, apart from its importance as the capital, it's also a major travel crossroads between the North and South islands.

The city is built around a fine harbour formed by the flooding of a long-extinct, and very large, volcano crater. The city runs up the hills on one side of the harbour, and so cramped is it for space that many Wellington workers live in two narrow urban valleys leading northwards between the steep, rugged hills – one is the Hutt Valley, and the other follows SH 1 northwards through Tawa and Porirua.

Wellington is undertaking a massive waterfront redevelopment programme, some of which has already been completed, like the new Frank Kitts Park, and some of which

is still in process, like the giant new building being constructed to house the National Museum Te Papa Tongarewa, scheduled to move to its new location in 1998.

The city's nickname is 'Windy Wellington'. You'll see why!

History

Traditionally, the Maoris maintain that the explorer, Kupe, was the first person to discover Wellington harbour. The original Maori name for the place was Te Whanga-Nui-a-Tara, Tara being the son of a Maori chief named Whatonga who had settled on the Hawke's Bay coast. Whatonga sent Tara and his half-brother off to explore the southern part of the North Island but it was over a year before they returned. When they did, their reports of the land were so favourable that Whatonga and his followers moved to the harbour, founding the Ngati Tara tribe.

The first European settlers arrived on 22

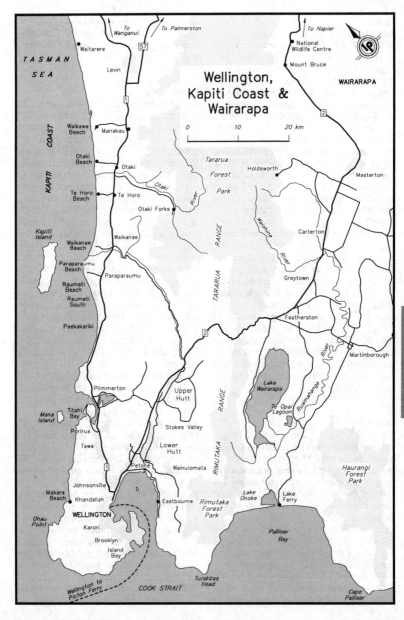

Wellington, Kapiti Coast & Wairarapa

0   10   20 km

To Wanganui
To Palmerston
To Napier

National Wildlife Centre
Mount Bruce

WAIRARAPA

TASMAN SEA

Waitarere

Levin

KAPITI COAST

Waikawa Beach
Manakau

Otaki Beach
Otaki

Te Horo Beach
Te Horo
Otaki Forks

Tararua Forest Park
Otaki River

Holdsworth
Masterton

Kapiti Island

Waikanae Beach
Waikanae
Paraparaumu Beach
Paraparaumu
Raumati Beach
Raumati South

Waiohine River
Carterton

TARARUA RANGE

Greytown

Paekakariki

Featherston

Mana Island
Titahi Bay
Plimmerton

Upper Hutt

RIMUTAKA RANGE

Lake Wairarapa
Te Opai Lagoon

Ruamahanga River
Martinborough

Porirua
Tawa

Stokes Valley

Lower Hutt

Wainuiomata

Makara Beach
Johnsonville
Khandallah

Ohau Point
WELLINGTON
Karori
Brooklyn
Island Bay

Petone
Eastbourne
Rimutaka Forest Park
Lake Onoke
Lake Ferry

Hauranga Forest Park

Palliser Bay

Wellington to Picton Ferry
COOK STRAIT
Turakirae Head
Cape Palliser

January 1840 in the New Zealand Company's ship *Aurora*, not long after Colonel William Wakefield had arrived to buy land from the Maoris. The idea was to build two cities: one would be a commercial centre by the harbour (Port Nicholson) and the other, further north, would be the agricultural hub. The settlers were to be allotted two blocks, a town section of an acre (less than half a hectare) and a back-country block worth $2 an acre. But the Maoris denied they had sold the land at Port Nicholson, or Poneke as they called it. The settlement was the result of hasty and illegal buying by the New Zealand Company and the start of land rights struggles which were to plague the country for the next 30 years and still affect it today.

Wellington began as a settlement with very little flat land. Originally the waterfront was along Lambton Quay, but reclamation of parts of the harbour began in 1852 and has continued ever since. In 1855 an earthquake razed part of the Hutt Rd and the area around Te Aro flat to the Basin Reserve, which initiated the first major reclamation.

In 1865 the seat of government was moved from Auckland to Wellington and since then it has gradually become the business centre of the country – most major organisations operating in New Zealand have their head office here. It is also the centre of the diplomatic corps.

Orientation

Lambton Quay, the main business street, wriggles along almost parallel to the seafront (which it once was). Many of the older buildings in Wellington have been demolished in the past few years and modern concrete and glass high-rises have sprung up in their place. The part of Wellington stretching from the railway station on the north end to Cambridge and Kent Terraces on the south end, known as the 'Miracle Mile', is the heart of the city. Thorndon is the historic area immediately north of the centre where you'll find a number of the major embassies. Mt Victoria is the area immediately south where you'll find good hostels and cheap places to

stay. In addition to Lambton Quay, Willis St, Cuba Mall, Manners Mall and Courtenay Place are all important streets for shopping and restaurants.

Information

Tourist Information The Wellington City Information Centre (☎ 801 4000; fax 801 3030) is in the Civic Square on Wakefield St. It's open every day from 9 am to 5 pm, with a wealth of information on Wellington and the surrounding area. They give out free city and country maps, provide information on events, accommodation, transport, etc. They also sell tickets for the Interislander ferry, trains, Newmans buses, South Island shuttle and backpacker bus services, and will make bookings for tours or anything else you might need.

The DOC Information Centre (☎ 471 0726) at 59 Boulcott St has information on walkways, parks, outdoor activities, camping, etc in the entire region. *Let's Do It! Your guide to the Outdoors*, a valuable publication with information on outdoor attractions in the Wellington-Wairarapa area, is available for $6. The office is open the usual DOC hours: Monday to Friday from 8.30 am to 4.30 pm.

The Automobile Association (AA) (☎ 473 8738) is upstairs on the 1st floor at 342 Lambton Quay. In addition to the usual AA maps and services it also offers an array of travel books on New Zealand and the world, DOSLI and Wises maps, road atlases and travel gear. All are available to AA members or non-members; members receive a 10% discount. It's open from 9 am to 5.30 pm Monday to Thursday, 9 am to 8.30 pm Friday, 9.30 am to 12.30 pm Saturday.

A number of useful free publications will tell you about attractions and events around Wellington. Look for the free weekly *Capital Times* newspaper and *What's On in the Harbour Capital*. Also check out the *Wellington Great Time Guide, Welcome to Wonderful Wellington, Discover Wellington* and *Wellington's Great Events*. All are freely available at the city information centre.

Money The American Express office (☎ 473 7766) in the Sun Alliance Centre on Lambton Quay at Grey St, near the lower cable car terminal, is open Monday to Friday from 8.30 am to 5 pm. Thomas Cook has a travel services office in Greenock House at 108 Lambton Quay (☎ 473 5167) and a Bureau de Change at 207 Lambton Quay (☎ 473 6267).

There are also plenty of banks where you can change money.

Post The main post office is in the railway station lobby. Poste restante mail can be collected here Monday to Friday, between 8.30 am and 5 pm. There are plenty of other post offices conveniently spread around the centre.

Foreign Embassies & Consulates As the capital city of New Zealand, Wellington is the base for consulates and embassies of many countries, including these and many others:

Australian High Commission
    72-78 Hobson St (☎ 473 6411)
Canadian High Commission
    61 Molesworth St (☎ 473 9577)
Danish Consulate General
    Marac House, 105-109 The Terrace (☎ 472 0020)
Fijian Embassy
    13th Floor, Plimmer City Centre, corner Boulcott St & Gilmer Terrace (☎ 473 5401/5402)
French Embassy
    Robert Jones House, 1-3 Willeston St (☎ 472 0200/0201)
German Embassy
    90-92 Hobson St (☎ 473 6063/6064)
Indonesian Embassy
    70 Glen Rd, Kelburn (☎ 475 8697–9)
Japanese Embassy
    7th Floor, Norwich Insurance House, 3-11 Hunter St (☎ 473 1540)
Netherlands Embassy
    10th Floor, Investment House, corner Featherston & Ballance Sts (☎ 473 8652)
Singapore High Commission
    17 Kabul St, Khandallah (☎ 479 2076/2077)
Swedish Embassy
    8th Floor, Greenock House, 39 The Terrace (☎ 472 0909/0910)
Swiss Embassy
    22 Panama St (☎ 472 1593/4)
Thai Embassy
    2 Cook St, Karori (☎ 476 8618/8619)
UK High Commission
    44 Hill St (☎ 472 6049)
US Embassy
    29 Fitzherbert Terrace (☎ 472 2068)

Cultural Centres A German cultural centre, Goethe Institut (☎ 499 2469) is at 150 Cuba St on the corner of Garret St, just south of Ghuznee St; the entrance to the building is around on the Garret St side. It's open Monday to Thursday from 9 am to 5 pm, Friday 9 am to 3 pm.

The Japan Information & Cultural Centre (☎ 472 7807) at 113 Customshouse Quay, near the corner of Lambton Quay, is open Monday to Friday from 9 am to 5 pm.

Travel Agencies There are plenty of travel agencies in Wellington. STA, specialising in student and youth travel, has an office at 207 Cuba St (☎ 385 0561) and another in the Student Union building at Victoria University (☎ 499 1017). They're open Monday to Friday from 9 am to 5 pm, Saturday 10 am to 12.30 pm.

The YHA travel agency (☎ 801 7238, 801 7280) is in the lobby of the YHA hostel on the corner of Wakefield St and Cambridge Terrace. It's open every day from 8 am to 8 pm and you don't have to be a YHA member to get their discounted rates. They specialise in backpacker services, selling tickets for transport and a variety of activities around New Zealand.

Books & Maps Wellington has some fine bookshops including Unity Books on the corner of Willis St and Manners Mall, Ahradsen's in the BNZ underground shopping centre with a good travel section, Pathfinder Books nearby at 142 Willis St, Whitcoulls at 312 Lambton Quay, and London Bookshops at 326 Lambton Quay and 89 Cuba Mall. Upstairs at 342 Lambton Quay, the AA shop has an excellent selection of travel books about New Zealand and other countries.

Bennett's Government Bookshop in the Bowen House, near the Beehive on the corner of Lambton Quay and Bowen St, has a great selection of books on New Zealand, both on travel and on other subjects (literature, poetry, nature, Maori subjects, etc), a good general travel section, plenty of maps including DOSLI maps, Wises maps, AA maps and road atlases, general fiction and a children's book section. It's open Monday to Friday, 8 am to 5.30 pm.

Bellamy's at 106 Cuba St is a good second-hand bookshop. A few others are found along Courtenay Place.

Metro Mags at 226 Lambton Quay has a mind-boggling selection of magazines and newspapers from around the world – about 4000 different titles. They're open Monday to Thursday from 7 am to 7 pm, Friday 7 am to 9 pm, Saturday 9 am to 4 pm and Sunday 10 am to 4 pm.

Tala's at 106 Victoria St is a South Pacific centre with a good selection of books on the Polynesian region plus Polynesian music, arts & crafts, and cloth.

The Map Shop at 103-115 Thorndon Quay is operated by the Department of Survey and Land Information (DOSLI) and carries their complete line of maps, including topographical, National Park, walking track, streetfinder and city maps, plus a line of aerial photographs. It's open Monday to Friday from 8.30 am to 5 pm.

The Beehive & Parliament

Three buildings form New Zealand's Parliament complex. By far the most distinctive and well known is the modernistic building known as the Beehive – because that is just what it looks like. Designed by British architect Sir Basil Spence, it was begun in 1969 and occupied in 1980. This is the executive wing of Parliament, housing the executive offices.

Next door, the Old Parliament Building, completed in 1922, was closed in 1990 for renovation due to more stringent earthquake safety standards. It is scheduled to re-open in 1995. Beside this, the neo-Gothic Parliamentary Library building is the oldest building in the Parliamentary complex.

While the repairs on the Old Parliament Building are being done, the House of Representatives meets in Bowen House, the pink-and-grey high-rise building opposite the Beehive on the corner of Bowen St and Lambton Quay.

Free public tours of the Beehive and the House of Representatives are offered most days, seven days a week, but the schedule depends on what functions or meetings are being held. Phone the Beehive (☎ 471 9999) to ask about tour times.

The public is also welcome to attend meetings of the House of Representatives. It usually meets three out of four weeks each month, with sessions Tuesday to Thursday

Windy Wellington

Wellington really can get windy. When the sun's shining it can be a very attractive city but it's not called the windy city for nothing – one of the local rock stations even calls itself Radio Windy.

Particularly as winter starts to arrive you've got a fair chance of experiencing some gale-force days. The sort of days when strong men get pinned up against walls and little old ladies, desperately clutching their umbrellas, can be seen floating by at skyscraper height. Seriously the flying grit and dust can be uncomfortable to the eyes and the flying rubbish can be a real mess. I was walking back from a restaurant late one windy night when a sudden gust blew several bags of garbage out of a doorway, a passing car hit one and a veritable snowstorm of soft drink cans, pizza boxes and assorted debris rushed down the street like tumbleweeds from an old western movie. The wind was blowing so hard that this blizzard of rubbish actually overtook the offending car!

One blustery day back in 1968 the wind blew so hard it pushed the almost new Wellington-to-Christchurch car ferry Wahine on to Barrett's Reef just outside the harbour entrance. The disabled ship later broke loose from the reef, drifted into the harbour and then sank with the loss of 51 lives. The Wellington Maritime Museum has a dramatic model and photographic display of the disaster. ■

from 2 to 5.30 pm and again from 7.30 to 10.30 pm, during which you are free to come and go as you please from the public gallery.

Old Government Building

Opposite the Beehive, at the northern end of Lambton Quay, stands the Old Government Building, one of the largest all-wooden buildings in the world – there's a wooden temple in Japan which beats it for 'the biggest' honours. The building was closed in 1992 due to a fire, with bids being taken for its restoration.

Wood was widely used in the construction of buildings in Wellington's early days. There are some fine old wooden houses still to be seen, especially along Tinakori Rd in the historic Thorndon area which was Wellington's first suburb, just uphill from the Parliament buildings.

National Library

Opposite the Beehive on the corner of Molesworth and Aitken Sts, the National Library Te Puna Matauranga o Aotearoa houses by far the most comprehensive book collection in New Zealand. Also at the National Library is the Alexander Turnbull Library, an early colonial collection complete with many historical photographs, often used for genealogical and other research on New Zealand.

The library hosts interesting art exhibits in the National Library Gallery, lectures and cultural events which are free and open to the public. Free tours are conducted weekly. The library is open Monday to Friday from 9 am to 5 pm, Saturday from 9 am to 1 pm.

National Archives

A block away, on Mulgrave St at the junction of Aitken St, the National Archives Te Whare Tohu Tuhituhinga o Aotearoa displays several interesting national treasures including the original Treaty of Waitangi and other historical treaties and documents. Also here are the New Zealand Portrait Gallery Te Pukenga Whakaata and other galleries with changing art exhibits. All can be visited for

free; open hours are Monday to Friday from 9 am to 5 pm, Saturday from 9 am to 1 pm.

Old St Paul's Church

Just a few doors up the hill on Mulgrave St is Old St Paul's Church. It was built from 1863 to 1864, and looks quaint from the outside, but take a look inside as the interior is a good example of Early English Gothic design in timber. Old St Paul's is open Monday to Saturday from 10 am to 4.30 pm, Sunday 1 to 4.30 pm, closed only on Good Friday and Christmas. Admission is free but donations are gratefully accepted.

National Museum & Art Gallery

The National Museum Te Papa Tongarewa (just look for the carillon on Buckle St) is a museum of art, history, Maori culture and the natural environment. It has a good Maori and Pacific Islands collection plus many other interesting exhibits; the National Art Gallery and New Zealand Academy of Fine Arts are also housed here. Admission is free (donations accepted) and it's open every day from 9 am to 5 pm. Get here on bus No 11.

The museum is scheduled to move to a much larger building, being built for it on Wellington's waterfront near the foot of Tory St, in 1998.

Maritime Museum

At Queen's Wharf and Jervois Quay is Wellington's interesting Maritime Museum. It has many relics of shipping associated with the city and a fine three-dimensional model of the harbour. The collection of ship models includes a great one of the interisland ferry, the *Wahine*, in the process of sinking, with a photo exhibit documenting the tragedy. The museum is open Monday to Friday from 9.30 am to 4 pm, Saturday and Sunday from noon to 4.30 pm; admission is $2 (student/unwaged $1, children 50c, family $5).

Other Museums

The **Colonial Cottage Museum** at 68 Nairn St is one of the oldest colonial cottages in Wellington, built in 1858 by local carpenter

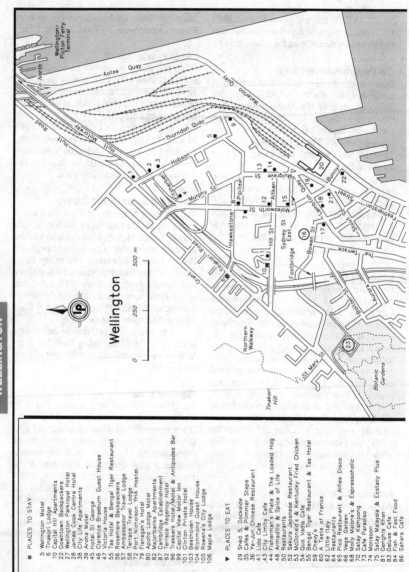

WELLINGTON

Wellington

■ PLACES TO STAY

5 Wellington Motel
6 Tinakori Lodge
10 Capital Hill Apartments
27 Downtown Backpackers
28 Wellington Parkroyal Hotel
38 James Cook Centra Hotel
39 City Life Apartments
39 Aroha Motel
45 Hotel St George
46 Clarence Braeburn Guest House
47 Victoria House
55 Tas Hotel & Bengal Tiger Restaurant
56 Rosemere Backpackers
57 Ambassador Travel Lodge
58 Terrace Travel Lodge
72 Port Nicholson YHA Hostel
79 Flanagan's Hotel
80 Apollo Lodge Motel
82 Majoribanks Apartments
87 Cambridge Establishment
92 Terrace Regency Hotel
96 Trekkers Hotel/Motel & Antipodes Bar
99 Capital View Motor Inn
101 Clinton Private Hotel
103 Beethoven House
104 Richmond Guest House
105 Rowena's City Lodge
106 Maple Lodge

▼ PLACES TO EAT

29 Shed 5, Dockside
35 Cafes & Plimmer Steps
36 Ye-Jun Chinese Restaurant
41 Lido Cafe
43 City Limits Cafe
47 Pharaohs Cafe & The Loaded Hog
48 Armadillo & Spice of Life
50 Restaurants
52 Sakura Japanese Restaurant
53 McDonald's & Kentucky Fried Chicken
54 Quo Vadis Cafe
55 Bengal Tiger Restaurant & Tas Hotel
59 Chevy's
60 A Taste of France
62 Little Italy
63 Restaurants
65 Pico Restaurant & Alfies Disco
66 Vege Garden
68 Molly Malone's & Espressoholic
70 Satay Kampong
73 Cafe Paradiso
74 Monsoon
75 Satay Malaysia & Ecstacy Plus
83 Genghis Khan
83 Deluxe Cafe
84 Fish & Fast Food
86 Sahara Cafe

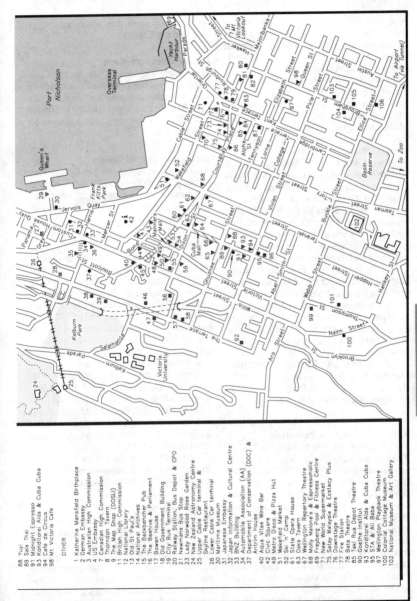

WELLINGTON

88 Yuyi
89 Sala Thai
91 Midnight Espresso
93 Konditorei Aida & Cuba Cuba
94 Cafe de Circus
98 Mt Victoria Cafe

OTHER

1 Katherine Mansfield Birthplace
2 German Embassy
3 Australian High Commission
4 US Embassy
7 Canadian High Commission
8 Thorndon Tavern
9 The Map Shop (DOSLI)
11 British High Commission
12 National Library
13 Old St Paul's
14 National Archives
15 The Backbencher Pub
16 The Beehive & Parliament
17 Bowen House
18 Old Government Building
19 City Bus Terminal
20 Railway Station, Bus Depot & CPO
21 Newmans Bus Stop
23 Lady Norwood Rose Garden
24 New Zealand Astronomy Centre
25 Upper Cable Car terminal &
   Skyline Restaurant
26 Lower Cable Car terminal
30 Maritime Museum
31 Japanese Embassy
32 Japan Information & Cultural Centre
33 BNZ Building
34 Automobile Association (AA)
37 Department of Conservation (DOC) &
   Antrim House
40 Aqua Vitae Wine Bar
42 Civic Square
49 Metro Disco & Pizza Hut
51 Wakefield Market
52 Ski 'n' Camp
61 State Opera House
63 Oaks Tavern
67 Wellington Repertory Theatre
68 Molly Malone's & Expressoholic
71 Freyberg Pool & Fitness Centre
75 New World Supermarket
75 Satay Malaysia & Ecstacy Plus
76 Downstage Theatre
77 Fire Station
78 Bats Theatre
85 Taki Rua Depot Theatre
90 Goethe Institut
95 Konditorei Aida & Cuba Cuba
96 STA & Ali Baba
97 Wellington Playback Theatre
100 Colonial Cottage Museum
102 National Museum & Art Gallery

William Wallis and lived in by his family until 1977. It's open from 10 am to 4 pm Monday to Friday, 1 to 4.30 pm on weekends and public holidays. Admission is $3 (children $1, students & seniors $2).

A Wellington's Heritage Concession Ticket for $7.50 entitles you to visit the Colonial Cottage Museum, the Maritime Museum and the Katherine Mansfield Birthplace, a savings if you're planning to visit all three. It is available at all three places and at the city information centre.

Other restored historic buildings include **Antrim House** at 63 Boulcott St, an Edwardian house built in 1905 for Robert Hannah, founder of the Hannah's footwear firm. It is now the headquarters of the New Zealand Historic Places Trust. It's open Monday to Friday from 8 am to 5 pm; you can visit it and admission is free, but remember this is an office building where people are working.

Sports fans might like the **National Cricket Museum**, in the Old Grandstand of the Basin Reserve. It's open October to April every day from 10.30 am to 3.30 pm; May to September it's open only on weekends, again from 10.30 am to 3.30 pm. Admission is $3 (children $1, but free if accompanied by an adult).

The **Alexander McKay Geological Museum** is in the Cotton Building at Victoria University. It's open from 9 am to 4 pm on weekdays; admission is free.

Katherine Mansfield Memorials

The Katherine Mansfield Birthplace at 25 Tinakori Rd is the house where this famous author was born in 1888 and lived for the first five years of her life; it is mentioned in her stories *The Aloe, Prelude* and *A Birthday*. The house has been restored and is open from 10 am to 4 pm every day except Monday; admission is $4 (students & seniors $2, children $1). Nearby, in the small park beside the fortress-like US Embassy building, is a memorial which Mansfield's father dedicated to her after her untimely death, at the age of 35, of tuberculosis.

You can also visit Days Bay, where Mansfield's family spent their summer holidays (see Harbour Cruises).

Capital Discovery Place

The Capital Discovery Place on the Civic Square behind the Town Hall is a hands-on science centre designed for children. It's open from 10 am to 5 pm Tuesday to Sunday and all public holidays; admission is $6 (children $4).

Wellington City Art Gallery

Also on Civic Square, in the Old Library building, the Wellington City Art Gallery is a contemporary art gallery open every day. The city information centre has details on other art galleries around town.

Cable Car

From a narrow alley off Lambton Quay a cable car runs up to Kelburn which overlooks the city. It's one of Wellington's historic attractions – the cable car service began in 1902, carried nearly half a million passengers in its first year and by 1912 was transporting a million passengers a year. In the late '70s the track was reconstructed and the two old wooden cable cars were replaced with shiny red Swiss-made ones.

A ride to the top costs $1.50 (children 70c) or $2.50 return (children $1.40, family $8). It operates at about 10-minute intervals from 7 am to 10 pm Monday to Friday; 9.30 am to 6 pm on Saturday; and 10.30 am to 6 pm on Sunday and public holidays. At the top terminal is a restaurant with a great view over the city and harbour, open every day from 11 am to 4 pm. From the top you can stroll back down through the Botanic Gardens.

Botanic Gardens

The tranquil Botanic Gardens are worth a visit, with 26 hectares of native bush and a wide variety of gardens including the Lady Norwood Rose Garden with over 100 kinds of roses, blooming from November to the end of April. Other gardens include succulents, ferns, threatened species, an Australian garden, rhododendrons, fuchsias, camellias, a begonia house, and herbs. The large gardens are always open.

New Zealand Astronomy Centre
The New Zealand Astronomy Centre is in the Botanic Garden near the top cable car terminal. It's open with displays, videos and computers relating to astronomy Monday to Friday from 9 am to 5 pm, Saturday and Sunday 1 to 4 pm; admission is $3 (children $1.50).

Hour-long planetarium programmes are presented on weekends, public and school holidays at 1.30, 2.30 and 3.30 pm; admission is $5 (children $2.50, family $12.50). They also hold evening public sessions which include a planetarium show and lecture on a topic of astronomy, plus telescope viewing (weather permitting). The evening sessions are held from March to October on Tuesday and Saturday evenings from 7.30 to 10 pm; admission is $6 (children $3, family $15).

Wellington Zoo
Wellington Zoo has a wide variety of native and other wildlife, including outdoor lion and chimpanzee parks plus a nocturnal kiwi house also housing tuataras and giant wetas. The kiwis are on view from 10 am to 4 pm daily but the best time to see them is from 10 am to noon.

The zoo is four km from the city centre, at the end of the Newtown Park bus route No 10. It is open daily from 8.30 am to 5 pm; admission is $7.50 (children $3.50).

Views
The best view of the entire city, harbour and surrounding region can be seen from the lookout at the top of Mt Victoria. It makes a good walk to get up there and it's well worth the effort; otherwise you can take bus No 20 departing from the railway station or Courtenay Place and walk or ride back down. To drive, head up the hill on Majoribanks St and follow the signs saying 'Lookout', turning left onto Hawker St.

Other good views are from the top cable car terminal and from the Northern, Southern and Eastern Walkways. The Majestic Building, near the corner of Willis and Boulcott Sts, is the tallest building in Wellington and it opens for sightseeing from time to time.

Walks
Wellington has numerous possibilities for enjoyable walks. Check with the city information centre for their brochures on walks in the city and surrounding areas. Ask for their leaflets on the Eastern, Northern and Southern Walkways, and on the Red Rocks Coastal Walk. *Walking Wellington* and *Women About Town* are also good brochures to guide you on theme-oriented city walking tours.

The DOC office on Boulcott St is another good source of information on walks. Their free brochure *Walking Around Wellington*, available at the DOC office or the city information centre, gives details on over 50 walks of all kinds and durations, from 15-minute walks to walks taking several hours, in the Wellington area including the city itself, the Kapiti Coast, the Hutt Valley and Wainuiomata on the eastern side of the harbour.

Walking is a popular activity in Wellington; the city information centre has info on walking groups, walking events and even walking festivals.

Some of our favourite walks in the city are the simplest and most obvious, like walking through the peaceful Botanic Garden, or along the waterfront.

Sports
Pools The Freyberg Swimming Pool & Fitness Centre (☎ 384 3107) at 139 Oriental Parade houses a large indoor pool, fitness centre and gymnasium. It's open every day from 6 am to 9 pm, except closing at 5 pm on Friday. Admission is $2.50 (children $1.50). The Silver Route No 14 bus stops at the door.

The Wellington Regional Aquatic Centre (☎ 387 8029) on Kilbirnie Crescent in Kilbirnie, a suburb out towards the airport, is open every day from 6 am to 9 pm. Facilities include a large indoor swimming pool (admission $2.50, children $1), sauna ($5 including swim) and spa pools ($3, children

$1.50), plus a fitness centre, coffee bar, creche and children's area. Bus No 2 stops at the door, Nos 11 and 12 nearby.

The city also has two large (30-metre) heated outdoor pools: the Thorndon Pool (☎ 472 8055) at 26 Murphy St, Thorndon, and the Karori Pool (☎ 476 6243) at 22 Donald St, Karori (take the Lyall Bay bus). They're open weekdays from around 6.30 am to 6.30 pm, weekends from around 8.30 am to 6.30 pm, but only from around November to the end of March.

North of the city, on the Johnsonville train line, are a couple of other pools. The Khandallah Pool is a large outdoor pool at Khandallah Park; from the Khandallah stop on the Johnsonville train, about 15 minutes from Wellington's railway station, the park is a 15-minute walk. Or there's an indoor heated pool in Johnsonville, opposite the Johnsonville railway station, about a 20 minutes' scenic train ride from Wellington.

Diving Contact the Wellington Regional Aquatic Centre, Kilbirnie (see Pools) or Aquaventure (☎ 232 6186).

Surfing & Windsurfing With all the wind, water and bays around, Wellington is a great place for windsurfing – take your choice of sheltered inlets, rough harbours, and wave-beaten coastal areas, all within half an hour's drive of the city and of one another. There are some good surf breaks around, too, including one near the airport.

The Stunned Mullet (☎ 382 8090, mobile (025) 450 603) on the corner of Tory and Vivian Sts is the centre for surfing and windsurfing in Wellington. They offer very reasonably priced windsurfing lessons (a two-hour 'taster session', a 10-hour beginner's course or private tuition), sailboard and surfboard hire, hire of gear such as wetsuits and roofracks, and sales of all the same. Phone them for a free recorded wind and surf report, updated daily.

Skating & Rollerblading You can't beat rollerblading along the waterfront on a sunny day. The 60 Cuba St shop (☎ 499 0455,

mobile (025) 436 848) at yes, 60 Cuba St, hires rollerblades from their shop or from their roving van, which is normally stationed at the foot of Taranaki St by the waterfront on weekends during the day and at Frank Kitts Park on Monday and Wednesday evenings, plus at evening roller hockey events where you can hire skates and play. You can phone the shop to ask where the van is; it only goes out in fine weather. The cost is $5/8/15 for half-hour/hourly/overnight hire.

There's indoor skating at the Valley Roller Rink (☎ 566 6677) and at the Kilbirnie Recreation Centre (☎ 387 7191).

Camping & Sports Gear If you need gear for camping, tramping or other sports, Wellington is a good place to buy it, with plenty of selection and shops to choose from. Second Wind Sports at 120 Wakefield St, opposite the Town Hall, sells both new and used sports equipment of all kinds – tents, packs, sleeping bags, tramping boots, camping gear, surfboards, wetsuits, kayaks, ski equipment, outdoor clothing and more. They have good prices on used stuff, or you can trade in. Ski 'n Camp at 181 Wakefield St is another shop worth checking out, especially if you're looking for a tent; their selection of tents is the biggest we've ever seen and they also specialise in all camping, tramping and skiing equipment. Other places include Gordon's on the corner of Wakefield and Cuba Sts, Doyles Army, Camping & Outdoor Store on the corner of Wakefield and Mercer Sts, and Kathmandu at 117 Lambton Quay.

Cycling See the Getting Around section for information on bicycle hire.

Cricket & Athletics The Basin Reserve (☎ 384 3171) is an international-standard cricket and athletics park; ring for information on cricket and other matches. The cricket season is in the summer from around October to April.

Tennis Renouf Tennis Centre (☎ 385 9709) on Brooklyn Rd, the uphill extension of

Willis St, is Wellington's principal tennis centre, both for spectator matches and for coming to play yourself. It's open every day from 8 am to 10 pm with both outdoor and indoor courts.

Horse Racing There's horse racing at the Hutt Park Raceway (☎ 568 5900) and at the Trentham Racecourse in Upper Hutt (☎ 528 9611).

Other The city information centre has information on any other sport you can think of. Check their monthly *What's On* publication for sporting events of all kinds.

Beaches
The best beaches around Wellington are at Days Bay (see Harbour Cruises) and on the Kapiti Coast (see Around Wellington).

Harbour & Fishing Cruises
Trips across the harbour to Days Bay are made on the *Trust Bank Ferry* (☎ 499 1282/ 1273). It's a 35-minute trip to Days Bay, where there are beaches, a fine park and a couple of houses which Katherine Mansfield's family kept for summer homes – her story *At the Bay* recalls summer holidays at Days Bay.

At Eastbourne village, a 15-minute walk from Days Bay, there's a pavilion popular with families for picnics and feeding the ducks; also at Eastbourne are a crafts shop and art gallery, restaurants and cafes and a branch of the *Rush-Munro's Ice Cream Garden* where you can sample the most famous ice cream in New Zealand. There's also a good swimming beach, kayaks for hire, and fishing off the wharf. At dusk, Little Blue Penguins come up from the sea and cross the road, going to their nests.

The *Trust Bank Ferry* catamaran goes to and fro on a regular daily schedule. The one-way fare is $6 (children and students $3, seniors $5) or there's a $33 family return fare. Departures are from Queens Wharf. The catamaran also does a special Starlight Cruise from 8 to 11 pm with dining and dancing; the cost is $40.

Bluefin Harbour Cruises (☎ 569 8203) does 1½ hour 'coffee cruises' around the harbour for $14, a 1½ hour Luncheon Cruise for $17, and two to three-hour dinner cruises for $25 to $30 (children half price on all tours). They depart from the wharf at the end of Whitmore St, between Queen's Wharf and the railway station.

Also departing from the same wharf, Lady Fisher Ltd (☎ 380 8888, mobile (025) 439 900) does reasonably priced fishing trips around the harbour and out into the Cook Strait. Four-hour weekend and holiday fishing trips around the harbour cost $25 (children $10 to $15); weekdays in summer, three-hour evening harbour fishing trips cost $20 (children $10 to $15). Or they do eight-hour fishing trips out into the Cook Strait for $50 (children $30). Fishing rods and tackle are for hire on the boat.

Tours
A number of interesting and worthwhile tours are offered in Wellington. Only a few of the more notable ones are mentioned here; the city information centre has details on these and several others.

City Scenic Tours (☎ 499 1282, after hours 387 8700) offers a 2½ hour bus tour that's a good introduction to the city, pointing out many of the major sights, heading up to the lookout at Mt Victoria and on around the coast past several of the area's bays. It departs from the city information centre every day at 10 am and 2 pm, or will pick you up and drop you off; the cost is $21 (children $10.50, family $52, with senior and YHA discounts).

Wally Hammond (☎ 472 0869) does similar 2½ hour city highlight tours, also departing at 10 am and 2 pm. The cost is $20 (children $10) with discounts for families, seniors, and a $5 discount for YHA members. Other Wally Hammond tours include a three-hour Kapiti Gold Coast Tour for $55 (children $26) and a full-day Wairarapa-Palliser Bay tour for $96 (children $48).

Unique Tours (☎ & fax 382 9850, after hours 389 2507) truly are unique, offering a Maori perspective on their 2½ to three-hour

Maori & European Heritage History Tours. The cost is $25 (children $12.50). Other Unique tours include a Vine Trail winery tour of the Martinborough area for $56 and a Progressive Restaurant Tour for $58.

Also emphasising the city's heritage, Newlands Coach Service (☎ 478 8315) operates a three-hour Wellington Heritage Highlights Tour with departures at 9.30 am and at 2 pm, with an optional harbour cruise and lunch. The cost is $33 (children $16.50) for the tour only, $64 (children $39) with the cruise and lunch.

Tours further afield include 4WD safaris with Discovery Tours (☎ 564 8176), tours of the Wairarapa, and more.

Festivals & Annual Events

It seems like Wellington is always celebrating one event or another; check the *What's On* from the city information centre for current happenings. Some of the more notable annual events include:

January
  BP Tennis Nationals – mid-January
  Wellington Anniversary Weekend – the Wellington Marathon and Half Marathon races, plus horse racing and Magic Millions yearling sales, are held on the Monday closest to the 22nd
February
  Wellington Big Coast Ride – late February, a two-day non-competitive mountain bike ride, starts from Rimutaka Incline in Maymorn, just north of Upper Hutt
February/March
  International Festival of the Arts – an entire month of national and international culture, including theatre, dance, music, opera and fringe activities (held only in even-numbered years)
March
  Irish Festival – first three weeks, leading up to St Patrick's Day on the 17th
  Bats Fringe Theatre Festival – two to three weeks of alternative theatre.
  Benson & Hedges Fashion Design Awards – mid to late-March, top New Zealand fashion show of the year, a glamour event
May
  Great Winter Show – trade show, side shows, etc during May school holidays, held for one week, mid-May

July
  International Film Festival – two week extravaganza
September
  Listener Women's Book Festival – week-long women's writing festival, mid-September
October
  Wine & Food Festival – held on Daylight Saving Day, 1st week in October
November
  Santa Festival & Parade – held on a Sunday in mid-November, attracts huge crowds
November/December
  Nissan Mobil 500 Waterfront St Race & Streets Ahead Festival – this race roars through the streets of Wellington on the last weekend of November or the first weekend in December.

Places to Stay

Wellington has a good selection of places to stay in all categories.

Hostels Most of the hostels offer free transport to and from the bus, ferry and railway stations; several also offer booking and ticketing services for buses, trains, ferries and transport in the South Island.

The *Port Nicholson YHA Hostel* (☎ 801 7280; fax 801 7278) on the corner of Cambridge Terrace and Wakefield St, is conveniently situated and quite a luxurious hostel. It moved here in 1991, occupying the former Port Nicholson Hotel, with a complete remodelling. Most rooms in this 98-bed hostel have good views right out over the harbour, and all have private bath. The cost is $17 in dorm rooms ($14 from May to November), $19 in triple and double rooms, or $24 in single rooms. The YHA travel agency is in the lobby.

Also convenient is *Downtown Backpackers* (☎ 473 8482; fax 471 1073) on the corner of Waterloo Quay and Bunny St, opposite the railway station, from where you can catch trains, buses, and a free shuttle bus to the ferry. It's a large hostel with a big-city feel; among its amenities are an in-house restaurant, a bar with billiards and other games, a pub next door, kitchen and lounge facilities, and a good information service. All rooms have private bathrooms; the cost is $15/

17.50/20 in dorm/double/single rooms, with $1 off for VIP members.

Trekkers Hotel/Motel (☎ 385 2153; fax 382 8873) is another central place, stretching through from Cuba St to Dunlop Terrace, just a few doors from the Cuba/Vivian St corner. While it also has hotel and motel rooms, it's a popular spot for backpackers, with 70 backpackers beds; the cost is $15 per person in double and triple rooms or $25 in single rooms if you bring your own sleeping bag, $5 extra with linen provided. Facilities include spa, sauna, laundry, guests' kitchen, restaurant, a bar with live music, and off-street parking.

These three (and Rowena's) are the 'big hostels' in Wellington; the others are smaller, with a more personal feel.

Rosemere Backpackers (☎ 384 3041) at 6 MacDonald Crescent is a short uphill walk from the centre, with good city views especially from the tiny 3rd-storey balcony. The cost is $13 in dorm rooms ($10 in winter), $16/20 in double/single rooms.

Several other hostels are found on and near Brougham St in the pleasant Mt Victoria section. To get there from the Railway Station end of town catch a bus No 2 or 5 to Brougham St, or a bus No 1 or 3 to the Kentucky Fried Chicken on Kent Terrace. From the Courtenay Place end of town it's only a five-minute walk.

Beethoven House (☎ 384 2226) at 89 Brougham St, Mt Victoria, is known for its eccentric atmosphere, largely due to the personality of its owner, Allen Goh ('don't mention my name'). He wakes the guests up to classical music each morning in time for a big communal breakfast at 8 am which on fine days is served out in the lush garden like a garden party – the $13 nightly rate includes breakfast. All birthdays, including Beethoven's, the house's, yours and Christmas are celebrated and there's a friendly communal atmosphere. Note however that this place inspires either love or hate and as many people positively hate it as love it! There's no prominent sign outside, just a small 'BH'. The No 2 Miramar bus stops on the corner of Brougham and Pirie Sts.

Nearby, *Rowena's City Lodge* (☎ & fax 385 7872) at 115 Brougham St is a larger hostel, up a driveway above the street with fine views down over the city. Specialities here include a $3 breakfast and $2 dinner, 'Nifty-fifty' hire scooters ($20/day), safe off-street parking, a BBQ area, three separate lounges and various things to play with such as billiards, a trampoline, a grand piano and more. Rates are $13 in dorm rooms, $16 in double or single rooms, $10 for tent sites.

Around the corner at 52 Ellice St is *Maple Lodge* (☎ 385 3771), a smaller 10-room hostel with rates of $13/15/17 in dorm/double/single rooms. It has safe off-street parking and the usual kitchen, lounge and laundry facilities.

Victoria House (☎ 384 3357), a university hostel at 282 The Terrace, has accommodation available during university holidays (mid-November to late February, mid-May and late August to early September). All the rooms are singles or doubles, with the cost the same in either: $10 with your own sleeping bag, $5 extra with linen provided. The one drawback is there is no hostellers' kitchen, but all meals are available in the cafeteria; you can get any meals you wish on a one-time basis, or pay $25 per day ($145 per week) for a room with three meals a day and linen provided.

If everything else is full, try the *Clarence Braeburn Guest House* (☎ 472 7547) at 253 and 260 The Terrace, with backpackers rates of $9.50 to $15 in single and double rooms. It's actually more of a boarding house, with mostly long-term tenants at $85 to $105 per week, but they do take the occasional backpacker.

Another *YHA Hostel* (☎ 526 4626) is at Kaitoke, 42 km north of Wellington at the top of the Hutt Valley, in Marchant Rd just off SH 2. The hostel, in hill country at the edge of the Tararua Forest Park, is 1.5 km from bushwalking tracks, swimming holes, horse and kayak hire, and 45 minutes' drive from Wellington – take the Masterton bus. Nightly cost is $9 in this rather basic hostel.

The *Clinton Private Hotel*, the *Ambassador Travel Lodge* and the *Terrace Travel*

Lodge are guesthouses but they also have backpackers rates (see Guesthouses).

Guesthouses Wellington has an excellent selection of guesthouses.

At 116 Brougham St in the Mt Victoria area, the *Richmond Guest House* (☎ 385 8529) is a clean, comfortable and friendly 'home away from home' with a guests' kitchen, laundry and TV lounge. B&B is $35/50 for single/double rooms with shared facilities, or $60 for double rooms with private bath.

Also on the south side of town, the *Clinton Private Hotel* (☎ 385 9515; fax 385 2695) at 35 Thompson St has singles/doubles at $30/45, with breakfast an extra $6.50, plus a backpackers rate of $15 in a five-bed dorm with linen provided. There's no guests' kitchen but you can request meals.

Up on The Terrace, the *Ambassador Travel Lodge* (☎ 384 5697; fax 385 7215) at 287 The Terrace has single/double rooms at $35/49 with shared bath or $49/65 with private bath, with substantial discounts if you stay by the week. They also have triple and family rooms, motel units, villas, a rental house, and a backpackers rate of $15 if you bring your own sleeping bag. There's no guest kitchen but continental/cooked breakfast is available for $5/10.

Nearby, the *Terrace Travel Lodge* (☎ 382 9506) at 291 The Terrace is a comfortable home-style guesthouse with single/double rooms at $40/60, all with private bath. Breakfast is $5 extra but there's also a guests' kitchen where you can do your own cooking. Out behind the house is a row of backpackers cabins where rates are $15 with your own sleeping bag, $5 extra with linen provided, in single or double cabins.

A bit more luxurious, the *Tinakori Lodge* (☎ 473 3478, 472 9697; fax 472 5554) at 182 Tinakori Rd in the historic Thorndon district offers attractive rooms, each with its own TV, with a lavish buffet breakfast at $66/80 for singles/doubles.

Hotels There are some cheap old hotels and plenty that head up towards the sky pricewise. Cheaper ones which are also central include the *Cambridge Establishment* (☎ 385 8829; fax 384 4500) at 28 Cambridge Terrace with rooms at $17/20 for singles/doubles, $30/44 with private bath. Nearby, *Flanagan's Hotel* (☎ 385 0216; fax 384 4500) on the corner of Kent Terrace and Majoribanks St has rooms at $40, $45 with private bath, and family rooms at $60.

The popular, centrally-situated *Trekkers Hotel* (see Hostels) has 100 hotel rooms, with simple rooms at $40/50 for singles/doubles or rooms with private bath, TV, telephone, clock radio and desk at $60/70.

On the corner of Willis and Boulcott Sts in the centre, the *Hotel St George* (☎ 473 9139; fax 473 9650) has single/double rooms at $60/75 from Friday to Sunday, rising to $75/95 Monday to Thursday. Also central, the *Tas Hotel* (☎ 385 1304; fax 385 1311) on the corner of Willis and Dixon Sts has a similar pricing arrangement, with singles/doubles at $60 on weekends, rising to $110/118 on weekdays.

Much more expensive hotels include the *Terrace Regency Hotel* (☎ 385 9829; fax 385 2119) at 345 The Terrace, with singles/doubles at $75/80 from Friday to Sunday, $120/128 from Monday to Thursday; the *James Cook Centra Hotel* (☎ 499 9500; fax 499 9800) at 147 The Terrace with singles/doubles at $113 from Friday to Sunday, $254 the rest of the week; and the *Wellington Parkroyal* (☎ 472 2722; fax 472 4724) on the corner of Grey and Featherston Sts with rooms starting at around $300.

Apartment Hotels Wellington has some apartment hotels, a cross between an apartment and a hotel. You can rent them nightly, and they often give discounts for longer-term stays.

Capital Hill Apartments (☎ 472 3716; fax 472 3887) at 54 Hill St, just behind the Beehive, has bedsit (studio) apartments at $80 Friday to Sunday nights, $90 Monday to Thursday; one-bedroom units at $90 Friday to Sunday, $110 Monday to Thursday nights; and two-bedroom family units at $135 per night. *Majoribanks Apartments* (☎ 385

7305; fax 385 1849) at 38 Majoribanks St has two-bedroom apartments at $85 per night for one or two people, $100 nightly for three or more.

Motels Apartments (☎ 389 7426; fax 472 8125) at 60 Rintoul St, Newtown, has one-bedroom apartments at $60/70 for one/two people, plus $10 for each extra adult or $6 per child. *City Life Apartments* (☎ 472 3413; fax 473 4804) at 202 The Terrace is at the top of the line, luxury-wise, with one, two and three-bedroom apartments starting at $180 per night; reductions for longer-term stays.

Motels The *Aroha Motel* (☎ 472 6206; fax 471 0634) at 222 The Terrace has single/double self-contained motel units at $79/96, plus family units for up to seven people at $135. The *Wellington Motel* (☎ 472 0334; fax 472 6825) at 14 Hobson is clean and comfortable with single/double studios at $87, or two-bedroom family units at $97.

Trekkers Hotel/Motel (see Hostels) is more centrally situated; one/two-bedroom motel units here are $89/99.

Other motels not too far from the centre include *Apollo Lodge Motel* (☎ & fax 385 1849) at 49 Majoribanks St, the *Capital View Motor Inn* (☎ & fax 385 0515) at 12 Thompson St, and *Academy Motor Lodge* (☎ 389 6166; fax 389 1761) at 327 Adelaide Rd.

Camping & Cabins If you're looking for a campsite you'll find Wellington a tough place – the only place we found to pitch a tent in the city centre was the little grassy area to one side of *Rowena's* (see Hostels). Otherwise you'll have to head a few km out of town.

Closest in is the *Hutt Park Holiday Village* (☎ 568 5913; fax 568 5914) at 95 Hutt Park Rd in Lower Hutt, 13 km from the centre of Wellington. It has tent sites at $16, powered sites at $18, standard cabins at $25, tourist cabins at $37, tourist flats at $48 and motel units at $63 (all prices the same for either one or two people). The camp is a 15-minute drive from the ferry terminal, a five-minute walk from the bus stop (take the Eastbourne

bus) or a 20-minute walk from the Woburn railway station.

The *Harcourt Holiday Park* (☎ 526 7400; fax 528 2652) at 45 Akatarawa Rd in Upper Hutt, about a 30-minute drive from Wellington, is in a lovely setting of native bush with a river running beside it, in the Harcourt family park. Tent and powered sites are $9 per person, tourist flats $48 for two.

A bit further out, about a 45-minute drive from Wellington, the *Rimutaka State Forest Park* (☎ 564 8551) has basic cold-water camping facilities at Catchpool Valley near the DOC's Catchpool Visitor Centre. The cost is $4/2 for adults/children.

There are also several camping grounds up along the Kapiti Coast; see the Around Wellington section.

Places to Eat

Wellington probably has the widest variety of international cuisines to be found in New Zealand and there are plenty of restaurants to choose from. Courtenay Place and Cuba St in particular are packed with restaurants.

Fast Food The American fast-food giants are well represented in Wellington. *McDonald's*, *Kentucky Fried Chicken* and *Pizza Hut* can all be found in Manners Mall in the centre. There's another *Kentucky Fried Chicken* on Kent Terrace on the corner of Pirie St. Another *McDonald's* is on Courtenay Place near the Cambridge Terrace junction and there's yet another on Lambton Quay near the lower cable car terminal.

Takeaways Wellington's a great place for a sandwich or snack at lunch time. You'll find lots of choices along Courtenay Place and Manners Mall, up Plimmer Steps and along Lambton Quay right in the centre, or along Cuba St and Cuba Mall.

Try the basement level under the BNZ building at the Willis St/Lambton Quay junction. This is the Wellington equivalent of the underground shopping centres of Montreal but while the French-Canadians go subterranean to escape the cold, the Wellingtonians do it to escape the wind. Several places here sell sandwiches, pizzas, Chinese food, doner kebab, fish & chips and other light meals.

Starting from the northern (Parliament and railway station) end of town and moving south, good sandwich places include *Stripes* in the Sun Alliance Centre on Lambton Quay; next door in the James Cook Arcade there's *Stickybun*. Climb Plimmer Steps off Lambton Quay and you'll come to the *Zephyr Cafe*, a bright and airy sit-down place open for breakfast too. Opposite this the *Cafe Mamba* is another lunch-time place. Or there's *Zoe's Cafe* (see Cafes).

At 101 Manners St, close to the Cuba St junction, *A Taste of France* French bakery has a variety of interesting sandwiches and baked goods. *Tastebuds Mexican* at 120 Victoria St, just off Manners Mall and opposite McDonald's, is one of a chain of good Mexican takeaways where you can get a good meal of tacos, enchiladas, etc for under $6.

At 203 Cuba St *Ali Baba* is a great place for a doner kebab, with salad and bread for around $6 or $7. It has both takeaway and restaurant sections and is open every day from 10.30 am to 9 pm, until 10 pm on Friday. Other places for a doner kebab are the *Sultan* at 39 Dixon St or the *Sahara Cafe* at 39 Courtenay Place. All of these places are Turkish restaurants with takeaway sections in front.

An important port like Wellington naturally has plenty of fish & chips specialists. At 12 Bond St in the city centre the *Fisherman's Plate* will dish you up a fine fish & chips or other seafood meal on a paper plate to eat there or take away. *Wellington Fish Supply* at 40 Molesworth St, opposite the Beehive, also has good fish & chips. On Courtenay Place near the corner of Cambridge Terrace are the *Capital Fish Shop* and *Courtenay Fish & Chips*, open every day from 11 am to 9.30 pm.

Also along Courtenay Place are innumerable Chinese takeaways.

Cafes Wellington has a number of enjoyable cafes for a rich cappuccino or a relaxed meal, snack or dessert. Typical cafe menus include selections like sandwiches, pizza, quiche, focaccia, muffins and rich cakes. There are plenty of cafes on Courtenay Place, on Cuba St and up Plimmer Steps.

Konditorei Aida at 181 Cuba St is a traditional Viennese-style cafe with rich Viennese pastries, chocolates, fruit cakes and coffees, open weekdays from 7.30 am to 5.30 pm, until 8 pm Friday, and Saturday from 9 am to 1 pm. It has another branch in Lambton Square on Lambton Quay.

Up on Plimmer Steps in the centre, *Zoe's Cafe* is a most enjoyable coffeehouse-restaurant with a great menu of focaccia, pasta, omelettes, espresso, wine and beer, and rich desserts. It's open Monday to Saturday from 9 am to 4.30 pm.

Other cafes in the centre include the licensed *Lido Cafe* on the corner of Victoria and Wakefield Sts, *City Limits Cafe* at 122 Wakefield St opposite the Old Town Hall, and the excellent *Clark's Cafe* upstairs on the mezzanine floor of the Public Library on Wakefield St. It's open Monday to Thursday 7.30 am to 7.45 pm, Friday 7.30 am to 9 pm, Saturday 9.30 am to 4.30 pm, Sunday from 1 to 4 pm and is worth a visit even if you weren't planning to go to the library.

The *Skyline* restaurant up at the top cable car terminal has a great view over the city and harbour; it's open every day from 11 am to 4 pm.

There are a number of hip cafes where the decor is graffiti, the music is underground, and the customers may include hipsters with spiky purple hair or dreadlocks down to their waists, international hitchhikers, visiting intergalactic guidebook researchers, or visiting librarians from Taupo.

If this is your thing there are a few places in town you can try. *Espressoholic* at 128 Courtenay Place near the corner of Taranaki St is trendy indeed and it's open long hours, beginning at 8 am every day and staying open until 1 am Sunday to Wednesday, to 3 am Thursday, and all the way until 5 am on Friday and Saturday nights.

Over on Cuba St are a couple of similar places. Check out the *Midnight Espresso* at 178 Cuba St near the corner of Vivian St, open from 9 am to 3 am Monday to Friday, 10.30 am to 3 am Saturday and Sunday, or *Cuba Cuba* opposite it at 179 Cuba St which is not only a cafe but also a bar with live music some nights (see Entertainment) and a courtyard out the back.

The *Deluxe Cafe* at 10 Kent Terrace, beside the Embassy Theatre and facing Courtenay Place, is a smaller and quieter but still hip little cafe, open weekdays from 7.30 am to midnight, weekends from around 10 am to midnight. *Kahlo's* upstairs at 103 Willis St, near Manners St, is also small and pleasant; it's open weekdays from 11 am to 6 pm, until midnight on Friday nights.

Pub Food The *Backbencher*, *Thorndon Tavern*, the *Victorian*, the *Bull & Bear*, the *Loaded Hog* and *Molly Malone's* are all good pubs serving pub food; see them under Pubs in the Entertainment section.

Vegetarian & Wholefood The *Mt Victoria Cafe* on the corner of Brougham and Queen Sts in the Mt Victoria district at the south end of town, is a pleasant vegetarian wholefood cafe with delicious food and live jazz and board games on Sunday evenings. It's open for lunch from 11 am to 2 pm Tuesday to Saturday, dinner from 6 to 10 pm every night except Monday. Art exhibits change monthly.

The *Quo Vadis Gourmet Vegetarian Cafe* at 145 Victoria St near the corner of Dixon St serves a variety of international vegetarian dishes; it's licensed and BYO for wine only. It's open every night for dinner from 5.30 to 10 pm, for lunch weekdays only from noon to 2 pm (except January and February).

Also vegetarian is the *Vege Garden* Chinese restaurant at 124 Cuba Mall. It's a simple little place where Chinese food is cooked with no MSG. Or there's the *Spice of Life* vegetarian cafe at 149 Willis St.

Restaurants Wellington has a great number of restaurants from which to choose, including many popular 'ethnic' ones. Typically they are open for lunch Monday to Friday and seven nights a week for dinner, except where noted. Possibilities are many but here are a few suggestions:

Malaysian One of the most delicious restaurants in Wellington is the *Satay Malaysia* upstairs at 46 Courtenay Place, with traditional Malaysian food. A giant feast will cost around $15 to $22 per person, or you can order from the à la carte menu (curry $7.50, roti chanai $2.50). It's open for dinner every night from 5.30 pm, for lunch Wednesday to Friday.

A cheaper but also good restaurant serving traditional Malaysian food is *Satay Kampong* at 262 Wakefield St, with nothing over $8 on the menu. The atmosphere is basic and functional, but the little restaurant is enormously popular. It's open Monday to Saturday from 10 am to 10 pm, Sunday 10 am to 3 pm.

Thai For Thai food head for Cuba St, where you'll find *Sala Thai* at No 134 and *Thiphayathep* at No 154.

Burmese At 34 Courtenay Place you'll find *Monsoon*, a Burmese curry restaurant. Burmese cuisine is nothing to get too excited about – just straightforward curries – but Burmese restaurants are rare, so this is a good opportunity. They also serve Singapore-Malaysian and Chinese dishes.

Chinese Wellington has an enormous number of Chinese restaurants – on Courtenay Place every block seems to have several Chinese restaurants and takeaways. With all the possibilities, one place stands out as a particularly good deal, but it's not on Courtenay Place. It is the *Ye-Jun* Cantonese restaurant upstairs at 40 Willis St, where an all-you-can-eat 10-course buffet with changing selections is served every evening at dinner for $12, weekdays at lunch time for $9.50. It's not gourmet food but the price and the all-you-can-eat aspect of it makes it especially popular with travellers.

Also don't forget the *Vege Garden* vegetarian Chinese restaurant (see Vegetarian).

Mongolian Yes there's a Mongolian restaurant in Wellington – the *Genghis Khan* at 25 Majoribanks St on the south end of town. Mongolian BBQ may not be your usual idea for a fancy night out – charcoal-broiled yak, anyone? – but this restaurant is very popular. No, not really for yak – the tasty food is beef, lamb, chicken and pork, choose any combination you like and it's barbecued before your eyes on a huge Mongolian-style BBQ. Soup, sauces and spices, vegetables and Mongolian rolls are included in the price of $16.50 (children $10) and it's 'bottomless portions' – keep going back as many times as you like. Dinner is served every night from 6 to 10.30 pm (to 9.30 pm on Sunday).

Japanese The *Donbeh Cafe* on Plimmer Steps is a Japanese snack and lunch bar, a tiny, casual cafe open from 8 am to 3 pm Monday to Thursday, 8 am to 8 pm Friday, and 10 am to 2 pm Saturday. Or there's the more expensive, licensed *Sakura* Japanese restaurant up on the third floor of the Japan Seamans' Insurance Hall at 181-195 Wakefield St, open for lunch and dinner Tuesday to Saturday.

Indian The *Bengal Tiger* at the Tas Hotel on the corner of Willis and Dixon Sts is a licensed, rather up-market Indian restaurant, notable for its Indian smorgasbord at $16.50 served every night for dinner.

Turkish *Ali Baba* at 203 Cuba St used to be mainly a takeaway with just a little alcove for seating, but now they've expanded the restaurant section into a very pleasant place to dine – sitting on Turkish pillows, of course, or chairs if you prefer. It's casual and great for an inexpensive meal, snack, or just a baklava and coffee, open every day from 10.30 am to 9 pm, until 10 pm Friday. Also on Cuba St at No 156 is *Cafe Istanbul*, another Turkish restaurant/cafe with a pleasant Turkish decor.

The *Sultan* at 39 Dixon St is a fancier Turkish restaurant, with a more complete menu, open Monday to Saturday from 11.30 am until late. The *Sahara Cafe* at 39 Court-enay Place is a similar place with Turkish, Lebanese and Syrian food, open weekdays from 11 am until late, weekends from 5 pm until late. All of these restaurants also have takeaways.

Italian Moving across the Mediterranean, Italian food is represented at several restaurants including *La Casa Pasta* upstairs at 37 Dixon St, with home-style Italian cuisine. *Mangiare*, another upstairs restaurant nearby at 35 Dixon St, was closed for remodelling the last time we checked, but it too is a long-standing favourite Italian restaurant in Wellington.

Other Italian restaurants include *Little Italy* at 125 Manners St and *Calzone* on the corner of Courtenay Place and Cambridge Terrace, a yuppie sort of place serving gourmet pizzas, pastas, salads and desserts, open every day from 10 am until 1 am. Or there's the candlelit *La Spaghettata* at 15 Edward St, beside the Mexican Cantina.

French The *Cafe Paradiso* on the corner of Courtenay Place and Blair St is an intimate, pleasant cafe with a 'mostly French' menu. With dinner main courses at around $20 it's not cheap, but it's an enjoyable place, with good music playing and candlelight on the tables, quite popular with the yuppie set. There's also a separate, cheaper bar menu for snacks.

Mexican The *Mexican Cantina* at 19 Edward St, just off Manners Mall, is a pleasant restaurant and good value for an enjoyable lunch or dinner out. They have all the usual Mexican dishes – enchiladas, tacos, etc – from around $4 to $6, main meals and combination plates for $13, and some choice for vegetarians. It's open for lunch on weekdays, for dinner every night except Sunday. On weekend evenings get there early as there may be a queue, it's a very popular spot.

Tex/Mex In the same area, *Armadillo* at 129 Willis St is another Wellington institution – a loud, Texas cowboy-style restaurant/bar specialising in American food like steaks, ribs, southern chicken, burgers, etc in Texas-size portions. It's not cheap at $18 for main courses, $9 for appetisers and desserts, but you get plenty of food and the place, complete with its John Wayne decor, is lots of fun. Dinner is every night, with an express lunch served from Wednesday to Friday.

Around the corner at 97 Dixon St, *Chevy's* is a colourful pseudo-US restaurant with fancy burgers, hot Texan chilli, and appetisers like chicken wings, nachos and potato skins, all from around $11 to $15. It's licensed and open long hours, from around 11.30 am to 11 pm, seven days a week.

Seafood The attractive, up-market *Shed 5* and *Dockside* restaurant/bars on Queen's Wharf are both fine places for seafood. Elegant and new, they have been opened as part of the city's waterfront redevelopment programme. *Shed 5* also has a cafe section, outdoor dining, and music for dancing on weekends.

Eclectic *Pico* is an elegant little restaurant that's a favourite with travellers, set back from the street at 60 Ghuznee St, near Cuba Mall. It serves an eclectic menu of delicious and interesting international foods, with plenty of choices for vegetarians, and accompanied by classical music. It's open for lunch and dinner every day except Sunday.

Cafe de Circus on the corner of Cuba and Vivian Sts is another place with an eclectic menu, with an emphasis on 'ethnic' foods and again, plenty of choices for vegetarians. It's licensed and open every day from 9 am until past midnight.

The *Dada* restaurant/bar at 9 Edward St is another trendy place with food from all over the world. Art exhibits are on display and sometimes they feature live jazz.

Entertainment

Pubs *The Loaded Hog* at 12-14 Bond St, just off Willis St, is one of the city's most popular pubs, with a lively atmosphere, live music Wednesday to Sunday nights with no cover

charge, and a good menu. They brew their own beers on the premises, including Red Dog draught beer, Hog's Head dark ale, Port Nick lager, and Weiss German-style lager. All are 100% natural and guaranteed to be hangover-free. Free brewery tours and beer tastings are given on Saturday and Sunday from 2 to 4 pm. It's open every day from 11 am until around midnight, until 2 am on Friday and Saturday nights, until 10 pm on Sunday.

Molly Malone's, an Irish pub at The Glass House on the corner of Courtenay Place and Taranaki St, is another rousing, good fun, popular pub. Live music is mostly Irish, playing Tuesday to Saturday nights with no cover charge; Sunday nights there's an Irish jam session where you're welcome to sit in. It's open from 11 am every day, until 11 pm Monday to Wednesday, to 1 am Thursday, Friday and Saturday, and until 9 pm on Sunday.

Another popular pub is *The Backbencher* on the corner of Molesworth St and Sydney St East, opposite the Beehive. It does a thriving business at lunch time, serving large portions of food, and dinners are becoming popular too. The atmosphere is casual, friendly and fun, with a decor and witty menu poking fun at the politicians who work across the street. It's open every day from 11 am until late.

Also on Molesworth St, a couple of blocks up the hill at No 110, the *Thorndon Tavern* is more of a sports bar, with a big screen sports TV, billiards, darts, plenty of room, TAB racing downstairs, and it also has pub food. Thursday, Friday and Saturday nights there's live music, mostly laid-back country style.

On Plimmer Steps in the centre off Lambton Quay, the *Bull & Bear* is a bar & grill pub, also with an emphasis on sports – they run buses to rugby games, you're welcome to go along – and live music Thursday, Friday and Saturday nights. Further along Lambton Quay at No 134-136 is the quieter *Victorian* pub.

The *Oaks Tavern* upstairs on Manners St near the corner of Cuba St has live music

WELLINGTON

Wednesday to Saturday nights, mainly blues bands for dancing. It's open every day except Sunday from 11 am, to 11 pm Monday to Wednesday, until 2 am Thursday to Saturday.

Wine buffs should check out the *Aqua Vitae Wine Bar* on the corner of Willis and Boulcott Sts, featuring over 100 wines.

Discos & Nightclubs There's dancing at several of the pubs mentioned above, and at other places around town.

Popular discos include the *Metro* on Manners St, on the underground floor below the Pizza Hut.

The *Antipodes Bar* in the Trekkers Hotel on Cuba St near Vivian St is popular with travellers and it has live music Thursday, Friday and Saturday nights. Another good place to meet other travellers is the upstairs *Globetrotters Bar* at the Downtown Backpackers opposite the railway station.

Cuba Cuba at 179 Cuba St is a hip coffeehouse/bar with live dance music Thursday, Friday and Saturday nights. Nearby, *Stax Nite Club* at 171 Cuba St is a nightclub open seven nights a week from around 8 pm until 8 or 10 am the next morning. It has live music Thursday, Friday and Saturday nights, disco music on other nights.

Shed 5 at Queen's Wharf and *Flanagan's* on the corner of Kent Terrace and Majoribanks St are both popular with the yuppie set for more up-market dancing (and dining if you like) on weekend nights.

The *Ecstacy Plus* bar/cafe on the corner of Courtenay Place and Tory St is the place people come to after the pubs shut down. Large and pleasant with an interesting decor and a long, twisted bar, it has live dance music on Wednesday nights, DJs on Thursday, Friday and Saturday nights. It's open from 11 am to 3 am Sunday to Tuesday, until 5 am Wednesday to Friday.

Euroclub, on Garret St just off Cuba Mall, just south of Ghuznee St, is a popular disco and bar for 'gays and friends'. *Alfie's* upstairs at 62 Dixon St near the corner of Cuba Mall is another gay disco, with live DJs on Thursday, Friday and Saturday nights until dawn.

Theatre Wellington is the most active place in New Zealand for live theatre, supporting a number of professional theatre companies and quality amateur companies.

Downstage Theatre (☎ 384 9639) presents plays in the Hannah Playhouse on the corner of Cambridge Terrace and Courtenay Place. *Circa Theatre* (☎ 385 0832) at 1-7 Harris St presents a variety of drama. The famous *Bats Theatre* (☎ 384 9507) at 1 Kent Terrace is a more avant-garde, alternative theatre.

The *Taki Rua Depot Theatre* (☎ 384 4531) at 12a Alpha St specialises in New Zealand drama, with new and Maori plays and local themes. The *Wellington Repertory Theatre* (☎ 385 4939/4247) at 13 Dixon St is a community theatre company.

The *Wellington Playback Theatre* (☎ 475 8643) based at the Tararua Tramping Club Hall at 4 Moncrieff St, a tiny street just off Elizabeth St in the Mt Victoria district, does spontaneous, improvised theatre on the last Saturday of each month. Half price theatre tickets for the Bats, Circa and Downstage Theatres are available at the city information centre Monday to Friday from noon to 4 pm, subject to availability.

The Wellington City Opera (☎ 384 4434) and the Royal New Zealand Ballet (☎ 238 5383) both perform in Wellington, usually at the State Opera House; ring for their current schedules.

Shows & Films The State Opera House (☎ 385 0832) in Manners St, the Michael Fowler Centre (☎ 471 1573) in Wakefield St, the Wellington Town Hall (☎ 471 1573) at Mercer and Wakefield Sts and the Victoria University Theatre (☎ 473 3120) are all popular performance venues. Check the newspapers or the city information centre for current shows. The amphitheatre at Frank Kitts Park on the waterfront and the Dell in the Botanic Garden are popular venues for outdoor concerts and shows.

The *Wellington Film Society* (☎ 384 6817) presents interesting international and art films at the Paramount Theatre, the National Library, and the Memorial Theatre at Victoria University's Student Union, phone for a current schedule. Some films are for members only, but others are open to the public.

Shopping

The Wakefield Market at the foot of Taranaki St, on the corner of Jervois Quay near the waterfront, is a large market with dozens of tiny shops selling everything from international arts & crafts to homemade jams, with several little restaurants for a snack. It's open Friday 11 am to 6 pm, weekends and holidays 10 am to 6 pm.

For fresh fruit and produce, check out Monty's Fresh Produce in the Wakefield Market building, or Vege King in the Shed 22 building opposite. They're open seven days a week, 9 am to 6 pm.

There's a large New World supermarket on the corner of Cambridge Terrace and Wakefield St.

Getting There & Away

Air The Wellington airport has two terminals, each with restaurants, gift shops, etc, and its own information centre. The Information Centre at the Air New Zealand/Domestic Terminal (☎ 388 6451) is open Monday to Friday from 7.30 am to 6 pm, 8 am to 4 pm Saturday and 9 am to 5 pm Sunday. The one at the Ansett/International Terminal (☎ 388 8289) is open similar hours. Left-luggage lockers are in the Domestic Terminal and are always available.

Wellington is served by two major international airlines, two major domestic airlines, and two small-craft airlines specialising in short flights across the Cook Strait.

Air New Zealand and Ansett offer direct domestic flights to many places in New Zealand, with connections to other centres. Air New Zealand's direct flights include Auckland, Blenheim, Christchurch, Dunedin, Gisborne, Hamilton, Motueka, Napier/Hastings, Nelson, New Plymouth, Palmerston North, Rotorua, Taupo, Tauranga, Timaru, Wanganui and Westport. Ansett has direct flights to Auckland, Blenheim, Christchurch, Dunedin, Invercargill, Nelson,

Palmerston North, Queenstown and Rotorua.

To get to the South Island you have to either take the ferry or fly. Some travellers take the ferry in one direction and fly in the other, to experience both – flying is not that much more expensive, plus you get a bird's-eye view of the Cook Strait and the Marlborough Sounds. The flight between Wellington and Picton takes 25 minutes in a small plane. Note that the strait can be just as bumpy up above as it often is at sea level.

Soundsair (☎ Wellington 388 2594, Picton (03) 573 6184) boasts that its Wellington-Picton flights cost only $14 more than the ferry; the cost is $42 (children $35) on a 10 or 14-seater aircraft. They also offer 'Whale of a Day' return flights to Kaikoura for $245 and return flights to the Heaphy Track (Abel Tasman National Park, Golden Bay and Karamea) for $294.

Float Air Picton (☎ Wellington 236 6870, Picton (03) 573 6433) operates from Porirua Harbour, a few km north of Wellington. Its planes are floatplanes, taking off and landing on the sea. The cost is $65 between Wellington and Picton.

Each of these small airlines also fly to any destination around the Marlborough Sounds, Float Air Picton in its floatplanes, Soundsair in small amphibious aircraft which can take off and set down on either land or sea. The cost is around $85 to $90 with either company for most flights, a bit more if you're going to a very remote sound.

International flights serving Wellington are limited to Air New Zealand and Qantas flights to/from Sydney, Brisbane and Melbourne. Though other international airlines do not fly from Wellington, many have offices here.

Airline offices in Wellington include:

Air New Zealand
    179 Featherston St (☎ 388 9737, 385 9911)
    79 Willis St (☎ 388 9737, 385 9911)
Ansett New Zealand
    69-71 Boulcott St (☎ 471 1146)
British Airways
    Royal Insurance Bldg, corner Featherston & Panama Sts (☎ 472 7327)

WELLINGTON

Continental Airlines
corner Featherston & Brandon Sts (☎ 472 5663)
Malaysia Airlines
DB Towers, 111 The Terrace (☎ 499 7744)
Mt Cook Airline
Mackay King Bldg, corner Taranaki St &
Courtenay Place (☎ 388 5020, 385 4130)
Qantas Airways
DFC Harbour Tower, corner Jervois Quay &
Hunter St (☎ 472 1100, freephone (0800) 808
767)
Singapore Airlines
Norwich Insurance House, 3-11 Hunter St
(☎ 473 9749)
United Airlines
26 Brandon St (☎ 473 8960)

Bus Wellington is an important junction for bus travel, with buses coming into and heading out of town on several major routes. Travel time from Wellington to some common destinations is: 1½ hours to Palmerston North, three hours to Wanganui, five hours to Napier, six hours to New Plymouth, seven hours to Taupo, eight hours to Rotorua, and 12 hours to Auckland.

InterCity buses (☎ 495 2443) depart from the railway station. Newmans buses (☎ 499 3261) depart from their bus stop on Strout St, opposite the railway station, as well as from the ferry terminal. Tickets for both bus lines are sold at the travel reservations & tickets centre in the railway station. Both have services to all the places mentioned above.

The Kiwi Experience (☎ 385 2153) and Magic Bus (☎ 387 2018) come in and out of Wellington. Bookings can be made at most Wellington hostels.

Train Wellington Railway Station (☎ 498 3999, freephone (0800) 802 802; fax 498 3721) is a large station with a travel centre offering reservations and tickets for trains, buses, the Interislander ferry, airlines, tours and more. Also here are Wellington's main post office, and luggage lockers open every day from 6 am to 10 pm.

A free shuttle bus operates between the railway station and the ferry terminal, departing from the railway station 35 minutes before each sailing and meeting each arriving ferry.

Two trains operate between Wellington and Auckland, running through the central North Island. The daytime Overlander train runs every day, departing each end in the morning. The overnight Northerner train runs every night except Saturday, departing each end in the evening and arriving early in the morning.

The Bay Express train operates daily between Wellington and Napier, departing from Wellington in the morning, arriving in Napier in the early afternoon, and departing from Napier an hour later to arrive back in Wellington in the evening.

In addition, four suburban electric train routes, with frequent trains every day from around 6 am to midnight, depart from the Wellington railway station: to Johnsonville, via Khandallah and Ngaio; to Paraparaumu, via Porirua and Paekakariki; to Melling, via Petone and Lower Hutt; and to Upper Hutt, going on to Masterton.

Phone Ridewell (☎ 801 7000) for questions on their services, or pick up a timetable from the railway station or city information centre. In addition to the regular fares there is also a day pass available which, for $15, allows two adults and two children (or one adult and three children) to ride these suburban trains anywhere, all day long.

Sea The Interislander ferry service shuttles back and forth between Wellington and Picton. There are usually four services daily in each direction and the crossing takes about three hours. The ferries are the *Aratika* and the newer *Arahura*. It can get pretty rough so if you're prone to seasickness come prepared. If it's not too crowded or the sea too rough the crossing can be quite comfortable. It's best to do the trip in daylight, if the weather's good, to see Wellington Harbour and the Marlborough Sounds. Watch out for dolphins during the crossing.

The fares vary with the seasons; normal fares are $28 during off-peak times, $36 during standard times. Off-peak means most of the time; standard means holiday periods, including Easter week, the May school holidays, the mid-August to mid-September school holidays, and the summer season from around the beginning of December until the end of February. Children aged four to 14 travel at half price; infants under four travel free. Return (round-trip) fares cost double the one-way fares.

Day excursion return fares cost the same as one-way fares and there is a variety of fares such as 'weekend savers', family, group, senior, fares and so on, which provide a substantial discount. Cars or motorhomes cost $90 to $112 off-peak fare, $112 to $150 standard fare. Bicycles cost $12, motorcycles $28, and it's $16 each for canoes, sailboards, hang-gliders or dogs.

At peak periods you must book well ahead – the ferries can be booked solid at certain popular holiday times, especially for the limited vehicle space, which can get booked up months in advance. In fact it's not a bad idea to book ahead anytime to be sure of getting on, especially if you're taking a vehicle. All the discount fares except the day excursions *must* be booked in advance, they are not available at the ferry terminal. You can book up to six months in advance, either directly (☎ 498 3999, freephone (0800) 802 802; fax 498 3721) or at railway stations, AA travel centres, or most travel agents and information centres throughout New Zealand.

A free shuttle bus service is provided for ferry sailings on either side of the strait. In Wellington it operates between the ferry and railway stations, departing from the railway station 35 minutes before each sailing. This is convenient for both train and bus connections, since the long-distance buses depart from either the ferry terminal or the railway station, as well as for just getting between town and the ferry. The shuttle meets all arriving ferries except the one late-night ferry on Monday nights. On the Picton side, a free shuttle is provided between the ferry and the Picton-Christchurch Coastal Pacific Express train.

A number of travellers have made recommendations about what to do with your baggage and how to make a quick exit after the ferry docks. 'Don't put your pack in the luggage vans if you can avoid it,' wrote one traveller. Because, 'if you are able to hang on to your pack, you can get off the other end without delays – no waiting around for hours until the luggage is unloaded'. Other travellers have reported that the luggage vans are off very quickly, however.

If you're planning to hitch out of Picton note that the cars are driving off the ferry almost as soon as the ferry docks. Foot passengers are likely to find every vehicle has gone by the time their feet hit terra firma! Try to hitch a ride while you're still at sea.

Hitching It's not easy to hitch out of Wellington because the highways heading out of the city, whether SH 1 heading up the Kapiti Coast or SH 2 heading up the Hutt Valley, are motorways for a long distance and it's illegal to hitch right on the motorway. It's best to catch a bus or train out to the Kapiti Coast or to Masterton and hitch from there.

Vehicle Storage If you need to store your vehicle while you go across on the ferry or for any other reason, Wellington has two reputable vehicle storage services. Shed 21 (☎ 472 3215) on Waterloo Quay charges $7 per day; Securaport (☎ 387 3700) at 57-61 Kingsford Smith St, Lyall Bay charges $10 per day. Both offer under-cover and fully insured storage, and will arrange for your transport between the car park and the airport or ferry terminal.

Getting Around
Airport Transport There are two types of shuttle service to the airport in Wellington, and two companies providing it: Johnston's Shuttle Express (☎ 384 7654) and Super Shuttle (☎ 387 8787), both with the same prices.

Door-to-door service to or from the airport costs $8 for one person, $10 for two people, $12 for three with either company, and they'll also go to the ferry and the bus or railway station. Less expensive at $4 per person, both companies also operate a shuttle directly from the railway station to the airport, departing from the railway station every half hour from 7.15 am to 5.45 pm, but note that this service operates only from Monday to Friday.

A taxi between the city centre and airport costs around $12 to $14.

Bus Wellington has a good city-and-suburbs bus system with frequent buses operating every day from around 7 am to 11 pm on most routes. Most routes depart from beside the railway station and from the major bus stop on Courtenay Place at the intersection of Cambridge Terrace. A complete line of useful colour-coded bus route maps and timetables is available at the visitor information centre.

Phone Busline (☎ 801 7000) for all questions about public transport around the Wellington area; the service operates Monday to Saturday from 7.30 am to 8.30 pm, Sunday from 9 am to 3 pm. They offer information on all bus and train schedules, fares, connections, etc.

Bus fares are determined by zones. The 'Miracle Mile', between the railway station and the Courtenay Place/Cambridge Terrace bus stops, costs $1; otherwise it's $1.10 to ride in one section, $1.70 to cross two sections, etc.

There's also a Daytripper Pass, good for riding all day and evening on any Big Red bus (most local buses); these passes can be used on weekdays from 9 am (after the rush hour), weekends at any time of day. The cost is $6.50, and two children can ride free with each adult.

Train City Rail operates the country's only electrified suburban train system, with quite good services along the two northern corridors. See Trains in the Getting There & Away section for details.

Bicycle Rental The Penny Farthing Cycle Shop (☎ 385 2279; fax 385 3733) at 89 Courtenay Place hires mountain bikes at $25/140/450 per day/week/month, plus a full range of panniers and other gear. They also have shops in Auckland and Christchurch, so

you can hire the bike at any of their shops and drop it off at any other.

Nearby, Bicycles Unlimited (☎ & fax 385 1233) at 65 Courtenay Place hires mountain bikes at $25/100 per day/week, road bikes (10-speeds, etc) at $15/60 per day/week, with special weekend rates of $25/40 for road/mountain bikes hired from Friday afternoon to Monday morning, and negotiable monthly rates. Both shops offer a full range of bicycle gear, clothing, bicycle repairs, and bicycles for sale.

The Stunned Mullet (☎ 382 8090) on the corner of Tory and Vivian Sts hires mountain bikes for $10/25 per hour/day.

Kiwi Experience (☎ 385 2153) also hires bicycles in conjunction with its bus services throughout both the North and South Islands; see the Getting Around chapter for details.

Kapiti Coast

The Kapiti Coast is an idyllic 30-km stretch of coastline along the west coast from Paekakariki (45 km north of Wellington) to Otaki (75 km north of Wellington).

The region takes its name from the large Kapiti Island five km offshore. The coast is known for its fine soft white sand beaches, all good for swimming and other water activities; other attractions are the island itself, which is a bird sanctuary on land and a marine sanctuary in the water around it, and the Tararua Forest Park in the Tararua Range, which forms a backdrop to the coastline all along its length. There are also a couple of interesting museums, a famous historic Maori church, and the Nga Manu bird sanctuary.

The Kapiti Coast is easily visited as a day trip from Wellington, providing a pleasant relief from the city. Or there are plenty of good places to stay along the coast, where you can spend some restful days.

PAEKAKARIKI
Paekakariki (population 2100) is a quiet seaside village with a lovely stretch of beach.

The railway station and the turn-off into town from the highway are two blocks from the beach. Most of the town is spread out along the beach, heading north from this turn-off. It's a great little town to rest and relax, and you might get the beach all to yourself.

The name Paekakariki means 'the perch (or the hill) of the parakeet' (*pae*, perch or hill; *kakariki*, parakeet).

Things to See & Do

The **Engine Shed Museum**, near the railway station and right on SH 1, contains several restored old steam locomotives. It's open from 10 am to 4.30 pm on Saturday only.

About five km north of Paekakariki at McKay's Crossing, just off SH 1, the **Tramway Museum** holds some old restored wooden trams which ran in Wellington until its tram system was shut down in 1964, plus some interesting photographs of old-time Wellington. A two-km track has been set up from the museum down to the beach, where there's a playground, good swimming and a number of walking tracks through the dunes. The cost for a return ride is $3 (children $1.50, family $8). The museum is open from 11 am to 5 pm on weekends and holidays only; admission is free.

About halfway between the Tramway Museum and the beach is the **Camp Russell Memorial**, an interesting little spot with historical photos and stories about the 20,000 US Marines who camped here during WW II, departing from here for the battle at Guadalcanal, in the Solomon Islands. The memorial was erected in 1992, on the 50th anniversary of the soldiers' arrival.

An alternative way to travel between Wellington and Paekakariki is over the scenic Paekakariki Hill Road. If you're cycling south, it's a steep climb for about three km and then smooth sailing all the way after that.

Places to Stay

Camping & Cabins *Batchelor's Holiday Park* (☎ 292 8292) is about 1.5 km north of the town, right on the beach in the Queen Elizabeth Park. Tent or powered sites are $8.50 per person, cabins $38 for two.

Hostels Up on a hill just one block from the beach and one block from the railway station and highway turn-off, *Paekakariki Backpackers* (☎ 292 8749) at 9 Wellington Rd is a small, friendly and relaxed hostel with a magnificent view of the sea and the sunset. Free use of surfboards, bicycles, and a courtesy car to take you to some of the area's attractions are all included in the cost of $14 in share rooms, $17.50 in twin or double rooms. The owner, Peter Mounsey, is the author of some excellent guidebooks on the Wellington, Kapiti Coast and Wairarapa region and can tell you all kinds of interesting things about the area.

PARAPARAUMU

Paraparaumu (population 3000) is the principal tourist town of the Kapiti Coast. It's actually two towns, not one: Paraparaumu on the main highway, and Paraparaumu Beach, a pleasant community on the beach three km to the west. The beach here is the most developed along the coast, with a beachside park, a big waterslide, playgrounds and plenty of water activities. Boat trips to Kapiti Island depart from here.

The name Paraparaumu is rather a mouthful, but not really difficult to pronounce ('para-para-umu'). Some of the locals affectionately call the town 'para-par-AM' for short, but this is a corruption of the original, and with New Zealand's renewing respect for the Maori language, it's polite to have the patience to call the town by its right name. The name means 'scraps from an oven' (*parapara*, scraps or waste fragments; *umu*, underground oven) and is said to have originated in the old days when a Maori war party attacked the settlement and found only scraps of food in the oven.

Orientation & Information

Most things you'll need in Paraparaumu town (the part by the highway) are right on the highway within a block or two of the one set of traffic lights. Just south of the lights on the inland side is the railway station, which also doubles as the bus station and taxi stand. Opposite this is a shopping centre with a post office, several banks, a supermarket, shops, and a row of fast-food diners.

Also in this shopping centre, the Kapiti Information Centre (☎ 298 5139) is open Monday to Saturday, from 9.30 am to 3.30 pm. On the highway just north of the traffic lights is an AA office (☎ 298 7026) open Monday to Friday, from 8.30 am to 5 pm.

Things to See & Do

The main attraction, of course, is **Paraparaumu Beach**, with its beachside park with good swimming, a big waterslide and other water activities (jet skiing, windsurfing, etc).

About halfway between Paraparaumu and Paraparaumu Beach is the **Paraparaumu Airport** (☎ 298 6536, mobile (025) 428 805) where you can arrange for scenic flights around Kapiti Island and further afield, flying lessons, tandem skydiving, and trial hang-glider flights.

On SH 1 about two km north of Paraparaumu, the **Linfield Farm Park** is where the famous Kapiti Cheese and Kapiti Ice Cream are made – drop in for a taste. There's also a deer and waterfowl park, crafts shops, and farm walks. On weekends and holidays there's a 2 pm farm show with sheep shearing, cow milking, etc – the cost is $5 (children $3, family $14) – plus horse-cart rides and farm-bike rides for the kids. It's open every day from 9 am to 5 pm.

About another km north, just off SH 1, the **Southward Car Museum** is one of the coast's main attractions. It holds the largest collection of antique and unusual cars in Austral-asia, with over 130 cars including the three oldest cars in New Zealand – the 1895 Benz 'horseless carriage' is the oldest of the lot – and an array of motorcycles, three-wheeled cars, inventive home-made vehicles, some antique airplanes, and bicycles including an 1863 Michaux Velocipede, known as 'the bone shaker'. It's open every day from 9 am to 4.30 pm; admission is $4 (children $1).

The **Nyco Chocolate Factory**, on SH 1

about a km south of the town, is open every day from 8 am to 5.30 pm with all kinds of chocolates and other confections.

Places to Stay

Camping & Cabins The *Lindale Motor Park* (☎ 298 8046) is about two km north of the town near SH 1, just south of the Lindale Farm Park. Rates are $8/14 for one/two people in tent sites, $13/16 in powered sites, $25/35 in cabins and $25/32 in on-site caravans.

Hostels Just opposite the beachside park at Paraparaumu Beach, the *Barnacles Seaside Inn* (☎ 298 6106) at 3 Marine Parade has a fine view of the sea and is convenient to everything (beach, shops, etc). The cost is $15 per person in single and double rooms.

Guesthouses The *Davy Gate Christian Guest House* (☎ & fax 297 2373) at 9 Moana Rd in Paraparaumu town is a 10-bed guesthouse with single, double and triple rooms. Bed & breakfast is $35 per person in a share room, $55 in a single room.

Motels There are plenty of motels both in Paraparaumu town and in Paraparaumu Beach; most cost around $60/70 a night. In Paraparaumu Beach there's the *Ocean Motel* (☎ & fax 298 6458) at 42-44 Ocean Rd, *Wright's by the Sea* (☎ 298 7646; fax 297 1511) at 387-389 Kapiti Rd, the *Kapiti Court Motel* (☎ 298 7982; fax 298 3028) at 341 Kapiti Rd, or the *Golf View Motel* (☎ & fax 298 6089) at 16 Golf Rd. Motels along SH 1 include the *Beechwood Motel* (☎ 298 8091), the *Belvedere Motel* (☎ 292 8478) and the *Paraparaumu Motel* (☎ & fax 298 4476).

Places to Eat

Restaurants, cafes and takeaways are plentiful near the beachside park at Paraparaumu Beach, to serve the beach crowd. Out on the highway, just south of the town's one traffic light, *Pizza Hut, Kentucky Fried Chicken* and *McDonald's* all do a thriving business.

KAPITI ISLAND

About 10 km long and two km wide, Kapiti Island is the coastline's dominant feature. Its name is short for Te-Waewae-Kapiti-o-Tara-raua-ko-Rangitane, meaning 'the place where the boundaries of Tara and Rangitane divide'; historically it formed the boundary between the Ngati Tara and Rangitane tribal lands. In the early 1800s the island was the base for Te Rauparaha, a mighty warrior who came down from Kawhia with his forces and took over the entire region. Later in the 19th century, the main island and the three small islands between it and the mainland became bases for seven whaling stations.

For almost a century, since 1897, the island has been a protected wildlife reserve. Many species of birds which are now rare or extinct on the mainland still thrive on Kapiti Island.

The island is maintained by DOC and access is extremely limited. To visit you must obtain a permit from the DOC office in Wellington. Permits are often booked solid for six months in advance; with luck, you might be able to grab a space at the last minute if a permit holder hasn't shown up, but of course you can't count on it. To arrange a permit, contact the Department of Conservation, Wellington Conservancy, 2nd floor, Bowen State Bldg, 58 Bowen St, Wellington (☎ 472 5821; fax 499 0077). Permits cost $15 per person and only day permits are issued (no overnight stays or camping allowed). The DOC office will advise you how to get out to the island; the boats depart from Paraparaumu Beach.

Although access to the island itself is restricted, there's no limitation on boat trips going *around* the island, or on diving in the marine reserve; these can be done anytime. A variety of tours around the island, lasting from 1½ hours to a full day, are offered by Kapiti Alive Tours (☎ 298 6044, 293 6126) in Paraparaumu; they also do fishing and diving trips. Dave Bennett (☎ 298 6085) offers scenic boat trips around the island and fishing trips. Or there's Chester Bellis (☎ 297 3573), offering diving and diving instruction trips, as well as fishing and scenic

round-the-island boat tours. All these trips depart from Paraparaumu Beach.

WAIKANAE

About five km north of Paraparaumu, Waikanae (population 5200) is another town with two sections, one on SH 1 and another by the beach.

Information

The Waikanae Field Centre (☎ 293 2191) at 10 Parata St is the main DOC office for the Kapiti Coast.

Nga Manu Sanctuary

Waikanae's main attraction is the Nga Manu Sanctuary, a 15-hectare bird sanctuary with habitats including ponds, swamp, scrubland, coastal and swamp forest, and birds including mute swans, keas, pied stilts, parakeets (kakariki), ducks and wood pigeons. Other features include picnic areas, a 15-minute bush walk and a nocturnal house with kiwis, owls and tuataras.

To reach the sanctuary, turn seaward from SH 1 onto Te Moana Rd and then follow the signs; the sanctuary is several km from the turn-off. It's open every day from 10 am to 5 pm; admission is $3 (children $1.50, family $6).

Places to Stay

Motels Waikanae has several motels including the *Safari Park Motel* (☎ 293 6053/4) on SH 1; the *Sand Castle Motel* (☎ 293 6072) on the beach at Paetawa Rd; the *Toledo Park Motel* (☎ 293 6199) at 95 Te Moana Rd and the *Ariki Lodge Motel* (☎ 293 6592) at 4 Omahi St.

OTAKI

Otaki (population 4400) is only a small town but it has three distinct sections. The section on SH 1 serves the passing traffic, with shops, takeaways, petrol stations and a railway station which doubles as the bus station. The main centre of Otaki, with the post office and more shops, is two km seawards. Three km further on the same road brings you to Otaki's beachside community.

Otaki is quiet and friendly, with a strong Maori history and influence: the little town has nine maraes, a Maori university and a historic Maori church. Its name means 'the place of sticking in' – relating to a story that this is the place where Hau stuck his staff in the ground when he was pursuing his wife.

Things to See & Do

The **Rangiatea Maori Church** in Otaki is one of the finest historic Maori churches in New Zealand. It is plain on the outside but elegant inside, with woven tukutuku panels, painted rafters, a carved pulpit and some giant totara trees – three supporting the long ridgepole tree on top – which were cut in the forest in 1844 and brought a long distance to build the church, which was completed in 1851. The name Rangiatea means 'the abode of the Absolute' – the house of God.

The church is open every day and you are welcome to visit it. To get there, turn seaward from SH 1 at the BP petrol station, then turn right at the post office onto Te Rauparaha St. The church is one block down, on your left. Opposite it are two large white obelisk monuments, one marking the grave of Te Rauparaha the great warrior, the other a monument to the arrival of Christianity in Otaki in 1840, which led to the cessation of war.

Two km south of the town, Otaki Gorge Road takes off inland from SH 1 and leads 19 km to **Otaki Forks**, the main western entrance to the Tararua Forest Park. The scenic half-hour drive up through the Otaki Gorge to the Forks has a number of posted walking tracks along the way. The road is sealed most of the way; the last five km is a gravel road.

Also along here is the **Tararua Outdoor Recreation Centre** (☎ (06) 364 3110) with canoe, kayak and rafting trips on the Grade Two Otaki River. You can hire the gear for a morning, afternoon or whole day, and they also offer guided river trips, abseiling, rock climbing, mountain biking, horse treks and other outdoor activities. It's open on weekends, school and public holidays, from October to April only.

At Otaki Forks there are picnic and swimming areas, camping areas and a hut, and a resident Conservation Officer (☎ (06) 364 3111) with maps and information on the Tararua Forest Park. Good tramping possibilities include bush walks from 30 minutes to 3½ hours in length around the immediate area, and longer tracks leading to huts. Ask for advice on longer tracks in the park – you could do some good tramps of several days. Bring adequate clothing if you're planning to do a lot of tramping as the weather can be changeable, and sign the tramping intentions book.

Places to Stay

Camping & Cabins Otaki has two motor camps just a block from the beach.

The *Capitol Seaside Resort* (☎ (06) 364 8121; fax 364 8123) at 20 Tasman Rd has tent sites at $8/14 for one/two people, powered sites at $13/17, tourist flats at $40/45 and motel units at $62/70. Facilities include a swimming pool, spa, sauna, tennis and other games courts, a trampoline and playgrounds.

The *Otaki Beach Holiday Camp* (☎ (06) 364 7107) on Moana St, is a simpler place with tent sites at $7/11, powered sites at $9.50/13.50, cabins and on-site caravans at $25 to $30.

You can also pitch a tent at the *Bridge Lodge* (see Hostels) or there's camping and a hut at Otaki Forks, half an hour's drive inland.

Hostels The *Otaki Oasis* (☎ (06) 364 6860) at 33 Rahui Rd is a small, pleasant well-tended home-style place with plenty of room and a rural atmosphere. Nonetheless it's not too remote; it's on the inland side of the railway tracks, about a block south of the railway station. If you're driving, turn inland at the BP petrol station on SH 1 and then right (south) just over the tracks. The cost is $15 per person in the bunkroom or $17.50 in the double room, but if you want to, you can work for your accommodation, or trade.

A bit farther from town, *Bridge Lodge* (☎ & fax (06) 364 5405) is on Otaki Gorge Road just inland from SH 1, about two km

Top: Abel Tasman National Park, Nelson (VB)
Bottom: Picton Harbour, Nelson (TW)

Top: Knights Point, West Coast (NK)
Bottom: Punakaiki Pancake Rocks, West Coast (JW)

south of the town. It's a large place with an attractive grounds which can sleep 130 people; they take mostly school groups and conferences but also backpackers. The cost is $13 per person in share rooms, $15 in single rooms, a bit extra with linen. To pitch a tent on the grounds costs $7.50 per person.

Hotels & Motels The *Family Hotel* (☎ (06) 364 7180) at 30 Main St in the centre of town, two km towards the sea from SH 1, has just 10 beds; the cost is $25/45 for singles/doubles.

The *Capitol Seaside Resort* has motel units (see Camping & Cabins); the *Otaki Motel* (☎ (06) 364 8469) on SH 1 is a little cheaper.

GETTING THERE & AWAY
Getting from Wellington to the coast is a breeze – this is the major route from Wellington to the rest of the North Island whether you're coming by bus, train or car.

Bus
InterCity, Newmans, Kiwi Experience and Magic Bus all stop at Paraparaumu and Otaki on their north-south routes between Wellington and the rest of the North Island. From Wellington it's about an hour to Otaki, 45 minutes to Paraparaumu.

Train
Trains between Wellington and the coast operate even more frequently than the buses. Coming from Wellington, the Paraparaumu electric train runs hourly in both directions every day from around 6 am to midnight, with stops at Paekakariki and Paraparaumu. From Wellington it's 50 minutes to Paekakariki, one hour to Paraparaumu.

All the long-distance trains serving Wellington stop at Paraparaumu and Otaki, making three trains a day in each direction. Travel time on these is 50 minutes to Paraparaumu, 1¼ hours to Otaki.

Hitching
Running along the coast, SH 1 is the principal route connecting Wellington to the rest

of the North Island, so there's plenty of traffic. Hitching is good anywhere along here.

The Wairarapa

The large region east and north-east of Wellington is known as the Wairarapa, taking its name from Lake Wairarapa ('shimmering waters'), a shallow but vast 8000-hectare lake. The Wairarapa is principally a sheep raising district – it boasts that it has three million sheep within a 16-km radius of Masterton, the region's principal centre. It also has a few interesting attractions for visitors including the National Wildlife Centre at Mt Bruce, wineries at Martinborough, and very good tramping and camping in several regional and forest parks.

MASTERTON
Principal centre of the Wairarapa, Masterton (population 22,500) is not a particularly exciting place, although it's a fair sized town. Probably its main claim to fame is the international Golden Shears competition held annually the first week in March, in which sheep shearing is raised to the level of sport and art, with some of the world's top shearers competing for finesse as well as speed.

You will pass through Masterton if you're travelling north-south on SH 2. The major bus and train routes serving Wellington don't come this way, though – they go along the Kapiti Coast. Masterton is 102 km north-east of Wellington.

Information
The information centre, Tourism Wairarapa (☎ & fax (06) 378 7373) is at 5 Dixon St. It's open weekdays from 8.30 am to 5 pm, Saturday and Sunday from 10 am to 4 pm, except in winter when the weekend hours are shortened to 10 am to noon on Saturday and 11 am to 3 pm on Sunday. It has information on the entire Wairarapa region.

There's a DOC field office (☎ (06) 378 2061) on the ground floor of the Departmen-

WAIRARAPA

tal Building in Chapel St, open Monday to Friday from 8.30 am to 5 pm. The AA (☎ (06) 378 2222) is on the corner of Chapel and Jackson Sts.

Things to See & Do

The large 32-hectare **Queen Elizabeth Park** in Park St off Queen St has sports grounds, an aviary, aquarium, deer park, small lake where boats are hired, children's playgrounds and a miniature railway where trains are run on weekends and holidays. Entry to the park is free.

The **Wairarapa Arts Centre** in Bruce St off Queen St has several galleries and the Stidolph Museum of Early Childhood, with a fascinating collection of antique items pertaining to childhood including antique dolls, toys, games, clothing and an array of teddy bears. Also at the centre is a historic 1878 Wesleyan church, with good acoustics which make it a popular venue for music concerts and theatre performances, plus a crafts shop, a coffee shop and a herb garden. The centre is open Monday to Friday from 9 am to 5 pm, Saturday and Sunday from 1 to 4.30 pm; admission is free, donations welcomed.

The **Memorial Recreation Centre** in Queen St has indoor and outdoor heated pools; it's open every day from around 6 am to 6 pm.

Places to Stay

The *Mawley Park Motor Camp* (☎ (06) 378 6454) is in Oxford St on the bank of the Waipoua River, about 800 metres from the CPO. Tent sites are $12 for two, powered sites $15 for two, and cabins are $24 and $31 for two.

Masterton Backpackers (☎ (06) 377 2228) at 22 Victoria St in the centre of town is a homely, colonial-style hostel with three dorm rooms each sleeping six. The cost is $14 per night.

The *Victoria House Guest House* (☎ (06) 377 0186) offers B&B at $35/56 for singles/doubles.

Inexpensive hotels and motels include the *Station Hotel* (☎ (06) 378 9319) at 145 Perry St with singles/doubles at $30/45, the *Colo-*

nial Cottage Motel (☎ (06) 377 0063; fax 377 0062) at 122 Chapel St with singles/doubles at $58/67 and the *Cornwall Park Motel* (☎ (06) 378 2939) at 119 Cornwall St with the same prices.

The information centre has referrals for farmstays throughout the Wairarapa region.

Getting There & Away

Tranzit Coachlines (☎ (06) 377 1227) on Queen St beside Woolworth's operates two buses daily between Wellington and Masterton, but only on weekdays – on weekends you'll have to take the train. The train service between the two cities is faster, cheaper and more frequent, with four trains a day on weekdays and two daily on weekends. Travel time is about two hours on the bus, 1½ hours on the train.

Tranzit Coachlines also operates buses between Masterton and Palmerston North, passing through Mt Bruce on the way.

MT BRUCE
National Wildlife Centre

Thirty km north of Masterton on SH 2, the National Wildlife Centre at Mt Bruce is a sanctuary for native New Zealand wildlife, mostly birds. Large aviaries and outdoor reserves feature some of the country's most rare and endangered species, which you probably won't get to see anywhere else, in addition to more common species and a nocturnal house with kiwis, tuataras and other endangered reptiles. There are breeding programmes of endangered species here. Each species is given as natural a habitat as possible, so you have to look closely to find the birds. The centre is open every day from 9 am to 4.30 pm; admission is $6 (children $1.50).

Both the Mt Bruce Pioneer Museum and the National Wildlife Centre are right on SH 2. Any bus going between Masterton and Palmerston North can drop you at the gates. It's also easy to hitchhike.

Mt Bruce Pioneer Museum

The Mt Bruce Pioneer Museum on SH 2, 10 km south of the National Wildlife Centre, is the largest private museum in the Wairarapa region, with over 3000 items including working displays of gramophones, milking machines, stationary engines and water-wheels, plus farming equipment and other interesting relics of New Zealand's pioneering days. The museum is open every day from 9 am to 4.30 pm; admission is $2.50 (children 50c).

TRAMPING

There are plenty of good opportunities for tramping in the Wairarapa, especially in the Tararua and Rimutaka Forest Parks in the Tararua and Rimutaka Ranges and in the Haurangi Forest Park. There are some fine coastal walks, too. Maps and information on tramping possibilities are available from the DOC offices in Wellington and Masterton.

A favourite spot for tramping in the Wairarapa is at Holdsworth, the principal eastern entrance to the Tararua Forest Park, where there is some beautiful virgin forest with pleasant streams running through. The park entrance has swimming, picnic and camping areas, a good hut and a number of fine walks including short, easy family walks, excellent one or two-day walks, and longer, more challenging treks for experienced mountaineers. A resident Conservation Officer (☎ (06) 377 0022) has maps and information on tramping in the area, and an intentions book where you can sign in. Ask there about current weather and track conditions before you set off, and come prepared for all weathers – weather in the Tararuas is notoriously changeable. The turn-off to Holdsworth is on SH 2, 35 km south of Masterton; from there it's 15 km to the park entrance.

Closer to Wellington, the Rimutaka In-cline walk is a five to seven-hour walk each way along a historic old railway line which operated trains between Wellington and the Wairarapa between 1878 and 1955; the walk begins from SH 2 (look for the signpost) nine km north of Upper Hutt. A little further north, 16 km north of Upper Hutt on SH 2, the Kaitoke Regional Park is good for swimming, rafting, camping, picnicking and a number of good walks ranging from 20 minutes to six hours. At Kaitoke there is camping and a basic YHA hostel (see Hostels in the Wellington section).

OTHER THINGS TO DO

Small boat (two-person) rafting tours on the Waiohine River, with an optional abseil in the afternoon, depart from Wellington every weekday; contact Venturebound Tours (☎ (06) 233 9034) or the Port Nicholson YHA hostel. For bungy jumping there's Zero Gravity (☎ (06) 292 8256), which does jumps from the Nagumu bridge 44 metres (131 feet) above the spectacular Deep Gorge, a 25-minute drive east of Masterton. Or you could try solo or tandem parachuting from the Hood Aerodrome in Masterton; contact Gold Coast Tandems at Paraparaumu Beach (☎ (06) 297 2600, mobile (025) 428 805).

For more sedate enjoyment of the Wairarapa, try a winery tour of the vineyards at Martinborough. The information centres in Wellington and Masterton have brochures on the vineyards so you can do your own tour, or there are organised tours available. Laura's Wairarapa Tours (☎ (06) 377 3534) is a local favourite, doing tours to wineries and to many other interesting places throughout the region.

WAIRARAPA

SOUTH ISLAND

Marlborough & Nelson

To some people, crossing Cook Strait from Wellington to Picton in the South Island is like entering a new country. Many visitors strike out further afield immediately after crossing, but there is much of interest in this area, in particular the inlets and bays of Marlborough Sounds. To the south of Picton is the sedate city of Blenheim, a great place for relaxing. Further south is the wildlife centre, Kaikoura. Here you can swim with hundreds of dolphins and seals or watch the mighty sperm whale surface, tail flukes first.

To the west is the Nelson region with great tramping possibilities in the North-west Nelson Forest Park, Nelson Lakes National Park and the splendid Abel Tasman National Park. Nelson is a great city to relax in, as too are the towns of Motueka and Takaka. If you are lucky to get right over to the west then you can make a trip up to Farewell Spit and observe the many varieties of birdlife in the important Golden Bay wetlands.

Information

All telephone numbers in the South Island have an 03 prefix if you are calling them from a long distance (even within the region).

Marlborough Sounds

The convoluted waterways of the Marlborough Sounds are the first sight of the South Island from the ferry. To get an idea of how convoluted the sounds are, Pelorus Sound is 42 km long but has 379 km of shoreline!

History

The first European to come across the Marlborough district was Abel Tasman, who spent five days sheltering on the eastern coast of D'Urville Island, in 1642. It was to be over 100 years before the next Pakeha, James Cook, turned up in January 1770,

remaining there for 23 days. Between 1770 and 1777 Cook made four visits to the stretch of water he named Queen Charlotte's (now Charlotte) Sound. Near the entrance of Ship Cove there's a monument which commemorates the explorer's visits. Because Cook spent so much time there he was able to make detailed reports of the area, so that it became the best known haven in the southern hemisphere. In 1827 the French navigator Jules Dumont d'Urville discovered the narrow strait now known as French Pass, and his officers named the island just north of there in his honour.

In the same year a whaling station was set up at Te Awaiti in Tory Channel, which brought about the first permanent European settlement in the district. In June 1840, Governor Hobson's envoy, Major Bunbury, arrived on the HMS *Herald* on the hunt for Maori signatures to the Treaty of Waitangi. On 17 June Bunbury proclaimed the British Queen's sovereignty over the South Island at

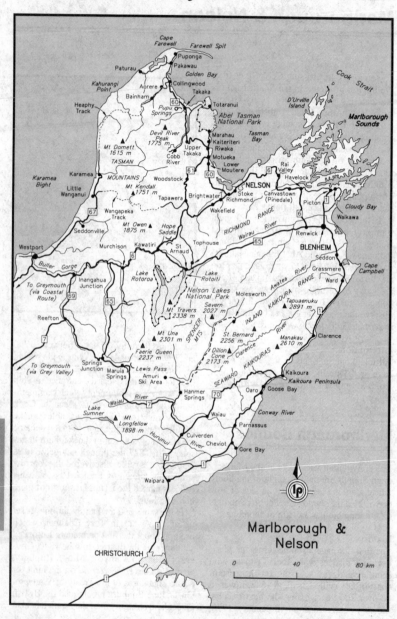

Marlborough &
Nelson

0   40   80 km

MARLBOROUGH

Horahora Kakahu Island. Towards the end of that year a Wesleyan mission was set up at Ngakuta Bay in the north-western corner of the port.

In spite of this, the Marlborough area was not the site of an organised company settlement; it was more an overflow of the Nelson colony. Around 1840 the opportunistic and unscrupulous New Zealand Company tried to settle part of the Wairau Plain after buying the alleged rights from the widow of a trader, John Blenkinsopp. He had claimed to have bought the land from the Maoris for one 16-pound cannon, and had obtained a dubious deed signed by Maori chiefs who couldn't read English. The cannon is now on display in Blenheim.

By 1843 the pressure for land from the Nelson settlers was so great that it led to conflict with the Maoris, who denied all knowledge that any part of Wairau was sold. Two Maori chiefs, Te Rauparaha and Te Rangihaeata, arrived from Kapiti to resist survey operations. The Pakehas sent out a hurriedly co-opted armed party led by Arthur Wakefield and Police Magistrate Thompson to arrest the chiefs. The party was met peacefully by the Maoris at Tuamarina, but the Pakehas precipitated a brief skirmish during which Te Rangihaeata's wife was shot. The Pakehas were then forced to surrender and Rangihaeata, mad with rage, demanded vengeance. Twenty-two of the party, including Wakefield and Thompson, were clubbed to death or shot; the rest escaped through the scrub and over the hills. The whole event came to be known as the Wairau Massacre.

Te Rauparaha was a formidable Ngati Toa chief who was, indirectly, a major reason for the British government taking control of New Zealand. He cultivated the captains and crews of visiting whaling ships (they nicknamed him the 'old sarpint') and, with muskets and other weapons he acquired, set out on the wholesale and horrific slaughter of other South Island tribes. In his most gruesome raid he was aided by a Pakeha trader, who transported his warriors and decoyed the opposing chiefs on board, where they were set upon by Te Rauparaha's men.

The ensuing slaughter virtually wiped out the local tribe. When news of this event and the captain's part in it reached Sydney, the British Government finally decided to bring some law and order to New Zealand and to their unruly citizens operating there.

A detailed account of Te Rauparaha's life can be found in a biography entitled *Te Rauparaha: A New Perspective* by Patricia Burns (paperback, 1988, Penguin).

In March 1847 Wairau was finally bought and added to the Nelson territory. It was not long before the place was deluged by people from Nelson and elsewhere. However, when the Wairau settlers realised that revenue from land sales in their area was being used to develop the Nelson district they petitioned for independence. The appeal was successful and the colonial government called the new region Marlborough and approved one of the two settlements, Waitohi (now Picton) as the capital. At the same time, the other settlement known as 'The Beaver' was renamed Blenheim. After a period of intense rivalry between the two towns, including legal action, the capital was transferred peacefully to Blenheim in 1865.

THE SOUNDS

The convoluted waters of the Marlborough Sounds have many bays, islands, coves and waterways, formed by the sea invading its deep valleys after the ice ages. Parts of the sounds are now included in the Marlborough Sounds Maritime Park. The park is actually many small reserves separated by private land. There is a small paperback, *Marlborough Sounds Maritime Park* (1989), which is a good introduction to the area; it costs $15.95.

Information

The best way to get around the sounds is still by boat, although the road system has been extended. Permits are required for hunting or camping and there's plenty of good swimming, tramping and fishing. Information on

MARLBOROUGH

the park is available in Picton from the visitor information centre and the DOC.

Queen Charlotte Walkway

Those put off by the hordes doing the Abel Tasman Track may wish to try this alternative. It is a 58-km-long track which connects historic Ship Cove with Anakiwa. You pass through privately owned land and DOC reserves. The coastal forest is lush, and from the ridges you can look down on either side to Queen Charlotte and Pelorus sounds.

You can arrange to complete the walk in sections (using local boat services – see Getting There & Away) or do the whole three to four-day journey. There are many campsites for those tenting it, as well as a number of hostels and hotels. Remember that you are here only through the cooperation of local landowners, so respect their property and carry out what you carry in.

The track is well defined and suitable for people of all ages and average fitness. Between Kenepuru Saddle and Portage Saddle you'll find the going toughest. Carry water between Kenepuru and Te Mahia saddles; this is available at the Bay of Many Coves Saddle campsite. For more information, get a copy of the pamphlet *The Queen Charlotte Track* from the DOC Information Centre. DOC provides the following information about distances and walking times:

Anakiwa-Te Mahia	9 km	4 hr
Te Mahia-Portage	8 km	4 hr
Portage-Bay of Many Coves Saddle	10 km	6 hr
Bay of Many Coves-Kenepuru Saddle	5 km	3 hr
Kenepuru Saddle-Endeavour Inlet	8 km	4 hr
Endeavour Inlet-Resolution Bay	6 km	3 hr
Resolution Bay-Ship Cove	3 km	2 hr

It may be possible to do a leg of the trip by sea kayak; contact Bruce Maunsell at Marlborough Sounds Adventure Company (☎ 573 6078) for possibilities.

Getting There & Away If you are planning to walk the whole track, Cougar Line (☎ 573 7925), 10 London Quay, Picton, operate a drop-off service at Ship Cove, the preferred starting end for the walk. The approximate

cost is $34 each. It leaves at 8.45 am and arrives at the drop-off point at about 10 am. At the Anakiwa end the mail van (☎ 577 8386, 573 6262) can pick you up from Monday to Friday, at approximately 10 to 10.15 am, for the return trip to Picton.

Sounds Outdoors (☎ 573 6175) conduct four-day guided walks along the walkway for $495 (minimum two persons); it is a good alternative for those wanting to do the walk in a leisurely manner, without having to carry equipment.

Sea Kayaking & Other Activities

The Marlborough Sounds Adventure Company (☎ 573 6078; fax 573 6982), Picton, organises sea-kayak trips and bush walks around the sounds. The kayak trips range from one day ($50) to four days ($350). Longer expeditions can be arranged but the complexity depends very much on the experience of the participants.

For example, you may catch the Cougar's water taxi to the outer sounds. From a base camp on Blumine Island you can explore the wildlife sanctuary and marine reserve, as well as the Maori pa on Motuara Island. Blumine has its own species of carnivorous snail and Motuara has saddlebacks transferred from Codfish Island (near Stewart Island).

Prices include the kayak, guide, camping equipment and all meals. They also hire kayaks for solo trips at a daily cost of $35 for a single kayak ($30 for each day after) or $65 for a double kayak. For $70 they will drive you and your kayaks to Tennyson Inlet.

Two other operators provide sea kayaking trips out of Picton. They are Sounds Experience (☎ 547 9436) and Waikawa Sea Kayaks (☎ 573 6800).

Places to Stay

There are plenty of places to stay on the sounds, although some are accessible only by boat or floatplane. Prices are usually fairly reasonable, and practically all offer free use of dinghies and other facilities. The fact that they are only accessible by boat means they're often in some beautiful settings.

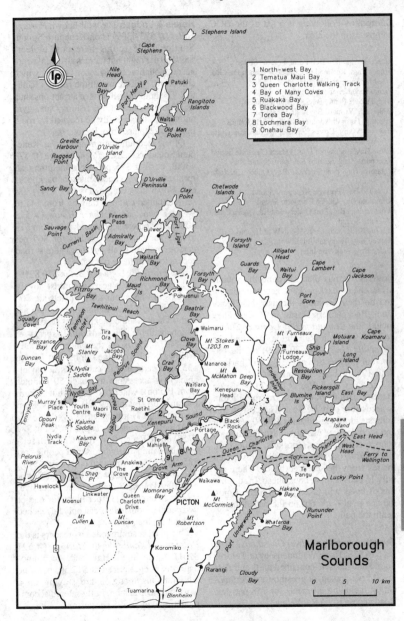

1 North-west Bay
2 Tematua Maui Bay
3 Queen Charlotte Walking Track
4 Bay of Many Coves
5 Ruakaka Bay
6 Blackwood Bay
7 Torea Bay
8 Lochmara Bay
9 Onahau Bay

Stephens Island
Cape Stephens
Nile Head
Otu Bay
Patuki
Port Hardy
Rangitoto Islands
Waitai
Old Man Point
Greville Harbour
D'Urville Island
Ragged Point
Sandy Bay
Kapowai
D'Urville Peninsula
Clay Point
Chetwode Islands
French Pass
Bulwer
Port Ligar
Forsyth Island
Alligator Head
Cape Lambert
Cape Jackson
Current Basin
Admiralty Bay
Waitata Bay
Forsyth Bay
Guards Bay
Waitui Bay
Sauvage Point
Richmond Bay
Maud Is
Pohuenui
Port Gore
Fitzroy Bay
Tawhitinui Reach
Beatrix Bay
Squally Cove
Tennyson Inlet
Waimaru
Mt Stokes 1203 m
Mt Furneaux
Motuara Island
Cape Koamaru
Penzance Bay
Mt Stanley
Tira Ora
Clova Bay
Furneaux Lodge
Ship Cove
Long Island
Duncan Bay
Nydia Saddle
Jacobs Bay
Pelorus Sound
Crail Bay
Manaroa
Mt McMahon
Deep Bay
Endeavour Inlet
Resolution Bay
Nydia Bay
Waitiara Bay
Kenepuru Head
Pickersgill Island
East Bay
Murray's Place
Youth Centre
Maori Bay
St Omer
Raetihi
Kenepuru Sound
Black Rock
Blumine Is
Arapawa Island
Opouri Peak
Kaiuma Saddle
4
East Head
Nydia Track
Kaiuma Bay
Te Mahia
Portage
5
Queen Charlotte Sound
Tory Channel
West Head
Ferry to Wellington
Pelorus River
9
8
6
Te Pangu
Lucky Point
Anakiwa
The Grove
Grove Arm
Waikawa
Shag Pt
Hakana Bay
Havelock
Linkwater
Momorangi Bay
Mt McCormick
Rununder Point
Moenui
Queen Charlotte Drive
PICTON
Mt Cullen
Mt Duncan
Mt Robertson
Port Underwood
Whataroa Bay
1
Koromiko

Marlborough Sounds

Rarangi
Cloudy Bay
0   5   10 km
Tuamarina
To Blenheim

MARLBOROUGH

Campsites Following is a list of the DOC campsites in the area:

Jacobs Bay, Dillon Bell Point, Pelorus Sound
French Pass, Roadend of Croiselles/French Pass Rd, Marlborough Sounds
Picnic Bay, Kenepuru Sound
Nikau Cove, Picnic Bay, Kenepuru Sound
Waimaru, Waimaru Bay, Pelorus Sound
Titirangi Farm Park, outer Marlborough Sounds
Bay of Many Coves Saddle, Queen Charlotte Walkway
Camp Bay, Endeavour Inlet, Queen Charlotte Sound
Kenepuru Head, head of Kenepuru Sound
Ratamira Bay, near Ruakaka Bay, Queen Charlotte Sound
Cowshed Bay, Portage, Kenepuru Sound
Kumutoto Bay, Queen Charlotte Sound
Whatamonga Bay, Port Underwood Rd, Queen Charlotte Sound
Pelorus Bridge, adjacent SH 6, NW of Havelock (FS)
Harvey Bay, Tennyson Inlet
Elaine Bay, Tennyson Inlet

Hostels Various places around the sounds offer cheap backpackers accommodation and do their bookings through the Plucky Duck Backpackers Hostel in Picton. They include the *Resolution Bay Camp & Cabins* (☎ 579 9411) in Resolution Bay and the *Furneaux Lodge* (☎ 579 8259) on the Endeavour Inlet section of the Queen Charlotte Sound Track, both charging just $10 a night.

The *Lazy Fish Hostel* (☎ 573 6055) on Queen Charlotte Sound, 12 km from Picton, is accessible only by boat. The cost in this homestead-turned-hostel is $17.50 per night and includes free use of windsurfer, dinghy, canoe, fishing gear, snorkels, volleyball, BBQ and so on. The front deck is just seven metres from the secluded beach. There are only 15 beds here, so book ahead. In summer lots of boats will take you out there. Enjoy the spa pool – it's out on the beach underneath the palm trees.

Guesthouses The *Bulwer Guesthouse* (☎ & fax 576 5285) is on Waihinau Bay on Pelorus Sound and has self-contained units and flats for $15 per person, or guesthouse accommodation including all meals for $58 per day. Road access is via Rai Valley.

Hotels & Lodges The well-known *Portage Hotel* (☎ 573 4309) is on Kenepuru Sound. Single/double rooms here cost at least $89/100 per night but there is also bunkroom accommodation for $22 per person, which still allows you to use all the resort's facilities. The hotel has all sorts of attractions such as sailing, windsurfing, fishing, spa, gym and tennis. It can easily be reached by road, boat or floatplane from Picton.

Other accommodation options at Kenepuru Sound include the *Raetihi Lodge* (☎ 573 4300), costing $75 per night including all meals; they have reduced rates for backpackers. *Hopewell Cottages* (☎ 573 4341) has self-contained cottages ranging from $41 to $49 for two, and *St Omer House* (☎ 573 4086) has cottage accommodation from $18 to $22 per person, or chalets for $65 per person including all meals. There's road access to all of these places.

The *Furneaux Lodge* (☎ & fax 579 8259) is a century-old place set amidst lovely gardens in Endeavour Inlet; chalets are $60 in winter and $70 in summer per couple per night. There is some backpackers accommodation available. The *Te Mahia Resort* (☎ & fax 573 4089) is on the Queen Charlotte Walkway. Self-contained units cost $30 to $35, and caravan and campsites are available. It is accessible by road (50 minutes from Picton), water taxi (20 minutes from Picton), or floatplane (30 minutes from Porirua in the North Island).

At the *Te-Pangu Bay Lodge* (☎ & fax 579 9755) on Te Pangu Bay, Tory Channel, self-contained units for two to seven people cost $25 per person (minimum unit charge $40). The *Tira-Ora Lodge* (☎ 579 8253) on Northwest Bay, Pelorus Sound, is more expensive; rooms there cost $112 per night for one or two people. Both lodges can only be reached by boat or floatplane.

One place recommended by readers is the *Pohuenui Island Sheep Station* (☎ 597 8161), Pohuenui, via Havelock. Accommodation is budget priced at $12.50, with the added bonus that you are staying on a working sheep station. Fully catered accommodation here is $95 per person.

On Kenepuru Sound there is *Mary's Holiday Cottage* (☎ 573 4376) at Waitaria Bay, 95 km from Picton via Linkwater, where an evening stay costs only $14. Check with the YHA in Havelock before going out there.

Resorts & Cabins There are cabins at *Gem Resort* (☎ 579 9771) at the Bay of Many Coves. Cabins for two cost between $46 and $61; there's no road access. The *Te Rawa Boatel* (☎ 579 8285), 27 km by launch from Havelock, is a bit cheaper, with rooms at $45 for two people. *Punga Cove Tourist Resort* (☎ 579 8561) on Endeavour Inlet, Charlotte Sound, is more expensive; double rooms cost between $68 and $115 per night; there is a licensed restaurant here. The *Endeavour Resort* (☎ 579 8381), also set in historic Endeavour Inlet, has chalets and units for $50 to $65 for two per night. You can get to it with the Cougar Line.

Getting Around

The 'mail run' boat runs to the Lazy Fish Hostel on Queen Charlotte Sound all year round on Tuesday and Friday, and costs about $11. A water taxi costs about the same if you have a group of four or five to split the fare; prices to accommodation in the area vary.

See the Picton and Havelock sections for information about transport around the sounds. Cougar Line run walkers out to the Queen Charlotte Walkway.

PICTON

The ferry from the North Island comes into Picton (population 3550), a pretty little port at the head of Queen Charlotte Sound. Picton, originally called Waitohi, is a small borough. It's a hive of activity when the ferry is in and during the peak of summer, but rather slow and sleepy any other time.

Information

The Picton Information Centre (☎ 573 8838) is in the Picton railway station between the ferry terminal and the town centre. Picton Information Services (☎ 573 6585) is located in the ferry terminal. Both have good maps, information on boats and walking in the sounds area, and some interesting exhibits. Opening hours vary depending on the time of year.

The DOC (☎ 573 7582) offices, on the 1st floor of the Mariners Mall on High St, are open from 8 am to 4.30 pm Monday to Friday. You can get information here on the Maritime Park, Mt Richmond Forest Park with its many walking tracks and huts, and the greater district. Picton Information Services has many of the DOC walkway leaflets. The CPO is also in the Mariner's Mall.

The ferry terminal in Picton has a convenience that you will not come across often in New Zealand – a laundromat – so if you've got a pile of dirty clothes in your backpack, take them along. The Marlin Motel (☎ 573 6784) at 33 Devon St is the AA agent.

Museum

The excellent little Picton Museum is on the foreshore, right below London Quay. The old building is being rebuilt with fancier quarters. There are a number of interesting whaling exhibits, including a harpoon gun, and numerous other unusual items such as an old Dursley Pederson bicycle built around 1890. The museum is open from 10 am to 4 pm daily; admission is $1 (children 50c).

The *Edwin Fox*

Between the museum and the ferry wharf is the battered, but still floating, hull of the old East Indiaman *Edwin Fox*, believed to be the ninth oldest ship in the world. Built of teak in the Bengal region of India, the 157-foot (48-metre), 760-ton vessel was launched in 1853 and in its long and varied career carried convicts to Perth, troops to the Crimean War and immigrants to New Zealand. Later it was one of the first vessels to operate as a cold store with the most up-to-date freezing machinery of the time. The ship arrived in Picton in 1897 and was used as a coal hulk for the Picton Freezing Works (meat-processing plant) until the mid-1950s. It sat unused next to the freezing works until it was towed to Shakespeare Bay in 1967. The

MARLBOROUGH

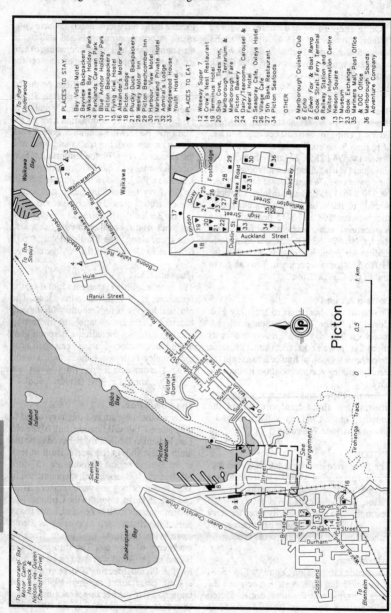

■ PLACES TO STAY

1 Bay Vista Motel
2 Bayview Backpackers
3 Waikawa Bay Holiday Park
4 Parklands Caravan Park
11 Blue Anchor Holiday Park
13 Picton Backpackers
15 Flying Kiwi Hostel
16 Alexander's Motor Park
18 Picton Lodge
21 Plucky Duck Backpackers
28 Wesley Motor Inn
29 Picton Beachcomber Inn
30 Harbour View Motel
31 Marineland Private Hotel
32 Admiral's Lodge
33 Wedgewood House
Youth Hostel

▼ PLACES TO EAT

12 Wiseway Super 7
14 Crow's Nest Restaurant
19 Terminus Hotel
20 Ship Cove, Tides Inn,
   Marlborough Terrarium &
   Marlborough Fare
22 Picton Bakery
24 Dairy/Tearooms, Carousel &
   Oxford Hotel
25 Seaspa Cafe, Oxleys Hotel
26 Village Cafe
27 5th Bank Restaurant
34 Picton Seafoods

OTHER

5 Marlborough Cruising Club
6 Echo
8 Edwin Fox & Boat Ramp
8 Cook Strait Ferry Terminal
9 Railway Station and
   Visitor Information Centre
17 Nelson Square
23 Museum
35 Book Exchange
   Marina Mall, Post Office
   & DOC Office
36 Marlborough Sounds
   Adventure Company

Edwin Fox remained a hulk on the beach there until 1986 when it was refloated and towed back to Picton.

Plans for the restoration of the *Edwin Fox* have now been drawn up. Progress has been impeded by lack of funding but work will begin when the funds are raised. The project will take at least 10 years to complete, and may cost several million dollars – but that should keep the boat in the water for another 200 years! All the original methods and materials will be used to restore the ship to its original condition, and it will remain open throughout the restoration process so you can see the work actually under way.

The metal-sheathed hull is open to visitors from 8.45 am to 5 pm every day (closing at 4.30 pm in winter) and admission is $4 (children $1, family $9). A small maritime museum has been started upstairs.

The *Echo*

On the other side of Shakespeare Bay, across the inlet from the town centre via the footbridge, is the scow *Echo*, now used as the clubrooms of the Marlborough Cruising Club. Built on the Wairau River in 1905, the *Echo* traded between Blenheim and Wellington, shipping around 14,000 tons of freight a year, and was only retired in 1965 after the railway ferries were introduced.

Walks

There are many scenic bush walks around Picton, as well as longer tramps. The information centre has a map showing several good walks in and near town, as well as others further afield in the sounds and the Maritime Park. DOC also has plenty of maps and leaflets on walks in the area.

An easy one-km track runs along the eastern side of Picton Harbour to Bob's Bay, where there's a BBQ area in a sheltered cove. Now added on to this is the Snout Walkway: carry on along the Bob's Bay path and follow it along the ridge. Allow three hours for the walk. There are great views of the length of Queen Charlotte Sound.

There's also the Tirohanga Walkway, beginning in Newgate St behind the hospital,

which takes about 45 minutes each way and offers a good view of Picton and the sounds.

Queen Charlotte Drive, the road between Picton and Havelock, has nice scenery but hostile sandflies. Walk up Queen Charlotte Drive for about five minutes for an excellent lookout over Picton.

Other Things to See

The New Zealand Experience audiovisual fantasia which used to be a 'highlight' in Piction has, fortunately, gone. There is an international weaving school (☎ 573 6966) at 22 Broadway, with a number of good quality items for sale.

Out of Picton is Port Underwood, the scene of a lot of whaling activity in the 19th century. The narrow winding road from Waikawa to Rarangi has magnificent views of the North Island silhouetted on the horizon.

Near Koromiko, six km south of Picton, is an alpaca park – complete with picnic area and children's playground. Tuamarina, 13 km further on, is historically interesting as the site of the Wairau Massacre. The tree near where the skirmish started still stands on the riverbank. In the cemetery, just above the road, is a Pakeha monument designed by Felix Wakefield, the youngest brother of Arthur Wakefield who was killed in the affray.

Tours

The main access around Queen Charlotte Sound is by water, which means there are innumerable cruises and fishing trips. Ask about them at the information centre, or take a stroll down by the wharf, where every operator seems to have a little office set up.

There are a number of round-the-bay cruises. Beachcomber Fun Cruises (☎ 573 6175) have popular cruises on the MV *Beachcomber*, including an all-day 'mail run' cruise around the sounds on Monday, Tuesday, Thursday and Friday for $36, and two-hour scenic cruises for $27. A full-day trip to the Portage Hotel on Kenepuru Sound is another possibility, for $30. Children

MARLBOROUGH

travel for half price on all the *Beachcomber* tours.

On land, Marlborough Scenic Tours (☎ 573 6262) and the Corgi Bus Company (☎ 573 7125) are two local (Picton) tour operators; winery visits are a speciality. Deluxe Coach-lines (☎ 578 5467) operate all-day wine-trail tours from Blenheim but they also make pick-ups in Picton.

Or you can get up above it all on floatplane flights. Float Air Picton (☎ 573 6433), between the *Edwin Fox* and the ferry termi-nal, does scenic flights and normal transport trips to any point around the sounds and also to Lake Rotoiti and Wellington.

The Picton Underwater Centre at 41 Wel-lington St hires diving equipment for under-water explorations. Divers World (☎ 573 7323), London Quay, also hire equipment and organise charters.

Places to Stay

Camping & Cabins The *Blue Anchor Holiday Park* (☎ 573 7212), on Waikawa Rd about 500 metres from the town centre, has campsites at $16 for two, various cabins for around $26 to $35 for two, and more expen-sive ($45) tourist flats. The *Alexander's Motor Park* (☎ 573 6378) is a km out on Canterbury St and has sites at $7 per person, plus a variety of cabins and on-site caravans at $24 to $28 for two.

The *Parklands Caravan Park* (☎ 573 6343) is on Beach Rd at Waikawa Bay, three km from town. Other possibilities include *Waikawa Bay Holiday Park* (☎ 573 7434) and *Momorangi Bay Motor Camp* (☎ 573 7865), on Queen Charlotte Drive, 13 km from Picton. The Momorangi Bay site has dinghies for hire.

Local DOC *campsites* are: Momorangi, Momo-rangi Bay, Queen Charlotte Drive (fully serviced); and Whites Bay, Port Underwood Rd, Rarangi.

Hostels The *Wedgwood House* (☎ 573 7797) is an Associate YHA Hostel at 10 Dublin St, close to the centre of town. It's a converted guesthouse with two, four or six beds to a room; the cost is $14 per night. YHA members get 'mail run' discounts (see the Tours section). You can stay here with or without a YHA card. The office stays open until 11 pm at night to cater for the passen-gers from the late ferry.

The *Plucky Duck Backpackers* (☎ & fax 573 6598), formerly Pavlova Backpackers, at 34 Auckland St has dorm beds for $14.50 or $16 each in double rooms. It's a well-equipped hostel which also serves as a centre for information and bookings for backpack-ers activities around Marlborough Sounds. They serve moa soup here (in name only!) and put on a BBQ on Saturday night.

The closest accommodation to the ferry terminal is *Picton Lodge* (☎ 573 7788; fax 573 8418) at 3 Auckland St. Dorm rooms (a bit sparse) are $14.50. Twins/doubles are $33 (low season) and $36 (high season). The facilities in this 54-bed place are good and they even have a smokers' terrace with harbour views. It is 200 metres from the ferry terminal (important if you are lugging a pack) and 20 metres from the railway station.

Another backpackers place is *Flying Kiwi Hostel* (☎ & fax 573 8126), at 2 Canterbury St, about a five-minute walk south of the city centre; rooms here are $13.50. This is a cosy place run by the Flying Kiwi bus people. They also rent out camping equipment for the Queen Charlotte Walkway and have a courtesy pick-up service.

On Waikawa Bay there is the impressive *Bayview Backpackers*, at 318 Waikawa Rd (☎ 573 7668). As they are four km from Picton town centre they offer free pick-up and drop-off services. There is a range of water sports equipment and bicycles avail-able for hire. Doubles and twins are $16 and the share rooms are $13.50. There are heaters in all the rooms, two kitchens, and two lounges.

Guesthouses Picton has a number of guest-houses and private hotels, including the *Marineland Guesthouse* (☎ 573 6429) at 28 Waikawa Rd which has a 'shark-free swim-ming pool'. Single/double rooms are $38/55 with breakfast or there are four self-contained motel units at $66 for two – the staff here are extremely friendly and helpful.

The *Admiral's Lodge* (☎ 573 6590) at 22 Waikawa Rd has single/double rooms for $45/72, and low-season discounts.

Motels Picton has plenty of motels, most priced at around $60 for two. The *Tourist Court Motels* (☎ 573 6331), in the centre of town at 45 High St, is a simple place with studio units from around $52 for two, or two-bedroom units for $63; low-season discounts might be available. The *Sunnyvale Motel* (☎ 573 6800), five km out at Waikawa Bay, is also good value at $60 for two. Highly recommended is the *Harbour View Motel* (☎ 573 6259) at 30 Waikawa Rd; the cost for two varies from $67 to $72 but there are also off-season reductions. As the name suggests, you get great views from here.

Hotels The *Federal Hotel* (☎ 573 6077) on the waterfront at 12 London Quay has single/double rooms at $28/40. Also very central is the *Terminus Hotel* (☎ 573 6452) at 1 High St, with singles/doubles for $50/60.

Places to Eat
Snacks & Fast Food Most food would be better than the indigestible cardboard you get tossed rudely at you on the ferry, but you're unlikely to find much on offer early in the morning or late at night. In any case Picton doesn't offer many real taste treats, although there are plenty of takeaways and fast-food places around the town centre.

The *Village Cafe* is on Wellington St; the sign announces 'A Good Eating Place' but a number of diners have suggested otherwise. There are several cafes along the waterfront including the attractive little *Seaspray Cafe*. Or there's the *London Quay Dairy & Tea Rooms* on the corner of London Quay and High St, and the *Carousel* takeaway next door.

The *Marlborough Fare* coffee lounge and restaurant on High St has strong coffee, good sit-down specials at lunch time, and takeaways.

Further down High St, *Picton Seafoods* has good fish & chips and pizzas, and it's one of the few places open late – until 8 pm from Sunday to Wednesday, 11 pm on Thursday, and until midnight on Friday and Saturday.

The *Picton Bakery*, on the corner of Dublin and Auckland Sts, has been recommended by an enthusiastic German traveller for its 'dark long-baked rye bread...real German style'. You'll also find that the doughnuts sold here have real cream in them.

Pub Food There are three pubs along London Quay and all three – the *Terminus*, the *Federal* and *Oxley* – have pub food, with bistro meals from about $6 to $8. On the south side of Nelson Square you will find the *Crow's Nest Restaurant* in the Crow Tavern – the seafood is good. Seafood is really the only decent choice in Picton!

Restaurants The *5th Bank*, at 33 Wellington St, is an expensive restaurant; if you feel like splashing out here then the mussels Creole at $19.50 is recommended. Around the corner, at 32 High St, is the *Americano Restaurant* where main courses are from $14.50: the great Ship 'n Shore (ribeye steak with scallops and mussels) is $22. A block away at 33 High St, the licensed *Ship Cove* and the BYO *Tides Inn* in the same Strand Arcade are both rather fancy, with main courses from about $12 to $16.

The *Terminus*, the *Federal* and *Oxley* hotels on London Quay all have licensed restaurants, in addition to the pub food mentioned earlier.

Some locals favour the *Marlborough Terranium*, at 31 High St, a sophisticated place which has a good wine selection. In this artistic interior an entrée costs about $9 and a main course $25.

Getting There & Away
Air Soundsair (☎ 573 6184) has a regular service across the strait to and from Wellington. The short flight costs $50 and operates about six times a day. The Picton airstrip is at Koromiko, eight km out of town, and a

MARLBOROUGH

shuttle bus connects to the flights for $5 (children $2).

The floatplane operated by Float Air Picton (☎ 573 6433) also flies to and from Wellington, where it lands at Porirua Harbour. The one-way fare is $65. It also does local and scenic flights around the Marlborough Sounds and to Lake Rotoiti.

Bus Skyline Connections (☎ 548 0285, 528 8850) runs a daily bus in summer from Picton to Motueka at 11.15 am and 1.35 pm, and Motueka to Picton at 6.45 and 7.45 am, and 1 and 3.15 pm. Similarly, they connect from the southern end of the Abel Tasman Track at Marahau at least a couple of times daily in each direction. There also are connections to Greymouth and Christchurch. Unlike InterCity and Mt Cook Landline, which go via Blenheim, this bus takes the more scenic Queen Charlotte Drive route.

There are a number of shuttles operating between Blenheim and Picton, as well as the major bus companies which head south. Blenheim Taxis travel between Picton and Blenheim at least twice a week. Cairns Coachlines make the trip to St Arnaud in the Nelson Lakes National Park on Monday and Friday. Because of the confusion of small operators, check details with the information centres; they will advise you on the best service and the current cheapest rate.

There are plenty of services from Picton to Christchurch. Mt Cook Landline buses (☎ 573 6687), also at the Ferry Terminal, continue all the way to Dunedin and Invercargill. There are connecting services through Blenheim around the northern coast to Havelock, Nelson, Motueka and Takaka, with connections to Collingwood. They also have buses heading south-west through Nelson to Westport and Greymouth, and south through Kaikoura to Christchurch and Dunedin.

InterCity (☎ 573 6855), also at the Ferry Terminal, has a bus route south to Christchurch with connections to Dunedin and Invercargill, and another route east to Nelson via Blenheim and Havelock with connec-

tions to Greymouth and the glaciers. At least one bus daily on each of these routes connects with a ferry sailing to and from Wellington.

The Flying Kiwi bus departs from Picton once a month for a tour of the South Island (more often in summer). See the 'Alternative' Buses section in the Getting Around chapter for details.

All buses serving Picton operate from the ferry terminal. It takes about three hours by bus from Picton to Nelson, two hours to Kaikoura, and five or six hours to Christchurch.

Train The train between Picton and Christchurch, via Blenheim and Kaikoura, operates daily in each direction and takes about 5½ hours. The train connects with the ferry and a free shuttle service is provided between the railway station and ferry terminal on both sides of the strait. This trip is recommended for its coastal scenery, especially around Kaikoura.

Car There are basically two directions you can take to the rest of the South Island from Picton: the west coast route and the east coast route. If you opt for the east coast route it's a straight run south from Picton through Blenheim and on down SH 1. If you're heading west, you can either take the scenic Queen Charlotte Drive westwards from Picton, or go south to Blenheim and head west from there.

Hitching Hitching out on SH 1 towards Blenheim is possible if you've got patience. It can take a few hours to get a ride or at other times you may not get one at all. Most traffic is on the road just after a ferry arrives – there is not much between sailings. The trouble with being on the road just after the ferry docks is that every other hitchhiker is there as well, so it doesn't necessarily make for easier hitching at that time.

If you're heading west, the best bet is to go south to Blenheim and head west from there.

On average it will take a day to reach Christchurch or Nelson. Queen Charlotte Drive between Picton and Havelock is the shortest way to Nelson but has little traffic, so it's easier to hitch via Blenheim on the Spring Creek bypass: follow the Blenheim road (SH 1) 22 km to Spring Creek, where you turn right towards Renwick.

Ferry The inter-island ferry service shuttles back and forth between Wellington and Picton. There are usually four services daily in each direction and the crossing takes about three hours. See the Getting There & Away section in the Wellington chapter for fares and details.

Boat Picton has several water taxis that can take you anywhere you want to go around the sounds, including the various out-of-the-way hotels and walking tracks that can be reached only by water. Check first, though, with the tour boat operators. Most tour boats will gladly take you along on the tour, dropping you off and picking you up wherever and whenever you wish; they can be cheaper than the taxis.

Getting Around

To/From the Airport A shuttle bus connects Picton with flights to and from the Picton airstrip at Koromiko for $5 (children $2).

Car Rental Avis, Hertz, Thrifty, Budget and Avon all have rental offices at the ferry terminal. Pegasus has an office at the railway station. Southern Cross has an office at 27 Auckland St.

Motorbike Rental Nifty-fifty (50 cc) motorbikes (no motorcycle licence needed) can be hired from the kiosk beside the MV *Beachcomber* office. The cost is $15 for the first hour and $10 per hour thereafter.

BLENHEIM

The largest town in the Marlborough Sounds region, Blenheim (population 19,000) is 29 km south of Picton, on the Wairau Plains – a contrasting landscape to the sounds – at the junction of the Taylor and Opawa rivers. The town is particularly well laid out, but more by accident than design as early development was confined to the high ground to avoid the swamp in the centre. The swamp has been reclaimed and is now Seymour Square with its attractive lawns and gardens.

During the second weekend in February Blenheim hosts the now-famous Marlborough Food & Wine Festival at Montana's Brancott Estate.

Information

The Blenheim Information Centre (☎ 578 9904) is at 1 Main St. It has a number of DOC maps and leaflets on the many walkways around the Marlborough Sounds and environs. The centre is open from 9 am to 5 pm Monday to Friday, seven days a week, and to 6.30 pm during summer. The AA office (☎ 578 3399) is at 23 Maxwell Rd on the corner of Seymour St.

Parks & Museums

The 5½-hectare Brayshaw Museum Park, off New Renwick Rd, has several attractions including a reconstructed village of colonial buildings designed to recreate colonial Blenheim. There's also some early farming equipment, a miniature railway, a model boating pond, and the Museum and Archives Building. The park is open during daylight hours and admission is free.

Pollard Park and Waterlea Gardens, off Parker St, have a children's playground and a fitness trail; flowers bloom all year here. The Blenheim Recreation Centre, near the town centre on Kinross and Scott Sts, has large indoor and outdoor swimming pools, a sauna, mini-golf and a roller-skating rink.

Near Seymour Square are relics of Blenheim's violent early history, including the old cannon known as Blenkinsopp's cannon which is on the corner of High and Seymour Sts. Originally part of the equipment of the whaling ship *Caroline* which Blenkinsopp captained, this is reputedly the cannon for which Te Rauparaha was persuaded to sign over the Wairau Plains, and is

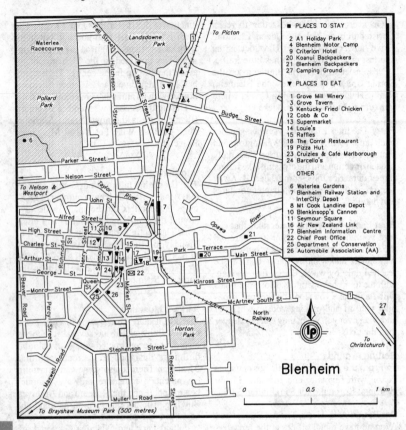

■ PLACES TO STAY

2 A1 Holiday Park
4 Blenheim Motor Camp
9 Criterion Hotel
20 Koanui Backpackers
21 Blenheim Backpackers
27 Camping Ground

▼ PLACES TO EAT

1 Grove Mill Winery
3 Grove Tavern
5 Kentucky Fried Chicken
12 Cobb & Co
13 Supermarket
14 Louie's
15 Raffles
18 The Corral Restaurant
19 Pizza Hut
23 Cruizies & Cafe Marlborough
24 Barcello's

OTHER

6 Waterlea Gardens
7 Blenheim Railway Station and
   InterCity Depot
8 Mt Cook Landline Depot
10 Blenkinsopp's Cannon
11 Seymour Square
16 Air New Zealand Link
17 Blenheim Information Centre
22 Chief Post Office
25 Department of Conservation
26 Automobile Association (AA)

Blenheim

0   0.5   1 km

thus one of the causes of the subsequent massacre at Tuamarina.

Walks

The information centre has details of some interesting walks in the Blenheim area, most some distance from town. About four km from the town centre the Wither Hills Walkway, off Taylor Pass Rd, has a view-point about 20 minutes from the roadside starting point with excellent views of the Wairau Plains and Cook Strait; on a clear day you can see all the way to the North Island.

Rainbow Ski Area

Rainbow ski area (☎ 521 1861), 130 km (1½ hours) west of Blenheim, has good skiing for families and beginners. Delta Landline buses from Blenheim stop at the ski area turn-off during the ski season, and a shuttle bus takes you from there up to the slopes.

Recreation Areas

There are many areas of public land where you can get away from the bustle of the larger towns. These places are outlined in the DOC pamphlet *Central Marlborough Recreation*

Areas, and have a variety of different flora and landforms. The Robertson Range and Whites Bay near Port Underwood are to the north of Blenheim – there are great vistas of Cloudy Bay from here. At the Wairau Lagoons, to the east of Blenheim, you can see some of the more than 70 bird species which frequent this area. Many of the areas have been set aside to preserve flora, such as native broom or prostrate kowhai.

Tours
Deluxe Coachlines (☎ 578 5467) has a six-hour 'Scenic Wine Trail' tour of local wineries which costs $34 (children $17, and $99 family concession). If you have your own wheels you can construct your own wine trail tour – pick up a copy of the *Marlborough Winemakers Wine Trail Guide* from the information centre, showing the location of 18 wineries around the Blenheim district.

White Water Rafting
The more adventurous could try rafting in some of the nearby rivers. Action in Marlborough Rafting (☎ 578 4531) at 59 Lakings Rd, Blenheim, can get you wet anytime! The costs range from about $60 for a half-day trip to over $400 for three-day expeditions. A number of their trips are focused on the Wairau River.

Places to Stay
Camping & Cabins The *A1 Holiday Park* (☎ 578 3667), at the northern end of town at 78 Grove Rd (SH 1), has campsites for $8 per person, cabins from $34 for two and tourist flats from $44. The *Blenheim Motor Camp* (☎ 578 7419) at 27 Budge St is one km from the town centre off SH 1. Campsites cost $7 per person ($9 with power); cabins are available from $30 to $35 for two, and tourist flats cost $45.

Camping grounds further out include *Duncannon Caravan Park* (☎ 578 8193), 1.2 km south of town, where caravan sites cost $7 per person and on-site caravans $15 per person. *Grenfelt Caravan Park* (☎ 578 1259) at 173 Middle Renwick Rd charges $14 for two people. The *Spring Creek Holi-*

day Park (☎ 570 5893), on Rapaura Rd six km out towards Picton and about 500 metres off SH 1, has campsites and cabins.

Hostels, Guesthouses & Hotels At present there are two backpackers establishments in Blenheim. *Blenheim Backpackers* (☎ 578 6062) is at 29 Park Terrace, Blenheim, in an old maternity home. Doubles are $15 each and share rooms $13.50, $12 for each subsequent night. The Opawa River runs behind the house and you can borrow canoes. At 33 Main St you will find *Koanui Backpackers* (☎ 578 7487). Here bunks are $13.50, and twins/doubles $15/16 each. This is a friendly place where a number of itinerant fruit pickers base themselves. It has washing facilities, bikes, pool table, TV and video, and there are electric blankets on all the beds.

The well-recommended *Maple Guesthouse* (☎ 578 7375) at 144 High St offers B&B for $28 per person.

Rooms at the *Criterion Hotel* (☎ 578 3299) on Market St cost $50/66 for singles/twins. Rooms at the *City Hotel* on High St are $45.

Homestays Two which are thoroughly recommended are *Glenrose* in its beautiful garden setting, and *Addiscombe*, five minutes south-west of the town centre. The latter offers a nostalgic journey into the past; a room in this well-restored house is $135 for dinner, bed & breakfast. Book at the information centre.

Motels Reasonably priced motels include the *Raymar Motor Inn* (☎ 578 5104) at 164 High St, where double rooms cost $55, and the similarly priced *Alpine Motel* (☎ 578 1604) at 148 Middle Renwick Rd. At most other motels doubles cost from about $60.

Places to Eat
Snacks & Fast Food There are plenty of takeaways and cafes around the centre, but this is another Kiwi town where they tend to produce the sort of sandwiches and snacks that give McDonald's a good name. No, McDonald's hasn't got to Blenheim (yet) but

there is a *Kentucky Fried Chicken* on the northern side of town and a *Pizza Hut* on Main St near the town centre.

Barcello's at 67 Queen St, is a small cafe and bar with ambience. Here you can get a good cup of real coffee – cappuccino and espresso. Try their great hot chocolate which is served in a huge cup with two equally large marshmallows. A plate of tagliatelle with salmon and prawns is good value at $14.

For fast food with class, try the *Bagel Bakery*, a tiny place with a big, successful product. You choose the filling for your bagel for about $3 – a little bit of New York in a provincial town. Then there's *Cruizies* at 10 Maxwell Rd, where you can buy filled rolls, bagels and giant muffins.

For self-caterers, there's a supermarket on the corner of Charles and Queen Sts.

Pub Food There's a *Cobb & Co* in the Grosvenor Establishment at 91 High St, on Seymour Square. It's open from 7.30 am to 10 pm every day. Reasonably priced bar meals are available there at lunch time. The *Criterion* on the corner of Market and Alfred Sts also does pub food. Don't forget to wash your meal down with either the fine Marlborough Dark or the Renwick Dark.

Restaurants A trusted restaurant in Blenheim is *Raffles* in the Raffles Hotel at 59 Market St, on the corner of Wynen St, which serves a variety of international dishes. Lunch (from $5) and dinner (from $10) are served every day. The *Cafe Marlborough*, also on Market St, is a licensed restaurant with a good reputation.

Those looking for spicy Tex-Mex food should try *The Corral* at 3 Main St, which is open for dinner every day from 6.30 pm. Chinese cuisine lovers should head to the *Bamboo Garden* at 53 Maxwell Rd, where there is a large selection of seafoods and authentic Cantonese dishes.

At the top of the dining tree are *Roccos'* at 5 Dodson St, serving international cuisine (main courses $16 to $26); *Seymour's* on the corner of Henry and Alfred Sts, the winner of Marlborough's Licensed Restaurant

Award in 1992 ($29.50 for the Captain Cook seafood platter); and *Louie's* at 57 Seymour St, which serves local seafood, Indonesian and Thai dishes (gai maprao $22.80, satch babi $24.80).

Wineries Several of the wineries around Blenheim also serve meals. The *Grove Mill Winery* north of town in Dodson St, off Grove Rd, has pretty good food. The *Hunters* and *Merlen* wineries on Rapaura Rd also serve food; at Hunters you can barbecue your own lunch. Jane Hunter, the winemaker at Hunters, was voted one of the world's top five women vignerons by the London *Sunday Times*. At Merlen's you can enjoy your German-style meal and wine in the Weingarten. Also recommended by a noted bon(ne) vivant is the *Twelve Trees Restaurant* at Allan Scott's winery in Jacksons Rd. Eat, drink and be merry.

For a map covering the wineries, get a copy of the *Marlborough Winemakers Wine Trail Guide* from the information centre.

Getting There & Away

Air Air New Zealand Link, in conjunction with Air Nelson (☎ 578 4059), at 29 Queen St, has direct flights to Wellington with connections to other centres. Ansett (☎ 578 7333) has flights to and from Wellington from Blenheim and Picton. Soundsair and Float Air also operate from Blenheim. The Marlborough Aero Club (☎ 578 5073), which operates from the Omaka Aerodrome, has cheap charter flights to Wellington and other places.

The Picton airstrip at Koromiko is about halfway between Blenheim and Picton. The Blenheim airport is on Middle Renwick Rd, about six km west of town.

Bus See the Picton Getting There & Away section for details of bus services. Deluxe Coachlines (☎ 578 5467) at 45 Main St has regular services between Blenheim and Picton. Both main companies, Mt Cook and InterCity, pass through Blenheim on their way to Christchurch and Nelson. Mt Cook Landline (☎ 578 0959) operates from an office on Grove Rd (opposite the railway station) and has a Picton-Blenheim-Christchurch service with connections to Dunedin and Invercargill.

InterCity (☎ 577 2890) buses operate from the Blenheim railway station in Sinclair St with services from Picton through Blenheim to Christchurch, Dunedin and Invercargill. West-bound InterCity buses from Picton stop at Blenheim on their way to Havelock, Nelson, Greymouth and the West Coast glaciers.

There are a number of shuttle buses; enquire at the information centre in town about prices and routes.

Train The daily Picton to Christchurch train stops at Blenheim. The reservations number at the station is 577 8777.

Getting Around
You can get a taxi to Blenheim airport from the town centre for about $8. You can also hire Nifty-fifties, cycles and tandems in town.

PICTON TO HAVELOCK
This scenic road takes in Queen Charlotte Drive and passes the picturesque Ngakuta and Momorangi Bays. There is budget accommodation at *Queen Charlotte Holiday Flats*, The Grove, and at Linkwater should you decide to stay here. Before reaching Havelock you pass through Mahakipawa Hill Scenic reserve and have the opportunity to stop at Cullen point lookout.

HAVELOCK
Heading west from Picton or Blenheim, the first town of any size you'll come to is Havelock (population 380).

Founded around 1860 and named after Sir Henry Havelock of Indian Mutiny fame, this attractive little town is situated at the confluence of the Pelorus and Kaiuma rivers, 43 km from Blenheim and 73 km from Nelson. It's the only place where a main road touches the Pelorus Sound.

Havelock was once the hub of the timber milling and export trade, and later became the service centre for gold-mining activities in the area. Today it's a thriving small-boat harbour and a pleasant place to drop off the planet for a couple of days. Havelock is also proud to be the 'green-lipped mussel capital of the world'; you can buy these mussels very cheaply at the packing plants down on the wharf, although purchase of these was somewhat hindered by a toxic algae ban at the time of our visit.

Information
Glenmore Cruises (☎ 574 2532) in the centre of town acts as the tourist information centre for Havelock. Peter Pannell and his son Aaron at the YHA hostel also have a wealth of information about the area. The DOC (☎ 574 2019) has a small office on Mahakipawa Rd.

The tiny museum is a good source of information on local history. It is open all day from 8 am to 5 pm; donations for its upkeep are gratefully accepted.

Walks
There's not much to do in the town itself but there are a number of good walks, including the four-hour return walk to Takorika Summit behind the township, and the half-hour walk to Cullen Point from where there are good views of Havelock and the sunset. Glenmore Cruises in Havelock provide boat access to the popular two-day Nydia Track (Tuesday only). The YHA hostel can supply information on these and other walks.

There are a number of extended walks in the area of Havelock. The Mt Stokes walk takes you to the 1204-metre summit, the highest point in the Marlborough Sounds. From here you can see the Kaikouras, Tararuas (in the North Island) and the Sounds below. Sounds Detours guide this walk for $50. Another walk is the three-day Pelorus Track to Nelson. This follows the Pelorus river, then heads over Dun Saddle via a historic railway line. Mountain bikers can test their pedal strength on the Maungatapu Track which passes through scenic Maitai Reserve. On the south side of the Nelson-Picton Rd is the Wakamarina Track. This

MARLBOROUGH

starts at the top of the Wakamarina valley (near the Trout Hotel) and heads to Onomalutu – it features an old gold-mining area.

Nydia Track The Nydia Track commences at Kaiuma and ends at Duncan Bay. The suggested walking time is two days or 10½ hours. There is cheap accommodation at Murray's Place ($10) about halfway. Nydia Bay was originally the site of a Maori pa and its Maori name meant 'place of sadness' – the DOC pamphlet explains why. The walk passes through different habitats of various species of birds. It is reputed to have fewer sandflies than the Abel Tasman National Park.

Getting There & Away It is best to get dropped off at Shag Point by water taxi ($10 per person) as it is only a five-minute trip past the mudflats. At the other end, Sounds Detours (☎ 574 214, 574 2104) can pick you up. The minimum cost is $60 so it pays to go with a few people. You can attempt the track in either direction; there is a phone at Murray's Place where you can contact either the water taxi or shuttle service.

Sea Kayaking
If you wish to try sea kayaking in Marlborough Sounds try Te Hoiere ('The Paddle') Sea Kayaks (☎ 574 2610) for daily or weekly rentals. Their trips leave from Havelock and go to Jacobs Bay, taking in bird and bush life; note that there is a four-person minimum. They rent all equipment for two days at $70, four days at $130.

Boat Trips
Glenmore Cruises take passengers along on the mail-run boat, stopping at isolated homesteads to deliver mail and supplies. Tea and coffee are available free on board. If you want to camp or tramp anywhere along the way you can get dropped off and collected again on a specified day. Once on land you're on your own, so take what you need. Fresh water is available in some places; ask the locals whether you need to take any.

The trips depart at 9.30 am on Tuesday,

Wednesday and Thursday, and then return between 5 and 6 pm. Between Christmas and Easter, Glenmore Cruises have various other trips every day except Monday, including an additional Friday sailing of the mail-run boat. The round-trip mail-run fare is $45 (children $20). There's a 10% discount to YHA members and other backpackers. For information and bookings check with the Glenmore Cruises office, or ask at the YHA hostel. Various other cruises and fishing trips are also available from Havelock, with costs ranging from $25.

There are a number of water taxis operating out of Havelock. Inquire about the hire of MVs *Reliance, Kanona* and *Ariki-Tai*. In particular, each January the *Ariki-Tai* makes five nature cruises to Maud Island, abode of the takahe, kakapo and Hamilton frog. Go to the YHA for information. Sounds Detours – surprise, they operate from the YHA – will drop off and pick up. They also rent mountain bikes and specialise in off-the-beaten-track drives to hidden parts of the Sounds.

Places to Stay
Camping & Cabins The *Havelock Motor Camp* (☎ 574 2339) on Inglis St has campsites from around $14 for two people ($16 with power). The *Chartridge Tourist Park* (☎ 574 2129), six km south of Havelock at Kaiuma Bridge on SH 6, has campsites at $8 per person and budget accommodation at about $10 per person in a primitive bunk room.

Hostels The *Havelock YHA Hostel* (☎ 574 2104) is on the corner of Lawrence St and Main Rd (No 46). The nightly cost is $14 in dorm or twin rooms. The hostel occupies an 1881 schoolhouse once attended by Lord Ernest Rutherford, who discovered the atomic nucleus. The manager has information on walks and other local activities including fishing, farmstays, explorations around the sounds, and more. The hostel is well-equipped with bicycles, billiards, volleyball, piano, guitar and so on.

Motels Havelock has a couple of small motels, both on the main road through town. The *Havelock Garden Motel* (☎ 574 2387) has units at $50 to $60 for two people, with low-season discounts available. The *Pelorus Tavern* (☎ 574 2412), which has a restaurant and pub, has motel units for about $55.

Places to Eat
The *tearoom* on the main road has snacks and light meals. You can get counter or restaurant meals at the *Pelorus Tavern* and dine overlooking the Havelock marina. Get a free feed of mussels at the YHA.

Getting There & Away
Mt Cook Landline and InterCity buses both have Picton-Blenheim-Nelson buses that stop at Glenmore Cruises in the centre of Havelock at least once each day. There's a minibus mail service along the Queen Charlotte Drive 'scenic route' between Picton and Havelock, making the return trip in the morning, Monday to Friday – when space is available, passengers are charged $8 each way. Check at the YHA hostel for departure times. A private bus company, the Skyline Connection, also stops at Havelock on its Picton-to-Nelson run. You can purchase tickets at the YHA; it is $11 each way or $8 if you arrange at the YHA for a discount.

HAVELOCK TO NELSON
The SH 6 from Havelock to Nelson is 75 km of scenic highway, passing the Wakamarina Valley, Pinedale (also known as Canvastown), the Pelorus Bridge Scenic Reserve and Rai Valley.

Pinedale (Canvastown)
The tiny township of Pinedale, in the Wakamarina Valley eight km west of Havelock, got the nickname Canvastown back in the 1860s – gold was discovered in the river in 1860 and by 1864 thousands of canvas tents had sprung up as miners flocked to the prosperous working goldfield, one of the richest in the country. By 1865 the boom was over. Nevertheless gold is still reputed to be in the area and in 1986 a tourist staying at the motor

camp panned a five-gram nugget from the river.

The Pinedale Motor Camp (☎ 574 2349) on Wakamarina Valley Rd, gives panning lessons ($6 for half an hour) – maybe you'll also find a nugget.

Things to See & Do
Visits to the interesting indoor-outdoor gold-mining museum, gold panning, horse-trekking, bushwalking and trout fishing are all popular activities. The Wakamarina Track, an old gold-miners' trail which passes through the Mt Richmond State Forest Park, begins from Butchers Flat, 15 km into the Wakamarina Valley on the metalled road from Pinedale.

Places to Stay
The *Trout Hotel* in the Wakamarina Valley (out from Canvastown) (☎ 574 2120) has single/double rooms at $25/40 and motel units at $50 for two. The *Pinedale Motor Camp* (☎ 574 2349) has campsites for $6 per person, $7 with power, and cabins from $25 to $33 for two; you can hire gold pans and other equipment there. *Wakavale Backpackers* is another cheap alternative here, and Butchers Flat, Roadend, Wakamarina Valley is a local DOC campsite.

Pelorus Bridge
The Pelorus Bridge Scenic Reserve, 18 km west of Havelock, has interesting walks of between 30 minutes and three hours on the Pelorus and Rai rivers, with waterfalls, a suspension bridge and the Pelorus Bridge itself. Within the reserve are tearooms, camp and caravan sites at $6 to $8, and some cabins for about $22 for two people. Ask for the ranger at the Rai Valley Tearoom (☎ 571 6019).

Rai Valley Pioneer Cottage
At Carluke, 1.5 km from the Rai Valley township on the road leading to Tennyson Inlet, is the Rai Valley Pioneer Cottage, built in 1881 when the area was still virgin bush. The cottage served as a home to its owner for

28 years and had been used as a sheep shed and chicken house before being restored in 1969 and given to the Historic Places Trust in 1980. There's no charge to see the cottage, but donations are appreciated.

South Marlborough

Many travellers head west or north-west from Picton to the walking tracks or the West Coast glaciers, but there are also a number of points of interest along the route south from the Marlborough district across the Seaward Kaikoura foothills to Christchurch.

KAIKOURA
Kaikoura (population 2010) is on SH 1, 133 km south of Blenheim and 180 km north of Christchurch. Just south of Kaikoura the road splits: SH 1 continues along the coast, while SH 70 branches off inland and later merges with SH 7 crossing over from the west coast.

Until early 1988 the sleepy little seaside town was noted mainly for its fishing and its fine setting on an incredibly beautiful bay backed by the steeply rising foothills of the Seaward Kaikoura Range, snow-capped in winter. It was also known for its crayfish (lobster) – Kaikoura means 'to eat crayfish' in Maori.

At Christmas 1987, Nature Watch Charters began making whale-watching trips – the first such commercial operation in New Zealand. The tours quickly became famous and put Kaikoura on the tourist map.

One whale-watch and two dolphin swimming companies are now operating very successfully. The host of other things to do in the area and the simple beauty of the town keep visitors around for days after they've gone to see the whales. There are many enjoyable and inexpensive tours, an interesting museum and some caves, and you'll pass some historic buildings if you walk out to the end of the peninsula to the seal and seabird colony and a small aquarium. Other good

walks in the area include Mt Fyffe and tracks in the State Forest. There's skiing in winter at the newly opened Mt Lyford ski field.

History
In Maori legend, the tiny Kaikoura Peninsula (or Taumanu-o-te-waka-a-Maui) was the seat upon which the demi-god Maui sat when he fished the North Island up from the depths of the sea. The area was heavily settled before Europeans came – at least 14 Maori pa sites have been identified.

Excavations near the Fyffe House show that the area was a moa-hunter settlement about 800 to 1000 years ago. In 1857 George Fyffe came upon an early moa-hunter burial site near the present Fyffe House and among other things he found an almost complete moa egg shell. It is the largest moa egg ever found (240 mm long and 178 mm in diameter) and is housed at the National Museum in Wellington. You can see a replica at the Kaikoura Museum.

In 1828 the beachfront of Kaikoura, now the site of the Garden of Memories, was the scene of a tremendous battle when a Ngati Toa war party led by the chief Te Rauparaha from Kapiti Island in the south of the North Island, bore down on Kaikoura armed with muskets, killing or capturing several hundred of the local Ngai Tahu tribe.

Captain Cook passed by here on 15 February 1770, but did not land. His journal states that 57 Maoris in four double-hulled canoes came out from shore towards the *Endeavour*, but 'would not be prevail'd upon to put along side'. Cook called the peninsula 'Lookers on', a name which was later mistakenly ascribed to the Seaward Kaikoura Range.

The first European to settle in Kaikoura was Robert Fyffe, who established a whaling station in 1842. Kaikoura was a whaling centre from 1843 until 1922. Meanwhile the land had been discovered to be rich for settlement and sheep-farming; even after Kaikoura's whaling era ended, the sea and the farmland continued to support the community.

Orientation

Kaikoura is a little town facing the sea. The main street curves along the seafront and is known variously as Beach Rd, West End, and The Esplanade; it's all one road. Kaikoura is on a peninsula and most of the town is built on the northern side. The southern side is called South Bay, and its main street is South Bay Parade – again, running right beside the sea. The whale watch and one dolphin swimming operation are based out at the railway (Whaleway) station.

Information

The Kaikoura Information Centre (☎ 319 5641), in West End by the car park (on the beach side), is open from 8.30 am to 6 pm every day in summer, and from 9 am to 5 pm in winter. Staff are very helpful and can make bookings for any tour.

The DOC office (☎ 319 5714) is on Ludstone Rd. Most of its information on walks, camping and so on is available at the information centre, but if you are planning an extended walk it may pay to call in here.

Museum

The Kaikoura Historical Society Museum on Ludstone Rd is not as small as it looks; it has several big sections out the back, including the old town jail, built in 1910. There are also many historical photographs, Maori and colonial artefacts, and an exhibit on the region's whaling era. The museum is open from 2 to 4 pm on weekends and during school holidays. It is open for a more extended period over the Christmas holidays. If it's not open and you want to have a look, there is a list of telephone numbers on the door – someone will gladly come and open it up. Admission is $1 (children 50c).

Fyffe House

George Fyffe, cousin of the first European settler, Robert Fyffe, came to Kaikoura from Scotland in 1854 and built Fyffe House around 1860. It is the only building remaining from the whaling days and is now under the protection of the Historic Places Trust. The house, on The Esplanade about two km east of the town centre, is open from 10 am to 5 pm, Thursday to Sunday. The curator, who lives in the house, will show you around at no charge; donations, however, are gratefully accepted.

Sea Aquarium

There's a tiny Sea Aquarium beside the YHA hostel on The Esplanade, with a single tank of sea animals and a video presentation on Kaikoura's ocean wildlife. It's run by the University of Canterbury Research Centre and is open most days; admission is free.

Maori Leap Cave

Tours of Maori Leap Cave, a limestone cave formed by the sea and discovered in 1958, take place several times daily and depart from the Caves Restaurant, three km south of the town centre on SH 1 (no bus to the restaurant, unfortunately). The 45-minute tour costs $7.50 (children $2.50); family and group discounts apply. Report 15 minutes before the tour times – 10.30 and 11.30 am, and 12.30, 1.45, 2.30 and 3.30 pm.

Other Things to See

On The Esplanade beachfront is the Garden of Memories, a pleasant garden with a walkway arched by giant whalebones. Further east along The Esplanade there's a seaside outdoor swimming pool; there is a small charge for its use.

Up on the hill at the eastern end of town there's a water tower which is a great lookout point; you can see both sides of the peninsula and all down the coast. Take the walking track up to the tower from The Esplanade or drive up Scarborough Terrace.

There are a few interesting art galleries, including a Maori gallery at the railway station run by the people who run Kaikoura Tours (both are operated by the local marae). The Sealside Gallery at 17 West End is a cooperative presenting the work of a number of Kaikoura artists, with a variety of arts & crafts. There are other galleries and workshops in town; ask the information centre for a list.

In winter there's skiing at the newly

MARLBOROUGH

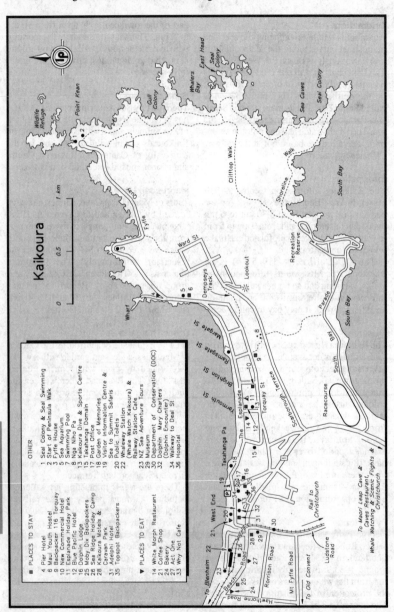

Kaikoura

■ PLACES TO STAY

4   Pier Hotel
6   Maui Youth Hostel
9   Backpacker 116 Torquay
10 Commercial Hotel
11 Esplanade Holiday Park
12 Blue Pacific Hotel
16 Dolphin Lodge
25 Moby Dix Backpackers
26 Sea Ridge Holiday Camp
28 Kaikoura Motels &
     Caravan Park
31 Adelphi Hotel
35 Topspot Backpackers

▼ PLACES TO EAT

14 White Morph Restaurant
21 Coffee Shop
27 Act One
33 Why Not Cafe

OTHER

1   Seal Colony & Seal Swimming
2   Start of Peninsula Walk
3   Fyffe House
5   Sea Aquarium
7   Swimming Pool
8   Nga Niho Pa
13 Kaikoura Dive & Sports Centre
15 Takahanga Domain
17 Post Office
18 Garden of Memories
19 Visitor Information Centre &
     Kaikoura Summit Safaris
20 Public Toilets
22 Whaleway Station Cafe
     (Whale Watch Kaikoura) &
     Railway Station Cafe
23 NZ Sea Adventure Tours
29 Museum
30 Department of Conservation (DOC)
32 Dolphin Mary Charters
     (Dolphin Encounter)
34 Walkway to Deal St
36 Hospital

opened Mt Lyford ski area. The daily use charges for the lifts are quite reasonable. Transport is available from Kaikoura with Sea to Summit Safaris (☎ 319 6182), for $20 return; this leaves in winter only at 8 am and returns about 6.30 pm.

Golf is very popular here. Clubs can be hired from the information centre at $10 per set; green fees are $10 for 18 holes.

Walks
There are a number of good walkways around the Kaikoura Peninsula. There are two walkways around the tip of the peninsula, one along the seashore and one above it along the clifftops. If you go on the seashore trail, check the tides beforehand! Both walks afford excellent views of the New Zealand fur seal and red-billed seagull colonies on the peninsula's rocky tip.

There are other walkways across the peninsula, from the northern side to the southern side, and to the water tower lookout point. A pamphlet on walks is available from the information centre and the DOC.

Other good walks in the area are at Mt Fyffe Forest, about nine km from Kaikoura; the Puhi Puhi Scenic Reserve, 18 km from town; and the Omihi Lookout, 19 km from town.

Mt Fyffe Walking Track Mt Fyffe (1602 metres), an outlier of the Seaward Kaikoura Range, dominates the narrow Kaikoura plain and the town. The eastern face of Fyffe is cloaked in forest and there's an enjoyable forest walk here. Information about history, vegetation, birds and the walking tracks is found in the NZ Forest Service publication *Mt Fyffe Forest: Kaikoura.*

One popular day or overnight walk is that to the summit of Fyffe and the hut of the same name. From here there are impressive views of the peninsula and plains; on a clear day you can see Banks Peninsula to the south and Cape Palliser in the North Island.

There are two means of access to the forest. The first is from the end of Mt Fyffe Rd, which leads to the short forest walk, and the second is from the western end of Post-

mans Rd and the access route to the Hinau Picnic area.

Swimming, Surfing & Fishing
There's safe swimming along the stretch of beach in front of The Esplanade and at Gooches Beach, Ingles Bay, Jimmy Armers Beach, and South Bay. The whole coastline, with its rocky formations and abundant marine life, makes for worthwhile snorkelling and diving. Mangamanu Beach, about 15 km north of Kaikoura, has good surfing.

Fishing is popular off the new and old wharves, at the Kahutara river mouth, or try surfcasting on the beach near the railway station. Several companies do fishing and diving trips from boats; see the Other Sea Tours entry in this section.

Snorkelling
With Seals Graeme Chambers of Sea to Summit Safaris (☎ 319 6182) can arrange for you to snorkel with NZ fur seals. These two-hour 'off-the-shore' guided snorkelling tours, which give you a great opportunity to view your mammalian cousins at close hand, commence at 9.30 am and 1.15 pm; sometimes there is a 4.30 pm trip. The cost is $30.

The seals may appear threatening if approached on land but underwater, in their element, they are completely passive.

You can also snorkel with the seals from a boat. From September to May, New Zealand Sea Adventures (☎ 319 6622), next door to the railway station, organise seal swimming and supply all equipment. The cost is $35, or $25 if watching from the boat.

Without Seals On the snorkelling trips you also see crayfish (lobster), paua (abalone) and other shellfish. The 3½-hour trips are available from November to April and cost $35, including the hire of a wetsuit and snorkelling gear, and a hot snack. Even non-swimmers can do this, wearing a special floating tube.

Boat Hire
Canoe hire is available at South Bay. Near

MARLBOROUGH

the seaside swimming pool, at 192 The Esplanade, Kaikoura Catamaran Rentals (☎ 319 5810) hire catamarans and give lessons.

Tours

Whale Watch Tours Only one company now operates daily whale watch tours: Whale Watch Kaikoura (☎ 319 5045; fax 319 6545) whose office is in the old railway (Whaleway) station. Most of the year the tours start at 5.30 am and continue through to 1.30 pm every day. Whale Watch has a free phone for reservations: ☎ (0800) 655 121. It is usually necessary to book three to four days in advance. Their boats, equipped with hydrophones (underwater microphones) to pick up the sounds of whales below the surface, set out to sea together and fan out in search of the whales and other wildlife.

The cost is $85 for a three-hour sea tour. There's a childrens' rate of $50, and a babysitting service is also provided if you want to leave the youngsters behind. The trips are not suitable for children under five.

For most people the tour is a thrilling experience. The main attraction is the sperm whale; and it just happens that Kaikoura is the most accessible spot on the planet for seeing them. The male can reach a length of 18 metres and a weight of 70 tons, making the sperm whale the largest toothed whale on the planet. Only the plankton-eating baleen whales, such as the blue whale, are bigger.

There are frequent sightings of other types of whales on these trips including the killer *orca* (actually a dolphin), minke, humpback and southern right. You may also see shearwaters, petrels, and royal and wandering albatross.

There is one really bad hitch to the whole whale watch experience – the weather. Nothing is more dismal than heading to a place for a special encounter with nature, then to have it stopped by the intervention of the uncontrollable. As Whale Watch depends on its spotter planes to locate the whales out at sea, they can't usually find them in foggy or wet conditions. What's more, the trip out to them in the inflatable naiads would not be fun. The booking clerk at the Whale Watch office then cancels line after line of disappointed customers. The town benefits each time this happens as many people stay on to try the next day. If this trip is a *must* for you, allow a few days.

Another way to see the whales is from an aircraft or helicopter. Whale Watch have their own plane which makes half-hour flights out over the whales. They guarantee that you see the 'whole whale' from the air. Helitours Kaikoura (☎ 319 6466) also offer flights out over the whales; the minimum time is 20 minutes and the cost is $120 each (three persons). Air Tours Kaikoura (☎ 319 5986; fax 319 5938) offer a Whale Explorer trip as well. Both Air Tours Kaikoura and Whale Watch charge $50 each (two persons) for a half-hour flight or $100 each for one hour (again, two persons).

Air Tours Kaikoura have been keeping statistics of their sightings. Interestingly, they have seen (in addition to sperm whales) humpback, fin, blue, southern right, south-

ern bottlenose, minky and pilot whales; orcas (killer whales); and dusky, bottlenose and Hector's dolphins – all in a one-year period!

For $245 you can fly between Wellington and Kaikoura with Soundsair (☎ 573 6184) – for this price you get the return flight, a three-hour whale watch trip or a dolphin swim, and ground transportation. A good option for those with limited time.

To know more before you go out whale watching (or even dolphin swimming), get a copy of the excellent publication *Whales & Dolphins of Kaikoura, New Zealand* by Barbara Todd.

Dolphin Swimming The original operators, Dolphin Mary Charters (Dolphin Encounter ☎ 319 6777; fax 319 6534) at 58 West End, offer you the opportunity to swim with the dolphins. They also provide wetsuits (essential in this water), masks and snorkels for $75 for a three-hour 'dolphin encounter'.

New Zealand Sea Adventures (☎ 319 6622), near the railway station, also operate dolphin swimming trips for the same price.

The dolphins are not fed (as they are at Monkey Mia in Australia), so the encounter is far more natural.

Nature in Bounty There's also a lot of other wildlife to be seen. The 'Big Five' most likely to be seen are the sperm whale, Hector's dolphin (the smallest and rarest of all dolphins, found only in NZ waters and now on the list of endangered species), the dusky dolphin (found only in the southern hemisphere, often in pods of more than 100 dolphins), the NZ fur seal, and the royal albatross. Other animals frequently seen include the orca or killer whale (the largest of all dolphins), bottlenose and common dolphins, pilot whales, blue penguins, and many sea birds.

There's no guarantee of seeing any spe-

Dolphin Swimming

I didn't quite know what to expect when I went dolphin swimming with Dolphin Encounter. At their office you are fitted out with a good quality wetsuit, flippers, face mask and snorkel. The early hour adds to the confusion and the only hint of what you are about to experience is given by the numerous photographs and postcards scattered around the office.

They head out in their shark cat to an area between Oaro and Goose Bay, the preferred feeding ground of the pods (groups) of dusky dolphins. There is no guarantee that the dolphins will be there but the skipper has successfully located many in the previous days. When the first pod is sighted the air on board the boat is electric. The skipper manoeuvres in front of the pod, which is zig-zag feeding on squid, and advises us to enter the water. The group of about eight people don their mask and flippers and jump in to the cold water. The initial shock is quickly overcome as streaks of quicksilver flash by. Before you know it a curious dusky circles below you and you gasp for air through your snorkel. You are witness to one of the most beautiful, stream-lined creatures of the sea. You raise your head out of the water to see another dolphin performing, circus-like, back flip after back flip – not one or two, but 10, 11, 12...

I dive down to show more of me to the curious duskys and for a brief instant I am an interloper in their underwater world. Down here you see better the graceful forms as they dart by. You feel as if there is communication in some way between human and dolphin, some inexplicable spiritual communication. When you surface for air you hope for a respite from the excitement but the pod is still passing.

Apparently on this day three pods of duskys, numbering in total some 450 dolphins, had joined together for mass feeding. Later they were joined by a pod of common dolphins. On the way back to Kaikoura, a lone bottlenose dolphin, Maui, comes to the boat. Three dolphin species in one day. The encounter is over and satisfaction is complete. I don't think I have experienced anything quite like this on any of five continents before, including weeks in the Galápagos Islands.

The next day my younger brother, Mark, fresh from a swim with the seals the previous day went for his dolphin swim. The joy on his face confirmed my experiences of the day before.

Jeff Williams

MARLBOROUGH

cific animal on any one tour, but it's fairly certain that something of interest will be out there any time you go. In general, the sperm whales are most likely to be seen from October to August, and orcas from December to March. Most of the other animals are seen all year round.

There's a reason why all these animals are found at Kaikoura. It is here that the continental shelf comes closest to land, just about 800 metres off the coast. From land, the shelf slopes gradually to a depth of about 90 metres and then drops abruptly to a depth of over 800 metres. Warm and cold currents converge here, and when the southerly current hits the continental shelf it creates an upswelling current, bringing nutrients up from the ocean floor and into the light zone. The nutrients attract small marine animals, which in turn attract larger fish and squid – the sperm whale's favourite food!

Other Sea Tours Ocean Experience have two-hour fishing trips for $40 per person. Dolphin Encounter also have glass-bottomed boats, ideal for families who want a short trip; price on application. Both New Zealand Sea Adventures and Ocean Experience offer diving trips; usually it is about $50 for one dive and $75 for two.

The Kaikoura Dive & Sports Centre on Yarmouth St is another place to ask about diving – it does diving trips, hires tanks, and has an air-filling station.

Tours on Land Sea-to-Summit Safaris (☎ 319 6182) are based at the Visitor Information Centre. They operate 4WD adventures on Mt Fyffe, up to a point 1080 metres above sea level, with a view of the sea and a portable telescope for spotting whales. In summer there are three-hour trips up there during the day, or sunset 'Alpine Wine & Dine Barbecues'. In winter they take up a toboggan for fun in the snow. The cost is $35, with a discount for hostellers and students. They also do visits to the seal and gull colonies and in winter 4WD trips to the Mt Lyford ski field for skiing, ice-skating and tobogganing; minimum of four people.

You can tour on horseback with Fyffe View Horse Treks (☎ 319 5069, 319 5641), which runs half-day guided horse treks for $30, and all-day adventure rides up Mt Fyffe for $60.

Aerial Sightseeing

The Kaikoura Aero Club (☎ 319 6132, 319 5371) has air tours ranging from 15 minutes to over one hour, carrying up to three passengers. A 15-minute flight costs around $47 and a 40-minute flight costs about $125 – not bad if split between two or three people. Aerial sightseeing tours are also operated by Air Kaikoura (☎ 319 5986, 319 5371) who specialise in whale-watching flights.

Places to Stay

Camping & Cabins *Kaikoura Motels & Caravan Park* (☎ 319 5999) at 11 Beach Rd, near the railway overpass, has tent sites costing $14 for two (powered sites $1 more). There are four rudimentary cabins which cost $20 for two. They also have a budget lodge with six rooms, each sleeping five people, at a cost of $28 for two plus $11 for each extra adult. Tourist flats at the park cost $45 for two and $10 each extra adult.

The *Sea Ridge Holiday Camp*, formerly the Kaikoura Holiday Camp (☎ 319 5362), on Beach Rd beside the railway station, has campsites for $6.50 per person (power $3 extra). A two-berth cabin costs $20 and a four-berth cabin costs $40. This used to be pretty bad but it is now under new management and should be much improved.

At the *Esplanade Holiday Park* (☎ 319 5947), 126 The Esplanade, powered campsites cost $14 for one or two people, cabins cost $28 for two, and on-site caravans cost $30 for two.

The DOC has two seaside camping grounds near Kaikoura: *Peketa Camping Ground* (☎ 319 6299), eight km south of Kaikoura, with 100 tent sites, 100 power points, 10 cabins and a camp shop; and *Goose Bay Camping Ground* (☎ 319 5348), 18 km south of Kaikoura, with 100 tent sites, 90 power points, and five cabins. The Goose Bay camp is actually several camping areas spread over

Top: Shantytown, Greymouth, West Coast (TW)
Bottom Left: Truck Home, Nelson (JW)
Bottom Right: Toilet entrance (lava-tory) at the Volcano, Lyttleton, Canterbury (JW)

Top: View from the Treble Cone Ski Area, Otago (RS)
Bottom: West Coast Express Bus, Nelson (JW)

a five-km stretch of coastline. The *Waipapa Bay Camping Ground* (☎ 319 4307), 32 km north of Kaikoura, with 25 tent sites and 26 power points, used to be run by DOC but it is now in private hands. Generally, the camp-sites at each camping ground cost $6 per adult (an extra $4 for power), and the cabins cost around $24 for two people.

The *Waitane Cabins* (☎ 319 5494) at Oaro, 22 km south of Kaikoura off SH 1, has just two self-contained cabins (you only need to bring linen), each costing $30 for two people. Also at Oaro is the *Ocean View Motel* (☎ 319 5454), where caravan sites cost $14 for two people and motel units cost $50 for two.

Hostels The *Maui YHA Hostel* (☎ 319 5931) at 270 The Esplanade is an attractive, modern hostel beside the sea about 1.5 km from the town centre. The common room is open all day and has a superb view along the bay to the mountains beyond. The cost is $14 per night in dorms or $16 per person in twin rooms. Mt Cook buses drop off and pick up passengers at the door. The hostel will send someone to pick you up from the railway station if you arrange it in advance.

Across the road from the whale-watching operations, at 65 Beach Rd, you'll find *Moby Dix's Backpackers* (☎ 319 6699) where dorms are $13.50, and twin/double rooms are $15 per person (60 beds in total). The people who run the place are extremely helpful and try hard to create a friendly atmosphere. It has all the necessary facilities, volleyball court, sundeck with a BBQ and a creek at the back. You can camp here for $7.

The *Topspot Backpackers* (☎ 319 5540) at 22 Deal St has space for 20 people and is a non-smokers' haven. There is a BBQ and sundeck here, they have a courtesy van, and the clean and tidy share rooms are $14, double units with ensuites from $32. There is a sign near the post office which indicates the path up to this place.

Another place which has received recommendations is *Kaikoura Backpackers* at 116 Torquay St (☎ 319 5899), where rooms are $15 on the first night and $12.50 thereafter.

Free bikes, TV and a fully equipped kitchen – competition is fierce in this town. They can only accommodate four people so ring ahead.

Hotels The *Adelphi Hotel* (☎ 319 5141) on West End has single/double rooms for $20 with shared bathrooms or $35/47 with private facilities. At the *New Commercial Hotel* (☎ 319 5018) on the corner of Torquay and Brighton Sts, B&B costs $33/54 for singles/doubles.

The *Pier Hotel* (☎ 319 5037) on Avoca St, near the wharf, has rooms for $25 per person, B&B for $30 per person, and B&B with dinner for $42 per person. Or there's the more modern *Blue Pacific Hotel* (☎ 319 5017) at 114 The Esplanade, where B&B costs $28 per person for singles/doubles. Budget accommodation is available here for $17/32 for singles/doubles.

Motels There are plenty of motels in Kaikoura, especially along The Esplanade. Most charge at least $55 to $65 per night for two, including the *Kaikoura Motels & Caravan Park* mentioned under Camping & Cabins ($55). *Panorama Motels* (☎ 319 5053) at 266 The Esplanade, *Clearwater Motels* (☎ 319 5326) at 168 The Esplanade, and *Oregon Court* (☎ 319 5623) at 169 Beach Rd are all similarly priced.

At the *Norfolk Pine Motor Inn* (☎ 319 5120), 124 The Esplanade, studio units cost $60 for two; two-bedroom units cost $80 for two; and a three-bedroom house sleeping eight people costs from $80 for two plus $14 for each extra adult and $11 for each extra child.

The *Old Convent* (☎ 319 6603), out on Mt Fyffe Rd (near the junction with Mill Rd) and about three minutes from the town, is neither a motel nor a convent. It is a highly regarded B&B where singles/doubles or twins/triples are $35/50/60 respectively.

Places to Eat
When in season, crayfish (lobster) are often featured in Kaikoura restaurants; you even find them in the local takeaways. Before the

whale-watching boom, the crayfish alone made Kaikoura a worthwhile stop! If you want to provide your own food you can try your luck fishing from the wharf.

Snacks & Fast Food There are many takeaways and coffee shops around town. *Why Not Cafe* in the town centre specialises in home-made food, with takeaways, pizza, sandwiches, salads and some health food selections. The fish shop down on the wharf sells cooked crayfish and many kinds of fish. Other places that have been mentioned by locals are *Suzy's Wok and Roll* for Chinese; *Station Cafe* for snacks while booking trips; *Changes Cafe* for cheap meals and late opening hours – Thai spring rolls or nachos and chilli sauce are both $8 per serve; and *Act One* for pizzas from $9, including the Shaftesbury special with chicken, brie and cranberries. There are also a number of fish & chip places scattered around town. The *bakery* out on Beach Rd (on the corner of Hawthorne Rd) is a good place to pick up a quick snack before ecotouring.

Pub Food Various hotels serve standard pub fare including the *Pier Hotel* near the wharf, *Adelphi Hotel, Blue Pacific* and *New Commercial Hotel*. To give you an idea, the roast of the day at the Adelphi costs $14; a steak at the New Commercial is $13.

Restaurants The *White Morph Restaurant* at 94 The Esplanade is housed in a stately old home and has both indoor and garden tables. In summer it's open every night from 6 to 9.30 pm. Devonshire teas are served all day, and there's seafood fresh from the local fishing boats for lunch and dinner. Main courses are $10.50 to $14 and there's a salad bar for $5.50 each serve.

The *Caves Restaurant*, next to the Maori Leap Cave three km south of the centre on SH 1, is open long hours – from 7 am to 6 pm during the week, sometimes later. Steak ($13) and seafood (light meals at around $9.50) are served in the restaurant, and there's also a separate takeaways counter.

Getting There & Away

Air There are no commercial airlines serving Kaikoura, but the local Aero Club fly to Wellington and other places. Contact the information centre for details. Soundsair (☎ 573 6184) do a special eco-flight from Wellington (see Whale-Watching earlier in this section). They are based at the Picton airstrip, Koromiko.

Bus The daily InterCity and Mt Cook Landline bus services operating between Picton and Christchurch all stop at Kaikoura. From Kaikoura it's about 2½ hours to either Picton or Christchurch. InterCity buses arrive and depart from Gilly & Marg's Four Square grocery (☎ 319 6160) on Beach Rd; tickets are sold at the shop. Mt Cook Landline buses arrive and depart from the car park on the beach side of West End in the centre of town. Mt Cook tickets are sold by the information centre and PGG Travel (☎ 319 5012). The Coffee Shop (☎ 319 5221) on West End in the centre of town is the only booking agent for Newmans (North Island only).

There are a number of shuttle buses taking off from West End, eg Compass Coachlines, South Island Connections, Southern Lake, NZ Coop and Nationwide which operate through Kaikoura; expect to pay about $15 to get to Christchurch.

Train One northbound and one southbound Coastal Pacific train between Picton and Christchurch stop at Kaikoura every day. The northbound arrives at about 11.10 am and the southbound at about 4.20 pm.

Getting Around
The Maui YHA Hostel hires out bicycles to hostellers. West End garage (Shell) hire out bikes as well.

Nelson

Nelson (population 47,800) is a pleasant, bright and active town. The surrounding area has some of the finest beaches in New

Zealand and more sunshine than any other part of the country so it's not surprising that it's a popular holiday area. Apart from beaches and bays, Nelson is noted for its fruit-growing industry and its very energetic local arts & crafts community.

History

The Maoris began to migrate to the South Island during the 16th century, and among the first to arrive in Nelson were the Ngati Tumatakokiri. By 1550 this tribe occupied most of the province, as Abel Tasman was to find out to his cost when he turned up at the place he later named Murderers' Bay. Other tribes followed the Tumatakokiri, settling at the mouth of the Waimea River. The Tumatakokiri remained supreme in Tasman Bay until the 18th century, when the Ngati-apa from Wanganui and the Ngai Tahu – the largest tribe in the South Island – got together in a devastating attack on the Tumatakokiri, who virtually ceased to exist as an independent tribe after 1800.

The Ngati-apa's victory was short-lived, because between 1828 and 1830 they were practically annihilated by armed tribes from Taranaki and Wellington who sailed into the bay in the largest fleet of canoes ever assembled in New Zealand.

By the time the European settlers arrived there were no Maoris living at Te Wakatu – the nearest pa being at Motueka – and the population of those that remained in the area was so decimated they put up no resistance. The first Pakeha settlers sailed in response to advertisements by the New Zealand Company, which was set up by Edward Gibbon Wakefield to colonise the country systematically. His grandiose scheme was to transplant a complete slice of English life from all social classes. In reality 'too few gentlemen with too little money' took up the challenge and the new colony almost foundered in its first few years from lack of money.

The settlement was planned to comprise small but workable farms grouped around central towns. However, the New Zealand Company's entitlement to the land was disputed and it was almost a year before this problem was sorted out. So while the land around the town had been distributed early, the farmland was not available for such a long time that landowners and labourers forced to live in town had whittled away their capital simply to survive.

The Wairau Massacre (described in the Marlborough Sounds History section) resulted in the deaths of 22 of Nelson's most able citizens, including Captain Wakefield whose leadership was irreplaceable, and plunged the colony into deep gloom. To make matters worse the New Zealand Company was declared bankrupt in April 1844 and, since nearly three-quarters of the population were dependent on it in some way or another, particularly for sustenance, the situation was so grim as to be near famine. Only the later arrival of hard-working German immigrants saved the region from economic ruin.

Information

The Nelson Visitor Centre (☎ 548 2304), on the corner of Trafalgar and Halifax Sts, is open from 7.30 am to 5 pm on weekdays and from 7.30 am to 1 pm on Saturday. From December to February it's open from 7.30 am to 5 pm every day, including Sunday. This office also acts as a travel agent and makes bookings for everything in town – accommodation, transport, tours and so on. It also serves as Nelson's Transit Centre – all buses serving Nelson arrive and depart from this office. Trafalgar St, which crosses the river just before the information centre and runs straight up to the cathedral, is the main street in Nelson. There is a very good *Visitor's Guide* published annually.

The AA office is nearby at 45 Halifax St. General inquiries about national parks and walks are fielded at the visitor information centre by 'DOC officials'. The DOC office (☎ 546 9335) is a couple of blocks away in the Monroe Building at 186 Bridge St. They have good topographical maps on the Nelson and Marlborough area, the Abel Tasman, Heaphy and Wangapeka tracks, and Nelson Lakes National Park. The office is open from 8 am to 4.35 pm Monday to Friday.

If you are on a working holiday there's fruit and tobacco picking and other agricultural work from February to May, and there may be some casual daily work at fisheries at the port. Contact the Employment NZ office or individual growers about picking work.

Cathedral

The focal point of Nelson is its cathedral, at the top of Trafalgar St. The present building has had a somewhat chequered career. The foundation stone for the cathedral was laid in 1925 but construction dragged on for many years and in the 1950s arguments raged over whether the building should be completed to its original design. Eventually construction recommenced to a modified design in the 1960s and was completed in 1967. When the cathedral was finally consecrated in 1972, no fewer than 47 years had passed since the foundation stone was laid! The cathedral is open from 8 am to 7 pm daily.

Bishop's School

For about 90 years from 1840, Bishop's School served Nelson as a school. It's on Nile St East and is open from 2 to 4 pm on Sunday, and on Tuesday and Thursday during holiday periods. If you don't find it open during these hours, ask at 28 Nile St. On display are the notes and textbooks used in the old days.

Arts & Crafts

The Suter Art Gallery adjoins Queen's Gardens on Bridge St and is open from 10.30 am to 4.30 pm every day. Entry is $1 (children 20c, family $2.20). As well as having a permanent art collection it has art exhibitions, musical, theatrical and dance performances, films and craft displays. The gallery takes its name from Bishop Suter, who formed the Bishopdale Sketching Club back in 1889.

Seven Weavers at 36 Collingwood St is a cooperative weavers' workshop where handwoven articles are designed and made on the premises, many with handspun wool. It's open from 10 am to 4 pm on weekdays.

If you're interested in pottery, visit the South St Gallery, close to the Cathedral on Nile St West. It's open from 10 am to 5 pm Monday to Thursday, 10 am to 7 pm on Friday, and 10 am to 4 pm on weekends and public holidays.

There are numerous other galleries in the area. Nelson's artistic reputation is partly due to the local clay which attracted many potters to the town. The Nelson Potters' Association has a leaflet showing where to find the potters in the Nelson area – get it from the visitor centre.

Museums

Founders Park, at 87 Atawhai Drive, is a collection of old Nelson buildings, reflecting the town's early history. It's open from 10 am to 4.30 pm daily and admission is $4 (children $2).

The Nelson Provincial Museum, at Isel Park in the nearby town of Stoke, has New Zealand's largest photographic collection, and exhibits on local and Maori history. It's open from 10 am to 4 pm Tuesday to Friday, and from 2 to 5 pm on Saturday, Sunday and holidays; it's closed on Monday. Admission is $2 for adults, $1 for children, and $5 for families. Also in Isel Park is the historic Isel House, open from 2 to 4 pm on Saturday and Sunday, but only from late October to Easter; admission is $1 for adults. You can get there on the bus to Stoke – see the Getting Around in this section.

Gardens & Walks

Nelson has some fine gardens, including the beautiful Botanic Gardens and Queens Gardens. In the Botanic Gardens there's a good lookout at the top of Botanical Hill, with a spire proclaiming it as the exact geographical centre of New Zealand.

The riverside footpath makes a pleasant stroll through the city and there are many other fine walks and tramps. The Maitai Valley is a particularly restful and beautiful area and the Maungatapu Track leads from here across to the Pelorus River. The information centre has a leaflet called 'Nelson, the City of Walks' outlining 17 good short walks in and around town, many of them good for an evening stroll.

Beaches
The best-known beach near Nelson is Tahunanui, five km from the town centre. Rabbit Island is another popular beach, with 13 km of undeveloped beach backed by forest. There's road access to the island but it's closed off after 9 pm daily, and camping is not allowed; the hours depend on the level of fire risk. You can get to Tahunanui on Nelson Suburban Bus Lines.

Adventure Activities
The Rapid River Rafting Company (☎ Nelson 542 3110) and the Nelson Raft Company (☎ 546 6212) both do white water rafting on the Buller and Gowan rivers. It costs about $55 for a half-day trip and $90 for the full day.

You can go parapenting with Sky High Parapentes (☎ 546 8711) or Airborn (☎ 543 2669), and the Nelson Aero Club (☎ 547 9643) offers a variety of scenic flights, very reasonably priced. The Nelson Visitor Centre has information on these and many other activities around Nelson.

For those with a little extra spending money try a tandem parachute jump with Tandem Skydive Nelson (☎ 548 2894). It costs $170 per person and this includes transport, 10 minutes' instruction, the free fall and parachute descent (what you came for) and a certificate.

Other Things to Do
The Riverside Pool on Halifax St, beside the river, is within walking distance of the town centre. It costs $1.80 (children $1) to swim in the large indoor heated pool, and there's also a spa pool which costs $3 (children $2) for 20 minutes. The pool is open from 7.30 am to 6 pm on Monday, Wednesday and Friday; from 7 am to 8 pm on Tuesday and Thursday; and from 11 am to 5 pm on weekends and holidays. It closes for 6 weeks in July and August.

Nelson offers a variety of less dangerous outdoor activities. At Tahunanui Beach, windsurfers, wave skis and body boards can be hired, and there's also a windsurfing school. Camping gear for trips on the Abel Tasman or other tracks can be hired in Nelson from many, in fact most, of the hostels, or from Alp Sports at 220 Hardy St (☎ 546 8536). Bruce Rollo Ltd (☎ 548 2363) at 12 Bridge St also has a more limited selection of gear for hire. Prices are usually quite reasonable, around $5 a day for packs and boots, $8 a day for tents. Just about every hostel will also store your excess luggage while you're away on the track, some for free and some for a small fee.

Tours
There are many tours around Nelson, all of which can be booked through the Nelson Visitor Centre. Some of the more popular are the Wine Trail tours ($30 to $35), Craft & Scenic Tours (from $18), and the Motueka Horticultural Tour ($18) which visits a number of unusual agricultural operations including tobacco, hop, green tea, kiwi fruit, nashi pear and other fruit farms, with their accompanying tobacco kilns, hop harvesters and packing houses. Farewell Spit Safari Tours ($33) are another popular attraction, departing from Collingwood; transport can be arranged from Nelson (see the Collingwood entry in the Nelson to Golden Bay section).

During the summer, day trips from Nelson to the Abel Tasman National Park are popular and good value. See the Abel Tasman National Park entry in the Nelson to Golden Bay section later in this chapter for details.

If you are into getting wet and frightened then go rafting with the Nelson Raft Co. They supply all the equipment you'll need for trips on the Buller, Wairau and Motueka rivers – costs vary from about $60 for a half-day trip to $100 for a full-day extravaganza.

Festivals
Nelson has many noteworthy events throughout the year. There's the Christmas

MARLBOROUGH

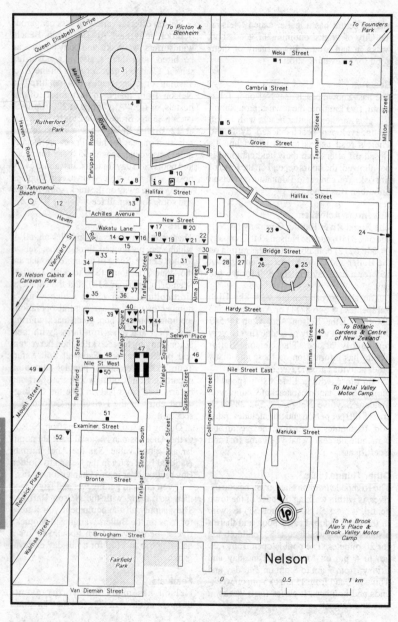

MARLBOROUGH

Nelson

■ PLACES TO STAY

1   Tasman Towers
2   Youth Hostel
4   Trafalgar Auto Lodge Motel
5   California House
6   Riverlodge Motel
10 AA Motor Lodge
18 Boots Backpackers
20 Sun City Backpackers'
24 Centre of New Zealand
    Backpackers Hostel
30 New Royal Hotel
33 Bumbles Hostel
37 Mid City Motor Lodge
45 Nelson Backpackers 125
48 Quality Inn
49 Dave's Palace
51 Lynton Lodge

▼ PLACES TO EAT

15 Valeno's Wine Bar
16 Cafe de Curb
17 Pizza My Heart
19 La Bonne Vie Seafood
21 Cactus Cantina
22 Hitching Post Pizza
28 Hotel Wakatu & Cobb & Co
29 Ciao, The More Italian Restaurant
31 Food with Attitude
34 Led Zebra

36 Cultured Cow Yoghurt
38 McDonalds
39 Jacksons
40 Burgerholics
41 Kaceys Restaurant & Nightclub
43 Chez Eelco & Pomeroy's
44 Victorian Rose
52 Pizza Hut

OTHER

3   Trafalgar Park
7   Horatio's Nightclub
8   Library
9   Nelson Visitor Centre & Mt Cook
    Landline and Other Buses
11 Automobile Association (AA)
12 Anzac Park
13 Chief Post Office
14 InterCity Depot & Suburban Bus Lines
23 Riverside Pool
25 Queen's Gardens
26 Suter Art Gallery
27 Department of Conservation (DOC)
32 Air New Zealand Link
35 Shakespearz Nightclub
42 Zhivago's Nightclub
46 Bishop's School
47 Cathedral
50 South Street Gallery, Historic South St

Carnival in Founders Park, the New Year Hops Festival, the Kaiteriteri Carnival in the first week of January and, in late February or early March, one of the most interesting of all, the 'Wearable Art Award' competitions. Also in early March is the Taste Nelson Festival for locally produced food and beverages, and an A&P (Agricultural and Pastoral) show on the third weekend in November.

Places to Stay

Camping & Cabins There are plenty of campsites around Nelson, including the *Tahuna Beach Holiday Park* (☎ 548 5159) near the airport and Tahuna Beach – the largest motor camp in Australasia! It can accommodate 4500 people and there are lots of camping places at $16 for two, cabins and

lodges from $25 to $38 for two, and tourist flats from $43 for two. Linen can be hired. The site is five km from the city centre and just a couple of minutes from the beach – but light sleepers, beware! It's also very near the airport. The convenient camp supermarket is open to campers and to the public every day of the year.

The *Brook Valley Motor Camp* (☎ 548 0399) in the upper Brook Valley is situated in a superb position near a stream and surrounded by rolling pastures and forested hills. It's about the same distance from the centre as Tahuna, but rather smaller and more personal. Camping costs $7 per person, or $9 with power. There are cabins from very basic four-bunk ones at $20 for two up to more luxurious ones at around $36 for two. The camp is a long way uphill if you're walking.

MARLBOROUGH

The *Maitai Valley Motor Camp* (☎ 548 7729) on Maitai Valley Rd is operated by the city council and is on the riverbank, six km from the centre. Sites are $14 for two people.

The *Nelson Cabins & Caravan Park* (☎ 548 1445) at 230 Vanguard St has cabins at $33.50 for two with cutlery and cooking utensils supplied, and you can hire linen if needed. Tourist flats are $45 for two. It's very central but there are no tent sites; powered caravan sites are $14.50 for two.

Other sites in the area include the *Richmond Holiday Park* (☎ 544 7323), 13 km from Nelson at Richmond, and the *Waimea Town & Country Club* (☎ 544 6476), also in Richmond, on Lower Queen St. There's also camping, caravan sites and cabins around Mapua (see the Motueka Places to Stay section for details). Back-to-nature *DOC campsites* in the region are at St Arnaud, Nelson Lakes National Park (fully serviced), and Lake Rotorua, Nelson Lakes National Park.

Hostels Hostels have been popping up like the proverbial mushrooms around Nelson, and the number has reached double figures – plenty to choose from in this not-so-large town!

The YHA hostel and a good backpackers are close to each other on Weka St about one km north of the town centre. The neat, clean and friendly *Nelson YHA Hostel* (☎ 548 8817) at 42 Weka St has room for 32 people at $14 per night. The hostel is in one of Nelson's original homesteads and it's loaded with information about tracks, transport and things to do in the area – the walls of the foyer are covered with information, and even as you sit on the toilet you can read a sign about transport to the Abel Tasman Track! The hostel hires out bicycles and camping equipment and will store your luggage if you go off tramping.

The *Tasman Towers* (☎ 548 7950) at 10 Weka St is a spacious, new purpose-built 50-bed hostel. Rooms are mainly for two, three or four people and there are plenty of doubles for couples. The cost is $15 per night

in any room and there are good kitchen and lounge facilities.

You can't miss the brightly coloured *Boots Backpackers*, formerly Pavlova City (☎ 548 9001), right in the centre of town on the corner of Trafalgar and Bridge Sts. There's room for 53 people in very ordinary, basic dorm, double and twin rooms. Dorms are $13.50 and the other rooms cost $15 per person. There's a special sound-proofed 'Party Room' where parties take place several times weekly. They give talks on the Abel Tasman and Nelson Lakes national parks every evening at 8 pm. Boots hire out motor scooters and camping equipment, store your excess luggage, and sell passes for the Abel Tasman Track and tickets for Mt Cook and InterCity buses. There is a climbing wall out the back for the really adventurous and it costs $7 a go.

Not far away from here is *Sun City Backpackers* (☎ 548 9905) at 131 Bridge St (enter from New St pub on Bridge St) in the former Metropolitan Hotel. They have full kitchen and laundry facilities and, according to their own literature, are the place to go if you want to party. They charge $13.50 per night in dorms and $15 in double or twin rooms, most with their own shower. A big drawback is the location above one of Nelson's less salubrious pubs, so quite often it is noisy.

In the centre of town, at 8 Bridge St, is *Bumbles* (☎ 548 2771), a former hotel with dorms for $14, triples for $16, and twin and double rooms for $18 per night. They have recycling facilities, a big common room, plenty of information, gas BBQ, video and helpful staff.

A little bit of an uphill walk away is a rambling building called *Dave's Palace* (☎ 548 4691) at 18 Mount St. Built in 1898 this was the original home of a jam and conserve bottling giant. It was left as an orphanage from 1925 and remained as such until Dave grabbed it in 1992. It has the air of an orphanage – this does not seem to deter its adoring travelling clientele, however, and its maze of rooms are more than likely to be full. Part of this has to do with the character of Dave, for sure. Beds in dorm rooms are

$13, and in twin or double rooms $15 per person. Be an orphan for the night in a single room for $15. Phone for free pick-up from the bus stop and railway station.

There are also two smaller hostels – Nelson Backpackers 125 and Alan's Place – set up in private homes. They can accommodate a maximum of 10 and 14 people respectively and although they are licensed hostels they have a more homely, personal atmosphere, with helpful and friendly hosts. Both have free bicycles to get around on, free luggage storage and so on. The owners work during the day; you can phone them in the evening and on weekends, but you're welcome to arrive anytime.

Nelson Backpackers 125 (☎ 548 7576) at 125 Tasman St is conveniently located and has beds for $14 in the downstairs of a pleasant two-storey home. *Alan's Place* (☎ 548 4854) at 42 Westbrook Terrace is a bit further out, but still a reasonable walk from town, and offers beds for $14 the first night, $12 each night after that, plus all the free tea you can drink. Alan may even take you for a free tour of town when you arrive, ending up at Chez Eelco where you can try one of his favourites, hot chocolate!

The newest hostel in town is the *Centre of New Zealand Backpackers Hostel* (☎ 546 6667; fax 546 6601) at 193 Milton St, centrally situated near the Queen's Gardens and the swimming pool. It occupies a beautiful large historic manor house, built in 1881, with ample space both inside and out around the grounds. Amenities include an outdoor BBQ, a large open fireplace, piano and guitar, a buy/sell backpackers car service, camping gear for hire, and much more. The cost is $14 in share and dorm rooms, $15 to $17 in double or twin rooms, or $20 for a single room. Or you can camp on the lawn.

The *Backpackers Beach Hostel* (☎ 548 6817) has recently moved to 25 Muritai St, Tahuna Beach. It's an enjoyable hostel, with free windsurfers, bicycles and luggage storage, and although it's four km from the town centre it's not inconvenient. Local and long-distance buses stop just around the corner, it's an easy hitch to town, and the

friendly owner Colin takes people along in the van whenever he goes to town. Phone for free pick-up when you arrive. All beds are $13 a night in dorms, double, twin and triple rooms. It is the closest hostel to the airport and there is a pub just across the road.

Guesthouses Nelson has plenty of B&B places, but you might still have difficulty finding somewhere to stay in the high season. Best known and probably most expensive is *California House* (☎ 548 4173) at 29 Collingwood St, just across the river from the town centre. It's run by Shelley & Neil, who provide a real Californian breakfast that might include orange juice, fresh berries and cream, ham and sour cream omelettes, apricot nut bread, apple and cheese blintzes, pancakes with maple syrup and coffee. The cost is $110 to $145 for a couple including that hearty breakfast. There are only double rooms; if you're by yourself it's going to cost $85, but you do get a double bed. California gets lots of recommendations but it's only open from September to May.

California is definitely a more expensive B&B but there are various other more conventional places in Nelson, all of which include breakfast in their tariff.

Further down the same street, at No 174, is *Collingwood House* (☎ 548 4481) where singles/doubles are $40/60. *Palm Grove* (☎ 548 4645), at 52 Cambria St, costs $40 per person or $60 a double. The *Abbey Lodge* (☎ 548 8816) at 84 Grove St and *Hunts Home Hosts* (☎ 548 0123) at 15 Riverside St both charge $40/60 for singles/doubles. There are several others in the area including the *Willowbank Guest House* (☎ 548 5041) at 71 Golf Rd, Tahunanui, and the *Bridge Guest House* (☎ 542 3301) at 141 Lightband Rd in Brightwater.

For real Kiwi hospitality stay with *Kay Morrison* (☎ 548 7993) at 81 Cleveland Terrace, on the eastern side of town, a 10-minute walk from the town centre. There's a self-contained unit set aside for guests, with two double bedrooms, for $14 per person.

Hotels There are plenty of regular hotels around Nelson. They include the *Dominion* (☎ 548 4984) at 2 Nile St West where singles cost $28.50 to $31.50 and doubles cost $43 to $47, and the *Star & Garter* (☎ 544 7391) out at 252 Queen St, Richmond, where singles/doubles cost $37/52. The *New Royal Hotel* (☎ 546 9279) at 152 Bridge St has rooms at $51 to $59 for doubles.

The more expensive 115-room *Quality Inn* (☎ 548 2299) is on Nile St West and has everything from a sauna and swimming pool to a spa and gym. The cheapest rooms cost about $125, with discounts on weekends.

Motels There are a great number of motels in Nelson, many of them near the airport at Tahunanui. Motels that are both fairly central and reasonably priced include the *Lynton Lodge Motel* (☎ 548 7112) at 25 Examiner St with double rooms for $62 to $73. The *Riverlodge Motel* (☎ 548 3094) is at 31 Collingwood St, on the corner with Grove St; double rooms cost $65 to $79. At the *Trafalgar Auto Lodge Motel* (☎ 548 3980), 46 Trafalgar St, motel units cost $55/65 for singles/doubles while B&B costs $35/55.

The *Mid City Motor Lodge* (☎ 546 9063; fax 548 3595), in the centre of town at 218 Trafalgar St, has rooms priced from $70 to $78 for doubles. By the river at 8 Ajax Ave the *AA Motor Lodge* (☎ 548 8214) is very conveniently located with rooms around $88 for two people.

Homestays Nelsonians are a friendly lot, and a number of private homes in the area offer accommodation for a maximum of four guests at a time, with rates usually about the same as the hostels. Ask for a referral at the Nelson Visitor Centre.

Places to Eat

It is the wealth of local produce that makes dining out in Nelson such a pleasure. Seafood is the main menu item as over 70% of the country's fishing quota is owned by Nelson businesses. Deep sea fish such as orange roughy and hoki, scallops from Tasman and Golden Bays, and mussels and

oysters harvested commercially are all available in the town's restaurants. These are complemented by a wide range of locally produced wines and beers. Get a copy of the latest *Nelson Regional Gourmet Guide*.

Snacks & Fast Food There are plenty of sandwich specialists around the centre and, a little further out, a *Pizza Hut* and a *Kentucky Fried Chicken*. *McDonald's* has also appeared in the centre of Nelson – it's on Rutherford St near the Hardy St corner. *Food with Attitude* serves great burgers.

The cafe at the *Suter Art Gallery* is worth considering for a more expensive but pleasant lunch – good food in an attractive setting; it's open daily.

The *Cafe de Curb* is a big white pie cart that has been serving mobile fast foods in Nelson since 1933. It's reputed to have the 'biggest burgers in New Zealand'. You can find it parked on Trafalgar St near Bridge St after 6 pm every day except Sunday. It's open until midnight on Monday and Tuesday, until 1.30 am on Wednesday and Thursday, and until 3.30 am on Friday and Saturday!

On Hardy St is *Burgerholics*, described by one traveller as 'fantastic'. Above their door is the sentence: 'World! The not yet famous Burgerholics'. Try the delicious char-grilled beef and bacon burger with whole-grained mustard.

Pub Food There's a *Cobb & Co* in the Wakatu Hotel on the corner of Collingwood and Bridge Sts, with the usual Cobb & Co menu and the usual opening hours – 7.30 am to 10 pm daily. *Kaceys*, on the corner of Trafalgar and Hardy Sts, also has a fairly standard pub-style menu.

Other hotels with pub food include the *New Royal Hotel* at 152 Bridge St, a rather trendy eatery where main courses cost $10 to $20, and the *Turf Hotel* in Stoke, which has the usual range of roasts, steaks and salads.

Restaurants The *Chez Eelco*, near the cathedral at 296 Trafalgar St, is a Nelson institution. It's a relaxed coffee bar and restaurant which stays open from 6 am to 11 pm, 7 days a week. They serve everything from strong coffee, croissants, sandwiches and fruit juices to regular restaurant meals. It's a popular meeting place and the front window is an equally popular local notice board. Give it a try. Next door, at 276 Trafalgar St, the place with a pervasive smell of fresh roasted coffee, is *Pomeroys*, where you can get good cakes, croissants and coffee.

Nearby and across the road, at 281 Trafalgar St, is the *Victorian Rose*, a pastiche of English/Irish pub styles in airy premises. The meals here are great – try the blue cod in filo pastry for $12.50. The Guinness is served with care and there is a varied selection of beers.

On Bridge St, at No 75, is *La Bonne Vie Seafood Restaurant*. It has been recommended widely for its good value seafood meals. A two-course Sunday lunch, served from 11.30 am onwards, is only $12. Usually a main course is about $15 to $18 and the famous green-lipped mussels feature heavily on the menu.

If you want good pizzas, try the popular *Hitching Post* at 145 Bridge St, which has 13 choices in three sizes; prices start at around $8. The menu goes much further, however, with main courses from $9 to $15, smorgasbord salads for $3.50, drinks, desserts and so on. The Post has a rustic decor and an open-air courtyard out the back.

Jacksons, at 142 Hardy St, is a glossy modern restaurant with a decidedly international menu including Greek, Californian, Mexican, Chinese – you name it – influences. Main courses cost $15 to $18, and it's open every day.

The Asian Gardens, once at 94 Collingwood St, has been replaced by *Ciao, The More Italian Restaurant*. They are open for lunch and dinner, Monday to Saturday, is BYO and a meal costs from $12 to $20. They use lots of fresh Nelson produce in their meals. With the gardens gone, don't despair. There are a number of other Asian places in town including *Thai Foods*, 105 Hardy St; *Chinatown*, 42 Tahunanui Drive, Tahunanui; *Hong Kong*, 65 Bridge St; *Jade Palace*

Chinese, 131 Trafalgar St, and *Nelson Oriental*, 105 Hardy St.

The *Samadhi*, an Indian vegetarian restaurant at 30 Washington Rd on the corner of Hastings St, isn't right in the town centre but it's well worth the short walk to reach it. Classic Indian dishes are served in the traditional thali style – all you can eat! – and cost from $12 to $19, with a good selection of sweets and drinks too. It's a non-smoking BYO which has become one of Nelson's favourites, open from 6 pm every day except Sunday.

Entertainment
Pubs Various pubs have entertainment including the *Turf Hotel* at Stoke or the *Ocean Lodge Hotel* at Tahunanui, both with discos. The *New Royal Hotel* and the glossy new *Kaceys* in the central city have entertainment on weekends.

Nightclubs Nelson also has several nightclubs. There's *Horatio's* in Halifax St near the CPO, *Zhivago's* in the City Centre shopping arcade, or *Shakespearz* on Hardy St near Rutherford. Downstairs is the *Officer's Club*; it isn't a nightclub as such but is a good place for a casual drink.

In New St off Trafalgar are three good places – *Maxine's*, the *Cactus Cantina*, and near these the *Bridge Cafe* also becomes a nightclub in the evening. Most nightclubs in town have one night during the week when they offer a special deal and become packed out with locals out for a good time.

Other Entertainment Wherever you're drinking in Nelson make it a point to try a Mac's beer. Nelson's own beer is brewed by an independent brewery and it's not bad. Another good local beer is the appropriately named Pink Elephant – it is reminiscent of some of the Belgian Trappist varieties. The Wine Trails Tour includes a tour of the brewery.

Also worth a mention is the evening entertainment at the Suter Art Gallery on Bridge St. Besides the theatre, music, dance and so on mentioned previously, they have the

Stage Two theatre with a top selection of popular and international art films, changing frequently.

Getting There & Away

Air The main office of Air New Zealand Link (which incorporates Air Nelson; ☎ 546 9300) is on the corner of Trafalgar and Bridge Sts. They have direct flights to Wellington, Auckland, Christchurch, Westport, and Palmerston North, again with connections to other cities. At the airport the contact number for Air Nelson is 547 6066. Mt Cook Airline (☎ 548 2329) does not have a service out of Nelson but you can book their other flights (eg to Mt Cook and Queenstown from Christchurch) here.

Bus All buses (except InterCity) serving Nelson arrive and depart from the Nelson Visitor Centre (☎ 548 2304) on the corner of Trafalgar and Halifax Sts. The office sells tickets for all bus lines. InterCity (☎ 548 1539) has a Travel Centre on Bridge St.

InterCity buses run daily east to Picton and south to Greymouth via Murchison and Westport, with connections to the Franz Josef and Fox glaciers. This is an interesting route to Greymouth as it goes via the Buller Gorge and the scenic coastal route, with a stop at Punakaiki (the Pancake Rocks).

Mt Cook Landline (☎ 548 8369) also has daily buses from Nelson to Picton, continuing south to Christchurch, and buses to Christchurch via the Lewis Pass.

Besides these two major bus lines, Nelson has a surprising number of more local operators. From Nelson to Picton there's the Skyline Connection, with three buses daily in each direction. Unlike Mt Cook and InterCity, which go via Blenheim, the Sky Connection bus goes via the scenic Queen Charlotte Drive coastal route, making stops at little towns and bays all along the way.

Heading west to Motueka and Golden Bay there's quite a variety of transport. Mt Cook Landline has buses to Motueka and Takaka. Golden Bay Connections (☎ 524 8188) has services from Nelson to Collingwood via Motueka and Takaka, connecting with Mt Cook buses at Takaka. It and other companies, such as Skyline Connections and Abel Tasman Enterprises, provide transport from Nelson, Motueka and Takaka to the Abel Tasman Track (see Abel Tasman National Park in the Nelson to Golden Bay section for details).

Several local companies have buses to the Nelson Lakes National Park. Nelson Lakes Transport (☎ 521 1858) runs a return bus between Nelson and St Arnaud daily except Sunday, connecting with other buses between Picton and Greymouth. Wadsworths Motors (☎ 522 4248) has thrice-weekly buses from Nelson to Lake Rotoiti and Tadmor, plus buses to Tapawera on weekdays.

Finally, Southern Sights (☎ 548 8901) is a good private bus and tour company providing transport to the Abel Tasman Track (northern or southern end), Nelson Lakes, the West Coast glaciers, Pancake Rocks, or any other place. It goes on demand, usually quite frequently – serving the YHA hostel and Tasman Towers regularly, but you can use the service no matter where you are staying; it will come to pick you up. Southern Sights goes anywhere, all year round, and provides not only transport but a scenic tour as well, stopping to see interesting things along the way. Trampers can arrange to be picked up at the end of a track at a specified time.

An alternative bus, the West Coast Express, departs from Nelson for six-day trips down the West Coast to Queenstown, with plenty of stops along the way. Since hitching is notoriously slow and seeing all the sights can be difficult travelling by public bus, this is a good way to see the West Coast if you don't have your own wheels. See the Getting Around chapter for details.

Boat You can now take a boat directly from Nelson to Abel Tasman National Park. Catalina Cruises (☎ 540 2759) go directly from Nelson to the start of the track. It costs $20 one-way and is a good alternative to the bus services offered.

Hitching Getting out of Nelson is not easy as the city sprawls so far. It's best to take a bus to the outskirts. Hitching to the West Coast can be hard going, so take a bus as far as Tapawera.

Getting Around

To/From the Airport The Airport Shuttle Service (☎ 546 7418) offers door-to-door service to and from the airport for $6. It operates from about 7 am to 6 pm on weekdays and from 8 am to 2 pm on Saturday, but not at all on Sunday. A taxi to the airport costs about $12.

Bus Nelson Suburban Bus Lines operates local services from its terminal on Lower Bridge St. They run out to Richmond via Tahuna and Stoke, and also to Wakefield. Buses operate during the day until about 5 or 6 pm on weekdays, with one later bus at about 7 pm on Friday nights. On Saturday a couple of buses run in the morning but there are no buses on Sunday.

The Airport Shuttle Service (see To/From the Airport) was set up to provide airport transport, but since it makes continuous return trips from Nelson to Tahuna Beach and on to the airport, many people use it to go just between Nelson and Tahuna. You can catch it from the Nelson Visitor Centre or the Quality Inn.

Bicycle & Motorbike Rental Bicycles can be hired from Stewart Cycles (☎ 548 4344) at 126 Hardy St, by the half-day, day, week or month, or from Greg Fraine Cycles Ltd (☎ 548 3877) at 105 Bridge St.

Mobile Mechanics (☎ 546 8001), out at the Tahunanui Beach car park, hire 50cc motorcycles (no special motorcycle licence needed) by the hour, half-day or full day.

AROUND NELSON
Nelson Lakes National Park

Nelson Lakes National Park is 118 km southwest of Nelson. There's good tramping, walking, lake scenery and also skiing (in winter) at the Rainbow and Mt Robert ski fields. Rainbow in particular is a good ski field for families and beginners. Here you have two beautiful glacial lakes fringed to the water's edge by beech forest and flax. The backdrop to these lakes consists of forested mountains. Information on the park is available at the Park Visitors' Centre (☎ 521 1806) in St Arnaud or at the Lake Rotoroa Ranger Station (☎ 523 9369) near the northern end of Lake Rotoroa.

The park is accessible from two different areas, lakes Rotoiti and Rotoroa. St Arnaud village, at Lake Rotoiti, is the main centre and Rotoroa receives far fewer visitors (mainly trampers and fishing groups). An excellent three-day tramp from St Arnaud takes you south along the eastern shore of Lake Rotoiti to Sabine Hut, across the Travers River and up the Cascade Track to Angelus Hut on beautiful alpine Lake Angelus. The trip back to St Arnaud takes you along Roberts Ridge to the Mt Robert ski field. On a clear day this ridge walk affords magnificent alpine views all along its length. The track descends steeply to the Mt Roberts car park, from where it's a seven-km road walk back to St Arnaud. Other walks at Rotoiti include Peninsula Nature walk (1½ hours), Black Hill track (1½ hours return), Mt Robert Lookout (20 minutes), St Arnaud Range Track (five hours), Loop Track (1½ hours return), Lakehead Track around the Lake (six hours) and Moraine walk (1½ hours).

There are a number of walks around Lake Rotoroa. Two short ones are the Short Loop Track (20 minutes) and the Flower walk (10 minutes). Medium ones include Porika Lookout (two-three hours), Lakeside Track (six hours) and Braeburn walk (two hours). The track along the eastern shore of the lake connects with the Sabine, Blue Lake and Lake Constance area of the walk described under Lake Rotoiti. For more information get a copy of the publication *Lake Rotoroa Nature Walks* – this has condensed much of the information you need to know about New Zealand forests into one tiny, excellent volume.

For information on other walks in Nelson Lakes National Park, ask at the ranger sta-

MARLBOROUGH

tions or refer to *Tramping in New Zealand* by Jim DuFresne (Lonely Planet).

Places to Stay & Eat – Lake Rotoiti The *Yellow House Guesthouse* (☎ 521 1887) in St Arnaud has hostel-style accommodation for $13 to $15 per night. It is only a five-minute walk to Lake Rotoiti, there is a spa pool, laundry facilities, drying room and TV lounge. *Alpine Lodge* (☎ 521 1869), a 10-minute walk from the lake, has 20 rooms for $80/85 for singles/doubles, but also some backpackers accommodation. There are also several camping grounds and lodges within the park itself – contact the Park Visitors' Centre. There's a restaurant at the Alpine Lodge, and a snack bar at the petrol station, which also sells limited supplies of groceries. The *Tophouse* (☎ 521 1848), eight km from St Arnaud, dates from the 1880s when it was a hotel. It is now a farmstay where you can get dinner, bed & breakfast for $45.

Places to Stay & Eat – Lake Rotoroa There are not many accommodation options here. There is a basic DOC camping ground by the lake where the facilities only extend to a toilet and a water point; it costs a mere $2 per person per night. At the *Retreat Camping Ground*, towards Gowan Bridge, campsites are $6 per night. The other two places, *Rotoroa Lodge* and *Braeburn Lodge* are both very expensive. At the Lodge expect to pay (for everything) about $290/480 for a single/double.

Getting There & Away Nelson Lakes Transport buses (☎ 521 1858) go to St Arnaud daily from Nelson. Wadsworths Motors (☎ 522 4248) of Tapawera operate a service between Nelson and St Arnaud on Monday, Wednesday and Friday, leaving St Arnaud at 8 am. In Nelson you get on this service at Beaurepaires car park. These services change all the time so ring and check with the operators. If you wish to get to Lake Rotoroa you will usually have to hitch from Gowan Bridge. Nelson Lakes Transport will pick up but it is expensive unless in a group.

The majority of visitors get here in their own cars.

Water taxis operate on both lakes Rotoiti and Rotoroa; these can be booked on (☎ 521 1894; Lake Rotoiti) or (☎ 521 523 9199; Lake Rotoroa). For the Lake Rotoroa run to the head of the lake from the village expect to pay $15 each if there are three passengers or $20 each if there are two.

Wakefield
South of Nelson, at Pigeon Valley, Wakefield, is the Waimea Steam Museum, with an interesting collection of vintage steam-driven machinery. It's open daily from 9 am to 4.30 pm.

Moutere Eels
On the back road route along Wilson's Rd to Motueka are the tame eels of the Moutere River. They're about 11 km from Upper Moutere village – look out for the signpost. Patient feeding over the years has made them so tame that they'll actually slither out of the water to take bits of meat from your hand. It's an unusual sight! Entry is $2 (children 50c) and feeding times are supposedly 10 am to noon and 1 to 4 pm, but they're fairly flexible. The eels hibernate over winter, from about late May to early August.

Wineries
There are a number of vineyards on the Nelson Wine Trail which you can follow by doing a loop from Nelson through Richmond to Motueka, following the SH 60 coast road in one direction and the inland Moutere River road in the other. Wineries which are open for visitors include Ruby Bay Wines, Neudorf Vineyards, Weingut Seifried, Redwood Cellars, Pelorus Vineyard, Robinson Brothers, Glover's Vineyard and Laska Cellars. Also McCashin's Brewery & Malthouse is nearby if you wish to sample the legendary Black Mac. You can get a Wine Trail map from the information centres in Nelson or Motueka.

Nelson to Golden Bay

MOTUEKA

Motueka (population 6210) is the centre of a tobacco, hops and fruit-growing area. People often come here for the summer-picking work and it's also a popular base for trampers en route to the walks in the Abel Tasman National Park and the Heaphy Track. The inhabitants are very cosmopolitan and include many craftspeople. In summer it's a bustling place, but in winter they say you could shoot a gun down the main street and not hit a thing!

Information

Motueka is essentially one long main street, High St, and just about every business in town is found along it.

At the Motueka Information Centre (☎ 528 7660), 236 High St, you can get information, make bookings and buy tickets for most things happening around town, including tours, kayaks, launches, transport and so on. It's open from 9 am to 5 pm every day, except during the Christmas holidays when it's open from 8.30 am to 7 pm on weekdays and 9 am to 7 pm weekends. There's an AA agent at 115 High St.

The DOC office (☎ 528 9117) is on the corner of High and King Edward Sts, and is open from 8 am to 4.30 pm on weekdays, and on weekends during the Christmas holidays. The office is an excellent source of information and maps on the Abel Tasman National Park and the North-West Nelson State Forest Park, which contains the Heaphy and Wangapeka tracks.

Facilities Use Passes for the Abel Tasman Track can be bought in Motueka at either the information centre or the DOC. Check with the DOC for tidal information.

Tramping

There are many tramping possibilities out of Motueka, especially in the North-West Nelson Forest Park. In particular the areas outlined in the DOC pamphlets, *Cobb Valley*

and *Mt Arthur Tablelands Walks*, offer plenty of scope.

Cobb Valley is 28 km from the Upper Takaka turn-off. You first drive up to the power station and from here it is another 13 km drive to the valley. Once in the valley there are a number of walks to choose from. These range from the 45-minute Mytton's Forest walk to others of a few hours' duration, eg Cobb Ridge to Peat Flat and Trilobite Hut to Chaffey Hut. Chaffey Hut, built in 1954, is constructed of split beech slabs.

To get to the Mt Arthur Tablelands you drive from Motueka south to Pokororo. From here take the Graham Rd into the Flora car park. From here there are a great number of walking possibilities. Walks include Mt Arthur Hut (three km, one hour), Mt Arthur (eight km, three hours), Mt Lodestone (five km, two hours) and Flora Hut (two km, half an hour). There are also a number of longer tramps from Flora car park, outlined in the pamphlet mentioned earlier. It is interesting to think that this tableland once lay under the sea and as a result still wears its mantle of limestone in places.

Tourist Transport (☎ 545 1055) in Nelson specialise in providing transport to and from walking tracks in the North-West Nelson Forest Park. The cost of a ride to the Cobb Valley is $30 and to the Mt Arthur Tablelands $20.

Things to See & Do

The interesting little Motueka District Museum is at 140 High St, in the same building as No 236/Annabelle's. It's open weekdays; admission is $1 (children 50c).

The Motueka Recreation Centre (☎ 528 8560) on Old Wharf Rd has lots going on including skating, a gym, aerobics, sports, and summer minibus tours.

Pretty's Tours (☎ 528 9480) offer a horticulture tour around Motueka. They operate from the Old Cederman House in Riwaka but can pick you up in Motueka. The tour costs $18 (children $10, discounts for families) and they also have a wine tour for $22.50.

The information centre has a *Motueka Valley Craft Trail* pamphlet with a map and

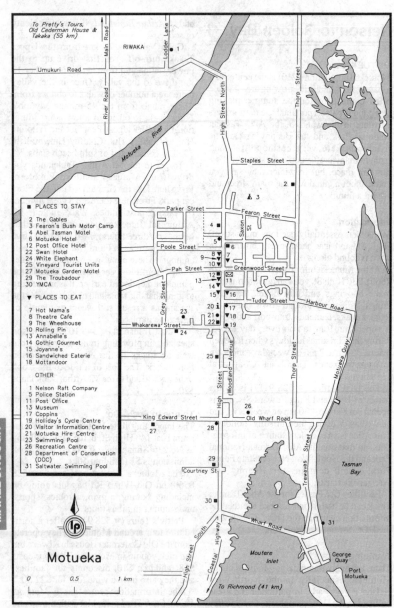

■ PLACES TO STAY

2   The Gables
3   Fearon's Bush Motor Camp
4   Abel Tasman Motel
6   Motueka Hotel
21 Post Office Hotel
22 Swan Hotel
24 White Elephant
25 Vineyard Tourist Units
27 Motueka Garden Motel
29 The Troubadour
30 YMCA

▼ PLACES TO EAT

7   Hot Mama's
8   Theatre Cafe
9   The Wheelhouse
10 Rolling Pin
13 Annabelle's
14 Gothic Gourmet
15 Joyanne's
16 Sandwiched Eaterie
18 Mottandoor

    OTHER

1   Nelson Raft Company
5   Police Station
11 Post Office
13 Museum
17 Coppins
19 Holliday's Cycle Centre
20 Visitor Information Centre
21 Motueka Hire Centre
23 Swimming Pool
26 Recreation Centre
28 Department of Conservation
    (DOC)
31 Saltwater Swimming Pool

Motueka

details on where to visit many artists and craftspeople in the area, and also a *Wine Trail* map.

There are good beaches near Motueka at Kaiteriteri, Marahau, and the dress optional Mapua Leisure Park. The best beach in the area is Kaiteriteri, north of Motueka on the road in to Abel Tasman National Park. At Ruby Bay, south of Motueka, a rock concert is held in March each year. The beaches along the Abel Tasman National Park coast can be easily reached on day launch trips; see the Abel Tasman National Park section in this chapter.

Rafting, Kayaks & Cruises

The Nelson Raft Company (☎ 528 6363) is based in Motueka and does white water rafting trips on the Buller and Gowan rivers. There's a half-day trip for $55 or an all-day trip for $90. There's also an easier 1½ hour trip on the Motueka River that's good for families, costing $28 (children $18).

You can hire sea kayaks from a number of places in the area. In the Motueka region, the Ocean River Adventure Company (☎ 527 8266) on Main Rd, Marahau Beach, rents sea kayaks for $80 per person for two days (two-day and two-person minimum). They also have one, two, three and six-day trips which vary in price from $75 to $1150 per person, depending on duration. Another operator out of Marahau is Abel Tasman Kayaks (☎ 527 8022), whose prices are similar to Ocean River Adventure Company. Both companies have a good selection of kayaks such as Southern Light (double), and single seater Puffin, Puysegur, Nordkapp and Arctic Raider sea kayaks. See Sea Kayaking in Abel Tasman National Park.

Launch trips off the Abel Tasman National Park coast are popular and good value; see the Abel Tasman National Park entry in this section for details.

Camping Gear

The Motueka Hire Centre (☎ 528 7296), beside the Shell service station at 255 High St, hires tents and backpacks for use on the Abel Tasman Track. Sleeping bags and cooking gear can be hired from the White Elephant hostel.

Places to Stay

Camping & Cabins The *Vineyard Tourist Units* (☎ 528 8550) are at 328 High St, near the centre of town. There's a variety of cabins and flats which are simple but good value, each with its own kitchen. Small cabins sleep up to four people for $31 to $36 for two; tourist units with private toilet facilities cost $41 to $48 for two.

Campsites include *Fearon's Bush Motor Camp* (☎ 528 7189) at the northern end of town, where tent and powered sites cost $9.50/16 for one/two people and cabins are $26 for two. The *Motueka Beach Reserve Camp* (☎ 528 7169) at Port Motueka has campsites at $9/14 for one/two people.

The *Peninsula Lodge* (☎ 526 8740) is a pleasant lodge on the bank of the Motueka River at Ngatimoti, 19 km from Motueka in the Motueka Valley. There's trout fishing, tramping, rafting and swimming. The cost is $35 per night for two people.

The *Mapua Leisure Park* (☎ 549 2666) at 33 Toru St, Mapua, 21 km south of Motueka, is 'New Zealand's first clothes-optional leisure park'! They have a private beach, nine-hole golf course, tennis and volleyball courts, swimming pool, sauna and spa, and a children's playground. Camping costs $9 per person for tent and $10 for powered sites and there are cabins for $14.50/29 for one/two people, on-site caravans and chalets at $42 for two, or more expensive tourist flats at $57 for two, with off-season reductions. Many people come over here just for the day, to enjoy the lovely beach.

The *McKee Memorial Reserve*, two km north of the leisure park and 19 km from town, is a very basic camping ground right on the water's edge. Water, toilets and barbecue pits are the only amenities, but rates are cheap at $5 per campsite.

Hostels A good backpackers, the *White Elephant* (☎ 528 6208) is at 55 Whakarewa St. It has room for 20 people in a big, comfortable old house set on almost one hectare of

MARLBOROUGH

land. It costs $14 in dorm rooms and $16 per person in double rooms, including linen. Bicycles and camping gear can be hired here for a minimal cost. The staff are friendly and informative.

At 16 Thorp St you can stay in Motueka's oldest colonial homestead, *The Gables* (☎ 528 6300). From the information centre cross the road, turn right into Tudor St and then left into Thorp. They boast all facilities including spa and BBQ. Private or shared rooms are advertised at $15 per person.

The *YMCA* (☎ 528 8652) has a hostel at 500 High St, on the Nelson side of town. Nightly costs in this pleasant and modern hostel are $12 to $13 per night plus a $5 key deposit, mostly in twin rooms. They also have tent sites at $7/12 for one/two people and if you don't have your own tent you can hire one for $1 per day. Bicycle hire costs $2 per day.

The *Riverside Community* (☎ 526 7805), seven km out of Motueka on the Moutere Highway, is a well-organised community that's been going since 1941 (it was set up by pacifists during WW II). Anyone can stay here for $11 a day, or $7 per person if you pitch your own tent, and the cost includes fresh milk and apples in season. Community meals are held several times weekly and they welcome visitors' involvement in the community. There's no difficulty in finding it – all the locals know it and there's a sign on the road.

Guesthouses *The Troubadour* (☎ 528 7318), formerly White's Guesthouse at 430 High St, is a friendly B&B in what used to be a nunnery! All rooms have a washbasin and there's a lounge with pleasant views. The cost is $45/67.50 per night for singles/doubles, with a substantial continental breakfast. You can get dinner here for under $20, with vegetables fresh from their organic garden.

Homestays Out at Thorpe, accessible from Motueka (30 km away), Richmond or Mapua, you can stay at a rural retreat, *Mountain Cottage* (☎ 543 3825; fax 543 3640), on

the Dovedale-Woodstock Rd. The 70-year-old cottage prices are $60 per weekend and $180 per week ($210 December-January); there is a maximum of three people. Dinners with the hosts are $15 per person. Nearby is *Doone Cottage* (☎ 526 8740), Woodstock, which has double/twin rooms with private bathrooms. It is close to some great fishing spots. On the way up Takaka Hill, 17 km north-west of Motueka, is a comfortable homestay, *Kairuru* (☎ 528 8091), where it is $60 for two, or $70 if you want breakfast. Their cottages sleep four so a group is charged $20 each for their use.

Holton House (☎ 554 2269) is situated in a historic home on eight hectares at Ruby Bay, just before Mapua. It costs $80 for two persons in doubles/twins and $60 for a single; dinner is $25 per person and special diets are catered for.

Hotels & Motels The *Post Office Hotel* (☎ 528 9890) in the centre of town has single/double rooms at $35/45. Other alternatives include the *Abel Tasman Motel* (☎ 528 7699) at 45 High St with double rooms at $63, and the *Motueka Garden Motel* (☎ 528 9299) at 71 King Edward St, near the clocktower, where rooms cost $62 to $70 for two.

Places to Eat
Snacks & Fast Food There's the usual string of takeaways and sandwich bars along Motueka's endless main street, including *The Wheelhouse*, oppsite the CPO, a three-part operation with takeaways at one end, fish & chips at the other, and an eat-in space in the middle. They have Chinese food as well as burgers and they're open until at least 8.30 pm every day; on Friday and Saturday they're open until midnight. For sandwiches and snacks try the *Rolling Pin* at 105 High St or the fancier *Sandwiched Eaterie* at 219 High St. *Joyannes*, also on High St (at No 180), has been recommended by locals.

Pub Food Opposite the CPO, next to the Wheelhouse, is the *Post Office Hotel*, serving lunch and dinner every day except Sunday. There's the regular pub menu with lunches for around $7.50 and dinners from $10 up to $16.50 for a big steak. The other two hotels – the *Motueka* and the *Swan* – also have pub food but the Post Office Hotel is the most serious about it, with a large dining area.

Restaurants Motueka's most interesting food question, however, is how did a little Kiwi country town end up with not one but five such interesting restaurants?

Smallest of all is the *Theatre Cafe* on High St, with some of the best pizza in New Zealand. The owner, Richard, has travelled in many countries and hundreds of photos and mementos of his travels that decorate the little place. It's open every day from 5 pm, with medium pizzas from $10 to $15 and large ones from $14 to $20.

Equally unusual is the *Gothic Gourmet* in the town centre. You can't miss the place; it's in what was formerly a Gothic-style Methodist church, now painted shocking pink with purple trim from steps to steeple! Walk in the side door and you enter the bar. The dining room is in the old sanctuary with its towering ceiling, and there's also a garden courtyard out the back. Decor aside, the gourmet-style meat and vegetarian dishes would be notable anywhere. Lunches are served daily and prices range from $8 to $11; dinners are served from Tuesday to Sunday, with main courses from $10 to $15; and there's a bar menu with selections from $4 to $10. The Sunday smorgasbord for $17.50 is good value.

At the southern end of the shopping area, at 265 High St, is *Mottandoor*, where the menu features a diverse array of Asian dishes. You can try a Burmese or Malay curry, an Indonesian satay, a Korean fried rice, or Indian dishes prepared in the tandoor oven. Starters cost $4 to $8, main courses $16 to $20, and desserts (also from all over Asia) $7. It's open from 6 pm every night (licensed or BYO) and has takeaways too.

Annabelle's, in the museum building in the centre of town, is both a cafe and an art gallery, with dining inside or out on the covered patio. They have particularly good salads, desserts and coffee – you can get a whole pot for $4.40 – and other tasty selections for lunch ($5 to $8) and the evening meal (main courses $12.50 to $16), with plenty for both meat-eaters and vegetarians. It is a favoured brunch place.

Finally, *Hot Mama's*, also on High St, keeps the best hours; when the others are closed queues of visitors and locals form. Here you can get spicy beef tacos for $5, hot chilli bean baked potato for $4.50 and follow it down with Pink Elephant beer or wine by the glass at $2.50.

Getting There & Away
Air Air New Zealand Link (incorporating Air Nelson; ☎ 528 6766) has direct flights to Nelson, Takaka and Wellington, with connections to other centres.

Bus Golden Bay Connections (☎ 528 7280), next to the information centre at 238 High St, operates buses from Nelson through Motueka to Takaka. The Collingwood buses go straight through to Collingwood; as this is operated in conjunction with Mt Cook Landline you can connect with services to many other parts of the South Island.

Skyline Connections (☎ 528 8850), on Wallace St, has daily buses to Nelson, Takaka, Totaranui, Kaiteriteri and Marahau, but only in summer. Also during the summer, Abel Tasman National Park Enterprises (☎ 528 7801) has buses linking Motueka with Nelson and Kaiteriteri, connecting in Kaiteriteri with their launch going up and down the coast following the Abel Tasman Track – but with this company you *must* book ahead.

Motueka Taxis (☎ 528 7900) at 108 High St, provide cheap transport all year round to the Abel Tasman track on their weekday mail run to Marahau. See the Abel Tasman National Park entry in this section for more information on transport to and from the track.

Getting Around
Holliday's Cycle Centre at 227 High St hires mountain bicycles. The White Elephant and

MARLBOROUGH

YMCA hostels also hire bicycles. This area is ideal to explore on bike, especially if you are going to the wineries or craft places. Think twice, however, about cycling up Takaka Hill to get the views.

MOTUEKA TO TAKAKA

From Motueka, SH 60 continues on over Takaka Hill to Takaka and Collingwood. Before ascending Takaka Hill you pass a turn-off on your right to Kaiteriteri and the southern end of Abel Tasman National Park, then a turn-off on your left to Riwaka Valley, a good area for picnicking, swimming in river pools, and walks. You can walk to the spring that is the source of the Riwaka River.

Takaka Hill, 791 metres high, separates Tasman Bay from Golden Bay. Near the summit are the Ngarua Caves (☎ 528 8093) where you can see moa bones. The caves are open from 10 am to 4 pm daily except Friday but are closed from mid-June to August. **Takaka Hill** is also known as Marble Mountain due to the large amounts of marble buried beneath the limestone that forms the hill's surface.

Also in the area is the biggest tomo (entrance or cave) in the southern hemisphere, **Harwood's Hole**. It is 400 metres deep and 70 metres wide. It will take you a full half day to get there from Motueka, as it is a half-hour walk one way from the carpark at the end of Canaan Rd, off SH 60. Exercise caution as you approach the lip of the hole; a rope is essential – accidents have occurred here.

As you cross the crest of the hill there are fine views from Harwood Lookout down the Takaka River Valley to Takaka and Golden Bay. There's an interesting explanation of the geography and geology of the area at the lookout. The view extends from the Northwest Nelson peneplain to the Anatoki Ranges. A peneplain, you ask? It is an area worn almost flat by erosion.

From the lookout you wind down through the beautiful Takaka Hill Scenic Reserve to the river valley, through Upper Takaka and on to Takaka itself.

Kaiteriteri Beach

This is one of the most popular beaches in the area, and it is just 13 km from Motueka on a sealed road. This beach has genuine golden sand. All water sports are available here as well as a great kids' playground complete with mini golf! Behind the camping ground you can try Withells Walk, a 45-minute excursion into native bush from where there are great views out across the bay. Or walk to Kaka Pah Point at the end of the beach and find some of the secluded little coves and hideaways.

Places to Stay & Eat Summer brings many holiday-makers to Kaiteriteri, mainly locals. Despite its popularity there are not a great number of accommodation options here.

The *Kimi Ora Holiday & Health Resort* (☎ 527 8027), Martin Farm Rd, has a number of choices. The time of year affects pricing markedly with about a 10% add-on for Christmas holidays. Twin/double rooms range from $55 to $69, four-bed units are from $55 to $89, and the four-bedroom house from $100 to $120. The *Kaiteriteri Motor Camp* (☎ 527 8010), adjacent to the beach, has facilities for over 450 caravans. There are, however, 12 cabins that cost from $22 and $30 for two persons, and 12 on-site caravans which cost $26.

Apart from the *Vegetarian Restaurant* at Kimi Ora there are not many dining choices here. Experiment with an eggplant, some kiwi fruit and seafood purchased in Motueka.

Getting There & Away If you have sufficient numbers to make the hire of a water taxi economical you could try the Water-Taxi Charter (☎ 528 7497) at Kaiteriteri Beach. They can drop off at various parts of the national park or even provide transport for diving trips.

ABEL TASMAN NATIONAL PARK

The coastal Abel Tasman National Park is a popular tramping area and the various walks include one around the coast – but beware of the sandflies! The park is at the northern end of a range of marble and limestone hills extending up from North-West Nelson State Forest Park, and the interior is honeycombed with caves and potholes. There are other tracks in the park, including an inland track, but the coastal track is the popular one. See Tramping in the Outdoor Activities chapter for more information.

Sea Kayaking

Some people prefer to follow the track around the coast by sea kayak. A traveller from Denmark, Steen Rasmussen, wrote to say:

I did the Abel Tasman National Park kayaking instead of walking, and can definitely recommend it. No overfilled tracks or huts, and you're alone with nature all the time. There're plenty of secluded beaches where trampers can't get access. No tiring hills, and possibility of bringing all you want. The beauty and the silence of the sea beats everything, and the seals playing below and around your boat are just amazing.

Kayak hire costs about $40 per day for a single and a double, including all gear. There are also guided sea kayaking trips at about $65 for a full day, including lunch. Two kayak operators are Ocean River Adventure (☎ 528 8823) and Abel Tasman Kayaks (☎ 527 8022).

Seal Swimming

Abel Tasman Seal Swim (☎ 527 8136) organise swimming trips with seals off Tonga Island; they have the DOC licence for this activity. They supply snorkel, mask, flippers and a snack for $65. If you prefer to just watch as the swimmers frolic with the seals it only costs $50.

Tours

Abel Tasman National Park Enterprises (☎ 87 801) has 6½-hour launch services departing from Kaiteriteri at 9 am, dropping off trampers in Totaranui (the northern end of the track) at 12.15 pm and picking up returning trampers, and arriving back at Kaiteriteri at about 3.30 or 4 pm.

The launch service doubles as trampers' transport and also a pleasant day cruise.

Along the way it stops at Tonga Bay, Bark Bay, Torrent Bay and Tinline Bay. You can easily combine a walk along part of the Abel Tasman track with the cruise, being dropped off at one bay and picked up later at another. There are several such options, the most popular being to disembark at Bark Bay, walk the track 2½ hours to Torrent Bay, have time on the beach for swimming, and be picked up there. The cost for either the full day cruise or a walk/cruise option is $33 (children $16.50).

The launch service operates on a scheduled route from 1 October to 31 May each year, but will go at any time of the year if it has enough bookings. From 26 December to 15 January there's also an evening cruise for $25 (children $12.50) and you can go in the morning, returning in the evening, to spend more time in the park.

All launch trips must be booked in advance, either directly with Abel Tasman National Park Enterprises or at the information centres in Nelson or Motueka. The same company operates a bus service from Nelson and Motueka which connects with the launch, making it an easy day trip from either town.

An alternative discussed earlier is Catalina Cruises which leave from Nelson and drop you right at the start of the track – see Getting There & Away for Nelson.

Places to Stay & Eat

At Awaroa Bay you can stay at the *Awaroa Lodge & Cafe* (☎ (025) 433 135) which is only 300 metres from the water. At this place, 200 metres off the track, share/twin accommodation is $15 per person per night and singles and twin/doubles are $30 and $45 respectively. Their cafe offers a range of health food, and the proprietors will also pack lunches. Stay a while to look at the birds – white faced herons, pied stilts, Caspian terns, tuis, bellbirds and moreporks are all found here. A great place to warm up your bird-watching skills before going to Farewell Spit. You have three ways of getting to Awaroa Lodge: by water taxi, walk part of

Sea Kayaking in Abel Tasman National Park

A lot of people choose to sea kayak around the relatively safe and definitely very scenic waters of Abel Tasman National Park. A popular starting point is Marahau at the southern end of the Abel Tasman Track. The peak season is from November to Easter but you can paddle all year round. Winter is a really good time as you will see more birdlife. Instruction is given to first timers. For those going on a day trip enough is provided, ie basic strokes, so you will manage a day's paddling. If renting, you will be given a couple of hour's briefing on tides, weather and basic strokes.

Firstly, a day trip. Typically from Marahau you are on the water by 9.30 am (depending on the tides). You can hope to get to Fisherman and Adele islands in about one hour of paddling. On the way you will see lagoons, an important part of the food chain, and several species of wading birds. If you are lucky when you head into the open sea you will spot Cook Strait penguins, black shags, Australasian gannets, black-backed gulls, crested and white-fronted terns, and sometimes black-fronted and Caspian terns. Often lunch is caught – mussels, pipis and scallops and complemented with pitta bread, salad, kebabs, orange juice, tea, coffee, and cake from the Park Cafe.

Longer trips, operated by the two main companies at Marahau, are typically two nights and three days; the cost is around $250. It may be a base camp trip returning to the same camp each night, say North Head or Bark Bay. From the base you will paddle out to Tonga to see fur seals, and tide permitting, into the lagoons. It would not be unusual to see a dolphin. The other type of trip would cover a set distance, eg Marahau to Onetahuti Beach, with two overnight stops at Te Puketea Bay/Anchorage and then Mosquito Bay/Tonga Quarry. Return is by water taxi to Marahau. Again, the paddlers see Tonga Island and fern-lined lagoons.

Save your feet for the bigger walks down south and paddle Abel Tasman National Park. ∎

the Abel Tasman Track from Totaranui, or drive to Awaroa car park then walk.

The *Marahau Beach Camp* (☎ 527 8176) at Marahau, 18 km north of Motueka, has tent and caravan sites for $9/14 for one/two people; cabins cost $25 for two and a self-contained flat is $35 for two.

There is also *The Barn* hostel and camping ground (☎ 527 8043) on Harvey Rd, Marahau, at the entrance to Abel Tasman National Park, where beds are $14. The hostel has 14 beds and there are 15 campsites at $8. They offer a range of supplies and activities including sea kayaking and horse-trekking. The bus service from Nelson drops you off at The Barn. There have been many readers' recommendations for this place. Nearby is the *Park Cafe* which has good food and a great atmosphere; gorge on cakes, muffins and blueberry milkshakes before heading out on the track.

There's a *DOC campsite* at Totaranui, Totaranui Rd, Abel Tasman National Park.

Getting There & Away

Abel Tasman National Park Enterprises (☎ 528 7801) operates buses from Motueka and Nelson to Kaiteriteri, from where its launch departs. You can take either the bus or the launch separately, but you must book this bus, as well as the launch, in advance. They depart from Nelson daily at 7.25 am and arrive at Totaranui at 11.10 am and at Marahau 9.30 am.

There's also land transport to either end of the track. Skyline Connections (☎ 548 0285 or 528 8850) operates buses between Nelson, Motueka, Kaiteriteri and Marahau from 19 October until 12 April. For the rest of the year there are also services to and from Takaka and Totaranui. Motueka Taxis (☎ 528 7900) have an inexpensive service to Marahau on their weekday mail run from Motueka, all year round.

Golden Bay Connection (☎ 524 8188) have services to and from the Totaranui end of the track, which run on demand and can be timed to connect with bus services to Nelson, Motueka, Takaka and Collingwood. You can phone and ask them to collect you from Totaranui (it is a free call).

TAKAKA

The small centre of Takaka (population

1215) is the last town of any size as you head towards the north-west corner of the South Island. It's the main centre for the beautiful Golden Bay area. It's also quite a hip little community – lots of '60s and artistic types have settled there. Pohara Beach is a popular summer resort near the town.

Orientation
Just about everything in Takaka is found along Commercial St, which is the main road through town, only a few blocks long.

Information
On the Motueka side of town there's a very helpful information centre (☎ 525 9136) open from 9 am to 5 pm in summer and 10 am to 4 pm in winter, seven days a week. Pick up a copy of their promotional booklet ($2) which has interesting articles about the many points of interest around Golden Bay.

There's a DOC office (☎ 525 8026) with information on the Abel Tasman, Heaphy and Kaituna tracks, Farewell Spit, Cobb Valley, the Aorere Goldfields and the Pupu Springs Scenic Reserve. It's open from 8.30 am to noon and 1 to 4 pm, Monday to Friday.

Facilities Use Passes for the Abel Tasman track are available in Takaka from the DOC office, the information centre, the Shady Rest Hostel, the Pohara Beach Camp and the bus depots. There's an AA agent in the centre of town.

Things to See
Takaka has a small museum, open daily (entry $1, children 50c). The Village Theatre brings in top quality popular and international films, with several different films showing each week. The Whole Meal Trading Company sometimes has live music. The Begonia House is open in summer to show off its colourful flowers.

Windsurfing is a popular activity on Golden Bay – all the local beaches are excellent – and windsurfers are available at the Shady Rest Hostel and the Pohara Beach Camp. There are tame eels in the Anatoki River, six km south of Takaka.

Arts & Crafts
Many artists and craftspeople are based in the Golden Bay area, including painters, potters, blacksmiths, screen printers, silversmiths and knitwear designers. Right in town, a cooperative of the Golden Bay craftspeople has established the large Artisans' Shop to display their wares. Many other artists and craftspeople are tucked away all around the bay. The *Golden Bay Craft Trail* leaflet gives directions to the galleries and workshops. The Whole Meal Trading Company also has art on display.

Rawhiti Caves
The Rawhiti Caves near Takaka are among the largest in New Zealand, well worth a look. A three-hour return guided tour of the caves costs $10 (children $4). To reach the caves you walk through stands of 400-year-old totara. It's an enjoyable and popular tour that's good value. Phone 525 9061 for bookings.

Pupu Springs
Pupu Springs (the full Maori name is Waikoropupu, but everyone calls it simply Pupu) are the largest freshwater springs in New Zealand and among the largest in the world. Many springs are dotted around the Pupu Springs Scenic Reserve, including one with 'dancing boulders' thrown upwards by the great volume of incredibly clear water emerging from the ground.

Walkways through the reserve take you to the various springs, passing by gold-mining works from last century – gold was discovered in Golden Bay in 1865, four years after the first NZ discovery in the Coromandel. The DOC produces an excellent leaflet about the reserve. To reach Pupu from Takaka, go four km north-west on SH 60, turn inland at Waitapu Bridge and continue another three km.

Places to Stay
Camping & Cabins The *Pohara Beach Camp* (☎ 525 9500) is 10 km from Takaka, right on the beach. Campsites are $13.50 for two ($1 more with power), and there are

cabins at $24 and $34 per night for two. On Tukurua Beach, 18 km north of Takaka and eight km south of Collingwood, the *Golden Bay Holiday Park* (☎ 525 9742) has campsites at $8/15 for single/doubles ($1 more with power) plus cabins at $26 for two people. Minimum unit rates apply during holidays.

The *Totaranui Beach Camp* (☎ 525 8026) at Totaranui, 33 km from Takaka in the Abel Tasman National Park, is administered by DOC, with campsites at $6.50 per person. Sites for the Christmas holidays can be reserved from July onwards.

There are far too many B&B places in this region to mention them all. They are listed in the pamphlet *Bed & Breakfast: Golden Bay Directory* available free from Visitor Information centres.

Hostels
The *Takaka Summer YHA Hostel* (☎ 525 8463) is in the Golden Bay High School on Meihana St. It's only open over the Christmas holiday period and costs $12 a night.

The *Shady Rest Hostel* is a hospitable and relaxed hostel in a big historic home on the main road (141 Commercial St), 400 metres from the town centre on the Collingwood side. Dorm rooms cost $14 per night, and there are twins/doubles listed at $17.50 per person, although you may get them for less. The hostel has windsurfers for hire, and you can spend some time feeding the tame eels, pukekos and ducks in the creek behind the house.

About 15 km west of Takaka you will find the *Shambhala Farm Hostel* (☎ 525 8463), on the beach at Onekaka. You just get off the Golden Bay Connection bus at the Mussel Inn at Onekaka or if driving take the right turn 50 metres before the Inn (coming from Takaka). It is only $13 per night and in this area there is snorkelling, windsurfing, swimming, boating, and party nights at the Mussell Inn.

Hotels & Motels
The *Junction Hotel* (☎ 525 9207) and *Telegraph Hotel* (☎ 525 9308) are both on the main road in Takaka and both

have rooms for around $34/50 for singles/doubles.

There are a number of motels in or around Takaka, particularly at Pohara Beach, all charging around $60 to $70 for two people. The *Golden Bay Motel* (☎ 525 9428) is on the main road in Takaka, and there's the *Tata Beach Motel* (☎ 525 9712) on Tata Beach. At Pohara the *Pohara Beachfront Motel* (☎ 525 9660) has units at $55 to $65 for two. Also on Pohara Beach, and slightly cheaper at $48 for two, is the *Sunflower Motel* (☎ 525 9075).

Places to Eat
Double back to Motueka (see Places to Eat in Motueka)! The *Whole Meal Trading Company* in the town centre is a local institution, an enjoyable wholefoods cafe, restaurant and art gallery which also sells bulk natural foods, has a community bulletin board, and sometimes has live music in the evenings.

Milliways further down the main road is another good spot with a relaxed atmosphere; it is licensed and open seven days. The *Takaka Restaurant & Tearooms* has an inexpensive Chinese takeaway to one side. The *Junction* and *Telegraph* hotels both have pubs with bistro meals.

Getting There & Away
Air Air New Zealand Link (incorporating Air Nelson) has direct flights to Motueka, with connecting flights to Wellington and Auckland; inquire at the information centre for latest schedules.

Bus The Golden Bay Connections bus service (☎ 525 9443) from Nelson through Motueka and Takaka terminates at Collingwood. See the Abel Tasman National Park entry in this section for details on bus services to and from the Abel Tasman Track, eg Skyline Connection and Abel Tasman National Park Enterprises.

COLLINGWOOD
The tiny township of Collingwood (population 220) is almost at the end of the line,

which is one of its main attractions. For most it's simply the jumping-off point for the Heaphy Track. From here you can head south-west to more caves and the Heaphy Track in the North-West Nelson State Forest Park, or north-east to the natural wonderland of Farewell Spit.

Farewell Spit

Farewell Spit is a wetland of international importance and a world-renowned bird sanctuary. It is the summer home to thousands of migratory waders from the Arctic tundra. The beach run is 26 km – here there are huge crescent-shaped sand dunes where you get panoramic views of the Spit, Golden Bay, and at low tide, the vast salt marsh is uncovered. This marsh is the feeding ground for huge flocks of waders. At low tide the swans feed on the eel grass, so-called because it wriggles when the water covers it at high tide.

At the car park before the closed section of road there are sperm whale bones from the largest-ever whale which beached here. You can look out over the eel grass flats and see many waders and seabirds such as pied and variable oystercatchers, turnstones, Caspian terns, eastern bar-tailed godwits, black and white-fronted terns, and big black shags.

From here the crossing to the north side of the Spit is made. The truck grinds up over the beach to about a km from Cape Farewell. Down towards the start of the sand are a number of fossilised shellfish. From this point it is 27 km to the end of the sandy spit. Again many species of birds are seen along the way and, often, a stranded pilot whale carcass. The normal trip ends at the old lighthouse compound. The metal lighthouse (it was once constructed of Australian hardwood) has an eight-sided light which flashes every 15 seconds. It is nearly100 years old.

Further east, up on the blown shell banks which comprise the far extremity of the Spit are colonies of Caspian terns and Australasian gannets. If you wish to get closer to the gannet colony, you can go with Collingwood Safari Tours.

At Puponga, near the southern base of the Spit (at the end of the public road) there is a visitors' centre. There is information available, as well as refreshments, and powerful binoculars are set up to view the wetlands and the many wading species.

Farewell Spit & Other Nature Tours

There are two options for visiting the remarkable Farewell Spit region – both guided tours. This is the only way you can visit the Spit, as it's a protected wildlife sanctuary and only licensed tour operators have permission to go onto it.

The original company which pioneered travel up the sandy beach to the lighthouse was Collingwood Safari Tours (☎ 524 8257) which commenced operations in 1948. Their five-hour Farewell Spit Safari Tours cost $42 (children $20), and you go up the beach in their 4WD vehicle. Tours leave daily on demand, timed to the tides. Collingwood Bus Services (☎ 524 8188) also conduct a tour to the lighthouse under the name Farewell Spit Nature Tours; it costs $48 and lunch is included.

If you want to visit the gannet colony, Collingwood Safari Tours are licensed by DOC to conduct two trips for 10 persons weekly. The trip involves a km walk from the lighthouse to the colony, where various features are pointed out. The guide knows his birds and the commentary is good. The 5½-hour tour costs $50. They are also operating a wader-watch tour on the inside of the sandy spit (the estuarine side). They travel about a third of the way along the inside beach three to four times per week; again it is a five-hour tour which is limited to 10 people. This is a must for twitchy birdwatchers.

Collingwood Safari Tours also does 2½ to three-hour trips to the Rebecca and Te Anaroa Caves for $11 (children $7).

In addition to their Farewell Spit tour, Collingwood Bus Service also does a couple of other good tours. The Scenic Mail Run tour visits isolated farming settlements and communities around Cape Farewell and the west coast. The driver points out many points of historical and contemporary interest along the way. The tour lasts five hours, departing

MARLBOROUGH

from the Collingwood CPO at 9.30 am Monday to Friday, and the cost of $25 ($15 for children under 12) includes a picnic lunch on a 1000-hectare farm.

Whararlki Beach

This beach is 29 km to the north of Collingwood and involves a 20-minute walk to the beach from the car park. It is a wild introduction to the West Coast with unusual dune formations, two looming, rock islets just out from shore, and a seal colony at its eastern end. A special place to get away entirely from the rat race of Collingwood.

Kaltuna Track

This track is situated west of Collingwood and the user is provided with two choices: a return walk of two to three hours through the old gold workings and bush scenery, and a longer track (five to seven hours, 12 km) which takes you to the West Coast at Whanganui Inlet.

The NZ Forest Service pamphlet *Kaituna Track* is most informative, outlining in detail flora & fauna to be seen along the way. Included is the nikau palm, the world's most southerly occurring and the crown fern.

Aorere Adventure Tramps & Walks (☎ 524 8040) run by the people from the Inn-let Accommodation House guide a one-day walk through the beautiful Wakamarama Range for $55.

Aorere Goldfields

The Aorere Goldfield was the first major goldfield in New Zealand. In February 1857, five ounces (142 grams) of Collingwood gold were auctioned in Nelson, precipitating a gold rush which lasted three years, although various companies continued to wrest gold from the soil by sluicing and stamping batteries right up until WW I. The old goldfields are now overgrown but the more durable features such as terraces, water races and mine shafts can still be seen.

The DOC office in Takaka has an excellent eight-page pamphlet, *Aorere Goldfields/ Caves Walk*, detailing the history of the gold-

fields and guiding you on a historical walk, with directions beginning from Collingwood. The walk takes most of a day to complete.

You can learn more about the local history at the small museum in town. Again, Aorere Adventure Tramps & Walks guide a one-day walk in the area for $55. With some luck you may even see the furtive fernbird.

Places to Stay

Camping & Cabins The *Collingwood Motor Camp* (☎ 524 8149), William St, near the centre of the tiny township has sites for $12 for two ($14 with power). Cabins cost $24 for two and tourist flats cost $30 and $40 for two. The *Pakawau Beach Motor Camp* (☎ 524 8327) is 13 km north of Collingwood, which means it's even closer to the end of the road. Campsites cost $6.75 per person ($7.75 with power), and there are also self-contained cottages at $30 and $35 for two.

Chalets & Motels The *Collingwood Vacations Chalets* (☎ 524 8221) in Tasman St have self-contained units at $40 for two. The *Collingwood Motel* (☎ 524 8224) in Haven Rd has units at $60 for two. In Tasman St, there are the *Beachcomber Chalets* (☎ 524 8499) where units are $45 for two persons.

There is a really friendly 'organic' accommodation house, *The Inn-let* (☎ 524 8040), on the way to Pakawau and about five km from Collingwood. It is the sort of place where you stay for a while, to relax by the Opua River which flows through the property, or to take walks along Golden Bay's beaches.

Jonathan and Katie are really attuned to their environment and are full of details about the surrounding area. Jonathan has plans for extending, but in time – crass commercialism before peace of mind, no way! Really comfortable beds in renovated rooms are from $15 upwards; make sure that you phone in advance. The owners pick up from Collingwood and also arrange excursions (with a difference) to nearby attractions. Incidentally, Opua means 'terrace', so sit on theirs above the river of that name, have a BBQ and relax in native bush surroundings.

Places to Eat

If you're not fixing your own food there's a pub opposite the CPO, or the *Collingwood Cafe*, a dairy and cafe that's open from 7.30 am to 8 or 9 pm every day.

Only halfway between Takaka (15 km) and Collingwood there is a new (modelled on a turn-of-the-century) alehouse, *The Mussell Inn*. Good meals are available eg pan-fried fish and salad or steak with mushroom sauce for $10. Although they only serve local boutique beers it seems a huge selection. The walls are adorned with local pottery.

Getting There & Away

Golden Bay Connections (☎ 524 8188) operates a bus from Collingwood to Nelson in the morning every day except Sunday, returning in the afternoon. It also has twice-daily buses from Collingwood connecting with Mt Cook Landline buses in Takaka and buses from Collingwood northwards around Cape Farewell or inland to Bainham, every day except Sunday.

Collingwood Bus Services also provides transport to and from the Totaranui (northern) end of the Abel Tasman Track and to the Browns Hut end of the Heaphy Track, 35 km from Collingwood (24 October – 30 May). These services run on demand; the cost is about $60 per trip for the minibus, or $12 per person if there are more than five people. Inward and outward trips can be arranged to connect with their buses onward to Nelson.

MARLBOROUGH

West Coast & Glaciers

The best thing about this coast is its ruggedness – the narrow coastal strip is still very much untamed. The pebbled and rocky beaches are wild, and from them the bush-clad hills sweep up to towering icy peaks. Often the narrow strip of land is *pakihi* (dried-up) swamp or second-class farmland, and everywhere studded by jewel-like lakes which mirror the peaks above.

Here and there are patches of native forest that have escaped the axe and fire. Scattered throughout the bush and by the rivers is the rusted debris of a hundred years of exploitative industry – gold and coal mining, and timber milling. The two glaciers, Fox and Franz Josef, are perhaps the major drawcards to the West Coast, but visitors soon find that the whole stretch from Karamea to Jacksons Bay is worth exploring.

The road hugs the coastline most of the way from Westport in the north to Hokitika, then runs inland until it finally joins the coast again for the last stretch, before turning east and heading over the Haast Pass. Not far inland from the coast, but a long way by road, is Mt Cook and the Tasman Glacier.

Most visitors come to the West Coast in summer, and the area is heavily visited from December to January. However, locals say that May to September is an excellent time to be on the coast. The days can often be warm and clear, with views of snow-capped peaks; there are no crowds and you can often get off-peak accommodation rates. Also there are no sandflies in winter!

Along the coastal beaches, the Fiordland crested penguin (*pokotiwha*) is found from June to November, and the seal colonies have the most seals from April to November. On the other hand, white herons (*kotuku*) are in residence at only one breeding site from November to February! Some of the organised activities take place only in summer, when the tourists are there in numbers. All in all, the West Coast is definitely worth a visit at any time of the year. Make sure you get

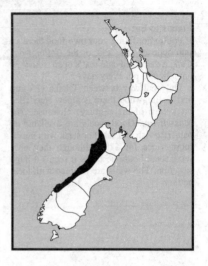

hold of the *West Coast Outdoor Recreation Guide*, available at a number of places for $1. It details all the areas where there are walks and points of interest along the Coast.

Weather

The West Coast could aptly be 'Wetland'. It rains a lot on the West Coast, five metres (200 inches) or more a year. A poetically inspired visitor to Hokitika earlier this century summed up the West Coast weather situation pretty well:

It rained and rained and rained
The average fall was well maintained
And when the tracks were simply bogs
It started raining cats and dogs
After a drought of half an hour
We had a most refreshing shower
And then the most curious thing of all
A gentle rain began to fall
Next day also was fairly dry
Save for a deluge from the sky
Which wetted the party to the skin
And after that the rain set in

Westland
(The West Coast)

0   40   80 km

MOUNTAINS

1   Rolleston 2272 m
2   Murchison 2400 m
3   Bryce 2188 m
4   Whitcombe 2638 m
5   Arrowsmith 2795 m
6   Tyndall 2524 m
7   Elie de Beaumont 3109 m
8   Malte Brun 3176 m
9   Tasman 3498 m
10 Cook 3764 m
11 La Perouse 3081 m
12 Sefton 3157 m
13 Ward 2646 m
14 Brewster 2519 m
15 Pollux 2542 m
16 Aspiring 3035 m

TASMAN MOUNTAINS

Heaphy Track

Mt Domett 1615 m

Whangapeka Track

Oparara
Karamea

Mt Kendall 1751 m

Karamea Bight

67

To Nelson

Seddonville

Denniston   Hector
                   Granity

WESTPORT

Cape Foulwind   Buller   Gorge   Murchison

                                                       6

Charleston   Inangahua
Nile River   Junction   69   65   Lake
                                                               Rotoroa
Paparoa   Mt
National Park   Uriah   Reefton

Punakaiki   6   Mt
Porarari River   Haast   Lewis
                   Mt   Ikamatua 1587 m   Pass
Barrytown   Ryall
Grey River   Blackball   Springs
Rapahoe   Junction
Runanga   Stillwater

GREYMOUTH   Moana
Brunner   Lake Brunner
                           (Moana Kotuku)
Kumara

Arahura
HOKITIKA   Arthurs Pass
                   Lake   Otira National Park
Mahinapua   Kaniere   Arthurs
                                  Pass
                         Ross   Arthurs Pass
Pukekura
                   ▲ 3   ▲ 2
Harihari   TASMAN
                  SEA

Whataroa   ▲ 4
Okarito   Mt   73
                 Adams ▲ 6   ▲ 5

Fox Glacier
Westland   Franz Josef Glacier
National Park   ▲ 7
                 ▲ 9 ▲ 8
Karangarua   ▲ 10
Bruce Bay   ▲ 11   Mt Cook
                   ▲ 12   National Park
Lake   To
Paringa   Paringa   Christchurch
Knights Point   Mt Cook Village
                 Copland   72   1
Lake   Track
Moeraki   ▲ 13   80   79
Haast
Jacksons   8
Bay   ▲ 14
                 Haast
                 Pass   PACIFIC
▲ 15   Mt Aspiring   OCEAN
              National Park
              Makarora   8
World
Heritage   Siberia   1
Area ▲ 16   Valley

Information

All telephone numbers in the South Island have an 03 prefix if you are calling them from a long distance (even within the region).

NELSON TO THE WEST COAST VIA BULLER GORGE

The road across from Nelson in the north to the coast is interesting and scenic. The Buller area is still scarred from the 1929 Murchison and 1968 Inangahua earthquakes. From Inangahua Junction you can head through the Lower Buller Gorge to the coast, or you can go on to Greymouth via Reefton on the inland route. The coastal route has more to offer but is a fair bit longer. Before you have to make the choice, however, the first town of any size that you will come to is Murchison.

Murchison

Murchison (population 700) is on the Buller Gorge Heritage Highway, some 125 km south of Nelson and 300 km north-west of Christchurch. It is an important service centre for the surrounding region and the starting point for a number of adventure activities. It is actually in Nelson Province but is included here as it is very much the gateway for travellers coming from the north to the West Coast.

Things to See & Do There is a great variety of recreational activities to be pursued in the Murchison area including fishing, rafting, kayaking, tramping, gold-panning, boating, mountain biking, caving and rock climbing.

Go West Rafting (☎ 523 9315), based at the Riverview Motor Camp, have a number of exciting rafting options. These range from their Two Rivers Fun Run on the Gowan and Buller (two-three hours, $65) to their Karamea Helirafting trip (full day, $150).

There are a number of mountain-bike trails in the area and popular rides include the west bank of the Matakitaki (16 km return) and the Upper Matakitaki (the return trip is 76 km).

The Lyell Walk (1½ hours, three km) is in the Upper Buller Gorge near the town of Lyell. It follows an old track to the town's cemetery, then joins a dray road to some old gold mines. Apart from its historic interest there are stands of beech forest and tree fern.

There is a small museum which is open Monday to Friday from 10 am to 4 pm.

Places to Stay There is a seasonal *YHA Hostel* (1 December – 31 March) in the hall at the Domain. It costs $9 per member and $13 for nonmembers. *Kiwi Park* (☎ 523 9248), Fairfax St, has cabins for $13 per person, a double-bed cabin at $30 for two, and self-contained units at $40 for two ($9 for each extra adult). The *Riverview Motor Camp & Cabins* (☎ 523 9315), two km north of the town, has tent sites at $7.50 per person, cabins at $26 for two, and self-contained tourist flats at $42 for two ($11 each extra adult). There are two motels in town: the *Murchison* (☎ 523 9026) and the *Mataki* (☎ 523 9088); expect to pay about $60 for two.

There's a DOC *campsite* at Lyell, Upper Buller Gorge, 10 km north-east of Inangahua.

Places to Eat There is not a great deal of choice here. There are two of the ubiquitous tearooms – *Collins Tearooms* and the *Murchison Tearooms*. The *Commercial Hotel* serves pub meals such as steak and fish for about $15 a meal. A feast at the luxury *Moonlight Lodge*, 32 km south of Murchison on SH 65, will set you back about $50 (per person).

Getting There & Away A number of bus services pass through Murchison. These include Nelson Lakes Transport, White Star, Blenheim Taxis, InterCity and Mt Cook Landline. Most of these stop at Collins Tearooms in Fairfax St. White Star, for instance, depart daily for Christchurch at 10.50 am and Nelson at 1.50 pm; on Sunday and Friday they depart for Westport and Greymouth at 10.50 am.

Buller Gorge

From Murchison to Westport takes about 1½ hours. To get on the Buller Gorge road you turn off at Sullivan's Bridge (the road straight ahead goes to Maruia Springs and the Lewis Pass). Just past the bridge look up the valley to the left to see **Old Man Mountain**. With imagination you see a pot-bellied supine fellow – the cloud above is smoke from his hidden pipe. Further on is New Zealand's longest swing bridge.

The road winds through the gorge to Inangahua Junction. This was the epicentre of a major earthquake in 1968 – over 7 on the Richter scale. The scarred hillsides still bear testimony to the power of nature.

The Buller Gorge itself is dark and forbidding, especially on a murky day – primeval ferns and cabbage trees cling to steep cliffs, toi toi flanks the road between gorge and river. The drive through the Buller Gorge Scenic Reserve itself is picturesque in any weather.

At **Hawks Crag** the road has been literally hacked out of the rock. Buses pass through it very slowly as the rock overhang comes extremely close to the top of the vehicle. It is named not after hawks but a goldminer, Robert Hawks, who prospected in the area.

WESTPORT

Westport (population 4570) is the major town at the northern end of Westland. Its prosperity is based on coal mining although the mining activity takes place some distance from the town. Westport is five km north from the turn-off south on the main coast road, SH 6. The SH 67 passes through Westport and terminates at Karamea.

Information

Palmerston St is the main street of Westport. The Buller Visitor & Information Centre (☎ 789 6658) is in Brougham St, a couple of doors from Palmerston St, open from 9 am to 5 pm every day. The DOC office (☎ 789 7742) in Palmerston St is open from 8 am to 4.30 pm on weekdays. It has information on the seal colony and the many tracks and walkways in the area. The main AA office is on Marine Parade in Carters Beach, and there is an agent on the corner of Queen and Wakefield Sts.

Coaltown Museum

Coaltown on Queen St is a well laid out museum reconstructing aspects of coal-mining life, including a walk through a simulated coal mine complete with authentic sound effects, two audiovisual presentations, coal-mining artefacts and some excellent photographic exhibits. It's open every day from 8.30 am to 4.30 pm (later in summer); admission is $4 (children $2).

Cape Foulwind Walkway

The four-km, 1½-hour Cape Foulwind Walkway is part of the New Zealand Walkway system and extends along the cape down to Tauranga Bay (see Surfing in the Outdoor Activities chapter), passing by a lighthouse site, a replica of Abel Tasman's *Astrolabe* and a seal colony. A brochure describing the walk is available from the information centre or the DOC office in Westport.

The Maoris knew the cape as Tauranga, meaning 'a sheltered anchorage or landing place'. The first European to reach the cape was the explorer Abel Tasman, who sighted it in December 1642 and named it 'Glyphaygen Hock' or Rocky Point. When Captain Cook anchored here in March 1770 his ship, the *Endeavour*, was rocked by a furious storm, so he gave it the apt name it retains today.

Seal Colony

There's a seal colony at Tauranga Bay, 12 km from Westport. It is on the southern end of the Cape Foulwind Walkway, which follows the coastline for four km from Cape Foulwind to Tauranga Bay. If you have wheels and you're not doing the walkway you can drive to the end (follow the signposted road to Carters Beach) and simply scale the bluff to look down on the colony.

Depending on the time of the year there may be anywhere from 20 to over 100 seals down on the rocks. Pups are born in late November to early December and for about a month afterwards the mothers stay on the rocks to tend the young before setting off to sea on feeding forays. Lookouts have been built to give you a good view of the seals; don't venture past the marked areas as the cliffs can be dangerous.

Karaka Tours (☎ 789 9869) take trips to the seal colony for $12 per person (minimum of three people). These take about two hours and include a scenic drive as well as a visit to the seal colony.

White Water Rafting

Buller Adventure Tours (☎ 789 7286) offer a variety of enjoyable and reasonably priced activities including white water rafting on the Buller, Mokihinui and Karamea rivers, jet-boating through the Buller Gorge, horse-trekking, coal-mining tours, gold panning, caving excursions and guided hunting and fishing trips.

The rafting is particularly good here with Grade Four trips on the Mokihinui and Buller, and Grade Five rapids on the Karamea. Pray you don't disappear in the Karamea's Landslip rapid or in Whopper Stopper and Rodeo, on the Buller. A day trip on the Buller costs $60; the Mokihinui (two-day) is $249, including a helicopter flight into the river headwaters; and the Karamea (one-day) is $169.

Buller Adventure Tours are located on the Buller Gorge Rd, SH 6 (on the right just past the Greymouth turn-off, if you're coming from Westport).

'Underworld' Rafting

This form of diversion has really caught on in New Zealand. In the Westport area Norwest Adventures Ltd (☎ 789 6686) run a number of trips into a place that could be the legendary reaches of Xanadu. For $60 they will take you down Coleridge's sacred river

(the Nile actually). In the lower, active levels of Metro Cave you sit in rubber rafts and paddle through spectacular glow worm-filled caverns. The trip ends in the rapids of the larger Nile River – definitely not for the usual air-conditioned bus set. They will take along any child over 10 who can walk for three hours. You can get in touch with them at Charleston or at 4 Dommett St, Westport.

There are two trips daily, departing Westport at 8.30 am and 2 pm; there is a limit of 36 persons and four guides on any one trip.

Adventure Caving

Another adventure activity started here by Norwest Adventures is adventure caving. This is a thrilling four-hour experience which starts with a 30-metre abseil into the Te Tahi tomo (hole). You then worm your way through rock squeezes and waterfalls, exploring prehistoric fossils and formations as you go (stalactites, stalagmites, straws and columns). In this cave system there is an embedded whale skeleton – it once used to span the full width of the cave. The cost of this trip is $95. There is even an option for those not keen on abseiling; you creep into the system via another entrance. After plumbing the depths, experience another sort of dark up at the bar in Charleston – they have an excellent dark ale on tap.

Other Things to See & Do

The information centre has brochures describing a number of bush walks in the region, many of which pass through old gold and coal-mining areas.

Other Westport activities include jet-boating on the Buller River or tramping, caving or fishing trips.

Norwest Adventures run two interesting adventure activities: adventure caving and 'underworld rafting' – see the separate entries later in this section.

Places to Stay

Camping & Cabins The *Howard Park Holiday Camp* (☎ 789 7043) is on Dommett St only a km from the post office. Camping

■ PLACES TO STAY

2 McManus Hotel
6 A1 Motels
7 Howard Park Holiday Camp
12 Bazil's Hostel
13 Marg's Hostel
15 Black & White Hotel
20 Tripinns
25 DB Westport Motor Hotel
26 Westport Motels
27 Buller Court Motels

▼ PLACES TO EAT

1 La'Sons Chinese Takeaway
4 Mandala Coffeehouse & Restaurant
5 Central Cafe
16 Bonanza Takeaways & Restaurant
19 Albion Hotel
22 Cristy's Restaurant

OTHER

3 Buller Hospital
5 White Star Transport
8 Norwest Adventures
9 Public Toilets
10 Heated Swimming Pool
11 Public Toilets
14 Visitor Information Centre
17 Post Office
18 Department of Conservation (DOC)
21 Automobile Association Agent (AA)
23 Cunningham's Coachlines
24 InterCity Bus Depot
28 Coaltown

Beach

Shellswell Street

Racecourse

Bright Street

Queen Street

Cobden Street

Orowaiti Road

Pakington Street

1 ▼   ■ 2

3 ✚

Henley Street

Hunter St

Domett Street

▲ 7

4 ▼
5 ▼

■ 6

Lyndhurst Street

Romily Street

Derby Street

● 8

12
14 ■   ■ 11   Victoria Square 9
i   13   10 ●

Brougham Street

Peel Street

Watson St

To Karamea

15 ■   ✉ 17   ▼ 19
16 ▼   ● 18   20

Wakefield Street   21
22 ●

● 23

Rintoul Street

Palmerston Street

Russell Street

Queen Street

Fonblanque Street

Colvin Street

● 24
■ 25

Mill Street

Haselden Street

Buller River

The Esplanade

Adderley Street

■ 26

■ 27

Bentham Street

Disraeli Street

Westport

0   125   250 m

Approximate Scale

To Cape Foulwind,
Carters Beach &
Seal Colony Tourist Park

Menzies Street

Roebuck Street

28

Stout Street

Westport Domain

Stafford Street

To Charleston,
Punakaiki & Greymouth
(Murchison & Nelson)

costs $7/14 a night for one/two people, or $8/15 with power. They also have chalets at $25 for two, on-site caravans at $28 for two and bunkroom accommodation at $10 per person.

The *Seal Colony Tourist Park* (☎ 789 8002) is six km from Westport, out towards (yes) the seal colony. Rates here for tent or powered sites are $18 for two, cabins are $36 for two and tourist flats are $52 for two, with discounts in the low season.

Hostels The *Tripinns* (☎ 789 7367; fax 789 6419) at 72 Queen St is a backpackers in a large old home built in 1870. Inside are about 38 beds and there are another 25 in newer units built to one side. Backpackers rates (with your own sleeping bag) are $13.50 per person, with linen singles/doubles cost $19.50 per person, and there's a variety of dorm, twin and double rooms. There is an outside area with BBQ which compensates for the rather run-down kitchen facilities.

Bazil's Hostel (☎ 789 6410), 54 Russell St, is a homely pleasant place and the regard in which the hosts are held is reflected in the visitors' book. Furnished rooms are $11 to $13.50 and the washing facilities are free. There is a large area of lawn where you can have a rest and, if you are lucky, soak in some rare sun.

Hotels & Motels Westport has a number of centrally located hotels along Palmerston St plus several motels from around $50 a night. On Palmerston St the *McManus Hotel* (☎ 789 6304) has singles/twins for $25/43. Also on Palmerston St, opposite the post office, the *Black & White Hotel* (☎ 789 7959) has B&B at $25/45 for a single/double. The *A1 Motels* (☎ 789 9808) at 63 Queen St has self-contained units at $65 to $75 for two.

Places to Eat
There are a number of takeaways and sandwich places along Palmerston St including *Bonanza Takeaways* near the Wakefield St corner; you can take food away or sit down and eat there. It's open from 8 am to 10 pm

on weekdays, until midnight on Friday and Saturday, and noon to 10 pm Sunday. There's pub food at several of the hotels including the *Black & White* and the restaurant in *Larsens Tavern*, on Palmerston St.

The *Mandala* on Palmerston St is a pleasant coffee house restaurant serving pizzas and takeaways, vegetable or meat burgers and dinner meals with main courses from around $12.50 to $16; pizzas range from $16 to $20. The burgers are absolutely huge, and range in price from $5 to $8; they also have good coffee, cold fruit drinks and desserts, and they're open every day of the week from 7 am until 10.30 pm.

Up-market *Cristy's* on Wakefield St is Westport's flashy licensed restaurant.

Getting There & Away
Air Air New Zealand Link (Air Nelson) (☎ 789 7209) have daily direct flights to Wellington (except on Saturday), with connections to other centres including Auckland, Christchurch, Dunedin, Nelson and Blenheim. Air West (☎ 789 7979) do charter flights.

Road InterCity buses make return trips between Westport and Greymouth (two hours) with a rest stop at the Pancake Rocks (Punakaiki) every day but Sunday. From Greymouth they have connecting buses heading north to Nelson and south to the glaciers, and both a bus and train to Christchurch. The Christchurch bus goes via Hanmer Springs, the largest thermal resort in the South Island.

White Star have a Nelson-Westport-Greymouth-Christchurch (via Springs Junction; connections with Nelson and Christchurch) service. This bus leaves for Greymouth at 2.30 pm every day except Saturday; the cost is $14. From Nelson they have connections to Motueka and Takaka, to Picton or to Christchurch.

East-West Express have a shuttle to Christchurch ($38 adult, $28 child). It leaves the information centre at 8 am and arrives in Christchurch at the railway station at 12.30

pm. It leaves the station at 2 pm and returns to Westport at 6.30 pm.

Heading north to Karamea for the Heaphy Track, Cunningham's buses make the return trip Monday to Friday, leaving Karamea in the morning and returning from Westport in the afternoon at 3 pm (it is the mail run). They also go to Springs Junction, connecting there with Mt Cook Landline buses to Christchurch, from Monday to Friday.

Getting Around

A taxi to the airport costs around $12. Bicycles can be hired from Beckers Cycles & Sports on Palmerston St, and also at Bazil's Hostel.

WESTPORT TO KARAMEA

This trip along SH 67 passes through a number of interesting towns. The first reached is Waimangaroa and the turn-off to **Denniston**. This town was once the largest producer of coal in New Zealand and it can be reached by the Denniston Walkway. The track follows the original path to the town and from it you get great views of the Denniston Incline. In its day this was acclaimed as a feat of engineering, as empty coal trucks were hauled back up the incline by the weight of the descending loaded trucks, sometimes at a gradient of one in one.

Four km north of Waimangaroa is the **Britannia Track**, a six-hour return walk to the Britannia battery and other remnants of the gold-mining era. Just near Granity there is another interesting walk at **Charming Creek**. This all-weather track follows an old coal line through the picturesque Ngakawau River gorge. Some of the features along the way are tunnels, Mangatini Falls, historic sites, a swing bridge and native bush; allow five hours return for this walk.

You could continue along the Charming Creek Walkway all the way to **Seddonville**, a town on the Mohikinui River about halfway between Westport and Karamea. This town, named after Richard John Seddon ('King Dick' – Liberal prime minister at the turn of the century), is surrounded by hill

covered in bush. You could choose either the *Motor Camp* (☎ 782 1816) or *Motor Hotel* (☎ 782 1828) to stay in – the hotel is $50 for two and the motor camp bunkrooms are $12 for two. There are three other walkways in the immediate vicinity of Seddonville – **Chasm Creek, Mohikinui River** and **Mt Glasgow**. Chasm Creek is suitable for families and has a glow-worm tunnel.

Between Mohikinui and Little Wanganui you pass over the **Karamea Bluff**, a great scenic drive through rata forest with views of the Tasman Sea below. There are also giant matai trees in this section of forest.

KARAMEA

From Westport, SH 67 continues 100 km north to Karamea, near the end of the Heaphy Track and the Wangapeka Track. Nearby is the beautiful Oparara forest, which should on no account be missed.

The Karamea River offers good swimming, fishing and canoeing. There are also good swimming holes on the Wanganui, Oparara and Kohaihai rivers. Swimming is dangerous in the open sea but there are tidal lagoons one km north and three km south of Karamea where swimming is good at high tide. There are lots of beautiful beaches around but the only drawback is the millions of sandflies. A long-running local saying is that 'sandflies work in pairs – one pulls back the sheets, while the other eats you alive'. Fishing is now popular with people from overseas, and the Last Resort will advise of places to go in the Karamea River (the locals have known about it since they first came here!).

Information on these and other natural attractions is available in Karamea at the DOC office (☎ 782 6852) or at the information centre at the Last Resort (☎ 782 6617; fax 782 6820).

Walks

Many good day walks are found in this area, including the five-hour Fenian Track into Adams Flat and the eight-hour return trek to the 1084-metre Mt Stormy. There's another walk to Lake Hanlon and the first leg of the

Wangepeka Track also makes a good day walk. Those not keen on walking the whole Heaphy Track may walk as far as Heaphy Hut and then return the same way. This walk includes what is considered by many to be the best part, the walk along the beach. For more information on the Heaphy and Whangapeka tracks, see Lonely Planet's *Tramping in New Zealand* by Jim DuFresne.

Honeycomb Caves & Oparara River

Several spectacular limestone arch formations are found in the Karamea area, 15 km from the North Beach turn-off – of particular interest are the Oparara Arch and Moria Gate in the Oparara River valley. You can actually canoe up to another arch, the Honeycomb (in fact it is the only means of access) with Adventures Unlimited (contact The Last Resort). The cost of the bus trip is $20 each way.

The Honeycomb Caves are also magnificent, with a collection of bones of moa and other extinct species. On a visit through these caves you will see bones of three of the five moa species found – slender, small and giant moas, *Megalapteryx didinus*, *Pachyornis elephantopus* and *Dinornis giganteus*. This is the cave where bones of the giant Haast eagle, the world's largest, were uncovered. This eagle was so large (with a three to four-metre wingspan) that it preyed on the moa. In all, the remains of 56 bird species have been uncovered including kakapo, bush wren, bush robin, kea and kaka.

The cave is also home to the cave dwelling spider, *gradungula*, unique to this area; it has a body length of 2.5 cm (about an inch) and leg span of 10 cm. If you are lucky you will also see the carnivorous snail, favourite food of the weka, called *Powelliphanta hochstetteri*. In addition to all this the largest deposit in the Southern Hemisphere of moon milk, a soft limestone deposit with a soapy feel, is found in the cave. Understandably, access is restricted to protect the caves, but you can go through them on a guided tour, again with Adventures Unlimited at The Last Resort.

Perhaps the greatest feature of the Honeycomb area is the primitive rainforest which has grown over the karst landscape. Moss-laden trees droop over the golden river water illuminated by light filtering through the dense forest canopy – for a mere $20 seeing this is alone worth the trip.

Places to Stay & Eat

Bravely, the local backpackers place here has the appellation *The Last Resort* (☎ 782 6617; fax 782 6820); it certainly is not, and would have to be one of the top backpackers in the South Island in my opinion, as it has been designed specifically for the budget traveller and incorporates many new features of communal living. In a single it will cost you $15 ($22 with linen) and a double is $20 for each person ($40 for the room). There is a fully licensed restaurant or you can cook for yourself. Tent sites are $6 per person. The food at the *Karamea Tavern* is also excellent; a large whitebait pattie with chips is about $4.50.

Kohaihai, 15 km north of Karamea, is the site of a DOC *camping area*.

Getting There & Away

From Westport you catch a Cunningham's bus at 3.45 pm. This arrives in Karamea at 5.30 or 6 pm. Air West has flights from Westport for about $35 per person each way. Many people end up in Karamea after walking either the Wangapeka or Heaphy tracks.

WESTPORT TO GREYMOUTH

This is an interesting stretch of road. Nowadays the towns along the way are extremely small – 10 or so inhabitants. It was a different story 130 years ago when the gold rush was in full swing. **Charleston** was a booming town with shantys all along the pack route and gold-diggers moving out to their claims on the Nile River. Today, the raucous pubs are all closed but you may find sanctuary in the *Charleston Motel* (☎ 728 7599) or *Motor Camp* (☎ 728 6773) – $50 for two in the motel and $24 for two in the motor camp cabins. Norwest Adventures run their

'Underworld' rafting and tomo exploring trips from here. **Constant Bay**, once the busy port for the mining settlement, is a pleasant picnic area nearby.

The coast from Fox River to Runanga is rugged and the road will remind west coast Americans of the Big Sur – and like the famous Californian coastline, it affords spectacular views. Woodpecker Bay, Tiromoana, Punakaiki, Barrytown, 14-mile, Motukiekie, 10-mile, nine-mile and seven-mile are all beaches sculpted by the relentless fury of the Roaring Forties.

Paparoa National Park & Punakaiki

Midway between Westport (57 km north) and Greymouth (47 km south) is Punakaiki and the Paparoa National Park, centred around the area better known as the **Pancake Rocks & Blowholes**. These limestone rocks at Dolomite Point have formed into what look like stacks of pancakes, through a weathering process known as stylobedding. If there's a good tide running here, the water surges into caverns below the rocks and squirts out in impressive geyser-like blowholes. During September and October white-fronted terns nest at Dolomite Point and pairs of banded dotterels nest near Porarari River mouth.

There's a 15-minute walk from the road, around the rocks and blowholes, and back again. It's best to go at high or a king tide when the blowholes really perform. Take heed of the signs warning you to keep on the track – people have been killed when they wandered off the track and fell over the cliffs.

There was pressure for years to have this area declared a national park and this was finally accomplished in December 1987, when the 30,000-hectare Paparoa National Park became the 12th national park in New Zealand. In addition to the rocks at Punakaiki it has many other natural attractions: mountains (the Paparoa Range), rivers, wilderness areas, limestone formations including cliffs and caves, diverse vegetation, and a black petrel colony, the only nesting area of this rare albatross-like bird. If you plan to go caving you need to know what you're doing – in some caves the water rises so fast after rain that you'd drown before you had a chance to get out.

The park has a number of interesting walks including the **Inland Pack Track**. This is a two-day track along a route established by miners around 1867 to circumvent the more rugged coastal route. The 25 km of track is divided into three distinct sections: Punakaiki/Pororari; Pororari/Bullock Creek; and Bullock Creek/Fox River. Also notable are the **Croesus Track**, a full-day or two-day

---

Westland Black Petrel (*Procellaria westlandica*)
Near Punakaiki are the world's only breeding grounds of the largest burrowing petrel.

Westland petrels come to land only during the breeding season from May to November. Eggs are laid in May/June and chicks hatch in July/August. From August to November the chicks are fed by one or other of the parents every three days. At the end of November the fledglings leave the colony and will not return for seven years.

The petrels spend the rest of the year at sea, roaming to South America and Australia. In season their daily flights to and from feeding grounds can best be observed from Razorback point, south of the Punakaiki river, or from near Nikau Scenic Reserve, four km further down the highway towards Greymouth. They fly out individually each morning but congregate offshore for the flight in at dusk. At the height of the season, between June and October, thousands can be seen at the colony en masse. Note that their webbed feet are positioned well back from their bodies, for ease of take-off from water.

Visiting times to the colony begin 30 minutes before sunset. They can only be undertaken with Paparoa Nature Tours (☎ 731 1826) and the cost of the tour, lasting about two hours, is $10. Paparoa Nature Tours also organise birdwatching trips – there are about 40 species in the area including the great spotted kiwi, NZ falcon, kaka, parakeet, fernbird, blue duck and a number of migratory wading birds. ■

tramp over the Paparoa Range from Blackball to Barrytown, and the **Moonlight Track** – both tracks pass through historic goldmining areas. There are also many shorter river and coast walks. If you're planning on walking or caving, register your intentions at the Park Visitor Centre. Guides are available for many activities within the park and its environs.

The Paparoa National Park Visitor Centre (☎ 731 1895) is next to the highway and it's open every day from 8.30 am to 6 pm. In summer it stays open until about 8 pm. It has interesting displays including an audiovisual, pamphlets and maps on all the park's walks and attractions, and can supply information on tides and current conditions throughout the park. Many of the inland walks are subject to river flooding and other conditions, so check here before setting out.

Places to Stay & Eat The *Punakaiki Camping Ground* (☎ 731 1894) has tent sites at $7 per person, powered sites at $15 for two, cabins at $26 for two, and bunkroom accommodation at $10 per person. It's operated by the DOC (☎ 731 1895). The *Punakaiki Motel* (☎ 731 1852) has a variety of accommodation from a family house to a bach (pronounced 'batch' – a getaway or holiday house).

The *Pancake Tearooms* opposite the Pancake Rocks are open from 9 am daily all year round. Also here is the very pleasant natural-foods *Nikau Palms Cafe*, which is open 'most of the time'.

At Barrytown, 16 km south of Punakaiki, the *All Nations Tavern* (☎ 731 1812) has bunkroom accommodation at $12 per person, double and twin rooms at $35, which one person can take for $17 if it's not busy. There's a fully equipped kitchen for guests' use and they also serve takeaways, breakfast and bistro meals.

At Motukiekie, about 20 km north of Greymouth, there is a B&B in an old miner's cottage, *Tiggers House* (☎ 731 1654), where rooms are $25 nightly. Ring beforehand and Jenny will pick you up from Punakaiki or Greymouth for a small fee. The view from

this small house is fantastic and the walks along Motukiekie Beach at sunset are truly memorable. Not far away, at 16-Mile, is *Sandie's Bed & Breakfast* (☎ 731 1889) where the rate is $20 for one or $35 for two; the backpackers rate is $12 for accommodation only.

Getting There & Away InterCity and White Star buses between Westport and Greymouth stop at Punakaiki every day except Sunday. Kea West Coast Tours (☎ 731 1802; 768 5101) have an 18-seater bus which goes from Greymouth to Punakaiki for $22 return.

Getting Around There are several options for getting around this beautiful region. Perhaps the most tranquil are by horse, bicycle or canoe. Bikes and canoes can be hired from Pororari Canoe and Cycle Hire (☎ 731 1870), and Waiwhero Pony Treks (☎ 731 1802) organise horse-trekking. You can observe the park from above in Coastwide Helicopters (☎ 731 1823); a short flight is $35 and a longer flight over the Inland Track is $65.

Runanga

The township of Runanga is about seven km north of Greymouth. It is not far from Rapahoe (Seven-Mile) Beach and there is a 1½-hour return walk to nearby Coal Creek falls. The monument a km south of town was erected in memory of two mine officials, murdered here in a robbery in 1917.

Places to Stay & Eat Try the solitude and splendour of the windswept *Rapahoe Hotel* (☎ 762 7701). It is about seven miles north of Greymouth at the northern terminus of the Point Elizabeth Track. A creek choked in raupo is out one door, the looming Paparoa's can be seen out the back and the driftwood-covered beach in front. Accommodation and the Sunday barbecues are priceless (actually $60 a double, B&B).

Also at Rapahoe, the *Rapahoe Motor Camp* (☎ 762 7337) has camp sites at $5 per person, $7 with power, and cabins which cost $15 to $20 for two.

NELSON TO GREYMOUTH VIA GREY VALLEY

After passing through Murchison you can elect to get to the West Coast via the Buller Gorge route and Westport, or you can turn off at Inangahua Junction and go inland via Reefton and the Grey Valley.

Reefton

If you choose to go via the inland route to the West Coast you will pass through Reefton (population 1180). Reefton's name comes from the gold-bearing quartz reefs in the region. As early as 1888 Reefton had its own electricity supply and street lighting, beating all other towns in New Zealand and many of the fashionable suburbs in places such as London and New York.

Two old buildings worth exploring are the **School of Mines** and **Blacks Point Museum**. In the surrounding area there are a number of interesting walks, including the **Powerhouse Walk**.

The North Westland Visitor Centre (☎ 732 8391) has opened on Broadway to rave reviews. The DOC office is out on Crampton Rd.

Places to Stay & Eat The *Reefton Domain Camp* (☎ 732 8477), Main St, has sites for $10 for two, $2 extra with power. There are also cabins for $25 for two. The *Bellbird Motel* (☎ 732 8444), Broadway, has rooms for two for $60 and the *Reefton Motel* (☎ 732 8574), Central Broadway, charges $46 for two. Rooms at the *Dawson Hotel* (☎ 732 8444), Broadway, are good value at $45 for two. There is a *tearooms* on Broadway but, alas, no gourmet restaurants.

The *DOC campsite* is nearby at Slab Hut Creek, 10 km south of Reefton.

Getting There & Away Cunningham's Coachlines operates a Christchurch to Westport bus service which passes through Reefton. A connection has to be made at Springs Junction.

The Grey Valley

From Reefton, SH 7 heads east via Springs Junction to Christchurch and south-west to Greymouth. For those heading towards Christchurch, there are two *DOC campsites* in the area via Lewis Pass: Marble Hill, 6½ km east of Springs Junction; and Deer Valley, Lewis Pass, 25 km east of Springs Junction

You can almost smell the sea as soon as you enter the Grey Valley. Despite the best efforts of a century of plunderers the green-cloaked hills have rejuvenated and the paddocks have fast become overgrown. Fuelled with an abundant rainfall the bush has grown back and the small towns are a vestige of futile attempts to tame the land. The valley is not grey, that is merely the name given by a temporary English population after a governor who has long gone.

At Hukarere, 21 km south of Reefton, you can turn east to visit **Waiuta**, now a ghost town but once the focus of the South Island's richest gold mine. Get the excellent DOC pamphlet *Waiuta: Victoria Forest Park* for help with your search through the past.

If you choose the inland route via Reefton you could stay at **Ikamatua**, at the local hotel *The Station* (☎ 732 3555) where share rooms are $13.50. Why Ikamatua? Just pop in and find out – there's no better introduction to the hidden delights of the Grey Valley. It is 50 km from Greymouth and a world away from anywhere.

Just before Ngahere, and 32 km from Greymouth, you can turn off to beautiful **Nelson Creek** and a great swimming hole. This area is full of reminders of the gold-mining era, with a number of walks including Callaghans which heads to a lookout, and the Tailrace Walk through old gold tailings. Nelson Creek has a DOC campsite.

After passing through the sawmilling town of Stillwater, the former coal mining town of Dobson and pastoral Kaiata, you arrive at the mouth of the Grey River near the Cobden Bridge and the Cobden Gap.

Blackball

This town, 25 km north of Greymouth on the road to Reefton, was established in 1866 as a provisioning centre for gold diggers. It was then a coal mining centre from the late 1880s until 1964, and the town in which the national Federation of Labour (organisation of trade unions) was born after two cataclysmic strikes in 1908 and 1931. The town is close to the start of the Croesus Track to Barrytown and to a number of other interesting areas. The *Blackball ex-Hilton* (☎ 732 4705) offers dormitory accommodation, double or twin rooms at $13 per person.

This huge pricing structure was obviously so much of a threat to a giant hotel chain that it mounted a challenge to force the little ol' now ex-Hilton in Blackball to change its name. The premises are now loosely termed the *Dominion* until the historiographers reveal that the name Hilton does not come from a multinational conglomerate but rather from an out-of-luck gold miner ('Darcno' Hilton) who first worked a claim near Darkies Terrace, Cobden, and then panned up near Croesus and Roa.

Blackball is an interesting old coal-mining town and the ex-Hilton is an equally interesting place to stay. The hotel went through a period of disrepair before its new owners lovingly restored it to some of its old glory and now it's been designated a New Zealand Historic Place.

The owners are friendly hosts with lots of information on the history of their hotel, the town, and things to do around Blackball. The ex-Hilton is full of character and has a billiards room, TV lounge, sauna and spa pool. They offer an excellent economical breakfast and dinner, or you can cook your own. They will pick up guests from Greymouth and there is no charge if there are two or more people.

Lake Brunner (Moana Kotuku)

At Stillwater you can turn off to Lake Brunner (also known as Moana Kotuku, 'Lake Heron'). The other points of access to the lake are near Jacksons on the Arthurs Pass road or near Kumara on the same road. If you have never baited a hook or gaffed an eel, then Lake Brunner offers you the big chance. They say that the trout here die of

old age – that is probably an age-old adage! The trout fishing certainly rivals that of Lake Taupo in the North Island. Fishing guides can be hired at Lake Brunner Lodge to show you the spots where the big ones shouldn't get away.

There is a wildlife park in the **Moana Reserve** with a large area devoted to natural species which can be viewed in their natural surroundings from the walkways. You are likely to see kereru (native pigeon), tui, bellbirds, fantails, and sometimes white heron (kotuku). The nearby Velenski Walk, which starts near the camping ground, leads through a remarkable selection of native bush consisting of totara, rimu and kahikatea. Unusual flora found here includes four varieties of native orchids.

Places to Stay & Eat The proprietors of the *Moana Adventure Lodge* (☎ 738 0101), at the Moana railway station, will serve you home brew after picking you up from Jacksons or Stillwater. The dorm is $15, and better singles are from $30 to $40 per person. The *Moana Camping Ground* is in the township on the shores of Lake Brunner (☎ 738 0543); a site is $10 for two, and cabins are $24 for two (each extra adult is $10). The Moana Hotel (☎ 738 0083) has singles/ doubles for $25/45 and cabins from $10 to $15 per person; they serve meals here as well. Across the far side of the lake is the upmarket *Lake Brunner Lodge* at Mitchells where meals are available.

GREYMOUTH

From Punakaiki it's another 47 km to Greymouth (population 9000), once the site of a Maori pa and known to its inhabitants as Mawhera, meaning 'widespread river mouth'. To the Ngai Tahu people, the Cobden Gap to the east of the town is where their ancestor Tuterakiwhanoa broke the side out of Te Waaka o Aoraki (the canoe of Aoraki) which released trapped rainwaters out to sea.

Greymouth is also a town with a long gold-mining history, and it still has a bit of gold town flavour today. It's the largest town on the West Coast despite its small population. It's located at the mouth of the Grey River – hence its name – and despite the high protective wall along the Mawhera Quay the river still manages to flood the town once in a while after periods of heavy rain. The quay walk from Cobden Bridge towards Blaketown is well worth doing.

The Grey River meets the sea at the 'bar' (an accumulation of sand just below the waterline) between the Cobden and Blaketown headlands. This area is dangerous in high seas but fishing boats, their crews eager to get to the comforts of home, run the huge, dangerous waves often with disastrous results. The seascapes here are phenomenal: to the south you can see a large sweep of beach which culminates in the faint outlines of Mt Cook and Mt Tasman, and to the north the rocky promontory of Point Elizabeth and Big Rock at the far end of Cobden Beach.

Information
There's an information centre (☎ 768 5101) in the Regent Theatre on the corner of Herbert and Mackay Sts. It's open from 8.30 am to 5 pm on weekdays only. There's an AA agent about a block away on Mackay St.

More information is obtainable at Ian Boustridge's greenstone carving premises, **The Jade Boulder Gallery**. Here, original jade sculpture and jewellery is crafted. Visit the gallery on the corner of Guinness and Tainui Sts from 8 am to 6 pm, 9 pm in summer.

Walks
The information centre has a leaflet produced by the Greymouth District Council with details of walks in and around the town. There are some fine walks around Blackball, an old mining town 25 km north-east of Greymouth.

The **Croesus Track** is a one or two-day walk from Blackball north over the Paparoa Range to Barrytown, on the coast south of Punakaiki. It can be walked in one long day but there's a good hut near the summit if you prefer to stay over. The five-hour **Point Elizabeth Track**, which passes through the Rapahoe Range Scenic Reserve, is six km

north of Greymouth. Both of these tracks go through interesting historic gold-mining areas. There are pamphlets available which describe both of these walks.

Taniwha Cave Rafting
Wild West Adventures (☎ 768 6649; fax 768 4413) has designed a subterranean adventure which is not for the faint-hearted. They take you into the Taniwha Cave either by walking in, abseiling or ladder. The trip begins with a 30-minute walk through native beech forest before a climb up to the 'Toilet Bowl' to see spectacular cave formations. Rushing waterfalls are visited before you float on inflated tubes down through a glow-worm gallery, ending the trip with an exhilarating ride down a 30-metre natural hydroslide.

The cost of this five-hour trip is $65, and they'll pick-up and drop-off from acommodation.

Other Tours
Interesting mining areas around Greymouth include the Brunner Mine Site, the Rewanui Mine Site and Nelson Creek. The information centre can give directions and historical information on all these sites, and on good spots where you might try panning for gold – there are many places along the West Coast where gold is still found. They also have details on many good scenic drives near Greymouth.

Wild West Adventures also does reasonably priced tours of gold and coal-mining sites, ghost towns, fishing, scenic rafting, transport to and from walking tracks, sailing trips on Lake Brunner, pub crawls off the main routes (three different watering holes), and more. Their 4WD gold-seekers' trip which includes a visit to the Wild West gold mine costs $75 for the full day. The principal of this company describes himself as a 'risk management facilitator' of the adventure you design yourself.

The Greymouth Aero Club (☎ 768 0407) does scenic flights around the area with rates starting from $20. There's surfing at Cobden Beach and at Seven-Mile Beach in Rapahoe. Fishing safaris are especially popular activi-

Greymouth

0   250   500 m

■ PLACES TO STAY

2 Royal Hotel
3 Railway Hotel
5 King's Motor Hotel
14 Revington's Hotel
16 Golden Coast Guest House
17 Ardwyn Homestay
18 Kaianga-Ra YHA Hostel
19 Noahs Ark Backpackers
22 Duke of Edinburgh Hotel
24 High Street Guest House
25 Living Streams Haven
     Backpackers
29 Seaside Holiday Park
30 Greymouth Motel
31 Australasian Hotel

▼ PLACES TO EAT

4 Cafe Collage & Out to Lunch
6 Bonzai Pizzeria
7 Richmond Hotel
8 Bakery
11 Steamers
12 Hideaway Tea & Coffee House
23 Union Hotel & Raceway Cavery
32 Cafe Brunner

    OTHER

1 TranzAlpine Express,
     InterCity Depot
9 Regent Theatre Visitor
     Information Centre
10 Library
13 Post Office
15 West Coast Motors &
     Public Toilets
20 St Patricks Church
21 Jade Boulder Gallery
26 Kowhai Bush Walk
27 Greymouth Aero Club
28 Grey Hospital

WEST COAST

ties from Greymouth. There's good fishing at Lake Brunner and in the Arnold, Orangepuke and Hohonu rivers.

Places to Stay

There is a wide range of accommodation choices in Greymouth. It is here that the *Aa*-motel prefix was invented so that a motel could be the first in a listing. A modern day gold rush of these occurred and *Aa*-names appeared like measles all over the South Island.

Hostels The *Kaianga-Ra YHA Hostel* (☎ 768 4951) 15 Alexander St, is housed in former Marist Brothers living quarters. It is a large, spacious place with dorm rooms for $13, and twins for $15 per person. The big 10-bed dorm used to be the chapel. There is a nature walk up behind the hostel and they have a BBQ, washing facilities, kitchen, TV and video player.

The *Noah's Ark Backpackers*, formerly Pavlova Backpackers (☎ & fax 768 4868) at 16 Chapel St, occupies a huge old edifice built in 1912 as the monastery for the St Patrick's Catholic Church next door. Dorm rooms cost $13.50 per person, double or twin rooms cost $15 per person. It is a typical backpackers, with murals in the walls, a large common room and adequate rooms.

The former youth hostel in Cowper St, directly opposite Buccleugh St, has metamorphosised into the *Living Streams Haven* (☎ 732 7272). In this quiet, nonsmoking atmosphere dorm beds are $11, and twins/doubles are $13/16 per person. Duvets and linen are supplied in the doubles. There are canoes, a dinghy and BBQs available as well.

Camping & Cabins The *Greymouth Seaside Holiday Park* (☎ 768 6618; fax 768 5873) is 2.5 km south of the centre on Chesterfield St. Camping charges for two people are $15.50, or with power $17. Cabins cost $30 to $37 for two, on-site caravans $32, and tourist flats $54. There's also bunkroom accommodation at $11. It's right beside the beach – and right at the end of the airport runway.

The *South Beach Motor Park* (☎ 762 6768) about five km south of Greymouth has camp sites at $7 per person, and $7.50 with power; happily it now has new kitchen and shower facilities.

Guesthouses There are guesthouses close to the town centre. The *Golden Coast Guest House* (☎ 768 7839), at 10 Smith St overlooking the river, is good value at $45 for singles, $66 for doubles, and $60 for twins, including breakfast. The *High St Guest Homestay* (☎ 768 7444) at 20 High St offers B&B at $47/68 for singles/doubles. *Ardwyn House* (☎ 768 6107), 48 Chapel St, has singles/doubles and twins for $35/60 with a cooked breakfast. A courtesy car will deliver you to this nice old blue house.

Motels There are plenty of motels in Greymouth but there's hardly anything under $65 a night! The *Willowbank Pacifica Lodge*(☎ 768 5339) on SH 6 two km from Greymouth, has two studio units at $78 for two, but their larger units cost $78 to $85. The *Riverview Motel* (☎ 768 6884) on Omoto Rd, also two km from the centre, has rooms from $65 to $73 for two. Others are the *South Beach Motel* (☎ 762 6768) at 318 Main South Rd and the *Greymouth Motel* (☎ 768 6090) at 195 High St, both with rooms at around $70 for two.

Hotels That gold-mining history shows in the number of hotels you'll find around central Greymouth. None of them are particularly special. You could try the *Duke of Edinburgh* (☎ 768 4020) in Guinness St with singles/doubles from $31/40 or the *Australasian Hotel* (☎ 768 4023) on Main South Rd about 2.5 km south of town, where singles/doubles cost from $25/45 or $44/65 for B&B. The *Royal Hotel* (☎ 768 4022), Mawhera Quay has singles/twins for $28/46.

There are other hotels around Greymouth but they are more expensive. The *Revington's Hotel* (☎ 768 7055) on Tainui St has rooms with attached bathroom for $50/70/76 for singles/doubles/triples – the Queen of England stayed here once and now backpackers can too as there are budget rooms from $20 per night. The *King's Motor Hotel* (☎ 768 5085; fax 768 5844) on Mawhera Quay has 100 singles or doubles ranging from around $70 to $99.

Places to Eat

There's the usual selection of cafes and sandwich places around the town centre. You could try the *Hideaway Tea & Coffee House* on Albert St or the *Out to Lunch* sandwich bar on Mackay St. The *Bonzai Pizzeria* at 29 Mackay St is a pleasant little place with 16 varieties of quite good pizza. Medium pizzas cost $9 to $16, large ones are $12 to $22, and they have tempting desserts too. They open at 11 am weekdays, 5 pm on weekends, and stay open every night until 10 or 11 pm.

At the *Union Hotel* on Herbert St near the railway line the *Raceway Carvery* is something of a local institution. The front is very unpromising but it's quite reasonable inside. The accent here is on low prices and big quantities; cuisine highlights are a definite second. It's open for breakfast, lunch and dinner daily. Dinner is served from around 5 to 8 pm Sunday to Thursday, to 9 pm Friday and Saturday. The menu has all the pub regulars from T-bones to chicken kiev at prices around $7 to $11.

Quite a few other pubs offer food, including the *Royal Hotel* on Mawhera Quay. Two flashier places are the *Cafe Brunner* in the Ashley Motor Inn on Tasman St, Karoro, and *Steamers* in Mackay St near the library. At the Brunner mains cost about $20; a venison steak with bacon batons and cranberry sauce will set you back about $24.50. Steamers, housed in a former shipping company office, is a pleasant cafe and bar. It keeps West Coast hours, ie stays open late like the pubs – here the roast of the day is $13 or so and a satay entrée about $6. What is more it is licensed with a good selection of beers.

For a fancier night out try the *Cafe Collage* on Mackay St. This is a BYO, quite expensive at $20 for a main but it offers a good choice of international cuisine; recommended is the whitebait (in season).

Getting There & Away

Air Air New Zealand Link (Air Nelson) flights operate from Hokitika although there is a small airport in Greymouth.

Bus White Star leave Greymouth for Nelson at 8 am daily and arrive in Nelson at 4 pm. They have connecting services to Takaka, Motueka and Picton. Information about White Star ticketing is available on (☎ 768 0596) or at Greymouth Taxis (☎ 768 7078); buses come and go from the taxi office on Mackay St.

InterCity buses depart from the railway station (☎ 768 4199) and they have daily services north to Westport and Nelson and south down the coast to the glaciers.

There is no longer an InterCity bus between Greymouth and Christchurch. The Coast to Coast Shuttle (☎ freephone (0800) 800 847) and Alpine Coach & Courier (☎ 769 5101) operate instead. Coast to Coast arrive at Greymouth at 12.30 pm and depart for Christchurch at 1 pm. Alpine Coach leaves the information centre at 8 am and arrives in Christchurch at 11.20 am. Christchurch to Arthurs Pass is $25 one way and Arthurs Pass to Greymouth is $15 one way; if you travel within four days from Christchurch to Greymouth and return, Coast to Coast have a discount fare of $60. Blenheim Taxis travel to Picton on Monday and Friday only for $49; they leave from the information centre at 1.15 pm.

Travel times are two hours to Westport, five hours to Nelson, four and five hours to the glaciers, and 4½ hours to Christchurch.

Train The TranzAlpine Express operates daily between Christchurch and Greymouth. The trip, which currently costs an exorbitant $60, takes about five hours and is notable for its spectacular scenery – it crosses some remarkable gorges on its climb through the Southern Alps, passing over numerous viaducts and bridges and through 19 tunnels, including the 8.5-km Otira Tunnel. Between Arthurs Pass and Greymouth the road and railway line take quite different routes. For

Whitebait

Whitebait is a translucent, small elongated fish, which is the imago (immature) stage of the river smelt. They swarm up the West Coast rivers in dense schools and are caught in set seine-net traps or large, round scoop nets. Many an argument has been had along a riverbank or near a river mouth as to the best rock to position yourself for catching the biggest haul. The season has been limited in recent years in an attempt to allow the declining stocks to breed. Usually it is September to mid-November, but may vary from year to year. Cooked in batter, these small fish are delicious and highly prized by Coasters.

After consulting one of the West Coast's doyennes of culinary expertise (my mum) I collected this perfect recipe for whitebait patties:

Take a pint (about half a litre – yes it is measured as a liquid rather than a solid as it used to be loaded into glass pint milk bottles for sale) of whitebait and pour it into a bowl. The batter: take one egg, about three tablespoons of flour, a pinch of salt, and a little milk to make a smooth paste. Mix this and then pour over the whitebait; cook in 'smoking hot' fat until golden brown and serve straight away with mint sauce and hot potato chips. Pickled onions are a fine accompaniment. ■

bookings contact InterCity travel centres NZ-wide (☎ freephone (0800) 802 802). The Greymouth centre's number is ☎ 768 1490. Various combination packages are offered.

Getting Around

Graeme Peter Cycle & Sport (☎ 768 6559), 34 Mackay St, rents bicycles, tandems, or baby push chairs. Greymouth Taxis (☎ 768 7078) goes to the airport for $10.

GREYMOUTH TO HOKITIKA

From Greymouth to Hokitika you get great views of the wild West Coast. If you deviate from the main road towards the beach you will see miles of salt spray and endless lines of driftwood. There are two very unusual bridges that you have to cross – **Taramakau** and **Arahura** (near a Maori settlement on the river, made famous by greenstone). A few years ago you may have met an oncoming train as these two bridges carry a railway line down the centre. Each bridge had its own gatekeeper.

Shantytown

This model village is eight km south of Greymouth and three km inland from the main road. Shantytown is a reconstruction of West Coast life in the gold rush days, with all the buildings a town of that era would have had. For many the prime attraction will

be the two 1897 steam locomotives taking you out for a short trip into the bush. You can also have a go at gold panning; there's an old fellow there to give you pointers and everyone is assured of coming up with at least a few flakes of gold to take away in a little bottle. It is advertised as 'NZ's most unique tourist attraction' – it is hardly that.

Shantytown is open 8.30 am to 5 pm daily and entry, including train rides, costs $7 (children with family $2). If you want to try panning for gold buy a combined ticket ($10), which includes the gold panning, at the entrance, otherwise it's an extra $4 at the pan.

Continuing 17 km inland from Shantytown through Marsden and Dunganville you come to the interesting **Woods Creek Track**, a very easy one-km loop walk through an old gold-mining area. There are a number of tunnels which you can enter if you have a torch (flashlight). A pamphlet about the track is available at Shantytown. If you have difficulty finding tracks take a tour with Out & About Tours for $35; the track is just part of this excursion.

Places to Stay & Eat You can't go past the *Paroa Hotel & Motel* (☎ 762 6860) for good old-fashioned West Coast hospitality. It is on the beach and the new Wintergarten offers a respite from the sandflies. Self-contained motel units cost $70 for two; there is budget accommodation available at $25 per person, and good hearty meals are available from the restaurant. All worth it just for an evening walk along the unspoilt Paroa Beach, about 100 metres from the hotel.

HOKITIKA

Hokitika, or Hoki as it is affectionately known to locals (population 3500), is 40 km south of Greymouth. It was settled in the 1860s after the discovery of gold in the region. It became a very busy port and ships often lay four abreast in the river by the wharf. The turn-around time was fast and life on the waterfront was hectic. In one busy five-day period 42 vessels entered the river. Locals used to watch ships attempt to run the bar and often saw them beached by tricky waves.

Hokitika is now a major centre for the working of greenstone and, for a while, its tourism resurgence was based on this. There is, however, far more to do in the region than look at stone being mass produced into bookends, tikis and taniwha. Hokitika is the centre of a region that is rich in history and nearby are a wealth of native forests, lakes and rivers.

Take the time to do the historical walk which is outlined in the museum pamphlet *Hokitika Historic Walk*. The Custom House and Gibson Quay are well worth looking at – it is not hard to imagine the river and wharf choked with sailing ships over a hundred years ago.

Information

The Hokitika Visitor Information Centre (☎ 755 8322) has moved to the corner of Weld and Sewell Sts in the Westland District Council offices, and is open weekdays from 9 am to 5 pm. From mid-December to March it's open on Saturday and Sunday too, also from 9 am to 5 pm.

Hokitika has several banks and, except for one branch of the Westland Bank in Harihari and an EFTPOS facility at Franz Josef, there are no more banks further south until you reach Wanaka. There's an AA agent beside

the Hokitika Motel in Fitzherbert St, on the outskirts of town.

Museum

The West Coast Historical Museum, on Tancred St, has many gold-mining relics. Medal collectors will revel in the hidden items here. It's open 9.30 am to 5 pm daily. Admission is $2.55 (children $1) including an audio-visual presentation. You can pan for gold at the museum for $5 and they have a good audiovisual on the gold rush.

Greenstone

Greenstone is big in Hoki. Historically, greenstone or jade was much treasured by the Maoris who used it for decorative jewellery – tikis – and for carving their lethal weapons – the flat war clubs known as meres – from the hard stone. Since greenstone is found predominantly on the West Coast, expeditions undertaken by the Maoris to collect it not only took months but were dangerous. Working the stone with their primitive equipment was no easy task either, but they managed to produce some exquisite items.

The legend of Tamatea explains why there are differing types of greenstone in the South Island. Tamatea's three wives were either abducted by Poutini (a taniwha) or they deserted him. At Anita Bay he found one wife turned into greenstone, and when he wept his tears entered it, giving it its flecked appearance; hence the name given to the stone is *tangiwai* ('water of weeping'). When travelling north he heard voices in the Arahura Valley and went to investigate. His companion, Tumuaki, breached tapu (law) by putting his burnt fingers in his mouth while cooking, so Tamatea was not able to find his other wives. Like his wife Hinetangiwai, the other wives were turned into greenstone – *auhanga* and *pounamu*.

Crafts

You can buy jewellery, tikis of course, and other greenstone ornaments from Westland Greenstone on Tancred St. It's open from 8 am to 5 pm daily. Whether you're buying or not you can visit the workshop and see greenstone being cut and carved. Even with modern tools and electric power, working greenstone is not simple and good greenstone pieces will not be cheap. Mountain Jade in Weld St specialises in jade sculpture as well as jewellery and is also open daily from 8 am to 5 pm.

There are several other craft outlets in Hokitika including the House of Wood and the Hokitika Craft Gallery almost opposite Westland Greenstone. Next door, The Gold Room sells handcrafted gold jewellery made from locally mined gold, with many specimens of the distinctively flat gold nuggets found in the region. Also in Tancred St is the Hokitika Glass Studio. All of these shops are open daily from 8.30 am to 5 pm. A block over on Revell St is Genesis Creations. Seaside Jade, next door to Genesis Creations, is another of the many such places in this area.

Tiki

Hokitika Tweed in Revell St also does some interesting work, weaving on Dobcross 1955 model looms imported from England. You'll find them weaving from 9 am to 4 pm on weekdays.

White Water Rafting

Alpine Rafts (☎ 755 4077) offers various rafting trips including all-day 'thrill seeker' trips down some of New Zealand's steepest rafting rivers. They use helicopters for access to the upper parts of the rivers, making the experience doubly exciting. A full day trip down the Wanganui River includes a dip in the hot pools on the riverbank, and a BBQ at the end; the cost is $185 per person. A two-day trip in the same area is available; the price is negotiable. They used to do the Frisco Canyon – inquire as to whether or not they still do this great piece of white water.

Walks

There are many walks in the area and detailed brochures outlining these are available from the information centre or the DOC office. A number of walks are near Lake Kaniere. Dorothy Falls, Kahikatea Forest and Canoe Cove are all short walks, but the Lake Kaniere Walkway is 13 km and takes about four hours. Longer walks include Mt Tahua and Mt Brown, both of seven hours duration. The Mahinapua Walkway which takes you through the scenic reserve to a swamp teeming with wildlife and to sand dunes takes two hours, covering 5.5 km.

The premier walk in the area is the Alps crossing via the three to five-day Three Pass (Browning-Whitehorn-Harman) route. You can choose to walk up either the Styx or Arahura rivers to start but it is for the experienced only – there are many steep climbs. The scenery, however, makes it worthwhile. Another option for experienced trampers is the five-day trip via the Whitcombe Pass to Canterbury.

Other Things to See

There's a glow-worm dell right beside the

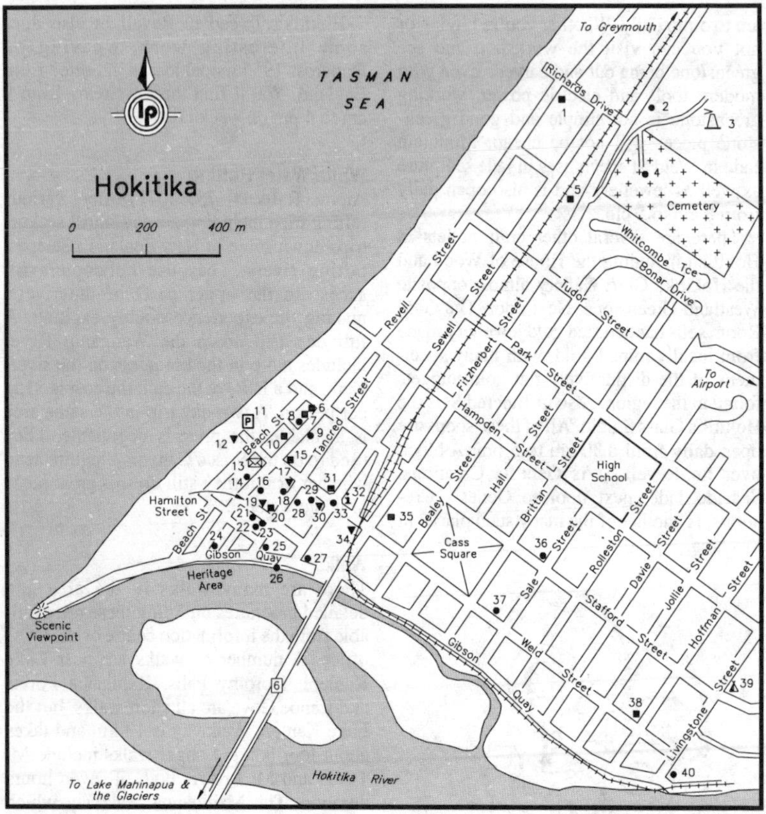

Hokitika

TASMAN SEA

0   200   400 m

road on the northern edge of the town. Hokitika has a number of historically interesting old buildings and a leaflet describing a historic walk is available at the information centre or the museum. In 1866 Revell St had no less than 84 hotels! Only six hotels are left in Hokitika.

The Heritage Hokitika group has recently renovated the historic old wharf along Gibson Quay, where there are historical buildings and various water activities.

There are a number of scenic areas around Hokitika including Lake Kaniere, Lake Mahinapua, the Hokitika Gorge, and Golds-

borough, with many interesting walking tracks, gold panning, camping, fishing, and so on. In 1991 the *Takutai Belle*, a paddle steamer, started operating on Mahinapua Creek taking visitors up to the lake and back. The information centre has details on the many other things to do in the region.

Places to Stay

Fortunately for the new breed of backpacker there are two suitable places. *Pete's Place* (☎ 755 8845) is opposite the turn into town at 40 Fitzherbert St. All options here are $15

■ PLACES TO STAY

1   Goldsborough Motels
5   Hokitika Motels
6   Beach House Backpacker
7   Club Hotel
10 Southland Hotel
15 Westland Hotel
20 Central Guesthouse
31 Railway Hotel
35 Pete's Place
38 Kiwi Motor Lodge
39 Hokitka Holiday Park

▼ PLACES TO EAT

10 Preston's Bakery & Tearooms
12 Tasman View Restaurant
17 PR's Coffee Shop
19 Café de Paris
30 Millie's Place
34 Porky's Takeaways

    OTHER

2   Glow-Worm Dell
8   Price Cutters Supermarket
9   New World Supermarket

11 Parking
13 Post Office
14 Genesis Creations
16 Westland Tweed
18 Hokitika Craft Gallery, The Gold Room
25 Hokitika Glass Studio
27 Department of Conservation (DOC)
28 Westland Greenstone
29 Ocean Paua
32 Visitor Information Centre
36 Petrol Station
37 Petrol Station
40 Westland Cooperative Dairy
    Milkpowder Factory

    HISTORIC TRAIL

3   Hokitika Lighthouse
4   Hokitika Cemetery & Explorers'
    Monument
21 Carnegie Building
22 West Coast Historical Museum &
    Public Toilets
23 Statue of 'Summer'
24 Site of Hokitika's First Store
26 Custom House
27 Government Building, Seddon Statue
33 Clock Tower

(linen supplied $20) and there is a females only dorm. Pete offers free tea and coffee and sometimes arranges visits to the local glow-worm dell. There is a car for hire at $30 per day. The place has good showers, a TV lounge and plenty of reading material. Nearly on the beach, at 137 Revell St, you'll find the *Beach House* (☎ 755 6589. Share rooms are $14 and doubles $16 for each person. This place has a great atmosphere – there are beach views from the back and mountain views from the front verandah. It is being upgraded bit by bit.

The *Hokitika Holiday Park* (☎ 755 8172), at 242 Stafford St, has a variety of accommodation possibilities. Camping is $14 a night for two people, $2 more with power. They also have a bunkhouse costing $9 per person, a selection of cabins priced from $22 to $36 for two, and tourist flats at $46 for two.

Hokitika has a number of motels, all from around $60 to $65 a night. There are also several hotels around the town centre. The big *Westland Hotel* (☎ 755 8411), on the corner of Weld and Revell Sts, has rooms at singles/doubles for $40/50. The *Club Hotel* (☎ 755 8170) at No 131 Revell St has rooms for $27/52. The *Southland Hotel* (☎ 755 8334), also on Revell St (No 111), has budget singles/doubles at about $35/45, in addition to their more expensive 'deluxe' rooms at $75/85.

The pleasant *Central Guesthouse* (☎ 755 8232) at 20 Hamilton St is a cosy place with rooms at $39/59 for singles/doubles. Meals are extra, but good value. The information centre has listings for farmstays around Hokitika and all around south West Coast.

There are *DOC campsites* at Goldsborough, 17 km from Hokitika; Hans Bay, Lake Kaniere, 18 km east of Hokitika; and Shanghai Bay, Lake Mahinapua, 16 km south of Hokitika.

WEST COAST

Places to Eat

For snacks and sandwiches you can try the *Preston Bakery & Tearoom* on Revell St, *Millie's Place* at 135 Weld St and *PR's Coffee Shop Bistro* in Tancred St. Millie's Place has a chef from Beijing who prepares huge Chinese dishes from $9 to $20. *Porky's Takeaways* by the railway tracks, on Weld St, does fish & chips.

In the pub food category, the *Westland Hotel* has a carvery for lunch and dinner. The *Central Restaurant* at 65 Fitzherbert St has a good range of pizzas.

Overlooking Hokitika's windswept and grey beach (this is the attraction for a lot of diners) is the *Tasman View* à la carte restaurant; they have a smorgasbord on Friday which is popular with locals. One reader recommended the French-style food at the *Cafe de Paris*, on Sewell St near the corner of Weld St, as the best food they had in NZ – venison, lamb, mussels, whitebait, etc.

Getting There & Away

Air Air New Zealand Link (incorporating Air Nelson; ☎ 755 8134) has three daily direct flights to Christchurch, with connections to other centres. WestAir (☎ mobile (025) 330 969; Franz Josef 752 0738) run an air taxi service from Hokitika to Greymouth ($50), Franz Josef Glacier ($125) and Fox Glacier ($150); all prices quoted are return and require a minimum of two passengers. They will even transport exhausted cyclists and their bikes up and down parts of the Coast. Their charter prices are available on request.

Bus The InterCity services down the coast from Greymouth to Fox Glacier pass through Hokitika at least once a day. Travel time is 40 minutes to Greymouth, and four hours to Fox Glacier. The InterCity agent is the Travel Centre at 65 Tancred St. Coast to Coast Shuttle, servicing Arthurs Pass and Christchurch, also calls into Hokitika; book at the Visitor Information Centre.

SOUTH FROM HOKITIKA

It's about 140 km south from Hokitika to the Franz Josef Glacier but you can make a few stops on the way. Hitching along this coast is notoriously bad, but the InterCity bus from Greymouth to the glaciers will stop anywhere along the highway. The Lake Mahinapua Hotel is a bit of a local institution – so much so that it rates its own entry here as a very typical West Coast pubs.

Ross

Ross, 30 km south of Hokitika, is a small, historic gold-mining township, and in fact gold is still mined in the town today. It was the place where New Zealand's largest gold nugget, the 99-ounce 'Honourable Roddy', was found in 1907. Currently Grimmond House, once the Bank of New Zealand in the gold rush era, is serving as the Visitors Information Centre. There's a small museum in an 1885 Miner's Cottage. It's supposed to be open from 8 am to 4 pm daily but if it's closed just ask around town and someone can easily be found to come and open it.

The Miner's Cottage sits at the beginning of two historic goldfield walkways, the Jones Flat Walk and the Water Race Walk. Each takes about one to 1½ hours and passes by numerous interesting features from the gold rush days. In the evening there are glow-worms on these walks but at any time, be very careful to stay on the walkway or you could find yourself down a mineshaft!

A long area along Jones Creek is open to the public for gold panning and pans may be hired from several businesses in town. Near the car park in front of the Miner's Cottage is a new working gold mine where you can stand and watch the operations from above. There's a small, but unusual, museum on the main street, which may be closed in winter. Also centrally located is a display of old gold-mining equipment and buildings.

At the Waitaha Valley, a few km south of Ross, South Westland Saddle Safaris (☎ 753 3095) conducts horse treks. Full-day treks cost $60 and they also do excursions up to 12 days long.

Places to Stay & Eat The atmospheric *Empire Hotel* (☎ 755 4005), 19 Aylmer St, has camp sites at $5 per person, cabins at $12 per person, B&B rooms at $40/80 for singles/doubles. Around the corner the *Ross Motel* (☎ 755 4022) has motel units at $58 a double, ask about them at the Manera Store. At the *City Hotel* (☎ 755 4104), 35 Moorhouse St, B&B is $30 per person.

The *Empire Hotel* has bar meals at lunch and dinner time and the *City Hotel* has a dining room. Or there's the *Nicada Tearooms & Restaurant* on the main street.

Pukekura to Okarito
From Ross it's another 109 km to Franz Josef, but there are plenty of bush tracks and lakes along the way if you want to break the journey and can stand the sandflies. Heading southwards the vegetation becomes more and more dense rainforest, in many parts it looks like you could walk right over the top of the forest easier than you could find a way through it!

There are many places along here where you can find low-cost accommodation. About 20 km south of Ross the *Lake Ianthe Cabins* (☎ 755 4032) near Pukekura has cabins at $27 for two and $11 for each additional person, with activities including boating, sailing, fishing and hunting. There is a giant matai tree about 100 metres south of the lake on the eastern side of the road. The short track to it is marked.

Harihari
The small town of Harihari is 22.5 km south of Lake Ianthe. Harihari made world headlines in 1931 when Guy Menzies completed the first solo flight across the Tasman Sea from Sydney, Australia. The landing was anything but smooth as he crash-landed *Southern Cross Junior* in the La Fontaine swamp. The aircraft turned over and when he undid his safety straps he fell head first in the mud. He had made the trip in 11¾ hours, 2½ hours less than Charles Kingsford Smith and his crew in 1928.

There are several interesting things to do around Harihari. The two to three-hour **Harihari Coastal Walkway** (also called the

Doughboy Walk) is a popular local attraction, with a lookout over the coastline, forest and mountains. You can also walk up into the Wilberg Range near the town. Other possibilities are an old goldminers' pack track, or rivermouth trout and salmon fishing and exploring of the estuaries and wetlands of the Poerua and Wanganui rivers. In a day of birdwatching you may be lucky to see native parrots, parakeets, herons, penguins, kakas and a number of migratory wading birds.

For specific information, try the Hokitika Visitor Information Centre.

Places to Stay & Eat The *Harihari Motor Inn* (☎ 753 3026) has motel units at $45/55 for a single/twin, and campervan sites at $12 per van, with free use of the hot spa pool. Across the road, *Tomasi's Motel* (☎ 753 3116) has cabins with private bathroom at $15 per person, and motel units at $50 a double. Neither one has kitchen facilities for the budget rooms, but there are several places in town where you can get inexpensive meals, including a *tearooms*, a *fish & chips shop*, and the *Motor Inn*, which has pub meals and takeaways plus a separate restaurant and two bars. If you wish to stay on a farm try *Muir's Farm Stay* (☎ 753 3074) at Harihari. Inquire about their rates and other farmstay possibilities.

The nearest *DOC campsite* is at Lake Ianthe, 18 km north of Harihari.

Whataroa & the Kotuku (White Heron) Sanctuary
Near Whataroa, 35 km south of Harihari, is a sanctuary for the kotuku (white herons), which nest here from November to February; it is the only NZ nesting site of this species. The herons then fly as individuals to winter throughout New Zealand. Royal spoonbills also nest here; their only two other nesting sites in New Zealand are near Moeraki and Green Island near Dunedin.

White Heron Sanctuary Tours (☎ 753 4120) at Whataroa operate jet-boat tours to see the birds in their colony beside the Waitangi-Taona River. Don't panic, bird lovers, as the jet-boat doesn't actually enter the nesting area. You walk along a boardwalk to the hide and are accompanied by a DOC officer. Cost is $60 (children $30) for the two-hour return trip. You can go in on your own but you must get permission from the DOC and check in with the warden at the sanctuary.

There is year-round accommodation behind the sanctuary tours office with White Heron Sanctuary Tours Motel & Cabins (☎ 753 4120) – part of this operation is called Whataroa Backpackers. Shared accommodation is $15 (you supply your own linen), motel-style doubles cost $55, or you can camp in a tent for $8 per person. Scenic jet-boat tours of the river operate all year round. The Whataroa Hotel (☎ 753 4076) charges $54 for B&B for two persons. They also have meals. Across the road from the tours office Country Fare Tearooms serve good West Coast tucker.

Okarito

Another 15 km south of Whataroa is The Forks. From here it's just 17 km to Franz Josef, but if you turn off here you will find peaceful Okarito, 13 km away on the coast. This is the hometown of writer Keri Hulme, the author of bestseller *The Bone People*, much of which is set in this region.

Okarito Lagoon is the feeding ground for the white heron and it's a good place for watching all kinds of birds in their natural habitat, including kiwis. There are lots of walks along the coast from Okarito – get hold of leaflets from the Visitor Information Centre in Hokitika or Franz Josef. Remember that the sanctuary tours only leave from Whataroa.

Okarito Nature Tours (☎ & fax 753 4014), The Strand, organise kayaking trips into the beautiful Okarito Lagoon. The lagoon is New Zealand's largest unmodified wetland and consists of shallow open water and tidal flats. This home to water birds, including the white heron, is surrounded by rimu and kahikatea rainforest. The operators of the nature tours provide a full species list. There is a pamphlet, *Okarito Walks*, which outlines

a number of excursions in the area. If you wish to paddle in the lagoon you can rent kayaks for $15 per day, or go on a guided boat tour for $50 with Okarito Nature Tours.

Places to Stay & Eat The small *Okarito YHA Hostel* (☎ 753 4082) was upgraded in late 1990. It now has electricity but costs $8 per night. Hot showers are available from the nearby caravan park for multiples of 50c. Originally the hostel was the schoolhouse, built in the 1870s when Okarito was a thriving gold town. Opposite the hostel is a very basic camping ground with BBQs and toilets, but it's a pleasant location and the price is right: just whatever you care to donate to the camp's upkeep. If you plan to stay at Okarito, bring your own food and sleeping bag, as supplies out there are limited. There is also a *DOC campsite* here.

Okarito to the Glaciers

Back towards the Forks turn-off, three km in from the highway, The Forks Lodge (☎ 753 4122) is an attractive little lodge with shared accommodation at $10 per person. It has everything you need – fully equipped kitchen, showers, etc – but bring your own bedding and food. They also have caravan power sites which cost $12 for two.

Soon after The Forks you reach Franz Josef, Westland National Park and the magnificent peaks of the Southern Alps.

The Glaciers

The two glaciers of the Westland National Park – the Fox and the Franz Josef – are among the most interesting sights in New Zealand. Nowhere else in the world, at this latitude, do glaciers approach so close to the sea. Unlike the Tasman Glacier, on the other side of the dividing range in Mt Cook National Park, these two are just what glaciers should be – mighty rivers of ice, tumbling down a valley towards the sea.

The reason for the glaciers' development is three-fold. The wet West Coast weather means there's a lot of snow on the mountain slopes. Secondly the zone where the ice accumulates on the glaciers is very large, so there's a lot of ice to push down the valley. Finally, they're very steep glaciers – the ice can get a long way before it finally melts. The rate of descent is staggering: a plane that crashed on the Franz Josef in 1943, 3.5 km from the terminal face, made it down to the bottom 6½ years later – a speed of 1.5 metres a day. At times the glacier can move at up to five metres a day, over 10 times as fast as glaciers in the Swiss Alps. More usually, it moves at about a metre a day.

Glaciers

You may find it useful to know some glacial terminology before visiting the Fox or Franz Josef glaciers, or any of the glaciers of the Mt Cook region (see the Canterbury chapter):

Accumulation zone – where the snow collects
Ablation zone – where the glacier melts
Bergschrund – large crevasse in the ice near the headwall or starting point of the glacier
Blue ice – as the accumulation zone or névé snow is compressed by subsequent snowfalls it becomes firn and then blue ice
Crevasses – as the glacial ice moves down the mountain it bends and cracks open in crevasses as it crosses irregularities
Dead ice – as a glacier retreats, isolated chunks of ice may be left behind. Sometimes these can remain for many years
Firn – partly compressed snow on the way to becoming glacial ice
Glacial flour – the river of melted ice that flows off glaciers is a milky colour from the suspension of finely ground rocks
Icefall – when a glacier descends so steeply that the upper ice breaks up in a jumble of iceblocks
Kettle lake – lake formed by the melt of an area of isolated dead ice
Lateral moraine – walls formed at the sides of the glacier
Névé – snowfield area where firn is formed
Seracs – ice pinnacles formed, like crevasses, by the glacier bending over irregularities
Terminal – the final ice face at the end of the glacier
Terminal moraine – mass of boulders and rocks marking the end point of the glacier, its final push down the valley

FRANZ JOSEF GLACIER

The Franz Josef was first explored in 1865 by Austrian Julius Haast, who named it after the Austrian emperor. Apart from short advances from 1907-09, 1921-34, 1946-59 and 1965-67, the glacier has generally been

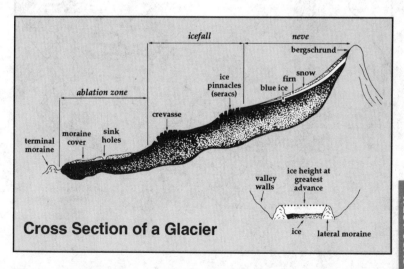

Cross Section of a Glacier

Glaciers & Westland National Park

0   5   10 km

WEST COAST

Advance & Retreat

Glaciers always advance, they never really retreat. The word 'retreat', with its image of the glacier pulling back up the valley, is rather a misnomer. The ice is always advancing, it's just that sometimes it melts even faster than it advances. And in that case the terminal or end face of the glacier moves back up the mountain.

Glacial ice, pulled by gravity, always advances downhill, but at the same time it melts. When advance exceeds melt the whole length of the glacier increases, when melt exceeds advance the length decreases. The great mass of ice higher up the mountain pushes the ice down the Fox and Franz Josef valleys at prodigious speeds but like most glaciers in the world this past century has been a story of steady retreat and only the odd short advance.

The last great ice age of 15,000 to 20,000 years ago saw the glaciers reach right down to the sea. Then warmer weather came and they may have retreated even further back than their current position. In the 14th century a new 'mini ice age' started and for centuries the glaciers advanced, reaching their greatest extent around 1750. At both the Fox and Franz Josef the terminal moraines from that last major advance can be clearly seen. In the nearly 250 years since then the glaciers have steadily retreated and the terminal face is now several km back from its first recorded position in the late 19th century or even from its position in the 1930s.

From 1965 to 1968 the Fox and Franz Josef glaciers made brief advances of about 180 metres and in 1985 they once again started to advance and have been moving forward steadily and fairly dramatically ever since. Nobody is quite sure why this advance is taking place. It could be cooler or more overcast summers or it could be the result of heavy snowfalls 10 or 15 years ago which are now working their way down to the bottom of the glacier. ■

in retreat since that time, although in 1985 it started advancing again and in early 1990 it was still moving down. It has progressed well over 1000 metres, moving forward by about 30 cm a day, although it is still several km back from the terminal point Haast first recorded.

Information

The Westland National Park Information Centre (☎ 752 0796; fax 752 0797) is open 8 am to 5 pm daily. The centre has leaflets on the many short walks around the glacier. In the summer they operate a free programme of guided walks and evening lectures and slide shows.

There is an EFTPOS facility at the local petrol station, Glacier Motors – at the time of writing there were not many of these south of Hokitika. DA's Restaurant acts as the local postal agency.

Walks

There are many walks to do around the glacier. Ask at the information centre for their excellent walk leaflets. There are several good glacier viewpoints close to the

road up to the glacier car park – including one from where the first photo of the glacier was taken, with a reproduction of that historic photo there so you can check how things have changed.

You can walk to the glacier from the car park, or you may find it worthwhile to fork out $32 (children $20) for a guided walk on the glacier ice with an experienced guide. In the high season there are guided walks departing twice daily from the Franz Josef Glacier Guides office (☎ 752 0763) in the village; equipment, including boots, is included.

Other walks require a little worthwhile footslogging. The loop track, off the Glacier Access Rd, is a 15-minute stroll by the terminal moraine from the 1750 advance and Peter's Pool – a small 'kettle lake' formed by the melting of ice buried and left by a retreating glacier. It's a longer walk (3½ hours) to Roberts Point, overlooking and quite close to the terminal face.

There is a pleasant one-hour round trip around the Terrace Track, which starts on the old Callery Track, scene of much gold-mining activity in earlier days, and leads up

WEST COAST

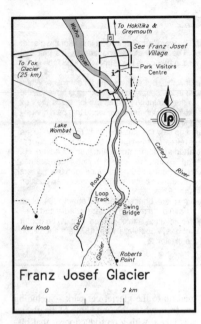

Franz Josef Glacier

onto a terrace at the back of the village, giving pleasant views down the Waiho River.

Aerial Sightseeing

Mt Cook Airline (☎ Franz Josef 752 0714; Fox 751 0812) has skiplane flights over both glaciers. You can fly over both glaciers for $88 (children $66), land on one of them for $90 ($68), visit the Tasman Glacier on the other side as well for $150 ($113) including a landing, or make the same Grand Circle route (three glaciers) but without a landing for $154 ($116).

The Helicopter Line (☎ 752 0767) flies from Franz Josef and has glacier flights from $65 (children under 14 half price) up to $106 ($50) for a snow landing, $140 ($90) for both glaciers and a landing on one, or $180 ($90) for the full Grand Circle across the divide and a landing. Franz Josef Heliservices (☎ Franz Josef 752 0793; Fox 751 0853) fly from both Fox and Franz Josef with roughly the same flights for roughly the same prices.

Flights up and over the glaciers are expensive but they're a superb experience – it's money well spent. You can also make helihikes with a flight up to the glacier and then a guided walk across the ice.

On the Grand Circle flights, done by several companies at both Franz Josef and Fox, you get to see not only the most famous glaciers but a number of others as well. The route passes over at least nine glaciers including the Fox, Franz Josef, Balfour, La Perouse, Hooker, Tasman, Rudolph, Albert and Victoria glaciers!

Glacier Rafting

From November to March there's milky white water rafting on the Waiho River, conducted by Glacier Rafting (part of Buller Adventure Tours; ☎ 752 0704). A 1½-hour trip costs $38 (minimum age 13) and wetsuits, etc are provided.

Tours

Stan Peterson operates Westland Guiding Services (☎ 752 0750), for guided fishing and hunting safaris. The fishing trips for salmon and trout are a good deal, the hourly cost of $45 for the boat can be shared by up to four people.

Waiho Stables (☎ 752 0747) conducts 2½-hour horse-riding tours through rainforest for $35; they also do an overnight trip for an additional $30 (six or more people).

White Heron Sanctuary Tours (☎ 753 4120) conduct tours of the white heron sanctuary near Whataroa during the herons' breeding season from November to February. See Whataroa for further details; note that they don't pick up from Franz Josef.

Places to Stay

Camping & Cabins The *Franz Josef Holiday Park* (☎ 752 0766) is a km or so south of the township, right beside the river. Tent sites are $7 per person, sites with power are $8 for one or $15 for two. There's a 12-bed dormitory with beds at $8, a lodge with double or twin rooms at $15 per person, cabins at $22 for one or two people, or cottages at $36 for two.

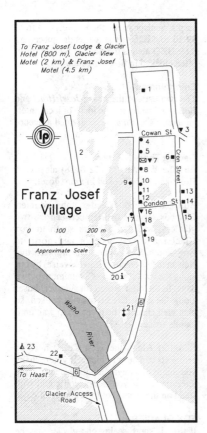

To Franz Josef Lodge & Glacier Hotel (800 m), Glacier View Motel (2 km) & Franz Josef Motel (4.5 km)

Franz Josef Village

0   100   200 m

Approximate Scale

Cowan St

Cron Street

Condon St

Waiho River

To Haast

Glacier Access Road

■ PLACES TO STAY

1   Westland Motor Inn
6   Rata Grove Motel
13 Bushland Court Motel
14 Chateau Franz Josef Backpackers
15 YHA Hostel
22 Glacier Gateway Motor Lodge
23 Franz Josef Holiday Park

▼ PLACES TO EAT

3   Batson's Tavern
7   DA's Restaurant & Tearoom
16 Blue Ice Pizza

OTHER

2   Helipad & Airstrip
4   Glacier Helicopters, Bicycle Hire
5   Mt Cook Airline
7   Taxi Depot, Postal Agency
8   Cardphones
9   Cardphones
10 Glacier Motors (EFTPOS Facility)
11 Glacier Guides
12 Helicopter Line
14 WestAir
17 Waiho Stables
18 Medical Centre
19 Catholic Church
20 Franz Josef DOC HQ & Visitor Centre
21 Anglican Church of St James

The Forks Lodge, 20 km north, also has caravan sites, and there's a minimal-facility camping ground at Okarito, 25 km north (see Okarito).

For a great *DOC campsite*, try McDonalds Creek, Lake Mapourika, 10 km north of Franz Josef.

Hostels The *Franz Josef Glacier YHA Hostel* (☎ 752 0754) is at 2-4 Cron St, just off the main road. It's a pleasant hostel and costs $14 a night. All rooms are centrally heated, with twin and family rooms available, and it's open all day. They have a small

shop, pool table, videos in the evenings, and a budget priced meal service from September to April.

Next door is the *Chateau Franz Josef Backpackers* (☎ & fax 752 0738) where share rooms are $13.50 and double/twins $16 per person; tent sites are $6. They have a number of facilities at this pleasant place including laundry, dryer, free video library, linen hire, and bicycle hire ($10 for a half day and $20 all day). The staff are extremely helpful.

On SH 6 is *Franz Josef Lodge – Backpackers* (☎ 752 0712) which has centrally heated rooms and a drying room. The rooms, all $14.50 per person in twins/quads, are in the former THC hotel's staff quarters, so it is

WEST COAST

close to the Franz Josef public bar and bistro. The lounge here has an open fire. You can purchase a discount meal voucher here for the bistro ($7.50).

Okarito, with its small YHA shelter hostel, is only 25 km north but it's a 13 km hitch from the highway. Or there's *The Forks Lodge*, three km from the same Okarito turn-off, 17 km north of Franz Josef. The Franz Josef Motor Camp also has some bunkroom accommodation.

Hotels & Motels There are half a dozen motels in Franz Josef, most with rooms from around $70 to $80 a night. *Bushland Court Motel* (☎ 752 0757) at 10 Cron St is the most economical of the lot, with units from $65 to $80 a night for two people. The *Westland Motor Inn* (☎ 752 0728) is rather more expensive as is the *Franz Josef Glacier Hotel* (☎ 752 0719) which is about a km north of the township and has double rooms from $120 to $140.

Places to Eat
The shops at Franz Josef have a good selection of food supplies. You can eat at the *Glacier Store & Tearoom* or at *DA's Restaurant & Tearoom*. Curiously, at DA's the cafe and takeaway section offers much the same menu as the proper restaurant side but at higher prices! In the restaurant there's a standard pub-style menu from chicken kiev to ham steak at around $14 to $20 including serve-yourself salads. Main courses in the coffee shop at the *Franz Josef Glacier Hotel* are also in the $14 to $20 range. The *Village Cafe*, upstairs in the Westland Motor Inn, has good meals and great views.

A local favourite is the *Blue Ice*, on SH 6, which is a pizza place and cafe. Small, medium and large pizzas are devoured here by a local population for too long starved of such delights. *Batson's Tavern & Grill Bar* on the corner of Cowan & Cron Sts, now saves the locals a trip down the road to the public bar at the Franz Josef Glacier Hotel. They have a good range of bistro meals (ham

steaks, venison, pork chops, beef, etc) from $9.50 to $12.50. It is a friendly place and their BBQ area is overlooked by rainforest, often cloaked in flowering rata.

Entertainment
The two bars, at the *Franz Josef Hotel* and *Batson's Tavern*, are the focus of local entertainment. The *Blue Ice*, if granted a licence in the near future, will join in as well.

Getting There & Away
Air The WestAir (☎ 752 0738) air taxi to Hokitika can be booked in Franz Josef.

Bus The northbound and southbound Inter-City bus services overlap between the two glaciers, with daily buses south to Fox Glacier and Queenstown and north to Greymouth. The connections are such that Nelson to Queenstown (or vice versa) by bus along the west coast takes a minimum of two days. In the high season (in summer) buses along the coast can be heavily booked, so plan well ahead or be prepared to wait until there's space.

Hitching Along the West Coast, hitching prospects can be very bleak. If you're lucky you might do Greymouth to Queenstown in three days – if you're not you could well stand on the same spot for a couple of days.

FOX GLACIER
If time is short, seeing one glacier may be enough, but if you have the time it's interesting to see both. Basically the same activities are offered at both glaciers – walks, glacier walks, flights and so on. Despite the consistent retreat throughout much of this century, the Fox Glacier, like the Franz Josef, has been on the advance since 1985. By 1987 it had moved forward a kilometre, and from May 1987 to October 1989 it advanced another 210 metres.

Information
The Fox Glacier Visitor Centre (☎ 751 0807) is open from 8.30 am to 4.30 pm daily. In the summer and during the holiday season it is

open much later and there are evening slide shows (sometimes there'll be a quick walk down to the glow-worm grotto afterwards). The centre has displays on the glaciers and natural environment of the area and leaflets on a number of interesting short walks around the glacier.

There's a petrol station in the town and if you're driving south, take note, this is the last fuel stop until you reach Haast, 120 km further on. Alpine Guides is the local postal agency, the stop for InterCity buses and Telecom phonecards are sold here.

Walks

The shortest and most popular walk at the Fox Glacier is the couple of minutes' stroll from the centre to the glow-worm grotto. It's close to the roadside just opposite the garage. Of course, you have to go in the dark of night in order to see the worms glowing! See the Waitomo section in the Waikato & the King Country chapter for more information on glow-worms.

Head towards the coast from the township for a viewpoint with superb views of the glacier and the whole mountain range. Before this viewpoint is the turn-off to **Lake Matheson** and one of the most famous panoramas in New Zealand. It's an hour's walk around the lake and at the far end you'll get a spectacular view of the mountains and their reflection in the lake. The best time to see the famed reflection is very early in the morning, when the lake is at its most mirror-like calm.

An almost equally famous viewpoint can be found off Glacier View Rd, by making the short climb up to **Cone Rock**, overlooking the glacier from a green and leafy lookout point, or the easier walk to Chalet lookout.

Mt Fox, off SH6 to Haast, is another excellent viewpoint – a three-hour walk one way.

There are many other interesting walks around the glacier, including the short moraine walk over the advance of 200 years ago, or forest walks on the Ngai Tahu Track, the short Minnehaha Walk or the River Walk. It takes something over an hour to walk from town to the glacier – it's 1½ km from town

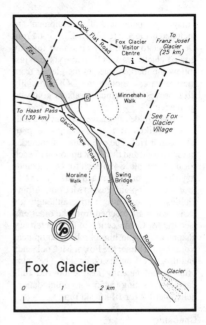

to the turn-off, and the glacier is another five km back from the main road.

A particularly interesting walk is the 1½ to two-hour coastal walk to the seal colony at **Gillespies Beach**. Up to 1500 seals can be seen here and the walk also passes an old miners' cemetery and the remains of gold dredges from the goldmining days. It is quite hazardous in places and not a suitable walk for children.

Another good walk takes you up to **Welcome Flat Hot Springs**, at the first hut on the Copland Track when entered from this side. It starts from the Copland Valley sign on the main road, 26 km south of town, from where it's an easy six-hour walk up the valley to the hot springs. The Welcome Flat Hut at the hot springs is an excellent modern hut, sleeping 40 people, and costing $8 per night.

As at the Franz Josef you can make guided walks up onto the glacier ice with Alpine Guides (☎ 751 0825; fax 751 0857). They leave at 9.30 am and 2 pm daily from the village, and boots and other equipment are included in the $32 (children $20) cost. From December to April they also have full-day guided glacier walks. Of course you can just follow the marked track to the glacier from the car park, although the DOC officially disapproves of unguided walkers going up on the ice.

Alpine Guides also have half-day and full-day helihikes and an overnight trip to Chancellor Hut. The overnight trip includes hut fees, food and the flight up for $415 each for three people, $495 each for two, including a helicopter trip on each end. If you want to cross the Copland Pass to Mt Cook, Alpine Guides will organise a trip, although it's easier when approached from the other end (see the Mt Cook section in the Canterbury chapter). You can hire climbing equipment from them at either the Fox or Mt Cook ends and drop it off on the other side. They also offer mountaineering instruction and full-day glacier skiing ($455 – accommodation, helicopter lift for 10-km ski run).

Canoeing

Canoe Fox (☎ 751 0825) based at the Alpine Guides building, organise canoeing trips to easy grade rivers such as the Jacobs and Papakeri Creek. The cost for a half-day trip is $45 (children $25). Jacobs River Canoe Hire (☎ 751 0871) conduct a one to two-hour trip through beautiful native forest on the Jacobs River; in calm places there are mirror reflections.

Aerial Sightseeing

Mt Cook Airline (☎ 751 0812) and Glacier Helicopters (☎ 751 0803) have the same flights from Fox Glacier as they do from Franz Josef – see the Franz Josef section for details. Both companies do landings around the tops of the glaciers.

Fox Glacier Helicopters (☎ 751 0866) at Fox also do glacier flights, with a 10-minute flight over the Fox Glacier for $66, a 20-minute flight over both Fox and Franz Josef for $120, a 15-minute landing flight at the top of Fox Glacier for $80, or a 40-minute Grand Circle flight for $170. As at the Franz

Josef Glacier these helicopter trips are expensive but a superb experience with quite amazing views.

Places to Stay

Camping & Cabins The *Fox Glacier Holiday Park* (☎ 751 0821) is a motor camp 400 metres down the Lake Matheson road from the town centre. Tent sites cost $7.75/15.50 for one/two people, powered sites are $8.50/17. It also has bunkroom accommodation at $11 per person, cabins at $28 for two, tourist cabins at $49 for two and motel units at the Alpine View Motel.

Hostels The *Ivory Towers* (☎ 751 0838) on Sullivans Rd, behind the Golden Glacier Motor Inn, is a friendly, well-equipped backpackers with rates of $13.50 a night in rooms sleeping four, or $16 a night each in twin rooms. There are heaters in all rooms – the types that allow you to dry clothes after a torrential downpour, and there are great views from the balcony. There is considerable renovation and upgrading taking place here.

The Fox Glacier Holiday Park, has bunkroom accommodation and inexpensive cabins, and you can also find cheap accommodation at the Fox Glacier Hotel (see Hotels & Motels).

B&B There are four B&B and farmstay places in the area. B&B in a twin is usually about $50 to $60. Ring these for more details: *Scott's* (☎ 751 0834), *Tucks* (☎ 751 0707), *Williams' Guesthouse* (☎ 751 0835) and *Homestyle B&B* (☎ 751 0895).

Hotels & Motels The elderly *Fox Glacier Hotel* (☎ 751 0839) in the centre of the village on Cook Flat Rd, has rooms with bathroom facilities for $85 per person. They also have a smaller number of cheaper rooms without attached bathrooms at $30 per person, or share budget rooms at $19 per person.

Close by, on the Lake Matheson road, is *Lake Matheson Motels* (☎ 751 0830) where the cost is $55 to $60 for two persons; they

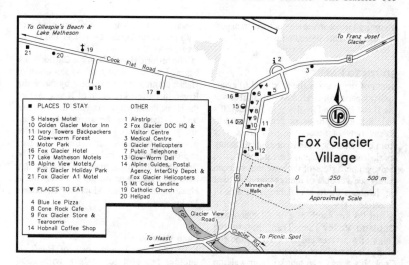

Fox Glacier Village

PLACES TO STAY

5 Halseys Motel
10 Golden Glacier Motor Inn
11 Ivory Towers Backpackers
12 Glow-worm Forest Motor Park
16 Fox Glacier Hotel
17 Lake Matheson Motels
18 Alpine View Motels/ Fox Glacier Holiday Park
21 Fox Glacier A1 Motel

PLACES TO EAT

4 Blue Ice Pizza
8 Cone Rock Cafe
9 Fox Glacier Store & Tearooms
14 Hobnail Coffee Shop

OTHER

1 Airstrip
2 Fox Glacier DOC HQ & Visitor Centre
3 Medical Centre
6 Glacier Helicopters
7 Public Telephone
13 Glow-Worm Dell
14 Alpine Guides, Postal Agency, InterCity Depot & Fox Glacier Helicopters
15 Mt Cook Landline
19 Catholic Church
20 Helipad

have a unit for the disabled. The *Golden Glacier Motor Inn* (☎ 751 0848) on the main road has rooms from $65 and upwards.

At the *Alpine View Motel* (☎ 751 0821), in the motor camp, units cost $64 for two. The small *Halseys Motel* (☎ 751 0833) is right in the township and a little cheaper, with rates at $50 for two.

Places to Eat
The shop in the town centre has a reasonable selection of essentials, although not as wide a choice as you'll find at the Franz Josef Glacier. You can eat at the *Cone Rock Cafe* or there are pretty good sandwiches and light meals at the *Hobnail Coffee Shop* in the Alpine Guides building. At the *Fox Glacier Hotel* there's a bar with good value bar meals from $5 to $11 and a restaurant with dinner main courses for $14, breakfast from $9 to $12.

Entertainment
Unlike the pub at the Franz Josef Glacier, the *Fox Glacier Hotel* is wonderfully central and you can sit with a jug of beer and talk about

where you've been and what you've seen during the day. If you want a more expensive, intimate cocktail try the bar at the *Golden Glacier Motor Inn*.

Getting There & Away
Air The WestAir (☎ 752 0738) air taxi to Hokitika, booked in Franz Josef, services Fox Glacier as well.

Bus The InterCity bus services overlap – southbound services from Greymouth start and finish at Fox Glacier, northbound ones from Queenstown continue to Franz Josef. Buses run every day to and from Greymouth (four hours) and Queenstown (eight hours). From Greymouth there are onward connections to Westport, Nelson, Picton and Christchurch.

See the Franz Josef section for the sad news on hitchhiking and a warning about the heavily booked bus services.

Getting Around
Mountain bicycles can be hired from Alpine Guides for $5 an hour, $15 for half a day or $25 for a full day; they provide helmets.

WEST COAST

There isn't much in the way of local transport services to sights so rent a bike.

SOUTH TO HAAST

South of the glaciers the road (SH 6) eventually departs from the coast and climbs over the Haast Pass and on down to Wanaka. It's a longish, all-day drive, presenting a remarkable variety of scenery as you cross over from one climatic zone to another. Heading south from the glaciers, the rainforest is so dense on both sides of the road that you can barely see a couple of metres into it. Further on, it opens up to reveal broad sweeps of coastline.

Just 26 km south of Fox Glacier is the **Copland Valley** (see Tramping in the Outdoor Activities chapter). This is the end of the Copland Track, coming over from Mt Cook. It's a very pleasant six-hour walk up the valley from the highway here to the first hut at Welcome Flat, where there are hot springs. A sign on the road marks the entrance to the valley and the track. There's transport from Fox Glacier to the Copland Valley by InterCity, but for the short length of journey it is expensive.

There are several possibilities for places to stay on the stretch of road between Fox Glacier and Haast to break up the journey. The *Pinegrove Motels* (☎ 751 0898), 35 km south of Fox Glacier, has a variety of accommodation including campervan sites at $7 per person, basic cabins at $15 per person, units at $45 for two in winter ($50 in summer).

Lake Paringa

Lake Paringa, about 70 km south of Fox Glacier and 50 km north of Haast, is a tranquil little trout-filled lake surrounded by forest, right beside the road. The Lake Paringa Heritage Lodge (☎ 751 0894) is on the lakeshore and has boats and canoes for hire. Rates are $15 per person in self-contained cabins if you supply your own bedding, or $60 for two in the larger motel units. About one km further south, still on the lakefront, is a free DOC camping area with just basic facilities – toilets and picnic areas.

The historic **Haast-Paringa Cattle Track** begins from the main road 43 km north of Haast, coming out at the coast by the Waita River, just a few km north of Haast. Before the Haast Pass road was opened in 1965, this trail was the only link between the Southland and the West Coast. It is being developed for tramping, with some huts already in place and others planned in the near future. The first leg of the track makes a pleasant day hike. Information on the track is available in Haast or at the Lake Moeraki Wilderness Lodge.

Lake Moeraki

Lake Moeraki, 31 km north of Haast, is another peaceful forest lake with good fishing, not far off the highway. It's also not far from the coast – just a 40-minute walk along a stream brings you to Monroe's Beach, where there's a breeding colony of Fiordland crested penguins, standing 70 cm tall, found there from July to November. Also at Monroe's Beach are fur seals and good snorkelling.

There are many other good short and long walks around the lake and the Moeraki River which runs from the lake to the sea. Fishing tackle, canoes and rowboats are available from the Lake Moeraki Wilderness Lodge.

The Lake Moeraki Wilderness Lodge (☎ Haast 750 0881; fax 750 0882), right on the highway and just 20 metres from the lakeside, has a variety of accommodation including lodge rooms at $89/99 for double/triple, and caravan sites at $25 for two persons. There's a riverside restaurant (a three-course dinner is $31.50), lots of help in organising outdoor and nature activities (these are expensive), and special indoor activities on rainy days. The owner of the lodge, Dr Gerry McSweeney, is the director of the New Zealand Forest and Bird Society, the country's largest conservation group. It was a co-winner of the 1992 NZ Ecotourism Awards.

Haast

This is a wildlife refuge where some of the biggest stands of rainforest survive alongside some of the most extensive wetlands. The kahikatea swamp forests, sand dune forests, seal and penguin colonies, the kaka, Red Hills and vast sweeeps of beach have ensured the preservation of this hauntingly beautiful place as a World Heritage area.

In the forests you will see the flaming red rimu in flower and kahikatea thriving in swampy lagoons. Birdlife abounds and the observant twitcher will see fantail, bellbird, native pigeon (kereru), falcons, kaka, kiwi and morepork. On the beaches you are likely to see blue penguins and Fiordland crested penguins. This is the home turf of legendary Arawata Bill who roamed this domain as a self-styled protector and explorer. Walk throught his incredible country and take a trip back hundreds of years – raupo, ferns and cabbage tree inhibit progress if you stray off the beaten track.

Haast Township

The tiny community of Haast is on the coast where the wide Haast River meets the sea, 120 km south of Fox Glacier. There's really not much to the town, although this is an area which has been targeted for tourist development, as it is now a World Heritage Area. Probably in the very near future there will be more activities including white water rafting, horse-trekking and so on, and more options in places to stay.

A series of tracks are being developed, including the **Hapuka Estuary Walk** leading from the motor camp, and a rainforest, seacoast and wetland walk along **Ship Creek**, halfway between Haast and Lake Moeraki. The aforementioned Haast-Paringa Cattle Track is also being upgraded.

A new DOC World Heritage Visitor Centre (☎ 750 0809) at the junction of SH 6 and Jackson Bay Rd on the southern bank of the Haast River, has current information on the area and on things to do, especially on nature-related activities.

Places to Stay & Eat

The *Haast Motor Camp* (☎ 750 0860) is at Okuru, 11 km south of Haast township on the road to Jackson Bay. Camping sites cost $15 for two, $15.50 with power, and there are various cabins at $30 or $38 for two, with linen for hire if needed. Closer to town is *Haast Highway Accommodation* (☎ 750 0703), at Marks Rd, three km east of the Visitor Centre and 200 metres from SH 6. There is a range of accommodation here: tent sites are $7 per person (extra $1 for powered site), a backpackers single is $14.50 and the motel units are from $55.

The *World Heritage Haast Hotel* (☎ 750 0828; fax 750 0827) has rooms from $49 to $69 for singles, and $59 to $79 for twins. There is a public bar nearby, a house bar and a good restaurant with a good selection of à la carte dishes. Two of their units are set up for disabled travellers.

Meals are served at the *restaurants* of both the Haast Hotel and the Lake Moeraki Wilderness Lodge, 31 km to the north.

HAAST PASS

Turning inland at Haast, snaking along beside the wide Haast River and climbing up the pass, you soon enter the Mt Aspiring National Park and the scenery changes again – the vegetation becomes much more sparse the further inland you proceed, until beyond the 563-metre summit you reach snow country covered only in tussock and scrub. Along the Haast Pass are many picturesque waterfalls, most of them just a couple of minutes' walk off the road.

The roadway over Haast Pass was opened in 1965. Prior to that the only southern link to the west coast was by the Haast-Paringa Cattle Track, walking or on horseback! The cattle track is now a historical walkway. On route to Wanaka you can see two sets of waterfalls close to the road – **Fantail** and **Thunder Creek falls**. See the DOC booklet *Haast Pass Highway*.

Heading south, the next town of any size you come to after Haast is Wanaka, a distance of 145 km, about 3½ hours by road (see the Otago & Southland chapter). If you're driving north, check your fuel gauge – the petrol station at Haast is the last one you'll come to until you reach Fox Glacier, 120 km north.

MAKARORA & THE SIBERIA VALLEY

When you reach Makarora you have left the West Coast. It has been included in this chapter as it still has a frontier feel about it, akin to the general atmosphere of the West Coast and it is the gateway to the Haast Pass and the West Coast for traffic heading up north.

It was a cruel early traveller who missed the point here. He called one of the world's most beautiful valleys Siberia and nearby Matterhornesque peaks Dreadful and Awful – he is not to be believed. Walk here in one of the last refuges of the blue duck and the rare orange-wattled South Island kokako (thought to be nearly extinct).

Makarora's permanent population is around 30. You really can't see the cluster of A-frame units from the road but they are capable of accommodating about 140 people, which can be useful from time to time when adventure-seekers arrive in town. Apart from these, there isn't much in this township, a fact from which it derives its charm. It is, however, the base for one of NZ's great outdoor adventures – the **Siberia Experience**. This is one of those Kiwi extravaganzas that combines thrill-seeking activities; in this case a small-plane flight (half an hour), a three-hour bush walk through a remote mountain valley, and a jet-boat trip (45 minutes) down a river valley completing the full-circle. Makarora Tourist Service (☎ 443 8372) operates the 'experience' from mid-October to mid-April and it costs $90.

Jet-Boating

Apart from the Siberia Experience (which includes jet-boating) there are plenty of other trips available. A 50-km return trip into Mt Aspiring National Park costs $40 if there is a minimum of 10 people. Contrast this to the 20-minute Shotover jet trip at $59. There is a transport service for trampers wishing to reach the top of the Wilkin River and a ferry service across from the Young River mouth when the Makarora is in flood.

For booking details, inquire at the Makarora Tourist Service.

Walks

There are many walks in the area. Shorter ones include the Old Bridal Track (1½ hours) which heads from the top of the Haast pass to Davis Flat; a 20-minute walk around Makarora; and the Blue Pools River Walk where you can see huge rainbow trout.

Two longer walks are the three-day Gillespies Pass trip and the head of the Wilkin River to Lake Castalia. The Gillespies Pass tramp goes via the Young, Siberia and Wilkin rivers (hopefully this will be further developed to take some of the heat off the Routeburn). With a jet-boat ride down the Wilkin to finish, this surely could rate alongside the Milford Track as one of the great tramps. The Wilkin Valley Track heads off from Kerin Forks Hut (where you can be dropped by jet-boat). It leads to Top Forks Hut, then the north branch of the Wilkin. Here you will see the picturesque lakes Diana, Lucidus and Castalia. These are one hour, 1½ hours and three-to-four hours respectively from Top Forks Hut.

If you want to stay in the Siberia Valley there is a 10-bed hut available; fees are payable at the ranger station at Makarora. For further independent possibilities in this region take a look at the Mt Aspiring National Park Service's brochure *Makarora Region*. There are DOC campsites at Cameron Flat, SH 6, 11 km north of Makarora, and Davis Flat, SH 6, 14 km north of Makarora.

Places to Stay & Eat

The Makarora Tourist Service operates the *A-Frame Motels & Cabins* (☎ 443 8372; fax 443 1082), in a bush setting. The cost is $55 for two people in the self-contained chalets,

Top: Cathedral Square, Christchurch (TW)
Bottom left: The Wizard, Cathedral Square, Christchurch (JW)

Top Left: Dune formation, Farewell Spit, Nelson (JW)
Top Right: Collecting water from Stirling Falls, the *Wanderer,* Milford Sound, Southland (JW)
Bottom: Fox Glacier, West Coast (HL)

$32 for two in the A-frame cabins, and $7 for a tent site. *Makarora House* (☎ 443 8255) was the first homestay in the valley; inquire at the Shell service station. B&B here costs $35/60 for a single/double.

There are *DOC campsites* at Cameron Flat, SH 6, 11 km north of Makarora, and Davis Flat, SH 6, 14 km north of Makarora

The *tearooms* are open from 8.30 am to 6 pm for lunch and snacks only, but the grocery stocks basic supplies.

Getting There & Away

West Coast Express, Fun Bus and Kiwi Experience buses regularly stop here. Inter-City have one northbound (to the Glaciers) and one southbound (to Hawea and Queenstown) coach per day.

Canterbury

Canterbury is the hub of the South Island. The large Canterbury region extends from near Kaikoura in the north to near Oamaru in the south, and from the Pacific coast to Arthurs Pass and Mt Cook in the Southern Alps.

This is one of the driest and flattest areas of New Zealand. The moisture-laden westerlies blowing in from the Tasman Sea are swept upwards by the Southern Alps, causing heavy rainfall on the South Island's West Coast – over five metres a year! When the winds continue east over Canterbury, they have lost most of their moisture, and the Canterbury region, though not so far from the West Coast distance-wise, has a markedly different climate, with an annual rainfall of only around 75 cm.

The predominant feature of the region is the Canterbury Plains, a large, flat area primarily devoted to farming and agriculture, which lies between the coast and the mountain foothills. Canterbury, however, contains the highest of New Zealand's mountains – Mt Cook, Mt Tasman, Mt Sefton, etc – so presents much more of a geographical contrast than any other part of New Zealand. This is perhaps the New Zealand – the blend of the rural and rugged – that is most often depicted to the overseas traveller. Christchurch, New Zealand's third largest city, is the centre for the region and, indeed, the South Island.

Information

All telephone numbers in the South Island have an 03 prefix if you are calling them from a long distance (even within the region).

Christchurch

The first Europeans in Christchurch began building huts along the Avon in 1851, but it

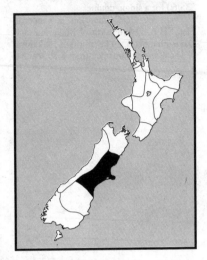

was not until March 1862 that it was incorporated as a city. The name Christchurch comes from Christ Church College at Oxford as one of the leaders of the early settlers was educated there. The Avon River which flows through Christchurch is named after a stream in Ayrshire, Scotland.

At the base of the hills of Banks Peninsula, Christchurch (population 308,200) is often described as the most English of New Zealand's cities. Many of the people represented by statues that dot the parks and boulevards are English, willows and oaks line the Avon where you may see someone in a boater steering a punt along, many schools still retain an English public-school style and the central square is dominated by a neo-Gothic cathedral in the fashion of English towns.

Get away from the square out to the western suburbs such as Fendalton, Avonhead, Bryndwr, Burnside and Ilam and you'll be struck by the tranquil atmosphere. Here are the exquisite gardens Christchurch

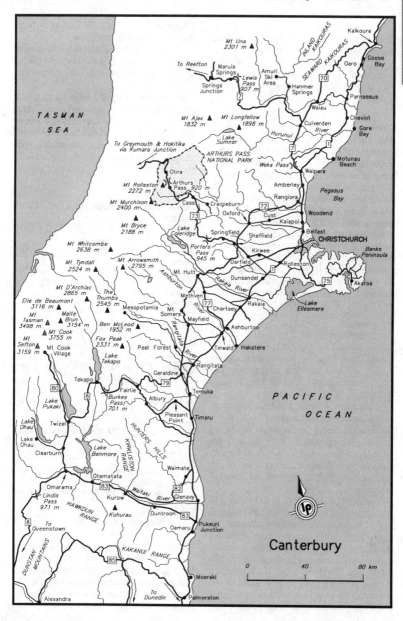

Canterbury

is famous for, gardens of geraniums, chrysanthemums and carefully edged lawns where not a blade of grass is out of place.

All this makes for a lovely city, relaxed, picturesque and with that pretty-as-a-postcard river winding its way right through the centre.

Orientation

The Cathedral Square is very much the centre of town. To find it, just look for the spire, and once there, climb to the top to get your orientation. The NZTP (New Zealand Tourism Promotions) and the CPO are both on the square. Christchurch is a compact city and walking around is easy, although slightly complicated by the river which twists and winds through the centre and crosses your path in disconcertingly varied directions. The network of one-way streets adds even more excitement if you're driving. Colombo St, running north-south through Cathedral Square, is the main shopping street.

Information

Tourist Information The NZTP (☎ 358 9888) is right on Cathedral Square in the Tower Court Building. It operates as a travel agency and also has local information. The NZTP is open from 8.30 am to 5 pm Monday to Friday.

Walk down Worcester St from the square to the Canterbury Information Centre (☎ 379 9629) by the river, on the corner of Oxford Terrace. It's open from 8.30 am to 5 pm Monday to Friday and from 9 am to 4 pm on Saturday and Sunday; it stays open later in the summer. This is the best bet for local information.

The DOC (☎ 379 9758) at 133 Victoria St has leaflets and information on most national parks, walkways and other outdoor attractions around the South Island. Opening hours are 8 am to 4.30 pm, Monday to Friday.

The AA District Headquarters (☎ 379 1280) is at 210 Hereford St. If Christchurch is your point of entry to New Zealand and you intend buying a car, you can have an AA inspection carried out in this city; contact the

AA for advice, and see the Getting Around chapter for more information.

Note that all bus numbers in this section refer to Canride (Canterbury Regional Council) buses unless indicated otherwise.

YHA The YHA national headquarters is in Christchurch. The office and Travel Centre (☎ 379 9970) is on the corner of Gloucester and Manchester Sts and handles YHA membership, takes passport photographs, sells camping equipment, packs, clothes and books and makes domestic and international travel reservations.

Consulates Consulates in Christchurch include:

Denmark	☎ 389 5134
Germany	☎ 379 3193
France	☎ 351 6280
Japan	☎ 366 5680
Finland	☎ 366 1653
Malaysia	
(Honorary Consul)	☎ 338 9059
Netherlands	☎ 366 9280
Sweden	☎ 365 0000
UK	☎ 379 6100
USA	☎ 379 0040

Airlines Offices Airline offices are generally close to Cathedral Square.

Air New Zealand
    156 Armagh St (☎ 379 7000)
Ansett New Zealand
    Clarendon Tower, 78 Worcester St (☎ 379 1300)
Mt Cook Airlines
    90 Worcester St (☎ 379 0690)
Qantas
    119 Armagh St (☎ 379 6500)
Singapore Airlines
    Ground Floor, AMP Bldg, Cathedral Square
    (☎ 366 8003)
United Airlines
    152 Hereford St (☎ 366 1736)

Bookshops Christchurch has numerous bookstores including the government-run GP Book Shop at 159 Hereford St, which carries government publications, DOSLI maps and books about New Zealand, including specialised guidebooks. Scorpio Books on the corner of Hereford St and Oxford Terrace has a wide range of books. Smith's Bookshop, at 133 Manchester St, is a classic secondhand bookshop which enjoys a good local reputation. One whole room is devoted to books on New Zealand, including Maori culture and art, and poetry and fiction by NZ authors.

Christchurch is the home town of detective fiction writer Dame Ngaio Marsh, born here in 1899, and this could be a good place to track down one of her many successful works.

Cathedral Square

Christchurch is calm, orderly and pancake flat so it's a good place to explore by bicycle. Start from the Cathedral Square where, for $2 (children $1), you can climb 133 steps to the viewing balconies 30 metres up the 63-metre-high spire of the cathedral. There you can study the cathedral bells and look around while you reflect that earthquakes have damaged the spire on several occasions, once toppling the very top into Cathedral Square! The pointed stone top was replaced with the green copper-skinned one after that incident. The cathedral is open from 9 am to 5 pm weekdays, noon to 5.30 pm on Sunday afternoon. Donations are gratefully accepted, especially now a comprehensive visitors' centre is being added to the northern side.

Inner City Walks (☎ 389 6475; 366 8243) run two-hour guided walks of the city, departing from their kiosk in the southwestern section of the square. These tours leave at 9.45 am and 1.45 pm daily, cost $8 and are most informative They're led by experienced guides who can reveal hidden aspects of the inner city, such as Rutherford's 'den' in the old university precinct.

The Wizard

Make sure you're around to hear the Wizard. He attempts to conquer gravity through levity, and can be seen and heard spouting in Cathedral Square at 1 pm from Monday to Friday. One of New Zealand's more amusing eccentrics, he dresses the part – long black velvet robes and cape in winter and white robes in summer – and plays it to the hilt. An extremely eloquent man, the Wizard has a line of glib patter – pet subjects are bureaucracy, the weakness of the male gender, Americans, priests, insurance companies and feminism – and a skilful way of playing with the hecklers. Whether you like what he has to say or not, it's a production you shouldn't miss.

Canterbury Museum

The fine Canterbury Museum on Rolleston Ave, at the entrance to the Botanic Gardens, is open daily from 9 am to 4.30 pm and admission is free. Free guided tours are held at 10.15 and 11.30 am, and 1.15 and 2.30 pm, and on Sunday there's a planetarium show at 3 pm.

Particularly interesting are the early colonists' exhibits featuring a century-old Christchurch street reconstruction, and the Antarctic exhibit. Christchurch is the HQ for 'Operation Deep Freeze', the supply link to Antarctica (see the International Antarctic Centre, later in this section, which should not be confused with this more historic exhibit).

There is a new gallery, Iwi Tawhito – Whenua Hou (Ancient People – New Land) which features displays of the now extinct moa and the early Polynesians who hunted them; included in this informative exhibit are three life-size dioramas, a walk-in (crawl-in) sinkhole cave, and computer information system.

Tucked away in a corner, close to the Antarctic exhibit, is Sir Edmund Hillary's beekeepers' hat and the oxygen bottles he wore on the first ascent of Mt Everest in 1953. There is also earlier climbing memorabilia relating to ascents in the Southern Alps.

Art Galleries

Behind the museum is the Robert McDougall Art Gallery. It has an extensive collection of NZ and international art and is open from 10 am to 4.30 pm daily; admission is free.

Other galleries are the Canterbury Society of Arts Gallery at 66 Gloucester St which specialises in New Zealand's arts & crafts; the Brooke/Gifford Gallery at 112 Manchester St which has contemporary NZ art; and the Gingko Gallery in the Arts Centre, which displays original prints and drawings. There's also the GEFN Crafts Co-Op on Cashel St Mall and a Crafts Gallery on Oxford Terrace near the boat sheds.

Arts Centre

The former University of Canterbury town site has been transformed into the biggest Arts Centre in New Zealand. (The university has been moved out to the suburb of Ilam.) It's worth a look, even if just to see the beautiful old buildings. New Zealand has a lot of good handicraft centres making some fine pottery, jewellery and other crafts, and Christchurch is particularly well represented. The Arts Centre has everything from handmade toys to Maori carvings, and a couple of good restaurants. An arts, crafts & antiques market, with live entertainment and plenty of exotic food, is held here Saturday and Sunday over the summer, usually just one or the other day in winter.

There are some beautiful old stone buildings around Christchurch, especially around the Arts Centre.

Botanic Gardens & Hagley Park

Beside the museum off Rolleston Ave the Botanic Gardens, open from 7 am to sunset, has 30 hectares of greenery beside the Avon River. The many floral show houses are open daily from 10.15 am to 4 pm, while tours leave from the cafe between 11 am and 4 pm when the weather is fine. There's an information centre open daily from 10.15 am to 4 pm September to April; 11 am to 3 pm May to August. The restaurant serves smorgasbord lunches from noon to 2 pm.

Town Hall

Christchurch citizens are justly proud of their modern riverbank town hall. Visitors are welcome from 9 am to 5 pm weekdays, 10 am to 5 pm on weekends and holidays; guided tours can be arranged. Outside is a fountain by the same designer as Sydney's Kings Cross Alamein Fountain.

Avon River

That invitingly calm Avon River obviously requires canoes, so head to the Antigua Boatsheds by the footbridge at the bottom of Rolleston Ave. One-person canoes are $4 an hour, two-person canoes $8 an hour. They also have paddle boats for $8 a half-hour. The boatshed is open from 9.30 am to 4 pm daily and there's a pretty good sandwich bar right by it.

If paddling a canoe sounds like too much effort you can relax and be punted along the river. Punts depart from the Worcester St Bridge Information Centre on the corner of Worcester St and Oxford Terrace, with departures and landings also available opposite the Town Hall Restaurant and the Thomas Edmonds (Band Rotunda) Restaurant. For a 20-minute trip it's $8 per person, for 30 minutes $10, and for 45 minutes it's $15 (children under 12 half price). The punts ply the river daily from 10 am, stopping at 6 pm from October to March, 5 pm in April and September, and 4 pm from May to August. Punts also operate from Mona Vale, on Fendalton Rd about 1.5 km from the city centre.

International Antarctic Centre

Out near the airport, on Orchard Rd, is the International Antarctic Centre (☎ 358 9896; fax 353 7799) which has only been open since September 1992. It is part of a huge complex built for the administration and warehousing for the New Zealand, US and Italian Antarctic Research programmes. The philosophy of the visitor centre is to allow the public to experience something of the Antarctic in an entertaining and informative manner.

Opened by naturalist Professor David Bellamy, the centre has hands-on exhibits, video presentations and the 'sights and sounds' of the vast continent. The first room you enter is the introductory 'Antarctic experience' which allows visitors to experience the four seasons, an aurora, changes in weather, and a penguin rookery, with the aid of special lighting, sound effects and holograms. The *Great White South* video presentation is marvellous.

The entry costs are $10 per adult and $6 per child; children under five get in for free and there is a family concession of $25 for two adults and two children.

There is a well-stocked souvenir shop and the 60° South Cafe & Bar. The centre is open October to March from 9.30 am to 8.30 pm; and April to September from 9.30 am to 5.30 pm. To get there catch a bus bound for the airport; ask for the visitors' centre. To get back to the square walk to Memorial Avenue then catch an airport bus heading for the city. The centre has a luggage room for storage of backpacks, and there are bicycle stands.

Air Force Museum

Opened in 1987 the RNZAF Museum is exceptionally well presented. On display are a variety of aircraft used by the RNZAF over the years, convincingly displayed with figures and background scenery. Antarctic aircraft sit in the snow, aircraft are serviced, a Canberra bomber of the 1950s taxis out at night, a WW II fighter is hidden in the jungle. There are also displays of air force memorabilia and many exceptionally good models.

The museum is at the former Wigram air base, which is quite close to the city centre. A courtesy bus runs from the Canterbury Information Centre in Worcester St, or it can be reached by a Hornby bus No 25 from Cathedral Square. It's open from 10 am to 4 pm Monday to Saturday, and from 1 to 4 pm on Sunday. Entry is $7 (children $2).

Mount Cavendish Gondola

For a cost of $12 for adults ($9 after 6 pm), $5 for children and $25 for families you can be whisked up from the Heathcote Valley terminal on a 945-metre, 4½-minute ride to a point somewhere above the Lyttleton Rd tunnel. There are great views at the top, and a Historic Time Tunnel, costing $4 adult, $2 child, $10 family.

The gondola whisks from 10 am daily, and the Gondola bus leaves regularly from the city centre and major hotels. Once up there, you can mountain-bike down with The Mountain Bike Adventure Company (☎ 329 9699; $22) or paraglide down with Clive Holgate Paragliding (☎ 332 2233).

Other Museums

South-east of the city centre is the 40-hectare **Ferrymead Historic Park** at 269 Bridle Path Rd, Heathcote. It's a working museum of transport and technology with incredibly varied exhibits including electric and steam locomotives, household appliances, cars and machinery of all types, plus hundreds of mechanical musical instruments. It's open from 10 am to 4.30 pm daily (in January it stays open until 6.30 pm). Entry is $7 for adults (children $3.50, family $19) including a ride on a steam train or tram. Canride buses Nos 3G, H, J or K all come from Christchurch.

The **Yaldhurst Transport Museum**, opposite the Yaldhurst Hotel on the Main West Rd, 11 km from the city centre, is open daily between 10 am and 5 pm. Displayed on the 14-hectare grounds of an attractive 1876 homestead is some of New Zealand's earliest transport, including horse-drawn vehicles, vintage cars, racing cars, motorcycles, steam engines and aircraft. Admission is $6 (children $2).

In the former railway station, on Moorhouse Avenue, you will find **Science Alive!**, an interesting hands-on science exhibit featuring 50 interactive stations. On Monday it is open from noon to 8 pm, and from Tuesday to Sunday 10 am to 8 pm. Its slogan is: 'If I wasn't meant to touch anything, what are these things on the end of my arms for?' A great place for kids willing to learn. Entry is $7 for adults, children $4 and a family of five $20.

Out at the Lancaster Park sports complex, three km from the square, you will find the **Rugby, Cricket & Sports Museum**. Much of the collection is the effort of one man, Russell Vine, who wandered NZ in search of

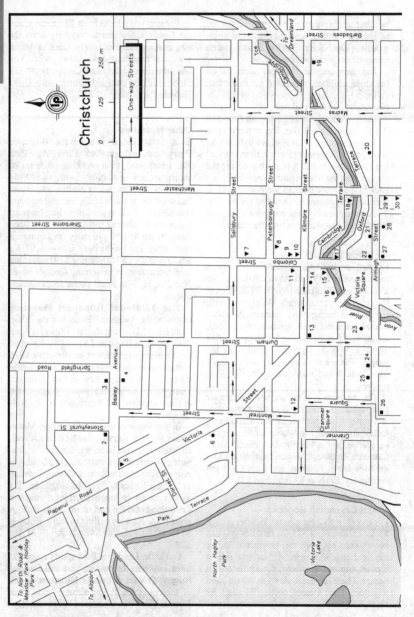

Christchurch

0 125 250 m

One-way Streets

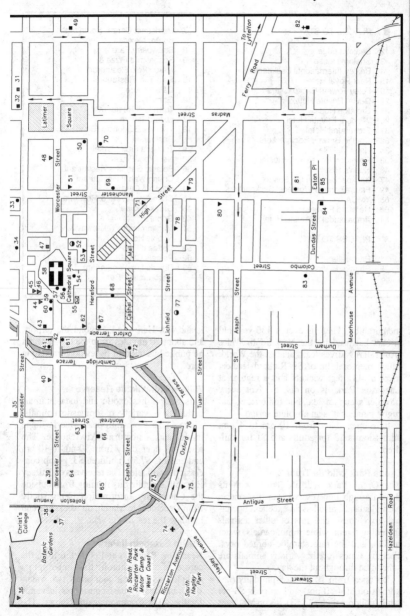

■ PLACES TO STAY

2 Bealey Lodge
3 Shalom House
4 Bealey International Backpackers
13 Park Royal Hotel
19 Foley Towers Backpackers
24 Devon Private Hotel
25 Croydon House
26 Windsor Private Hotel
31 Stonehurst Hotel
32 Charlie Browns Backpackers
35 Hotel Melville
39 Rolleston House YHA Hostel
43 Noah's Hotel
47 Backpackers Inn the Square
49 Fraureisehaus Womens' Backpackers
65 YMCA
66 Hereford Private Hotel
84 Ambassador's Private Hotel

▼ PLACES TO EAT

1 Pastarella
5 Saggio de Vino

7 Mainstreet Cafe & South of the Border Mexican
8 Strawberry Fare
9 Spagalimi's Pizza & Marco Polo Restaurant
10 Sala Thai Restaurant
11 Cafe Revere
12 Grimsby's
15 Town Hall Restaurant
17 Oxford Tavern
18 Thomas Edmond's (Band Rotunda) Restaurant
29 Tanner's Fruit Market
30 New York Pizzeria
36 Botanic Gardens Restaurant
40 Chung Wah II Restaurant
44 Gaslight Cafe
45 Chancery Tavern & Restaurant
46 Greek Recipe
48 Gopal's
51 Mediterranean Takeaway & Noodle House
53 Coffee d'Fafo
62 Pastels Cafe
63 Dux de Lux Vegetarian Restaurant & Bar

memorabilia. There is even a 130-year-old cricket bat used by the New South Wales (Australia) Natives team against the World. Much memorabilia of Sir Richard Hadlee, taker of 431 test wickets and a regular at Lancaster Park, is on display. Not every traveller's cup of tea, but for cricket and rugby fanatics it is an absolute shrine.

It is open daily from 10 am to 4 pm; admission is $3 for adults and $1 for children.

Orana Park Wildlife Trust

The Orana Park Wildlife Trust, with its drive-through lion reserve (the first one in New Zealand), also has an excellent nocturnal kiwi house and lots of other animals including tigers, white rhino, camels, water buffalo and the rare scimitar-horned oryx. Feeding times for the various animals are scheduled throughout the day.

It's open from 10 am to 5 pm daily (last admission at 4.30 pm) and entry is $8 per adult (children under 15 $3). It's on McLeans Island Rd, Harewood, beyond the airport, and about 20 minutes from the city. There's no public bus but tour buses do come along here.

Willowbank Wildlife Reserve

This reserve has exotic and local animals including a variety of domestic animals. There's also a pre-European Maori village model and a nocturnal kiwi house. The reserve is open daily from 10 am to 10 pm and entry is $7.50 (children $3, group concessions available). The reserve is on Hussey Rd, with a public bus running from outside the Canterbury Information Centre daily from December to March, on weekends and holidays the rest of the year.

Queen Elizabeth II Park

Near New Brighton and eight km from the centre of Christchurch, this huge sports complex, with four indoor pools, two waterslides and seven squash courts was the venue for the 1974 Commonwealth Games. The

71	Mirado Japanese Restaurant		54	Inner City Walks
75	Pegasus Arms		55	Post Office
78	Tre Gatti's		56	The Wizard
79	The Excelsior		57	Canride Bus Information Kiosk
80	Sahara Middle Eastern Restaurant		58	Cathedral
			59	New Zealand Tourism Promotion Office
	OTHER		60	Ansett New Zealand & Mt Cook Airline
6	Department of Conservation (DOC)		61	Robert Falcon Scott Statue
14	Town Hall		64	Arts Centre
16	Dandelion Fountain		67	Scorpio Books
20	Centennial Pool		68	Shades Arcade
21	Qantas House		69	Cat's NiteClub
22	Thomas Cook Forex		70	Automobile Association (Canterbury)
23	Floral Clock		72	Bridge of Remembrance
27	Trust Bank Forex		73	Antigua Boat Sheds
28	Air New Zealand		74	Public Hospital
33	YHA Headquarters		76	Craft Gallery
34	Rent-a-Cycle		77	Mt Cook Landline
37	Robert McDougall Art Gallery		81	Coker's Hotel
38	Canterbury Museum		82	Roman Catholic Cathedral
41	Avon Punting		83	South City Supermarket
42	Canterbury Information Centre		85	Lone Star Cafe
50	Eastside Saloon		86	Railway Station, InterCity, Science Alive! & TranzAlpine Express
52	Great Sights Buses			

Leisure Centre has a variety of amusement park attractions and is open from 10 am to 5 pm daily. To get there take Canride bus No 19 from Christchurch.

Mona Vale

The enchanting grounds of Mona Vale, an Elizabethan-style riverside homestead with 4½ hectares of richly landscaped gardens, ponds and fountains, are open every day from 8 am to 7.30 pm October to March, and from 8.30 am to 5.30 pm April to September. Tea and a smorgasbord lunch are served here from Sunday to Friday, and there's punting on the Avon River. It's just 1.5 km from the city centre, on Fendalton Rd (bus No 9).

Other Things to See & Do

There's an aquarium and zoo at 155 Beach Rd, North Beach. It's open daily from 10 am to 5 pm, admission is $3 (children $1.50) and you can get there on bus No 19.

Just over the Ferrymead Bridge on the main road to Sumner, Cob Cottage is a restored sod hut from the 1860s. Deans Bush and Homestead on Kauri St, built in 1843, is the oldest building in the province and is now a private museum, standing amidst a native bush reserve.

The Waimakariri River, about 15 km north of the city centre, is a popular river for jet-boating. Day trips to the Waimakariri Gorge are made from Christchurch. Longer rafting trips are also made on this river. Also about 1½ hours away are the Rangitata and Rakaia rivers where you can go kayaking, rafting and jet-boating.

Beaches

The closest beaches to the city are North Beach (10 km, bus No 19), South Brighton beach (10 km, bus No 5), Sumner (11 km, bus No 3), Waimairi (10 km, bus No 19), New Brighton (eight km, bus No 5) and Taylors Mistake – a pleasant sheltered beach further out from Sumner and popular for surfing. All bus numbers refer to Canride (Canterbury Regional Council) buses.

CANTERBURY

Walks

Visit the Canterbury Information Centre for details and leaflets about walks around Christchurch. The bus information kiosk has a leaflet on bus access to the various walks.

Starting in the city are the **Riverside Walk** – the leaflet on this is packed with information – and various city historical walks. For great views of the city, there is a walkway from the **Sign of the Takahe**. The various 'Sign of...' places in this area were originally roadhouses built during the depression as rest stops. Now they vary from the impressive tearooms at the Sign of the Takahe to a simple shelter at the Sign of the Bellbird, and are referred to primarily as landmarks. This walk leads up to the Sign of the Kiwi through Victoria Park, and then along near the Summit Rd to Scott Reserve – there are several lookout points along the way. The walk is accessible by bus No 2 from Victoria Square near the Town Hall.

How about walking one way to Lyttelton on the **Bridle Path**? It leads from Heathcote Valley to Lyttelton and takes one to 1½ hours at an easy pace. To get to Heath-cote Valley, take bus Nos 3G, H, J or K. The **Godley Head Walkway** is a two-hour round trip from Taylors Mistake, crossing then recrossing Summit Rd with beautiful views on a clear day. The **Rapaki Track** is an excellent walk taking just a couple of hours and offering fine views of the whole city and of Lyttelton. For information on these walks, inquire at the Canterbury Information Centre.

The **Crater Rim Walkway** around Lyttelton Harbour goes some 14 km from the Bridle Path to the Ahuriri Scenic Reserve, passing through a number of scenic reserves along the way, plus the Sign of the Bellbird and the Sign of the Kiwi. The walkway can easily be done in several short stages.

There are a number of shorter walks in and around **Nicholson Park & Sumner Head**, about 25 minutes by car from the square, or catch a No 3 bus. Here you'll see many inshore birds, such as the eastern bar-tailed godwit, gulls, spotted shags and black swans. Common plants include poroporo, ngaio, pohuehue and ice plant.

Skiing

There are several ski areas within a 2-hour drive of Christchurch. For more information see Skiing in the Outdoor Activities chapter and individual entries for each of the resorts. The ski areas are:

Porter Heights – near Porters Pass (89 km, one-hour drive from Christchurch)
Mt Hutt – near Methven (104 km, 1½ hours)
Broken River, Craigieburn Valley and Mt Cheeseman – all between Porters Pass and Arthurs Pass (122 km, 1½ hours)
Mt Olympus – near Lake Ida (132 km, two hours)
Amuri – near Hanmer Springs (150 km, two hours)
Fox Peak – near Fairlie (153 km, 2½ hours)
Temple Basin – near Arthurs Pass (163 km, two hours)
Erewhon – Upper Rangitata River (185 km, 2¼ hours)
Mt Dobson – near Fairlie (200 km, 2½ hours)
Mt Lyford – near Hanmer Springs (143 km, two hours)

Information on all ski areas is available in Christchurch from the NZTP and the Canterbury Information Centre. The ski season is generally from June to November at Mt Hutt, from June or July to September or October at the other areas.

Tours & Trips

Bus Tours Christchurch Transport Limited (☎ 366 1661) operate four tours which are good value. There's a 9 am three-hour tour of the city which costs $24 (children $12), and a three-hour afternoon tour of the hills, coast and harbour, including a short harbour cruise and a stop for tea at the Sign of the Takahe. This one costs $29 (children $14.50), tea extra. They also have two full-day tours to Akaroa ($55, children half) and the high country ($125, children half). The high country trip includes a jet-boat trip on the Waimakariri and a short bush walk at Grey-neys Flat near Arthurs Pass.

Gray Line (☎ 343 3874) have a three-hour morning sights tour which includes Mona Vale and the Port Hills ($23, children half), an afternoon sights tour to Sumner, Lyttleton Harbour (launch cruise) and the Port Hills ($29, children half); an afternoon sights tour with the gondola ride thrown in ($46, children half) and a foothills experience tour which includes the Mayfield Sheep show near Methven, horse-riding, Mt Hutt Station and a jet-boat ride ($165, $130 for children).They have three interesting day tours: to Akaroa ($49), to Mt Cook ($124) and a TranzAlpine tour ($225); children half price in all cases.

Canterbury Day Tripper (☎ 349 3558) have more expensive tours but a lot more activities, with entry fees included. Their day trip City Top Spots is $130; Night View and Dinner Evening tour is $99; and the full-day Akaroa Resort Farm Visit & Cruise is $185 (includes a trip on the *Canterbury Cat*).

Travel Pioneer (☎ 388 2042) have interesting trips to Akaroa via the coastal back roads ($44 return); Arthurs Pass and the Otira Gorge ($48 return); and Hanmer Springs via the Waipara Gorge back road ($44 return): you can go one way on these trips for about $25. All trips depart at 8.30 am and return about 6 pm.

From December to February the English Connection red double-decker bus does a couple of very economical short city tours. The 40-minute Inner City tour departs daily at 10.30 and 11.30 am, and 2.30 pm, and if you like you can jump off at the Canterbury Museum, Arts Centre or Botanic Gardens, and rejoin the bus when it comes past again. The cost is $4 (children $2). Their two-hour Mona Vale tour includes the Inner City tour. The cost for this one is $5 (children $2.50) and it departs daily at 12.30 pm. The English Connection buses depart from bus stop No 16 in Cathedral Square and bookings can be made at the Bus Information Kiosk in the square.

Canterbury Scenic Tours (☎ 366 9660) offer half-day city tours ($23) and full-day tours to Akaroa or Hanmer Springs.

South Island Canoe Expeditions (☎ 364 8887) take canoeing trips (in Canadian canoes) to lakes and rivers near Christchurch. You are able to canoe, fish and walk in a pristine alpine environment, and transport to and from the lake is included. A full-day trip is $75 and a two-day overnight trip is $195.

Places to Stay

Christchurch is the major city and the only international arrival point on the South Island. As a result it has many accommodation options.

Distances quoted here are taken from Cathedral Square as the centre of town.

Camping & Cabins There are plenty of campsites, some very conveniently located. The *Showground Motor Camp* (☎ 338 9770), at 47-51 Whiteleigh Rd off Lincoln Rd, is only three km from the city centre and has campsites at $6.35 per person, or with power at $10.15/14.65 for one/two people. It also has a variety of cabins from as little as $22.80 for two people. Other cabins are $29 for two, or $42.75 with fully equipped cooking facilities, private shower and toilet. It's conveniently located, comfortable and cheap – but closed for two weeks during the show in early November. Get there on bus No 7.

The *Riccarton Park Motor Camp* (☎ 348 5690) at 19 Main South Rd, Upper Riccarton, is six km from the city centre. Tent sites are about $7, cabins are $24 for two people, or there are on-site caravans. Take bus No 8.

The *Meadow Park Holiday Park* (☎ 352 9176) at 39 Meadow St off the Main North Rd, is five km out. Camping, with power, costs $9 per person. There are cabins from $30 to $47 for two, tourist flats at $55 for two and a hostel with 22 units which sleep two to five at $43 for two, each extra adult $11. The camp has a covered heated swimming pool, a spa, children's playground equipment and a recreation hall. Take bus No 4.

Russley Park Motor Camp (☎ 342 7021) is at 372 Yaldhurst Rd, opposite Riccarton Racecourse about 10 km from Cathedral Square or five km from the airport. Campsites cost $8 per person, or $14/18 with power. The camp also has on-site vans at $30 to $34 for two, chalet cabins from $34 to $38 and some fancier tourist flats from $48. Take bus No 8.

South New Brighton Park (☎ 388 9844), in Halsey St off Estuary Rd, is another attractive park, also 10 km out, heading north-east.

Caravan sites cost $9.50/17 or there are a few on-site caravans at $15 plus the site charges. Take bus No 5.

The *All Seasons Holiday Park* (☎ 384 9490) is at 5 Kidbrooke St, Linwood. In this new park tent sites are $7 (with power $11), budget cabins are $15/25 for singles/doubles, cabins are $25/35 for single/doubles, and tourist flats $50 for two people.

Amber Park Caravan Park (☎ 348 3327) is conveniently located at 308 Blenheim Rd, only five km south of the city centre. There are no tent sites here, caravan sites cost $13/16 for one/two people. Tourist flats, which share the camp kitchen facilities but have their own showers and toilets, cost $44 to $50 for two. Bus No 25 will get you there.

Other camping grounds include *Prebbleton Holiday Park* (☎ 349 7861) at 18 Blakes Rd, Prebbleton, 12 km out; and *Spencer Park Holiday Camp* (☎ 329 8721) in Heyders Rd, Spencerville, 14 km north.

Hostels Christchurch has two YHA hostels and some popular backpackers. *Rolleston House YHA Hostel* (☎ 366 6564; fax 365 5589) at 5 Worcester St is opposite the Canterbury Museum, the Arts Centre and the Botanic Gardens, and only 700 metres from the city centre (about eight minutes' walk to Cathedral Square) so it's very conveniently located. There are 48 beds at $16/18 a night for singles/doubles or twins. The hostel and office are open all day but it's very popular so booking ahead is a good idea. Close by is Dux de Lux if you need a feed and a beer.

The other YHA hostel, *Cora Wilding* (☎ 389 9199), at 9 Evelyn Couzins Ave, Richmond, is five km from the city centre and has 40 beds. To get there catch a bus No 10 from Cathedral Square to Tweed St. The cost here is $14 a night and the place is quite elegant, being a former mansion in a well-cared-for city park. The office shuts during the day but the rest of the hostel remains open.

The popular *Foley Towers Backpackers – Avon View* (☎ 366 9720) is at 208 Kilmore St near the Madras St end. It's a straight-forward travellers' hostel with plenty of space. You may have trouble getting a bed here so phone ahead. There's a pleasant little garden at the back, the usual kitchen and laundry facilities and a bed on average costs $13 a night. The rooms are for two to five, with plenty of new twin and double rooms at $16 per person. It's run by the organiser of the NZ Backpackers Accommodation 'Blue Book', who is au fait with travellers' needs.

Bealey International Backpackers (☎ & fax 366 6760) at 70 Bealey Ave (between Montreal and Durham Sts), is a smaller place with a friendly atmosphere, an outdoor garden and BBQ area, and a cosy log fire in winter. They offer a free pick-up service and luggage storage. Rates are $14 for a share room, or $15 per person for a twin/double.

The *Backpackers Inn the Square* formerly Pavlova Backpackers (☎ 366 5158; fax same), located in the old Warners Hotel right in Cathedral Square, has accommodation starting at $14.50 per person (some equipped with bed linen). Singles are $25, double/twins are $15, and dorm rooms are $10 to $13.50 per person. The hostel is open 24 hours. The benefit of this place is its proximity to Bailies Bar (see Entertainment).

Dreamland (☎ 366 3206), 50 Perth St, is a very small hostel on an 1100 sq metre section. They have some tent sites ($8.50) or twin rooms at $15. It is particularly well set up for non-smoking, teetotalling cyclists as the demon drink and weed are forbidden and there is a cyclist's workshop.

The *YMCA* (☎ 366 0689) is at 12 Hereford St, a few steps from the Botanic Gardens, the Arts Centre and Canterbury Museum. There are over 250 beds in this new hostel! And a wide variety of accommodation with singles from $30 to $50, twins and doubles from $40 to $65. They also have one and two-bedroom apartments at $85 and $100, and substantially discounted rates for stays of two weeks or longer. There's a cafeteria serving inexpensive meals, plus a hostellers' kitchen to do your own cooking. During the school terms most of the single and double plain rooms may be full of students, but there should always be some room for casuals. The hostel is open 24 hours a day and they take both men and women.

Charlie Brown's, formerly the Latimer Hostel, (☎ 379 8429) is centrally located on the corner of Madras and Gloucester Sts. Prices have gone down in a war to lure backpackers through the door. The cheapest dorm rooms are $8 and you get what you pay for. It is $10 per person in triples/quads, and $22 for doubles/twins ($15 for a single). There's a courtesy van and drop-off, cooking, laundry and ironing facilities, a games room, Sky TV, videos, BBQ and off-street parking.

Fraureisehaus – The Homestead (☎ 366 2585), located at 272 Barbadoes St, only five minutes' walk from the central city, is a women-only backpackers. They offer courtesy transport and have a fully equipped kitchen and laundry, TV and video, games room, library and free linen. Bikes are available and there is a vegetable and herb garden. Double, twin and bunk (four-bed) rooms are only $10 per person. Phone Sandra beforehand or just turn up.

The *YWCA* (☎ 355 4903, 385 4594) at 93 Harewood Rd is away from the city centre, about five km from the airport, in a quiet area, with a park-like setting and it takes women only. Bus Nos 1 and 4 run frequently from Cathedral Square, stopping at the gate. The cost of $20/30 for single/twin rooms includes a light breakfast, or there's a weekly rate of $80/120. You can get both lunch and dinner for an extra $7 per day, or cook in the hostellers' kitchen.

Rooms & Hostel-Style Accommodation
There are several places providing good accommodation at hostel rates in addition to regular rooms.

The *Hereford Private Hotel* (☎ 379 9536) at 36 Hereford St is opposite the Arts Centre and Dux de Lux, and very close to the YMCA and YHA hostel. Bunkroom accommodation is $15, singles $25, doubles or twins $35, and all rooms come equipped with bed linen, towels and soap. It's very plain and straightforward but excellent value. There are laundry facilities for guests' use but no kitch-

ens. This is made up for by a restaurant which serves very economical meals – continental breakfast for $4.50, or a Kiwi breakfast (bacon, eggs, etc) for $6.50. This place has had strong recommendations from several travellers.

The *Ambassadors Hotel* (☎ 366 7808) at 19 Manchester St is a five-minute walk south of the city centre and very close to the railway station and InterCity and Mt Cook bus depots. It's quite a flash old hotel, with leadlight windows, a lovely lounge area and deep velvety carpets. Upstairs the B&B rates are $35/55 for single/double rooms, but downstairs there's another section where beds in a five-bed dorm are $12.50. Or pay $20 per person in single, twin or double rooms. All the beds are nicely made up – no need for your own linen! The one drawback is that there's no kitchen, although there's free tea and coffee anytime, and continental breakfast for $3 or a giant cooked breakfast for $6.

Shalom House (☎ 366 6770) is at 69 Bealey Ave on the corner of Stoneyhurst St, near the Bealey International Backpackers Hostel. It's a small, quiet and very pleasant guesthouse with rooms at $30/52. If you bring your own bedding it's just $15 per person in twin rooms, and they'll provide breakfast for an extra $4 or you can cook in the upstairs kitchen; bedding can be hired.

Thistle Private Hotel (☎ 348 1499) at 21 Main South Rd, near the junction of Riccarton and Yaldhurst roads, is near the airport, with frequent buses to town. Rooms are $28/40, but if you provide your own bedding it's $10 to $17 per person in singles or doubles. Breakfast is available and there's a kitchen, laundry and off-street parking.

Built in 1885, *Turret House* (☎ 365 3900), 435 Durham St (Nth), has been elegantly restored. The $85 room charge for two includes a continental breakfast, and private bathroom.

A couple of other places have separate hostel and regular sections. Not as central, but in a pleasant location near Hagley Park, is *Aarangi Backpackers* (☎ 348 3584), 15 Riccarton Rd. They are close to all major bus routes, or getting to the Square is simply a walk through Hagley park. Share rooms are $14 and doubles/twins are $16 per person. There's also a B&B guesthouse section upstairs, where the cost is $48/58 for singles/doubles. They have a courtesy bus for pick up and drop off; bicycles are lent out free.

Stonehurst Hotel (☎ 379 4620) at 241 Gloucester St is just around the corner from Charlie Brown's, very close to the city centre, and it has a separate building with all the usual hostel facilities (kitchen, laundry, etc). Bunkroom beds are $14 per person (provide your own bedding) or there are double rooms (linen provided) at $32 for two; backpackers singles are $25. Hostellers are welcome to use the garden, house bars and TV and billiards rooms of the hotel next door. There's a courtesy van and the hostel is open 24 hours. Room rates in the hotel are $50 for doubles.

As in other major cities it may be possible to find accommodation at the university during student vacations. You can call the student association on 348 7069.

Guesthouses The *Windsor Private Hotel* (☎ 366 1503) at 52 Armagh St is just five to 10 minutes' walk from the city centre. It's meticulously clean and orderly and rooms cost about $50/78 including a traditional cooked breakfast and private bathroom.

There are other places near the Windsor, such as the *Hotel Melville* (☎ 379 8956) at 49 Gloucester St. It's not quite as neat and tidy but most rooms have washbasins. B&B costs $33/55.

Two km north-west of Cathedral Square the *Wolseley Lodge* (☎ 355 6202) at 107 Papanui Rd is an old-fashioned place in a quiet setting with rooms at $25/50 including breakfast. A few doors down at No 121 the *Highway Lodge* (☎ 355 5418) has rooms at $40/65 plus $5 for breakfast. It's also an olde-worlde place, and you can get to both these lodges on a No 1 bus.

Closer in, the *New City Hotel* (☎ 366 0769) at 527 Colombo St offers rooms including breakfast at $34/49. At 82 Bealey Ave is the elegantly restored *Eliza's Manor House*

(☎ 366 8584; fax 366 4946) with 10 bed-rooms (eight with en suite bathrooms) from $65 to $125. They have fully licensed restaurant and bar facilities. *Dublin House* (☎ 366 1861), 12 Dublin St, in a turn-of-the-century home, has B&B singles/doubles for $30/60.

Motels Christchurch is well-equipped with motels, most of them costing from $70 to $90 a double. The Motel Association of NZ puts out the *Christchurch Motel Guide* annually; get a copy from tourist information centres. As in other towns there are bargains to be found at the campsites, which often have motels, tourist flats and cabins as well as sites for camping or campervans.

Better priced motels include:

Achilles Motel (☎ 379 9688), 118 Sherbourne St, on SH 1, doubles $66 to $79
Adelphi Motel (☎ 355 6037), 49 Papanui Rd, doubles $56 to $69
Adorian Motel (☎ 366 7626), 47 Worcester St, Linwood, doubles $75
Avalon Motel (☎ 379 9681), corner Bealey Ave and Geraldine St, doubles $68 to $80
Avon City Motel (☎ 352 6079), 402 Main North Rd, doubles $63
Avonhead Lodge Motel (☎ 348 1309), 168 Yaldhurst Rd, doubles $60 to $69
Bluegum Lodge Motel (☎ 347 8658), Main South Rd, Templeton, doubles $68
Canterbury Court Motel (☎ 738 8351), 140 Lincoln Rd, swimming pool, doubles $72
Cashel Court Motel (☎ 389 2768), 457 Cashel St, swimming pool, doubles $58 to $70 with cooking facilities
City Worcester Motel (☎ 366 4491), 336 Worcester St, doubles $59 to $75
Colombo Travel Lodge (☎ 366 3029), 965 Colombo St, one km north of Cathedral Square, singles/doubles $55/60
Cranford Court Motel (☎ 379 2406), 63 Cranford St, doubles $66 to $75
Earnslaw Motel (☎ 348 6387), 288 Blenheim Rd, double $60 to $70
Fairlane Court (☎ 389 4943), 69 Linwood Ave, doubles $54
Golden Mile Motor Lodge (☎ 349 6153), Main South Rd, singles/doubles $50 to $60/58 to $68
Golden Sands Beach Motel (☎ 388 7996), 121 Estuary Rd, double $65
Hillvue Court Motel (☎ 338 5112), 37 Hillier Place, Spreydon, doubles $60

Holiday Lodge Motel (☎ 366 6584), 862 Colombo St, doubles $58

Middlepark Motel & Kowhai Lodge (☎ 348 7320), 120 Main South Rd, Upper Riccarton, doubles $62 to $70

Northcote Motel (☎ 352 8417), 309 Main North Rd, doubles $66

Riccarton Motel Ltd (☎ 348 7127), 92 Main South Rd, Upper Riccarton, doubles $64.50

Tall Trees Motel (☎ 352 6681), 454 Papanui Rd, doubles $59 to $79

Hotels Top-bracket Christchurch hotels include the *Christchurch City Travelodge* (☎ 379 1180) at 356 Oxford Terrace, the *Quality Inn Chateau* (☎ 348 8999) on the corner of Deans Ave and Kilmarnock St, *Noah's* (☎ 379 4700) on the corner of Worcester St and Oxford Terrace, and out at the airport the *Christchurch Airport Travelodge* (☎ 358 3139). At all these hotels doubles are in the $150 and up range. Right at the top of the price scale is the imaginatively designed and wonderfully situated *Park Royal Hotel* (☎ 365 7799), corner of Durham and Kilmore Sts, where a double costs nearly $315, with great views.

Places to Eat

It is unbelievable how the food options have improved in this town in recent years. You can find whatever you want – even Cajun food is no problem! These days you can eat in Christchurch every day and at all hours. There are a number of restaurants, luncheon places and takeaways around Cathedral Square, and the two-block stretch of Colombo St just north of the river has interesting restaurants.

There are a number of tourist newspapers which advertise restaurants such as the *Official Visitors Guide* and *Christchurch Tourist Times*. Many restaurants distribute their own 'dodgers' or 'flyers' to the tourist centres; let their glossy photographs tempt you. The information centre has a complete restaurant guide, available for $3.95.

Fast Food & Takeaways There are various places around Cathedral Square, including

Warners, a 24-hour takeaway bar right behind Warners Hotel, in the north-east corner. If you would rather sit at the base of one of the statues, or on a bench in the square then go to one of the many takeaway food stalls in the square selling a variety of international cuisine. A reader, describing himself as one of 'the fussiest and most hopelessly addicted drinkers of gourmet speciality coffees' recommends *Coffee d'Fafo*, 137 Hereford St, for its authentic products.

Apart from the usual sandwich places there are some more exotic takeaways around Cathedral Square. *The Greek Recipe* at 55 Cathedral Square, beside the West End Theatre, has authentic, inexpensive Greek takeaways and is open from 10 am to 10 pm every day but Sunday. Only a block from the square at 176A Manchester St the *Mediterranean Take Away* has that eastern Med blend of Turkish/Greek/Lebanese food, such as doner kebabs. It's a good place to get food to eat in the square. On the corner of Oxford and Hereford Sts, close to the information centre, you'll find *Pastels Cafe*. Here, in a pastel setting, you get views of the Avon whilst sipping a reasonable brew.

Gaslight Cafe in the Chancery Lane Arcade is a cosy little cafe, open from 6 am to 4 pm Monday to Thursday, until 9 pm on Friday. There's an economically priced cafeteria at the *YMCA*, opposite the Arts Centre on Hereford St. The coffee bar in the foyer of the *Town Hall* is open every day and in the evening whenever there's a concert.

If you are visiting the YHA headquarters in Gloucester St, pop around the corner to the *New York Pizzeria*, 265 Manchester St, for a slice of the genuine product. There is a great *fruiterer* just a couple of doors down and to the north.

Pub Food On Colombo St by the river, the conveniently located Oxford Tavern has a family restaurant called the *Major Bunbury*. It's open daily from 11 am to 9 pm, until 10 pm on Friday and Saturday. Main courses, which span the pub-food universe from family roasts to T-bone steaks, are in the $10 to $15 range, and there's also a cheaper children's menu.

Other places with pub food include the *Excelsior* on the corner of High and Manchester Sts with main courses in the $12 to $15 range and again it's open for lunch and dinner every day.

There are *Cobb & Co's* at the Caledonian Hotel, 101 Caledonian Rd, north of Cathedral Square, and at the Bush Inn, 364 Riccarton Rd, south of the square. Cobb & Co's are all open every day until 10 pm at night and have a standard and highly consistent pub food menu. Other pub food possibilities include the *Carlton Hotel* on the corner of Papanui Rd and Bealey Ave; the *Coachman Inn*, at 144 Gloucester St, with a theatre restaurant set-up; the *Pegasus Arms*, 14 Oxford Terrace near the hospital, for a bistro lunch and a view out over the 1886 topsail cutter *Pastime*; and *Chancery Tavern & Restaurant* in Chancery Lane, which features roasts.

Restaurants The *Gardens Restaurant* in Christchurch's wonderful Botanic Gardens is renowned for its excellent smorgasbord which costs $12.50 including coffee. It's served from noon to 2 pm daily. The restaurant is open from 10 am for snacks and other light meals.

The riverside setting of the *Town Hall Restaurant* makes it a popular place to eat. There's a weekday lunch-time smorgasbord for $20, a Sunday smorgasbord lunch or dinner for $22, and a regular à la carte menu for dinner or late supper, with main courses from $12 to $30. Across the plaza at the ultra-modern, ultra-expensive *Park Royal Hotel*, the inner courtyard is given over to a rather elegant cafe/restaurant which is not as expensive as it looks – main courses, both meat and vegetarian, cost around $9 to $16, and there's an attractive salad bar. The wine list is about as long as the menu!

The riverside *Thomas Edmonds Band Rotunda Restaurant* is housed in what used to be a band rotunda by the river on Cambridge Terrace. It's a great position and you could complement the romantic atmosphere

by arriving by punt! It's reasonably priced with main courses for lunch at around $10, for dinner from $15, with both meat and vegetarian selections. The orange roughy is superb as are the desserts (including delicious homemade ice cream), and it is BYO. It's open for lunch from Tuesday to Friday and again on Sunday; in the evening from Wednesday to Sunday.

The Chancery in Gloucester St has a carvery with lamb, pork, and beef featured daily ($9.95 lunch, $11.95 dinner) and a good selection of desserts. A number of locals recommended the very chic *Expresso 124*, at 124 Oxford Terrace, for breakfast, lunch and dinner – it is open six days a week from 10 am to 2 am.

The restaurant blocks off Colombo St offer good dining possibilities. These include the Oxford Tavern just south of the river (see Pub Food) and the Mainstreet Cafe, with its smoke-free bar, further north (see Vegetarian). Or try *Marco Polo's* at No 812 with an interesting mix of Indonesian and Indian dishes. It's open from Monday to Saturday evenings, with main courses from $15.50 to $18. At No 818 try a burrita at *Rita's Burritas*. *Cafe Valentino* at 813 Colombo St is a casual restaurant with a spacious woodbeam and brick decor. It serves mainly Italian food and is open Tuesday to Sunday from 5.30 pm until late, with live music on Friday and Saturday.

Strawberry Fare at 114 Peterborough St, a few steps off Colombo St, is a restaurant famed for its desserts, such as the ubiquitous Death by Chocolate. They also serve great breakfasts including a Parisian special; meals are served from 7 am to midnight daily, except weekends when it opens at the more respectable hour of 8 am. Also in the same area, not far off Colombo in the Gloucester Arcade, Gloucester St, is *Britas Restaurant* which has hot roast meals with four vegetables from $9.

There is a good representation of quality Italian restaurants in Christchurch, in addition to Cafe Valentino mentioned earlier. *Spagalimi's Italian Pizza Restaurant* on the corner of Dorset and Victoria Sts is a very popular place with takeaways as well. At 76 Lichfield St, just south of the city centre, *Tre Gatti's* has reasonable standard Italian dishes and is open commendably late at night. An up-market place is *Saggio di Vino*, at 185 Victoria St (corner of Bealey Ave), which has a great wine selection; more than 50 are available by the glass. Light meals are served here also. Popular with locals is *Bardelli's*, in the centre at 98 Cashel St, specialising in Mediterranean and Asian food.

There are plenty of Chinese restaurants around Christchurch including the imposing *Chung Wah II* at 61-63 Worcester St. At the *Mongolian Marquee*, at 154 Durham St, eat as much of this barbecued food as you can for a set price. It is open Tuesday to Sunday from 6 pm until late.

The *Sign of the Takahe*, out of the city at Cashmere Hills, is in an impressive old stone building, with fine views of the city, a great setting, careful service and quite high prices to go with it. It's open daily for Devonshire teas ($6) and smorgasbord lunches ($23), Tuesday to Saturday for dinner ($20 or more for a main course). You can get there on bus No 2.

Similar in style to the Sign of the Takahe, is *Grimsby's*, opposite Cranmer Square, on the corner of Kilmore and Montreal Sts. This is considered by locals to be a pinnacle of dining in this town, and is definitely not in the budget category.

Vegetarian Vegetarians are well catered for in Christchurch with good food in all price categories. *Gopals* at 143 Worcester St is another of the excellent Hare Krishna-run restaurants. It's open for lunch on weekdays and on Friday evenings.

Exceptionally good vegetarian food can be found at the *Mainstreet Cafe* on Colombo St by the corner with Salisbury St. Mainstreet is a relaxed and very popular place with an open-air courtyard at the back. Imaginative main courses are around $16.50 or you could have bread and salad for $5. The salads are good and the desserts, particularly their varied selection of cheesecakes, are

mouthwatering. It's open long hours, from 7 am to 11 pm daily.

Dux de Lux is another very popular place for gourmet vegetarian taste treats. It's in the Arts Centre, on Montreal St near Hereford St. There's a green outdoor courtyard and service is counter style, with main courses around $7 or $8 (lunch) or $13.50 (dinner). They're licensed, with their own bar and brewery, and live music four nights a week. Dux de Lux is open from around 11.30 am until midnight, every day. The beers are excellent – Hereford Bitter, Sou'wester, Nor'wester and Blue Duck Draught.

Entertainment
Pub Music There are a few pubs with rock music at night, particularly on the weekends. Popular ones include *Dux de Lux* with its own brewery and bar (see Vegetarian Restaurants) and *Bush Inn* at 364 Riccarton Rd, which has a small cover charge. The *Carlton*, on the corner of Bealey Ave and Papanui Rd, also has weekend entertainment. Or there's the *Star & Garter* at 332 Oxford Terrace, the *Imperial* on the corner of St Asaph and Barbadoes Sts, the *Ferrymead Tavern*, the *Bishopdale Tavern*, the *Eastside Tavern*, the *Lancaster Park Hotel* and plenty of others.

An old favourite is *Bailies* at Backpackers Inn the Square. In here smoke fills the room, the Guinness is carefully decanted into pint glasses, and boiled eggs and salt are left on the bar for patrons.

Dance & Music There's rock all week at *The Playroom* on the corner of Cuffs Rd and Pages Rd. The *Firehouse* at 293 Colombo St in the city centre is a nightclub. Other Christchurch nightclubs are *Cats*, on Manchester St, the *Palladium* on Gloucester St, and *Warners*, in Cathedral Square, which has folk music. The *Loft Bar* in Gloucester St, part of the Coachman Inn complex, has Irish folk music on occasions.

Two other places in the south part of town, down towards the railway station are *The Loaded Hog*, at 39 Dundas St off Manchester St, with its own brewery and excellent Weiss

Beer; and *The Lone Star Cafe & Bar*, on the corner of Manchester and Eaton Sts. The latter is one of those Tex-Mex saloons with a great 'Wild West' atmosphere.

Getting There & Away

Air Christchurch is the only international arrival and departure point on the South Island. Qantas, Air New Zealand, British Airways, Singapore Airlines and Thai Airlines all fly here. Mt Cook Airline flies between Christchurch and the Chatham Islands.

Air New Zealand have their Christchurch office (☎ 379 5200) at 156 Armagh St. There are connections between Christchurch and most destinations in the North and South Islands including Auckland (1½ hours), Dunedin (45 minutes), Invercargill (one hour) and Wellington (45 minutes). There are as many as eight to 10 flights daily to Auckland or Wellington.

Ansett New Zealand (☎ 371 1146) and Mt Cook Airlines (☎ 379 0690) also fly into and out of Christchurch. Ansett have flights to Auckland, Dunedin, Invercargill, Queenstown and Rotorua.

Mt Cook Airline fly between Kerikeri, Auckland, Hamilton, Rotorua, Taupo, Palmerston North, Wellington and Christchurch. In the South Island, they fly to Mt Cook, Nelson, Queenstown, Te Anau and Wanaka. They also have a flight to the Chathams (see Getting There & Away in the Chatham Islands section). Air New Zealand Link (incorporating Air Nelson, ☎ 358 5112) have flights to Nelson, Hokitika and Timaru.

Smaller airlines operating out of Christchurch include Associated Air which fly to Blenheim and on to Paraparaumu near Wellington on the North Island. Wairarapa Airlines fly between Christchurch and Nelson or Masterton on the North Island.

The airport is modern and has an information centre (☎ 358 5029) open every day. There are luggage lockers at 50c for eight hours, $1.50 for 24 hours. Ask about storing luggage for longer periods. Don't forget your $20 departure tax on international flights.

Bus InterCity buses (☎ 372 8534) depart from the InterCity Travel Centre at the railway station on Moorhouse Ave. Mt Cook Landline buses (☎ 379 0690) go from 40 Lichfield St, near Cathedral Square, and pick up at their depot on Riccarton Rd.

Christchurch to Picton is a trip of about five to six hours, with Kaikoura an interesting midway stopping point. Both InterCity and Mt Cook Landline do this route. Both also operate south to Dunedin – about 6½ hours, and continue south from Dunedin to Invercargill, another three hours. Mt Cook have a Christchurch to Nelson service (via either Lewis Pass or Picton) with connections through to Westport and Greymouth on the West Coast, or another route to Westport running more directly across the island.

InterCity also have services from Greymouth south to the glaciers three times a week, but this requires a stopover in Greymouth as the schedules of the two routes are not timed to connect. The trip across the South Island via Arthurs Pass is not serviced by the major companies but rather by two smaller operators, Coast to Coast Shuttle and Alpine Coach & Courier (see Getting There & Away for Greymouth for more details). This route is a stunningly beautiful journey, not to be missed. From Christchurch it's about 2½ hours to Arthurs Pass, and another 1¾ hours on to Greymouth.

InterCity and Mt Cook also have daily bus services to Mt Cook (five hours) and Queenstown. The shortest in time is Mt Cook if going direct to Queenstown. If you wish to go to the village with Mt Cook you would change at Twizel. From November to April Mt Cook has an additional daily Christchurch-Queenstown excursion bus which makes a 3½ hour stopover at Mt Cook; this can make either a day trip (Christchurch to Mt Cook and return) or an attractive way of getting to Queenstown. InterCity buses take the same route daily all year round (to Queenstown via Mt Cook) but with only a 40-minute stopover at Mt Cook. Mt Cook's year-round daily buses from Christchurch to Mt Cook connect through Twizel; their year-round buses to Queenstown continue on to Te Anau. Another bus to Queenstown with a brief stopover at Mt Cook is operated by Great Sights Gray Line (☎ 343 3874).

Other InterCity services from Christchurch include buses to Akaroa (two hours), Hanmer Springs (two hours), Tekapo (3½ hours) and Wanaka (nine hours).

The Kiwi Experience bus passes through Christchurch, and the Flying Kiwi bus can also be picked up here as well as from Picton. In addition a number of shuttle operators pass through on their way elsewhere. See the Getting Around chapter for details on these 'alternative' buses.

Train The railway station (☎ 379 9020) is on Clarence St in Addington, some way out of the city and no public transport linking to it. There are luggage lockers in the station costing $1 for 24 hours.

Trains run daily each way between Christchurch and Picton, connecting with the ferry across to Wellington. There's also a Monday to Saturday service each way between Christchurch and Invercargill via Dunedin. The TranzAlpine Express train runs daily between Christchurch and Greymouth via Arthurs Pass. Crossing over to the west coast the section of railway through the Waimakariri Gorge (above Springfield) has interesting scenery, but the road follows a different and even more spectacular route.

Car From Christchurch it's 340 km north to Picton, 362 km south to Dunedin, about four or five hours' drive in either direction. Westbound it's 150 km to Arthurs Pass, 248 km to Greymouth, 331 km to Mt Cook or 486 km to Queenstown.

Hitching It's pretty good hitching on the whole but Christchurch to Dunedin can be a long day. Generally it gets harder the further south you go, then easier as you approach Dunedin. Catch a Templeton bus (Nos 25 or 8) to get out of the city. It's also possible to hitch between Christchurch and Picton in a day although there can be long waits in some places. If you're hitching northwards take a Christchurch bus to Woodend to get you on your way.

To hitch west take a bus No 8 (Yaldhurst) – then keep your fingers crossed; it can be a long hard haul, say a two-day trip. Pick up the train somewhere along the way if you become despondent. The first part of this trip is easily hitched, but once you leave SH 1 it gets steadily harder.

Getting Around
To/From the Airport The public bus service to the airport is operated by Canride from Worcester St, just off Cathedral Square. Going out to the airport it's bus No 24, coming in it's bus No 28. Buses depart about every half-hour from around 6 am to nearly 6 pm, then less frequently until the last at 9.45 pm on weekdays; they're also less frequent on Saturday and Sunday. The cost is $3.

There are several door-to-door airport shuttle buses. Super Shuttle (☎ 365 5655) operates 24 hours a day, serving not only the airport ($5) but also the bus and railway stations. Another shuttle is operated by Canterbury Scenic Tours (☎ 366 9660) and also costs $5. A taxi to or from the airport will cost about $14 to $18 depending on the time you go, so it can work out cheaper than the shuttles with several people.

Bus Most city buses are operated by Canride and run from Cathedral Square. Unlike most NZ urban bus services, Christchurch's is good, cheap and well organised. For bus information phone Bus Info (☎ 366 8855). Fares start at 50c and step up 50c for each additional section, to $2.50. Note the Christchurch tradition of hanging baby strollers and pushchairs off the back of the buses.

Taxi There are plenty of taxis in Christchurch but, as with other places in New Zealand, they don't cruise. You have to find them on taxi ranks or phone for them.

Car & Campervan Rental The major operators all have offices in Christchurch, as do numerous smaller local companies. With the smaller operators, unlimited km rates start from around $50 a day plus about $12 per day for insurance, for rental periods of three days or more.

Avis
26 Lichfield St (☎ 379 6133)
Avon Rent-a-Car
corner of Tuam & Antigua Sts (☎ 379 3822)
Budget Rent-a-Car
corner Oxford Terrace & Lichfield St (☎ 366 0072)
Economy Rental Cars
518 Wairakei Rd, Burnside (☎ 359 7410)
Hertz
48-50 Lichfield St (☎ 379 9888)
Percy Rent-a-Car
154 Durham St (☎ 379 3466)
Renny Rent-a-Car
156 Tuam St (☎ 366 6790)
Southern Cross Rental Cars
23 Sheffield Crescent, Burnside (☎ 358 9681)
Thrifty Car Rental
574 Wairakei Rd, Burnside (☎ 358 7533)

Wheels (☎ 366 4855) at 20 Manchester St hires cars at about $250 per week, everything included, but they also have a programme whereby they sell you a car and buy it back again at a pre-agreed price.

There are also many campervan rentals available in Christchurch. Campervan companies include:

Horizon
530-544 Memorial Ave (☎ 353 5600)
Maui Campavans
530 Memorial Ave (☎ 358 4159)
Mt Cook Line Motorhomes
47 Riccarton Rd (☎ 348 2099)

Motorcycle Rental Motorcycles can be hired from Phil Payne's Cycletreads (☎ 379 7382) at 50 Tuam St, Eric Wood Suzuki (☎ 366 0129) at 35 Manchester St, or from Te Waipounamu Motorcycle Tours.

Bicycle Rental Bicycles are ideal for Christchurch as it is nice and flat. There are cycling lanes on many roads, and Hagley Park, which encompasses the Botanical Gardens, has many cycling paths. You can pedal away from Rent-a-Cycle (☎ 365 7589) in the Avon Car Park Building, 139 Gloucester St; it's open Monday to Thursday from 8.30 am to 6 pm, 8.30 am to 11 pm on Friday. Single-speed bikes rent for $2 an hour, $10 a day, or $54 a week. Three-speed bikes are $3/15/70.

Sam's Bike Shop (☎ 384 2549) at 636 Ferry Rd, Woolston, has 18-speed mountain bikes at $7 an hour, $20 a day or $90 a week. Insurance is $1.50 a day. Contact the Recreational Cycling Club if you'd like to join the club's Sunday tours.

There's even a Penny Farthing bike shop in Christchurch.

North of Christchurch

SH 1 heads north from Christchurch through the towns of Belfast, Kaiapoi and Woodend. The large market town of Rangiora is six km west of Woodend. At Waipara, 57 km north of Christchurch SH 1 splits – the left highway, SH7, heads via Hurunui and Culverden to the Red Post Corner where it too splits. The westerly choice leads to the Lewis Pass, Maruia Springs, and eventually either the West Coast or Nelson. If you proceed north from Red Post Corner you will reach Kaikoura either by the inland or coastal routes. About 23 km from Red Post, on the Lewis Pass route, there is a right-hand turn to Hanmer Springs, a thermal area and resort.

KAIAPOI

Kaiapoi (population 5400), on the coast 20 km north of Christchurch, is noted for its wool mills. The Kaiapoi Museum in the Old Courthouse on Williams St has exhibits on local history. It's open from 2 to 4 pm on Sunday and Thursday; entry is $1 (children 20c or free with an adult).

From Kaiapoi you can make trips on the MV *Tuhoe*, an old steamer, which sails most Sundays to Kairaki and back. It doesn't sail every Sunday; tickets are on sail one hour before sailing and sailings are subject to weather conditions. The return trip costs $8 (children $4) and takes 1¼ hours.

There's fishing for trout, salmon and whitebait on the Kaiapoi River. You can reach Kaiapoi from Christchurch on a Kaiapoi bus Nos 1 or 4, Waikuku bus Nos 1 or 4, or Rangiora bus No 4; it's a 35-minute trip. For times and points of departure, phone Bus Info (☎ 366 8855).

Places to Stay & Eat

There are a couple of places to stay in Kaiapoi. *Pineacres Holiday Park* (☎ & fax 327 7421) is two km north. Basic sites are $7.50 per person ($1 more with power), cabins $22 for two, tourist flats $45 for two and motel units $65 for two. There are two other camping places nearby: *Kairaki Camping Ground* (☎ 327 7335) and *Blueskies* (☎ 327 8007); the hostel at Blueskies costs $6.60 per person and camping at Kairaki is $9 per person.

As far as food goes there is not a great selection here; drive to Christchurch. If your car breaks down then try the *Taurus Restaurant*, 134 William St, which serves good old favourites for $12 to $22 depending on how fancy you want your food while the car is being repaired. Dinner is served every evening from about 5.30 to 8.30 pm, and it stays open later on Friday and Saturday nights.

Heading further north, past Woodend, there is a *DOC campsite* at Mt Thomas, Hayland Rd, 30 km north-west of Rangiora

HANMER SPRINGS

Hanmer Springs (population 1240), the main thermal resort in the South Island, is about 10 km off SH 7, the highway to the West Coast. It's popular for a variety of outdoor activities including forest walks, horse treks, river and lake fishing, jet-boating, rafting, bungy jumping from the Waiau ferry bridge, skiing in winter and golfing at the 18-hole course. And of course, the hot pools!

Information

There's an information centre, run by DOC (☎ & fax 315 7128) on the corner of Amuri Rd and Jacks Pass Rd. It's open from 9 am to 5.30 pm Monday to Friday. There are a number of other centres where you can get information, such as the Hanmer Springs Visitor Centre (☎ 315 7323) on Conical Hill Rd opposite the Lodge Hotel, and The Log Cabin (☎ 315 7192) on Amuri Rd opposite the thermal reserve. The BNZ is in the Mall on Conical Hill Rd and the Price Cutter Supermarket has an EFTPOS facility.

Thermal Reserve

For over a hundred years, maybe more, Hanmer Springs has been renowned for its thermal waters. The springs are part of the legend of the fires of Tamatea. It is said that they are a piece of the fire dropped from the sky after an eruption of Mt Ngauruhoe's volcanic ridge. William Jones, in April 1859, was reputed to be the first Pakeha to see them. He tried unsuccessfully to arouse local interest in their development. From 1916 to 1971, Queen Mary Hospital functioned here as a hydrotherapy centre and, later, a centre for the treatment of alcoholics.

It is now the Hanmer Springs Thermal Reserve (☎ 315 7239), open daily from 10 am to 8 pm, and a far cry from the grubby appearance of a few years ago. There are three 'relaxer' pools (temperatures range from 37° to 40°C); four rock pools connected by a rock stream; private pools (39°C); a fresh-water 25-metre pool; and a toddlers' pool (34°C). Admission is $4.80 for adults, $2.50 for children, preschoolers free, and spectators $2.

Bungy Jumping

This takes place at the Thrillseekers Canyon where the Waiau ferry bridge crosses the river of the same name. It costs $89 to hurl yourself from this bridge (37 metres high), money better saved for the more aesthetic surrounds of the Kawarau or Shotover rivers and bridges which are higher. If it's your only chance however, being the closest to Christchurch, the reservation number is 315 7046; they operate from 9 am to 5.30 pm.

Skiing

There are three skiing areas near Hanmer Springs. Amuri is the closest as it is only 27

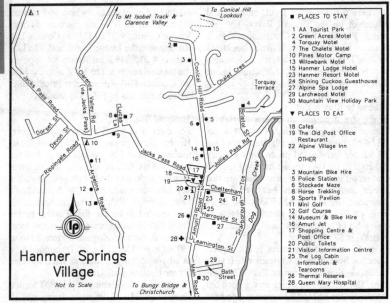

Hanmer Springs Village
Not to Scale

■ PLACES TO STAY

1 AA Tourist Park
2 Green Acres Motel
4 Torquay Motel
7 The Chalets Motel
10 Pines Motor Camp
11 Willowbank Motel
15 Hanmer Lodge Hotel
23 Hanmer Resort Motel
24 Shining Cuckoo Guesthouse
27 Alpine Spa Lodge
29 Larchwood Motel
30 Mountain View Holiday Park

▼ PLACES TO EAT

18 Cafes
19 The Old Post Office Restaurant
22 Alpine Village Inn

OTHER

3 Mountain Bike Hire
5 Police Station
6 Stockade Maze
8 Horse Trekking
9 Sports Pavilion
12 Mini Golf
12 Golf Course
13 Museum & Bike Hire
16 Amuri Jet
17 Shopping Centre & Post Office
20 Public Toilets
21 Visitor Information Centre
25 The Log Cabin Information & Tearooms
26 Thermal Reserve
28 Queen Mary Hospital

km from Hanmer and Lyford, a new area in the early developmental stages, is 75 km away. In comparison to the larger resorts they are not nearly as expensive. Mt Lyford also offers nordic skiing at the base of the area, and Mt Terako is being developed nearby. See the Outdoor Activities chapter for more details.

Rafting & Jet-boating

There are two companies operating jet-boat trips through the Waiau Gorge. They are Thrill-seekers Jet (☎ 315 7046) and Amuri Jet (☎ 315 7323); both charge about $45 for adults and $20 for children. You can raft the gorge for the same price with Waiau River Rafting Adventures (☎ 315 7401), who offer a three-hour trip twice daily (9.30 am, 1 pm) for $45 per person.

Other Things to Do

There are two companies providing safaris to Molesworth Station, the largest in NZ's high country. They are Trailways Safaris (☎ 315 7401) and Alpine Adventures (☎ 315 7323); the cost is $45 for a half-day tour. Trailways take a full-day tour and provide lunch for $75. You can also do a flightseeing tour over Molesworth Station in a helicopter or light plane – get advice and prices from the Hanmer Springs Visitor Centre.

Rainbow Adventures (☎ 315 7444) at the Stables at Jacks Pass Rd take trail rides around Hanmer; one hour is $25, half day $45 and a full day is $90.

Places to Stay

Camping & Cabins The *Mountain View Holiday Park* (☎ 315 7113), on the south edge of town, has campsites at $7.50/15 for one/two people ($1 more with power). There's also a variety of cabins at $31 to $39 for two people and fully equipped tourist flats at $49 to $54 for two.

The *AA (Central) Tourist Park* (☎ 315 7112) is on Jacks Pass Rd, three km from the town centre, with campsites at $15 for two, cabins at $37 for two and tourist flats at $52 for two, with a small discount for AA members. Also on Jacks Pass Rd, adjacent to the golf course, is the *Pines Motor Camp* (☎ 315 7152) where campsites cost $6 per person ($7 with power); there is a self-contained backpackers bunkroom where beds are $12.50 per person. At the *Hanmer Alpine Village* (☎ 315 7111), six km from town, on-site caravans cost $22 for two people, cabins cost $30 for two, and tourist flats cost $35 for two.

Hotels & Guesthouses The *Hanmer Lodge Hotel* (☎ 315 7021) is a fine old hotel right in the centre of town. Rooms cost $40/60 for singles/doubles or twin; some with private bathroom facilities. There's also a swimming pool. The *Shining Cuckoo Guesthouse* (☎ 315 7095) at 6 Cheltenham St has B&B for $35/50. It's conveniently close to the town centre and just a three-minute walk from the hot pools.

Motels There are numerous motels, most costing at least $65 per night. The *Willowbank Motel* (☎ 315 7211) on Argelins Rd is less expensive; units cost from $49 to $59 for two. At the *Forest Peak Motel* (☎ 315 7132) on Bristol St rooms cost $58 for two. The height of motel luxury is the *Alpine Spa Lodge* (☎ 315 7311), on the corner of Amuri Rd and Harrogate St, where four of their units have circular beds and spa baths, for a cool $180. There are other units for $66 to $90 for two persons.

Places to Eat
The *Village Plus*, on the corner of Conical Hill and Jacks Pass Rd is a good place for a cup of coffee. The *Alpine Restaurant*, around the corner from the CPO, sells basic takeaways. The *Old Post Office Restaurant* is quite expensive but the dishes are tasy NZ fare: Canterbury lamb topside baked in the oven with berry mint sauce is $21.50; entrees are about $9.50. It is open from 6 pm for dinner.

Getting There & Away
InterCity buses run twice daily (once on Sundays) between Hanmer Springs and Christchurch; it's a two to three-hour trip depending on which bus you take! Mt Cook Landline buses go from Christchurch to the Hanmer turn-off (from where it is 10 km to the town) Monday to Friday, connecting at Springs Junction with Cunningham's 'Buller Connection' buses to and from Westport (two hours) and Karamea (four hours). Remember, these buses, unlike the InterCity ones, just drop you at the junction and you have to make your own way into the town. There are a number of tour operators to Hanmer from Christchurch; inquire at the Christchurch-Canterbury Information Centre.

BEYOND HANMER SPRINGS
SH 7 continues from the Hanmer Springs turn-off to Lewis Pass, Maruia Springs and Springs Junction. From Lewis Pass (907 metres) there are a number of interesting walks – these are outlined in the pamphlet *Guide to Tracks and Walks in the Lewis Pass Region*. Most of the tracks pass through beautiful beech forest. Snow-capped mountains form the backdrop and there are lakes, alpine tarns and mountain rivers.

Maruia Springs is 69 km from the Hanmer turn-off. It is nowhere near as developed as its Hanmer cousin. From Maruia the road continues to Springs Junction where it splits. SH 65 heads north to the Buller Gorge and SH 6 to Nelson. SH 7 continues west from here to Reefton, then down the Grey Valley to Greymouth and the West Coast.

Banks Peninsula

Near Christchurch, Banks Peninsula makes an interesting side trip. A change from the flat area around the city itself, this hilly peninsula was formed by two giant volcanic eruptions in the distant past. The many tiny inlets and bays all around the peninsula's coast make for some pleasant explorations.

Smaller harbours such as Le Bons, Pigeon and Little Akaroa bays radiate out from the centre of the peninsula and give the peninsula a cog-wheel shape.

The peninsula has a chequered history of settlement. Captain Cook first sighted the peninsula in 1770, although he thought it was an island. He named it after naturalist Sir Joseph Banks. The Maori Ngai Tahu tribe, who then occupied the peninsula, were attacked by Te Rauparaha in 1831 and suffered a severe decline in numbers. A few years later, in 1836, the British established a whaling station at Peraki.

Two years later, in 1838, the French captain Jean Langlois chose the site of Akaroa as an attractive spot for French settlement. He returned to France and in 1840 a group of 63 French settlers set out in the *Comte de Paris* from Rochefort. Meanwhile, also in 1840, the Treaty of Waitangi was signed, bringing all New Zealand under British sovereignty. The French, however, did go ahead with their plans to settle at Akaroa. In 1849 the French land claim was sold to the New Zealand Company and the following year the French were joined by a large group of British settlers. The small

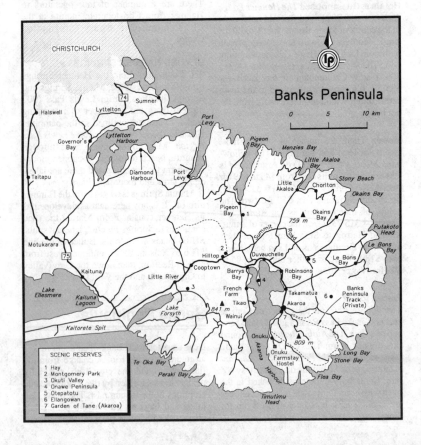

Banks Peninsula

0   5   10 km

SCENIC RESERVES
1 Hay
2 Montgomery Park
3 Okuti Valley
4 Onawe Peninsula
5 Otepatotu
6 Ellangowan
7 Garden of Tane (Akaroa)

group of French colonists have clearly stamped their mark on this place. Many streets (rues Jolie, Lavaud, Balguerie) and houses (Langlois-Etevenaux) have French names, and descendants of the original French settlers reside in the town.

Originally heavily forested, the land was cleared for timber, and dairy farming, later supplanted by sheep farming, became the main industry of the peninsula. A good account of the peninsula's history is found in *Banks Peninsula: Cradle of Canterbury* by Gordon Ogilvie (GP Books, 1990).

LYTTELTON

To the south-east of Christchurch are the prominent hills, and behind them Lyttelton Harbour, Christchurch's port. Like Wellington Harbour it is the drowned crater of a long extinct volcano. Drive on from Lyttelton and up over the Port Hills to Sumner. The narrow road is compensated for by breathtaking views of the azure waters of Lyttelton Harbour, contrasted to the golden brown sweep of the bare Port Hills. Read more of its history in the *Port Hills of Christchurch* by Gordon Ogilvie (AH & AW Reed, 1978).

Harbour Trips

There are all sorts of boat trips on Lyttelton Harbour, starting from as low as $4 (children $2) for the one-way trip to Diamond Harbour and Quail Island. The turn-of-the-century steam tug *Lyttelton* does two-hour harbour cruises from January to April every Sunday at 2 pm. It departs from No 2 Wharf and the cost is about $12 (children $6). Lyttelton Harbour Cruises (☎ 328 8368) also cruise every day at 2 pm from Jetty B to Ripapa Island Historic Reserve, also for about $12 (children $6).

Museum

The Lyttelton Museum has displays on colonial Lyttelton, a maritime gallery and an Antarctic gallery. It's in the centre of Lyttelton on Gladstone Quay and is open from 2 to 4 pm on weekends all year round; from 2 to 4 pm on weekends, Tuesday and Thursday from December to February. A self-guided historic walk begins from the museum and guided tours are available.

Timeball Station

In Reserve Terrace, Lyttelton, is the Timeball Station, one of the few remaining in the world. Built in 1876, it once fulfilled an important maritime duty. Every day, for 58 years at 1 pm, Greenwich Time was signalled to all ships in the harbour, thus allowing their captains to calculate their longitude accurately. It's open from 10 am to 5 pm daily, and entry is $3 (children $1, family $6).

Places to Stay & Eat

There are no places to stay in Lyttelton apart from basic pub accommodation. If you happen to be visiting Lyttelton at lunch time there are plenty of places to take a bite to eat. There's *Noko's Restaurant* on the corner of London and Oxford Sts. It was once the scene of the Great Fire of Lyttelton, where the three-storied wooden Queen's Hotel stood. On 24 October 1870 a fire started in the building and quickly spread to adjacent buildings until the business area of town was completely destroyed. In all some 74 buildings in all were razed. Crayfish bisque at Noko's is $7.50 and delicious whitebait is $12.50.

Close together, almost in a row, are *Volcano Cafe*, a nameless *fish & chip* shop, *Harbour Light Theatre & Cafe Bar, Deluxe Cafe, Mickey's Ice Cream, Waterfront Wholefoods* and *Smail's Wine Bar & Cafe*.

The Volcano Cafe is a quaint place with artwork adorning the walls and the quirkiest toilet entry you are likely to see. Someone with a cheeky sense of humour designed this. You can relax with a drink here or enjoy a good range of food. Enchiladas are $7.50 as an entree or $18.50 as a main with salad, and smoked salmon in fresh filo is $18.50.

For those who enjoy a drink with a view try out the *Wunderbar*, rather hidden and with a convoluted stairway entry – ask for directions as all the locals will know it; it only opened recently. From here you can look out over the docks area with the ragged

Port Hills behind and listen to mellow jazz playing in the background as the sun sets.

Getting There & Away

Bus No 28 from Cathedral Square take you to Lyttelton. From Christchurch there are three roads to Lyttelton. The quickest way is through the road tunnel (12 km).

Alternatively, you can go via Sumner and Evans Pass (19 km) or head straight down Colombo St from the square, and continue up over Dyers Pass (22 km). The Dyers Pass route passes the Sign of the Takahe, an impressive Gothic-style stone building, now housing an olde-English tea house. There is also a road along the summit of the hills.

AKAROA

Akaroa, meaning 'long harbour' in Maori, is 82 km from Christchurch on the Banks Peninsula. It's good value for day trips – there are boats for rent, horse-riding and 'the best fish & chips in NZ'. The Summit road back to Christchurch is amazingly winding. The best way to get around this small, intriguing village is on foot.

Orientation & Information

Most of the places of interest are concentrated along the waterfront from where SH 75 enters the township in the north, to the lighthouse at the south end of town. SH 75 merges into Rue Lavaud which then becomes Beach Rd. The Akaroa Information Centre (☎ 377 1755) is in the Gaiety Centre on Rue Jolie and the post office is on the corner of rues Lavaud and Balguerie.

Museum & Lighthouse

The Akaroa Museum, on the corner of Rue Lavaud and Rue Balguerie, has a 20-minute audiovisual presentation on the Maori history of Banks Peninsula, exhibits on the whaling industry which attracted the French to settle Akaroa in 1840, and the British settlers who came along in 1850. The Langlois-Eteveneaux Cottage in front of the museum also contains exhibits – it's one of the oldest houses in New Zealand and was partly prefabricated in France. The Customs

House by Daly's Wharf has been restored and is also part of the museum complex. The museum is open daily from 10.30 am to 4.30 pm (4 pm in winter); admission is $2.50 (children 50c).

The historic Akaroa Lighthouse is open on Sunday from 1 to 4 pm, daily during January.

Walking Tour

The Akaroa Civic Trust produces an excellent pamphlet: *Akaroa Historic Village Walk*. The walk starts at Waeckerle Cottage at the northern end of town, follows Rue Lavaud then Rue Brittan up to L'Aube Hill Reserve, the first consecrated Pakeha burial ground in Canterbury. It then returns to Rue Lavaud to take in such fine buildings as the Town Hall, Courthouse, St Peter's Anglican Church, Langlois-Eteveneaux House, the Custom House and the Church of St Patrick. Continue along Rue Jolie as there are a number of interesting houses in this main wharf locality, such as Glencarrig, built in 1852 for Akaroa's first Anglican vicar. Return to the start of the walk via the waterfront and perhaps wander out on to Daly's wharf to get a different aspect of the town.

Harbour Cruises

Daily harbour cruises are operated on the *Canterbury Cat* (☎ 304 7641), departing from the Main Wharf at 11 am and 1.30 pm, except from April to November when only the 1.30-pm trip departs. The cost is $23 (children $10). You can buy tickets from their office opposite the wharf at the Akaroa Village Inn (☎ & fax 304 7641).

The *Canterbury Clipper*, an inflatable naiad (☎ 304 7641), does an outer bays' tour where you may see Hector's dolphins, little blue penguins and seal colonies. It departs at 1.15 pm – the cost for adults is $29 and children are $20. Hector's dolphins are the world's rarest and smallest, and they just love to surf in the bow waves of boats. It is not unusual for them to beach themselves after surfing a particularly tricky shore break.

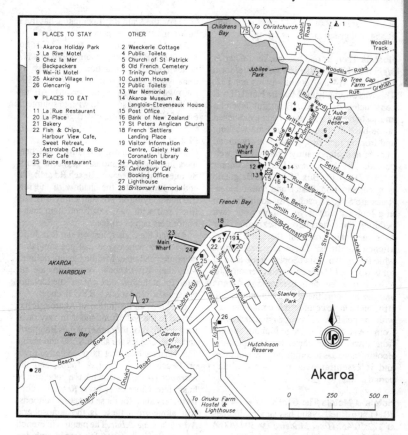

Akaroa

Banks Peninsula Track

Advertised as 'Four nights, four days, four beaches, four bays', this track allows you to make a two to four-day walk across private farmland and then around the dramatic coastline of Banks Peninsula. It starts and ends in Akaroa.

The night stops are in Trampers' Hut, Onuku Farm; Flea Bay Cottage; Macrocarpa Cottage; and Otanerito Cabins. A package tour which includes transport from Akaroa to the first hut, four nights' hut accommodation, landowners' fees, track registration and a booklet which describes features of the track and the history, is $90 to $100; the two-day option is $75. Telephone 304 7612 for more information; booking is essential.

Get hold of a copy of *Banks Peninsula Track: A guide to the route, natural features and human history*. This is gratis if you have paid to walk the track and it includes heaps of good information about the area and features along the way.

Places to Stay

Camping & Cabins The *Akaroa Holiday Park* (☎ 304 7471) on Morgans Rd, off Old Coach Rd, has sites at $16, on-site caravans at $32, cabins at $40 to $42 and tourist flats at $54. All prices are for two people.

Hostels There is one backpackers, *Chez la Mer* (☎ 304 7024), Rue Lavaud. Share/dorm rooms are $14 and doubles/twins are $32. This was originally the Madeira Hotel (it was constructed of wood). Beautiful lavender and jasmine gardens have been established at the back of the house, there are washing and ironing facilities, a common room and kitchen and, importantly, children are welcomed. The *Mt Vernon Lodge & Stables* (☎ 304 7180), PO Box 51, on Rue Balguerie is a combination hostel and guest lodge. Rates are $40 ($5 each extra adult) for two in a four-bed unit if you supply your own bedding. The rooms have a mezzanine floor over the main area and there are share-kitchen facilities. There are two cabins which sleep two to six people – these are $45 for two and $7.50 for each extra person. The lodge is in a deer farm overlooking Akaroa and the harbour; there's a swimming pool, BBQ and a large comfortable common room with an open fire, and you can ride the horses from the stables. The lodge is about one km from town, phone ahead for free pick-up. Booking ahead is recommended all summer, and is essential over the busy holiday periods.

Hotels & Motels The *Grand Hotel* (☎ 304 7011) at 6 Rue Lavaud has singles/doubles at $22.50/45. *Hotel Madeira* (☎ 304 7009) at 48 Rue Lavaud has rooms at $20 per person. *Mt Vernon Lodge & Stables* (see Hostels) is not only an associate YHA hostel but also a regular lodge.

Cheaper motels include *La Rive Motel* (☎ 304 7651) at 1 Rue Lavaud and the *Waiiti Motel* (☎ 304 7292) at 64 Rue Jolie, with rooms from $60 to $75. Not far from town there is a delightful B&B place. *Glencarrig* (☎ 304 7008) is a listed historic house at 7 Percy St. Here, in the town's first vicarage, you can stay in a tranquil garden setting. They have a swimming pool and the rooms, centrally heated, cost $45, with breakfast included. For a farm setting *The Barn* (☎ 304

7671) on the Main Rd, Takamatua, has three bedrooms at $25 per person.

The *Akaroa Village Inn* (☎ 304 7421; fax 304 7423), Beach Rd, is something of a NZ honeymooners' destination. They have 17 units which sleep a maximum of six at $90 for two ($10 each extra person). All the facilities are here so if you wish to splurge in one of NZ's great little towns go for it.

Places to Eat

Options for purchasing quality food here have increased enormously in recent years. Sit outside the *Bakery* on Beach Rd at the far end of town under the shadow of the few tricolours flying in NZ and enjoy a hearty filled roll with egg, salad and ham and a bottomless cup of coffee.

Around the corner, just off the Rue Jolie, is *La Place*, where you can get souvlakis, tabbouleh and other Middle Eastern delights – try their Kiwi kebab. Vegetarians are catered for at the *Atomic Cafe* on Rue Lavaud, vegans also, and it has a BYO licence.

La Rue is an institution in Akaroa. It has moved to the waterfront and is in very ordinary premises on the corner of rues Balguerie and Jolie; entrees are about $7.50 and mains $15. Near each other at the other end of town on Beach Rd are *Fish & Chips*, and the *Harbour View Cafe* which has a good mix of lunch fare. Close by is *Sweet Retreat*, a confectionery shop for those tempting bonbons. Just along from these is the atmospheric *Astrolabe Cafe & Bar*. The menu is in French but they will translate for free. Lamb leg roasted with herbs and served with kiwi fruit chutney is $16.50. Akaroa salmon with asparagus and melon salad is $12.50, and they have a range of calzone and pizza.

A place with a great setting is the *Pier Cafe*. Akaroa cod and French fries are $11.95 and breast of chicken with pocketed cheese and crayfish wrapped in filo pastry and served with plum sauce is $18.95. The top of the dining tree is *Relais Roquefort*, in Ngaio Grove, Duvauchelle, which is open winter and summer Thursday to Monday from 10 am (breakfast and earlier opening in summer only), with great views all year round.

The Akaroa Village Inn has its own bar, the *Jacques*, and restaurant *Bruce* – a worthy blend of the French and New Zealand.

At the end of the 1½-hour Woodills track there is the quaint *Tree Crop Farm* where you can relax with a rather expensive juice – extras are served but seem to be factored into the $5 price. There is a good selection of reading material here.

Getting There & Away

Akaroa is only 82 km from Christchurch and there are regular buses, as well as daily excursions available through Jenkins Motors (InterCity) (☎ 372 8534), Great Sights/Gray Line (☎ 343 3874), Canterbury Day Tripper (☎ 349 3558) and Christchurch Transport Limited (☎ 366 1661). Depending on the operator and the amount of extras thrown in (such as a trip on the *Canterbury Cat*, entrance fees, lunch and afternoon tea) these tours can cost from $55 to $185. Akaroa Tours (☎ Akaroa 304 7609 or 304 7421; Christchurch 379 9629) operate an Akaroa Shuttle minibus, departing from the post office in Akaroa and from the information centre in Christchurch; the cost of a ticket is $10. The InterCity depot in Akaroa is on Aubrey St close to the centre.

PLACES TO STAY

Most of the places to stay on the Banks Peninsula are in or near Akaroa, the peninsula's principal (though tiny) town, but a few other possibilities are scattered around the various bays.

Camping & Cabins

Duvauchelle Reserve Board Camp (☎ 304 5777) is eight km from Akaroa off SH 75. Tent sites are $4.50 per person, add an extra $1.50 per site for power.

The *Le Bons Bay Motor Camp* (☎ 304 8533), on Le Bons Bay Valley Rd about 22 km from Akaroa, has tent and powered sites at about $8 per person, on-site caravans at $30 for two.

Hostels

Six km south of Akaroa at Onuku, the *Onuku*

Farm Hostel (☎ 304 7612), PO Box 50, is beside the bay on a 400-hectare sheep farm. It's a friendly and relaxed place with a good library. Nightly costs are $12 in the house, $10 in summer huts, or $7 for campsites. They will pick you up from Akaroa. It is close to the start of the Banks Peninsula Walk and a good place to be if you want to get away from it all.

The *Kukupa Hostel* (☎ 304 6823) at Pettigrew's Rd, Pigeon Bay was the first YHA Hostel in New Zealand, though it's now privately owned. There are just two bunkrooms at this small hostel; the cost is $9 for YHA members, $10 for everyone else, or $30 for families. Set in magnificent bush, it's a bit far from everything if you don't have your own wheels – Pigeon Bay is about 35 km from Akaroa and very remote. To get there from Christchurch, take a bus to Duvauchelle or Akaroa and then transfer to the Jenkins Travel bus, which operates every day except Sunday and stops near the hostel. The nonresident manager lives in the second house on the left up Starvation Gully Rd.

Le Bons Bay Backpackers (☎ 304 8582), is quite out of the way – it is on the right-hand side of the hill about six km before Le Bons Bay. The cost here is $12/15 per night in single/double rooms, including breakfast. The farm house is in a great location with commanding views down the Le Bons Valley. An evening meal costs $8 and you can choose from the menu – when we were there, a selection included freshly caught crayfish with salad and mayonnaise. It is a suitable place for people with cars but the proprietors do pick up from Akaroa. Boat and fishing trips on secluded Le Bons Bay can be organised from here. Ring in advance as places are limited.

West of Christchurch

Heading west from Christchurch on SH 73, it's about a 2½-hour trip to Arthurs Pass and the Arthurs Pass National Park, at the summit of the Southern Alps. If you keep going west past the summit, you're in Westland. (See Arthurs Pass in this chapter.) The crossing from Christchurch to Greymouth, over the Alpine summit at Arthurs Pass, is a spectacular route covered by shuttle buses and the TranzAlpine Express train.

Nowhere in New Zealand do you get a better picture of the climb from the sea to mountains than on SH 73 to the West Coast via Arthurs Pass National Park. From Christchurch and almost at sea level, the road cuts through the flat Canterbury Plains, through rural towns such as Kirwee, Darfield, Racecourse Hill, Sheffield and Springfield. The road then winds up into the skiing areas of Porters Pass and Craigieburn before following the Waimakariri and Bealey rivers to Arthurs Pass. Two picturesque lakes are passed on the way, lakes Pearson and Grassmere.

Skiing
Craigieburn is described as one of the best skiing areas in the country, as it has a vertical rise of 503 metres. It is set in wild country and suits the advanced skier. You can ski tour from here to the club area at Broken River where Craigieburn tickets are accepted and there's a vertical rise of 360 metres. The other ski area in the vicinity is Mt Cheeseman, 120 km from Christchurch, is more suitable for beginners.

Craigieburn Forest Park
This forest park is 110 km north-west of Christchurch and 42 km south of Arthurs Pass, on SH 73. There is a good system of walking tracks in the park, and in the valleys west of the Craigieburn Range longer tramps are possible. The nearby country is suitable for rock climbing and skiing. In winter two areas – the Broken River and Craigieburn – operate in the eastern sector of the park. Broken River is particularly suitable for cross-country skiing. The predominant vegetation types are beech, alpine tussock, snow totara, mountain toatoa and turpentine scrub. If you are lucky you may see patches of South Island edelweiss *Leucogenes grandiceps*. Good longer walks are the Craigieburn

Valley Walking Track (1½ hours) and Camp Saddle Track (1½ hours). Get a copy of the DOC pamphlet *Craigieburn Forest Park Walks* for details.

The *Flock Hill Lodge* (☎ 318 8196) is a high country sheep station 35 km east of Arthurs Pass on SH 73, adjacent to Lake Pearson and the Craigieburn Forest Park. It can accommodate 36 people in twin or bunkrooms for $22 per person and there's a fully equipped communal kitchen. Activities include tramping and forest walks, canoeing, windsurfing, swimming, fishing, horseriding, skiing and ice skating.

Bealey
About 16 km east of Arthurs Pass is the now legendary *Bealey Hotel* (☎ 318 9277) with rooms for $70 a double. This is the location of a recent hoax, which led people across the nation to believe that a live moa (that large and long-extinct bird) had been sighted in the area. The publican at this hotel had his sighting confirmed by two German tourists...and business is booming.

ARTHURS PASS
The small settlement of Arthurs Pass is four km from the pass of the same name. The 924-metre pass was on the route used by the Maoris to reach Westland, but its European discovery was made by Arthur Dobson in 1864, when the Westland gold rush created enormous pressure to find a crossing over the Southern Alps from Christchurch. A coach road was completed within a year of Dobson's discovery. Later on, the coal and timber trade demanded a railway, which was completed in 1923.

The town is a fine base for walks, climbs, views and winter-time skiing (at Temple Basin) in Arthurs Pass National Park, and you can go there on a day trip from Greymouth or Christchurch.

Information
There's a National Park Visitor Centre (☎ 318 9211) in the town, open from 8 am to 5 pm every day. It has information on all the park

Top: Queenstown and the Remarkables, Otago (RS)
Bottom Left: TSS *Earnslaw,* Queenstown, Otago (TW)
Bottom Right: Bungy Jumping near Queenstown, Otago (TC)

Top: Lake Tekapo, Canterbury (TW)
Bottom Left: Mt Cook, Canterbury (TW)
Bottom Right: Copland River, West Coast (VB)

walks, with pamphlets on many good day walks and also topographical maps and route guides for 11 longer tramps with huts. They can also offer valuable advice on the park's often savagely changeable weather conditions – check here before you go on any walk, and fill out an intentions card. Be sure to sign out again when you leave, otherwise they'll send a search party out to find you! The rangers can help you to choose a walk that is safe at the time and suitable for your experience and abilities.

The visitor centre is also a park museum, with excellent displays, an audiovisual presentation, and a three-dimensional model of the park. In January there's a summer programme of guided walks and evening talks, discussions, films and slide shows.

Arthurs Pass National Park

There are day walks in the park which offer 360° views of the snow-capped peaks. Many of these peaks are over 2000 metres, the highest being Mt Murchison at 2400 metres. One of the most spectacular views to be had from the road is of the Bealey Face of Mt Rolleston.

The park has huts on the tramping tracks and also several areas suitable for camping. The day walks leaflet from the Visitor Centre lists half-day walks of one to four hours and day walks of five to eight hours. The two-hour (one-way) walk to Temple Basin provides superb views of the surrounding peaks. There's skiing at Temple Basin; the ski season is usually from June to September.

Places to Stay

The *Sir Arthur Dudley Dobson Memorial YHA Hostel* (☎ 318 9230) has bunkroom accommodation at $18 a night. Across the road is *Mountain House* (☎ 318 9258), a good backpackers which has bunks for $15 – from June to August (the best time to be here) stay three nights for the price of two. The *Alpine Motel* (☎ 318 9233) has double rooms at $65 and some simpler rooms from $50. The *Chalet Guest House* (☎ 318 9236)

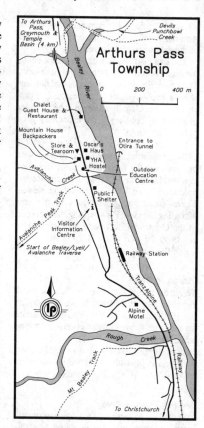

offers B&B for $75 double with shared facilities or $85 a double with private facilities.

The *Oscar's Haus Alpine Crafts* (☎ 318 9234) has a fully equipped Alpine-style house behind the shop with double rates of $65 for the first night, $55 the second night and $50 for each night thereafter. They also have a few campervan sites at $15. One small place is the *Snow Grass Cabin* which has one unit: a double and two bunks, bathroom, kitchen and TV; it costs $50 for two and $5 each additional person

You can camp at the Public Shelter for $3 per night; the facilities at this price are understandably basic, cold water and a flush toilet. Another place to try is Maori Flat, east out of the village, which is free.

You can also check with the visitor centre for other accommodation in and near town. They have listings of club and social huts and private baches which are sometimes available for hire. Usually these must be arranged in advance, but they're an especially good option for groups.

Outside town, the *Otira Hotel* (☎ 738 2802) in the township of Otira, 14.5 km west of, and over the other side of Arthurs Pass, has singles from $25, backpackers accommodation from $12 and meals are served. There are some great walks in the area including the Goat Pass trip which forms part of the Coast to Coast endurance race. Also nearby is the start of the Harpers Pass crossing of the Alps.

Places to Eat

You can eat in the *Arthurs Pass Store & Tearoom* or in the *Chalet Restaurant*, which has a cheaper coffee bar beyond its restaurant area. The restaurant itself has very good food and a bar.

If you're preparing your own food bring it with you if possible, as groceries are more expensive in Arthurs Pass than elsewhere.

Getting There & Away

You can get to Arthurs Pass by road or rail. InterCity buses no longer operate on this route and their service has been superseded by Alpine Coach & Courier and Coast to Coast Shuttle (see getting There & Away for Greymouth). The TranzAlpine Express daily train between Greymouth and Christchurch also stops here. Both are priced about the same. Bus and train tickets are sold at the Arthurs Pass Store.

Between Arthurs Pass and Christchurch, the train takes the more scenic route; on to Greymouth they both offer great views of the Otira Gorge, although the road goes over the top of the pass, rather more spectacular than the rail route which goes through the 8.5 km Otira tunnel immediately upon leaving town.

Getting Around

The Arthurs Pass Passenger Service (☎ 318 9233) offers minibus transport to the ski areas and walking tracks. If you're going tramping you can arrange for them to pick you up at the other end when you finish. This cost will vary depending on the walk that you do.

South Canterbury

If you head south from Christchurch there are basically two routes through the South Canterbury region. Taking SH 1 straight south along the coast you come to Ashburton, Timaru, Oamaru and then Dunedin. Or you can head inland, crossing the MacKenzie Country and heading towards the Southern Alps. This route between Christchurch and Queenstown, passing Lake Tekapo and Mt Cook along the way, is a much travelled road.

Methven and Geraldine are each a short distance off the road, whether you're taking the inland or coastal routes.

METHVEN

Inland from Ashburton and about 35 minutes below Mt Hutt is Methven (population 920), a good centre for the Canterbury Plains or the mountains. A small town, Methven is very quiet for most of the year, coming alive only during the winter when it fills up with skiers using it as a base for Mt Hutt and other ski areas. There is a world-class 18-hole golf course nearby.

Orientation & Information

The Methven Information Centre (☎ 302 8955) is on Mt Hutt Rd next to the Mt Hutt Ski Area office. The staff here are very helpful and do all they can to promote Methven and the surrounding district. They can make bookings for accommodation, skiing packages and other activities throughout this area.

A number of the restaurants and services

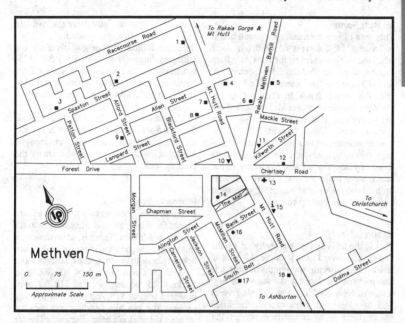

Methven

0   75   150 m

Approximate Scale

To Rakaia Gorge &
Mt Hutt

To
Christchurch

To Ashburton

■ PLACES TO STAY

1   Mountain View & Mt Hutt Motels
2   Aorangi Lodge
3   Mt Hutt Chalets
4   Koromiko Lodge
5   Methven Caravan Park
6   Mt Hutt Country Club
7   Mt Hutt Accommodation
    (Bedpost Budget)
8   Mt Hutt Bunkhouse & Lampard Lodge
9   Pinedale Lodge
17 Redwood Backpackers Lodge
18 Centrepoint Resort Hotel

▼ PLACES TO EAT

10 Canterbury Hotel
11 Blue Pub
15 Vee Tee's Bar & Bistro

OTHER

10 Ultimate Jump Booking Office
12 Police Station
13 Medical Centre
14 Shopping Centre
15 Methven Information Centre
16 Methven Historical Museum

---

are concentrated around the Mall and the adjacent shopping centre at the intersection of Chertsey and Mt Hutt Rds and Forest Drive. There are two banks near the Mall and the medical centre is opposite, on the corner of Chertsey and Mt Hutt Rds.

The number for ski information, especially mountain weather on Mt Hutt, is (☎ 302 8605).

Mayfield Merino Show

Out at Mayfield township, not far from Methven there is Rural Promotions (☎ 303 6142). Every day at 10 am and 2 pm daily they conduct a one-hour comprehensive sheep show which includes a demonstration by a top shearer; there are a range of sheep-involved activities which you can share in for $5 (children $2).

Mt Hutt Forest

This area of predominantly mountain beech is located 14 km west of Methven. It is adjoined by two reserves, the Awa Awa Rata Reserve and the Pudding Hill Scenic Reserve. There are two access roads, Pudding Hill Rd which leads to foot access for Pudding Hill Stream; and McLennan's Bush Rd to Pudding Hill Reserve and Awa Awa Rata Reserve. The Pudding Hill Stream Route, which requires many stream crossings, takes 2½ hours, and the Awa Awa Rata Reserve Loop Track takes 1½ hours. In the rata reserve there are many short walks set up to show the diverse nature of vegetation within the surrounding forest.

Skiing

This is the activity that has really set Methven on an upward growth curve. Mt Hutt is nearby and, offering six months of skiing, it has perhaps the longest ski season of any resort in New Zealand. The skiable area is 365 hectares and snow-making facilities ensure there is an adequate cover for the whole season. All levels of alpine skiing, snow-boarding, telemarking and recreational racing are catered for. The *Beaches Restaurant* in the mountain complex is the highest dining establishment in Australasia.

See Skiing in the Outdoor Activities chapter for more details.

Jet-Boating

Two operators take trips in this area. White Water Jets (☎ 318 6574) and Rakaia Gorge Scenic Jet (☎ 318 6515) zip up to the Rakaia Gorge, every day or on demand. You can only see this area from the river, so a jet-boat is the obvious choice of transportation in this braided river system.

Air Activities

If you want to see what the Canterbury Plains look like while you are looping the loop, barrel rolling and stall turning in a Pitts Special aerobatic aircraft, ring Four Season Tours (☎ 308 8787). They also cover flights over other parts of Canterbury that you are unlikely to see from the ground.

If free-falling is your bag then try the Ultimate Jump (☎ mobile (025) 321 135) which is based at Pudding Hill, five km from Methven. You leap out of a plane attached to a competent instructor and free-fall before engaging a special tandem parachute.

More sedate is a balloon flight organised through Aoraki Balloon Safaris (☎ & fax 302 8172); includes a traditional 'champagne breakfast' with the farmer who owns the landing spot.

Places to Stay

Most of the accommodation places are geared for winter tourists who are here to ski on nearby Mt Hutt. There is, nevertheless, a full range of accommodation available, from budget places to international quality resorts.

Methven Caravan Park (☎ 302 8005) on Barkers Rd has tent sites at $10 for two, powered sites at $15, and cabins at $12 per person. You can hire bedding and cooking utensils if you don't have your own. The *Mt Hutt Accommodation – The Bedpost* (☎ 302 8508/8585) near the corner of Mt Hutt Rd and Lampard St in central Methven has hostel-style accommodation from $14 ($16 to $18 in winter), with facilities including twin, double and multiple-bed rooms in lodges, cottages and bunk houses. If you don't have your own bedding you can hire it for $2.

On the corner of Alford and Allen Sts is *Pinedale Lodge* (☎ & fax 302 8621) where share rooms are $12 (summer October to April) and $16 (winter May to September). There is a large open fire, a fully equipped kitchen and lock-up ski storage. A courtesy van will pick-up from the local bus stop. Another budget place, the *Redwood Backpackers Lodge* (☎ 302 8287), is near the corner of South Belt Rd and Jackson St. It has a well-equipped kitchen, log fire, stereo and TV, and linen is supplied. In summer it costs a very reasonable $8 (winter is $16) per person in share rooms; there is storage available.

Pudding Hill Chalets (☎ 302 8416) five km from town on SH 72 has campsites at $12/20 for one/two people, and chalets where B&B is $30 per person in twin rooms, $39 per person in larger rooms (lower off-season,September to June). They have lots of enjoyable extras including sauna, spa pool, swimming pool, a children's play area, billiards, a ski room and drying room. This is also the base for the Ultimate Jump tandem parachuting.

Aorangi Lodge (☎ 302 8482) is at 38 Spaxton St and has double or twin/triple/quad rooms at $80/108/132 during the ski season, with off-season reductions. *Mt Hutt Homestead* (☎ 302 8130) is part of a high country sheep and deer station just outside Methven. B&B is not cheap at singles $90 to $105, doubles $102 to $130, but the food is excellent and it's an interesting place to stay. There are other motels and hotels, such as the comfortable *Koromiko Lodge* (☎ 302 8165) on SH 77 (Mt Hutt Rd), where a share twin is $94 in winter.

Places to Eat

In the Mall and shopping centre there are a number of takeaways including *Mac's Place*, *Munchies* and *The Hard Wok Cafe*. Additionally, there are a number of good restaurants in Methven. *Vee Tees Bar & Bistro*, above the information centre on Mt Hutt Rd serves good family meals. There are two pubs, the *Canterbury Hotel* and the famous *Blue Pub*, on the corner of Mt Hutt Rd and Forest Drive. The latter is very popular with ski bums during winter, but both serve good pub meals. Good seafood meals are available at the *Centrepoint Resort Hotel* on Mt Hutt Rd. There is lots of entertainment in winter when the skiers converge back on the town after a day on the slopes.

Getting There & Away

There is an InterCity bus service summer and winter to Methven; the cost to Christchurch Airport return is $40. Also Value Tours (☎ 302 8112) and Allan's Bus (☎ Christchurch 359 3199) will pick you up from the Christchurch airport and will drop you off at your accommodation. Value Tours and Guthreys usually include ski hire, transport and accommodation in a package.

Getting Around

As it is such a compact town most people walk to get around. Many accommodation places have courtesy vehicles; ask when you book in. A village shuttle will be in operation in winter from May to October.

GERALDINE

Off the main Christchurch-Timaru road on the road inland to Mt Cook is Geraldine (population 2200), a picturesque town with a country village atmosphere. Geraldine was not settled until 1854 when Samuel Hewlings built the first bark hut in Talbot St; a totara tree planted at that time still survives today. There are a number of early settlers' cottages still remaining.

Vintage Car & Machinery Museum

This interesting museum, on Lower Talbot St, includes a De Dion Bouton (1907), an International Motor Buggy (1908), a couple of 1910 Model Ts and lots of cars from the 1900s, '20s and '30s. The huge shed at the back houses about 60 tractors, dating back to the 1920s; the tractors are entered in the annual Geraldine tractor races and competitions. There's also a single aircraft and a large amount of rather rusty agricultural machinery. The museum is open from 10 am to 4.30 pm on Saturday and Sunday all year, daily during school holidays, and entry is $2 (children free).

Barker's Wines (☎ 693 8969) is eight km out of Geraldine, off SH 79 towards Mt Cook, and is open for tasting Monday to Saturday until 6 pm. It specialises in elderberry and other berry wines.

There is an information centre (☎ 693 8636) in the Geraldine Borough Council Chambers, near the corner of Cox and Talbot Sts.

White Water Rafting

Two rafting companies operate in the nearby Rangitata River. The main one is Mt Peel-based Rangitata Rafts (☎ 696 3735; Christchurch 366 9731; mobile (025) 332 449); they have budget accommodation at Mt Peel where you can get a bunk bed for $10. Christchurch-based Rapid Action (☎ 377 1929) operate on the Hurunui, Clarence and Rangitata rivers. Rafters who have done a number of trips say that the Rangitata Gorge is one of the best, because of the exhilarating Grade Five rapids. Rangitata rafts charge $89 per person for the Rangitata Gorge and $45 for the Grade Two-to-Three lower river. The trips depart from Christchurch at 9.30 am and arrive at the river base at 11 am. The trip on the river is about three hours and return to Christchurch is about 7 pm.

Peel Forest & Mt Somers

The Peel Forest, 19 km from Geraldine, is one of New Zealand's most important areas of indigenous podocarp forest. Mt Peel station is nearby, and the road from it leads to Mesopotamia, once the run of the English writer, Samuel Butler, in the 1860s. Before heading in to the park stop at the Peel Forest Park DOC office (☎ 696 3826) and obtain more information. Particularly good is the pamphlet *Peel Forest Park: Track Information*. They also take bookings for the excellent *camping ground* on the banks of the Rangitata River; $6.50 each adult, and an extra $2.50 for power.

You are only minutes away from a magnificent native podocarp (conifer) forest of totara, kahikatea and matai. One fine example of totara can be seen on the Big Tree Walk – it is nine metres in circumference and over 1000 years old. The birdlife attracted to this forest includes the rifleman, kereru (native pigeon), bellbird, fantail and grey warbler. There are nesting New Zealand falcons on the higher reaches of Mt Peel. There are also picturesque waterfalls in the park – Emily Falls (1½ hours return), Rata Falls (two hours return) and Acland Falls (20 minutes).

The 10-hour Mt Somers Alpine Walkway traverses the northern face of Mt Somers, linking the Sharplin Falls with Woolshed Creek. The highlight of this trip is the several altitudinal plant sequences which walkers pass through, although there is also plenty of regenerating beech forest. Two huts, the Pinnacles and Mt Somers, are available on the walk; $4 each adult. Be warned that this subalpine route is subject to sudden changes in weather and all normal tramping precautions should be taken.

Places to Stay & Eat

The *Geraldine Motor Camp* (☎ 693 8860), Hislop Rd, has tent sites for $7, and cabins for $14 per person. At the *Farmyard Holiday Park* (☎ 693 9355), seven km from Geraldine you can get cabins for $22 for two. There is now a backpackers here: *The Olde Presbytery* (☎ 693 8308) at 13 Jollie St; a bed here costs $13 per night.

The Crossing (☎ 693 9689), Woodbury Rd, is a pretty B&B with a licensed restaurant. Standard rooms are $58/70 for doubles/twins. On Talbot St there is the *Crown Hotel* (☎ 693 8458) where B&B is $30/50 for singles/doubles or twins; this hotel has a restaurant. The two motels, the *Geraldine* and the *Andorra* both charge about $65 and up for a unit. For a good breakfast go to *Robbie's Tearooms & Restaurant* in Talbot St. *The Oaks*, unashamedly established to entice the bus trade, has opened on the corner of Talbot and Cox Sts – all the usual travellers delights are available here from greasies to classy restaurant fare.

DOC campsites in this region can be found at Peel Forest, 22 km north of Geraldine (full services); Orari Gorge, Yates Rd, 12 km northwest of Geraldine; Waihi Gorge, Waihi Gorge Rd, 14 km northwest of Geraldine; and Pioneer Park, Home Bush Rd, 14 km west of Geraldine

MACKENZIE COUNTRY

The high country from which the Mt Cook park rises is known as the MacKenzie country after a legendary sheep rustler, Jock McKenzie, who is said to have run his stolen flocks in that uninhabited region around 1843. When he was finally caught other settlers realised the potential of the land and followed in his footsteps. The first people to

The Legend of Jock McKenzie

Legend this rightly is as many subsequent investigations have only helped cloud or confuse the truth. It is thought that James (Jock) McKenzie was born in 1820 in Scotland. In his short time in this country (date of arrival unknown), possibly only two years, he achieved great notoriety. In March 1855 he was caught near present day MacKenzie Pass in possession of 1000 sheep which had been stolen from the Levels run, north-west of Timaru.

It was believed at the time that he had stolen the sheep to stock a run he had purchased in Otago, and that he was aided only by his remarkable dog, Friday. He was captured near the pass by the Levels overseer and two Maori shepherds. He escaped and made his way to Lyttleton where he was recaptured, by a police sergeant, while hiding in a loft. He was then tried for sheepstealing and sentenced to five years' imprisonment. Throughout the trial McKenzie had pleaded not guilty and nine months after the trial was granted a pardon. He had escaped from prison three times, it is reputed, during his nine month incarceration, always proclaiming his innocence. Even the then Superintendent of Canterbury, James Fitzgerald, added: 'I am inclined to believe his story'. Popular myth has it that he was then ordered to leave the country, but there is no evidence to back this up.

Lyttleton's town clock now covers the foundations of the gaol that once held McKenzie; he was interned here after the only Supreme Court trial ever held in the town. It is believed by some that James McKenzies' 'treasure', well his savings anyway, are concealed in a bush near Edendale, 39 km north of Invercargill. He supposedly selected the bush as it was tapu to the local Maoris. As legend had it McKenzie was only pardoned on the condition that he leave New Zealand for ever. So he never returned to pick up his savings.

If heading to Timaru via MacKenzie Pass there is a monument erected near the spot where McKenzie was apprehended, although who really knows. The pass is said to be named after McKenzie as the discoverer, but it is now believed that it had appeared on an earlier map in the late 1840s. Similarly there is no proof that he had ever purchased land in Otago to stock with either stolen or bought sheep. His date of death and indeed much at all about his later life is mystery. More fuel to the legend. ■

traverse the MacKenzie were the Maoris who used to trek across the country from Banks Peninsula to Otago hundreds of years ago.

FAIRLIE

This town (population 870) is often described as 'the gateway to the MacKenzie' because, just west of here, the landscape changes dramatically as the road mounts Burkes Pass to the open spaces of the Mac-Kenzie Country. It was named after the town of Fairlie in Ayrshire, Scotland, the birthplace of the first hotel owner to set up in the NZ Fairlie in 1865.

One legacy of the early residents is the tree-lined avenues. The colonial Mabel Binney cottage and Vintage Machinery Museum are on the main highway, just west of the town centre. There is a horse-drawn covered wagon and traction engine at the museum. A few minutes' drive west of Fairlie is the historic limestone woolshed of the Three Springs Sheep Station, which once had space on its floor for nine blade shearers.

There is a good scenic drive of 1½ hours just out from Fairlie which takes in the spectacular Opihi Gorge. The drive takes you to Allandale, then along Middle Valley Rd and Spur Rd to Opihi, and back to Fairlie – it is 38 km in length. You can get information on Fairlie and the surrounding area from the Sunflower Centre (☎ 685 8258) at 31 Main St.

Skiing

There are two skiing areas near Fairlie. Fox Peak (☎ 685 8539), located in the Two Thumb Range north-west of Fairlie, is a club ski area which offers skiers a vertical run of 680 metres top to bottom. More adventurous skiers can climb all the way to the top of Fox Peak and ski from there; lift fees are about $25 per day.

Mt Dobson (☎ 685 8039), also northwest (26 km) of Fairlie, has an adult lift rate of $32 daily. The ski area is situated in a basin three km wide, accessed from the highest car park in NZ (1692 metres). Mt Cook and the Southern Alps are clearly viewed while skiing here. Daily transport is offered from the ski shop in Fairlie.

Places to Stay & Eat
The *Fairlie Motor Camp* (☎ 685 8375), Allandale Rd, has campsites for $6 each adult, cabins for $23 for two and a family unit. One of the local hotels, probably the *Fairlie* (☎ 685 8061) was setting up as a backpackers with economical rates – their normal singles/doubles are $25/50; inquire at the Sunflower Centre.

The *Aorangi Motel* (☎ 685 8340), 26 Denmark St, and the *Rimuwhare Motor Inn* (☎ 685 8058), 53 Mt Cook Rd, have units for between $58 and $65 for two; there is a restaurant in the latter which is open for breakfast, lunch and dinner. Try the hot smoked lamb of Ambrosia and red currants, or lamb rump filled with peppered cheese and spinach.

The *Sunflower Centre* serves good whole-food meals; *Fairlie Stores* and *Tom's*, both on Main St, cater for the fast food and fish & chip cravers; and the local pubs have pub food.

Getting There & Away
Both InterCity and Mt Cook Landline have depots in Fairlie. The InterCity depot is at the BB Stop (☎ 685 8139), 81 Main St and Mt Cook (☎ 685 8311) have a depot on Main St as well.

Getting Around
One unusual way of getting around is in a horse-drawn wagon. The horse power comes from two Clydesdales. The route follows a mountain stream to a campsite near Mac-Kenzie Pass. The evening meal is cooked for you before you turn in to a comfortable bed in one of the wagons. Contact Fairlie Creek Waggon Company (☎ 685 8336).

TEKAPO
At the southern end of Lake Tekapo the small settlement of Tekapo (population 520) is a popular rest stop for buses heading to or from Mt Cook or Queenstown. It derives its name from *taka* meaning 'sleeping mat' and *po* meaning 'night'.

There's a little cluster of businesses by the main road, from where there are sweeping views across the lake with the hills and mountains as a backdrop. It is a place to avoid when the buses arrive at meal times and, fortunately, it does not take much to get away from the scene.

The lake, walks and, in winter, skiing are the Lake Tekapo attractions. The turquoise colour of the lake is created by 'rock flour', which is finely ground particles of rock held in suspension in the glacial melt water.

Church of the Good Shepherd
The picturesque little church beside the lake was built of stone and oak in 1935. Further along is a statue of a collie dog, a touching tribute to the sheep dogs which made the development of the MacKenzie country possible. It is not, as a lot of people believe, the infamous dog Friday of James McKenzie. Again, walk down here when the last bus departs. It is a peaceful place and probably just as its founders intended.

Walks
It's an hour's walk to the top of Mt John and you can continue on to lakes Alexandrina and McGregor, an all day walk. Other walks are along the eastern side of the lake to the ski area road, the one-hour return walk to the Tekapo Lookout or 1½ hours to the power station.

Aerial Sightseeing
Air Safaris (☎ 680 6880) operate flights from Tekapo over Mt Cook and its glaciers for $125 (children $88). The flights do not land on the glacier, but Air Safari's 'Grand Traverse' takes you up the Tasman Glacier, over the upper part of the Fox and Franz Josef glaciers, and by Mt Cook and Mt Tasman. Air Safaris operates the same flights

from Glentanner, near Mt Cook for the same price ($125, children $88), but YHA members can get a 10% discount from Tekapo, not available from Glentanner. They are much cheaper than similar flights offered by other airlines from Mt Cook itself.

Other Things to Do

Other popular activities around Lake Tekapo include fishing, boating, kayaking and bicycle touring, horse trekking and hang-gliding. In winter, Tekapo is the base for downhill skiing at Round Hill (beginners) or Mt Dobson (intermediates), or cross-country skiing on Two Thumb Range. There's ski area transport and ski hire in season. Tekapo also has an open-air ice skating rink.

Places to Stay

Camping & Cabins Beside the lake the *Tekapo Camp* (☎ 680 6825) has tent or powered sites at $8 per person, cabins at $12 per person, cottages with cooking facilities (everything supplied except bed linen) at $46 for two, and motel units from $68 for two.

Hostels The *Tekapo YHA Hostel* (☎ 680 6857), PO Box 38, is beyond the post office, restaurants and shops on the Mt Cook side of town, down towards the water. It's a well-equipped, friendly little hostel sleeping 24 people and with great views across the lake to the mountains beyond. It's open all day and the nightly cost is $14, or there are limited tent sites beside it for about half that price ($7.50).

Wilma and Michael, who advertise themselves as 'can do' people (and obviously read ee cummings at school) run *tailor-made-tekapo backpackers* (☎ 680 6700) where their 11 rooms (two triple, three doubles and six twins) all cost $14 per person. It has full kitchen facilities, a laundry and, importantly, caring owners. It is in Aorangi Crescent, not far from the highway where all the buses stop.

Hotels & Motels The *Lake Tekapo Hotel* (☎ 680 6808) has singles/doubles at $30/65. The *Lake Tekapo Alpine Inn* (☎ 680 6848)

has budget rooms at about $55, standard rooms at $75, and superior (lake view) rooms at about $100, all for two people. The Tekapo Camp also has motel units, see Camping & Cabins.

Places to Eat

There are takeaways and cafes, as well as a bakery, in the business centre by the main road. The *Lake Tekapo Hotel* has reasonably priced bistro meals for lunch and dinner every day except Sunday. The *Alpine Inn Family Restaurant* is open daily for all three meals. During the summer season they serve a daily hot buffet lunch ($13.50) and dinner ($23). *Cassinia Cafe* is a more up-market coffee shop with vegetarian alternatives; lunch is $6 to $8. The *Cassinia Carvery* is a restaurant next door with a range of take-aways during the day, and meals during the evening. The *Golden Fleece* service station also does sandwiches during the day and meals at night.

Getting There & Away

The InterCity and Mt Cook Landline south-bound services to Queenstown (3½ hours), Wanaka (five hours) and Mt Cook (1¼ hours) come through every day, as do the northbound services to Timaru (three hours) and Christchurch (3½ hours). Book at the petrol station. Nationwide Shuttles & Buses (☎ Christchurch 474 3300) include Tekapo on their route. They pick up at the Kahurangi Craft Shop or the YHA. See the Getting There & Away section for Twizel.

Hitching in or out of Tekapo can sometimes be difficult as there is not much traffic; but once you've got a ride it will probably be going a fair way.

TWIZEL

Slightly south of Lake Pukaki, Twizel (population 1170) is at a conveniently central location for the whole area. By car it's only about 30 minutes from Mt Cook. Nearby Lake Ruataniwha has an international rowing centre, fishing, boating and windsurfing. In the Ben Ohau ranges there is heli-skiing in winter. And there's a huge hydroelectric power station; you can arrange a free tour through the town's information centre.

There is a black stilt captive breeding centre near Twizel. The black stilt is the rarest wader species in the world.

Information

The Twizel Information and Display Centre (☎ 435 0802) on Wairepo Rd is open from 9 am to 4 pm daily. It also houses the DOC and is the headquarters of the very important black stilt breeding programme. Informative tours to the black stilt hide leave from here.

Lake Ohau & Ohau Forest

There are six forests in the Ohau area – Dobson, Hopkins, Huxley, Temple, Ohau and Ahuriri, all administered by DOC. The walks in this vast area are too numerous to mention but you will find them outlined in the DOC pamphlet *Ohau Forests Recreation Guide*. There are many huts scattered throughout the region for the more adventurous trampers. The less adventurous can stay in the *Lake Ohau Lodge* (☎ & fax 438 9885) on the western shore of Lake Ohau. Powered campsites cost $7 per person, beds in the Huxley wing are $15, and double accommodation in the Maitland wing $45, and the Temple wing $65. The Temple wing has views of the lake and mountains. This is a

great base for walks into this tramper's paradise.

Places to Stay

The *Basil Lodge* (☎ 435 0671) has all sorts of accommodation starting with hostel-style bunks (only two beds to a room, though) at $13.50, doubles/twins at $15 per person and singles/doubles at $27/39. Family rooms are $39 plus $5 per child. Linen is provided in all rooms except the backpackers. Another cheap alternative is *Mountain Chalets Lodge* (☎ 435 0785; fax 435 0551), Wairepo Rd; twin rooms in the 12-person lodge are $13 each adult. This is a very comfortable place and would work out cheaply for a group. The lodge is in a new A-frame building and kitchen facilities, lounge area with TV and bathrooms are available. Separate motel units (in the A-frame style) are $75 per double; an extra adult is $14.

At the edge of town the *MacKenzie Country Inn* (☎ 435 0869) has rooms at $105 a double. Right beside the lake, four km out of town, the *Ruataniwha Motor Camp* (☎ 435 0613) has tent or powered sites at $8.50 per person and cheap, although fairly basic, cabins at $12.50 per person.

Glenbrook Station (☎ 438 9407) is a high-country sheep station between Twizel and Omarama on SH 8, eight km south of Twizel

---

Black Stilt
The MacKenzie country of South Canterbury is the home of one of the world's rarest wading birds – the black stilt *(Himantopus novaezelandiae* – Maori: Kaki). It is found in swamps and beside riverbeds in the Waitaki River system, Otago. A single remnant population of 70 adults (11 breeding pairs) survives in the wild. The Department of Conservation has established a captive breeding and release programme for this endangered species near Twizel. Three large enclosures house five breeding pairs in a semi-natural environment, where they hatch and rear their chicks. Approximately 30 juvenile birds have also been hand-reared (in isolation of humans) and will be released into the wild at nine months of age. Public viewing of these captive birds is welcome and guided tours leave from the DOC Information Centre in Twizel daily. A specially designed hide allows visitors to view the breeding birds without disturbance, and displays provide information on management of this unique bird. Bookings are essential.

It would be an indictment on the collective conscience of NZ if this species was allowed to become extinct. Every effort should be undertaken to preserve them, as it was the hydroelectric scheme and the introduction of predators that has led to their threatened status. One sure way to keep them in the limelight is to visit the centre – numbers of interested observers, especially committed birders, are the sort of raw material that galvanises DOC into action. ∎

and 22 km north of Omarama. Accommodation includes four bunkrooms, each with kitchen and bathroom and sleeping up to 10 people, at $12 per person; motel units each sleeping up to six people at $50 per unit, or at $75/125 for one/two people including breakfast and dinner. It's an interesting place to stay, with horse-riding, cross-country trail riding, bush walks and hunting among the activities.

There's also homestead accommodation on the 72-sq-km *Rhoboro Downs Sheep Station* (☎ 438 9509), 15 km from Twizel near the SH 8 and SH 80 junction. Here there's just one twin room and one double room, and rates including breakfast and dinner are about $100 a night for two people.

There's a *DOC campsite* in Temple Forest, Lake Ohau Rd, 50 km west of Twizel

Places to Eat

The licensed Basil Lodge *Rumbles* restaurant serves breakfast ($5.50 to $11.50), lunch ($5 to $7) and dinner (main courses $10 to $17.50). They also have a cheaper takeaway counter.

In the small shopping centre the plain *Black Stilt Cafe* offers takeaways, burgers at $3 to $4.50, cooked breakfast at $7 and meals at around $10. Also in the shopping centre the *Lunch Box* has takeaways and outdoor tables. For higher class dining there's the restaurant at the *MacKenzie Country Motor Inn*, which also serves less expensive bistro meals; open for breakfast, and for dinner from 6.30 to 9 pm.

Getting There & Away

The InterCity and Mt Cook Landline buses serving Mt Cook all stop at Twizel, with additional buses shuttling between Twizel and Mt Cook; it's about a 50-minute bus ride. Leisuretime Activities (☎ 680 6732) operate a Tekapo-Twizel-Mt Cook shuttle bus every day. The cost from Tekapo to Mt Cook is $15 or $25 return the same day. From Tekapo to Twizel is $10, Twizel to Mt Cook $10 and Twizel to Glentanner $7.50. They also carry bikes for $5 each.

MT COOK NATIONAL PARK

Mt Cook National Park, along with Fiordland, Aspiring and Westland national parks, has been incorporated into a World Heritage area which extends from the Cook River in Westland down to the base of Fiordland. The Mt Cook National Park is 700 sq km in size and one of the most spectacular parks in a country famous for them. Encompassed by the main divide, the Two Thumb, Liebig and Ben Ohau ranges, more than one third of the park is in permanent snow and glacial ice.

Of the 27 New Zealand mountains over 3050 metres, 22 are in this park including the mighty Mt Cook – at 3755 metres the highest peak in New Zealand and Australasia.

Known to the Maoris as Aoraki, after the name of a god, the tent-shaped Mt Cook was named after Captain James Cook by Captain Stokes of the survey ship HMS *Acheron*. It was first climbed on Christmas Day 1894 (by local mountaineers Jack Clarke, Tom Fyfe and George Graham) and many famous climbers, including Sir Edmund Hillary, have sharpened their skills on this formidable peak. It dominates the park and is the centre of a great vista from the famed Hermitage Hotel.

In the early hours of 14 December 1991, a substantial piece of the east face (around 14 million cubic metres) fell away in a massive landslide. Debris spewed out over the surrounding glaciers for 7.3 kilometres, following a path down the Grand Plateau and Hochestetter Icefall and reaching as far as the Tasman Glacier. Miraculously, no one was killed, although there were climbers nearby at the time; the last climber up the old face was Geoff Wayatt from the Mountain Recreation School of Mountaineering in Wanaka – only the day before! (see Mountaineering in the Outdoor Activities chapter.)

The best introduction to this park is the beautifully illustrated *The Alpine World of Mount Cook National Park* by Andy Dennis and Craig Potton (Department of Lands & Survey). It has sections on high country weather, avalanches and glaciers in addition to the detailed descriptions of flora & fauna, walks and history of the park.

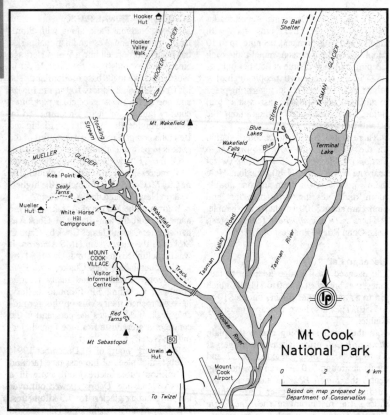

Orientation & Information

The National Park Visitor Centre (☎ 435 1818/1819), open daily from 8 am to 5 pm, will advise you on what guided tours are available and on tramping routes. For information before you arrive write to: The Field Centre Manager, PO Box 5, Mt Cook. They screen a dated but excellent audiovisual on the history, mountaineering and human occupation in the Mt Cook region at 8.30 and 10.30 am and 1.30 and 3.30 pm; the cost is $2.

A new post office and general store was opened in 1992. Travellers' cheques can be cashed at the Hermitage.

The Alpine Guides Mountain Shop (☎ 435 1834) sells equipment for skiing and mountaineering, or you can rent a variety of equipment including boots, parkas, ice axes, crampons, packs, rain pants, day packs and gaiters. It's open every day from 8 am to 5.30 pm.

The Hermitage

Skiing on the Tasman Glacier, and the crossing to Westland via the Copland Pass Track (see the Outdoor Activities chapter) are two of the energetic attractions of the park, but one of the park's chief attractions is rather

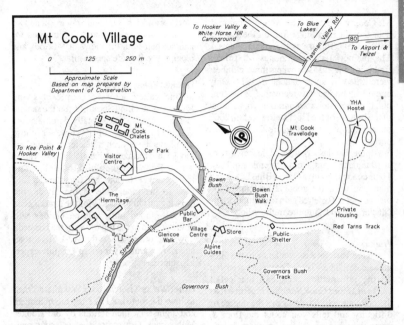

more sedentary. The Hermitage is the most famous hotel in New Zealand – principally for its location and the fantastic views out to Mt Cook. Originally constructed in 1884, when the trip up here from Christchurch took several days, the first hotel was destroyed in a flash flood in 1913. You can see the foundations about a km from the current Hermitage. Rebuilt, it survived until 1957 when it was totally burnt out and the present Hermitage was built on the same site.

Even if your budget is not up to staying here, make sure you come in for a beer so you can relax and look out the huge windows straight up to Mt Cook.

Tasman Glacier

Higher up, the Tasman Glacier is a spectacular sweep of ice just like a glacier should be, but further down it's ugly. Glaciers in New Zealand (and elsewhere in the world) have generally been retreating all this century, although they are advancing now. Normally

as a glacier retreats it melts back up the mountain, but the Tasman is unusual because its last few km are almost horizontal. In the process of melting over the last 75-or-so years it has contracted vertically rather than horizontally: the stones, rocks and boulders it carried down the mountain are left on top as the ice around them melts. So the Tasman in its 'ablation zone' (the region it melts in) is covered in a more or less solid mass of debris – which slows down its melting rate and makes it look pretty unpleasant.

Despite this considerable melt the ice by the site of the old Ball Hut is still estimated to be over 600 metres thick. In its last major advance, 17,000 years ago, the glacier crept right down to Pukaki, carving out Lake Pukaki in the process. A later advance didn't reach out to the valley sides, so the Ball Hut Rd runs between the outer valley walls and the lateral moraines of this later advance.

Like the Fox and Franz Josef glaciers on the other side of the divide the glaciers from

Mt Cook move fast. The Alpine Memorial, near the old Hermitage Site on the Hooker Valley Walk, illustrates the glaciers' speed. The memorial commemorates Mt Cook's first climbing disaster when three climbers were killed by an avalanche in 1914. Only one of the bodies was recovered at the time but 12 years later a second body melted out of the bottom of the Hochstetter Icefall, 2000 metres below the spot where the party was buried.

Alpine Guides organise sightseeing trips at 10 am and 2 pm, from September to May. Their coach goes up as far as Blue Lakes and then you walk for about 20 minutes (500 metres, but 100 metres gain in altitude) to the Glacier Lookout; inquire in the village.

Walks

There are various easy walks from the Hermitage area. The Visitor Centre can give you all the information including the leaflet *Walks in Mount Cook National Park* that lists the main attractions, describes the degree of difficulty and tells you about the flora & fauna in the area. If you're there in the summer keep a look out for the large mountain buttercup, often called the Mt Cook lily. There are also mountain daisies, gentians and edelweiss. Among the animals you may see are the thar, a goatlike mammal and excellent climber; the chamois, smaller and of lighter build than the thar but an agile climber; and red deer.

Kea Point An easy two-three hour (return) walk with much native plant life and fine views of Mt Cook, the Hooker Valley and the ice faces of Mt Sefton and the Footstool to the south of Copland Pass. There are plenty of opportunities to see keas here as well as at the Fox and Franz Josef glaciers.

Sealy Tarns This is a three-to-four hour return walk from the village, that branches off the Kea Point track. If the weather is warm and you're feeling brave you can swim in the tarns.

Red Tarns This is a good way to spend two to three hours (return) and if you climb for another half-hour the views of Mt Cook and along the valley are spectacular.

Hooker Valley It is a four-hour return walk up the valley across a couple of swing bridges to Stocking Stream. After the second swing bridge Mt Cook totally dominates the valley and there are superb views. For those who have never seen a glacier 'calving' ice blocks into the azure blue glacial lake, this is a must. From here the alpine route climbs up to the Hooker Hut and then over the Copland Pass to the other side of the divide, but crossing this high pass is for the experienced or well-guided only. Alpine Guides will guide you up to the top of the pass. The walk down the other side to the West Coast road and Karangarua River doesn't require expert assistance.

Other Walks The two-hour Wakefield Track follows the route used by early mountaineers and sightseers, then returns by the Hooker Valley track. Governors Bush is a short one-hour walk through one of the last stands of silver beech in the park. A special brochure on native plants in Governors Bush is available at the Visitor Centre. Shorter walks include the 10-minute Bowen Bush Walk through a small patch of totara trees near the Alpine Guides shop. The 15-minute Glencoe Walk, beginning from the rear of the Hermitage, ascends through totara forest to a lookout point facing Mt Cook and the Hooker Valley.

Tasman Valley Rd Tracks A number of short tracks branch off from the Tasman Valley Rd including a track to view the Wakefield Falls, another to overlook the five Blue Lakes, and various tracks providing different viewpoints of the Tasman Glacier. All are signposted from the road.

Overnight If you're well enough equipped you can tramp up to Hooker or Mueller huts, the closest huts to the village, and spend the night there. Both are three to four hours each way from the village.

Guided Walks Alpine Recreation Canterbury (☎ 680 6736; fax 680 6765) offer two high altitude guided walks in the area. The Ball Pass trip is a two-to-three day crossing over Ball Pass (2130 metres) from the Tasman to the Hooker valleys; it allows you to get close to Mt Cook without requiring mountaineering experience (with a group of six to eight people it would cost $275 each). The MacKenzie High Country Walk is a three-day easy alpine walk through open tussock country from which you get superb views of the Southern Alps and MacKenzie Basin. The highest point reached is Mt Hope (2073 metres). With a group of eight or more it would cost each person $195.

Climbing

There is unlimited scope here for climbing for the experienced, but beware, there have been over 160 people killed in climbing accidents in the park, with an average of five deaths each year! The Copland Pass track is a particularly problematic track, as it is well known and is too often attempted by people who are not sufficiently experienced to handle it safely.

Ice axes and crampons are a necessity, but you must know how to use them. Ropes are recommended, but there have been cases of several climbers tying themselves together and when one falls over a ledge, they have all been pulled over.

The highly changeable weather is an important factor around here – Mt Cook is only 44 km from the Tasman coast, catching the weather conditions blowing in over the Tasman Sea. The weather can change abruptly and a storm be upon you before you know it. Unless you are experienced in these types of conditions, don't attempt to climb anywhere without a guide.

It's important to check with the park rangers before attempting any climb, and not only to check with them, but to heed their advice! Fill in a climber's intentions card before starting out on any climb, so someone

can check on you if you are overdue coming out.

Alpine Guides have ski-touring and mountaineering courses but they are costly. A one-week Mountain Experience course is $1075, a 10-day Technical Mountaineering Course $1975, other courses and expeditions are around $2000. They also provide guides for the Copland Track, see the Outdoor Activities chapter.

Heliskiing in the Ben Ohau Range is $440, and to go skiing on the glacier it's a cool $425 by skiplane.

Aerial Sightseeing

The skies above Mt Cook are alive with the sound of aircraft. This is the antipodean equivalent of the Grand Canyon in the USA although fortunately the skies are not yet that crowded. The views are superb and glacier landings are a great experience.

Air trips are operated by Mt Cook Airlines from Mt Cook, or by Air Safaris from Tekapo (see Tekapo in this chapter) and Glentanner, and the Helicopter Line from Glentanner. YHA members get a 10% discount on the Air Safaris flights if taken from Tekapo, a saving not offered from Glentanner.

The Mt Cook skiplane landing flights are the most expensive. They have a 30-minute Skiplane Fun flight at $120 (children $89); a 40-minute Glacier Highlights flight at $167 ($125); and a 55-minute Grand Circle flight at $237 ($178).

The Helicopter Line has a 30-minute Trans Glacier flight at $108; a 30-minute flight over the Richardson Glacier at $180; and a 45-minute Mountains High flight over the Tasman Glacier and by Mt Cook with a glacier landing for $252. These flights depart from Glentanner Park as do the Air Safaris flights, which are probably the best value although they do not actually land on the glacier. Air Safaris' Grand Traverse takes you up the Tasman Glacier, over the upper part of the Fox and Franz Josef glaciers, by Mt Cook and Mt Tasman and generally gives you your fill of mountain scenery for $125 (children $88). Transport is available to Glentanner Park from Mt Cook village.

Other Things to Do

From the Glentanner camp you can go on horse treks from $14 for half an hour to $72.50 for four hours. There are 4WD trips for $22 per person, lasting about an hour. They also do a one-hour tour of the Glentanner Station farm, which for $14 includes a sheep shearing and sheepdog demonstration. Or you can combine the farm tour and the 4WD trip and pay $35 (children $17.50), the whole thing takes about 2½ hours. They also do fishing safaris. A minimum of four people is required for all the Glentanner trips.

Tours

The interesting (but at $24 rather expensive) two-hour Tasman Glacier Guided Coach Tour is operated two or three times a day in season – check at the Hermitage or Travelodge about bookings and tour times. The rocky road follows the lateral moraines of the Tasman Glacier and the bus stops several times to see this mighty river of ice. Part of the tour involves an optional 15-minute walk to view the glacier (see Tasman Glacier in this chapter).

Places to Stay

Camping & Cabins Camping is allowed at the White Horse Hill *camping area* at the old Hermitage site, the starting point for the Hooker Valley track, 1.8 km from Mt Cook Village. There's running water and toilets but no electricity, showers or other luxuries you find at motor camps. It's run by DOC on a first-come, first-served basis (no advance bookings) and the cost is $3 per night for each adult (children $1). For more information contact the Park Visitor Centre.

The nearest motor camp to the park is 23 km down the valley on the shores of Lake Pukaki at *Glentanner Park* (☎ 435 1855). Facilities are good and campervan sites with power cost $6.50 per person. There are also on-site vans at $12 per person, basic cabins at $30 for two, and deluxe cabins at $55 for two. Note that the camp store here is only open from 8 am to 5 pm. The only other store is up at Mt Cook, so if you're going to arrive

late bring supplies with you, or prepare to starve!

If you are hiking or mountaineering there are many huts scattered around the park, but some are only accessible to the experienced climber. The Park Visitor Centre can tell you where they are and advise you on good walks. Hut fees are generally $14 a night, except for the very basic shelters, which are free.

Hostels The excellent *Mt Cook YHA Hostel* (☎ 435 1820), on the corner of Bowen and Kitchener Drives, has lots more room than the small old one. Nevertheless it can still get crowded in the high season, from December to April, so try to book at least four days in advance. It's well equipped, with a sauna, BBQ, and disabled facilities. It's also conveniently located, has a friendly atmosphere, and is open all day. The cost is $17 per night.

Chalets, Hotels & Motels These are all run by the THC and booked by phoning Mt Cook on ☎ 435 1809.

At the bottom of the price range are the *Mt Cook Chalets* which cost $106 for up to four persons, then $17 for each child. They have two mini-bedrooms and a fold-down double bed-sofa, so between six people they can be reasonably economical. Well-equipped kitchens and a dining table add to the convenience. They may be closed in the winter season though.

Above this, the prices become expensive. The *Travelodge (Mt Cook)*, open only during the summer season from September to April, costs $185 for doubles; the rooms have no cooking facilities but the price includes breakfast. The *Hermitage* has prices and services in line with its fame – from about $214 to $270 for a double or twin.

Places to Eat

The only way to eat economically at Mt Cook is to prepare your own food. There's a small, but well-stocked, store and prices aren't too out of line, although you'll save a bit by bringing food up with you. The Glentanner motor camp has a small store and cafe.

There's also a little coffee shop at the Mt Cook airport.

Otherwise you have three choices at the Hermitage and one at the Travelodge. The Hermitage base line is their *coffee shop* which is usually open from 9 am to 5 pm but sometimes closes earlier. It does very unexciting sandwiches and pies.

Then there's the *Alpine Room* where main courses are around $15 to $19 (but if you want vegetables or a salad, that's a few dollars extra) and desserts are around $6. For breakfast and lunch the Alpine Room does buffets – $17 for breakfast, $25 for lunch. The *Travelodge (Mt Cook)* has a similarly priced restaurant but it's open only for dinner in the evening. Finally there's the Hermitage's *Panorama Room* where two people can spend well over $100 – starters are $9 to $13.50, main courses $20 to $40, desserts $7.50 to $11. The surroundings and the view must be amongst the best in the world – Sefton to your left, Cook in the centre and the Ben Ohau's, brown dark and forbidding to your right.

Entertainment
There's a *village tavern* where you can drink at the bar, sit around and talk, or there's the occasional disco at the village tavern on Friday evenings during the busy season. The Hermitage sometimes has a pianist.

Getting There & Away
Air Mt Cook Airlines (☎ 435 1848) have daily direct flights to and from Queenstown and Christchurch, with connections to other centres. At certain times of the year they also have daily flights to and from Te Anau. Mt Cook provides bus services to and from the airport.

There's no scheduled air service to Fox or Franz Josef but you can fly over one way if you like. It's a way of combining transport with a scenic flight and means you can avoid the difficult Haast route if hitching. But you can't rely on the weather and may get held up at Mt Cook for quite a while waiting for suitable conditions to get across.

Bus Mt Cook Landline (☎ 435 1849) has daily buses to Queenstown, Te Anau and Christchurch. Most of their services connect with the longer routes through Twizel, 70 km (an hour's drive) from Mt Cook. There are year round daily buses, but in summer they add extra, more direct services, making travel time quicker. From November to April they run special excursion buses between Christchurch and Queenstown, or day trips out of Christchurch, all allowing about 3½ hours stopover time at Mt Cook.

InterCity also has a daily Queenstown-Christchurch route with a 40-minute stop at Mt Cook. The Mt Cook and InterCity buses both stop at the front door of the Mt Cook YHA Hostel.

Hitching It's over five hours' drive from Christchurch or Queenstown. Hitching is hard – expect long waits once you leave SH 1 if coming from Christchurch or Dunedin and long waits all the way if coming from Queenstown. Hardest of all, though, is simply getting out of Mt Cook itself since the road is a dead end. It's worth considering taking the bus down to Twizel, where there's much more traffic.

Christchurch to Dunedin

The SH 1, south of Christchurch, is very flat and boring as you cross the Canterbury Plains. There are long straight stretches and one town looks much like another. Being in a truck, or even a bus, makes all the difference to your view, allowing you to see over the nearby hedges and obstructions. In clear weather there are some magnificent views to be seen of the distant Southern Alps and their foothills.

South of Christchurch you drive through plantation forests that were flattened by a storm some years ago. The remnants of these forests are still being picked through, though much has merely been bulldozed into long mounds and new trees planted. The first town of any size that you come to is Ashburton.

There are many wide, glacial-fed rivers to be crossed – quite a sight in flood, though you don't see much water at other times. The Rakaia River Bridge is about two km long and this river is popular for jet-boating; the Rangitata River popular for white water rafting; and salmon fishing is popular in South Canterbury. When you reach the Waitaki River you cross into North Otago.

ASHBURTON
Ashburton (population 14,200) is very much the service centre for the surrounding district and its population of 25,000. It is about 85 km south of Christchurch and lies between the Rakaia and Rangitata rivers. There are six museums in this town – the Plains Museum in nearby Tinwald, the Station Museum, an Aviation Museum, Museum of Woodwork & Ornamental Turning, Vintage Car Club Museum and the Ashburton Museum. The Ashburton Walkway is an easy walk of 19 km from the town to the coast at Hakatere; there is a free campsite along the way. For information on other activities in the area contact the Ashburton Information Centre (☎ 308 1064) on the corner of East and Burnett Sts. The AA area office (☎ 308 7128) is at 119 Tancred St.

Places to Stay & Eat
There is a full range of all types of accommodation in Ashburton. The *Coronation Caravan Park* (☎ 308 6603), 780 East St, has tent sites for $12, on-site caravans for $25 and cabins for $40; all costs are for two people. Next door is the *Academy Lodge Motel* (☎ 308 5503) for $60 to $65 for two. There are at least seven other motels typically charging from $55 to $70 for a unit; inquire at the information centre. They also have a list of farmstays that are available in the mid-Canterbury region.

There is a *KFC* in Ashburton for fast-food freaks. Other dining possibilities are the licensed *Chandler House*, 9 Mona Square, where all sorts of delights can be sampled in

this Edwardian two-storey house; *100 Pipers Restaurant & Bakery*, The Arcade; for Chinese meals the *Jade Garden*, 148 East St; and *The Stables*, one km south in the Tinwald Tavern.

Getting There & Away
Both InterCity and Mt Cook Landline pass through Ashburton on their way south to Dunedin or north to Christchurch. InterCity's depot is Ashburton Station Souvenirs (☎ 308 5178), East St, and Mt Cook's is Farmers Corner Tearooms, 208 Havelock St (☎ 308 8332). In winter, Mountain Transport (☎ 302 8443) operate a bus service to Mt Hutt.

Temuka
In 1853 William Hornbrook settled on his run Arowhenua, on the south bank of the Temuka River. His wife, who settled there a year later, was the first Pakeha female pioneer in South Canterbury. Arowhenua had long been a pa site of the Ngai Tahu people. Their earth ovens, *te umu kaha* or 'fierce strong ovens', gave Tumukaha, later Temuka, its name. A number of relics of early settlement survive, including middens, Old Hope Cottage, Mendelssohn House and the magnificent redwood trees on the corner of King St and Wilmhurst Rd. The site of pioneer aviator Richard Pearse's first attempted flight is out on Main Waitohi Rd, 13.5 km from Temuka towards Hanging Rock Bridge. He took off from the road but crashed into a nearby hedge, which has long since been removed. The District Council Service Centre (☎ 615 9537), Domain Avenue, acts as an information centre.

Places to Stay & Eat The *Temuka Holiday Park* (☎ 615 7241), 1 Ferguson Drive, has sites for $7.50 and cabins for $26 for one or two persons. Temuka has five hotels and four motels. The *Royal Hotel* (☎ 615 7507) has B&B for $27. The *A and A Motel* (☎615 8004), 54 King St, has reasonable rates: $36/45 for singles/doubles.

You shouldn't have any problem finding food along King St as there are pubs serving meals, a number of takeaways and the omni-present tearooms. The local cheese products – edam, cheddar, colby, gouda and high cream cheddar – are superb.

TIMARU

Timaru (population 28,000) is a pleasant little port about halfway between Christ-church (164 km) and Dunedin (202 km), a convenient stopping point with an especially attractive beach at Caroline Bay. The Christ-mas Carnival at Caroline Bay, beginning on 26 December and continuing for about 10 days, is superb.

Timaru comes from the Maori name Te Maru, meaning 'the place of shelter', but there was no permanent Maori settlement here when the first Europeans, the Weller brothers of Sydney, set up a whaling station in 1839. The *Caroline*, one of the sailing ships which picked up whale oil, gave the picturesque bay its name.

The town really began to boom when a landing service was established at the foot of Strathallan St. Later a better landing service building was established in 1868 in George St and is still there, now renovated into a restaurant and boutique brewery. After about 30 vessels were wrecked between the mid-1860s and 1880s attempting to berth near Timaru, the decision was made to establish an artificial harbour. The end result is the excellent port which stands there today and Caroline Bay's beach which has resulted from the construction of breakwaters.

Orientation & Information

Timaru's main road, SH 1, is a road of many names – the Hilton Highway north of town, Evans St as it enters town and Stafford St as it goes through the town centre. Most busi-nesses are on or near Stafford St. Continuing south, it becomes King St and then SH 1 as it emerges from town heading south.

The South Canterbury/Timaru Informa-tion Centre (☎ 688 6163; fax 688 6162) on lower George St, diagonally across from the railway station, is minded by zealous staff.

It's open from 8.30 am to 5 pm Monday to Friday, and on Saturday morning in summer. The AA is on the corner of Church and Bank Sts. A street map and the interesting pamph-let *Timaru City Historic Walk* are available from the information centre. The public library is on Sophia St, and is open Monday to Saturday (check the varying daily hours).

Caroline Bay & Other Parks

Caroline Bay is one of the few safe, sheltered beaches along the east coast and it attracts windsurfers, swimmers and sunbathers. The park along the beach has a walk-through aviary, a maze, a pleasant walkway and other attractions. The Christmas Carnival is held here. A pleasant walk heads north from town along Caroline Bay, past the Benvenue Cliffs and on to the Dashing Rocks and rock pools at the northern point of the bay. Caroline Bay is sheltered and calm but there's good surfing south of town. There is an easy 45-minute walk around the bay outlined in an old Timaru City Council pamphlet; it should still be available from the information centre.

Timaru has other good parks including Centennial Park along the Otipua Creek with a pleasant 3.5 km walkway along the stream bed. Timaru Gardens has gardens, duck ponds and a statue of Robert Burns overlook-ing the Queen St entrance. The information centre has leaflets outlining a scenic drive.

Museum & Art Gallery

The South Canterbury Museum, in the Pioneer Hall on Perth St, is the main regional museum, with exhibits on the whalers and early settlers. Admission is free and it's open daily from 1.30 to 4 pm except Monday and Saturday. One fascinating exhibit is a replica of the aeroplane designed and flown by early South Canterbury aviator, Richard Pearse, in 1903 (some nine months before Orville Wright in the USA). Pearse died in Sunny-side Psychiatric Hospital in 1953, virtually unknown to the outside world.

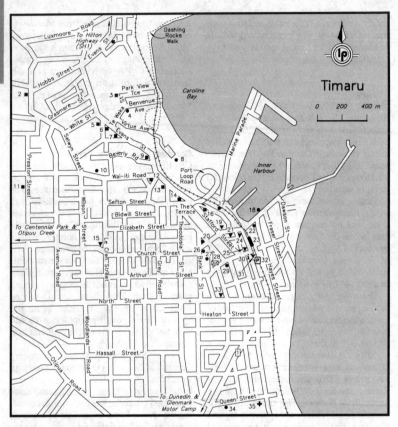

Timaru

Over 900 works of art, plus changing exhibits, are featured at the Aigantighe Art Gallery at 49 Wai-iti Rd. The gallery (Aigantighe is derived from a Scots Gaelic phrase meaning 'come in') is open from 11 am to 4.30 pm from Tuesday to Friday, and from 2 to 4.30 pm on Saturday and Sunday; admission is free but any donation would be welcomed.

Other Things to See & Do

The DB Brewery, Sheffield St, Washdyke, on the northern outskirts of town, gives free tours at 10.30 am and 2 pm Monday to Thursday. Enclosed footwear must be worn; just turn up.

There are also outdoor and indoor swimming pools and horse-riding, or Mt Cook flights can be arranged.

Interesting day trips can be made from Timaru if you have private transport. There are Maori rock carvings on the back road from Pleasant Point to Fairlie, an interesting two-hour round trip. The winery and museum at Geraldine are popular excursions while Peel Forest Park Scenic Reserve and Mt Nimrod have camping and many good

■ PLACES TO STAY

1   Al Casa Motel
2   Selwyn Holiday Park
3   Ashbury House
5   White Star Motel
6   Caroline Motel
7   Anchor Motel & Timaru Backpackers
9   Trailways Motor Inn
11 Wai-iti Court Motel
12 Bay Motel
13 Dominion Hotel
14 Hydro Grand Hotel
16 DB Grosvenor Hotel

▼ PLACES TO EAT

15 The Tavern
16 Boat House Restaurant
19 Bsunders Restaurant
21 Vienna Cafe
23 Railways Cafeteria
24 Casa Italia Restaurant
25 Annette's Kitchen
31 Loaded Hog Brewery
33 Hibernian Hotel

OTHER

4   Maori Park Swimming Pool
8   Caroline Bay Amusement Playground
10 Aigantighe Art Gallery
17 Terrace Footbridge
18 No 1 Wharf
20 Library
22 Footbridge
23 Railway Station & Railways Cafeteria
    Booking Office
26 Automobile Association (AA)
27 South Canterbury Museum
28 Post Office
29 Council Chambers
30 South Canterbury/Timaru
    Information Centre
31 Historic Landing Service
32 Free Car parking
    (behind Loaded Hog)
34 Timaru Gardens, Statue of Robbie
    Burns
35 Public Hospital

bush walks. Inquire at the information centre for details.

Places to Stay

Camping & Cabins The *Selwyn Holiday Park* (☎ 684 7690) on Selwyn St, two km north of the town centre, has sites from $6 per person, powered sites at $8.50/14 for one/two people, cabins at $19 for two, cottages and on-site caravans at $25 for two, and tourist flats at $50 for two. There's also the *Glenmark Motor Camp* (☎ 684 3682), on Beaconsfield Rd south of the town centre, where campsites are $12 for two ($2 more with power), cabins and on-site caravans are $25 for two.

The *Seadown Holiday Village* (☎ & fax 688 2657), on the corner of Divan Rd and SH 1, six km north of Timaru, has sites for $6.50 per person (with power it's $9/14 for one/two people), and motel units for $30/45 for one/two people. The *Hibernian* (☎ 688 8125), 4 Latter St, has been recommended by readers, but we haven't tried it out.

DOC campsites are at Mt Nimrod, Back Line Rd, 32 km southwest of Timaru, and Otaio Gorge, Back Line Rd, 29 km southwest of Timaru

Hostels At 44 Evans St in the Anchor Motel is *Timaru Backpackers* (☎ 684 5067). The variety of rooms here are all $12 per person (10 person capacity). Double rooms are available with TV, radio and toaster.

Guesthouses & Hotels *Jan's Place* (☎ 688 4589) at 4A Rose St offers B&B at $25 per person; there are backpackers beds for $15 per person. *Ashbury House* (☎ 684 3396) at 30 Te Weka St has rooms at $30/55 including a big cooked breakfast. The *Dominion Hotel* (☎ 688 6189) on Stafford St North has rooms at $25 per person or $30 with breakfast. On the same street the *Hydro Grand Hotel* (☎ 684 7059) is somewhat grander and costs $28/36 or $40/46 with bathroom. The *DB Grosvenor Hotel* (☎ 688 3129) on Cains Terrace is more expensive at $74/80. The

Trailways Motor Inn (☎ 688 4049), 16-22 Evans St, has a flat room rate of $79 (for as many as you can fit in, but usually four).

Motels Timaru has numerous motels, especially along Evans St (SH 1) on the northern end of town. Most cost from around $65 a night but the *Anchor Motel* (☎ 684 5067) at 42 Evans St (see Guesthouses & Hostels) is marginally cheaper. Also reasonable are the *Bay Motel* (☎ 684 3267) at 9 Hewlings St; *Al Casa* (☎ 684 7071) at 131 Evans St; the *Caroline* (☎ 684 4155) at 48 Evans St; *White Star Motel* (☎ 684 7509) at 12 White St, and *Wai-iti Court Motel* (☎ 688 8447) at 5 Preston St.

Homestays & Farmstays The information centre has listings for private homestays and farmstays.

Places to Eat

The dining scene has improved markedly in this town and few its size could boast their own gourmet's guide. Get a copy of the *Timaru Diners Guide* from the information centre – in a few years, with patience and the inculcation of culinary excellence this town could rival Motueka. The *Vienna Cafe* at 17 Biswick St is a pleasant European-style coffee shop, with fresh flowers on red-checked tablecloths, serving good cappuccino but rather bland lunches and light meals. The *Richard Pearse Restaurant* in The Tavern on Le Cren St and the *Hibernian* at 4 Latter St offer pub food.

Near the railway station *Annette's Kitchen* at 5 George St is an excellent licensed vegetarian restaurant with main courses from $7 (lunch) and $12.50 (dinner), starters and desserts at $4.50. It's open from 8 am to 3.30 pm Monday to Friday, from 11.30 am for brunch on Sunday, and from 6.30 pm for dinner Wednesday to Saturday.

For a more expensive night out *BSunders* at 247 Stafford St is operated by a Swiss couple and has an accent on French cuisine. At *The Boat House*, 1st floor at 335 Stafford St on the corner of Sefton St, seafood and steak are the specialities and it has a great view all the way from the bay to the mountains. Both are licensed.

A welcome addition to the international line-up is *Casa Italia*, Strathallan St. It is housed in a beautiful building, has an excellent winelist and serves authentic Italian cuisine – bellissimo. What is more, it is open from 6 pm to late every day. (It is pleasing to see that this operation has branched out to Dunedin.)

A boutique brewery and bistro has opened in the former Landing Service building in George St – the *Loaded Hog* has a veritable trough of selections for the beer lover. Sample one of each of Plains Lager, Red Dog Draught, Hogs Head Dark Ale and Weiss beer, then hand your car keys to someone more sober.

Getting There & Away

Air Air New Zealand Link (incorporating Air Nelson, ☎ freephone (0800) 652 881) have daily flights to Christchurch and Wellington with onward connections.

Bus The InterCity depot (☎ 684 7199) at the railway station has buses through Timaru on their Christchurch-Dunedin-Invercargill route at least twice daily. Mt Cook Landline also use the railway station on their daily Picton-Christchurch-Dunedin-Invercargill and Christchurch-Tekapo-Mt Cook route. Their tickets are sold from the cafeteria at the railway station. Tek Tours go from Tekapo to Timaru and return on Monday, Wednesday and Friday; the cost is $10 one way or $19 return. Several shuttle buses pass through Timaru such as Catch-a-Bus (☎ freephone (0800) 508 000) and Coop Shuttles (☎ freephone (0800) 805 505).

From Timaru it's two hours to Christchurch, three hours to Dunedin, and four hours to Mt Cook.

Train Timaru is on the Christchurch-Dunedin-Invercargill railway route, with a train in each direction daily except Saturday.

Hitching For hitching north get a Grants Rd bus to Jellicoe St and save yourself a walk.

Getting Around

For a taxi to Timaru airport, contact Timaru Taxis (☎ 684 8899); it costs about $16. They also offer tours for up to eight people, contact them for current rates.

WAIMATE

This town (population 4850) is 45 km south of Timaru near the Waitaki River. The tourist literature neglects to mention that its name translates as 'stagnant water' although there is little hint of it today. Here you will find instead the historic 'Cuddy', a thatched cottage constructed from a single totara tree. For a tour, which includes the woolshed, phone 689 8737. A monument to NZ's first practising woman doctor, Margaret Cruickshank, is on the corner of Queen St and Seddon Square. Dr Cruickshank graduated from Otago University in 1897.

You can obtain information about the town from the Waimate Information Centre (☎ 689 8097), Queen St.

Don't be surprised if you see wallabys in the nearby hills, as they breed like rabbits here since they were released from that Australian land of marsupials. Unfortunately, they are now hunted in the same fashion as rabbits since they are considered a noxious introduced species.

Places to Stay & Eat

Waimate has a number of accommodation options, more favoured by holidaying locals than international visitors. At the *Waimate Motor Camp* (☎ 689 7387), Victoria Park, a site is $7 per person, and basic cabins are $8 per adult. A room in the *New Criterion* (☎ 689 8069), corner of Mill Rd and Queen St, will cost $28/45 for a single/double. The *Lochiel Motel* (☎ 689 7570), 100 Shearman St, charges $25 for B&B in simple rooms, and their units are $52 for two.

There are plenty of places where you can get a meal along Queen St. Tea rooms, grill rooms and the inevitable *Country Kitchen* open their doors to the weary traveller. The *Te Kiteroa Lodge*, on Bush Point Rd, has a silver service restaurant – it specialises in local produce, especially salmon.

North Otago

When you cross the Waitaki River south of Waimate you have entered North Otago. Continue south from the Waitaki to reach the administrative hub of North Otago, Oamaru. Follow either SH 82 from Waimate or SH 83 from Pukeuri Junction (just north of Oamaru), to reach Kurow and the Waitaki Valley. From here SH 83 continues to Omarama via the hydroelectric lakes of Waitaki, Aviemore and Benmore.

WAITAKI VALLEY

There is quite a lot to see and do in the Waitaki Valley and there are a number of interesting towns between the turn-offs on SH 1 and Omarama: Glenavy, Duntroon, Kurow and Otematata. **Duntroon** was established in 1859 by Robert Campbell, owner of Otekaieke Station, as a village for his workers. It was named after Duntroon Castle in Scotland. In addition to an authentic blacksmith shop in the town, there is trout and salmon fishing nearby and jet-boating in the Waitaki; accommodation is available at the motor camps (including Dansey Pass) and food is served at the Duntroon tavern.

Kurow is at the junction of the Waitaki and Hakataramea rivers. Loosely translated the name means a 'hundred mists' as nearby Mt Bitterness is often covered with fog. From 1928, when the Waitaki power station was built, Kurow has been a service centre for hydroelectric development in the Waitaki. **Benmore power station** was constructed from 1956 to 1965 and Aviemore in 1968. There is fishing, boating and snow skiing all within a relatively short distance. For accommodation there are motels in the town and nearby farm stays; contact the Kurow Community Centre (☎ 436 0812) for more information.

Omarama is at the head of the Waitaki Valley, 119 km north-west of Oamaru, at the junction of SH 8 and 83. Not far from Omarama are the Paritea or **Clay Cliffs**, formed by the active Osler fault line which continually exposes clay and gravel cliffs. These clay pinnacles change colour during the day and are quite spectacular to see. Omarama has a world-wide reputation for gliding due to the north-west thermals – gliding world championships have been held here. Omarama has hotels, a motel and two motor camps (including Glenburn, seven km from town); food is available from a number of tearooms.

OAMARU

Visitors to Oamaru (population 12,500) prepare to be surprised, as this is an extremely pretty town centred in a region where there is a lot to do. Oamaru was first settled by Europeans in 1853. By the 1870s and early 1880s it was the seventh largest town in New Zealand. The Otago goldfields had a lot to do with its early prosperity, and this factor, allied with the availability of sandstone in the area, resulted in the erection of a number of imposing and enduring buildings.

In addition, Oamaru has beaches, the Forrester Art Gallery, a museum, a heated swimming pool and the large Oamaru Gardens. Colonies of the rare yellow-eyed penguins and little blue penguins live on one of the beaches – ask at the Information Centre for directions to a hidden observation spot. They also have maps for the Oamaru Walkway and for directions to the Parkside Quarry, seven km out of town at Weston, where you can make a self-guided tour to see how the soft, white Oamaru limestone is quarried. Clark's Mill Historic Site is at Maheno, 13 km south, and the mill (built in 1866) has been restored to full working order.

The Totara Estate Centennial Park is about eight km south of Oamaru and it was from here that the first NZ frozen meat was shipped to England in 1882. It took over three months to reach England but arrived in good condition and thus began New Zealand's most important industry. It's a New Zealand Historic Place and is open from 1 to 4 pm on Sunday, 10 am to 4 pm on school and public holidays, and other days by arrangement. Admission is $3.50 (children $1).

There's a 30-minute walkway to Brydone Monument on nearby Sebastopol Hill. Oamaru has a well-organised walkway within the town which comprises the South Hill Walk (7.8 km) and the Skyline Walk (5 km). The walkway traverses a large proportion of Oamaru's park system and many of Oamaru's scenic attractions. See the information centre for details.

Orientation & Information

Thames St is the main street through town. The Information Centre (☎ 434 5643) on Severn St, opposite the police station, is open from 9 am to 5 pm Monday to Friday. The extremely helpful staff vigorously promote their area, and at the time of research, plans were to have the centre open for seven days a week by 1994 . There's an AA agent on the corner of Thames and Usk Sts.

Harbour-Tyne Historic Precinct

Oamaru boasts the best preserved collection of historic commercial buildings in New Zealand. Nowhere better is this seen than in the Harbour-Tyne Street Precinct; in all, 22 buildings have been classified for preservation. Oamaru architecture, as in many NZ towns, is a mosaic of styles. Expect to find Gothic revival alongside neo-classic (Italianate and Greek) styles. The local limestone could be sawn (it hardened later when it was exposed to the air) so it was readily accepted as the most convenient building material.

There's an excellent brochure *Historic Oamaru* which outlines a walk through the 19th-century commercial area of town, and it is available free from the information centre. The leaflet gives background details on each of the town's main architects.

Penguins

Both the yellow-eyed penguin (hoiho) and little blue penguin (koroa) are found in close proximity to Oamaru. It is probably one of the few towns where you can actually walk out to the colonies from the town centre. The yellow-eyed is one of the world's rarest pen-

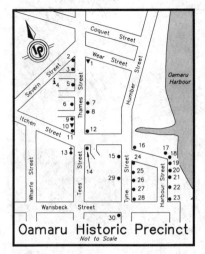

Oamaru Historic Precinct
Not to Scale

guins and the reason for their decline is thought to be the loss of coastal forest where they breed. Bushy Beach, close to Oamaru, has good natural vegetation and efforts are being made to extend it.

Importantly, a hide has been constructed so these beautiful birds can be observed without being disturbed. The yellow-eyeds are shy and easily upset, so on no account disturb them either with your presence or loud noises. The best time to view them is in the late afternoon when they come ashore to feed their chicks.

The little blue penguins nest right around the Oamaru Harbour area; they couldn't be closer to human habitation. One area of the foreshore is now a penguin refuge, native shrubs have been planted in the nesting area and nesting boxes have been provided. The best viewing of their return from fishing at sea, usually on dusk, is from the car park at the end of Waterfront Rd. Again, in no way disturb these birds and keep the most deadly of predators, dogs, well away from the area. Cameras with a flash are an absolute no-no; while binoculars can be useful even in dull light. Oamaru has got a great natural asset here so enjoy it.

Oamaru Public Gardens

Another one of the surprises in this town is its fine public gardens. They date back to 1876 and have been improved upon since. There is a Japanese red bridge which crosses Oamaru Creek, an Oriental Garden, Fragrant Garden, Rhododendron Dell, Cactus House, Azalea Lawn and so on. Flora-philes will adore this place. The main entrance gates are on Severn St where SH 1 crosses the railway

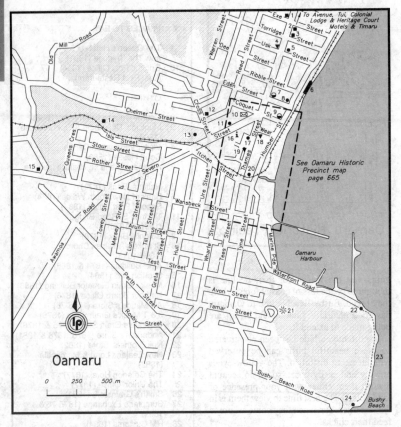

Oamaru

0   250   500 m

line. On weekend, October through March, you can go on a Clydesdale & Wagon Tour for $2.50 (children $1.50).

Places to Stay

Camping & Cabins The *Oamaru Gardens Holiday Park* (☎ 434 7666) is in Chelmer St, adjacent to the large Oamaru Gardens domain. Tent or powered sites cost $8.50 per person and there are various cabins from $25 to $38 per night for two. At the south side of the Waitaki bridge, on SH1, there is the *Waitaki Mouth Motor Camp* (☎ 431 3880); sites are $6 per person ($14 for two with

power), and cabins are $15/25 for one/two people.

There's a *DOC campsite* at Glencoe Reserve, adjacent SH 1, two km south of Herbert.

Hostels The Oamaru *Red Kettle Seasonal Hostel* (☎ 434 5008), corner Reed & Cross Sts, is a seasonal YHA hostel open approximately from mid-October to mid or late April; the nightly cost is $14.

Motels The *Alpine Motel* (☎ 434 5038) at 285 Thames St is conveniently located and

■ PLACES TO STAY

1   Thames Court Motel
2   Midway Motel
3   Alpine Motel
12 Red Kettle Seasonal Motel
14 Oamaru Gardens Holiday Park
15 Holmes Hill Motel

▼ PLACES TO EAT

4   Kentucky Fried Chicken
18 Brydone Hotel
19 Last Post Restaurant

OTHER

5   Automobile Association (AA)
6   Railway Station
7   Mt Cook Landline Depot
8   Taxis
9   InterCity Depot
10 Post Office
11 Police Station
13 Oamaru Public Gardens
16 Visitor Information Centre
17 Library
20 Forrester Art Gallery
21 Lookout Point
22 Little Blue Penguin Reserve
23 Graves Walkway
24 Yellow-eyed Penguin Hide

has units sleeping one to seven people from $64 to $68 for two. The *Thames Court Motel* (☎ 434 6963) at 252 Thames St is similarly priced ($59 for two). At the *Avenue Motel* (☎ 437 0091) at 473 Thames St rooms range from $52 to $63 a night for two, while the *Tui Motels* (☎ 437 1443) at 469 Thames St charges $49. The *Alma Motels* (☎ 434 6531), five km south on SH 1, are $42/52 for singles/doubles or twins. There are a number of others in town; inquire at the information centre.

Places to Eat

Oamaru has its fair share of restaurants, tearooms and takeaways, most of which are concentrated along Thames St and the Thames Highway. Recommended are *Harvey's Restaurant*, at 419 Thames Highway for its presentation and service; hearty meals of fish and venison are $14 for a main course. Also on Thames St is the town's first post office now revived as the *Last Post*, a restaurant serving continental fare. Good meals are served at the *Brydone Hotel* on the corner of Wear and Thames Sts. Out at Waianakaura, 27 km south of town, is the *Mill House*, where the food is excellent but expensive. There are about a dozen *tearooms*, two-thirds of which are on Thames St. Similarly, there are about a dozen takeaways, including *KFC*, on the corner of Usk and Thames Sts.

Getting There & Away

Air The air service is no longer around but there's hope that Oamaru will be relinked into the national network in the future. The House of Travel (☎ 434 9960) at 61 Thames St is the centre for air reservations for other centres.

Bus The InterCity and Mt Cook Landline bus services between Christchurch and Dunedin all stop at Oamaru. From Oamaru it's one hour to Timaru, three hours to Christchurch and two hours to Dunedin. Shuttles which pass through are generally cheaper but not as reliable. Nationwide (Christchurch (☎ 474 3300) and Catch-a-Bus (☎ freephone (0800) 508 000) charge about $10 one way to Dunedin. From Christchurch it is about $20 for pick up only and $35 for door to door.

Train The Christchurch-Dunedin-Invercargill rail service also stops at Oamaru, with a train in each direction every day except Saturday. Trains depart for Invercargill at 11.45 am and for Christchurch at 1.40 pm.

Getting Around

There is a taxi service (☎ 434 8790). Perhaps the best way to see the old part of town, indeed most of the town, is on foot (see Harbour-Tyne Historic Precinct).

TAKIROA

There are Maori rock drawings at Takiroa, 50 km east of Oamaru on SH 83. The sandstone cliff drawings were done with red ochre and charcoal and may date back to the moa-hunting period (between 1000 and 1500 AD). Some were cut out of the sandstone in 1916 and are now in museums at Dunedin, Wanganui and Auckland.

Other rock art sites in the region portray humans, moas, dogs, birds and fish as well as unrecognisable or simple geometrical shapes. Most of the sites are on private land and can only be visited with permission from the owners but there are several on public land, in addition to the ones at Takiroa. These include Timpendean, at the Weka Pass in North Canterbury; Raincliff and Frenchman's Gully in South Canterbury; and Maerewhenua which, like Takiroa, is in North Otago. Local information centres can give directions or you can contact the New Zealand Historic Places Trust in Wellington (☎ (04) 472 4341). All these sites are protected by the Historic Places Act; don't touch or modify the drawings in any way.

For more information on this subject read the monograph *Prehistoric Rock Art of New Zealand* by Michael Trotter & Beverley McCulloch (Longman Paul, 1981).

MOERAKI

At Moeraki, 30 km south of Oamaru, there are extraordinary spherical boulders rather like giant marbles. There are others further south at Kaitiki and Shag Point. The Ngai Tahu people relate the boulders to the cargo which washed ashore from the canoe *Arai Te Uru*. The canoe, on a voyage in search of the prized stone of *te wai pounamu* (greenstone), was wrecked near Shag Point. The round boulders at Moeraki are baskets and gourds (*te kai hinaki*, 'food baskets'), and the irregularly shaped boulders to the south are kumara (sweet potatoes). The reef which extends seaward from Shag Point is the wreck of the canoe.

Scientists have a different, less romantic explanation. The boulders were not washed up onto the beach, but rather eroded from the mudstone cliffs behind. They were not moulded by the surf but were formed into their spherical shape in the mudstone. Geologists refer to the boulders as septarian concretions, formed when minerals crystallised equally in all directions from an organic nuclei. Subsequent erosion often exposes an internal network of veins, which look like a turtle's shell, hence the name 'turtle back'. Further down the beach two concretions have been found to contain the bones of a seven-metre plesiosaur and a smaller mosasaur, both extinct marine reptiles. The Institute of Geological and Nuclear Sciences publish an informative information sheet, *The Moeraki Boulders*.

Places to Stay & Eat

At the friendly *Moeraki Motor Camp* (☎ 439 4759), 37 km south of Oamaru and less than an hour's walk from the boulders, sites are $6.50 each person, $14 for two with power, standard cabins $20 for two, better cabins from $24 to $29 for two, and tourist flats $37 to $40, again for two. Nearby, the *Motel Moeraki* (☎ 439 4862) has units at $35 for two. Food is available from the architectural representation of the boulders at the end of the road near the car park.

SOUTH TO DUNEDIN

Past Shag Point the high, pointed hill with a phallic-shaped symbol on top is a monument to Sir John MacKenzie, the Member of Parliament responsible for splitting large farms into smaller holdings, farms that are now being bought up again. The hill is called **Puketapu** and there's a track to the top signposted from the northern end of Palmerston. Every Labour Weekend there is a race up the hill (19 minutes is the record), known as 'Kelly's Canter' because, during the war, Kelly, the local policeman, had to climb it every day to keep an eye out for shipping. **Palmerston** has a number of places where you can get food for the road, such as *Locomotion No 1* at the railway station and *McGregor's Bakery* at 126 Ronaldsay St.

From Palmerston the **'Pigroot'** to Central Otago leaves SH 1, the name probably having to do with the early road's condition. Gold miners preferred this route into the Maniototo as it was far more sheltered than the Old Dunstan Rd. The road is now much improved and offers a scenic trip into Central Otago (see the Otago chapter).

About 34 km north of Dunedin is the town of **Karitane**, which overlooks part of the Waikouaiti estuary. Up on the cliff is the two-storey house, 'King's Cliff', where in 1907 Sir Truby King founded the Plunket Society, whose nurses continue today to care for the country's babies. King revolutionised child care and in his lifetime saw infant mortality in New Zealand drop by two-thirds from about 90 to 30 deaths per thousand births. King was also active in many other fields including the 'open ward' treatment of psychiatric patients.

As you approach Dunedin it gets hillier. You pass over the Kilmog, then the Northern Motorway hill, and you're in Dunedin.

Otago

Otago has come of age. Two pearls have been created in this once hoary oyster – Queenstown and its adrenaline activities, and the Otago Peninsula with New Zealand's first real foray into ecotourism. Otago is a must for any visitor to New Zealand. And Dunedin, now one of the great surprises for its architecture, nightlife, band scene and proximity to many eco-activities, should not be missed.

There are several sides to this fascinating region and none more interesting than the history of the gold rushes. The Arrowtown you relax in today, the tunnel on the Shotover you raft through, and the Kawarau and Shotover bridges you bungy jump off all hark back to the era of prosperity when the rivers and creeks swarmed with humans in search of gold.

As Otago occupies a central position in the South Island it can be approached from a number of directions. The main route is SH 1 from Christchurch to Dunedin along the east coast. If coming from Southland you can approach it via the Southern Scenic route, through the Catlins or via SH 1 from Invercargill, and chances are you have already been through part of Otago to get to Southland. The most scenic way is via the West Coast (SH 6) and across Haast Pass. If you choose this route, the first sizeable town you'll reach is Wanaka, after passing between lakes Wanaka and Hawea at the Neck (see Makarora & the Siberia Experience in the Westland & Glaciers chapters).

Information

All telephone numbers in the South Island have an 03 prefix if you are calling them from a long distance (even within the region).

HAWEA

Lake Hawea, which is separated from Lake Wanaka by a narrow isthmus, is 35 km long; it is extremely deep, reaching a depth of 410

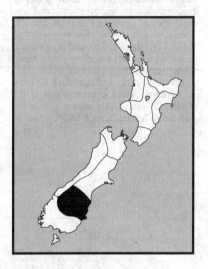

metres. The lake was raised 20 metres in 1958 to provide those important cusecs for power stations downriver. Trout and land-locked salmon can be caught in its waters. Hawea has a hotel, motel and motor camp. At the *Hawea Hotel* (☎ 443 1224) there is a 10-room hostel where a bed in a four-bed room costs $15. The *Glenruth Lakeview Motel* (☎ 443 1440) has rooms for $63 to $68 for two. At the Lake Hawea Motor Camp powered sites are $7 per person and cabins $27 for two. The pub puts on a good meal, or you can arrange with someone to cook the fish you caught in the lake.

WANAKA

Wanaka (population 1130) is nirvana for those seeking to combine the adrenaline buzz with fine living while overdosing on scenery and the outdoors. Just over 100 km from Queenstown, at the southern end of Lake Wanaka, Wanaka is the gateway to the Mt Aspiring National Park and the Cardrona,

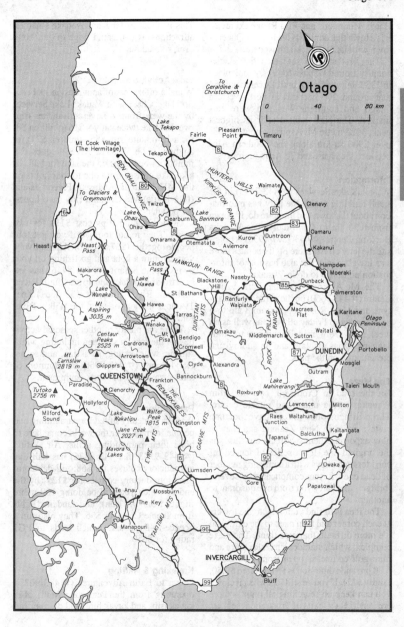

OTAGO

Otago

0   40   80 km

To Geraldine &
Christchurch

Lake
Tekapo

Fairlie

Pleasant
Point

Timaru

Mt Cook Village
(The Hermitage)

Tekapo

8

HUNTERS HILLS

KIRKLISTON RANGE

Waimate

BEN OHAU RANGE

80

Twizel

Glenavy

82

To Glaciers &
Greymouth

6

Lake
Ohau

Clearburn

Lake
Benmore

83

Oamaru

Ohau

8

Omarama

Otematata

Kurow

Duntroon

Kakanui

Haast

Haast
Pass

Aviemore

HAWKDUN RANGE

Hampden
Moeraki

Makarora

Lindis
Pass

Naseby

Dunback

85

Palmerston

Lake
Wanaka

Lake
Hawea

Blackstone
Hill

St Bathans

Mt
Aspiring
▲ 3035 m

Hawea

Ranfurly
Waipiata

Macraes
Flat

Karitane

Otago
Peninsula

Tarras

DUNSTAN MTS

Wanaka

Centaur
Peaks
2525 m

Cardrona

Mt
Pisa

Bendigo

Omakau

Middlemarch

PILLAR RANGE

Waitati

Portobello

87

DUNEDIN

Mt
Earnslaw
2819 m ▲

Arrowtown

Cromwell

Sutton

ROCK & PILLAR RANGE

Skippers

Clyde

Alexandra

Mosgiel

Tutoko
2756 m

Paradise

QUEENSTOWN

Frankton

Bannockburn

8

Outram

Taieri Mouth

Milford
Sound

Hollyford

Glenorchy

THE REMARKABLES

Roxburgh

Lake
Mahinerangi

Lawrence

Milton

Lake
Wakatipu

Walter
Peak
1815 m

Kingston

GARVIE MTS

Raes Waitahuna
Junction

Kaitangata

Jane Peak
2027 m

EYRE MTS

Tapanui

Balclutha

Mavora
Lakes

Lumsden

90

1

Owaka

Te Anau

Mossburn

Gore

Papatowai

The Key

TAKITIMU MTS

Manapouri

96

92

INVERCARGILL

99

Bluff

Harris Mountains and Pisa Range ski areas. It is a town that contrasts the hype of Queenstown with its laid-back atmosphere.

The first step to set aside the glacier country around Wanaka for a park took place in 1935, but it was not until December 1964 that around 200 hectares in north-western Otago and southern Westland were earmarked. The park, named after its highest peak, 3027 metre Mt Aspiring, now extends over 2900 sq km along the Southern Alps between the Haast and Te Anau highways.

Information

Wanaka Lake Services (☎ 443 7495) in the small building beside the jetty has information about the town and things to do. It's open from 8.30 am to 6 pm daily. The Wanaka Booking Centre (☎ 443 7277/7930) is opposite the jetty on Ardmore St. It operates more as a travel agency but also has lots of information on things to do in Wanaka.

The Mt Aspiring National Park Visitor Centre (☎ 443 7660) on the corner of Ballantyne and Main Rds is open from 8 am to 5 pm Monday to Friday all year, as well as on weekends from mid-December to mid-January. It has displays and an audiovisual presentation on the park.

The Maze

On the road to Cromwell, two km from Wanaka, is the maze and puzzle centre. Three-dimensional mazes have become quite a craze in New Zealand and they're now exporting them overseas, but this was the original one. It's a series of fenced-off corridors and alleys with a confusing number of dead ends, further complicated by several 'bridges' that carry you from one quadrant to another.

The idea is to find your way to the towers at each corner and then back to the exit. And it's more difficult than you think. The maze complex, which includes a puzzle centre and mini-golf course, is open from 8.30 am to 5.30 pm and admission is $5 (children $2.50, family $12). If you're still lost when it closes you can keep on searching all night – there are emergency exits if frustration sets in.

This is about as far from Wanaka's natural attractions as you could hope to get, however, so read on.

Lake Activities

Wanaka offers lots of activities on its beautiful lake. Check with Wanaka Lake Services by the waterfront. A hovercraft makes trips over the lake twice daily – $16 (children $8) for a 15-minute trip, $55 (children $27) for an hour. The Wanaka Riverjet does 50-minute jet-boat trips on the lake for $38. Or take lake cruises from one to four hours on the MV *Paranui* – trips to Pigeon Island (four hours) and Glendhu Bay (two hours) are popular.

Guided fishing trips cost $110 for two hours. They're not too bad if you get four people together ($27.50 each). Alternatively, you can hire a boat and go fishing on your own. Alpine Safaris (☎ 443 8446) has jet-boat trips on the lake and up the Clutha River. Makaroa River Tours (☎ 433 8351) does 1¼ hour jet-boat rides on the Wilkin River for $36.

There are plenty of other seasonal activities on the lake in summer, including windsurfing, water-skiing, jet-skiing, and so on. Good Sports (☎ 443 7966) on Dunmore St hires a vast array of sports equipment.

Paragliding

Wanaka is ideally suited for paragliding and people from all over the world come here to hone their paragliding skills. Air Action (☎ 443 9193; fax 443 8876) has half-day introductory courses for $68; full-day complete introductory courses for $125 (by the end of which you will be doing 100-metre flights from Mt Iron); and tandem flights from Treble Cone for $96. They also run a licence-to-fly course which leads to PG1 rating for $350.

Kayaking & Rafting

Down to Earth Adventures (☎ 443 9023), operating from the Pembroke Mall, offer kayak trips and kayak hire, and do river raft

Top: Lake Hawea, Otago (RS)
Bottom: Dart River, Otago (JW)

Top: Moeraki Boulders, South of Oamaru, Canterbury (TC)
Bottom: Hot air ballooning, near Queenstown, Otago (RS)

trips on local rivers and in Mt Aspiring National Park. There are kayak trips on the Matukituki or Makarora rivers in a park, both of which take the better part of the day. The Matukituki River trip starts at the put-in point at Raspberry Creek, after the guides have gone through the rudiments of kayaking. Occasionally there are trips on the Clutha and Hawea rivers. All these trips have been LP tested and come highly recommended. A full day out (well, about seven hours) costs $75 and is well worth it. The main guide, Graeme, is one of NZ's true characters or 'dudes'.

Walks & Tramps

You don't have to be a physical fitness freak to attempt the fairly gentle climb up Mt Iron (527 metres) near the Maze. It is 45 minutes from the road to the top and the view of the rivers, lakes and mountains is worth the effort.

More exhausting is the trek up Mt Roy (1585 metres). It will take about three hours from the road to the top if you're fit – longer if you're the sedentary type. The track winds every step of the eight km from base to peak, but Mt Aspiring is quite a knockout from here.

The 2½ to three-hour Rob Roy Walk is a popular bush walk with good views. It's a one-hour drive up the Matukituki Valley (in summer you can bus up there with Matuki Services), from where the walk goes up the Rob Roy Stream to a point below the Rob Roy Glacier.

There are lots of places to go tramping in Mt Aspiring National Park and the Matukituki, Motatapu, Makarora, Blue and Wilkin valleys. You can get all the information you need on these walks and tramps from the National Park Visitor Information Centre (see Information in this section).

Easiest of all is the lakeside walk which starts along the grassy lakefront in town and runs around to Eely Point and on to Bremner Bay, about a 30-minute walk from town.

Get hold of the pamphlet *Wanaka Walks* from the DOC office at the Visitor Informa-

tion Centre; it has a good map showing the location of seven walks.

For a tramp with a difference, billed as 'just a taste of mountaineering', contact Mountain Recreation (☎ 443 7330). The director, Geoff Wayatt, has worked out a number of spectacular treks in the region of Mt Aspiring. The Matukituki Valley trek involves a helicopter flight to base camp, treks up to the valley head where you see glaciers and waterfalls, and a rafting trip down the Matukituki to finish.

He is now specialising in guided trips over Cascade Saddle for those wanting to connect with the Rees-Dart; this is one of the great tramps in New Zealand.

Horse-Trekking

NZ Backcountry Saddle Expeditions (☎ 443 8151), based 26 km from Wanaka on the Cardrona Valley Rd (SH 89), offer two-hour horse treks for $45 (children $30) and overnight wilderness pack trips from $130. Hawea Horse-Trekking (☎ 443 1059), just out of Hawea on the way to Wanaka, have two-hour mountain and river treks for $40 (children $25).

Aerial Sightseeing

Aspiring Air (☎ 443 7943) has scenic flights ranging from a 15-minute jaunt over Ruby Island, Glendhu Bay, Matukituki River and other local beauty spots costing $50, to a 45-minute flight over Mt Aspiring and the glacier and alpine country for $110. There are also flights to Mt Cook for about $200 or Milford Sound for around $180 to $190. With a launch trip as well the Milford trip costs $230. Children travel for half price on all these trips. Wanaka Aviation (☎ 443 1385; fax 443 8244) offer the same sort of trips for about the same price.

For those who want to see the scenery from an upside-down vantage point there are joy-rides in either Tiger Moths or a Pitts Special stunt plane. These are operated by Biplane Adventures (☎ 443 1000; mobile (025) 323 121) at Wanaka Airport. The Helicopter Line (☎ 752 0767) also has flights in the Wanaka area.

OTAGO

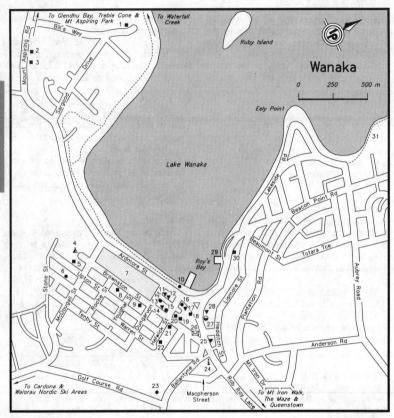

Other Things to Do

Matuki Services (☎ 443 7135) offers various bus trips and provides access to the tramping tracks; for example, $100 for 10 people to Matukituki roadend. Wanaka Taxis (☎ 443 7999) also provide transport to various trampers' destinations. Edgewater Resort Adventures (☎ 443 8311) does 4WD trips in the area at a cost of around $60.

Makarora Tourist Service (☎ 433 8351, 443 8372) offers an interesting trip, the 'Siberia Experience' – see Makarora & the Siberia Valley in the Westland chapter.

The Wanaka and Hawea lakes are good for trout and salmon fishing. Hawea is about 16 km from Wanaka.

Down to Earth Adventures offers instruction in rock climbing – as mentioned before, the guide Graeme is one of the most delightful people you could meet and his sense of humour is infectious. Good Sports also offers mountaineering instruction and they have a 'climbing wall' for practising your climbing techniques. Out on a Thread (☎ 443 9418) offer rock climbing and rap jumping trips, including a 90-metre extravaganza. They also give lessons in windsurfing and kayaking.

■ PLACES TO STAY

1	Edgewater Resort Hotel
2	Altamont Lodge
3	Wanaka Motor Inn & Rafters Restaurant
4	Wanaka Motor Camp
5	YHA Hostel
8	Wunderview Motel
9	Pembroke Inn
18	Clifford's Resort Hotel
19	Clifford's Backpackers
20	McThrifty's & Brookvale Manor
21	Matterhorn South
22	Creekside Guesthouse
30	Wanaka Bakpaka

▼ PLACES TO EAT

11	Kai Whaka Pai & Snack Shack
12	Capriccio's, Ripples Restaurant
14	Te Kano Cafe
17	Relishes
25	Barrow's Tavern
28	First Cafe

OTHER

6	Mountain Recreation (Geoff Wayatt)
7	Pembroke Park
10	Wanaka Lake Services
12	The Pembroke Mall, Air Action & Down to Earth Adventures
13	Good Sports
15	Matuki Services
16	Wanaka Booking Centre, Aspiring Guides & Mt Cook Landline Depot
23	Golf Course
24	Wanaka Visitor Information Centre & Department of Conservation (DOC)
26	Post Office
27	InterCity Bus Depot
29	Jetty
31	Walk to Beacon Point

Cycling is another popular activity around Wanaka and mountain bikes can be hired at many places around town.

Wanaka is near several good ski areas – Treble Cone, Cardrona, the Pisa Range Nordic Ski Area for cross-country skiing, and Harris Mountain heli-skiing. Cardrona has the longest ski season in New Zealand (June-July to September). Wanaka is the

base for all of these areas during the ski season, with ski hire, ski field transport, etc readily available. Daily shuttle buses also operate from Queenstown, 1½ hours away, to these slopes during ski season. (See the Skiing section in the Outdoor Activities chapter for more details.)

Wanaka is a good place to learn the skills required to reach some of the spectacular peaks in the area (see Mountaineering in the Outdoor Activities chapter).

Places to Stay

Camping & Cabins The *Wanaka Motor Park* (☎ 443 7883) is on Brownston St, about one km from the town centre. Camping costs $8 per person with power. A bunkroom costs $11.50 per person, cabins cost $27 for two and tourist flats cost $45 for two. The *Pleasant Lodge Holiday Park* (☎ 443 7360), three km from Wanaka on Glendhu Bay Rd, has cabins and tourist flats at similar prices.

Adjacent to Lake Wanaka, 13 km out of town on the Treble Cone road, is the *Glendhu Bay Camp* (☎ 443 7243), again with camping for $6.50 per person and cabins at $25 for two. Finally, *Penrith Motor Camp* (☎ 443 7009) is at Beacon Point and has camping, cabins and a bunkroom.

DOC campsites are to be found in the area at: Wharf Creek Reserve, adjacent SH 6, at the head of Lake Wanaka; Kidds Bush Reserve, Hunter Valley Rd, west of The Neck between lakes Hawea and Wanaka; and Albert Town reserve, adjacent to SH 6, five km north of Wanaka.

Hostels The *Wanaka YHA Hostel* (☎ 443 7405) at 181 Upton St has a relaxed, friendly atmosphere and its facilities are open all day. The cost is $14 per night. Mountain bikes are available from the hostel, which also sponsors many other activities. YHA members receive discounts on various activities around town.

At the back of Clifford's Resort Hotel (☎ 443 7826) there is a backpackers, *Cliffords*, in the old staff quarters. Comfortable singles are $13.50 and twins/doubles are $20 (all with heating). There is a large central common room with kitchen facilities, TV and reading material. The hostel is not far from the public bar and nearby is a short-cut down to the business area of town.

The *Wanaka Bakpaka* (☎ 443 7837) at 117 Lakeside Rd is opposite the jetty on the northern side of Roys Bay, just a few metres from the lake. It's on a hill with a great view of the lake, town, and mountains. Formerly a hotel, it opened as a backpackers in April 1990. There's a hot spa pool (only open during the ski season) and you can hire mountain bikes, kayaks and a Canadian canoe. The cost per person is $13.50 in dorm rooms, $15 in twins or $16 in doubles.

At 56 Brownston St is *Matterhorn South* (☎ 443 1119), a small homely 20-bed hostel with a cosy log fire. Here, share rooms are $13.50 and double/twins are $15. There is a great selection of reading material and the owners, Marleen and Rudy, are friendly and informative. They are also involved in booking white water sledging trips for Thierry Huet (Frogz Have More Fun). They hire mountain bikes for $15 per day, and can provide transport to Treble Cone in winter.

Guesthouses There are several small B&B places in Wanaka. The small *Creekside Guesthouse* (☎ 443 7834) at 84 Helwick St has just three rooms with B&B at around $25/50.

The *Altamont Lodge* (☎ 443 8864) on Mt Aspiring Rd, had just opened to casual visitors when we were there. This ski lodge is good value, offering very comfortable accommodation; the rooms are $22 per person and linen is supplied for an extra $2.50. It has a fully equipped modern kitchen, private tennis court, TV/video room, reading room, playground, BBQ, spa pool, and is only 25 minutes from Treble Cone. As it is over a km from the centre of town it suits those with their own transport.

Perhaps the most exciting accommodation choice in the region is the *Minaret Mountain Resort* (☎ 443 7590; fax 443 7823). For $225 you get flown into the resort by Wanaka Aviation and two nights in a secluded lodge in its mountain location.

Hotels & Motels There are plenty of places in this category in Wanaka and you can also find such accommodation at the campsites.

At *McThrifty's Motel* (☎ 443 8333) on the corner of Brownston and Helwick Sts, you can get a room with a private bathroom, fridge, and tea and coffee-making facilities at $44 for one to four people. It's run by the *Brookvale Manor* (☎ 443 8333) next door, where double rooms cost $66.

Other cheaper motels include the *All Seasons Motel* (☎ 433 7530), five km from town on the Haast Highway. Rooms there cost $54 for two. More centrally located are the similarly priced *Wunderview Motel* (☎ 433 7480) and *Pembroke Inn* (☎ 433 7296), both on Brownston St.

At the top of the market are the *Clifford's Resort Hotel* (☎ 433 7826) on Ardmore St with rooms for $65 to $75 and the *Edgewater Resort* (☎ 433 8311) on Sargood Drive with rooms for $130 to $200. The *Wanaka Motor Inn* (☎ 443 8216; fax 443 9108) at Mt Aspiring Rd is a very swish establishment with singles/doubles for $90 to $126.50 for two; they have their own restaurant (see Places to Eat in this section).

Places to Eat
Snacks & Fast Food The *Snack Shack* on Ardmore St, by the Mall, has pizzas and the usual takeaway food. Next door is *Kai Whaka Pai*, a pleasant cafe where good cheap food, such as doner kebabs, are served; imaginative food at low prices. In the Mall are the *Freshwater Cafe*, the *Coffee Shop* which is open reasonably early for breakfast, and the *Doughbin* for bread and baked food. The *Chiu Po* on Helwick St has a Chinese and English takeaway counter and a restaurant to one side.

Pub Food & Restaurants The *Clifford's Resort Hotel* has a bistro restaurant with pub-style meals, and a restaurant with a Sunday buffet for $19. *Barrow's Tavern*, Ardmore St, also serves good pub fare – hoki & chips, for instance.

Wanaka is surprisingly well equipped with restaurants, including the *Te Kano Cafe* on Brownston St. This little cottage has wonderful vegetarian food and pizzas – well prepared, imaginative, filling and delicious. Soup costs $4.50, starters around $7.50, and main courses $13.50 to $17.50. In winter you can get gluhwein (hot spiced red wine). A 10% discount is offered to YHA members.

The *First Cafe* on Ardmore St is an interesting little place where the menu includes spaghetti, dishes with an Indonesian or Chinese flavour, and steaks. Starters cost around $5.50 and all the main courses cost either $10 or $17.50. *Relishes Cafe* on Ardmore St is also pleasant and has dinner main courses for around $15; lunches are cheaper. It is a great place to relax with a piece of country-style baked cake, muffins and a frothy cappuccino.

In the Mall, the up-market BYO *Ripples Restaurant* offers 'al fresco' dining on the verandah with good views of the lake and mountains. The food here has a good reputation, and a full three-course meal will cost about $30 to $40. *Capriccio Restaurant* is a licensed Italian restaurant, also in the Mall, which sometimes has intriguingly un-Italian 'Chinese nights'! It has several award-winning specialities but it's not cheap – main courses are in the $20 to $27 range. The *Edgewater Resort Hotel* on Sargood Drive has its own brasserie. Try the rack of lamb with herbed breadcrumbs, honey and kiwi fruit sauce; wash it down with one of their fine selection of NZ wines. At the Wanaka Motor Inn is the licensed *Rafters Restaurant* where there is a blackboard menu listing their wholesome food.

Finally there's the well-restored *Cardrona Restaurant*, 30 km from town in the Cardrona Valley. This is a place for splurges – it's licensed.

Getting There & Away
Air Aspiring Air (☎ 443 7943) has flights to Queenstown up to four times daily, connecting there with Mt Cook Airlines and Ansett New Zealand flights to other centres.

Bus The InterCity bus depot is on Ardmore St, opposite the Clifford's Resort Hotel. Daily buses from Queenstown stop at Wanaka on the way to the glaciers via Haast Pass, as does a connecting bus from Tarras on InterCity's daily service from Queenstown to Christchurch via Mt Cook. InterCity also has a connecting bus from Cromwell on the Queenstown to Dunedin route every day except Sunday.

Mt Cook Landline buses operate from the Wanaka Travel Centre (☎ 443 7414) on Dunmore St in the town centre. Buses run every day to Christchurch, Dunedin and Mt Cook, daily except Saturday to Queenstown, and on weekdays to Invercargill.

Travel times from Wanaka are: Queenstown (two hours); glaciers (six hours); Mt Cook (4¼ hours); Christchurch (10 hours); and Dunedin (seven hours).

Car Although the Cardrona road to Queenstown looks much shorter than the route via Cromwell on the map, it's a winding, twisting, climbing, unsealed mountain road so travel is unlikely to be quicker. Rental cars and campervans are banned from this road, and a large sign at each end announces that caravans are also banned.

Hitching If you're heading out of Queenstown to the Haast Pass and glacier country you could try hitching to Wanaka, but you will have to be very patient. Hitching out of Queenstown is difficult and hitching through the Haast Pass to Fox or Franz Josef is almost impossible because of the light traffic, although once you're offered a lift you're more than likely to get one going the whole way. The Haast Pass road branches off the Cromwell road about two km from Wanaka, just beyond the Maze. Hitchhikers have written, on stones by the roadside, the sorry stories of their long waits.

Getting Around
Matuki Services (☎ 443 7135) offers minibus transport to various places within Mt Aspiring National Park, including the

OTAGO

White Water Sledging

This new adrenaline sport is for the fit and adventurous. Relatively new to New Zealand, white water sledging is already very popular in France and Switzerland. Equipped with sledge, six mm padded wet-suit, flippers, lifejacket and helmet the sledger takes control – the sort of control that you don't get if you are a passenger in a raft. Yes, you are alone (solo!) in raging white water and you do the steering through the rapids. The guide leads the way of course and points out the best route but it is you who has to flipper into the rapid facing the right direction.

The 10 minutes of instruction on the river bank not enough? Well, by the end of the trip you are either scared out of your wits (which is why you came in the first place) or finning into eddies and surfing waves with the ease of a master kayaker.

The person responsible for this year's new 'buzz' is Thierry Huet, a Frenchman, and his company is Frogz Have More Fun (mobile phone (025) 338 737). He has sussed out three rivers to sledge: the Clutha, a 2½-hour scenic and gentle trip; the Hawea, a two-hour gentle trip of medium grade; and the Kawarau, a raging 1½-hour trip. The last-mentioned is the best as it is challenging and exciting, especially the Grade Four-plus Chinese Dogleg rapid. You also get to pass under the bungy bridge and see the fear in the eyes of the jumpers from below. Fun in a raft? It's even more fun at eye level on a polystyrene sledge. The cost is $65 for the Kawarau (half day), or $120 for a full day (this may include the Roaring Meg section and the Chinese Dogleg); lunch, if you can contain it, is also thrown in with the full-day option. ■

Matukituki Valley and Cameron Flat. There are regular services from mid-December to mid-March, but minibuses also go at other times (and to other places) if there are at least three passengers. Wanaka Taxis (☎ 443 7999) also offer trampers transport, local scenic trips, airport transport and ski field transport in winter.

A few years ago somebody got the idea of hiring mountain bikes in Wanaka and now there are about as many mountain bikes for hire as there are people in the town! You can hire them from the YHA hostel (whether or not you're staying there) for $20 per day or $15 for half a day. In the town centre, Good Sports, Racer's Edge and Ski 47, to name a few, also hire mountain bikes.

Central Otago

Most of the present-day towns in Central Otago owe their origin to about 40 years of gold-mining last century. The goldfields heritage area extends from Wanaka down to Queenstown and Glenorchy, east through Alexandra to the coast at Palmerston, and south-east from Alexandra to Milton on the sea. There are several interpretive pamphlets available which show towns and gold-mining areas, such as *NZ's Otago Goldfields: Heritage Highway*. June Wood's *Gold Trails of Otago* (AH & AW Reed, Wellington, reprinted several times since 1970) has a wealth of old photographs and some interesting historical snippets from the gold-rush period.

Throughout this area you will stumble across evidence of the gold rush – stone buildings, equipment and machinery, and miles of tailings (waste left over from mining). Queenstown, once a focal town during Otago's golden days, maintains its importance in a modern gold rush – tourism.

There are many arts & crafts places in Central Otago and these are listed in the pamphlet *Central Otago Arts & Crafts Trail* available in Alexandra and Cromwell.

CROMWELL

This pleasant little town on the main route between Wanaka and Queenstown is a good place for a short pause. The Cromwell Information Centre (☎ 445 0212) in the Cromwell Mall, has some excellent displays and slide presentations on the hydroelectric power projects in the Clutha Valley. It's open daily from 10 am to 4 pm. Get a copy of the

Cromwell and Districts: Guide to Walks and Outings here.

Cromwell has a museum with artefacts of local mining, including a section on the Chinese miners. It's open from 10 am to 4 pm daily. In Melmore Terrace several historic buildings, some made of stone, are being restored to recreate a main street of 'Old Cromwell'. They were painstakingly removed from the real Old Cromwell which is now covered by the waters of the Dunstan Dam.

Cromwell is the heart of apricot country. There are a number of roadside stalls here where you can buy apricots, peaches, nectarines, plums, cherries, apples and pears. Try some – you'll probably be tempted after seeing the Carmen Miranda's hat display in front of the town.

The Kawarau Gorge between here and Queenstown is spectacular and you can pause to watch the bungy jumping at the interesting old Kawarau suspension bridge. The bridge was built in 1880 for access to the Wakatipu goldfields and used right up until 1963.

There are a number of gold-mining sites around Cromwell – Bannockburn, Bendigo and the Kawarau. You can see a working exhibition of gold-mining technology at the Kawarau Gorge Mining Centre (Hidden Valley Goldmine). Access is across a walking bridge which spans the Kawarau.

If you want to see all this at river level, raft it, boogey board it or (if you are really daring) white water sledge it (see White Water Sledging in this chapter).

Bendigo

This town is 18 km from Cromwell on the Bendigo Loop Rd. Quartz was successfully mined here for 50 years. Bendigo is the classic ghost town these days and if you hunt around in the scrub you will find ruins of stone cottages and huts. There are also many mine shafts so stick to obvious tracks when exploring.

Places to Stay & Eat

The *Sunhaven Motor Camp* (☎ 445 0164) on Alpha St, about two km from the town centre, has campsites and cabins; camping costs $6 per person ($7 with power) and cabins cost $20 to $30 for two. There are also hotels and motels, including the newer *Golden Gate Lodge* with restaurant, lounge and public bars.

There are a number of sandwich places in the Cromwell Mall. You can try the *Gold Mine Restaurant*, which has good food, or the pricier *Daniel's*. The *Golden Gate Lodge* has bistro food in the pub and also a restaurant.

ARROWTOWN

Between Cromwell and Queenstown (not far past the bungy jump bridge) is the loop road turn-off to Arrowtown. Arrowtown (population 1100) is a faithfully restored early gold-mining settlement and you can still find gold in the river there. The Lake District Centennial Museum, which also acts as the local information office, has displays on gold mining and local history. It's open from 9 am to 5 pm and admission is $3 (children 50c). Get a copy of *Historic Arrowtown* or the photocopied *Arrowtown Walks* from the museum – the latter has information about getting to Macetown as well as historic notes about the area.

There are many shops, eating places, a range of accommodation, and a beautiful main street, part of which is lined with deciduous trees.

Chinese Settlement

Perhaps the best remaining example of a Chinese goldfields settlement in New Zealand is near Bush creek, at the top end of Buckingham St. A store and two huts have been restored as a reminder of the role played by many Chinese 'diggers' during and after the gold rush. The Chinese were subjected to prejudice, especially during the economic depression of the 1880s. More often than not they did not seek new gold claims but worked through the tailings looking for the fine gold which had been undetected by

OTAGO

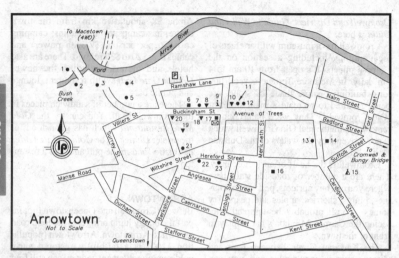

Arrowtown
Not to Scale

PLACES TO STAY	
6	New Orleans Hotel
14	Mace Motel
15	Arrowtown Camping Ground
16	Settlers Motel
17	Postmaster's Guest House

▼ PLACES TO EAT

8	Grannies Kitchen
10	Stone Cottage
18	Royal Oak Hotel
19	Stables Restaurant
20	Lieber's Bakery

OTHER

17	Post Office
22	Fire Station
23	Swimming Pool

HISTORIC WALK

1	Miners' Monument (1962)
2	Chinese Settlement (from 1866)
3	Butler's Cottage (early 1870s)
4	Police Camp Building (1863)
5	Butler's Wall (1866)
6	New Orleans Hotel
7	Athenaeum Hall (1932 after last one burnt down)
9	Lakes District Museum & Information Centre (1875)
10	The Stone Cottage (c 1870)
11	Borough Council Office (1877)
12	Granny Jones Cottage (1860s)
13	Arrowtown Jail (1876)
17	Post Office (1863)
18	Royal Oak Hotel (original site)
19	Stables Restaurant (1860s) & Village Green
21	King Edward VII Street Lamp

earlier miners. The Lakes District Historical Museum sell an excellent brochure, *The Arrowtown Chinese Settlement*, for $2.50.

Macetown

Beyond Arrowtown is Macetown, a gold-mining ghost town. It can be reached only by

going down a long, unimproved and flood-prone road – the original miners' wagon track – which crosses the Arrow River 44 times! Trips are made from Queenstown on horseback or by 4WD vehicle, and allow time to do some gold panning.

The two tour operators are Outback Tours

(☎ 442 7386) and New Zealand Nomad Safaris (☎ 442 6699).

Places to Stay

Arrowtown district has a wide variety of accommodation, including two camping grounds in the town. At the *Arrowtown Camping Ground* (☎ 442 1825), entrance off Suffolk St, sites are $8 per person, on-site caravans from $26 to $30 for two, and cabins $16/28 for one/two. Sites are the same price at the *Arrowtown Caravan Park* (☎ 442 1838) at 47 Devon St; on-site caravans are $30 for two persons.

At the *New Orleans Hotel* (☎ 442 1745) singles/doubles are $25/50. Nearby is the historic *Postmaster's Guest House* (☎ 442 1204) where singles/doubles are $45/65. Out of town, on the Speargrass Flat Rd, four minutes' walk to picturesque Lake Hayes, is the *Speargrass Lodge* (☎ & fax 442 1411); B&B singles/doubles are $50/95 and dinner is provided by arrangement for $28.

Arrowtown has four motels. Three of them cost between $60 and $70 – *Golden View Motel* (☎ 442 1833) at 48 Adamson Drive; *Mace Motel* (☎ 442 1825) at 13 Cardigan St; and *Viking Lodge* (☎ & fax 442 1765). Top of the range is the *Settlers Motel* (☎ & fax 442 1734) at 20-22 Hereford St, where rooms are $80 to $86.

Places to Eat

There are a number of places along Buckingham St where you can get either a snack or a meal. Best value is *Lieber's Bakery*, purveyors of excellent bolognaise mince pies, rolls, and German-style bread. Both the *New Orleans* and *Royal Oak* hotels have bistros where you can get the usual pub fare. Three restaurants, housed in gold-rush-era houses are *Granny's Kitchen*, *The Stables* and *The Stone Cottage*. The Stables serves Thai cuisine and is licensed or BYO. In the Mall there is the *Courtyard*, winner of a Taste NZ Award, which is open every day. About 400 metres from the bungy bridge is the *Gibbston Valley Winery* which has a cellar restaurant and outdoor courtyard set amongst the vines; the blackboard menu is changed daily and

the food receives rave reviews. Dine *after* your bungy jump.

Getting There & Away

Arrowtown is served from Queenstown by a scheduled bus, the Arrow Express (☎ 442 1535). It can be picked up outside the library in Buckingham St or at the top of the Mall in Queenstown (it is a 25-minute journey). Twice a day The Double Decker (☎ 442 6067) leaves Queenstown for a 2½-hour return trip via Arrowtown. Arrowtown can easily be reached by Nifty-fifties (motorbikes) from Queenstown, or even by bicycle. Both Viking Lodge and Arrow Stores hire mountain bikes.

ALEXANDRA

Heading eastwards from Cromwell it is not far to Alexandra (population 4700), the hub of Central Otago. It was the lure of gold that brought thousands of diggers here to the Dunstan goldfields. The town, however, owes its permanence to the dredging boom of the 1890s that followed the rush. The names of the dredges are recorded in some of the street names in modern Alexandra – Enterprise and Eureka for instance. Next to move in were the orchardists and it is to them that Alexandra owes its prosperity today.

The Alexandra & Districts Promotion Centre (☎ 448 9515) at 22 Centennial Ave, provides maps and plenty of information on things to see and do in the region. The DOC office (☎ 448 8874) is at 45 Centennial Ave. The Sir William Bodkin Museum on the corner of Thompson and Walton Sts houses a comprehensive collection of mining relics; it is open Monday to Friday from 2 to 4 pm.

Clyde

This former gold town is only 10 km from Alexandra. It was once the centre of the Dunstan Goldfields, and historic stone buildings still line the streets. Clyde has two museums: the Clyde Museum, in Blythe St, is housed in the historic Magistrate's Court House and features exhibits depicting domestic life on the early goldfields; and the Stationary Engine Display, Upper Fraser St, includes all sorts of rural machinery. The Clyde Lookout Point, accessible from a signposted road, affords great views out over the once bustling goldfields.

Places to Stay

Alexandra has a full range of accommodation options. There are two camping grounds in town and one in nearby Clyde. The *Alexandra Camping Ground* (☎ 448 8297) at Manuherikia Rd, has sites for $6.50 per person and basic cabins for $22 for two. The *Pine Lodge Holiday Camp* (☎ 448 8861) at Ngapara St, has sites for $7 per person, basic units at $26 for two, and cabins at $30 for two. In nearby Clyde the *Clyde Holiday Park* (☎ 449 2713) has powered sites for $6.50 per person and on-site caravans for $26 for two.

There is one budget hostel in town – the *Alexandra Riverside Associate YHA Hostel* (☎ 448 8152) at 4 Dunorling St. At this hostel, which overlooks the Clutha River, a bed in a twin room will cost $12. *The Willows Guest House* (☎ 449 2231) at 3 Young Lane (off SH 8 to Clyde), has singles/doubles for $35/60. Clyde has two guesthouses at different ends of the price spectrum. *Dunstan House* (☎ 449 2701) at 29 Sunderland St has beds for $25 per person. *Oliver's Lodge* (☎ 449 2860) at Main St, has stables for $106 and lodges for $151; and there's a great restaurant attached to this lodge.

The two motels in Alexandra and four in Clyde each charge around $60 per room.

Places to Eat

There are a few bakeries such as the *Avenue* and *The Bakery* on Centennial Ave, and the *Clydesdale Bakery* in the Centrepoint Mall. In Tarbert St there are a number of takeaway and sandwich places including *Gobble & Go*, *Pulsarts* and the *Cobblestone Cafe*. Pub food is available from the *Bendigo Hotel*, Tarbert St; and a good up-market restaurant is *Stepping Out* – this is situated in a renovated stone house and is noted for dishes prepared with Koenig Smokehouse smoked salmon and salmon caviar.

The renowned *Oliver's Restaurant*, 34 Sunderland St, Clyde, is where you can enjoy scrumptious grilled fillet steak with pickled walnuts. This great restaurant is open for lunch and dinner, Monday to Saturday.

Getting There & Away

Both InterCity and Mt Cook Landline buses have services which pass through Alexandra. The Mt Cook landline agent is Bees Knees (☎ 448 7348) at 56 Centennial Ave. InterCity's agent is Gourlay's (☎ 448 9421) at 4 Centennial Ave.

THE GOLDFIELDS: ALEXANDRA TO PALMERSTON

To the north-east of Alexandra lies the Manuherikia Valley, which is rich in evidence of Otago's golden age. At Blackstone Hill the road, SH 85, swings south-east to the Maniototo plain and out via the Pigroot to the sea and Palmerston.

About 27 km north of Alexandra, and a small sidetrip from Omakau on the main highway is the small township of **Ophir**. Today peacefulness belies its once bustling past. There is a restored post and telegraph building, dating from 1886, in the town. The Manuherikia River is spanned by the Dan O'Connell bridge, built in the 1870s and still in use today. The town has the widest temperature range of any in NZ; from -20°C in winter to 35°C in summer.

At the town of Becks the road forks. The left fork leads to **St Bathans**, once also a thriving gold-mining town with a population of 2000 – today there are less than 20. This is a real get-away sort of place and the visitor is able to enjoy a peaceful stroll through a town which retains a number of original buildings. The *Vulcan Hotel* (☎ 447 3629) is a quaint living museum, and is the only remainder of the town's 14 hotels. Here B&B is $38 per person (dinner is $20 extra). In winter the curling teams compete on frozen ponds near the town. The Blue Lake, formed entirely by sluicing activity, is a popular picnic spot not far from town.

Back on SH 85, past Blackstone Hill and heading east, the next main town reached is Ranfurly (88 km from Alexandra). Thirteen km north of Ranfurly is **Naseby**, once the largest gold-mining town on the Maniototo. There's an Early Settlers Association Museum here, and the area has some great walking country. From May to September the Maniototo Ice Rink (☎ 444 9270) in town is used for skating, curling and ice hockey. From Ranfurly there are two choices to reach SH 1 on the coast: either via the Pigroot and Dunback, on SH 85, to Palmerston, or via Hyde, Middlemarch and MacRaes Flat to Dunback.

Ranfurly

This town (population 960) is the hub of the Maniototo region. Nearby Naseby with its goldfields, and the more luckless Hamiltons, were the original reasons for Europeans coming to this part of New Zealand. The vast inland plain is now referred to as the Maniototo and is the site of a number of stud farms.

Places to Stay & Eat Campsites at the *Ranfurly Motor Camp* (☎ 444 9144) at Reade St, are $9.50 for two ($11 with power), and cabins are $20 for two. You can actually stay on a farm in the Maniototo and not ransom your own station to do it. *Peter's Farm Hostel* (☎ 444 9083), is in a 100-year-old homestead, three km from Waipiata and 12 km from Ranfurly (on Highway 85, Central Otago). Hamiltons goldmine is actually located on the farm. The farm offers kitchen and bathroom facilities, open log fire, and a number of activities; all for $12 per night. If you ring in advance Peter may be able to assist with transport from Dunedin. If you head out this way, do so for a couple of days or more to make the trip worthwhile.

The *Ranfurly Lion* (☎ 444 9140) at Charlemont St East, has singles/doubles for $35/60 (the waterbed suite is $5 extra!). The *Lion Hotel Restaurant* is the best of the town's eateries, with chicken, steak and fish dishes.

THE GOLDFIELDS: ALEXANDRA TO DUNEDIN

If you head south-east from Alexandra via SH 8 to Dunedin you get the opportunity to see more evidence of the gold seekers of last century. **Fruitlands** is the first place of interest and there is a restored pub, dating from 1866, where food and crafts are sold. One km away, via Symes Rd, is the restored **Mitchells Cottage**, a fine example of the Shetland Island stone masons' building skills.

The next town of any size is Roxburgh, 40 km south of Alexandra. The area is known for fruit growing, and sales begin in early December, continuing until early winter. There is a motor camp and a couple of motels in this town of 900 people.

Between Roxburgh and Milton, near the town of Lawrence, is **Gabriels Gully**, the site of a frenzied stampede for gold by 10,000 miners in July 1861, after Gabriel Read discovered gold in the Tuapeka River. In Lawrence, you can get cheap accommodation at *Oban Guest House – Backpackers*, 1 Oban St, (☎ 485 9101) for $13 in share/dorms and $15 for twins/doubles. There is a *takeaway* in Ross Place and a bistro in the *Coach & Horses Tavern*, also in Ross Place. There are also a number of interesting walks in the vicinity of the town, including that up Gabriel's Gully to Jacobs Ladder.

At Lawrence the road splits and you have the choice of reaching the coast and SH 1 to Dunedin by one of two ways: either to Milton on SH 1 or by Lake Mahinerangi and

Gold panning

the Waipori goldfield (and Waipori Falls) where there are more relics of the gold rushes. Dunedin is 55 km north of Milton or about half that distance from where the Waipori Falls road meets SH 1.

Queenstown

Queenstown is situated on the shores of beautiful Lake Wakatipu in what is surely one of the most scenic settings in the world. There is great skiing in winter, with two ranges – Coronet Peak and The Remarkables within 30 km.

In summer there are a great deal of adrenaline activities to compensate for the lack of snow. A lot of these are centred around the lake and in the many rivers nearby, especially the Dart, Shotover and Kawarau. White water rafting, jet-boating, boogey boarding, and this years' ultra high buzz, white water sledging, are all great ways to get wet. Bungy jumping, tandem parachute jumping, and parapenting are all exciting ways to fly through the air – and they let you get wet dangling from the end of your bungy cord if you wish! You can always be assured of finding something exhilarating that suits you.

If you would rather relax and move at a much more leisurely pace you too are catered for. Take a trip on the TSS *Earnslaw* to Walter Peak Station, stroll through golden Arrowtown in autumn, fossick for gold near Macetown, or shop in one of Queenstown's many (expensive) boutiques.

It's extremely easy to go through a lot of money here but Queenstown is a 'doing' place and sometimes you just have to forget the cost and 'do' it. So relax and enjoy the fantastic setting; there's lots to do, a large and transient work population and more nightlife than most places in New Zealand.

History

There is evidence that Queenstown was once the site of a Maori settlement. However, when the Pakehas began arriving in the mid-

1850s the region was deserted. The first Pakehas to settle the area were sheep farmers, but in 1862 two shearers, Thomas Arthur and Harry Redfern, discovered gold on the banks of the Shotover River, precipitating a rush of prospectors to the area. Queenstown fast developed into a mining town and by early 1863 streets had been laid out and permanent buildings established. Then the gold petered out and by 1900 the population had dropped from several thousand to a mere 190 people.

During this era the lake was the principal means of communication and at the height of the mining boom there were four paddle steamers and about 30 other craft plying the waters. One of those early steamers, still in use today, was the TSS *Earnslaw*, which was prefabricated in Dunedin, carted overland in sections, and rebuilt at Kingston in 1912. The highway skirting the lake between Queenstown and Glenorchy was only completed in 1962, the centenary of the founding of the township. There are several theories on how Queenstown got its name, but the most popular is that it commemorates the town of the same name on Great Island in Cork Harbour, Ireland, probably because most of the diggers were Irish.

Orientation

Queenstown is a growing, but compact township on the shores of beautiful Lake Wakatipu, and backed by equally beautiful hills. The main streets are the pedestrians-only Mall and Shotover St, where the Bungy centre and a number of raft operators are located.

Information

Tourist Information The Visitor Information Centre/InterCity travel (☎ 442 8238) is close to the lake in the Clocktower Centre, on the corner of Shotover and Camp Sts. The office is open from 7 am to 7 pm every day. The InterCity office is part of this complex and there is a foreign currency exchange, Travelex, in the office.

The Queenstown Information Centre

(☎ 442 7318) on the corner of Shotover and Camp Sts (diagonally opposite the Visitor Information Centre) is another source of information and also makes bookings for local activities. The office is open in winter from 7.30 am to 8 pm and in summer from 7.30 am to 10 pm, every day. There's an AA agent in the AMI office about four doors away, on Shotover St.

Also on Shotover St is the Information & Track Walking Centre (☎ 442 9708). They do bookings for the Routeburn, Greenstone-Caples, Kepler, Milford and Rees-Dart tracks. They know all the transport options, especially for the back-road trip via Lake Wakatipu and the Mavora lakes. They are open in summer from 8 am to 8 pm, and in winter until 7 pm.

The DOC (☎ 442 7933) is on Shotover St opposite the Trust Bank; there's also one in Ballarat St. It has information on the many natural attractions of the area, long and short drives and walks, including the Milford, Kepler, Routeburn and other tracks. It has interesting displays and a summer programme of nature walks. It's open from 9 am to 4.30 pm Monday to Friday all year round, and also from 10 am to 3 pm on Saturday and Sunday from mid-December to mid-February.

There is a 24-hour free information service, Infophone (☎ 442 5000) which lists a variety of activities. You are talked through the options – ask for a listing at your backpackers, motel or hotel desk.

Tour Agencies Plenty of places make bookings for Queenstown's multitude of activities, including the Visitor Information Centre and the Queenstown Information Centre already mentioned, or there's Fiordland Travel and the InterCity office by the *Earnslaw* wharf, Mt Cook Travel at the end of the Mall and plenty of others. The Southern World Vacations (formerly Newmans) office is on Church St opposite the Mt Cook Landline depot.

Other Information There's a useful notice stand right in the middle of the Mall. If you have plenty of dirty clothes and nowhere to wash them head for the Alpine Laundrette on Shotover St near the Athol St junction.

Views
Try starting at, literally, the top of the town. Catch the Skyline Gondola to the summit of the hill overlooking the town for incredible views over the lake – well worth the $9 (children $3, family $20). There's a licensed cafe up at the top which is not bad and a more expensive restaurant for dinner. If you're more energetic you can walk up the vehicle track to Skyline from Lomond Crescent, but the ride is worth experiencing. The lift operates from 10 am to 10 pm daily.

Another good viewpoint is Coronet Peak, 18 km from the town centre. There's skiing in winter but it also stays open in summer, when you can ride the chairlift to the top for $12 (children $6) and shoot back down in a little cart on the Cresta Slide. One ride down is $4 (children $3), five rides are $12 ($8), and you can go up and down the chairlift as many times as you like.

What really makes Queenstown's setting is the Remarkables to the east and the Eyre Mountains to the south-west. A written description can hardly do the Remarkables justice. They're especially beautiful capped with snow, at sunrise or in the after-glow of dusk. If you're super fit it's a long, hard, steep climb to the top, 2000 metres above the lake level – very energy-sapping in the hot Central Otago sun.

If you want to get views in the other direction you can drive up to the back of the ski field. A short track leads past Lake Alta to a viewpoint at the top of The Remarkables. From here you look down over the lake back to a diminutive Queenstown.

Queenstown Motor Museum
The motor museum just below the lower gondola terminal has a fine collection of cars, all well restored and in running order. There's also a motorcycle collection upstairs and a fine old Tiger Moth suspended over-

OTAGO

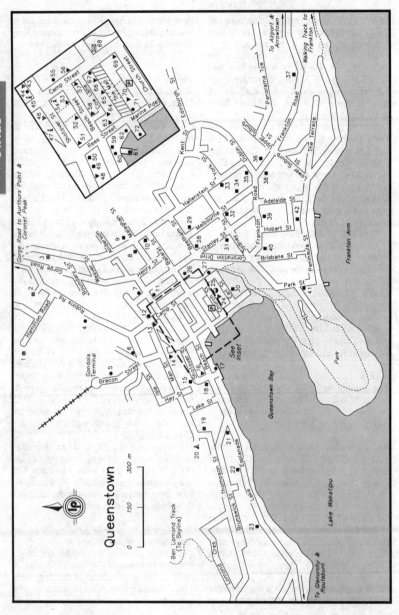

Queenstown

OTAGO

head. The museum is open 9 am to 5.30 pm daily, admission is $5 (children $2.50).

Kiwi & Birdlife Park

Also below the gondola terminal is the kiwi and birdlife park. It has what is becoming a NZ standard – the nocturnal kiwi house. Keas and a variety of other birds (including endangered species) can also be seen in the pleasant park. The park is open from 9 am to 5 pm daily and admission is $7 (children $2.50, family $16).

The Queenstown Farm Fun Park, next

door, is very popular with children. The cost is $5 for adults and $3 for children.

The TSS *Earnslaw*
The stately old coal-burning TSS (Twin Screw Steamer) *Earnslaw* is the most famous of Queenstown's many lake cruise boats. There's a daily three-hour cruise at 2 pm which goes out to the Walter Peak sheep station and back. On the way you can sip a beer, watch the activity in the immaculate engine room or sing along with a pianist. At the station you see a sheep dog demonstration and sheep shearing. The cost is $37 (children $10).

The *Earnslaw* also operates a short lunchtime cruise at 12.30 pm which costs $21 ($10), not including lunch, which is available on board for an additional $3 to $6. There's an evening dinner cruise at 5.30 pm, cost is $25 ($10) for the 1½ hour cruise and the buffet is an extra $25 ($18). The main dining excursion includes a meal at Walter Peak ($52). In winter the expensive-to-run *Earnslaw* used to be parked in favour of a smaller modern boat but these days it only takes one month off in June for its annual overhaul.

The *Earnslaw* is steel-hulled and weighs 330 tons. At full speed it churns across the lake at 13 knots, burning a ton of coal an hour. Measuring 51 metres in length and 7.3 metres across the beam, it is licensed to carry 810 passengers and at one time was the major means of transport on the lake. The development of modern roads ended its career with New Zealand Railways and it has been used for lake cruises since 1969.

The *City of Dunedin*
The *City of Dunedin* was the sole NZ craft in the 1982 single-handed round the world yacht race. She was one of only a few vessels to complete the 43,470 km (27,000 mile) voyage, taking nine months to reach the finish line, with many adventures along the way. The *City* is now based at Queenstown and does two-hour sailings in which every passenger (maximum 19) can become part of the crew and participate in the sail. She sails

at 10.30 am, 1 and 4 pm daily from the water taxi jetty opposite the Park Royal Hotel; the cost is $29 (children $15).

Other Lake Cruises
There are various other lake cruises to choose from, including a half-hour zip round the lake by hydrofoil every hour for $22 (children free). It departs from the pier at the end of the Mall. Fiordland Travel operate a three-hour morning launch tour at 9.30 am, morning tea is included in the price.

Jet-Boat Trips
Hurtling up the rivers around Queenstown in jet-boats or down them in inflatable rafts, on boogey boards or polystyrene sleds, are all popular activities. The Shotover and Kawarau rivers are the popular jet-boat rivers, with the Dart River less travelled but also good. Trips either depart straight from Queenstown or go by minibus to the river and then by boat. The jet-boat trips generally take about an hour and cost around $50 to $55.

The Shotover Jet (☎ 442 8570) is one of the most popular; the narrow and shallow Shotover River is particularly exciting for jet-boating. Be prepared to get wet but it's great fun.

For a full-on blast of shallow water jet-boating, try Twin Rivers Jet (☎ 442 3257; fax 442 3830), which takes you on both the Upper Kawarau and Lower Shotover rivers in the one trip.

The Kawarau Jet (☎ 442 6142) departs from the town wharf and crosses the lake to the Kawarau River; the trip costs $55. People who really want to do everything can combine helicopter and jet-boat rides (from $75) or three-in-one trips combining helicopters, jet-boats and raft rides ($110 on the Kawarau River, or from $139 to $154 on the Shotover).

Trips on the Dart River with Dart River Jet-boat Safari are also excellent, passing parts of the Routeburn and Dart-Rees tracks. Bookings for their trips can be made in Queenstown (☎ 442 7318), the office being on the corner of Shotover and Camp Sts (see

OTAGO

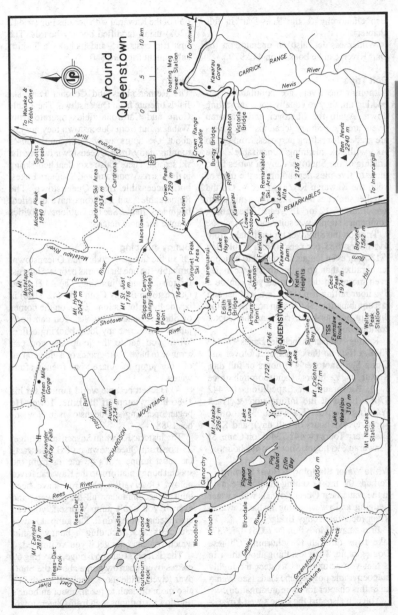

Around Queenstown

0   5   10 km

OTAGO

also Glenorchy & the Rees-Dart in this chapter).

Wilderness Jet, also an operator on the Dart River, can be booked on 442 9792.

Raft Trips

Although the rivers are popular for jet-boating up, they're equally good for rafting down. Again the Shotover and Kawarau rivers are the primary locations. The rivers are graded, for rafting purposes, from one to six, with six meaning 'unraftable'. The grading of the Shotover canyon varies from three to five-plus depending on the time of year, the Kawarau River is rated 4. On the rougher stretches there's usually a minimum age limit of 12 or 13 years. The rafting companies supply wet suits and life jackets.

Trips on the Shotover typically take from 4½ hours ($85 per person) to a whole day ($130), or even longer. If you opt to helicopter in rather than go by minibus you can pay even more. On the Kawarau you can do a 3½ hour rafting trip ($65) or a jet-boat and raft combination ($85) or, on both rivers, the three-in-one jet-boat, raft and helicopter combination trips.

Rafting companies include: Danes, (☎ 442 7318) office on the corner of Shotover and Camp Sts (Shotover 4½ hours or full day, Kawarau 3½ hours, Landsborough three day); Kawarau Raft Expeditions (☎ 442 9708), based at the Information & Track Walking Centre (Ka-warau 3½ hours, Shotover 4½ hours or full day); and Kiwi Discovery Tours (☎ 442 7340), on Camp St (Kawarau 3½ hours, Shotover 4½ hours).

White Water Sledging & River Surfing

Perhaps the most exciting thing you can do in the water near Queenstown is white water sledging and river surfing in the Kawarau River (near the Bungy Bridge).

Frogz have More Fun (☎ (025) 338 737) take trips through the churning Chinese Dogleg rapid. The great thing about this trip is that you actually get to steer the highly manoeuvrable polystyrene sleds (see Wanaka in this chapter for more information).

You can also surf the same seven-km sec-

tion of the Kawarau with Serious Fun (☎ 442 6207) using modified boogey boards. The first trip costs $75 and includes a T-shirt; subsequent trips are $40.

Skiing

The Remarkables and Coronet Peak ski fields operate from Queenstown. The Treble Cone and Cardrona fields operate from Wanaka, but from Queenstown they are just about 1½ hours away, with shuttle buses running daily from Queenstown during the ski season. There's also excellent heli-skiing in the Harris Mountains and Southern Lakes, both accessible from Queenstown. The Remarkables and Cardrona have excellent beginners' fields. See the Outdoor Activities chapter for more details.

Bungy Jumping

Of all the things to do around Queenstown, probably the one that sparks people's interest the most is bungy jumping. The AJ Hackett Queenstown Bungy Centre (☎ 442 7100) is beside the Information Centre on the corner of Shotover and Camp Sts. You can book jumps there or at any local booking office. When you get to the jump site you can arrange to have photographs or a video taken of your jump to amaze your friends afterwards.

AJ Hackett became world-famous for his 1986 bungy jump off the Eiffel Tower. He began operating at Queenstown in November 1988.

The historic Kawarau Suspension Bridge, 23 km from Queenstown on SH 6, attracts the most jumpers; it's 43 metres from the special bungy platform to the Kawarau River below. Observation platforms have been built to accommodate all the viewers, and even if you don't jump yourself, you can enjoy seeing others do it. The jump at Kawarau costs $85, including a bungy T-shirt which you can only get if you've jumped.

The Skippers Canyon Bridge, towering 69 metres over a narrow gorge above the Shotover River, is the more spectacular site. It's also more difficult to reach, about an hour's ride down a tortuous road from Queenstown.

Several packages have been arranged for jumping at Skippers. The 'Barefoot Special – Big Thrills, No Frills' package costs $129, with a shuttle van taking you out to the bridge and back, and the optional T-shirt is an extra $25. Other packages include the 'Heli-Bungy' for $199 where you helicopter to and from the bridge, or the 'Canyon Classic' for $245 where you do basically the same but with a champagne lunch thrown in. Or there's the 'White Water Bungy' for $241 where you shuttle into the canyon, do the jump, and then do some white water rafting out down the Shotover River, with a lunch stop on the way.

Aerial Sightseeing

No possibility is ignored at Queenstown – if you can't boat up it, down it or across it, walk around it, or get a chairlift over it, then you can still fly above it. There are all sorts of flights from Queenstown, from short helicopter flights over Queenstown (from $55) to flights to Milford Sound (from $100). More expensive flights to Milford include a brief landing, or a one or two-hour launch cruise on the sound. Mt Cook, Fiordland Travel, Air Fiordland and Air Wakatipu are some of the operators.

If you are up to it, let yourself be tempted into an tandem aerial parapente jump from Bob's Peak. Two operators are Max Air (☎ 442 7770) and Flying Cow (☎ 442 8636); both charge $100 for a tandem flight.

Paraflying on the lake is another way to see the sights from the air. Contact Paraflying (☎ 442 8501); an eight-minute flight behind their boat is $49.

Finally, and pardon the pun, why not take the Ultimate Jump (☎ (025) 325 961). For $245 you can tandem freefall at your 'terminal' velocity before your 'chute is opened and you are nursed safely to ground.

Walks

Many of Queenstown's activities are decidedly expensive but the walks cost nothing. Stroll along the waterfront through town and keep going to the park on the peninsula. It's a peaceful place. There's now a lakeshore walkway from Queenstown beginning at the end of Peninsula St; it takes about 1¼ hours each way.

One of the shortest climbs around Queenstown is Queenstown Hill, overlooking the town. It's 900 metres high, and a comfortable climb with good views – two to three hours return. For a more spectacular view, climb Ben Lomond (1746 metres) – it takes five hours there and back. Follow the Skyline vehicle track for half an hour until you get to a small rock cairn, which marks a turn-off on your left. When you reach the saddle, head west to the top of Ben Lomond. During the summer you can start walking about midnight and have a spectacular view of the sunrise.

There are many other walks in the area, especially from Arthurs Point and Arrowtown, areas rich in history of the gold days – consult the DOC office for information.

If you're planning on longer walks there are several places in town where you can hire camping equipment. Replay Sports (☎ 442 6590) at the Windsurf Mania house, 27 Shotover St, hires camping equipment in addition to fishing tackle, goldpans, mopeds, bicycles, canoes and, of course, windsurfers. They also buy and sell used camping and sports equipment. Other places to hire camping equipment are Bill Lacheny Sports (☎ 442 8438) in the Mall, and Kiwi Discovery (☎ 442 7340) in Camp St.

Bus Trips

There are all sorts of bus trips from Queenstown:

Arrowtown The red Double Decker bus makes a 2½-hour trip to Arrowtown at 10 am and 2 pm daily; the cost is $16 (children $8). It leaves from several points around town, including near the Mall. There is also the Arrow Express (☎ 442 1535) scheduled service. InterCity and Mt Cook long-distance buses from Queenstown also stop at Arrowtown (see Arrowtown in this chapter).

Skippers Canyon Nomad Safaris (☎ 442 6699), Outback Tours (☎ 442 7386) and Great Sights Gray Line (☎ 442) all do 4½-

hour bus trips up the winding road above the Shotover River. The scenery is spectacular, the road's hair-raising, and there's plenty of historical interest as well. The cost is about $39 (children $19), including a stop to try your luck panning for gold.

Milford Sound & Elsewhere Day trips via Te Anau to Milford Sound are operated by Fiordland, Mt Cook, Great Sights and Inter-City. They take 12 to 13 hours and cost from $99 (children about half price) including a two-hour launch cruise on the sound. The Queenstown-Milford Sound trip makes a very long day, so if you're going to Te Anau it makes a lot more sense to make the trip from there. The same is true for trips to Doubtful Sound, which cost $128 (children $74) from Queenstown.

From October to March Fiordland Travel, in conjunction with Kiwi Experience, has a 'backpackers alternative' trip to Milford which takes two days and costs $176. The first day you go from Queenstown to Walter Peak on the MV *Walter Peak*, then a bus takes you to Te Anau via the back road; you stay there overnight on the *Milford Wanderer*. On the second day the bus takes you from Milford back to Queenstown via the back road and Mavora lakes. You board the TSS *Earnslaw* for the return trip across Lake Wakatipu (see Milford Sound in the Southland chapter for more details).

Backpacker Express (☎ 442 9939) has trampers' transport to the Routeburn, Greenstone, Caples and Dart-Rees tracks. If you're not tramping you can still go along on the bus and make a day trip of it. They also go between Queenstown and Milford, leaving in the morning and arriving in the afternoon, with a stopover in Te Anau.

Other Things to Do
Still more Queenstown activities? Well, you can go fishing, water-skiing, windsurfing, charter a yacht, hire a catamaran, ride a horse, play squash, rap jump, try a space shuttle simulator, ride a water-bike, visit the amusement park or underwater observatory, or hire a moped or mountain bike.

The two rap jumping companies are Rap Jumping (☎ 442 9708) and Rap Jump NZ Ltd (☎ 442 7391). Abseil face first, but under complete control, and learn the finer points of rope handling with these people.

There are three companies which specialise in mountain-bike trips with a difference. They cover the usual strenuous uphill pedalling by taking you and your bike to a suitable high point. From there you can glide back to Queenstown in less than two hours. Try the Mountain Bike Cruising Co (☎ 442 6827), Remarkable Downhill Mountain-bike Cruise (☎ (025) 335 674), or Zany Mountain Byke Adventure Tours (☎ 442 7340).

At the opposite end of the scale, you can see how dried flowers are grown, harvested and processed at Queenstown Dried Flowers, near the Shotover River. Guided tours, from Queenstown, run through summer, starting around mid-November.

The Skyline Showscan Theatre at the top gondola terminal shows 'Kiwi Magic', a film on the scenery of New Zealand. The wraparound screen and a dynamic sound system give the feeling of being inside the action.

On the pier at the end of the Mall, near the centre of Queenstown, is Underwater World, a submerged observation gallery where you can look out and see eels and trout in the clear waters of Lake Wakatipu. The agile little scaup or 'diving' ducks also make periodic appearances outside the windows. Entry is $5 (children $2.50).

Places to Stay
Despite the multitude of accommodation possibilities in Queenstown you will probably have trouble finding a room at peak periods. Try the Visitor Information Centre or the Queenstown Information Centre if you're stuck. Prices vary with the season, they go sky high at the peak summer period or in the middle of the ski season, then drop in between (high-season prices for Queenstown are given here). There's a lot of overlap between accommodation types in Queenstown – some of the guesthouses and campsites also have cabins, bunkrooms and motel rooms, for example.

Forgive local accommodation owners if they squeeze a number of you into a small room or on to a miniscule campsite – it will be all that they have left.

Camping & Cabins There are plenty of campsites in and around Queenstown, all with cabins. The closest in is the *Queenstown Motor Park* (☎ 442 72524), less than one km from the town centre at the end of Man St. Camping costs $8 per person ($8.50 with power). There are also cabins from $30 for one or two people, tourist flats from $52, and motel flats from $70. As well as being so conveniently located, the camp is very well equipped – good kitchen, coin-operated laundry, TV room and so on.

The *Creeksyde Campervan Park* (☎ 442 9447) on Robins Rd is a very modern, comfortable place. It has campervan sites for $10 per person, and a very limited number of tent sites for $8.50 per person. There's also just one self-contained cottage for $50 for two, with the possibility of a cheaper rate for families.

The *Mountain View Lodge Holiday Park* (☎ 442 8246) is on Frankton Rd, just over one km from the town centre on the Frankton side. Camping costs $11 per night for two, with or without power. There's also a lodge with 10 rooms, each sleeping two to four people, that costs $36 for two. Bedding is supplied in the lodge and you have your own toilet, but you need your own cooking equipment for the communal kitchens. The camp also has a restaurant and bar.

At *Frankton Motor Camp* (☎ 442 2079), six km from town, camping costs $7 per person ($8 with power). Cabins cost $31 for two. The *Kawarau Falls Lodge & Motor Camp* (☎ 442 3510), also at Frankton, has campsites for $7.50 per person ($8.50 with power) plus a variety of indoor accommodation, including a hostel-style lodge and cabins for $15.50 per person. *Arthurs Point Camping Ground* (☎ 442 9306) at Arthurs Point, has camping for $7.50 per person and cabins for $28 for two.

The *Closeburn Alpine Park* (☎ 442 6073) is about seven km south of town in a particularly peaceful and attractive forest setting overlooking the lake. Its campsites cost $8 for each person ($17 for two with power) or $22 for two with private toilet and shower. On-site caravans with attached bathrooms cost $35 for two, and a hostel-style lodge with bunks costs $14 per night.

There's a *DOC campsite* at 12-Mile Creek Reserve, Glenorchy Rd, just five km from Queenstown.

Hostels The *Wakatipu Lodge – YHA Hostel* (☎ 442 8413; fax 442 6561) is right by the lake at 80 Lake Esplanade. It's a large hostel with beds for 100 people; the cost is $16 per night. The night-time curfew at the hostel has been extended until 3 am and you can also get tasty food here – a huge lasagne, for example, for $6.50. In winter the hostel can get hopelessly booked out due to all the skiers.

Also along Lake Esplanade beside the lake are two other hostels. *Bumbles* (☎ 442 6298) on the corner of Brunswick St, has dorm beds for $14, twins for $15 and double rooms for $16 per person. It's a comfortable, friendly hostel with good cheap meals. This is one of the closest hostels to town, and it's enormously popular.

The *Lakeside Motel* (☎ 442 8976) at 18 Lake Esplanade has hostel-style accommodation in the buildings behind the large and fancy motel. The cost is $13 per person for a dorm room, or $28 for a double/twin for two.

In the town itself, there is *Thomas's Hotel & Backpackers* (☎ 442 7180) at 50 Beach St. It has a first-floor kitchen and lounge with views of Lake Wakatipu. All rooms are heated and have their own bathrooms. Here share rooms are $15 and doubles are $17.50. Their gimmick – free chocolate bars when you book a tour.

The former Mountaineer is no longer. It has been split into two. *McFee's Waterfront Hotel* (☎ 442 7400; fax 442 7403) at 48a Shotover St, has great real estate value (as the name suggests). Share rooms are $14 and doubles are $16 per person, and all have ensuite bathrooms. *Backpackers Downtown*

OTAGO

(☎ 442 7384) at 48 Shotover St, is the other part of the Mountaineer. Dorm beds are $15, and twins/doubles are $16 per person (with facilities $17). Pay $3 once for linen; blankets are provided. The Downtown has a laundry, kitchen and dining area with a TV.

A few minutes with pack (the management boast one minute) from town is *Deco Backpackers* (☎ 442 7384) at 52 Man St. It is in a restored art deco building (hence its name), sleeps 20 and share rooms are $14, twins $15 and doubles $16 per person. It is opposite the entrance to the central camping ground. This is a clean, pleasant place with full facilities and, importantly, a happy staff. They are expanding next door and have a great (public) recreation area overlooking the lake.

Bungi Backpackers (☎ 442 8725; fax same) on the corner of Sydney and Stanley Sts have share rooms for $14 and double/twins for $16. This, the town's old maternity hospital, has full laundry and kitchen facilities and is just off the main road out of and into town. They have a large common room with a separate area for smokers; there is a large garden area out the back of the building from where you get a glimpse of Lake Wakatipu.

There are a few other backpackers close to the town centre. The *Redwood Lodge* (☎ 442 9116), just above the town centre at 8 Lower Malaghan St, has great views over the town and lake. It's a small place with beds for $12 – supply your own bedding as usual – or fancier rooms upstairs for $15 or $20 per person, linen included.

The *Pinewood Lodge* (☎ 442 8273) is a little further from the centre at 48 Hamilton Rd. It used to offer motel-style accommodation but it's now a hostel with several units of two or three rooms that share a lounge, kitchen and bathroom. If you supply your own bedding the nightly cost is $14 per person in a dorm room or $16 per person in a twin or double room; you can hire linen and blankets if needed. There's a free pick-up service from all transport terminals.

Just a bit further out and south of the centre, *FAB Accommodation – Families &*

Backpackers (☎ 442 6095) at 42 Frankton Rd is also a former motel; in fact it still has some motel units, at $50 for doubles. Shared accommodation is $14 in dorm rooms (up to five people) or $15 per person in twin rooms. Each room has its own fully-equipped kitchen and bathroom with shower and tub.

Another possibility is the *Queenstown Lodge* (☎ 442 7107) on Sainsbury Rd in Fernhill, about two km from the centre, with a magnificent view of the lake. Rooms (with linen service and bathroom en suite) are $35 per person, and rooms without en suite bathrooms are $25 per person; basic backpackers accommodation is $15 per person. The lodge has budget meals, a licensed restaurant and bar, games and various activities including party nights.

Guesthouses The pleasant *Queenstown House* (☎ 442 9043) at 69 Hallenstein St, on the corner of Malaghan St, has B&B for $45/65. There are good views over the town and lake from the balcony and it's close to the town centre.

Nearby is *Melbourne House* (☎ 442 9043) at Melbourne St, where B&B costs $49.50/ 76.50 for singles/twins (this is part of the Melbourne Motor Lodge – see Motels).

Between Melbourne House and Queenstown House is the wonderful old *Hulbert House* (☎ 442-8767) at 68 Ballarat St. This is upper class B&B; just a handful of very gracious rooms, wonderful views and a cost of $90 to $125 for a single and $125 to $145 for a double per night. There is, however, just one very cheap cabin-style room separate from the main house. It has its own restaurant, The Tutulia.

The *Goldfields Breakfast Inn* (☎ 442 7211) is at 41 Frankton Rd (see The Goldfields Motel in Motels). B&B is $48/62 for one/two persons.

Motels Queenstown has plenty of motels and motel flats including some at the various campsites and guesthouses; see those sections for details. Motel prices in Queenstown are not cheap but they tend to fluctuate with the seasons.

The *Mountain View Lodge* (☎ 442 8246) on Frankton Rd is a good example – there are cabins and motel-style rooms as well as the adjoining camping facilities. The main building is known as the bottle house – nearly 15,000 bottles (none of them beer bottles!) are set into the walls.

The *Goldfields Motel* (☎ 442 7211) is at 41 Frankton Rd. Like the Melbourne Motor Lodge it has a variety of accommodation. Motel rates are $60 to $76.50 for two.

At *Melbourne Motor Lodge* (☎ 442 8431; see also Melbourne House) 35 Melbourne St, rooms are from $95 to $105 for two. It's a friendly and well-organised place with laundry facilities and a guest lounge, and it's conveniently close to the town centre.

There are quite a few other motels in and around Queenstown, generally costing from $60 to $80 per night.

Some of the reasonably priced ones are:

A1 Queenstown Motel (☎ 442 7289), 13 Frankton Rd
Alpine Sun Motel (☎ 442 8482), 14 Hallenstein St
Amber Motor Lodge (☎ 442 8480), corner of Shotover St & Gorge Rd
Autoline Motel (☎ 442 8734), corner of Frankton Rd & Dublin St
Blue Peaks Lodge (☎ 442 9224), corner of Stanley & Sydney Sts
Colonial Village Motel (☎ 442 7629), 100 Frankton Rd
Hillside Motel (☎ 442 9280), 35 Gorge Rd
Lakeside Motel (☎ 442 8976), 18 Lake Esplanade

Hotels At the *Hotel Esplanade* (☎ 442 8611), overlooking the lake at 32 Peninsula St, a room with a bathroom costs $28/44/51 for singles/doubles/triples. Breakfast is available for $5 (continental) or $7 (cooked) and there's an indoor pool and sauna.

In addition to backpackers beds, *McFee's Waterfront Hotel* (☎ 442 7400) on Beach St, has rooms for $59/69 for singles/twins.

Some of the top-range establishments are the *Earnslaw Motor Lodge* (☎ 442 8728) at 53 Frankton Rd; *Holiday Inn Queenstown* (☎ & fax 442 7354) at Sainsbury Rd, Fernhill; the *Kingsgate Queenstown Hotel* (☎ 442 8123) at Frankton Rd; and the *Queenstown Parkroyal* (☎ 442 7800) at Beach St.

Places to Eat

Queenstown has its share of pricey restaurants (well, it *is* a ski resort) but there are plenty of places with reasonably priced good-value food. The centre is very compact so it's no problem walking to these places.

Snacks & Fast Food There is an assortment of the usual snacks – sandwiches, fish & chips, and the like. For coffee-bar food, pancakes and light meals (breakfast, lunch and early dinner) try the *Cardrona Cafe* in the Mall where you can sit down and watch the Mall activity. A mixed grill is just over $10 and vegetarian lasagne about $12. Next door is *Sweet Memories*, a patisserie and chocolate shop with tasty sandwiches.

A block away at 5 Beach St, *Down to Earth Natural Foods*, as its title suggests, has good sandwiches and excellent wholemeal munchies. *The Bakery*, at 11 Shotover St just beyond Camp St, has baked food, sandwiches and pizzas. For a good fish meal go to the *Fishbone Grill* on Beach St – the fish is fresh. The tiny *Habebe's Lebanese Takeaways* is near the waterfront in the arcade on the corner of Rees and Beach Sts (opposite McFee's Waterfront Hotel).

Three American fast-food giants have set up their predictable outlets in Queenstown. *Pizza Hut* and *Kentucky Fried Chicken* are on Camp St, and *McDonald's* is in O'Connell's Pavilion. The *Gourmet Express*, on Shotover St towards the waterfront in the Bay Centre, looks very American – like a Denny's. It's very popular for breakfast; you can get pancakes or a continental breakfast for $5. The menu features the fast food regulars including a variety of tasty looking burgers from $4 to $7. It's open from 7 am to 9 pm daily.

O'Connell's Foodhall, in the O'Connell's Pavilion in Beach St, is the place to go if you want to confuse yourself with choice. There are chicken, international (eg Chinese, Mexican), sandwich and ice cream outlets here, and a lunch bar called *The Sardine*

OTAGO

Factory. Nature's Pantry is great for really healthy food. The foodhall is open from 9 am to 9 pm daily.

If you want the definitive cup of coffee, go to *Naff Caff* at 62 Shotover St. They have their own coffee roaster; fresh croissants make the perfect accompaniment. Not since Coffee d'Fafo in Christchurch will you have spaced out so well on caffeine.

Restaurants The *Cow Restaurant* in Cow Lane is something of a Queenstown institution, a tiny old stone-walled building with a roaring fire (in winter) and excellent pizzas and pastas. It's an atmospheric little BYO with the emphasis on little. You'll probably have to queue for a table although they do takeaways as well. The pizzas cost $8 to $11 for small ones and $11 to $17 for the large size. Either way they're substantial, so bring an appetite. Spaghetti costs around $9 to $13. When you have finished your meal, however, be prepared to be asked to leave as turnover is fast here.

Over on the Mall is *Avanti*, a straightforward Italian BYO with pizzas from $5 to $22, pastas and Italian main courses from $9.50 to $12.50, and desserts for $4 – nothing special but good value and with a pleasant courtyard at the back. Directly opposite, the *Stonewall Cafe* is a pleasant place for snacks, lunch, dinner, desserts and cappuccino. Tasty food with a variety of international dishes is served at tables inside, out on the Mall, and in the little rear courtyard. It's a good place for people-watching. Another Mall establishment is *HMS Britannia*, nautically set up as an English galleon. The emphasis is on seafood but there are plenty of other choices on the menu. Also in the centre of town is *The Jazz Bar* where food is '...healthy, good value and nicely presented'. Next door to Eichardt's is the *Continental Cafe & Bar*. This place has a regularly changed blackboard menu which features fresh seafood, pasta dishes and good salads. At the *Pot au Feu* (☎ 442 8333), on Camp St, food is consistently good; reservations are essential.

The *Lone Star Cafe & Bar* at 14 Brecon St is a great place to dine and enjoy a drink. The food is Tex-Mex in style. A plate of nachos here is large enough to serve as a whole meal for two people. It is a rowdy place, both upstairs and downstairs, as it serves to bring out the nocturnal twitchings of the town's vast battalions of adrenaline junkies.

Upstairs in the SSB Arcade, at 13-23 Beach St, *Saguaro* has Mexican food – enchiladas, tacos, burritos, fajitas – for around $16, with lunch-time specials for $5.50, all served with Mexican rice and beans. It's open until late every night. For those who can afford a sushi/sashimi feast try *Minami Jujisei Japanese Restaurant* on Rees St.

There are plenty of more expensive restaurants. Facing each other across Shotover St are *Upstairs, Downstairs* and *Roaring Megs*, two of Queenstown's better and pricier BYO eating places with main courses in the $18 to $25 range. Roaring Megs is an old miner's cottage.

Right at the top, altitude-wise at least, would have to be dinner at the *Skyline Restaurant*. Including the gondola ride to the top, a big carvery buffet dinner costs $35 (children $17.50). It has great views and nightly entertainment.

A number of the more swish hotels have their own restaurants. The Lakeland Hotel has *Clancy's*, the Queenstown Parkroyal *Bentley's Brasserie*, The Terraces Hotel *Hillarys Restaurant*, the Quality Inn *The Hillside Brasserie*, and the Holiday Inn *Reflections*. If your tastebuds are up to sampling muttonbird then try the award-winning *Treetops of Queenstown* (☎ 442 7328) at Sunshine Bay. Treetops have a courtesy vehicle which delivers you right to the door of this Japanese-style teahouse – dining in this style does not come cheaply.

Entertainment
Queenstown is a small place but there's a reasonable variety of night-time activities. In the Mall near the waterfront is *Eichardt's*,

which has been around for a long time –
during the 1879 floods, hard-drinking
miners are said to have paddled up to the bar
in rowboats! During the Franco-Prussian
war, 1870 to 1871, Herr Eichardt, being a
good Prussian nationalist, ran the German
flag up the flagpole after every German
victory. Meanwhile, down the road at Mon-
sieur Francois St Omer's bakery, the
tricolour flew every time the French won.
The public bar is a popular local meeting and
drinking place. Upstairs you'll find activity
until late at night in the rather run-down
Penthouse nightclub.

Around the corner on Church St, near the
Mt Cook Landline terminal, is *McNeill's
Brewery & Bar*. The beer here is good and
costs between $2 and $3 for a half-pint; try
the dark McNeill's Classic or savour the
Moonlight or Wakatipu Gold. On Upper
Camp St is the *Red Rock Cafe & Bar*, where
the locals sip aperitifs before going out for
dinner or home to Channel One. They also
serve generous lunches and dinners. A little
later, the stayers will have gravitated to
Solera Vino, a tapas bar, at 25 Beach St. They
serve 40 wines by the glass or bottle and open
from 4 pm until late; lunch is served at noon
from Wednesday to Saturday.

. *Wicked Willies* on Beach St has recently
had a major rebuild. Or ride the gondola to
the *Skyline Restaurant* where there's entertainment with dinner each night and impressive views back down to the lights of Queenstown.

Getting There & Away
Air Air New Zealand, Mt Cook Airlines and
Ansett New Zealand all fly into Queenstown.
Mt Cook Airline (☎ 442 7650) has daily
direct flights to Auckland, Christchurch,
Dunedin, Te Anau, Milford Sound, Wanaka,
Mt Cook, Nelson and Rotorua, with additional connecting flights from Christchurch
to Wellington, Auckland and Nelson. It also
has scenic flights to Milford Sound. The Mt
Cook office is in Rees St next to the pier at
the end of the mall; Ansett New Zealand is
at the airport.

Ansett New Zealand (☎ 442 6161) has

daily direct flights to Christchurch with connections to Wellington, Auckland and
Rotorua. Air New Zealand operate one daily
jet service Christchurch-Queenstown.

Bus The InterCity booking office (☎ 442
7420) is on the corner of Shotover and Camp
Sts, next to the Visitor Information Centre.
Mt Cook buses leave from the depot on
Church St (☎ 442 7650). Great Sights Gray
Line buses (☎ 442 7028) depart from the Mt
Cook Landline depot. Backpacker Express
(☎ 442 9940) departs from the Information
and Track Walking Centre on Shotover St,
but will pick up from anywhere in Queenstown.

InterCity buses have several daily routes
to and from Queenstown. The route to
Christchurch (10 hours) goes via Mt Cook
(4¼ hours). Other routes are to Te Anau
(2½ hours) and Milford Sound (five hours),
Invercargill (3½ hours) and Dunedin (5¼
hours).

InterCity also has a daily West Coast
service to the West Coast glaciers via
Wanaka and the Haast Pass, taking two hours
to Wanaka, 7½ hours to Fox Glacier and
eight hours to Franz Josef Glacier. If you
want to continue up the coast from the glaciers you have to stay overnight at Fox or
Franz Josef. It takes a minimum of two days
(longer if you want to see more than a bus
window) to get up the West Coast to Nelson.

If you want to go up the coast to Nelson
by bus, the West Coast Express, Kiwi Experience or the Flying Kiwi are probably the
best alternatives, particularly if you have the
time and you want to get out and see things.
See the Getting Around chapter for details on
these 'alternative' bus lines.

Mt Cook Landline also has several bus
routes from Queenstown, with daily buses to
Christchurch, Wanaka, Mt Cook and Te
Anau. From November to April it has a
special daily bus route to Christchurch which
includes a 3½-hour stopover at Mt Cook. Mt
Cook buses to Dunedin run daily except
Sunday, and to Invercargill daily except Sat-
urday. Great Sights operates tourist buses to
Christchurch.

Several companies have buses to Milford via Te Anau, including InterCity and Fiordland Travel. For an interesting variation on travel to Milford Sound from Queenstown see MV *Wanderer* in the Milford Sound section of the Southland chapter.

Tramping Transport Backpackers Express (☎ 442 9939; fax 442 9940) runs to and from the Routeburn, Greenstone, Caples, and Rees-Dart tracks, all via Glenorchy. If you are taking a Fun Yak trip as a conclusion to the Rees-Dart Track, transport is included. Approximate prices for the Backpackers Express are:

Queenstown to the Routeburn $20
Queenstown to the Greenstone-Caples $25
Glenorchy to the Rees $12
Glenorchy to the Greenstone-Caples $15
Queenstown to the Rees $22
Queenstown to Glenorchy $10
Dart to Glenorchy $12
Greenstone-Caples to Glenorchy $15

Amazing Tours (contact Dave McDonald on 442 9437) go to Milford every day and stop at the western end of the Routeburn.

The services between Queenstown and Milford via Te Anau can be used for track transport or simply as a way to get to or from Milford. Buses generally run two or three times weekly but the schedule varies according to demand, with extra trips in summer and possibly none at all in winter. Fiordland Travel and InterCity also have buses to and from the Routeburn, Greenstone, Caples, Hollyford and Rees-Dart tracks during the tramping season. Transport to Glade House on the Milford Track departs from Te Anau.

Hitching Hitching into Queenstown is relatively easy, but getting out may require real patience. Be prepared for very long waits, and remember big wet packs are a real deterrent.

Getting Around
To/From the Airport The Airporter Shuttle (☎ 442 9803) meets all incoming and outgoing flights and costs $5 each way per person,

picking you up and dropping you off wherever you wish. A taxi, either Economy Taxis (☎ 442 6666) or Queenstown Taxis (☎ 442 7788), is just as good a deal for two people and even better for a larger group, charging $12 for up to five people.

Bicycle Rental You can rent bicycles at Queenstown Bike Hire, 23 Beach St. They have single-speed and 10-speed bikes, tandems, triples, side-by-side bikes, and 10, 12 and 18-speed mountain bikes. Mountain bikes can also be hired from Replay Sports in the Windsurf Mania house at 27 Shotover St, and from Kiwi Discovery in Camp St.

Moped Rental Queenstown Bike Hire at 23 Beach St also hires mopeds. Replay Sports at 27 Shotover St, and Letz Rent-a-Car on Camp St near the corner of Shotover St, beside the Information Centre, also hire mopeds.

GLENORCHY & THE REES-DART
The town of Glenorchy (population 125), which lies at the head of Lake Wakatipu, is only 47 km or a 40-minute drive from Queenstown. If you are looking for some tranquility after Queenstown, then Glenorchy may well be what you are looking for. A great many pass through briefly in their rush to knock off the Routeburn Track, and thus bypass perhaps one of the greatest tramping opportunities – the Rees and Dart river valleys. Glenorchy was once the terminus for the TSS *Earnslaw* – now a stream of buses and helicopters make the trip.

Jet-Boating
The Dart River jet-boat trip is one of the best value for money in New Zealand. It, along with those in the Makarora region, offers a scenic trip into the heart of New Zealand wilderness which lasts for a couple of hours. Sure they will spin the boat and pretend to almost crash into river obstacles, but this is only a small portion of the experience. The Dart River must be one of New Zealand's most beautiful places. Spin a couple of times but savour the grandeur of the slopes of Mt

Earnslaw and the bush that cascades down from the mountain walls on both sides of the river. You are in this breathtaking scenery for 2½ hours, and the driver even stops to let you take a brief walk through the beech forest at Beansburn, downriver from the turnaround point.

The founder of Dart River Jetboat Safari (DRJS) is sheepfarmer complete with full length gumboots, Neil Ross. He has been racing jet-boats for as long as he can remember. DRJS (☎ 442 9992) depart from Queenstown 8 and 11 am, and 2 pm in summer; check departure times in winter. The cost is $95 for a five-hour trip from Queenstown.

Neil has teamed up with Fun Yaks to offer a great return downriver option to the Dart River trip or finale to the Rees-Dart Track. Wilderness Jet (☎ 442 9792) have recently commenced trips from the Dart River bridge.

Fun Yaks

A novel way to finish the Rees-Dart Track is to kayak the last day of the walk. Eric Billoud drives you to the start of the Rees (saving you normal transport costs), then you walk independently for three days through the scenery of the Rees and Upper Dart Valley. On the fourth day Eric meets you at Sandy Bluff. From there you travel in an inflatable canoe down the Dart to the Dart River bridge near Glenorchy, where you are taken by courtesy vehicle back to Queenstown. Book with Danes (☎ 442 7318), corner of Shotover & Camp Sts; the cost is $79 from Queenstown, and $59 from Glenorchy.

There is also a day trip – jet-boat up with Neil Ross and canoe down with Eric. You get the opportunity to canoe through the Rockburn Chasm. No experience is necessary and the return cost from Queenstown is $149.

A Trip to Paradise

Glenorchy is the jumping-off point for a number of New Zealand's famous walks (see the Outdoor Activities chapter).

Perhaps some of the best alternatives for eco-tourists are the wilderness walks offered by Earthfirst Enterprises (Wilderness Expe-ditions) (☎ 442 8542). These walks range in duration from one hour to three days and include: Bobs Cove to Twelve Mile Reserve, Mt Crighton Loop, Lake Sylvan Wilderness Walk, and Paradise and Beyond. To go to Paradise costs $48/68 for a half/full day.

Other Things to Do

A good way to see this spectacular country is on horseback. Dart Stables (☎ 442 9968) have two two-hour trips daily at 9 am and 1 pm, and the Glenorchy Cafe (☎ 442 9915) hires out horses by the hour or day.

Glenorchy Air (☎ 442 2207) have a local scenic flight around Mt Earnslaw and the Routeburn; the cost is $80 for 20 minutes. If you wish to see Mt Aspiring and the Olivine Ice Plateau as well, the cost is $149 (45 minutes).

Places to Stay & Eat

Glenorchy is small and there is a limited choice of places to stay. The *Glenorchy Holiday Park* (☎ 442 9939; fax 442 9940) at 2 Oban St, Glenorchy, offers camping either by itself or in combination with transport to various walking tracks; see the Getting There & Away section for details. Normally, camp-sites are $6 per person, cabins and hostel are $12 for one, and the units are $60 for four people. It is really well set up for those doing the Greenstone-Caples, Rees-Dart and Route-burn tracks.

Next door to the Glenorchy Hotel (and part of it) is the *Glenorchy Backpackers Retreat* (☎ 442 9902) where a bed costs between $13 and $15 per night. The *Glenorchy Hotel* (☎ 442 9902; fax 442 9912) has B&B for $25/70 a single/double. The hotel has a restaurant, lounge bar and public bar. Not far away is the *Glen Roydon Outdoor Lodge* (☎ 442 9968) with rooms for the same price as the hotel.

The *Glenorchy Cafe* is the local hangout as they have fresh baked bread, organic salads and vegetables and home-cooked meals.

Getting There & Away

The Glenorchy Holiday Park is conveniently

near many of the walks and offers packages of transport to their camp, overnight accommodation and transport the next morning to the walks. This is a good way to make an early start. The cost for the Routeburn or Dart-Rees packages is $25 for campers and $30 for those staying in their lodge. For the Greenstone/Caples package the cost is $30 and $35.

If you are doing the Fun Yak trip then transport is included in the price.

Dunedin

Dunedin (population 114,500) is predominantly a student town. There are about 12,000 students attending the tertiary institutions here and the local entertainment scene, cafe and pub life, and arts are a consequence of this. Another very evident feature is Dunedin's distinct Scottishness – not surprising considering the name is Celtic for Edinburgh. It's a solid, no nonsense sort of place – second city of the South Island, home of New Zealand's first university and at one time (during the gold rush days) the largest city in New Zealand.

The city is situated in a kind of natural amphitheatre at the head of Otago Harbour, a long fiord-like inlet. It has become the hub for many eco-tourism activities, especially on the peninsula and in nearby coastal areas. There are a great many historic buildings in this town and efforts have been made to preserve the architectural heritage. Dunedin is also the gateway to Otago with its many lakes, mountain resorts and historic goldfields.

History
The early Maori history of the Dunedin area was particularly bloody, with a three-way feud between tribes occupying the Otago Peninsula. *Utu* (revenge) followed attack as the feud between the Ngai Tahu and the Ngatimamoe tribes escalated at the end of the 1800s. With the advent of sealing and whaling along the coast the Maori popula-

tion was ravaged by disease; by 1848 the once considerable population of Otakau Pa was just over 100.

The first permanent European settlers arrived at Port Chalmers in March 1848, six years after the plan for a Presbyterian settlement on the east coast of the South Island was initially mooted. Not long after the settlers' arrival in Dunedin, gold was discovered in Otago and the province quickly became the richest and most influential in the colony. In 1879 it was the first city outside the USA to have its own tram system, and this remained working until the last one was phased out in 1957.

Orientation
The eight-sided Octagon – really more of a circle – marks the centre of Dunedin. The main street runs through it, changing name from Princes St on the southern side to George St on the northern side.

Information
The well-organised and extremely helpful Dunedin Visitor Centre (☎ 474 3300; fax 474 3311) is at 48 The Octagon, in the magnificently restored Municipal Chambers. It's open from 8.30 am to 5 pm on weekdays and from 9 am to 5 pm on weekends, with extended hours in summer. As well as providing a great deal of information and advice, the centre books tours.

The DOC (☎ 477 0677) is at 77 Stuart St. It has pamphlets and information on walking tracks but most of their information is also available from the Dunedin Visitor Centre. The AA (☎ 477 5945) at 450 Moray Place just east of Princes St (opposite First Church), is open from 8.30 am to 5 pm Monday to Friday.

Brochures The very informative, and free, *Focus on Dunedin* is widely available.

The Visitor Centre also has other interesting pamphlets on places you can visit, including *Historic Dunedin* published by the New Zealand Historic Places Trust. There are many other old churches and stone buildings worth a look. The public library at the back of the Octagon is quite impressive.

Olveston

Olveston is a fine old turn-of-the-century house at 42 Royal Terrace, preserved as it was when lived in by the wealthy and cultured Theomin family of the early 1900s. Olveston was designed by a London architect and built between 1904 and 1906. It is lavishly furnished with a wealth of items, especially decorative art from East Asia, collected by David Theomin on his extensive travels. The guided tour is a real education. There are six tours daily – phone ahead (☎ 477 3320) to reserve a place; admission is $9 (children $3).

Chocolate Factory

A tour of the Cadbury's chocolate factory is a major attraction – in fact it's so popular that you have to book well in advance and you can give up all hope during school holidays! The one-hour tour shows you how all the chocolates are made and concludes with a free sample of the delicious stuff. Tours are held twice daily from Monday to Thursday and can be booked at the Visitor Centre or by phoning 474 1126. The entrance to the factory is on Cumberland St. The factory closes to give its workers a break over the Christmas holiday period.

Wilson's Distillers

Wilson's (☎ 474 3300 for bookings) on George St, is New Zealand's only 'legal' whisky distillery and the southernmost distillery in the world. All aspects of distillation are covered in the informative 1½-hour guided tour. An excellent video is screened and, importantly, the product is sampled. The whisky is made entirely from local products – pure water piped from the Lammerlaw range, and malting barley from Otago, Southland and South Canterbury. Tours run at 1 and 2.30 pm, Monday to Friday, and you book at the Visitor Centre. Enjoy your 'wee dram'.

Speight's Brewery

When you've overdosed on chocolate (but hopefully not whisky) you can head to Speight's Brewery in Rattray St for a tour at 10.30 am Monday to Friday. It costs $5 (children free), and you must book in advance by phoning 477 9480. Tours start from the visitors centre at the brewery. The brewery is one of the smallest in the country and the 1¾-hour tour concludes with a glass of beer in the company board room.

There have been complaints about the lack of enthusiasm by tour guides on this tour – hopefully this attitude would have changed by now with the increasing emphasis on gracious Kiwi-Hosting.

Otago Museum

The Otago Museum on the corner of Great King and Union Sts has a large and varied collection including Maori and South Pacific exhibits; items from ancient Egypt, Greece, Rome, Japan, China, Tibet, South-East Asia, a marine and maritime hall; wildlife and ceramics exhibits; jewellery and art; and a lot more.

Particularly good are the natural history displays featuring penguins and moas. There is a hands-on science centre (Discovery World) for children. Exhibits relate to the present as well as the past. Admission is free and it's open from 10 am to 5 pm on weekdays, 1 to 5 pm on Saturday, and 2 to 5 pm on Sunday. The museum has a cafe and a craft shop.

Early Settlers Museum

The Early Settlers Museum (☎ 4¯7 5052) at 220 Cumberland St, between the railway station and the InterCity bus depot, has a fine collection relating to the early settlement of the region. At the railway station end of the museum there are a couple of old steam locomotives in glassed-in display rooms. These include *Josephine*, the first engine to run between Dunedin and Port Chalmers. The museum's open from 10 am to 5 pm on weekdays, 1 to 5 pm on Saturday and Sunday. Admission is $4 (students $3, accompanied children free).

OTAGO

Dunedin

OTAGO

PLACES TO STAY

4	Sahara Guesthouse
23	Hotel Branson
24	Quality Inn
34	Law Courts Establishment
41	YMCA
45	Elm Lodge
47	Leviathan Hotel
53	Southern Cross Hotel
54	Penguin Place Backpackers
58	Wains Boutique Hotel
62	Chalet Backpackers
64	Stafford Gables YHA Hostel
65	Manor House International Backpackers

PLACES TO EAT

3	Santa Fe
6	Captain Cook Hotel
8	Blades Restaurant & Epi D'or
9	Capers
12	Mega Bite & Robbie Burns Hotel
13	Albert Arms
14	Huntsman Chargrill Steak House
17	McDonalds
18	Little India
22	Bentleys Restaurant & Bar
30	Parisettes
31	Tapestry Restaurant
35	Potpourri
36	Bagdad Cafe
38	Sidewalk Cafe
40	Out on a Limb Cafe
44	Smithies Pizza
50	Palms Cafe
51	Ma Cuisine
55	Monarch Sunset Smorgasbord Cruise
56	Wharf Street Restaurant

60	Provincial Hotel
63	Rogano's Seafood Restaurant

OTHER

1	Dunedin Public Art Gallery
2	University & Hocken Library
5	Otago Museum
7	Olveston
10	Taxi Stand
11	Public Hospital
15	Taxi Stand
16	Moana Pool
19	Suburban Bus Lines
20	Supermarket
21	Mt Cook Landline
25	Library
26	Town Hall
27	Dunedin Visitor Centre
28	Supermarket
29	Cadbury Chocolate Factory
32	Railway Station & Taieri Gorge Railway
33	Police Station
35	Department of Conservation (DOC)
37	Automobile Association (AA)
39	Air New Zealand
42	Stuart Street Terrace Houses
43	Fortune Theatre
46	First Church
48	Early Settlers Museum
49	InterCity Travel Centre
52	Speight's Brewery
55	MV *Monarch*
57	Central Post Office
59	Taxi Stand
60	Provincial Hotel
61	Royal Terrace & High Street
66	Newton's Tours
67	Harbour Cruise

Other Museums & Galleries

The Dunedin Public Art Gallery is in Logan Park, near the university at the northern end of Anzac Ave. It's open from 10 am to 5 pm on weekdays and 2 to 5 pm on weekends; admission is free. It's the oldest art gallery in New Zealand and has an extensive collection of international and NZ art.

The Otago Military Museum is at the Army headquarters Drill Hall in Bridgman St. Admission is free, and the museum is open by arrangement (☎ 455 1099).

University of Otago

The Geology Museum of the University of Otago has displays illustrating mineral types and NZ fossils. Admission is free and it's open from 9 am to 5 pm on weekdays during teaching time, and by arrangement at other times (☎ 479 1100).

Also in the university is the Hocken Library (☎ 479 1100), founded by Dr T M Hocken (1836-1910). It has an extensive collection of books, manuscripts, paintings and photographs relating to New Zealand

and the Pacific. This library is open from 9.30 am to 5 pm, Monday to Friday, and 9 am to noon Saturday.

The university itself is worth a walk around. It was founded in 1869, 25 years after the settlement of Otago, with 81 students. Today it has 12,000; more than two-thirds coming from outside Otago. There's a wide variety of old and new styles of architecture on the campus. Dunedin, more than any other NZ city, is a university town.

Surf Rafting

The new addition to Dunedin's long list of attractions and activities is surf rafting. Surf Rafting NZ Ltd (☎ 455 0066) have devised a trip that is both exhilarating and educational. They operate from their beach-side premises between St Kilda and St Clair at Middle Beach, on Moana Rua Rd. First they penetrate the breakers in inflatable, motorised rubber boats, often in spectacular fashion with the boat flying into the air.

Beyond the breakers the adventure starts. It can be broken into two parts: wildlife observation, and a historical and scenic spectacle. The boat powers past the towering cliffs south of Dunedin towards two islands where you are likely to see fur seals, little blue penguins, Stewart Island shags, pied shags, yellow-eyed penguin (hoiho), royal spoonbills, white-faced herons, sooty shearwaters, and pelagic species. Occasionally dolphins are seen in the water near the boat.

After viewing a host of fauna at a safe and not intrusive range the driver turns the raft towards land, and the cliffs and formations which can only be viewed from the sea.

This is part two of a great trip – thrills and history. If sea conditions permit, the raft goes through the hole in Johnson's Rock or into the Amphitheatre. Perhaps the highlight is the tricky entry into the huge cathedral-like cave, only accessible by boat. In here there is graffiti dating back to 1872, as well as freshwater springs.

The trip can be undertaken by all except young children. All safety matters are attended to and the drivers cut their teeth as surf lifesavers, using similar equipment. There are back-up boats and the rafts are in radio contact with base. The cost is \$29.50 (through surf, tunnels and into the Cave), \$39.50 (all except one of the wildlife islands), and \$59.50 (complete). They surf raft all summer, and from May to October trips take place on demand.

Parks & Pools

Dunedin has plenty of parks, including the Botanical Gardens at the northern end of the city on the lower slopes of Signal Hill. The hothouse there is open from 10 am to 4.30 pm. Rhododendron Week, the third week in October, is a big deal at the gardens. There is also an aviary, with keas and other native birds.

In Upper Stuart St on the corner of Littlebourne Rd is a fine Olympic swimming pool, Moana Pool (☎ 474 3513), with hydroslides and heated to 27°C. Phone first to check on opening hours.

Stargazing

If the night is clear it's possible to do a little stargazing at the Beverley Begg Observatory (☎ 477 7683), in the Robin Hood Ground – it's off to your left across the lawn when you reach the top (western end) of Rattray St.

There's usually viewing on clear Sunday nights at around 7.30 pm, but may be later or not at all during summer when it gets dark as late as 10 pm. The cost is only around \$2. Public meetings are held at the observatory on the first and third Tuesday of every month, and visitors are welcome. Tours are by arrangement.

Taieri River Gorge Railway

There are four-hour train excursions through the Taieri River Gorge from October to April, departing from Dunedin Station on various days at 3.30 pm and returning by 7.30 pm. Some visitors have rated this one of the great train journeys of the world, similar to the Silverton to Durango line in Colorado. The cost is around \$40 (student ID cardholders \$31.50) and one child can ride for free with

Top: Lake Manapouri, Southland (TW)
Bottom Left: Ancient tree trunk fossil, Curio Bay, Catlins, Southland (JW)
Bottom Right: Viewing a Sperm Whale on a Nature Watch Tour (BT)

Top: Otago University, Dunedin (RS)
Bottom: Olveston, Dunedin (TW)

each paying adult. Phone 477 4449 for a schedule and reservations.

The Taieri Gorge Limited Trust publishes the excellent pamphlet *Your Guide to the Taieri Railway*. Remember to bring an empty bottle because just before Salisbury Tunnel there are huge soda springs. With luck you will be able to collect some.

Ocean Beach Railway

During the week you can sometimes see restoration work in progress at the Ocean Beach Railway (☎ 455 2798). From 2 to 5 pm on certain Sunday you can have a ride but phone to check what's going on before you go out. Catch the St Kilda bus from John Wickliffe House in town to its terminus.

Other Things to See

Other activities around Dunedin include golf (there are three 18-hole golf courses), tennis, 10-pin bowling, and horse trail riding. There are three flightseeing companies: the Otago Aero Club (☎ 489 4006), Beck Aviation – Helicopters (☎ 489 7322), and Mainland Air Services (☎ 486 2200).

The Otago Tramping & Mountaineering Club have regular weekly meetings and discuss their walking and climbing trips. You can get information on all these activities through the Visitor Centre.

Cruises

You can take 2½ to four-hour cruises with Otago Harbour Cruises (☎ 477 4276; fax 477 4216) on the MV *Monarch* from Rattray St Wharf. Among the *Monarch* cruises is one out along Otago Harbour, passing seal, shag and gull colonies and the royal albatross colony at Taiaroa Head. This half-day full harbour cruise costs $37 (children half price). Their 75-minute cruise to Wellers Rock, which takes in Taiaroa Head, is $15, and the six-hour cruise/coach option is $55. They also run evening supper cruises and the smorgasbord is, by all reports, quite good.

The 57-foot (17½-metre) *Southern Spirit* (☎ 477 1031) sails daily on a similar five-hour harbour cruise to Taiaroa Head, departing from the Harbour Board Basin Marina in

Birch St. The cost is $40. Also available are two-hour ($45) and four-hour ($75) salmon fishing trips. This is a participatory activity as you have a hand in sailing the yacht.

Beaches & Walks

On the headland at the end of St Clair Beach is a heated outdoor saltwater pool. It's open only in the summer – catch bus No 7. St Clair and St Kilda are good beaches to walk along or if you happen to be there on the shortest day (the middle of the winter) you can join the famous Shortest Day Swim (in the sea, not the heated pool!).

There is a 1.5-km walkway to Tunnel Beach. Catch a Corstorphine bus from the Octagon to Stenhope Crescent and walk along Blackhead Rd until you reach a 'no exit' road leading towards the coast. Head towards the triangular promontory, where you'll find a handcarved stone tunnel leading towards a secluded beach. The walkway is closed in September and October for the lambing season. For more information get a copy of the *D3 Information Sheet* from the Visitor Centre.

If you catch a Dunedin City Council Normandy bus to the start of Norwood Rd, you can walk up the road to the Mt Cargill-Bethunes Gully Walkway. It takes two hours uphill, and 1½ down. The highlight is the view from Mt Cargill, which is accessible by car. In Maori legend the three peaks of Cargill represent the petrified head and feet of a princess of an early Otakau tribe. 'Cargill' actually comes from Captain William Cargill, a leader of the early Otago colonists. Take warm clothes as it gets very windy at the top.

The walkway continues from Mt Cargill to the Organ Pipes (1½ hours return). These formations are about 10 million years old and were formed during the cooling of lavas which flowed across here.

Up behind Dunedin is the five-km Pineapple Flagstaff Walk, which is not accessible by public transport. There are great views of the harbour, coastline and inland ranges from this walk. You can get leaflets on these walks from the Visitor Centre.

One shorter but definitely more strenuous walk is that up Baldwin St. It is listed in the Guinness Book of records as the steepest street in the world with a gradient of 1 in 1.266. Ask at the Visitor Centre for directions.

Tours

There are numerous tours to choose from. See also the bus tours detailed in the Otago Peninsula section.

Silverpeaks Tours (☎ 489 6167) has jet-boating and white water rafting trips on the Taieri River.

Gold Trail Mini Tours (☎ 474 3300) take visitors via the Pigroot to the Macraes gold mine and the historic Golden Point Battery. Lunch is at the Stanleys Hotel in Macraes Flat. The tour connects with the Taieri Gorge Limited for the return trip to Dunedin, and the cost of this trip is $67.50. There is also a two-day trip for $123.75 which takes in much of the Central Otago goldfields (see Central Otago in this chapter).

If you wish to go horse-trekking there are a number of choices: in the Taieri Gorge with Ardachy Treks (☎ 489 1499); from Broad Bay to Larnach's Castle with Castle Discovery Horse Treks (☎ 478 0592); and, as the name says, Horse Riding on the Otago Peninsula (☎ 476 1198).

One highly recommended operation for small group eco-tours is Wings of Kotuku (☎ & fax 473 0077). They offer three trips concentrating on wildlife and history: the Early Bird, which includes the albatross colony ($45); Otago Peninsula, with visits to the albatross and yellow-eyed penguin colonies ($53, but May to August $42); and the Moeraki Boulders ($40).

Peninsula Mountain Bikes will drive you out to the high point of the Otago Peninsula, where you then bike back to the city via a scenic route.

Places to Stay

As well as the following places to stay in Dunedin, there are a few places on the Otago Peninsula; they're listed in the Otago Peninsula section.

Camping & Cabins The *Tahuna Park Seaside Camp* (☎ 455 4690) is by the beach, near the showgrounds at St Kilda. You can get there on a St Kilda bus. Sites cost $8 per person, powered sites are $16.50 for two. There is a variety of cabins from $26 for two in the simplest ones to $42 for two in the best ones.

At the *Aaron Lodge Motor Camp* (☎ 476 4725) at 162 Kaikorai Valley Rd, sites cost $15.50 for two ($17 with power). Cabins are $27 to $30 for two, and blankets and utensils are available for hire. They also have tourist flats at $50 for two. You can get there on a Bradford bus, and the Brockville bus also goes nearby on some runs.

The *Leith Valley Touring Park* (☎ 467 9936) is at 103 Malvern St, Woodhaugh. Powered sites are $8.50 per person; there are on-site caravans which cost $12; and there is the basic campsite fee – you supply your bedding but everything else is provided.

The *Farmlands Caravan Park* (☎ 482 2730) is on Waitati Valley Rd, 13 km north of Dunedin off SH 1. There are no tent sites, caravan sites are $8 per person, cabins cost $26 for two, and on-site caravans cost $26 for two. There's an adventure playground with pony rides, a flying fox and farm animals.

The *Brighton Motor Camp* (☎ 481 1404) is at 1044 Brighton Rd, Brighton, about 10 km south of Dunedin. The cost is $7.50 per person in tent or powered sites, on-site caravans are $27 for two, and there are boats available for hire.

Hostels The *Stafford Gables YHA Hostel* (☎ 474 1919) is at 71 Stafford St, only about a five minute walk from the CPO. It's a very elegant and sprawling old building, once used as a private hotel before being converted to a YHA hostel. The cost is $14 for a bed in a dorm room, or $16 per person in twins/doubles. There are good laundry facilities here, and cheap meals are available in the evening all year round ($6 upwards, guests only); order the good value $5 continental breakfast the evening before. The hostel rents out 10-speed bikes ($15 per day) and books tours of the Otago Peninsula. The hostel and office are open all day.

At 296 High St there is *Chalet Backpackers* (☎ 479 2075) where share rooms are $14.50, singles $25, twins $17 and doubles $18 per person. It is both centrally heated and located, which is a big plus, however this place is austere. It was purpose-built in the 1930s as a hospital, and looks and smells like one.

The *Elm Lodge* (☎ 474 1872) at 74 Elm Row, 10 minutes uphill (five back down) from the Octagon, is a backpackers situated in a fine old family home, with a smaller, homely atmosphere. It costs $13 in dorm rooms and $15 in twin/double rooms. There's free pick-up from central locations, and the lodge rents out bicycles. Despite its central location, Elm Lodge has great harbour views. This is a great backpackers, made such a success by Brian, Lesley and Dave. They pick up and drop off visitors (but within reason) and often look for another hostel if theirs is full.

In one of Dunedin's old stately homes is *Manor House International Backpackers* (☎ 477 0484; fax 477 8145) at 28 Manor Place, where dorms are $13 to $14, twins $15 and singles $17.50 per person; tent sites are $8. The management is very helpful and they operate a courtesy vehicle.

Right in the centre of Dunedin is *Penguin Palace Backpackers*, formerly Pavlova Backpackers (☎ 479 2175; fax same) on the corner of Rattray and Vogel Sts, a city-style hostel with accommodation for 60 people for $13.50 in dorms or $15 in double or twin rooms. You can't miss it – the outside is painted bright lavender and green! It's very close to various attractions including the brewery and the chocolate factory. It was a bit run down when we were there but the new owners assured us that there were plans to fix it up, including the building of a decent common area upstairs. Bikes are available for hire at $18 per day.

The *YMCA* (☎ 477 9555) at 54 Moray Place, just off the Octagon, is also very centrally located. It generally caters for permanents, but will take casuals when there's room. It's shared accommodation – six people to a flat in singles and doubles, sharing a lounge and kitchen. The nightly cost is $14/22 for one/two people if you use your own bedding, or $16/24 with sheets supplied (blankets are free). There's also a weekly rate of $90 per person. The Y takes in both men and women, and doesn't segregate them. The *YWCA*, taking only women, is just across the road.

Guesthouses The *Sahara Guesthouse & Motel* (☎ 477 6662) is at 619 George St, quite close to the university. Singles/doubles cost $45/69, including breakfast, and there are some motel units for $69 for two.

At *Magnolia House* (☎ 467 5999), a Victorian villa on Grendon St, B&B costs $40/65 for singles/doubles. It's a very pleasant place but all bookings must be made by phone – don't just turn up – and it's strictly non-smoking. One place recommended by readers is *Alvand House* (☎ 477 7379) at 3 Union St (off George St). All rooms have colour TV, tea and coffee making facilities, electric blankets and radio clock and cost $45 for a single or $65 for a double or twin ($15 for each extra person).

Motels There are a number of moderately priced motels along Musselburgh Rise, on the Otago Peninsula side of town. They include the *Arcadian Motel* (☎ 455 0992) at Nos 85-89, the *Chequers Motel* (☎ 455 0778) at No 119, and the *Bayfield Motel* (☎ 455 0756) at No 210. Double rooms cost around $55 to $60 at each of these places.

Others to try include the *Aaron Lodge Motel* (see Camping & Cabins) and the *Sahara Motel* (see Guesthouses). The *Dunedin Motel* (☎ 477 7692) at 624 George St has double rooms from $70. The *Argyle Court Motel* (☎ 477 5129) on the corner of Duke and George Sts is slightly cheaper, as is the *St Kilda Motel* (☎ 455 1151) on the corner of Victoria Rd and Queens Drive. There are plenty of other motels (see the free publication *Focus on Dunedin* for a fuller listing).

Hotels Hotels in the relatively cheap bracket in Dunedin include the small *Hotel Branson* (formerly O'Brien's Hotel, ☎ 477 8411) at 91 St Andrew St. Single/double rooms cost $25/50, although they may sometimes have special deals. Breakfast is an extra $5 (continental) or $10 (cooked) and cheap bistro meals are also available. The *Wharf Hotel* (☎ 477 1233) at 25 Fryatt St offers rooms for $35/50 for singles/twins, the B&B rate is $40 for one, and dinner is an extra $5.

The *Beach Hotel* (☎ 455 4642) on the corner of Prince Albert and Victoria Rds at St Kilda, has single/double rooms with private facilities for $36/50. *Wains Boutique Hotel* (☎ 477 9283) at 310 Princes St is a great-looking old place close to the town centre, with B&B at $60/75 for singles/doubles. Out at Port Chalmers, *Chicks Hotel* (☎ 472 8736) at 2 Mount St is a classic old stone building with B&B at $25 per person.

The solid, reliable, old-fashioned and central *Leviathan Hotel* (☎ 477 3160) on the corner of Cumberland and High Sts, opposite the railway station, is a Dunedin landmark. In budget rooms singles/twins are $45/50, the standard rate is $65/69, and the studio units are $79 for one or two persons (all rooms have bathrooms); there are also motel units for $76.

Right up at the top of the Dunedin hotel list are the *Quality Inn Dunedin* (☎ 477 6784) on Upper Moray Place and the *Southern Cross* (☎ 477 0752), with its excellent DeliCafe, at 118 High St. Both start from the high side of $125 and both are centrally located. Costing about the same is *Cargill's Motor Inn* (☎ 477 7983) at 678 George St.

Places to Eat
Dunedin's a surprisingly good place for eating out in just about all categories. There is plenty of restaurant and dining information available from the Visitor Centre. The centre also has free leaflets on restaurants and on places which are open on Sunday.

Snacks & Fast Food Dunedin has a excellent selection of places for a sandwich or for lunch, many located along George St and around Moray Place. *Ma Cuisine*, a wholefood cafe with quiches, spinach pies, sandwiches and so on is at 102 Princes St. A mixed salad costs $4 and there are also inexpensive rolls and vegetarian pizzas. Just around the corner is the spacious *Purple Sage*, at 111 Moray St, equally well priced and also a relaxed place to sit and eat.

You might also try the *Sidewalk Cafe* at 480 Moray Place. It's open from 10 am to 4 pm daily and on Wednesday to Saturday nights for dinner. The cafe has an excellent selection of sandwiches and light meals and it's a popular and pleasant place to eat them. *Potpourri* at 97 Stuart St is another good wholefood place open for lunch Monday to Saturday, and also for dinner from 5 to 8 pm Monday to Friday. It has salads, tacos, quiche and other light meals. The sister cafe to Potpourri is *Mega Bite* (formerly The Larder) at 388 George St; its menu is similar.

There are several other sandwich or light lunch possibilities in George St. The *Upper Crust* at 263 George St is open for lunch every day except Sunday and has salads, sandwiches and baked food. A bit further down, at 351 George St, is *Partners*. It's a bit more expensive than some of the other lunch-time cafes but the food is excellent. You can have a big bowl of soup with French bread, open sandwiches, larger meals and diet-blowing (but superb-tasting) cakes.

There's *Epi d'Or*, a French bakery at 430 George St, and at the other end of the George St culinary spectrum is the *McDonald's*, just north of The Octagon. *Stewarts Coffee House*, downstairs at 12 Lower Octagon, has cheap sandwiches and excellent coffee. The *Bakers Oven* at 11 Lower Octagon is a big bakery. Good food is also available from *Botanica*, in the Botanic Gardens, which is open from 10 am to 4 pm daily. It receives many good comments about its service and food.

The *DeliCafe* on the ground floor of the Southern Cross Hotel at 118 High St is open 24 hours. *Doug's Diner* at 116 Lower Rattray

St is a straightforward place for grilled food and takeaways but it opens early and closes late. If you want to start the day with bacon and eggs and finish it with a late-night burger then this is the place.

For a sumptuous breakfast, such as a ham, cheese and pineapple Spanish omelette ($6.50) and good cafelatte ($2.50) go to *Capers*, on George St opposite Knox Church. On the subject of coffee – *Out on a Limb Cafe*, 56 Princes St, has a great selection of coffee, served with a smile. Top of the cafe tree is *Parisettes*, 368 Moray Place, where they seem to have got the cafe/eatery mix just right; they have an extensive blackboard menu.

Pub Food The *Albert Arms Hotel*, on the corner of George and London Sts, is open every day for good bistro meals – steak and seafood – for under $10. And there's the *Bowling Green* at 71 Frederick St, open for lunch from Monday to Saturday and for dinner on Friday, Saturday and Sunday.

The *Exchange Brasserie* in the Southern Cross Hotel, corner of Princes and High Sts, has fish, chicken, seafood and vegetarian dishes; expect to pay $12 on for a main meal. The brasserie is open from 11 am to 10 pm for bar meals.

Well north at 370 George St, *Foxy's Cafe* in the Robbie Burns Hotel has pub food regulars for $15 to $18 or cheaper dishes like curried lamb or pasta. Downstairs there is the *Cafe Society Wine Bar*. The *Leviathan Hotel* has a fully licensed restaurant which is open every day.

The *Captain Cook* is a popular student pub and has good food upstairs – if you can get in the door – and also a beer garden. It's round the corner from the Robbie Burns at the intersection of Albany and Great Kings Sts.

Restaurants *Palms Cafe* on the corner of Dowling and Lower High Sts is a very pleasant and deservedly popular place, open from 6 to 9 pm Wednesday to Sunday. It has good salads, pastas for $8 to $10, main courses for

$10 to $14 and desserts for around $5; it is also non-smoking. *Tapestry*, 366 Moray Place and right next to Parisettes, has a good international menu which includes vegetarian dishes. Entrees start at $5, mains are from $16, and desserts from $5; it is BYO.

At *Santa Fe*, 629 George St, you can get great Mexican and Cajun food – chicken and pork ribs, jambalaya gumbo, enchiladas and tacos. A great replacement for the former Los Gatos which rated as one of the most authentic Mexican establishments in New Zealand. The restaurant is open from 6 pm Wednesday to Monday; main courses cost from around $12 and up. More Cajun food can be had at *Bagdad Cafe*, 401 Moray Place from Wednesday to Sunday, 6 pm until late.

For Italian go to the *Peppermill Italian Restaurant*, on the west corner of The Octagon and Stuart St. All the faves are here including antipasti, pasta, and a variety of sauces and salads. Dessert is, of course, delicious cassata. Italian in name but not necessarily food is *Rogano's Seafood Restaurant*, upstairs at 388 Princes St. They feature fresh daily market specials, a full range of seafood dishes, and they are BYO.

Casa Italia Ristorante, in the Municipal Building on The Octagon just west of the Dunedin Visitor Centre, is an elegant restaurant with fine cuisine, and priced accordingly.

Two recommended Indian eateries are *Prasad's Place*, 466 George St, and *Little India*, 82 St Andrew St. At the latter try the nargisi kofta (finely shredded lamb wrapped around an egg and deep fried) sautéed in onions and fresh spices (to make a thick gravy).

Steak lovers head to the *Huntsman Chargrill Steak House*, 311 George St – can't go wrong with 20 steak dishes to choose from. More steak (and other dishes) are on offer at *Bentley's Restaurant & Bar*, near the corner of Cumberland and St Andrew Sts.

If you're looking for an expensive night out at the best Dunedin has to offer then two places to try are *Blades*, way up at 450 George St, or *95 Filleul* at 95 Filleul St. The latter has green lipped mussels in spicy sauce

OTAGO

for $6.50, ratatouille and potato gnocci for $17.50.

Entertainment

Pubs Dunedin is a drinkers' town and there are plenty of places to slake that thirst. They include several of the places mentioned under Pub Food, such as the *Provincial*, *Albert Arms* or the *Captain Cook*.

In particular, the Captain Cook, on the corner of Albany and Great Kings Sts near the university, is a very popular student pub. It gets so crowded that you can hardly get in the door sometimes. There's a pleasant garden bar which is great in summer.

Pubs with music, particularly in the evenings, include the *Beach Hotel* at St Kilda, the Albert Arms, the Provincial, *Foxy's Cafe* at the Robbie Burns and a great many others. Check the *Otago Daily Times* on Sunday for what's on.

Other Entertainment Dunedin has a number of theatres including the professional Fortune Theatre and several amateur companies. The New Edinburgh Folk Club meets at 6 Carroll St at 8 pm on Friday. Dunedin is the capital of New Zealand's live music scene (see The Dunedin Sound below) and a number of pubs specialise in featuring new as well as proven acts.

Getting There & Away

Air Air New Zealand's office (☎ 477 5769) is on the corner of Princes St and the Upper Octagon. There are daily direct flights to Auckland, Christchurch, Invercargill and Wellington, with connections to other centres. Ansett New Zealand (☎ 479 2146) at 1 George St (on The Octagon) has flights to Auckland, Christchurch, Wellington and Invercargill. At present, there is no flight link to Central Otago.

Bus InterCity buses depart from the Inter-City Travel Centre (☎ 477 8860) on Cumberland St, only a couple of blocks from The Octagon and a short distance from the railway station. It's a fine example of art deco architecture. They have services north to Christchurch, south to Invercargill and west to Queenstown, Te Anau, Milford Sound,

---

The Dunedin Sound

Dunedin has achieved the status of being the most active place in the New Zealand music scene. In the past dozen or so years Dunedin has produced a number of successful bands, many of which have achieved international recognition. A lot of this has had to do with the success of the Flying Nun (FN) record label and their successful promotion of FN overseas. Although the label has now moved to Auckland, it has been replaced with the Port Chalmers-based Xpressway label.

In fact, so many of the Dunedin 'gig goers' have affiliations with musicians that it led one American observer to say of Dunedin that '...it's just a town full of band members'. A lot of really good bands evolve in this town, make an album which receives a small local following, perhaps get recognition overseas, then disband. As soon as they have gone the vast resource pool of student musicians and songwriters in town throws up another band to fill the void.

Some North Americans equate Dunedin, a relatively small city, with Athens, Georgia, home of the B-52s and now-mega band REM. Bands from Dunedin which have been or are popular on the college airwaves in the USA are the Verlaines, Straitjacket Fits, The Clean and perhaps most popular of all, The Chills.

Ten years of Flying Nun and a large chunk of the Dunedin band scene was celebrated with the release of *Getting Older*, which featured the four bands mentioned earlier, along with other well-known acts such as the Able Tasmans, the Bats, and the Headless Chickens. Another compilation album, *Pink Flying Saucers over the Southern Alps* covered a more recent selection and included the Dunedin's 3Ds, which in 1993 were getting good press overseas.

So while in Dunedin head out to one of the pubs where a band is playing – there are a number of them. Maybe one of next year's super groups will be playing, and you saw them for the price of a couple of beers. ■

Wanaka and the West Coast. There are several buses daily to Christchurch and Invercargill. Travel times from Dunedin are six hours to Christchurch, 3½ hours to Invercargill, six hours to Queenstown, six hours to Te Anau and five hours to Wanaka.

Mt Cook Landline (☎ 474 0674; fax 479 0298) at 205 St Andrew St, has daily services up and down the east coast of the South Island, all the way from Picton to Invercargill via Christchurch and Dunedin. It takes 15½ hours from end to end.

Nationwide Shuttles & Buses (☎ 474 3300) is at 215 Gloucester St. They have a daily service from Dunedin to Christchurch. Some of their services pass through Central Otago.

Train Stuart St, which runs through The Octagon, continues down to the railway station on Anzac Ave. The Christchurch-Invercargill train passes through in both directions every day except Saturday. The train to Christchurch takes about six hours, to Invercargill about 3½ hours. The railway station is a local landmark, an example of Dunedin architecture at its most imposing and confident. Tickets are sold at the railway station and the Dunedin Visitor Centre. The InterIslander can also be booked at the Visitor Centre.

Hitching To hitch northwards you can get a Pinehill bus to the beginning of the motorway or a Normandy bus to the Gardens from The Octagon, or walk there in about 30 or 40 minutes. You can get an InterCity Cherry Farm bus to Waitati and avoid the city and the motorway. Hitching south, you can take an Otago Road Services bus from Lower High St (opposite Queens Gardens) to Fairfield. Alternatively take an InterCity bus to Mosgiel, alighting at the turn-off or, if it's a long-distance bus, at East Taieri.

Getting Around

To/From the Airport Five companies offer door-to-door service to and from the airport. Dunedin Airport Shuttle (☎ 477 7777), Airporter Express (☎ 476 2519) and Ritchies

Coachlines (☎ 477 9238) cost around $10 per person, The 31-km trip to the airport takes around 40 minutes. If you have a long wait at the airport you can eat at the airport restaurant, which is better than most.

Bus City buses leave from The Octagon area and suburban buses leave from Cumberland St (behind Centre City). The local buses are operated by the Dunedin City Council. Unlike most places in New Zealand, they run every day including weekends, although buses are more frequent during the week.

Bicycle Rental You can rent bicycles from Recycled Recreation (☎ 474 1211) at 77 Lower Stuart St. Little Rainbow Bikes (☎ 474 3300), operating from the Visitor Centre, also rents bicycles. From Dunedin down the peninsula all the way to the albatross colony is a good ride.

OTAGO PENINSULA

The Otago Peninsula is one of the most significant wildlife areas in the South Island. You can spend a pleasant afternoon or longer tripping around this peninsula. Stops can be made at Glenfalloch Woodland Gardens, the Trust Bank (Portobello) Aquarium and Marine Biological Station, and Otakou Marae where there's a Maori church and meeting house with a small museum. There are many other historical sites, walkways, natural formations, and so on dotted around the peninsula, making for an interesting trip. The *Otago Peninsula* brochure and map, published by the Otago Peninsula Trust and available at the Dunedin Visitor Centre for 90c, lists 41 different things to see and do on the peninsula.

Glenfalloch Woodland Gardens

About nine km from Dunedin, the Glenfalloch Woodland Gardens are noted for their rhododendrons and azaleas and for domestic birds which wander freely in the grounds. The gardens are open from 9.30 am until dusk every day. There's a restaurant and tearoom there too (the restaurant is open

OTAGO

from Tuesday to Saturday). You can get to Glenfalloch on a Portobello bus.

Larnach Castle

The highlight of the peninsula is probably Larnach Castle (☎ 476 1616), a conglomeration of architectural styles and fantasies on the highest point of the peninsula. It's open to the public from 9 am to 5 pm (longer from December to May). Built by J W M Larnach in 1871, it is said to be the most expensive house in the southern hemisphere – its construction cost over $10 million by today's standards. Its owner, a politician, committed suicide in a Parliament House committee room in 1898.

You can get to Larnach Castle, 15 km from central Dunedin, by taking the Newtons Peninsula bus to Company Bay, from where it's a four km uphill walk, or you can come on a tour from Dunedin. Entry to the castle and gardens is $9.50 (children $3.50), or $4 (children $1) to visit only the gardens, stable and ballroom. A cafe in the castle ballroom does Devonshire teas or light lunches. Accommodation is also available (see Places to Stay).

Taiaroa Head & Albatross Colony

At the end of the peninsula is Taiaroa Head where the only northern royal albatross colony in the world close to human habitation can be seen. Public access is allowed only by purchasing a permit for $15 (children $7) from the Visitor Centre in Dunedin, entitling you to a one-hour conducted visit. Visiting hours are from 8.30 am to 5 pm daily except on weekends, when it's open from 9 am to 5 pm. Access to the colony is closed between 31 August and 24 November but this varies.

To get to the albatross colony, catch a Newtons Peninsula bus to Portobello, then walk or hitch the remaining 11 km through beautiful scenery to the colony. Otherwise you can come on any of several tours from Dunedin. There is an element of chance in what you will see – in calm weather it's unlikely you'll see an albatross flying. The later you get there the more likely you are to

see them fly as there's usually more wind later in the day.

The northern royal albatross is the largest sea bird in the world with a wingspan which can exceed three metres. Because of their great size, these birds nest only where there are the high winds and favourable updrafts that they need to get airborne. The birds arrive at the nesting site in September, court and mate in October, lay eggs in November, then incubate the eggs until January when the chicks hatch. Between March and September the chicks are left alone at the colony while their parents collect food for them, returning only for feeding. By September the fully grown chicks depart, and the cycle begins again.

The albatross tour is extremely popular and bus tour operators often snap up places in advance, leaving independent travellers (many who have hitched out here) to be turned away. The moral: book in advance (☎ 478 0499, 474 3300). The Monarch cruise is a good alternative way of seeing these birds.

Fort Taiaroa

A tour to the historic 6-inch Armstrong Disappearing Gun at Fort Taiaroa can be combined with the visit to the albatross colony (an extra $3 if you have a ticket to the albatross colony).

Penguins & Seals

Penguins and seals are also to be found on the peninsula. The local yellow-eyed penguin (hoiho), the rarest penguin on earth, can be seen at close quarters here. To visit the penguin and seal colonies you have three options.

You can go up to Penguin Place on Harington Point Rd, off Portobello Rd. You need to obtain a key to the gate just past the albatross colony from McGrouther's Farm ($4 and a key deposit to be paid). This leads to a colony of yellow-eyed penguins which you view from a distance; bring binoculars.

The other two ways are connected to a unique wildlife conservation project. At McGrouther's Farm, just off the Portobello

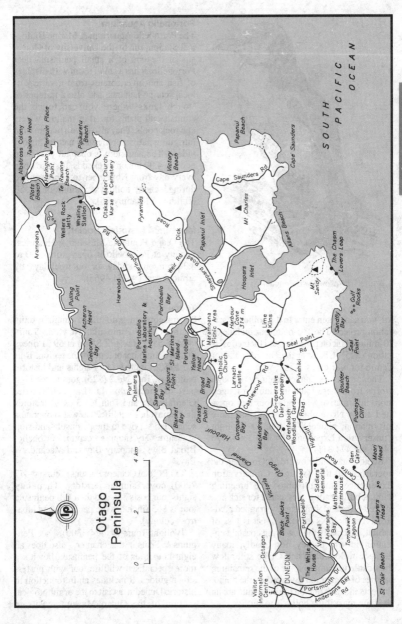

SOUTH PACIFIC OCEAN

Otago Peninsula

Albatross Colony
Taiaroa Head
Penguin Place
Pilots Beach
Harington Point
Pipikaretu Beach
Te Rauone Beach
Weilers Rock Jetty
Whaling Station
Aramoana
Otakou Maori Church, Marae & Cemetery
Victory Beach
Papanui Beach
Cape Saunders
Cape Saunders Rd
Mt Charles
Pulling Point
Acheron Head
Harwood
Pyramids
Weir Rd
Harington Point Rd
Dick Road
Shepperds Road
Papanui Inlet
Allans Beach
Hoopers Inlet
Deborah Bay
Portobello Bay
Mt Sandy
The Chasm
Lovers Leap
Port Chalmers
Portobello Marine Laboratory & Aquarium
St Martins Island
Kilgours Point
Portobello
Yellow Head
Maramoana Picnic Area
Harbour Cone 314 m
Lime Kilns
Gull Rocks
Sandfly Bay
Seal Point
Seal Point Rd
Seal Point
Sawyers Bay
Broad Bay
Catholic Church
Larnach Castle
Castlewood
Pukehiki
Boulder Beach
Blanket Bay
Grassy Point
Company Bay
MacAndrew Bay
Glenfalloch Woodland Gardens
Co-operative Dairy Company
Road
Highcliff Road
Pudneys Cliff
Otago Harbour Channel
Victoria Road
Portobello Road
Centre Road
Highcliff
Glen Cairn
Maori Head
Black Jacks Point
Soldiers' Memorial
Mathieson Farmhouse
Lawyers Head
Vauxhall
Andersons Bay
Tomahawk Lagoon
Visitor Information Centre
Octagon
DUNEDIN
The White House
Portsmouth Dr
Andersons Bay Rd
St Clair Beach
St Kilda Beach

0   2   4 km

Yellow-eyed Penguin

Rd, you can obtain entry to the hoiho conservation project. The 1½-hour tour includes a 20-minute talk on penguins and their conservation ($15). Check at the Dunedin Visitor Centre for tour times.

The project is funded entirely through profits from these tours including a longer, more informative $46 eight-hour tour operated from November to May. For more information, phone Wild South's Twilight Conservation Experience (☎ 474 3300, 476 1443; fax 474 3111).

Scott Clarke and Howard McGrouther, the operators of the Twilight Conservation Experience have replanted the breeding habitat, built nesting sites, cared for sick and injured birds and, importantly, trapped predators. The hoiho's greatest threat is loss of habitat, especially the low lying coastal vegetation in which they nest. Sadly, many farmers in Southland and Otago still allow their cattle to trample some of the remaining patches of vegetation favoured by the hoiho. Projects like this one on the peninsula are an absolute must if the hoiho is to survive.

Portobello Aquarium
The Portobello Aquarium & Marine Biological Station, run by the University of Otago, sits at the end of a small peninsula near Portobello. It has a small room with displays of fish and invertebrates from a variety of local marine habitats, and also a number of 'touch tanks' where you can touch the animals and plants found in shallow waters and rock pools. They also have a tuatara (that intriguing native reptile) and natural history videos. The aquarium is open all year from noon to 4.30 pm on weekends. It's also open every day from November to February and during school holidays. Admission is $3 (children $1, family $6).

Museum & Historical Society
The Otago Peninsula Museum & Historical Society at Portobello is open from 1.30 to 4.30 pm on Sunday, or on weekdays by arrangement (☎ 454 4965).

Tours
Several companies do full-day minibus tours of the Otago Peninsula. Newtons Tours (☎ 477 5577; fax 477 8147) at 595 Princes St, have a number of tours in the region. Tour No 1 ($20) includes city sights and historic buildings, Tour No 2 ($25) goes to the high part of the peninsula (Larnach Castle, Glenfalloch), and Tour No 3 ($39) features the peninsula's wildlife. They also operate a scheduled service to the peninsula and stop at Centre City shopping centre, Portobello, Broad Bay, Company Bay and Macandrew Bay.

T.O.P (Total Outdoor Pursuits) Tours (☎ 477 7200) cover similar territory. Their city sights tour costs $25 and their full peninsula tour is $65 (includes the penguins and albatross colony).

Twilight Tours (☎ 474 3300) – see Penguins & Seals in this chapter – also does an eight-hour tour of the peninsula but it's a more specialised wildlife tour with professional guides. It includes an introduction to historic Dunedin, a visit to the ornithological section of the Otago Museum, visits to beaches where many bird species can be seen, seal and shag colonies, the albatross colony (entry optional) and the hoiho conservation area. The cost is $46, but students and hostellers receive a substantial discount.

Places to Stay & Eat

There are a few places where you can stay on the peninsula. The *Portobello Village Tourist Park* (☎ 478 0359) is at 27 Hereweka St in Portobello township. Tent sites are $7.50 per person and powered sites $16 for two.

At *McGrouther's Farm* (☎ 780-286) you can stay in former army barracks which have everything you need, including a lounge and fully equipped kitchen; you only need supply your bedding and food. The cost is $7 per person.

The *Larnach Castle Lodge* (☎ 476 1616) is on the grounds of the famous castle. Bedrooms in the historic stable building cost $30

for two, and hotel-style rooms cost $49 for two (or $74 with private facilities).

There are two recommended restaurants (by happy readers): *Harbour Lights Seafood Restarant*, 494 Portobello Rd, Macandrew Bay is moderately priced and has good tableside views; *1908 Cafe on Portobello* serves a variety of seafood – blue cod, bay clams, mussels and other delights such as 'Kid Curry & the Poppadom Kid' and 'Honey, You're Nuts'. It is not cheap.

At the historic *Glenfalloch Homestead*, 430 Portobello Rd, there is a restaurant which has a full à la carte menu.

Getting Around

As well as the tour bus services already mentioned under Tours, Newtons Coach Tours (☎ 477 5577) run buses up as far as Portobello.

The peninsula is very easy to cycle around, but be careful on blind corners on Portobello Rd.

OTAGO

Southland

Southland is a captivating place, with eye-catching scenery and an abundance of flora & fauna, which is too often left out of travellers' itineraries. Many make it to the north-western reaches of Milford Sound and Te Anau in one or two-day trips from Queenstown and get no further into this mountainous province. They have definitely missed out as some of New Zealand's best scenery is found east of Invercargill.

Southland has a predominantly Scottish heritage and many of its inhabitants speak with a distinctive rolling of their 'r's. There is also a considerable Maori and Islander population, and maraes are being re-established throughout the region.

The weather is a bit of a deterrent but if you come prepared for it, you'll enjoy the experience much more. There are three main routes into Southland; via Queenstown to Fiordland, from Queenstown down SH 6 to Invercargill, or from Dunedin to Invercargill on SH 1. All three, however, miss out spectacular scenery, so some more local routes with far more to see along them have been described in this chapter.

Information

All telephone numbers in the South Island have an 03 prefix if you are calling them from a long distance (even within the region).

Te Anau & Fiordland

Te Anau is the jumping-off point for visits to the Fiordland National Park and World Heritage area and for some of New Zealand's most famous walks, including the best known of the lot, the Milford Track. Information on these walks can be found in the Outdoor Activities chapter. The two main towns in the area are Te Anau and, a little to the south, Manapouri on Lake Manapouri.

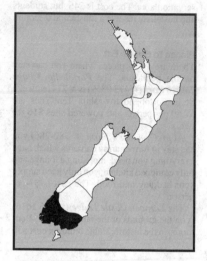

TE ANAU

Lake Te Anau, and its three arms which penetrate into the mountainous forested shore, was gouged out by a huge glacier. It is 417 metres at its deepest, and is New Zealand's second largest lake after Taupo in the North Island; it is 53 km long and 10 km across at its widest. The lake takes its name from the caves discovered on its western shore, Te Ana-au or 'cave of rushing water'.

The township is beautifully situated on the shores of Lake Te Anau, and is a bit like a smaller, low-key version of Queenstown. Like Queenstown there are all manner of activities and trips here to keep you busy, although for many visitors the town is just a jumping-off point for trips to Milford and the Milford Track.

Orientation

Most of the activities and businesses in Te Anau are found along two streets – Te Anau Terrace, which runs along the lakefront, and Milford Rd.

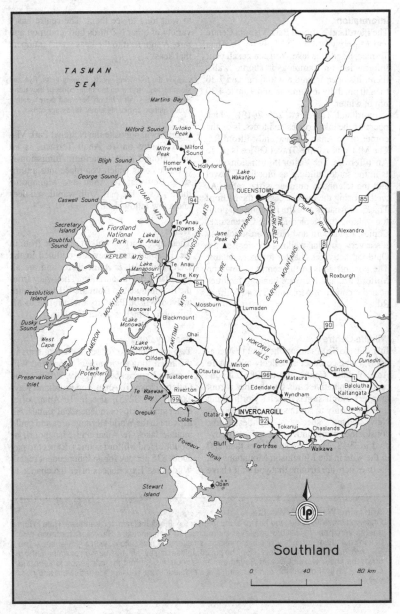

SOUTHLAND

TASMAN SEA

Martins Bay

Milford Sound
Tutoko Peak
Mitre Peak
Milford Sound
Bligh Sound
Homer Tunnel
Hollyford
Lake Wakatipu
George Sound

Caswell Sound

Secretary Island
Fiordland National Park
Lake Te Anau
Te Anau Downs
Jane Peak
QUEENSTOWN
THE REMARKABLES
Clutha River
Alexandra

Doubtful Sound
KEPLER MTS
Lake Manapouri
Te Anau
The Key
Roxburgh

Resolution Island
Manapouri
Monowai
Lake Monowai
Blackmount
Mossburn
Lumsden
GARVIE MOUNTAINS

Dusky Sound
CAMERON MOUNTAINS
TAKITIMU MTS
Ohai
HOKONUI HILLS
Gore

West Cape
Lake Hauroko
Winton
To Dunedin

Preservation Inlet
Lake Poteriteri
Clifden
Te Waewae
Otautau
Mataura
Clinton

Te Waewae Bay
Tuatapere
Riverton
Edendale
Wyndham
Balclutha
Kaitangata

Orepuki
Colac
Otatara
INVERCARGILL
Tokanui
Owaka

Bluff
Fortrose
Chaslands
Waikawa

Foveaux Strait

Stewart Island
Oban

Southland

0   40   80 km

SOUTHLAND

Information

The Fiordland National Park Visitors Centre and Museum (☎ 249 7921) is on Te Anau Terrace, beside the lake. You can get all your information on tramping or shorter walks there. It's open from 8 am to 6 pm and 7.30 to 9.30 pm daily in summer, and 9 am to 4.30 pm in winter.

Fiordland Travel (☎ 249 7419), which operates the lake cruises and tours, is on the corner of Te Anau Terrace and Milford Rd. The Mt Cook Airline Travel Office is on Te Anau Terrace. The Visitor Information office is in the same building as Fiordland Travel and the telephone number is the same. As well as being the main access to the Milford Track, Te Anau is also the jumping-off point for walking the Kepler, Dusky, Greenstone, Caples, Routeburn and Hollyford tracks, so it's a very popular walking locale. See the Outdoor Activities chapter for more details. The post office is in the centre of town on Milford Rd, and there are banking facilities near the corner of Mokonui St and Milford Rd.

Wildlife Centre

Just outside Te Anau, on the road to Manapouri, is the compact and nicely laid out Te Anau Wildlife Centre, run by DOC. It concentrates on native birds but also has a trout hatchery. Admission is free. It's worth taking time out if only to see the rare takahe, one of New Zealand's species of flightless birds, considered extinct until a colony was discovered in 1948. There are still fewer than 200 in the wild in the Murchison Mountains but the ones here are so tame that you won't have

to wait long to see them. The centre has a variety of other NZ birds both common and rare. A sign next to the keas warns trampers that keas:

...enjoy the following sports: ripping tents, flys and sleeping bags, trying on tramping boots (if they don't fit they usually cut a bit off here and there), eating your supplies, criticising alpine landscape artists...

In the town, opposite the National Park Visitors Centre on Te Anau Terrace, is an underground trout aquarium. Admission is two 50c coins which you place into a turnstile. Between Te Anau and Manapouri there's a wildlife park with wapiti, red deer and a few fallow deer.

Walks

There are plenty of walks to choose from in the Te Anau area; they are outlined in the DOC pamphlet *Te Anau Walks* and are all less than a day in duration. They vary from the five-minute trip from the Visitors Centre to Ivon Wilson Park, to a return trip to Mt Luxmore, which is about 10 hours.

Sea Kayaking

Two companies offer sea kayaking trips in this interesting environment. Fiordland Wilderness Experiences (☎ 249 7700) at 66 Quintin Drive, Te Anau, and Fiordland Kayaks (☎ 249 8275), also in Te Anau, offer either guided trips or independent rentals. All trips are in the World Heritage area and could include lakes Te Anau and Manapouri, or Doubtful and Milford sounds. Expect to pay about $35 per day for an independent rental. Wilderness Experiences offer the chance to

---

Annoying Weather & Wildlife

Once you leave Te Anau, you hit two of the menaces of Fiordland: rain and sandflies. Rain in this area is very heavy – Milford gets over six metres (20 feet) annually! Sandflies, for those who haven't met them, are nasty little biting insects, smaller than mosquitoes, with a similar bite – you will see clouds of them at Milford. Don't be put off sightseeing by rain, the masses of water hurtling down the sheer walls of Milford Sound are an incredible sight and the rain tends to keep the sandflies away. For walking and tramping it is a different story, causing flooded rivers and poor visibility. ■

paddle to the start of the Kepler Track for $18 per person. Both could arrange for a paddling prelude to the Milford Track or a trip into the silence of Doubtful Sound. One company offers the chance to see '...virginal rainforest'; here, virgin or not, the bush, lakes, waterfalls and fiords will overwhelm.

Te Ana-au Caves

The Te Ana-au caves are not old geologically, but they possess an energy that is immediately apparent when you go underground. They are located on the Tunnel Burn stream at the foot of and below the Murchison Mountains, which are the last refuge of the takahe.

These caves, which gave the lake and the town its name, were mentioned in Maori legends and rediscovered in 1948 by Lawson Burrows who had searched for them for several years. On the shores of the lake and accessible only by boat, the 200 metres of active cave system is magical with waterfalls, whirlpools and glow-worm grotto in the inner reaches. In order to get into the heart of the caves a system of walkways and two short punt journeys are used.

The 2½-hour trip costs $31 (children $10); departures are at 2 and 8.15 pm. Book at Fiordland Travel, on the corner of Te Anau Terrace and Milford Rd.

Cruises & Trips

There are all manner of cruises and trips from Te Anau. Fiordland Travel has trips to Milford Sound, Doubtful Sound, the Manapouri Power Station and the Te Ana-au Caves, all of which can be taken from Te Anau. See the following sections on Milford Sound and Manapouri for details of the trips in these areas.

Cruises on Lake Te Anau are very popular. One of the cheaper trips goes to the incredible Te Ana-au Caves (described earlier in this section).

You can also go to Glade House at the northern end of the lake, the starting point for the Milford Track. From November to April, when the Milford track is open, Fiord-

land Travel boats run from Te Anau Downs to Glade House for the Milford Track trampers. They run at 2 pm every day during the season, and as advertised at 8.30 am during school holidays. You can go on the 2 pm boat only if there is extra space, and you'll have to come straight back if you're not doing the track. However, going on the morning boat gives you about a five-hour stopover – enough time to walk from Glade House to Clinton Forks, the first hut on the Milford track, and be back at Glade House to meet the afternoon boat on its homeward trip.

InterCity buses to Te Anau Downs connect with the 2 pm boat trip but not with the morning trip – you may have to take a taxi. The boat trip costs $37 (children $10). Other boats also go to Glade House.

Discounts are available on Fiordland Travel trips by combining more than one trip. If you do both the Milford Sound and Doubtful Sound trips, the total cost comes to $155 (seasonal as advertised).

Yacht charters and scenic cruises on the lake are also made by Sinbad Cruises (☎ 249 7106) on the gaff ketch *Manuska*, sailing to Glade House for $50 or Brod Bay for $12 ($20 return).

Lakeland Boat Hire/Te Anau Lake Services (☎ 249 7495) goes to Glade House, and also rents out rowing boats, outboard motors, pedal boats, catamarans, canoes or jet skis from a little caravan beside the lake. They also do guided fishing trips on the lake at a cost of $60 per hour for a boat for four people.

Trips 'n Tramps (☎ 249 7081) offers a variety of things to do around Te Anau, including half-day and all-day guided walks, farm visits, photographic safaris, backpackers transport and leisurely Milford Road explorations.

Milford Sound Adventure Tours (☎ 249 7227) has full-day mountain bike trips, beginning from the Homer Tunnel on the road to Milford, descending to the Cleddau Valley and then going on a cruise of the sound. The cost is $75 (children $37.50) including mountain bikes and gear.

There are many interesting things to see

SOUTHLAND

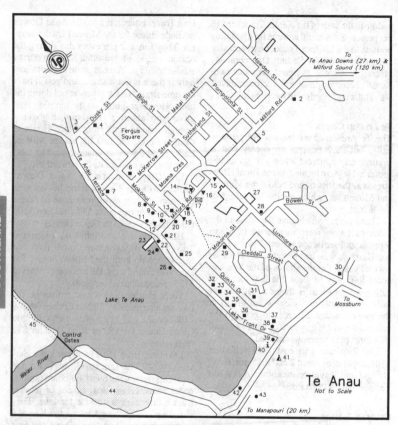

Te Anau
Not to Scale

along the road to Milford. Fiordland Travel has a free map pointing out the many scenic wonders along the route.

Aerial Sightseeing

There are plenty of flightseeing opportunities around Te Anau. Waterwings Airways (☎ 249 7405) has floatplane flights from right off Te Anau Terrace in the town centre. There's a quick zip around the area for $36, a flight to Lake Manapouri and Doubtful Sound for $84, one over the Kepler Track for $66, a day excursion to Queenstown for $108, and to Doubtful Sound for $131.

Waterwings also has a variety of Milford Sound flights including morning and afternoon fly/cruise/fly tours for $195, a coach/cruise/fly tour for about $220, a one-way flight between Milford Sound and Te Anau for $139, a Milford Sound landing flight for $139 (one way, return is $184), or a one-hour flight to Milford Sound without landing at the sound for $154. Children's fares are 60% of adult fares. All the flights can be made either by floatplane or normal plane, and there are other scenic flights from Milford.

Air Fiordland (☎ 249 7505) has short scenic flights from Milford for $46, flights

---

■ PLACES TO STAY

2   Te Anau YHA Hostel
4   Shakespeare House
6   Matai Lodge
7   Mountain View Cabin & Caravan Park
13   Luxmore Resort Hotel
25   THC Te Anau Travelodge
29   Explorer Motel
30   Fiordland Resort Hotel &
     Te Anau Club
31   Aden Motel
32   Edgewater XL Motel
33   Te Anau Backpackers
34   Campbell Autolodge
35   Lakeside Motel
36   Kingsgate Motel
37   Amber Court Motel
41   Te Anau Motor Park

▼ PLACES TO EAT

12   Pop Inn Tearoom & Bakery
13   Baileys & Luxmore Bistro
14   Ming Gardens Restaurant
15   Keplers
16   La Toscana
19   Jailhouse Cafe
25   Henry's Restaurant &
     The Mackinnon Room
41   Jintz Restaurant

OTHER

1   Swimming Pool
3   Public Toilets
5   Police Station
8   Bicycle Hire
9   Trips 'n Tramps
10   Petrol Station
11   Public Toilets
14   InterCity Depot
17   Post Office
18   Milford Sound Adventure Tours
20   Bank of New Zealand
21   Mt Cook Lines Booking Office
22   Fiordland Travel & *Manuska*
23   Lakeland Boat Hire
24   Southern Lakes Helicopters
26   Waterwings Airways
27   Medical Centre
28   Petrol Station
38   Trout Observatory
39   Public Toilets
40   Visitor Information Centre, DOC &
     Museum
42   Wildlife Centre (Takahe Display)
43   Ivon Wilson Park
44   Te Anau Golf Course
45   Kepler Track

---

to Milford Sound from Te Anau for $139 and to Doubtful Sound for $108, or a 1½-hour tour over both sounds and the Fiordland National Park for $230. The trips to Milford include a fly/cruise/fly for $232 and a coach/cruise/fly for $217. Children's fares are 60% of adult fares. The flight to Milford Sound goes over the Milford Track, with views of the amazing drop of the Sutherland Falls and Lake Quill. They can do cheaper scenic flights from Milford as they have a plane based there in summer. There is a big range of flights available, Sutherland Falls, for instance, is $69 for a 25-minute flight. Charters are also available. Hollyford's Martins Bay would be $250 for charter of a plane.

Southern Lakes Helicopters (☎ 249 7167) also has flights around the area. On one combination trip, similar but not as good as the Siberia Experience (see Makarora in the West Coast & Glaciers chapter), you can 'heli-trek-sail' for $85. Southern Lakes take you up to Mt Luxmore, then you walk to Brod Bay (about three hours) and then return to Te Anau by sail on the *Manuska*.

Places to Stay
Camping & Cabins The *Te Anau Motor Park* (☎ 249 7457/7695), opposite the lake just one km from Te Anau on the road to Manapouri, has sites for $8.50 per person ($9 with power). There's also a bunkhouse with beds for $11, standard cabins at $30 (jug, heater, toaster provided), tourist cabins at $38 for two, tourist flats from $49.50, and motel units. It's a large, well-equipped camp with attractive surroundings and a very pleasant atmosphere. Car, van and gear storage is available for trampers. They

provide the Kepler Track Shuttle Service – to the Control Gates it is $5 and return, from the swing bridge is $8. If you're lucky you may see the Southern Lights (Aurora Australis) from this campsite.

The *Mountain View Cabins & Caravan Park* (☎ 249 7462) on Mokonui St has cabins and on-site caravans from $40 for two, but there are no facilities for tent campers. Powered caravan sites cost $9 per person.

About 1.5 km north of town on the Milford Rd is the *Fiordland Holiday Park* (☎ 249 7457). Campsites are $7 for one (power is 50c extra), the one cabin is $32 for two and on-site caravans are $28.

There are many of the basic *DOC campsites* in this region:

Lake Gunn, adjacent SH 94, 81 km north of Te Anau
Cascade Creek, adjacent SH 94, 78 km north of Te Anau
Upper Eglinton, adjacent SH 94, 71 km north of Te Anau
Smithy Creek, adjacent SH 94, 67 km north of Te Anau
Deer Flat, adjacent SH 94, 62 km north of Te Anau
Kiosk Creek, adjacent SH 94, 65 km north of Te Anau
East Branch Eglinton, adjacent SH 94, 56 km north of Te Anau
McKay Creek, adjacent SH 94, 53 km north of Te Anau
Totara Creek, adjacent SH 94, 53 km north of Te Anau
Walker Creek, adjacent SH 94, 49 km north of Te Anau
Boyd Creek, adjacent SH 94, 45 km north of Te Anau
Henry Creek, adjacent SH 94, 25 km north of Te Anau
Ten Mile Bush, adjacent SH 94, 17 km north of Te Anau

Hostels The *Te Anau YHA Hostel* (☎ 249 7847), about 1.5 km out of town on Milford Rd, has room for 40 people. The cost is $15 per night and you can hire camping equipment, leave gear here while you're away tramping, and get YHA discounts on cruises, bus trips and so on. The hostel stores gear for you while you are away tramping, for $2 per item.

The *Fiordland Resort Hotel* (☎ 249 7113) located on Luxmore Drive, has two sets of backpackers accommodation – in the main block twin rooms are $34, and in the Kepler

Block $45 for a triple. Other options are double rooms with linen supplied for $45 to $50, and kitchen units for $65 a double. The resort has plenty of more expensive rooms as well. All rooms have private bathrooms and you can do your own cooking or eat in the licensed restaurant. A swimming pool and sauna all make this an enormously popular place, so it's a good idea to book ahead.

Te Anau Backpackers (☎ 249 7713) at 48 Lake Front Drive, have dorms and share rooms for $14 and twins/doubles for $16. They can help arrange transport to the Kepler Track, have complimentary bikes and gear storage, dinghies for hire and there is a garden to relax in. There is a summer-only pool here also. The upstairs dorm room has an excellent view; there are kitchen facilities, a small lounge and a radio up here so book ahead if you want it.

Guesthouses Te Anau has a couple of well-kept B&B places. *Shakespeare House* (☎ 249 7349) at 10 Dusky St offers B&B accommodation 'as you like it' but the prices have risen considerably. The quiet and pleasant rooms are off a bright, covered-in verandah and the breakfast is a substantial one – you're fixed up for the day! Rooms cost $66 to 72 for a single and $82 to $112 for doubles from December to March. At other times of the year they're a bit cheaper. The hosts, Mike and Rosina, claim they are related to William Shakespeare – prepare for soliloquies in the conservatory.

At the *Matai Lodge* (☎ 249 7360) on the corner of Matai and Mokonui Sts, B&B costs $55/60 for singles/doubles in the high season and a bit less during the rest of the year.

The *Southern Lakes Vacation Units* (☎ 249 7307) at 162 Milford Rd, have units for $50/60 for one to two/three persons.

Hotels & Motels The *Edgewater XL Motel* (☎ 249 7258) at 52 Te Anau Terrace has rooms for $65 to $70 per night for two. There's a small one-night surcharge and lower off-season rates. The *Lakeside Motel*

(☎ 249 7435) at 36 Te Anau Terrace is about $5 more than the Edgewater.

Another moderately priced motel is the *Anchorage* (☎ 249 7256) at 47 Quintin Drive with rooms for $60 to $72 for a double. There are numerous other motels at similar or higher prices. If you're aiming for the top, the *THC Te Anau Travelodge* (☎ 249 7411) is on Te Anau Terrace right in the town centre; rooms range from $115 to around $210.

Places to Eat
Snacks & Fast Food The *Pop Inn Tearoom*, close to Fiordland Travel near the lakefront, has light snacks and sandwiches; there's a pleasant outdoor eating area looking out over the lake. The *Burger Bus* appears nearby at night to dispense burgers and other fast food.

There are several places along Milford Rd in the town centre with snacks and take-aways – try the *Jailhouse Cafe* which has good sandwiches, the popular *Te Anau Dairy*, or the *Fiordland Bakery*.

If you're going to Milford take some supplies with you, there's not much available there in the cheap eats department.

Pub Food & Restaurants *Henry's Family Restaurant & Bar* at the Te Anau Travelodge has main courses for $12 to $18 and a Sunday evening buffet for $17.50 (children $8); it is open for lunch, and for dinner from 5 to 9.30 pm. Their specialities include Fiordland venison, Southland lamb noisettes and Stewart Island salmon. *Keplers* on Milford Rd features venison and seafood on its menu, with main courses from $14 to $21.

Bailey's Restaurant & Coffee Shop on the corner of Milford Rd and Mokonui St serves breakfast all day, bistro lunches, morning and afternoon teas, and an evening menu with selections which can be ordered as a starter for $8 to $11 or as a main course with potatoes and salad bar for $14 to $22.

On the main street in the town centre is *La Toscana*, a BYO place which has Italian food. The *Pop-Inn* has been recommended for its barbecued venison steak ($9.50) and

one kg of butcher's venison sausages for $5.50 a kg.

At the Te Anau Motor Park there is the licensed *Jintz Restaurant*, open only from 6 to 9 pm. It serves a range of food; a mixed grill is about $20 and a big T-bone is also $20 with a selection from a range of toppings, which themselves range from $4 to $5. The annoying thing about this place is that they charge an additional $4.50 for salad and $3.50 for a bowl of fries; ipso facto steak with a sauce, salad and chips costs well over $30.

At the Kingsgate Hotel, Te Anau Terrace, there are two restaurants, *The Bluestone Room* and *The Gallery*. A seafood medley in The Gallery is $13.50 and meals in The Bluestone probably suit those with fat wallets; $22.50 for a steak and $49.50 for 'Fiordland' crayfish. There is also the *Mac-Kinnon Room Restaurant* at the Te Anau Travelodge with all the usual Te Anau selections plus West Coast whitebait. Around the corner, on Mokoroa St, is *The Village Inn*, where the up-market restaurant serves continental food. The *Ming Gardens*, on Loop Rd, is the local Chinese and a favourite.

Getting There & Away
Air Mt Cook Airline (☎ 249 7516) has daily flights to Queenstown and Mt Cook, with connections to other centres. Waterwings Airways (☎ 249 7405), an agent for Ansett New Zealand, has flights to Queenstown and Milford. Air Fiordland (☎ 249 7505) also has flights to Queenstown, Milford and Mt Cook.

Bus InterCity (☎ 249 7559) has daily bus services between Queenstown and Milford via Te Anau, taking 2½ hours from Te Anau to either Queenstown or Milford. There's also a daily service to Invercargill (three hours) and Dunedin (six hours), involving a half-hour transfer stop in Lumsden. Buses arrive and depart from the InterCity depot on Milford Rd.

Mt Cook Landline (☎ 249 7516) also has daily buses between Queenstown and

Milford via Te Anau, and a weekday bus from Te Anau to Invercargill.

Topline Tours (☎ 249 8059), 80 Quintin Drive, operate a daily service between Te Anau and Queenstown. It departs from Te Anau at 10 am and Queenstown at 2 pm.

Fiordland Travel (☎ 249 7419) on the lakefront has buses to Queenstown and Milford. It also has a special bus, launch, steamship and *Milford Wanderer* combination which goes between Queenstown and Milford Sound. Part of the journey is made by launch to the western shores of Lake Wakatipu, then it's by coach on the back road to Te Anau and Milford, overnight on the *Milford Wanderer*, bus again on the back-roads via Mavora Lakes to Walter Peak, and finally, on the TSS *Earnslaw* to Queenstown. The cost is $176 (children $102); see also Queenstown in the Otago chapter.

A good way of getting around this region is in the 16-seater bus Southern Explorer (☎ 249 7820; fax 249 7536). It has a fixed weekly itinerary (Wednesday to Sunday) and you can do all of it or just a one-day section: Queenstown to Dunedin is $110; Queenstown to Queenstown is $130. One-day sections are: Queenstown to Te Anau back road $36, direct $18; Te Anau to Milford return $30; Te Anau to Invercargill and Bluff $25; Invercargill to Dunedin via the Catlins $30; and Dunedin through Central Otago goldfields to Queenstown (or Te Anau) $30.

Hitching Hitching in and out is a bit easier than to Milford, though still fairly hard. Hitching between Manapouri and Te Anau is good if you go there for a day trip.

Getting Around
For trampers intending to do the Kepler Track there is the shuttle service operated from the Te Anau Motor Park (☎ 249 7457). Their transport package includes (for $17) a 9 am departure on the *Manuska* to Brod Bay or 10.30 am and 3 pm departures from the Waiau River swing bridge. Sinbad cruises have a number of options for transport around the lake, especially to the Brod Bay end of the Kepler Track.

You can hire bicycles from Little Golf & Bike Hire (☎ 249 7959) just off Milford Rd, on Mokonui St.

MANAPOURI
Just 19 km south of Te Anau, on the shores of the lake of the same name, Manapouri (population 400) is a popular centre for trips, cruises and walking expeditions into the Fiordland World Heritage area. The lake is in a spectacular setting, surrounded by mountains which are, in their lower reaches, covered by native bush. The town exists on a combination of hydroelectricity generation and tourism, an incongruous and volatile mix at the best of times. Here, because the greenies work hand in hand with the red-necks, there seems to be some sort of homeostasis. The damage has been done and now all are attempting to preserve their live-lihoods.

Orientation & Information
Fiordland Travel (☎ 249 7416) is the main information and tour centre here – the office on the waterfront organises most of the trips. Pick your times as they won't have time to help you just prior to a boat leaving. Although the Manapouri Power Station and Doubtful Sound trips depart from Mana-pouri, there are connecting buses from Te Anau for these trips.

Doubtful Sound
The popular cruise from Manapouri with Fiordland Travel heads across the lake to Doubtful Sound. Their boat takes you across the lake to visit the hydroelectric power station on West Arm. The Doubtful Sound trip follows the power station visit with a drive over Wilmot Pass to Deep Cove on Doubtful Sound and then a cruise on Doubt-ful Sound up Hall Arm.

The power station on West Arm was built primarily to provide power for the Comalco aluminium smelter near Bluff. It generates 760,000 kW and discharges 19 million litres of water per minute from Lake Manapouri into Doubtful Sound. Not surprisingly, the project was the focus of intense environmental battles in the 1970s. At one time it was planned to considerably raise the level of the lake but this plan was defeated by the Save Manapouri Petition – the longest petition in NZ history. When you see the beauty of what has been described as 'New Zealand's loveliest lake' it's hard to imagine that anyone would want to destroy it. Lake Manapouri is the second-deepest lake in New Zealand after Lake Hauroko.

The cruise across the lake from Manapouri is followed by a bus trip down a two-km spiral tunnel to the power station machine hall, about two-km underground – a long way! From there the water is passed through a 10-km-long tailrace to Deep Cove in Doubtful Sound. The road from West Arm over the Wilmot Pass to Doubtful Sound, built during the construction of the powerhouse, is totally isolated from the rest of the NZ road system.

Before the road was built in 1959 only the most intrepid tramper or sailor entered the inner reaches of Doubtful Sound. Even Captain Cook, who named it, did not enter it – when he observed it from off the coast in 1770 he was 'doubtful' whether the winds in the sound would be sufficient to blow the ship back out to sea. He consequently named the place Doubtful Sound and continued sailing up the coast.

In 1793 the Spanish entered the Sound, and Malsapina Reach is named after one of the leaders of this expedition; Bauza Island after another.

Today Doubtful Sound is an exquisitely peaceful place. Bottlenose and dusky dolphins can be seen in its waters, and there's also a small colony of fur seals. The Fiordland crested penguin nests in the sound for about six to eight weeks in October and November. Life is also abundant below the surface, with black coral growing at an unusually shallow depth due to the fresh water on the surface, brought down by the power station and darkening the water. 1993 was the bicentenary of the Spanish exploration of Doubtful Sound.

The power station visit takes nearly four hours and costs $40 (children $10), book at Fiordland Travel. If you want to continue on to Deep Cove and go on the Doubtful Sound cruise it'll cost you $105 (children $30) for the all-day excursion. You can order lunch on the trip when you book or take your own. It costs less if you combine several Fiordland Travel trips; see Queenstown in the Otago chapter and Te Anau in this chapter for details.

An Ecology Holiday

Fiordland Ecology Holidays (☎ 249 6600) at 1 Home St, set out to offer a completely different type of experience to a small number of clients. These tours are run by Lance and Ruth Shaw; for the last 12 years Lance was the skipper of the DOC research vessel MV *Renown* and as such became very familiar with the flora & fauna of the area from Martins Bay, at the north end of the World Heritage area, to the Subantarctic islands. Ruth has been equally as active in the same fields and both are committed to showing the special features of the fiords' environment to others who care. They use the 82-foot (25-metre) yacht *Evohe* to take trips into parts of the World Heritage area that are only now being discovered. You will have the chance to dive, as many visiting marine biologists do, in a 40-metre depth of fresh water in the fiords that reveals deep water species you couldn't hope to see elsewhere.

Their onshore B&B accommodation is $40/60 for a single/double. Perhaps take the opportunity to stay with them before you discuss the more exciting explorations in Fiordland and, remember, it will always be less expensive in a manageable group of six or so people, and over a period of three to five days. There is every chance on these tours to sit amidst the fur seals and swim with the resident pod of dolphins.

Walks

The National Park Visitors Centre in Te Anau has a leaflet on short Manapouri walks ranging from one to four hours. They're all across the Lower Waiau River from Manapouri, so you have to row across to the

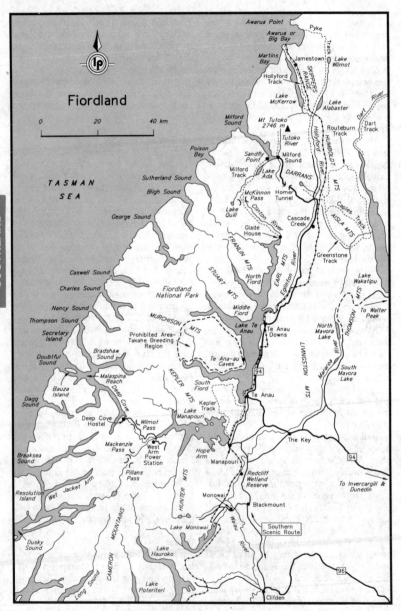

SOUTHLAND

starting point. (See Getting Around in this section.)

Places to Stay
Camping & Cabins The *Lakeview Motel* (☎ 249 6624), one km from the post office on the Te Anau road, has campsites at $15 for two ($17 with power) and cabins from $28 for two. The motor park has a sauna and spa pool.

The *Manapouri Glade Motel and Motor Park* (☎ 249 6623), on a stunning site adjacent to the river and lake, has campsites at $15 per night for two and cabins at $26 for two. There's a spa pool here, and it's only a five-minute walk to Doubtful Sound cruise departures.

Hostels There are no hostels in Manapouri but you can stay at the *Deep Cove Hostel* at Deep Cove on Doubtful Sound for $17 per person. The hostel has dinghies, fishing lines, lifejackets and wet-weather gear for hire, and there are a number of good walks in the vicinity. For most of the year it also hosts school groups, which come for four-day park outings. Arrangements must be made through the Fiordland National Park Visitors Centre in Te Anau.

The only way to get there is with Fiordland Travel. If you wish to stay in the DOC Deep Cove Hostel, you have to buy sector fares of the Doubtful Cruise: Manapouri-Deep Cove is $47 (one way) and if you want the cruise on Doubtful Sound it is $29 extra (bookings can be made at Fiordland Travel at the Manapouri wharf).

Guesthouses & Motels The fine old *Murrell's Grand View House* (☎ 249 6642), built in 1889, has B&B at $50/90 for singles/doubles with a shared bathroom or $70/120 with a private bathroom. Good dinners are available here as well.

There are motels next to both camping grounds. The *Lakeview Motel* (☎ 249 6624) has units for $58 to $70 and the *Manapouri Glade Motel* (☎ 249 6623) has units for $60.

Places to Eat
The coffee lounge at the *Pearl Harbour Coffee Bar* has good sandwiches and other snacks. If you're going on a day trip it's probably better putting something together here (or before you arrive) rather than paying $8 for a Fiordland Travel lunch pack. Meals are available at *Murrell's Grand View* and the *Fiordland Lakeside Lodge*; there is ordinary service, very much so, compensated for by great views at the latter.

Getting There & Away
InterCity used to have buses to Manapouri but they seem to have been discontinued. Fiordland Travel has lots of people going from Manapouri to Te Anau to hook up with their Te Anau trips and vice versa so they operate a Te Anau-Manapouri bus service for $5 (children $2.50) one way. Many other tour buses bring groups in here. Te Anau Motor Park operates a service to Manapouri for $39 return.

Getting Around
You can rent rowing boats from Manapouri Motors (☎ 249 6644) at Waiau St, for $4 per person per day, plus $2 a night if you keep it overnight, while you go on the walking tracks across the river. The hitching between Te Anau and Manapouri is OK if you don't rely on it to make a connection with the Doubtful Sound cruises.

THE ROAD TO MILFORD
It is 119 km from Te Anau to Milford on one of the most scenic roads you could hope to travel along. The first part of the road is through relatively undulating farmland which sits atop the lateral moraine of the glacier that once gouged out the lake. At 16 km the road enters a patch of mountain beech forest, passes the **Te Anau Downs Harbour** at 29 km and heads towards the entrance of Fiordland National Park and the Eglinton valley. Again, patches of beech – red, silver and mountain – are passed through, as well as alluvial flats and meadows. Two interesting sights on the way are the **Avenue of the Disappearing Mountain** and the **Mirror**

Lakes; the latter are 58 km from Te Anau, about halfway to Milford Sound.

At the 77 km mark is the locale referred to now as O Tapara, but known more commonly as **Cascade Creek**. O Tapara is the original name for nearby Lake Gunn, and refers to a Ngai Tahu ancestor Tapara. The lake was a stopover for parties heading to Anita Bay in search of greenstone. There is an excellent nature walk to the lake which starts from the O Tapara Lodge. The 40-minute track passes through tall red beech forest which shelters a variety of birdlife such as fantails, tomtits, bellbirds, parakeets, chaffinches, kereru and riflemen. On the lake paradise ducks and New Zealand scaup are often seen. Lake Gunn is the largest of the Eglinton Valley lakes but Fergus and Lochie are higher. The forest floor is an array of mosses, ferns and lichens. In Cascade Creek you may see long-tail bats, New Zealand's only native land mammal. For more fascinating background to the human story in this area read *Aotea: A History of the South Westland Maori* (Paul Madgwick, 1992).

The vegetation alters significantly as **The Divide** is approached. The size of the bush is reduced and ribbonwood and fuchsia are prominent. The Divide is the lowest east-west pass in the Southern Alps, and there is a good shelter here for walkers either finishing or commencing the Routeburn and Greenstone tracks. About a 1½-hour walk along the Routeburn brings you to **Key Summit**, where there are numerous tarns and patches of alpine bog. Three river systems – the Hollyford, Greenstone/Clutha and Eglinton/Waiau – start from the sides of this feature and radiate out to the west, east and south coasts of the island.

From the Divide the road falls into the beech forest of the **Hollyford Valley** and there is an interesting turn-off to Hollyford (Gunn's) Camp and the start of the Hollyford Track to the West Coast at Martins Bay. Have a yarn with Murray Gunn, and if you are lucky you will meet the oldest horse in the world – Jane. The views either side of the road are stupendous. One km down the Lower Hollyford road from Marian Corner,

where the avalanche barriers are, there is a track leading to **Lake Marian** and splendid views; it is four hours return.

From the corner the road rises up to the east portal of the **Homer Tunnel**, 101 km from Te Anau. The tunnel is named after Harry Homer who discovered the Homer Saddle in 1889; however work on the tunnel didn't begin until 1935 (to provide relief work for the unemployed after the Depression), and it wasn't finished until 1952. Rough-hewn, it has a steep east to west gradient of one in 11, but emerges into the spectacular **Cleddau Canyon** on the Milford side. At each portal there are short nature walks which describe alpine species found here.

Until recently the tunnel was too narrow to allow traffic to travel in both directions at the same time. Now it has been widened and sealed and you no longer need to plan your trip to arrive at the tunnel at the right time to be able to go straight through without waiting. The road is normally open all year, but may occasionally be closed in winter due to heavy snow and avalanches. About 10 km before Milford is the **Chasm Walk**. The Cleddau River plunges through eroded boulders in a narrow chasm, the Upper Fall, which is 22 metres deep. About 16 metres lower it cascades under a natural rock bridge to another waterfall.

There are views of **Mt Tutoko**, Fiordland's proudest and highest peak, glimpsed above the beech forest just before you arrive in Milford.

The scenery of the Milford Track is only just 'interesting' to those who have been lucky enough to explore north of the Milford Rd. In this area lie the majestic Darrans and Mt Tutoko. A track leads off from the western side of the bridge over Tutoko River. The scenery in here, after a two-hour walk through bush, is overpowering. The trail to Turner Bivvy (a rock shelter) is dangerous and hard to find – for the adventurous only. If you see a blue duck or rock wren here it will only serve to reinforce the specialness of the area. There is no fear of overdevelopment in this part of the bush – nature, swarms of human-devouring sandflies and the rainfall seem to retort 'Just you try'.

Places to Stay & Eat

There are a number of camping areas along the Milford road between Te Anau and the Eglinton Valley – check with the Park Visitors Centre in Te Anau.

At Te Anau Downs, 27 km on the road to Milford, there is the *Te Anau Downs Motor Inn* (☎ 249 7811; fax 249 7753); there are 52 units (20 with kitchen) and the rate is $57 to $89 for two. It is closed from June to August.

At Cascade Creek you can stay at the *O Tapara Lodge* (☎ 249 7335; fax 249 8151) for $60/75 for singles/twins or doubles. This lodge is in one of the most idyllic spots in the South Island and is a haven for birdwatchers; get a copy of the very informative *Fiordland Birds and Where to Find Them in Fiordland National Park*, as it clearly explains the habitats favoured by various species.

You can also camp at *Hollyford Camp*, formerly Gunn's Camp, in the Hollyford Valley for $3.50 per person. The camp also has rustic cabins (innersprung mattresses, wood and coal-burning stoves, separate kitchen, hand basins; you supply the rest) at $14/24/39 for one/two/three people. The camp has a shop with basic trampers' supplies (sorted into 'pack-friendly' bags), and also an interesting little museum, the very personal creation of owner Murray Gunn, who has been finding things in the hills around here for nearly 40 years and saving mementoes of the area's history; entry is free if you stay in his cabins. Jane, his 38-year-old brown horse, the product of a half-draught mare and a well-bred racing stallion, will come to greet you in expectation of a meal of bread.

Just before the Homer Tunnel is a turn-off to the hidden Homer Hut, the property of the New Zealand Alpine Club. They may take casual guests here during the week for a minimal fee; check with the caretaker at the hut – if one has been taken on for the season.

MILFORD SOUND

Whether or not you walk the Milford Track, you should make a visit to Milford Sound, the 22-km-long fiord that marks the end of the walk and beside which rises the beautiful, 1695-metre-high Mitre Peak. The fiord is really breathtaking. The water, usually calm, mirrors the sheer peaks that rise all around.

There's a small but very interesting display on the history of Milford Sound in the foyer of the Milford Sound Hotel, with photographs and stories relating to the geology and the glacial formation of the fiords, the long efforts to find a pass and then to construct a roadway from Te Anau to Milford, and the arduous construction of the Homer Tunnel. There are also photographs and stories of Donald Sutherland, 'the Hermit of Milford' who lived from 1843 to 1919 and ran the first accommodation place at Milford Sound. The Sutherland Falls are named after him. You can see his grave out behind the hotel.

Cruises & Trips

Cruises on Milford Sound are very popular so it's a good idea to book a few days ahead. There are a great number of alternatives for cruising Milford and they are listed here. On all of the trips you can expect to see Bowen Falls, Mitre Peak, The Elephant, Anita Bay and Stirling Falls. A number of the cruises are linked to package trips from Te Anau and Queenstown.

All cruises leave from the new wharf complex, which is a vast improvement on the old model. No longer do you have to rush across from the hotel in a Fiordland downpour to get on the boats; there is a covered and elevated walkway through a patch of Fiordland bush from the overnight car park to the wharf.

Fiordland Travel The Fiordland Travel cruise on the MV *Milford Haven* lasts a little over 1½ hours and costs $36 (children $10). You can have a buffet lunch for $20 (children $10) or you can get a packed lunch for $8 from Fiordland Travel, or bring your own. Free tea and coffee are served on all the Fiordland Travel cruises.

Fiordland Travel also has a 2½-hour

fishing cruise on a smaller boat, the *Queens-towner*, which goes on exactly the same route as the *Milford Haven* – all the way out to the Tasman Sea – but is a more relaxed cruise, with the opportunity to catch some fish along the way. The cost is the same as for the *Milford Haven* cruise.

Their jet-boat trip to the Tasman Sea is one hour long and costs $25 (children $10); this is probably too short a time to fully appreciate the sound but is an option if you are in a rush.

So Fiordland Travel certainly have an eclectic mix of cruises: the *Milford Haven*, *Milford Flyer* (a catamaran), a 30-seat jet-boat, the sailing vessel *Milford Wanderer* and the fishing vessel *Queenstowner* – take your pick! They have a mix 'n match Take Five Pack for $149 (children $50); inquire at their offices about the savings you can make if you use this.

If going to Milford Sound by bus pay a little extra for Fiordland Travel's glass roof coaches so that you can fully appreciate the scenery on both sides of the Homer Tunnel.

Red Boats The Milford Sound Hotel (☎ 249 7926) also operates cruise boats on the sound in their Red Boats. They take basically the same route as the Fiordland Travel boats and they cost the same. Red Boats operate the *Lady of the Sounds*, a 85-foot (26-metre) catamaran, MVs *Mitre Peak II* and *Lady Bowen*.

The prices quoted in this section are for the simple cruise. Various cruise packages involving busing or flying into and out of Milford are available from Queenstown and Te Anau; see those sections for details.

The *Milford Wanderer* A new initiative of Fiordland Travel is the *Milford Wanderer*, designed to carry 150 passengers on daytime cruises, and 70 passengers overnight. The overnight cruise, on board a vessel reminiscent of NZ's early coastal traders, gives you the opportunity to take in the awesome views from the Sound at a time when there is very little water traffic and definitely no sightseeing flights, omnipresent during the day. If you are extra lucky you will probably see a

pod of dolphins while the *Wanderer* is moored in Harrison Cove, feeding near the mouth of the Harrison River. The *Wanderer* is impressive when the sails are unfurled but realise it is still under power as it heaves its way through the Tasman swell out from Milford Sound. The small crew of four perform miracles when feeding a full passenger quota of 70.

Usually passengers on the *Wanderer* have arrived on a package trip, via back roads from Queenstown, which includes launch, bus and the TSS *Earnslaw* as components.

MV *Tutoko* If you prefer to be part of a smaller group try the MV Tutoko, an ex-Red Boat. It takes 44 passengers during the day and 10 overnight; the four-hour day trip is $36 and the overnight option $96. From November to March, it leaves at 5 pm from Milford wharf and passengers can bushwalk, dive and fish for as long as daylight allows. Breakfast is provided in the morning before the return to Milford Wharf. The *Tutoko* is hired out from April to October and operates in Dusky or Doubtful sounds. To book on this contact Kawarau Rafts (☎ 442 9792) or the Information & Track Centre (☎ Queenstown 442 9708) in Queenstown.

The *Milford Explorer* A number of readers have recommended a fishing trip on the smaller fishing boat *Milford Explorer*. For $35 they take a maximum of 12 passengers for 3½ hours out to the Tasman Sea; you can even fish if you like. You can book through the Milford Lodge (☎ 249 8071).

MV *Pembroke* The operators of the *Pembroke* (☎ & fax 249 8833), operating as Fiordland Fish 'n Dive, offer tours with a difference. They concentrate on the natural history of the Sound – they offer swimming with dolphins and seals, scuba diving with experienced guides to view red and black corals, fishing outside the Sound, and walking on the beach at Anita Bay and to St Ann's lighthouse. Anita Bay is the place where 'tangiwai' greenstone is found.

From June to October they offer extended trips to Doubtful and Dusky sounds, Stewart Island, and to the North Island (Great Barrier Island, Moko Hinau and the Poor Knights).

Places to Stay

Accommodation at Milford Sound is very limited, so it's a good idea to book ahead if you want to stay there.

The hostel-style *Milford Lodge* (☎ & fax 249 8071) has beds for $16 in two to six-person rooms, four twins for $40 a room, two doubles at $45 for two, tent sites for $8 per person, and campervan sites for $9 per person. It's open all year but it's especially busy from December to April, when there's a free sauna, daily budget transport to and from walking tracks, and the evening meal is served from a little cafe counter (or you can cook your own). A casual shower for track finishers is $3 with an extra $1 for soap. This was once the worst accommodation in the country, but management has changed and the new broom has swept clean, making it a pleasant place to stay. No longer do you have to rush to get the early bus to Te Anau.

The other accommodation option at Milford is the *Milford Sound Hotel* (☎ 249 7926), where even the 'economy' rooms are $57/85 for singles/doubles and the standard rooms are $135 for one, two or three people. The hotel is attractively situated at the tip of the sound and has great views, but it's becoming rather elderly and frayed – hopefully the new management will spruce it up. The booking offices for Mt Cook Landline, Mt Cook Airline, Ansett and Milford Sound scenic flights are in the foyer.

Places to Eat

The *Milford Sound Hotel* has a restaurant and the pub serves basic pub food – well only pies at the last check. If the wallet allows try the restaurant – salmon resting (dead) on lettuce with cream sauce is $23 and venison and wild boar in red-wine glaze is $29. Next to the pub is the *Exchange Cafe* where you can get sandwiches and coffee. The *Milford Lodge* serves good evening meals at its little

restaurant counter from December to April, and it also has a small shop.

Getting There & Away

You can reach Milford Sound by four methods, all interesting: hike, fly, bus, and drive or hitch. The first, the Milford Track route, is detailed in the Tramping section in the Outdoor Activities chapter. Currently the guided walk is $1355 – yes, you read correctly. Book well in advance, perhaps a year, to 'freedom walk' the Track but realise that the title is a misnomer as it is still quite costly.

Air Probably the most spectacular way to go is to fly there. Flights operate from Queenstown and Te Anau; see those sections for details. A good combination trip is to go to Milford by bus and return by air.

Bus You can do the return trip by bus from Te Anau or further afield. Making the return trip from Queenstown in one day involves a lot of bus travel, so Te Anau is a better jumping-off point; a day trip from Queenstown means about 10 hours of bus travel, but from Te Anau it's only about five hours. The 120-km trip by road is spectacular, and Inter-City, Mt Cook Landline and Fiordland Travel all run daily bus services from Te Anau for $34 one way or $68 return (children half price).

The one-day Fiordland Travel coach/cruise/coach excursion, leaving Te Anau at 8 am and returning at 5 pm, costs $78 (children $38.50). From Queenstown it departs at 7.15 am and returns at 7.45 pm. InterCity has basically the same excursion at the same price, except the cruise is on the THC Red Boats. It's essential to book in advance for the Milford excursions during the high season.

Car If you're driving to Milford, stop by Fiordland Travel in Te Anau for a copy of their free map of the road to Milford, which points out sights along the way (see The Road to Milford earlier in this chapter). If you go by car the drive itself should take about 2½ hours, but make sure you allow extra time to stop off on the way, especially if you're planning to take photographs.

Hitching Hitching on the Milford road is possible but hard going. There's little traffic and nearly all of it is tourist traffic which is unlikely to stop. There are walks off the Milford road, including walks close to both ends of the tunnel, and also walks off the Lower Hollyford road which branches off the Milford road.

THE SOUTHERN SCENIC ROUTE

The Southern Scenic Route is only now being discovered and appreciated by travellers. It starts in Te Anau and goes via Manapouri, Blackmount and Clifden to Tuatapere. At Tuatapere SH 99 is followed to Invercargill via Colac Bay and Riverton. From Invercargill to Dunedin the road, SH 99, hugs the south-east coast. Many of the attractions in the Invercargill-Dunedin portion of the scenic route are covered in The Catlins section of this chapter.

From Te Anau to Invercargill there are a number of interesting features along the way. Between Manapouri and Blackmount watch out for the one sign indicating the **Redcliff Wetland Reserve** – birdwatchers will be particularly pleased as they observe a predatory bush falcon in action. Just before Blackmount there is a turn-off to the right to **Lake Monowai** and Borland Lodge. Monowai even stands today as testament to blunder – it was flooded in 1925 for a very small power station and the lake is still unsightly all these years later.

The town of **Clifden** has a cave system nearby and the Clifden Suspension Bridge, built in 1902. About 16 km from Clifden there is a walk to 1000-year-old totara trees. From Clifden you can drive out on 30 km of unsealed road to **Lake Hauroko**, the deepest in NZ. Hauroko lies in a beautiful bush setting, with precipitous slopes on its sides. In 1967, out on Mary Island a good example of a Maori cave burial was discovered. In this tapu place a woman of high rank was buried, sitting upright, in about 1660.

The three-day tramp to Supper Cove on Dusky Sound starts at Hauroko Burn. For more information on this tramp read Lonely Planet's *Tramping in New Zealand* by Jim DuFresne. Lake Hauroko Tours (☎ 226 6681), based near Tuatapere organise four and eight-day tramps from Hauroko to Lake Manapouri; they also specialise in the Hump Track, South Coast Track, Monowai and Green Lake.

The Southern Coastal Track and the Hump Track are described in the DOC pamphlet *Waitutu Tracks*; both commence at Te Waewae Bay. The coastal track goes via Port Craig (where there is a deserted schoolhouse) to Lake Hakapoua, and the Hump to Teal Bay at the base of Lake Hauroko and then via the lake's eastern shore to the Hauroko roadhead.

Tuatapere

Once a timber milling town, Tuatapere (population 900) is now a farming centre on the banks of the Waiau River. It is a good base for trips to Hauroko or Te Waewae Bay and beyond. To check out how effective the woodchoppers were, look at the small remnant of native forest in the town's domain – once most of the area looked like this!

About 10 km south of Tuatapere the scenic route reaches the cliffs above Te Waewae Bay, where Hectors dolphins and southern right whales are sometimes seen. In this bay, at the eastern end, is Monkey Island or Te Poka a Takatimu (anchor stone of the *Takatimu* canoe). Nearby is Orepuki, where the strong southerlies have had a dramatic effect on the growth of macrocarpas, trees windshorn so that they grow in a direction away from the shore. A little further on, the next point on the coast reached is Colac Bay, an old Maori settlement and now a popular holiday spot for Southlanders.

Places to Stay & Eat

There is a holiday park, hotel and motel in Tuatapere. At the *Five Mountains Holiday Park* (☎ 226 6418) at 14 Clifden Rd, twin units are $10 per person and self-contained doubles are $35 for two. Bedrooms at the

Waiau Hotel (☎ 226 6409) at 47 Main St, are $45/75 for singles/doubles, and the *Tuatapere Motel* (☎ 226 6593) at 41 Orawia Rd, has rooms for two at $60. Good solid country fare is to be had at the Waiau Hotel or from one of the other places – the *Waiau Restaurant, D's Dairy* or *Heather's Coffee Shop*, all in Bob Seager's immortal words 'down on Main St'.

Riverton

Riverton (population 1700), 38 km west of Invercargill and at the mouths of the Aparima and Pourakino rivers, is considered to be one of the oldest settlements in New Zealand, dating from the sealing and whaling days. There is an Early Settlers Museum on Palmerston St; and, in the town of Thornbury, close by, there is a Vintage Machinery Museum. The Riverton Rocks area is a popular local beach and holiday resort, and Taramea Bay is a safe place to swim.

Places to Stay & Eat

At the *Riverton Motor Camp* (☎ 234 8526), off Roy and Hamlet Sts, tent sites are $6 per person, powered sites $7, cabins $20 for two and the cottages $40 for four people. The *Riverton Beach Motel* (☎ 234 8181) at 4 Marne St, has singles/doubles for $45/50. The two hotels, the *Carriers Arms* and the *Globe* are on Palmerston St. Also on Palmerston St are the eateries, including *Ricardo's Pizzeria* at No 135, and *Pioneer Food Bar* at No 118.

The *Rivertonian Restaurant* at 102 Palmerston St has achieved a more than local reputation with excellently prepared local food including Bluff oysters and Aparima whitebait.

Invercargill

Invercargill (population 57,000), the southernmost city in New Zealand, is very much a farm-service community, with a surprising amount of wealth (you notice more Jags here than anywhere else in New Zealand). It is often claimed to be the southernmost city in the world but has probably been eclipsed by Ushuaia in Argentina. In fact, relative to South America it's at the northern end of Patagonia rather than the southern end.

To many travellers coming here it's just a jumping-off point for the tramping tracks of Stewart Island. As the main city of Southland, however, it offers a great deal of other possibilities including the nearby Catlins and the wild areas of southern Fiordland. It is a remarkably ordered city based on a grid pattern reminiscent of Melbourne, Australia. Its biggest drawback is the lack of any break in the geometricity of its surroundings. It is built on a plain and is 'flat as a tack'.

History

When the Chief Surveyor of Otago, JT Thomson, travelled south to settle on a site for Invercargill the region was uninhabited and covered in a dense forest known as Taurakitewaru Wood, which stretched from the Otepuni Stream (then known as the Otarewa) in the south to the Waihopai River in the north. Realising that ships of 500 tons could sail up the estuary to the mouth of the Otepuni Stream, Thomson chose Taurakitewaru Wood as the best site for the new town. It was laid out over 'a mile square' with four reserves just inside its boundaries and a fifth one running down the banks of the Otepuni Stream. Originally, Queens Park was just over the northern boundary and 200 acres (80 hectares) of forest was set aside for it. Today the only part of the forest that remains is a small area known as Thomsons Bush.

Orientation

The locals staunchly defend their city, despite snide comments from the rest of the country about its backwardness. There are minor variations in speech and language throughout New Zealand, but in Southland the difference is most marked. Listen for the 'Southland drawl', with its rolled 'r' – more pronounced in the isolated rural areas.

The two major streets are Tay St, which is the main road in from Dunedin and the east, and Dee St which meets Tay St at right

SOUTHLAND

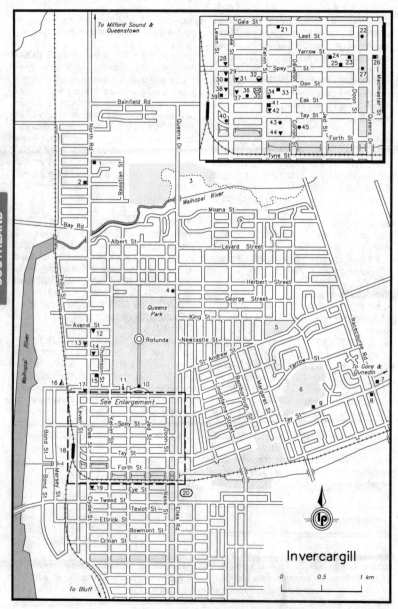

To Milford Sound & Queenstown

Gala St
Leet St
Yarrow St
Spey
St
Don St
Esk St
Tay St
Forth St
Tyne St

Leven St
Dee St
Kelvin St
Deveron St
Doon St
Macmaster St
Queens Dr

21
22
24
25 23
26
27
28
29
30
31 32
38 36
37 35
34 33
40
41
42
43
44 45
39

Bainfield Rd

Queens Dr

Waihopai River

North Rd

Basstian St

Bay Rd

Albert St

Philip St

Waihopai River

Moana St
Layard Street
Herbert Street
George Street
King St
Newcastle St
St Andrew

Queens Park

Rotunda

Avenel St
Thomson St
Leven St
Dee St
Kelvin St
Spey St
Doon St
Tay St
Forth St
Eye St
Tweed St
Teviot St
Ettrick St
Bowmont St
Crinan St
Clyde St

Bond St
Mersey St
Ness St
Elles Rd

Lindisfarne Street
Bamborough St
Margaret St
Yarrow St
Tay St

Racecourse Rd

To Gore & Dunedin

See Enlargement

1
2
3
4
5
6
7
8
9
10
11
12
13
14
15
16
17
18
19
20

Invercargill

0   0.5   1 km

To Bluff

■ PLACES TO STAY

1   Garden Grove Motel
2   YHA Hostel
7   Ascot Hotel
8   Coachman's Inn & Coachman's
    Caravan Park
9   Moana Court Motel
15 Southern Comfort Backpackers
16 Invercargill Caravan Park
23 Yarrow Motel
24 Aachen Motel
25 Montecillo Travel Lodge
26 Ashlar Motel
30 Grand Hotel
33 Don Lodge
39 Gerrard's Hotel
41 Kelvin Hotel

▼ PLACES TO EAT

12 Avenal Homestead Family Restaurant
13 Pizza Hut & Willow Chinese
    Restaurant
14 Kentucky Fried Chicken
17 McDonalds
19 Clyde Tavern
28 Moa's Restaurant, Joy's Gourmet
    Kitchen & Fresh Sea Food
29 Corner Cafe

31 Tillerman's Restaurant
37 Nobles
38 The Office Bar &
    Brasserie
42 HMS King's Restaurant
44 Boulevard Hotel

OTHER

3   Waihopai Walkway
4   Queens Park Swimming Pool &
    Hydroslide
5   Waverley Park
6   Surrey Park
10 Queens Park (Entrance)
11 Southland Museum & Art Gallery &
    Southland Information Centre
18 Railway Station
20 Rugby Park
21 Automobile Association (AA)
22 Water Tower
27 Otakaro Park
32 Mt Cook Landline Depot
34 Bank of New Zealand
35 Chief Post Office & Department of
    Conservation (DOC)
36 Air New Zealand
40 Telecom
43 Pak 'n Save
45 Conon St Swimming Pool

SOUTHLAND

angles. The shopping centre is between them, north of Tay and east of Dee St. Invercargill really sprawls – they had lots of room to build it and they used it all!

Information

There's a Visitors Information Centre (☎ & fax 218 5793) in the museum building near the entrance to Queen's Park in Gala St. For most of the year it's only open from 10 am to 4.30 pm on weekdays, but during holiday periods it's also open from 1 to 5 pm on Saturday and Sunday. The CPO, with its strange purple-and-white colour scheme, is at the bottom of Dee St, but postal services are in a separate building on Don St.

The AA Southland office (☎ 218 9033) is at 47 Gala St and the DOC (☎ 214 4589) is in the State Insurance Building on Don St. If you're going to Stewart Island it's a good idea to drop in at the DOC office to pick up all the details on walks. The Visitors Information Centre also has information on Stewart Island.

There is an excellent public library on Dee St, open from 8 am to 9.30 pm Monday to Friday.

Museum & Art Gallery

Invercargill's main attraction is the Southland Museum & Art Gallery, near the entrance to Queens Park in Gala St. It has been redeveloped as an interpretation centre for the Subantarctic. The first two stages – an audiovisual theatre and a subantarctic garden – are ready, as is the book sales area. The Roaring Forties gallery, the last part of the redevelopment, will be open in 1995. The

Roaring Forties Experience audiovisual takes you on a 25-minute journey to the Subantarctic islands administered by New Zealand. As you watch you feel the chill wind, thunderstorms and horizontal rain that has shaped these islands. Walk amidst the rookeries, dodge elephant seals and climb up to the exposed nests of shy mollymawks. Andris Apse's photography captures the remote and surreal atmosphere of the last stands of the great untouched. It is well worth the $2 (50c children) entrance fee. There is a book for sale at the museum which contains more information than you are presented with in the audiovisual.

The museum building itself is of interest. It's been rebuilt in the shape of a pyramid, and they say that at 26 metres high, with a base of 42 by 52 metres, it's the largest pyramid to be constructed in the Southern Hemisphere, and even larger than the glass one in Paris.

There's also a tuatara house, where several of the ancient and rare NZ reptiles are on display. Some are about 100 years old (they can live to about 150 years), and new ones are being born here – some of the young ones are on display. Other features include a Maori gallery, a natural history gallery, a gallery on the history and technology of the Southland, and three art galleries.

The museum's astronomical observatory is open from 7 to 9 pm on Wednesday nights from April to September – good fun on a starry night.

The museum itself is open from 10 am to 4.30 pm Monday to Friday and from 1 to 5 pm on weekends. Admission is free, but all the restoration is costing a lot of money and donations are very gratefully accepted. While you are there, the 80-hectare Queens Park itself is worth a quiet wander. The cafe here is open daily.

The Anderson Park Art Gallery (☎ 215 7432) is seven km north. Turn off the main road to Queenstown onto McIvor Rd and drive down it for three km; it is signposted. It's open from 2 to 4.30 pm daily except Monday and Friday; afternoon tea is available at this elegant Georgian house.

Beaches & Pools

There are two heated indoor swimming pools in Invercargill, one on Conon St, just off Tay St, and one on Queens Drive at the end of Queen's Park. The one on Queen's Drive has a waterslide too.

Invercargill's beach is Oreti, 9.5 km west of the city. It's a long sweeping beach and the water is much milder than in most of the South Island beaches because a warm current sweeps across from Australia. If you've got a car, you can drive along this beach and find a really secluded spot.

Other Things to See

Queens Park is the town's principal park. Among its attractions are various animals, an aviary, duck ponds, rose gardens, a tea kiosk open daily from 10 am to 5 pm, and a swimming pool and waterslide complex, in addition to the Museum & Art Gallery mentioned earlier. The curious water tower at the bottom of Leet St was built in 1889. Climb up to the top for a bird's-eye appreciation of the town's flatness. If you want to go horse-riding contact the Invercargill Riding Centre (☎ 213 0781) on Oreti Rd. It's open every day, but bookings are essential. There's 10-pin bowling at Super Bowl, on the corner of Kelvin and Leet Sts.

Walks

For local sites of interest, pick up a walking-tour leaflet of Invercargill's historical places from the museum.

Waihopai Walkway, along the banks of the Waihopai River, is only 10 minutes from the YHA hostel. Thomson's bush, on Queens Drive, is the last remnant of Taurakitewaru Wood, the forest which once covered the site of Invercargill. It is 3.5 km north of the CPO.

Seaward Bush, eight km south-east of the CPO (signed from the junction of Rockdale and Mason Rds), was once part of the much larger Seaward Forest which was extensively milled for house-building timber in the late 19th century. The reserve still contains a good range of native trees and shrubs

– kamahi, rimu, kahikatea and matai. There are several other walks; ask at the Visitors Information Centre or the DOC, and see the DOC booklet *Get Out & Walk – a guide to walking tracks in Southland*. The Museum & Art Gallery has a walking-tour leaflet for historical places around Invercargill.

Tours

H&H Travel Lines (☎ 218 2419) offers a city sights tour whenever there are three or more people who want to go. It takes a couple of hours and you get a running commentary on all the historical, cultural and beauty spots of Invercargill. The tour leaves from the terminal on the corner of Don and Kelvin Sts and costs $15. Blue Star Taxis (☎ 218 6079) offer tours for smaller groups. AB Mini Tours (☎ 218 7704) offers trips further afield, including farm visits, jet-boating, fishing and so on.

Places to Stay

Camping & Cabins The *Invercargill Caravan Park* (☎ 218 8787) is at the A&P Showgrounds on Victoria Ave off Dee St, only one km from the centre. It's closed during showtime (the first two weeks in December) but the rest of the year tent sites are $7 per person, or $11/16 for one/two people with power. They also have cabins from $22 to $26 for two.

The *Coachman's Caravan Park* (☎ 217 6046) at 705 Tay St has sites for $6 per person, or $16 with power for one or two persons. There are also cabins at $27.50 for two.

The *Beach Road Motor Camp* (☎ 213 0400), out towards Oreti Beach eight km from the centre, has sites for $6 per person ($8 with power), cabins from $24 for two, and tourist flats at $38 for two.

Hostels The world's southernmost *YHA Hostel* (☎ 215 9344) is at 122 North Rd (on the corner of Bullar St), Waikiwi, about three km from the town centre. It costs $14 per night and sleeps 28. See the manager if you're interested in backpackers accommodation on Stewart Island. Apparently, they offer a special discount on plane flights to Stewart Island ($33.75). It is rumoured that this hostel will be moved closer to town in the future.

The YMCA (☎ 218 2989) on Tay St doesn't have any accommodation, although it does have squash courts. There are two backpackers. *Southern Comfort* (☎ 218 3838) at 30 Thomson St, has share/dorms for $15 and twins (and one double) at $17 per person. This 20-bed backpackers is housed in a turn-of-the-century art nouveau villa, with beautifully manicured gardens and pleasant, clean dorms. The kitchen is modern and the dining room excellent. It's only five minutes to the Information Centre although you probably won't need to go there as the hosts, Willie and Valerie, give away a wealth of information.

The *Coachmans Inn* (☎ 217 6046; fax 217 6045), is at 705 Tay St, where share rooms are $15 in basic cabins.

Hotels & Motels The *Montecillo Travel Lodge* (☎ 218 2503; fax 218 2506) at 240 Spey St is a friendly place with hotel and motel rooms. The old part is 90 years old, and bedrooms have been restored to their original condition. Including breakfast the hotel rooms are $59/74 for singles/doubles without private facilities. The motel units cost $54/64 for singles/doubles, without breakfast. The Montecillo is a straightforward but well-kept place conveniently close to the town centre (about a 10-minute walk).

At the *Coachman's Inn* tourist flats are $50 to $69 and motels are $60 to $73. Other reasonably cheap motels include the *Ashlar Motel* (☎ 217 9093) at 81 Queens Drive, singles/doubles are $60/70; *Garden Grove Motel* (☎ 215 9555) at 161 North Rd, singles/doubles are $55/65; *Moana Court Motel* (☎ 217 8443) at 554 Tay St, $66 for two; and *Yarrow Motel* (☎ 218 2797) at on Yarrow St, singles/doubles are $54/66. There are numerous other motels, typically from around $70.

The *Gerrard's Hotel* (☎ 218 3406; fax 214 4567) is on the corner of Esk and Leven Sts, opposite the railway station. It's an ornate 1896 building (with additions in 1907)

SOUTHLAND

which has been renovated. It also houses one of the town's best licensed restaurants. Single/double rooms with private facilities cost $66/70, B&B costs $49 for singles and $70 for doubles or twins.

On Dee St, opposite the end of Don St, is the imposing old *Grand Hotel* (☎ 218 8059) where singles cost $45 to $65, depending on their size, and doubles or twins cost $76. The restaurant there is open every day. The *Kelvin Hotel* (☎ 218 2829) on Kelvin St in the town centre is the largest hotel in Invercargill. It's well kept but bland and costs a hefty $100/105 for singles/doubles.

Places to Eat

Because Invercargill is the centre of an important fishing area there's lots of seafood for sale – particularly crayfish, cod, and the superb Bluff oysters for less than $3 a dozen. It's also the home of mutton birds. The local Maoris are allowed to collect them from small islands off Stewart Island at certain times of the year. They keep the best ones and sell the rest through the shops. But make sure you know how to cook them or they'll taste revolting!

Snacks & Fast Food Along Dee St and around the town centre there's the usual collection of fast food places and a number of sandwich places.

Nobles at 47 Dee St serves good 'mousetraps' (onion, cheese and bacon) but on our last visit we were given the wateriest cappuccino in the South Island. It's open from 7 am to 4 pm Monday to Friday, and closes a little later on Friday. *Joy's Gourmet Kitchen* at 122 Dee St has a good selection of salads, wholemeal goodies, sandwiches, quiches, wholemeal pizzas and budget hot roast meals. You can eat in or take away.

A good vegetarian/wholemeal/health food place in Invercargill is *Tillerman's*, upstairs at 16 Don St. It's quite a gathering spot locally and is open from 10 am to 3 pm Monday to Friday. It also opens from 5 to 7 pm on Friday and then from 9.15 pm until late for coffees/teas and snacks.

Despite its plain appearance, *Moa's Res-taurant* is something of a local institution and is open commendably long hours. It's at 142 Dee St and serves straightforward food in large quantities – this is the sort of place where the plate disappears under the steak and chips. Grills cost around $8 to $11 and lighter meals such as egg & chips cost $6 or $7.

Further north up Dee St, about halfway to the YHA, there's a *Pizza Hut*, *McDonald's*, *Kentucky Fried Chicken* and several other big drive-in takeaways. Next to the Pizza Hut, the *Willow* does Chinese takeaways, with a bargain lunch-time special for just $3.50. The takeaways counter is beside the fancier Chinese restaurant of the same name. *Enter the Dragon* at 107 Tay St is another Chinese takeaways although you can get burgers there too.

Pub Food Like Dunedin, there are plenty of pubs here and most of them serve food as well. The *Boulevard Licensed Restaurant* in the Boulevard Hotel at 50 Tay St is a popular place, serving breakfast and brunch all day long, with pancakes or bacon and eggs for $5. Of course they serve lunch and dinner meals too, with plenty of seafood on the menu as well as steak, venison, roasts and the like, with main courses from about $12.50 to $20. It's open from 7.30 am to 8.30 pm Monday to Thursday and from 7.30 am to 9.30 pm on Friday and Saturday; it's closed on Sunday. *Molly O'Grady's*, in the Kelvin Hotel on the corner of Esk and Kelvin Sts, has smorgasbord meals at lunch-time and for dinner; these are good value.

The *Avenal Homestead Family Restaurant*, on the corner of Dee and Avenal Sts, has the usual bars and a good restaurant, very much in the Cobb & Co mould. It's a modern, pleasant place with the standard pub food (roast of the day, fresh fish) for $12 to $17. It's open for dinner every day except Saturday, after the bars open at 4.30 pm.

The licensed *Galaxy Family Restaurant* at the Waikiwi Family Inn is even more modern with its shiny, blinking-light space-age setting. The food, however, is more down to earth. All the regular pub fare is on the menu with main courses in the $11 to $14 bracket, including a trip to the salad bar. There's a children's menu for about $5. It's around the corner from the Homestead, on Gimblett St, very close to the YHA hostel.

The Office Bar & Brasserie is a barn-like establishment on Dee St in the centre of town. Bar food is reasonably priced and you can get a salad plate for lunch for $5. One of its big pluses is the Guinness on tap – long overdue in all NZ towns. You can barbecue your own food here; a fillet steak would cost $13.50. Similar to the Office but with a more intimate atmosphere is *Zookeepers*. It is the sort of place you go to, if for no other reason, to buy the establishment's T-shirt. The 'Zoo' has really good value meals, laid-back staff, some of Invercargill's brighter patrons and corrugated iron statuary.

Restaurants Most of the restaurants in Invercargill are pretty mundane. You could try the simple and straightforward *Ainos Steak House* at the Waikiwi Shopping Centre on Dee St, seven blocks north of the YHA hostel. It's open for dinner every day except Sunday and Monday, from 6 to 10 pm.

The *Willow* at 232 Dee St, next to the Pizza Hut, is an attractive licensed Chinese restaurant with six-course meals for $13 at lunch time and around $20 to $24 in the evening. On Sunday there's a six-course 'family special' for $18 (children half price). A separate takeaways section is off to one side.

Back in the centre, *Gerrard's* at the Railway Hotel, opposite the railway station, is one local restaurant which does seem to have a good reputation. It's open every night; if you'd like a really flashy night out in Invercargill this could be the place.

The Coachman's Inn, located near SH 1, has its own *Stable Restaurant & Bar*.

If you want to sample some of the local fish, try *HMS Kings Restaurant*, home of the 'famous fisherman's platter' (who was he?) at 83 Tay St. Oysters, whitebait, blue cod, crayfish, all feature here. It is open Monday to Saturday, from 11.30 am to 2.30 pm, and 5 to 9.30 pm. It has the atmosphere of an old sailing ship.

Entertainment
There is entertainment in the town centre, which ostensibly closes with a bang after 9 pm, if you are willing to search it out. There is the odd nightclub such as *Crazy Horse* on Dee St which buzzes until the early hours. A lot is happening out in the suburbs, but you need to ask around.

The weekend editions of the *Southland Times* will tell you what's on. The *Rafters Bar* at the Whitehouse Hotel is possibly the best place to go to, but it's right out at Lorneville, eight km north of Waikiwi (a left turn towards Riverton). There's a cover charge. The *Waikiwi Tavern*, on Gimblett St just off Dee St, is at least handy to the YHA hostel, and there's now a nightclub, *Lazers*, in the rear of the same large building. Other pubs with entertainment include the *Ascot Park Motor Hotel* on the corner of Tay St and Racecourse Rd, and the *Southland Hotel* on Elles Rd.

Getting There & Away
Air Air New Zealand (☎ 214 4737) has an office at 46 Esk St. It has daily direct flights to Dunedin, Christchurch, Auckland and Wellington, although not all flights to Auckland and Wellington are direct. From these four cities there are connections to many other centres.

Ansett New Zealand (☎ 214 4644), at Invercargill Airport, has daily flights to and from Christchurch, Wellington, Palmerston North and Auckland, also with connections to other centres.

Flights to Stewart Island are made with Southern Air (☎ 218 9129). See the Stewart Island section for details. Make sure that you get a copy of their informative free booklet. The airport is spacious, new and very much the transport hub of this city.

In 1984 Invercargill had bad floods which caused immense destruction throughout the region, isolating it from the rest of New Zealand – and the world – for several weeks. The airport was completely flooded and there's a high water marker two metres above floor level in the terminal building. Despite extensive flood prevention measures there was a repeat performance in 1987 and again the airport was inundated, although this time only one metre or so. Air New Zealand flights were halted for weeks but flights for Stewart Island operated from the local race course.

Bus InterCity buses are based at the railway station (☎ 218 1837, 214 0598), behind the CPO in Leven St. Daily buses run from Invercargill to Te Anau, Queenstown and Christchurch, with more frequent buses to Dunedin.

The Mt Cook Landline bus depot (☎ 218 2419) is on the corner of Don and Kelvin Sts. It has daily buses up the coast through Dunedin (three hours), Christchurch (nine hours) and on to Picton (16 hours). The Picton bus connects with the ferry to Wellington. Other services include buses to and from Queenstown (2½ hours) every day except Saturday, and to Te Anau (2¾ hours) and Wanaka (5¼ hours) Monday to Friday. Mt Cook Landline also has local services to Bluff, Gore and other centres further afield in Southland; see the Getting Around section for details.

Colin Horn (Invercargill; ☎ 218 8145) has a scheduled service between Invercargill and Dunedin, which leaves Invercargill at 7 am and Dunedin at 3 pm, going via Gore and Balclutha. You can arrange to go to Christchurch and Picton on connecting services.

Train The Southerner Christchurch-Dunedin-Invercargill train operates every day except Saturday and Sunday, departing from each end of the line at around 8.50 am and arriving on the other end around 6.30 pm. It's about 3½ hours from Invercargill to Dunedin and 9½ hours to Christchurch. Call (☎ 218 1837) for bookings and information.

Car For details on the coastal road between the two cities, crossing the region known as the Catlins, see the Catlins section later in this chapter. Since this route is not covered by public buses, and light traffic makes it difficult for hitching, the best way to see this part of the country is with your own wheels.

Hitching Hitching between Dunedin and Invercargill is usually fairly simple and should only take about half a day. If you're on your way to Queenstown or Te Anau it gets steadily harder the further you go, and many people get stuck overnight in Lumsden. Without transport the coastal route between Dunedin and Invercargill is pretty hard – public transport is almost non-existent and there's little traffic for hitching. The same is true for the coast road heading west towards Te Anau.

Getting Around
To/From the Airport The airport is 2.5 km from the centre and you can get there by taxi for around $9. Spitfire Shuttle go to the airport for $3. They will pick up from your accommodation.

Bus Invercargill City Bus Lines (☎ 218 7108) puts out a timetable with a colour-coded map of bus routes. Pick up a copy from the Visitors Information Centre at the museum. The buses run only from around 7 am to 6 pm Monday to Friday, or until around 9 or 10 pm on late shopping nights. There are no city buses on weekends. Local bus trips cost $1.20.

Campbelltown Bus and Foveaux Express Bus Services both offer a ferry connection and will pick up from backpackers, etc, for $6 per person.

Taxis There are two taxi companies: A Cabs (☎ 216 0186) and Blue Star (☎ 218 6079).

Bicycles Mike Hughes Triathlon Shop (☎ 218 4865), Kelvin St, hires out 10-speed and cruiser bikes.

BLUFF
Invercargill's port, and the departure point for the Stewart Island catamaran, is Bluff, 27 km to the south. There's an observation point at the top of 265-metre Bluff Hill – you can drive all the way to the top, or walk it in a half hour or so – from where you can see the Island Harbour, Foveaux Strait, Stewart

Island and the Tiwai Point aluminium smelter. Hills being quite a rare physical feature in this area, it's one of the better vantage spots. On Blackwater St, you will find the statue of Australian-born Sir Joseph Ward, Mayor of Bluff, before he became Prime Minister in 1906. He was PM from 1906 to 1911 and again from 1928 to 1930.

Also at Bluff is Fred & Myrtle's Paua Shell House, at 258 Marine Parade. It has an amazing array of shells collected from all over the world, and the entire front room is lined from floor to ceiling with brilliantly polished paua (abalone) shells. It's all set up in the friendly old couple's private home and Fred, who personally collected the shells from more countries than he can remember, is on hand to show you around. Visitors are welcome from 9 am to 5 pm every day; there's no admission fee, but you could make a donation.

Further on past the Paua Shell House is an ocean lookout with a sign indicating your distance to the South Pole, the equator, and many other places around the world.

Across the harbour from Bluff is the Tiwai aluminium smelter, the eighth largest in the world. The overseas owners were attracted to Bluff by promises of cheap power; the Manapouri Power Scheme was built to feed it, and if there hadn't been such a public outcry Lake Manapouri would have been raised and destroyed to cater for the hunger for electricity. The smelter is now a major source of employment for Invercargill's citizens – around 1600 jobs – and they get mighty sensitive to any hint of criticism about it. Aluminium is NZ's fifth ranked principal export, after meat, wool, dairy and forest products. Free tours can be arranged by phoning ☎ 218 5999 in advance. The tours are at 2 pm on Tuesday and Thursday, and daily during holiday periods, but you need your own transport to get out there.

Foveaux Walk is a 6.6 km walkway from the southern end of SH 1 to Ocean Beach, where it emerges at a bus stop. It takes about 2½ hours. Don't be misled by the name 'Ocean Beach' – what you will find there is a smelly freezing works. Glory Track leaves

from Gunpot Rd and passes through Bluff Hill's only remaining stand of native bush, connecting with the main walkway (35 minutes).

Places to Stay & Eat

The four budget options are *Flynn's Club Hotel*, 100 Gore St (☎ 212 8124), where all rooms are $28; *Bay View* (☎ 212 8615) at Gore St, where singles/doubles are $25/50; the *Camping Ground*, Gregory St (☎ 212 8722); and *Property Arcade Backpackers* (☎ 212 8074) at 120 Gore St (share/dorm rooms are $14 here). At Property Arcade, which is situated 100 metres from the wharf, there are good cooking facilities and security lock-up for vehicles. Their minibus departs at regular intervals and connects with airport transport and northbound buses and trains.

Try the *Stirling Point Tearooms* for a meal. Their restaurant is open on Saturday and Sunday evenings for seafood meals and grills.

Getting There & Away

See the Stewart Island section for details on getting to and from Stewart Island.

INVERCARGILL TO DUNEDIN

There are two ways of getting from Invercargill to Dunedin: either by SH 1 via Gore and Balclutha, or by the continuation of the Southern Scenic Route, SH 92, via the coastal road through the Catlins. The state highway is utilitarian and passes through predominantly rural scenery which you may just have had enough of by now. If so read about the Catlins and plan to spend some extra time there – you won't regret it. The two sizeable towns on the SH 1 route are Gore, home of the Big Brown Trout and country music, and Balclutha.

Gore

Despite the 'trout' this farming community service town (population 8650) is actually not in such a bad locale. It spans the Mataura River, and the Hokonui Hills are a great backdrop. In June Gore hosts the New Zealand Gold Guitars, an annual country &

western festival. The place is booked out at this time, so lovers of country & western music should plan well ahead.

Find the trout and you will find the Gore Information Centre (☎ 208 9908), near the Mataura River bridge.

The Eastern Southland Museum & Art Gallery is on the corner of Main and Norfolk Sts, and is open Monday to Friday from 10 am to 5 pm, and Sunday from 2 to 4.30 pm.

Hopefully you will catch a trout the size of the 'big one' in one of the many (40 or so) excellent streams, including the Pomahaka, Mataura, Waimea, Otamita and Waipahi. If the anglers are drinking more Hokonui moonshine than the trout you never know what stories you will hear.

Places to Stay & Eat
At the south end of town you will find the *Gore Motor Camp* (☎ 208 4919) where sites are $7 per person, $10/16 for one/two with power, and cabins at $26 for two. The *Charlton Motel* (☎ 208 9733) at 9 Charlton Rd, has rooms for $66 and the *Oakleigh Motel* (☎ 208 4863) at 70 Hokonui Drive, has rooms for $68 for two.

There are a number of places which help you keep the wolf from the door along Main St. These range from the *Gore Pie Cart*, beside the old railway station to *Bridget's BYO Restaurant*, Main St. The *Croydon Lodge Motor Hotel*, Waimea St, has two dining rooms, a house bar and a public bar.

The Catlins

'The coast is picturesque, being precipitous with numerous indentations'. So said Sir James Hector in 1863. If you've got your own transport and you're travelling between Invercargill and Dunedin, take the longer coastal route allowing a couple of days for stopovers. The distance is pretty similar to the inland route although it's somewhat slower since some of the road is unsealed. The route goes through the region known as the Catlins, which stretches from Waipapa

Point in Southland to Nugget Point in South Otago. It includes the Western Catlins Forest (22,250 hectares) and a number of other forests and scenic reserves – it is the largest remaining area of native forest on the east coast of the South Island. The Catlins is a totally absorbing area.

History
The area was once inhabited by the moa hunters and evidence of their campsites and middens have beeng found at Papatowai. Sometime between 1600 and 1800 the Maori population thinned out; attributable to the decline of the moa, no kumara cultivation and fear of the *Maeroero* (the wild yeti-like creature of the Tautuku bush), a bald hairy creature reputed to snatch children and young women.

Later, whalers occupied sites along the shoreline such as at Waikawa Harbour, Tautuku Peninsula and Port Molyneaux. Then timber millers, providing the Dunedin market, moved into the dense stands of beech forest in the 1860s. For many years the millers kept scows, and later the railway, busy with loads of timber for the Port Chalmers area, and at the height of logging there were about 30 mills in the area. Incidentally, the railway was commenced in 1879 but did not reach Owaka for another 25 years and Tahakopa, where it ended, until 36 years later; it was finally closed in 1971. Like many other parts of New Zealand the final wave were the pastoralists.

Flora & Fauna
There are still reserves of podocarp forests in the Catlins, containing trees such as kahikatea, totara, rimu and miro. Behind the sand dunes of Tahakopa and Tautuku bays there are excellent examples of native forest which extend several km inland. The vegetation zones are best seen at Tautuku: sand dune plants (marram, lupin, flax) are found near the beach; behind are low trees such as rata, kamahi and five-finger; in the peaty sands behind the dunes is young podocarp forest; and then there is mature forest with emergent rimu and miro and a main canopy of kamahi.

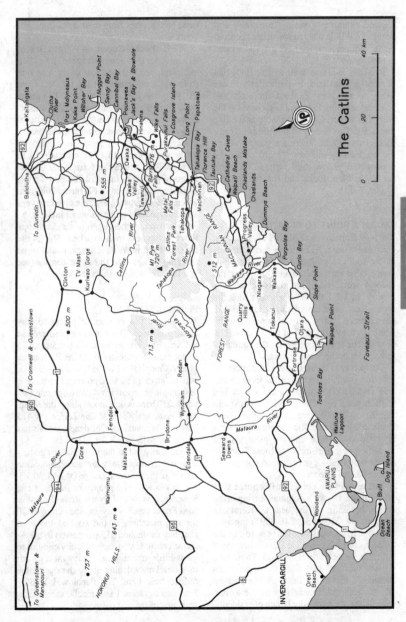

The Catlins

A good example of young forest is found near Lake Wilkie where growth has occurred on the sediments which have gradually filled in the lagoon.

It is the fauna as well as the flora that attracts people here. In particular you are likely to see New Zealand fur seals and Hookers sea lion. Elephant seals breed at the Nuggets, a series of remarkable wave-like pinnacles. The variety of birdlife is an ornithologist's delight. There are many birds of the sea, estuary and forest. Included are the endangered yellow-eyed penguin (hoi-ho), the kaka, blue ducks and the rare mohua (yellowhead).

WAIPAPA POINT TO PAPATOWAI
The road from Invercargill, SH 92, meets the coast at Fortrose. At Fortrose, take a turn off to the south to **Waipapa Point**. The lighthouse here was erected in 1884 after the second worst maritime disaster in NZ's history. In 1881 the SS *Tararua* struck the Otara Reef, one km offshore. Of the 151 passengers and crew only 20 survived; in the nearby graveyard are 65 of the victims. The next detour is to Slope Point, the southernmost point in the South Island.

Curio Bay is the next point of interest. At low tide you can see one of the most extensive fossil forests in the world – it is 160 million years old. The petrified stumps and fallen log fossils are evidence of New Zealand's location in the ancient supercontinent Gondwanaland and the plant species identified here are similar to those found in South America – cycads, treeferns, matai-like and kauri-like trees.

Just around the corner in **Porpoise Bay** you may see Hector's dolphins surfing in the waves breaking on the beach. Koramika Charters (☎ 216 5931, 246 8897) organise trips out from Waikawa Harbour to see the dolphins, which come close into shore over summer to rear their young. Their two cruises are $35 and $55; the latter price includes a trip to the Brothers Point where NZ fur seals and Hooker's sea lions are often seen. They are a friendly bunch of residents,

must be the vibes from their dolphin neighbours.

The **Cathedral Caves**, on Waipati Beach, so named for their resemblance to an English cathedral, are only accessible at low tide (tide-tables are posted at the turn-off from SH 92). The caves are about a 40-minute walk from the road, but part of the walk is through beautiful native forest. At **Tautuku Bay** there is a 15-minute walk to the beach, a stunning sweep of sand punctuated by drifts of seaweed, and a five-minute walk to **Lake Wilkie**, where there are some unique forms of plant life. Just past Tautuku there is a good vantage point at **Florence Hill** from where you can distinguish the different vegetation types and other points of interest.

Papatowai, at the mouth of the Tahakopa River is the next town reached. This is the base for Catlins Wildlife Trackers and some amazing forays into the close forests (see Wildlife Tracking in this section).

Places to Stay & Eat
You have a few choices of places to stay along this route. There is a *camping ground* at Curio Bay, *campsites* at Waipohatu, and a motor camp at Papatowai. At the *Papatowai Motor Camp* (☎ 415 8063) a site is $5 per person (an extra $2 with power), and there is one on-site caravan for $12/16 for one/two persons. There is one motel along the route, the *Chaslands Farm Motor Lodge* (☎ 415 8501) at Waipati Rd, Chaslands, which has double or twin rooms for $48.

One really out of the way place to go to – if you can organise your accommodation here – is the *Tautuku Lodge* (☎ 415 8024), six km south of Papatowai in the Lenz Reserve. It is owned by the Royal Forest & Bird Protection Society and they charge $20 for non-members in the six-bed lodge or four-bed cabin, and $15 per person in the A-frame cabin. If you are not lucky enough to go wildlife tracking in Papatowai try your own hand at twitching along the tracks that radiate from here. The Papatowai Trading Post can organise basic meals, sandwiches and cups of tea and coffee.

There are *DOC campsites* at the folling areas in the Catlins: Tawanui, Catlins Forest Park, SE Otago; Purakaunui Bay, Catlins Forest Park, SE Otago; and Papatowai, 24 km from Owaka, SE Otago (fully serviced).

PAPATOWAI TO BALCLUTHA

Between Papatowai and the regional centre of Owaka there are many interesting places to visit. First, follow SH 92 east to **Matai Falls** on the Maclennan River. After looking at these, head south on the signposted road to the more scenic **Purakaunui Falls**. It is only a short walk through bush to these tiered falls, best viewed from a platform at their base.

In the **Catlins State Forest Park** you can do the river walk, a good day trip out of Owaka. There is a track to Tawanui from the Wisp camping area – observant walkers may see the rare mohua (yellowhead) here. Out near the mouth of the Catlins River, on the western side, is **Jack's Blowhole**, a 55-metre deep hole in the middle of paddocks. It is 200 metres from the sea but connected by a subterranean cavern.

On the eastern side of the river, south of Owaka, is the **Pounawea Nature Walk**, a 45-minute loop through kahikatea, ferns, kamahi, rimu, totara and southern rata. There is a salt marsh near the Catlins River estuary which features plants suited to that environment.

To the east of Owaka at **Tunnel Hill** there is a short track which leads to NZ's most southerly railway tunnel, excavated by hand in 1893 as part of the Catlins Branch Railway (see History in this section).

The road leading south from Tunnel Hill heads to **Cannibal Bay** where Hooker's sea lions sometimes beach themselves; if you are extra lucky you may see a grey-coated female. The bay gets its name from the fact that the surveyor Hector discovered human bones in a midden here, and assumed it was part of a feast. Also Te Rauparaha popped up here and exacted revenge which may have included acts of cannibalism – which part of the NZ coastline remained immune from his attacks?

Further around the coast, on a not-to-be-missed sidetrack from the Kaka Point road is **Nugget Point**. This is one of NZ's special places. The islands sitting out from the lighthouse promontory seem to lead off to the very edge of the world. Fur seals bask below on the rocks, as do Hooker's sea lions and elephant seals on occasions. There is a wealth of birdlife – yellow-eyed and little blue penguins, gannets, shags and sooty shearwaters breed here and many other pelagic species such as the cape pigeon pass by. The lighthouse, constructed of stone, was built in 1869. Avoid the temptation to leave the track – observe only from above with binoculars so as not to disturb the birds.

From Nugget Point the road loops back around through Kaka Point and Port Molyneaux to SH 92. Balclutha is not far up the road.

Owaka

Owaka is the main town of the Catlins area and has a population of 380. The DOC office (☎ 415 8341), on the corner of Ryley and Campbell Sts has information about the area. The Owaka Museum (☎ 415 8136) is open from 1.30 to 4 pm Thursday or by appointment. There are a number of craft shops in this small town.

Places to Stay & Eat Close to Owaka are two good camping options. The *Pounawea Motor Camp* (☎ 415 8483) has sites for $5 per person ($13 for two with power) and cabins for $12.50 per person. The *Kaka Point Camping Ground* (☎ 412 8814) has sites for one/two for $6/10 (with power $12 for two) and one cabin which is $18 for two.

There's a *DOC campsite*, with full services, at Papatowai, 24 km from Owaka, SE Otago.

There are two sets of motels in town: *Highview Motels* (☎ 415 8686) at 23 Royal Terrace; and *Owaka Lodge Motels* (☎ 415 8728) on the corner of Ryley and Campbell Sts. You can eat out at the *Catlins Diner* on Main St or at the *Catlins Inn*, 21 Ryley St.

SOUTHLAND

Wildlife Tracking

One highly recommended operation that will assist in your search for the ultimate 'twitch' is *Catlins Wildlife Trackers* (☎ 455 2681). They offer a 'total' unified eco-experience. The natural history, landforms and geology are interwoven with recent history; the secrets of the sea, littoral, rainforest, wetlands and sky are all gathered together, dissected and meticulously explained; and nature's rare and timid creatures are revealed. Delicious stuff for the voracious eco-tourist anxious to learn more about the interrelationship between themselves and their environment.

It is run by two dedicated conservationists, Fergus and Mary Sutherland, who are extremely knowledgeable about wildlife in the area. They organise food, transport and accommodation in their superbly sited crib (home) overlooking the estuary of the Tahakopa River and the sweep of Tahakopa Bay, at Papatowai. From here you can observe many species of birds, see a Hooker's sea lion swim into the estuary, and watch the changing moods of the southern ocean. Most importantly they supply binoculars, torches (flashlights) and snorkels, masks, flippers and wet suits. The meals, including the picnic lunches they take to their observation sites, are the best you are likely to get in the region.

The cost for this tour is $170 for two days, ex Dunedin (they have their own vehicle). New Zealand's ex-best kept secret!

If for some reason you can't get them on their home number you can book through the Visitor Information Centre in Dunedin.

DOC campsites can be found at Tawanui and Purakaunui Bay, Catlins Forest Park.

Stewart, Chatham & Other Islands

Information
All telephone numbers in the South Island have an 03 prefix if you are calling them from a long distance (even within the region).

Stewart Island

Called Rakiura by the Maoris, New Zealand's third largest island is often not even considered by travellers as a potential destination. Rakiura means 'heavenly glow' in Maori, perhaps referring to the aurora australis which is often seen in this southern sky, or the spectacular blood red sunsets that are witnessed here. The island is thought of as being isolated and suffering the battering of harsh southern winds. Actually Stewart Island is not as inhospitable as that, but it most definitely is an unspoilt, unhurried getaway-from-it-all type of place.

The minuscule population of 450 is congregated in the one town of any size, Oban, on Halfmoon Bay. Half an hour's walk from there and you enter a sanctuary of forest, sea, beaches and hills.

The people are hardy, independent, insular and suspicious of mainlanders, the law and bureaucracy. The weather is incredibly changeable – brilliant sunshine one minute, pouring rain the next. Conditions can be very muddy underfoot and you will need boots and waterproof clothing, but the temperature is much milder than you would expect.

Ann Pullen, a resident of the island, has pointed out that the island's rainforest *is*, after all, more beautiful in the rain – and that mud is 'great character-building stuff'!

History
There is all sorts of evidence that parts of Stewart Island were occupied by moa hunters as early as the 13th century AD. According to Polynesian mythology New

Zealand was hauled up from the depths of the South Pacific Ocean by Maui who said 'Let us go out of sight of land and when we have quite lost sight of it, then let the anchor be dropped; but let it be very far off – quite out in the open sea'. One interpretation of this myth is that the North Island was a great flat fish caught by Maui; the South Island his canoe and Stewart Island the anchor – 'Te Punga o te Waka a Maui' being the legendary name for the latter.

The first Pakeha to come across Stewart Island was good old Captain Cook in 1770, who sailed around the eastern, southern and western coasts but could not make up his mind whether it was an island or a peninsula. Deciding it was part of the South Island mainland he called it Cape South. Several

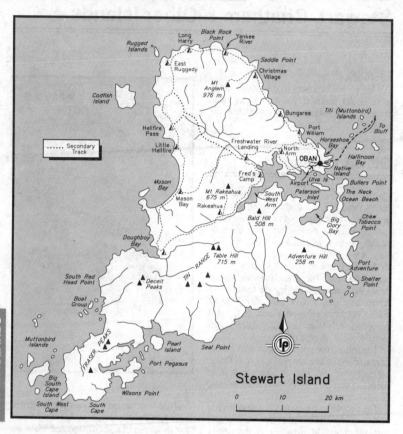

OUTER ISLANDS

decades later his theory was disproved when the sealing vessel *Pegasus*, under the command of Captain Chase, circumnavigated Stewart Island – presumably becoming the first European ship to do so. The island was named after William Stewart, first officer of the *Pegasus*, who charted the southern coast of the island in detail.

In June 1864 Stewart and the adjacent islands were bought from the Maoris for the sum of £6000. Early industries consisted of sealing, timber milling, fish curing and ship building. The discovery of gold and tin towards the end of the 19th century also led to an increase in settlement but the rush didn't last long and today the island's economy is based on fishing – crayfish and cod – and tourism.

Orientation

Stewart Island is 64 km long and 40 km across at its widest, has less than 15 km of roads and its rocky coastline is incised by numerous inlets, the largest of these being Paterson. The highest point on the island is Mt Anglem at 976 metres. The principal settlement is Oban, which takes its name from a place in Scotland, around Halfmoon

Bay, with roads extending only a few km further out from there.

Two essential reading companions (if you can get them) are *Birds in New Zealand* by CJ Robertson and *Rakiura* by Basil Howard.

Information

For information on tracks and tramping you can contact DOC (☎ 214 4589) in the State Insurance Building on Don St, Invercargill, before you take off for the island. The Southland Museum Visitors Information Centre (☎ 218 9753) at 82 Dee St also has information on Stewart Island.

On the island there's a DOC Stewart Island Visitor Centre (☎ 219 1218; for DOC matters 219 1130) beside the deer park on Main Rd in Halfmoon Bay. It's very close to both the Stewart Island Travel office (where you'll arrive if you come by plane) and the ferry wharf. In addition to much useful information on the island it has good displays on flora, fauna, walks and so on, and a summer activities programme in January. It publishes several handy cheap pamphlets on tramps on the island, including *Halfmoon Bay Walks*; *Rakiura Track* and *North West Circuit Tracks* – $1 each. Fossick around and you might be lucky to uncover some of the Stewart Island Natural History series including *Key to Common Sea Birds*, *Guide to Common Sea Weeds* and *Geology*. You can store gear at the DOC centre while you're walking ($2.50 small locker, $5 large). Lesley and Ann go out of their way to welcome you to their island and fill your head with many ideas of how to spend your time here.

The Stewart Island Promotion Association appreciate it if you fill in their 'departure card'. This is an extremely important survey as it allows them to assess the need for future developments and improvements in the island's facilities.

There is a general store at Halfmoon Bay which is open from 9 am to 5.30 pm during the week, 10 am until noon on Saturday and Sunday, and 4 to 5 pm Saturday (only in the busy period). Make sure you order bread, milk, eggs and newspapers in advance if you want them. The Lettuce Inn sells fruit and vegetables, sweets, films, rents videos, and has bulk bins of dried food for trampers.

There is a postal and banking agency where you can cash travellers' cheques – the locals are praying for their first automatic teller machine. Meanwhile, the agency is on Elgin Terrace, Halfmoon Bay, about five minutes' walk from the wharf. Stewart Island is a local (not long-distance) telephone call from Invercargill. There are public toilets at DOC, the South Sea Hotel, the wharf and the public hall.

Flora & Fauna

If you know anything about trees the first thing you'll notice is that, unlike the North and South islands, there is no beech forest on Stewart Island. The predominant lowland vegetation is hardwood but there are also lots of tree ferns, a variety of ground ferns and several different kinds of orchid, including three species of lady's slipper, two earinas and a number of spider orchids. Along the coast the vegetation consists of muttonbird scrub, grass tree, tree daisies, jack vine and leatherwood. You need a trusty machete to hack through the last two if there are no defined tramping tracks! You are warned, however, not to go tramping off the beaten track.

Stewart Island is an ornithologist's delight. Apart from the numerous seabirds that breed here, bush birds such as tuis, parakeets, kakas, bellbirds, fernbirds, robins – the last two are found near Freshwater Flats – dotterels and kiwis abound. The much rarer orange-wattled kokako, kakapo and weka can sometimes be seen, and the Fiordland crested penguin, the yellow-eyed penguin, and the little blue penguin are also found here (see Ulva Island in this section).

Two species of deer were introduced to the island early in the 20th century. They are the red deer found mainly around Mt Anglem, in the Freshwater and Rakeahua valleys and at Toi Toi Flat in the south-east, and the Virginia (whitetail) deer which inhabits the coastal areas of the island. Also introduced were brush-tailed possums, which are particularly numerous in the northern half of the

OUTER ISLANDS

island and rather destructive to the native bush. Stewart Island has lots of seals too.

Around the shores there are clusters of bull kelp, common kelp, fine red weeds, delicate green thallus and bladders of all shapes and sizes.

Ulva Island

Ever dreamed of paradise? Likely you would find the subject of your dreams here on Ulva Island. It is only 260 hectares, but a lot is packed into it. An early naturalist, Charles Traill, was honorary postmaster. He would hoist a flag to signal to other islands including Stewart that the mail had arrived and hopefuls would come from everywhere. It fell out of favour however, being replaced by a postal service at Oban, and a year later the island was declared a bird sanctuary in 1922, and the post office closed.

Nowadays Ulva remains as a birder's paradise. As soon as you get off the launch the air is alive with the song of tuis and bellbirds. You see kaka, weka, kakariki and kereru (native pigeon). This has a lot to do with the absence of predators and it is believed (in 1993) there is only one rat left on the island.

The forest on the island has a mossy floor and many tracks intersect the stands of rimu, miro, totara and rata – all of which, added to the delight of the birdsong, create a setting you won't forget. The birds come so close that you don't even need a telephoto lens.

A number of tour operators pass here on their way to view salmon farms. If you would rather follow tracks to quiet, private beaches than visit a commercial salmon farm in Big Glory Bay, ask to be left here while the launch excursion visits the farms. They will pick you when they stop on the return trip to let passengers explore the island for all too brief a time.

Walks

If you want to visit Stewart Island, plan on spending a few days so you can enjoy the beaches, seals, rare bird and plant life. There are many walks on the island; although some take only a couple of hours, a day trip to

Stewart Island is hardly worthwhile as it is a tramper's paradise. You could spend weeks tramping here.

There is a good network of tracks and huts in the northern part of the island, but the southern part is undeveloped and can be very desolate and isolated. Visit the DOC office and get hold of their booklets before you set off. They have detailed information on the walks, the time they take, when to go and accommodation facilities. A number of the longer walks are covered in detail in Lonely Planet's *Tramping in New Zealand* by Jim DuFresne.

You are advised not to go off on your own – particularly from the established walks – unless you have discussed your itinerary with someone beforehand. Foam rubber mattresses, camp ovens and billies are provided at each hut but you need to take food, sleeping bags, ground sheets, eating and cooking utensils, first-aid equipment and so on with you and, if you have them, a tent and portable gas stove may be useful as the huts can get packed out at certain times of the year. The stove is a useful insurance against finding wet firewood.

The first huts on the North West Circuit Track are about four to 5½ hours from Halfmoon Bay, and a lot of people just take the circuit to them. The track's well-defined and it's an easy walk, the major drawback being that it gets very crowded in the summer. There's a maximum stay of two nights in a hut. Hut fees for most huts on the island are $4 (children $2) per night. The tracks further away from Halfmoon Bay can be very muddy and quite steep in places.

Around Halfmoon Bay there are a number of shorter walks. Take the 15-minute walk to Observation Rock which affords a good view over the island's main settlement. You can continue past the Stone House at Harrold Bay to Ackers Point, where are good views of Foveaux Strait, and seals, penguins and dolphins can be seen near the rocks. This is the site of the only shearwater colony on the main island. There are many other possible walks outlined in the DOC pamphlet *Halfmoon Bay Walks*.

Museum & Other Things to See

The **Rakiura Museum** on Ayr St is no Victoria & Albert but it's worth a visit if you're interested in the history of the island – it features whaling, sealing, tin mining, timber milling and fishing. It's open from 10 am to noon Tuesday and Thursday; 10 am to 2 pm on Monday, Wednesday and Friday; 11 am to noon Saturday and 1 to 2.30 pm Sunday. Entry costs $1, children 50c.

Particularly interesting is the section dealing with the Maori heritage. It is believed that Maoris have lived on Rakiura for 800 years or more. The muttonbirds (titi) on the islands adjacent to Stewart Island were an important seasonal food source for the southern Maori. The modern Maori population in the southern region is predominantly Ngai Tahu, with earlier lineages to Kati Mamoe and Waitaho.

There is a dolphin teeth necklace on display, alongside a collection of adzes and barter goods traded between Maoris and whalers, such as pipes from The Neck. In the collection of shipping memorabilia there is scrimshaw and photographs of the ferries that plied across Foveaux Strait – *Awarua, Theresa Ward, Matai, Tamatea* and *Southland*.

Also on Ayr St is a **library** which is open for even less time, from 2 to 3 pm on Wednesday and 11 am to noon on Friday. On your way to the Visitors Centre, look into the **deer park** to see whitetail deer. It's not far along Main Rd.

There is a craft shop & gallery, **The Fernery** (☎ 219 1453), about 400 metres from town in a bush setting, and housed in an old-time island crib. It has been extensively renovated and the interior belies the bush clad exterior. Elspeth Tindal, the owner, propogates fern from spore in a fashion discovered accidentally in 1830 by a London doctor. Tiny fernlets from the hen-and-chicken fern *Aplenium bulbiferum* are placed in small egg-shaped containers and grow, ultimately to four or five feet tall. The items for sale in the shop have been selected for their relevance to Stewart Island's flora & fauna. There is a variety of beautiful cards,

exquisite prints, bookmarks and pottery available.

At Harrold Bay, about three km from town, is an **old stone house** built by Lewis Acker around 1835. It's one of the oldest stone buildings in New Zealand – probably the second-oldest after the famous Stone Store in Kerikeri which dates from 1833. You can make arrangements to look inside if you wish. A track leads from Harrold Bay to the beacon at Ackers Point where there is a viewing and interpretation platform.

Tours

In summer there are minibus tours around Halfmoon Bay, Horseshoe Bay and various other places. They're zippy little trips – only about an hour – because there really isn't very far you can drive on Stewart Island! There are also boat trips to Ulva Island (a great bird sanctuary) and Ocean Beach (for kiwi spotting). Check with the Fox at Stewart Island Travel (☎ 219 1269; fax 219 1355), or check the notice boards next to the store, for more detailed information. Fishing trips are other popular activities.

Every second night Matangi Charters (☎ 219 1144) offer you the chance to see kiwis in the wild for $45. Their daily cruises to Ulva Island, and salmon farms are $35. Moana Charters (☎ 219 1202) take half-day fishing and sightseeing trips for up to 21 persons for $35 a head. Thorfinn Charters (☎ 219 1210) have a 30-foot (nine-metre) launch available for half-day and full-day cruises; fishing trips are their speciality. They also provide a water taxi service for birdwatchers and backpackers.

Kiwi Spotting

This is one of the best eco-activities of New Zealand. The search for *Apteryx australis lawryi* would be a difficult one if you did not know where to look. The Stewart Island kiwi is a distinct sub-species of the brown kiwi, with longer legs and beak than its northern cousins. These kiwis are common over much of the island, particularly around beaches where they forage for sandhoppers under washed-up kelp. Unusually, *apt.aus.law.* is

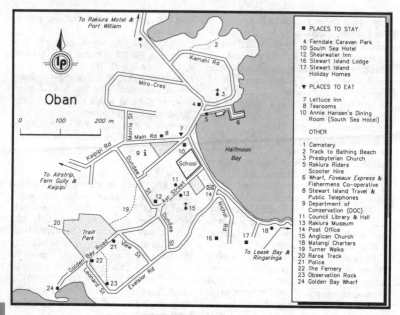

■ PLACES TO STAY
4 Ferndale Caravan Park
10 South Sea Hotel
12 Shearwater Inn
16 Stewart Island Lodge
17 Stewart Island
 Holiday Homes

▼ PLACES TO EAT
7 Lettuce Inn
8 Tearooms
10 Annie Hansen's Dining
 Room (South Sea Hotel)

OTHER
1 Cemetery
2 Track to Bathing Beach
3 Presbyterian Church
5 Rakiura Riders
 Scooter Hire
6 Wharf, *Foveaux Express* &
 Fishermens Co-operative
8 Stewart Island Travel &
 Public Telephones
9 Department of
 Conservation (DOC)
11 Council Library & Hall
13 Rakiura Museum
14 Post Office
15 Anglican Church
18 Matangi Charters
19 Turner Walks
20 Raroa Track
21 Police
22 The Fernery
23 Observation Rock
24 Golden Bay Wharf

active during the day as well as night, as they are forced to forage for longer to attain breeding condition. Many walkers on the Rakiura Track and North West Circuit Track spot them, especially at Mason Bay.

On any one night in summer you will probably see about three to five kiwis on Ocean Beach. Nowadays, they are quite used to human voyeurs and they even let people close enough to take video footage. If you're lucky you'll also see a morepork and penguins on the way to the beach.

Phillip Smith, a local, was first to see that people were coming to Stewart Island to see wildlife in isolation. Phillip is a descendant of Yankee Smith, a shipwright on a whaling vessel out of Nantucket, who bore children with one of the Maori women of Rakiura. His head just hums with information about the local flora & fauna. An ex-fisherman, Phillip has two boats – the *Volantis* and the *Matangi*, to make the trips to the kiwi-spotting beach.

There is one huge insurmountable factor

to this whole exercise, and some far-sighted official has implemented it for the kiwis' protection. Only 12 humans, on any consecutive day, can accompany Phillip to view this flightless marvel. Demand outstrips supply, so book ahead (☎ 249 1144) to avoid disappointment. The tours, which run from 8.30 pm to 1 am cost $45, but in actuality are priceless.

Sea Kayaking
Kayaks are available to rent for freedom kayaking in Paterson Inlet. See the visitor centre for information. The inlet is 100 sq km of bush-clad sheltered waterways, with 20 islands, DOC huts and two navigable rivers. A popular trip is a paddle to Freshwater River Landing (seven km upriver from the inlet) followed by a three to four-hour walk to Mason Bay to see kiwis in the wild.

Places to Stay
The DOC Stewart Island Visitor Centre

(☎ 219 1218) has information on all accommodation options.

Camping & Cabins There is a free campsite at Apple Bridge, Fern Tree Gully, but it's definitely basic, with a fireplace, wood and water supply and pit toilets only. It's about a half-hour walk from the wharf along Main Rd.

The *Ferndale Caravan Park* (☎ 219 1176) at Halfmoon Bay has tent sites for $5 – it has an ablution block with one coin-operated shower ($2 for six minutes), picnic tables and rubbish collection.

Backpackers Ann Pullen of *Ann's Place* (☎ 219 1065) offers tramping-style accommodation in a small house behind the main house for $8 per night. It's very basic, but then the price is basic too, and it's a supremely friendly place to stay. Bring your own sleeping bag and food.

Hotels & Motels The *Shearwater Inn* (☎ 219 1114), Ayr St, in the centre of the township has rooms (linen included) at $28/ 52 for singles/doubles, or $20 per person in larger shared rooms (three or four people). The inn has a restaurant serving breakfast and dinner, or you can cook your own meals – it costs 50c for half an hour to use the hot plate. The kitchen facilities are really limited here.

A room at the *Rakiura Motel* (☎ 219 1096), 1.5 km from the township, costs $60 per night for doubles/twins ($15 each extra adult). The *South Sea Hotel* (☎ 219 1059; fax 219 1120), close to the wharf, costs $50/75 for singles/doubles; there are also less expensive share twin rooms for $40 for a twin.

The *Stewart Island Lodge* (☎ 219 1085) is much more expensive. Its four rooms all have private facilities and cost about $175 per person in share twin rooms (or $210 for a single), including all meals – it is about 75% of this in winter.

Homestays An excellent alternative is to stay in one of the several homes on the island offering hostel-style accommodation at

hostel (or lower) rates. Ask at the visitor centre for the latest information.

A couple of other places offer very cheap homestays. *Michael Squires* (☎ 219 1425) can accommodate up to four people in his 'house hostel' at the start of the Golden Bay Rd. The cost is $15; bring your own sleeping bag and food. With *Andy & Jo Riksem* (☎ 219 1230), on the corner of Main Rd and Morris St, you stay in the family home (they can accommodate up to five guests) and the nightly cost of $12 per person includes a cooked breakfast each morning! If you don't have your own bedding they will provide it for an extra $3.

There are quite a few other places offering this type of accommodation: *Russell & Carolyn's* (☎ 219 1353) is a flat under the family home where a maximum of five pay $12 each; *Heti & Trevor Atkins* (☎ 219 1274), who enjoy the company of travellers, have a self-contained flat which costs $12 per person (maximum of five); *Joy's Place* (☎ 219 1376) has bunkroom beds for $10, but there is definitely no drinking or smoking here; *Iris & Mick Gibb* (☎ 219 1575) also have a flat for five for $12 each; and at *Dave's Place* (☎ 219 1078) five people can stop over for $10 each. Check in the book kept by the DOC staff when you get to Halfmoon Bay.

Holiday Homes Another option on Stewart Island is to hire a holiday home. There are several available. Stewart Island Travel (☎ 219 1269) has a couple for around $46 for two people, plus $13 each additional adult; families are especially welcome. Jeanette and Peter Goomes (☎ 217 6585) of *Stewart Island Holiday Homes* have two homes, each sleeping up to 10 people, about a five-minute walk from the town. The cost is $60 per night for two plus $15 for each extra adult (children $7.50).

Places to Eat

There's not much choice of eating places on Stewart Island. It comes down to the *Travel Inn* tearoom or the *South Sea Hotel* where meals are available by prior arrangement. The South Sea's meals can vary in quality

OUTER ISLANDS

depending on the stress on the kitchen – perhaps 10 diners is the maximum in Annie Hansen's dining room. The plus about this place is the sheer weight of seafood, locally caught, which features on the menu; fortunately for us bird lovers, the crisp-roasted muttonbird with apple sauce was not available when we ate there. The *Shearwater Inn* has a restaurant where breakfast and dinner are served daily. You should expect prices to be higher than the mainland due to freight costs.

Why Not? – this cafe has gone and the town is desperately calling out for something similar, as a great cup of coffee is hard to come by round here.

You can get basic necessities from the general store, fruit and vegetables from the Lettuce Inn, buy fresh fish and crayfish from the locals (it's the main industry of the island so there should be no shortage), catch your own fish or bring food across from Invercargill and prepare meals yourself. Often the Stewart Island Fishermens Co-operative has crayfish for sale – yum!

Entertainment

The only place to go for any nightlife here is the pub – there is only one. If you're tired of conversation, escape to the TV room with some takeaways and locally brewed ale. Return to the bar when you can't stand the video any more and start the evening life cycle of the Stewart Islander again.

Getting There & Away

Air Southern Air (☎ 218 9129; fax 214 4681) flies from Invercargill to Stewart Island for $67.50 one-way and $118 return (children half price). They also have a student/YHA standby fare of $33.75 (return $67.50); you must present either a YHA or a student card. They like you to be at the airport 30 minutes before departure; it's a good idea to telephone ahead to see how many seats may be available before going out to the airport. Flights supposedly go three or four times a day and take 20 minutes to hop over the narrow strait, but in actual fact they put on as many flights as necessary. Sometimes they shuttle back and forth all day in their Britten Norman Islander.

Southern Air sends a minibus once a day to pick up passengers from the YHA hostel in Invercargill. Other than that, you'll have to make your own way to the airport. The bus from the airstrip to 'town' on Stewart Island is included in the airfare. The free baggage allowance is only 15 kg per person, which is very little if you're carrying camping or tramping gear – if you exceed 20 kg or so you'll be charged extra. Southern Air also produce a handy brochure for their passengers which explains the topography you see as you pass over Bluff and approach Stewart Island.

Ferry Stewart Island Marine Services (☎ 219 1327 or 212 8376) operates the *Foveaux Express* from Bluff to Stewart Island for $37/74 one-way/return (children 15 and under half price). There are departures every day except Saturday in summer – Tuesday, Friday and Sunday during the winter. There are often extra sailings on public holidays. It's wise to book at least a few days ahead, especially in summer. In winter it's not so busy.

The crossing takes one hour across Foveaux Strait, noted for its often stormy weather – it can be a rough trip, so take some seasickness pills with you. You'll see a lot of sea birds on the crossing.

Two local buses go to the ferry these days. Campbelltown Passenger (☎ 212 7404) and Foveaux Express Bus Services (Bluff Motors, ☎ 212 8709) connect with the ferry. They pick up from anywhere in Invercargill. Unlike past times, the ferry operator offers no discounts or standby fares – if you go standby on the plane it actually works out cheaper. Fly!

If you wish to experience a blast from the past, go over on a slower boat. Southern Charter & Marine Ltd (☎ 212 7070) operate the MV *Deepstar*, which, because of its speed, is the suitable birdwatchers' alternative. It is not scheduled but will sail with a minimum of six passengers.

Getting Around

Stewart Island Travel, (☎ 219 1269; fax 219 1355) arrange bus tours, taxis and accommodation. They are agents for Southern Air. They also brew and bottle their own beer – Roaring Forties Ale. See them for travel advice, especially air and boat charters. On this island, with its lack of roads, a boat trip is a viable option to get a feel for the place.

Thorfinn Charters (☎ 219 1210) provide a water taxi service for birdwatchers and backpackers. See also under Tours in this section.

Rakiura Riders (☎ 219 1011) near the wharf rents motor scooters for about $15 per hour or $40 per day. A free tank of petrol is included with every hire, as are helmets and gloves; just remember to bring your driving licence.

Subantarctic Islands

New Zealand administers a number of Subantarctic islands – the Snares, Campbell, Auckland, Bounty and Antipodes islands – where there are established nature reserves. Entry is restricted to three of the five island groups and is by permit only. To get some idea of this wild environment go to the Southland Museum & Art Gallery in Invercargill and watch their Roaring Forties Experience audiovisual presentation. If you want first-hand experience it is going to be very expensive, as the islands are a long way from New Zealand's main islands.

The islands have a colourful human history – sealing, ship wrecks and forlorn attempts at farming. Now the islands are important as a reserve for remaining areas of vegetation unmodified by humans and breeding grounds for seabirds, penguins and mammals such as the elephant seal. Few are fortunate enough to visit these remote islands but increasing eco-tourism possibilities, well-managed and guided, are being created.

SNARES ISLANDS

The Snares are famous for the incredible number of sooty shearwaters (muttonbirds) which breed there. It has been estimated that on any one evening during the season there will be six million in the air before they crash land to find their burrows. Other birds found on the Snares include the endemic Snares crested penguin, cape pigeon and Bullers mollymawks.

AUCKLAND ISLANDS

These are probably the most accessible of the islands, especially Enderby Island. At Sandy Bay on Enderby you will be able to see the rare Hooker's sea lion. Many species of birds also make Enderby their home (either temporary or permanent), including endemic shags, the flightless teal and the royal albatross. Skuas (gull-like birds) are everpresent in the skies above the sea lion colony. Settlement was attempted in Erebus Cove, and it was not until 1992 that the last introduced cattle were destroyed. On Disappointment Island there are approximately 50,000 white-capped mollymawks.

CAMPBELL ISLAND

This is the only inhabited island in the New Zealand subantarctic islands, as there is a contingent from the NZ meteorological service stationed here. Apart from a few humans it is the true domain of pelagic bird species. It is estimated that there are over 7500 pairs of southern royal albatross here, as well as colonies of greyheaded and black-browed mollymawks. The vegetation of the island has been divided into three distinct zones: upper alpine, lower alpine, and subalpine.

ANTIPODES ISLANDS

These islands get their name from the fact that they are opposite latitude 0° at Greenwich, England. The real treat on this island is the endemic Antipodes Island parakeet, which is found with, but does not breed with, the red-crowned parakeet (similar to the New Zealand species of parakeet). In the shorter grasses at the top of the islands wandering albatross nest. Landing is not permitted on the Antipodes so viewing is from zodiacs.

BOUNTY ISLANDS

Landing is not permitted on any of the 13 Bounty Islands – there is a good chance that you would step on the wildlife anyway, as the 135 hectares of land that makes up these granite islands is covered with mammals or birds. There are literally thousands of erect crested penguins, fulmar prions and salvins mollymawks clustered in crevices, near the lower slopes and on all other available pieces of real estate.

GETTING THERE & AWAY

At the moment there is really only one way of getting to the Subantarctic Islands – by boat on an expensive tour. Southern Heritage Expeditions (☎ 314 4393; fax 314 4137), 1992 Winner of the New Zealand Ecotourism Award, have about four trips a year to these islands aboard the MY *Pacific Ruby*. For a 15-day cruise, which takes in all the islands, it will cost you about $4500; all inclusive. If you have the money you will consider it well spent, because of the rich variety of flora & fauna you will see. As two of the islands are off-limits, cruises past them are made in zodiac inflatables.

Their trips usually include Macquarie Island, which is administered by Australia. The highlights of this island are the four species of penguin: the rockhopper, king, gentoo and royal – it is estimated that there are three to four million on the island!

In the USA, contact them through New Zealand Central Reservations Office (☎ (213) 338 1538), 6033 West Century Blvd # 1270, Los Angeles CA 90045.

Chatham Islands

Way out in the Pacific, about 770 km east of Christchurch, the Chatham Islands (population 750) are among the most remote parts of New Zealand. There are 10 islands in the group but apart from the 50 or so people on Pitt Island, only Chatham Island is populated. It's a wild and attractive place, and very much off the beaten track. The islands offer a world of contrast – rugged coastlines and towering cliffs, volcanic peaks, lagoons and peat bogs, sweeping beaches devoid of human habitation, isolated farms, wind-stunted vegetation and dense patches of forest. Apart from farming and tourism, the other main industry is crayfish processing and there are plants at Waitangi, Kaingaroa, Owenga and Port Hutt.

History

Chatham Island is renowned for being the last home of the Moriori, an isolated group of Polynesians. They were here before the Maori settlement of New Zealand, but with the arrival of Europeans things rapidly began to go wrong.

A British expedition commanded by Lieutenant Broughton first arrived at the island in 1791 and even that initial visit resulted in a clash, at aptly named Skirmish Bay (now Kaingaroa), and one Moriori was killed. There are two memorials at this spot to this day. In the 1820s and 1830s European and American whalers and sealers began to arrive and then, in 1835, a Maori tribe, the Ngati-awa, was resettled in the Chathams. The impact on the peaceable Moriorios was dramatic as the Ngati-awa, under Chief Pomare, established themselves by right of conquest; the Moriori population crashed from around 2000 at the time of the first European arrival in 1791 to only about 100 in the 1860s. By the beginning of the 20th century there were just 12 full-blooded Moriorios left. The last local Moriori, Tommy Solomon, died in March 1933 and there is a statue of him at Owenga in the south-east of Chatham.

The Maori leader and prophet Te Kooti was imprisoned here last century, after he had eluded the British troops and officials on the mainland for many years. He turned to peace and established the Ringatu faith while incarcerated here.

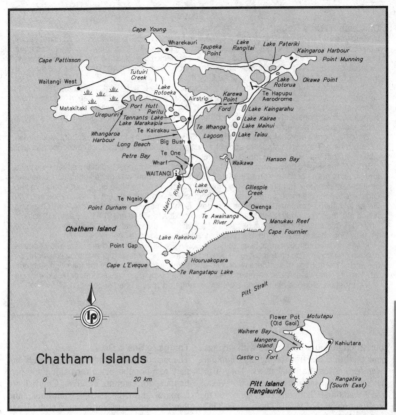

Chatham Islands

Fauna

There are 18 species of bird unique to the islands, and because of the isolation there is a large degree of endemism, as with the local tit, pigeon and robin. Entry to the sanctuaries, such as those near Pitt, and Rangatira (South East) Island, is prohibited but many species can still be seen. DOC staff will outline the best viewing spots for birdwatchers. There are numerous rare and unusual birds to be seen. The birds include the endangered black robin, which at one stage was perilously close to extinction in its last refuge, Little Mangere Island near Pitt Island (read more about the Black Robin story in this chapter). Black swans, many species of ducks, pukekos and wekas are common.

There is a private fur seal colony near Kaingaroa in the north-east of Chatham Island. Southern Heritage Expeditions (see the Subantarctic Islands section in this chapter) take eight-day tours to the islands.

Information

Waitangi is the only town on the islands. There are a couple of shops, a hotel, motel,

Chatham Islands Robin

In 1980 there were only five black robins in the world. Such a small population would usually spell extinction of the species, but as a last resort, wildlife authorities began a cross-fostering programme to save them. This entailed the transfer of black robin eggs to nests of another species for incubation and hatching, in order to make the black robins re-nest and produce more eggs. At the time this technique was new and potentially risky.

The main reason for the demise of the black robin was loss of habitat. Since the 1900s they had been confined to Little Mangere Island, an exposed volcanic rockstack 22 km from the main Chatham island. A small patch of scrub, about five hectares. in all, was the robins' home. A combination of shearwaters excavating burrows, dry seasons and the building of an illegal helicopter pad, all served to reduce the breeding area.

By 1972 there were only 18 black robins left. This was a far cry from the numbers recorded in 1871 by Henry Travers on Mangere and Little Mangere islands; archaeological evidence has also confirmed that they were once found on the main Chatham island.

In 1976 there were only seven left. That year wildlife officers caught five of the seven (two pairs and an extra male) and transferred them to Mangere where there was more vegetation. Later the other two males were transferred. In the next four years two of the older birds died – only five left. Cross-fostering was then started using Chatham Islands warblers. As soon as Old Blue and Old Green laid, their eggs were transferred and, despite many upsets, four chicks survived. Chatham Island tits, found on South East Island, were used next. At the end of 1977 there were 12 robins. The next season was disastrous because of appalling weather and the population was back to 11, only one chick had survived. By 1980 they were back down to five.

It was decided to move adult black robins to South East Island where there were 100 hectares of bush and scrub. The birds must have sensed that the time for their reemergence was right. By the end of the 1984 summer there were 19 black robins, and at the end of the following summer, 38. The tits were ideal foster parents. The future of the black robin was no longer bleak and one of the most courageous attempts to save an endangered species had succeeded. ∎

tourist lodge and a post office with savings bank facilities. The free fortnightly *Chatham Islander* carries the local news. They also have their own radio station, Radio Weka, and TV station (Chathams Television) run in conjunction with TVNZ. There is an STD and facsimile link with the mainland.

Information on the islands is available from Air New Zealand or, more particularly, from Mt Cook Airlines. *A Land Apart*, by Michael King & Robin Morrison (Random Century, 1992) provides a wealth of information about the islands.

The Chatham Islands, because of their location, are very exposed but they have a temperate climate. Temperature variations are 12°C to 18°C in February and 6°C to 10°C in July. The best time to visit is in December and January; often the temperatures then reach 23°C to 24°C.

Chatham Islands time is 45 minutes ahead of mainland New Zealand time.

Things to See & Do

The islands have plenty of fine beaches and they're a popular place for fishing and particularly for catching crayfish. Crayfish are a major industry in the Chathams, and they're exported to North America and Japan (six crayfish can be caught per person per day and 10 paua are allowed each person; check with DOC). Scuba divers can explore the shipwrecks around the islands while trampers will also find interesting country to explore, particularly at the southern end of Chatham Island. DOC have set up six formal reserves, developed with walking tracks of anything from an hour to full day in duration. The northern end of Chatham is flat and windswept. There's a small museum with Moriori artefacts in the council offices.

Two unusual attractions to be seen are the tree carvings and fossilised black sharks' teeth. The 200-year-old Moriori tree carvings (dendroglyphs) can be found in a grove adjacent to the old Te Hapupu aerodrome, in a signposted and fenced-off area. These mysterious carvings are gradually disappearing. The fossilised sharks' teeth can be found at Blind Jim's Creek, on the shores of Te Whanga Lagoon. The teeth are about 40 million years old and a local heritage – please leave them where you see them. Their appearance here, pushed up by the waves of the lagoon, has not yet been fully explained.

Places to Stay & Eat

The *Hotel Chathams* (☎ 305 0048; fax 305 0097), Waterfront Rd, has single/double rooms for $45/50, or $35 per person for twin share rooms; meals are available.

The newer and more up-market *Chathams Tourist Lodge* (☎ 305 0196) has single/double rooms for $66/78, or $106/150 per day including all meals (which you can also arrange separately). There's also a twin share rate of $38.50 per person, or $75 including all meals. The lodge hires out 4WDs and boats and can arrange a variety of activities including diving, fishing, boating, horse-riding and tramping.

Rooms at the *Tuanui Motel* (☎ 305 0150) cost $30 per person for a bed only or $60 per person including all meals; single meals can be arranged separately. Unlike the hotel and the lodge, there are kitchens here where you can prepare your own meals.

Homestays with locals are also possible, especially when all other accommodation is booked up. The cost is usually around $55 per person, meals included. There is no accommodation on Pitt Island so take a tent if you manage to make it out there. Ask permission from the locals before camping anywhere.

You can buy crayfish and blue cod at the packaging factory in Waitangi. Flounder and whitebait can be caught in the lagoon, and

paua and kina gathered just offshore. For the true gourmets there are swan egg omelettes and roast weka – yes the weka is consumed here as it is not native to the islands. It has almost assumed the status of introduced pest. Entertainment – bring your own or head to the *Waitangi pub* to listen to a few yarns.

Getting There & Away

Apart from a periodic freight-only cargo ship, the only transport to the islands is provided by Mt Cook Airlines (whose agents are Air New Zealand) using Bae 748 aircraft, or Air Chathams (fax 305 0209) using a Beech 99. The MCA 44-seater goes from Wellington and Christchurch, and the Air Chathams flight from Napier; the fare is $342 one way (children $228). The flight takes three hours and since there are only minimal seats available it's wise to book well ahead. Bookings for Air Chathams are handled through Ansett. Aircraft are met by a bus which transfers the passengers the 19 km to Waitangi.

Getting Around

Beyond Waitangi most roads are unsealed and there is no public transport. Val Croon (fax 305 0097) of the Hotel Chathams will pick you up from Karewa Airport if he knows of your arrival. Chatham Motors (☎ 305 0093) hires small 4WDs for $60 per day plus 21 cents per km, or larger ones for $82 per day plus 26 cents per km. There are at least three other operators (Black Robin Rentals, Chathams Tourist Lodge, Hotel Chathams) hiring vehicles. It's also quite easy to hitch around the island.

Air Chathams (☎ 305 0126) operates a light aircraft (five-seat Cessna) for flightseeing and for trips to Pitt Island. It may be possible to hitch a ride with fishing vessels across to Pitt Island, but the seas are very rough, often with mountainous waves.

OUTER ISLANDS

Index

MAPS

TEXT

Thanks

Thanks to the many travellers who wrote in with helpful hints, useful advice and interesting and funny stories:

Jeff Ainge (NZ), Adele Alexander (NZ), David Allen (UK), Bryan Alvis (NZ), Sophia Andras-Shadboet (C), Peter Andrews (NZ), Vaughan Andrews (Aus), Lucy Appleton (NZ), Ian Armstrong (NZ), Katherine & Derek Arnold (UK), Noeline Arnold (NZ), Heidi Arntzen (NL), Robert Aronoff (USA), Peter Attwell (NZ)

Jane Baird (NZ), Declan Ball, David Bargery (UK), Deborah Barker (NZ), Ross Barnett (NZ), Jenny Barratt (NZ), T W Bateman (NZ), Mary & Roger Batkins (UK), Chris Batten (NZ), Robert Behrendt (USA), Kirk Bendall (Aus), Johann Bernhardt, Danielle Bernstein (USA), M & G Berrini (I), Barbara & Dan Biggs (Aus), Eric Billoud (NZ), Junie Birch (NZ), Grant L Bisset (NZ), Katie Bizzey (UK), Bruce Black (NZ), Rick Blackburn (NZ), Mark Blackham (Aus), Dirk Bocques (NZ), Anne Bogle (NZ), Jan Bolton (NZ), Jane Bonnesen (USA), Malcolm Booth (UK), Robert Bowler (USA), Philip Bowtell (Aus), Mark Brabyn (NZ), Ute Bradter (D), Anna Bray (Aus), Iris & Rene Brazerol (CH), Mark Breen (NZ), Eric Bronson (USA), Stephanie Brookes (Aus), Chris Brown (NZ), Joan Brown (Aus), Mrs Jean Brown (NZ), Greg Brown, Katie Bryan-Brown (UK), Andrew Bullock (UK), Kathleen & David Burford (NZ), Kevin Burns (NZ), Charles Burrows (UK), Ann Burton (UK), Nicholas Bush (UK)

John Cairns (NZ), Robin & Daphne Calder (NZ), S C Callaway (USA), Amy Campbell (NZ), Miss Val Campbell (UK), Biddy Canard (NZ), Colin & Sara Carey (NZ), Roger Carnachan (NZ), Colin Carr (UK), Phyllis Carroll (USA), Roy Carter (NZ), Catherine Christie (UK), Christine Chryssouergis (USA), John Clere (NZ), Ken & Pearl Coatsworth (NZ), Melissa Combley (Aus), Peter Cook (NZ), Catherine Cooper (UK), Ethne & Graham Copp (NZ), G B Copp (NZ), Alison Corich (NZ), Dave & Paddy Corneby (NZ), Diane Cornelius (NZ), Jane Craig, Richard Craik (UK), Marlene Crapper (NZ), Brenda Crocker (NZ), Alison Crowe (UK), Mac Cubitt (UK)

Ruth Dalley (NZ), Peter Daniliuc (Aus), Kathy Davies (UK), Joe Davis (NZ), Tim de Jong (NZ), Ernst Debets (NL), Mary Dell (UK), Dr Susan De Marinis (USA), Kaye Dennison (NZ), Paul Denton (UK), Karen Devine (Aus), Paul Dick (UK), Braden Dickson (NZ), Christine Diesel (D), P Dimond (NZ), Diana Dobson (C), Anita Doraisami (Aus), Barbara Doyle (NZ), Phillip Du Val (NZ), Peter & Dianne Dudfield (NZ), Arthur Dudley (UK), Gavin Duncan (UK), James Dunne (NZ), John Durley (C), Jennifer Dykes (UK)

John Eames (NZ), Steffen Emvich (D), Philip &
Angela England (NZ), Dieter Ettl (Aus), Ngaire Evans (NZ), S Everson (NZ)

Mari Fagin (USA), Rebecca Ferguson (UK), R S Findlay (UK), Keith Fisher (NZ), C R Ford (NZ), Simon Fowler (UK), Sheila Fox (US), Warwick Franklin (NZ)

Horst Geerken (D), Sue Gibbson, David Gilhooley (Aus), Philippa Gilmour (NZ), Stephen Gorman, Diane Gorman (NZ), Cornelius Gorres (D), B Graham (UK), Jacqie Grant (NZ), Paul Greening (UK), Emily Greenleaf (USA), Clare Greenwood (NZ), K A Griffiths (UK), Dion Grooten (NZ), Jan & Jim Grounds (NZ), Steve Grove (NZ), Ian Grundy (UK), Christine Gruttke, Lisa Guiliani (USA), Alison Gunn (Aus), Birgit Gutberlett (D)

Michael & Diana Haizelden (UK), Elaine Hall (Aus), Mrs S Hall (Aus), Jorg Hammerschmidt (D), Chris Hanham (NZ), Pia Trine Hansen (Dk), Ian Harrison (Aus), Marilyn Hart (C), Alfred & Heidi Hassencamp (NZ), Heike Haug (Aus), Amy Haus (USA), D J Hawkey (NZ), Anne Hawthorn (NZ), Des and Gill Heath (NZ), Hans Heidensleben (Dk), F C Heimberg (NZ), Geert Jan Heusuinkueld (NL), Irene Heydkamp (CH), Tony Hobbs (Aus), Bert Hoffeman (NL), Peter Hoffman (D), Karin Hogan (UK), Andrea & Chris Hogg (Aus), Ruth Holman, Sarah Holman (NZ), Gill Holmes (UK), Catherine Hood (NZ), Trudi Hopping (NZ), Christopher Horn (UK), Mrs Nita Horne (NZ), Donald Horner (USA), Chip Houde (USA), Kay Howe (NZ), Winona Hubbard (USA), K W Hubbard (USA), Chris Huggett (UK), E Hunter (UK), Iain Hutchison (UK), Sylvia Huxtable (NZ), Monique Huystens (Aus)

Judith Irving (UK), John Irwin (NZ), Guy Irwin (NZ), Richard Israel (NZ), Richard & Pam Ivory (NZ), Kathy Jamieson (NZ), Paul Jidges (UK), Dr Neil Johnson (UK), Neil & Shelley Johnstone (NZ), Kirsty Joiner (NZ), Mrs Edna Jones (UK), Breck Jones (USA), Loreley Jorgensen (Aus), Laurie Joyce (USA)

Marion Kaglund (NZ), Miss M Kaiarama (NZ), Robert Kaspar (NZ), Sandra Kavraikis (NZ), Kevin Kelly (Aus), Gary Kelsberg (USA), Ralph Kent (UK), Ashley King (NZ), R E King (NZ), Ray King (NZ), Hanne Kingma (NL), Michael Krulik (USA), Lutz Krummreich (D), Lucy Kunkel (USA), Anna Kurmann (NZ)

Johnny Lake (USA), Stuart Landsborough, Valeria Lane (NZ), C & A Langpape (D), Ary Laufer (Aus), Bitten Laursen (Dk), Shaun Laws (UK), Bill Lawson (NZ), Kevin Lee (Sin), Michael & Hanka Lee, Julia Legg (NZ), Thomas Lejre (Dk), Nigel Levick (NZ), Stephan Lieden (S), Victor Lim (Tai), Nicholas Lincoln (UK), Sarah Lodge (NZ), John & Ruth Loebl (UK), Patrick Logan (USA), Gabor Lovei (NZ), Debbie Loveridge (NZ), Audrey Lowe (C)

P & C MacDonald (C), Mary Mackey (NZ), Gail Marmont (NZ), J Marsh (UK), Heather Martin (Aus), Jean & Ken Martin (UK), Patrick Martin (USA),

Anne-Marie Mastaglio (UK), Jane Matthews (NZ), Bruce Maunsell (NZ), Clarice & Bill May (NZ), Toireasa McCann (UK), Murray McCarthy (NZ), Kim McConkey (NZ), Kirstine McCulloch (NZ), Neville McGill (NZ), R B McGregor (NZ), Patrick McGuire (UK), Laura McKay, Bev McLeay (NZ), Jim McNair (NZ), Alan McQuarters (NZ), Ronda McRae (NZ), Frederico Medici (I), Michael Midgley (NZ), Suzy Miller (NZ), Janice Milligan (C), Y Mimran (Isr), Harry Mirick (USA), Scott Moeller (NZ), Marylise Montandon (CH), Peter Moore (Aus), Vanda Moss (UK), Douglas Mullett (Aus), Victoria Murray (NZ)

Kevin Narramore (USA), Leigh Neighbour (NZ), Mrs F Neumann (NZ), Jeff Neumann (NZ), Allan & Marilyn Nicklin (NZ), Anna Noelle (Sp), Holly Nosaztki (USA), Neil O'Callaghan (UK), Colleen Oakley (NZ), Richard Oddy (NZ), Peter One (NZ), Shelley Osborne (C), David Osmers (NZ), Manfred Ossendorf (D), Craig Ow (USA)

Jos van der Palen (NL), Lucinda Pallis (Aus), Peter Pannell (NZ), Lyne Pare (C), Helen Paterson (NZ), David Patrick (C), Peggy Paulhus (C), Gordon & Janet Pearce (NZ), Michael Pearson (UK), Brendan Peet (NZ), Lois Penno (NZ), Mattys Peridech (Aus), James & Shelley Peters (USA), Karen Pettigrew (USA), Mark Pettit (Aus), Mr & Mrs P G Phillips (UK), Lisa Pittar (NZ), Jackie Plusch (USA), Doug Portnow (Aus), Joan Potts (Aus), Capt Ivan Preston (NZ), Christian W Pruchnic (USA), Aloys Pruente (D), Charles Puckle (NZ), Danny & Julie Quant (HK)

Paul Radcliffs (NZ), Mike Raddock (NZ), Gareth & Suzy Ralphs (UK), Alan Ramsbottom (NZ), Felicia Rasheed, Heather Renton (Aus), Ann & Mark Restad (USA), Trevor Reynolds (C), Patricia Rhodes (UK), John Richards (Aus), Sue Rigby (Aus), Sandy Robinson (USA), Margaret Robson (NZ), Susan Rogers (USA), Jo Ronan (NZ), Tony Rook (UK), Marty Rosenfeld (NZ), Kevin Ross (NZ), Bob & Louise Rowley (NZ)

Stephen Salzano (NZ), C N Sammons (NZ), Cindy Schneider (USA), Jill Schou (NZ), Edith Schowalter (D), Dr Rainer Schumacher (D), J R Scott (NZ), Loh Boon Seah (Sin), Jacquie Shartier (C), T A Short (NZ), Gil Sittoz (Isr), M A Sixtus (NZ), Jude Smith (NZ), Judi Smythe (NZ), Sunny Soon (Aus), Grant Southy (NZ), Paul Spence (NZ), Silke & Tanja Speth (D), Doris Spratley (C), John D St Clair Brown (NZ), Michael Stewart (USA), Sylvia Stockli (CH), Kay Stokes (NZ), Bunny Stoufull (USA), Debbie Strong (NZ), Bruce Stuart-Monteath (NZ), Fleur Sullivan (NZ), Joan & George Sutherland (NZ), Fergus Sutherland (NZ), Michael & Julia Sweet (UK)

Mike Tamaki (NZ), W Tapanila (C), Chris & Emma Tatton (UK), Clint Tauri (NZ), Daphne Taylor (NZ), Rob Temple (Aus), Saxon Templeton (NZ), Nicola Thomas (UK), Ian Thomas (UK), Carl Thompson (NZ), Susan Thompson (NZ), Grant Thomson (NZ), Kurt Tobuck (USA), Sally Tomlins (NZ), Mrs M Turner (Aus), Sarah Turtill (UK)

Armin Uhlig (B), John Urbana (USA), Marma Van Valkenburgh (USA), Raymond L Valle (USA), Adrian & Marg van Dooren (NZ), Mike Vaughan (UK), Jacques Vauthier, Rene Visser (UK), P M Voermanek (NZ)

M Walensky (USA), M Ward (Aus), Susan Ward (NZ), Linda Ward (UK), Geoff Wayatt (NZ), Pat John Webb (Aus), Doug Weihing (C), Janet Wells (USA), Bradley Wenman (Aus), Emma Weston (UK), Rick Whittiker (C), Elisabeth Widmer (CH), Lesley Wilkins (NZ), Pam & David Williams (NZ), David Willis (UK), David Wilson (NZ), Mary Wilson (USA), Nick Wilton, Amanda Withers (UK), Patricia Wood (UK), Eyal & Rivki Yatuv (Isr), Lisa Choy Zafra (USA), Tony Zimmerman (NZ)

Keep in touch!

We love hearing from you and think you'd like to hear from us.

The Lonely Planet Newsletter covers the when, where, how and what of travel (AND it's free!).

When...is the right time to see reindeer in Finland?
Where...can you hear the best palm-wine music in Ghana?
How...do you get from Asunción to Areguá by steam train?
What...should you leave behind to avoid hassles with customs in Iran?

To join our mailing list just contact us at any of our offices (details below).

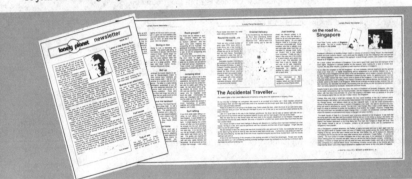

Every issue includes:

- *a letter from Lonely Planet founders Tony and Maureen Wheeler*
- *travel diary from a Lonely Planet author - find out what it's really like out on the road*
- *feature article on an important and topical travel issue*
- *a selection of recent letters from our readers*
- *the latest travel news from all over the world*
- *details on Lonely Planet's new and forthcoming releases*

Also available Lonely Planet T-shirts. 100% heavyweight cotton (S, M, L, XL)

LONELY PLANET PUBLICATIONS
Australia: PO Box 617, Hawthorn 3122, Victoria (tel: 03-819 1877)
USA: Embarcadero West, 155 Filbert St, Suite 251, Oakland, CA 94607 (tel: 510-893 8555)
UK: Devonshire House, 12 Barley Mow Passage, Chiswick, London W4 4PH (tel: 081-742 3161)

Guides to the Pacific

Australia – a travel survival kit
The complete low-down on Down Under – home of Ayers Rock, the Great Barrier Reef, extraordinary animals, cosmopolitan cities, rainforests, beaches ... and Lonely Planet!

Bushwalking in Australia
Two experienced and respected walkers give details of the best walks in every state, covering many different terrains and climates.

Bushwalking in Papua New Guinea
The best way to get to know Papua New Guinea is from the ground up, which is just as well as bushwalking is the best way to travel around the rugged and varied landscape of this island.

Islands of Australia's Great Barrier Reef – a travel survival kit
The Great Barrier Reef is one of the wonders of the world – and one of the great travel destinations! Whether you're looking for a tropical island resort or a secluded island hideaway, this guide has all the facts you'll need.

Melbourne city guide
From historic houses to fascinating churches and famous nudes to tapas bars, cafés and bistros – Melbourne is a dream for gourmands and a paradise for party goers.

Sydney city guide
A wealth of information on Australia's most exciting city; all in a handy pocket-sized format.

Victoria – Australia guide
From the high country to the coast and from the cities to tranquil country retreats, Australia's most compact state is packed with attractions and activities for everyone.

Fiji – a travel survival kit
Whether you prefer to stay in camping grounds, international hotels, or something in-between, this comprehensive guide will help you to enjoy the beautiful Fijian archipelago.

Hawaii – a travel survival kit
Share in the delights of this island paradise – and avoid some of its high prices – with this practical guide. Covers all of Hawaii's well-known attractions, plus plenty of uncrowded sights and activities.

Micronesia – a travel survival kit
The glorious beaches, lagoons and reefs of these 2100 islands would dazzle even the most jaded traveller. This guide has all the details on island-hopping across the north Pacific.

New Caledonia – a travel survival kit
This guide shows how to discover all that he idyllic islands of New Caledonia have to offer – from French colonial culture to traditional Melanesian life.

Tramping in New Zealand
Call it tramping, hiking, walking, bushwalking, or trekking – travelling by foot is the best way to explore New Zealand's natural beauty. Detailed descriptions of 20 walks of varying length and difficulty.

Papua New Guinea – a travel survival kit
With its coastal cities, villages perched beside mighty rivers, palm-fringed beaches and rushing mountain streams, Papua New Guinea promises memorable travel.

Rarotonga & the Cook Islands – a travel survival kit
Rarotonga and the Cook Islands have history, beauty and magic to rival the better-known islands of Hawaii and Tahiti, but the world has virtually passed them by.

Samoa – a travel survival kit
Two remarkably different countries, Western Samoa and American Samoa offer some wonderful island escapes, and Polynesian culture at its best..

Solomon Islands – a travel survival kit
The Solomon Islands are the best-kept secret of the Pacific. Discover remote tropical islands, jungle covered volcanoes and traditional Melanesian villages with this detailed guide.

Tahiti & French Polynesia – a travel survival kit
Tahiti's idyllic beauty has seduced sailors, artists and traveller for generations. The latest edition provides full details on the main island of Tahiti, the Tuamotos, Marquesas and other island groups. Invaluable information for independent travellers and package tourists alike.

Tonga – a travel survival kit
The only South Pacific country never to be colonised by Europeans, Tonga has also been ignored by tourists. The people of this far-flung island group offer some of the most sincere and unconditional hospitality in the world.

Vanuatu – a travel survival kit
Discover superb beaches, lush rainforests, dazzling coral reefs and traditional Melanesian customs in this glorious Pacific Ocean archipelago.

Also available:
Pidgin phrasebook.

Lonely Planet Guidebooks

Lonely Planet guidebooks cover every accessible part of Asia as well as Australia, the Pacific, South America, Africa, the Middle East, Europe and parts of North America. There are five series: *travel survival kits*, covering a country for a range of budgets; *shoestring guides* with compact information for low-budget travel in a major region; *walking guides*; *city guides* and *phrasebooks*.

Australia & the Pacific
Australia
Bushwalking in Australia
Islands of Australia's Great Barrier Reef
Fiji
Melbourne city guide
Micronesia
New Caledonia
New Zealand
Tramping in New Zealand
Papua New Guinea
Bushwalking in Papua New Guinea
Papua New Guinea phrasebook
Rarotonga & the Cook Islands
Samoa
Solomon Islands
Sydney city guide
Tahiti & French Polynesia
Tonga
Vanuatu
Victoria

South-East Asia
Bali & Lombok
Bangkok city guide
Cambodia
Indonesia
Indonesia phrasebook
Laos
Malaysia, Singapore & Brunei
Myanmar (Burma)
Burmese phrasebook
Philippines
Pilipino phrasebook
Singapore city guide
South-East Asia on a shoestring
Thailand
Thai phrasebook
Vietnam
Vietnamese phrasebook

North-East Asia
China
Beijing city guide
Mandarin Chinese phrasebook
Hong Kong, Macau & Canton
Japan
Japanese phrasebook
Korea
Korean phrasebook
Mongolia
North-East Asia on a shoestring
Seoul city guide
Taiwan
Tibet
Tibet phrasebook
Tokyo city guide

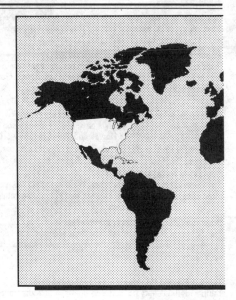

West Asia
Trekking in Turkey
Turkey
Turkish phrasebook
West Asia on a shoestring

Middle East
Arab Gulf States
Egypt & the Sudan
Arabic (Egyptian) phrasebook
Iran
Israel
Jordan & Syria
Yemen

Indian Ocean
Madagascar & Comoros
Maldives & Islands of the East Indian Ocean
Mauritius, Réunion & Seychelles

Mail Order

Lonely Planet guidebooks are distributed worldwide. They are also available by mail order from Lonely Planet, so if you have difficulty finding a title please write to us. US and Canadian residents should write to Embarcadero West, 155 Filbert St, Suite 251, Oakland CA 94607, USA ; European residents should write to Devonshire House, 12 Barley Mow Passage, Chiswick, London W4 4PH; and residents of other countries to PO Box 617, Hawthorn, Victoria 3122, Australia.

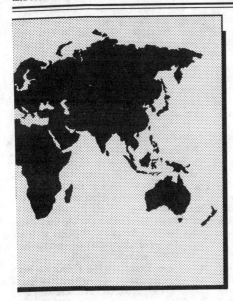

Indian Subcontinent
Bangladesh
India
Hindi/Urdu phrasebook
Trekking in the Indian Himalaya
Karakoram Highway
Kashmir, Ladakh & Zanskar
Nepal
Trekking in the Nepal Himalaya
Nepali phrasebook
Pakistan
Sri Lanka
Sri Lanka phrasebook

Africa
Africa on a shoestring
Central Africa
East Africa
Trekking in East Africa
Kenya
Swahili phrasebook
Morocco, Algeria & Tunisia
Arabic (Moroccan) phrasebook
South Africa, Lesotho & Swaziland
Zimbabwe, Botswana & Namibia
West Africa

Central America
Baja California
Central America on a shoestring
Costa Rica
La Ruta Maya
Mexico

North America
Alaska
Canada
Hawaii

Europe
Baltic States & Kaliningrad
Dublin city guide
Eastern Europe on a shoestring
Eastern Europe phrasebook
Finland
Greece
Hungary
Iceland, Greenland & the Faroe Islands
Ireland
Italy
Mediterranean Europe on a shoestring
Mediterranean Europe phrasebook
Poland
Scandinavian & Baltic Europe on a shoestring
Scandinavian Europe phrasebook
Switzerland
Trekking in Spain
Trekking in Greece
USSR
Russian phrasebook
Western Europe on a shoestring
Western Europe phrasebook

South America
Argentina, Uruguay & Paraguay
Bolivia
Brazil
Brazilian phrasebook
Chile & Easter Island
Colombia
Ecuador & the Galápagos Islands
Latin American Spanish phrasebook
Peru
Quechua phrasebook
South America on a shoestring
Trekking in the Patagonian Andes

The Lonely Planet Story

Lonely Planet published its first book in 1973 in response to the numerous 'How did you do it?' questions Maureen and Tony Wheeler were asked after driving, bussing, hitching, sailing and railing their way from England to Australia.

Written at a kitchen table and hand collated, trimmed and stapled, *Across Asia on the Cheap* became an instant local bestseller, inspiring thoughts of another book.

Eighteen months in South-East Asia resulted in their second guide, *South-East Asia on a shoestring*, which they put together in a backstreet Chinese hotel in Singapore in 1975. The 'yellow bible' as it quickly became known to backpackers around the world, soon became *the* guide to the region. It has sold well over half a million copies and is now in its 7th edition, still retaining its familiar yellow cover.

Today there are over 120 Lonely Planet titles in print – books that have that same adventurous approach to travel as those early guides; books that 'assume you know how to get your luggage off the carousel' as one reviewer put it.

Although Lonely Planet initially specialised in guides to Asia, they now cover most regions of the world, including the Pacific, South America, Africa, the Middle East and Europe. The list of *walking guides* and *phrasebooks* (for 'unusual' languages such as Quechua, Swahili, Nepalese and Egyptian Arabic) is also growing rapidly.

The emphasis continues to be on travel for independent travellers. Tony and Maureen still travel for several months of each year and play an active part in the writing, updating and quality control of Lonely Planet's guides.

They have been joined by over 50 authors, 54 staff – mainly editors, cartographers, & designers – at our office in Melbourne, Australia, 10 at our US office in Oakland, California and another three at our office in London to handle sales for Britain, Europe and Africa. In 1992 Lonely Planet opened an editorial office in Paris. Travellers themselves also make a valuable contribution to the guides through the feedback we receive in thousands of letters each year.

The people at Lonely Planet strongly believe that travellers can make a positive contribution to the countries they visit, both through their appreciation of the countries' culture, wildlife and natural features, and through the money they spend. In addition, the company makes a direct contribution to the countries and regions it covers. Since 1986 a percentage of the income from each book has been donated to ventures such as famine relief in Africa; aid projects in India; agricultural projects in Central America; Greenpeace's efforts to halt French nuclear testing in the Pacific and Amnesty International. In 1993 $100,000 was donated to such causes.

Lonely Planet's basic travel philosophy is summed up in Tony Wheeler's comment, 'Don't worry about whether your trip will work out. Just go!'